The Cambridge Handbook of Areal Linguistics

Providing a contemporary and comprehensive view of the topical field of areal linguistics, this book looks systematically at different regions of the world whilst presenting a focused and informed overview of the theory behind research into areal linguistics and language contact. The topicality of areal linguistics is thoroughly documented by a wealth of case studies from all major regions of the world and, with chapters from scholars with a broad spectrum of language expertise, it offers insights into the mechanisms of external language change. With no book currently like this in the market, *The Cambridge Handbook of Areal Linguistics* will be welcomed by students and scholars working on the history of language families, documentation and classification, and will help readers to understand the key field of areal linguistics within a broader linguistic context.

RAYMOND HICKEY is Professor of English Linguistics, University of Duisburg and Essen, Germany. His main research interests are varieties of English (especially Irish English and Dublin English) and general questions of language contact, variation and change. Among his recent book publications are *Motives for Language Change* (2003), *A Sound Atlas of Irish English* (2004), *Legacies of Colonial English* (2004), *Dublin English: Evolution and Change* (2005), *Irish English: History and Present-day Forms* (2007), *The Handbook of Language Contact* (2010), *Eighteenth-Century English* (2010), *Varieties of English in Writing* (2010), *Areal Features of the Anglophone World* (2012), *The Sound Structure of Modern Irish* (2014), *A Dictionary of Varieties of English* (2014), *Sociolinguistics in Ireland* (2016) and *Listening to the Past: Audio Records of Accents of English* (2016).

CAMBRIDGE HANDBOOKS IN LANGUAGE AND LINGUISTICS

Genuinely broad in scope, each handbook in this series provides a complete state-of-the-field overview of a major sub-discipline within language study and research. Grouped into broad thematic areas, the chapters in each volume encompass the most important issues and topics within each subject, offering a coherent picture of the latest theories and findings. Together, the volumes will build into an integrated overview of the discipline in its entirety.

Published titles

The Cambridge Handbook of Phonology, edited by Paul de Lacy

The Cambridge Handbook of Linguistic Code-switching, edited by Barbara E. Bullock and Almeida Jacqueline Toribio

The Cambridge Handbook of Child Language, Second Edition, edited by Edith L. Bavin and Letitia Naigles

The Cambridge Handbook of Endangered Languages, edited by Peter K. Austin and Julia Sallabank

The Cambridge Handbook of Sociolinguistics, edited by Rajend Mesthrie

The Cambridge Handbook of Pragmatics, edited by Keith Allan and Kasia M. Jaszczolt

The Cambridge Handbook of Language Policy, edited by Bernard Spolsky

The Cambridge Handbook of Second Language Acquisition, edited by Julia Herschensohn and Martha Young-Scholten

The Cambridge Handbook of Biolinguistics, edited by Cedric Boeckx and Kleanthes K. Grohmann

The Cambridge Handbook of Generative Syntax, edited by Marcel den Dikken

The Cambridge Handbook of Communication Disorders, edited by Louise Cummings

The Cambridge Handbook of Stylistics, edited by Peter Stockwell and Sara Whiteley

The Cambridge Handbook of Linguistic Anthropology, edited by N.J. Enfield, Paul Kockelman and Jack Sidnell

The Cambridge Handbook of English Corpus Linguistics, edited by Douglas Biber and Randi Reppen

The Cambridge Handbook of Bilingual Processing, edited by John W. Schwieter

The Cambridge Handbook of Learner Corpus Research, edited by Sylviane Granger, Gaëtanelle Gilquin and Fanny Meunier

The Cambridge Handbook of English Historical Linguistics, edited by Merja Kytö and Päivi Pahta

The Cambridge Handbook of Linguistic Multicompetence, edited by Li Wei and Vivian Cook

Forthcoming

The Cambridge Handbook of Formal Semantics, edited by Maria Aloni and Paul Dekker

The Cambridge Handbook of Linguistic Typology, edited by Alexandra Aikhenvald and R. M. W. Dixon

The Cambridge Handbook of Areal Linguistics

Edited by
Raymond Hickey

CAMBRIDGE
UNIVERSITY PRESS

CAMBRIDGE
UNIVERSITY PRESS

University Printing House, Cambridge CB2 8BS, United Kingdom

Cambridge University Press is part of the University of Cambridge.

It furthers the University's mission by disseminating knowledge in the pursuit of education, learning, and research at the highest international levels of excellence.

www.cambridge.org
Information on this title: www.cambridge.org/9781107051614

© Cambridge University Press 2017

First published 2017

Printed in the United Kingdom by TJ International Ltd., Padstow, Cornwall

A catalogue record for this publication is available from the British Library.

Library of Congress Cataloging-in-Publication Data
Hickey, Raymond, 1954– editor.
The Cambridge handbook of areal linguistics / edited by Raymond Hickey.
Handbook of areal linguistics
Cambridge, United Kingdom : University Printing House, [2017] |
Series: Cambridge handbooks in language and linguistics
LCCN 2016024593 | ISBN 9781107051614
LCSH: Areal linguistics – Handbooks, manuals, etc. | Linguistic geography – Handbooks, manuals, etc.
LCC P130 .C36 2017 | DDC 409–dc23
LC record available at https://lccn.loc.gov/2016024593

ISBN 978-1-107-05161-4 Hardback

Contents

Figures

Maps

Tables

Contributors

Gregory D. S. Anderson is Lead Scientist and President at the Living Tongues Institute for Endangered Languages and Research Fellow at the University of South Africa (UNISA). His main research interests are linguistic typology and historical linguistics, with particular focus on the languages of Siberia, Papua New Guinea, Africa, and the Munda and Tibeto-Burman languages of India. Recent publications include his monograph on Auxiliary Verb Constructions, as well as articles on Indian linguistics, language and education, and studies on African linguistics, linguistic typology and Oceanic linguistics. Current research projects include descriptive grammars with text collections and dictionaries for the Munda language Gta' of India and the Turkic language Xyzyl of Siberia, a monograph on language extinction, electronic online dictionaries and ethno-biological compendia for several languages of Papua New Guinea.

Umberto Ansaldo is Professor of Linguistics at The University of Hong Kong. His interests include contact linguistics, linguistic typology and language evolution. He specializes in languages of East, South and Southeast Asia as well as pidgin and creole studies. His most recent publication is *Languages in Contact* (with Lisa Lim, 2015).

Johan van der Auwera is Professor of English and General Linguistics at the University of Antwerp in Belgium. His main research interests are the grammar and the semantics of modality, mood, negation and indefiniteness, both from language-specific, areal and typological as well as synchronic and diachronic perspectives. Publications relevant to this chapter include *The Germanic Languages* (with Ekkehard König, 1994), 'English *do*: on the convergence of languages and linguists' (with Inge Genee, *English Language and Linguistics* 6, 283–307, 2002), *The Languages and Linguistics of Europe: A Comprehensive Guide* (with Bernd Kortmann, 2011) and 'Modality and mood in Standard Average

European' in *The Oxford Handbook of Mood and Modality*, edited by Jan Nuyts and Johan van der Auwera (with Daniël Van Olmen, 2016).

Balthasar Bickel holds the Chair of General Linguistics at the University of Zurich. Before this, he was a postdoctoral researcher at the University of California, Berkeley, and then a professor of general linguistics at the University of Leipzig. His core interests are the regional and universal factors shaping the distribution of linguistic diversity over time. For this, Bickel applies methods ranging from the statistical analysis of typological databases and corpora to ethnolinguistic fieldwork and experimental methods. A special focus area is the Himalayas, where Bickel has been engaged in interdisciplinary projects on endangered languages and developing and analysing corpora of them. He has been editor of the journal *Studies of Language* and co-edited the volume *Language Typology and Historical Contingency* (2013).

Juliette Blevins is Professor of Linguistics at The Graduate Center, City University of New York, and was previously a senior research scientist at the Max Planck Institute for Evolutionary Anthropology in Leipzig. Her main research interests are sound patterns and sound change, with a special focus on phonological typology, as detailed in her chapter 'Evolutionary Phonology: A holistic approach to sound change typology', in *The Oxford Handbook of Historical Phonology* (2015). She is currently working on a new reconstruction of Proto-Basque.

Marc Brunelle is Associate Professor in Linguistics at the University of Ottawa. His main research interests are the phonetics and phonology of Southeast Asian languages, with a special emphasis on tones and prosody. His research mostly focuses on Vietnamese and Eastern Cham. His work has been published in a variety of journals including *Journal of Phonetics*, *Phonetica*, *Journal of the Acoustical Society of America*, *Diachronica* and *The Linguistic Review*.

Lyle Campbell (PhD, University of California, Los Angeles), Professor of Linguistics, University of Hawaiʻi, Mānoa, has held appointments in anthropology, behavioural research, Latin American studies, linguistics, and Spanish, and has taught in Australia, Brazil, Canada, Finland, Germany, Mexico, New Zealand and Spain. His specializations are: language documentation, historical linguistics, American Indian languages, and typology. He has published 20 books and about 200 articles, and won the Linguistic Society of America's 'Leonard Bloomfield Book Award' twice, for *American Indian Languages* (1997) and *Historical Syntax in Cross-linguistic Perspective* (with Alice Harris, 1995). His current projects include the *Catalogue of Endangered Languages* (www.endangeredlanguages.com) and documentation of several indigenous languages of Latin America.

Hilary Chappell holds a Research Chair as Professor in Linguistic Typology of East Asian Languages at the Ecole des Hautes Etudes en Sciences Sociales in Paris, an appointment she took up in 2005 after teaching in the Linguistics Department at La Trobe University in Melbourne for 18 years. She was originally awarded her doctoral degree in 1984 by the Australian National University in Canberra for her thesis, *A Semantic Analysis of Passive, Causative and Dative Constructions in Standard Chinese*, and has over 60 publications on Chinese linguistics and typology, with a book, *A Grammar and Lexicon of Hakka* (with Christine Lamarre), and four edited volumes, including *The Grammar of Inalienability* (with William McGregor, 1996), *Sinitic Grammar: Synchronic and Diachronic Perspectives* (2001) and *Diversity in Sinitic Languages* (2015). Her main research interests are (1) rethinking the typological profile of Sinitic languages on the basis of in-depth explorations of their diversity, and (2) studying the diachronic grammar of the Southern Min or Hokkien dialect, using a corpus of late sixteenth and early seventeenth century materials.

Alan Dench is Pro Vice-Chancellor of Humanities at Curtin University, Western Australia. His principal area of expertise lies in the documentation and grammatical description of Australian Aboriginal languages, especially those of Western Australia. He has written grammars of three languages of the Pilbara – Panyjima, Martuthunira and Yingkarta – and is working towards a description of Nyamal. In addition to primary grammatical description he has made contributions to the historical and comparative analysis of Australian languages, and has written in the general area of ethnolinguistics. His work also includes contributions to studies of language contact.

Gerrit J. Dimmendaal is Professor of African Studies at the University of Cologne. His main research interests are the comparative study of African languages, language typology and anthropological linguistics. Recent publications include *Historical Linguistics and the Comparative Study of African Languages* (2011), *Number: Constructions and Semantics. Case Studies from Africa, Amazonia, India and Oceania* (with Anne Storch, 2014) and *The Leopard's Spots: Essays on Language, Cognition and Culture* (2015).

N. J. Enfield is Professor and Chair of Linguistics at the University of Sydney, and a Research Associate at the Max Planck Institute for Psycholinguistics in Nijmegen, the Netherlands. His research on language and cognition in social and cultural context is based on long-term field work in Mainland Southeast Asia, especially Laos. His books include *A Grammar of Lao* (2007), *Dynamics of Human Diversity: The Case of Mainland Southeast Asia* (2011), *The Cambridge Handbook of Linguistic Anthropology* (with Paul Kockelman and Jack Sidnell, 2014) and *Mainland Southeast Asian Languages: The State of the Art* (with Bernard Comrie, 2015).

Patience Epps is Professor of Linguistics at the University of Texas at Austin. Her research focuses on indigenous languages of Amazonia, particularly involving description/documentation and the study of

language contact and change. Recent publications include
A Grammar of Hup (2008) and articles in *Linguistic Typology, International Journal of American Linguistics, Journal of Ethnobiology* and *Journal of Language Contact.*

Anne-Maria Fehn holds a PhD in African Studies from the University of Cologne. She is currently affiliated to the Goethe University of Frankfurt and the Max Planck Institute for the Science of Human History, Jena. She was part of the multidisciplinary research projects 'Kalahari Basin Area' (Humboldt University of Berlin) and 'Towards a multidisciplinary population profiling of southern Angola' (CIBIO-InBIO, Porto). Her research interests include language documentation and areal linguistics. She is currently working on 'Khoisan' languages of Botswana and Angola, and on varieties of Himba and Kuvale spoken in southwestern Angola.

Victor A. Friedman (PhD, University of Chicago, 1975) is Andrew W. Mellon Distinguished Service Professor Emeritus in the Department of Linguistics at the University of Chicago and is president of the US National Committee of the International Association for Southeast European Studies. He has held Guggenheim, Fulbright-Hays, ACLS, IREX, NEH and other fellowships. His publications include *The Grammatical Categories of the Macedonian Indicative* (1977; second revised edition, 2014), *Turkish in Macedonia and Beyond* (2003), *Studies in Albanian and Other Balkan Languages* (2004), *Očerki lakskogo jazyka* (2011) and *Makedonistički Studii* I, II (2011, 2015), as well as more than 200 scholarly articles. His main research interests are grammatical categories and sociolinguistic issues related to contact, standardization, ideology and identity in the languages of the Balkans and the Caucasus.

Paul Geraghty graduated from Cambridge with an MA in Modern Languages (French and German), and earned his PhD from the University of Hawai'i with a dissertation on the history of the Fijian languages. He was Director of the Institute of Fijian Language and Culture in Suva from 1986 to 2001, and is currently Associate Professor in Linguistics at the University of the South Pacific and Adjunct Associate Professor at the University of New England in Australia. He is author and editor of several books, including *The History of the Fijian Languages* (1983), *Fijian Phrasebook* (1994), *Borrowing: A Pacific Perspective* (with Jan Tent, 2004) and *The Macquarie Dictionary of English for the Fiji Islands* (2006), and numerous articles in professional journals and newspapers on Fijian and Pacific languages, culture and history. He is also well known in Fiji as a newspaper columnist and radio and TV presenter.

Rik van Gijn is postdoctoral researcher at the University of Zurich. His main research interests are South American languages, areal typology, morphology and complex sentences. Recent publications include co-edited volumes *Subordination Strategies in Native South American Languages*

(2011) and *Information Structure and Reference Tracking in Complex Sentences* (2014). Current research projects look at areal distributions of subordination strategies and morphological patterns.

Rob Goedemans is presently employed as Information Manager at the Humanities Faculty of Leiden University. He is associated with the Leiden University Centre for Linguistics as a guest researcher. His main research interests are the phonology, phonetics and typology of stress and accent. He is currently involved in a research project, funded by the National Science Foundation, with Harry van der Hulst (University of Connecticut) and Jeff Heinz (University of Delaware). The goal of this project is to merge and enhance two large databases on stress to facilitate the advance of research in stress typology.

Jeff Good is Associate Professor of Linguistics at the University at Buffalo. His research interests centre around comparative Benue-Congo linguistics, morphosyntactic typology, and the documentation of underdescribed Bantoid languages. His recent publications include *The Linguistic Typology of Templates* (2015) and articles in *Language, Morphology, Diachronica, Studies in Language*, the *Journal of Pidgin and Creole Languages*, and *Language Documentation and Conservation*. He is currently heading a research project investigating the relationship between multilingualism and language change in rural areas of the Cameroonian Grassfields.

Anthony P. Grant is Professor of Historical Linguistics and Language Contact at Edge Hill University, having studied at York under Robert Le Page, defending his PhD at the University of Bradford in 1995 on *Agglutinated Nominals in Creole French*, and having previously worked at the Universities of Manchester, Sheffield, Southampton and St Andrews. A native Bradfordian and author of over four dozen books, articles and chapters, his special research interests are Native North American languages, Austronesian languages, Romani, creoles and pidgins, and issues in language documentation. He is editor of the forthcoming *Oxford Handbook of Language Contact*, and is completing a monograph on intimate language contact.

Sven Grawunder has been working since 2005 as a postdoctorate researcher at the Max Planck Institute for Evolutionary Anthropology in Leipzig. His main research topics are phonetic motivations of sound change with an areal perspective, and voice (production and perception) from an evolutionary perspective. Current projects involve the assessment of phonetic speaker variability in processes of neutralization as well as areal phonetic typology of glottalization, ejective stops, germination, palatalization and pharyngealization (mainly) in languages of the Caucasus.

Tom Güldemann is Professor of African Linguistics at the Department of African Studies of the Humboldt University of Berlin. His main research interests are language description and typology as well as historical and areal linguistics. Major publications include *Quotative Indexes in African Languages: A Synchronic and Diachronic Survey* (2008) and *Beyond 'Khoisan': Historical Relations in the Kalahari Basin* (with Anne-Maria Fehn, 2014). Current research projects deal with macro-areal linguistics in Africa in general and the linguistic and population history of southern Africa in particular.

Geoffrey Haig is Professor of General Linguistics at the Institute for Oriental Studies at the University of Bamberg. His main areas of research are the languages of the Middle East with a focus on Iranian languages, areal linguistics, documentary linguistics, and language typology, in particular corpus-based typology.

Harald Hammarström studied Computer Science and Linguistics at the University of Uppsala (1997–2003). He then went on to do a PhD in Computational Linguistics at Chalmers University (2004–2009), focusing on computational models that cater to diverse kinds of languages. In his postdoctoral work he started documentation of the endangered language isolate Mor in Papua, Indonesia. At present he is research staff at the Max Planck Institute for Psycholinguistics in Nijmegen, where he is engaged in empirical and computational approaches to linguistic diversity, genealogical/areal relationships and language universals.

Bernd Heine is Emeritus Professor at the Institute of African Studies (Institut für Afrikanistik), University of Cologne, Germany. He is presently Yunshan Chair Professor at Guangdong University of Foreign Studies, China. His 33 books include *Possession: Cognitive Sources, Forces, and Grammaticalization* (1997), *Auxiliaries: Cognitive Forces and Grammaticalization* (1993), *Cognitive Foundations of Grammar* (1997); with Derek Nurse, *African Languages: An Introduction* (2000), *A Linguistic Geography of Africa* (2008); with Tania Kuteva, *World Lexicon of Grammaticalization* (2002), *Language Contact and Grammatical Change* (2005), *The Changing Languages of Europe* (2006), *The Genesis of Grammar: A Reconstruction* (2007). He has held visiting professorships and appointments in several countries in Europe, Eastern Asia, Australia, Africa, North America and South America. His present main research areas are discourse grammar and grammaticalization theory.

Raymond Hickey is Professor of English Linguistics at the University of Duisburg and Essen. His main research interests are varieties of English, Late Modern English and general questions of language contact, variation and change. Among his recent book publications are *Motives for Language Change* (2003), *A Sound Atlas of Irish English* (2004), *Legacies of Colonial English* (2004), *Dublin English: Evolution and Change* (2005), *Irish English: History and Present-day Forms* (2007), *The Handbook of Language Contact* (2010), *Eighteenth-Century English* (2010), *Varieties of English in Writing* (2010), *Areal Features of the Anglophone World* (2012), *The Sound Structure of Modern Irish* (2014), *A Dictionary of Varieties of English* (2014),

Sociolinguistics in Ireland (2016) and *Listening to the Past: Audio Records of Accents of English* (2016).

Harry van der Hulst is Professor in Linguistics at the University of Connecticut. His main area of research is phonology (of both spoken and sign languages). He is the author of *Syllable Structure and Stress in Dutch* (1984) and *The Phonological Structure of Words: An Introduction* (with Colin Ewen, 2001) as well as some 30 edited books and 160 articles/book chapters. He is also the editor-in-chief of *The Linguistic Review* (since 1990).

Brian D. Joseph is Distinguished University Professor of Linguistics and The Kenneth E. Naylor Professor of South Slavic Linguistics at The Ohio State University, where he has taught since 1979. He received his PhD from Harvard University in 1978, writing his dissertation on syntactic change between Medieval and Modern Greek. Brian Joseph specializes in historical linguistics, Greek linguistics, and Balkan linguistics, and has published extensively in these areas, including the monograph *The Synchrony and Diachrony of the Balkan Infinitive: A Study in Areal, General, and Historical Linguistics* (1983). He served as editor of *Diachronica* from 1999 to 2001 and as editor of *Language* from 2002 to 2008.

Simon van de Kerke is a retired senior lecturer at Leiden University and a specialist in the indigenous languages of Bolivia. He wrote his thesis on the morphological structure of the verb in Bolivian Quechua. Currently he is working on Pukina and Leko in particular. He wrote the grammatical sketches of these languages for the first volume of the *Lenguas de Bolivia* series (edited by Emily Irene Crevels and Pieter Muysken; the sketch of Pukina with Willem Adelaar as co-author).

James Kirby is a Reader in Phonetics at the University of Edinburgh. His research is on the phonetics and phonological underpinnings of sound change, with particular attention to tonogenesis and the phonetic mechanisms involved in the production and perception of tone and voice quality.

Maria Koptjevskaja-Tamm is Professor of Linguistics at Stockholm University. She has published extensively on various aspects of semantically oriented typology, combining synchronic and diachronic approaches across many languages. A large portion of her work focuses on the interplay between lexical and grammatical semantics. An important direction in her work has been areal typology, with the main focus on the European and, particularly, the circum-Baltic languages: see *The Circum-Baltic Languages: Typology and Contact* (with Östen Dahl, 2001). More recent publications include *New Directions in Lexical Typology* (special issue of *Linguistics*, 2013, co-edited with Martine Vanhove) and *The Linguistics of Temperature* (2015).

Bernd Kortmann is Full Professor in English Language and Linguistics at the University of Freiburg, Germany, and Director of the Freiburg

Institute for Advanced Studies. His main research interests include the areal typology of Europe, grammaticalization, language complexity, and grammatical variation across non-standard varieties of English. His publications include four monographs, nine edited volumes, two handbooks, one print and one open-access online atlas on grammatical variation in the Anglophone world (2012/2013), and about 90 research articles and reviews in journals and collective volumes. He is co-editor of the journal *English Language and Linguistics* and co-editor of two international book series.

Olga Krasnoukhova received her PhD at the Centre for Language Studies of Radboud University Nijmegen, the Netherlands. From 2017, she is postdoctoral researcher at the University of Antwerp in Belgium. Her research interests include South American languages, areal typology and morphology. She has publications on noun phrase structure, demonstratives and attributive possession in South American languages. Her current research focus is negation in South American languages.

Nataliya Levkovych is Senior Researcher in General Linguistics at the University of Bremen. Her main research interests are language contact, areal linguistics and typology. Recent publications include *Po-russki in Deutschland: Russisch und Deutsch als Konkurrenten in der Kommunikation mehrsprachiger Gruppen von Personen mit postsowjetischem Hintergrund in Deutschland* (2012).

Henrik Liljegren is Associate Professor in Linguistics at Stockholm University. He is a co-founder of Forum for Language Initiatives, a resource and training centre for the many language communities in Pakistan's mountainous north, where he carried out linguistic fieldwork, primarily in the Indo-Aryan Palula community. His main research interests are areal-linguistic typology, Indo-Iranian languages (in particular in the northwest of the Indian subcontinent), case alignment, phonology and lexicography. He has also been engaged in revitalization efforts, mentoring language activists in local communities. He is presently leading a Swedish Research Council project, investigating language contact and relatedness in the Hindu Kush region.

Rajend Mesthrie is Professor of Linguistics at the University of Cape Town where he teaches sociolinguistics, including language contact and variation. He was head of the Linguistics Section (1998–2009), and currently holds a National Research Foundation research chair in migration, language and social change. He was President of the Linguistics Society of Southern Africa (2002–2009) and co-editor of *English Today* (2008–2012). Amongst his book publications are *Introducing Sociolinguistics* (with Joan Swann, Ana Deumert and William Leap, 2009), *Language in South Africa* (2002), *A Dictionary of South African Indian English* (2010) and *The Cambridge Handbook of Sociolinguistics* (2011).

Luisa Miceli is an Associate Lecturer in Linguistics at the University of Western Australia. Her research interests include methodological issues in historical linguistics, the role of bilingualism in language change, and Australian languages (in particular Pama-Nyungan languages). She is currently collaborating on a research project investigating bilingual-led form differentiation in language contact.

Lev Michael is Associate Professor of Linguistics at the University of California, Berkeley. With a methodological grounding in language documentation, his research focuses on the sociocultural dimensions of grammar and language use, typology, language contact in South America, and the historical linguistics of Arawak, Tupí-Guaraní, and Zaparoan languages. His recent publications include *Evidentiality in Interaction* (with Janis Nuckolls, 2012) and *Negation in Arawak Languages* (with Tania Granadillo, 2014).

Marianne Mithun is Professor of Linguistics at the University of California, Santa Barbara. Her main research interests are morphology, syntax, discourse, prosody, and their interrelations; language contact and language change; typology and universals; language documentation; North American Indian linguistics; and Austronesian linguistics. Among her major publications is *The Languages of Native North America* (1999).

Pieter Muysken is Professor of Linguistics at Radboud University Nijmegen, the Netherlands. His main research interests are language contact, Andean linguistics, and Creole studies. Recent publications include *The Native Languages of South America: Origins, Development, Typology* (with Loretta O'Connor, 2014) and *Surviving Middle Passage: The West Africa–Surinam Sprachbund* (with Norval Smith, 2014). Earlier books include *The Languages of the Andes* (Willem Adelaar with Pieter Muysken 2004).

John Peterson is Professor in General Linguistics at the University of Kiel in Germany. His areas of specialization include language description, especially with respect to the Munda and Indo-Aryan languages of eastern-central India, multilingualism and linguistic theory. He is editor of the series *Brill's Studies in South and Southwestern Asian Languages* (BSSAL) and is a member of the editorial board of the *Journal of South Asian Languages and Linguistics*.

Keren Rice is University Professor and Canada Research Chair in Linguistics and Aboriginal Studies at the University of Toronto. Her major research interests are in phonology (with a focus on markedness), morphology, indigenous languages of North America (in particular Dene [Athabaskan] languages), and fieldwork. Recent publications include papers on accent systems in North American indigenous languages, accent and language contact in North America, derivational morphology in Athabaskan languages, and sounds in grammar writing. She is one of the co-editors of the *Blackwell Companion to Phonology*.

Martine Robbeets is Associate Professor of Japanese Linguistics at Leiden University. Her main research interests are historical comparative linguistics, areal linguistics, diachronic typology, grammaticalization theory, morphology and interdisciplinary research of linguistic prehistory. Recent publications include *Diachrony of Verb Morphology: Japanese and the Other Transeurasian Languages* (2015) and various edited volumes such as *Copies versus Cognates in Bound Morphology* (with Lars Johanson, 2012), *Shared Grammaticalization* (with Hubert Cuyckens, 2013) and *Paradigm Change* (with Walter Bisang, 2014). Since September 2015 she has been conducting an interdisciplinary research project on the dispersal of the Transeurasian languages, funded by a Consolidator Grant from the European Research Council.

Malcolm Ross is Emeritus Professor in Linguistics at the Australian National University, where he held various positions from 1986 until his retirement in 2007. His main research interests are the histories of the languages of New Guinea and the Pacific, the study of language contact, and the methodologies of historical linguistics. Recent articles have appeared in *Oceanic Linguistics*, the *Journal of Historical Linguistics* and the *Journal of Language Contact*. He is co-editor with Andrew Pawley and Meredith Osmond of the volumes (four to date) of *The Lexicon of Proto Oceanic*. Current research projects include the Oceanic Lexicon Project (reconstructing the lexicon of the language ancestral to the Oceanic group of Austronesian languages) and reconstructing the history of the Trans New Guinea family of Papuan languages.

Verena Schröter studied English language and literature and philosophy at the University of Freiburg, and completed her MA in 2010. She is a part-time lecturer at the English Department of the University of Freiburg, and is currently working on her PhD, exploring morphosyntactic variation in Southeast Asian varieties of English.

Thomas Stolz is Full Professor of General and Comparative Linguistics at the University of Bremen (Germany). His main research interests are areal linguistics, language contact, morphology and language typology. Recent publications include *Competing Comparative Constructions in Europe* (2013), *The Crosslinguistics of Zero-marking of Spatial Relations* (with Sander Lestrade and Christel Stolz, 2014), and articles in *Linguistics, Studies in Language*, and *Sprachtypologie und Universalienforschung*. Current research projects include the areal linguistics and typology of spatial interrogatives as well as the morphosyntax of place names in cross-linguistic perspective.

Alan Timberlake is Professor of Slavic Linguistics and Director of the East Central European Center at Columbia University. A long-term research concern of his is the integration of sociolinguistic/communicative approaches and structural analysis. Recent publications include two articles on historical syntax for the volume on Slavic languages in the series *Handbücher zur Sprach- und Kommunikationswissenschaft* and three studies on the legends of Wenceslaus of Bohemia.

Daniël Van Olmen is lecturer in historical linguistics and linguistic typology at Lancaster University. His main research interests are tense, mood, modality and pragmatic markers from a West Germanic, Standard Average European and typological perspective.

Preface

The current book aims at presenting a focused and clearly structured volume on a topical field of linguistics, that of areal linguistics. This relates to many other fields such as language contact, typology and historical linguistics, to mention the three most directly involved. However, areal linguistics is more than each of these, and unifies research into how languages come to share features diachronically and the manner in which this takes place. Areal linguistics is thus both an intersection between different subfields of linguistics and a domain of research in its own right.

For the current book a team of forty-seven scholars came together to discuss issues surrounding areal linguistics in their particular fields of expertise. The editor is grateful to these colleagues for agreeing to contribute to this volume, helping to make it a comprehensive and linguistically insightful work on a topical subject in present-day linguistics.

In the preparation of this book Helen Barton, commissioning editor for linguistics at Cambridge University Press, was a great source of assistance and encouragement and ready to answer any questions which arose in the course of the project, so my thanks also go to her and her colleagues at the press, as well as to my copy-editor Glennis Starling, who all worked as a team to transform the manuscripts of authors into finished products in print.

1

Areas, Areal Features and Areality

Raymond Hickey

1.1 Introduction

The clustering of linguistic features in geographically delimited areas has long been recognized by researchers on a wide range of languages. In the course of the twentieth century this recognition gave rise to the notion of 'linguistic area' (Emeneau 1980; Matras, McMahon and Vincent 2006), a region in which shared features among a number of languages are found with more than chance probability. The reason for such sharing lies in contact[1] between speakers whose own language comes under the influence of others in their environment. Admittedly, this view is simplistic, but it is useful as a first approximation because it focuses attention on speaker contact. Of course, there are many contact scenarios and many situations of bi- or multilingualism (Field 2002) in which individuals speak different languages to varying extents. In such cases the contact is speaker-internal, so to speak.

1.1.1 Areal Linguistics and Linguistic Areas

The term 'linguistic area' is a useful conceptual aid, and in the early days of research it helped to heighten scholars' awareness of shared structural features among not necessarily related languages in circumscribed geographical areas. However, the term came to dominate research

---

[1] There is a wealth of literature on language contact, much of which is recent, e.g. Adamou (2016), Bakker and Matras (2013), Deumert and Durrleman (2006), Gilbers, Nerbonne and Schaeken (2000), Goebl, Nelde, Stary and Wölck (1996), Grant (in press), Hickey (2010), Matras (2009), Moravcsik (1978), Myers-Scotton (2002), Siemund and Kintana (2008), Thomason (1997, 2001), Winford (2003, 2005, 2013). A well-known monograph on language contact is Weinreich (1953). Van Coetsem (2000) is a more recent study offering a classification of contact. The following is a representative selection of works dealing with language contact in specific language scenarios: Aikhenvald (2002), Ansaldo (2009), Clyne (2003), Dutton and Tryon (1994), Filppula, Klemola and Paulasto (2008), Hickey (1995), Isaac (2003), Johanson (2002), Loveday (1996), Matras (1995), Mesthrie (1992), Siegel (2000), Silva-Corvalán (1994).

(Campbell 2006), so that scholars often felt that a binary decision had to be made as to whether a given geographical area could be classified as a linguistic area or not. This concern has not always proved to be fruitful. What can be more significant is research into the forces and mechanisms which lead to languages in a given area coming to share features. This approach would highlight the scholarly concern with areality, that is, the areal concentration of linguistic features. How this concentration emerges and continues to develop is centre stage, not the attempt to attach the label 'linguistic area' to any given region.

1.1.2   Areal Concentrations and Geography

For areal concentrations to arise, many centuries of prolonged contact and population interaction are usually required, especially as the common features of such areas usually belong to the closed classes of the languages involved, typically to the phonology and morphosyntax (Matras and Sakel 2007). Furthermore, the languages of a putative area show not only internal coherence but also recognizable external boundaries with languages immediately outside the area. So feature clustering is both positive within an area and negative vis-à-vis adjoining regions. The non-linguistic characteristics of an area involve its geography: regions bounded by mountain ranges, large rivers, the sea on two or three sides (peninsulas) are all candidates for locations with areal concentrations of linguistic features.

   The number of features which an area shares is a much-discussed matter in linguistic typology (Campbell, Chapter 2, this volume; Croft 1990; Haspelmath, König, Oesterreicher and Raible 2001; Hickey 2001, 2003a). However, the number does not need to be great, and there are cases where single features are involved. In the main one can contend that the fewer the features shared in an area the more these must be typologically unusual (statistically rare across the world's languages) for them to be areally significant.

1.1.3   Areality, Contact and Language Change

An areal view of a region is a description of its language configuration at a certain point in time. Areal considerations become dynamic once processes of language change[2] are considered. Generally in studies of change there is a tension between possible internal versus external factors (Hickey 2012). Some authors see internal causes as primary unless there is no other possible account, in which case contact may then be appealed to; see Lass

---

[2] Change as a result of contact is treated in virtually all textbooks on language change. The following works are examples of studies in which contact-induced change occupies a central position: Jones and Esch (2002), Mufwene (2008), Nichols (1992), Sankoff (2002), Trudgill (1986).

and Wright (1986) as a clear demonstration of this stance. Other authors, e.g. Vennemann (2002), see contact, i.e. external causes, as equally possible for change and by no means secondary to internal causes. The weighting of internal and external factors in contact and change has consequences for the classification of languages: see McMahon (2013). It can also be significant in accounting for how not just single features but structural patterns arose in languages, as in the discussion of possible contact-induced grammaticalization (Heine and Kuteva 2003, 2005). However, not all discussions of contact-induced change involve an areal dimension. For instance, the literature on creolization and contact – e.g. Holm (2004), Huber and Velupillai (2007), McWhorter (2000), Migge (2003), Siegel (1987), Thomason and Kaufman (1988) – does not generally include considerations of areality.

1.1.4 The Dynamics of Areality

The basis for areality is obviously language contact, which leads to different degrees of feature transfer between languages. Certain developments in a language, and the community which speaks it, can be viewed as areality-enhancing and others as areality-diminishing. For instance, accommodation (Trudgill 1986) is areality-enhancing but dissociation (Hickey 2013) is areality-diminishing.

Dynamics of areality

Areality-enhancing
accommodation during contact (without shift)
increase in bi-/multilingualism with sharing
feature transfer during language shift leading to sharing across at least two
 languages

Areality-diminishing
dissociation between languages or varieties
decrease in bi-/multilingualism with loss of shared features
processes of standardization or de-creolization
importation of outside features to only some of the languages/varieties in
 an area

1.1.5 Changes in Areality

The degree of areality within a region is not constant. The processes outlined above can lead to changes in the level of areality. This means that investigations of putative feature-sharing areas at present are just snapshots in a historical development which began in the past, in most cases in the deep past. And if a region has a high level of areality this does not mean that it will maintain this level: see the areality-diminishing processes listed above.

Figures 1.1–1.4 offer more details of some of the processes which can lead to a change in the areality of a region containing different languages, whether genetically related or not.

1.2 Issues in Areal Linguistics

Linguistic levels are affected to different degrees in regions sharing languages. It would seem that grammar is least affected in areal contact because it is the core of a language and consists of closed classes acquired in early childhood: see Figure 1.5. However, as researchers on language contact have pointed out (Hickey 2010; Thomason 2001), there is no part of a language which cannot in principle be borrowed by speakers of another language. The details of this borrowing process, above all whether between speakers or internally for single bilingual speakers (Matras 2009), is a matter of discussion in the literature.

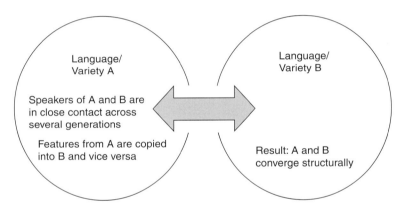

Figure 1.1 Increase in areality due to close contact

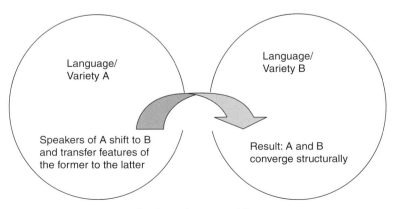

Figure 1.2 Increase in areality due to language shift

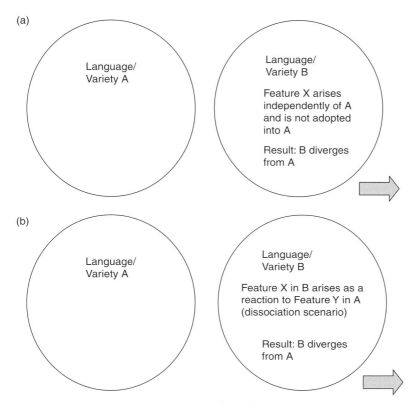

Figure 1.3 Feature development: decrease in areality

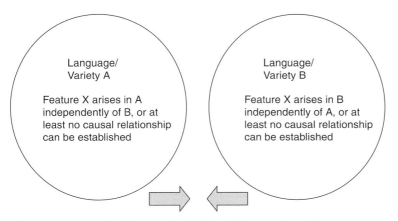

Figure 1.4 Feature development: (coincidental) increase in areality

1.2.1 Levels of Language

Sound variation can be used to differentiate quite small areas, as opposed to grammatical variation which tends to be typical of larger regions. The reason is probably that phonetic variation is immediately available for

Levels most affected

Vocabulary (loanwords, phrases)
Sounds (present in loanwords)
Speech habits (general pronunciation, suprasegmentals [stress, intonation])
Sentence structure, word-order
Grammar (morphology: inflections)

Levels least affected

Figure 1.5 Levels of language and borrowing

assessment in anyone's speech whereas grammatical features might not occur in any given stretch of discourse and so are not so suitable for fine differentiation, either spatially or socially.

The development of inflectional morphology is generally a community-internal phenomenon which takes several centuries to mature: consider the extensive morphology in many Indo-European languages. With adult language contact, morphological features are not usually transferred unless they are transparent, productive and easily separable from lexical bases. However, with child language learners, morphology can be borrowed with ease.

Syntactic transfer across speech communities can result via bilingualism and/or language shift, but whether it can result from adult contact among speakers of different languages is disputed in the literature; see the discussion of the rise of the progressive in English (Hickey, Chapter 10, this volume). The structures in question may be those used to express the same category or which represent the same organizational principle in two or more languages but where there is a difference in exponence, such as the change from one canonical word order to another, e.g. the rise of SOV in a language which previously had VSO as basic order. Probably the earliest example of contact-induced syntactic change shows just this: despite the posited verb-initial syntax of Proto-Semitic, Akkadian shows verb-final position, which is assumed to be an areal influence from Sumerian (Zólyomi 2012: 402). Syntactic transfer is also common in cases of language shift, where the original language of a speech community is abandoned and (nearly) all the speakers shift to the new language within a fairly well delimited period of time, a few centuries at most. In such situations speakers search for equivalents to structures in the target language which they are familiar with from their native language (Hickey 2001).

As an open class which speakers are consciously aware of, the lexicon is usually the first to experience transfer in adult language contact. All languages with a documented history exhibit lexical borrowings in their textual record, although the amount of borrowing can vary. For instance, Irish throughout its history has experienced many borrowings from Latin, Old Norse, Anglo-Norman and English, whereas Icelandic has relatively few borrowings (Kvaran 2004: 145–149).

There is, however, an important caveat here: if the speakers of languages in contact have a negative attitude towards each other, then lexical borrowings become unlikely. But if the contact is very prolonged then structural transfer from closed classes, which show less conscious awareness among speakers, can occur: see the examples discussed in Epps and Michael (Chapter 32, this volume).

1.3 Structure of the Current Volume

Part I of this volume is concerned with general issues in areal linguistics. The opening chapter by Lyle Campbell, 'Why is it so hard to define a linguistic area?', considers the pitfalls in defining linguistic areas and discusses a large number of suggested areas while examining the features they contain and the languages spoken there.

In his contribution 'Areas and universals', Balthasar Bickel addresses the relationship of language universals to linguistic areas. The former has been researched intensively in recent years (Comrie and Dahl 1984; Good 2008; Mairal and Gil 2006), and Bickel emphasizes the necessity for this research to be coupled to areal linguistics in order to increase the linguistic reliability of statements concerning areal features.[3]

In the field of areal linguistics, the Balkans is regarded as one of the classic cases of a linguistic area (Joseph 1983). In their chapter 'Reassessing sprachbunds: A view from the Balkans', Victor A. Friedman and Brian D. Joseph re-examine the evidence put forward for the Balkans and discuss the general relevance of these arguments. They also consider what features can be regarded as defining for a linguistic area, and in what combinations.

The level of phonology, both segmental and suprasegmental, is catered for in three chapters. The first, by Juliette Blevins, 'Areal sound patterns: From perceptual magnets to stone soup', highlights the similarities between internal mechanisms for first language acquisition of phonology and external mechanisms by which sounds are borrowed and diffuse areally.

The chapter by Thomas Stolz and Nataliya Levkovych, 'Convergence and divergence in the phonology of the languages of Europe', reports on a large-scale typological study of sound systems across Europe and parts of Western Asia with a view to recognizing and accounting for macro-patterns in sound systems, especially those which are probably triggered by language contact.

Suprasegmental phonology and contact (Clements and Gooden 2009) is addressed by Harry van der Hulst, Rob Goedemans and Keren Rice in their

---

[3] There is also a body of literature on 'vernacular universals' in the context of English studies, so-called Angloversals (Filppula, Klemola and Paulasto 2009).

contribution 'Word prominence and areal linguistics'. The authors present three case studies and attempt to link the observations made in their attested data with those gleaned in second language phonology and loan phonology studies.

The areal linguistics of semantics is covered by Maria Koptjevskaja-Tamm and Henrik Liljegren in their chapter 'Semantic patterns from an areal perspective', in which they offer a typological classification of areal semantics determined on the basis of a number of lexico-semantic databases.

Contact studies in the European context are well established (Dahl and Koptjevskaja-Tamm 2001; Fisiak 1995; Kastovsky and Mettinger 2001; Ureland and Broderick 1991), and the chapters presented at the outset of Part II examine and re-evaluate insights and conclusions reached about the areality of the Germanic and the Slavic languages. Johan van der Auwera and Daniël Van Olmen, in 'The Germanic languages and areal linguistics', examine the Germanic languages as a whole, focusing on linguistic contacts with non-Germanic languages. The areality of English is the concern of both Raymond Hickey's chapter on 'Britain and Ireland' as well as Bernd Kortmann and Verena Schröter's contribution on 'Varieties of English'. The approaches are somewhat different. Hickey looks at the diachrony of English in Britain and Ireland and considers historical contact with Celtic in some detail, while Kortmann and Schröter cast a much wider net and classify the varieties of English worldwide from a typological perspective. The two chapters thus provide complementary views of developments within the English language.

Alan Timberlake's chapter 'Slavic languages' considers the large family of Slavic languages with regard to the various types and periods of contact they experienced over their long recorded history. Here the role of external history and social structure on language development is given particular attention.

The Caucasus and Western Asia (Haig and Khan 2015) are treated in two dedicated chapters: 'The Caucasus' by Sven Grawunder and 'Western Asia: East Anatolia as a transition zone' by Geoffrey Haig. Both authors offer fine-grained presentations of language contact and contact-induced change in their respective areas in the modern era, and present classifications of highly complex language regions based on the results of their research.

The areal linguistics of Africa (Güldemann 2016) begins with the overview chapter by Bernd Heine and Anne-Maria Fehn, 'An areal view of Africa', in which the authors deal with various classification proposals and assess their merit in the light of the most recent research into Africa, especially from a typological perspective. This approach is continued by Gerrit Dimmendaal in 'Areal contact in Nilo-Saharan', where he looks at morphological structures, notably case systems, to attempt a classification of this large phylum in Eastern and Central Africa. The largest language group in Africa is scrutinized in Jeff Good's chapter 'Niger-Congo languages'. In particular he addresses questions concerning the internal composition of the family and the proposals for various subgroupings. He stresses the importance of understanding the relationship between Niger-Congo cultures and the Niger-Congo languages.

Southern Africa is the subject of two chapters. The first is 'The Kalahari Basin area as a "sprachbund" before the Bantu expansion', by Tom Güldemann and Anne-Maria Fehn, which examines the evidence for linguistic groupings in the Kalahari Basin, which stretches from southern Namibia through Botswana to southwest Zambia, before the Bantu migrations into southern Africa which affected the distribution of pre-Bantu languages in the region due to contact and mixture. The second chapter, 'South Africa and areal linguistics' by Rajend Mesthrie, considers both native Bantu languages of South Africa and the two major European descendant languages, English and Afrikaans, and considers the possible cases of transfer across linguistic boundaries in South Africa among these languages in the centuries of the colonial and the more recent post-colonial period.

South Asia (Hock and Bashir 2016) is represented in this volume by two chapters. The first, by John Peterson, is 'Jharkhand as a "linguistic area"', in which he investigates contact across the Indo-Aryan/Munda family border. The observable convergence is not just in the lexical area but encompasses many features of morphosyntax as well. In 'Sri Lanka and South India', Umberto Ansaldo investigates the predominance of a number of typological profiles for languages in different parts of the world and then applies the insights from this research to the linguistic situation in Sri Lanka.

The region of northern Siberia, stretching to the far east of Northern Asia, is the topic of Martine Robbeets' chapter on 'The Transeurasian languages', in which she takes a fresh look at areality over this vast area by examining the realization of a set of 27 features which show parallels among languages as far apart as Uralic in the west and Nivkh and Ainu in the east. A specific linguistic subsystem, that of case-marking, is examined by Gregory Anderson for languages of Northeastern Siberia – 'The changing profile of case marking in the Northeastern Siberia area'. He notes that the system of case-marked clausal subordination is gradually being replaced by another case system under the influence of contact with Russian.

The main language families of China are outlined in Hilary Chappell's 'Languages of China in their East and Southeast Asian context', in which she examines the areal linguistics of these large groupings. She then scrutinizes three small clusters in which contact and transfer from non-Sinitic languages have occurred.

The convergence experienced by the languages of Southeast Asia is examined in the chapter by N. J. Enfield, 'Language in the Mainland Southeast Asia area'. He reports on the confirmation of standard wisdoms concerning these mainland languages, e.g. their structural similarities, as well as on newer research which challenges orthodox views such as how the noted convergence took place during historical social contact. A more specific investigation is offered by James Kirby and Marc Brunelle, who look at phonological tone in the same group of languages in their chapter 'Southeast Asian tone in areal perspective'. They describe the diverse kinds of tone systems found in Mainland Southeast Asia and question whether tone is indeed a strong indicator of convergence in this area.

Australia and the Pacific is dealt with in a series of four chapters. The first of these, 'The areal linguistics of Australia' by Luisa Miceli and Alan Dench, looks at standard views on areal groupings in Australia against the background of their own detailed research in the Pilbara region of Western Australia. This work confirms the complex interaction of genetic relationship and language contact in the areal settings of Australia.

An in-depth examination of classification proposals for the languages of New Guinea (Palmer 2015) and some neighbouring regions is given by Malcolm Ross in 'Languages of the New Guinea Region'. He specifically addresses the question of whether a typological profile can be established for New Guinea languages, or any subsection of these, which could account for structural similarities over and beyond those established by phylogenetic connections. By looking at a predetermined set of variables across a wide range of languages, Ross was able to establish that while the occurrence of variables was not always in geographically contiguous areas, nonetheless constellations of variable values were recognized which were hardly the outcome of chance.

Languages from two of the major cultural zones of the island Pacific are examined in two subsequent chapters. In 'Languages of Eastern Melanesia' Paul Geraghty examines the historical evidence for Melanesian languages and for Papuan languages in the area, and considers the complex landscape of present-day Vanuatu and other locations such as the Solomon Islands and New Caledonia. The linguistic features he scrutinized cross-linguistically include serial verbs and numeral systems. In 'The Western Micronesian sprachbund' Anthony Grant examines the field of lexical borrowings, and classifies the languages of the area as lexical donors and lexical recipients, or indeed both.

The areal linguistics of the Americas is covered by the final three chapters. The first is 'Native North American languages', a tour de force by Marianne Mithun in which she brings her great expertise in this area to bear on issues of classification and cross-influence in a vast and complex language region. No less complex, but with different ecologies, are the areas of South America, which are examined in two dedicated chapters. 'The areal linguistics of Amazonia', by Patience Epps and Lev Michael, considers the role of languages functioning as linguae francae and examines various contact zones in South America, dealing with language shift and borrowing which has led to grammatical diffusion (Aikhenvald and Dixon 2001), often of bound morphology. The final chapter is 'Linguistic areas, linguistic convergence and river systems in South America' by Rik van Gijn, Harald Hammarström, Simon van de Kerke, Olga Krasnoukhova and Pieter Muysken, who consider the role played by the large rivers of South America in determining the linguistic landscape of this continent, especially where rivers have led to contact and convergence.

1.4   Outlook

The diversity of contributions in the present volume attests to the vitality of the field of areal linguistics. Furthermore, the range of perspectives on data is wide indeed and the interpretations of features found in these data are various, showing how actively issues of language contact and development in geographically defined regions are discussed in the scholarly community today. It is hoped that this volume will add to the knowledge and insights in areal linguistics and provide an impetus for further research in this field in the foreseeable future.

References

Adamou, Evangelia, 2016. *A Corpus-Driven Approach to Language Contact: Endangered Languages in a Comparative Perspective*. Berlin: de Gruyter Mouton.

Aikhenvald, Alexandra Y., 2002. *Language Contact in Amazonia*. Oxford: Oxford University Press.

Aikhenvald, Alexandra Y. and Robert M. W. Dixon (eds), 2001. *Areal Diffusion and Genetic Inheritance*. Oxford: Oxford University Press.

Ansaldo, Umberto, 2009. *Contact Languages: Ecology and Evolution in Asia*. Cambridge University Press.

Bakker, Peter and Yaron Matras (eds), 2013. *Contact Languages: A Comprehensive Guide*. Berlin: de Gruyter Mouton.

Campbell, Lyle, 2006. Areal linguistics: A closer scrutiny. In Matras, McMahon and Vincent (eds), pp. 1–31.

Clements, J. Clancy and Shelome Gooden (eds), 2009. *Language Change in Contact Languages: Grammatical and Prosodic Considerations*. Special issue of *Studies in Language* 33 (2). Amsterdam: John Benjamins.

Clyne, Michael, 2003. *Dynamics of Language Contact: English and Immigrant Languages*. Cambridge: Cambridge University Press.

Comrie, Bernard and Östen Dahl (eds), 1984. *Explanations for Language Universals*. Berlin: Mouton.

Croft, William, 1990. *Typology and Universals*. Cambridge: Cambridge University Press.

Dahl, Östen and Maria Koptjevskaja-Tamm (eds), 2001. *The Circum-Baltic Languages: Typology and Contact*. Amsterdam: John Benjamins.

Deumert, Ana and Stephanie Durrleman (eds), 2006. *Structure and Variation in Language Contact*. Amsterdam: John Benjamins.

Deutscher, Guy, 2007. *Syntactic Change in Akkadian: The Evolution of Sentential Complementation*. Oxford: Oxford University Press.

Dutton, Thomas E. and Darrell T. Tryon (eds), 1994. *Language Contact and Change in the Austronesian World*. Berlin: Mouton de Gruyter.

Emeneau, Murray B., 1980. *Language and Linguistic Area*, edited by Anwar S. Dil. Stanford, CA: Stanford University Press.

Field, Frederic W., 2002. *Linguistic Borrowing in Bilingual Contexts*. Amsterdam: John Benjamins.

Filppula, Markku, Juhani Klemola and Heli Paulasto, 2008. *English and Celtic in Contact*. London: Routledge.

Filppula, Markku, Juhani Klemola and Heli Paulasto (eds), 2009. *Vernacular Universals and Language Contacts: Evidence from Varieties of English and Beyond*. London: Routledge.

Fisiak, Jacek (ed.), 1995. *Language Change under Contact Conditions*. Berlin: Mouton de Gruyter.

Gilbers, Dicky G., John Nerbonne and Jos Schaeken (eds), 2000. *Languages in Contact*. Amsterdam: Rodopi.

Goebl, Hans, Peter H. Nelde, Zdenek Stary and Wolfgang Wölck (eds), 1996. *Kontaktlinguistik / Contact Linguistics / Linguistique de Contact*, two volumes. Berlin: Mouton de Gruyter.

Good, Jeff (ed.), 2008. *Linguistic Universals and Language Change*. Oxford: Oxford University Press.

Grant, Anthony, in press. *The Oxford Handbook of Language Contact*. Oxford: Oxford University Press.

Güldemann, Tom (ed.), 2016. *The Language and Linguistics of Africa*. Berlin: de Gruyter Mouton.

Haig, Geoffrey and Geoffrey Khan (eds), 2015. *The Language and Linguistics of Western Asia*. Berlin: de Gruyter Mouton.

Haspelmath, Martin, Ekkehard König, Wulf Oesterreicher and Wolfgang Raible (eds), 2001. *Language Typology and Language Universals*. Berlin: de Gruyter.

Heine, Bernd and Tania Kuteva, 2003. On contact-induced grammaticalization. *Studies in Language* 27: 529–572.

Heine, Bernd and Tania Kuteva, 2005. *Language Contact and Grammatical Change*. Cambridge: Cambridge University Press.

Hickey, Raymond, 1995. An assessment of language contact in the development of Irish English. In Fisiak (ed.), pp. 109–130.

Hickey, Raymond, 2001. Language contact and typological difference: Transfer between Irish and Irish English. In Kastovsky and Mettinger (eds), pp. 131–169.

Hickey, Raymond, 2003a. Reanalysis and typological change. In Hickey (ed.), pp. 258–278.

Hickey, Raymond (ed.), 2003b. *Motives for Language Change*. Cambridge: Cambridge University Press.

Hickey, Raymond (ed.), 2010. *The Handbook of Language Contact*. Malden, MA: Wiley Blackwell.

Hickey, Raymond, 2012. Internally and externally motivated language change. In Juan Manuel Hernández-Campoy and Juan Camilo Conde-Silvestre (eds), *The Handbook of Historical Sociolinguistics*, pp. 401–421. Malden, MA: Wiley-Blackwell.

Hickey, Raymond, 2013. Supraregionalisation and dissociation. In J. K. Chambers and Natalie Schilling (eds), *The Handbook of Language Variation and Change*, second edition, pp. 537–554. Wiley-Blackwell.

Hock, Hans Heinrich and Elena Bashir (eds), 2016. *The Language and Linguistics of South Asia*. Berlin: de Gruyter Mouton.

Holm, John, 2004. *Languages in Contact: The Partial Restructuring of Vernaculars*. Cambridge: Cambridge University Press.

Huber, Magnus and Viveka Velupillai (eds), 2007. *Synchronic and Diachronic Perspectives on Contact Languages*. Amsterdam: John Benjamins.

Isaac, Graham, 2003. Diagnosing the symptoms of contact: Some Celtic–English case histories. In Hildegard L. C. Tristram (ed.), *The Celtic Englishes III*, pp. 46–64. Heidelberg: Winter.

Johanson, Lars, 2002. *Structural Factors in Turkic Language Contacts*. London: Curzon.

Jones, Mari C. and Edith Esch (eds), 2002. *Language Change: The Interplay of Internal, External and Extra-linguistic Factors*. Berlin: Mouton de Gruyter.

Joseph, Brian D., 1983. *The Balkan Infinitive*. Cambridge: Cambridge University Press.

Kastovsky, Dieter and Arthur Mettinger (eds), 2001. *Language Contact in the History of English*. Berlin: Mouton de Gruyter.

Kvaran, Guðrún, 2004. English influence on the Icelandic lexicon. *Nordic Journal of English Studies* 3 (2): 142–152.

Lass, Roger and Susan Wright, 1986. Endogeny vs. contact: Afrikaans influence on South African English. *English World-Wide* 7: 201–223.

Loveday, Leo J., 1996. *Language Contact in Japan: A Socio-linguistic History*. Oxford: Clarendon Press.

Mairal, Ricardo and Juana Gil (eds), 2006. *Linguistic Universals*. Cambridge: Cambridge University Press.

Matras, Yaron (ed.), 1995. *Romani in Contact: The History, Structure and Sociology of a Language*. Amsterdam: John Benjamins.

Matras, Yaron, 2009. *Language Contact*. Cambridge: Cambridge University Press.

Matras, Yaron, April McMahon and Nigel Vincent (eds), 2006. *Linguistic Areas: Convergence in Historical and Typological Perspective*. Basingstoke, UK: Palgrave Macmillan.

Matras, Yaron and Jeanette Sakel (eds), 2007. *Grammatical Borrowing in Cross-linguistic Perspective*. Berlin: Mouton de Gruyter.

McMahon, April, 2013. Issues in the genetic classification of contact languages. In Bakker and Matras (eds), pp. 333–362.

McWhorter, John H. (ed.), 2000. *Language Change and Language Contact in Pidgins and Creoles*. Amsterdam: John Benjamins.

Mesthrie, Rajend, 1992. *English in Language Shift: The History, Structure and Sociolinguistics of South African Indian English*. Cambridge: Cambridge University Press.

Migge, Bettina, 2003. *Creole Formation as Language Contact*. Amsterdam: John Benjamins.

Moravcsik, Edith A., 1978. Language contact. In Joseph H. Greenberg (ed.), *Universals of Human Language,* vol. 1: *Method and Theory*, pp. 94–122. Stanford, CA: Stanford University Press.

Mufwene, Salikoko S., 2008. *Language Evolution: Contact, Competition and Change*. London: Continuum International Publishing Group.

Myers-Scotton, Carol, 2002. *Contact Linguistics: Bilingual Encounters and Grammatical Outcomes*. Oxford: Oxford University Press.

Nichols, Johanna, 1992. *Linguistic Diversity in Space and Time*. Chicago: University of Chicago Press.

Palmer, Bill (ed.), 2015. *The Language and Linguistics of the New Guinea Area*. Berlin: de Gruyter Mouton.

Sankoff, Gillian, 2002. Linguistic outcomes of language contact. In J. K. Chambers et al. (eds), *The Handbook of Language Variation and Change*, first edition, pp. 638–668. Oxford: Blackwell.

Siegel, Jeff, 1987. *Language Contact in a Plantation Environment*. Cambridge: Cambridge University Press.

Siegel, Jeff, 2000. Substrate influence in Hawai'i Creole English. *Language in Society* 29: 197–236.

Siemund, Peter and Noemi Kintana (eds), 2008. *Language Contact and Contact Languages*. Amsterdam: John Benjamins.

Silva-Corvalán, Carmen, 1994. *Language Contact and Change: Spanish in Los Angeles*. Oxford: Clarendon Press.

Thomason, Sarah G. (ed.), 1997. *Contact Languages: A Wider Perspective*. Amsterdam: John Benjamins.

Thomason, Sarah G., 2001. *Language Contact: An Introduction*. Edinburgh: Edinburgh University Press.

Thomason, Sarah G. and Terrence Kaufman, 1988. *Language Contact, Creolization, and Genetic Linguistics*. Berkeley, CA: University of California Press.

Trudgill, Peter, 1986. *Dialects in Contact*. Oxford: Blackwell.

Ureland, P. Sture and George Broderick (eds), 1991. *Language Contact in the British Isles: Proceedings of the 8th International Symposium on Language Contact in Europe*. Tübingen: Niemeyer.

Van Coetsem, Frans, 2000. *A General and Unified Theory of the Transmission Process in Language Contact*. Heidelberg: Winter.

Vennemann, Theo, 2002. Semitic > Celtic > English: The transitivity of language contact. In Markku Filppula, Juhani Klemola and Heli Pitkänen (eds), *The Celtic Roots of English*, pp. 295–330. Studies in Language, vol. 37. University of Joensuu: Faculty of Humanities.

Weinreich, Uriel, 1953. *Languages in Contact*. The Hague: Mouton.

Winford, Donald, 2003. *An Introduction to Contact Linguistics*. Oxford: Blackwell.

Winford, Donald, 2005. Contact-induced changes: Classification and processes. *Diachronica* 22 (2): 373–427.

Winford, Donald, 2013. Social factors in contact languages. In Bakker and Matras (eds), pp. 363–416.

Zólyomi, Gábor, 2012. Akkadian and Sumerian language contact. In Stefan Weninger, Geoffrey Khan, Michael P. Streck and Janet C. E. Watson (eds), *The Semitic Languages: An International Handbook*, pp. 396–404. Berlin: de Gruyter.

Part I

Issues in Areal Linguistics

2

Why is it so Hard to Define a Linguistic Area?

Lyle Campbell

2.1 Introduction

This chapter examines the criteria that have been used to define linguistic areas, with the goal of determining the adequacy of these criteria for the task. It evaluates general recommendations in the literature for how to establish linguistic areas, and it looks to see how they work with respect to several of the most widely acknowledged linguistic areas. It recommends new ways of looking at the overall enterprise of areal linguistics, and illustrates both the recommended approach and the problems in defining linguistic areas through a case study of the Chaco as a potential linguistic area. It is generally acknowledged that linguistic areas are 'notoriously messy', 'notoriously fuzzy' things (Heine and Kuteva 2001: 396; Thomason and Kaufman 1988: 95; Tosco 2000: 332), and that 'what we understand about linguistic areas is depressingly meager' (Thomason 2001: 99). I argue that the reason for this is because the focus has misleadingly been on geography rather than on the diffused changes themselves. The goal of this chapter is to re-examine areal linguistics and in so doing to arrive at a clearer understanding of the notion 'linguistic area'. The conclusion reached is that it is individual historical events of diffusion that count, not the *post hoc* attempts to impose geographical order on varied conglomerations of these borrowings.

2.2 Proposed Linguistic Areas

Scholars have struggled with both the definition of the concept 'linguistic area' and with determining what criteria might be valid or most useful for establishing linguistic areas; the two are closely interrelated, and we need to examine both. We could approach our task of examining these two vexed but key topics in one or both of two ways: (1) by examining the linguistic areas that have been proposed to see what they have in common (for the definition of the concept 'linguistic area') and what defines them (for perspectives on the criteria for establishing linguistic areas), or (2) by examining the shared traits upon which each linguistic area is based and then applying the criteria proposed in the linguistic literature for determining the validity or the strength of each linguistic area, to see how effective the criteria may be in determining the various proposed linguistic areas.

The exercise of trying to approach areal linguistics in these two ways, however, runs into obstacles from the outset. Not everything that has been proposed as a linguistic area is necessarily accepted by knowledgeable linguists, and not all the criteria that have been proposed may be generally accepted, either. This makes the task of trying to understand the concept of linguistic area and the criteria for establishing linguistic areas seem circular. On the one hand, the linguistic areas – whether solid ones or not – depend on the criteria utilized to establish them. On the other hand, the criteria are arrived at by examining the linguistic areas – whether generally accepted or not. This makes it unclear whether the areas can tell us what the criteria should be or the criteria can tell us what the areas should be.

The difficulty can be understood more fully from a quick look at a list of some of the linguistic areas that have been proposed in the linguistic literature. These include but are not limited to the following.

Proposed linguistic areas
 1 Africa as a linguistic area
 2 Ethiopia, or the Ethiopian Highlands
 3 Southern Africa
 4 Macro-Sudan Belt
 5 West African Sahel sprachbund
 6 The Cape linguistic area
 7 Yobe State (Nigeria) linguistic area
 8 Benin-Surinam Transatlantic sprachbund
 9 Trans-Atlantic sprachbund
10 European sprachbund (Standard Average European linguistic area)
11 Ireland (see Hickey 1999, 2012)
12 Scotland
13 Basque and its neighbours
14 Balkans
15 Baltic
16 Karelian sprachbund (see Sarhimaa 1991)
17 Uralic-Siberian linguistic area
18 Uralo-Altaic sprachbund
19 Sumero-Akkadian, Ancient Near East
20 Anatolian area

21 Carpathian (Danube) linguistic area
22 Onogur sprachbund
23 Rossic sprachbund
24 Siberian linguistic area
25 Upper Yenisei sprachbund (Yenisei-Kirgiz area)
26 Volga-Kama sprachbund
27 Ostyak (Ob-Yeniseic) sprachbund
28 Volga-Oka sprachbund ?
29 Yeniseic sprachbund
30 Ob-Ugric sprachbund
31 Core Uralic (Central Uralic) sprachbund
32 Peripheral Uralic (Lateral Uralic) sprachbund
33 Eastern Uralic sprachbund
34 South Asian linguistic area (Indian subcontinent)
35 Sri Lanka sprachbund
36 Caucasus
37 Northern Asia
38 Amdo sprachbund (Qinghai-Gansu sprachbund)
39 Northwest China sprachbund
40 Mainland Southeast Asia
41 Sepik River Basin
42 Bird's Head sprachbund
43 East Nusantara area (Eastern Indonesian linguistic area)
44 Timoric (Timor Leste)
45 North Vanuatu sprachbund
46 The Pacific linguistic area
47 Australia as a linguistic area
48 Northwest Coast of North America
49 Northern Northwest Coast linguistic area
50 Northern California
51 Clear Lake area (California)
52 South Coast Range area (California)
53 California linguistic area
54 Southern California/Western Arizona area
55 Plateau linguistic area
56 Great Basin area
57 Pueblo linguistic area
58 Plains area
59 Southeast linguistic area
60 Northeast linguistic area
61 Mesoamerica
62 Lowland Maya diffusion area
63 The Huehuetenango sprachbund
64 Guaporé-Mamoré linguistic area
65 Vaupés(-Içana Basin) linguistic area

66 The Chaco
67 Amazonia, Amazonian linguistic area
68 Upper Xingu incipient linguistic area
69 Orinoco-Amazon linguistic area
70 Venezuelan-Antillean linguistic area
71 Andes linguistic area (Andean area)
72 Colombian–Central American linguistic area
73 Lower Central America linguistic area
74 Lowland South American linguistic area
75 Southern Cone linguistic area

It might be thought that a good number of these proposed linguistic areas do not have general acceptance, and that therefore perhaps we could gain traction on our task by considering only the best established, most widely accepted linguistic areas. However, even this tactic is unclear, since it would reduce the task to examining the very small number of areas that enjoy a reasonable measure of general acceptance: the Balkans, South Asia (Indian subcontinent), Baltic, Mesoamerica, and perhaps the Northwest Coast of North America, plus or minus one or two. (For the traits shared in each of these areas, see, for example, Campbell 2013: 298–305.) However, the task gets even bleaker: even in the case of these most widely acknowledged linguistic areas, there is no general agreement upon exactly which languages belong to each linguistic area, nor on what the traits of the areas are, nor on what the geographical extent of each is. Nevertheless, let's look further.

2.3   Different Kinds of Linguistic Areas

The tasks to be tackled are made all the more complicated because of the differing sorts of linguistic areas talked about in the literature: not all areas are equal, or even similar, in their histories or composition. Things called 'linguistic areas' have included entities of widely divergent character and historical backgrounds, differing in social, cultural, political, geographical, attitudinal, historical and other factors; see Aikhenvald and Dixon (2001b: 11, 13), Dahl (2001: 1458), Kuteva (1998: 308–309). As Thomason (2001: 104) explains, '[linguistic areas] arise in any of several ways – through social networks established by such interactions as trade and exogamy, through the shift by indigenous peoples in a region to the language(s) of invaders, through repeated instances of movement by small groups to different places within the area.' The different sorts of linguistic areas found in the literature include: incipient ones, only beginning to form and with as yet few shared traits; moribund and decaying ones, where due to many changes after the area was actively formed, fewer traits are currently recognizable among the languages than would formerly have been the case; layered ones (with new layers and old layers of diffusion from different sources); overlapping ones, where different areas formed on top of one another or overlapping one another at different times for different reasons; multilateral versus unilateral areas; areas with some nuclear (core) languages and other peripheral ones; areas resulting from rapid conquest, from population spread and migration (traits moving with movement of speakers), and others through home-grown, stay-in-place contact (movement of traits but not of peoples); disrupted areas with 'latecomers, earlier drop-outs, and temporary passers-by' (Stolz 2002: 265); and so on.

Clearly then, '"linguistic area" is not a uniform phenomenon, either socially or linguistically' (Thomason 2001: 115). These different kinds of linguistic areas raise doubts about the utility of the whole concept 'linguistic area'. Are all these different kinds of things legitimate linguistic areas, given their very different make-up and the large differences in the circumstances of their origins and histories? It appears that there is little in the notion 'linguistic area' to unite these different sorts of linguistic areas other than the fact that they all involve borrowing in some way, but borrowings of different sorts, for different reasons, in different settings, and at different times. This leads me to agree with Dahl's (2001) conclusion:

> In the end, we are led to the following more far-going question about the notion of area: to what extent do areas . . . have a reality of their own and to what extent are they just convenient ways of summarizing certain phenomena? At the most basic level, linguistic contact relationships are binary: one language influences another. An area is then simply the sum of many such binary relationships.   *(Dahl 2001: 1458)*

I argue here that a linguistic area, to the extent that the concept may be of any value, is merely the sum of borrowings among individual languages in contact situations. If we abandon the search for an adequate geographically oriented definition of the concept and for criteria for establishing linguistic areas, and instead focus on understanding the borrowings, those contingent historical facts and the difficulty of determining what qualifies as a legitimate linguistic area cease to be problems.

With this discussion in mind, let us turn now to look at the vexed problem of attempts at defining the notion 'linguistic area'.

2.4   The Concept 'Linguistic Area'

In broad terms, we might think that a general definition of the term 'linguistic area' would contain reference to a geographical area in which, due to language contact, languages of a region come to share certain structural features. Linguistic areas are also referred to at times by the

terms *sprachbund, diffusion area, adstratum relationship* and *convergence area.*
The central feature of a linguistic area is generally held to be the existence
of structural similarities shared among languages of the geographical area
in question, usually coupled with the assumption that the reason the
languages of the area share these traits is because at least some of them
are borrowed. This definition or something similar to it is characteristic of
the notion employed in much of the work in areal linguistics. However, it
is not that simple, and there are many disagreements, which make even
this notional definition, however appealing, unacceptable to some scholars who work in areal linguistics, and it does not fit all the entities called
'linguistic areas' in the literature.

   Different approaches have been taken in attempts to establish linguistic
areas, with different implications for the definition of the concept. The
circumstantialist approach (see Campbell 1985) mostly just lists similarities
found in the languages of a geographical area and allows the list of shared
traits to suggest diffusion and to define the linguistic area accordingly.
Here, concrete evidence that the shared traits are diffused is not required.
Circumstantialist areal linguistics has been criticized for not eliminating
chance, universals, and possibly undetected genetic relationships among
the languages as other possible explanations for shared traits. The *histori-
cist* approach (Campbell 1985) seeks concrete evidence that the shared
traits of an area are diffused (borrowed). This approach is more rigorous,
although the lack of clear historical information in many cases has often
led scholars to rely on the less trustworthy circumstantialist approach.
Linguistic areas are often defined, surprisingly, on the basis of a rather
small number of shared linguistic traits.

2.5   Criteria for Determining Linguistic Areas

The following criteria are the major ones that have been utilized to define
linguistic areas: the number of traits shared by languages in the area,
bundling of the shared traits (clustering at geographical boundaries), and
different weights attributed to different areal traits (under the assumption
that some kinds of diffused changes constitute stronger evidence than
others of areal affiliation). Let's look at these a bit more closely.

2.5.1   Number of Shared Traits

There is no general agreement on the number of areal traits necessary to
justify calling something a linguistic area (see Campbell 2006a; Katz 1975:
16; Schaller 1975: 54, 58; Thomason 2001: 99). For views on trait weighting, see Aikhenvald and Dixon (2001b), Campbell (1985, 1996a, 1996b,
2002: 732), Campbell, Kaufman and Smith-Stark (1986: 535–536),
Curnow (2001), Giannini and Scaglione (2002), Haig (2001: 218–222),

Heath (1978: 104–107), Katz (1975), Stolz (2002: 264–265) and van der Auwera (1998), among others. I have argued that it is not a matter of some minimum number of shared traits, but rather the more, the merrier: some areas are more securely established because they contain many shared diffused traits, and other areas with fewer shared traits are weaker (Campbell 1985, 2006a). In the linguistic areas considered above, we see considerable variation in the number and kind of traits they share and which define them.

2.5.2   Number of Language Families

The number of language families involved has played a role in some scholars' ideas about the criteria for linguistic areas. Some have required that two or more language families be involved to define a linguistic area: see Aikhenvald and Dixon (2001b: 11), Emeneau (1980 [1956]: 124; 1980 [1965]: 127; 1980 [1978]: 1), Schaller (1975: 58), Tosco (2000), van der Auwera (1998: 260). However, this appears not to be a strong requirement, since the Balkan Linguistic Area, probably the best-known and most widely accepted of all linguistic areas, involves only Indo-European languages for most scholars (though some include also Turkish in the area): see Masica (1992: 110). Some scholars temper the multiple language family requirement, suggesting instead that at least some of the languages of an area should not be closely related if only languages from one family are involved, although details of what 'not closely related' means in this context has been left unaddressed: see Campbell (1985: 25; 1994: 1471), Matthews (1997: 351), Stolz (2002: 261). Nevertheless, the idea of some minimum level of required linguistic diversity among the languages of a linguistic area has not really been a focus of attention.

2.5.3   Trait Weight

It is easy to see the value of the relatively greater weight or importance attributed to some traits than to others for defining linguistic areas, but how to assign weight is not clear. For instance, the borrowed word order patterns in the Ethiopian linguistic area provide an instructive example. Ethiopian Semitic languages exhibit a number of areal traits diffused from neighbouring Cushitic languages. Several of these individual traits, however, are interconnected due to the borrowing of the SOV (subject–object–verb) basic word order patterns of Cushitic languages into the formerly VSO Ethiopian Semitic languages (Campbell et al. 1988). Typologically, the orders noun–postposition, verb–auxiliary, relative clause–head noun and adjective–noun all tend to correlate with one another and to co-occur with SOV order cross-linguistically. If the expected correlations among these constructions are not taken into account, we might be tempted to count each one of these as a separate shared areal trait. Their presence in

Ethiopian Semitic languages might seem to reflect several different diffused traits (SOV counted as one, noun–postposition as another, and so on), and they could be taken as several independent pieces of evidence defining a linguistic area. However, from the perspective of expected word order pattern co-occurrences, these word order arrangements are not independent traits, but may be viewed as the diffusion of a single complex feature, the overall SOV word order type with its various expected coordinated orderings of typologically interrelated constructions. However, even though the borrowing of the SOV basic word order type may count only as a single diffused areal trait, many scholars would rank it as counting for far more than many other less complex individual traits, based on the knowledge of how difficult it is for a language to change so much of its basic word order.[1]

2.5.4   Trait Bundling

With respect to the criterion of the bundling of areal traits, some scholars had thought that such clustering at the borders of a linguistic area might be necessary for defining linguistic areas correctly. However, linguistic areas are not typically viewed this way. Rather, they are similar to traditional dialects in this regard. Often, one trait may spread out and extend across a greater territory than another trait, whose territory may be more limited, so that traits' territories do not coincide, they do not 'bundle' together at some border. Some would distinguish different kinds of traits based on their belief that some kinds of linguistic features, such as phonological ones, may be able to diffuse more easily and thus cover more terrain than others, such as grammatical features. The most typical pattern is where languages within the core of an area may share a number of features, but the geographical expanses of the individual traits may vary considerably one from another. However, in a situation where the traits do coincide at a clear boundary, rare though this may be, the definition of a linguistic area which matches their boundary is considered relatively secure. An additional complication (pointed out to me by Ray Hickey) is that even where a few features might coincide – especially ones that diffuse more easily – the apparent bundling could be simply due to coincidence. Unfortunately, however, in most linguistic areas, the areal traits do not have the same boundaries, offering no clearly identifiable outer border of the linguistic area in question. As Emeneau (1980 [1965]: 1366) said, 'in linguistic area studies it is doubtful if there will ever emerge isogloss-bundles.'

---

[1] As Raymond Hickey points out (personal communication, 2015), the apparent difficulty of borrowing basic word order is supported by Irish. Despite the enormous influence from English on Irish (seen in many syntactic features), the English SVO word order has not made a single dent in Irish, which staunchly maintains VSO basic word order (with correlated N+Adj, Nom+Gen, etc.); see Hickey (2010: 13).

2.6 Defining 'Linguistic Area'

A common perception is that the term 'linguistic area' is difficult to define (see Heine and Kuteva 2001: 409). As Thomason (2001: 99) observes, 'linguistics has struggled to define the concept [linguistic area] ever since [Trubetzkoy 1928], mainly because it isn't always easy to decide whether a particular region constitutes a linguistic area or not.' The principal definitions that have been given of the notion 'linguistic area' (or of related and more or less synonymous terms, *sprachbund, diffusion area, convergence area,* etc.) are surveyed in Campbell (2006a), and are not repeated here in the interest of space. In spite of prolonged efforts to define 'linguistic area', there is no general agreement on its definition, and even for the most widely accepted linguistic areas, such as the Balkans, scholars do not agree wholly on which languages belong to the area, what linguistic traits characterize the area, and what its precise geographical extent is. In Stolz's (2002: 260) words, 'these terms [sprachbund, linguistic area and areal type] seem to invite as many meanings and readings as there are linguistic minds to contemplate them.' Stolz (2002: 259) is correct that 'the search for clearcut definitions [of sprachbund, linguistic area and areal type] has been largely futile and will probably never come to a really satisfying conclusion.'

I argue that too much effort has been wasted on trying to define the concept, that little progress has been made, and that it would be more productive to investigate the facts of linguistic diffusion without the concern for defining linguistic areas. Every 'linguistic area', to the extent that the notion has any meaning at all, arises from an accumulation of individual cases of 'localized diffusion'; it is the investigation of these specific instances of diffusion, and not the pursuit of defining properties for linguistic areas, that will increase our understanding and will explain the historical facts. With the focus rather on specific instances of borrowing, many of the unresolved issues and indeterminacies which have dogged areal linguistics from the outset cease to be relevant questions.

2.7 New Concept

Areal linguistics might appear to have been somewhat schizophrenic, sometimes concentrating on situations like set intersection and at other times on situations like set union. We have sought to define linguistic areas in a *set-intersection*-like manner, based mainly on traits shared by all the members of the thing being designated a linguistic area, but we have also set up linguistic areas in a more *set-union*-like way, seeing anything whatsoever found in the thing being designated a linguistic area as evidence defining that area so long as that trait is found in more than one language in the region. Some might say we prefer the former, with set-intersection-like traits as the main protagonists in our cast of characters, but that at the same time we also call upon the latter, with the set-union-like traits as supporting cast members. However, because we have not sorted out the consequences from inclusion of these different kinds of traits, the definitional muddle has persisted. It could be argued that our interests are better served by making the differences explicit, with appropriate terminology to help avoid confusion. We might reserve the term *linguistic area sensu stricto* (LASS) for a geographical region defined by shared diffused traits mostly contained within and shared across the languages of a clearly delimited geographical space (set-intersection-like). We need a different term for the entity that focuses more on the shared traits themselves regardless of whether they show up in all the languages thereabouts or coincide in their distribution within some bounded geographical space – the set-union-like situations. I suggest for this the term *trait-sprawl area* (TSA). The word 'sprawl' here reflects the fact that the individual traits can pattern in disordered ways, with some crisscrossing some languages while others crisscross other languages, with some extending in one direction, others in another direction, with some partially overlapping others in part of their distribution but also not coinciding in other parts of their geographical distribution.[2] The focus of the TSA is the actual diffused traits themselves, with the emphasis on answering the question which is the prime directive for historical linguists, 'What happened?' – that is, with focus on what changes took place, rather than on defining some geographical area itself. To the extent that any clear LASSes with geographical focus may be established, we will still want to answer the same question – 'What happened?' –about the linguistic traits shared by the languages of the LASS.

For TSA, what I have in mind are the cases where clearly there is considerable sharing of linguistic traits in some region, even though by applying the usual criteria for setting up linguistic areas it is difficult to determine whether the case in question can legitimately be defined as a linguistic area. I have in mind cases where different traits are shared by some adjacent languages, but the set of individual traits can vary greatly in terms of which languages may share which ones and how different they can be in their territorial expanse. In order to illustrate the notion of TSA and what it means for the problems of defining linguistic areas, I will use a brief case study, the Grand Chaco of South America.

Others have observed similar difficulties in defining linguistic areas due to different behaviour with respect to which languages share which traits, though not conceptualized precisely as proposed here. Daumé (2009) has developed a Bayesian approach to attempt to quantify traits and thus kinds of linguistic areas. Muysken et al. (2015: 209), following Lindstedt (2000), note that 'a Sprachbund may exhibit gradience in language membership, from "core" languages in the Sprachbund to "non-core" languages ... thus

---

[2] Note here also the belief of some linguists, mentioned earlier, that phonological features might sprawl differently from grammatical or lexical traits.

the Balkans can be characterized as a Sprachbund with "soft" boundaries: there is no sharp transition from Sprachbund to Sprachbund.' They explore possible quantitative definitions of linguistic areas, though their areal traits are not weighted.

2.8   Is the Gran Chaco a Linguistic Area?

The Gran Chaco is the extensive dry lowland plain of northern Argentina, Paraguay, southeastern Bolivia and southern Brazil. It has been considered a culture area characterized by cultural traits shared across ethnic boundaries (Miller 1999; Murdock 1951), and it has sometimes been considered a linguistic area, too, although the evidence has not been clear: see Adelaar with Muysken (2004: 386, 499), Aikhenvald (2011), Campbell and Grondona (2012a), Grondona (2003), Kirtchuk (1996), Messineo (2011), Rona (1969–1972), Tovar (1961), Viegas Barros (2002: 140). More than twenty languages from six language families are found in the Chaco region (see Campbell and Grondona 2012a for details). The language families are Guaicuruan (Waykuruan), Matacoan (Mataco-Mataguayan), Mascoyan (Mascoian, Maskoyan, Lengua-Mascoy, Enlhet-Enenlhet), Lule-Vilelan, Zamucoan and Tupí-Guaranían (a branch of Tupían). There were also a number of poorly known extinct languages in the region that are not dealt with here (see Campbell 2012a for details). A look at what makes it difficult to determine whether the Chaco is a linguistic area will help to clarify central issues addressed in this chapter and the concept of TSA. Details of the Chaco linguistic traits are not repeated here (for that see Campbell and Grondona 2012a), but some of the main ones are discussed sufficiently to help clarify what is at stake here.

2.8.1   SVO Word Order

Shared basic word order has been cited as a trait of Chaco languages: see Adelaar with Muysken (2004: 499), Campbell (2012b), Messineo (2011), Tovar (1961: 195), Tovar and Tovar (1984: 202). SVO basic word order is found in Matacoan and Guaicuruan languages, and Ayoreo (Zamucoan). SVO basic word order may be characteristic of several Chaco languages, but not of all of them; Lule and Vilela have SOV (with Noun–Adjective, Modifier–Head) (Comrie et al. 2010: 91–92). Moreover, SVO does not set Chaco languages clearly apart from languages of neighbouring parts of South America.

2.8.2   Gender

Grammatical gender has been suggested as a Chaco areal trait: see Aikhenvald (2000: 80), Tovar (1961). Matacoan, Guaicuruan, Zamucoan and Mascoyan languages have a masculine–feminine gender distinction.

However, gender as a grammatical category is also found widely elsewhere in South America, but, again, not in all languages of the Chaco.

2.8.3   Genitive Classifiers

Matacoan, Guaicuruan, Maskoyan and Zamucoan languages have a genitive (or possessive) noun classifier construction for possessed domestic animals (Campbell 2012b; Fabre 2007; Messineo 2011). In these languages it is not possible to say directly, for example, 'my cow'; rather, a 'possessive domestic animal classifier' that bears a possessive pronominal prefix is necessary. Genitive classifiers are rare though several other South American Indian languages also have them, but in these languages it is usually a member of a larger classifier system with several other noun classifiers. These Chaco languages typically have only the genitive classifiers, not other kinds of noun classifiers, and this may distinguish them from languages of other areas.

2.8.4   Rich Set of Demonstratives

Chaco languages typically have a rich system of demonstratives, with forms distinguished on a number of different semantic parameters which include visible versus not visible, often also proximate, distal, extended horizontally, extended vertically, three-dimensional, known from first-hand experience, known from hearsay, no longer existent, and so on; see Campbell (2012b), Campbell and Grondona (2012a), Messineo et al. (2011). However, this is far from unique to Chaco languages; numerous other South American languages also have complex demonstrative systems.

2.8.5   Active–Stative Verb Alignment

Active–stative alignment characterizes many Chaco languages and may be an area-defining feature (Adelaar with Muysken 2004: 499; Grondona 2003). Matacoan and Guaicuruan languages are clearly active–stative; Enlhet (Maskoyan) appears to be (Grubb 1914: 319). Guaranían is well known for having active–stative alignment. Active–inactive languages which operate on the semantic criterion of event (for active) and non-event or stative (for inactive) seem to be limited mostly to the Chaco and adjacent regions – though not exclusively; for example Tunica, an extinct language isolate of Louisiana, also has active–stative alignment (Heaton in press). This feature, however, also extends beyond the Chaco, found in several Tupí-Guaranían languages. Thus it is an important feature of the Chaco, but not limited to the Chaco region alone.

2.8.6   Lack of Verbal Tense

Matacoan, Guaicuruan, Ayoreo and Guaraní for the most part do not mark tense on verbs: tense in these languages is either determined from context or signalled by adverbials, demonstratives or directionals. Several have nominal tense (instances where a nominal or part of a noun phrase, not the verb, carries the tense information for the proposition); see Campbell (2012b), Tonhauser (2007, 2008); Vidal and Gutiérrez (2010). Nevertheless, nominal tense is also found in several other South American languages, not just in the Chaco (Campbell 2012a).

2.8.7 Directional Verbal Affixes

Chaco languages typically have a complex set of directional verbal affixes, found for example in Matacoan, Guaicuruan, Maskoyan, Zamucoan and Chiriguano (Tupí-Guaranían); see Campbell and Grondona (2012a), Messineo (2011). This trait may characterize most Chaco languages. Again it is not limited to the Chaco, however. Many other languages in southern South America have directional affixes on verbs (Campbell 2012b).

2.8.9 Other Postulated Areal Traits in the Chaco

A number of other traits have been mentioned as possibly diffused among Chaco languages. Most of these, however, are not compelling as evidence for a Chaco linguistic area (assessed in Campbell and Grondona 2012a). Several are commonplace and can be found easily in languages around the world. Others are found not just in the Chaco but also widely in other areas of South America. This does not mean these traits are not diffused, but only that they provide no strong evidence for designating the Chaco as a clearly delineated linguistic area, since they do not distinguish Chaco languages from languages in neighbouring areas that also bear these traits. In other cases, the trait in question is limited to only a few languages of the Chaco and so does not provide evidence of the area as a whole.

All the phonological traits that have been mentioned as possibly diffused in the Chaco are either widely spread beyond the Chaco or are limited to only a few of the Chaco languages. These include the following: lack of voiced stops; simple vowel systems; voiceless bilabial fricative [ɸ] (Gerzenstein 2004); vowel nasalization (Adelaar with Muysken 2004: 499); vowel harmony (Adelaar with Muysken 2004: 499; cf. Gerzenstein and Gualdieri 2003); palatalization (Messineo 2003: 36; Messineo 2011 limits it to palatalization of coronal consonants); glottalized (ejective) consonants (only in a few Chaco languages, Matacoan and Vilela-Lule) (Campbell 2006b; Campbell and Grondona 2012a; Comrie et al. 2010: 93–94); uvular (postvelar) consonants (Campbell 2006b; Campbell and Grondona 2012a; Comrie et al. 2010); voiceless 'l' (Campbell and Grondona 2012a; Comrie et al. 2010); simple consonant clusters (Adelaar with Muysken 2004: 499). Other suggested areal traits in the Chaco that are either widely spread in languages beyond the Chaco or found only in some of the Chaco languages, or both, include: prefixing (versus only suffixing); alienable/inalienable possessive marking (see Comrie et al. 2010; dismissed as not very significant by Campbell and Grondona 2012a); unspecified possessor marker (denoting unpossessed forms: Campbell 2012b;

Grondona 2003); plural object suffixes on verbs (Grondona 2003); inclusive/ exclusive contrast in first person plural pronominal forms; negated adjectives for antonyms (for example, Nivaclé *nipitexa* 'short' [*ni-* N E G + *pitex* 'tall, long' + *-a* N E G]). (See Campbell 2012b.)

2.8.10   Is the Chaco a Linguistic Area?

Most of the diffused traits involving languages of the Chaco do not provide strong support for a Chaco linguistic area, particularly not as a LASS. Most are found extending also into languages beyond the Chaco, and others are characteristic of only a few of the languages within the region. Only a few of the traits seem true of a majority of Chaco languages, but none of these is unique to the area and some are quite commonplace in the world, for example SVO word order. This raises the question about whether or how a Chaco linguistic area might be defined. Tupí-Guaranían illustrates the problem. Opinion has diverged about whether Tupí-Guaranían languages should be considered members of a Chaco linguistic area, and no grounds for excluding Chiriguano and Tapiete have as yet been found: see Comrie et al. (2010: 86) for discussion. Tupí-Guaranían shares most of the Chaco traits just listed. Since Tupí-Guaranían extends far beyond the Chaco region, though it has representatives also in the Chaco, its inclusion in a Chaco linguistic area would extend the linguistic area way beyond the geographical extent of the Chaco region – hardly a 'Chaco' area if defined in that way. If Tupí-Guaranían is included, since these languages also share many traits with languages of the Amazonian area (see Campbell 2006b or Campbell and Grondona 2012a for details), how could we establish what belongs to the Chaco linguistic area and what to the Amazonian linguistic area and how are the two areas distinguished? If Tupí-Guaranían is not included, the areal definition of the Chaco as defined on the basis of shared traits is compromised, since many of the traits seemingly reflective of a Chaco area are also found in neighbouring languages well beyond the Chaco region. This sprawling, overlapping or intertwining of shared traits among Chaco languages and languages of the Andes, of Amazonia, and elsewhere complicates any attempt to define a Chaco linguistic area with recognizable boundaries. In short, the Chaco is a good example of a TSA, but does not qualify as a LASS – in fact hardly any proposed linguistic area qualifies well as a LASS.

Interestingly, Comrie et al. (2010) declare their faith that the Chaco is a linguistic area by acknowledging but dismissing the complications just discussed. They say:

> From our theoretical perspective, the existence of phonological, grammatical or lexical features in the languages of the Chaco that are repeated in other areas of South America does not invalidate the characterization of the Chaco region as a linguistic area. The identification of linguistic areas in other geographical regions of South America has shown that often the traits listed are very general and are found widespread throughout South

America; see for example the list of traits of Amazonian languages in Dixon and Aikhenvald (1999). Therefore, not only is the identification of common traits important, but also their overall manifestation in a given area, in non-related languages (Aikhenvald and Dixon 2006).

(Comrie et al. 2010: 89)[3]

I take this statement not as a defence of the Chaco as a true linguistic area, but as a declaration of interest in shared traits found in and around Chaco languages, no matter what the ultimate geographical distribution of the various traits might be. That is, I take this to be an endorsement of the argument put forward here that what is important are the diffused changes themselves, not attempts to set up linguistic areas defined by the overall reach of these traits. That is, I take the statement as a tacit acknowledgement of the Chaco as a TSA, only. More precisely, Comrie et al. (2010: 125) conclude that the Chaco is a core–periphery (núcleo–periferia) type linguistics area (see also Campbell 2006a), with Guaicuruan and Matacoan languages at the core and Vilela (Lule-Vilelan) and Tapiete (Tupí-Guaraníán) on the periphery. This view, unfortunately, suffers from the fact that even the so-called core languages do not have several of the traits talked about as areal ones, as well as the acknowledged inconvenience that most of these traits extend far beyond the Chaco to languages of other areas. The notion of a core–periphery type language area is an interesting one, but does not seem to have overcome the problems in defining linguistic areas. Since it is not clear that the 'core' hangs together in this case, we appear to be left with a lot of trait-sprawling, a TSA at best.

There does appear to be considerable diffusion of structural traits involving Chaco languages, but these do not come together in such a way as to suggest a cohesive geographical area. Rather, they show varying linkages with languages and regions outside the Chaco on all sides, while at the same time often not linking all Chaco languages. This is not a surprising finding, since the Chaco as a cultural area is also not distinguished clearly from surrounding regions, and Chaco groups underwent cultural influences from many directions (see Métraux 1946: 210).[4] The linguistic traits shared among and beyond the Chaco languages appear to parallel the

---

[3] 'Desde nuestra perspectiva teórica, la existencia de características fonológicas, gramaticales o léxicas en las lenguas del Chaco que se repiten en otras áreas de América del Sur no invalida la caracterización de la región chaqueña como área lingüística. La identificación de áreas lingüísticas en otras regiones geográficas de América del Sur ha mostrado que muchas veces los rasgos señalados son muy generales y se encuentran extendidos a lo largo de América del Sur – véase, por ejemplo, la enumeración de rasgos de las lenguas amazónicas en Dixon y Aikhenvald (1999). Por lo tanto, no importa sólo la identificación de los rasgos comunes, sino su manifestación en conjunto en un área determinada, en lenguas no emparentadas (Aikhenvald y Dixon, 2006)'.

[4] As Raymond Hickey pointed out to me, the topography in the case of the Chaco region also favours the spread of cultural traits and linguistic traits in and from various directions. Since there are no sharp geographical features that set the Chaco off from neighbouring regions, presumably movement on dry lowland plains of peoples with contact among their cultures and their languages is easier, not as impeded as would be the case if mountains or other geographical barriers were involved.

distribution of the cultural traits. This evidence is too weak to declare a Chaco linguistic area *sensu stricto*, a LASS. However, the sprawling of traits among Chaco languages and beyond is a good example of a *trait-sprawling area* (TSA), the concept advocated here to avoid definitional problems with the concept of linguistic area, focusing on actual diffused traits and on answering the question, 'What happened?', rather than on fixing a geographical area to be defined by its shared linguistic traits.

2.9   Conclusions

So, what does all this mean? The goal should be to understand the changes themselves, in particular in this instance the changes diffused across languages. It is not important nor practical to try to force the various sprawling, overlapping, and intertwining diffused traits to fit together into coherent geographical spaces with clearly defined borders. If we succeed in finding out what happened, we will know which changes are due to borrowing and which to other factors, and we will know how the changes are distributed among the languages involved. Whatever geographical patterning there may be will fall out naturally from this fuller historical account. There is no longer any need to continue to struggle over the intractability of defining the concept 'linguistic area' and the specific 'linguistic areas'.

References

Adelaar, Willem F. H. (with Pieter C. Muysken), 2004. *The Languages of the Andes*. Cambridge: Cambridge University Press.

Aikhenvald, Alexandra Y., 2000. *Classifiers: A Typology of Noun Categorization Devices*. Oxford: Oxford University Press.

Aikhenvald, Alexandra Y., 2011. The wonders of the Gran Chaco: Setting the scene. *Indiana* 28: 171–181.

Aikhenvald, Alexandra Y. and R. M. W. Dixon (eds), 2001a. *Areal Diffusion and Genetic Inheritance: Problems in Comparative Linguistics*. Oxford: Oxford University Press.

Aikhenvald, Alexandra Y. and R. M. W. Dixon, 2001b. Introduction. In Aikhenvald and Dixon (eds), pp. 1–26.

van der Auwera, Johan, 1998. Revisiting the Balkan and Meso-American linguistic areas. *Language Sciences* 20: 259–270.

Campbell, Lyle, 1985. Areal linguistics and its implications for historical linguistic theory. In Jacek Fisiak (ed.), *Proceedings of the Sixth International Conference of Historical Linguistics*, pp. 25–56. Amsterdam: John Benjamins.

Campbell, Lyle, 1994. Grammar: Typological and areal issues. In R. E. Asher and J. M. Y. Simpson (eds), *Encyclopedia of Language and Linguistics*, vol. 3, pp. 1471–1474. London: Pergamon Press.

Campbell, Lyle, 1996a. Typological and areal issues. In Keith Brown and Jim Miller (eds), *Concise Encyclopedia of Syntactic Theories*, pp. 339–343. Oxford: Pergamon Press. Reprint of 1994, in *Encyclopedia of Language and Linguistics*.

Campbell, Lyle, 1996b. Phonetics and phonology. In Hans Goebl, Peter H. Nelde, Zdenek Stary and Wolfgang Wölck (eds), *An International Handbook of Contemporary Research*, vol. 14: *Contact Linguistics*, pp. 98–103. Berlin: Walter de Gruyter.

Campbell, Lyle, 2002. Areal linguistics. In Neil J. Smelser and Paul B. Balte (eds), *International Encyclopedia of Social and Behavioral Sciences*, pp. 729–733, volume edited by Bernard Comrie. Oxford: Pergamon.

Campbell, Lyle, 2006a. Areal linguistics: A closer scrutiny. In Yaron Matras, April McMahon and Nigel Vincent (eds), *Linguistic Areas: Convergence in Historical and Typological Perspective*, pp. 1–31. Houndmills, Basingstoke, UK: Palgrave Macmillan.

Campbell, Lyle, 2006b. Contacto lingüístico entre las lenguas del Gran Chaco: Existe una area lingüística chaqueña? Paper presented at the symposium *Advances in South American Historical Linguistics*, 52nd International Congress of Americanists, Seville, Spain, 17–21 July 2006.

Campbell, Lyle, 2012a. The classification of South American indigenous languages. In Campbell and Grondona (eds), pp. 59–166.

Campbell, Lyle, 2012b. Typological characteristics of South American indigenous languages. In Campbell and Grondona (eds), pp. 259–330.

Campbell, Lyle, 2013. *Historical Linguistics: An Introduction*, third edition. Edinburgh: Edinburgh University Press, and Cambridge, MA: The MIT Press.

Campbell, Lyle, Vit Bubenik and Leslie Saxon, 1988. Word order universals: Refinements and clarifications. *Canadian Journal of Linguistics* 33: 209–230.

Campbell, Lyle and Verónica Grondona, 2012a. Languages of the Chaco and Southern Cone. In Campbell and Grondona (eds), pp. 625–668.

Campbell, Lyle and Verónica Grondona (eds), 2012b. *The Indigenous Languages of South America: A Comprehensive Guide*. Berlin: Mouton de Gruyter.

Campbell, Lyle, Terrence Kaufman and Thomas Smith-Stark, 1986. Mesoamerica as a linguistic area. *Language* 62: 530–570.

Comrie, Bernard, Lucía A. Golluscio, Hebe González and Alejandra Vidal, 2010. El Chaco como área lingüística. In Zarina Estrada Fernández and Ramón Arzápalo Marín (eds), *Estudios de Lenguas Amerindias 2: Contribuciones al Estudio de las Lenguas Originarias de América*, pp. 85–132. Hermosillo, Sonora, Mexico: Editorial Universidad de Sonora.

Curnow, Timothy Jowan, 2001. What language features can be 'borrowed'? In Aikhenvald and Dixon (eds), pp. 412–436.

Dahl, Östen, 2001. Principles of areal typology. In Martin Haspelmath, Ekkehard König, Wulf Oesterreicher and Wolfgang Raible (eds), *Language Typology and Language Universals: An International Handbook*, vol. 2, pp. 1456–1470. Berlin: Mouton de Gruyter.

Daumé, Hal, III, 2009. Non-parametric Bayesian areal linguistics. In *Proceedings of Human Language Technologies: The 2009 Annual Conference of the North American Chapter of the Association for Computational Linguistics (NAACL '09)*, pp. 593–601. Morristown, NJ: Association for Computational Linguistics.

Emeneau, Murray B., 1956. India as a linguistic area. *Language* 32: 3–16. Reprinted in Emeneau 1980, pp. 38–65.

Emeneau, Murray B., 1965. India and linguistic areas. In *India and Historical Grammar*. Ammamalai University, Department of Linguistics, pub. no. 5, pp. 25–75. Reprinted in Emeneau 1980, pp. 126–166.

Emeneau, Murray B., 1978. Review of *Defining a Linguistic Area*, by Colin P. Masica. *Language* 54: 201–210. Reprinted with additions in Emeneau 1980, pp. 1–18.

Emeneau, Murray B., 1980. *Language and Linguistic Area*, essays by Murray B. Emeneau, selected and introduced by Anwar S. Dil. Stanford, CA: Stanford University Press.

Fabre, Alain, 2007. Morfosintaxis de los clasificadores posesivos en las lenguas del Gran Chaco (Argentina, Bolivia y Paraguay). *UniverSOS: Revista de lenguas indígenas y universos culturales* 4: 67–85.

Gerzenstein, Ana, 2004. Las consonantes laterales y labializadas en lenguas mataguayas del Chaco argentino paraguayo. In Zarina Estrada Fernández, Ana V. Fernández Garay and A. Álvarez González (eds), *Estudios en Lenguas Amerindias: Homenaje a Ken L. Hale*, pp. 183–197. Hermosillo, Sonora, Mexico: Editorial Universidad de Sonora.

Gerzenstein, Ana and Beatriz Gualdieri, 2003. La armonía vocálica en lenguas chaqueñas de las familias Guaicurú y Mataguaya. *LIAMES* 3: 99–112.

Giannini, Stefania and Stefania Scaglione, 2002. On defining the notion of areality coefficient: The diagnostic value of quantitative criteria. In Paolo Ramat and Thomas Stolz (eds), *Mediterranean Languages: Papers from the MEDTYP Workshop, Tirrenia, June 2000*, pp. 151–170. Bochum: Brockmeyer.

Grondona, Verónica, 2003. Are Guaycuruan and Matacoan languages related? A preliminary account. Paper presented at the 17th International Congress of Linguists, July 2003, Prague.

Grubb, W. Barbrooke, 1914. *An Unknown People in an Unknown Land*. London: Seeley, Service & Co.

Haig, Jeffrey, 2001. Linguistic diffusion in present-day East Anatolia: From top to bottom. In Aikhenvald and Dixon (eds), pp. 195–224.

Heath, Jeffrey, 1978. *Linguistic Diffusion in Arnhem Land*. Canberra: Australian Institute of Aboriginal Studies.

Heaton, Raina, in press. Active–stative agreement in Tunica. *Anthropological Linguistics*.

Heine, Bernd and Tania Kuteva, 2001. Convergence and divergence in the development of African languages. In Aikhenvald and Dixon (eds), pp. 393–411.

Hickey, Raymond, 1999. Ireland as a linguistic area. In J. P. Mallory (ed.), *Language in Ulster*, pp. 36–53. Special issue of *Ulster Folklife* 45. Holywood, Co. Down, Northern Ireland: Ulster Folk and Transport Museum.

Hickey, Raymond, 2010. Language contact: Reassessment and reconsideration. In Raymond Hickey (ed.), *The Handbook of Language Contact*, pp. 1–28. Malden, MA: Wiley-Blackwell.

Hickey, Raymond, 2012. English in Ireland. In Raymond Hickey (ed.), *Areal Features of the Anglophone World*, pp. 79–107. Berlin: de Gruyter Mouton.

Katz, Harmut, 1975. *Generative Phonologie und Phonologische Sprachbünde des Ostjakischen und Samojedischen*. Munich: Wilhelm Fink.

Kirtchuk, Pablo, 1996. Lingüística areal: Deixis y clasificación nominal en lenguas del Gran Chaco. In Eusebia H. Martín and Andrés Pérez Diez (eds), *Lenguas Indígenas de Argentina 1492–1992*, pp. 19–32. (Instituto de Investigaciones Lingüísticas y Filológicas 'Manuel Alvar'.) San Juan: Editorial Fundación Universidad Nacional de San Juan.

Kuteva, Tania, 1998. Large linguistic areas in grammaticalization: Auxiliation in Europe. *Language Sciences* 20: 289–311.

Lindstedt, Jouko, 2000. Linguistic Balkanization: Contact-induced change by mutual reinforcement. In Dicky Gilbers, John Nerbonne and Jos Schaeken (eds), *Languages in Contact*, pp. 231–246. Amsterdam: Rodopi.

Masica, Colin P., 1992. Areal linguistics. In William Bright (ed.), *International Encyclopedia of Linguistics*, pp. 108–112. Oxford: Oxford University Press.

Matthews, Peter, 1997. *The Concise Oxford Dictionary of Linguistics*. Oxford: Oxford University Press.

Messineo, Cristina, 2003. *Lengua toba (guaycurú): Aspectos gramaticales y discursivos*. Munich: LINCOM Europa.

Messineo, Cristina, 2011. Aproximación tipológica a las lenguas indígenas del Gran Chaco: Rasgos compartidos entre toba (familia guaycurú) y maká (familia mataco-mataguayo). *Indiana* 28: 183–225.

Messineo, Cristina, Javier Carol and Harriet Manelis Klein, 2011. Los determinantes demostrativos en las lenguas guaycurúes y mataguayas (Región del Gran Chaco). Paper presented at the *Memorias del V Congreso de Idiomas Indígenas de Latinoamérica*, 6–8 October 2011, University of Texas, Austin.

Métraux, Alfred, 1946. Ethnography of the Chaco. In Julian H. Steward (ed.), *Handbook of South American Indians,* vol. 1: *The Marginal Tribes,* pp. 197–370. Smithsonian Institution Bureau of American Ethnology, Bulletin 143. Washington, DC: Government Printing Office.

Miller, Elmer S. (ed.), 1999. *Peoples of the Gran Chaco*. Westport, CT: Bergin & Garvey.

Murdock, George P., 1951. *Outline of South American Cultures*. New Haven: Human Relations Area Files, Inc.

Muysken, Pieter, Harald Hammarström, Joshua Birchall, Rik van Gijn, Olga Krasnoukhova and Neele Müller, 2015. Linguistic areas, bottom-up or top-down? The case of the Guaporé-Mamoré. In Bernard Comrie and Lucia Golluscio (eds), *Language Contact and Documentation*, pp. 205–238. Berlin: de Gruyter.

Rona, José Pedro, 1969–1972. Extensión del tipo chaqueño de lenguas. *Revista de Antropología* 17/20: 93–103.

Sarhimaa, Anneli, 1991. Karelian Sprachbund? Theoretical basis of the study of Russian/Baltic–Finnic contacts. *Finnisch-Ugrische Forschungen* 50: 209–219.

Schaller, Helmut Wilhelm, 1975. *Die Balkansprachen: Eine Einführung in die Balkanphilologie*. Heidelberg: Winter.

Stolz, Thomas, 2002. No sprachbund beyond this line! On the age-old discussion of how to define a linguistic area. In Paolo Ramat and Thomas Stolz (eds), *Mediterranean Languages: Papers from the MEDTYP Workshop, Tirrenia, June 2000*, pp. 259–281. Bochum: Brockmeyer.

Thomason, Sarah G., 2001. *Language Contact: An Introduction*. Edinburgh: Edinburgh University Press.

Thomason, Sarah G. and Terrence Kaufman, 1988. *Language Contact, Creolization, and Genetic Linguistics*. Berkeley, CA: University of California Press.

Tonhauser, Judith, 2007. Nominal tense? The meaning of Guaraní nominal temporal markers. *Language* 83: 831–869.

Tonhauser, Judith, 2008. Defining crosslinguistic categories: The case of nominal tense (Reply to Nordlinger and Sadler). *Language* 84: 332–342.

Tosco, M., 2000. Is there an Ethiopian language area? *Anthropological Linguistics* 42: 329–365.

Tovar, Antonio, 1961. *Catálogo de las lenguas de América del Sur*. Buenos Aires: Editorial Sudamericana.

Tovar, Antonio and Consuelo Larrucea de Tovar, 1984. *Catálogo de las lenguas de América del Sur*. Madrid: Editorial Gredos.

Trubetzkoy, Nikolai Sergeevich, 1928. Proposition 16. In *Acts of the First International Congress of Linguists*, pp. 17–18. Leiden.

Vidal, Alejandra and Analía Gutiérrez, 2010. La categoría de 'tiempo nominal' en las lenguas chaqueñas. In V. M. Castel and L. Cubo (eds), *La Renovación de la Palabra en el Bicentenario de la Argentina: 1348–1355*. Mendoza: Universidad Nacional de Cuyo.

Viegas Barros, José Pedro, 2002. Fonología del proto-mataguayo. In Mily Crevels, Hein van der Voort, Sérgio Meira and Simon van de Kerke (eds), *Current Studies on South American Languages: Contributions to the 50th International Congress of Americanists*, pp. 137–148. Indigenous Languages of Latin America Series, vol. 3. Leiden: Research School CNWS of Asian, African and Amerindian Studies.

3

Areas and Universals

Balthasar Bickel

3.1 Introduction

In explanations of how linguistic structures are distributed in the world, the pendulum has swung back from an emphasis on universals, which dominated the second half of the twentieth century, to a renewed emphasis on local developments and areal diffusion. This shift in emphasis started over twenty years ago with Dryer (1989), who drew attention to large-scale diffusion as an important possible confounding factor in the statistics of universals, and with Nichols (1992), who set out to test universals but instead discovered an intriguing set of large-scale areal patterns. The general shift has gained further impetus with Maslova (2000), who raised the possibility that the current distribution of linguistic structures does not so much reflect universal tendencies but rather accidental skewings during the early developments of language, including skewings due to areal diffusion. Dediu and Levinson (2013) even suggest that the current distribution might reveal signals from ancient contacts with now-extinct sister lineages (Neanderthals, Denisovans and perhaps other unknown lineages) in Eurasia and the Sahul area.

The shift in emphasis has considerably challenged prospects for the discovery of universals. It has become clear that the sheer frequency of some patterns in the world does not in itself suggest effects from a universal principle of language: a pattern can be dominant in frequency worldwide just because it spread around the world through historically contingent cases of areal diffusion. For example, the fact that non-verb-initial languages are far more frequent than verb-initial languages does not necessarily suggest that the former are preferred as a matter of principle, for example because of a processing principle. The observed frequency

My thanks go to Johanna Nichols and Raymond Hickey for helpful comments on an earlier draft of this chapter. The chapter was written in January 2014 and revised in early 2015. It thus reflects the state of areal linguistics at that time. All shortcomings are my own.

distribution could just as well reflect a multitude of far-reaching but accidental spreads in the distant past, for example, expansion of verb-final structure in the Eurasian steppe, spread of verb-medial order in Southeast Asia in the wake of Tai migrations, or spread of verb-medial order together with the Bantu expansion.

But how can we assess and demonstrate such kinds of areal diffusion? The problems here are by no means smaller than the challenges facing research on universals. First, the repeated spread of some pattern might itself be driven by universal forces: if a structure is universally preferred by some principle (e.g. by processing ease), we would in fact expect it to diffuse in contact situations more easily than universally dispreferred structures. For example, there is growing evidence that simple morphology, for example in case marking, is favoured by adult learners (Bentz and Winter 2013, summarizing earlier work), and there is tentative evidence from Artificial Language Learning experiments that certain word order patterns are more easily acquired by adults than others (Culbertson et al. 2012). Findings like these imply that some patterns spread more easily in the wake of second language learning, i.e. in contact situations, than other patterns, possibly resulting in large-scale areal spreads.

A second problem is similar in kind to the possible fallacies when interpreting worldwide frequencies as universal preferences: if a pattern is more frequent in an area than outside it, this can be attributed to diffusion in contact only to the extent that we can be sure that the pattern did not arise many times independently because of some universal principle. For example, dependent marking on arguments (by case or adpositions) is known to occur with increased frequency throughout Eurasia, with only a few exceptions in Southeast Asia (Bickel and Nichols 2009). This does not by itself establish that dependent marking spread in this area: it is equally possible that dependent marking is favoured in the area independently in each family. This could be caused by the fact that dependent marking here is mostly embedded in verb-final sentence structures. These structures are expected to favour dependent marking universally (Greenberg 1963; Nichols 1992; Siewierska 1996), because this kind of marking makes sentence processing (Hawkins 2004) and/or transmission of meaning more efficient (Gibson et al. 2013; Hall et al. 2013).

Obviously, none of these problems can be solved by keeping the pendulum of emphasis active, sometimes attributing frequency patterns to areal diffusion, sometimes to universal trends. What is needed instead is an approach that focuses on the *interaction* between area formation and universals, seeking to identify the extent to which the two explain how linguistic structures are distributed in the world. This chapter discusses some possible ways of making progress in this question, drawing mostly on the theoretical framework of Distributional Typology (Bickel 2015).

In the following, I begin the discussion by exploring the kinds of processes that lead to area formation and universal patterns (Section 3.2). This leads me to suggest ways of distinguishing the statistical footprint of the relevant processes (Section 3.3). Section 3.4 illustrates the methods via recent case studies, and Section 3.5 concludes the chapter.

3.2 Functional and Event-based Triggers of Language Change

As already noted, one of the key challenges in understanding areal patterns is that they need not result from historical contingencies but can just as well reflect universally preferred patterns of areal diffusion. The traditional opposition between areas and universals fails to capture the underlying processes and causes here.

As an alternative conceptual opposition, genetics offers the contrast between 'horizontal' and 'vertical' transfer, but these notions do not help much either: linguistic diffusion is always a vertical, diachronic process (Croft et al. 2011). When we say that a structure (say, verb-final order) has spread in an area, what is meant is that the languages in this area changed their structure so as to mirror the structure of their neighbours, or that they selectively kept structures that mirror those of their neighbours. Such processes can easily take several generations before their results stabilize in a community, and as Johanson (1992) emphasized some time ago, these processes are fundamentally based on copying and imitating (calquing). Horizontal transfer in genetics, by contrast, involves the direct transfer of concrete genetic material across synchronically co-existing individuals (as is common in bacteria).[1]

Given these conceptual problems, it is advisable to replace the traditional opposition between areas and universals by one that is grounded in the causes and conditions of distributional patterns. Approached from this perspective, the main contrast turns out to be between *functional* and *event-based* triggers (inducers) of language change.

Functional triggers are grounded in the biological/cognitive or social/communicative conditions of language, such as specific processing preferences (e.g. Bickel et al. 2015; Christiansen and Chater 2008; Hawkins 2004) or specific sociolinguistic constellations (e.g. Lupyan and Dale 2010; Trudgill 2011) that systematically bias the way linguistic structures evolve. The defining property of functional triggers is that they affect transition probabilities universally, independent of concrete historical events. For example, if it is true that processing principles cause verb-final word order to associate with dependent marking, we expect this to cause a higher probability of

---

[1] Lexical borrowing would seem more similar to horizontal transfer than structural copying, but even lexical borrowing does not involve the direct transfer of Saussurian signs. Rather, the recipient language imitates a foreign word, using its own phonology, and so the process is more similar to the creation of a new word, inspired by a foreign model, but firmly under the constraints of the native sound inventory.

languages changing towards than away from this association, and this transition probability is the same in any language, at any time.

But note that such kinds of universally fixed transition probabilities do not always result in universally widespread patterns: a functional trigger may be tied to a biological or social condition that itself has a limited distribution in the world. Possible such cases are discussed by Dediu and Ladd (2007) for genetic and Everett et al. (2015) for environmental factors in phonological tone, and by Evans (2003) for specific social structures favouring specific grammars and lexicalizations in kinship expressions (known as 'kintax'). To the extent that the underlying functional trigger is indeed real, the probabilities of developing and maintaining the relevant structures (tone, kintax) are universally fixed even if they cannot yield the same results all over the world because the conditions do not obtain everywhere. When the conditions are met, however, functional triggers are expected to yield systematic, replicated patterns. Therefore, such triggers can also be called *principles*.

The expected systematicity of effects also entails that a functionally preferred structure can easily spread when languages are in contact, leading to area formation: if a certain structure, or a certain association between structures, is preferred by processing mechanisms or a certain sociolinguistic setting, there is every reason to expect that when speakers can select between variants in multilingual settings, they select the variant that complies with the preferred structure or the preferred association of structures.

Event-based triggers are tied to single historical events, leading to idiosyncratic, one-off changes. A classic example is the RUKI rule of Indo-European which retracted *s after *r, *u, *k and *i at some point in the history of the family. Event-based triggers are especially prominent in language contact situations, when a structure is copied not because it has a universally high probability of developing, but simply out of fashion. For example, relative pronouns and 'have'-based perfect tenses appear to have a very low probability of developing, as suggested by their extremely rare occurrence (see Comrie and Kuteva 2013 and Dahl and Velupillai 2013, respectively). As far as we know, the structures do not seem to be particularly preferred by either processing or social conditions of language use. However, where they occur, they appear to have spread in the wake of intensive language contact events, that is, in Europe during the transition period between Antiquity and the Middle Ages (Haspelmath 1998; Heine and Kuteva 2006). Another example is the finding by Bickel et al. (2014) that differential object and differential subject marking are strongly dispreferred worldwide, but spread widely (to different extents) in two hotbeds, one in Southwestern Eurasia and the other in Australia.

In these cases, event-based area formation rests mostly on the preferred development (grammaticalization) of a structure inside an area. But as in other diachronic processes, the key effect can also be the preferred maintenance, rather than innovation, of a structure. Examples of this are ergative case alignment or pronominal gender. These structures have been observed to emerge rarely, but when they do emerge, they tend to persist in areal clusters: see Bickel et al. (2015) and Nichols (1993) on ergativity, and Bickel (2013) and Nichols (1992) on gender.

What these examples suggest is that both functional and event-based triggers can lead to area formation. However, because functional triggers come with universally fixed transition probabilities, they can be expected to leave a different statistical footprint in the typological record than event-based triggers. Specifically, functional triggers can be expected to leave the same footprint across geographical regions. Event-based triggers, by contrast, are tied to specific historical contingencies, and so they are expected to leave signals only in single regions.

Quantification of this contrast is challenging because the relevant regions are often unknown. Since Dryer (1989) and Nichols (1992), typologists usually operate with a predefined set of regions (e.g. Africa, Eurasia, New Guinea/Australia and the Americas, or more fine-grained distinctions). Functional triggers are then expected to leave the same statistical signal across all these regions while event-based triggers are expected to leave statistically different signals in each region. This is the basic state-of-the-art model in which we can test the effects of functional versus event-based triggers, and I will discuss the relevant methods for this model and case study applications below. Before getting there, however, I wish to elaborate a bit further the challenges posed by the definition of regions.

Humans, linguists among them, are good at detecting spatial patterns. Browsing *The World Atlas of Language Structures* (WALS: Dryer and Haspelmath 2013), for example, one can easily discern dozens of potentially interesting clusterings in space. What is not so easy is to tease apart genuine from spurious clusters. Statistical methods are only of limited help here because a statistical correlation can of course itself be spurious (as was recently highlighted for typological data by Roberts and Winters 2013). What is needed is robust causal theories that motivate specific scenarios of event-based triggers and the distributional patterns that can be predicted from these scenarios, that is, what Bickel and Nichols (2006) call *Predictive Areality Theories*. The key idea of Predictive Areality Theories is that areal patterns are predicted by what is known from social/cultural history and archaeology, from language spreads and contact events, and from migration patterns as revealed for example through molecular anthropology. An example is the Predictive Areality Theory of the Eurasian area, which has good support in both the historical record of ancient migrations and language spreads and the population genetic record. Together, these records suggest multiple waves of intensive language contact events over at least the past 14,000–19,000 years; for a summary of the historical record, see Nichols (1998), and for the genetic record, Rootsi et al. (2007) and Ilumäe et al. (2016).

3.3 Methods

The discussion so far suggests that the relative impact of functional and event-based triggers can be best evaluated through statistical modelling, following the well-established framework of *Generalized Linear Models* (see Baayen 2008 and Johnson 2008 for linguistically oriented introductions): the distribution of a particular structure (say a specific word order) is predicted by the interaction of the conditions that are caused by the assumed triggers, for example, conditions of area formation that are caused by specific historical contact events (e.g. Eurasia) and conditions of universal preferences that are caused by functional triggers (e.g. verb-final clause structures favouring certain argument-marking patterns, or social organization types favouring certain 'kintax' patterns).

There are various ways of implementing such models, and there is no consensus yet as to which implementation is most suitable. The literature includes logistic (Sinnemäki 2010) as well as log-linear (Poisson) models (Bickel 2011; Cysouw 2010a), and some authors model areas as random factors (Cysouw 2010a; Jaeger et al. 2011), others as fixed factors (Bickel et al. 2009; Sinnemäki 2010). In practice, these choices often have relatively little impact on results. Still, we clearly need more 'meta-typological' research of the kind presented in Maslova (2008) and Cysouw (2010b) to resolve the underlying issues.

What is far more pressing, however, is the question of how one can in fact assess whether a hypothesized diachronic process – functional or event-based, alone or through interaction – leaves a signal in the typological record. Synchronic frequency counts can be deceptive because we cannot assume that the distributions of our samples have reached what is known as stationarity (Cysouw 2011; Dediu and Cysouw 2013; Maslova 2000). Stationarity means that when individual languages change types, this is compensated for by other changes elsewhere in the population of languages so that the total frequencies of types remain the same. If this is the case, synchronic frequencies can provide a direct and reliable estimate of transition probabilities (if well sampled). But such a situation cannot be assumed *a priori* for typological data, especially since event-based triggers do not lead to universally fixed and constant transition probabilities (Maslova 2000). Further, empirical studies of large families have shown that synchronic frequency distributions can indeed sometimes differ markedly from the frequencies that one would expect under stationarity; see for example Cysouw (2011) for a demonstration of this with regard to word order and adposition patterns in Austronesian.

In response to these challenges, current approaches have moved away from interpreting raw synchronic frequency patterns and now aim at estimating trends in transition probabilities within individual families (from which in turn one can calculate the expected stationary distribution for each family). There is a number of proposals that are currently being explored, but they all share the basic insight that differences and trends in transition probabilities can be estimated from languages that belong to the same family. If we know that some languages belong to the same family (because the family has been demonstrated using the comparative method), we know that the properties of these languages have developed through a chain of innovation and retention from a single proto-language (corresponding to what is known as a Markov chain in mathematics). The challenge then is to estimate the development of this chain. Some methods rely on pairs of languages that belong to the same family, each sampled at the same time depth (Dediu and Cysouw 2013; Maslova 2004; Maslova and Nikitina 2007); others rely on exhaustive samples of languages in each family, at variable time depths (Bickel 2011, 2013); still others rely on estimated or reconstructed tree topologies, of variable size and time depth (Dediu and Levinson 2012; Dunn et al. 2011).[2]

Each method has its advantages and disadvantages. Pairwise methods make the problematic assumption that, within an assumed time depth, there was at most one change and no reticulation (Dediu and Cysouw 2013), but they have the advantage that one needs to sample only two languages per family. Exhaustive-sample methods require more data. This is an apparent disadvantage, but it has the advantage that the method can pick up more signals. Tree-based methods have the highest resolution, but they limit historical models to trees and exclude the possibility of wave and network models, although such models are often plausible, especially from the point of view of areal diffusion processes (François 2014). Another requirement of tree-based methods is estimates of branch lengths, as these provide the relevant time intervals within which rates of change are calculated. This can be problematic when, as is usually done, branch length estimates are gained from lexical data (cognate replacements), because lexical change is not necessarily a good calibration stick for structural change. After all, lexical stems can be conservative while syntax may at the same time change rapidly, precisely as one would in fact expect for substrate effects (Thomason and Kaufman 1988).

A key problem faced by all methods is that they require samples from within families. Yet about half of the known families on our planet are represented in available databases by only a single member – either because no other members are known at all or because no relevant data are available. When testing theories with universal scope or large-scale area effects, data from these single-member families can be absolutely critical. The only proposal so far that attempts to solve this problem is based on an extrapolation algorithm (Bickel 2013).

---

[2] Software implementation is available and documented for all methods. Maslova's pairwise method is available via Dediu and Cysouw (2013); my own exhaustive-sample-based Family Bias Method via Bickel (2013). Tree-based methods rely on software developed for genetics, such as BayesTraits (Pagel and Meade 2013), MrBayes (Ronquist and Huelsenbeck 2003) or GEIGER (Harmon et al. 2008).

The basic strategy is to first perform estimates on diachronic biases (differences in transition probabilities) within larger families, using one of the methods mentioned above. This results in an overall estimate of the probability that a family will show a diachronic bias (i.e. a significant difference in estimated transition probabilities) as opposed to being diverse (with no significant difference in the direction of estimated transition probabilities). For the typological variable of agent-before-patient versus patient-before-agent order, for example, there is a 0.69 probability of families showing a bias (in one of the two possible directions) and a 0.31 probability of being diverse (Bickel 2013). Extrapolation then proceeds by randomly selecting 69 per cent of the small families (with between one and, say, four languages) and declaring them as stemming from an unknown larger family with a bias. The actual value of the bias is read off the data: for example, if Basque happens to be picked up as belonging to an unknown biased family, it would be taken to reflect a bias towards agent-before-patient order, since this is the pattern shown by Basque. Allowing for statistical deviation (the sole known survivor of a family may be the odd one out, having undergone atypical development) and resampling the extrapolations in order to assess error margins, the algorithm then yields estimates of how many families are likely to have been biased versus not biased diachronically, when they are estimated to have been biased, and how many families have been biased in which direction.

Another important challenge for all methods is that the statistical signals of diachronic biases are often very weak: functional principles and historical contact events can only ever trigger possible diachronies, but they do not themselves guarantee the emergence of actual developments: the actualization of a possible diachrony is entirely a matter of social propagation within a speech community. This process is fraught with multiple confounding factors, ranging from competing functional principles and competing contact events to matters of social prestige and language ideology in a given community. Consequently, it often takes many functionally driven or event-based processes in individuals before the result can be detected in the diachronic biases of a language family.

3.4 Areal Signals of Eurasia, Hidden Behind Universals

A number of recent studies have reassessed the evidence for functional principles that have been hypothesized to underlie statistical universals in the literature. While controlling for areal patterns, some of these studies have revealed evidence for event-based triggers of change that have affected distributions in addition to, but independently of, the relevant functional principles. These studies are interesting for the purposes of the present chapter because they suggest that evidence for event-based area formation can come from research into universals. I focus here on two recent case studies that concern the Eurasian area.[3]

Performing log-linear analyses on diachronic biases, Bickel (2015) reports that families within Eurasia are significantly more likely to be biased towards developing and maintaining dependent marking on arguments (specifically, towards formal distinctions between agent and patient noun phrases of two-argument clauses) than families outside Eurasia. This difference is independent of the equally significant effect that leads verb-final families or subfamilies[4] to biases towards dependent marking. In other words, the event-based diachrony that favours the emergence and maintenance of dependent marking in Eurasia is statistically independent of the functional principles that make verb-final structures easier to process and/or transmit in communication if there is dependent marking than if there is no such marking (Gibson et al. 2013; Hall et al. 2013; Hawkins 2004).

An earlier study (Bickel 2011) looked at the Greenbergian correlation between the order of dependent noun phrases with respect to the head noun (left-branching [[NP] N] versus right-branching [N [NP]]) and the order of patient noun phrases with respect to the verb (left-branching [[NP] V] versus right-branching [V [NP]]), relying on Dryer's data in WALS (Dryer 2005a, 2005b). The study controlled for various continent-sized areal patterns. However, since left-branching NPs are particularly frequent in the core of Eurasia (Masica's 2001 'Indo-Turanian' area), it is possible that any areal effect on NP order is specifically caused by the difference between diachronic biases within versus outside Eurasia. The Eurasian peripheries in Europe and Southeast Asia tend to show deviating NP orders (e.g. right-branching dependent NPs in French and Thai, respectively), but as argued in Bickel (2015) for other parts of grammar, deviating patterns like these may represent younger developments than those that shaped the Eurasian area as a whole. Incipient evidence for this possibility comes from the fact that left-branching NPs are attested even in the peripheries, sometimes as the dominant structure (Basque in Europe, Karen in Southeast Asia) and sometimes as an alternative pattern (English left-branching *John's house* versus right-branching *the house of John*).

Based on these considerations, I estimated family biases in NP orders and performed a log-linear analysis of the association of these biases with VP order and the location within versus outside Eurasia. The results are given in Table 3.1.

The statistical analysis suggests that both area and VP order are significant and at the same time independent of each other.[5] This means that the

---

[3] See Sinnemäki (2010) for a case study showing evidence for Southeast Asia and for what Güldemann (2008) calls the 'Macro-Sudan Belt' in Africa, while testing a functional theory relating zero-marking and SVO order.

[4] When families are split with regard to word order, as is the case for Indo-European or Sino-Tibetan, the study estimated biases within homogeneous subgroups of the family. See the original study for details, and Bickel (2013) for theoretical justification.

[5] This can be tested using a likelihood ratio test to compare models with versus without the relevant interaction between variables: AREA × NP ORDER BIAS $\chi^2 = 4.96, p = 0.03$; VP ORDER × NP ORDER BIAS $\chi^2 = 112.2, p < 0.001$. The three-way interaction is not significant ($\chi^2 = 1.79, p = 0.18$), suggesting independence of the area and order effects.

Table 3.1 *Mean estimated diachronic biases of NP order in families with right-branching versus left-branching VPs, inside versus outside Eurasia (data from Dryer 2005a, 2005b; estimation method from Bickel 2013 with extrapolation to isolates and small families)*

| Area | VP order | Biased families | | | Ratio of biases |
		No bias	[[NP] N]	[N [NP]]	[[NP] N] / [N [NP]]
Inside Eurasia	[V [NP]]	3.67	7.93	14.40	0.55
	[[NP] V]	6.86	45.30	0.84	53.93
Outside Eurasia	[V [NP]]	10.61	36.92	66.47	0.56
	[[NP] V]	37.76	97.42	8.83	11.03

family biases are best modelled by effects both from functional principles preferring harmony in branching direction and an event-based process that increases the number of families that are diachronically biased towards left-branching NPs in Eurasia. This can also be seen directly in the differences between the ratio of left-branching versus right-branching families in the last column of Table 3.1. Inside Eurasia, families biased towards left-branching NPs outnumber families biased towards right-branching NPs by a factor of almost 54. Outside Eurasia this factor is only about 11. No comparable difference can be observed with biases in right-branching NPs. This confirms the hypothesis that the Eurasian spreads specifically targeted left-branching NPs – not as a structure with a universal preference but as something that happened to be locally attractive for copying, a mere fashion.

The two case studies reported here show that critical evidence for event-based area formation can sometimes come from research on universal correlations. In both case studies, a hypothesized functional principle is confirmed by looking at estimates of diachronic biases in families. But the functional principles alone fail to explain the distribution sufficiently. In addition, there is evidence that event-based triggers of language change also significantly contributed to the observed spatial distribution.

3.5 Conclusions

Research on areas and research on universals have long been considered to be irreconcilable opposites. The studies surveyed in this chapter have shown that the two strands of research require one another. Research on areas is needed in order to control for alternative explanations when studying universals. Conversely, research on universals sometimes

---

Family biases in NP order were estimated using the familybias function that is made available at https://github.com/IVS-UZH/familybias for use in R (R Development Core Team 2014), with default parameter settings. When families are split in VP order, biases are estimated within non-split subgroups, just as in the other case study (see the previous note).

provides critical evidence for areal developments in particular regions. Progress in each domain requires a deeper and better understanding of the relevant trigger that causes the observed distributions: in-depth research on the cognitive/biological and social/communicative principles that favour the development and maintenance of specific structures, and at the same time, in-depth research on the historical and population-genetic events that intensified language contact during specific periods in specific regions.

Good causal theories in these domains make clear predictions on likely or less likely pathways of diachronic development. We now have a range of estimation techniques and databases at our disposal that make it possible to test these predictions. Good theories bring with them higher resolution in their predictions and modern estimation techniques require dense samples. This means that for all the methodological and theoretical progress that has been made on the question of areas and universals, the most urgent task remains the empirical groundwork of analysing ever-larger arrays of languages across the world and making these analyses available in databases.

References

Baayen, R. Harald, 2008. *Analyzing Linguistic Data*. Cambridge: Cambridge University Press.

Bentz, Christian and Bodo Winter, 2013. Languages with more second language learners tend to lose nominal case. *Language Dynamics and Change* 3: 1–27.

Bickel, Balthasar, 2011. Statistical modeling of language universals. *Linguistic Typology* 15: 401–414.

Bickel, Balthasar, 2013. Distributional biases in language families. In Balthasar Bickel, Lenore A. Grenoble, David A. Peterson and Alan Timberlake (eds), *Language Typology and Historical Contingency*, pp. 415–444. Amsterdam: John Benjamins.

Bickel, Balthasar, 2015. Distributional Typology: Statistical inquiries into the dynamics of linguistic diversity. In Bernd Heine and Heiko Narrog (eds), *The Oxford Handbook of Linguistic Analysis*, second edition, pp. 901–923. Oxford: Oxford University Press.

Bickel, Balthasar, Kristine Hildebrandt and René Schiering, 2009. The distribution of phonological word domains: A probabilistic typology. In Janet Grijzenhout and Bariş Kabak (eds), *Phonological Domains: Universals and Deviations*, pp. 47–75. Berlin: Mouton de Gruyter.

Bickel, Balthasar and Johanna Nichols, 2006. Oceania, the Pacific Rim, and the theory of linguistic areas. *Proc. Berkeley Linguistics Society* 32: 3–15.

Bickel, Balthasar and Johanna Nichols, 2009. The geography of case. In Andrej Malchukov and Andrew Spencer (eds), *The Oxford Handbook of Case*, pp. 479–493. Oxford: Oxford University Press.

Bickel, Balthasar, Alena Witzlack-Makarevich and Taras Zakharko, 2014. Typological evidence against universal effects of referential scales on case alignment. In Ina Bornkessel-Schlesewsky, Andrej Malchukov and Marc Richards (eds), *Scales: A Cross-Disciplinary Perspective on Referential Hierarchies*, pp. 7–43. Berlin: de Gruyter Mouton.

Bickel, Balthasar, Alena Witzlack-Makarevich, Kamal K. Choudhary, Matthias Schlesewsky and Ina Bornkessel-Schlesewsky, 2015. The neurophysiology of language processing shapes the evolution of grammar: Evidence from case marking. *PLoS ONE* 10: e0132819.

Christiansen, Morten H. and Nick Chater, 2008. Language as shaped by the brain. *Behavioral and Brain Sciences* 31: 489–509.

Comrie, Bernard and Tania Kuteva, 2013. Relativization strategies. In Matthew S. Dryer and Martin Haspelmath (eds), *The World Atlas of Language Structures Online*. Leipzig: Max Planck Institute for Evolutionary Anthropology. http://wals.info/chapter/s8

Croft, William, Tanmoy Bhattacharya, Dave Kleinschmidt, Eric D. Smith and T. Florian Jaeger, 2011. Greenbergian universals, diachrony and statistical analysis. *Linguistic Typology* 15: 433–453.

Culbertson, Jennifer, Paul Smolensky and Géraldine Legendre, 2012. Learning biases predict a word order universal. *Cognition* 122: 306–329.

Cysouw, Michael, 2010a. Dealing with diversity: Towards an explanation of NP-internal word order frequencies. *Linguistic Typology* 14: 253–286.

Cysouw, Michael, 2010b. On the probability distribution of typological frequencies. In Christian Ebert, Gerhard Jäger and Jens Michaelis (eds), *The Mathematics of Language*, pp. 29–35. Berlin: Springer.

Cysouw, Michael, 2011. Understanding transition probabilities. *Linguistic Typology* 15: 415–431.

Dahl, Östen and Viveka Velupillai, 2013. The Perfect. In Matthew S. Dryer and Martin Haspelmath (eds), *The World Atlas of Language Structures Online*. Leipzig: Max Planck Institute for Evolutionary Anthropology. http://wals.info/chapter/68

Dediu, Dan and Michael Cysouw, 2013. Some structural aspects of language are more stable than others: A comparison of seven methods. *PLoS ONE* 8: e55009.

Dediu, Dan and Robert D. Ladd, 2007. Linguistic tone is related to the population frequency of the adaptive haplogroups of two brain size genes, *ASPM* and *Microcephalin*. *Proceedings of the National Academy of Sciences of the USA* 104: 10944–10949.

Dediu, Dan and Stephen C. Levinson, 2012. Abstract profiles of structural stability point to universal tendencies, family-specific factors, and ancient connections between languages. *PLoS ONE* 7: e45198.

Dediu, Dan and Stephen C. Levinson, 2013. On the antiquity of language: The reinterpretation of Neandertal linguistic capacities and its consequences. *Frontiers in Psychology* 4 (397): 1–17.

Dryer, Matthew S., 1989. Large linguistic areas and language sampling. *Studies in Language* 13: 257–292.

Dryer, Matthew S., 2005a. Order of genitive and noun. In Martin Haspelmath, Matthew S. Dryer, David Gil and Bernard Comrie (eds), *The World Atlas of Language Structures*, pp. 350–353. Oxford University Press.

Dryer, Matthew S., 2005b. Order of subject, object, and verb. In Martin Haspelmath, Matthew S. Dryer, David Gil and Bernard Comrie (eds), *The World Atlas of Language Structures*, pp. 330–341. Oxford University Press.

Dryer, Matthew S. and Martin Haspelmath (eds), 2013. *The World Atlas of Language Structures Online*. Leipzig: Max Planck Institute for Evolutionary Anthropology. http://wals.info

Dunn, Michael J., Simon J. Greenhill, Stephen C. Levinson and Russell D. Gray, 2011. Evolved structure of language shows lineage-specific trends in word-order universals. *Nature* 473: 79–82.

Evans, Nicholas, 2003. Context, culture, and structuration in the languages of Australia. *Annual Review of Anthropology* 32: 13–40.

Everett, Caleb, Damián E. Blasi and Seán G. Roberts, 2015. Climate, vocal folds, and tonal languages: Connecting the physiological and geographic dots. *Proceedings of the National Academy of Sciences* 112: 1322–1327.

François, Alexandre, 2014. Trees, waves and linkages: Models of language diversification. In Claire Bowern and Bethwyn Evans (eds), *The Routledge Handbook of Historical Linguistics*, pp. 161–189. London: Routledge.

Gibson, Edward, Steven T. Piantadosi, Kimberly Brink et al., 2013. A noisy-channel account of crosslinguistic word-order variation. *Psychological Science* 24: 1079–1088.

Greenberg, Joseph H., 1963. Some universals of grammar with particular reference to the order of meaningful elements. In Joseph H. Greenberg (ed.), *Universals of Language*, pp. 73–113. Cambridge, MA: The MIT Press.

Güldemann, Tom, 2008. The Macro-Sudan Belt: Towards identifying a linguistic area in northern sub-Saharan Africa. In Bernd Heine (ed.), *A Linguistic Geography of Africa*, pp. 151–185. Cambridge: Cambridge University Press.

Hall, Matthew L., Rachel I. Mayberry and Victor S. Ferreira, 2013. Cognitive constraints on constituent order: Evidence from elicited pantomime. *Cognition* 129: 1–17.

Harmon, Luke J., Jason T. Weir, Chad D. Brock, Richard E. Glor and Wendell Challenger, 2008. GEIGER: Investigating evolutionary radiations. *Bioinformatics* 24: 129–131.

Haspelmath, Martin, 1998. How young is Standard Average European? *Language Sciences* 20: 271–287.

Hawkins, John A., 2004. *Efficiency and Complexity in Grammars*. Oxford: Oxford University Press.

Heine, Bernd and Tania Kuteva, 2006. *The Changing Languages of Europe*. Oxford: Oxford University Press.

Ilumäe, Anne-Mai, Maere Reidla, Marina Chukhryaeva et al., 2016. Human Y chromosome haplogroup N: A non-trivial time-resolved phylogeography that cuts across language families. *The American Journal of Human Genetics* 99: 163–173.

Jaeger, T. Florian, Peter Graff, William Croft and Daniel Pontillo, 2011. Mixed effect models for genetic and areal dependencies in linguistic typology. *Linguistic Typology* 15: 281–320.

Johanson, Lars, 1992. *Strukturelle Faktoren in türkischen Sprachkontakten*. Stuttgart: Steiner.

Johnson, Keith, 2008. *Quantitative Methods in Linguistics*. London: Blackwell.

Lupyan, Gary and Rick Dale, 2010. Language structure is partly determined by social structure. *PLoS ONE* 5: e8559.

Masica, Colin, 2001. The definition and significance of linguistic areas: Methods, pitfalls, and possibilities (with special reference to the validity of South Asia as a linguistic area). In Peri Bhaskararao and Karumuri Venkata Subbarao (eds), *Tokyo Symposium on South Asian Languages: Contact, Convergence, and Typology (The Yearbook of South Asian Languages and Linguistics 2001)*, pp. 205–267. New Delhi: Sage Publications.

Maslova, Elena, 2000. A dynamic approach to the verification of distributional universals. *Linguistic Typology* 4: 307–333.

Maslova, Elena, 2004. Dinamika tipologičeskix raspredelenij i stabil'nost' jazykovyx tipov. *Voprosy Jazykoznanija* 2004: 3–16.

Maslova, Elena, 2008. Meta-typological distributions. *Language Typology and Universals* 61: 199–207.

Maslova, Elena and Tatiana Nikitina, 2007. Stochastic universals and dynamics of cross-linguistic distributions: The case of alignment types. Manuscript, Stanford University. http://anothersumma.net/Publications/Ergativity.pdf

Nichols, Johanna, 1992. *Linguistic Diversity in Space and Time*. Chicago: University of Chicago Press.

Nichols, Johanna, 1993. Ergativity and linguistic geography. *Australian Journal of Linguistics* 13: 39–89.

Nichols, Johanna, 1998. The Eurasian spread zone and the Indo-European dispersal. In Roger Blench and Matthew Spriggs (eds), *Archaeology and Language,* vol. II: *Archaeological Data and Linguistic Hypotheses*, pp. 220–266. London: Routledge.

Pagel, Mark and Andrew Meade, 2013. BayesTraits V2: Software and manual. www.evolution.rdg.ac.uk/BayesTraitsV2Beta.html

R Development Core Team, 2014. *R: A Language and Environment for Statistical Computing*. Vienna: R Foundation for Statistical Computing. www.r-project.org

Roberts, Seán and James Winters, 2013. Linguistic diversity and traffic accidents: Lessons from statistical studies of cultural traits. *PLoS ONE* 8: e70902.

Ronquist, Fredrik and John P. Huelsenbeck, 2003. MrBayes 3: Bayesian phylogenetic inference under mixed models. *Bioinformatics* 19: 1572–1574.

Rootsi, S., L. A. Zhivotovsky, M. Baldovic et al., 2007. A counter-clockwise northern route of the Y-chromosome haplogroup N from Southeast Asia towards Europe. *European Journal of Human Genetics* 15: 204–211.

Siewierska, Anna, 1996. Word order type and alignment. *Language Typology and Universals* 49: 149–176.

Sinnemäki, Kaius, 2010. Word order in zero-marking languages. *Studies in Language* 34: 869–912.

Thomason, Sarah Grey and Terrence Kaufman, 1988. *Language Contact, Creolization, and Genetic Linguistics*. Berkeley, CA: University of California Press.

Trudgill, Peter, 2011. *Sociolinguistic Typology: Social Determinants of Linguistic Complexity*. Oxford: Oxford University Press.

4

Reassessing Sprachbunds: A View from the Balkans

Victor A. Friedman and Brian D. Joseph

4.1 Basic Facts about Sprachbunds, in the Balkans and Elsewhere

It is almost impossible to talk about the Balkans from a linguistic standpoint and not utter the term 'sprachbund' or one of the variously used English counterparts, such as 'linguistic area', 'linguistic union', 'convergence area' or 'linguistic league'.[1] Indeed, among linguists, one of the things that the Balkans are best known for is being a sprachbund, that is to say, a zone – a geographic grouping – of languages with similarities, especially of a structural nature, that are the result of language contact rather than descent from a common ancestor or typological universals.

The Balkan sprachbund, taking in Albanian, Greek, the South Slavic languages Bulgarian, Macedonian, and some dialects of the Bosnian-Croatian-Serbian-Montenegrin (BCSM) complex, the Eastern Romance languages Aromanian, Romanian and Meglenoromanian, the co-territorial dialects of the Indic language Romani, and to some extent the co-territorial dialects of Judezmo (brought to the Ottoman Balkans by Jews expelled from the Iberian peninsula) and Turkic (especially West Rumelian and Gagauz), is noted for a large number of 'areal features' – first called 'Balkanisms' by Seliščev (1925) – covering aspects of phonology, morphology, syntax, semantics and lexicon. For concise overviews of these Balkan features, one can consult Friedman (2006a, 2006b, 2011a), Joseph (2003) or Joseph (2010), with more details to be found in handbook-like presentations such as Sandfeld (1930), Schaller (1975), Feuillet (2012), Asenova

---

[1] The German *Sprachbund* means literally 'language-union'; none of the English terms proposed in its place has really caught on, so we use here the German word as a borrowing into English, and we nativize it. We therefore write it with a lower-case initial letter and form the plural as *sprachbunds*, not *Sprachbünde*, except when citing the explicit usage of another scholar; in this way, it is like *pretzel* or other German loanwords in English (plural *pretzels*, not **Pretzeln*). As is seen below, just as English *pretzel* has similar but not identical connotations to its German source, so, too, our understanding of sprachbund is not the literal translation from German that has disturbed scholars such as Stolz (2006).

(2002), Demiraj (2004) and in the compendious Friedman and Joseph (in press b).

The result of this linguistic convergence is that, in many instances, one can map between Balkan languages simply by taking note of relevant vocabulary differences.[2] For instance, many Balkan languages converge in using impersonal (third person singular) non-active verb forms (involving either medio-passive (MP) morphology or reflexive marking (RX)) with a dative experiencer in the sense 'X feels like …' (literally 'to-X$_{DAT}$ VERB$_{NONACT.3SG}$ …'), as illustrated in (1) for the meaning 'I feel like eating burek' (see Friedman and Joseph in press a):

(1) Macedonian   *Mi*   *se jade*   *(burek)*
     Aromanian   *Nji*   *-si mãcã*   *(burec)*
     Meglenoromanian   *Ăń*   *-ţi máncă*   *(burec)*
                       me.DAT RX eat.3SG.PRS   (burek)
     Albanian   *Më*   *hahet*   *(byrek)*
                       me.DAT eat.3SG.PRS.MP   (burek)
     Bulgarian   *Jade*   *mi se*   *(bjurek)*
                       eats.3SG.PRS me.DAT RX   (burek)
     Romani   *Hala*   *pe mange*   *(bureko)*
                       eat.3SG.PRS RX me.DAT   (burek)
     Kastoria Greek   *Mi*   *trójiti*   (brek)[3]
                       me.ACC eat.3SG.PRS.MP   (burek)
                       'I feel like eating (burek)'

Similarly, several of the languages converge in the order of elements marking negation, future tense, mood and argument structure in the verbal complex, as in (2):[4]

(2) Macedonian   ne   ḱe   (da)   mu   go   davam[5]
     Albanian   s'   do   të   j+   a   jep
     Romanian   nu   o   să   i+   l   dau
     Dialectal Greek: ðe   θe   na   tu   to   ðóso[6]
                     NEG   FUT   SBJV   3SG.DAT/3SG.ACC   give.1SG
                     'I will not give it to him.'

This word-by-word or even morpheme-by-morpheme 'translatability' between languages is what led Jernej Kopitar (1829: 86) to famously characterize the Balkans as an area where '*nur eine Sprachform herrscht, aber mit dreyerley Sprachmaterie.*'[7] Similarly, Miklosich (1861: 6–8) remarked on the convergence by noting such features as:

(3)   a. future with 'want'+ infinitive[8]
       b. lack of infinitive, with replacement by a finite verb preceded by a conjunction[9]
       c. merger of genitive and dative
       d. the un-Romance postposing of the definite article

It was Trubetzkoy, writing in 1923, who took such observations and coined the notion of *jazykovoj sojuz* 'linguistic union' in Russian and the German *Sprachbund*, in his more famous 1928 formulation (Trubetzkoy 1930).

In subsequent years, the features in Miklosich's (1861) account were significantly expanded and elaborated, especially in Sandfeld's (1930) classic study, Asenova (2002) and other works, and further features were taken as characteristic of the Balkan sprachbund, as given in (3, continued):

(3)   e. replacement of conditional by anterior future
       f. object reduplication (proleptic use of clitic pronouns)
       g. simplification of the declensional system
       h. replacement of synthetic comparatives by analytic ones
       i. development of a perfect using the auxiliary 'have'
       j. the so-called narrative imperative[10]
       k. evidential forms or usages
       l. certain types of dative subject constructions
       m. shared lexicon from Turkish, Romance, Slavic, Greek and a presumed ancestor of Albanian.

The isoglosses for these and other important features are complex. For example, there are various remnants of person marking for some future markers; remnants of the infinitive survive to varying degrees; the conditional meaning of the anterior future extends into the BCSM of Montenegro and Bosnia; the postposed definite article is absent from some regions that have the other features; evidentials sometimes come

---

[7] 'Only one grammar dominates but with three lexicons (literally: "language material")'.

[8] Most of these features were also noted by Kopitar. *Infinitive* here is to be understood only in historical terms. Synchronically, the formulation is 'future marked by a particle descended from "want" plus finite form (with or without the so-called subjunctive marker)'. Miklosich (1861) noted other features, especially phonological ones such as the 'prominence' of stressed schwa, and some of these phonological features are repeated in modern surveys. In terms of contact-induced change, however, many of these features represent parallel historical developments rather than convergence; see Hamp (1977) on the need to distinguish the areal from the typological, and Friedman (2008) on Balkan phonologies versus Balkan phonology (but see also Sawicka 1997).

[9] In modern terms, a subjunctive particle. The item in question can also mark independent clauses, generally with a modal sense, as in wishes and polite commands.

[10] This is a construction wherein an imperative, a form ostensibly co-indexing a second person subject, can be used with a first or a third person subject, to render narration more vivid.

from perfects and sometimes from futures, and so on (Belyavski-Frank 2003; Friedman 2006b; Greenberg 2000; Hamp 1989; Joseph 1983).[11]

The notion of a geographic area characterized by languages that are similar in various ways owing to contact rather than genealogical heritage has been extended to groupings in other parts of the world, including South Asia (Emeneau 1956; Masica 1976), the Pacific Northwest (Beck 2000), Mesoamerica (Campbell, Kaufman and Smith-Stark 1986), the Vaupés River region in the Amazon (Aikhenvald 2006b; Epps 2006), the Caucasus (Grawunder, Chapter 13, this volume; but see also Tuite 1999), Ethiopia (Bisang 2006, but see Masica 2001) and Mainland Southeast Asia (Enfield 2005).

In each case studied, there are languages occupying the same space for a reasonably long time, there are various convergent features, and there is the clear evidence of lexical borrowings showing contact among speakers of the different languages. Putting all that together – especially if there is evidence of divergence in at least some of the languages from earlier stages without the convergent features – one is led to the conclusion that the speaker interactions in the region in question are the reason for the convergence. Thus, one indeed has a geographic grouping of languages showing structural convergences as a result of contact: a sprachbund.

But, there are reasons to think that identifying a sprachbund is not as simple as might appear at first glance. In this respect, Tuite (1999) on the Caucasus is highly instructive. He argues that while glottalization and certain phraseological calques do indeed appear to be areal in the Caucasus, on careful examination the oft-cited feature of ergativity is in fact realized in such different ways that it cannot be taken as a commonality, and that the Caucasus region does not, therefore, represent a sprachbund in Trubetzkoy's original sense. In Section 4.2, therefore, we outline some key questions concerning the identification of a sprachbund and then turn to a consideration of how one might answer those questions in general in Sections 4.3–4.6, looking to the Balkans in particular throughout.

4.2   Interrogating the 'Sprachbund'

Although a well-established concept in contact linguistics and historical linguistics, the notion of 'sprachbund' is not without problems. In

---

[11] Phonological features do not figure significantly in this list. While there are some shared phonological innovations among co-territorial dialects of different languages, they are too localized, diverse and diffuse to be generalized in the same way as morphosyntactic features and the lexicon (Friedman 2008; see also Hamp 1977 on schwa as a [non-] Balkanism). This difference may be because getting phonology right is less relevant to second language users, whereas syntactic and morphosyntactic issues are more likely to hinder communicative acts. Moreover, phonology tends to function as an emblematic identity marker. The sort of deeper familiarity with another language that would foster phonological convergence generally occurs at the local level.

particular, the following questions are among those that need to be addressed when considering the utility and validity of this construct. These questions pertain to the nature of the languages involved, in (4a), to the nature of the features involved, in (4b), and to the nature of the causes, in (4c). Moreover, there are others involved in the problematization of the notion of 'sprachbund' that concern the delineation of the region and the groups, as in (4d), and with the assessment of the construct, as in (4e).

(4)   Questions to ask concerning 'sprachbund' as a viable notion
      a. Language-based issues
             i. Is there a minimum number of languages needed to identify a sprachbund?
            ii. Must the languages be unrelated to one another? If relatedness is allowed, how closely related can they be?

      b. Feature-based issues
           iii. Is there a minimum number of features needed to identify a sprachbund?
            iv. How should the features be distributed across the languages? Must all features be found in all the languages? Do some features characterize some languages as forming the 'core' of the sprachbund? If so, how does one assess the contribution of the non-core – peripheral or marginal – features or languages?

      c. Cause-based issues
             v. If contact is the basis for the convergence at issue in an area (and not some other causal factor or mere chance), is there a type of contact that is needed to create a sprachbund?
            vi. What else might play a role in the formation of a sprachbund?

      d. Delineational issues
           vii. How do we identify the boundaries of a sprachbund, if any? Are there different degrees of membership, as suggested by the core/periphery distinction in (iv)?

      e. Assessment issues
          viii. Is the evidence giving a basis for identifying a sprachbund the effects of past sprachbund construction or is the sprachbund an on-going phenomenon?

In what follows, these questions are elaborated upon and some answers given.[12]

---

[12] Much of the material in Sections 4.3 and 4.4 is adapted from Chapter 3 of Friedman and Joseph (in press b), and much of Sections 4.5–4.7 is from Chapter 8.

4.3   Answering the Language-based Issues

First, to address (4a.i), since language contact is involved in the basic definition of a sprachbund, clearly the minimum number of languages necessarily involved is greater than one, but that provokes another question, namely how much greater? Two languages would necessarily constitute the logical minimum for a sprachbund, just as the minimum needed in genetic linguistics for a language family – i.e., a grouping for which contact is irrelevant – is one, as in the case of so-called *isolates*, languages not demonstrably related to any other.[13] While for a sprachbund, one has to have at least two to tango, i.e. at least some contact between speakers of historically distinct systems, Thomason (2001: 99) is among those who insist that a sprachbund must be at least a *ménage à trois*, a point to which we return below.

Trubetzkoy (1930), in his formulation of the difference between the *Sprachfamilie* and the *Sprachbund*, made no mention of boundaries or numbers. He was attempting both to account for and to distinguish the two diachronic ways languages come to resemble one another, what Labov (2007) has termed *transmission* and *diffusion* (see also Hamp 1977). As Trubetzkoy recognized, the *Sprachfamilie* is distinguished by the existence of regular sound correspondences across the member languages, deriving from regular sound changes each underwent, as can be determined using the comparative method and as are found in both grammatical morphemes and core vocabulary. The *Sprachbund*, on the other hand, as Trubetzkoy defined it, was characterized by shared syntax and morphosyntax, non-systematic phonological correspondences, and common 'culture words' (*Kulturwörter*).

While the regularity of sound correspondences has a predictability that neatly parallels the scientific method, the distinction between *core vocabulary* and *culture words* is not uniform and is susceptible to social manipulation. Thus, for example, in the Pomak dialects of Greece, numerals and basic kinship terms are Turkish loanwords, even though the dialects are clearly Slavic in origin, arguably because the speakers of these dialects view Turkish as having importance to their identity as Muslims.[14] Thus, any given body part or basic verb of motion, feeling, bodily function, etc.,

---

[13]   For example, Sumerian, Zuñi and Basque, to name a few. Such isolates of course can have internal dialect diversity – quite rich in the case of Basque, cf. Trask (1996) – a situation that stretches the notion of 'language isolate' through its intersection with the vexing language-versus-dialect question. Also, known isolates may in fact form a stock or phylum with some other existing language, but such connections are not demonstrable given our current state of knowledge and methodology.

[14]   Likewise both Albanian and Bosnian, with their significant numbers of Muslim speakers, use more Turkish kinship terms than co-territorial or neighbouring Macedonian, Serbian or Croatian. On the one hand, Romani dialects in these regions, whose speakers are predominantly Muslim, have native (or Slavic) kinship terms for these relations, arguably as a boundary-marking device. On the other hand, Bulgarian-speaking Christians from Thrace used Turkish numerals like their Pomak neighbours (Kodov 1935). Thus numerals can be highly conservative, but they are also subject to lexical borrowing.

representing words that would certainly be part of any lexical 'core', has the potential to be replaced by a loan.[15] In this respect, Romani is illustrative, perhaps precisely because of its massive multilateral contact. Romani has a pre-Byzantine, mostly Indic, core that accords remarkably well with the notional concept in its basics.

The usefulness of the concept of language family is considered to be self-evident since it provides a historical basis for accounting for language resemblances and relations. Still, as noted above, in the absence of evidence demonstrating a relationship of a given language to any other, the existence of a family with only a single member poses no problem to the concept of language family. Similarly, for defining a given language family, it is precisely the shared history of regular sound change combined with notions of core vocabulary and basic grammar that enable us to speak of boundedness, although Thomason and Kaufman (1988) cogently question the rigidity of such conceptions. It can be argued that nineteenth and early twentieth century ideas connected with the need to establish purities of lineage in 'races' were carried over to languages as well, whence Schleicher's (1850: 143) characterization of the Balkan languages as 'misbegotten sons' [*missrathenen Söhne*] that are 'the most corrupt [*die verdorbensten*] in their families' and Whitney's (1868: 199) characterization of structural borrowing as a 'monstrosity'. In a world suffering anxieties about 'purity' of race and origin, and one in which political (national) boundaries were in the process of being drawn and redrawn, it is not surprising that such concerns would also permeate academic discourse.

Moreover, the difference between a language and a dialect or the definition of a dialect boundary remains, to some extent, a social or political artefact. A particularly telling example from the Balkans is the way in which conflicting Serbian and Bulgarian territorial claims to Macedonia in the nineteenth and first half of the twentieth centuries were bolstered by the selection of different isoglosses in the South Slavic dialect continuum. Serbian linguists chose the monophonemic (versus diphonemic) reflex of Common Slavic *tj/dj*, while Bulgarian linguists chose the isogloss for the presence of a postposed definite article (see Friedman 2003). Even after the recognition of Macedonian as a separate language within Yugoslavia, Yugoslav linguists continued to treat all dialects with /u/ from the Common Slavic back nasal as at least 'transitional' to Serbian.

In the case of the sprachbund, however, Trubetzkoy's intent is sometimes forgotten or misunderstood. He was not talking about any situation of bilingual contact but rather those in which there was a range of similarities in syntax, lexicon, morphosyntax and even phonology, but precisely without regular sound correspondences and shared core vocabulary. An

---

[15] This includes closed word classes that are generally felt to be resistant to borrowing, such as pronouns, complementizers or conjunctions; see Section 4.4 on 'ERIC' (conversationally based) loanwords, which defy common assumptions about such resistance.

underlying assumption was areal contiguity, but it is the very nature of areality that raises the question of defining the 'area'. Masica (1976: 11) writes:

> Some [instances of convergence] . . . involve only two or three contiguous languages. These may merely be instances of what is possibly a tendency for contiguous languages anywhere in the world – or at least contiguous dialects of contiguous languages – to resemble each other in some way or another. Even if every Indian language turns out to be linked to its neighbors by special two-by-two relationships, forming a continuous network covering the subcontinent, this in itself would not establish India as a special area, especially if similar *arbitrary* [our emphasis VAF/BDJ] linkages continue beyond India . . .[16]

And Thomason (2001: 99) is explicit about numbers:

> The general idea is clear enough: a linguistic area is a geographical region containing a group of three or more languages that share some structural features as a result of contact rather than as a result of accident or inheritance from a common ancestor. The reason for requiring three or more languages is that calling two-language contact situations linguistic areas would trivialize the notion of a linguistic area, which would then include all of the world's contact situations except long-distance contacts (via religious language . . . etc.) . . . the linguistic results of contact [among more than two languages] may differ in certain respects.

But, as Hamp (1989) had already pointed out with respect to the former Yugoslavia, even the Balkans can be understood as part of a 'crossroads of *Sprachbünde*', with 'a spectrum of differential bindings, a spectrum that extends in different densities across the whole of Europe and beyond'. A crucial characteristic of the Balkan sprachbund, and by extension, of any sprachbund, is that it is, in the words of Thomason and Kaufman (1988: 95), 'messy', i.e. directionality of the sharing can be difficult to determine. In fact, it is precisely the 'messiness' of multiple causation and mutual reinforcement that is characteristic of a sprachbund such as the Balkans. We have enough historical data to know that certain features are innovations in all of the languages for which there are attestations. While hints may occur in this or that earlier stage of this or that language, and typological parallels may exist elsewhere, in the end we have a situation in which languages underwent the same innovation in the same place at the same time, under known conditions of mutual multilingualism. Under such circumstances, attempting to locate a single cause may not be merely futile, it may in fact smack of the same nineteenth century anxieties about purity alluded to above. Thus, for example, Leake (1814) attributed the commonalities of the Balkan languages to Slavic, Kopitar (1829), Miklosich (1861) and others to a substratum of one or more of the

---

[16] A problematic aspect of Masica's formulation is the assumption that contiguity entails communication. This is not necessarily always the case.

unattested or poorly attested ancient languages of the Balkans (by definition unprovable), Sandfeld (1930) to Byzantine Greek, and Solta (1980) to
Balkan Latin (chiefly). Nonetheless, given the complexity of the evidence,
the attempt to identify a single source for all the Balkan commonalities is
downright wrong, and the attempt to prove that each innovation arose
completely independently in each language strains credulity; see Joseph
(1983) on multiple causation, Friedman (2007) on the irrelevance of identifying a single source for each and every phenomenon, and below on the
Janus face of genealogical and areal linguistics. A sprachbund is thus a
stable situation of mutual multilingualism (see also Aikhenvald 2006a), as
opposed to, for example, unidirectional multilingualism such as the vertical multilingualism of the Caucasus (Nichols 1997).[17] A bilingual situation in which the two languages were more or less socially equal and stable
would indeed be a type of sprachbund situation.

For example, the Geg (northern) Albanian variety spoken in the town of
Debar in Macedonia matches the local Macedonian dialect in having no
vowel nasalization, a phonological detail which occurs in no other Geg
dialect. However, other Albanian dialects northeast of Debar have only one
nasal vowel, which is a severely reduced inventory for Geg. To this can be
added the fact that the peculiar rounded reflex of the Common Slavic back
nasal in the Debar region matches exactly the reflex of the equivalent vowel
in Albanian. To exclude Debar Macedonian and Albanian from consideration
in the overall convergence of Macedonian and Albanian, and to treat their
localized phonological convergence as irrelevant to convergences found
across other Balkan languages, would simply be an arbitrary decision rooted
in an aprioristic minimum number of languages needed for a sprachbund.

We are then faced with two problems: the problem of 'boundaries'
(which subsumes both the territorial implication of 'area' and the membership implications of 'union' and 'league') and the problem of 'number'.
These problems are reminiscent of the difficulties in defining concepts
such as 'nation', 'empire', 'state', 'ethnicity' or 'culture' as well as 'language', 'dialect', 'pidgin' and 'creole'. What level of control constitutes a
'state'? How big must a 'state' be to be an 'empire'? How many 'nations'
must it comprise? When is the speech of a community a 'dialect' of
another 'language' and when is it a separate 'language'? What is 'separate'
and how much intelligibility is required before it is 'mutual'?[18] From a
general theoretical point of view, it does not actually seem that the kind of
diffusion that takes place among three or more languages is in any way
qualitatively different from diffusion that is possible between two languages. For a speaker of a given language – and the role of speakers in
language contact must never be ignored – diffusion involves the entry of

---

[17] In vertical multilingualism, people in higher villages know the languages of those down the mountain, but those in the
lowlands do not bother to learn highland languages.

[18] Haugen (1966) remains a classic account of this issue and should be read by those who write about the Balkans
regardless of their field.

an extra-systemic feature into their existing system; whether a feature of system X that comes into X from system Y was original to Y or entered Y from another system Z is irrelevant to the reality of the presence of that feature in X and Y (and possibly Z); in either case, contact and diffusion between X and Y were responsible for the shared presence of that feature. Thus, it is important not to confuse a methodological issue for linguists with the realities of a contact situation for speakers.

Moreover, contact phenomena are never arbitrary. They are embedded in social relations as well as the structures of the languages that manifest them. In a sense, the village of Kupwar in Maharashtra state in India (Gumperz and Wilson 1971; also Masica 1976: 11), with its convergence among Marathi, Urdu and Kannada, is a linguistic area, albeit one that is part of a larger area, just as the dialects spoken in it are parts of larger languages. If Marathi, Urdu and Kannada can be shown to converge over a broader region at least to some extent, then we can say that in a sense, Kupwar is the Debar of India (or vice versa).

Trubetzkoy's original motivation for the terminological distinction between *Sprachfamilie* and *Sprachbund* means that two languages related by diffusion can constitute a *Sprachbund* just as two languages related by transmission from a common source can constitute a *Sprachfamilie*. The crucial difference is that the *Sprachfamilie* can involve an isolate, while the *Sprachbund* by definition requires more than one member for diffusion to take place. There is, however, another issue in the definition of a *Sprachbund* as understood by Thomason and Kaufman (1988: 95) – who, unlike Thomason 2001 (see above), do not explicitly impose a tripartite requirement on the concept – namely that of directionality. It is generally agreed that in bilateral language contact situations, there is usually asymmetry in the direction of transfer. As argued above, if two languages were demonstrably genetically different enough that similarities resulting from diffusion could be identified but not the directionality (or if the directionality is symmetric), such a unit could arguably be described as a sprachbund. On the other hand, a situation such as that which we find in the Balkans clearly involves diffusion, but directionality can be variable. For our purposes here, determining directionality is desirable but not requisite, and it can even be argued that it is ultimately irrelevant (see Ilievski 1988 [1973] on internal versus external factors). Moreover, in the end the size question does not affect the Balkans: regardless of any minimum considered necessary for a sprachbund, the Balkans, with up to six distinct contributing language groups (Albanic, Indic, Hellenic, Romance, Slavic and Turkic), would qualify.

As to question (4a.ii) regarding relatedness, these six contributing language groups constitute only two different language families, Indo-European for the first five and also Turkic.[19] Does the relatedness of five of the six groups vitiate the sprachbund in this case? Most assuredly not, if

---

[19] Leaving aside here the vexed question of whether Turkic fits into a larger language grouping such as Altaic.

the evident convergence is there and is contact-related. The task of identifying the source of features in a given language potentially involved in a convergence is complicated by the possibility of (genealogical) inheritance being responsible for the feature occurring in two related languages rather than diffusion (contact), but this methodological issue for linguists – ease of analysis – should not be equated with realities for speakers.

4.4 Answering the Feature-based Issues

Points similar to those in Section 4.3 can be made in response to question (4b.iii), regarding the number of features for determining a sprachbund. All researchers here are non-committal: note Thomason's reference to '*some* [our emphasis, VAF/BDJ] structural features'. Clearly, the more convergent features one can find, the more compelling the case becomes for a convergence area, but could a single feature constitute the basis for a sprachbund? Here again we can refer to Trubetzkoy's original idea, which specified convergences at various levels. There is a parallel to be drawn here with a key aspect of genetic (genealogical) linguistics, namely dialect subgrouping. A single highly significant feature, i.e. non-trivial and unlikely to arise independently, can be taken as diagnostic or emblematic for distinguishing one dialect from another and at the same time for establishing subgrouping. The rhoticization of Proto-Albanian *n* intervocalically to *r* is perhaps the single most salient feature distinguishing Tosk (southern) dialects of Albanian from Geg (northern), although the isoglosses for the development of stressed schwa from the low nasal vowel, the general loss of nasality, *va* from original *vo* in initial position, and *ua* from *ue* all coincide with the *r/n* isogloss or deviate from it by no more than 20 kilometres.[20] Similarly, Joseph and Wallace (1987) argue that the parallelism in the first person singular of the verb 'to be' in Latin and Oscan, with both showing a reflex of an enclitic allomorph of a strong form **esom*, even though a single innovation, is diagnostic of the existence of an Italic branch within Indo-European subsuming these two languages of ancient Italy.

Moreover, simply totting up the presence of some set of features and, based on that, scoring the languages as to their degree of membership, as in Campbell, Kaufman and Smith-Stark (1986), Haspelmath (1998), Lindstedt (2000), Reiter (1994) and van der Auwera (1998a), fails to provide an accurate picture of a linguistic area. When applied to the Balkans, complex phenomena are treated as unitary, so that the facts 'on the ground' disappear from view. And what it means to 'count' a feature as

---

[20] On the level of morphosyntax, there are Tosk dialects with infinitives marked with *me*, usually thought of as a Geg feature. In this case, the *me*-marked infinitives are best viewed as reflecting the proto-Albanian infinitive (so Altimari 2011). This helps support an argument that while regular sound change is genealogically diagnostic, morphosyntax can be more problematic.

present in some language is far from trivial. For instance, the 'feels-like' construction in (1) is absent from Standard Modern Greek and occurs only in some dialects, specifically those in areas where the majority of the population spoke Macedonian, Albanian and Aromanian into the mid-twentieth century. Does Greek count as a language with this construction? Yes and no. Yes, in that it is found in *some* variety of Greek, but no, in that it is not widespread across all of Greek. How would that fact, and the fact of the specific dialect distribution of that feature within Greek, be reflected in the scoring? A binary assignment of 1 (presence) or 0 (absence) would not reflect the facts well, nor would a percentage-based score, e.g. 0.1, to signal presence in a small percentage of dialects. And in any case, does the absence across most of Greek render the Kastoria Greek use of that construction any less significant for the speakers of that dialect? We think not.

Even if in principle one should pay attention to a single feature, it is certainly true that the more features one can conclusively identify as convergent due to contact, the stronger the case is for a sprachbund. Nonetheless, when speaking of features we cannot really give a quantifiable threshold, a magic number metric for how much shared vocabulary or how many shared features determine a sprachbund. In this regard, areal linguistics is like its Janus-twin of genealogical linguistics: the criterion for relatedness is simply that the systematic and correspondent similarities are too many to be a coincidence, but attempts to quantify what would constitute coincidence (e.g. Ringe 1992) have been problematic and are not widely recognized as valid.[21]

In the case of the Balkans, for reaching any conclusions about the sprachbund, we also have two advantages. First, there is historical documentation for long stretches of time for most of the languages.[22] Second, there is comparative evidence in the form of related languages, both within the most immediate genealogical groups (e.g. for comparisons with Balkan Romance, not only Italian within Eastern Romance, but beyond that, within Romance more generally, also Spanish and French as well as the non-Balkan dialects of Judezmo) and across more distant relatives (e.g. Celtic and Germanic for comparisons involving the Indo-European branches in the Balkans). There is also a qualitative side that cannot be ignored in the assessment of any given feature.

Related to the issue of the number of features is the question (see 4b.iv) of what distribution of features is needed in the group to permit classification as a sprachbund. In particular, must the features identified as diagnostic be present in all of the languages? Belić (1936) and Mladenov (1939)

---

[21] Chang, Cathcart, Hall and Garrett (2015) show that certain more sophisticated and refined statistical methods, while still not replacing what traditional methods show, offer promise of enhancing historical understanding in situations where ancient records are lacking.

[22] The historical record for Greek begins in ancient (BCE) times, and so also for Indic (in the form of Sanskrit) and Romance (in the form of Latin); Turkish is attested from the eighth century and Slavic from the ninth/tenth centuries, and Albanian has extended texts starting in the sixteenth century CE.

adduce the piecemeal geographic distribution of some Balkan features as a problem for the sprachbund construct (so also Birnbaum 1968). The discussion above in Section 4.3 addresses that criticism, since a cluster-based approach means that features need not be widespread to be relevant.[23] Smaller convergence areas that nonetheless overlap, when taken together, determine more extensive geographic zones in which convergence is to be found. The convergent phonological features of Debar Albanian and Macedonian, for instance, when joined with other features the languages share, obviously form a wider area of convergence involving these two languages. So too, the Kastoria Greek convergence with Albanian, Macedonian and Aromanian seen in (1) overlaps with the distribution of the 'want'-based future, found across all of Balkan Greek, and thus adds to the strength of the sprachbund as far as these languages are concerned.

As with other issues, here too a comparison with genealogical linguistics is instructive. According to Bird's (1982) compilation of the distribution of roots reconstructed for Proto-Indo-European in the various branches of that family – Bird operates with 14 such branches – only one root, *tēu- 'swell', is found in all 14 branches. Moreover, there are only eight roots that occur in 13 branches. The number of non-isolated roots increases as the threshold for distributions decreases, so there are 28 roots attested in 12 of the branches, and so on. Taken in this light, the absence of post-positioning for the definite article in Greek, for example, is much less important than its absence in the non-Torlak dialects of former Serbo-Croatian. Similarly, the distributions of 'have' and 'want' futures take on different meanings in different geographic contexts. The point is that it is not the absolute totality of features that all languages share but rather the cumulative effect of smaller convergence zones that justifies the concept of sprachbund.

Having determined that distribution need not be uniform and that the quest for an absolute minimum of determining features is unrealistic without a qualitative assessment of each feature, the next question is whether certain types of features are more relevant than others. The methodological issue of the sprachbund as a consistently definable unit is that despite the parallel first drawn by Trubetzkoy (1923) between the genealogical-linguistic family and the areal-linguistic league, the manner of selecting the correspondences used to define the latter has not been systematized. Contact phenomena, however, do not have the type of systemic invariance found in regular sound change or shared morphology, the bedrock of demonstrable genealogical origin. Contact-induced change, by its very nature, involves a complex ecology of choices among competing systems (see Mufwene 2001). Trubetzkoy recognized all types of features,

---

[23] See also articles such as Steinke (1999) and Reiter (1999) and the discussion of defining features mentioned in Section 4.1 (and in footnote 8). Note also Masica (1976), whose approach to mapping South Asian features involves selecting a few morphosyntactic features and mapping them in all directions as far as possible.

and earlier works, e.g. Miklosich (1861), gave prominence to the lexicon while more recent works, e.g. Thomason (2001: 100), give primacy to structural commonalities. Within the group of non-lexical features taken to be more important, calques are especially significant.[24] Campbell et al. (1986) use evidence from calques and shared metaphors in Mesoamerican languages to argue for a Mesoamerican sprachbund, since some degree of bilingualism is needed for calquing to occur and to spread (see also Ross 2001 on metatypy).[25] Likewise, especially crucial are intimate borrowings and in particular conversationally based loans – 'ERIC' loans (those that are 'essentially rooted in conversation') as defined and discussed in Friedman and Joseph (2014, in press b: Chapter 4). ERIC loans include closed classes and generally borrowing-resistant items including kinship terms, numerals and pronouns, conversationally based elements such as greetings, idioms and phraseology, and discourse elements such as connectives and interjections. These are important as they are precisely the lexical items that depend on – and thus demonstrate – close, intimate and sustained everyday interactions among speakers. They give direct evidence of communication between speakers that is not 'object' oriented, not purely aimed at satisfying the needs one speaker may have.

Since contact is involved, except for cases of shared retentions, defining a sprachbund presupposes an innovation and thus a drift away from a prior state and toward a state resembling that occurring in another language; in this way, sprachbund phenomena typically involve not only convergence on a new type by two or more languages but also concomitant divergence from earlier types (possibly preserved in genealogically related languages outside the sprachbund) as well. In numerous oral presentations, Andrei N. Sobolev (University of St Petersburg, Marburg University) has claimed that the definition of Balkanisms is circular: Balkan languages have certain features and those features constitute the Balkan sprachbund. This is an unfair, even inaccurate characterization. One must begin with the fact that a variety of languages have been spoken in a multilingual environment for a long time. For most of these languages the previous stages are well attested. If we omit this starting point, then it is indeed possible to accuse Balkan linguistics of circularity. However, it is precisely the diachrony at our disposal that enables us to identify convergent features among the Balkan languages. This is Ilievski's (1988 [1973]) point, alluded to above, when he argues that what is important is not the source of convergence but the fact of convergence.

---

[24] We call calques 'non-lexical' here since they involve the transfer/copying not of specific lexical material but rather of conceptual structures; there is often a lexical dimension too, but it is not requisite (see Enfield 2005, 2008 on linguistic epidemiology).

[25] Other cases where calques have been used in arguing for a sprachbund include Nuckols (2000) with regard to a Central European area taking in Hungarian, Czech, Slovak and German, and Gil (2011) with regard to a Mekong-Mamberamo linguistic area (from the Mekong river area in Southeast Asia, and southeast along the Malay archipelago to the Mamberamo river in western New Guinea), where part of the evidence was the shared phraseology of 'EYE-DAY' meaning SUN.

If not all features one is considering must be found in all the languages being assessed, then the next relevant question is to query, as in (4b.iv), whether some set of features, and thus some set of languages, constitute the core of the sprachbund, i.e. the most prototypical members as revealed by their incorporation of features x, y, z etc. This is a reasonable question, and would seem to lend itself to the quantitative approaches discussed above, assessing strength of membership by occurrence of features. Many scholars who have addressed the Balkan sprachbund have in fact written in terms of different gradations of 'membership' in the sprachbund. Schaller (1975), for instance, classifies Balkan languages as 'ersten Grades' ('of the first order') and 'zweiten Grades' ('of the second order'), where some features are taken as more telling than others. Schaller's approach has been seriously criticized (e.g. by Joseph 1987). Not all features are found to the same extent in all languages. Thus, for example, Schaller classifies Greek as a 'second degree' Balkan language, but Joseph (1983) demonstrates that the loss of the infinitive is not realized uniformly across the various Balkan languages, with Macedonian and Greek both showing the total loss of the infinitive while the other languages show infinitives to varying, often limited, degrees.

However, the cluster approach as envisioned by Hamp (1989) and outlined in Section 4.3 above provides a basis for understanding the variable realization of given features across the Balkans: each feature has its own spatial trajectory of diffusion, and thus it is unrealistic to expect full 'compliance', so to speak, by all languages on all features. The diffusion takes place between speakers, not between languages in some abstract sense, and moreover, it takes place in socially and geographically defined space; this is the 'speaker-plus-dialect approach' advocated in Friedman and Joseph (in press b: Chapter 3.3).[26] Furthermore, given that each feature could have a different point of origin, it is evident that some features will have different distributions from others. Thus the cluster approach in a sense means that no particular feature or set of features is privileged as diagnostic for the sprachbund but rather all convergent features contribute to the sprachbund, each in its own locale. The more locales a feature occurs in, the more salient it becomes to the linguist, though not necessarily to the speaker. Thus, as in other cases discussed already, the needs and interests of the linguist and those of the speaker do not necessarily coincide.

4.5   Answering the Cause-based Questions

Turning now to the questions pertaining to cause, the response must start with an acknowledgement that speaker-to-speaker contact is responsible

---

[26] 'Dialect' is meant in the sense of regional or social dialect, distinguished from the standard varieties of the languages in question, which, as noted below, are too often the basis for comparisons and judgements concerning a sprachbund, at least for the Balkans.

for the diffusion of features in the Balkans, as in any sprachbund, and it is therefore responsible for the convergence observed therein. But, as (4c.v) asks, it must be considered whether there is a particular type of contact that is needed. Based on what is seen in the Balkans, the relevant contact is not casual contact but intense contact, specifically, in the typical case, multilateral, multidirectional, mutual multilingualism. This 'Four-M' model means that several languages are involved (minimally two – see Section 4.3 – but typically more) and that speakers are multilingual, each speaking some version of the language of others, and overall it is mutually so, in that speakers of language X know language Y and speakers of Y know X, with the result that features can flow in either direction from one language to another. The qualifier 'some version of' is important because the speakers are not necessarily perfect bilinguals, but rather have sufficient knowledge of the other language(s) to communicate, and their interlocutors presumably alter aspects of their own usage in the direction of these imperfect speakers. The multilingualism could be stable, or could be a first step towards wholesale language shift, but in either case, an imperfect knowledge of the other language(s) could be involved, knowledge to the extent needed for the relevant communicative acts.

Moreover, as noted in Section 4.4 regarding the sorts of features that are significant, what we have defined as ERIC loans give evidence of the intense, mutual and sustained contact needed for a sprachbund. The ability of speakers of different languages to interact on a regular basis in non-need-based ways was fostered by a particular sociohistoric milieu, and we turn to that to answer question (4c.vi), regarding other factors that might figure in the development of a sprachbund.[27]

Based on our available documentation, processes that may have been set in motion, or at the very least begun to be reinforced during the Middle Ages, and even features that may have appeared in the written record at earlier dates, achieved their current state during the five-century period of control of the Balkans by the Ottoman Turks, referred to as the *Pax Ottomanica*.[28] Ottoman rule created a political and socioeconomic stability in the central Balkans that allowed for the stable multilingualism necessary for the convergence effects that constitute the 'sprachbund'. Some comparisons with other contact situations are especially helpful for pinning down what it was about the Balkans that led to the massive observed convergence.

Heath (1984: 378) presents an interesting view: 'It now seems that the extent of borrowing in the Balkans is not especially spectacular; ongoing mixing involving superimposed European languages vs. native vernaculars in (former) colonies such as [the] Philippines and Morocco is, overall, at

---

[27] The response that follows draws heavily on Friedman (2014).

[28] In Bulgarian this period is referred to as *turskoto igo* 'the Turkish yoke'. In a similarly telling example of differences of point of view, the Byzantine Empire is sometimes referred to in Bulgarian as *vizantijskoto igo* 'the Byzantine yoke'.

least as extensive as in the Balkan case even when (as in Morocco) the diffusion only began in earnest in the present century.' Heath's observations are important for several reasons. On the one hand, the point that significant change can take place rapidly concurs with the view that it was precisely during the Ottoman empire that the Balkan sprachbund was formed.[29] The examples from Morocco and the Philippines, however, all involve lexical items or reinterpreted morphemes rather than morphosyntactic patterns. Moreover, the relationship of colonial languages to indigenous ones is roughly equivalent to that of Turkish to the Balkan Indo-European languages at the beginning of the Ottoman conquest. While Turkish did maintain a certain social prestige owing to unequal power relations, there is nonetheless a significant difference between recent European colonial settings lasting a century or so and the five centuries of Turkish settlement in the Balkans during which the language became indigenized and members of all social classes were Turkish speakers. To this we can add that the complexity of indigenous power relations prior to conquest is another part of the picture that is easier to tease out in the Balkans than in European colonies owing to longer histories of documentation of the languages prior to conquest. It is precisely this background of long-term, stable language contact with significant documented history that makes the Balkans an interesting model for comparing and contrasting with other contact situations.

It has been noted above in Section 4.4 that a strictly quantitative approach to the Balkans, or really any sprachbund, is fraught with problems. Further consideration of numbers leads to another telling comparison with the Balkans. Hamp (1977) includes a critique of the conflation of areal and typological linguistics seen in Sherzer (1976) in describing indigenous languages of North America. Among Hamp's (1977: 282) points is that which he refers to as 'gross inventorizing' of what he characterizes as 'a Procrustean bed of parameters' (Hamp 1977: 283) which cannot capture the historical depth and specificity that gives meaning to areal developments. Such number games played with a small set of features, characterized by Donohue (2012) as 'cherry picking', can produce maps in which languages seem to mimic modern politics, e.g. Haspelmath (1998: 23), showing a French–German–Dutch–North Italian 'nucleus' for a presumed 'Standard Average European', with the Indo-European Balkan languages at the next level once removed, and with Turkish entirely outside 'Europe'. A subsequent representation (Haspelmath 2001: 107) has only French and German at its core, with Albanian and Romanian as part of the next closest level, Bulgarian and the former Serbo-Croatian entity beyond that, and Turkish still totally outside. Van der Auwera (1998b: 825–827) has dubbed such constructs the 'Charlemagne sprachbund' on the assumption that

---

[29] On rapidity of change see Mufwene (2004: 203) and Dixon (1997), regarding 'punctuated equilibrium', but on this latter, see also Joseph (2001a).

Charlemagne's short-lived (800–814) empire, or its successor, the Holy Roman Empire, was the nucleus for a linguistically unified Europe whose influence is detectable today in the mapping out of synchronic feature points. This is, in essence, an extension of Sherzer's (1976) methodology in Europe (see also König 1998: v–vi), and is best seen in the work of the EUROTYP project. To be sure, as with Sherzer (1976), the assembled data are welcome. The over-arching quasi-historical conclusion, however, is misleading and the lack of attention to historical and dialectological detail of the type called for by Hamp (1977) is problematic.

Van der Auwera's (1998b: 827) formulation that on the basis of EUROTYP's investigations 'the Balkans do indeed get their *Sprachbund* status confirmed' still gives the impression of the Balkan languages being defined vis-à-vis (the rest of) Europe. But the linguistic realities of the Balkan sprachbund (as identified by Trubetzkoy) took their modern shape internal to the Ottoman Empire – not Obolensky's (1971) Byzantine Commonwealth – in the regions that were part of the Ottoman Empire from the fourteenth to the early twentieth centuries. This area, during this period, was where, as Olivera Jašar-Nasteva said, with one *teskere* (travel document) you could travel the whole (Balkan) peninsula.

Hamp (1977: 280) recognizes that areal features 'may be crudely labeled Post-Roman European', but, for example, the spread of the perfect in 'have' into the Balkans has nothing to do with Charlemagne. The construction was a Late Latin innovation, whose origins are already apparent in Cicero and Julius Caesar (Allen 1916: 313), and it made its way into the Balkans with the Roman armies, settlers and Romanized indigenous populations. It became the preterite of choice – independently – in French and Romanian (except in the south: see Pană Dindelegan 2013: 33), and continues to displace the aorist in other parts of both Western and Eastern Romance. In Balkan Slavic it was precisely those populations in most intensive contact with the Balkan Romance that became Aromanian which developed independent *have*-perfect paradigms, namely those in what is today the southwest of the Republic of Macedonia and adjacent areas in Greece and Albania (for details see Gołąb 1976, 1984: 134–136). Moreover, it is hardly coincidental that in Bulgarian dialects, it is precisely those that were spoken along the route of the Via Egnatia where similar perfect paradigms developed. As for Greek, as Joseph (2000a and references therein) makes abundantly clear, the use of 'have' as a perfect auxiliary is in fact of very different, albeit also Roman, origin. The use of 'have' plus a petrified infinitival form as a future in post-Classical Greek – itself a Latin-influenced innovation – gave rise to an anterior future with the imperfect of 'have' that became a conditional and then a pluperfect. This pluperfect then provided the model for the formation of the perfect using a present of 'have'. This stands in stark contrast to the Romance perfect, which began as 'have' plus past passive participle, the participle then abandoning agreement, which is exactly the construction that was calqued into Macedonian (and some Thracian Bulgarian). On the other hand, the perfect in the Romani dialect of Parakalamos in Epirus (Matras 2004) is clearly calqued on Greek, as is the very innovation of a verb meaning 'have'. Albanian also has a perfect in 'have' plus participle, and the participle itself is historically of the past passive type found in Romance and Slavic. The directionality is difficult to judge. The Albanian perfect was securely in place by the time of the first significant texts in the sixteenth century – a time when it was still not well established in Greek – but the relationship to Latin or Romance influence is difficult to tease out. Such perfects are not found in the Torlak dialects of former Serbo-Croatian, a region where early contact was likely with populations whose languages are presumed to have been ancestral to Albanian and modern Balkan Romance, and where there were significant Albanian-speaking populations until 1878 (Vermeer 1992: 107–108). The Slavic dialects of Kosovo and southern Montenegro – where contact with Romance lasted into the twentieth century[30] and where it is on-going with Albanian, albeit strained – do not show such developments. This fact itself may be due to the importance of social factors in language change. Living in close proximity does not necessarily produce shared linguistic structures. A certain level of coexistential communication must also involve social acceptance. On the western end of the old Roman Empire, Breton is the only Celtic language with a 'have' perfect, and the directionality is clear. Still to describe all these perfects as part of a 'Charlemagne sprachbund' is to do violence to historical facts.

The spread of *have*-perfects exemplifies linguistic epidemiology in Enfield's (2008) sense. And thanks to the depth and detail of our historical records, we can tease out the facts. Thus, for example, Donohue (2012) showed that WALS (2005) features for the main territorial languages of Europe, when 'decoded' into binary format, then pushed through computational algorithms (Splitstree) that cluster languages on the basis of 'best shared similarity' produce groupings for Germanic, Slavic, Balkan, Romance and Celtic. These clusters, Donohue is careful to point out, are explicitly synchronic and not diachronic, and details within groupings are interesting only because we already know the history. Thus, Icelandic and Faroese come out closer to German than to Scandinavian, while Afrikaans is closer to Scandinavian than to Dutch; Polish comes between Belarusian and Ukrainian, on the one hand, and Russian, on the other, while Portuguese is much closer to French than to Spanish. Moreover, the ability to differentiate areal from genealogical causality – what prompted Trubetzkoy's sprachbund in the first place – is missing. These results demonstrate clearly Hamp's (1977) point: typological, areal and genealogical linguistics are independent disciplines, the former achronic, the latter two 'twin faces of diachronic linguistics' (Hamp 1977: 279). Nonetheless, despite its many sins of omission and commission

---

[30] According to Rexhep Ismajli (personal communication), when Pavle Ivić was conducting field work on the old town former Serbo-Croatian dialect of Prizren (southern Kosovo) in the mid-twentieth century, he asked a group of old women to count in the old-fashioned way (*po-starinski*) and they began: *unā, dao, trei, patru* . . . 'one, two three, four' (counting in Aromanian).

(under-representation of so-called non-territorial languages, itself a problematic, almost bureaucratic notion, absence of crucial dialect facts, misanalyses, misleading generalizations, etc.), WALS (2005) is a blunt instrument that, if wielded with care and sensitivity, can at least spur us to consider other approaches, as Donohue (2012) has productively done in his discussion of Australia.

In the context of the putative Charlemagne sprachbund, it is instructive to cite here Jakobson's (1931/1971) concept of the Eurasian sprachbund. Jakobson deviated significantly from Trubetzkoy's (1930) emphasis on morphosyntactic structure by positing phonologically based sprachbunds, specifically a Eurasian one, concentrating on consonantal timbre (meaning here palatalization) and prosody (meaning here pitch-accent or tone), with nominal declension mentioned in a footnote. Eurasia was the centre. For nominal declension, Germano-Romance Europe and South and Southeast Asia were the peripheries. For phonological tone, the Baltic and Pacific areas were the peripheries (with West South Slavic, most of Serbo-Croatian and Slovenian, as a relic island), while for palatalization the core was roughly the boundaries of the Russian Empire, with the inclusion of eastern Bulgaria (imagined as Russia's potential *zadunajskaja gubernaja* 'trans-Danubian province' during the nineteenth and into the twentieth century). He even suggested that palatalization finds its most complete expression in Great Russian [*sic*], and it is thus no coincidence that it is the basis of the Russian literary language, i.e. the language with a pan-Eurasian cultural mission (Jakobson 1931/1971: 191).

It is also important to remember that, while Masica (2001: 239) warns against confusing 'recent political configurations' with 'linguistic areas', it is precisely the legacy of political configurations such as the Ottoman Empire that created the conditions for the emergence of the Balkan sprachbund as it was identified by Trubetzkoy. It is here that the German *Bund* 'union' in *Sprachbund* (*sojuz* in Trubetzkoy's 1923 Russian formulation) has misled scholars such as Stolz (2006), who suggests that since sprachbunds do not have clearly definable boundaries the concept should be discarded. His 'all or nothing' methodology misses Trubetzkoy's original point that the sprachbund is fundamentally different from a linguistic family, and it fails to take into account the basic historical fact that the 'boundaries' of a sprachbund are consequences of on-going multilingual processes (Friedman 2012). In Hamp's (1989: 47) words, they are 'a spectrum of differential bindings' rather than 'compact borders', a point also alluded to in Hamp (1977: 282). It is also important to remember that Trubetzkoy first proposed the term at a time when the *Sprachfamilie* 'language family' was widely considered the only legitimate unit of historical linguistics, while resemblances that resulted from the diffusion of contact-induced changes were described in terms such as those used by Schleicher (1850: 143), who described Albanian, Balkan Romance and Balkan Slavic as 'agree[ing] only in the fact that they are the most corrupt in their families'. Trubetzkoy explicitly wanted to avoid the confusion more recently generated by conflations of areal and typological linguistics, although in his time the issues involved areal and genealogical linguistics.

Turning now to language ideology in the Balkans itself, the difference between Greek and other languages is striking. It is certainly the case that multilingualism itself does not guarantee the formation of a sprachbund. As Ball (2007: 7–25) makes clear, in the multilingual Upper Xingu, multilingualism, while necessary for dealing with outsiders, is viewed as polluting, and monolingualism is considered a requisite for high status. This endogamous region is quite different from exogamous ones in other parts of Amazonia, where multilingualism is an expected norm, and lexical mixing is viewed negatively, but morphosyntactic convergence is rampant (Aikhenvald 2006b; Epps and Michael, Chapter 32, this volume). Consider also the vertical multilingualism that Nichols (1997) has identified in the Caucasus, which is similar to various Balkan multilingual practices, where specific types of multilingualism index different types of social status.[31] Ideologies that consider contact-induced change as symptomatic of pollution and equate isolation and archaism with purity were at work in the nineteenth century too, as seen in Schleicher's formulation above.

4.6   Answering the Delineational and Assessment issues[32]

We are now in a position to address the last of the issues by which the notion of 'sprachbund' has been problematized. Question (4d.vii) in a sense restates an issue dealt with earlier, namely that of setting the boundaries of the sprachbund and recognizing different degrees of 'participation' in the sprachbund on the part of speakers of the various languages involved. The answer emerges from the foregoing discussion: the boundaries are as elastic as the micro-zones of convergence that add up to the larger convergence area. There is nothing fixed, and even political boundaries, while convenient, are relevant only insofar as they correspond to sociohistorical realities that might promote the sort of contact necessary for sprachbund formation. Geography is no accident as far as the Balkans are concerned, in that for most of the features recognized as important regarding structural convergence in this region, the more geographically peripheral the language, the less likely it is to demonstrate the feature fully, and the more centrally located a language or dialect is in the Balkans, the more fully it shows the feature. This is especially clear in the replacement of the infinitive by finite subordination. Particularly telling from a geographic standpoint are the comparisons in Table 4.1, where

---

[31] See footnote 17. Nonetheless, as Tuite (1999) makes clear, aside from shared glottalized consonants and some phraseological calques, a Caucasian sprachbund, when examined closely, vanishes like a mirage. Hamp (1977), too, noted that glottalization in Armenian and Ossetian, respectively, must have distinct areal diachronic explanations.

[32] The discussion in this section draws on Friedman and Joseph (in press b), especially Chapter 7.7.2 and Chapter 8.

Table 4.1 *Distribution of infinitival markers*

[+infinitival]	[–infinitival]
Romeyka Greek (eastern Turkey)	mainland Greek
Southern Italy Greek	mainland Greek
Arbëresh Tosk Albanian (So. Italy)	mainland Tosk Albanian
Geg Albanian	most of Tosk
West South Slavic (BCSM, Slovene)	East South Slavic (Macedonian/Bulgarian)
Bulgarian	Macedonian
Maleshevo-Pirin, Lower Vardar Mac.	the rest of Eastern Mac.
non-Torlak former Serbo-Croatian	Torlak former Serbo-Croatian
Istro-Romanian	Balkan Romance (Aromanian, Meglenoromanian, Romanian[a])
Romanian	Aromanian/Meglenoromanian
East Rumelian and Anatolian Turkish	Western Rumelian Turkish
Modern Indo-Aryan (e.g. Hindi)	Romani
some of non-Balkan Romani	Balkan Romani

[a]   Romanian is mentioned on both sides of the table as it is 'less infinitival' than Istro-Romanian but 'more infinitival' than Aromanian or Megleno-Romanian.

[+infinitival] means that the infinitive is alive – or remained alive longer – in the language to some (not insignificant) degree and [–infinitival] means that there essentially is no infinitive.[33]

The generalization emerging from such comparisons is that the more deeply embedded a language (or dialect) is in the Balkans, the weaker is its category of infinitive. Admittedly, there are some exceptions to this generalization: for example, Cypriot Greek is geographically peripheral but lacks the infinitive to the same degree as mainland Greek, and Geg Albanian is relatively central in the Balkans but has an infinitive. However, Tosk is arguably more central and does not have an infinitive, or at least did not for some stretch of time. While there may be other forces at work in such cases that can help to explain exceptions to the generalization, even with them, it nonetheless holds true in the vast majority of cases and thus provides support for the notion that there is something characteristically Balkan about the loss of the infinitive and its replacement by finite forms.[34]

Peripherality in Table 4.1 is geographic in nature, but there can be chronological peripherality as well. Judezmo offers a striking example here. As noted in Friedman and Joseph (2014), Judezmo entered the Balkans rather late, only after Sephardic Jews were expelled from Spain and Portugal after 1492, and some of the ways in which Judezmo appears to be non-Balkan can be attributed to this chronological dimension. For instance, Judezmo speakers arrived in the Balkans with a fully functioning

[33]   See Friedman and Joseph (in press b: Chapter 7.7.2) for details on the various languages that inform this table; most of the relevant facts can also be found in Joseph (1983).

[34]   For instance, contact between Greeks of the mainland and Cypriot Greeks – note that the Cypriots have a separate word for mainlander Greek (*kalamaristika*), suggesting on-going contact – may have helped to spread the lack of an infinitive to the Cypriots.

preposed definite article so absence of the enclitic Balkan definite article can be explained by the fact that an article had already developed in Judezmo (from a Latin starting point without an article); that is, Judezmo came to the Balkans at a point when, in terms of its own development, the issue of a definite article had already been settled. The situation of Judezmo vis-à-vis the infinitival developments is another, perhaps even stronger, case in point. That is, although the ultimate loss of the infinitive in some of the languages is late, or has not yet occurred – Romanian, for instance, preserves the infinitive as an option even in contemporary usage – it can be localized temporally in the sixteenth or seventeenth century for the languages that lack it most fully, especially Greek, Macedonian and Tosk Albanian.[35] Thus the relative robustness of the infinitive in Balkan Judezmo, as compared to its linguistic neighbours in the Balkans, especially Greek and Macedonian, may in part be due to chronology. That is, the entry of Iberian Jews into the Balkans came at the end of the period when the infinitive was lost in this region. One can speculate, then, that being peripheral to the temporal period most associated with strong loss of the infinitive may have played a role in the survival of the Judezmo infinitive even into contemporary usage (see especially Dobreva 2016).

Another factor affecting the degree of participation in the convergence builds on the observation in Section 4.5 concerning sociohistorical factors. That is, there is also a social dimension to peripherality. Once again, this can be seen with Judezmo and the infinitive. As discussed in Friedman and Joseph (2014, 2016: Chapter 7.7.2), Balkan Judezmo shows contradictory tendencies regarding the infinitive, with both innovative finite subjunctive usage and conservative infinitival usage. The sociolinguistics of Jewish languages provides a basis for an explanation here. Jewish languages in general are likely to preserve archaisms different from those of co-territorial languages (see Wexler 1981), and given the local and social segregation of Jewish communities, Jewish speakers would have had less exposure to linguistic innovations found in the usage of co-territorial non-Jewish speakers. The Judeo-Greek of sixteenth century Constantinople, for instance, shows archaic infinitival usage paralleling that of New Testament Greek (Joseph 2000b). Moreover, as documented in Friedman (1995), Jews were linguistically peripheral as shown by the absence of Judezmo from nineteenth century Macedonian code-switching anecdotes, where Jews, who speak Turkish, are the only ethnic group that does not switch into its own language. While it is true that non-Jewish merchants in the bazaars often had some knowledge of Judezmo (and, as with Yiddish, Hebraisms were used as cryptolectal elements in such circumstances; Benor 2009), multilingualism, as with Romani, tended to be unidirectional (Friedman 2000). Thus the persistence of the

---

[35] Tosk Albanian has developed a new infinitival construction, e.g. *për të punuar* '(for) to work', apparently composed of a preposition (*për* 'for') with a nominalized participle (*të punuar*), but this seems to be a relatively recent development, after a period without an infinitive in the language.

use of infinitives in at least some Balkan Judezmo varieties seems to be an important reflection of a lesser degree of contact between Jews and non-Jews in the Balkans than among he non-Jewish speakers of various languages in the region. By contrast, Romani was in intimate contact with Greek for hundreds of years beginning no later than the eleventh century or so. And while we cannot know what Proto-Romani looked like at that time, Romani is as dependent as Greek and Macedonian on its analytic subjunctive to perform infinitival functions.[36]

Thus peripherality can be measured spatially, temporally and socially, of which social factors are the most important. Geography can help or hinder such interactions, and chronology is insurmountable but also instrumental in that speakers can only be in a place when they have come to that place. As the lesson of the *Pax Ottomanica* shows, political conditions – which are a macrosocial phenomenon in any case – can also serve as a contributing factor. In the end, then, social factors, aided and abetted by various other external conditions, determine participation and boundaries.

Andriotis and Kourmoulis (1968: 30) maintain that the Balkan sprachbund is 'une fiction qui n'est perceptible que de très loin' and that the commonalities are 'tout à fait inorganiques et superficielles'. Their view – no doubt influenced by Greek nation-state ideology – addresses the final question, (4e. viii), that is, whether the Balkan sprachbund, or any sprachbund that might be identified, is an on-going concern or just an artefact of the past.

Contrary to the challenge posed by Andriotis and Kourmoulis, one can argue that Balkan linguistic diversity occurs within the context of a set of structural similarities that constitute a framework of contact-induced change. Moreover, it is important to distinguish between 'superficial' and 'surface'. As Joseph (2001b) argued, surface realizations constitute the locus of language contact, and therefore accounts that are concerned with typological aspects of universal grammar (including formalist descriptions) do not address the mechanisms of language contact.[37] Also, surface realizations are by no means 'inorganic': they represent convergences that are evidence of the multilingualism that we know existed for centuries and even millennia, and which thrived and developed into the 'Four-M' (multilateral, multidirectional, mutual multilingualism) set of conditions under Ottoman rule.

Moreover, and this may be the real source of Andriotis and Kourmoulis's position, when one compares just the standard national languages of the Balkans (as does Asenova 2002, leaving out Macedonian, however), one can get a sense of language states frozen in time, fixed in a form that might reflect a structural state of affairs from several centuries back, affected somewhat by the process of standardization. Or then again, the literary

---

[36] Relatively recently, Romani dialects outside the Balkans have begun developing new infinitival constructions in contact with European languages that do have infinitives (Boretzky 1996).

[37] Aikhenvald (2006b) makes a similar point.

language might reflect a state of affairs that never existed in the spoken language, but has been borrowed from some prestigious language outside the Balkans. As for Greek, for instance, it is instructive to examine Thumb (1895) for the state of the language as recently as the late nineteenth century and to see regular Demotic forms given that exist today only in regional dialects, forced out of the emerging standard language by the onslaught of puristic pressures, overt and covert; for example, *práɣma* 'thing', currently with a genitive *práɣmatos*, forms that match Ancient Greek except for the realization of the velar as a fricative, is given as *práma* (still an accepted variant today) but with a genitive *pramátu*, a form found now in such outlying dialects as Cappadocian but not in the standard language. And the effects of lexical purism affecting the ERIC loans are evident in a look through Grannes et al. (2002), where so many of the Turkisms recorded there for Bulgarian are artefacts of the nineteenth century, considered now, in present-day Bulgarian, to be obsolete or else serving only to lend an archaic flavour to literary works. Such is also the case in all the other Balkan languages (Friedman 1996, but see Friedman 2005 on the resurgence of Turkisms in ex-communist countries as a badge of democracy). These examples teach two important lessons.

First, there is the important injunction of Bailey, Maynor and Cukor-Avila (1989: 299) regarding vernaculars and standard languages:

> [T]he history of ... language is the history of vernaculars rather than standard languages. Present-day vernaculars evolved from earlier ones that differed remarkably from present-day textbook[-varieties] ... These earlier vernaculars, rather than the standard, clearly must be ... the focus of research into the history of ... [languages].

This holds true for the Balkans, and the difference between the crystallized structure of the standard languages, with some Balkan convergent structure intact but not going anywhere, gives a sense of déjà vu to the sprachbund if one looks only at these standard languages. They are based on speech forms that were affected by the intense contact of the Ottoman period, and therefore show Balkanisms. But the 'present-day vernaculars' are the regional dialects, so the second key lesson is that the dialects and not the standard languages are where Balkan linguistic processes continue. The example in (1) of the 'feels-like' construction in Kastoria Greek but not elsewhere in Greek is a case in point. On-going contact among speakers of regional varieties of Greek, Macedonian, Balkan Romance, Romani, Albanian and so on, continues to occur in northern Greece, in the Republic of Macedonia, in parts of Albania and elsewhere in the Balkans, in cities and in rural areas. This contact continues the 'Four-M' model conditions (see Friedman 2011b). In that sense, the Balkan sprachbund is alive and developing as contact among speakers continues.

For sprachbunds that have no standard languages and no literary tradition, the vitality of the convergence zone as a living and on-going entity will depend on the health of the languages involved, that is, of the speakers' commitment to and ability to use their languages, and the extent to which contact and mutual multilingualism continue. Here the Republic of Macedonia presents a considerably more promising picture than the Hellenic Republic, although both countries are still home to speakers of languages from all the major Balkan linguistic groups. But in principle, a sprachbund is not a relic of the past; under the right conditions, the necessary type of contact renders the processes of convergence on-going.

We see the Balkan sprachbund as crucial to placing the differences in the context of the similarities. That is, there are certain cleavages within the Balkans that are particularly revealing, e.g. between 'have'-based futures and 'want'-based futures, or between the presence of systematic marking for evidentiality and the absence of such marking, that yield a crisscross pattern over the whole of the sprachbund area. Paying attention to such features and their distribution offers a more nuanced picture of the sprachbund, one based in part on the recognition that, like all language change, degrees of convergence can take place at varying speeds. And, as with other aspects of the present discussion, social conditions are the crucial factor.

4.7 Conclusion

The problematization and interrogation of the notion of 'sprachbund' offered here come down to a single issue: Do sprachbunds exist as a distinct entity in the context of contact-induced change?

Our answer is 'yes'. Insofar as we can speak of 'language' as both a linguistic and a social fact, so too can we speak of a sprachbund as a linguistic and social result of a particular kind of language contact. Such contact reflects the effects of intense multilateral, multidirectional, mutual multilingualism. A sprachbund is no more a linguist's construct than is a language. Just as a language, in the external sense of a medium of communication shared in a speech community, is the creation of its speakers, so, too, speakers are involved in forging the convergent structures that define a sprachbund. The sprachbund is a well-instantiated and distinctly observable entity shaped by space, time and social conditions, and it is necessarily based on contact between speakers of distinct 'languages' in a geographical space. This answer leads to an additional question: Are the Balkans an instance of a sprachbund? Again, the answer is 'yes'. Whether the region that was once a sprachbund still is depends on whether one focuses on achronic comparisons involving current standard languages or instead looks to see the forces that shaped the standard languages structurally and that are still observable in on-going contact situations outside the standard varieties.

Finally, does a sprachbund represent the outcome of a special *type* of contact, different from that found in casual borrowing, trade contexts, learnèd borrowing or creolization? The answer is still 'yes'. A sprachbund reflects aspects of contact found in other contexts such as multilingualism, but the type of stable, relatively egalitarian multilingualism we discuss here, with intense and sustained contact on an everyday basis, is arguably diagnostic. The sprachbund, therefore, even if it raises important questions, is a useful construct, which contact linguistics needs to recognize within the overall scope of contact-induced linguistic developments.

References

Aikhenvald, Alexandra Y., 2006a. Grammars in contact: A cross-linguistic perspective. In Aikhenvald and Dixon (eds), pp. 1–66.

Aikhenvald, Alexandra Y., 2006b. Semantics and pragmatics of grammatical relations in the Vaupés linguistic area. In Aikhenvald and Dixon (eds), pp. 237–266.

Aikhenvald, Alexandra and R. M. W. Dixon (eds), 2006. *Grammars in Contact: A Cross-linguistic Typology*. Oxford: Oxford University Press.

Allen, Joseph H., 1916. *Allen and Greenough's New Latin Grammar*. New York: Ginn & Company.

Altimari, Francesco, 2011. Traces d'infinitifs anciens appartenant à l'albanais dans la langue arbërisht d'Italie. In Hélène Antoniadis-Bibicou, Maurice Aymard and André Guillou (eds), *L'homme et son environnement dans le Sud-Est européen: Actes du Xe Congrès de l'Association internationale du Sud-Est européen*, pp. 445–455. Paris: Association Pierre Belon.

Andriotis, Nikolaos and Georgios Kourmoulis, 1968. Questions de la linguistique balkanique et l'apport de la langue grecque. In I. Gălăbov et al. (eds), *Actes du Premier Congrès International des Études Balkaniques et Sud-est Européennes*, vol. 6, pp. 21–30. Sofia: BAN.

Asenova, Petja, 2002. *Balkansko ezikoznanie [Balkan Linguistics]*, second edition. Veliko Tărnovo: Faber.

van der Auwera, Johan, 1998a. Revisiting the Balkan and Meso-American linguistic areas. *Language Sciences* 20 (3): 259–270.

van der Auwera, Johan, 1998b. Conclusions. In Johan van der Auwera (ed.), *Adverbial Constructions in the Languages of Europe*, pp. 813–836. Berlin: Mouton de Gruyter.

Bailey, Guy, Natalie Maynor and Patricia Cukor-Avila, 1989. Variation in subject–verb concord in early Modern English. *Language Variation and Change* 1 (3): 285–300.

Ball, Christopher G., 2007. *Out of the Park: Trajectories of Wauja (Xingu Arawak) Language and Culture*. PhD thesis, University of Chicago.

Beck, David, 2000. Grammatical convergence and the genesis of diversity in the Northwest coast Sprachbund. *Anthropological Linguistics* 42: 147–213

Belić, Aleksandar, 1936. La linguistique balkanique aux congrès internationaux des linguistes. *Revue Internationale des Etudes Balkaniques* 2 (3/4): 167–171.

Belyavski-Frank, Masha, 2003. *The Balkan Conditional in South Slavic*. Munich: Otto Sagner.

Benor, Sarah Bunin, 2009. Lexical othering in Judezmo: How Ottoman Sephardim refer to non-Jews. In David M. Bunis (ed.), *Languages and Literatures of Sephardic and Oriental Jews*, pp. 65–85. Jerusalem: The Bialik Institute & Misgav Yerushalayim.

Bird, Norman, 1982. *The Distribution of Indo-European Root Morphemes (A Checklist for Philologists)*. Wiesbaden: Harrassowitz.

Birnbaum, Henrik, 1968. Slavjanskie jazyki na Balkanax i ponjatie tak nazyvaemyx jazykovyx sojuzov. *Glossa* 2 (1): 70–92.

Bisang, Walter, 2006. Linguistic areas, language contact and typology: Some implications from the case of Ethiopia as a linguistic area. In Yaron Matras, April McMahon and Nigel Vincent (eds), *Linguistic Areas: Convergence in Historical and Typological Perspective*, pp. 75–98. London: Palgrave.

Boretzky, Norbert, 1996. The new infinitive in Romani. *Journal of the Gypsy Lore Society, Fifth Series* 6: 1–51.

Campbell, Lyle, Terrence Kaufman and Thomas C. Smith-Stark, 1986. Meso-America as a linguistic area. *Language* 62: 530–570.

Chang, Will, Chundra Cathcart, David Hall and Andrew Garrett, 2015. Ancestry-constrained phylogenetic analysis supports the Indo-European steppe hypothesis. *Language* 91: 194–244.

Demiraj, Shaban, 2004. *Gjuhësi ballkanike*, second edition. Tiranë: Akademia e Shkencave e Republikës së Shqipërise (Instituti i Gjuhësisë dhe i Letërisë).

Dixon, R. M. W., 1997. *The Rise and Fall of Languages*. Cambridge: Cambridge University Press.

Dobreva, Iskra. 2016. Préstam panbalcanicos en judeoespañol / Panbalkanski zaemki v sefardski ezik. Doctoral dissertation, University of Sofia.

Donohue, Mark, 2012. Studying contact without detailed studies of the languages involved: A non-philological approach to language contact. Paper presented at the 38th Annual Meeting of the Berkeley Linguistics Society, Berkeley, CA, 10–12 February 2012.

Emeneau, Murray, B., 1956. India as a linguistic area. *Language* 32: 3–16.

Enfield, Nick, 2005. Areal linguistics and mainland Southeast Asia. *Annual Review of Anthropology* 34: 181–206.

Enfield, Nick J., 2008. Transmission biases in linguistic epidemiology. *Journal of Language Contact, Thema* 2: 297–306.

Epps, Patience, 2006. The Vaupés melting pot: Tucanoan influence on Hup. In Aikhenvald and Dixon (eds), pp. 267–289.

Feuillet, Jack, 2012. *Linguistique comparée des langues balkaniques*. Paris: Institut d'études slaves.

Friedman, Victor A., 1995. Persistence and change in Ottoman patterns of codeswitching in the Republic of Macedonia: Nostalgia, duress and language shift in contemporary Southeastern Europe. In Durk Gorter et al. (eds), *Summer School: Code-switching and Language Contact*, pp. 58–67. Ljouwert/Leeuwarden: Fryske Akademy.

Friedman, Victor A., 1996. The Turkish lexical element in the languages of the Republic of Macedonia from the Ottoman period to independence. *Zeitschrift für Balkanologie* 32 (1): 133–150

Friedman, Victor A., 2000. After 170 years of Balkan linguistics: Whither the millennium? *Mediterranean Language Review* 12: 1–15.

Friedman, Victor A., 2003. Language in Macedonia as an identity construction site. In Brian Joseph, Johanna DeStefano, Neil Jacobs and Ilse Lehiste (eds), *When Languages Collide: Perspectives on Language Conflict, Language Competition, and Language Coexistence*, pp. 257–295. Columbus, OH: Ohio State University Press.

Friedman, Victor A., 2005. From orientalism to democracy and back again. In Raymond Detrez and Pieter Plas (eds), *Developing Cultural Identity in the Balkans: Convergence vs. Divergence*, pp. 25–43. Berlin: Peter Lang.

Friedman, Victor A., 2006a. Balkanizing the Balkan sprachbund: A closer look at grammatical permeability and feature distribution. In Aikhenvald and Dixon (eds), pp. 201–219.

Friedman, Victor A., 2006b. The Balkans as a linguistic area. In Keith Brown (Editor-in-Chief), *Elsevier Encyclopedia of Language and Linguistics*, vol. 1, pp. 657–672. Oxford: Elsevier.

Friedman, Victor A., 2007. Udvojuvanjeto na objektot vo balkanskite jazici vo minatoto i denes [Macedonian: Object reduplication in Balkan languages in the past and today]. In Zuzana Topolińska et al. (eds), *Klasika – Balkanistika – Paleoslavistika: Festschrift in Honor of the 85th Birthday and 60th Anniversary of Scholarly Activity of Acad. Petar Ilievski*, pp. 235–249. Skopje: Macedonian Academy of Arts and Sciences.

Friedman, Victor A., 2008. Balkan Slavic dialectology and Balkan linguistics: Periphery as center. In Christina Bethin (ed.), *American Contributions to the Fourteenth International Congress of Slavists*, pp. 131–148. Bloomington, IN: Slavica.

Friedman, Victor A., 2011a. The Balkan languages and Balkan linguistics. *Annual Review of Anthropology* 40: 275–291.

Friedman, Victor A., 2011b. Le multilinguisme en République de Macédoine et l'union balkanique aujourd'hui. In Hélène Antoniadis-Bibicou, Maurice Aymard and André Guillou (eds), *L'homme et son environnement dans le Sud-Est européen: Actes du Xe Congrès de l'Association internationale du Sud-Est européen*, pp. 479–481. Paris: Association Pierre Belon.

Friedman, Victor A., 2012. Conjunction calquing: A heartland Balkanism. In Thede Kahl, Michael Metzelin and Helmut Schaller (eds), *Balkanismen heute / Balkanisms Today / Balkanizmy segodnja*, pp. 31–37. Vienna: LIT Verlag.

Friedman, Victor A., 2014. Languages are wealth: The Sprachbund as linguistic capital. In Florian Lionnet, Kayla Carpenter, Oana David, Tammy Stark, Vivian Wauters and Christine Sheil (eds), *Proceedings of the 38th*

Annual Meeting of the Berkeley Linguistics Society. Berkeley, CA: Berkeley Linguistics Society.

Friedman, Victor A. and Brian D. Joseph, 2014. Lessons from Judezmo about the Balkan sprachbund and contact linguistics. *International Journal of the Sociology of Language* 226: 3–23. Special issue on Jewish Language Contact, edited by Ghil'ad Zuckermann.

Friedman, Victor A. and Brian D. Joseph, in press a. Non-nominative and depersonalized subjects in the Balkans: Areality vs. genealogy. In Jóhanna Barðdal, Stephen Mark Carey, Thórhallur Eythórsson and Na'ama Pat-El (eds), *Non-Canonically Case-Marked Subjects within and across Languages and Language Families: The Reykjavík–Eyjafjallajökull Papers*. Amsterdam: John Benjamins.

Friedman, Victor A. and Brian D. Joseph, in press b. *The Balkan Languages*. Cambridge: Cambridge University Press.

Gil, David, 2011. Obligatory vs. optional tense-aspect-mood marking. Paper presented at ICHL 20 (20th International Conference on Historical Linguistics), Osaka, 28 July 2011.

Gołąb, Zbigniew, 1976. On the mechanism of Slavic–Rumanian linguistic interference in the Balkans. In Thomas Butler (ed.), *Bulgaria, Past and Present: Studies in History, Literature, Economics, Music, Sociology, Folklore and Linguistics*, pp. 296–309. Columbus, OH: AAASS.

Gołąb, Zbigniew, 1984. *The Arumanian Dialect of Kruševo in SR Macedonia SFR Yugoslavia*. Skopje: MANU.

Grannes, Alf, Kjetil Rå Hauge and Hayriye Süleymenoğlu, 2002. *A Dictionary of Turkisms in Bulgarian*. Oslo: Novus.

Greenberg, Robert, 2000. The dialects of Macedonia and Montenegro: Random linguistic parallels or evidence of a sprachbund? *Južnoslovenski Filolog* 56: 295–300.

Gumperz, J. J. and R. Wilson, 1971. Convergence and creolization: A case from the Indo-Aryan / Dravidian border in India. In Dell Hymes (ed.), *Pidginization and Creolization of Languages*, pp. 151–167. Cambridge: Cambridge University Press.

Hamp, Eric P., 1977. On some questions of areal linguistics. In Kenneth Whistler, Robert D. Van Valin, Chris Chiarello, Jeri J. Jaeger, Miriam Petruck, Henry Thompson, Ronya Javkin and Anthony Woodbury (eds), *Proceedings of the Third Annual Meeting of the Berkeley Linguistics Society*, pp. 279–282. Berkeley, CA: Berkeley Linguistics Society.

Hamp, Eric P., 1989. Yugoslavia crossroads of Sprachbünde. *Zeitschrift für Balkanologie* 25 (1): 44–47.

Haspelmath Martin, 1998. How young is Standard Average European? *Language Sciences* 20 (3): 271–287.

Haspelmath, Martin, 2001. The European linguistic area: Standard Average European. In Martin Haspelmath (ed.), *Language Typology and Language Universals*, vol. 2, pp. 1492–1551. Berlin: Mouton de Gruyter.

Haugen, Einar, 1966. Semicommunication: The language gap in Scandinavia. *Sociological Inquiry* 36: 280–297.

Heath, Jeffrey, 1984. Language contact and language change. *Annual Review of Anthropology* 13: 367–384.

Ilievski, Petar, 1972. Kon interpretacijata na modelot na udvoeniot objekt vo makedonskiot jazik. In *Godišen zbornik, Filozofski fakultet na Univerzitetot Skopje*, pp. 205–220. Reprinted in Ilievski 1988, pp. 167–182.

Ilievski, Petar, 1988 [1973]. *Balkanološki Lingvistički Studii*. Skopje: Institut za makedonski Jazik.

Jakobson, Roman, 1931/1971. Harakteristike evrazijskogo jazykovogo sojuza [Characteristics of the Eurasian sprachbund]. In *Selected Writings*, second edition, vol. 1, pp. 143–201. The Hague: Mouton.

Joseph, Brian D., 1983. *The Synchrony and Diachrony of the Balkan Infinitive: A Study in Areal, General, and Historical Linguistics*. Cambridge: Cambridge University Press. Reissued in paperback, 2009.

Joseph, Brian, 1987. A fresh look at the Balkan sprachbund: Some observations on H. W. Schaller's Die Balkansprachen. *Mediterranean Language Review* 3: 105–114.

Joseph, Brian D., 2000a. Textual authenticity: Evidence from Medieval Greek. In Susan C. Herring, Pieter van Reenen and Lene Schøsler (eds), *Textual Parameters in Older Languages*, pp. 309–329. Amsterdam: John Benjamins.

Joseph, Brian D., 2000b. Processes of spread for syntactic constructions in the Balkans. In Christos Tzitzilis and Charalambos Symeonidis (eds), *Balkan Linguistik: Synchronie und Diachronie*, pp. 139–150. Thessaloniki: Aristotle University of Thessaloniki.

Joseph, Brian D., 2001a. Review of R. M. W. Dixon, The Rise and Fall of Languages. *Journal of Linguistics* 37: 180–186.

Joseph, Brian D., 2001b. Is Balkan comparative syntax possible? In Maria L. Rivero and Angela Ralli (eds), *Comparative Syntax of Balkan Languages*, pp. 17–43. Oxford: Oxford University Press.

Joseph, Brian D., 2003. The Balkan languages. In William Frawley (ed.), *International Encyclopedia of Linguistics*, second edition, pp. 194–196. Oxford: Oxford University Press.

Joseph, Brian D., 2010. Language contact in the Balkans. In Raymond Hickey (ed.), *The Handbook of Language Contact*, pp. 618–633. Oxford: Wiley-Blackwell.

Joseph, Brian D. and Rex E. Wallace, 1987. Latin *sum* / Oscan *súm, sim*, esum. *American Journal of Philology* 108: 675–693.

Kodov, Hr., 1935. *Ezikăt na trakijskite bălgari [The Language of the Thracian Bulgarians]*. Sofia: Trakijskijăt naučen institut.

König, Ekkehard, 1998. General preface. In Johan van der Auwera (ed.), *Adverbial Constructions in the Languages of Europe*, pp. v–vii. Berlin: Mouton de Gruyter.

Kopitar, Jernej, 1829. Albanische, walachische und bulgarische Sprache. *Jahrbücher der Literatur* 46: 59–106.

Labov, William, 2007. Transmission and diffusion. *Language* 83 (2): 344–387.

Leake, William Martin, 1814. *Researches in Greece*. London: John Booth.

Lindstedt, Jouko, 2000. Linguistic Balkanization: Contact-induced change by mutual reinforcement. In Dicky Gilbers, John Nerbonne and Jos Schaeken (eds), *Languages in Contact*, pp. 231–246. Amsterdam: Rodopi.

Masica, Colin, 1976. *South Asia as a Linguistic Area*. Chicago: University of Chicago.

Masica, Colin, 2001. The definition and significance of linguistic areas: Methods, pitfalls, and possibilities (with special reference to the validity of South Asia as a linguistic area). In P. Bhaskararao and K. Subbarao (eds), *The Yearbook of South Asian Languages and Linguistics 2001*, pp. 205–268. New Delhi: Sage.

Matras, Yaron, 2004. Romacilikanes: The Romani dialect of Parakalamos. *Romani Studies* 14 (1): 59–109.

Miklosich, Franz, 1861. Die slavischen Elemente im Rumunischen. *Denkschriften der Kaiserlichen Akademie der Wissenschaften, Philosophisch-historische Klasse* 12: 1–70.

Mladenov, Stefan, 1939. Bălgarskijat ezik v svetlinata na balkanistika. *Godišnik na Sofijskija Universitet, Istor.-filol. fakultet*, 35.13.1ff.

Mufwene, Salikoko, 2001. *The Ecology of Language Evolution*. Cambridge: Cambridge University.

Mufwene, Salikoko, 2004. Language birth and death. *Annual Review of Anthropology* 33: 201–222.

Nichols, Johanna, 1997. Modeling ancient population structures and movements in linguistics. *Annual Review of Anthropology* 26: 359–284.

Nuckols, Mark, 2000. *Examination of the case for a Central European Sprachbund of Czech, German, Hungarian and Slovak*. MA thesis, The Ohio State University, Columbus, OH.

Obolensky, Dimitri, 1971. *The Byzantine Commonwealth*. New York: Praeger.

Pană Dindelegan, Gabriela, 2013. *The Grammar of Romanian*. Oxford: Oxford University Press.

Reiter, Norbert, 1994. *Grundzüge der Balkanologie: Ein Schritt in die Eurolinguistik*. Wiesbaden: Harrassowitz.

Reiter, Norbert, 1999. Von der Balkanologie zur Eurolinguistik. In Uwe Hinrichs (ed.), *Handbuch der Südosteuropa–Linguistik*, pp. 19–26. Wiesbaden: Harrassowitz.

Ringe, Donald A., 1992. On calculating the factor of chance in language comparison. *Transactions of the American Philosophical Society* 82 (1): 1–110.

Ross, Malcolm, 2001. Contact-induced language change in north-west Melanesia. In Alexandra Aikhenvald and R. M. W. Dixon (eds), *Areal Diffusion and Genetic Inheritance*, pp. 134–166. Oxford: Oxford University Press.

Sandfeld, Kristian, 1930. *Linguistique balkanique*. Paris: Klinksieck.

Sawicka, Irena, 1997. *The Balkan Sprachbund in the Light of Phonetic Features*. Toruń: Energeia.

Schaller, Helmut W., 1975. *Die Balkansprachen: Eine Einführung in die Balkanphilologie*. Heidelberg: Carl Winter.

Schleicher, August, 1850. *Die Sprachen Europas in systematischer Übersicht*. Bonn: König.

Seliščev, A., 1925. Des traits linguistiques communs aux langues balkaniques: Un balkanisme ancien en bulgare. *Révue des Études Slaves* 5: 38–57.

Sherzer, Joel, 1976. *An Areal-Typological Study of American Indian Languages North of Mexico*. Amsterdam: North-Holland.

Solta, Georg R., 1980. *Einführung in die Balkanlinguistik mit besonderer Berücksichtigung des Substrats und des Balkanlateinischen*. Darmstadt: Wissenschaftliche Buchgesellschaft.

Steinke, Klaus, 1999. Zur theoretischen Grundlegung der Südosteuropa-Linguistik. In Uwe Hinrichs (ed.), *Handbuch der Südosteuropa-Linguistik*, pp. 67–90. Wiesbaden: Harrassowitz.

Stolz, Thomas, 2006. Europe as a linguistic area. In Keith Brown et al. (eds), *Encyclopedia of Language and Linguistics*, vol. IV, pp. 278–295. Amsterdam: Elsevier.

Thomason, Sarah G., 2001. *Language Contact: An Introduction*. Washington, DC: Georgetown University Press.

Thomason, Sarah G. and Terrence Kaufman, 1988. *Language Contact, Creolization, and Genetic Linguistics*. Berkeley, CA: University of California Press.

Thumb, Albert, 1895. *Handbuch der neugriechischen Volkssprache: Grammatik, Texte, Glossar*. Strasbourg: Trübner.

Trask, Robert Lawrence, 1996. *Historical Linguistics*. London: Arnold.

Trubetzkoy, Nikolai S., 1923. Vavilonskaja bašnja i smešenie jazykov. [The tower of Babel and the confusion of languages]. *Evrazijskij vremennik* 3: 107–124.

Trubetzkoy, Nikolai S., 1930. Proposition 16. In Cornelis de Boer, Jacobus van Ginneken and Anton G. van Hamel (eds), *Actes du Premier Congrès International des Linguistes à La Haye, du 10–15 Avril 1928*, pp. 17–18. Leiden, the Netherlands: A. W. Sijthoff.

Tuite, Kevin, 1999. The myth of the Caucasian sprachbund: The case of ergativity. *Lingua* 108: 1–26.

Vermeer, Willem, 1992. Serbs and Albanians in Yugoslavia. *Yearbook of European Studies* 5: 101–124.

Vinožito, 2006. *Bukvar/Anagnōstiko ['Primer' Macedonian/Greek]*. Thessaloniki: Batavia.

WALS, 2005. *The World Atlas of Language Structures*, edited by Martin Haspelmath, Matthew Dryer, David Gil and Bernard Comrie. Oxford: Oxford University Press.

Wexler, Paul, 1981. Jewish interlinguistics: Facts and conceptual framework. *Language* 57: 99–149.

Whitney, William D., 1868. *Language and the Study of Language: Twelve Lectures on the Principles of Linguistic Science*. New York: C. Scribner & Co.

5

Areal Sound Patterns: From Perceptual Magnets to Stone Soup

Juliette Blevins

5.1 Defining Areal Sound Patterns

Linguistic areas are geographic regions where languages share character-istics as a result of language contact and not as a consequence of shared inheritance, general linguistic tendencies, linguistic universals or chance.[1] Though there is controversy over the precise set of grammatical characteristics that can spread via language contact (see Campbell, Chapter 2, this volume), recognition and study of linguistic areas in the modern era continues to reaffirm that sound patterns can and do spread in this way (Aikhenvald 2002; Boas 1911, 1920, 1929; Emeneau 1956; Heath 1978; Trubetzkoy 1939). Given this general outline, we can define areal sound patterns as in (1).

(1)   Areal sound pattern: a definition

An areal sound pattern is a sound pattern shared by two or more languages in a designated geographic region that: (i) does not result from shared inheritance for at least one pair of languages; (ii) is not a consequence of general linguistic tendencies alone for at least one language; and (iii) cannot be attributed to chance for at least one lan-guage. An areal sound pattern results from language contact when speakers of a language that lacks a particular sound pattern come to acquire a sound pattern in their speech from extensive contact with a distinct language that has that pattern.

---

[1] Within some phonological frameworks, like Optimality Theory, linguistic universals are encoded as markedness constraints, while general linguistic tendencies are not (Kiparsky 2006; Prince and Smolensky 2004). In other frameworks, like Evolutionary Phonology, there is no clear categorical distinction between statistical tendencies and phonological universals, with apparent universals exhibiting extreme instances of statistical tendencies (Blevins 2004, 2006, 2009a, 2015). In the remainder of this chapter, I do not distinguish between general linguistic tendencies and linguistic universals, since, in both cases, what is relevant is a strong statistical tendency for a particular sound pattern to occur cross-linguistically, independent, for the most part, of inherited features. For cases where strong statistical tendencies do appear to correlate with other inherited sound patterns, see Blevins (2009b) and Blevins and Grawunder (2009).

The notion of sound pattern in (1) is a general one. It includes: overall properties of contrastive sound inventories such as vowel, consonant and tone inventories; patterns determining the distribution of sounds or contrastive features of sounds, including the distribution of stress, tone, length, laryngeal features and consonant clusters; and the variable realization of sounds in different contexts that constitute phonological alternations. We will look at cases of each of these types in the sections that follow.

The definition in (1) defines an areal sound pattern as a sound pattern shared minimally by two languages, having arguably diffused from one into the other. Though linguistic areas as large as the Australian continent have been proposed (Dixon 2002), looking only at sound patterns, we find many cases of areal sound patterns limited to small geographic areas and to a small number of languages.[2]

Within the large and widely dispersed Austronesian language family, an areal sound pattern is found in a small region of central Taiwan as shown in Map 5.1.

Three geographically contiguous Formosan languages – Thao, Bunun and Tsou – show pre-glottalization of voiced stops /b/ and /d/ as [ˀb] and [ˀd] respectively (Blust 2009: 52, 165, 641–642). Blust (2009: 641) suggests that the innovation occurred in Bunun and spread to both Tsou and Thao. Pre-glottalization is not a feature of Proto-Austronesian – the only common ancestor from which these three languages descend.[3] Therefore, shared inheritance is ruled out.[4] Assessing whether pre-glottalization of /b/ and /d/ in three distinct Formosan subgroups could be attributed to phonetic naturalness or chance is more complex. If we look at the distribution of pre-glottalization and implosion of voiced stops throughout the Austronesian language family, we find it occurring in approximately 20/1,000 or 2 per cent of languages,[5] while cross-linguistically, based on modern sampling of the WALS database, implosives occur in 77/567 or approximately 13.5 per cent of languages, but in less than 10 per cent of languages that do not also have ejectives or glottalized sonorants

---

[2] Macro-areas and micro-areas for sound patterns may be more common than those for other levels of languages for the simple fact that the phonetics of one language is immediately accessible to speakers of another in a language contact zone, while aspects of morphology and syntax are not.

[3] I follow Blust's (2009, 2013) Proto-Austronesian (PAN) reconstructions here. However, the possibility that PAN did indeed have (phonetically) preglottalized [ˀb] and [ˀd] that were retained in at least one Formosan language, Bunun, might be considered: Proto-Mon-Khmer is reconstructed with preglottalized stops */ˀb/ and /ˀd / (Diffloth 1976; Haudricourt 1965) which were maintained in Mon, Palaungic, Katuic and Bahnaric, but lost in Khmer, Pearic and Khmuic (Diffloth 1976; Haudricourt 1965).

[4] Under Blust's (1999, 2009) classification, Bunun is an immediate daughter of Proto-Austronesian, while Thao is a member of the Western Plains group and Tsou a member of the Tsouic subgroup. Since no other Western Plains or Tsouic language has pre-glottalization, this feature appears to post-date the diversification of these subgroups.

[5] Implosives are found in Bintulu, Lowland Kenyah dialects, languages of the western Lesser Sundas and languages of southeast Sulawesi (Blust 2009: 176, 188). If these additional cases are not included, the figure may be under 1 per cent. However, even in the language count, implosion is likely over-represented, since, as noted by Blust, implosion appears to be an areal feature in the western Lesser Sundas and southeast Sulawesi as well.

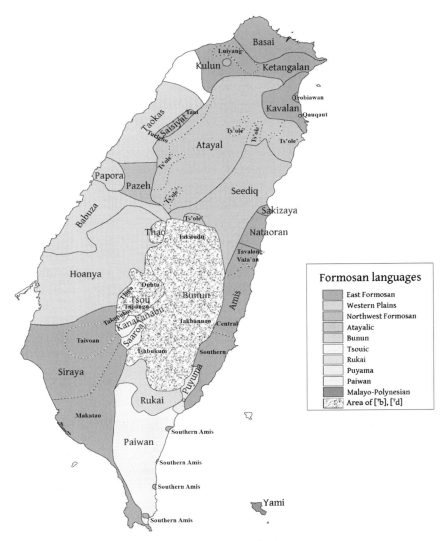

Map 5.1 Pre-glottalization in a micro-area of central Taiwan

(Maddieson 2013a). The chance, then, of three randomly chosen Austronesian languages having this property is 0.00008, while the chance of any three randomly chosen languages having this property is 0.001. Pre-glottalization/implosion is also clearly under-represented within the Austronesian family. The occurrence of this feature in 3/24 or 12.5 per cent of known indigenous languages of Taiwan at a shallow time depth (see note 3) and in a contiguous area, then, does not appear to reflect the general tendencies for these sounds to develop within Austronesian languages, but, as Blust suggests, is best attributed to diffusion of pre-glotta-lization from Bunun to neighbouring languages of central Taiwan.

Since areal sound patterns must be distinguished from sound patterns resulting from shared inheritance, general linguistic tendencies, or chance, the establishment of an areal feature cannot be based simply on the association of a geographically defined region with a linguistic feature that crosses language boundaries, no matter how vast the geographic region is, or how uncommon the linguistic feature is outside this region. In this context, consider Dixon's (2002) proposal that the entire continent of pre-contact Australia is a linguistic area, including more than 200 indigenous Aboriginal languages. While this area might be defended on other grounds, proposed areal sound patterns do not meet the criteria set out in (1) because direct inheritance cannot be ruled out. The clearest example involves the contrast between retroflex and non-retroflex apical stops found in more than two-thirds of the indigenous languages.[6] Cross-linguistically, contrastive retroflexion for oral and nasal stops ranges from about 5 to 7 per cent in the UPSID database sample of 451 languages (Maddieson 1984; Maddieson and Precoda 1989), so the much higher rates of this feature across Australia are suggestive. A further suggestion of areality is the band of Pama-Nyungan languages lacking retroflexes, stretching along the eastern coast of the continent, from Cape York south, as shown in Map 5.2 (after Dixon 2002: 66).

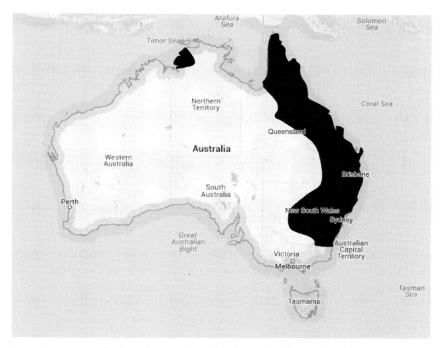

Map 5.2 Areas on the Australian continent lacking contrastive retroflexion

---

[6] Australian languages with a retroflex contrast are often referred to as 'double apical' languages in contrast to 'single apical' languages that lack it. We return to consonant retroflexion as an areal feature in Section 5.2.

However, contrastive retroflexion is reconstructed for Proto-Pama-Nyungan (Bowern and Koch 2004), the mother language of approximately 75 per cent of Aboriginal languages. The remaining Aboriginal languages fall into approximately 27 families/isolates. While detailed historical work on many of these is in the early stages, at least some non-Pama-Nyungan proto-languages, like Proto-Tangkic, are reconstructed with contrastive retroflexion as well (Evans 1995; Round 2011). Given these historical proposals, the high frequency of contrastive retroflexion in Australian Aboriginal languages seems due to inheritance or shared inheritance within recognized language families.[7] If any areal feature needs to be explained, it is the band of Pama-Nyungan languages on the east coast that appear to have lost this contrast.

In regions where significant historical work has been done, shared inheritance is usually the easiest factor to rule out as a source of phonological convergence. For example, in assessing whether the occurrence of glottalized consonants in Yurok, an Algic language of Northwestern California, may constitute part of an areal sound pattern in Northwestern California (Haas 1976) or part of a larger identifiable areal pattern of high-frequency glottalized consonants on the Northwest Coast of North America (Maddieson 2013a), we can rule out shared inheritance. This areal pattern is shown in Map 5.3, where only the northernmost language, Alutiq (1), and two southern fringe languages, Karok (48) and Wiyot (51), lack ejectives.

Glottalized consonants are found in Yurok (49), as well as in neighbouring Hupa (50) and Tolowa (47), two Athabaskan languages, Chimariko, an isolate, in slightly more distant Shasta, another isolate, and in Wintu, a Wintuan language. Since Yurok is unrelated to all of these languages, the glottalized consonants in Yurok are not due to shared inheritance. Further, Yurok is unique among Algic languages in having ejectives /p', t', k', tʃ'/.[8] The development of ejectives in Yurok is, apparently, unique within its language family.

However, ruling out general linguistic tendencies or chance may be more difficult in this case. Ejectives, or ejective-like consonants, are found in 92/566 or 16.3 per cent of languages in WALS (Maddieson 2013a). Since Yurok is one of approximately 32 Algic languages, and the only one with ejectives, how can we rule this out as a chance event within Algic? If a particular sound change or sound pattern is common, or simply attested in some significant percentage of the world's languages, how can

---

[7] In support of this, one can look at other apparent areal features of the Australian continent that are typologically unusual, like the occurrence of non-homorganic NC clusters. These are also arguably inherited, not diffused (Blevins 2004: 209–211).

[8] The development of ejectives does not appear to be a natural one within the Algic family. No other languages have glottalized obstruents. Wiyot, a neighbour of Yurok, has some evidence of glottalized sonorants, but not obstruents. In Algonquian proper, aspiration and spread glottal gestures are more common accompaniments to the voiceless stop series.

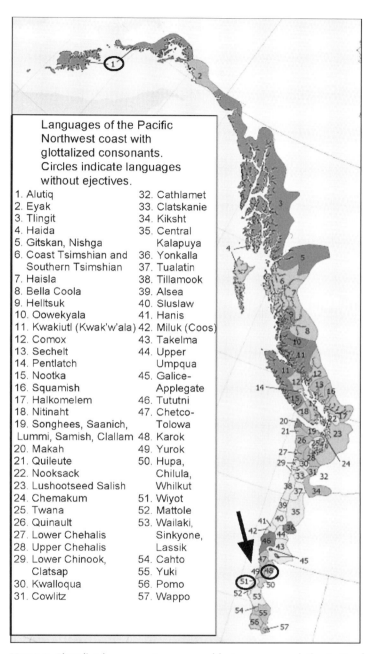

Languages of the Pacific Northwest coast with glottalized consonants. Circles indicate languages without ejectives.

1. Alutiq
2. Eyak
3. Tlingit
4. Haida
5. Gitskan, Nishga
6. Coast Tsimshian and Southern Tsimshian
7. Haisla
8. Bella Coola
9. Helltsuk
10. Oowekyala
11. Kwakiutl (Kwak'w'ala)
12. Comox
13. Sechelt
14. Pentlatch
15. Nootka
16. Squamish
17. Halkomelem
18. Nitinaht
19. Songhees, Saanich, Lummi, Samish, Clallam
20. Makah
21. Quileute
22. Nooksack
23. Lushootseed Salish
24. Chemakum
25. Twana
26. Quinault
27. Lower Chehalis
28. Upper Chehalis
29. Lower Chinook, Clatsap
30. Kwalloqua
31. Cowlitz
32. Cathlamet
33. Clatskanie
34. Kiksht
35. Central Kalapuya
36. Yonkalla
37. Tualatin
38. Tillamook
39. Alsea
40. Sluslaw
41. Hanis
42. Miluk (Coos)
43. Takelma
44. Upper Umpqua
45. Galice-Applegate
46. Tututni
47. Chetco-Tolowa
48. Karok
49. Yurok
50. Hupa, Chilula, Whilkut
51. Wiyot
52. Mattole
53. Wailaki, Sinkyone, Lassik
54. Cahto
55. Yuki
56. Pomo
57. Wappo

Map 5.3 Glottalized consonants as an areal feature, arrow pointing to Yurok

we determine whether its occurrence in what could be a linguistic area is independent or due to contact?

To appreciate the problems involved, let us consider a more common sound pattern, like final obstruent devoicing. Final obstruent devoicing refers to sound patterns where an obstruent voicing contrast is neutralized to the voiceless series in word-final position.[9] Devoicing is widespread in the world's languages and has a well-understood natural phonetic basis (Blevins 2006). An area with a high frequency of final devoicing sound patterns is Europe as illustrated in Map 5.4.

This sound pattern stretches from East Slavic (Russian) to West Slavic (Polish), north and west into Germanic languages (German, Dutch), and farther west and south into Romance (Picard, Romansh, Camuno). Proto-Indo-European, as well as Proto-Slavic, Proto-Germanic and Proto-Italic, are all reconstructed with voicing contrasts in initial, medial and final position. As a consequence, final devoicing sound patterns are not due to shared inheritance. Independent developments must be posited within each subgroup, and could reflect parallel evolution of a phonetically based sound change, or diffusions. In cases like this, a useful heuristic for diffusion is the occurrence of closely related dialects or languages, where one, arguably within the contact zone, shows the areal feature, and another, outside it, does not. Within the swathe of European devoicing, at least a few cases in the literature show this profile. In the central area, for example, we find that Standard Albanian maintains voicing contrasts finally, while Northern Tosk and transitional Southern Geg dialects exhibit final devoicing, shared with adjacent Montenegrin dialects. In this case, Friedman (2004) attributes Albanian devoicing to diffusion, due to historical contact with Macedonian (South Slavic) speakers. Many cases of final devoicing in Romance are also attributed to contact, usually with Germanic languages. For example, final devoicing in Old French is attributed to contact with Frankish (Posner 1995: 219–220).[10]

In the discussion that follows, we will use the range of criteria in (1) to define areal sound patterns so as to ensure that the sound pattern in question is not likely to have resulted from (shared) inheritance, general linguistic tendencies or chance. Though some of these criteria may prove too restrictive, eliminating some cases of areal sound patterns, they will provide us with a working base of areal patterns from which we may be able to extract interesting generalizations. It should be kept in mind that databases on sound pattern frequency are limited, so that all references to general distributions noted in the typological literature should be

---

[9] The term is used to refer to other kinds of laryngeal neutralization in final position as well. In German, for example, many varieties show a contrast between fortis aspirated and lenis unaspirated series, with neutralization to the aspirated series in final position (Iverson and Salmons 2006). See Jansen (2004) for phonetically based definitions of obstruent voicing versus VOT contrasts in a range of European languages. This is perhaps the best place to point out that the classic Balkan Sprachbund (Joseph 1983, 1992), on which the notion of linguistic areas is based, is not securely associated with areal-phonological features as defined in (1). Some features (like *n > r in Tosk Albanian and Romanian) are found in only a small subset of the languages involved. Others, like the existence of a central unrounded vowel, are common sound patterns, and could therefore result from natural parallel developments, or chance. See Vaux (2002) for further discussion.

[10] Diffusion of apparent regular sound changes leads one to question their usefulness in subgrouping. In a recent study of Western Numic dialects, Babel et al. (2013) show that all of the six regular sound changes identified show evidence of diffusion. They conclude that, like parallel natural sound changes in distinct lines of descent, 'phonological diffusion too can confound cladistic analysis' (p. 482).

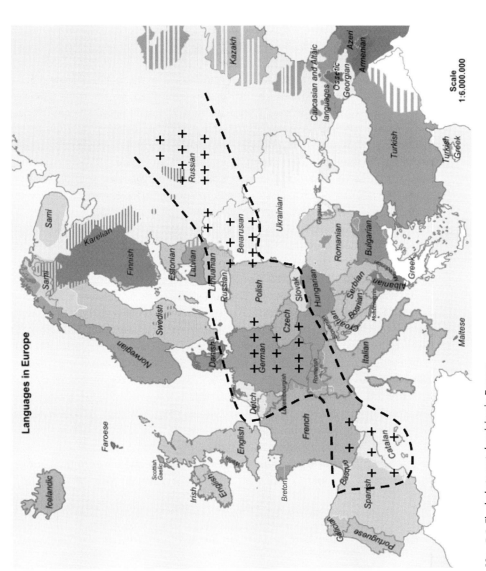

Map 5.4 Final obstruent devoicing in Europe

taken as preliminary. For general statistical approaches to linguistic typology, and the problem of ruling out chance in the assessment of areal features, see Bickel (2015). For the purposes of this chapter, we classify a sound pattern as uncommon if it occurs in less than 25 per cent of the world's languages, and as rare if it occurs in less than 5 per cent of the world's languages based on the UPSID (Maddieson 1984) and WALS (Dryer and Haspelmath 2013) survey data. A sound pattern like final obstruent devoicing, then, is not rare, and the areal devoicing illustrated in Map 5.4 could well be a consequence of parallel evolution, diffusion, or some combination of the two.

5.2 The Evolution of Areal Sound Patterns: Stone Soup and the Perceptual Magnet Effect

How do sound patterns spread from one language to another? How does a language without consonant implosion or retroflexion acquire these features by osmosis? How do new sound patterns materialize as speakers, exposed to these sound patterns in another language, continue to speak their own?

Though it was once commonly believed that areal sound patterns diffused primarily through lexical borrowing, as early as Emeneau (1956), it was clear that a process of 'acculturation' occurred, whereby native sounds became more like sounds of contact languages, without, or independent of, lexical borrowing. A case where this is particularly clear is the linguistic area of Northwestern California, mentioned earlier with respect to the areal distribution of glottalized consonants illustrated in Map 5.3. The Northwestern California culture area is home to at least four distinct language families/isolates: Karuk (isolate), Yurok and Wiyot (Algic), Hupa and Tolowa (Athabaskan), and Chimariko (isolate). As detailed in Conathan (2004), hundreds of years of multilingualism, intermarriage and cross-cultural exchange have led to linguistic convergence in many areas of grammar. However, in this linguistic area, lexical borrowing is very rare (Conathan 2004: 80–81). Not only are borrowings rare, but we are hard-pressed to find even one word that was borrowed into Yurok with /p'/ or /k'/; the most likely instances of borrowed words with ejectives involve /t'/ and /tʃ'/ (Blevins 2002).[11] Given that ejectives like /p'/ and /k'/ are thought to be areal features, and to have arisen in Yurok as a consequence of language contact, we cannot attribute the source of the sounds themselves to lexical borrowing.[12] For at least some ejectives, an internal historical source has been identified. A sequence of regular sound changes takes *Ct clusters to ejectives as shown in (2) (Blevins 2002).

[11] The most likely borrowings with ejectives are Yurok /tʃʼutʃʼiʃ/ 'bird', /tʃʼek/ 'wren', /tʃʼiʃah/ 'dog' (Blevins 2002: 11–12). Internal to Yurok, the primary source of glottal stop and ejection, is Proto-Algic *t.

[12] Indeed, Yurok pronominal prefixes 'ne- first person, k'e- second person, 'we- third person, that are cognate with Wiyot and more distant Algonquian languages, and that form the basis of the established genetic relationship of these languages, show glottalization, including the ejective /k'/ in the second person.

(2)   One source of glottalization in Pre-Yurok
         *Ct [Ct, C$^{\textrm{?}}$t, Ct$^{\textrm{?}}$] > C? > C'

Yurok ejectives, then, appear to be triggered by areal contact with neigh-bouring languages that have ejectives. Yet, they appear to evolve via natural phonetically motivated sound change. This observation is just one instantiation of what we might call the 'Areal Sound Pattern Paradox': areal sound patterns are paradoxical, in that their primary cata-lyst is external, and yet they often take the form of regular internally motivated sound change. How can this be?

A useful comparison is to the making of stone soup in the well-known European folktale, *Stone Soup*:[13]

> A poor peasant has been travelling for days through rugged land. He is hungry. When he arrives at the next village, he begs for food, first at one door, then at the next, and the next. But no one obliges. 'Ah' he tells them, 'then I will have to make a delicious stone soup like no other', and he collects wood, makes a fire, fills his black pot with water from the stream, sets it on the flames, and, with the villagers all looking on, drops one large stone into the pot and begins to stir. 'Go away,' he says to them. 'It will take some time to cook. I will tell you when it is ready.' But the villagers are curious, and, one by one, they return. First a woman comes by. 'What kind of soup is this, made from a stone?' the woman asks. 'Ah,' he tells her, taking a taste, 'you will see, it is a delicious soup, like no other, and only needs a bit of carrot to be just right.' The woman gives a carrot from her basket, and the peasant drops it in. Soon the woman's daughter comes by. 'What kind of soup is this, made from a stone?' the girl asks. 'Ah,' he tells her, taking a taste, 'you will see, it is a delicious soup, like no other, and only needs a bit of onion to be just right.' The girl takes an onion from her skirt pocket, and the peasant drops it in. Soon the suitor of the girl arrives and asks 'What kind of soup is this, made from a stone?' 'Ah,' he tells the boy, taking a taste, 'you will see, it is a delicious soup, like no other, and only needs a bit of mushroom to be just right.' The boy gives what he has gathered, and the peasant drops it in. Soon the father of the boy comes around, a farmer. 'What kind of soup is this, made from a stone?' the farmer asks. 'Ah,' he tells the farmer, taking a taste, 'you will see, it is a delicious soup, like no other, and only needs a bit of barley to be just right.' The farmer digs in his bag for a pouch of barley, and the peasant drops it in. Soon the farmer's wife arrives. 'What kind of soup is this, made from a stone?' she asks. 'Ah,' he tells her, taking a taste, 'you will see, it is a delicious soup, like no other, and only needs a bit of herbs to be just right.' The farmer's wife gives what she has just picked, and the peasant drops it in. When the peasant declares the soup 'just right', he shares it with the entire village, and all agree that it is a most delicious soup, like no other. All are well fed and rejoice.

---

[13] This folktale has many different variants, including those where the hungry travellers making the soup are peasants, beggars, monks or soldiers, and where the initial ingredient is a stone, a piece of wood, a nail, or some other non-foodstuff. The version here is the one I heard most often as a child.

While there are many ways of reading this tale, the features that most versions share are that of a hungry stranger coming into new country with nothing. From nothing, he makes a delicious soup. In essence, the soup is made from contributions of the surrounding villagers, but since each contribution is small, none of them notice that the soup is made from their own contributions, and not from the original stone. Clearly the stone is not the central ingredient, in fact, in the culinary sense, it is not an ingredient at all. It is a tool which mobilizes external ingredients, and these are what make the soup.

This, I suggest, is a useful metaphor for how areal sound patterns arise. The 'stone' in the linguistic scenario of language contact is the contact sound pattern that ultimately spreads: it is the main ingredient of something new, different and delicious, that people speaking their own language want to experience, but, in reality, it is completely inert. Areal sound patterns are not the result of phonetic borrowing or contamination. Under the view outlined below, the contact language serves as catalyst, but salient features of the new sound pattern come from the indigenous language, naturally and unknowingly. In the same way that stone soup has the same active ingredients as other soups, areal sound patterns have similar language-internal phonetic trajectories as non-areal sound patterns. The external stimulus of a contact sound pattern shifts the odds of the same pattern evolving in a neighbouring language, but it could have evolved in that language independently of contact, only with much lower probability.[14]

To make this comparison more concrete, I propose the *Areal Sound Pattern Hypothesis*:

> Areal sound patterns are due to perceptual magnet effects within one language, where the perceptual magnets themselves are sounds from another language. As a consequence, their evolution may mimic that of internal phonetically based sound change.

The notion that language experience alters phonetic perception is central in the field of language acquisition, where it is often referred to as the 'perceptual magnet effect' (e.g. Kuhl 1991, 2000; Kuhl and Iverson 1995). The central finding in this research paradigm is that exposure to a specific language results in the warping of perceived distances or similarities between phonetic stimuli. In experiments with children and adults, listeners judge similar acoustic differences as being perceptually closer when the tokens include a prototype or best instance of a particular phonological category. In the course of language acquisition, as proto-categories are established, they

---

[14] Taking some of the frequencies introduced earlier, recall that ejectives, worldwide, occur in approximately 13.5 per cent of languages. In contrast, in the Pacific Northwest culture zone depicted in Map 5.3, 94 per cent of languages have ejectives (3/50 do not). Since these languages represent many distinct families, inheritance cannot explain the discrepancy between 13.5 and 94 per cent. The hypothesis is that the odds of a language like Yurok developing consonant glottalization are skewed because of the external stimuli of ejectives in neighbouring languages, as detailed below.

function as perceptual magnets, making stimuli in their vicinity seem more like them, and drawing tokens into the evolving category.

Areal sound patterns can be viewed as long-term consequences of a special case of the perceptual magnet effect. In the case of an areal sound pattern, an external phonetic prototype is internalized by a speaker on the basis of data external to the language being acquired. In contact situations where bilingualism is the norm, the phonetic prototype established for one language may have a magnet effect in another. In the mind of the speaker, the two languages are distinct; however, phonetic categories may move towards each other due to the perceptual magnet effect. While this process may have the greatest impact in the early years of language acquisition, there is growing evidence that, at least for fluent bilinguals, these effects may continue into adulthood (Simonet 2014).

This model of areal sound patterns does not require lexical borrowing for sound pattern spread. Further, with phonetic prototypes from one language acting as magnets in another, a prediction is that areal sound patterns will evolve incrementally via one or more seemingly natural phonetically based sound changes, since perceptual magnet effects are natural movements of categories in the perceptual/acoustic space.

Three additional concrete conditions can be identified from the empirical case studies summarized in this chapter as stated in (3).

(3)   Sound pattern spread by the perceptual magnet effect: three variables
    i. Establishment of a phonetic prototype requires *phonetic saliency*: the more salient the phonetic pattern, the more likely it will spread areally.
    ii. Establishment of a phonetic prototype requires *significant exposure*: the more intense the language contact, the more likely it will result in diffusion of a sound pattern. The perceptual magnet effect works on phonetic prototypes, and may take several generations to yield sound patterns that are recognizable instances of sound change. For this reason, exposure must not only be intense, but span several generations of language learners.
    iii. The perceptual magnet effect requires *phonetic proximity* between the prototype and language-internal tokens, and draws phonetically similar tokens closer to the phonetic prototype. If there are such tokens in the neighbourhood, sound change will appear to be natural and phonetically motivated, and indistinguishable from internal developments. If the phonetic prototype is far from similar tokens, there may be no effect, and no new category will evolve.

Within this model, perceptual saliency is critical to sound pattern diffusion (3i). Articulation plays little role in the spread of sound patterns. If the difference between an apical dental stop and an apical alveolar stop is not phonetically salient, this articulatory feature is unlikely to diffuse. Other features that may be less likely to diffuse under (3i) are within-category differences: for example, if two neighbouring languages both have a plain voiceless versus voiceless aspirated contrast that is cued by positive VOT, but one language has significantly longer VOT than the other, the difference in positive VOT is less likely to diffuse than an unshared phonetic feature, because perception of VOT will already itself be active in warping the perceptual space.

At the same time, perceptual saliency is not enough for a sound pattern to diffuse, even if exposure is significant. If the phonetic prototype is too far from native sounds, magnet effects will not result in new categories. One perceptually salient sound pattern that may resist diffusion for this reason is the occurrence of clicks. Clicks, or consonant sounds made with the ingressive velaric airstream mechanism, are rare sounds occurring in less than 1 per cent of the world's languages, and in 1.8 per cent of the WALS sample of 567 (Maddieson 2013b). They are primarily restricted to the Khoisan languages (including Sandawe) where they are believed to be directly inherited, but they are also found in Hadza of Tanzania, and clearly borrowed into some unrelated Bantu languages like Xhosa and Zulu. Areally, however, it is clear that clicks did not spread widely outside the Khoisan zone. The few languages such as Zulu that show borrowed clicks have them through two processes: lexical borrowing, and *hlonipha* vocabulary – a process of taboo word formation where clicks can be replaced by non-clicks and vice versa (Faye 1923–1925). In short, there is no evidence of perceptual magnet effects yielding diffusion of clicks. Within this model, the failure of clicks to establish themselves as an areal feature is not due to lack of phonetic saliency (3i) or to insignificant contact (3ii); on the contrary, both of these conditions are strongly met. It is the actual mechanism of sound change (3iii) that renders clicks ineffective as perceptual magnets in Bantu. Most Bantu languages reflect the simple Proto-Bantu consonant system with /p t c k b d j g m n ɲ/ combining into CV or NCV syllables. The problem seems to be that from this Bantu language type, no phonetic categories are particularly close to clicks. As perceptually robust as clicks are, there is nothing to draw into their sphere. They can be borrowed in specific lexical items, and they can replace sounds in taboo word formation, but they remain inert within the phonological system due to their phonetic distance from other consonants.[15]

---

[15] Another segment type that rarely, if ever, takes part in areal sound patterns is pharyngeals. Pharyngeals and pharyngealized sounds are perceptually salient. However, significant contact between languages with pharyngeals and those lacking them is not enough to induce areal pharyngealization, since it is rare that a language will have a phonetic pattern that approaches the characteristic F2 lowering of adjacent vowels triggered by pharyngeals. For example, languages in contact with varieties of Arabic rarely show sound changes shifting other sounds to pharyngeals. One possible case of pharyngealization as an areal feature is nomadic Northern Songhay Tasawaq, that might have acquired pharyngealization via contact with Tuareg (Kossmann 2012).

In contrast, the ejective consonants of many North American languages seem to be close enough to distinct sound patterns to serve as perceptual magnets. Recall that Yurok is unique among Algic languages in having ejective or glottalized consonants /p', t', k', tʃ'/.[16] The evolution of ejectives via the sound changes in (2) appears to be due to contact. Glottalized consonants are an areal feature of Northwestern America, and Northwest California, the region where Yurok is spoken, is a genetically diverse micro-area within this greater macro-area. How did Yurok acquire ejectives? What triggered the sound changes in (2)? Adhering to the model in (3), we suggest that ejectives, as pronounced in the American Northwest, are perceptually salient sounds (3i). Further, these ejectives were established as phonetic prototypes in Pre-Yurok due to sustained contact and multilingualism with languages having these sounds (3ii). Finally, given certain contexts where consonants were produced with glottalization, perceptual space between these sounds and ejectives was compressed, giving rise to the sequence of changes in (2) where a glottal stop and an adjacent oral stop are produced as a single glottalized consonant (3iii).

One striking aspect of the evolution of areal sound patterns within this model is that the sound changes involved, like those in (2) above, are, for the most part, indistinguishable from phonetically based sound changes elsewhere in the world that appear to be internally motivated. For example, the association of glottalization with /t/, and a sound change of *t [t, ʔt, tʔ] > ʔ, has occurred in many varieties of English (Wells 1982), especially in the syllable coda, with no apparent external conditioning, while similar neutralization of glottalized codas to glottal stop is found in the transition from Middle Chinese to Fuzhou (Blevins 2004: 120–121). At the same time, the regular Pre-Yurok fusional development Cʔ > C' is the diachronic source of ejectives in widespread unrelated languages, including Caddo of the American central plains, and Yapese, an Austronesian language with a long independent history (Fallon 2002: 303).

If ejectives can propagate in the Pacific Northwest through the process described, then, given significant contact in other parts of the world, ejectives are expected to show areal distributions in these regions as well. A survey of the high-density pockets of languages with glottalized consonants in the world shows that this is indeed the case. For example, as illustrated in Map 5.5, in the Caucasus region, ejectives are found in four different language families: in Nakh-Daghestani languages (e.g. Archi, Lak); in Northwest Caucasian languages (e.g. Kabardian); in South Caucasian languages (e.g. Georgian, Laz); and in two distinct subgroups of Indo-European – Armenian (Eastern Armenian) and Iranian (Ossetic).

---

[16] The development of ejectives does not appear to be a natural one within the Algic family. No other languages have glottalized obstruents. Wiyot, a neighbour of Yurok, has some evidence of glottalized sonorants, but not obstruents. In Algonquian proper, aspiration and spread glottal gestures are more common accompaniments to the voiceless stop series.

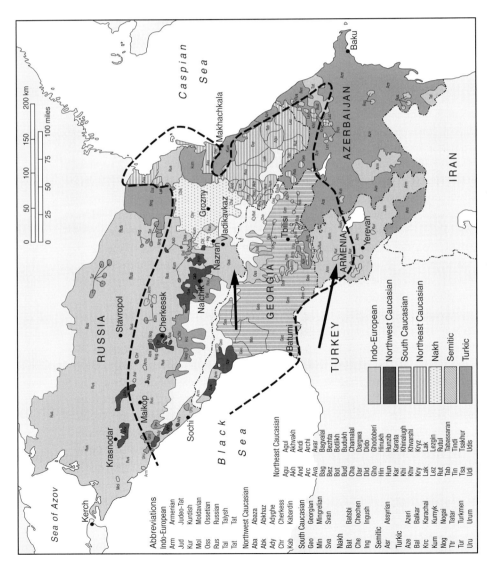

Map 5.5 Ejectives of the Caucasus region including Ossetic and Eastern Armenian

Abbreviations

Indo-European
Arm   Armenian
Jud   Judeo-Tat
Kur   Kurdish
Mol   Moldavian
Oss   Ossetian
Rus   Russian
Tal   Talysh
Tat   Tat

Northwest Caucasian
Aba   Abaza
Abk   Abkhaz
Adk   Adyghe
Chr   Cherkess
Kab   Kabardin

South Caucasian
Geo   Georgian
Min   Mingrelian
Sva   Svan

Nakh
Bat   Batsbi
Che   Chechen
Ing   Ingush

Semitic
Asr   Assyrian

Turkic
Aze   Azeri
Bal   Balkar
Krc   Karachai
Kum   Kumyk
Nog   Nogai
Ttr   Tatar
Tur   Turkmen
Uru   Urum

Northeast Caucasian
Agu   Agul
Akh   Akhwakh
And   Andi
Arc   Archi
Ava   Avar
Bag   Bagvalal
Bez   Bezhta
Bot   Botlikh
Bud   Budukh
Cha   Chamalal
Dar   Dargwa
Did   Dido
Gho   Ghodoberi
Hin   Hinukh
Hun   Hunzib
Kar   Karata
Khi   Khinalugh
Khv   Khwarshi
Kry   Kryz
Lak   Lak
Lez   Lezgin
Rut   Rutul
Tab   Tabassaran
Tin   Tindi
Tsa   Tsakhur
Udi   Udis

Indo-European
Northwest Caucasian
South Caucasian
Northeast Caucasian
Nakh
Semitic
Turkic

While ejectives may be inherited in Caucasian languages, their occurrence in Armenian and Ossetic stands out in the same way Yurok glottalized consonants do: within the Indo-European language family, ejectives are only found in these two languages. In Ossetic, unlike Yurok, loanwords are the primary source of ejectives (Thordarson 2009). These include Caucasian loans, where ejection is preserved, and Russian loans, where voiceless stops can be replaced with ejectives.[17] However, there is at least one environment in Ossetic where ejectives have arisen in native words: in final -sC clusters, e.g. *xuisk', xusk'* 'dry' (< Old Iranian *huʃka-*). Again, it appears that perceptual magnet effects may be at work, drawing a final [k] with heavy release and surrounding noise into the /k'/ category.

The phonetic naturalness and regularity of internal sound changes giving rise to areal sound patterns (3iii) is central to Hamp's (1996) account of the origins of the retroflex contrast in Sanskrit. As first detailed by Emeneau (1956) in his influential paper 'India as a linguistic area', the contrast between retroflex and non-retroflex apical stops is a striking feature of India and surrounding areas that cannot be attributed to direct inheritance and defies chance. Within the area, illustrated in Map 5.6, the contrast is found in languages of the four major language families represented: Dravidian, Indo-Aryan, Austroasiatic (Munda) and Sino-Tibetan (e.g. Ladakhi).

As one moves east and north through Pakistan, retroflexion can be found in Burushaski, an isolate, and in Iranian languages (e.g. Wakhi). Retroflexion is not reconstructed for Proto-Indo-European, Proto-Austroasiatic or Proto-Sino-Tibetan, but it is a contrastive feature of Proto-Dravidian. For this reason, Emeneau (1956) and others attribute the feature in Indo-Aryan languages to early contact with Dravidian languages, which clearly had a wider distribution than they do at present.[18]

In trying to pin down the precise source of retroflexion, Emeneau (1956) suggests that bilingualism allowed 'allophones to be redistributed as retroflex phonemes'. Hamp (1996) attempts to be more precise about the mechanisms giving rise to Sanskrit retroflexion, justifying the level of detail in terms of providing a clear explanation of 'the development and spread of an important trait of the South Asian *Sprachbund . . .* [and] one of the clearest, most fully documented, and most internally complex cases known to us of what appears as areally induced phonological diffusion.' Hamp's focus is on the internal evolution of retroflexion by natural means (3iii). The evolution of retroflex consonants within Indic begins with the birth of Indo-Iranian *ʃ, which had several sources, including the 'RUKI

---

[17]   In the case of Russian loans, ejection may be used to mark words as foreign, and could be unrelated to perceptual magnet effects.

[18]   Brahui, a Dravidian language, is spoken in the modern Balochistan region of eastern Iran and Pakistan, almost one thousand miles from the closest Dravidian speaking regions of southern India. Kurukh, another Northern Dravidian language, is spoken hundreds of miles to the east, in Odisha, and Malto, another, is spoken mostly in East India.

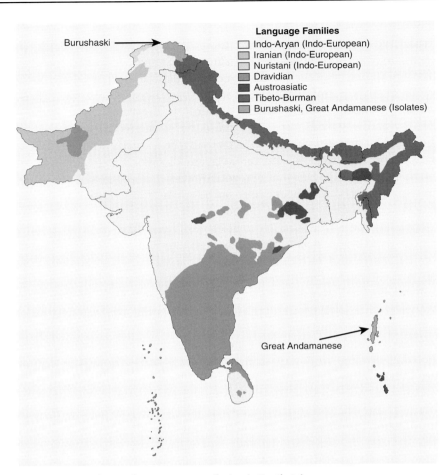

Map 5.6 General area of consonant retroflexion in South Asia

rule', whereby *s > ʃ / {r, u, k, i}___.[19] A rule of voice assimilation in clusters results in a further split, so that Proto-Indo-Iranian has both *ʃ and *ʒ. In Indic, these sounds shift to retroflex articulations. In terms of the model in (3), exposure to Dravidian retroflexion seems to draw the 'closest' Indic sounds towards the retroflex category, giving rise to an internal context-free *ʃ, *ʒ > ʂ, ʐ sound change.[20] After the evolution of [ʂ], [ʐ] in Indic, local and long-distance assimilations between /t, d, n, l/ and these retroflex sibilants give rise to retroflex oral stops, nasals and laterals. Since these assimilations, are, by their very nature, natural and phonetically motivated, the key step in the infiltration of retroflexion into the Indic system appears to be the initial *ʃ, *ʒ > ʂ, ʐ sound change, itself a clear example of the perceptual magnet effect.[21]

Other languages with distinct sound patterns within this greater India area have alternative means of fabricating retroflex obstruents from scratch. For example, in Ladakhi, a Tibetan language of Ladakh, India, retroflex oral stops have developed from fusion of earlier *tr and *dr clusters, as in truk > ʈuk 'six', dre > ɖe 'devil', etc. (Śarmā 2004: 30).

An interesting question one can pose in this context is how common or rare a sound pattern is aside from cases where it appears to arise through contact. Consider, for example the case of front rounded vowels. Maddieson (2013c) finds that 37/562 languages or only 6.6 per cent of languages in the WALS survey have front rounded vowels. This suggests that front rounded vowels are relatively rare features in the world's languages. However, when one looks at the distribution of the vowels in the sample, one finds that the majority of languages with front rounded vowels (29/37 or 78 per cent) are spoken in the north-central area of the Eurasian continent, and further, that outside this region very few languages with front rounded vowels are found, and they are widely scattered (Maddieson 2013c).

Within Eurasia front rounded vowels appear to be directly inherited within Uralic and Turkic, but elsewhere, the result of widespread diffusion. Map 5.7 illustrates some of the languages of Europe with front rounded vowels, and shows that they constitute a near-continuous stretch, from Hungarian in the east, north to Finnish, Norwegian and Swedish, south to Albanian and Greek, and west and south to Gallo-Romance, including Camuno, a Gallo-Italic language of northern Italy (Cresci 2013).

From Gallo-Romance, front rounded vowels have diffused even farther west, from French to Breton, and farther south, from French to eastern varieties of Basque, including Souletin, where they are attested in the earliest written documents (Egurtzegi 2013, 2014).[22] Of Proto-Indo-European, Proto-Uralic and Proto-Basque, only Proto-Uralic is reconstructed with front rounded vowels. Within Indo-European, front rounded vowels arose in: Germanic (excluding Gothic) via umlaut; in Albanian; in South Slavic (Vermeer 1979); and in Gallo-Romance.[23] We suspect that

---

[21] Typological evidence for context free *ʃ, *ʒ > ʂ, ʐ as an areally induced perceptual magnet effect would come from statistical evaluation of the probability of this change occurring without an 'external' perceptual magnet. How common is it for this context-free sound change to occur in the isolated development of a language? These kinds of questions are difficult to evaluate at present, since a comprehensive inventory of context-free sound changes has not been compiled. Other areally induced examples of this change appear in Eastern Iranian languages like Pashto (Henderson, no date).

[22] See Trudgill (2011: 120–121) for related discussion.

[23] In South Slavic, front rounded vowels are still found in some Kajkavian dialects (Vermeer 1979). Greek is also thought to have had front rounded *y (Allen 1987). Under this view, it would be typologically highly unusual in lacking a back rounded counterpart.

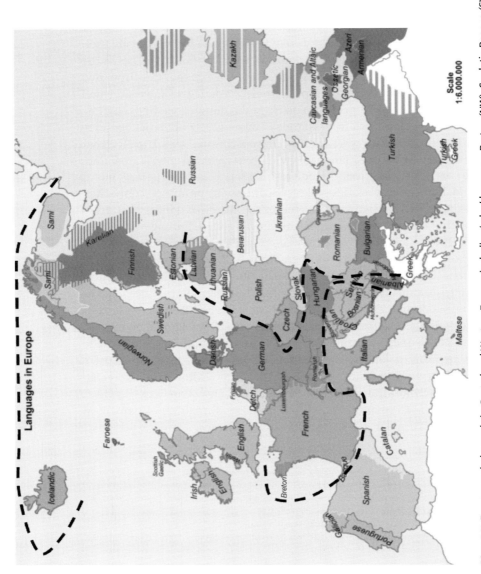

Map 5.7 Front rounded vowels in Central and Western Europe, including 'edge' languages Breton (NW), Souletin Basque (SW), Albanian (SE), Finnish (NE)

many of these cases were also contact-induced, given the rarity of front rounded vowels outside this zone. If we eliminate front rounded vowels that are clear areal features of Western Europe from the WALS database, the sound pattern falls from 6.6 to 5.6 per cent, and if inherited cases are eliminated in Uralic and Turkic, the figure falls to below 5 per cent. By our gross measures above, front rounded vowels would be rare features.

As with Indic retroflexion, details of the evolution of front rounded vowels support a model incorporating the perceptual magnet effect. Front rounded vowels are perceptually salient, and can result in phonetic prototypes when a speaker of a language without them has sustained and significant contact with a language making use of them. As perceptual magnets, front rounded vowels draw phonetically similar tokens closer to the prototype. And, if there are such tokens in the neighbourhood, sound change will appear to be natural and phonetically motivated (3).[24] In Germanic and Albanian, front rounded vowels are a consequence of anticipatory coarticulation in _C₀i sequences, while in Gallo-Romance and Souletin Basque, we see context-free changes of u: > y and u > y respectively; in Souletin and Camuno, subsequent vowel to vowel harmonic sound changes take more vowels to /y/. While all of these are natural, phonetically motivated changes, they appear to be extremely rare without pre-existing front rounded vowels as perceptual magnets.[25]

However, at least one areal sound pattern leads one to question whether perceptual saliency is central to all cases of phonetic diffusion. The feature of interest is preaspiration, an areal feature of medial tense voiceless stops in northern Europe, especially Scandinavia and areas where Old Norse was once spoken (Hansson 1999; Helgason 2002). Preaspiration is a rare phonetic feature cross-linguistically, occurring in only 4/451 languages of UPSID, and is typically an allophonic variant of post-aspiration in voiceless stops.[26] It is even rarer as a contrastive feature of oral stops, with Ojibwe being the only UPSID language with this property. Bladon (1986) has suggested that the rarity of preaspiration is due to its low perceptual saliency. If this is the case, then, preaspiration should be less likely to diffuse by (3i) than other more salient phonetic properties. Helgason's (2002) detailed study of preaspiration in Nordic languages, shown in Map 5.8, provides confirmation of the model in (3) in two ways.

---

[24] Slavic speakers consistently unround rounded vowels when speaking German (Raymond Hickey, personal communication). Recall that contact must be sustained for the perceptual magnet effects hypothesized here to take effect.

[25] Maddieson's (2013c) remarks are in line with this hypothesis. With respect to the distribution of front rounded vowels, he remarks 'it is quite striking that their occurrence is so relatively concentrated in a particular geographical area. It seems likely that the *hearing of sounds of this sort in some languages of the area may have given further support to phonetically natural processes in other languages* [my emphasis, JB], with the end result being the addition of front rounded vowels to the inventory of more of the languages.'

[26] Tarascan (aka P'urhépecha), an isolate of Michoacan, Mexico, is classified by UPSID as a language with (post-) aspirated stops, though these are preaspirated in predictable environments (Friedrich 1971, 1975; Lluvia Camacho, 2013, personal communication). Counting Tarascan as a preaspirating language would make the figure 5/451 languages in UPSID.

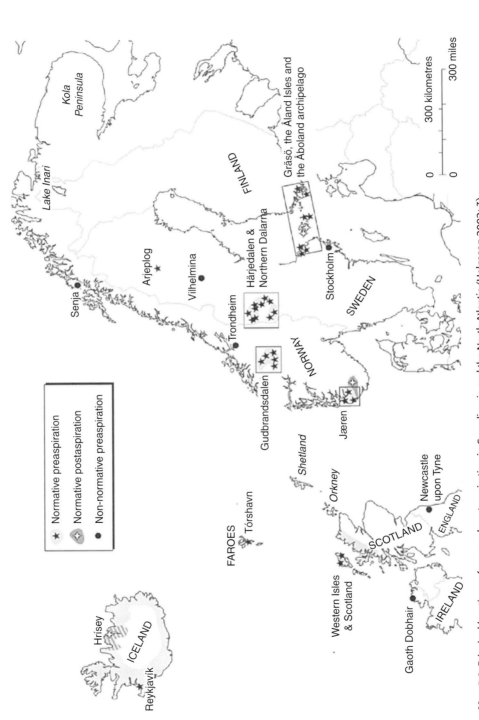

Map 5.8 Principal locations of pre- and post-aspiration in Scandinavia and the North Atlantic (Helgason 2002: 3)

First, it demonstrates that the strongest instances of preaspiration, cases where it is a language-specific phonetic feature, or 'normative' in his terms, are those directly inherited from Old Norse.[27] In these cases, direct inheritance accounts for the common feature of preaspiration and its distribution. In cases where preaspiration has diffused into other language families, it is either highly variable and non-contrastive, or strengthened to be more perceptually salient. In the first case, exemplified by Saami varieties and Tyneside English, the weak perceptual saliency of preaspiration results in spotty diffusion, with variability across speakers, and what Helgason refers to as 'non-normative' phonetics.[28] In contrast, a stronger percept is associated with Helgason's category of 'normative' phonetics. The spread of preaspiration from North Germanic languages into Celtic has given rise to many Scottish Gaelic dialects where Common Gaelic /p, t, k/ are realized as preaspirated stops. In areas where pronunciation appears to be the most 'normative', preaspirates are strengthened to velar fricatives, resulting in pronunciations like [xp], [xt] and [xk]. It appears then that where preaspiration diffuses and becomes a regular allophonic pattern, it is more perceptually salient than elsewhere.[29]

5.3   Radical Areal Spread, and Tone as an Areal Feature

To this point, the areal sound patterns under discussion have involved single features or segment types: pre-glottalization of voiced consonants; ejectives; retroflexion; click sounds; front rounded vowels; and preaspiration. Recall that part of the reason for focusing on less common phonological features was to rule out chance, or parallel evolution (i.e. natural internal developments) of more common sound patterns. However, another way of ruling out chance or parallel evolution is to show that a group of features is shared between neighbouring languages, and that this group of features cannot be the consequence of shared inheritance. In cases where multiple aspects of sound patterns spread, radical changes to the typological profile of a language are possible.

---

[27] Helgason's definitions of normative versus non-normative phonetic traits are as follows: 'If the absence (or presence) of a particular phonetic trait leads to a pronunciation that is considered deviant by the speakers of a given dialect, that trait can be classified as normative (or normatively absent) in that dialect. Conversely, a trait whose absence or presence does not lead to deviant pronunciation can be classified as non-normative in that dialect' (Helgason 2002: 21). There may be some circularity in these terms, and I have taken the liberty of paraphrasing them in the text.

[28] The phrase-final distribution of preaspiration in Tyneside English is consistent with perceptual magnet effects: in this variety, which lacks a geminate/singleton or tense/lax obstruent contrast, preaspirates, as perceptual magnets, might be expected to draw in phrase-final obstruents due to the effects of phrase-final spread-glottal gestures (Blevins 2006).

[29] A final aspect of preaspiration that should be kept in mind in assessing its perceptual saliency is what it contrasts with. In typical cases, the phonetic contrast is between long voiceless stop closure preceded by modal voicing versus shorter voiceless stop closure preceded by a period of glottal friction, e.g. Vt:V versus VhtV. The relevant question that must be asked then is how perceptually salient this contrast is for speakers of different language types.

One of the most striking instances of this kind of radical areal spread is found in Southeast Asia. Matisoff (2006) catalogues numerous instances of this kind of profound structural and prosodic influence, including: Chinese phonotactic and prosodic influence on Vietnamese, Tai and Hmong-Mien; Mon phonational influence on Burmese with subsequent Burmese tonal influence on Karenic; and the influence of Mon-Khmer and Sinitic on the evolution of tone and register in Chamic, a subgroup of Austronesian. This last case is, perhaps, the best documented of all instances of radical phonological areal diffusion, being the subject of Thurgood's (1999) monograph, *From Ancient Cham to Modern Dialects: Two Thousand Years of Language Contact and Change*. The level of detail in terms of social and linguistic history is remarkable, and the stages and range of areal-phonological features are audible to this day in the Chamic languages still spoken.

Chamic, and its sister Malayic, are subgroups of Western Malayo-Polynesian, within the expansive Austronesian language family. The history of Chamic-speaking people over the last 2,000 years involves movement from insular Asia to the Southeast Asian mainland as early as 500 BCE, and involves initial and sustained contact with speakers of Mon-Khmer languages, with the exception of Achenese speakers, who returned to northern Sumatra (Map 5.9a).

Subsequent movements of distinct groups of Chamic-speaking peoples resulted in later intense contact with Vietnamese, and with Min speakers

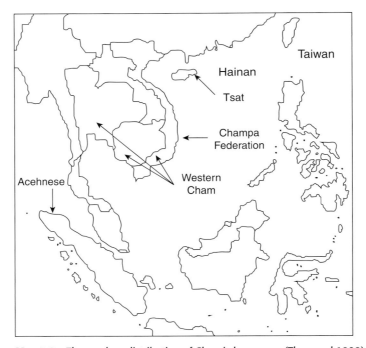

Map 5.9a The modern distribution of Chamic languages (Thurgood 1999)

on the island of Hainan (Maps 5.9a, 5.9b). Thurgood's (1999: 6) summary of the general tendencies in sound change under the influence of these languages is given in (4).

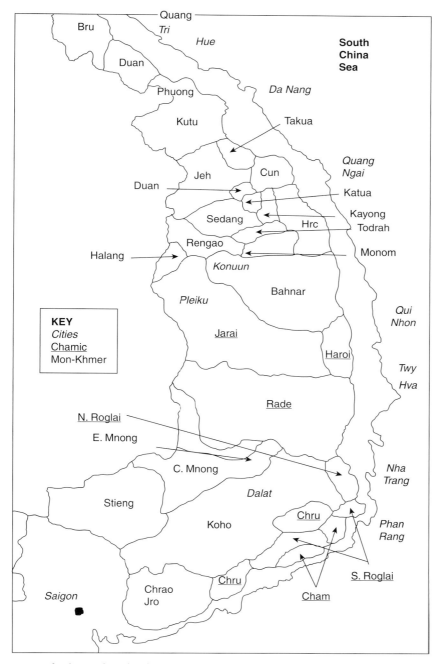

Map 5.9b The modern distribution of Cham and Mon-Khmer languages (Thurgood 1999)

Table 5.1 *Radical phonological change in two Chamic languages: Rade of South Vietnam, and Tsat of Hainan Island (based on Thurgood 1999)*

Mostly disyllabic		Mostly sesquisyllabic	Mostly monosyllabic	
no tone no register	no tone no register	no tone no register	tone	
PMP	**Malay**	**Rade**	**Tsat**	**gloss**
*mamaq	mamah	məmah	ma⁵⁵	'chew'
*qumah	huma	həmah	ma³³	'dry field'
*taŋan	taŋan	kəŋan	ŋa:ŋ³³	'hand; arm'
*panaq	panah	mənah	na⁵⁵	'shoot (bow)'
*baseq	basah	məsah	sa⁵⁵	'wet; damp'
*m-uda	muda	məda	tha¹¹	'young, tender'
*daRaq	darah	ərah	sia⁵⁵	'blood'
*bulan	bulan	mlan	-phian¹¹	'moon'
*qabu	abu	hbao	phə¹¹	'ashes'

(4)   Radical areal sound patterns in Chamic
 i. Templatic modification: disyllabic > sesquisyllabic > monosyllabic
 ii. Restructuring of segment inventories
  a. new consonant series
  b. proliferation of vowel contrasts
 iii. Syllabic modification
  c. merger and loss of final consonants
  d. neutralization of voicing and vowel-quality in pre-syllable

Prosodic innovation: neutral > register complex > tone

Table 5.1 illustrates the shift from disyllabic to sesquisyllabic to monosyllabic/tonal with Austronesian cognate sets. The shift to sesquisyllabic or iambic words was due to contact with Mon-Khmer languages that are sesquisyllabic; the further reduction to monosyllables in Phan Rang Cham was due to contact with Vietnamese, a monosyllabic language, while for Tsat, monosyllabism resulted from contact with the monosyllabic Sinitic languages of Hainan.

As with other cases of areal sound patterns discussed above, Thurgood demonstrates that the contact-induced sound patterns that arise in Chamic do so through natural, phonetically based regular sound change. While substantial loans undoubtedly played a role in seeding sesquisyllabic structure, register and tone in these languages, the internal developments support the model in (3), where a perceptual magnet effect gives rise to new categories from old cloth. In the shift from disyllables to sesquisyllables, the iambic prosody of Mon-Khmer languages draws similar disyllables toward it, resulting in wholesale reduction of initial vowels as seen in Rade (Table 5.1). In Western Cham, contact with neighbouring Mon-Khmer register languages has additional effects. Proto-Chamic *b-, *d-, *g- and *j- and their transitions into following vowels are perceptually close to the breathy voiced register of contact languages, and it is this register which is found in syllables with these initials. In the Tsat case, Min tones act as perceptual magnets drawing F0 perturbations, originally due to laryngeal aspects of consonants, in to be reinterpreted as tones.

Thurgood's (1999) case study of the areal diffusion of multiple sound patterns, including tone and register, has serious implications for general typological work on tone. It is widely recognized that about half of the world's languages are tone languages.[30] Most of these tone languages are centred in three large zones: Southeast Asia, New Guinea and equatorial Africa, as illustrated in Map 5.10, where 'simple tone systems' are those with an H versus L contrast, and 'complex tone systems' are all the others (Maddieson 2013d).

Within Africa, most of the tonal languages are found within the Niger-Congo family, and tone is assumed to be an inherited feature there. However, the situation in Southeast Asia is very different. Though tone and register are pervasive, the largest language families in the area, Proto-Austroasiatic and Proto-Sino-Tibetan, are reconstructed as non-tonal languages. It could well be that tone has evolved through contact more than any other phonological feature, both within Southeast Asia and within the New Guinea area.

Potential support for the rarity of non-contact-induced tonogenesis can be found in the wider history of the Austronesian family, a family of approximately 1,000 languages. Proto-Austronesian was thought to be spoken approximately 6,000 years ago in what is now Taiwan. Proto-Austronesian had no register or tone contrasts and fairly simple CVC(C)V(C) stem structure. Over the course of thousands of years, as populations moved and split and moved and split, thousands of sound changes occurred. However, nearly all cases of tonogenesis within the Austronesian family can be attributed to contact-induced change: tonogenesis in Tsat occurred under Min influence as outlined above; tone in a dialect of Moken, and in Pattani Malay are due to heavy contact with southern Thai (Blust 2009: 181); and there are scattered cases of tonogenesis in the New Guinea area, including the Raja Empat languages of western Papua (Remijsen 2003), Jabem and Bukawa of the coastal Huon Gulf area (Ross 1993), and Kara of New Ireland (Hajek and Stevens 2004), which occur in Papuan contact zones. The one apparent exception to contact-induced change is tonogenesis in New Caledonia, resulting in 5 (of 28) tone languages (Rivierre 1993). Assuming that the islands of this chain were uninhabited when settled by Austronesian speakers, tonogenesis in New Caledonia is the sole instance of an internal development leading to contrastive tone over thousands of years of development, and thousands of languages.

Implications of tone as a common areal sound pattern, however, go beyond linguistic typology. It has been hypothesized by Dediu and Ladd

---

[30] Maddieson's (2013d) WALS figure is 58.2 non-tonal versus 41.8 tonal; however, in the text he suggests that if Niger-Congo languages were not under-represented, the figure would be closer to 50/50.

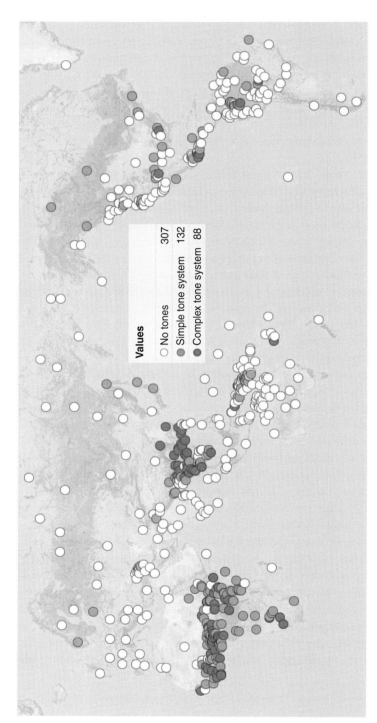

Values

○ No tones   307
◐ Simple tone system   132
● Complex tone system   88

Map 5.10 Tone as an areal feature of Sub-Saharan Africa, Southeast Asia and New Guinea (Maddieson 2013d)

(2007) that the global distribution of tone languages is related to a negative correlation between the linguistic feature of tone and population frequency of the derived haplogroups of two brain size genes in human populations, ASPM and Microcephalin. Evidence that tone can and does spread areally, and that the tone languages of Southeast Asia represent a linguistic area, seems incompatible with a hypothesis that the distribution of tone (or absence of tone) in the world's languages is related to an inherited genetic feature of human brains.[31]

5.4 Concluding Remarks

Areal sound patterns are easy to define but not always easy to identify. This is because they appear to mimic internal developments. The perceptual magnet model of sound pattern diffusion makes use of the same mechanisms needed in first language acquisition, and therefore predicts the similarity between regular sound changes with internal perceptual magnets and those whose perceptual magnets are external. Sound patterns that diffuse must be perceptually salient, but how salient? It was suggested that category-internal divisions are unlikely to propagate, but a more positive proposal is possible. Phonetic features that are not central to signalling contrast in a language are more likely to be co-opted into new category formation than others, and the great majority of areal sound patterns are additive, as opposed to neutralizing. Because areal sound patterns require extensive periods of significant language contact, they could, in theory, be used to reconstruct ancient population movements and prehistoric contact zones. In this area, countless mysteries present themselves. Consider, for example, the geographic distribution of rare word-final pre-stopped (pre-ploded) nasals, found in some Austronesian languages of Borneo, Chamic languages, and some Mon-Khmer languages of the Malaysian peninsula (Blust 1991: 149). Does this distribution reflect prehistoric contact between Austronesian and Mon-Khmer speakers in Borneo? Another mysterious but well-studied sound pattern is the Proto-Aztecan sound change of $*t > t\dashv /\_a$ (Campbell and Langacker 1978). Since the evolution of lateral affricates from /t/ before low vowels appears to be unknown outside of this case, could areal influence from languages with lateral fricatives or affricates have played a role? Could this unusual sound change provide evidence for early contact between Proto-Aztecan speakers and speakers of Proto-Totonaco-Tepehua? The Areal Sound Pattern Hypothesis together with other tools of analysis offered in this volume should bring us closer to answering these questions and many more.

---

[31] A serious problem is raised by Wong et al. (2012), in an fMRI study of brain function, where a positive relationship between ASPM and lexical tone perception is found, in contrast to the opposite pattern predicted by Dediu and Ladd (2007).

References

Aikhenvald, Alexandra, 2002. *Language Contact in Amazonia*. Oxford: Oxford University Press.

Aikhenvald, Alexandra and R. M. W. Dixon, 2006. *Areal Diffusion and Genetic Inheritance: Problems in Comparative Linguistics*. Oxford: Oxford University Press.

Allen, W. Sidney, 1987. *Vox Graeca: The Pronunciation of Classical Greek*, third edition. Cambridge: Cambridge University Press.

Babel, Molly, Andrew Garrett, Michael J. Houser and Maziar Toosarvandani, 2013. Descent and diffusion in language diversification: A study in Western Numic dialectology. *International Journal of American Linguistics* 79: 445–489.

Bickel, Balthasar, 2015. Distributional Typology: Statistical inquiries into the dynamics of linguistic diversity. In Bernd Heine and Heiko Narrog (eds), *The Oxford Handbook of Linguistic Analysis*, second edition, pp. 901–924. Oxford: Oxford University Press.

Bladon, Anthony, 1986. Phonetics for hearers. In Graham McGregor (ed.), *Language for Hearers*, pp. 1–24. Oxford: Pergamon Press.

Blevins, James P. and Juliette Blevins (eds), 2009. *Analogy in Grammar: Form and Acquisition*. Oxford: Oxford University Press.

Blevins, Juliette, 2002. Notes on Yurok glottalized consonants. In Laura Buszard-Welcher and Leanne Hinton (eds), *Proceedings of the Meeting of the Hokan-Penutian Workshop: Survey of California and Other Indian Languages*, report 11, pp. 1–18. Berkeley, CA: University of California.

Blevins, Juliette, 2003. The phonology of Yurok glottalized sonorants: Segmental fission under syllabification. *International Journal of American Linguistics* 69: 371–396.

Blevins, Juliette, 2004. *Evolutionary Phonology: The Emergence of Sound Patterns*. Cambridge: Cambridge University Press.

Blevins, Juliette, 2006. A theoretical synopsis of Evolutionary Phonology. *Theoretical Linguistics* 32: 117–165.

Blevins, Juliette, 2007. The importance of typology in explaining recurrent sound patterns. *Linguistic Typology* 11: 107–113.

Blevins, Juliette, 2008. Natural and unnatural sound patterns: A pocket field guide. In Klaas Willems and Ludovic De Cuypere (eds), *Naturalness and Iconicity in Language*, pp. 121–148. Amsterdam: John Benjamins.

Blevins, Juliette, 2009a. Another universal bites the dust: Northwest Mekeo lacks coronal phonemes. *Oceanic Linguistics* 48: 264–273.

Blevins, Juliette, 2009b. Structure-preserving sound change: A look at unstressed vowel syncope in Austronesian. In Alexander Adelaar and Andrew Pawley (eds), *Austronesian Historical Linguistics and Culture History: A Festschrift for Bob Blust*, pp. 33–49. Canberra: Pacific Linguistics.

Blevins, Juliette, 2015. Evolutionary Phonology: A holistic approach to sound change typology. In Patrick Honeybone and Joseph Salmons (eds), *The Oxford Handbook of Historical Phonology*, pp. 485–500. Oxford: Oxford University Press.

Blevins, Juliette and Sven Grawunder, 2009. *Kl > Tl sound change in Germanic and elsewhere: Descriptions, explanations, and implications. *Linguistic Typology* 13: 267–303.

Blust, Robert, 1991. Patterns of sound change in the Austronesian languages. In Philip Baldi (ed.), *Patterns of Change, Change of Patterns: Linguistic Change and Reconstruction Methodology*, pp. 129–165. Berlin: Mouton de Gruyter.

Blust, Robert, 1999. Subgrouping, circularity and extinction: Some issues in Austronesian comparative linguistics. In Elizabeth Zeitoun and Paul J. K. Li (eds), *Selected Papers from the Eighth International Conference on Austronesian Linguistics*, pp. 31–94. Taipei: Academia Sinica.

Blust, Robert, 2009. *The Austronesian Languages*. Canberra: Pacific Linguistics.

Blust, Robert, 2013. *The Austronesian Languages*, revised edition. Canberra: Australian National University.

Boas, Franz, 1911. Introduction. In Franz Boas (ed.), *Handbook of American Indian Languages*, part 1, pp. 5–83. Washington, DC: Government Printing Office.

Boas, Franz, 1920. The classification of American languages. *American Anthropologist* 22: 367–376.

Boas, Franz, 1929. Classification of American Indian Languages. *Language* 5: 1–7.

Bowern, Claire and Harold Koch (eds), 2004. *Australian Languages: Classification and the Comparative Method*. Amsterdam: John Benjamins.

Campbell, Lyle, 2004. *Historical Linguistics: An Introduction*, second edition. Cambridge, MA: The MIT Press.

Campbell, Lyle, Terrence Kaufman and Thomas Smith-Stark, 1986. Meso-America as a linguistic area. *Language* 62: 530–570.

Campbell, Lyle and Ronald Langacker, 1978. Proto-Aztecan vowels: part I. *International Journal of American Linguistics* 44: 85–102

Conathan, Lisa, 2004. *Linguistic Ecology of Northwestern California: Contact, Functional Convergence and Dialectology*. PhD dissertation, University of California, Berkeley.

Cresci, Michela, 2013. *Camuno Sound Patterns*. PhD dissertation, CUNY Graduate Center, New York.

Dediu, Dan and D. Robert Ladd, 2007. Linguistic tone is related to the population frequency of the adaptive haplogroups of two brain size genes, ASPM and Microcephalin. *Proceedings of the National Academy of Sciences* 104: 10944–10949.

Difloth, Gérard, 1976. Minor-syllable vocalism in Senoic languages. In Philip N. Jenner, Laurence C. Thompson and Stanley Starosta (eds), *Austroasiatic Studies*, vol. I, pp. 229–248. Oceanic Linguistics Special Publication, vol. 13. Honolulu: University of Hawai'i Press.

Dixon, R. M. W., 2002. *The Australian Languages: Their Nature and Development.* Cambridge: Cambridge University Press.

Dryer, Matthew S. and Martin Haspelmath (eds), 2013. *The World Atlas of Language Structures Online.* Munich: Max Planck Digital Library.

Edmondson, Jerold and Kenneth Gregerson (eds), 1993. *Tonality in Austronesian Languages.* Honolulu: University of Hawai'i Press.

Egurtzegi, Ander, 2013. Back vowel fronting in Souletin Basque. Manuscript, University of the Basque Country.

Egurtzegi, Ander, 2014. *Towards a Phonetically Grounded Diachronic Phonology of Basque.* PhD dissertation, University of the Basque Country.

Emeneau, Murray B., 1956. India as a linguistic area. *Language* 32: 3–16.

Evans, Nicholas, 1995. *A Grammar of Kayardild.* Berlin: Mouton de Gruyter.

Fallon, Paul D., 2002. *The Synchronic and Diachronic Phonology of Ejectives.* London: Routledge.

Faye, C. U., 1923-1925. The influence of the 'Hlonipa' on the Zulu clicks. *Bulletin of the School of Oriental and African Studies* 3: 757–782.

Friedman, Victor, 2004. Geg Albanian and Balkan dialectology. Paper presented at the 14th Biennial Conference on Balkan and South Slavic Linguistics, Literature and Folklore.

Friedrich, Paul, 1971. Dialectal variation in Tarascan phonology. *International Journal of American Linguistics* 37: 164–187.

Friedrich, Paul, 1975. *A Phonology of Tarascan.* Chicago: University of Chicago, Department of Anthropology.

Goddard, Ives, 1979. Comparative Algonquian. In Lyle Campbell and Marianne Mithun (eds), *The Languages of Native America: Historical and Comparative Assessment*, pp. 70–132. Austin, TX: University of Texas Press.

Haas, Mary R., 1976. The Northern Californian Linguistic Area. In Margaret Langdon and Shirley Silver (eds), *Hokan Studies: Papers from the First Conference on Hokan Languages*, pp. 347–359. The Hague: Mouton.

Hajek, John and Mary Stevens, 2004. Tonal activity in Kara, an Austronesian language spoken in New Britain. In *Proceedings of the 10th Australian International Conference on Speech Science and Technology, Macquarie University, Sydney, December 8 to 10, 2004.* Australian Speech Science and Technology Association Inc.

Hall, Alan T., 1997. The historical development of retroflex consonants in Indo-Aryan. *Lingua* 102: 203–221.

Hamp, Eric, 1996. On the Indo-European origins of the retroflexes in Sanskrit. *Journal of the American Oriental Society* 116: 719–723.

Hansson, Gunnar, 1999. Remains of a submerged continent: Preaspiration in the languages of Northwest Europe. In Laurel J. Brinton (ed.), *Historical Linguistics 1999: Selected Papers from the 14th International Conference on Historical Linguistics, Vancouver, 9–13 August 1999*, pp. 157–173. Amsterdam: John Benjamins.

Haudricourt, André-Georges, 1965. Les mutations consonantiques des occlusives initiales en mon-khmer. *Bulletin de la Société de Linguistique de Paris* 60: 160–172.

Heath, Jeffrey, 1978. *Linguistic Diffusion in Arnhem Land*. Canberra: Australian Institute of Aboriginal Studies.

Helgason, Pétur, 2002. *Preaspiration in the Nordic Languages: Synchronic and Diachronic Aspects*. PhD dissertation, Department of Linguistics, Stockholm University.

Henderson, Michael M. T. Some 'Indic' features in Pashto. Manuscript, University of Wisconsin-Madison.

Iverson, Gregory K. and Joseph Salmons, 2006. On the typology of final laryngeal neutralization: Evolutionary Phonology and laryngeal realism. *Theoretical Linguistics* 32: 205–216.

Jansen, Wouter, 2004. *Laryngeal Contrast and Phonetic Voicing: A Laboratory Phonology Approach to English, Hungarian, and Dutch*. PhD dissertation, University of Gröningen.

Joseph, Brian, 1983. *The Synchrony and Diachrony of the Balkan Infinitive*. Cambridge: Cambridge University Press.

Joseph, Brian, 1992. The Balkan languages. In William Bright (ed.), *International Encyclopedia of Linguistics*, pp. 153–155. Oxford: Oxford University Press.

Kiparsky, Paul, 2006. The amphichronic problem vs. Evolutionary Phonology. *Theoretical Linguistics* 32: 217–236.

Kossmann, Maarten, 2012. Pharyngealization and the vowel system of Tasawaq (Northern Songhay). *Nordic Journal of African Studies* 21: 21–33.

Kuhl, Patricia K., 1991. Human adults and human infants show a 'perceptual magnet effect' for the prototypes of speech categories, monkeys do not. *Perception and Psychophysics* 50 (2): 93–107.

Kuhl, Patricia K., 2000. Language, mind, and brain: Experience alters perception. In Michael S. Gazzaniga (ed.), *The New Cognitive Neurosciences*, second edition, pp. 99–115. Cambridge, MA: The MIT Press.

Kuhl, Patricia K. and Paul Iverson, 1995. Linguistic experience and the 'perceptual magnet effect'. In Winifried Strange (ed.), *Speech Perception and Linguistic Experience: Issues in Cross-language Research*, pp. 121–154. Baltimore, MD: York Press.

Kuhl, Patricia K., Erica Stevens, Akiko Hayashi et al., 2006. Infants show a facilitation effect for native language phonetic perception between 6 and 12 months. *Developmental Science* 9, F13–F21.

Kuhl, Patricia K., Karen A. Williams, Francisco Lacerda, Kenneth N. Stevens and Björn Lindblom, 1992. Linguistic experience alters phonetic perception in infants by 6 months of age. *Science* 255: 606–608.

Labov, William, 2007. Transmission and diffusion. *Language* 83: 344–387.

Ladefoged, Peter and Ian Maddieson, 1996. *Sounds of the World's Languages*. Oxford: Blackwell.

Longerich, Linda, 1998. *Acoustic Conditioning for the RUKI Rule*. Master's thesis, Department of Linguistics, Memorial University of Newfoundland.

Maddieson, Ian, 1984. *Patterns of Sounds*. Cambridge: Cambridge University Press.

Maddieson, Ian, 2013a. Glottalized consonants. In Dryer and Haspelmath (eds). http://wals.info/chapter/7

Maddieson, Ian, 2013b. Presence of uncommon consonants. In Dryer and Haspelmath (eds). http://wals.info/chapter/19

Maddieson, Ian, 2013c. Front rounded vowels. In Dryer and Haspelmath (eds). http://wals.info/chapter/11

Maddieson, Ian, 2013d. Tone. In Dryer and Haspelmath (eds). http://wals.info/chapter/13

Maddieson, Ian and Kristin Precoda, 1989. Updating UPSID. *Journal of the Acoustical Society of America*, Suppl. 1, 86: S19.

Matisoff, James A., 2006. Genetic vs. contact relationship: Prosodic diffusion in South-East Asian languages. In Aikhenvald and Dixon (eds), pp. 291–327.

Posner, Rebecca, 1995. Contact, social variants, parameter setting, and pragmatic function: An example from the history of French syntax. In Jacek Fisiak (ed.), *Language Change under Contact Conditions*, pp. 217–236. Berlin: Mouton de Gruyter.

Prince, Alan and Paul Smolensky, 2004. *Optimality Theory: Constraint Interaction in Generative Grammar*. Oxford: Blackwell.

Remijsen, B., 2003. *Word-prosodic Systems of Raja Ampat Languages*. Utrecht: LOT.

Rivierre, Jean-Claude, 1993. Tonogenesis in New Caledonia. In Edmondson and Gregerson (eds), pp. 155–173.

Ross, Malcolm, 1993. Tonogenesis in the North Huon Gulf Chain. In Edmondson and Gregerson (eds), pp. 133–145.

Round, Erich R., 2011. Apical obstruents in pre-Proto-Tangkic and the origins of the non-zero absolute. *Proceedings of Berkeley Linguistics Society* 32: 109–121.

Śarmā, Devīdatta, 2004. *Tribal Languages of Ladakh*, part III. New Delhi: Mittal Publications.

Simonet, Miquel, 2014. Phonetic consequences of dynamic cross-linguistic interference in proficient bilinguals. *Journal of Phonetics* 43: 26–37.

Thomason, Sarah G. and Terrence Kaufman, 1988. *Language Contact, Creolization, and Genetic Linguistics*. Berkeley, CA: University of California Press.

Thordarson, Fridrik, 2009. Ossetic Language. In *Encyclopedia Iranica OnLine*. www.iranicaonline.org/articles/ossetic

Thurgood, Graham, 1999. *From Ancient Cham to Modern Dialects: Two Thousand Years of Language Contact and Change: With an Appendix of Chamic Reconstructions and Loanwords*. Oceanic Linguistics Special Publications, no. 28. Honolulu: University of Hawai'i Press.

Trubetzkoy, Nikolai Sergei, 1939. Gedanken über das Indogermanenproblem. *Acta Linguistica* 1: 81–89.

Trudgill, Peter, 2011. *Sociolinguistic Typology: Social Determinants of Linguistic Complexity*. Oxford: Oxford University Press.

Tsao, Feng-Ming, Huai-Mai Liu and Patricia K. Kuhl, 2006. Perception of native and non-native affricate-fricative contrasts: Cross-language tests on adults and infants. *Journal of the Acoustical Society of America* 120: 2285–2294.

Vaux, Bert, 2002. There was and wasn't a Balkan Sprachbund. Paper presented at AIEA, Würzburg.

Vermeer, Willem R., 1979. Proto-Slavonic *u in Kajkavian. *Zbornik za Filologiju i Lingvistiku* 22 (1): 171–177.

Wagner, Heinrich, 1964. Nordeuropäische Lautgeographie. *Zeitschrift für celtische Philologie* 29: 224–298.

Weinreich, Uriel, 1953. *Language in Contact: Findings and Problems.* The Hague: Mouton.

Wells, John C., 1982. *Accents of English*, three volumes. Cambridge: Cambridge University Press.

Wong, Patrick C. M., Barath Chandrasekaran and Jing Zheng, 2012. The derived allele of ASPM is associated with lexical tone perception. *PLoS ONE* 7 (4): e34243.

6

Convergence and Divergence in the Phonology of the Languages of Europe

Thomas Stolz and Nataliya Levkovych

6.1 Introduction

This chapter addresses the synchronic structural similarity and dissimilarity of languages in general by way of discussing selected phenomena of the segmental phonology of the languages of Europe in particular. Our guiding question is whether or not the distribution of certain properties of phonological systems provides at least circumstantial evidence of areal-linguistically meaningful patterns. We start from the assumption that the phonological profile of Europe provides sufficiently interesting data to feed the debate on the comparability of language structures.

Before we present, discuss and evaluate the phonological phenomena, it is necessary to clarify a small set of basic notions which are essential for the understanding of our line of argumentation. Similarity and dissimilarity are synchronic properties of many languages. The degrees of similarity and dissimilarity among languages serve as indicators of structural unity and diversity, respectively. Positive similarity is equivalent to the presence of a given phenomenon in the languages compared whereas the parallel absence of a given phenomenon constitutes a case of negative similarity, i.e. dissimilarity. Convergence and divergence, on the other hand, are dynamic concepts which presuppose processes of language change in the course of which the degree of similarity or dissimilarity of a given set of languages increases or decreases. Increasing similarity is tantamount to the strengthening of structural unity whereas decreasing similarity results from the growth of diversity. The convergence of languages A and B may trigger the divergence of languages A and C and vice versa. In this chapter, we adopt an exclusively synchronic perspective which needs to be complemented by a diachronic interpretation in follow-up studies. Thus, discounting the occasional digression and the concluding section, we do not directly address the issue of language contact and independent parallel development in this contribution.

The identification of linguistic areas is not a primary goal of ours since we subscribe to Campbell's (2006) critical assessment of the sprachbund debate. Instead we apply the principles laid down in Bechert ([1981] 1998: 14), according to which the determination of the full extension of isoglosses has to precede the construction of linguistic areas and not vice versa. In this study, only the outer boundaries of Europe impose restrictions on the possibility of tracking some of the isoglosses in their entirety. What we expect to find are bundles of isoglosses (isopleths in the sense of van der Auwera 1998) and/or different statistically noticeable preferences in different parts of the continent under scrutiny. To this end, we frequently employ simple dichotomies such as periphery versus centre/interior, east versus west, etc. The geolinguistic interpretation of the results is supported by maps throughout this chapter.

As to the geographical limits of Europe, we follow the lead of the EUROTYP-inspired maximalist interpretation in Kortmann and van der Auwera (2011), so that the westernmost parts of Kazakhstan, Transcaucasia and Anatolia belong to Europe. To make the endeavour more interesting, we add Greenland as the northwesternmost extension to the area under scrutiny. Our sample comprises Afroasiatic, Eskimo-Aleutic, Indo-European, Mongolian, Northeast Caucasian, Northwest Caucasian, South Caucasian, Turkic and Uralic languages as well as the isolate Basque (see the Appendix). For reasons of space, the focus is on consonantal phonemes and some of their prominent properties, which we check for in an as yet unbalanced pan-European sample of 185 languages including non-standard varieties. We discuss both selected qualitative and quantitative aspects of the systems of phonemic consonants.

In terms of phonological theory and methodology, we are indebted to functional typology (Velupillai 2012: 61–87) and to the 'received' structuralist tradition (Hall 2011: 37–99). As to terminology and classification we largely adopt the distinctions introduced by Ladefoged and Maddieson (1996).

Notwithstanding the previous areal-linguistically minded research of phonological issues in European languages (see Section 6.2), the project into which this study is embedded is a first, since there is as yet no comprehensive areal-linguistic account of the phonologies of the languages of Europe. Only one of the eight volumes which document the achievements of the EUROTYP project displays an orientation towards phonology, namely van der Hulst (1999) on word-prosodic systems. A distant forerunner, the volume on sandhi phenomena in the languages of Europe edited by Andersen (1986), covers an important aspect of phonotactics (also across word boundaries). Proper segmental phonology, however, has clearly not been fully studied in the many post-EUROTYP spin-offs which continue to refine our knowledge of the areal character-istics of the European linguistic landscape. According to Haspelmath (2001: 1493), there are two possible explanations for this apparent neglect. Either the phonological properties of the languages of Europe are too trivial to justify being studied in-depth, or phonologists 'have not looked hard enough' to discover geolinguistically meaningful patterns. The most likely reason for this gap is given by Haarmann (1976a: 115), who states that the phonological systems of the languages of Europe still need to be described according to one and the same model. Since the extant descrip-tions of the individual sample languages apply different phonological models, the compatibility of the results is severely restricted. This is why we have to reanalyse (many of) the sources in order to fit the data into a common format.

Problems arise also from the different goals and motivations of the scholars to argue for or against diversity or unity. For the now largely outdated pioneer Lewy (1964 [1942]: 107–108), for instance, it was impor-tant to establish the existence of structural diversity to prove his *Völkerpsychological* idea that people in different parts of Europe think differently. Conversely, Décsy (2000b) needs structural unity to support his idea that there is a 'common European mind-set'. In the light of van Pottelberge's (2005) criticism of the ideology behind many areal-linguistic accounts of the European situation, we attempt to establish – as objectively as is possible with a constructed category – the distribution of (classes of) phonemes across the European linguistic landscape. In brief, we assume that structural similarity applies if the phonological phenom-ena in different languages are identical.

There is a plethora of options for how to determine whether languages are structurally similar or dissimilar. For the purpose at hand, we stipulate three different levels on which similarity and dissimilarity can be checked. On the macro-level, phonological classes and other over-arching principles of the organization of phonological systems are compared to each other. The meso-level is reserved for the comparison of phonemes as (moder-ately) abstract members of systems, whereas the concrete realizations of phonemes, i.e. the phonetics, are studied on the micro-level. Macro-level similarity does not automatically correspond to micro-level similarity. For the purpose at hand, we focus especially on the macro-level and check the meso-level only for primary articulations (see Section 6.3.2) to the exclu-sion of the micro-level, since the range of variation on the micro-level is considerably more complex than on the two higher levels and would demand separate investigation.

For genetically closely related languages it is assumed, as an initial premise, that they are structurally similar to each other. The data discussed in this study suggest that this assumption is not borne out by the facts. What we will often find instead are areally based preferences which cut across genetic boundaries. Since two of the above three levels are checked for similarity and dissimilarity, we make a selection from the wealth of data to keep the presentation within reasonable bounds. This is why we comment on the heterogeneity or homogeneity of language families only in passing. A brief excursus highlights aspects of internal diversity for four selected families. Our main interest, however, is to determine to what extent diversity and unity in the realm of phonology is dependent upon areal considerations.

We are aware of the limitations of our endeavour. The study of a narrowly circumscribed fragment of the phonology of our sample languages does not allow us to classify these languages holistically. Even if it can be shown that certain languages are similar in their phoneme inventories, the chances are that the same languages differ markedly in other aspects of phonology (such as phonotactics). We intend to fill in the many gaps in the future and thus to complement the present explorative study.

The chapter is organized as follows. In Section 6.2, we first report briefly on the role phonological issues have played in recent areal-linguistic research, and then we zoom in on Europe. To this end we consider the views on the interrelationship between phonology and areal factors in the languages of Europe. With this background information, we can view the empirical side of the areal phonology of Europe in Section 6.3 and its subsections. The excursus on diversity in genetic families is presented in Section 6.3.3. Section 6.4 contains the conclusions, including the general evaluation of our findings and an outlook on future research. Restriction of space does not allow us to do justice to all of the interesting hypotheses suggested for phonological systems in areal perspective and/or under conditions of language contact. In the subsequent parts of this chapter, we therefore content ourselves with referring to a small selection of the contributions on this topic. We restrict the cartographic illustration of the distribution of phonological properties of our sample languages to a selection of those cases in which the isoglosses do not single out particularly small subareas of Europe but yield a different picture with two or more major subareas.

6.2   Areal Phonology – With a Special Focus on Europe

Jakobson ([1930] 1971) coined the term *Phonologischer Sprachbund* in the early 1930s. The existence of phonological areas – sometimes of considerable extent – is corroborated by *The World Atlas of Language Structures* (WALS), which contains nineteen chapters devoted to phonological problems (Anderson 2005; Goedemans and van der Hulst 2005a–d; Hajek 2005; Maddieson 2005a–m). The maps which accompany these chapters illustrate that most of the properties offer evidence of areal preferences, some of which involve Europe or parts thereof. Phonological issues are also relevant to all of the eight linguistic areas discussed in Matras, McMahon and Vincent (2006). Accordingly, one would expect that phonology also features prominently when it comes to determining areal properties of European languages. However, the situation is by no means as clear as that.

The prior work on areal-phonological issues in Europe can be divided informally into several strands of research. First of all, a distinction must be made between essentialist and descriptive approaches. The former aim at identifying the common (and, if possible, distinctive) phonological properties shared by all of the languages of Europe or a subregion of the continent. On the descriptive side, scholars ideally take stock of all phonological phenomena which occur in (a subregion of) Europe independent of their areal typicality. Both these perspectives are well represented in the relevant literature.

Wagner (2002 [1964]) and Ewels (2009), for instance, scrutinize two contiguous regions – northern Europe and the Baltic – regarding the diffusion of selected phonological phenomena over groups of genetically diverse languages. In this way they contribute to characterizing two potential subareas of Europe phonologically. The accessibility of several other studies of this kind dedicated to further subareas of the continent notwithstanding, it is practically impossible to paint a linguistically satisfactory picture of the areal phonology of Europe by way of simply adding up the results of the investigations of specific subareas. Some of the phonological isoglosses cross the borders of, or occur in several (not necessarily contiguous) subareas, other properties are not shared by all members of a supposed subarea, and still other phenomena are passed over tacitly because they do not count among the characteristics of a given subarea. For example, a stable site for word stress is considered a characteristic not only of the Danube sprachbund but also of the Baltic sprachbund (Haarmann 1976b: 100–101 and 110).

Haarmann (1976a), Ternes (1998, 2010) and Décsy (2000a, 2000b) are examples of investigations which combine essentialist and descriptivist elements. In their search for pan-Europeanisms, these authors come up with a variety of solutions. Haarmann (1976a: 108–109) postulates so-called 'Europemes', the first four of which belong to the realm of phonology. These phonological Europemes can be shown to reflect language-independent universal trends and thus fail to be distinctive (Stolz 2006). This result is largely in line with the results of the two studies by Ternes (1998, 2010), who surveys the phonological typology of the languages of Europe with a view to formulating generalizations of pan-European dimensions. According to this author, the European languages do not stand out in any way in a cross-linguistic perspective (Ternes 2010: 594). Décsy (2000b: 341–353) tries to reconstruct the set of phonemes common to all contemporary languages of Europe without judging the distinctiveness of the set in comparison to non-European languages. In general, essentialist models do not inform us sufficiently about the areal phonology of the European continent because they gloss over all aspects of structural diversity to the benefit of unity.

On the other hand, Haarmann (1976a: 116) and Ternes (2010: 584–586) observe that there is variation on other parameters, and some of the phenomena can be interpreted as being areally (and to some extent also genetically) biased. This observation suggests that, phonologically, Europe is probably more interesting in terms of its internal diversity than it is in a global perspective. As Comrie (1993) maintains, it is important to study the linguistic variation that occurs within a relatively limited geographical space, for instance that in Europe in comparison to more sizable continents like Africa, Asia and the Americas. The extent of the structural diversity across Europe on the phonological level still needs to be determined.

In this context, studies like that of Stadnik (2002) on the areal aspects of palatalization correlations in Europe and Asia are especially helpful since they focus on well-defined structural phenomena without having to prove an *idée fixe* as to the areal subdivision of the European continent. Distributions which are independent of the putative boundaries of internal subareas are identified in this approach to the areal phonology of Europe. In a similar vein, Stolz (2007, 2010) and Stolz, Urdze and Otsuka (2010, 2011, 2012) check the distribution of the structures of monosyllables, sibilants and affricates, along with velar and postvelar fricatives, liquids, and phonological rara and rarissima in Europe. In most of the cases areal patterns are discernible, so it is very probable that similarly meaningful results can be achieved by way of scrutinizing further phonological phenomena. This potential of our project is illustrated below by the aspects of the phonemics of European languages we discuss in Section 6.3.

6.3 The Areal Phonemics of Europe

This section contains two subsections: Section 6.3.1 is dedicated to the macro-level and Section 6.3.2 deals with the meso-level. In these subsections we discuss the phenomena connected to structural unity and structural diversity. These aspects are checked for areally remarkable results, with the occasional comment on diversity and unity within genetically defined groups of languages. We look at both positive similarity and negative similarity without aiming at a balanced treatment of either. Furthermore, most of the data we analyse in this section will be evaluated quantitatively without addressing qualitative aspects systematically. Since our study looks exclusively at consonants, we do not make any statements about the consonant–vowel ratio of our sample languages – a topic that is important for Haarmann (1976a: 113–114) and Ternes (2010: 579–580). Furthermore, Ternes (2010: 578), for phonological reasons to be explained below, excludes the languages of the Caucasus region from his sample of European languages. Our study – which also covers the languages of the Caucasus – is designed to check whether or not Ternes' decision is justified.

Throughout this chapter we provide maps which reflect the geolinguistic distribution of selected phenomena discussed in the subsequent paragraphs. To guarantee easy readability, the maps are kept as simple as possible, i.e. we restrict the number of features whose distribution is represented on a given map to two or three. More often than not the map is based on the dichotomy of the presence versus absence of a phonological phenomenon. For the purposes of areal-linguistic cartography, we focus on those features for which there is a statistically significant majority distribution and a (set of) undisputable minority distribution(s).

We start with a straightforward working definition of the segmental phoneme, which we conceive of as a countable unit that serves to distinguish meaningful elements in a given language. We discount geminates because their phonological status is too controversial to allow for their consideration. The presentation largely follows a top-down pattern.

The frame of reference for the empirical part of this study is the chart of consonants of the International Phonetic Alphabet (IPA) provided by the International Phonetic Association (1999: ix). There are 58 simple symbols for pulmonic consonants, 16 symbols for ejectives and implosives, and 9 additional symbols including those for epiglottal consonants and clicks. Affricates are represented by complex symbols (mostly ligatures). On the basis of our prior investigations, we have identified a set of 76 simple IPA symbols that are required for the languages of Europe. For convenience, we term the phonological units represented by these symbols 'cardinal phonemes', segments which involve primary articulations. In the IPA system, secondary articulations are represented by diacritics which turn simple symbols into complex symbols. In our terminology, complex symbols of this kind represent 'extended cardinal phonemes'. Cardinal and extended cardinal phonemes conform to the structuralist definition of the phoneme insofar as their feature specifications contain only those elements which are distinctive systemically. If the secondary articulations are merely phonetics, they are ignored in this study.

6.3.1   Macro-level: Phonological Classes

In this subsection we determine the areal distribution of phonological classes. For a phonological class to be attested in a given language, the presence of a single phonemic representative of this class is sufficient.

We start on the highest levels of the phonological matrix by way of checking whether or not the parameters of airstream mechanisms, manner of articulation, place of articulation, and phonation (Sections 6.3.1.1–6.3.1.4) are subject to geolinguistic variation in Europe. Section 6.3.1 comes to a close with the discussion of secondary articulations. Owing to the general systematicity of phonological phenomena, Section 6.3.1.5 bears a resemblance to the organization of the studies by Ternes (1998, 2010).

6.3.1.1　Airstream Mechanisms

The initial observation is trivial, of course, because it states that all 185 languages of our sample are equipped with pulmonic consonants. Since this is a universal property of human languages, the common behaviour of our sample languages is predictable. What is much less trivial, however, is the existence of additional non-pulmonic consonants in a sizable minority of the sample. Non-pulmonic classes such as clicks and implosives are unknown in Europe. In contrast, ejectives are attested in the Caucasus region, i.e. in a narrowly delimited geographical part of Europe. Thus, the distinction of pulmonic versus non-pulmonic consonants is areally significant because it divides Europe into a large area of languages which only admit pulmonic consonants and a much smaller southeastern area in which pulmonic consonants coexist with non-pulmonic consonants (see Table 6.1).

The pulmonic consonants constitute an expected element of structural unity whereas the existence of non-pulmonic consonants is an element of structural diversity. The vast majority of our sample languages show only one airstream mechanism; there is a minority of languages in which two modes of airstream mechanisms are phonologically relevant.

It is exactly the existence of ejectives in the languages of the Caucasus which motivates Ternes (2010: 578) to exclude the Caucasus region from his account of the phonological typology of the languages of Europe, because the Caucasian propensity for ejectives would jeopardize

Table 6.1 *Unity and diversity with regard to airstream mechanism*

Airstream mechanism	Unity	Diversity
Pulmonic	+ pulmonic	–
Non-pulmonic	– clicks – implosives	+ ejectives 　1. Genetic: 　• Northwest Caucasian 　• Northeast Caucasian 　• South Caucasian 　2. Areal: 　• Caucasus

the supposedly homogeneous picture of the areal phonology of Europe.[1] Ejectives are a common feature of all members of the genetically unrelated phyla Northwest Caucasian, Northeast Caucasian and South Caucasian. However, ejectives are also an areal feature of the Caucasus region since this airstream mechanism is phonemically relevant in Indo-European languages as well (Eastern Armenian and Ossetic) and regional varieties of Turkic languages (Kumyk, Azeri, Karachay-Balkar and Turkish) spoken in the Caucasus as well as in the geographically slightly more remote Neo-Aramaic (i.e. Semitic) varieties of Urmia, Van and Mosul (Chirikba 2008: 44–45).[2] This means that the diffusion of the feature of non-pulmonic airstream mechanisms across genetic boundaries has contributed to the structural unity of genetically unrelated neighbours and at the same time those non-Caucasian languages which have converged on this parameter with their Caucasian neighbours have become dissimilar to their next-of-kin outside the Caucasus region. Therefore, the increase of similarity in areal perspective triggers the decrease of similarity in genetic perspective.

In what follows we pay special attention to the behaviour of the languages of the Caucasus if it is at variance with that of the bulk of our sample languages.

6.3.1.2 Manner of Articulation

As to the manner of articulation, the distinction of obstruents versus sonorants is a common European feature because both these classes occur in all of our sample languages. This omnipresence also holds for the majority of distinctions on the next level. In terms of phonological classes, stops, fricatives, nasals, liquids and approximants are indeed attested across the board in Europe. There are three cases however, for which the analysis is not so straightforward.

The class of liquids can be further subdivided into laterals and rhotics. All 185 of our sample languages offer evidence of both these subclasses. The phonemes which are often subsumed under the class of rhotics (= /r/, /ɾ/, /ɹ/, /ɽ/, /ɻ/, /ʀ/, /ʁ/, /ɭ/) do not form a natural class because by no means all of them share the necessary minimum of features (Ladefoged and Maddieson 1996: 215–217). In terms of the manner of articulation, different rhotics belong to different phonological classes, namely approximants, taps/flaps or trills. Given that approximants occur in all of our sample languages, only the distribution of taps/flaps and trills as classes is of interest for the topic of this subsection. With attestations in 167 languages (90 per cent of the sample), trills represent the more widespread of the two classes. In contrast, taps are reported for

---

[1] The Caucasus region is also excluded from the studies by Lewy ([1942] 1964), Haarmann (1976b) and Décsy (2000a, 2000b), though mostly for extra-linguistic reasons, some of which are of a dubious nature.

[2] Not all of the varieties equipped with ejectives form part of our sample.

Table 6.2 *Diversity in the realm of rhotics*

Rhotics	Attested		Unattested	
	absolute	share	absolute	share
Taps/flaps	24	13%	161	87%
Approximants	39	21%	146	79%
Trills	167	90%	18	10%

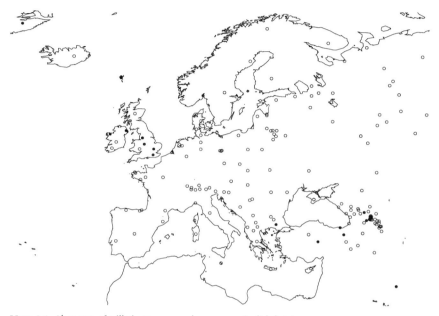

Map 6.1 Absence of trills in European languages (solid dots)

a minority of 24 languages or 13 per cent of the sample. A total of 178 languages show either taps/flaps or trills, which is equivalent to 96 per cent of the sample. The erstwhile cover term for the two classes of taps/flaps and trills is vibrants, that is, 96 per cent of our sample languages offer evidence of vibrants. Moreover, this means that there are 11 languages (6 per cent of the sample) in which phonemic taps/flaps coexist with and are distinct from phonemic trills. Thus, there are four groups of languages, namely those which only show trills, those which only allow for taps/flaps, those which contrast phonemic taps/flaps with phonemic trills, and finally those three languages (< 2 per cent of the sample) from which these classes of rhotics are absent. Since 39 languages (21 per cent) also show the voiced uvular approximant /ʁ/ (sometimes classified as a fricative), there must be 36 languages in which this approximant forms a phonological opposition with trills or taps/flaps or both (see Table 6.2). Map 6.1 shows the distribution of those sample languages which lack the class of trills.

Table 6.3 *Unity and diversity in the realm of laterals*

Laterals	Unity	Diversity
Approximants	+ approximants	
Fricative		+ fricative
		1. Areal:
		• Caucasus
		2. Genetic:
		• Northwest Caucasian
		• Northeast Caucasian
		3. Isolate:
		• Welsh
Affricate		+ affricate
		1. Areal:
		• Caucasus
		2. Genetic:
		• Northwest Caucasian
		• Northeast Caucasian

Areally significant results are yielded by the distribution of lateral fricatives and lateral affricates, which are somewhat special in comparison to the lateral approximants (Ladefoged and Maddieson 1996: 197). All of the sample languages give evidence of the phonological class of laterals. Only a relatively small segment of the sample, however, provides evidence of lateral fricatives, namely 22 languages (11 per cent), with Welsh being the sole example of a language outside the Caucasus region to employ a lateral fricative phoneme. The Caucasian monopoly is even more pronounced with the lateral affricates, which are attested in 16 languages (9 per cent), all of which belong to either the Northwest Caucasian or the Northeast Caucasian phylum. There is thus a clear pattern of structural diversity which is areally and genetically based at the same time. The above Northwest Caucasian and Northeast Caucasian languages display several phonemic laterals which belong to different manners of articulation (see Table 6.3).

The geolinguistic facts are, however, different with affricates (Ternes 2010: 585) because only 160 out of 185 sample languages offer evidence of phonemic affricates.[3] This corresponds to 86 per cent of our sample. There is thus a bipartition of the sample into a majority formed by those languages which distinguish six phonemic manners of articulation and a minority of those languages which make do with five phonemic manners of articulation. Stolz (2010: 616–619) provides several maps showing that the distribution of affricates follows an areal logic, in the sense that the languages that display phonemic affricates occupy a huge uninterrupted central territory surrounded by those languages which lack phonemic affricates. The latter are thus situated on the periphery: see Map 6.2.

---

[3] Haarmann (1976a: 116) does not recognize any areally significant pattern, and erroneously assumes that Portuguese too has phonemic affricates.

Map 6.2 Absence of affricates in European languages (solid dots)

Both positive similarity and negative similarity cut across some genetic boundaries since we find members of the Germanic, Romance, Turkic and Uralic phyla in both classes. In sum, European languages tend to have phonemic affricates if their neighbours have them. They tend to lack phonemic affricates if their neighbours lack them too. The distribution of the phonological class of affricates thus illustrates diversity. Genetic unity characterizes the Slavic, Baltic, Northwest Caucasian, Northeast Caucasian and South Caucasian languages because all of these languages count affricates among their phonemes. On the other hand, none of the Celtic languages in our sample shows phonemic affricates. Some language families or their branches behave homogeneously whereas others do not.

6.3.1.3   Place of Articulation

As to the places of articulation, Ternes (2010: 584) assumes that the globally most widespread categories are also represented throughout Europe. This view of the facts is corroborated by the statistics for the ternary distinction of labial, coronal and dorsal places of articulation, all of which are present in each of the 185 sample languages. This means that all of our sample languages make use of labial and lingual places of articulation. If we exclude the affricates and focus on the tongue as active articulator, it is evident that the root position does not score as high as either the coronal or the dorsal positions. There are 24 languages (13 per cent of the sample) in which the root of the tongue is the active articulator (for pharyngeals

Table 6.4 *Unity versus diversity with major places of articulation (tongue positions)*

Place of articulation	Present		Absent	
	absolute	share	absolute	share
Coronal	185	100%	0	0%
Dorsal	185	100%	0	0%
Radical	24	13%	161	87%

Table 6.5 *Unity versus diversity with major places of articulation (non-tongue positions)*

Place of articulation	Present		Absent	
	absolute	share	absolute	share
Labial	185	100%	0	0%
Laryngeal	119	64%	66	36%

and epiglottals). Table 6.4 shows that unity is characteristic of the places of articulation that involve the front half of the tongue as active articulator.

The picture becomes more varied if we include the non-tongue positions. On the one hand, the omnipresence of labial places of articulation fits in with the above preference for places of articulation located in the front part of the oral cavity. However, this tendency is counterbalanced by the remarkably high share of the glottal (laryngeal) place of articulation among our sample languages (see Table 6.5).

The high number of languages with laryngeal places of articulation notwithstanding, the values in Tables 6.4 and 6.5 suggest a bipartition of the following kind. With regard to those places of articulation which are situated in the front part of the oral cavity, the languages of Europe behave homogeneously in the sense that all of them offer evidence of the phonological classes concerned. Structural diversity is largely a matter of those places of articulation which are located in the back part of the oral cavity or beyond. In particular, the feature 'tongue root' is associated with the languages of the Caucasus whereas the absence of the feature 'laryngeal' is areally less clearly distributed.

For the subdivisions of the major categories of place, the picture is even more varied. The highest rates are reported for bilabials, alveolars and velars with a share of 100 per cent for each of the three places of articulation. As Table 6.6 shows, there are only a further three places of articulation – palatal, labio-dental and palato-alveolar – which are attested in significantly more than two-thirds of the sample languages. The glottal place of articulation is attested in slightly less than two-thirds of the sample languages. All other places of articulation are minority

Table 6.6 *Unity versus diversity with places of articulation (primary subdivisions)*

Place of articulation	Present		Absent	
	absolute	share	absolute	share
Bilabial	185	100%	0	0%
Alveolar	185	100%	0	0%
Velar	185	100%	0	0%
Palatal	176	95%	9	5%
Labio-dental	165	89%	20	11%
Palato-alveolar	165	89%	20	11%
Glottal	119	64%	66	36%
Labio-velar	69	37%	116	63%
Uvular	63	34%	122	66%
Alveo-palatal	27	15%	158	85%
Pharyngeal	21	11%	164	89%
Interdental	19	10%	166	90%
Epiglottal	8	4%	177	96%
Retroflex	3	2%	182	98%
Labio-palatal	1	< 1%	184	> 99%

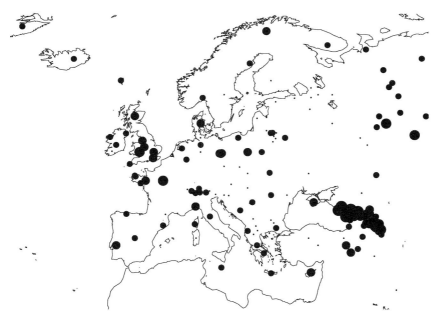

Map 6.3 Attested minority configurations (place of articulation, Table 6.6). Size of dot represents number of configurations attested; tiny dot indicates no configurations attested

configurations, none of which comes near the 40 per cent mark. Map 6.3 indicates the location of those languages which realize one or several of the minority configurations given in Table 6.6. Map 6.4 shows the geolinguistic position of those languages which do not partake in one or more of the majority configurations.

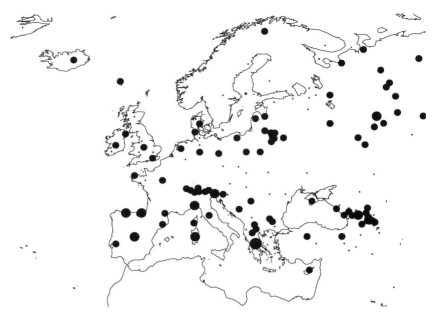

Map 6.4 Absence of majority configurations (place of articulation, Table 6.6). Size of dot represents number of configurations absent; tiny dot indicates no configurations absent

The palatal place of articulation is absent from nine languages, which do not belong together either genetically or areally. Seven of these languages are situated on the periphery of the continent. As to the absence of the labio-dental place of articulation, the overall distribution yields a very clear pattern. Apart from Basque, 19 of the 20 languages which lack labio-dentals are located in eastern Europe. With 16 Northeast Caucasian languages and one South Caucasian language, there is an indisputable areal and genetic bias. No Indo-European language reflects this negative feature.

The palato-alveolar place of articulation is not made use of in a variety of Indo-European and Uralic languages. These languages form a string of languages on the periphery of a large and compact area of genetically diverse languages which are equipped with palato-alveolar phonemes.

Both the presence and absence of the glottal place of articulation cut across the boundaries of language families. Members of the Indo-European family are found in both groups; the same division holds for Turkic, Uralic, Afroasiatic and Northwest Caucasian languages. In terms of the areal distribution, it is possible to distinguish two regions from which the glottal place of articulation is absent, namely a long southern stretch along the Mediterranean and a huge territory which covers eastern-central Europe and much of Eurasia. In contrast, northern Europe and the southeasternmost parts of the continent host the bulk of those languages which make use of the glottal place of articulation for phonological distinctions.

Double articulation is a rarity in Europe. The labio-velar place of articulation stands out statistically in the sense that it is attested in slightly more than a third of the sample languages. In practically all of these cases we are dealing with a voiced labio-velar approximant /w/. Of the 69 languages which offer evidence of labio-velars, 28 (41 per cent) belong to the three Caucasian families. Another 10 non-Indo-European languages display labio-velars, so the 31 Indo-European languages with labio-velars account for only 45 per cent of this group of languages. The phenomenon is absent from most of the languages of eastern-central Europe and Eurasia.

Ternes (2010: 584) assumes that uvular and pharyngeal places of articulation are excluded from the repertoire of the languages of Europe (with the putative exception of Maltese). This statement needs to be revised. It is true that 37 of the 63 languages which have uvulars belong to the Caucasian language families. Another eight languages are situated outside Ternes' conception of Europe. However, there are 18 languages (29 per cent) which are located inside the area under scrutiny and which nevertheless display uvulars. Many of these languages show the uvular trill /ʀ/ or the uvular fricative /ʁ/. Ternes (2010: 586) concedes that the geolinguistic distribution of these uvular rhotics yields an areally significant pattern with a centre of diffusion in the so-called 'Charlemagne sprachbund' (van der Auwera 1998).

Alveo-palatal places of articulation are reported for 27 languages, 11 of which are members of the Indo-European language family. With 18 languages, the two-thirds majority of the languages equipped with alveo-palatal phonemes are well established in eastern Europe. Six of these languages belong to the Northwest Caucasian family. In the western half of the continent, the languages with alveo-palatal phonemes are not connected to each other, either genetically or areally.

Except for Cypriot Arabic, those languages which make use of the pharyngeal place of articulation are situated in the Caucasus and belong to the Northwest Caucasian and the Northeast Caucasian phyla. Similarly, the very small number of languages attesting to the epiglottal place of articulation – all of them are members of Northeast Caucasian – lends support to the idea that in the bulk of the languages of Europe, the back part of the oral cavity is disfavoured as an area in which to produce speech sounds.

The interdental place of articulation is largely absent from the huge central and eastern area. None of the Caucasian languages testify to phonemic interdentals. Similarly, Slavic and Baltic languages do not employ this place of articulation. Interdentals are attested in a variety of languages in the south (including Albanian, Greek and Cypriot Arabic) and in the northwest of the continent. There are also three languages on the eastern fringe of Europe which employ interdentals. Germanic, Celtic, Romance, Semitic, Turkic and Uralic languages behave heterogeneously with regard to the interdental place of articulation, because some of them have interdental phonemes whereas their sister languages lack this phonological class altogether; for example, Welsh has interdental phonemes but Irish no longer has them.

The two remaining places of articulation – retroflex and labio-palatal – are only marginally represented in Europe. For retroflexion, caution is necessary since it is not always clear whether we are dealing with a phonemic property or an allophonic realization, for example in Faroese. Ternes (2010: 584) assumes a northwest European isogloss of retroflexion, whereas the labio-palatal place of articulation is unique to French which has phonemic /ɥ/. These rarities single out small numbers of languages from their families and thus contribute to the structural diversity of these families.

6.3.1.4 Phonation

Ternes (2010: 587) observes that the opposition voiced versus voiceless is very common throughout Europe. As a matter of fact, the feature [+voice] is present in each of the 185 sample languages. However, in two of the languages in the east – Chuvash (Turkic) and Karelian (Uralic) – this feature is not properly phonemic since there is no voiced counterpart. Both languages show /v/ but lack */f/. In 183 languages, that is, in 99 per cent of the European languages, phonation is phonologically distinctive.

It remains to be seen over which phonological classes the domain of the voice correlation extends. With reference to manners of articulation, Ternes (2010: 587) states that the classes of stops and fricatives are the most likely manners of articulation which are subject to voice distinctions. This statement is corroborated by the behaviour of our sample languages. There are only 11 languages (6 per cent) which do not have phonemic voice distinctions with fricatives. With just eight languages (4 per cent), the group of languages which lack evidence of the voice correlation with stops is even smaller. It is thus absolutely exceptional for a language of Europe to lack the voice correlation in these phonological classes, the Karelian variety of Archangelsk and Chuvash being the only examples of languages which do not have phonemic voice distinctions in both of the classes. Affricates, however, tell a different story because 41 languages (22 per cent of the entire sample) allow for voiceless affricates only. This is equivalent to a share of 26 per cent of the 160 languages which show the phonological class of affricates.

In areal terms, the absence of the voice correlation with stops and fricatives is largely confined to languages which are situated on the periphery. In the case of the stops, there is an accumulation in the east, with four Uralic and Turkic languages of Eurasia. For the fricatives, the Iberian Peninsula seems to be largely excluded from the voice correlation isogloss. These two areal centres are also included in the geolinguistic domain characterized by the absence of voiced affricates (in languages with affricates). Twenty-nine or 71 per cent of the 41 languages are located

Table 6.7 *Unity versus diversity in the realm of phonation (manner of articulation)*

Manner of articulation	Present		Absent	
	absolute	share	absolute	share
General	183	99%	2	1%
Stops	177	96%	8	4%
Fricatives	174	94%	11	6%
Affricates	41	22% (of 185)	144	78%
		26% (of 160)	119	74%
Sonorants	6	3%	179	97%

in the eastern half of the European continent. Another three are at home on the Iberian Peninsula. With 14 languages, the North Caucasian family accounts for 34 per cent of the languages without voiced affricates. Twenty-three (56 per cent) of these languages are non-Indo-European (Northeast Caucasian, Uralic, Turkic, Basque). There is thus a clear areal ratio behind the distribution of the negative property under scrutiny.

In Europe, voiceless sonorants belong among the rara and rarissima (Ternes 2010: 587). Some of the reported cases are doubtful insofar as the voiceless units might perhaps be better analysed as allophones. The indisputable cases are represented by the Uralic languages Erzya and Mokša Mordvin, Kildin and North Saami, which show phonemic voice contrasts with laterals, nasals and rhotics. Chechen and Welsh illustrate the opposition of voiced and voiceless rhotics.

Table 6.7 provides a summary of the findings regarding the distribution of the voice correlation over manners of articulation. The absence of voice contrasts is infrequent in general and especially rare with obstruents. This does not hold for affricates, for which the reverse is true. Note, however, that affricates themselves are not attested as widely as stops or fricatives, that is, they constitute a cross-linguistically marked phonological class which displays marked behaviour insofar as it does not allow for distinctions made with other obstruent classes.

Is there a correlation between place of articulation and the presence or absence of the voice? The various places of articulation behave differently as to the susceptibility to voice contrasts. If we ask whether or not the distinction of voiceless versus voiced is phonemic with a given place of articulation in the languages of our sample, we get the results shown in Table 6.8.

In the table, the places of articulation come in the order of increasing shares for those languages which lack voice contrasts. Since the languages differ as to the absence/presence of many of the places of articulation in their phonological system, the figures for sharing are calculated on the basis of the number of languages which make use of a given place of articulation. Except

Table 6.8 *Unity versus diversity in the realm of phonation (place of articulation)*

Place of articulation	Absent		Total of place
	absolute	share of place	absolute
Alveolar	5	3%	185
Palatal	7	4%	176
Velar	8	4%	185
Bilabial	8	4%	185
Alveo-palatal	4	15%	27
Palato-alveolar	31	19%	165
Labio-dental	35	21%	165
Interdental	5	26%	19
Pharyngeal	6	29%	21
Retroflex	1	33%	3
Uvular	21	33%	63
Epiglottal	3	38%	8
Labio-palatal	0	100%	1
Labio-velar	0	100%	69
Glottal	0	100%	119

for the three categories at the bottom of Table 6.8, all the values are indicative of a preference for phonemic voice contrasts. The highest rate of absence of voice contrasts – apart from the final three places of articulation – exceeds a third of the languages involved by only a narrow margin. For the four places of articulation which are attested in over 90 per cent of the sample languages, the absence of the voice correlation is minimal. Among the eleven places of articulation with higher absence rates for voice contrasts, eight categories belong to the minority configurations. Voice is phonologically not distinctive in three cases. The labio-palatal approximant is a trivial case because, phonetically, it is exempt from voice contrasts. For labio-velars and glottals, however, it is phonetically possible to distinguish voiced from voiceless realizations. Nevertheless, in our sample, all labio-velars represent voiced /w/ (and never voiceless /ʍ/ except in conservative varieties of Scottish and rural Irish English which have both /w/ and /ʍ/, i.e. in varieties not included in our sample). For the glottals, there are examples of voiced and voiceless phonemes. However, they never co-occur in phonemic oppositions in one and the same language.

Unsurprisingly, the absence of voice contrasts with pharyngeal and epiglottal places of articulation has a relatively clear areal foundation. Since these places of articulation are almost a 100 per cent monopoly of the Caucasian families, it is only logical that the eight out of nine languages which lack voiceless/voiced pairs of phonemes with these places of articulation are spoken in the Caucasus. Six of them belong to the Northeast Caucasian family and two others to the Northwest Caucasian family; the only non-Caucasian language without voiceless/voiced pairs within

Map 6.5 Absence of voice correlation with bilabials (solid dots)

pharyngeal and epiglottal consonants is Cypriot Arabic (Afroasiatic phylum, Semitic branch). In all other cases, the genetic composition of the groups of languages which lack phonemic voice contrasts is considerably more heterogeneous. However, for at least some of the places of articulation, an areal factor is discernible. This is the case with the bilabials, for instance. The eight languages without an opposition of voiceless versus voiced bilabials are all situated on the periphery of the European continent: see Map 6.5.

This peripheral location also holds for the 21 languages which lack voice contrasts with uvulars: see Map 6.6.

The situation is similar – though not identical – for the places of articulation alveo-palatal, palatal, velar and uvular, which lack voice distinctions mostly in languages which are located on the northern, southern or eastern rim of the continents: see Map 6.7.

In each of these categories, however, there is also an example of a language – Danish twice, Swedish, Franco-Provençal and the German variety of Brig once each – which is located closer to the interior of the area under scrutiny. For labio-dentals and palato-alveolars, the facts are more complex. Twenty-five, i.e. 71 per cent, of the languages without voice contrasts in the class of labio-dentals are located in the eastern part of Europe: see Map 6.8.

Twenty-one, i.e. 60 per cent, of the same group of languages are non-Indo-European languages. There is also a majority of languages (63 per cent) which are located on the periphery of the European map. In the case of the palato-alveolar place of articulation, the distribution is

Map 6.6 Absence of voice correlation with uvulars (solid dots)

Map 6.7 Absence of voice correlation with alveo-palatals/palatals/velars (solid dots)

more balanced genetically as well as areally, although there is a slight majority of 58 per cent for peripheral languages: see Map 6.9.

From an overall perspective, the contrast voiced versus voiceless is a majority situation. The size of its domain varies with manner and place

Map 6.8 Absence of voice correlation with labio-dentals (solid dots)

Map 6.9 Absence of voice correlation with palato-alveolars (solid dots)

of articulation. Languages in the interior of Europe are more likely to employ phonemic voice contrasts, whereas with peripheral languages the probability that the voiceless/voiced opposition is phonologically relevant diminishes.

6.3.1.5 Secondary Articulation

According to Ternes (2010: 586–587), secondary articulations are not prominently represented among the languages of Europe. The author discounts labialization and glottalization as European features because he excludes the Caucasus region from his version of Europe. For our project, however, labialization is a characteristic trait of the Northwest Caucasian and Northeast Caucasian families. Moreover, 'glottalization' (in Ternes' terms) is treated as an equivalent of the non-pulmonic class of ejectives in the present chapter. This class is again typical of the Caucasus region (see discussion in Section 6.3.1.1).

Our own count yields 73 languages that make use of phonemic secondary articulations. This corresponds to a share of 40 per cent of the sample, which is not a negligible quantity. The genetic affiliation of these 73 languages is given in Table 6.9. For convenience, Northeast and Northwest Caucasian languages are lumped together to form a fictitious Caucasian phylum. There is no evidence of secondary articulations with phonemic status in the South Caucasian languages of our sample. Map 6.10 captures the geographical distribution of languages which display phonemic secondary articulations.

Going by the standards in Ternes (2010), the only secondary articulation that yields statistically significant values is palatalization. Stadnik (2002) demonstrates that phonemic palatalization is an areal feature of the European east and Eurasia which is shared by Indo-European, Uralic, Turkic and Mongolian languages of these regions (see also Haarmann 1976a: 116). The presence or absence of the palatalization correlation splits genetic families into two branches; in the Baltic phylum, for example, Lithuanian displays phonemic palatalization whereas its next-of-kin Latvian lacks palatalization. Outside the compact eastern area there is a much smaller island of palatalization which comprises the Goidelic languages Irish and Scottish Gaelic in the far northwest (Ternes 2010: 586).

Table 6.10 proves the dominance of palatalization among the types of phonemic secondary articulations. Almost three-quarters of all instances of phonemic secondary articulations are covered by palatalization alone.

Table 6.9 *Genetic affiliation of languages with phonemic secondary articulations*

Affiliation	Absolute	Share (of 73)
Indo-European	40	55%
Caucasian (Northeast, Northwest)	16	22%
Uralic	12	16%
Turkic and Mongolic	5	7%
Total	73	100%

Map 6.10 Phonemic secondary articulation (solid dots)

Table 6.10 *Types of phonemic secondary articulations (statistics)*

Secondary articulation	absolute	share (of 73)	Caucasian languages	
			absolute	share (of type)
Palatalization	56	77%	7	13%
Labialization	15	21%	15	100%
Aspiration	11	15%	2	18%
Velarization	6	8%	0	0%
Pharyngealization	4	6%	4	100%

At the same time, the values featured in Table 6.10 are also indicative of genetically based preferences since labialization and pharyngealization are exclusive to Northeast and Northwest Caucasian languages, whereas these two families account for relatively small shares with palatalization and aspiration, and do not partake in the velarization isogloss at all. It is worth noting, however, that even without the contribution of the 18 Caucasian languages, there is a clear preference for phonemic secondary articulations to occur in languages of the European east. Of the 73 languages with phonemic secondary articulations, only seven (10 per cent of this class) are located in the western half of Europe whereas 66 (90 per cent) are to be found on the other side of the vertical dividing line. Those western languages which show phonemic secondary articulations are members of the Celtic branch of Indo-European.

Table 6.11 *Secondary articulations and manner of articulation*

Manner of articulation	Absolute	Share of manner	Total of manner
Stops	61	33%	185
Fricatives	49	27%	185
Laterals	48	26%	185
Nasals	45	24%	185
Affricates	35	22%	160
Rhotics (trills, taps/flaps)	27	15%	178
(Labio-velar) approximants	6	9%	69

Table 6.12 *Secondary articulations and place of articulation*

Place of articulation	Absolute	Share of place	Total of place
Alveolar	67	36%	185
Velar	45	24%	185
Bilabial	42	23%	185
Uvular	14	22%	63
Labio-dental	25	15%	165
Palato-alveolar	15	9%	165
Labio-velar	6	9%	69
Pharyngeal	2	10%	21
Glottal	8	7%	119
Palatal	1	< 1%	176

The strong position of phonemic secondary articulations in the east is in line with Haarmann's (1976a: 114) observation that the number of phonemes per language is noticeably higher in the European east than in the west.

As can be seen in Table 6.11, the different manners of articulation are affected by secondary articulations to a relatively low degree.

The upper limit is a third of the sample languages. For those manners of articulation which are not attested in all the sample languages, the share of secondary articulations is even more restricted. The geographic picture is largely inconclusive in the sense that there is no clear areal preference for any manner of articulation. Therefore we do not provide a separate map for this issue.

The question arises whether or not similar patterns can be observed in correlation to the places of articulation. Our sample languages do not allow secondary articulations with the following places of articulation: interdental, alveo-palatal, retroflex, labio-palatal and epiglottal. For the remaining ten places of articulation, the statistics yield results which are reminiscent of those of manner of articulation: see Table 6.12.

The three places of articulation which are attested universally in our sample also document the highest degree of secondary articulation. The shares are comparable to those of the top-ranking manners of articulation in Table 6.11. Since palatalization is the most important type of secondary articulation, it is hardly surprising that the palatal place cf articulation is subject to phonemic secondary articulation only marginally.

Glottal, pharyngeal and uvular places of articulation are susceptible to secondary articulations predominantly in Northeast and Northwest Caucasian languages. For the remaining places of articulation, the geolinguistic distribution is random, that is, no areal foci can be identified.

6.3.2   Meso-level: Primary Articulations

Haarmann (1976a: 115–116) makes several unsystematic observations about the geolinguistic distribution of certain individual phonemes. He mentions the absence of single phonemes from the phoneme systems cf individual languages and remarks on the commonality of a variety of other phonemes. Ternes (2010: 583–587) comments briefly upon a selection cf specific phonemes and their presence or absence in some of the languages of Europe. On closer inspection, the statistics of the phonemic units reveals rather interesting patterns of structural unity and diversity: see Tables 6.13–6.14.

For expository reasons, we have done statistics only for primary articulations (i.e. secondary articulations were not counted separately). On purely statistical grounds, the phonemes are divided into two classes. Table 6.13 provides the rank order of those phonemic primary articulations which are attested in more than half of our sample languages. This

Table 6.13 *Statistics of phonemic primary articulations which occur in more than half of the sample languages*

Rank	Languages	Share	Phonemes
1–4	185	100%	/p/, /t/, /m/, /n/
5–6	184	99%	/k/, /s/
7	181	98%	/l/
8–9	177	96%	/b/, /d/
10	174	94%	/g/
11	163	88%	/ʃ/
12	160	86%	/r/
13–14	159	86%	/z/, /j/
15	149	81%	/f/
16	146	79%	/v/
17	140	76%	/tʃ/
18	136	74%	/ʒ/
19	133	72%	/ts/
20	117	63%	/x/
21	109	59%	/h/
22	107	58%	/dʒ/

Table 6.14 *Statistics of phonemic primary articulations which occur in less than half of the sample languages*

Rank	Languages	Share	Phonemes
23	69	37%	/w/
24	66	36%	/ʣ/
25	52	28%	/ɲ/
26	48	26%	/ɣ/
27	44	24%	/q/
28	40	22%	/ŋ/
29	39	21%	/ʁ/
30	38	21%	/c/
31	36	19%	/ʝ/
32–33	35	19%	/ʔ/, /χ/
34	34	18%	/ʎ/
35	27	15%	/ɕ/
36	25	14%	/tɕ/
37	24	13%	/ɾ/
38	23	12%	/ʑ/
39	21	11%	/ɬ/
40–41	20	11%	/ç/, /ħ/
42	18	10%	/ʤ/
43	17	9%	/ð/
44–46	16	9%	/θ/, /ʃ/, /tɬ/
47	14	8%	/ɟ/
48	8	4%	/ʀ/
49	7	4%	/ɻ/
50–54	6	3%	/β/, /ʡ/, /ɦ/, /ʧ/, /kx/
55	5	3%	/ɢ/
56	4	2%	/ʊ/
57–59	3	2%	/ʕ/, /qχ/, /ʔħ/
60–62	2	1%	/ʂ/, /ʜ/, /pf/
63–76	1	< 1%	/ɸ/, /ʈ/, /ɖ/, /ɳ/, /ɴ/, /ʐ/, /ɰ/, /ʟ/, /ɥ/, /ʦ/, /ʣ/, /tɕ/, /ɢʁ/, /ʔʜ/

survey is complemented by Table 6.14, which contains the statistical information about those phonemic primary articulations which are attested in less than half of the sample languages.

What strikes the eye immediately is the huge gap of 21 points which separates the last entry of Table 6.13 from the first entry of Table 6.14. This clear-cut distinction of majority and minority configurations precludes the possibility of treating the above data as a continuum. Equally noteworthy is the surprisingly small number of phonemic primary articulations which can be termed truly pan-European, since only four units are reported for each of the 185 sample languages. This means that, already on the meso-level, structural unity is restricted. Diversity is connected to 72 out of 76 phonemic primary articulations (including affricates). 95 per cent of the phonemic primary articulations are attested in fewer than 185 languages, that is, cross-linguistic variation is the rule and not the exception. This observation holds both for positive and negative phenomena.

From an overall perspective, one may say that for the top-ranking 10 per cent in Table 6.13 there is a strong tendency towards positive structural unity. Conversely, the final 10 per cent of Table 6.14 is suggestive of an equally strong tendency towards negative structural unity, because the phonemic primary articulations found at the bottom of Table 6.14 are avoided by 90 per cent or more of the sample languages.

The group of languages which lack one or more of the ten most frequently attested primary articulations overlaps with that of the languages which attest one or more of the 35 least frequently attested primary articulations. Fifteen languages are represented in both groups. Seven of these languages are situated in the Caucasus region, 11 languages are non-Indo-European. Twenty-one of the 35 least frequently attested primary articulations are attested in Northeast and/or Northwest Caucasian languages: see Map 6.11.

Twenty-six of the same class are attested in non-Indo-European languages. On the European map (see Map 6.12), a relatively clear areal pattern emerges regarding those languages which lack one or more of the most frequently attested primary articulations are overwhelmingly peripheral.

Sixteen of these languages are located on the eastern or northern rim of the continent. Superficially, the geographical distribution of the languages which show rare primary articulations does not seem to

Map 6.11 Presence of ranks 42–76 (Table 6.14). Size of dot represents number of features attested; tiny dot indicates no features attested

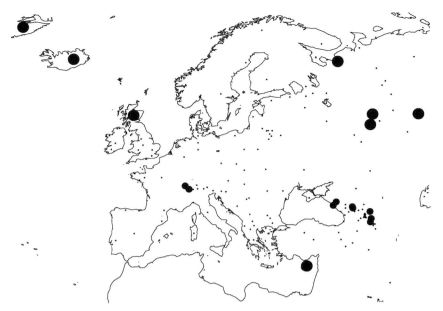

Map 6.12 Absence of ranks 1–10 (Table 6.13). Size of dot represents number of features absent; tiny dot indicates no features absent

be remarkable. However, if we concentrate on those languages which are repeatedly involved with infrequent primary articulations, the situation changes drastically. Languages which show two or more of the rare primary articulations form a chain which encircles the large central region from which rare primary articulations are absent or where they are attested only occasionally. Map 6.13 accounts for the geographical location of those languages which combine the attestation of minority configurations with the absence of majority configurations.

Haarmann (1976a: 116) claims that most of the majority and minority configurations fail to yield an areally significant distribution. Only for a small number of individual phonemes does he assume that there are restrictions on their occurrence in the phonological systems of the languages of Europe such that their absence from certain regions gives rise to a negatively defined area. Our own results, however, are indicative of a considerably higher degree of areal sensitivity of the phonological phenomena under scrutiny than Haarmann admits.

6.3.3 Excursus: Glimpses of Phylum-internal Diversity

In the previous subsections we have alluded repeatedly to aspects of phonological homogeneity versus heterogeneity within language families. To emphasize that genetic relatives do not necessarily behave absolutely the same phonologically, we provide statistical information

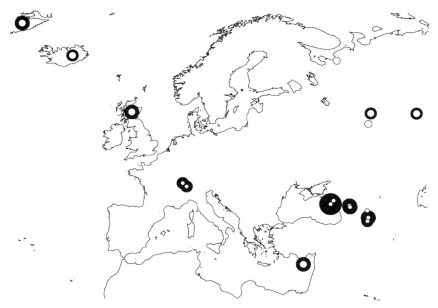

Map 6.13 Attestation of minority configurations (ranks 42–76) and absence of majority configurations (ranks 1–10) in combination. Size of circle represents number of minority configurations attested (black) or number of majority configurations absent (white)

Table 6.15 *Diversity within language families (manner of articulation)*

Family	Trills	Taps	Affricates
Slavic (27)	27 = 100%	0 = 0%	27 = 100%
Uralic (24)	24 = 100%	0 = 0%	22 = 92%
Romance (20)	20 = 100%	4 = 20%	17 = 85%
Germanic (17)	11 = 65%	1 = 6%	10 = 59%

about the structural variation within three branches of the Indo-European language family (Slavic, Romance and Germanic) and the Uralic language family.

In Table 6.15 we determine how many of the members of a given phylum show a given manner of articulation. Since all of the languages have stops, fricatives, nasals and approximants, and lack lateral fricatives as well as lateral affricates, we take account only of those manners of articulation for which variation can be expected. The languages are ordered according to their decreasing size. The values indicate how many of the languages of a phylum/family document the manner of articulation under scrutiny.

There is a marked difference between eastern European languages and western European languages. The Slavic group offers evidence of

Table 6.16 *Diversity within language families (place of articulation)*

Place of articulation	Slavic (27)	Uralic (24)	Romance (20)	Germanic (17)
Labio-dental	27 = 100%	23 = 96%	20 = 100%	17 = 100%
Interdental	0 = 0%	3 = 13%	2 = 10%	5 = 29%
Palato-alveolar	27 = 100%	21 = 88%	9 = 45%	14 = 82%
Retroflex	0 = 0%	0 = 0%	0 = 0%	2 = 12%
Alveo-palatal	3 = 11%	8 = 33%	6 = 30%	1 = 6%
Palatal	27 = 100%	24 = 100%	20 = 100%	14 = 82%
Uvular	1 = 4%	0 = 0%	2 = 10%	5 = 29%
Glottal	8 = 30%	14 = 58%	7 = 35%	14 = 82%
Labio-velar	7 = 26%	2 = 8%	7 = 35%	4 = 24%
Labio-palatal	0 = 0%	0 = 0%	1 = 5%	0 = 0%

homogeneity because all of its members either attest a manner of articulation or lack it altogether. Uralic languages behave similarly regarding trills and taps but fail to reach full homogeneity with affricates. For Romance languages, homogeneity is restricted to the class of trills, whereas there is variation in connection with the other two phonological classes. The Germanic branch of Indo-European is characterized by diversity in all three categories.

We conclude this section with a brief look at the variation within language families concerning place of articulation. Since all the languages show bilabials, alveolars and velars while lacking evidence of pharyngeals and epiglottals, Table 6.16 informs us only about the ten places of articulation which are subject to dissimilarity.

This time the picture is not as straightforward as with manner of articulation. The Slavic languages are especially homogeneous as a group because in six out of ten categories they display absolute solidarity, either by attesting or by failing to attest a given category. In the case of Uralic, solidarity is restricted to four categories. In three of these cases, it is the absence of the place of articulation which unites the languages of this family. Germanic (with two cases of solidarity) and Romance (with three cases of solidarity) tend towards heterogeneity.

The considerations here show that identical genetic affiliation does not guarantee that languages are very similar phonologically. The language families differ, however, as to the degree of structural variation of their members. In comparison to the Slavic languages, Germanic languages, for instance, are relatively dissimilar from each other.

6.4   Conclusions

The conclusions for this chapter are divided into two subsections. Section 6.4.1 provides a discussion of the major insights gained from evaluating the above data. Section 6.4.2 outlines a possible continuation of the project outlined in this study.

6.4.1 Evaluation

It is necessary to state that the languages of Europe are neither all the same phonologically nor do they offer evidence of an overdose of diversity in the realm of phonology. The distribution of phonological properties over the languages of our sample is not entirely random. On the contrary, the above presentation suggests that there are areal factors which shape the phonological diversity or unity of Europe.

We have to state the obvious by saying that the higher the degree of generalization and/or abstraction, the higher the degree of similarity. The more concrete the units are that are compared to each other, the higher is the degree of dissimilarity. The languages of Europe thus are very similar to each other on the highest level whereas they tend to be dissimilar on the lowest level of comparison.

Diversity comes into play on the highest possible level, since languages with two airstream mechanisms can be distinguished from those with only one airstream mechanism. With every subsequent level the degree of structural variation over the sample increases, to culminate at the level of primary articulations. Thus, it can be said that, independent of the macro-level and meso-level, Europe is never fully homogeneous in phonological terms.

At the same time, there is a common core shared by all of the sample languages on all of the levels. This basis of structural similarity shrinks with every step we take in the direction of the micro-level. On the highest level, one of two options – pulmonic versus non-pulmonic – is chosen by 100 per cent of the sample languages. With primary articulations, however, only four out of 76 options are represented in each of the sample languages. Dissimilarity is a crucial factor not only on the level of primary articulations. The differences of the sample languages are not random, however.

The principal differences we observe reflect areal biases. First of all, Ternes' (1998, 2010) assumption that the Caucasian languages display characteristic traits which separate them from the bulk of the European languages finds corroboration in a variety of cases, starting with the non-pulmonic airstream mechanism via the pharyngeal and epiglottal places of articulation down to the many examples of rara and rarissima with primary articulations attested in the Northeast and Northwest Caucasian languages – either exclusively or nearly so. In several cases there is thus a bipartition of Europe, with the Caucasus hosting the representatives of the minority configuration as opposed to the majority configuration which dominates outside this region.

However, this does not mean that the inclusion of the languages of the Caucasus distorts the picture of the areal-phonological composition of Europe. Even if we subtract the Caucasian languages from the sample, Europe does not turn into a fully homogeneous entity. *Mutatis mutandis* the position of Greenlandic in our sample is similar to that of the Caucasian languages, since this member of the Eskimo-Aleut language family behaves largely like other languages situated on the periphery of the continent.

In point of fact, the geolinguistic distribution of the phonological phenomena often corresponds to a distinction of periphery versus centre/interior. Minority configurations tend to occur in languages that are remote from the centre of the European continent. More often than not, these languages are situated on the outskirts or near to the boundaries of Europe. In contrast, majority configurations are found frequently in languages which occupy a sizable portion of the interior of the continent. The territory these languages claim is not only larger than that of the minority configurations but normally also forms an extended and uninterrupted contiguous neighbourhood, whereas the languages which reflect minority configurations may not always be direct neighbours of each other on the periphery.

These distribution patterns are reminiscent of the isoglosses identified by Haspelmath (2001) in his search for evidence of the *Standard Average European* linguistic area. We are hesitant to claim that our data confirm this supposed sprachbund, which has been postulated almost exclusively on the basis of non-phonological phenomena. Nevertheless, several of the phonological properties discussed above yield distribution patterns which reflect a cline from east to west, in the sense that the eastern half of the continent is characterized by preferences which differ from those which are most typical of the western half and vice versa. This rule of thumb holds even if we discount the evidence provided by the languages of the Caucasus region. The overwhelmingly eastern basis of the secondary articulations is a showcase of the east/west divide.

The latter case is also a paradigm case of an areal preference that disregards genetically defined boundaries. The further to the west a Slavonic language is located, the less likely it is to employ phonemic palatalization. In its eastern sister languages, however, palatalization is the rule. Genetically unrelated or only distantly related languages in the Eurasian region behave like their Slavonic neighbours and distinguish plain from palatalized consonants. On a minor scale, similar areal preferences of genetically mixed groups of languages can also be identified with other phonological properties. No language family is absolutely homogeneous. Their internal diversity can often be connected to areal factors.

Yet these are all comparatively vague observations which need to stand the test of dedicated in-depth studies in the future. We are still largely in the dark as to the possibility of identifying correlations and implications. It is of course clear that in the top-down architecture of phonology the lower levels and higher levels are logically connected to each other. However, how categories of the same rank – say, manner of articulation and place of articulation – interact is a problem that calls for closer scrutiny. The catalogue of open questions is large.

6.4.2   Towards Contact Phonology

If genetically unrelated or only distantly related neighbouring languages share phonological properties which are unknown in their closest relatives, what comes to mind first is an explanation which assumes diffusion via language contact. In this study, we have refrained from any kind of explanation of the distribution patterns we have observed. That language contact must be a strong factor in the areal phonology of Europe is beyond doubt. However, there is as yet no fully developed framework within which phonological convergence can be studied systematically.

According to Thomason's (2001: 70–71) borrowing scale, phonological systems are affected by language contact from stage 2 onwards. The processes become linguistically interesting mostly in the final stages, that is, when the degree of bilingualism with the donor language is very high among replica-language speakers. There is ample evidence of the transfer of phonological properties in language contact situations world-wide (Matras 2007: 36–40). Nonetheless, a full-blown linguistic paradigm of contact phonology has yet to be developed. Research into loan phonology mainly enquires into the mechanisms of phonological adaptation of loan-words (Calabrese and Wetzels 2009: 1; Uffmann 2015). However, the phonological treatment of loanwords does not exhaust the phenomenology of phonologies under the conditions of language contact.

When studying the areal diffusion of phonological properties, the distinction of direct and indirect borrowing introduced by Aikhenvald (2002: 33–50) is helpful. However, as Sakel (2007: 17–18) shows, it is relatively difficult to disentangle (overt) matter replication from (covert) pattern replication in the realm of phonology.

The European facts outlined above invite an interpretation that is inspired by insights from the study of language contact. However, one should not mistake any kind of similarity as proof of contact-induced convergence. Owing to the universal constraints on phonological systems, there are far too many chances that structural similarities of languages of the same geographic region arise from general phonological principles and not from language contact. To determine the correct interpretation, it is urgent that the similarities and dissimilarities of the phonologies (not only) of the languages of Europe be recorded and evaluated as completely as possible. It is hoped that this chapter has shown this to be feasible and promising for the field of areal linguistics in general.

Acknowledgements

This study is intended as a preliminary to our project *The Areal-Phonological Atlas of the Languages of Europe* (abbreviated to *Europhonology*). We are grateful to Darja Appelganz, Sonja Hauser, Julia Nintemann, Robin Okrongli and Benjamin Saade for their kind support in technical matters and logistics. We thank Raymond Hickey for inviting us to contribute to *The Cambridge Handbook of Areal Linguistics*. The responsibility for what is said in this chapter is exclusively ours.

Appendix

Sample (185)

Indo-European (98)
Germanic (17) Danish (Standard), Dutch (Standard), English (Standard), English (Cockney), English (Cannock), English (Bolton area), Faroese (Standard), German (Standard), German (Cologne), German (Brig), German (Ladelund), Icelandic (Standard), Low German (East Frisian), Low German (Northern Low Saxon), Norwegian Bokmål (Standard), Swedish (Standard), Yiddish (Standard)

Romance (20) Asturian (Standard), Catalan (Standard), Corsican (Standard), Franco-Provençal (Standard), French (Standard), Friulian (Udine), Italian (Standard), Italian (Genovese), Ladin (Standard), Ladino (Standard), Portuguese (Standard), Romanian (Standard), Romanian (Megleno), Romansch (Puter), Romansch (Surmeiran), Romansch (Sursilvan), Romansch (Sutselvan), Romansch (Vallader), Sardinian (Standard), Spanish (Standard)

Slavic (27) Belorusian (Standard), Belorusian (Dieveniškės), Belorusian (Gervjaty), Belorusian (Lazduny), Belorusian (Zetela), Bosnian (Standard), Bulgarian (Standard), Bulgarian (Dimitrovgrad), Croatian (Standard), Czech (Standard), Czech (Moravian-Slovak), Kashubian (Standard), Macedonian (Standard), Macedonian (Kostur-Korča), Polish (Standard), Polish (Dieveniškės), Polish (Gervjaty), Polish (Lazduny), Polish (Zetela), Russian (Standard), Serbian (Standard), Slovak (Standard), Slovene (Standard), Sorbian Lower (Standard), Sorbian Lower (Vetschau), Sorbian Upper (Standard), Ukrainian (Standard)

Baltic (7) Latvian (Standard), Latvian (Skrunda), Lithuanian (Standard), Lithuanian (Dieveniškės), Lithuanian (Gervjaty), Lithuanian (Lazduny), Lithuanian (Zetela)

Celtic (11) Breton (Standard), Breton (Léonais), Breton (Trégorois), Breton (Vannetais), Cornish (Standard), Irish (Standard), Irish (Northern), Irish (Western), Irish (Southern), Scottish Gaelic (Leurbost), Welsh (Standard)

Indo-Iranian (10) Kurmanji (Standard), Ossetic (Standard), Romani Ajia Varvara (Standard), Romani Bugurdzi (Standard), Romani Burgenland (Standard), Romani Kalderash (Standard), Romani Lithuanian (Standard), Romani North Russian (Standard), Romani Sepecides (Standard), Zaza (Northern)

Others (6) Albanian (Standard), Albanian (Mandrica), Albanian (Salamis), Armenian East (Standard), Armenian West (Standard), Greek (Standard)

Non-Indo-European (87)

Uralic (24) Estonian (Standard), Finnish (Standard), Hungarian (Standard), Karelian (Archangelsk), Karelian (Tikhvin), Karelian (Livvi), Karelian (Valdai), Komi-Permyak (Jaźva), Komi-Zyrian (Standard), Komi-Zyrian (Middle Sysola), Komi-Zyrian (Pečora), Komi-Zyrian (Udora), Livonian (Standard), Mari Hill (Standard), Mari Meadow (Standard), Mordvin Erzya (Standard), Mordvin Moksha (Standard), Nenets (Western Tundra), Saami Central-South (Standard), Saami Kildin (Standard), Saami Northern (Enontekiö), Udmurt (Standard), Veps (Standard), Votic (West)

Turkic (17) Azerbaijani (Standard), Azerbaijani (Iranian), Azerbaijani (Khalaj), Bashkir (Standard), Chuvash (Standard), Crimean Tatar (Standard), Gagauz (Standard), Karachay-Balkar (Standard), Karaim (Galits), Karaim (Eastern), Karaim (Trakai), Kazakh (Standard), Kumyk (Standard), Noghay (Standard), Tatar (Standard), Turkish (Standard), Turkish (Trabzon)

South Caucasian (5) Georgian (Standard), Laz (Standard), Laz (Mutafi), Mingrelian (Standard), Svan (Standard)

Northeast Caucasian (28) Aghul (Standard), Akhvakh (Standard), Andi (Standard), Archi (Standard), Avar (Standard), Bagvalal (Standard), Bezhta (Tlyadal), Botlikh (Standard), Budukh (Standard), Chamalal (Standard), Chechen (Standard), Dargwa (Icari), Godoberi (Standard), Hinukh (Standard), Hunzib (Standard), Ingush (Standard), Karata (Standard), Khinalug (Standard), Khvarshi (Standard), Kryts (Standard), Lak (Standard), Lezgian (Standard), Rutul (Standard), Tabasaran (Standard), Tindi (Standard), Tsakhur (Standard), Tsova-Tush (Standard), Udi (Standard)

Northwest Caucasian (6) Abaza (Standard), Abkhaz (Standard), Adyghe (Standard), Kabardian (Standard), Kabardian (Baksan), Ubykh (Standard)

Others (7) Arabic (Cypriot/Kormakiti), Maltese (Standard), West Greenlandic (Standard), Kalmyk (Standard), Basque (Standard), Basque (Lekeitio), Basque (Marquina)

References

Aikhenvald, Alexandra Y., 2002. *Language Contact in Amazonia*. Oxford: Oxford University Press.

Andersen, Henning, 1986. *Sandhi Phenomena in the Languages of Europe*. Berlin and New York: Mouton de Gruyter.

Anderson, Gregory D. S., 2005. The velar nasal (ŋ). In Haspelmath et al. (eds), pp. 42–45.

van der Auwera, Johan, 1998. Conclusions. In Johan van der Auwera (ed.) with Dónall Ó Baoill, *Adverbial Constructions in the Languages of Europe*. Berlin and New York: Mouton de Gruyter, pp. 813–836.

Bechert, Johannes, [1981] 1998. Notiz über eine Möglichkeit, die historisch-vergleichende Sprachwissenschaft zu vervollständigen, oder: Lesefrüchte zur Verbesserung Mitteleuropas und anderer Weltgegenden. In Winfried Boeder (ed.), *Sprache in Raum und Zeit: Beiträge zur empirischen Sprachwissenschaft*, pp. 13–16. Tübingen: Narr.

Calabrese, Andrea and W. Leo Wetzels (eds), 2009. *Loan Phonology*. Amsterdam and Philadelphia: John Benjamins.

Campbell, Lyle, 2006. Areal linguistics: A closer scrutiny. In Yaron Matras, April McMahon and Nigel Vincent (eds), *Linguistic Areas: Convergence in Historical and Typological Perspective*, pp. 1–30. Houndmills, Basingstoke, UK: Palgrave.

Chirikba, Viacheslav, 2008. The problem of the Caucasian Sprachbund. In Pieter Muysken (ed.), *From Linguistic Areas to Areal Linguistics*, pp. 25–94. Amsterdam and Philadelphia: John Benjamins.

Comrie, Bernard, 1993. Language universals and linguistic typology: Data-bases and explanations. *Sprachtypologie und Universalienforschung* 46: 3–14.

Décsy, Gyula, 2000a. *The Linguistic Identity of Europe,* part 1: *The 62 Languages of Europe Classified in Functional Zones*. Bloomington, IN: EUROLINGUA.

Décsy, Gyula, 2000b. *The Linguistic Identity of Europe,* part 2: *Macrolinguistics and Demostatistics of Europe*. Bloomington, IN: EUROLINGUA.

Ewels, Andrea-Eva, 2009. *Areallinguistik und Sprachtypologie im Ostseeraum: Die phonologisch relevante Vokal- und Konsonantenquantität*. Frankfurt am Main: Lang.

Goedemans, Rob and Harry van der Hulst, 2005. (a) Fixed stress locations; (b) Weight-sensitive stress; (c) Weight factors in weight-sensitive stress systems; (d) Rhythm types. In Haspelmath et al. (eds), pp. 62–77.

Haarmann, Harald, 1976a. *Grundzüge der Sprachtypologie*. Stuttgart: Kohlhammer.

Haarmann, Harald, 1976b. *Aspekte der Arealtypologie: Die Problematik der europäischen Sprachbünde*. Tübingen: Narr.

Hajek, John, 2005. Vowel nasalization. In Haspelmath et al. (eds), pp. 46–49.

Hall, T. Alan, 2011. *Phonologie: Eine Einführung*. Berlin and New York: de Gruyter.

Haspelmath, Martin, 2001. The European linguistic area: Standard Average European. In Martin Haspelmath et al. (eds), *Language Typology and Language Universals*, pp. 1492–1510. Berlin: Mouton de Gruyter.

Haspelmath, Martin, Matthew S. Dryer, David Gil and Bernard Comrie (eds), 2005. *The World Atlas of Language Structures*. Oxford: Oxford University Press.

van der Hulst, Harry (ed.), 1999. *Word Prosodic Systems in the Languages of Europe*. Berlin: Mouton de Gruyter.

IPA, 1999. *Handbook of the International Phonetic Association: A Guide to the Use of the International Phonetic Alphabet*. Cambridge: Cambridge University Press.

Jakobson, Roman, [1930] 1971. *Selected Writings. Phonological Studies*. Berlin, New York and Amsterdam: Mouton de Gruyter.

Kortmann, Bernd and Johan van der Auwera (eds), 2011. *The Languages and Linguistics of Europe: A Comprehensive Guide*. Berlin and New York: de Gruyter Mouton.

Ladefoged, Peter and Ian Maddieson, 1996. *The Sounds of the World's Languages*. Oxford: Blackwell.

Lewy, Ernst, [1942] 1964. *Der Bau der europäischen Sprachen*. Tübingen: Niemeyer.

Maddieson, Ian, 2005. (a) Consonant inventories; (b) Vowel quality inventories; (c) Consonant–vowel ratio; (d) Voicing in plosives and fricatives; (e) Voicing and gaps in plosive systems; (f) Uvular consonants; (g) Glottalized consonants; (h) Lateral consonants; (i) Front rounded vowels; (j) Syllable structure; (k) Tone; (l) Absence of common consonants; (m) Presence of uncommon consonants. In Haspelmath et al. (eds), pp. 10–41, 50–61, 78–85.

Matras, Yaron, 2007. The borrowability of structural categories. In Yaron Matras and Jeanette Sakel (eds), *Grammatical Borrowing in Cross-linguistic Perspective*, pp. 31–74. New York: Mouton de Gruyter.

Matras, Yaron, April M. S. McMahon and Nigel Vincent, 2006. *Linguistic Areas: Convergence in Historical and Typological Perspective*. New York: Palgrave Macmillan.

van Pottelberge, Jeroen, 2005. Ist jedes grammatische Verfahren Ergebnis eines Grammatikalisierungsprozesses? Fragen zur Entwicklung des *am*-Progressivs. In Torsten Leuschner, Tanja Mortelmans and Sarah De Groodt (eds), *Grammatikalisierung im Deutschen*, pp. 169–191. Berlin and New York: Walter de Gruyter.

Sakel, Jeanette, 2007. Types of loan: Matter and pattern. In Yaron Matras and Jeanette Sakel (eds), *Grammatical Borrowing in Cross-linguistic Perspective*, pp. 15–30. New York: Mouton de Gruyter.

Stadnik, Elena, 2002. *Die Palatalisierung in den Sprachen Europas und Asiens: Eine areal-typologische Untersuchung*. Tübingen: Narr.

Stolz, Thomas, 2006. Europe as a linguistic area. In Keith Brown et al. (eds), *Encyclopedia of Language and Linguistics*, vol. IV, pp. 278–295. Amsterdam: Elsevier.

Stolz, Thomas, 2007. Being monosyllabic in Europe: An areal-typological project in statu nascendi. In Andreas Ammann (ed.), *Linguistics Festival: May 2006, Bremen*, pp. 97–134. Bochum: Brockmeyer.

Stolz, Thomas, 2010. Phonologie und areal Europa. In Uwe Hinrichs (ed.), *Handbuch der Eurolinguistik*, pp. 597–622. Wiesbaden: Harrassowitz.

Stolz, Thomas, Aina Urdze and Hitomi Otsuka, 2010. Europäische Liquiden: Rhotische und laterale Phoneme – sprachgeographisch betrachtet. In Cornelia Stroh (ed.), *Von Katastrophen, Zeichen und vom Ursprung der menschlichen Sprache: Würdigung eines vielseitigen Linguisten, Wolfgang Wildgen zur Emeritierung*, pp. 93–114. Bochum: Brockmeyer.

Stolz, Thomas, Aina Urdze and Hitomi Otsuka, 2011. The sounds of Europe: Velar and post-velar fricatives in areal perspective. *Lingua Posnaniensis* 53 (1): 87–108.

Stolz, Thomas, Aina Urdze and Hitomi Otsuka, 2012. Seltene Klänge: Zu den Marginalien der arealen Phonologie Europas. In Cornelia Stroh (ed.), *Neues aus der Bremer Linguistikwerkstatt: Aktuelle Themen und Projekte*, pp. 1–22. Bochum: Brockmeyer.

Ternes, Elmar, 1998. Lauttypologie der Sprachen Europas. In Winfried Boeder et al. (eds), *Sprache in Raum und Zeit: Beiträge zur empirischen Sprachwissenschaft*, pp. 139–152. Tübingen: Narr.

Ternes, Elmar, 2010. Phonetische Eigenschaften der Sprachen Europas. In Uwe Hinrichs (ed.), *Handbuch der Eurolinguistik*, pp. 577–596. Wiesbaden: Harrassowitz.

Thomason, Sarah Grey, 2001. *Language Contact: An Introduction*. Washington, DC: Georgetown University Press.

Uffmann, Christian, 2015. Loanword adaptation. In Patrick Honeybone and Joseph Salmons (eds), *The Oxford Handbook of Historical Phonology*, pp. 644–666. Oxford: Oxford University Press.

Velupillai, Viveka, 2012. *An Introduction to Linguistic Typology*. Amsterdam and Philadelphia: John Benjamins.

Wagner, Heinrich, 2002 [1964]. Nordeuropäische Lautgeographie. In Birgit Benes, Uta Fromherz and Fredy Gröbli (eds), *Heinrich Wagner: Beiträge zur typologischen Sprachgeographie*, pp. 19–88. Bern: Peter Lang.

7

Word Prominence and Areal Linguistics

Harry van der Hulst, Rob Goedemans and Keren Rice

7.1 Introduction

The goal of this chapter is to present an overview of the consequences of language contact, with the understanding that linguistic areas arise through contact (Hickey 2010), focusing on word prominence (i.e. stress and pitch-accent). Section 7.2 deals with preliminary issues which are relevant to the study of contact-induced change. In Section 7.3 we briefly present some cases of convergence involving changes in word prominence attributable to contact. Section 7.4 makes the point that language contact often leads to hybrid systems. Realizing that language contact can lead to both convergence (linguistic areas) and divergence, Section 7.5 focuses on divergence of an ancestral system, partly due to language contact, into a variety of closely related systems, taking Basque as a case study. Given the rather limited availability of systematic studies of contact-induced change in word prominence, in Sections 7.6 and 7.7 we present two detailed original case studies. Section 7.6 deals with the languages of North America where, drawing on Rice (2010, 2014), but based on a larger sample of languages, various instances of language contact are studied, focusing on areal distributions that cut across language families. Section 7.7, drawing on Goedemans (2010a), offers a case study concerning the aboriginal languages of Australia, in which we find variation between initial stress and penultimate stress in a geographically concise contact area. Section 7.8 presents some conclusions and directions for further research.

7.2 Preliminaries

7.2.1 What is a Linguistic Area?

The definition of 'linguistic area' as the domain of study of 'areal linguistics' has been the subject of much debate. We accept the conclusion of

We would like to thank Ksenia Bogomolets, Matthew Gordon, Raymond Hickey, José Hualde, Larry Hyman, Sarah Thomason and Victor Friedman for valuable comments and suggestions.

Campbell (2006) that the notion 'linguistic area' refers to the epipheno-menal result of an accumulation of linguistic changes that are due to *language contact*. Convergence of properties in 'a couple of' languages that are 'not too closely related' points the linguist in the direction of suspect-ing the influence of language contact and thus offers an opportunity to study the manner in which languages acquire properties *laterally*, or due to external factors, as opposed to *vertically*, or due to inheritance, as expressed in the family tree model.[1]

7.2.2   Word Prominence

The phrase 'word prominence' covers a wide variety of properties that can vary independently. A number of terms are used in the literature, includ-ing (word) prominence, (word) accent, tone, stress and pitch-accent.

(1)   Dimensions of word prominence (see van der Hulst 1999b, 2012, 2014b)
        a. Presence/absence of word accent (or word stress[2])
        b. Location of accent (word edge, weight sensitivity, boundedness)
        c. Phonetic correlates of accent (e.g. enhanced duration, amplitude, pitch; taken separately or together often referred to as 'stress' or, if pitch is prevalent, as 'pitch-accent')
        d. Phonotactic correlates of accent (e.g. richer vowel contrast, more complex syllable structure, tonal contrast exclusively or richer on the accented syllable)
        e. Presence/absence of word rhythm
        f. Type of rhythm (edge prominence, direction, weight sensitivity)

Given this 'deconstruction' of word prominence, it is clear that changes in this aspect of language, whether attributed to internal or external causes, can be of many different kinds. Limiting our attention to effects of language contact, we expect languages to potentially influence each other in many different ways, even with reference to such a 'limited' aspect as word prominence.

Word prominence is an especially worthwhile area to study, as it has often been noted in the literature that it 'proves particularly vulnerable to systemic reshaping within language contact' (Salmons 1992: 7). Similarly, Matras (2009: 231) remarks that, within phonology, 'prosody seems to be

---

[1] Vertical and lateral effects are not mutually exclusive. An internally driven change might be enhanced by contact with a language that has already implemented this change or is more advanced in implementing it.

[2] Many linguists use the terms 'accent' and 'stress' interchangeably. We here follow a tradition that regards 'accent' as the abstract lexical mark and 'stress' as a particular bundle of phonetic properties (e.g. duration, amplitude, fundamental frequency) that realize accent. This gives a stress-accent language. If accent is realized mainly in terms of F0, we speak of a pitch-accent language. Languages that have fully predictable occurrences of prominence peaks can be said to have 'stress' that does not realize a lexical accent mark, although we believe that such cases are rare and, if seemingly occurring, 'stress' in those cases may be due to 'edge prominence' and phrasal rhythm.

more prone to cross-linguistic replication in contact situations than segmental phonology, with stress figuring in-between the two.'[3]

7.2.3 The Distribution of Stress/Accent Systems in the Languages of the World

Various examples of linguistic areas that display convergence of word prominence have been mentioned in the literature (e.g. Hayes 1995; Jakobson 1971; Salmons 1992).

(2)   Areas of convergence
   a. The area around the Baltic with languages from different families having initial stress (Dogil 1999a)
   b. Afroasiatic languages like Hausa (and other Chadic languages) which got tone from neighbouring Niger-Kordofanian languages (Ruhlen 1975: 62)
   c. Areas in Southeast Asia sharing tonal properties (Benedict 1948)
   d. Occurrence of iambic word rhythm in North American languages (Hayes 1995)

Since Salmons' study, which focuses on (2a), more typological surveys of word prominence systems have become available. One such source is StressTyp2, a database that contains information on stress systems of over 700 languages.[4] For reference to general characteristics regarding the distribution of word prominence see Goedemans and van der Hulst (2005a, 2005b, 2005c, 2005d) and Goedemans (2010b), which are based on a subset of the current StressTyp dataset. Comparing these distributions with the geographical spread of language families, two types of findings can be reported. On the one hand, word prominence properties often do cut across language families that are spoken in contiguous areas (possible evidence of convergence), while on the other hand, we also see several examples of rich diversity within language families (evidence of divergence). In particular, van der Hulst and Goedemans identify a number of general areal tendencies (corroborated by the studies in van der Hulst, Goedemans and van Zanten 2010) in the distribution of prominence.

(3)   Areas of convergence
   a. European systems that are not sensitive to weight tend to have initial stress (see van der Hulst 2010)
   b. Austronesian systems tend to have penultimate stress (see Section 7.7 and Goedemans 2010b)

---

[3] 'Word prominence' can be subsumed under the more general phrase 'word prosody' which covers all phonetic and phonological properties that are dependent on the 'word domain' such as lenition and fortition processes that mark word edges, and vowel harmony.
[4] See Goedemans and van der Hulst (2009); URL of StressTyp2: http://st2.ullet.net.

    c. Arabic dialects are generally sensitive to weight (see Hayes 1995; van der Hulst and Hellmuth 2010)

    d. South American languages are generally insensitive to weight, with stress near the right edge of the word (see Wetzels and Meira 2010)

    e. Australian languages generally have initial stress (except in the north) and are not weight-sensitive (see Section 7.7 and Goedemans 2010b)

Section 7.7 offers an in-depth discussion of Australian patterns. For additional information we also refer to van der Hulst, Goedemans and van Zanten (2010), which contains extensive chapters of word prominence patterns in all continents of the world, with occasional explicit references to areal characteristics.

7.2.4　Loan Phonology

Before turning to linguistic areas in particular, it is worthwhile mentioning some aspects of loan phonology (Kang 2010, 2011; Uffmann 2015), as the incidental patterns that we find in borrowing form a foundation for looking at more extensive patterning that might arise through contact and the formation of what we call linguistic areas. When words are borrowed, the pattern of the source language may be respected (preservative borrowing) or not (neglectful borrowing). We identify a number of possible scenarios that have been reported in the relevant literature (Broselow 2009; Davis, Tsujimura and Tu 2012; Kang 2010, 2011; Kubozono 2006) in (4).[5]

(4)　Borrowing scenarios
    A. Preservative borrowing
        a. Pattern of source language fits the pattern of recipient language: words are adopted with no change
        b. Pattern of source language differs from pattern of recipient language: foreign words are admitted into recipient language as exceptional pattern
    B. Neglectful borrowing:
        a. Pattern of source language and recipient language differs: the recipient system is imposed on borrowings from source language[6]
        b. Creation of a default pattern specific to loans

The list in (5) presents illustrative examples that we collected from the literature (in particular Davis, Tsujimura and Tu 2012; Kang 2010, 2011),

---

[5] In this discussion we ignore the important distinction between contact among adults and among child language learners.

[6] Sometimes foreign words may be clipped so that their stress pattern will fit the receiving language.

identifying the specific realization of word prominence (involving tone, pitch-accent and stress-accent) in both the source and the recipient language.[7]

(5)　　Borrowing word prosody
　　　　A. Source (tone) / Recipient (tone)
　　　　　　Preservation of tone in tone language: Hausa > Gwari
　　　　　　Neglect of tone in tone language: Mandarin > Lhasa Tibetan
　　　　B. Source (tone) / Recipient (pitch-accent)
　　　　　　Preservation of tone in pitch-accent language: Mandarin > Yanbian Korean
　　　　　　Neglect of tone in pitch-accent language: Chinese > Japanese
　　　　C. Source (tone) / Recipient (stress)
　　　　　　Preservation of tone in stress language: not attested
　　　　　　Neglect of tone in stress language: Chinese > English
　　　　D. Source (pitch-accent) / Recipient (tone)
　　　　　　Preservation of pitch-accent in tone language: not attested
　　　　　　Neglect of pitch-accent in tone language: Japanese > Thai
　　　　E. Source (pitch-accent) / Recipient (pitch-accent)
　　　　　　Preservation of pitch-accent in pitch-accent language: not attested
　　　　　　Neglect of pitch-accent in pitch-accent language: Japanese > Korean
　　　　F. Source (pitch-accent) / Recipient (stress)
　　　　　　Preservation of pitch-accent in stress language: not attested
　　　　　　Neglect of pitch-accent in stress language: Japanese > English
　　　　G. Source (stress) / Recipient (tone)
　　　　　　Preservation of stress in tone language: English > Cantonese
　　　　　　Neglect of stress in tone language: French/English > Vietnamese
　　　　H. Source (stress) / Recipient (pitch-accent)
　　　　　　Preservation of stress in pitch-accent language: not attested
　　　　　　Neglect of stress in pitch-accent language: French/English > Japanese
　　　　 I. Source (stress) / Recipient (stress)
　　　　　　Preservation of stress in stress language: very common
　　　　　　Neglect of stress in stress language: default stress English > Finnish

Where a property is said to be preserved from one prosodic type into another type, this implies that the location of a property is preserved but not necessarily its phonetic cues. Thus, if stress is preserved in a tone system, the stress cue is reinterpreted as a tone and vice versa. The summary in (5) is, we believe, useful in providing clear illustrations of

---

[7] Here we mention the examples found in these sources, without taking issue with specific cases.

the consequences of borrowing, which, then, might also be expected to show up in linguistic areas.[8]

7.2.5   A Theory of Word Prominence Change

In this section we briefly survey some of the kinds of changes that have been identified in word prominence, whether attributable to vertical or lateral factors. As pointed out in Section 7.2.2, the holistic notion 'word prominence' comprises numerous smaller properties which, independently, can be subject to change; we will consider some of these here.

   Taking 'primary accent/stress' and rhythm to be the main components of many prominence systems, we first mention factors that give rise to the notion of primary accent/stress. It has been suggested (see for example Hyman 1977 and Gordon 2014) that word accent/stress may result as the reanalysis of intonational peaks as properties of word edges. Penultimate accent systems are common in languages of the world (Goedemans and van der Hulst 2005a). Hyman (1977) suggests that the preponderance of this accent location may be due to the occurrence of an intonation pitch-accent H+L on the right edge of the rightmost word in an intonational phrase. To avoid tonal crowding on the final syllable, the HL melody would spread out over the final two syllables, giving the penultimate syllable the appearance of prominence due to bearing the H-tone. This then may lead to interpretation of this syllable as being accented at the word level. Gordon (2014) pays special attention to the development of word prominence from phrasal intonation and suggests that, even synchronically, some cases of alleged word accent may be more properly analysed in terms of intonational structure.[9]

   Another source for the emergence of an accentual system is tone (see Ratliff 2015 about tonal change in general). Salmons (1992) in particular discusses the change from tonal to accentual systems, resulting from the fact that the distribution of specifically high tones may develop constraints (up to the maximal occurrence of one H tone per word) which, then, trigger a reinterpretation of tone and pitch-accent and eventually stress-accent.

   Once accent is present, changes in the factors that determine accent location may be related to, or caused by, changes in another component of the phonology or the grammar at large. In classical Latin, accent

---

[8] In addition to loan phonology, another area of research that is relevant to the study of language contact is second language phonology. There is a considerable literature on how speakers perceive and produce word prominence patterns of languages that they are learning: see, for instance, Altmann (2006), Altmann and Kabak (2011), Kijak (2009), Peperkamp and Dupoux (2002), and for the relation between second language acquisition and phonological change, Eckman and Iverson (2015). The three areas of loan phonology, second language phonology and language contact share a number of interesting common results, but space limitations prevent us from discussing these here.

[9] While the languages discussed above involve reanalysis where the changes appear to arise internal to the system, reanalysis may also be triggered from outside the system. Reanalysis may also lie behind the change from Germanic initial accent to right-edge accent, due to the presence of Latin loans (Lahiri, Riad and Jacobs 1999).

placement was sensitive to vowel length (among other factors). Contrastive vowel length was lost in Romance languages such as Italian and Spanish, but vowels that were long kept the accent. Accent placement thus became partially lexicalized, with specification of these unpredictable accents in the lexicon (see Roca 1999).

Another important factor that can change the determination of accent location is emergence of syllable weight, when intrinsic properties of syllables (in particular syllable rhymes) phonologize by becoming determinants in stress location. Penultimate heavy syllables (containing a long vowel or coda consonant) can influence the relocation of final accent (which is already somewhat disfavoured) to penultimate accent.

Another kind of accentual change involves an edge switch for accent, as can be seen by reference to two Slavic languages, Polish and Czech. Polish has penultimate accent, while Czech has initial accent. Many languages with penultimate accent have an initial edge prominence ('secondary stress') on the first syllable, which in specific contexts might be the locus of an intonational pitch-accent (see van der Hulst 2014b). This may motivate the learner to regard the initial rather than the penultimate syllable as accented. Such a change can then be said to be caused by the intonational system.

Regarding rhythm, we suggest that this aspect of word prominence may arise as the result of grammaticalizing low-level phonetic properties. For instance, a language can acquire 'notable' rhythm when low-level rhythm (which we take to be a universal property of all languages) is exaggerated and causes allophonic changes in phonemes. It is even possible for rhythm to fully lexicalize (and lose some of its 'natural' phonetic properties) becoming 'abstract', still guiding for example allomorphic choice and phonotactic asymmetries, while the language has meanwhile been subjected to a new kind of rhythm. Such mismatches, which reflect a form of hybridity and which underscore the need for a 'deconstructed' analysis (see Section 7.4), are discussed in Gordon (2014, 2016).

Changes in rhythm type may arise due to the influence of the same intrinsic properties of syllables that can affect the location or primary accent/stress.

Given the deconstruction of word prominence into several factors (see 1), a few other patterns of change would have to be considered in a fuller account.[10] Many of these changes can be seen as motivated by grammar-internal factors or in terms of acquisition strategies. This leaves a small remnant for changes that could be said to rely crucially on language contact, but, of course, even internally motivated changes

---

[10] Another area of change concerns the distinction between bounded and unbounded systems, which we omit here for reasons of space.

can be triggered or enhanced by external influences due to languages in which such factors play a role. Illustrating the potentially complex interaction of internal and external factors, Salmons (1992) offers extensive discussion of specific patterns of change that involve the transition from tonal systems to pitch-accent systems to stress systems, which he sees as potentially resulting from internal factors and reanalysis, although language contact may contribute to such internally motivated changes. Moravcsik (1978) also remarks that changes in word prominence, whether potentially internally driven or not, are often probably due to language contact, precisely, as we have already mentioned, because they are the first to be affected by such contact.

7.3 Convergence

Salmons (1992) focuses on language contact in early northern Europe, especially between Germanic and Celtic, but including Italic, Finnish, Saami and other Finno-Ugric languages which together, he argues, form an areal fixed initial stress group. He pays particular attention to the joint Germanic–Celtic shift to initial accent (shared with Italic). It has been debated whether this shift is attributable to language contact with an unknown substrate language in northern Europe or to Finno-Ugric. Salmons opts for the latter.[11]

  Salmons' conclusion that the presence of initial stress in this area is due to language contact receives support, he argues, when one considers the distribution of stress patterns in the languages of the world. Based on Ruhlen (1975, 1977), Salmons finds that initial accent is absent in 16 of Ruhlen's 28 genetic groupings (including Austroasiatic, Nilo-Saharan, Sino-Tibetan and Palaeosiberian). In many other families the average number of languages with initial stress is under 7 per cent. The bulk of initial stress systems come from Australian (Section 7.7) and Uralic (with 16 out of 23 languages listed in Ruhlen having initial stress). Interestingly, the six Indo-European languages in his survey (Latvian, Czech, Irish,[12] Swedish, Danish, Dutch) all belong to the linguistic area that forms the subject of Salmons' survey. Final stress also has a biased genetic distribution, with '63.9 per cent' of the languages with this stress system coming from three families (Penutian, Altaic, Indo-European) based on Ruhlen's counts. The Indo-European languages in this group are French, Armenian and Iranian languages, and the latter form part of a linguistic area with Altaic languages. Penultimate stress appears to have a much more equal

---

[11] For reviews of Salmons' book see Peter (1994), Greiner (1994) and Lehiste (1994).

[12] Only Northern and Western Irish have initial stress. Southern Irish has a complicated system determined by vowel length and syllable weight which attracts stress to non-initial syllables. This may have been due to contact with Anglo-Norman after the late twelfth century or to internal tensions due to the rise of long vowels in non-initial syllables in Middle Irish (or due to a combination of both). See Hickey (1997, 2014).

distribution in language families (which correlates with its preponderance as a fixed accent type: Goedemans and van der Hulst 2005a; Hyman 1977).

Results such as these show that accentual types can run in families (as might be expected). This makes resemblances *across* families more likely to be the result of language contact than of independent development toward certain common types. Thus, the widespread occurrence of initial stress in the northern European initial stress area proposed by Salmons is therefore plausibly the result of language contact.[13]

Salmons includes a survey of examples of accentual change due to language contact; to these we add further examples in the list below.[14] We suspect that a broader survey of the literature might reveal many more of these examples.

(6)   Examples of contact-induced changes in word prominence
   a. Scandinavian tonal systems lost in the dialects spoken in Finland, a non-tonal language (Haugen 1970)
   b. Within Bantu, languages range from fully tonal to restricted tone or pitch-accent systems, to stress systems (as in Swahili) (Salmons 1992)
   c. Loss of tone in African pidgins (Fanagalo, Town-Bemba, pidgin Hausa) (Heine 1973)
   d. Presence of fixed stress in African pidgins (Kituba) (Heine 1973)
   e. Loss of tone in some Caribbean pidgins and creoles (Alleyne 1980)[15]
   f. Loss of tone in Danish in contact with Low German (Gårding 1977)
   g. Loss of tone in Swedish spoken in the United States (Ureland 1971)
   h. Russian dialects bordering on Karelian-Olonec-Vepsian speaking areas show a tendency toward initial stress (Veenker 1967)
   i. Hungarian may have influenced the emergence of initial accent in Czech and Slovak (Thomason and Kaufman 1988; Veenker 1967)
   j. Boanon, a Mongolian language, acquiring tone under the influence of Linxia, a Chinese language (Li 1986)
   k. Transfer of a stress system in Iroquoian languages Cayuga to Onondaga and Seneca (Michelson 1988)
   l. Influence of penultimate stress in a dialect of French spoken in Brittany as a possible influence on penultimate stress in Breton (Sommerfelt 1962)
   m. Final stress in Turkic languages, Armenian, Iranian languages (Hyman 1977)

---

[13] Peters (1994), in his review of Salmons (1992), criticized Salmons' use of percentages to make this point.

[14] We thank Sally Thomason for bringing some of these examples to our attention. See Thomason and Kaufman (1988) for other examples.

[15] Island Caribbean. Sranan and Saramaccan in Surinam are exceptions.

> n. English influence on Stoney Dakota (Siouan) in having right-edge stress patterns similar to English in addition to the expected second-syllable Dakota stress pattern (Shaw 1985)
>
> o. Germanic initial primary accent added accent determined from the right edge, as in Romance with French loanwords (van der Hulst, Hendriks and van de Weijer 1999)
>
> p. Cree-Montagnais-Naskapi (Algonquian) final stress attributed to French (Mackenzie 1980)
>
> q. Shift in Hungarian dialects near the former Yugoslavia border from initial stress to fixed penultimate stress (Thomason 2001: 143) (note that Serbo-Croatian varieties generally have free stress, but in this dialect there is also fixed penultimate stress)
>
> r. Latvian complex accent system replaced by first-syllable stress under influence of Livonian (Finnic) (Thomason 2001)

Clearly, a list like this does not allow for any general conclusions or hypotheses. What is missing in most cases are detailed analyses of the circumstances and mechanisms involved. Thus, while there is no shortage of reported cases of accentual change due to language contact, there is a clear need for more detailed studies of specific cases and we will offer two such studies in Sections 7.6 and 7.7.

7.4　Hybridity

Although, as argued in Section 7.2.5, in general it is difficult to determine whether change in a word accent system is motivated by contact or not, we take hybridity to be an indication of contact-induced change. By hybridity we mean that a system clearly incorporates aspects of systems that are, under usual assumptions, compatible with one another (i.e. can be shown to follow from a single uniform analysis). Languages can be hybrid in their prominence system in many ways; several of these types of hybridity will be illustrated in our case studies in Sections 7.6 and 7.7.

(7)　Types of hybridity
　　　A. Competing patterns
　　　　　a. Due to loans, a regular pattern may have a limited number of exceptions
　　　　　b. Exceptions may increase in number and, if originating from a single language, form a second pattern, that may be restricted to an independently identifiable lexical stratum
　　　　　c. The new (default) pattern may start being applied to non-loans, but not all
　　　　　d. The change may lead to variability

B. Deviant patterns
   a. Due to contact, a pattern may change one of its parameters, leading to a theoretically possible yet more marked pattern
   b. Due to contact, words of different lengths may have different patterns
C. Incomplete patterns
   a. Due to contact with other patterns, a pattern may display incompleteness in that certain parameters are not set, e.g. absence of primary stress

An example of a stratal effect (7Ab) is found in European languages belonging to the Germanic group which, as a whole, have Romance-influenced right-edge stress, while also maintaining traits of the Germanic initial stress. The Romance influence on Germanic languages (partly via English) has given rise to a 'pan-European right-edge stress pattern, from which only Icelandic has escaped' (van der Hulst, Hendriks and van de Weijer 1999; Lahiri 2015).

While hybridity can be a sign of language contact, we must realize that hybridity can also result from the synchronic presence of different stages of historical developments. As mentioned in Section 7.2.5, when a language changes its rhythmic bias, a synchronic accent of certain phonological regularities may require the postulation of the older pattern at a deeper level of analysis, while the new pattern is accounted for at a later stratum (see Gordon 2014). In a general sense, hybridity results from the presence of two (or more) systems, whether originating from different stages of a single language or from different languages that are in contact.[16]

7.5   Divergence: The Case of Basque

In Section 7.2.1 we noted that contact-induced change can result in cases in which a set of closely related languages displays a wide variety of word prominence systems, although it is likely that such fragmentation can also result without much external influence. There are several cases with a sometimes strikingly rich proliferation of word prominence types within one language family.

(8)   Examples of divergence
   a. Basque dialects (see below)
   b. Bantu dialects/languages (Carter 1973; Clements and Goldsmith 1984; Goldsmith 1988; Hyman 1989; Odden 1988; Salmons 1992: 46 ff.)
   c. Japanese dialects (Haraguchi 1979; Uwano 1999, 2012)

---

[16] Dresher and Lahiri (1991) speak of metrical incoherence to characterize such cases.

    d. Arabic dialects (Hayes 1995; van der Hulst and Hellmuth 2010)
    e. Scandinavian dialects (Bye 2004; Gårding 1977; Riad 1998)

Modern-day Slavic languages exhibit quite a bit of diversity (see Dogil 1999b; Salmons 1992: 49). To this, we add the languages spoken in Mesoamerica, which show a rich variety of tonal accentual systems, although in these cases several language families have been claimed to be involved (see van der Hulst, Rice and Wetzels 2010). Several more examples of divergence can be found in van der Hulst, Goedemans and van Zanten (2010), which offers an overview of the distribution of word prominence systems in all language families of the world.

    In all these cases, a group of languages belonging to a single (macro-) family display an enormous amount of diversity, while preserving certain common properties. We suggest that it would be very interesting to look into the internal and external causes that result in the divergence processes that lead to such diversity. As an example of such an approach we discuss the case of Basque.

    Hualde (1999) presents an overview of the different contemporary accentual systems found in Basque dialects.[17] The Basque dialects present a great diversity of word-prosodic systems, especially when one takes into account the size of the area in which Basque is spoken (only about 135 × 35 km.). This area shows many patterns of convergence and divergence: see Hualde (2007). The Basque word-prosodic systems range from lexical pitch-accent and stress-accent systems in the Western dialects to weight-insensitive accent on the second syllable in some Central Basque dialects and weight-insensitive accent on the penultimate syllable in, for instance, the High Navarrese variety of Baztan. Thus, there is not only a distinction between pitch-accent and stress-accent systems and between weight-sensitive and weight-insensitive systems, but also, within the weight-insensitive accent systems, accent can be assigned from either the right or the left edge.[18] Hualde distinguishes the following main accentual types.

(9)   Basque word prominence systems
    a. the *Western* type, which is a lexical system with unaccented and accented stems and affixes, and prominence in accented words realized as pitch drop or stress, depending on region (types: Markina, Gernika-Getxo, Antzuola)
    b. the *Central* type, in which accent is assigned from the left word edge
    c. the *Hondarribia/Old Labourdian* type, in which accent seems to be assigned from the right word edge, with variety between dialects

---

[17] We thank José Hualde for additional information and helpful comments on this section of our chapter.

[18] The scope and nature of this enormous variety in such a small territory is reminiscent of the situation in the Caucasus (see Kodzasov 1999).

    d. the *Souletin* type (with unmarked final and marked penultimate stress) as a special type

    e. the *Western Navarrese* type represented by Goizueta, with both lexical stress *and* lexical pitch-accent

In this subsection we focus on some changes that have occurred in Western varieties of Basque which Hualde (2003) attributes to contact with Spanish. This case reveals a number of subtle and perhaps unexpected responses to confrontation with a prominence system that is different from the influenced dialects.

As a point of departure, Hualde takes the Western Basque dialects (spoken in the provinces of Bizkaia and Gipuzkoa and neighbouring areas), and, in particular, the Northern or Coastal Bizkaian pitch-accent type. A hypothesis for how the Western Navarrese (Goizueta) type may be historically related to Northern Bizkaian is developed in Hualde (2012). Western Basque is a system with accented and unaccented morphemes, the majority being unaccented. A pitch pattern is associated with phrases. In particular, Hualde proposes initial %LH and final H*L accentual patterns, the former distributed over two syllables and the latter on the final syllable. A phrase final unaccented word in the Gernika-Getxo type receives a *derived accent* on the final syllable (the Markina type has a penultimate default; see (14)). In (10) and (11) we illustrate the Gernika-Getxo type:

(10)   %L H-   H*L
           | | | /
        [la gu nen] [a ma ri]   'to the friend-SING's mother'

(11)   %L H*L   H*L
           | | / | /
        [la gú nen] [a ma ri]   'to the friend-PLURs' mother'

The plural has a morphologically determined accent, in particular the plural suffix is pre-accenting; see Hualde (1999) for paradigms showing this. On the surface, all lexical accents are on a non-final syllable because the accented suffixes are actually pre-accenting. For lexical roots there are some tendencies for their location depending on the local dialect. For instance in three-syllable accented roots, the accent is generally on the first syllable in some dialects (e.g. *bélarri* 'ear', *tómate* 'tomato', *pátata* 'potato'), but on the second in other towns (*belárri, tomáte, patáta*). We refer to Hualde (2012) for details.

Hualde (2003) shows how this Western type has developed into different kinds of systems under the possible influence of Spanish. All Western Basque speakers are Basque/Spanish bilinguals.

The Western pattern has given rise to two responses, shown in (12) and (13).

(12)   Reanalysis
Response A. In Bilbao Basque (as well as in varieties of the Central type) the initial LH in (11) has been reanalysed as the phonetic realization of a pitch-accent on the second syllable, attributed to the fact that in Spanish a comparable pitch rise is an important cue to its stress-accent.

(13)   Pitch rise ⟹ accent
Response B. In the Antzuola dialect, the initial H is suppressed, and there is a high pitch-accent on the penultimate syllable followed by a low on the final syllable.

(14)   Accent ⟹ pitch rise

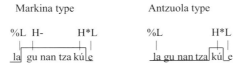

'the one for the friend'

This change makes the Antzuola type sound much more like Spanish.

All responses reflect an influence of the Spanish stress cue, a rise to high pitch on the stress-accented syllable. In response A it is the initial rise that is identified with the accent (because rises identify accent location in Spanish), whereas in response B the accent location is identified with a rise (again because rises identify accent location in Spanish). Hualde suggests that the change in the Antzuola system with penultimate accent led to changes in Azkoitia and other cases, giving rise to third syllable stress-accent [+3] (with non-finality, i.e. avoidance of final accent), a reinterpretation that can easily result from the ambiguity that is caused by words of up to four syllables where a penultimate location could be reinterpreted as a third syllable location. The difference would only be clear in words with five syllables or more.

For younger speakers in Getaria the [+3] system is changing to [+2]. The change from [−2] to [+3] and the change from [+3] to [+2] could be influenced by the existence of [+2] dialects (see above).

Summarizing (broken lines indicate influence, solid lines indicate change):[19]

(15)

---

[19] '+2' means second syllable accent, etc. '−2' means penultimate accent.

This case study shows how language contact, including contact between dialects, can lead to surprising consequences. In particular, Spanish contact triggered changes that in one case (response A) caused an analysis of a non-accentual pitch rise as accentual and in another case (response B) a change in the pitch realization of the accent (and the entire word contour). Both responses are based on identification of accents with pitch rises.[20]

7.6 North American Linguistic Areas: Evidence for Convergence?

Several linguistic areas have been identified in North America, but accent has not been considered as a factor that defines these areas. In this section we first present three case studies of accent patterns in areas that are argued to be linguistic areas, asking what these areas reveal about contact-induced change. We then look more broadly at the continent as a whole, asking whether there is support for the observation that North America might be a linguistic area in terms of accent patterns.

7.6.1 Three Areas of Convergence

In this section we offer a study of three linguistic areas of California for which evidence of convergence has been given (see discussions in Campbell 1997 and Mithun 1999; see Haynie 2012 for the most recent discussion of two of these areas). The grounds for speaking of convergence for these linguistic areas are quite different. In two cases there is evidence for the borrowing of words, while in the third there is no such evidence, and the linguistic factors that define this third area are quite different. We will ask what these areas tell us about word prominence and areal phenomena more broadly rather than about contact-induced change specifically.

   It is important to keep in mind that we do not have detailed descriptions of accentual systems for many of the languages addressed in this section. We can, generally, refer to the placement of 'primary stress', but often not to 'secondary stress'. Also, there is no detailed discussion of the realization of accent available for many of the languages. As Golla (2011: 209) points out, 'Accentual uses of pitch and tonal phenomena occur widely in the languages of the northern part of the California region, but in most instances the documentation is poor.'

7.6.1.1 Clear Lake Linguistic Area (California)

One well-defined linguistic area in California is Clear Lake, located approximately 100 miles north of San Francisco. This area includes the

---

[20] See Hualde (2000) and Hualde et al. (2002) for additional details.

following languages (the language family is given in parentheses): Lake Miwok (Utian), Patwin (Wintuan), Eastern Pomo (Pomoan), Southeastern Pomo (Pomoan) and Wappo (isolate, or Yukian, see Campbell 1997: 132, Golla 2011: 192–193, Mithun 1999: 554 for discussions and different perspectives). This list of languages is taken from Campbell (1997: 336); Mithun (1999: 317) includes examples from a second Wintuan language, Nomlaki.

Campbell and Mithun identify a number of phonological characteristics shared by languages of the Clear Lake area. Their particular focus is on how Lake Miwok, part of the Clear Lake area, differs from genealogically related languages. For instance, Lake Miwok, like its neighbours, has contrasting phonation types in stops and affricates, while other Miwok languages do not. Lake Miwok and some of the other languages in the area have a voiceless lateral and a lateral affricate; other Miwok languages do not; Lake Miwok and other Clear Lake languages all have five short and five long vowels, while other Miwok languages have six short and six long vowels. The source of innovation in Lake Miwok, discussed by Callaghan (1964), is borrowing: Lake Miwok borrowed words from Hill Patwin and from Southeastern Pomo, with the sounds not found in other Miwok languages introduced through those borrowings. Campbell (1997: 129) notes that Lake Miwok is geographically isolated from the other Miwok languages, and speakers had frequent contact with speakers of Eastern Pomo, Southeastern Pomo, Foothills Patwin, and Wappo, as reflected in loanwords. Golla (2011: 107) reports on the relationship between Patwin and Southeastern Pomo, noting that Patwin influence was strong in the Southeastern Pomo area, with Patwin-Pomo bilingualism common.

We now examine word accent in this area, asking if it too shows areal characteristics. In order to discuss word accent in most of these languages, it is necessary to say something about morphology, so information about this is included in the discussion below.

Word stress in Wappo appears on the first syllable of the stem. The language has some prefixes as well as derivational and aspectual suffixes.

We have not found sources that discuss stress in the Wintuan language Patwin. In Wintu (Pitkin 1984), stress is described as falling on one of the first two syllables of the stem – the first heavy syllable, with the first syllable if neither is heavy. Golla (2011: 146) notes that both Wintu and Patwin have prefixes indicating location and direction; both languages also have suffixes.

The position of word accent in the Pomoan languages is addressed in Moshinsky (1974). Moshinsky (1974: 56) proposes that stress was predictable in Proto-Pomoan, falling on the first stem vowel. The stem was frequently preceded by a monosyllabic prefix, so stress was often on the second syllable. Languages in the family developed in different ways.

In Eastern, Central and Northern Pomo, this pattern was usually maintained, with stress generally on the second syllable, although there is not always clear evidence for a synchronic morphological analysis. McLendon (1975: 12) notes that in Eastern Pomo, stress falls on the root, with second syllable stress being the predominant pattern. Northeastern Pomo often moved stress on to a previously unstressed syllable.

Kashaya, another Pomoan language, has a complex system. Basically, primary stress can appear on one of the first three syllables of the word. Buckley (2013) treats the language as quantity-sensitive and iambic, with the first syllable invisible for purposes of stress. Moshinsky (1974) notes that Southern Pomo has the most aberrant stress pattern, with stress on the penultimate syllable of a phrase; see Walker (2013), who also finds penultimate stress on words and phrases and secondary stress on the first syllable. Southeastern Pomo is regarded by Moshinky as having regular stress (1974: 57), with word stress generally on the first syllable of nouns, verbs and adjectives. While Moshinsky notes that there are a few exceptions where it does not fall on the first vowel (it is on the second vowel if there is a directional prefix or if the first vowel is a part of reduplication), Buckley (2013) argues that primary stress falls on the first syllable, while directional prefixes and the first vowel of the stem may have secondary stress.

While the Pomoan languages in question differ in detail, there is in general morphological sensitivity, with stress attracted to the root in most of the languages. The position of primary stress is determined from the left edge, and is near the left edge of the word in languages of this family. Even in Northern Pomo, there is secondary stress on the first syllable.

The Miwok languages are largely suffixing, with pronominal prefixes that fall outside the domain of stress. Word accent appears on one of the first two syllables of the root, being attracted to heavy syllables, with heaviness defined slightly differently depending on the language. Lake Miwok has word stress on the first or second syllable of the root; prefixes do not take stress (Callaghan 1964). In particular, primary stress falls on the second root syllable if it is heavy, and otherwise on the first syllable.

The languages of the Clear Lake area (Lake Miwok, Patwin, Eastern Pomo, Southeastern Pomo, Wappo) share several characteristics with respect to accent. Most noticeable is that primary stress occurs near the left edge of either the word or the root/stem. Given that these languages are largely suffixing (as are Miwok, Wintuan and Pomoan languages that are not in the area), stress is quite likely to fall on one of the first two syllables. In general, all the languages under consideration have the root as the domain of stress (Southeastern Pomo is the exception). Some of the languages show quantity sensitivity (Lake Miwok, other Miwok, Kashaya), and some do not (Eastern Pomo, Southeastern Pomo, Wappo).

The left-edge orientation of primary stress is clearly a characteristic that defines this linguistic area, and thus can be considered an areal phenomenon. Whether this is a result of contact is not certain, since the major languages that border the Clear Lake area are genealogically related to languages of the area and generally share the same orientation of stress. It is possible that the languages of the area retained similar accent patterns because they form an area. Kashaya, geographically the most remote member, has the most divergent pattern in the Pomoan family, although it maintains much of the basic pattern of the related languages with the position of accent determined from the left edge. The homogeneity that is found in word accent could result from convergence, or from inheritance, with the areal effects inhibiting change.

7.6.1.2 Northwestern California

Another part of California that has been identified as a linguistic area is Northwestern California. Haynie (2012), based on Conathan (2004) and others, notes good evidence for areal feature spread in Northern California, and particularly in the Northwestern California area.

The Northwestern California area differs from the Clear Lake area in several ways. While in the Clear Lake area, there is evidence for lexical borrowing between languages, this is not so in the Northwestern California area. Conathan (2004) argues that the Northwestern California area is characterized by functional convergence, but not by actual borrowing or calquing.

Conathan defines the Northwestern California area as consisting of the following languages: Tolowa (Athabaskan), Hupa (Athabaskan), Karuk (isolate), Chimariko (isolate), Yurok (Algic) and Wiyot (Algic). Karuk and Chimariko are sometimes grouped together in the Hokan stock. Conathan notes that the language group is somewhat controversial, and that she could have included Shasta (Hokan) and Wintu (Wintuan) as well.

Haynie (2012) examines several phonological and morphological characteristics that are claimed to mark an even broader area, Northern California, based on a spatial autocorrelation technique that examines features likely to have diffused geographically rather than genealogically or by chance, to determine whether feature diffusion is a likely scenario in this area (Haynie 2012: 88). Haynie concludes that the Northwestern California area, discussed in this section, and the Clear Lake area, discussed in Section 7.6.1.1, show evidence for feature diffusion, while Northern California as a whole is 'more like a collection of smaller diffusion zones' (Haynie 2012: 89).

The phonological characteristics of Northwestern California that Haynie discusses are summarized below, with some additional characteristics discussed in Jany (2009). Several of the languages have plain, ejective and aspirated stops (Tolowa, Hupa, Chimariko); Yurok has plain and ejective stops; Wiyot has plain and aspirated stops; Karuk has plain stops. Hupa and Chimariko have a back velar; the others do not. Tolowa and Wiyot have a lateral fricative; Yurok has both a plain and ejective lateral fricative; Hupa has a lateral fricative and ejective affricate; Karuk and Yurok have neither. Hupa has a velar nasal; none of the other languages do. Tolowa, Hupa, Yurok and Wiyot have labialized consonants, while the other languages do not (Jany 2009); Tolowa has retroflex consonants while the others do not (Jany 2009). The languages also differ in their vowel inventories (ranging from three to six vowels; some have length contrasts, some have nasalized vowels). There are clearly considerable phonological differences between the languages in this group, as Conathan (2004) and Haynie (2012) conclude.

Turning to word accent, there are also differences between the languages. In terms of domain, Tolowa, Karuk, Yurok and probably Wiyot take the word as the domain, Hupa has the word as the domain of accent with the morpheme also playing a role, while Chimariko takes the root as the domain of accent. Wiyot determines the location of accent from the left edge, as does Hupa as recorded by Sapir; later Hupa has accent on the first long vowel and on the root if there is no prefix long vowel (see Gordon and Luna 2004 on Hupa). Karuk is similar, with accent on the first long vowel, with default to the last vowel. In Chimariko, accent is generally on the penultimate syllable of the root. The various languages are quantity-sensitive. In terms of morphology, Yurok and Wiyot are largely suffixing, with some prefixes; the others are largely prefixing; Karuk has both prefixes and suffixes.

Languages in this group may have lexical accent (Tolowa), or the position of accent may be predictable. Accent may take the word or the root as its domain and it might respond to weight (Yurok, Shasta). It may appear near the left edge (Hupa, Wiyot, Karuk), but stress can also be near the end of the word (Hupa default in the later recordings; Karuk default).

Jany (2009: 32) comments extensively on similarities in stress systems in these and a few other languages:

> Stress systems are often described in detail in the grammars consulted. However, the phonetic correlates of stress are not always mentioned. In general, stress patterns show many similarities in Northern California. Immediate neighbours of Chimariko, Hupa, Shasta, and Wintu, all show weight-sensitive stress systems. While their weight hierarchies are slightly different, all have CVV as their heaviest syllable. Root stress, as well as penultimate stress and leftward attraction of stress, are also very common in the area. Shasta, for example, has penultimate stress, but moves the stress in longer sequences to the first preceding heavy syllable. Acoustic correlates of stress include pitch and intensity for Hupa. For Shasta, a high–low pitch tonal accent has been described. Hence the acoustic correlate of stress in Chimariko, which is pitch, is also attested in other languages of the area. Given that stress is easily

transferred through language contact, it is likely that the languages in Northern California have shifted their stress patterns as a result of multilingualism in the area. For Chimariko it can be speculated that vowel length on stressed syllables was developing as a contact phenomenon given the weight-sensitive stress systems of neighbouring languages with CVV as the heaviest syllable type.

Conathan (2004) takes a different perspective in her discussion of the area. She notes that this is an area of intense cultural interaction, but with little lexical borrowing. She says specifically that 'Local convergence of phonological features is conspicuous in its absence' (2004: 167). Conathan remarks that the three languages Karuk, Hupa and Yurok, all genealogically distinct, are the 'core' members of this area, and their inventories are quite different; she attributes this to lack of lexical borrowing between these languages (Conathan 2004: 169). Golla (2011) remarks that, given the close social and ceremonial ties, intergroup marriage and a moderate degree of multilingualism, 'it is surprising how few of the distinctive phonological, lexical, or grammatical features of Hupa-Chilula can be attributed to direct Yurok influence', further noting that lexical borrowings are almost non-existent. What Conathan finds most noteworthy about the Northwestern California linguistic area is the existence of grammatical borrowing without lexical borrowing. Thus, she finds evidence of contact effects in certain components of the grammar – tense and aspect marking, classifier systems, second person prominence in argument marking, loan translations, word order – but she does not find loanwords and phonological convergence. Mithun (2010) too notes a number of structural parallels in languages of this area (and in North America more broadly).

Conathan (2004: 175–179) identifies a variety of reasons for why there might be an absence of lexical borrowing, including the absence of a dominant language in terms of population size, the overall rarity of bilingualism, an overall egalitarian society with multidirectional bilingualism combined with the absence of language shift or a lingua franca, and efforts to avoid mixing languages. With respect to multilingualism, she points out that it arose largely from interlingual marriages.

These languages, unlike those of the Clear Lake area, do not show many similarities in their word accent systems. Perhaps the commonalities that Jany (2009) identifies – weight sensitivity, realization as pitch – are the phonological parallels to the kinds of contact effects that Conathan identifies in the Northwestern Californian languages. Within the phonological domain, a study of intonational patterns would be worthwhile, as this might be an area where convergence would be more likely. Matras (2009: 231–233) specifically notes the susceptibility of prosody, referring largely to word-level prosody, to shift under contact conditions. He suggests that prosody is peripheral in conveying meaning, being prototypically a form of expression of emotive modes, and thus operating at the level of the speech act rather than the word level. He further notes that 'This allows speakers to mentally disconnect prosody more easily from the matter or shape of words', making it prone to change.

While the Clear Lake area likely involves both areal and genetic changes, this is less clear in the Northwestern California area, where even between genetically related languages there are several differences, there is no clear evidence of areal convergence, and absence of clear genetic relationships between other languages makes it difficult to ascertain if there are divergences.

7.6.1.3 Yuman-Takic

Hinton (1991) presents a detailed study of a group of languages in southern California, making the case that Yuman languages and a class of Uto-Aztecan languages known as Cupan formed a linguistic area at some point. Hinton argues that Yuman languages had a major influence on the Cupan language group (1991: 148), with the Cupan languages (Luiseño, Cupeño, Cahuilla) evolving to resemble the Yuman languages phonologically under the influence of a Yuman substratum that was replaced by the Cupan languages. Hinton shows that there are several characteristics that are shared by Yuman and Cupan languages, but are not reconstructed for Proto-Uto-Aztecan and are generally not present in the neighbouring Esselen, Chumashan and Salinan languages. The traits that Hinton examines are segmental, with a focus on unusual segments that are reconstructed for Proto-Yuman but not for Proto-Uto-Aztecan, and are found in Cupan languages but not in other Uto-Aztecan languages of the area. These include a kw/qw distinction, phonemic in Proto-Yuman and in Luiseño and allophonic in Cahuilla and Cupeño. Other characteristics found in Proto-Yuman, not in Proto-Uto-Aztecan, and in Cupan languages but not in other nearby Uto-Aztecan languages, include a distinction between s and retroflex s (also in a nearby Uto-Aztecan language, Serrano), xw, ñ (not in Luiseño), ly (not in Luiseño), r/l. Hinton further notes that Cahuilla and Cupeño share a small vowel inventory with Proto-Yuman (three vowels with allophonic variation), while Proto-Uto-Aztecan and most Uto-Aztecan have a larger vowel inventory (five vowels).

What about word accent? Yuman languages have accent near the right edge of the word. There is variation across Uto-Aztecan in terms of stress placement, but Cahuilla, Cupeño and Luiseño, while they differ in their patterns, all have primary stress near the left edge of the word. Of the other Takic languages, a larger group in which the Cupan languages fall, Tübatulabal has no main stress, with the placement of stress determined from the right edge of the word, and Chemehuevi has stress on the second syllable. We have not found information on Serrano and Gabrielino, two other Takic languages. While there are clearly segmental influences of Yuman languages on the Cupan languages, as detailed by Hinton (1991), it does not appear that the accent system was subject to contact effects in terms of merging. Thus, this area suggests that, while stress is viewed as subject to borrowing (see Matras 2009), borrowing of segmental features may occur without borrowing of the stress system.

7.6.1.4   Summary: Linguistic Areas of California

We have surveyed three areas of California that have been identified as linguistic areas. The three different areas investigated lead us to different conclusions. In one, Clear Lake, word accent is a factor that contributes to the linguistic area, although its origin (genealogy, contact, both) is not clear. In another, Northwestern California, accent resembles segmental properties in not showing obvious areal effects. In a third case, Yuman-Takic, several segmental features suggest an area, but accent does not appear to be involved in defining this area.

7.6.2   A Survey of Accent Patterns in North America

Hayes (1995) remarks on the distribution of iambicity in North America, noting that iambic patterns are more common in North America than elsewhere in the world. Mithun (2010) looks at a number of parallels in morphosyntactic patterns across North America, arguing that 'The Americas provide rich examples of language contact' in terms of structural parallelisms 'even in the absence of borrowed words and morphemes' (Mithun 2010: 691). In this section we examine some of the similarities in accent patterns in languages of North America in order to study whether there are any broad generalizations that might be drawn.

First we report on findings related to a study of word prominence systems in languages around the world, drawing on Goedemans' (2010b) study of cross-linguistic patterns of stress, which are based on the StressTyp database.

We begin with fixed versus variable (weight-sensitive) stress. Due to limitations of space, we do not provide details, but simply summarize findings.

Based on language family (a total of 40 families; within a family, languages may fall into both categories), 24 families have languages that are quantity-insensitive (fixed stress), and 26 of the families have languages that are quantity-sensitive (variable) with respect to primary stress. Goedemans (2010b: 651) reports that in the StressTyp survey, 278 languages (55.5 per cent) showed fixed, or quantity-insensitive, stress, while 222, or 44.5 per cent, have variable, or quantity-sensitive, stress. The difference between the numbers of North American families showing fixed and variable stress is probably not significant (recall that the count is based on families, not on languages).

The specific location of primary stress in quantity-sensitive languages is also of interest. In the 222 quantity-sensitive languages examined by

Goedemans, primary stress is located on one of the leftmost two syllables in around 15 per cent and on one of the rightmost two syllables in around 30 per cent of the languages (2010b: 655); the next most common pattern is stress located on any syllable (unbounded), followed by stress on the right edge, but not restricted to the rightmost two syllables (~13 per cent) and then by stress location being unpredictable (e.g., lexical, irregular, no primary stress). This suggests that the most common pattern is for variable stress to be determined from the right (around 43 per cent of the languages in the survey).

The numbers for North America are by family unless there are differences between languages within the family, in which case the family is counted in both categories left and right. Languages that are considered to be count systems within StressTyp – foot assignment starts at one edge, but primary stress occurs on the other edge – are considered in terms of the position of primary stress, not in terms of the edge from which it is determined. Given this, 11 of the families in North America have languages with primary stress near the left edge, while six have it near the right edge. Since we are not counting individual languages, but rather patterns within a language family, it is not clear whether the numbers are comparable with those in Goedemans (2010b). If they are, languages of North America exhibit a different bias in terms of the placement of primary stress than Goedemans found, with a preference for left-edge primary stress in North America but right edge generally.

We next consider the edge at which primary accent occurs in the quantity-insensitive languages, conflating word edge and root/stem edge. In the sample, 12 families have languages with stress on the final or penultimate syllable, while 11 have left-edge oriented primary stress. For quantity-insensitive languages, Goedemans (2010b) includes information about whether stress is initial, second syllable, antepenultimate, penultimate or final. In the StressTyp survey, at the left edge, stress is more likely to fall on the first syllable – around 32 per cent of the languages – than on the second syllable – around 4 per cent of the languages, while at the right edge, stress is more likely to fall on the penultimate syllable (around 37 per cent of the languages) than the final syllable (around 17 per cent). In the North American survey, there are slightly more families with languages that mark stress at the end of the word, although the sample size is quite small and the difference is very small and most likely not significant.

Compared then with the StressTyp survey, North America shows some differences. Approximately equal numbers of families have languages with quantity-insensitive and quantity-sensitive stress systems, while the StressTyp survey finds more quantity-insensitive languages. Furthermore, there appears to be a preference for accent falling near the left edge in quantity-sensitive North America, but near the right edge generally. Finally, in quantity-insensitive languages, somewhat more languages show final stress, in keeping with patterns noted in StressTyp. Based on this evidence, it appears that North America as a whole shows some distinct patterns when compared with other languages in StressTyp; more careful study with counts based on similar criteria would clearly be worthwhile to determine whether accent patterns indeed define North America as a linguistic area.

7.7 Australia (the Arnhem Land Clash)

A particularly striking example of an areal phenomenon related to stress (reported in Goedemans 2010a) can be found in Arnhem Land and neighbouring areas in the Northern Territory of Australia.[21] In this section, the case will be presented anew, drawing from additional examples found in continued research on the stress systems of languages in the area.

   Australia is divided into two linguistic areas. Across most of the continent, languages from only one family are spoken. We refer to these as the Pama-Nyungan languages, a term coined by Ken Hale (see Dixon 1980) from the word for 'man' in the languages spoken in the northeast and southwest of Australia. Opposed to this continent-wide unity we find an area in the northern parts of the Northern Territory and Western Australia in which linguistic diversity is abundant. Languages from no fewer than 15 different families, the so-called non-Pama-Nyungan languages, are spoken there.[22] Moreover, a few isolated 'pockets' of the Pama-Nyungan group can be found there as well.

7.7.1 Two Different Patterns: Initial and Penultimate Stress

When we look at the stress systems of the languages in these two areas, we observe a striking difference. The dominant stress pattern for Australian Aboriginal languages is one of the most common patterns we find in the languages of the world (see Goedemans 2010b). Although minor variations and exceptions exist, almost all Pama-Nyungan languages place primary stress on the first syllable and secondary stress on all odd syllables to the right of that primary stress (Initial stress: shorthand 'I'). The pattern is illustrated in (16) with some examples from Djambarrpuyngu, a language spoken on Elcho Island off the northeast coast of the Northern Territory (Wilkinson 1991).

(16)   Djambarrpuyngu
          ˈputuru   'ear'
          ˈŋurru ˌpandala   'bush apple'
          ˈlithan ˌmara ˌnhamirr   'dry CAUS+FOURTH+PROP'

---

[21] Although not geographically correct, we will refer to this area as Arnhem Land for the sake of convenience.

[22] *Ethnologue*, 17th edition, Lewis et al. (2013).

This language does not place a secondary stress on the final syllable, producing a final lapse in words with an odd number of syllables. In a common variant on the pattern exemplified in (16) a secondary stress is placed on the final syllable of words with an odd number of syllables. Maranunggu (Daly River, Tryon 1970) stresses the final syllable of *lángkaratetì* 'prawn', while in Djambarrpuyngu it remains unstressed in *púthuru*.

Among the non-Pama-Nyungan languages, however, many languages place the primary stress on the penultimate syllable, while secondary stresses appear on even syllables before the penult (penultimate stress: shorthand 'P'). The examples in (17) from Limilngan, another Arnhem Land language (Harvey 2001), illustrate the pattern.

(17)   Limilngan
     uˈwagi   'fire'
     ˌlatdinˈyayan   'crocodile'
     ˌuruˌgalitjˈbagi 'bandicoot'

The cases that are most interesting to us appear in the border areas between groups of languages with penultimate stress and those featuring initial stress. It is quite clear that in the hotbed of diffusional activity that Arnhem Land is (Heath 1978, Dixon 1980), languages influence each other on many linguistic fronts, and stress is no exception. We observe a host of patterns that seem to have features of both the patterns in (16) and (17), but which are in fact different from both. We will call these systems 'hybrids' and we will show below that these hybrids do not randomly select features from contact stress patterns. Rather, there is a distinct order to their behaviour which allows us to draw a continuum between the patterns in (16) and (17) with discrete steps, all but one of which can be filled with an example language from the Arnhem Land area. Moreover, we will show why these hybrids are of considerable theoretical importance. To understand this fully, we must first briefly explain the basics of the theory that students of stress use in their field.

7.7.2   Deriving the Patterns

To represent the Djambarrpuyngu pattern in (16) we adopt the so-called metrical approach (Hayes 1995; Liberman and Prince 1977), in which patterns like those in (16) can be derived in two steps. First, syllables are grouped into binary feet (from right to left or from left to right). These feet can be left strong (trochaic) or right strong (iambic). In words that contain an odd number of syllables the left-over syllable at the end of the parse can be left unparsed or form a monosyllabic foot. After footing, a second step (called the End Rule) promotes the leftmost or rightmost strong syllable to the status of primary word stress. Given these parameters, the patterns illustrated in (16) can be analysed as shown in (18). For Djambarrpuyngu we assign trochees from left to right and apply the End Rule left. A final left-over syllable remains unparsed.

(18)   Djambarrpuyngu
    a.   *   b.   *
      (* .) (* .) (* .)   (* .) (* .)
      ˈlithan ˌmara ˌnhamirr   ˈŋurru ˌpaṇḍala

Maranunggu is identical, except for the fact that a left-over syllable will be parsed as a monosyllabic foot. In Limilngan we assign trochees from right to left and apply the End Rule right. In this case, an initial left-over syllable cannot be parsed as a monosyllabic foot because this would create a stress clash, which is universally disallowed (see van der Hulst 2014c). In (19) we summarize the three analyses.

(19)

Parameters	Djambarrpuyngu	Maranunggu	Limilngan
Footing (LR/RL)	LR	LR	RL
Foot type (trochee/iamb)	trochee	trochee	trochee
Monosyllabic foot (yes/no)	no	yes	(no)
End rule (L/R)	L	L	R

Let us now turn to the hybrid systems. Looking at these parameters, we could envisage a continuum between true I (initial) languages like Djambarrpuyngu and true P (penultimate) languages like Limilngan. A small change (as a result of diffusional pressure) in parameter settings with respect to the values that deliver true right-edge or true left-edge patterns in (19) will alter the stress system of the language in question, moving it towards the other end of the continuum, slightly changing the orientation of stress to one of the word edges. The striking observation with respect to the Arnhem Land contact area is that we find example languages for the full range of possible changes in parameter settings. Before we present those languages, we must address one more theoretical problem which we encounter when we consider a language like Nakara (Eather 1990). This language only deviates from Djambarrpuyngu in that it assigns secondary stress from right to left instead of left to right. The primary stress remains firmly on the first syllable, as shown in (20).

(20)   Nakara
      ˈdiɟːaɽaˌbaga 'he emerges'

We observe that, although the step that Nakara takes towards the right edge of the continuum is a minor one, we run into a theoretical problem. The Nakara pattern is not a logical option, given the set of parameters available to us. In a standard metrical system, we should assign feet starting at either the right or the left edge and then promote one of the feet to primary stress. Nakara seems to indicate that the choice of edge for primary stress and the starting edge of footing for secondary stresses must be stated separately. Cases like Nakara, as well as many other considerations, have prompted van der Hulst (1996) to deviate from standard metrical theory, as explained above, by separating the algorithms for the assignment of primary and secondary stress. Contrary to standard metrical practice, he claims that primary stress is assigned first, after which secondary stress is assigned using its own set of rules (see Goedemans and van der Hulst 2014 for supporting arguments for this position). In quantity-insensitive languages[23] primary and secondary stress may be assigned along the following lines.[24]

(21)   *Parameters for primary stress*: Create a bisyllabic domain (|...|)
          Edge (L/R)
          Type (trochee/iamb)
       Parameters for secondary stress: ((...))
          Footing (LR/RL)
          Foot type (trochee/iamb)
          Assign more than one foot (iterative: yes/no)
          Monosyllabic foot (yes/no)

There is no need for an End Rule in this approach because as a matter of principle the strong syllable in the primary stress domain is the primary stress. Application of these principles to (20) leads to the representation in (22).

(22) |ˈ* .| (* .)
          ˈdiɟːaɾaˌbaga

Adopting this alternative model, Table 7.1 presents the Arnhem Land hybrid stress languages in a logical step-by-step 'tour' of parametrical changes from Djambarrpuyngu-type languages to Limilngan-type languages (each parameter represented in bold indicates the crucial change with respect to the languages above it; iterative foot assignment is indicated by an asterisk * after the direction setting, and we leave out the settings for monosyllabic feet since they are not relevant to the discussion).[25]

   We can see that the large variety[26] of intermediate stress systems on our continuum can be straightforwardly analysed once we adopt the

---

[23] These are languages not using the internal make-up of syllables in the stress assignment rules.

[24] These distinctions refer to the parameters we use in the StressTyp database to describe the stress patterns of the world's languages. We ignore some parameters that we do not need in this section.

[25] Languages in an area that is as diffusionally active as this one will have scores of exceptions to regular patterns. Large subsets of exceptions might be seen as 'a first step' towards the other end of the continuum. There are example languages in this respect, but for reasons of space, we will not discuss them here. See Section 7.7.3, however, for a discussion of exceptions as a sign of instability.

[26] Note that one logical variety is missing in the scheme. There are R and L mirror images for most patterns, but not for Ngankikurrungkurr. This conspicuous absence is theoretically relevant and we will come back to it in Section 7.7.5.

Table 7.1 *Arnhem Land hybrid stress languages*

Main | Secondary	Description, language and example
L/tr | LR*/tr	Primary stress on the first syllable, secondary on alternates after it. **Dyambarrpuyngu** ˈlithan ˌmara ˌnhamirr
L/tr | **RL***/tr	Primary stress on the first, but secondary on the penult and alternates before it. **Nakara** ˈdiɟːaɽa ˌbaga
L/tr | **RL**/tr	Primary stress on the first, but only one secondary stress at the right edge. **Waanyi** (Osbourne 1966) ˈwabinbara ˌulu 'for turtles'
L/**Ø**[27] | RL*/tr	Secondary stress on the penult and alternates before it. Primary stress on the first or second, depending on which is stressed based on the RL rhythm. **Ngankikurrungkurr** (Hoddinott and Kofod 1988) ˈweri ˌfepi 'cave' aˈnimpirr ˌmire 'firefly'
none | LR*/tr	Secondary stress on the first and alternates after it. No primary stress. **Rembarrnga** (McKay 1975) ˌkamu ˌnuŋku 'white ochre'
LR/tr | RL*/tr	Secondary stress on the penult and alternates before it *and* one secondary stress on the first (for which we use the primary stress domain). **Anindilyakwa** (Leeding 1989) ˌningkwirri ˌpwikwi ˌrriwa 'you three'
RL/tr | LR*/tr	Secondary stress on the first and alternates after it *and* one secondary stress on the penult. **Yanyuwa** (Kirton 1977) ˌmaɽuwa ˌṛala 'cousin'
none | RL*/tr	Secondary stress on the penult and alternates before it. No primary stress. **Wardaman** (Merlan 1994) ja ˌwarrga 'liver'
R/tr | LR/tr	Primary stress on the penult and only one secondary stress on the first. **Umbugarla** (Davies 1989) no example available
R/tr | **LR***/tr	Primary stress on the penult, secondary stress on the first and alternates after it. **Nunggubuyu** (Hore 1981) ˌrawu ˌrrumuguˈrrumu plant species
R/tr | **RL***/tr	Primary stress on the penult, secondary stress on alternates before it. **Limilngan** ˌuru ˌgalitjˈbagi 'bandicoot'

theoretical separation of primary and secondary stress. Without it, the analyses for all these hybrid patterns form a much greater challenge. It would seem, then, that Arnhem Land is a show case for the validity of this separation.

---

[27] The unspecified main stress domain allows main stress to end up on the first or second syllable, whichever one is made 'strong' by iterative secondary stress assignment from right to left (see Goedemans, van der Hulst and Visch 1996 for a discussion of this unusual type of stress system called a count system; see also note 26 and the discussion in Section 7.6.2). In our view, count systems are hybrids situated well towards the centre of the left-to-right spectrum. One could say that languages like Ngankikurrungkurr are still within the left half, since the primary stress domain is located there, but they obviously occupy a niche one step further to the right than, for example, Waanyi, in that they have got rid of the fixed initial primary stress. Interestingly, Ngan'gityemerri (Reid 1990), a dialect of Ngankikurrungkurr, is of the Djambarrpuyngu type, placing primary stress on initial syllables, while alternates thereafter carry secondary stress. However, that language also shows distinct signs of right-edge diffusional pressure, since in many five-syllable words secondary stress occurs on the penult or final instead of the third syllable.

7.7.3 Exceptions and Other Signs of Instability

The first possibility that comes to mind when we think of languages that adopt specific features from neighbouring languages involves plain exceptions due to the borrowing of words with preservation of their original stress pattern. When that effect becomes so large that significant parts of the lexicon exhibit the alternative pattern (or a common variant of it) we should include that pattern in the stress description of the language as belonging to a set of 'regular' exceptions. In our view, abundance of exceptions in many languages in the area may point to high diffusional activity. We have seen in Section 7.7.2 that there is an abundance of hybrid stress types in Arnhem Land that form intermediate stages between true I and true P languages. Add to that the fact that most of the languages we looked at have scores of exceptions, and we have all the ingredients for a boiling cauldron of metrical activity. This might mean that some (or all) of the hybrid patterns we have encountered are unstable; they are transitional, and 'on the move' along the suggested continuum, and are therefore more weakly anchored in the phonology of the language than the patterns of languages with more common single-edge fixed-stress locations. Such systems might be more susceptible to outside influence in the form of (a) relatively swift changes in the rules, (b) harbouring a wealth of exceptions, (c) variability of stressing within single words, and (d) maybe even some unexplained metrical effects. Such instability has indeed been reported for Arnhem Land languages, and we review some cases below.

Many of the penultimate stress languages have scores of initial stress exceptions. Two cases in point are Ngalakan and Mangarayi (Merlan 1983, 1989). Some examples are presented in (23).

(23) Ngalakan   Mangarayi
      ˈdakbaˌrara 'green tree frog'   ˈwuruˌmumu 'hornet'
      ˌmiliˈbalkiñ 'salt water'   ˌwarinˈjalan '*Exocarpos latifolius*'

Merlan notes that these languages even show exceptions that go beyond penultimate or initial stress. Antepenultimate stress is not at all hard to find. It is clear that the stress patterns of these two languages are anything but stable.

In another type of hybrid, stressing in longer words may be relatively uniform, while three-syllable words, often quite susceptible to variation, show alternation between the initial and the penultimate pattern. The pattern is exemplified in (24) by Alawa (Sharpe 1972), spoken in the southern end of the region, to the west of Yanyuwa. In Maung, a language from the north coast (Capell and Hinch 1970) however, a radically different solution is chosen. Three-syllable words in this language reportedly have primary stress on the initial *and* the penultimate syllable.

(24) Alawa   Maung
      aˈlawal 'properly'   ˈbaˈladji   'bag'
      ˈpařakal 'spear'   ˈmaˈmiŋa   'clam shell'

The Maung examples exhibit what we called 'unexplained metrical effects' above. Whereas languages without primary stress, only employing several equal secondary stresses, occur frequently, languages with 'more than one primary stress' would appear to be impossible from a theoretical point of view. We do not attempt to solve that issue here. Whatever is going on in Maung three-syllable words, it is clearly not common, and in our view it is a sure sign of the instability of its hybrid stress pattern.

Another sign of the instability of hybrids we mentioned above is that, in some languages, changes in the stress pattern could occur relatively swiftly. Such changes are perhaps difficult to capture in grammatical descriptions, which may not be based on contact with the speakers that is long enough to reveal metrical transitions. Yet, we might have cases in Ngalkbun (Capell 1962; Sandefur and Jenhan 1977) and Ndjébanna (McKay 1975, 2000), two languages spoken on the northeastern fringe of the penultimate area, near the border with the predominantly left-oriented Yolngu languages. Capell classifies Ngalkbun as a typical initial stress language that has the same pattern as Djambarrpuyngu. However, 15 years later, Sandefur and Jenhan wrote that the pattern in words longer than three syllables is to stress the penult and alternates before it. Three-syllable words also stress the penult, and place a secondary stress on the initial syllable that remains 'stranded' in bisyllabic parsing. Some examples from Sandefur and Jenhan are presented in (25).

(25)   Ngalkbun
        a. ˌwulkunˈtjaŋŋan   'my younger sister'
        b. ˌŋaʔyenjyenjtjuˈŋiyan   'I will talk'
        c. naˈkomtutj ~ ˈnakomtutj   'little boy'

Example (25a) shows the pattern claimed by Sandefur and Jenhan to apply to most Ngalkbun words. Example (25b), however, reveals the Umbugarla pattern, with only one secondary stress located on the left-hand side. Example (25c) shows that Ngalkbun is also an example of the last sign of instability we mentioned above: variation of stressing *within* the word. The language as described by Sandefur and Jenhan unmistakably shows signs of affinity with the edge Capell designated as the location for primary stress. Even though we might suspect that one of the descriptions is just wrong, all the signs point to a much more enticing possibility: the sources have captured Ngalkbun at two different stages in its transition from a left-oriented to a right-oriented stress system. Similarly, in a few scant remarks about stress in Ndjébanna, McKay (1975) sketches a left-oriented system, while in a much later source (McKay 2000) a right-oriented pattern seems to dominate the scene.

With this discussion on exceptions and their signal function for instability we conclude the overview of Arnhem Land stress types. We have seen what all these hybrid patterns tell us theoretically.

They strongly support van der Hulst's claim that the algorithms for the assignment of primary and secondary stress must be separated. What we have not yet seen is how these languages are located with respect to each other. In Section 7.7.4 we will check whether the hybrid patterns have something to tell us when we look at their geographical locations.

7.7.4 Geographical Distribution

To create an easily understood map, we have taken the geographical language data for Google Earth that were created in the AUTOTYP project (www.autotyp.uzh.ch/). We have excluded all the languages for which we had no stress data, and divided the others into three categories, as shown in (26).

(26)   i. Predominantly initial stress (Djambarrpuyngu type, white dots)
       ii. Predominantly penultimate stress (Limilngan type, black dots)
      iii. Hybrids (grey dots)

In categories i and ii, we have incorporated languages that are of the prototypical type but which do have exceptions. Even though we introduced these as having taken the first step towards the other edge, and therefore hybridity, we felt it would be more revealing to include only the languages for which hybridity is more prominently present in category iii. The cleaned-up AUTOTYP map is shown in Map 7.1.

What strikes us immediately is that the black dots split the area down the middle. A pocket of white initial stress languages is isolated in the northeast, while some other white dots are located in the west. In the southeast, not visible on the map, some Pama-Nyungan initial stress languages are the closest neighbours of Yanyuwa, Garawa and Waanyi. Most hybrids are located in the border areas, where the initial and penultimate stress systems collide. We already noted in the introduction to Section 7.7 that this contact area is where almost all hybrids appear, but their exact locations with respect to I, P and the other hybrids only now becomes clear. Perhaps most noteworthy in this respect is the fact that we do not see any hybrids in the south. We do not know the reason for this. There are Pama-Nyungan languages there, but diffusional forces between these and Djingulu and Gudanji, if any, have not (yet) resulted in any overtly hybrid stress patterns.

7.7.5 Going Left or Going Right? Innovation or Remnant?

In this case study, we have discussed a journey along a continuum from initial (I) to penultimate (P) stress, as if that were the direction in which the languages in the Arnhem Land area are evolving. But we have in fact thus far made no claim regarding the issue of the direction of diffusion. This is, however, a most intriguing question, and we endeavour to answer it in this section.

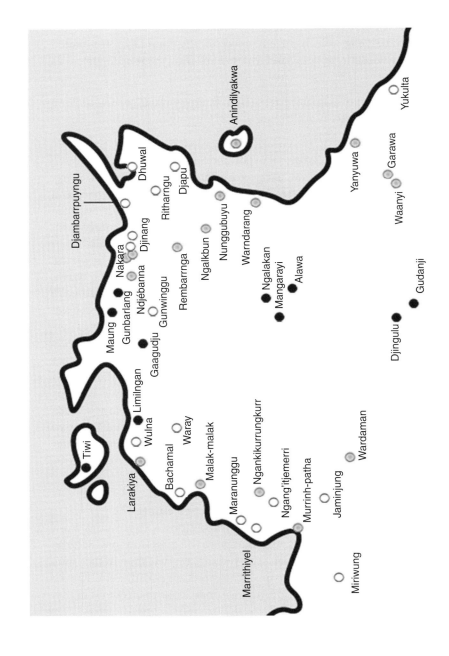

Map 7.1 Arnhem Land area with P, I and hybrids

What is really happening in Arnhem Land? Has the P stress innovation invaded the area, forcing back the native I pattern to the northeast and the west? Or was the P pattern once used across the board in all non-Pama-Nyungan languages and is it now being slowly mopped up by the Pama-Nyungan I forces? Or is our impression of a 'journey' that languages can make to either end of our spectrum a false one? Maybe the intermediate hybrid 'states' that we have found above are in fact stable stress patterns and no evolution of stress patterns to more left- or right-oriented versions has taken place at all. Even though it is difficult to be certain, given the highly volatile nature of most of the data we have found, we do believe that we can answer these questions.[28] It is our firm belief that the metrical scene in the Arnhem Land area is in turmoil. Almost all the data we have found in grammars point to systems that are changing. A myriad of exceptions to patterns and rules reflects a situation of great instability. Also on theoretical grounds, as we noted in Section 7.4, we could assume that hybrids will not always remain hybrids, but are on the move towards more common stress patterns. Therefore, firstly, we propose here that these languages *are* changing as the result of diffusional pressure, and secondly, that they are going rightward to become more and more P-like. For the second claim, we have not yet given the arguments. We now review what evidence is available.

Our first piece of evidence concerns the northeast of Arnhem Land, the isolated 'white pocket' in Map 7.1. The suggestion that this group of Pama-Nyungan languages is slowly giving in to pressure of the P languages to the west turns out to be correct in the light of claims made by Dixon (1980). Dixon shows that the Yolngu tribes speaking the languages in the area moved there only recently, and notes that after the migration, considerable diffusional pressure towards the Yolngu languages (I languages) originated from the P languages to the west. It is therefore most likely that the stress patterns of languages like Nakara developed from true I patterns through influence of P languages, and not the other way around.

Evidence for the same direction of diffusion can be found in Yanyuwa (Kirton 1977). In long polymorphemic words, a tendency is developing to replace the stress on the initial syllable of a word-internal morpheme by a stress on the pre-antepenultimate syllable. Compare the alternatives in (27).

(27)   Yanyuwa
      ˌgumbaˌramandaˌninjdja   'he was hitting himself'
      ˌgumbaraˌmandaˌninjdja

---

[28] Note that we can do nothing but make claims about *tendencies* here. In an area as diffusionally active as this one, pressure may well work both ways, and some stress systems might evolve leftward, while others go to the right, and some may even go back and forth between directions before they make their final choice. The case made here will simply concern the direction in which the languages are generally going.

The top pattern is the traditional one, the bottom word represents the tendency. Clearly, this tendency reflects a movement to a more rigid right-to-left way of assigning secondary stresses. This is the only language-internal evidence available in favour of movement towards penultimate stress.

A theoretical argument for the movement towards penultimate rather than initial stress can be found when we consider the absence of left-to-right count systems[29] in the diffusional melting pot of Arnhem Land that we noted in Section 7.7.2. In this chapter we cannot delve into the full arguments,[30] so we must summarize. To derive a right-to-left count system from a basic non-count pattern we can walk two very different paths: (1) we could start out with a basic initial stress pattern and switch the starting edge of footing from the left to the right side *while leaving the primary stress domain where it is*, or (2) starting with the domain at the right edge in a penultimate stress system, we could derive the desired count system if we *flipped the domain* to the left while leaving the starting edge of footing at the right. However, in our view such a movement of the domain is far too drastic to constitute the first reaction of a language to diffusional pressure, and once other, less drastic, evolutionary steps have been taken, the right-to-left count system can no longer be derived. Therefore, we submit that I-systems are the point of departure for Arnhem Land hybrids. For left-to-right count systems, the argument would be the inverse of the above, with P-systems forming a point of departure. We propose, therefore, that the absence of such left-to-right count systems in the area can be interpreted as evidence for the claim that, in principle, Arnhem Land languages do not move from P to I-systems.

Two scenarios for the development of diffusional pressure in Arnhem Land were sketched above. P-systems could be relatively new on the scene, expanding their influence on the much older I-systems. Alternatively, P-systems could be remnants of a much older pattern that is on the retreat under the pressure of the I-systems. There is no doubt that P-systems are indeed an innovation with respect to Proto-Australian, which had simple initial stress across the board (Dixon 1980). But that may still mean that P-systems could have arisen long ago and are now slowly fading away. To choose between the two scenarios, we need to look for a trigger, a relatively recent development that could have caused the genesis of P-systems or be the agent of their demise. It so happens that the former is easy to find. Both Heath (1978) and Dixon (1980) report prefixing as a rather new phenomenon among the non-Pama-Nyungan languages. It is quite likely that the penultimate stress pattern arose as the result of the

---

[29] In a count system the starting edge for footing is opposite to the edge selected by the End Rule; see van der Hulst (2014c).

[30] The interested reader is referred to Goedemans (2010a).

addition of prefixes to stress initial stems, many of which will have been bisyllabic. A penultimate, or at least a more right-oriented, primary stress, perhaps already with some secondary stresses on the chain of prefixes, might have been the result.[31] This pattern may have spread rapidly among the non-Pama-Nyungan languages, in the wake of the prefixing innovation. In this scenario, penultimate stress has become more regular over time and is now exerting its influence over non-prefixing neighbouring languages. The fact that a trigger for P-innovation can be found so easily adds to the evidence for the claim that hybrids become more P-like through pressure from the penultimate stress systems.

The evidence presented above does not make a rock-solid case for the claim that diffusion indeed pushes back the I-languages in Arnhem Land. It does, however, provide some fairly firm ground to walk on when we take new steps towards understanding the metrical upheaval that these languages are subject to. Much more scrutiny of linguistic data is needed before we can say anything more definitive. We hope that such data will become readily available in the near future.

7.8   Conclusions

While this chapter has referenced different approaches and studies concerning contact-induced change, linguistic areas and word-prosodic systems, our main conclusion is that the study of these topics is largely an under-investigated area. There are challenges in identifying whether similarity of stress systems in an area is due to independent factors or is contact-induced. We definitely see areal effects and many very likely cases have long been identified. In this chapter we have provided information and references concerning the typological distribution of word prominence systems in selected languages and language families of the world in the hope that proper considerations of these will lead to the identification of additional linguistic areas. However, we believe that the study of contact-induced change in word prominence systems is still largely dominated by anecdotal reports, and much is uncertain about the precise mechanisms that are at play. (A notable exception is the detailed study of Salmons 1992.) This, in part, is caused by a typical holistic approach to stress/accent that does not take into account that these notions more often than not cover a package of properties at both the phonological and the phonetic levels (see Section 7.2.2). We have also suggested that when moving toward an understanding of the mechanisms of contact-induced changes much can be learned from descriptive and experimental work on loan phonology and second language phonology (see Section 7.2.4).

---

[31] See Goedemans (2010a) for a more in-depth discussion.

By looking at three cases in more detail, we have tried to move beyond anecdotal reports. In Section 7.5 we discussed the case of Basque dialects, based on the work of José Hualde. This shows how a prominence system can respond to language contact in various different ways. It would clearly be desirable to have more studies of this kind within the context of specific modular theories of word prominence systems which also take into account the interplay between word prominence and intonation (Gordon 2014). Section 7.6 discussed in detail the word prominence evidence for considering certain previously identified language clusters in North America as linguistic areas, showing that prominence is an areal indicator in some areas but not in others. Finally, Section 7.7 offered a detailed case study of the consequences of language contact in northern Australia, clearly showing that a modular, parametric analysis of word prominence systems provides insights into the myriad of attested systems. Overall, we have argued that contact situations can create hybrid systems which provide clear descriptive and theoretical challenges for areal linguistics.

References

Alleyne, Mervyn, 1980. *Comparative Afro-American: An Historical-comparative Study of English-based Afro-American Dialects of the New World*. Ann Arbor, MI: Karoma.

Altmann, Heidi, 2006. *The Perception and Production of Second Language Stress: A Cross-linguistic Experimental Study*. Unpublished PhD dissertation, University of Delaware.

Altmann, Heidi and Bari Kabak, 2011. Second language phonology. In Nancy C. Kula, Bert Botma and Kuniya Nasukawa (eds), *The Continuum Companion to Phonology*, pp. 298–319. London: Continuum.

Benedict, Paul K., 1948. Tonal systems in Southeast Asia. *Journal of the American Oriental Society* 68: 18491.

Broselow, Ellen, 2009. Stress adaptation in loanword phonology: Perception and learnability. In Paul Boersma and Silke Hamann (eds), *Phonology in Perception*, pp. 191–234. Berlin: Mouton de Gruyter.

Buckley, Eugene, 2013. Prosodic systems in Southeastern Pomo stress. Talk presented at the Society for the Study of the Indigenous Languages of the Americas, Boston, January 2013.

Bye, Patrick, 2004. Evolutionary typology and Scandinavian pitch accent. Manuscript, University of Tromsø/CASTL.

Callaghan, Catherine A., 1964. *A Grammar of the Lake Miwok Language*. PhD dissertation, University of California, Berkeley.

Campbell, Lyle, 1997. *American Indian Languages: The Historical Linguistics of Native America*. Oxford: Oxford University Press.

Campbell, Lyle, 2006. Areal linguistics: A closer scrutiny. In Yaron Matras, April McMahon and Nigel Vincent (eds), *Linguistic Areas: Convergence in Historical and Typological Perspective*, pp. 1–31. Basingstoke, UK: Palgrave Macmillan.

Capell, Arthur, 1962. *Some Linguistic Types in Australia.* Oceania Linguistic Monographs, no. 7. University of Sydney.

Capell, Arthur and Heather E. Hinch, 1970. *Maung Grammar: Text and Vocabulary.* The Hague: Mouton.

Carter, Hazel, 1973. Tonal data in comparative Bantu. *African Language Studies* 14: 3652.

Clements, George N. and John Goldsmith, 1984. Autosegmental studies in Bantu tone: Introduction. In George Clements and John Goldsmith (eds), *Autosegmental Studies in Bantu Tone*, pp. 1–17. Dordrecht: Foris.

Conathan, Lisa, 2004. *The Linguistic Ecology of Northwestern California: Contact, Functional Convergence, and Dialectology.* PhD dissertation, University of California, Berkeley.

Davies, J., 1989. *Umbugarla: A Sketch Grammar.* BA (Hons) thesis, University of Melbourne.

Davis, Stuart, Natsuko Tsujimura and Jung-yueh Tu, 2012. Toward a taxonomy of loanword prosody. *Catalan Journal of Linguistics* 11: 13–39

Dixon, Robert M. W., 1980. *The Languages of Australia.* Cambridge: Cambridge University Press.

Dogil, Grzegorz, 1999a. Baltic languages. In van der Hulst (ed.), *Word Prosodic Systems in the Languages of Europe*, pp. 877–896.

Dogil, Grzegorz, 1999b. West Slavic [languages]. In van der Hulst (ed.), *Word Prosodic Systems in the Languages of Europe*, pp. 813–838.

Dresher, B. Elan and Aditi Lahiri, 1991. The Germanic foot: Metrical coherence in Old English. *Linguistic Inquiry* 22 (2): 251–286.

Eather, Bronwyn, 1990. *A Grammar of Nakkara (Central Arnhem Land Coast).* PhD dissertation, Australian National University. Reprinted in 2011 in series Outstanding Grammars from Australia, vol. 7, LINCOM.

Eckman, Fred R. and Gregory Iverson, 2015. Second language acquisition and phonological change. In Honeybone and Salmons (eds), pp. 637–643.

Gårding, Eva, 1977. *Scandinavian Word Accents.* Lund: Travaux de L'Institut de Linguistique de Lund.

Goedemans, Rob, 2010a. A typology of stress patterns. In van der Hulst et al. (eds), *A Survey of Word Accentual Systems in the Languages of the World*, pp. 647–666.

Goedemans, Rob, 2010b. An overview of word stress in Australian Aboriginal languages. In van der Hulst et al. (eds), *A Survey of Word Accentual Systems in the Languages of the World*, pp. 55–86.

Goedemans, Rob and Harry van der Hulst, 2005a. Fixed stress locations. In Haspelmath et al. (eds), *The World Atlas of Language Structures*, pp. 62–65.

Goedemans, Rob and Harry van der Hulst, 2005b. Weight-sensitive stress. In Haspelmath et al. (eds), *The World Atlas of Language Structures*, pp. 66–69.

Goedemans, Rob and Harry van der Hulst, 2005c. Weight factors in weight-sensitive stress systems. In Haspelmath et al. (eds), *The World Atlas of Language Structures*, pp. 70–73.

Goedemans, Rob and Harry van der Hulst, 2005d. Rhythm types. In Haspelmath et al. (eds), *The World Atlas of Language Structures*, pp. 74–77.

Goedemans, Rob and Harry van der Hulst, 2009. StressTyp: A database for word accentual patterns in the world's languages. In Martin Everaert and Simon Musgrave (eds), *The Use of Databases in Cross-linguistic Research*, pp. 235–282. Berlin: Mouton de Gruyter.

Goedemans, Rob and Harry van der Hulst, 2014. The separation of accent and rhythm: Evidence from StressTyp. In van der Hulst (ed.), *Word Stress: Theoretical and Typological Issues*, pp. 119–148.

Goedemans, Rob, Harry van der Hulst and Ellis Visch (eds), 1996. *Stress Patterns of the World*. HIL Publications, vol. 2. The Hague: Holland Academic Graphics.

Goldsmith, John, 1988. Prosodic trends in the Bantu languages. In Harry van der Hulst and Norval Smith (eds), *Autosegmental Studies on Pitch Accent*, pp. 81–94. Dordrecht: Foris publications.

Golla, Victor, 2011. *California Indian Languages*. Berkeley, CA: University of California Press.

Gordon, Matthew, 2014. Disentangling stress and pitch accent: Toward a typology of prominence at different prosodic levels. In van der Hulst (ed.), *Word Stress: Theoretical and Typological Issues*, pp. 83–118.

Gordon, Matthew, 2016. Metrical incoherence: Diachronic sources and synchronic analysis. In Jeff Heinz, Rob Goedemans and Harry van der Hulst (eds), *Dimensions of Phonological Stress*, pp. 9–48. Cambridge: Cambridge University Press.

Gordon, Matthew and Edmundo Luna, 2004. An intergenerational investigation of Hupa stress. In *Proceedings of the 30th Annual Meeting of the Berkeley Linguistics Society*, pp. 105–117. Berkeley, CA: Berkeley Linguistics Society.

Greiner, Paul, 1994. Review of Salmons 1994. *American Journal of Germanic Linguistics and Literatures* 6 (2): 259–266.

Haraguchi, Shoshuke, 1979. *The Tone Pattern of Japanese: An Autosegmental Theory of Tonology*. Tokyo: Kaitakusha.

Harvey, Mark, 2001. *A Grammar of Limilngan*. Pacific Linguistics, vol. 516. Canberra: Australian National University.

Haspelmath, Martin, Matthew Dryer, David Gil and Bernard Comrie (eds), 2005. *The World Atlas of Language Structures*. Oxford: Oxford University Press.

Haugen, Einer, 1970. The language history of Scandinavia: A profile of problems. In Hreinn Beneddiktsson (ed.), *The Nordic Languages and Modern Linguistics*, pp. 41–86. Reykjavik: Visindafelag.

Hayes, Bruce, 1995. *Metrical Stress Theory*. Chicago: University of Chicago Press.

Haynie, Hannah Jane, 2012. *Studies in the History and Geography of California Languages*. PhD dissertation, University of California, Berkeley.

Heath, Jeffrey, 1978. *Linguistic Diffusion in Arnhem Land*. Canberra: AIATSIS.

Heine, Bernd, 1973. *Pidgin-Sprachen im Bantu-Bereich*. Berlin: Reimer.

Hickey, Raymond, 1997. Assessing the relative status of languages in medieval Ireland. In Jacek Fisiak (ed.), *Studies in Middle English Linguistics*, pp. 181–205. Berlin: Mouton.

Hickey, Raymond, 2010. Language contact: Reassessment and reconsideration. In Raymond Hickey (ed.), *The Handbook of Language Contact*, pp. 1–28. Malden, MA: Wiley-Blackwell.

Hickey, Raymond, 2014. *The Sound Structure of Modern Irish*. Berlin: de Gruyter Mouton.

Hinton, Leanne, 1991. Takic and Yuman: A study in phonological convergence. *International Journal of American Linguistics* 57 (2): 133–157.

Hoddinott, W. G. and F. M. Kofod, 1988. *The Ngankikurungkurr Language (Daly river area, Northern Territory)*. Pacific Linguistics, vol. D-77. Canberra: Australian National University.

Honeybone, Patrick and Joseph Salmons (eds), 2015. *The Oxford Handbook of Historical Phonology*. Oxford: Oxford University Press.

Hore, Michael, 1981. Syllable length and stress in Nunggubuyu. In B. Waters (ed.), *AAB SIL Working papers*, series A5, pp. 1–62.

Hualde, José Ignacio, 1999. Basque accentuation. In van der Hulst (ed.), *Word Prosodic Systems in the Languages of Europe*, pp. 947–994.

Hualde, José Ignacio, 2000. On system-driven sound change: Accent shift in Markina Basque. *Lingua* 110: 99–129.

Hualde, José Ignacio, 2003. From phrase-final to post-initial accent in Western Basque. In Paula Fikkert and Heike Jacobs (eds), *Development in Prosodic Systems*, pp. 249–281. Berlin: Mouton de Gruyter.

Hualde, José Ignacio, 2007. Historical convergence and divergence in Basque accentuation. In Tomas Riad and Carlos Gussenhoven (eds), *Tones and Tunes*, pp. 291–322. Berlin: Mouton de Gruyter.

Hualde, José Ignacio, 2012. Two Basque accentual systems and word-prosodic typology. *Lingua* 122: 1335–1351.

Hualde, José Ignacio, Gorka Elordieta, Iñaki Gaminde and Rajka Smiljanic, 2002. From pitch accent to stress accent in Basque. In Carlos Gussenhoven and Natasha Warner (eds), *Laboratory Phonology*, vol. 7, pp. 547–584. Berlin: Mouton de Gruyter.

van der Hulst, Harry, 1996. Primary accent is non-metrical. *Revista de Linguistica* 9 (1): 1–119.

van der Hulst, Harry (ed.), 1999a. *Word Prosodic Systems in the Languages of Europe*. Berlin: Mouton de Gruyter.

van der Hulst, Harry, 1999b. Word accent. In van der Hulst (ed.), *Word Prosodic Systems in the Languages of Europe*, pp. 3–116.

van der Hulst, Harry, 2010. Word accent systems in the languages of Europe. In van der Hulst et al. (eds), *A Survey of Word Accentual Systems in the Languages of the World*, pp. 429–508.

van der Hulst, Harry, 2012. Deconstructing stress. *Lingua* 122: 1494–1521.

van der Hulst, Harry (ed.), 2014a. *Word Stress: Theoretical and Typological Issues*. Cambridge: Cambridge University Press

van der Hulst, Harry, 2014b. Word stress: Past, present and future. In van der Hulst (ed.), *Word Stress: Theoretical and Typological Issues*, pp. 3–55.

van der Hulst, Harry, 2014c. Representing rhythm. In van der Hulst (ed.), *Word Stress: Theoretical and Typological Issues*, pp. 325–365.

van der Hulst, Harry, Rob Goedemans and Ellen van Zanten (eds), 2010. *A Survey of Word Accentual Systems in the Languages of the World*. Berlin: Mouton de Gruyter.

van der Hulst, Harry and Sam Hellmuth, 2010. Word accent systems in the Middle Eastern languages. In van der Hulst et al. (eds), *A Survey of Word Accentual Systems in the Languages of the World*, pp. 615–648.

van der Hulst, Harry, Bernadet Hendriks and Jeroen van de Weijer, 1999. A survey of European word prosodic systems. In van der Hulst (ed.), *Word Prosodic Systems in the Languages of Europe*, pp. 425–476.

van der Hulst, Harry, Keren Rice and Leo Wetzels, 2010. Word accent systems in the languages of Middle America. In van der Hulst et al. (eds), *A Survey of Word Accentual Systems in the Languages of the World*, pp. 313–380.

Hyman, Larry M., 1977. On the nature of linguistic stress. In Larry M. Hyman (ed.), *Studies in Stress and Accent*, pp. 37–82. Los Angeles: Department of Linguistics, University of Southern California.

Hyman, Larry M., 1989. Accent in Bantu: An appraisal. *Studies in the Linguistic Sciences* 19: 115–134.

Jakobson, Roman, 1971. Über die phonologischen Sprachbünde. In *Selected Works: Phonological Studies*, pp. 137–144. The Hague: Mouton.

Jany, Carmen, 2009. *Chimariko Grammar: Areal and Typological Perspective*. University of California Papers in Linguistics, vol. 142. Berkeley, CA: University of California Press.

Kang, Yoonjung, 2010. Tutorial overview: Suprasegmental adaptation in loanwords. *Lingua* 120: 2295–2310.

Kang, Yoonjung, 2011. Loanword phonology. In Marc van Oostendorp, Colin Ewen, Elizabeth Hume and Keren Rice (eds), *Companion to Phonology*, pp. 2258–2282. Malden, MA: Wiley-Blackwell.

Kijak, Anna M., 2009. *A Cross-linguistic Study of L2 Perception and Production of Metrical Systems*. Dissertation, University of Utrecht.

Kirton, J. F., 1977. *Anyula Phonology*. Pacific Linguistics, vol. A-10. Canberra: Australian National University.

Kodzasov, Sandro, 1999. Caucasian: The Daghestanian languages. In van der Hulst (ed.), *Word Prosodic Systems in the Languages of Europe*, pp. 995–1020.

Kubozono, Haruo, 2006. Where does loanword prosody come from? A case study of Japanese loanword accent. *Lingua* 116: 1140–1170.

Lahiri, Aditi, 2015. Change in word prosody: Stress and quantity. In Honeybone and Salmons (eds), pp. 219–244.

Lahiri, Aditi, Tomas Riad and Haike Jacobs, 1999. Diachronic prosody. In van der Hulst (ed.), *Word Prosodic Systems in the Languages of Europe*, pp. 335–424.

Leeding V. L., 1989. *Anindilyakwa Phonology and Morphology*. PhD dissertation, University of Sydney. http://ses.library.usyd.edu.au/handle/2123/1558

Lehiste, Ilse, 1994. Review of *Accentual Change and Language Contact: Comparative Survey and a Case Study of Early Northern Europe* (Joe Salmons). *Diachronica* 11 (1): 126–130.

Lewis, M. P. et al. (eds), 2013. *Ethnologue: Languages of the World*, 17th edition. Dallas, TX: SIL International. www.ethnologue.com

Li, Charles N., 1986. The rise and fall of tones through diffusion. In *Proceedings of the Twelfth Annual Meeting of the Berkeley Linguistics Society*, pp. 173–185. Berkeley, CA: Berkeley Linguistics Society.

Liberman, Mark and Alan Prince, 1977. On stress and linguistic rhythm. *Linguistic Inquiry* 8: 249–336.

Mackenzie, Marguerite, 1980. *Towards a Dialectology of Cree-Montagnais-Naskapi*. Doctoral dissertation, University of Toronto.

Matras, Yaron, 2009. *Language Contact*. Cambridge: Cambridge University Press.

McKay, G. R., 1975. *Rembarnga, a Language of Central Arnhem Land*. PhD dissertation, Australian National University. Reprinted in 2011 in series Outstanding Grammars from Australia, vol. 5, LINCOM.

McKay, G. R., 2000. Ndjébanna. In R. M. W. Dixon and B. Blake (eds), *The Handbook of Australian Languages*, vol. 5, pp. 155–356. Oxford: Oxford University Press.

McLendon, Sally, 1975. *A Grammar of Eastern Pomo*. University of California Publications in Linguistics, vol. 74. Berkeley, CA: University of California Press.

Merlan, Francesca, 1983. *Ngalakan Grammar Texts and Vocabulary*. Pacific Linguistics, vol. B-89. Canberra: Australian National University.

Merlan, Francesca, 1989. *Mangarayi*. New York: Routledge.

Merlan, Francesca, 1994. *A Grammar of Wardaman*. Berlin: Mouton de Gruyter.

Michelson, Karin, 1988. *A Comparative Study of Lake-Iroquian Accent*. Dordrecht: Kluwer Academic Publishers.

Mithun, Marianne, 1999. *The Languages of Native North America*. Cambridge: Cambridge University Press.

Mithun, Marianne, 2010. Contact and North American languages. In Raymond Hickey (ed.), *The Handbook of Language Contact*, pp. 673–694. Wiley-Blackwell.

Moravcsik, Edith, 1978. Universals of language contact. In *Universals 79: Germanen und Kelten*. Also in Bruno Krüger (ed.) 1983, *Die Germanen: Geschichte und Kultur der germanischen Stämme bis zum 2. Jahrhundert unserer Zeitrechnung*, pp. 232–254. Berlin: Akademie Verlag.

Moshinsky, Julius, 1974. *A Grammar of Southeastern Pomo*. University of California Publications in Linguistics, vol. 72. Berkeley, CA: University of California Press.

Odden, David, 1988. Predictable tone systems in Bantu. In Harry van der Hulst and Norval Smith (eds), *Autosegmental Studies on Pitch Accent*, pp. 225–251. Dordrecht: Foris.

Osbourne, C. R., 1966. A tentative description of the Waanji language. Manuscript, Australian National University.

Peperkamp, Sharon and Emmanuel Dupoux, 2002. A typological study of stress 'deafness'. In Carlos Gussenhoven and Natasha Warner (eds), *Laboratory Phonology*, vol. 7, pp. 203–240. Berlin: Mouton de Gruyter.

Peter, Steve, 1994. Review of Salmons 1994. *Language* 70 (1): 182–184.

Pitkin, Harvey, 1984. *Wintu Grammar*. University of California Publications in Linguistics, vol. 94. Berkeley, CA: University of California Press.

Ratliff, Martha, 2015. Tonoexodus, tonogenesis, and tone change. In Honeybone and Salmons (eds), pp. 245–261.

Reid, Nicholas J., 1990. *Nagan'gityemerri: A Language of the Daly River Region, Northern Territory of Australia*. Reprinted in 2011 in series Outstanding Grammars from Australia, vol. 6, LINCOM.

Riad, Tomas, 1998. Toward a Scandinavian accent typology. In Wolfgang Kehrein and Richard Wiese (eds), *Phonology and Morphology of the Germanic Languages*, pp. 77–112. Tübingen: Niemeyer.

Rice, Keren, 2010. Accent in the native languages of North America. In van der Hulst et al. (eds), *A Survey of Word Accentual Systems in the Languages of the World*, pp. 155–248.

Rice, Keren, 2014. Convergence of prominence systems? In van der Hulst (ed.), *Word Stress: Theoretical and Typological Issues*, pp. 194–227.

Roca, Iggy, 1999. Stress in the Romance languages. In van der Hulst (ed.), *Word Prosodic Systems in the Languages of Europe*, pp. 659–812.

Ruhlen, Merritt, 1975. *A Guide to the Languages of the World*. Stanford, CA: Language Universals Project.

Ruhlen, Merritt, 1977. The geographical and genetic distribution of linguistic features. In Alphonse Juilland (ed.), *Linguistic Studies Offered to Joseph Greenberg*, vol. 1: *General Linguistics*, pp. 137–160. Saratoga, CA: Anma Libri.

Salmons, Joseph, 1992. *Accentual Change and Language Contact: Comparative Survey and a Case Study of Early Northern Europe*. Stanford, CA: Stanford University Press.

Sandefur, John and David Jenhan, 1977. A tentative description of the phonemes of the Ngalkbun language. *Work Papers of the SIL-AAB*, series A1: 57–96. Darwin.

Sharpe, Margaret C., 1972. *Alawa Phonology and Grammar*. Canberra: AIATSIS.

Shaw, Patricia, 1985. Coexistent and competing stress rules. *International Journal of American Linguistics* 51: 1–18.

Sommerfelt, Alf, 1962. *Diachronic and Synchronic Linguistics*. The Hague: Mouton.

Thomason, Sarah G., 2001. *Language Contact: An Introduction*. Washington, DC: Georgetown University Press.

Thomason, Sarah G. and Terrence Kaufman, 1988. *Language Contact, Creolization, and Genetic Linguistics*. Berkeley, CA: University of California Press.

Tryon, Darrel T., 1970. *An Introduction to Maranungku*. Pacific Linguistics, vol. B-14. Canberra: Australian National University.

Uffmann, Christian, 2015. Loanword adaptation. In Honeybone and Salmons (eds), pp. 644–666.

Ureland, Sture, 1971. Observations on Texas–Swedish phonology. *Studia Linguistica* 25: 69–110.

Uwano, Zendo, 1999. Classification of Japanese accent systems. In Shigeki Kaji (ed.), *Proceedings of the Symposium 'Cross-Linguistic Studies on Tonal Phenomena, Tonogenesis, Typology, and Related Topics'*, pp. 151–186. Tokyo: ILCAA.

Uwano, Zendo, 2012. Three types of accent kernels in Japanese. *Lingua* 122: 1415–1440.

Veenker, Wolfgang, 1967. *Die Frage des finnougrischen Substrats in der russischen Sprache*. Bloomington, IN: Indiana University Publications.

Walker, Neil, 2013. *A Grammar of Southern Pomo: An Indigenous Language of California*. PhD dissertation, University of California, Santa Barbara.

Wetzels, Leo and Sergio Meira, 2010. A survey of South American stress systems. In van der Hulst et al. (eds), *A Survey of Word Accentual Systems in the Languages of the World*, pp. 313–380.

Wilkinson, Melanie P., 1991. *Djambarrpuyngu: A Yolngu Variety of Northern Australia*. PhD dissertation, University of Sydney.

8

Semantic Patterns from an Areal Perspective

Maria Koptjevskaja-Tamm and Henrik Liljegren

8.1 Introduction

The aim of this chapter is to define, exemplify and problematize the lexico-semantic aspects of areality / language convergence. Just as with areal linguistics in general, this subfield is an intersection of a number of more general approaches: the study of language contact, language change and typological research. Particularly prominent in our treatment is the cross-fertilization of meticulous documentation of linguistic features in specific geographical regions or areas, often grounded in fieldwork, and large-scale cross-linguistic findings and generalizations.

Areal semantics, in its concern with the diffusion of semantic features across language boundaries in a geographical area, is a potentially vast field, spanning the convergence of individual lexemes, through the structuring of entire semantic domains, to the organization of complete lexicons. For practical reasons we have largely excluded the two extreme ends of that continuum. At the lower end, the subject of loanwords, or the spread of individual vocabulary forms, will only feature when it also involves co-lexicalization or the diffusion of area-specific concepts. At the higher end, we will usually exclude features defining the lexicon at large, such as very general derivational mechanisms or the proportion of verbs versus nouns, sometimes referred to as the lexical profile of a language. The latter is related to an attempt to uphold a distinction between grammar and lexicon, also reflected in our decision to exclude grammaticalization *per se* from our discussion.

Our choice of focus for the chapter is to a large degree motivated by a desire to attend to the issues that have so far received relatively little attention in theoretical discussions in areal linguistics (Ameka and Wilkins 1996; Matisoff 2004). As a consequence, we will not be able to report on generalizations comparable to those accumulated in research on 'material' borrowings or on contact-induced grammaticalization, such as constraints on borrowability or correlations between the socio-linguistic parameters of contact situations and possible contact-induced change. The main part of this chapter is an overview of a number of lexico-semantic phenomena that have been shown, or at least suggested, to serve as indicators of areality. The phenomena dealt with are lexico-semantic parallels, in turn subdivided into polysemy calquing and lexico-constructional calquing (Section 8.2), shared formu-laic expressions (Section 8.3), area-specific lexicalizations and a shared or similar-looking internal organization of certain semantic domains (Section 8.4). Section 8.5 is a case study of semantic patterns in the Hindu Kush region. After that (Section 8.6) follows a discussion of causality and possible mechanisms behind obvious correlations between lexico-semantic phenomena and geographically contiguous areas: inheritance, diffusion, shared environment and independent innovation. Section 8.7 offers a conclusion.

8.2 Lexico-semantic Parallels (Calques)

The two traditionally distinguished groups of contact phenomena in the lexicon are loanwords and calques – the distinction parallelled by contact phenomena at other levels ('replication of matter' versus 'pattern replication' in Matras and Sakel 2007; see also Croft's 2000 distinction between 'substance linguemes' and 'schematic linguemes', and Heine and Kuteva's 2005 notion of 'polysemy copying'). Calques encompass a broad group of lexico-semantic parallels between two or more languages with respect to the range of meaning(s) of the expressions that may count as interlingual matches (see the notion of 'interlingual identification' in Weinreich 1953: 7–8, 32), as well as their internal structure, as will be clarified and exemplified later.

8.2.1 Polysemy Calquing

The first subtype of these phenomena includes polysemy calquing, or polysemy copying (Heine and Kuteva 2003, 2005), also called 'semantic borrowing', 'semantic loan', 'semantic shift' or 'loan synonym' (see Urban 2012 for the terminology). In polysemy copying the same two meanings are expressed by the same form in each of the languages (normally by different forms in different languages), or are 'colexified', to use François' (2008) term. For instance, the Spanish *verde* 'green, unripe', is semantically extended to also mean 'raw' in the speech of the Acatec on the model of the Acatec (a Mayan language of Guatemala) word *yaaš* (Smith-Stark 1994). Here the semantic extension is triggered by the interlingual identification of *verde* and *yaaš* by the bilingual Acatec–Spanish speakers on the basis of their two overlapping meanings – 'green' (colour) and 'unripe'. However,

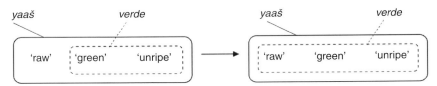

Figure 8.1 The process of polysemy copying: Spanish *verde* and Acatec *yaaš* in the speech of Acatec–Spanish bilinguals (after Smith-Stark 1994)

since *yaaš*, in addition, has the meaning 'raw', *verde* has extended its semantic range to 'properly' align with its interlingual match, which leads to the convergence of the two languages with respect to the semantic structure of these two lexical items. The whole process is visualized in Figure 8.1, inspired by Gast and van der Auwera's (2012) notion of 'semantic map assimilation'.

In the *verde–yaaš* example we can easily identify the model and the replica language, given the general knowledge about both languages involved and the contact situations. Since things are often much more complicated, especially when many languages are involved, in the rest of the chapter we will be talking about 'shared polysemies' or 'shared colexification patterns', rather than about 'polysemy copying / calquing', without making any further commitments about the possible reasons for these similarities. Examples (1)–(3) illustrate some patterns of polysemy shared among the languages spoken in the same area.

Polysemy sharing across languages

(1)   'draw water' = 'copy, imitate' in the languages of Ethiopia–Eritrea: *k'ädda* in Amharic (Afroasiatic, Semitic), *waraabe* in Oromo (Afroasiatic, Cushitic) and *duuk'k'ides* in Gamo (Afroasiatic, Omotic) (Hayward 1991, 2000)

(2)   'child' = 'fruit' in West African languages: *díŋ* in Mandinka (Mande, West Mande) and in several other Mande languages, *doom* in Wolof (Niger-Congo, Atlantic), *ízè* in Songhay (Nilo-Saharan, Songai), *fidju* in Kabuverdianu (Portuguese-based creole), *obi* in Sɛlɛɛ (Niger-Congo, Kwa)

(3)   'eat' = 'drink' in many Papuan and Australian Aboriginal languages, e.g. *kə-* in Manambu (Ndu) or *a* in Kwoma (Kwoma-Nukuma) (Aikhenvald 2009), as well as in a number of other languages of the world (Vanhove 2008a).

8.2.2   Lexico-constructional Calquing

For the other subtype of calquing, which we will call lexico-constructional calquing (also called 'translation loans'), it is both the meaning and the internal structure of the expressions that is in focus. What matters here is that expressions that constitute interlingual matches show the same

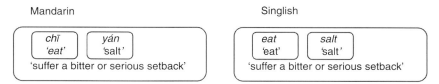

Figure 8.2 Lexico-constructional parallels: Mandarin *chī yán* and Singlish *eat salt*

semantic and structural patterning, i.e. are made up of parts that match each other across the languages. The term 'calque' was for a long time exclusively or mainly used for exactly such cases, with only a recent inclusion of polysemy copying into its scope. For instance, Singlish (or Singapore English) abounds in lexicalized phrases that clearly replicate the model of the local languages, as in the following two examples of loan translations from Mandarin, visualized in Figure 8.2:

(4)　Singlish versus Mandarin
　　　a. *eat salt* versus *chī* 'eat' + *yán* 'salt' – 'suffer a bitter or serious setback'
　　　b. *give face* versus *gěi* 'give, grant' + *miàn* 'face; reputation, prestige' – 'show due respect for one's feelings' (http://www.singlishdictionary.com/)

Again, since in most areal contexts it is difficult or even impossible to identify the model and the replica languages, we will be using a more neutral term 'shared lexico-constructional patterns'. Examples in (5)–(8) illustrate several types of lexico-constructional patterns shared among the languages in the same area, ranging from derivational patterns to collocations.

Lexico-constructional parallels across languages

(5)　'need' = causative of 'want' (a shared derivational pattern) in the Ethio-Eritrean languages: *asfälläägä* (from *fällägä*) in Amharic, *barbaachise* (from *barbaade*) in Omoro and *kosshides* (from *koyides*) in Gamo (Hayward 1991, 2000)

(6)　'sun' = 'eye of the day' (a shared compounding pattern) in Mainland Southeast Asia and parts of Oceania: *mata hari* in Malay/Indonesian (Austronesian, Malayo-Polynesian), *wangere ma la'o* 'day POSS eye' in Sahu (Papuan, North Halmahera), *mata-ni-siga* 'eye/face-POSS-day /sun' in Fijian (Austronesian, Malayo-Polynesian), *masonàndro* (*màso-nàndro*) in Malagasy (Austronesian, Malayo-Polynesian) (Blust 2011; Urban 2010, 2012)

(7)　'people' = 'man' + 'woman' (a shared compounding pattern) in the languages of New Guinea: *man-meri* in Tok Pisin, *uwr-sa* in Abau (Sepik), *oná-aa* in East Kewa (Nuclear Trans New Guinea, West-Central East New Guinea Highlands), *nɨbi bɨ* in Kobon (Nuclear Trans New Guinea, Madang) (Wälchli 2015), *kadi-imet* in Waskia (Nuclear

Trans New Guinea, Madang) or *tamol-pein* in Takia (Austronesian, Oceanic) (Ross 2007: 122)

(8)   'to obey someone' = 'to follow someone's mouth' (a shared collocational pattern) in the languages of Karkar island (Papua New Guinea): *awa-n ŋa-ri* 'mouth-3SG.POSS 1SG.S-follow' in Takia (Austronesian, Oceanic) versus *kurŋ karotu-sam* 'mouth:3SG.POSS follow-1SG.S' in Waskia (Nuclear Trans New Guinea, Madang) (Ross 2007: 122)

Polysemy sharing and lexico-semantic sharing are different manifestations of *lexico-semantic parallels* among languages, but there is no strict borderline between the two. Different meanings of a polysemous lexeme are normally associated with different constrictions, and polysemy in fact often arises due to the ellipsis of additional disambiguating material. To give a simple example, some languages share the polysemy 'child' = 'fruit', as in (2). In some other languages, however, the latter meaning requires a combination with 'tree', such as 'child of tree', resulting in a shared lexico-constructional pattern. However, even in the languages with the 'child'='fruit' polysemy the latter meaning may also be prevalent in combinations with 'tree', which makes it difficult to draw a strict line between shared polysemy and shared lexico-constructional patterns. The common denominator here is the shared *semantic association* between 'child' and 'fruit' (Matisoff 2004; Urban 2012; Vanhove 2008a).

8.2.3   Lexico-semantic Parallels as Areality Indicators: Mesoamerica and Ethiopia–Eritrea

Examples of lexico-semantic parallels abound in the literature on contact phenomena; among others, they figure prominently in discussions of metatypy (e.g. Ross 2007). Some have been discussed or at least mentioned in connection with various regions of different sizes and significance. A few of these have been attested and described across a large number of languages. Schapper et al.'s (2016) careful study of the different colexification patterns between 'tree', 'firewood' and 'fire' includes 275 languages spoken in Sahul, i.e. Australia, New Guinea and surrounding islands; Aikhenvald's (2009) sample for the 'eat' = 'drink' polysemy includes 36 languages from the same region (28 Papuan and eight Australian aboriginal languages). Other lexico-semantic parallels are often mentioned in a more implicit way. Our impression is that there is much knowledge on such shared patterns among experts on particular languages, language families and linguistic areas, which often remains concealed to outsiders.

There is surprisingly little discussion of the role of lexico-semantic parallels in areal linguistics. Some of the exceptions, in addition to the above-mentioned studies by Schapper et al. and by Aikhenvald, include

Austin et al. (1976) and Evans (1992), who discuss or at least mention a number of semantic associations shared by the aboriginal languages of Australia, Matisoff (1978, 2004), who focuses on various semantic associations in Southeast Asian languages, and Pardeshi et al. (2006), who deal with the meanings, functions and structure of expressions involving the verb 'eat' across the Asian languages. Vanhove 2008a (see also www.typologie.cnrs.fr/spip.php?rubrique131) focuses on several cross-linguistically recurrent patterns in polysemy and semantic change across 45 languages. Heine and Leyew (2005) and Güldemann and Fehn (Chapter 18, this volume) mention some lexico-semantic parallels of potential relevance for Africa, including the Kalahari Basin, as a group of linguistic areas. Enfield's (2003) excellent study of the multi-functionality of 'acquire' in the languages of Mainland Southeast Asia is mainly concerned with patterns crossing the border between lexicon and grammar.

We are aware of only two linguistic areas where lexico-semantic parallels have been systematically used as areality indicators: the Mesoamerican and the Ethio-Eritrean languages. Each of the cases involves a list of lexico-semantic parallels that have been checked both for the languages belonging to the presumed linguistic area and for those that do not.

For the Mesoamerican languages the discussion of lexico-semantic parallels as evidence for linguistic contact and, further, as indicators of linguistic areas, goes back at least to the 1970s and has involved such prominent linguists as Kaufman, Campbell, Smith-Stark and Brown. In the present context, the two most relevant publications are Smith-Stark (1994) and Brown (2011).

Smith-Stark (1994) tests to what extent 52 lexico-semantic parallels, previously detected in the Mesoamerican languages, may in fact count as strong areality indicators. The study embraces 46 languages, of which 25 come from Mesoamerica (MA) and represent its genetic and geographic diversity, 11 languages border the region, and 10 languages comprise five North American and five South American languages well removed from the Mesoamerican area. The procedure takes into consideration three parameters: to what extent the feature occurs throughout the region, its frequency in MA, and its limitation to MA (within the Americas). Fourteen lexico-semantic parallels turn out to be bound to MA, where they are widely distributed. Among these ten occur in at least four language families: 'boa' = 'deer snake', 'lime(stone)' = 'rock ashes', 'wrist' = 'neck (of hand)', 'molar' = 'grind-stone', 'mouth' = 'edge', 'thumb' = 'mother (of hand)', 'finger' = 'child (of hand)', 'poor' = 'widow' = 'orphan', 'alive' = 'awake', 'marry' = 'find/meet'.

Cross-linguistic similarities are of course particularly valuable as areality indicators whenever it is possible to trace their origin and the details of their diffusion, and to link them to the history of the linguistic contacts in an area. While this is often a relatively easy task for lexical borrowings, where the forms may betray their origin, finding out the history of lexico-semantic parallels is a much trickier endeavour. This step is undertaken by Brown (2011), who attempts to account for the circumstances behind the shared lexical traits in Mesoamerica, such as which languages acted as donors, when the traits spread, and so on. To this end he further tested 13 of the suggested Mesoamerican lexico-semantic parallels in a sample of 70 Native American languages in other areas. According to his conclusions, only five of these most probably originated in a single area language from where they diffused across Mesoamerica (among others, 'boa' = 'deer snake' and 'lime(stone)' = 'ashes'). Brown attributes the decisive role here to Nahuatl, the major lingua franca in Mesoamerica (first in the Aztec empire and later in New Spain). Although this conclusion is far from certain, the study is an impressive attempt to put areal lexico-semantic parallels in a larger historical framework.

The systematic research on lexico-semantic parallels in the Ethio-Eritrean languages has so far been relatively modest in that it only covers four languages (see, however, Treis 2010, mentioned in Section 8.6, for an update). Hayward's (1991, 2000) list contains 40 lexico-semantic parallels, among others 'draw water' = 'copy, imitate' in example (1), 'need' = causative of 'want' (5), or 'foreign country' = 'land of man/person'. These are shared by three languages representing the three main groups of the Ethio-Eritrean languages: Amharic (Semitic), Oromo (Cushitic) and Gamo (Omotic), all belonging to the Afroasiatic phylum. The list has also been tested for another East Lowland Cushitic language, Somali, which is both closely related to many of the languages in the Ethio-Eritrean area and is also spoken in their vicinity. Strikingly, Somali shares only four of the 40 patterns in the list, which fits into the accepted view of the history of the Somali within the Horn of Africa. In a nutshell, Somali groups have not had enough time to develop close contact with the speakers of the other languages more deeply integrated into the Ethio-Eritrean sprachbund, since they arrived there relatively late (most probably from northern Kenya). In addition, most of their social networks have been within the larger Muslim context, rather than with the other ethnic groups within Ethiopia and Eritrea.

Summarizing, Smith-Stark's (1994), Brown's (2011) and Hayward's (1991, 2000) studies of the Mesoamerican and the Ethio-Eritrean languages suggest that lexico-semantic parallels are a powerful tool for measuring membership of a linguistic area. As emphasized in these studies, the idiosyncratic nature of lexico-semantic parallels, their potential multiplicity and logical independence of each other lead to a great increase in the number of quantifiable properties. This makes them potentially more advantageous as areality indicators than the seemingly more important structural properties that are often listed as indicators of language convergence, such as word order or phonological contrasts. These latter features may show various interdependencies and in the long run be reducible to too few independent properties for quantifying convergence. However, evaluating any cross-linguistic similarities as areal indicators is always a challenge, and the same goes for lexico-semantic parallels (see the discussion in Section 8.6). Similar lexico-semantic parallelisms may be found in other regions of the world for different language groups. What often counts is that they are found in contiguous zones and in bundles with others.

8.3   Shared Formulaic Expressions

Conventionalized formulaic expressions used for particular pragmatic functions (e.g. greetings, curses, proverbs) represent a special case among shared lexico-constructional patterns; cf. the familiar farewell expressions *au revoir* (French), *auf Wiedersehen* (German), *på återseende* (Swedish), *do svidanija* (Russian), *näkemiin* (Finnish), that follow the same model across a number of European languages. Such conventionalized formulae are occasionally mentioned as areality indicators, as, for instance, the curse 'eat earth!', included in Hayward's (1991, 2000) list over the lexico-semantic parallels in the Ethio-Eritrean area. Ameka (2006, 2011) quotes several interactional routines including proverbs shared among the West African languages, primarily those in the Volta Basin, e.g. good-night wishes ('sleep/lie well'), thanking or leave-taking expressions. The formula 'When I die don't cry (i.e. don't mourn for me)' as expression of extreme gratitude in (9) builds on the West African cultural requirement to publicly show sorrow during the funeral by crying and wailing, and people who do not participate in this public display of sorrow are viewed with greatest suspicion. However, 'when someone does something very good for you, by absolving them from doing the things that one is expected to do when other people die, one is saying that the favour that has been received is like the ultimate thing or even more than it' (Ameka 2011: 253). The leave-taking expressions in (10) reflect the common West African cultural model that a visitor cannot just leave without first asking the host for a permission to do so. Pre-closing requests ('I am asking for a way/road') are genuine requests that can be answered both positively and negatively, initiating a whole chain of further communicative exchanges between the host and the visitor (Ameka and Breedveld 2004: 171–172).

(9)   Expressions of extreme gratitude in West Africa / in the languages of the Volta Basin
       a. Ewe (Niger-Congo, Kwa, Gbe; Ghana and Togo)
          Né   me-kú   lá,   me-ga-fa   aví   o.
          COND 1SG-die   TP   2SG:NEG-REP-shed   cry   NEG
          'When I die, don't cry.'

b. Akan (Niger-Congo, Kwa, Tano; Ghana)
   Se   ma-wu-a,   n-su.
   COND 1SG-die-TP   2SG:NEG-cry.
   'When I die, don't cry.'

c. Dagaare (Niger-Congo, Gur, Oti-Volta; N Ghana, Burkina Faso)
   Ka maa wa   kpi tɔɔ   kono.
   If 1SG come die NEG:IMP cry
   'When I die, don't cry.'

d. Gã (Niger-Congo, Kwa, Ga-Dengme; SE Ghana)
   Kɛ   o-nu   akɛ   ŋ-gbó-ɛ   kaa fo.
   COND 2SG-hear QUOT 1SG-die-TP NEG cry
   'When you hear that I am dead, don't cry.'

e. Moore (Niger-Congo, Gur, Oti-Volta; Burkina Faso)
   M   sã   nki bi   y   ra   yâb ye.
   1SG COND die that 2:POLITE   NEG cry NEG
   'When I die, please don't cry.'

(Ameka 2011: 232, 254)

(10) Pre-closing requests in the languages of Volta Basin
      a. Likpe   ń-tɔ   ku-sú ló
                 1SG-ask   CM-way UFP
      b. Akan   yɛ-srɛ   ᴋwan
                 1PL-beg   road
      c. Ewe   ma-biá   mɔ́
                 1SG:POT-ask way
                 'I ask permission to leave'

(Ameka 2006: 138–139)

Formulaic expressions are of great potential value as areality indicators, in particular due to their idiosyncratic properties. First, since their meaning is normally not compositional in the normal sense, their chances of being shared as a result of independent innovation is in general lower than for many other expressions. Second, speakers have to learn additional conversational routines and conventions as to which formulae should be appropriate for which pragmatic functions. These are therefore normally shared via socialization and repeated communication across languages, which implies more than sporadic language contact.

   Formulaic expressions are often permeated with shared cultural scripts and values and may bear testimony to the shared cultural history of the area. This is amply demonstrated in Piirainen's (2012) study of European figurative idioms, or items of phraseology. Piirainen, in collaboration with numerous colleagues (about 250) and experts spread over Europe, collected data on idioms in 73 linguistic varieties spoken in Europe, 17 non-European languages and Esperanto. As the result of this unprecedented effort she was able to identify 380 widespread European idioms. These can be traced to various sources, such as texts of ancient writers, the Bible, post-classical literature, proverbial units of medieval and reformation times, and fables, tales and legends. The six most widely spread European idioms (the number of the languages using them are in square brackets) are *night and day* [69], *to be/fight like cat and dog* [68], *to be someone's right hand* [64], *to play with fire* [64], *to take someone under one's wings* [62], and *to tear/ pull one's hair out* [62]. Interestingly, the European area, as defined by its core lexicon of idioms, is organized somewhat differently from that defined by shared grammatical structures. Whereas structural features place West Romance in the prototypical Standard Average European area and Slavic in its periphery (see van der Auwera 2011), it is the Slavic languages that share the European figurative lexicon to a greater extent than West Romance. Likewise, while both Armenian and Arabic are quite non-European from the structural point of view, they turn out to be much more 'European' in their idioms than the receding languages West Frisian and Kashubian, spoken in the core of Europe.

8.4 Area-specific Lexicalizations and Shared Organization of Semantic Domains

Experts occasionally mention area-specific concepts, i.e. concepts that are lexicalized across languages in a particular area but strike outsiders as very specific and curious. The extent to which these testify to language contact is, of course, not always clear. Some of them may be rooted in the shared physical environment, others bear witness to shared material culture and/ or cultural values and practices, which may go hand in hand with language contact but do not have to. To give a few examples, the languages of Ethiopia–Eritrea lexicalize the same four seasons of the year, similar categories of terrain, similar skin colour classification and particular kinds of artefacts (like a wooden chair). Another shared lexicalization is 'die without ritual slaughter (of cattle)', implying that the meat is unfit for consumption – *bäkkätä* in Amharic, *rak'e* in Oromo and *bawutides* in Gamo (Hayward 1991, 2000). West African languages sometimes have a special unanalysable lexeme for 'joking-relative', a notion which has no equivalent in European cultures. The joking relationship may be of three kinds: between ethnic groups, between clans, or between kinspersons of certain categories (for example, between a woman and the younger brothers of her husband) – all of them are covered by the word *sànáwú* in Mandinka (Niger-Congo, Mande; Senegal), *gaammu* in Wolof (Niger-Congo, Atlantic; Senegal) or *bárírá* in Bomu (Niger-Congo, Gur; Mali, Burkina Faso) (Denis Creissels and Martine Vanhove, personal communication). Matisoff (2004) quotes the Jingpo (Sino-Tibetan, Tibeto-Burman) expression *my ìt ʔəwām~ my ìt ʔəwām* 'to be deterred by feelings of respect, embarrassment, fear of offending; be generally restrained in one's interpersonal behaviour by the knowledge that self-assertiveness is not socially approved' as parallelled by Thai (Tai-Kadai, Kam-Tai) *krɛɛŋ-caj*, Burmese (Sino-Tibetan, Tibeto-Burman) *ʔâ-na*, Japanese (Japonic) *enryō suru*, 'reflecting a mind-set more typical of the [Southeast Asian] region than the more aggressive interpersonal ideal in Western competitive societies' (Matisoff 2004: 369; see also Markan 1979).

Shared areal lexicalizations pertaining to shared physical environment, material culture and cultural values and practices, are, of course, extremely valuable for areal studies. From a theoretical-linguistic point of view, however, it is even more interesting to ask whether areal convergence can lead to similar lexicalizations within more 'universal' lexical semantic domains. Some of Hayward's (1991, 2000) shared lexicalizations in the Ethio-Eritrean area may be included in this category, for instance, the adjectives *t'äfäff yalä* in Amharic, *kafaffa* in Oromo and *ts'izʔa* in Gamo, which all mean 'dry enough for use' (clothes that have been washed for wearing, a road for travelling, firewood to be used as fuel, etc.), or the two different verbs for 'borrowing something to be returned in kind only (like money)' and 'borrowing which is itself to be returned'.

A fundamental issue here is whether and/or to what extent languages can in general lexically converge in a particular semantic domain. Ricca's (1993) study of deictic verbs in the European languages is interesting here. The twenty languages in the sample fall into three groups depending on the extent to which they make a systematic distinction between verbs showing centripetal (to the deictic centre) versus centrifugal (from the deictic centre) motion. Significantly, the distribution of the types across the sample is dependent on a combination of genetic and areal factors, where the *fully deictic* languages are mainly found in southwestern and southern Europe (Portuguese, Spanish, Italian, Albanian, Modern Greek, with the two Finno-Ugric outliers Hungarian and Finnish), the *non-deictic* languages are Western and Eastern Slavic and Baltic, while the *predominantly deictic* ones are Germanic, along with French and the two Southern Slavic languages Serbo-Croatian and Slovenian.

Another instructive example is provided by van der Auwera's (1998) research on phasal adverbials, again in the European languages. These languages normally have systems that contrast the four adverbials *still, no longer, not yet, already* with each other, which is by no means universal and is also lacking in a few languages on the fringes of Europe. The languages with four adverbials fall further into two large groups, depending on how they express *no longer*. English, French (*ne plus*) or Swedish (*inte längre*) use a comparative here, which is also true for many (but not all) languages in Western and Central Europe. Spanish (*ya no*), Russian (*uže ne*) and most of the languages in Eastern Europe and on the Iberian peninsula show a different pattern, by combining 'already' with negation. Since both these large areas contain languages of distinct or at least distant genetic affiliation, the similarities in the semantic organization of their systems of phasal adverbials are largely attributable to convergence. All in all, van der Auwera (1998) has twelve properties for identifying the typical Standard Average European system, and their different subsets are particularly useful for zooming in on various convergence areas among the European languages.

8.5 The Greater Hindu Kush: A Case Study

In this section we attempt to outline the lexico-semantic profile of one particular 'linguistic area', the Greater Hindu Kush, focusing on the groups of lexico-semantic parallels discussed in the preceding sections. The Greater Hindu Kush (henceforth GHK) is the mountainous region comprising northern Pakistan, northeastern Afghanistan and the northernmost part of Indian Kashmir. There are 40–50 languages belonging to six different genera spoken here: Indo-Aryan (the largest component both demographically and in terms of the number of individual varieties), Iranian, Nuristani, Tibeto-Burman, Turkic and the isolate Burushaski. Areality research in the Greater Hindu Kush is only in its early stages, and although its significance as a convergence area has been suggested by several scholars for at least a few decades (Baart 2003; Bashir 1996, 2003: 823; Edelman 1980, 1983: 16; Tikkanen 1999, 2008; Toporov 1970), only a few features – primarily phonological and grammatical – have been studied in a more systematic fashion. GHK shares a number of features with the South Asian sprachbund at large, some others with languages spoken in the adjacent regions of Central Asia to the north of the Greater Hindu Kush, while still others might be typical of the region itself or of a significant subdivision of it. The region has probably never been united politically in its entirety, but has for a long time been at the periphery of a few larger contending political forces, while also maintaining cultural homogeneity and collective identity (Cacopardo and Cacopardo 2001: 251–252). Areal features in the realm of semantics in the GHK are found on multiple levels, and it is likely that higher-level convergence is an effect of prolonged and massive lower-level convergence, and that higher-level convergence in its turn functions as a catalyst for even more pervasive lower-level convergence. The following inventory should be read as an indication of semantic convergence rather than as a set of firm results from empirical study; our main focus here is to point to features bundled with one another in contiguous geographical areas or zones. Neither does it exclude the possibility of similar parallelisms in other regions of the world – a point that we will return to at the end of this section. Indeed, all of the subfields exemplified would benefit from further research.

The most visible signs of areal convergence are seen in the identical, or at least significantly similar, semantic structure of individual lexemes (or lexicalized phrases) across languages. To begin with, the shared loan vocabulary often comes from more prestigious languages (primarily Persian, Arabic, Portuguese and English). Some examples of polysemy copying or polysemy sharing across languages in the GHK (and most likely well beyond) are given in (11)–(13).

(11) 'Take' = 'buy' (widespread and old in the entire Indo-Aryan family, Turner 1966: 4236): *griik* in Kalasha (Trail and Cooper 1999), *ghína* in Palula, *gi~gig* in Dameli (Perder 2013: 207), *lenma* in Balti (Read 1934), *ŋaa* in Kamviri (Nuristani: Strand 2013), *axistəl* in Pashto. Interestingly, the semantically related notions of 'sell' and 'give' are normally kept apart in the same set of languages: e.g. *warkawəl* 'give' versus *xartsawəl* 'sell' (Pashto).

(12) 'Whiten/bleach/whitewash' = 'peel/rinse': *spinawəl* in Pashto, *paṇaróo* in Palula; cf. *goor* 'peel' and *goora/goori* 'white' in Dameli (Emil Perder p.c.).

(13) 'Heavy' = 'important, honourable': *drund* in Pashto, *gúraka* in Kalasha (Trail and Cooper 1999).

Related to that are shared metaphorical extensions, such as Kashmiri *toṛon* 'cold' -> 'hostile, unkind'. There are also a few widespread metonymical shifts, such as from 'house' to 'household' and by extension to a taboo-avoiding mechanism for enquiring about someone's wife (which is considered inappropriate in an environment where women observe *purdah*, i.e. seclusion) without actually using the word 'wife'. The phenomenon as such is of course even more widespread, particularly across the Muslim world.

Some of the shared lexico-constructional patterns in the region (and, again, most likely with an even wider distribution) are listed in (14)–(16).

(14) 'Parent' = 'mother-father': *mor-plaar* in Pashto, *yeei-baabu* in Palula, *yii-dadi* in Dameli (Emil Perder p.c.), *nan-tat* in Khowar, *nua-tot* in Kamviri (Strand 2013), *ata-ama* (lit. father-mother, i.e. the reverse order) in Purik (Tibeto-Burman: Marius Zemp p.c.).

(15) 'Elder' = 'white-beard': *spin-giraay* in Pashto, *paṇar-dóoṛu* in Palula, *paṇar-daa* in Indus Kohistani (Claus Peter Zoller p.c.).

(16) 'Beef' = 'big meat': *yəṭa ɣwaxa* in Pashto, *uyúm čhap* in Burushaski, *ghav masii* in Indus Kohistani (Claus Peter Zoller p.c.); cf. 'mutton' = 'small/narrow meat': *narəy ɣwaxa* in Pashto, *ǰoṭ čhap* in Burushaski.

Examples (17)–(18) (also known from many other, individual, languages and parts of the world – see below) show a shared semantic association that manifests itself as polysemy in some languages and as a lexico-constructional pattern in others.

(17)   'Finger' = 'toe': *aaŋür* in Kamviri (Strand 2013), *čamút* in Khowar, *aaŋguẉi* in Dameli (Emil Perder p.c.), *senmo* in Balti (Read 1934), *zuu~zuɣu* in Purik (Marius Zemp p.c.), *émiṣ* in Burushaski (Willson 1999).

(18)   'Toe' = 'foot's finger': *póngo čamúṭ* in Khowar, *kɔ̀s ongɔ̌j* in Kashmiri, *khuray angui* in Indus Kohistani (Claus Peter Zoller p.c.), *kangmi senmo* in Balti (Read 1934), *yuútise émiṣ* in Burushaski, *paaes anguuriikii* in Degano Pashai (Indo-Aryan: Strand 2013).

Many of the GHK languages have a basic kinship term covering both 'father' and 'father's brother' (often lexically distinct from 'mother's brother'). However, the latter meaning is probably becoming lexicalized in combinations with qualifying adjectives 'big' and 'small', where BIG FATHER is one's father's older brother and SMALL FATHER is one's father's younger brother: see examples (19)–(23). Similarly, there is a widespread polysemy pattern for 'mother' and 'mother's sister', but again with 'big' and 'small' only used for 'mother's sister'.

(19)   Burushaski (Parkin 1987: 161; Willson 1999): *áya* 'father', *(uyúm) áya* '(his) father's older brother (lit. big father)'.

(20)   Balti (Read 1934): *ata* 'father', *ata tsharma* 'father's older brother (lit. big father)', *ata tshuntse* 'father's younger brother (lit. small father)'; cf. *momo* 'mother's brother'.

(21)   Kati (Strand 2013): *to* 'father', *aalto* 'father's oldest brother (lit. big father)', *maaǰam to* 'father's middle brother (lit. middle father)', *křašto* 'father's youngest brother (lit. youngest father)'.

(22)   Palula: *báabu* 'father', *gaaḍbáabu* 'father's older brother (lit. big father)', *lhookbáabu* 'father's younger brother (lit. small father)'; cf. *máamu* 'mother's brother'; *pitrí* 'father's brother (generic)'.

(23)   Dameli (Perder 2013: 67): *dadi* 'father', *ǰeṣṭadadi* 'father's older brother (lit. older father)', *mažumadadi* 'father's middle brother (lit. middle father)', *sureedadi~učuṭadadi* 'father's younger brother (lit. young father, small father, respectively)'; cf. *mam* 'mother's brother'; *pitri* 'father's brother (generic)'.

Area-specific lexicalizations that do not easily translate into European languages (or even into any language outside the region) are often found in those domains which play a prominent role in the shared Hindu Kush culture, shaped by a similar mountainous environment, by traditional economies, and by similar-looking world views (some of them rooted in Islam, others in similar-looking and still pervasive pre-Islamic values and beliefs, yet others in a common pan-South Asian culture). Some of the more promising domains for further research are marriage, kinship, animal husbandry and supernatural beings.

Marriage in the region (and again, as in many other, primarily non-Western, societies) is never an individual affair: when you marry, you marry an entire family, and a large number of people are involved in the arrangements. A wedding, here exemplified from Khowar (Akhunzada and Liljegren 2009: 88–97), is a whole series of events or stages: *veçik* 'confirmation of engagement, betrothal'; *žaqdoyo* 'the party arriving from afar prior to the first day of the wedding'; *nikah/xotbal* 'the official signing of the marriage contract conducted by a religious scholar in the house of the bride'; *šištu* 'the procession taking the bride to the groom's house', *ɣečinisik* 'the groom's visiting his father-in-law three days after the wedding'; *mari* 'a party given by the groom to which the relatives of the bride are invited a few days after the wedding'. Many of those stages involve a specified kind of gift-giving or financial transaction: *mahar* 'bride price, as negotiated between the families of the bride and the groom'; *hosti çakhelik* 'engagement gifts, partly monetary, handed over by the groom's father to the bride and her family'; *maal* 'food items for the wedding supplied by the groom'; *ṣabokaan* 'wedding clothes (for the bride and groom) supplied by the groom's family'; *pandaar* 'gifts from relatives and villagers'; *išpeeri* 'food-gifts (sweets, sugar, etc.) given to the new couple at their arrival at the groom's place'.

An example of area-specific lexicalization (although far from being limited to the GHK) from the domain of kinship is a lexeme, mostly synchronically non-analysable, referring to a 'co-wife, a rival wife' in a situation where a man has more than one wife: *abeeni* in Dameli (Perder 2013: 69), *iaarí* in Kamviri (Strand 2013), *son* in Kashmiri (Khawaja Rehman, personal communication), *ambax* in Degano Pashai (Strand 2013).

The domain of animal husbandry has a highly specialized vocabulary describing dairy practices and dairy products. Some examples (in this case from Nuristan, in the eastern part of GHK) are 'buttermilk' (*niwo* in Kati, *trawəl* in Ashkun, *wašip* in Waigali), 'clarified butter' (*anðu* in Kati, *učo* in Prasuni, *anaa* in Ashkun), 'butter churn made from inflated goat skin' (*üzuu* in Prasuni, *maṇa* in Ashkun, *mõka* in Waigali), 'whey from buttermilk' (*skülåå* in Kati, *čiikəl* in Ashkun, *kütegaaw* in Waigali), 'cheese whey from milk curdled with rennet' (*elə* in Kati, *astoo* in Ashkun, *uštuwä* in Waigali), 'whey cheese' (*skürə* in Kati, *tskir* in Prasuni, *tsikarə* in Ashkun), 'fat rennet cheese made by the rennet poured directly into the milk' (*šipuu* in Ashkun/Waigali), 'soft rennet cheese (type 1)' (*tsila* in Ashkun, *kilaa* in Waigali), 'soft rennet cheese (type 2)' (*aməṣ* in Ashkun, *amüṣ* in Waigali), the difference between the latter two only in the boiling and use of the sack (Edelberg and Jones 1979, 74–91).

Some clearly pre-Islamic beliefs are still deeply rooted in the region, quite a few of them even amalgamated with the new religion or re-interpreted though its lens. This is particularly relevant from an areal-semantic viewpoint in the identification of a number of supernatural or 'not-quite-human' beings that have parallels in various languages across the region (Cacopardo and Cacopardo 2001: 140–143). First and foremost, there is the category of fairies, often, but not necessarily referred to with a word related to Persian *parii* 'winged; a good genius, a fairy' (Steingass 2000): *perē̃* in Dameli, *pari* in Khowar, *peereeṇ̃ii* or *peerái* in Palula, *súci* or *parí* in Kalasha, *pʌ̀yɽ ̣ⁱ* or *rʌçīⁱⁱ* in Indus Kohistani. Secondly, there is a rather different category of beings that are extremely dangerous; they are described as man-eating monsters, often living out in the wilderness: *ṭhaaṭáaku* (or *ṭhaaṭéeki* in their female form) in Palula, *balah* in Khowar (Akhunzada and Liljegren 2009: 106) and *ḍaaṇḍik* in Dameli (Emil Perder, personal communication). A third category comprises a witch-like creature, who, although often described as decidedly human, is also endowed with clearly supernatural powers or characteristics – *rui* in Shina-varieties, *goorvav* in Khowar, *šišeki* or possibly *runzi* in Dameli and *ruikúri* (i.e. *rui* woman) or *šišáki* in Palula (also a Shina variety). According to some 'modernist' accounts, she is a real, living woman who has abandoned society and gone into the forest or, alternatively, has taken residence in the ruins of an old house. Other, probably more 'traditional' accounts hold that she is a spirit who appears in the form of an old woman, sometimes seen with her feet turned backwards and with long breasts. Like the *ṭhaaṭéeki*, she drinks blood and eats people (Akhunzada and Liljegren 2009: 107–108; Cacopardo and Cacopardo 2001: 140–141, 170).

Shared formulaic expressions also deserve further research. Common greetings, farewell expressions and a number of other interactional routines (exclamations, congratulations, etc.) are to a very large extent Islamicized, based on Arabic or Persian expressions, and are therefore often also formally identical or near-identical across language boundaries. However, many of these are supplemented with language-specific expressions that nevertheless follow a rather uniform pattern, with a quick succession of polite questions and answers. An older layer of greetings seems to contain a distinct element of congratulation and well-wishing. Before the conversion to Islam (and probably a long time even after), Palula speakers greeted each other with an initial *wháatuee* 'Didn't you come down?' if the other person came down from a higher elevation, or *ukháatuee* 'Didn't you come up?' if he happened to have ascended from a place further down the valley or the slope; cf. Dameli *ageepi* 'Have you come?' (Emil Perder, personal communication). Although framed as questions, these formulae were really expressions of congratulation to the other person having safely reached his destination. This is still reflected in the Palula expression *tu xeera sangi phediluee* 'Did you arrive safely (lit. with happiness)?' A simple *kíi biáanu* 'Where are you going?' or *kíi gúum de* 'Where did you go?' is still frequently heard, and is as much a greeting in itself as an actual enquiry for information. The polite, traditional, exchange between Pashto speakers meeting each other contains paired expressions of (more or less) set well-wishes, such as *pə xer raayle* 'May you come in peace!', triggering the reply *pə xer use* 'May you live in peace!' or *stəray məše* 'May you not be tired!' answered with *xwaar məše* 'May you not be poor!' Similar

Table 8.1 *Calendrical expressions in Kamviri (Strand 2013), Burushaski (Berger 1998: 103), Dameli (Morgenstierne 1942: 137–178; Emil Perder, personal communication) and Balti (Read 1934: 30–31)*

Kamviri	Burushaski	Dameli	Balti	
nučút		učoot/čoot diyoo	dunma jaq	three days ago
nutrí	yáarbulto	itrii	karchaqla	the day before yesterday
dus	sabuúr	doos	gonde	yesterday
strák gaaǰaar	khúulto	mudya	diring	today
daalkě	jímale	beraa	bela, haske	tomorrow
aatrí	hípulto	truida	snangla	the day after tomorrow
aačův	máalto	čoot/čoova ki	rzesla	three days hence

Table 8.2 *Numerals in Burushaski (isolate: Berger 1998: 100–101), Balti (Tibeto-Burman: Bielmeier 1985; Read 1934: 24–25) and Ashkun (Nuristani: Strand 2013)*

Numeral	Burushaski		Balti	Ashkun
10	tóorumo		phcū	dos
20	áltar		ɲīšu	viši
30	áltar-tóorumo	20 + 10	xsumču	višiā dos
40	altó-áltar	2 × 20	ɲīšu ɲīs	du-viši
50	altó-áltar tóorumo	(2 × 20) + 10	ɲīšu ɲīs na phču / γaphču	du-višiā-dos
60	iskí-áltar	3 × 20	ɲīšu xsum	tra-viši
70	iskí-áltar tóorumo	(3 × 20) + 10	ɲīšu xsum na phču / dun-ču na phču	tra-višiā-dos
80	wálti-áltar	4 × 20	ɲīšu bjī	čā tā-viši
80	wálti-áltar tóorumo	(4 × 20) + 10	ɲīšu bjī na phču / bgya na phču	čā tā-višiā-dos
100	tha		bgya	pōč-viši

to the observations about West African leave-taking in Section 8.3, the guest in the GHK also explicitly asks for permission to leave, not infrequently by using the word *ijaazat* 'permission': *ijaazat day* 'Is there permission [to leave] (Pashto)?'

Another level of convergence has to do with shared organization of entire semantic domains, as for instance within calendrical expressions that include distinct lexical items for 'three days ago', 'the day before yesterday', 'yesterday', 'today', 'tomorrow', 'the day after tomorrow' and 'three days from now': see Table 8.1.

Another example of organizational patterns, this one affecting an entire part of speech, is the structure of numeral systems. Virtually all languages in the region, regardless of genealogical affiliation, have a vigesimal system, or numeral systems that are primarily vigesimal, i.e. based on 'twenty', although they differ in the details and the extent to which more peripheral decimal features have been added (often affecting

Table 8.3 *Sets of pro-forms in GHK languages (Bashir 2003, 2009; Berger 1998; Koul 2003; Strand 2013; Zemp 2013). Morphemes entailing emphasis (either in combination with a non-emphatic pro-form or in contrast with it) are indicated within parentheses*

	Proximate (visible)	Remote visible	Remote non-visible
Kashmiri	*yi(hoy)*	*hu(hay)*	*su(y)*
Palula	*(ee)nu*	*(ee)ro*	*(ee)so*
Kalasha	*(š)íya*	*(š)ása*	*(ša)se*
Burushaski	*in(é)*	*khin(é)*	*khin(é)*
Wakhi	*(ha)yem*	*(ha)yet*	*(ha)ya*
Kamviri	*(o)iná*	*(o)iá*	*(o)aaská*
Purik	*dyu*	*ao – (odoo)*	*eu*

Table 8.4 *Extended (but incomplete) set of Kashmiri pro-forms (Koul 2003)*

	Proximate	Remote within sight	Remote out of sight	Interrogative
Nominal	*yi*	*hu*	*su*	*kus* (an); *k'a* (inan)
Location	*yeti*	*hoti*	*tati*	*kati*
Direction	*yapōr'*	*hɔpōr'*	*tapōr'*	*kapōr'*
Manner	*yithi kin'*	*huthi kin'*	*tithi kin'*	*kithi kin'*
Quantity	*yūtāh*	*hūtāh*	*t'ūtāh*	*kūtāh*

numerals above 100): see Table 8.2. Tibeto-Burman varieties related to Balti and those spoken further to the south and southeast are entirely decimal, and so are most of the major languages surrounding the region, such as Hindi-Urdu, Persian, Turkic, etc. Massive Urdu influence in today's Pakistan leads to a gradual replacement of numerals above ten in the local languages by Urdu numerals.

Areally shared patterns have a bearing on the overall organization of the lexicon. Dimensions in time, space and discourse make use of similar multi-dimensional and multi-degree deictic contrasts in many GHK languages (some exemplified in the simplified paradigm in Table 8.3).

It seems that lexical material for such extensive (and to some extent symmetrical, and not seldom rhyming) sets of pro-forms has been recruited from various language-internal sources. A slightly more extended set is displayed for Kashmiri (Table 8.4); this set is, however, in no way unique to this particular language but shows a common structure found in most of the languages of the region, regardless of their genealogical classification.

The distinctions made in such sets (although not all of them are shared by all languages in the region) include emphatic / non-emphatic, proximate / remote, visible / invisible, interrogative / demonstrative / relative, nominal / adnominal. Some of the deictic values, usually the remote-within-sight ones, are further specified for distance, direction and angle,

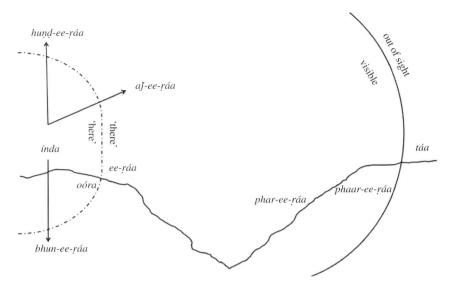

Figure 8.3 Palula spatial pro-forms

especially relevant in a mountainous region as this one (Bashir 2003): *paár ajóo* 'over there where I point', *paár adí* 'right over there', *paár asdí* 'right over there somewhere', *pér adí* 'over there (near, known but invisible)', *pér asdí* 'over there (out of sight)' in Kohistani Shina (Schmidt and Kohistani 2008, 97–98). Many of those, for example in Indo-Aryan Palula and Gawri (Baart 1999: 175–196), in Iranian Wakhi (Bashir 2009: 230–232), in the isolate Burushaski (Berger 1998: 78–97), as well as in Tibeto-Burman Purik (Zemp 2013: 235–242), can be used adverbially ('that place down there'), pronominally ('she down there') as well as adnominally ('that x down there'): see Figure 8.3. This might also be reflected in verbal specifications such as distinct lexical items for 'come up', 'come down', 'come out'; 'take up', 'take down'. The same, or a similar phenomenon, referred to as 'vertical case' and 'vertical verbs' (Noonan 2003), is characteristic of a group of languages spoken in the Nepal Himalayas, an adjacent mountainous region located to the east of the GHK.

An example that is difficult to place in any of the hitherto mentioned categories, is the prevalence of co-lexicalized intensifiers: Burushaski (Berger 1998: 226–227) *qhal-matúm* 'pitch black'; Gilgiti Shina (Carla Radloff, personal communication) *khutún šaróo* 'full autumn', *brang sang* 'very bright'; Kalasha (Trail and Cooper 1999) *ṭam laṭóra* 'perfectly round'; Kashmiri (Khawaja Rehman, personal communication) *sia krio-hon/kriohon sia* 'pitch black'. Curiously, for Indo-Aryan Palula, such intensifiers are almost exclusively made up of a single closed syllable, CVC(C): see Table 8.5. Characteristically, the intensifier is a unique lexical unit, compatible with a single head, or in some cases with a limited set of those.

Table 8.5 *Palula co-lexicalized intensifiers*

phaṣ *paṇáaru*	white as a sheet	**tap** *c̣hiṇ*	pitch dark
kham *kiṣinu*	pitch black	**bak** *práal*	shining bright
čáw *lhóilu*	bright red	**ḍang** *khilayí*	all alone
tak *zeṛ*	bright yellow		

As indicated in the beginning of this section, the inventory presented here should be taken with a certain degree of caution. For instance, neither of the lexical parallels 'toe' = '(foot's) finger', 'take' = 'buy' or 'parent' = 'mother-father', is unique to the Hindu Kush region. 'Parent' = 'mother-father' or 'father-mother' is mentioned by Wälchli (2005, 2015) as the most reliable single-word indicator for co-compounding (dwandwa-compounds) in Eurasia, in the sense that if a Eurasian language will have co-compounding at all, it will necessarily express 'parent' as 'mother-father' or 'father-mother'. The sequence of the components differs areally in various unpredictable ways: see Map 6.2 in Wälchli (2005: 218) for the occurrence of this pattern in the languages of Eurasia. 'Toe' = '(foot's) finger' is found in such familiar languages as Russian (*palec (na noge)*) or Italian (*dito (del piede)*), but is also well attested elsewhere. The online database CLIS (http://clics.lingpy.org/direct.php) lists 51 occurrences of 'toe'/'finger' colexifications and 38 'take' = 'buy' colexifications among the 221 languages in the database, both in Eurasia and in other parts of the world. Conspicuously, most of the examples for 'take' = 'buy' come from the Northern Caucasus, but these languages are also heavily represented in the database.

Vigesimal systems, or numeral systems that are primarily vigesimal, are found in various parts of the world, but are also being replaced by decimal systems. In Comrie's (2013) 196-language sample, Asia is indeed populated by decimal systems, with Burushaski as one of the very rare exceptions (none of the other Hindu Kush languages are included in the sample).

An evaluation of the systems of calendrical expressions as an isogloss is not straightforward. On the one hand, the systems with at least three distinctions in both the future and the past are not very rare and occur in 44 languages (28 per cent) in Tent's (1998) global 157-language sample. On the other hand, systems based on monomorphemic (non-transparent) expressions are only found in 16 languages (10 per cent) within Tent's sample, including Hindi. Some of these, however, have fewer semantic distinctions than the Hindu Kush languages. Interestingly, the calendrical expressions in the other Indo-Iranian language in Tent's study, Farsi, involve transparent polymorphemic structures.

Evaluation of most of the other properties, suggested as areal indicators for the Hindu Kush languages, is currently not possible due to lack of reliable data and would require further systematic research, both within the region and outside it.

8.6 Causation and Mechanisms: Inheritance, Diffusion, Shared Environment or Independent Innovation?

A central issue in all research concerned with cross-linguistic comparison is to what extent an observed cross-linguistic similarity may be explained by accident, inheritance, contacts, universal tendencies, or a combination of these factors. Certainly, when many languages belonging to different families within a more or less well-defined region share a property that is very rare in other parts of the world, language contact suggests itself as a likely explanation. However, as is evident from our discussion of the potential areal Hindu Kush traits, such an exercise is normally much more complicated than expected, in particular when most (or all) languages in the area are closely related to each other, which is in fact a frequent complication in presumed linguistic areas (most of the Ethio-Eritrean languages are Afroasiatic, most of the languages in the Volta basin are Niger-Congo or even Kwa, etc.). François (2010) exhibits the intricacies embedded in such an enterprise for the Oceanic languages of Northern Vanuatu, while Epps (2013) demonstrates how a careful and well-informed argumentation may be used for evaluating the relative probability of the different factors behind the lexico-constructional similarities, in this case the morphologically complex numeral expressions, in the Amazonian languages of the Vaupés region (see Epps and Michael, Chapter 32, this volume).

Like areal linguistics in general, a quest for areal lexico-semantic parallels faces various potential fallacies, which are often rooted in the researchers' natural bias to notice and overestimate the importance of patterns that strike them as unusual. However, most contact-induced change is not particularly spectacular, and most isoglosses are probably neither unique to an area nor skewed in their distribution so much that they will 'betray' the area in a large-scale sample. Isoglosses rooted in language contacts will, thus, often 'stand out' only within a particular area but will not necessarily be noticeable from a large-scale typological perspective. To identify them as areal properties requires, among other things, that they have been systematically tested both across the languages of the region and across the languages outside it, ideally across a large sample of the world's languages (with a combination of micro- and macrotypological methods: Koptjevskaja-Tamm 2011). A systematic large-scale investigation gives an important evaluation of how frequent or unique a particular property is among the languages of the world and provides an indication of the areas in which it might be found. By zooming in on a particular area with the help of a fine-grained sample it is possible to further estimate to what extent this property is systematically represented in the area rather than, say, appearing here and there.

In what follows we will illustrate the complexity of these issues with a few examples of relevant recent and on-going research related to the evaluation of particular lexico-semantic parallels as areal indicators.

Cross-linguistic research on semantic associations between verbs of perception and cognition provides an excellent example of how data based on different language samples may affect our understanding of what is universal, genetic and areal in a particular lexico-semantic field. In her influential study, mainly based on the Indo-European languages, Sweetser (1990) suggests that the metaphorical extension from vision to knowledge ('know', 'think') may 'be fairly common crossculturally, if not universal' (Sweetser 1990: 45), while the cognitive extension of hearing may be limited to 'understand'. These putatively universal connections are questioned by Evans and Wilkins (2000) in their study of about 60 Australian aboriginal languages, where the most frequent semantic extension is from hearing to cognition, and in particular, to knowledge ('know', 'think', 'remember'). Vision, on the contrary, mainly gives rise to social interaction readings such as desire and sexual attraction, aggression and negative social interactions, etc. Evans and Wilkins provide numerous arguments for showing that the connection between perception and cognition in the Australian aboriginal languages is rooted in various social and cultural practices of their speakers, without, however, ruling out that some of these may find parallels in other parts of the world.

Vanhove's (2008b) typological follow-up demonstrates that Evans and Wilkins's findings hold more generally. For instance, all the 25 languages of her genetically and geographically diverse sample have semantic extensions from hearing to cognition – to internal reception ('heed', 'obey'), often to intellectual perceptions and cognition ('understand', 'learn', 'know'), and, more rarely, to 'think' and 'remember'. The shift to cognitive meanings from vision is far less common, and most of the languages concerned have the same cognitive extensions for both 'hear' and 'see'.

Summarizing, the semantic associations that were believed to be (almost) universal have later turned out to be mainly genetic, while those that were believed to be genetic / areal have later proved to be much more widespread.

The most significant large-scale investigations of cross-linguistically recurrent semantic associations are reported in Urban (2012; also 2009, 2010). Urban's goal is to detect the semantic and structural patterns among the terms for 160 nominal concepts contained in a global sample of 109 languages. To give an idea of what is at stake, consider the concepts 'sun', 'moon' and 'day'. These are expressed by three different morphologically simple (indivisible) terms in English. Some languages, however, associate 'sun' and 'moon' in various ways, either by colexifying them within the same lexeme or by deriving the word for 'moon' from 'sun' in patterns like 'night sun'. Many languages associate 'sun' and 'day' by either using the same word for both (sometimes colexifying all the three concepts) or by deriving the term for 'sun' from 'day'. Languages differ therefore as to whether they express comparable concepts by unanalysable terms and as to which concepts are semantically associated with each other, either by polysemy or by various lexico-constructional patterns. There are both remarkable cross-linguistic dissimilarities and striking cross-linguistically recurrent patterns, that may be accounted for by a complex interplay among universal tendencies and genetic versus areal relations among the involved languages. A balanced global sample of this scale is, however, often too sparse a net to catch significant areal lexico-semantic parallels, and should be complemented by a more fine-grained sample covering many language varieties within the relevant area.

To continue with the 'sun'/'day'/'moon' example, the pattern 'sun' = 'eye of day' is very rare in the balanced global 214-language sample, but shows a remarkably high presence in the Austroasiatic, Tai-Kadai and Austronesian languages of Southeast Asia and Oceania, as demonstrated in the additional augmented 154-language sample for this part of the world (Urban 2010, 2012). Urban himself suggests two possible contact scenarios for this situation, while Gil (2015) mentions this skewed distribution as one of the areal properties of what he calls the Mekong-Mamberamo linguistic area, consisting of Mainland Southeast Asia, the Nusantara archipelago in Indonesia and parts of New Guinea. However, to complicate the issue, the reliability of Urban's data and his explanations is still contested by Blust (2011), who makes a case for the universality of this pattern by adding parallels from other languages.

The cross-linguistic distribution of the 'sun' = 'moon' colexification presents another challenge for historical linguistics. As Urban (2009, 2012) shows, the pattern is very unevenly distributed among the languages of the world. It is richly represented in the Americas, but is also found in the Palaeosiberian languages (the indigenous languages of northeastern Eurasia) and among the languages of New Guinea. Urban further argues that this distribution strongly correlates with the large Circum-Pacific area, suggested by Nichols and her collaborators (e.g. Bickel and Nichols 2006; Nichols 1995). This very old area is believed to have resulted from the large-scale population movement out of coastal Southeast Asia during the last glaciation. At such a great time depth 'historical' relatedness among languages may be detected by means of careful statistical analysis of the observed cross-linguistic patterns (Nichols and Peterson 1996), but it is not possible to further distinguish between genetic and areal relatedness.

Our next example concerns formulaic expressions used for particular pragmatic functions. Although their chances of being shared by languages as a result of independent innovation is in general lower than for many other expressions, this possibility should not be neglected either. In his inspiring paper 'Areal semantics: Is there such a thing?' Matisoff

(2004: 369) mentions typically Southeast Asian greetings such as 'Where are you going?' and 'Have you eaten yet?': see the examples in (24).

(24)   Conventionalized direction 'where'-greetings
       a. Vietnamese (Austroasiatic, Mon-Khmer)
          Đi đâu?
          go where
       b. Jakarta Indonesian (Austronesian, Malayo-Polynesian)
          Mau ke mana?
          want to where
          'How are you?' (lit. 'Where are you going?')

                                                                (Gil 2015)

Such greetings do not presuppose any precise reply, like 'I am going to my mother', in the same way as 'How do you do?' does not presuppose any real report on the interlocutor's life situation. Somewhat surprisingly, conventionalized greetings with 'directional where' (i.e. 'Where are you going?' or 'Where are you coming from?') are much more spread than Matisoff suggests: they occur in 65 per cent of the 363 languages in Gil's (2015) global sample, including the Greater Hindu Kush languages, as shown in Section 8.5. It remains unclear, though, whether all these languages use such expressions to the same extent. As Gil comments, 'where'-greetings are often restricted to outdoor contexts, but in some cases can also be heard indoors. Obviously, greeting someone outdoors often presupposes that at least one of the interlocutors is on their way from one place to another. Under such circumstances the *where*-questions have a reasonable source, and different languages may have independently developed their conventionalized greetings on the basis of this universally recurrent situation. However, as Gil (2015) argues, directional 'where'-greetings are not equally well spread across the world: in some areas they are used just in few languages, whereas in others they are the rule. The latter is the case in the Mekong-Mamberamo area (see above), but this isogloss covers a larger area, extending, among other things, into the Himalayas in South Asia.

Our final reflections concern the issue of whether and/or to what extent languages can in general converge in their lexical systems used for a particular semantic domain. The phasal adverbs and deictic verbs in the European languages (Section 8.4) or the calendrical expressions in the Greater Hindu Kush region (Section 8.5) are excellent examples of convergence in the conceptual organization of entire lexical semantic systems. However, in all these cases the lexical systems are relatively closed and/or organized according to comparatively simple oppositions, bordering on grammatical phenomena. The question is to what extent convergence may involve more typical lexical systems, corresponding to complex semantic domains which in principle allow for greater freedom in categorization. The evidence so far is very sketchy and partly contradictory.

There are, in fact, some examples of shared organization in lexical domains that have been attributed to areal forces. Particularly inspiring for these suggestions is Viberg's (1984) widely quoted lexico-typological study of PERCEPTION verbs. Güldemann and Fehn (Chapter 18, this volume) show that the conflation of HEARING, TOUCH, TASTE and SMELL in one verb as opposed to SIGHT is found in languages of all the different families in Central Kalahari, while the languages in other parts of the Kalahari Basin show more elaborated systems. Also Treis (2010) provisionally suggests that some particular conflations of perception verbs (such as one verb for 'hear' and 'listen' or the use of the passive form of the hearing verbs for TOUCH and TASTE) and taste adjectives may be added to the lexico-semantic parallels within the Ethio-Eritrean area (see the discussion of Hayward 1991, 2000 in Section 8.2). Enfield (2011: 31) asks whether language contact can 'permeate the conceptual organization of lexical semantic domains' in relation to the domain of TASTE and FLAVOUR in two Southeast Asian languages: Lao (a southwest Tai-Kadai language spoken by 25 million people in Laos, Thailand and Cambodia) and Kri (an Austroasiatic language with 300 speakers in upland central Laos). His answer is positive, in that the two languages turn out to divide the domain in similar ways, i.e. organize it into similar categories. Since Tai languages were adopted by pre-existing Austroasiatic-speaking populations, Enfield (2011: 36) hypothesizes that perhaps the ancestors of modern-day Lao speakers 'once learned an earlier form of Lao as their second language, and in shifting toward using it as their first language introduced semantic distinctions that were encoded in their original language'.

However, while Enfield's results are striking, they are also somewhat questionable, given the knowledge accumulated in cross-linguistic research into the lexicon. In a nutshell, the lexicon is subject to relatively rapid changes, which often lead to restructuring of lexical semantic domains. As a result, even closely related languages often display significant typological differences in how they categorize and organize similar cognitive domains, often by means of cognates: see Majid et al. (2007) for the CUT and BREAK domain in Germanic, and Koptjevskaja-Tamm et al. (2011) for the AQUAMOTION domain in Germanic and Slavic. The same is also true for lexical systems in closely related languages that have been spoken in close contact with each other for any considerable time. For instance, the Timor-Alor-Pantar languages Abui and Kamang (Schapper 2015) or the Kwa languages Ewe, Likpe and Sɛlɛɛ (Agbetsoamedo and Di Garbo 2015; Ameka 2015) show significant dissimilarities in their categorization and lexicalization of the TEMPERATURE domain. Against this background it is hardly plausible that languages would keep the same lexical distinctions for such a long time period as is invoked by Enfield.

There may, however, be a 'milder' version of lexical convergence having to do with the general level of elaboration within a particular lexical system, rather than with the distinctions themselves. For instance, according to Matisoff (2004: 366), the Southeast Asian lexico-semantic areal features include a rich lexicon of verbs of manipulation within such domains as CARRYING or CUTTING. And at least for CARRYING this is confirmed by Wälchli's (2009: 35–39) study of 'carry' verbs in the parallel corpus of the Mark New Testament in 100 languages, where Southeast Asia and Oceania show the highest presence of body-specific 'carry'-verbs. These are largely absent from some other areas (such as Europe) or are sometimes restricted to 'carrying on head', as, for instance, in a number of African languages.

8.7 Final Words

Lexical phenomena do of course have a long-standing record in research on language contact and linguistic areas. However, the recent developments in areal linguistics and areal typology have, with a few exceptions, mainly concerned grammatical phenomena. This is not at all surprising given the central place of this research in modern linguistics of all denominations, including typology, where the rapidly developing field of areal typology has encouraged and facilitated serious research on the relative role of universal, genetic and areal factors for many grammatical (and phonetic phenomena). Further, loanwords have been studied from a more systematic cross-linguistic perspective, where the core issue has been the varying borrowability of various words, seen as belonging to different parts of speech and/or coming from different semantic domains (Haspelmath and Tadmor 2009; Wohlgemuth 2009). The interesting research angles here, as elsewhere in research on contact phenomena and in (areal-) typological research (see Koptjevskaja-Tamm 2011), are (i) possible outcomes of language contact in the realm of the lexicon, and (ii) the possibility of using lexical phenomena to reconstruct contact.

As we hope to have shown in this chapter, lexical semantics in language contact and diffusion of lexico-semantic phenomena across language boundaries in a geographical area has a great potential for historical and areal linguistics, but is still awaiting systematic research. This is partly related to the relatively limited cross-linguistic research on lexical issues in general, which may impede evaluation of particular lexico-semantic parallels as areal indicators and obstruct informed attempts to find reasonable explanations for their origin.

The following two enterprises directed at unveiling cross-linguistically recurrent patterns of polysemy and lexico-constructional patterns deserve special mention.

1 The *Database of Semantic Shifts in the Languages of the World* (http://semshifts
   .iling-ran.ru/), at the Institute of Linguistics, Russian Academy of
   Sciences in Moscow, is a searchable computer database (not yet fully
   implemented online) that currently contains more than 3,000 semantic
   shifts found in 319 languages (Zalizniak 2008; Zalizniak et al. 2012).

2 *CLICS: Database of Cross-Linguistic Colexifications* (List et al., http://clics
   .lingpy.org/main.php) is an online database of colexifications in 221
   languages. It is based on four different freely available online resources
   and contains 16,239 different links among the 1,280 concepts it operates with (all in all 45,667 cases of colexification).

The information accumulated in these databases provides a valuable cross-
linguistic complement to many of the lexico-semantic parallels that have
been mentioned in connection with different areas.

The good news is that lexical typology is currently on the rise: see
Koptjevskaja-Tamm et al. (2015) for a recent review. We are therefore
looking forward to more cross-linguistic research on the categorization
of lexical semantic domains, polysemy patterns, semantic associations
and lexico-constructional patterns, complemented by detailed case studies
of these phenomena in languages in various contact situations. This
knowledge is essential for gaining a better understanding of what happens
with semantics in language contact.

References

Agbetsoamedo, Yvonne and Francesca Di Garbo, 2015. Unravelling tem-
   perature terms in Sɛlɛɛ. In Koptjevskaja-Tamm (ed.), pp. 107–127.
Aikhenvald, Aleksandra Y., 2009. 'Eating', 'drinking' and 'smoking': A generic
   verb and its semantics in Manambu. In John Newman (ed.), *The Linguistics of
   Eating and Drinking*, pp. 91–108. Amsterdam: John Benjamins.
Akhunzada, Fakhruddin and Maarit Liljegren, 2009. *Kalkatak: A Crossroads of
   Cultures in Chitral*. FLI Language and Culture Series, vol. 4. Islamabad:
   Forum for Language Initiatives.
Ameka, Felix K., 2006. Grammars in contact in the Volta Basin (West Africa):
   On contact induced grammatical change in Likpe. In
   Aleksandra Y. Aikhenvald and R. M. W. Dixon (eds), *Grammars in Contact:
   A Cross-Linguistic Typology*, pp. 114–142. Oxford: Oxford University Press.
Ameka, Felix K., 2011. 'When I die don't cry': The ethnopragmatics of
   'gratitude' in West African languages. In Cliff Goddard (ed.),
   Ethnopragmatics: Understanding Discourse in Natural Context, pp. 231–266.
   Berlin: de Gruyter Mouton.
Ameka, Felix K., 2015. 'Hard sun, hot weather, skin pain': The cultural
   semantics of temperature expressions in Ewe and Likpe (West Africa).
   In Koptjevskaja-Tamm (ed.), pp. 43–72.

Ameka, Felix K. and Anneke Breedveld, 2004. Areal cultural scripts for social interaction in West African communities. *Intercultural Pragmatics* 1 (2): 167–187.

Ameka, Felix K. and David P. Wilkins, 1996. Semantics. In Hans Goebl, Peter H. Nelde, Zdeněk Starý and Wolfgang Wölck (eds), *Contact Linguistics: An International Handbook of Contemporary Research*, pp. 130–138. Berlin: Walter de Gruyter.

Austin, Peter, Robert Ellis and Luise Hercus, 1976. 'Fruit of the eyes': Semantic diffusion in the Lakes languages of South Australia. *Papers in Australian Linguistics* 10: 51–77.

van der Auwera, Johan, 1998. Phasal adverbials. In Johan van der Auwera (ed.) with Dónall P. Ó Baoill, *Adverbial Constructions in the Languages of Europe*, pp. 25–145. Berlin: Mouton de Gruyter.

van der Auwera, Johan, 2011. Standard Average European. In Bernd Kortmann and Johan van der Auwera (eds), *The Languages and Linguistics of Europe: A Comprehensive Guide*, pp. 291–306. Berlin: de Gruyter Mouton.

Baart, Joan L. G., 1999. *A Sketch of Kalam Kohistani Grammar*. Studies in Languages of Northern Pakistan, vol. 5. Islamabad: National Institute of Pakistan Studies and Summer Institute of Linguistics.

Baart, Joan L. G., 2003. Tonal features in languages of Northern Pakistan. In Joan L. G. Baart and Ghulam Hyder Sindhi (eds), *Pakistani Languages and Society: Problems and Prospects*, pp. 132–144. Islamabad and High Wycombe: National Institute of Pakistan Studies, Quaid-i-Azam University and Summer Institute of Linguistics.

Bashir, Elena, 1996. The areal position of Khowar: South Asian and other affinities. In Elena Bashir and Israr-ud-Din (eds), *Proceedings of the Second International Hindukush Cultural Conference*, pp. 167–179. Hindukush and Karakoram Studies, vol. 1. Karachi: Oxford University Press.

Bashir, Elena, 2003. Dardic. In George Cardona and Danesh Jain (eds), *The Indo-Aryan Languages*, pp. 818–894. London: Routledge.

Bashir, Elena, 2009. Wakhi. In Gernot Windfuhr (ed.), *The Iranian Languages*, pp. 825–862. London: Routledge.

Berger, Hermann, 1998. *Die Burushaski-Sprache von Hunza und Nager*, vol. 1: *Grammatik*. Neuindische Studien, vol. 13. Wiesbaden: Harrassowitz.

Bickel, Balthasar and Johanna Nichols, 2006. Oceania, the Pacific Rim, and the theory of linguistic areas. *Proceedings of the Annual Meeting of the Berkeley Linguistics Society* 32: 3–15.

Bielmeier, Roland, 1985. *Das Märchen vom Prinzen Čobzaṅ: Eine tibetische Erzählung aus Baltistan: Text, Übersetzung, Grammatik und Westtibetisch vergleichendes Glossar*. Beiträge zur Tibetischen Erzählforschung, vol. 6. Sankt Augustin: VGH Wissenschaftsverlag.

Blust, Robert, 2011. 'Eye of the day': A response to Urban (2010). *Oceanic Linguistics* 50 (2): 524–535.

Boyeldieu, Pascal, 2008. From semantic change to polysemy: The cases of 'meat/animal' and 'drink'. In Vanhove (ed.), pp. 303–315.

Brown, Cecil, 2011. The role of Nahuatl in the formation of Mesoamerica as a linguistic area. *Language Dynamics and Change* 1: 171–204.

Cacopardo, Alberto M. and Augusto S. Cacopardo, 2001. *Gates of Peristan: History, Religion and Society in the Hindu Kush*. Reports and Memoirs, vol. 5. Rome: IsIAO.

Comrie, Bernard, 2013. Numeral bases. In Matthew S. Dryer and Martin Haspelmath (eds), *The World Atlas of Language Structures Online*. Leipzig: Max Planck Institute for Evolutionary Anthropology. http://wals.info/chapter/131

Croft, William, 2000. *Explaining Language Change: An Evolutionary Approach*. Harlow, UK: Pearson Education Limited.

Edelberg, Lennart and Schuyler Jones, 1979. *Nuristan*. Graz: Akadem. Druck- u. Verlagsanst.

Edelman, Dzhoi Iosifovna, 1980. K substratnomu naslediju Central'no-Asiatskogo jazykogo sojuza [Towards the substrate heritage of the Central Asian Sprachbund]. *Voprosy Jazykoznanija* 5: 21–32.

Edelman, Dzhoi Iosifovna, 1983. *The Dardic and Nuristani Languages*, translated from Russian by E. H. Tsipan. Moscow: Nauka, Central Department of Oriental Literature.

Enfield, Nicholas J. (ed.), 2003. *Linguistic Epidemiology: Semantics and Grammar of Language Contact in Mainland Southeast Asia*. London: Routledge Curzon.

Enfield, Nicholas J., 2011. Taste in two tongues: A Southeast Asian study of semantic convergence. In Asifa Majid and Stephen C. Levinson (eds), *The Senses in Language and Culture*, pp. 30–37. Special issue of *The Senses and Society* 6 (1).

Epps, Patience, 2013. Inheritance, calquing or independent innovation? Reconstructing morphological complexity in Amazonian numerals. *Journal of Language Contact* 6: 329–357.

Evans, Nicholas, 1992. Multiple semiotic systems, hyperpolysemy, and the reconstruction of semantic change in Australian languages. In Peter Austin, R. M. W. Dixon, Tom Dutton and Isobel White (eds), *Language and History: Essays in Honour of Luise A. Hercus*, pp. 137–155. Pacific Linguistics, vol. C-116. Canberra: Australian National University.

Evans, Nicholas and David P. Wilkins, 2000. In the mind's ear: The semantic extensions of perception verbs in Australian languages. *Language* 76: 546–592.

François, Alexandre, 2008. Semantic maps and the typology of colexification: Intertwining polysemous networks across languages. In Vanhove (ed.), pp. 163–215.

François, Alexandre, 2010. Des valeurs en héritage: Les isomorphismes sémantiques et la reconstruction des langues. In Injoo Choi-Jonin,

Marc Duval and Olivier Soutet (eds), *Typologie et comparatisme*, pp. 129–145. Orbis-Supplementa, vol. 29. Louvain: Peeters.

Gast, Volker and Johan van der Auwera, 2012. What is contact-induced grammaticalization? Evidence from Mayan and Mixe-Zoquean languages. In Björn Wiemer, Bernhard Wälchli and Björn Hansen (eds), *Grammatical Replication and Borrowability in Language Contact*, pp. 381–426. Berlin: de Gruyter Mouton.

Gil, David, 2015. The Mekong-Mamberamo linguistic area. In Nicholas Enfield and Bernard Comrie (eds), *The Languages of Mainland Southeast Asia: The State of the Art*, pp. 266–355. Pacific Linguistics, vol. 649. Berlin: de Gruyter Mouton.

Haspelmath, Martin and Uri Tadmor (eds), 2009. *Loanwords in the World's Languages: A Comparative Handbook*. Berlin: Mouton de Gruyter.

Hayward, Richard J., 1991. A propos patterns of lexicalization in the Ethiopian language area. In Daniela Mendel and Ulrike Claudi (eds), *Ägypten im afro-orientalischen Kontext*, pp. 139–156. Special issue of *Afrikanistische Arbeitspapiere*. Köln: Institute of African Studies.

Hayward, Richard J., 2000. Is there a metric for convergence? In Colin Renfrew, April McMahon and R. L. Trask (eds), *Time Depth in Historical Linguistics*, pp. 621–640. Papers in the Prehistory of Languages, vol. 2. Cambridge: McDonald Institute for Archaeological Research.

Heine, Bernd and Tania Kuteva, 2003. On contact-induced grammaticalization. *Studies in Language* 27 (3): 529–572.

Heine, Bernd and Tania Kuteva, 2005. *Language Contact and Grammatical Change*. Cambridge: Cambridge University Press.

Heine, Bernd and Zelealem Leyew, 2008. Is Africa a linguistic area? In Bernd Heine and Derek Nurse (eds), *A Linguistic Geography of Africa*, pp. 15–35. Cambridge: Cambridge University Press.

Koptjevskaja-Tamm, Maria, 2011. Linguistic typology and language contact. In Jae Jung Song (ed.), *The Oxford Handbook of Linguistic Typology*, pp. 568–590. Oxford: Oxford University Press.

Koptjevskaja-Tamm, Maria (ed.), 2015. *The Linguistics of Temperature*. Amsterdam: John Benjamins.

Koptjevskaja-Tamm, Maria, Dagmar Divjak and Ekaterina V. Rakhilina. 2010. Aquamotion verbs in Slavic and Germanic: A case study in lexical typology. In Victoria Hasko and Renee Perelmutter (eds), *New Approaches to Slavic Verbs of Motion*, pp. 315–341. Amsterdam: John Benjamins.

Koptjevskaja-Tamm, Maria, Ekaterina V. Rakhilina and Martine Vanhove. 2015. The semantics of lexical typology. In Nick Riemer (ed.), *The Routledge Handbook of Semantics*, pp. 434–454. London: Routledge.

Koul, Omkar N., 2003. Kashmiri. In George Cardona and Danesh Jain (eds), *The Indo-Aryan Languages*, pp. 895–952. London: Routledge.

List, Johann-Mattis, Thomas Mayer, Anselm Terhalle and Matthias Urban, 2014. *Database of Cross-Linguistic Colexifications*, Version 1.0. Marburg: Forschungszentrum Deutscher Sprachatlas. http://CLICS.lingpy.org

Majid, Asifa, Marianne Gullberg, Miriam van Staden and Melissa Bowerman, 2007. How similar are semantic categories in closely related languages? A comparison of cutting and breaking in four Germanic languages. In Asifa Majid and Melissa Bowerman (eds), *Cutting and Breaking Events: A Cross-linguistic Perspective*, pp. 179–194. Special issue of *Cognitive Linguistics* 18 (2).

Markan, LaRaw, 1979. A dictionary of modern Jinghpaw. Unpublished manuscript, quoted in Matisoff (2004).

Matisoff, James A., 1978. *Variational Semantics in Tibeto-Burman: The 'Organic' Approach to Linguistic Comparison*. Philadelphia: Institute for the Study of Human Issues.

Matisoff, James A., 2004. Areal semantics: Is there such a thing? In Anju Saxena (ed.), *Himalayan Languages: Past and Present*, pp. 347–393. Berlin: Mouton de Gruyter.

Matras, Yaron and Jeanette Sakel, 2007. Investigating the mechanisms of pattern replication in language convergence, *Studies in Language* 31: 829–865.

Morgenstierne, Georg, 1942. Notes on Dameli: A Kafir-Dardic dialect of Chitral. *Norsk Tidsskrift for Sprogvidenskap* 12: 115–198.

Nichols, Johanna, 1995. The spread of language around the Pacific Rim. *Evolutionary Anthropology* 3: 206–215.

Nichols, Johanna and David A. Petterson, 1996. The Amerind personal pronouns. *Language* 72: 336–371.

Noonan, Michael, 2003. Recent language contact in the Nepal Himalaya. In David Bradley, Randy LaPolla, Boyd Michailovsky and Graham Thurgood (eds), *Language Variation: Papers on Variation and Change in the Sinosphere and in the Indosphere in Honour of James A. Matisoff*, pp. 65–87. Canberra: Pacific Linguistics.

Pardeshi, Prashant, Peter Hook, Colin P. Masica et al., 2006. Toward a geotypology of EAT-expressions in the languages of Asia: Visualizing areal patterns through WALS. *Gengo Kenkyu* 130: 89–108.

Parkin, Robert, 1987. Kin classification in the Karakorum. *Man* 22 (1): 157–170.

Perder, Emil, 2013. *A Grammatical Description of Dameli*. PhD dissertation, Stockholm University.

Piirainen, Elisabeth, 2012. *Widespread Idioms in Europe and Beyond: Toward a Lexicon of Common Figurative Units*. New York: Peter Lang.

Read, Alfred F. C., 1934. *Balti Grammar*. London: James G. Forlong Fund.

Ricca, Davide, 1993. *I verbi deittici di movimento in Europa: Una ricerca inter-linguistica*. Firenze: La Nuova Italia Editrice.

Ross, Malcolm, 2007. Calquing and metatypy. *Journal of Language Contact* 1 (1): 116–143.

Schapper, Antoinette, 2015. Temperature terms in Kamang and Abui, two Papuan languages of the Timor-Alor-Pantar family. In Koptjevskaja-Tamm (ed.), pp. 860–887.

Schapper, Antoinette, Lila San Roque and Rachel Hendery, 2016. *Tree, firewood* and *fire* in the languages of Sahul. In Päivi Juvonen and Maria Koptjevskaja-Tamm (eds), *The Lexical Typology of Semantic Shifts*, pp. 355–422. Berlin: de Gruyter Mouton.

Schmidt, Ruth Laila and Razwal Kohistani, 2008. *A Grammar of the Shina Language of Indus Kohistan*. Beiträge zur Kenntnis Südasiatischer Sprachen und Literaturen, vol. 17. Wiesbaden: Harrassowitz.

Smith-Stark, Thomas C., 1994. Mesoamerican calques. In Carolyn J. MacKay and Verónica Vásques (eds), *Investigaciones lingüísticas en Mesoamérica*, pp. 15–50. Mexico: Universidad Nacional Autónoma de México.

Steingass, Francis Joseph, 2000. *A Comprehensive Persian, English Dictionary: Including the Arabic Words and Phrases to Be Met with in Persian Literature Being Johnson and Richardson's Persian, Arabic and English Dictionary*. Lahore: Sang-e-Meel Publications.

Strand, Richard F., 2013. Richard Strand's Nuristân Site: Lexicons of Kâmviri, Khowar, and Other Hindu-Kush Languages. http://nuristan.info/lngFrameL.html

Sweetser, Eve, 1990. *From Etymology to Pragmatics: Metaphorical and Cultural Aspects of Semantic Structure*. Cambridge: Cambridge University Press.

Tent, Jan, 1998. The structure of deictic day-name systems. *Studia Linguistica* 52 (2): 112–148.

Tikkanen, Bertil, 1999. Archaeological-linguistic correlations in the formation of retroflex typologies and correlating areal features in South Asia. In Roger Blench (ed.), *Archaeology and Language*, pp. 138–148. London: Routledge.

Tikkanen, Bertil, 2008. Some areal phonological isoglosses in the transit zone between South and Central Asia. In Israr-ud-Din (ed.), *Proceedings of the Third International Hindu Kush Cultural Conference*, pp. 250–262. Karachi: Oxford University Press.

Toporov, Vladimir Nikolayevich, 1970. About the phonological typology of Burushaski. In Roman Jakobson and Shigeo Kawamoto (eds), *Studies in General and Oriental Linguistics Presented to Shiro Hattori on the Occasion of his Sixtieth Birthday*, pp. 632–647. Tokyo: TEC Corporation for Language and Educational Research.

Trail, Ronald L. and Gregory R. Cooper, 1999. *Kalasha Dictionary with English and Urdu*. Islamabad and High Wycombe: National Institute of Pakistan Studies, Quaid-i-Azam University and Summer Institute of Linguistics.

Treis, Yvonne, 2010. Perception verbs and taste adjectives in Kambaata and beyond. In Anne Storch (ed.), *Perception of the Invisible: Religion, Historical Semantics and the Role of Perceptive Verbs*, pp. 313–346. Sprache und Geschichte in Afrika, vol. 21. Köln: Köppe.

Turner, Sir Ralph Lilley, 1966. *A Comparative Dictionary of the Indo-Aryan Languages*. Oxford: Oxford University Press.

Urban, Matthias, 2009. 'Sun' and 'moon' in the Circum-Pacific language area. *Anthropological Linguistics* 51 (3/4): 328–346.

Urban, Matthias, 2010. 'Sun' = 'Eye of the day': A linguistic pattern of Southeast Asia and Oceania. *Oceanic Linguistics* 49 (2): 568–579.

Urban, Matthias, 2012. *Analyzability and Semantic Associations in Referring Expressions: A Study in Comparative Lexicology*. PhD dissertation, Leiden University.

Vanhove, Martine (ed.), 2008a. *From Polysemy to Semantic Change: Towards a Typology of Lexical Semantic Associations*. Amsterdam: John Benjamins.

Vanhove, Martine, 2008b. Semantic associations between sensory modalities, prehension and mental perceptions: A cross-linguistic perspective. In Vanhove (ed.), pp. 341–370.

Viberg, Åke, 1984. The verbs of perception: A typological study. In Brian Butterworth, Bernard Comrie and Östen Dahl (eds), *Explanations for Language Universals*, pp. 123–162. Berlin: Mouton.

Wälchli, Bernhard, 2005. *Co-Compounds and Natural Coordination*. Oxford: Oxford University Press.

Wälchli, Bernhard, 2009. *Motion Events in Parallel Texts*. Habilitationsschrift, Philosophisch-historische Fakultät der Universität Bern.

Wälchli, Bernhard, 2015. Co-compounds. In Peter O. Müller, Ingeborg Ohnheiser, Susan Olsen and Franz Rainer (eds), *Word Formation: An International Handbook of the Languages of Europe*, vol. 1, pp. 707–726. Berlin: de Gruyter Mouton.

Weinreich, Uriel, 1953. *Languages in Contact: Findings and Problems*. New York: Linguistic Circle of New York. Reprinted 1963, The Hague: Mouton.

Willson, Stephen R., 1999. *Basic Burushaski Vocabulary*. Islamabad and High Wycombe: National Institute of Pakistan Studies, Quaid-i-Azam University and Summer Institute of Linguistics.

Wohlgemuth, Jan, 2009. *A Typology of Verbal Borrowings*. Berlin: Mouton de Gruyter.

Zalizniak, Anna A., 2008. A catalogue of semantic shifts: Towards a typology of semantic derivation. In Vanhove (ed.), pp. 217–238.

Zalizniak, Anna A., Maria Bulakh, Dmitrij Ganenkov et al., 2012. The catalogue of semantic shifts as a database for lexical semantic typology. In Maria Koptjevskaja-Tamm and Martine Vanhove (eds), *New Directions in Lexical Typology*, pp. 633–669. Special issue of *Linguistics* 50 (3).

Zemp, Marius, 2013. *A Historical Grammar of the Tibetan Dialect spoken in Kargil (Purik)*. PhD Dissertation, University of Bern.

Part II

Case Studies for Areal Linguistics

9

The Germanic Languages and Areal Linguistics

Johan van der Auwera and Daniël Van Olmen

9.1 Introduction

The Germanic languages have most likely been 'areal' since prehistoric times. When Germanic split off from Indo-European, it was probably in part due to contact with non-Indo-European languages. And if we time-travel straight to the present, we see that the most successful Germanic language, with success defined in terms of global societal relevance and the number of first or second language speakers, i.e. English, is also very 'areal' (Hickey 2012a). For one thing, English is very Romance, arguably also partly Celtic and, though it is a West Germanic language, it is also North Germanic to an appreciable extent. And for another thing, due to its worldwide geographical spread, English is now giving rise to a large number of contact varieties. English is indeed areally unique, but the stories of the other Germanic languages also have important areal dimensions, for example with Low German shaping Continental North Germanic, Danish splitting away from Norwegian, or Dutch giving rise to Afrikaans. The current chapter sketches the research and issues in the areal linguistics of the Germanic languages. In Section 9.2 some general notions are introduced. Section 9.3 deals with areality within Germanic and Section 9.4 with areality involving Germanic and non-Germanic. Section 9.5 is the conclusion.

Note that the current chapter overlaps with several others, namely the chapter by Stolz and Levkovych on the phonologies of languages in Europe (Chapter 6), that by Kortmann and Schröter on varieties of English (Chapter 11), that by Hickey on the British Isles (Chapter 10) and that by Mesthrie on South Africa (Chapter 19). The volume-wide presence of English is partially a result of the areal success of the language, but not entirely. English is clearly the best-studied language in the world, but that does not

Thanks are due to Markku Filppula (University of Eastern Finland), Hartmut Haberland (Roskilde University) and Axel Holvoet (Universities of Vilnius and Warsaw).

mean that its areal linguistics has been attended to sufficiently. In fact, for a long time it was not, but recent years have seen a drastic change (e.g. Hickey 2012a; Miller 2012; Schreier and Hundt 2013). Although this chapter cannot focus on English, the language cannot be absent either, for we may not always agree with our fellow linguists. We will also take special care to compare the areal linguistics of English with that of the other Germanic languages.

9.2   Concepts, Dimensions and Restrictions

Firstly, to describe the dimensions of contact change, various terms and concepts are at our disposal. The first is 'areality'. We use the term in a rather strict but also standard way, i.e. to refer to similarities between languages used in the same or an adjacent geographical area which are due not (only) to chance, universal formal/functional tendencies or genetic affiliation but (at least partially) to contact. The more the languages resemble each other, the more the similarity concerns grammar rather than the lexicon. The more the similarities are typologically unusual and the more languages the contact involves, the more interesting are the phenomena, and the more linguists are inclined to refer to the languages as a *Sprachbund* (Trubetzkoy 1930) or – the standard rendering in English – a 'linguistic area'.[1] Of the linguistic areas discussed in the current literature, three are relevant for Germanic, that is, 'Standard Average European' (van der Auwera 1998b, 2011; Haspelmath 1998, 2001; Heine and Kuteva 2006), 'Circum-Baltic' (Koptjevskaja-Tamm and Wälchli 2001; Wälchli 2011),[2] and 'British Isles' (Filppula, Klemola and Paulasto 2008; Tristram 1999; see also Hickey, Chapter 10, this volume).[3] These areas are old and the first two are very large, loose and multi-causal. In what follows we will refer to these linguistic areas, but the areality of Germanic languages is by no means confined to these or to the periods in which they arose. Areality is also found in Germanic linguistic enclaves (*Sprachinseln*), that is, relatively small areas in which a Germanic vernacular – (nearly?) always a non-standard variety – is surrounded by other languages, or in border areas, in which a Germanic language – again (nearly?) always a non-standard variety – is adjacent to another language.[4] For both situations it would be justified to

---

[1] With this correlative statement (*the more . . . the more*) we imply that the notion of linguistic area is a fuzzy concept (see Campbell 2006 and Stolz 2006).

[2] Koptjevskaja-Tamm and Wälchli (2001) and Wälchli (2011) suggest that the concept of 'linguistic area' is not appropriate for the Circum-Baltic languages and propose 'contact superposition zone' instead, rather similar to Weinreich's (1958b: 378–379) proposal of 'convergence area'. We will gloss over these largely terminological proposals here (van der Auwera 2011: 297–298; Östman 2011: 374).

[3] They are not the only ones: see e.g. Hickey (1999) on considering Ireland as a linguistic area or Wehr (2001) for a 'West-Atlantic' linguistic area, comprising Celtic, French and Portuguese.

[4] Even though there is a large literature on linguistic enclave and border situations, it generally focuses on sociolinguistic aspects, and to the extent that it deals with language, it tends to focus on the lexicon (see the point below about the levels of contact influence).

bring in a notion of 'linguistic area', but it is not clear how much that would advance our knowledge (see Matras 2009: 265–277). Note that these two situations feature non-standard languages, and it is increasingly stressed that areality studies should indeed focus on such varieties (e.g. Murelli and Kortmann 2011; Wälchli 2011: 339). This is not in conflict with the fact that the current chapter often discusses the standard varieties, the reason being that their areal properties arose in the period before they were standardized.

Secondly, the traditional notions of 'superstrate', 'substrate' and 'adstrate' (coming from Romance linguistics, Kontzi 1982: 4, 9–10) remain useful. They reflect differences of prestige, with 'super' pointing to more prestige, 'sub' with less prestige, and 'ad' with equal prestige. The distinction also relates to registers, at least for the notions of superstrate and substrate, with superstrate influence being associated with the written and more formal registers and substrate with the spoken and more informal registers.

Thirdly, we will use 'borrowing' versus 'shift', and distinguish between them along the lines of Thomason and Kaufman (1988) and Van Coetsem (1988). On the level of the languages involved, these processes are alike: one language, the target language, changes through interference from another language, the source language. On the level of the speakers involved, however, the processes are different. In borrowing the target language speakers are more active, in the sense that they take something from the source language, either a relatively concrete linguistic entity such as a sound or a morpheme or something more abstract such as a word order pattern – in the terms of Matras and Sakel (2007), either 'MAT' ('matter') or 'PAT' ('pattern'). In shift, however, the source language speakers are the more active ones, as they learn the target language. They can then bring in features from the source language, but the very fact of acquisition, typically imperfect, may also give the target language new properties, which themselves are not found in the source language and which typically make the target language in some respects either more simple or more complex. Note that a language shift scenario can, of course, lead to the disappearance of the source language. In that case, one ends up not with a linguistic area but with a contact-influenced new language. Of course, if the shifting language is documented and/or a closely related language is spoken in the same region, we may still observe areality: similarities of the target language with the disappearing source language or a language related to the source language. Note also that when shift itself simplifies or complexifies a target source, there may be no areal effect, because the simple or complex properties of the target language do not come from the source language.

Characterizing a change in terms of borrowing versus shift or superstratal versus substratal versus adstratal is, of course, a simplification. The source language may be partly adstratal and partly superstratal, and the contact change may partly involve borrowing and partly shift. Also, as already adumbrated with the definition of the notion of 'areality', a change may be partially contact-based and partially 'something else'.

A few more general considerations are in order. Thus it is important to realize that there is a geographical dimension in the study of language which this chapter will not deal with. The Germanic family was once a dialect continuum stretching over an 'area' and this geographical dimension is reflected in the branching of the family into North, West and East Germanic. When the language family broke up into different languages, in part due to standardization, the languages that developed out of erstwhile neighbouring dialects may still betray common features, either in the standard languages or in their dialects. A good illustration are the 'Ingvaeonic'[5] features of Dutch, Frisian and English. They include the absence of a nasal in English *five*, Dutch *vijf* and West Frisian *fiif* and the presence of one in German *fünf*, and the existence of *h*-pronouns such as English *he*, Dutch *hij* and Frisian *hy* versus German *er*. These kinds of commonalities, reflecting erstwhile – or for that matter, current – dialect continua, remain outside the scope of this chapter. This does not mean, however, that when two languages are closely related and spoken next to each other, it is always easy to distinguish between similarities due to contact and similarities due to the fact they once formed a dialect chain.

Another kind of areality that we will largely leave undiscussed is the fact that a language may have acquired an international status through culture or religion and have influenced languages within that sphere. What we have in mind is Latin, later also French and German, mostly in Europe, and now English, not just in Europe but in the entire world.

A further point concerns the number of languages that are involved in the contact situation. The paragraph clarifying the distinction between borrowing and shift was phrased in terms of 'the' target language and 'the' source language. It is correct that many contact scenarios figure just two languages. But this is a simplification: in any one area more than two languages could be spoken and influence each other and the speakers involved may be, to some extent, multilingual rather than bilingual. Thus the East Frisian contact situation involves East Frisian and both Low German and High German, and for North Frisian the speakers closest to the Danish border may have Danish as the fourth language (Århammar 2007). Nevertheless, for any one item of structure that switches between languages, the transfer probably always just happens between two languages; it is not or rarely the case that during the transfer part of that item or structure comes from one language and another part from a third one.

Also, in the research reflected in this chapter, there is a strong focus on the target language. This is understandable. In the case of borrowing it is

---

[5] The term 'Ingvaeonic' is typical of Dutch and German linguistics and refers to the division of the Germanic tribes into Ingvaeones, Istvaeones and Erminones in Tacitus' *Germania*. One also finds the term 'North Sea Germanic' (Nielsen 1985).

only the target language that changes, and in the case of language shift the source language may disappear (at least the variant that is involved in the shift scenario) and leave few or no traces. But one must be aware of simplification here too. A transfer could be reciprocal, with, for example, German borrowing Danish and Danish borrowing German along the Danish–German language border. In that case both Danish and German are target languages. For some such pairs, both scenarios have been studied, but often independently. In the case of language shift – as already remarked in the above – the disappearance of the source language by no means implies that its transitional stage is not documented. Thus the Norman French that influenced English during the Middle English period did indeed disappear – at least in England – but not without leaving an enormous literature (e.g. Wogan-Browne 2009).

A last point but one is this: areal and contact linguistics is often concerned with what could be called the linguistic level(s) at which matter or patterns converge between languages, and, very specifically, whether there is a hierarchy of 'affectability' or 'borrowability' (Hickey, Chapter 1, this volume; Matras 2009: 153–165). Thus, uncontroversially, lexical items, and in particular content words, are more malleable than inflectional morphemes and quite often more so than syntactic patterns. In what follows we will try to give a general feeling for the levels affected in the various contact scenarios, but we will give pride of place to morpho-syntax. It is more interesting, precisely because – thanks to its lower malleability and its lesser visibility – it is also more controversial.

Finally, and obviously, the discussion cannot be complete. Although the survey touches upon a great many contact situations, some will not even be mentioned, in part because not much is known about them (e.g. Crimean Gothic, Swedish Walloon or Ukrainian Swedish), and of the 'great many' that do pass the test for inclusion, the discussion will be superficial. Nonetheless, this chapter should make it clear that the Germanic languages offer an extremely rich dataset, from Proto-Germanic prehistory to the present day. In what follows, the more detailed discussion will involve hypotheses about the areal modification of the grammars of current languages, that is, English, Continental North Germanic, Dutch, Afrikaans and, surprisingly perhaps, French. A moderate amount will also be devoted to the three partially Germanic 'mixed languages'.

9.3 Areality within Germanic

An important early contact situation within Germanic concerns the Viking settlement in the British Isles (in the smaller Northern Isles but also in a large northeastern part of England called the 'Danelaw') during the fourth quarter of the first millennium. The languages of the Vikings (varieties of Old Norse) were close to Old and later Middle English, and they were predominantly adstratal. There was both borrowing and shift, with the speakers of Old and Middle English borrowing a lot of Old Norse lexicon and the Viking settlers taking Old Norse lexicon with them into the Old and Middle English they were switching to. The lexical interference was aptly described by Otto Jespersen more than a century ago: '[A]n Englishman cannot *thrive* or *die* or be *ill* without Scandinavian words: *they* are to the language what *bread* and *eggs* are to the daily fare' (Jespersen 1905: 80).The italics are Jespersen's and indicate words taken from Scandinavian. These words include grammatical formatives such as *they*, and to that extent Old Norse influenced the grammar too. It is a matter of debate whether the substantial morphosyntactic simplification of English, as compared to its West Germanic sister languages, could, at least in part, be due to contact with the Vikings. Fischer (2013: 31–37) reviews this debate. From the fact that the loss of morphosyntactic variation happened faster in the North than in the South of England, she concludes that it is imperfect learning in the shift from Old Norse to English that simplified English (a point already made by Jespersen 1922: 214 and repeated many times).

The influence of Old Norse on English is thus considerable, but because it is predominantly lexical and because the impact is not normally considered to have made English very similar to North Germanic (but see Emonds 2011 and Emonds and Faarlund 2014 for the opposite view), it would not be appropriate to consider English and (some of) North Germanic to constitute a linguistic area. Probably during the time that Old Norse was receding in English, Scandinavianized English and Anglicized Old Norse did form a small linguistic area, but this Anglicized Old Norse is not documented very well (but see Hofmann 1955). It is slightly different in the extreme north, for the Vikings also settled on Orkney, Shetland and the northern coast of Scotland. Here the shift happened much later, not to English but to Scots. The Old Norse, known as 'Norn' survived until the eighteenth century, in a progressively Scots-influenced version (Barnes 1998), and it left its mark on the local dialects, primarily their lexicons (Melchers and Sundkvist 2010).

While the preceding paragraphs have briefly touched upon North Germanic impinging on West Germanic, in this paragraph we focus on the reverse process. In the second half of the twentieth century the West Germanic language exerting influence on North Germanic is English, but that is not particular to the Germanic family given that English, due to its global role, exerts influence in the world at large. From the Reformation to the nineteenth century, High German was the most important, but the greatest impact of West Germanic dates back to the thirteenth to early sixteenth centuries, when Low German was the language of the Hanseatic League. This commercial enterprise took substantial numbers of speakers to mainland Scandinavian cities, more so in the Baltic south than in the north, both as transient and as resident traders. There Low German acted as superstrate but also as an adstrate, to the extent that Low German functioned as the Baltic lingua franca. Like adstratal Old Norse in England it contributed mainly to lexical MAT borrowing. The quotation from Jespersen about the influence of Scandinavian on English is matched by one from his Norwegian colleague Didrik Arup Seip (1931: 102–103): 'Two Norwegians cannot in our day carry on a conversation of two to three minutes without using L[ow] G[erman] loanwords . . . of course without knowing that they are doing so. It is the same with Swedish and Danish.'[6] As in the English scenario, some of the material serves a grammatical purpose, particularly derivational affixes (see Diercks 1993). The influence also extended to morphology, with a change from a three-gender system to a two-gender system in the Hanseatic Norwegian town of Bergen (Östman 2011: 371), and to syntax, with, for example, the replacement of Swedish *varda* by the Low German loan *bli(va)* for the pseudo-copula 'become' (Markey 1969). Moreover, the contact itself, with language mixing and imperfect learning, has been held responsible for the simplification in the grammars of Continental North Germanic, compared with Insular North Germanic, or in those of the southern Swedish dialects, as compared to the northern ones (Haugen 1976: 285; Östman 2011: 371; Wessén 1929: 272). But there is also evidence for complexification. For the replacement of *varda* by *bliva*, Dahl (2009: 46) shows that it is complete in both the south, closer to the Hanseatic Baltic sphere of action, and the written standard, and that it is absent from the conservative northern vernaculars. In the central dialects, however, Swedish has a complex system with *varda* and *bliva* competing depending on the form of verb it accompanies. Interestingly, Dahl (2009: 46) mentions that the original meaning of Low German *bliva* is not 'become', but 'stay' – as it still is in modern German and Dutch – and that a similar semantic shift can be found in Polish, Lithuanian, Latvian and Estonian. This puts the contact influence from Low German on North Germanic into the wider picture of the Circum-Baltic linguistic area. For this reason and also because the Low German influence had a considerable impact on morphology, one may invoke a notion of 'linguistic area' here, while there is no reason to invoke one for aligning English and North Germanic.

Interestingly, both English and Continental North Germanic are morphologically simple as compared to German (for English) and Icelandic (for Continental North Germanic). In that sense, they have become similar. Although there is a contact explanation for both processes of simplification, involving the Vikings for English and Low German Hanse traders for Continental North Germanic, the similarities are not a matter of areal convergence: the morphological simplicity of either English or Continental North Germanic is not due to the morphological simplicity of the other language(s). Moreover, some of the parallels between North

---

[6] The original is in Norwegian. The translation is ours, but for the first sentence we follow Haugen (1976: 316), who is responsible for sharing this line with a larger audience.

Germanic and English may also be due to the fact that both English and North Germanic are arguably not part of the core of the Standard Average European linguistic area and thus missed out on the convergence characterizing this core: see van der Auwera (1998a) for an illustration involving phasal adverbials such as *already, yet, still, not yet, no longer*.

What is also interesting about the Low German contact in the north is that there is some documentation of Scandinavian Low German. There may not be many studies, but see Carlie (1925) and Brattegard (1945) on the Low German of Bergen and Copenhagen, respectively. It seems that the influence of the North Germanic languages on Scandinavian Low German is modest in that it primarily concerned the orthography and the lexicon. At least part of the reason must be that Hanseatic Low German was after all a language of traders and travellers, not of migrants losing contact with the homeland.

During the Middle Ages, inner-Germanic contact influence in Scandinavia did not only involve Low German, but also the vernacular and standardizing North Germanic languages. The most important source language was Danish and the strongest contact influence, in the form of a superstrate, relates to Norwegian. Norway was ruled by Denmark from 1380 to 1814, and from the sixteenth century onwards the main written language in Norway was Danish. This written Danish-in-Norway gave rise to a spoken variety as well, and today Dano-Norwegian or *Bokmål* 'book language', the current official term (earlier also *Riksmål* 'kingdom's language'), is still one of the two official Norwegian languages. The other is 'New Norwegian' (*Nynorsk*) (earlier *landsmål* 'country language'), a standard created in the nineteenth century and based on Norwegian dialects. The twentieth century saw an attempt to unite the two standards – the *Samnorsk* 'pan-Norwegian' project. The two varieties did converge somewhat, but they nevertheless remain distinct (Jahr 2004), and in the spoken register, *Nynorsk* exists in more than one variety. Through *Bokmål* Norwegian thus belongs to a true but small linguistic area, a 'Danosphere',[7] a part of the Circum-Baltic area.

There is also a Danish contact story to be told for Swedish, but it is of a different nature. The dialects in the southern part of Sweden, Scania (*Skåne*), were more Danish than Swedish in the dialect continuum between the two languages. Politically, the area was Danish until 1658. After the annexation by the Swedes, a Swedification process started, with Swedish as the superstrate. This process appears to have been successful surprisingly fast (Haugen 1976: 351; Ohlsson 2004: 1367). Nevertheless, the Scanian dialects today still retain Danish features, and there is a Scanian variant of standard Swedish. The Danish dialects native to the area now only survive on the island of Bornholm – off the Scanian coast, closer to Sweden than to Denmark, but protected from Swedification because it belongs to Denmark. Scanian is thus not Swedish that fell into the

---

[7] The term is inspired by Matisoff's (1991) use of the terms 'Sinosphere' and 'Indosphere'.

Danosphere, as Norwegian did. It is the opposite: it is Danish that entered the 'Swedosphere'.[8]

Danish also served as the superstrate language for Faroese and Icelandic. Iceland was under Danish sovereignty from the Middle Ages until 1943 while the Faroe Islands are still part of the Kingdom of Denmark, though with 'home rule' since 1948. Due to its isolation, its larger population, its earlier and complete independence from Denmark as well as its early writing tradition (twelfth to fourteenth centuries), the impact of Danish is less strong in Icelandic than in Faroese (Worren 2004: 2037–2038) and less strong than that of Low German on mainland Scandinavian, thus placing Faroese in the middle of a west-to-east cline from Iceland to mainland Scandinavian (O'Neil 1978: 277–281; Van Coetsem 1988: 52). The Faroese also have a distinct Faro-Danish variety, which differs from Danish not just in the lexicon but also in the grammar. The Danosphere therefore extends to the west too. Does it extend to the south as well?

In the south, North Germanic Danish borders on West Germanic German and Frisian, but, as the North/West Germanic division suggests, there is no dialect continuum, probably because the region had no or few inhabitants at the end of the period of the Germanic migrations (Walker 2001: 266). There are, however, various border effects, maybe already in existence in the fifteenth century (Pedersen 2009: 312) and definitely in the nineteenth and twentieth centuries, with *Petuhtantendeutsch* or *Petuhsnak*. This variety was named after ladies (*Tanten* 'aunts') that had *Partout* tickets on the ferries. It has a predominantly (High) German lexicon and a Low German and Danish (standard as well as dialectal) grammar (Faatz 2009; http:/petuhsch nacker.de). The border area, Schleswig/Slesvig, was partitioned between a German and a Danish part in the aftermath of the First World War. As a result there is now a small German minority in the Danish part and a somewhat bigger Danish minority in the German part. Both the German and Danish vernaculars show influence from their respective co-territorial languages (High German, Low German, Standard Danish and dialectal Danish, North Frisian) in lexicon, pronunciation and grammar (Kühl and Petersen 2009; Pedersen 2000: 212–214; Pedersen 2009: 306–307).

Within West Germanic there is more contact influence, and sometimes true contact varieties, on the borders between North and East Frisian and (Low) German (various chapters in Munske 2001), between West Frisian and Dutch (see below), between Low and High German, between German and Dutch (Smits 2009) and between German and Western Yiddish (Reershemius 2007). The most interesting variety might well be the one called *Stadsfries* in Dutch, literally 'Town Frisian'. It is not actually Frisian, and, in a sense, not really Dutch either. It is indeed a language of towns, more particularly of some of the towns in the province of Frisia in the

---

[8] In prehistoric times, however, central Swedish may well have been in the Danosphere – to the extent that Dahl (2001) raises the flippant question of why Swedes speak Danish.

Netherlands. Van Bree and Versloot (2008) convincingly argue that it arose in the sixteenth century when native West Frisian speakers learnt Dutch, the more prestigious language, but imperfectly so. To the extent that the original speakers intended to speak Dutch, their language can be considered to be a variety of Dutch with Frisian as a substrate. However, this substrate is so strong that *Stadsfries* became a language of its own, a 'mixed language' (Matras and Bakker 2003). Its accent, syntax, regular inflection and function words are mainly of West Frisian origin while its derivation, composition, irregular inflection and content words are primarily Dutch. No wonder there is some disagreement as to whether the language is 'basically' Frisian or 'basically' Dutch (Van Bree and Versloot 2008: 35–46). *Stadsfries* thus has a contact-based similarity to both Dutch and Frisian, but interestingly, it did not lead to one *Stadsfries* area, but to several ones, that is, the various Frisian towns.

Interestingly, the grammar of Dutch, as compared to that of English and German, has also been approached from a contact perspective. Comparing the three languages, English is morphologically simplest, German most complex and Dutch is in between. According to some, the demise of inflection in English is due to language contact: the Vikings. Weerman (2006) (and earlier but less explicitly also O'Neil 1978: 281) agrees, and claims that the moderate reduction of inflection seen in Dutch is also due to contact, that is, the influx of migrants into sixteenth and seventeenth century Amsterdam, the time and the place where the modern standard finds its origin. We thus see a geographical west-to-east gradient in West Germanic, similar to the North Germanic one (from Iceland over the Faroese Islands to mainland Scandinavia). Note, however, that both the demise of inflection in English and in Dutch, though each arguably resulting from contact, do not constitute a case of areal convergence in the sense employed in this chapter. They are independent processes, just like those of mainland North Germanic and Faroese.

So much for a brief discussion of at least the most prominent areality effects involving the Germanic languages in Europe. But, of course, when the Europeans colonized the world, they took their languages with them and they interacted not only with the indigenous population but also with each other.[9] In this way Germanic languages met outside Europe too. Usually we find contact scenarios with English as one of the partners, especially in the United States and in South Africa. In the United States most contact scenarios resulted in the disappearance of the 'other' Germanic language, although this process often took a few generations and the 'life and death' of such languages is sometimes well documented (e.g. the 200 years of Texas German, Boas 2009). The two Germanic languages that still resist having their speakers shift to English are Pennsylvania German and, less

---

[9] They typically took different dialects with them. This interdialect contact – contact again! – then led to dialect levelling and the formation of a new dialect, possibly out of line with the regular dialect continuum back home.

successfully, Yiddish. It is religion and culture as well as the size of the community that keep the languages alive and the contact influence from English relatively modest: compare the size and the fate of the two West Virginia communities studied by Van Ness (1990) to the size and the fate of the Pennsylvania communities studied by Meister Ferré (1994). American English did not undergo much influence from them either – perhaps the most visible influence being some Yiddish-derived lexical items ('Yinglish', Gold 1985). In South Africa, it is Afrikaans, the 'colonial offshoot' of Dutch, that has resisted the language shift to English. The two languages have been in contact (of various types) for more than two centuries and have influenced each other at the lexical and the grammatical level (Bowerman 2004; Donaldson 1991). But the Afrikaans impact on South African English phonology and morphosyntax, though significant, should not be exaggerated (Lass and Wright 1986) (e.g. progressive *busy X-ing* was once considered a pure calque of Afrikaans *besig om te* but has recently been linked to Settler English: Mesthrie 2002). In the same vein, it is tempting to attribute English-like aspects of Afrikaans to influence from English, but such similarities may well be the result of independent developments (e.g. Colleman 2013): as the Germanic 'contact languages *par excellence*' (Van Coetsem 1988: 137), English and Afrikaans have both undergone extreme loss of inflection (see also Section 9.4.3) and it is possible that they have developed, and will perhaps continue to develop, in comparable ways.

9.4 Areality with Germanic and Non-Germanic

In one sense, contact-based similarities between Germanic and non-Germanic should be easier to detect than inner-Germanic ones: the intrusion of non-Germanic sounds, words or patterns should be clearly visible, and vice versa for the intrusion of Germanic into non-Germanic. However, to describe the finer details one needs a knowledge of (at least) two language families, for example Germanic and Celtic; see Hickey (2007: Chapter 4) for a detailed discussion of the case for contact between Irish and English in Ireland during the past few centuries. Some instances of language contact may also date back a long way, which makes the detection of the similarity very difficult, as we see in the first contact situation to be discussed now.

9.4.1 Semitic

In prehistoric Europe (from the fifth millennium BCE extending into our era), Vennemann claims – in two collections (2003, 2012) with the titles *Europa Vasconica – Europa Semitica* and *Germania Semitica*, echoing Gamillscheg's *Romania Germanica* (1934–1936) – speakers of Semitic languages (probably Phoenician) were present on the Atlantic coast of Europe and exerted a superstrate influence on Indo-European. This influence particularly targeted the languages that were to become 'Germanic'. The argumentation is based on cultural and mythological similarities as well as linguistic ones. Thus Germanic verbal ablaut (i.e. the Germanic strong verb system) and a good part of the 'sizable'[10] non-European lexicon of Germanic would be due to this superstrate influence. According to Vennemann (2003, 2012), Indo-European also underwent a prehistoric, substratal influence from Vasconic (the family that Basque is the sole survivor of), but this influence did not specifically target Germanic. Despite the great depth of the hypothesized contact influence, the argumentation is rather detailed, but also speculative, and it competes with Nostratic attempts to explain Indo-European Semitic similarities (Bomhard and Kerns 1994).

A modern Semiticized Germanic language is Yiddish, with superstrate input mainly in the vocabulary of about 12–20 per cent (Jacobs et al. 1994: 417) and marginally also in morphology (with the nominal pluralizer -*im* in *profesoyrim* 'professors', a pejorative alternative for *profesorn*: Jacobs, Prince and van der Auwera 1994: 402). One would not, however, resort to the notion of 'linguistic area' to explain the similarity. The Semitic superstrate effect does not, of course, come from an adjacent or co-territorial group of speakers of Aramaic and Hebrew. It is a subset of the speakers of Yiddish themselves that also speak or at least use Aramaic and Hebrew. The Semitic effect on Yiddish is thus similar to the Latin and Greek effect on European languages.[11]

9.4.2 Finno-Ugric

Vennemann's hypothesis that earliest Germanic was a contact language relates to Vasconic and Semitic. But there is another view on the contact language status of Germanic, based on phonetics, which takes Germanic to have involved a Finno-Ugric substrate and a language shift from Finno-Ugric speakers (Wiik 1997). This view is also contested, though not the less radical claim that Finno-Ugric and Germanic have been in contact for a long time (Koivulehto 2002), to some extent as part of the Circum-Baltic area (Wälchli 2011: 326). And instead of contact, a common origin, in Nostratic, might explain some of the similarities.

In historical times, Finno-Ugric interacted with both North Germanic and West Germanic. Both Norwegian and Swedish interacted with Saami languages (e.g. Bergsland 1992) and with Finnish. In addition, Swedish

---

[10] The size of this part of the lexicon is unclear: for Polomé (1972: 45) it is 'substantial', for Hawkins (1987: 74–75) it could be a 'full one third' and for Vennemann (e.g. 2012: 257) even 'close to two thirds'.

[11] The areal effect of Latin and Greek on European languages and that of Hebrew and Aramaic on Yiddish is not quite the same, though. Thus Kortmann (1998) does give Latin and Greek a role in the formation of linguistic areas, i.e. the Balkan one for Greek and Standard Average European for Latin, and Drinka (2013) does the same with Carolingian Latin in relation to the Charlemagne core of Standard Average European.

interacted with Estonian and some minor Finnic languages, which in turn (except for Saami) interacted with Low German and later High German – and often also a Baltic and/or Slavic language. In Norway and Sweden, the Finno-Ugric languages are minority languages, and in Finland and earlier also Estonia, it is the other way round. The Finnish–Swedish contact is described best (see Lagman, Ohlsson and Voodla 2002 and Ohlsson 2004 for references to other situations) and it is also rather special, in the sense that Swedish used to be the only 'official' and high-prestige language in Finland, and that the minority that speaks it as a native language is not so small (some 290,000 speakers). In its written form Finland Swedish is very similar to Sweden Swedish. The spoken variants are rather different, both because of their dialect base and because of the influence from Finnish. The latter is especially clear in the pronunciation, prosody (e.g. Helgason, Ringen and Suomi 2013) and the lexicon, with so many intrusions from Finnish that they have been the target of purists for more than a century (Östman 2011: 366). This variant of Swedish is the one that is best described. Others include the Finland Swedish used by native speakers of Finnish and the Swedish spoken by the sizable Finnish immigrant community in Sweden.

The other major Finno-Ugric language of Europe, i.e. Hungarian, interacted with Germanic, too, in this case, German. Most of the Hungarian Germans trace their ancestry to migration waves of the late seventeenth and most of the eighteenth century, taking settlers into present-day Hungary, but also into present-day Romania and Serbia, when these areas fell under the Habsburg monarchy. The villagewise settlement created linguistic enclaves, a phenomenon for which German linguistics has appropriated the term *Sprachinsel* (lit. 'language island'). In these enclaves contact influence went in both directions, mostly, as expected, involving lexicon and pronunciation (Knipf-Komlósi 2006; Manherz and Wild 1987).

9.4.3 Romance

English is the most Romance of the major Germanic languages. This is due in part to Latin, which influenced its lexicon – though this happened for all the Germanic languages – but primarily to French, which acted as a superstrate as a consequence of the invasion by William the Conqueror in 1066 and the ensuing colonization of the British Isles. The influence is visible in the lexicon (with an estimated 38 per cent of the 4,000 most common words: Durkin 2014: 254–280; Lutz 2002: 147; Scheler 1977: 70–77) and in derivational morphology (e.g. *-ment* or *-(a)tion-*: Dalton-Puffer 1996).[12] Syntax has largely remained untouched, as Miller (2012:

---

[12] If the morphological attrition of English is associated with language contact, it is probably the contact with Old Norse that is relevant here, as mentioned above. But Norman French is also associated with it (e.g. Mossé 1952: 44; Wessén 1929: 272).

185–186) and Fischer (2013: 38–40) argue after a scrutiny of the literature. The impact on the lexicon, it should be noted, was partially a matter of replacing Anglo-Saxon and partially a matter of enriching it. As a result, the lexicon became more complex. The now obligatory choice between *sheep* and *mutton* is a case in point: the former comes from Anglo-Saxon, the latter from French. Another example is the stylistic difference between Anglo-Saxon *help* and 'French' *aid* or *assist*. The variety of French that crossed the channel with the Normans was 'Norman French', itself a contact variety of French with minor lexical input from Old Norse. Once settled on the British Isles, it can be called 'Anglo-Norman'. It initially functioned as the mother tongue of the invaders and it progressively became a language learned through instruction. Because the language left a large body of texts from the Conquest in 1066 until the fifteenth century, we can see it change throughout the centuries. Thus Ingham (2012) focuses on the grammar and shows how Anglo-Norman diverged from continental French first in the phonology, then the morphology, and finally and only marginally the syntax.

With this clear areal influence from (a kind of) French on English and back, there is some temptation to 'gild' it with the concept of 'linguistic area'. But this is not done. English, different from French, is also strongly influenced by North Germanic (see above) and probably also by Celtic (see below). Interestingly, there are two parallels to the English–French contact scenario just sketched. For the first, we have to go to the Channel Isles of Jersey, Guernsey and Sark, where something like Anglo-Norman French still survives – though probably not for much longer. These dialects are similar to those of the Norman mainland, but they have more Anglicisms, given that the standard superstrate language of the islands is English and that of the mainland is French (Spence 1984). They also coloured, as a substrate, the English spoken there, 'Channel Island English' (Jones 2010). For the second parallel, we have to go to the French mainland.

If English is the most Romance of the Germanic languages, French has been called 'the most Germanic of the Romance languages' (Hélix 2011: 12; Walter 1994: 225). This 'Germanization' is a result of the migrations of Germanic tribes into the (Gallo-) Romance lands that were part of the Roman Empire, involving Goths, Lombards, Burgundians, Saxons and Franks.[13] The effect on the Romance lexicon and toponymy is well described (Gamillscheg 1934–1936). The language most affected by the migrations was French and, as the name of this language already suggests, the crucial Germanic language was Frankish (Franconian), most clearly surviving as Dutch and the Franconian dialects of German. The Franks conquered parts of present-day France, settled in the north amidst the

---

[13] These languages are West Germanic (Frankish, Lombardic, Saxon) or East Germanic (Gothic, Burgundian). But as mentioned earlier, North Germanic Old Norse also infiltrated Romance, i.e. Norman French, and thus, to a lesser extent, later Standard French.

Gallo-Romance population, and ruled a mixed Romance–Germanic area, with more Germanic in the north, from the end of the fifth century. In this bilingual area Frankish was a superstrate – we have to wait until king Hugh Capet in the second half of the tenth century to have a ruler that did not have Frankish as a mother tongue (Picoche and Marchello-Nizia 1994: 13) – and probably also an adstrate, in the northern areas with the denser Frankish settlement. The Frankish influence on the Gallo-Romance of the north (the *langue d'oïl* as opposed to the *langue d'oc* or Occitan of the south), which was to become Standard French, did not only concern toponymy and the lexicon. According to Mitterand (1968: 18), about 35 of the 1,000 most common current French words come from Frankish or some other older Germanic language. But the influence is also evident in phonology (e.g. the diphthongization of Latin *tres* 'three' into French *trois*) and grammar. For grammar the literature usually mentions the more frequent anteposition of the attributive adjective in Old French – still reflected in toponyms (e.g. northern *Neufchatel* 'new castle' versus southern *Châteuneuf*) – and the entry of some morphology (e.g. the suffix *-ard*). The most interesting 'Germanic-like' features are (1) the non-pro-drop character of French, that is, the requirement of a non-emphatic subject pronoun in French *je t'aime* (lit.) 'I you love' (compare Italian *ti amo* (lit.) 'you love.1st-person-singular'), and (2) the fact that Old French was a 'verb-second' language, requiring a verb in the second slot of the sentence. Interestingly, the view that these two features are not only superficially Germanic but at least in part due to contact influence from Germanic (with a language shift scenario) has not been given much attention in recent years. Thus it is not discussed by Picoche and Marchello-Nizia (1994) or Marchello-Nizia (1995),[14] for instance, or scholars are content with observing the similarity between French and Germanic (Rainsford et al. 2012: 175). This stance contrasts with that of earlier linguists (particularly von Wartburg 1946: 66 and 1967: 102–104, but also Hilty 1968: 507–511) and of linguists that have tried to define 'Standard Average European' and even posit a Charlemagne area as its core (van der Auwera 1998b, and implicitly Haspelmath 1998, 2001; see also Drinka 2013). The parallel with the French influence on English is clear, but partial. In both cases the language that arrived later, French in England and Frankish in France, came in as a superstrate. But in the north of France the incoming language must have been adstratal as well. It led to a wider bilingualism and to a slow language shift. In that sense the scenario is closer to that of the North Germanic contact influence on English, which was also adstratal and involved bilingualism and language shift. Interestingly, in France this kind of contact led to the calquing of syntax. This is not clear in England,

---

[14] Marchello-Nizia (1995: 61–65) surveys the various explanations of the V2 character of Old French, starting with Le Coultre (1875), considered typical of the period in which linguists were discussing to what extent French was 'Germanized'. In later research, she does not mention the contact influence hypothesis (Marchello-Nizia 1995: 62).

but the reason is perhaps that the syntax of Old and Middle English and Old Norse was already very similar. In English, the language shift is taken to have led to morphological simplification. Interestingly, such a claim is not unreasonable for French either. In many ways French is phonetically and morphologically simpler than the other Romance languages. To some extent this difference is similar to the way English is phonetically and morphologically simpler than the other West Germanic languages (Lamiroy 2011) and – a further parallel – to the way Continental North Germanic is simpler than Icelandic and Faroese. If the simplification of English and that of Continental North Germanic are at least partially due to language contact, it is tempting to investigate whether a similar claim would make sense for French.

The interaction of Frankish and French did not stop when Hugh Capet ascended the French throne more than a millennium ago. Dutch descends from Frankish and it never stopped interacting with French. A very special case is Luxembourgish, now the national language of Luxembourg (functioning alongside French and German as 'administrative languages'): it is a Frankish variety with a lexicon particularly receptive to French.[15] Going south along the Romance–Germanic language border and into Switzerland and Italy brings us to many more German–Romance contact varieties. Some are German-influenced Romance, such as the Rhaeto-Romance of the Swiss Canton of Graubünden/Grischun, which has verb-second word order, at least partially due to German (Kaiser and Scholze 2009), and there is also Romance-influenced German, such as Cimbrian. Cimbrian refers to German enclaves in the north of Italy, with a strongly Italian-influenced Bavarian brought by eleventh and twelfth century migrants (Bidese, Dow and Stolz 2005). In the Balkans German interacted with Romanian (Gadeanu 1998), and outside Europe, English and French interact(ed) in Canada and in the USA (e.g. King 2000 on English influence on Acadian French morphosyntax, and Poplack 2008 and Boberg 2012 on the predominantly lexical influence of French on Quebec English), in the USA English interacts with Spanish (e.g. Roca and Lipski 1993, and Otheguy and Zentella 2012 on the presence/absence of subject pronouns in Spanish in New York), and in Latin America the Low German of the Mennonites interacts with Spanish and Portuguese (Kaufmann 2011).

9.4.4 Celtic

When Germanic tribes, in this case Saxons, Angles and Jutes, settled in the British Isles in the fifth century, the population they met spoke Celtic languages. The two groups mixed and by the end of the first millennium Anglo-Saxon had replaced Celtic in most of England. This process would

---

[15] The study of the synchronic and diachronic grammar of Luxembourgish has only just started (Moulin and Nübling 2006).

continue – but not to completion – in Ireland, Scotland and Wales. Celtic was the substrate, responsible for toponyms and a very small set of lexical items and no more needs to be said. At least, that was the agreed opinion until recently and to some extent it still is: when Fischer (2013) discusses the role of contact for syntax in the Old and Middle English periods Celtic is not mentioned and Townend (2012: 104) writes that 'sadly the possible influence of Celtic on English (besides the handful of loanwords …) remains obscure and disputed'. But the view that Celtic did play an important role in shaping English grammar has gained ground (Filppula, Klemola and Pitkänen 2002; Hickey 2012b), with McWhorter (2008: 61) echoing Jespersen on North Germanic in English and Seip on Low German in North Germanic when he describes English as a language 'whose speakers today use Celtic-derived constructions almost every time they open their mouths for longer than a couple of seconds. *Do you want to leave now? What's he doing? Did he even know? What are you thinking? I don't care. She's talking to the manager.*' The constructions he refers to are *do* periphrasis and the progressive (van der Auwera and Genee 2002; Filppula 2002). The list is not restricted to these two features: White (2002: 169–170) lists as many as 52 possible 'Brittonicisms',[16] as good a prospect as any for daring to advance a sprachbund hypothesis (Tristram 1999; Filppula, Klemola and Paulasto 2008: 228–229) and for keeping both English and Celtic out of the Standard Average European core (van der Auwera 1998b). Similar to the Frankish influence on French syntax, the process deemed responsible is language shift (Hickey 2007: Chapter 4), with Celtic learners of English calquing features of Celtic.

Again, just like Romance–Germanic contact on the continent, Celtic and English have continued to interact until today, in the regional varieties of English spoken close to or in areas with modern or earlier speakers of Welsh, Irish, Scottish Gaelic, Cornish and Manx (Filppula, Klemola and Paulasto 2008: 135–220). The opposite contact influence is also very real but it is less well described (e.g. Jones 1973 for Welsh, and Stenson 1993 for Irish).

9.4.5   Balto-Slavic

We have already discussed that the Baltic area was the stage for interaction between Low German and later High German with North Germanic and Finno-Ugric. The contact also involved Slavic and Baltic languages and among the latter Latvian stands out, a contact which gave rise to the Latvian (and Estonian) influenced *Baltendeutsch* of the German settlers and the *Halbdeutsch* of the mother tongue speakers of primarily Latvian and Estonian but other languages too (e.g. Polish, Russian). Best described are the influences on the pronunciation and the lexicon (see

---

[16] This list includes morphological attrition, more commonly associated with Scandinavian contact (see above), rarely with Norman French contact (note 13). See also Tristram (2002).

Polanska 2002 for Latvian-in-German, and Jordan 1995 for German-in-Latvian). Further east and south, German interacted with Slavic languages, especially North and East Slavic but also South Slavic (especially Slovenian), not necessarily co-territorial, with mutual lexical enrichment, even in the realm of function words (e.g. the modal verb *müssen* 'must', Hansen 2000). The influence can also be more subtle, such as when one expresses uncertainty with either a verb meaning 'may' – the western, Standard Average European strategy – or with an adverb meaning 'maybe' – the eastern strategy (van der Auwera, Schalley and Nuyts 2005). Apart from the contacts along the German–Slavic line, there is also the typically German *Sprachinsel* phenomenon. Thus German settlers created small and large German enclaves in Russia, starting in 1765, the most well-known being that of the Volga Germans, creating varieties of Russian German (Berend and Jedig 1991). A particular twist to the contact history of this variant is that many of the 'Russian Germans' have now remigrated to Germany, allowing their Russian German – as well as their German Russian – to be influenced by varieties of 'German German' (Berend 1998, 2009). There are also two Slavic enclaves in German-speaking areas, namely the West Slavic enclaves of Sorbian in the eastern part of Germany (Scholze 2008) and the South Slavic enclaves of Burgenland Croatian in eastern Austria (e.g. Pawischitz 2009). We should also mention Yiddish, in its eastern variety, interacting with Baltic (especially Lithuanian) and Slavic (especially non-standard varieties of Polish, Ukrainian, Belarusian and Russian), mainly in the lexicon – including grammatical formatives such as the question particle *czy* and the conjunction *abi* 'if only' – but also in the phonology and morphosyntax (Eggers 1998; Jacobs 2001; Weinreich 1958a) – with, for example, the Slavic-style reanalysis of verbal prefixes (Kiefer 2010; Talmy 1972). There is also a claim that Yiddish is basically Slavic (Sorbian, Ukrainian and Belarusian), relexified into High German and, as the process continued, Yiddish-*in-statu-nascendi* (Wexler 2002).

9.4.6 Indo-Aryan

A particularly interesting case is the contact of Germanic with the Indo-Aryan language Romani, the language of the Roma. The Romani varieties of groups that lived in or passed through Germanic lands show influence from the Germanic languages, particularly German. But in two cases the contact also led to mixed languages, called 'Para-Romani' in Romani scholarship. One is Angloromani (Hancock 2010) and the other Scandoromani (Hancock 1992; Lindell and Thorbjörnsson-Djerf 2008). In both cases the grammar is strongly Germanic while the lexicon is Romani. In this respect the languages are like *Stadsfries*, and a further similarity is that the languages are not confined to one area but to many small ones, not in cities this time but in diaspora. But there is an interesting difference too. For

Stadsfries the substrate (Frisian) is prominent in the grammar; for Para-Romani the substrate (Romani) is prominent in the lexicon. This difference may be related to their different origin. Whether Para-Romani is a late stage of the abandonment of the 'real' Romani, surviving mostly in lexical items (Matras 2009: 295) or a consequence of an effort to create a secret language (Hancock 1992: 43–44) or even partially both (Hancock 2010: 374), these scenarios are irrelevant for *Stadsfries* and Frisian.

9.4.7 Other

Germanic interacted with other families too, e.g. Eskimo-Aleut languages (Danish in Greenland, and English in Alaska and Canada) or American Indian languages in the US and Canada. In South Africa we find Dutch interacting with a number of language families. When Dutch was stabilizing and nativizing there, it was in immediate contact not only with the Khoisan language of the indigenous population but also with the languages of the Asian and African slaves that were brought to the Cape, in particular Malay and Creole Portuguese (as well as with the French, German and English of other migrants from Europe). Later on, it also interacted with the Bantu languages spoken in the rest of South Africa (van Rensburg 2012). The lexical influence on the language cannot be denied; for example, the Afrikaans words *dagga* 'cannabis', *baie* 'very, much', *mielie* 'corn/maize' and *babelas* 'hangover' come from Khoisan, Malay, Creole Portuguese and Bantu respectively. The impact on the grammar, however, has been the subject of debate for a long time, as it relates directly to the question of the origin of Afrikaans: is it (like) a creole (e.g. Hesseling 1923) or has it developed out of Dutch autonomously (e.g. Smith 1952), possibly with some dialect levelling and convergence? These two extreme positions seem untenable, however. First, Afrikaans exhibits only a few of the 'typical' features of creoles (Markey 1982) and has preserved the Dutch word order rules of verb-second in main clauses and verb-final in subordinate clauses, unlike 'real' creoles based on the language (Biberauer 2009: 9). Second, the autonomous evolution view cannot explain the drastic changes that Dutch underwent between 1652, when the settlers arrived, and the end of the eighteenth century, when the Europeans as well as the Khoi and the slaves already spoke something very Afrikaans-like (Raidt 1983). A more likely account involves the interaction of, on the one hand, the Dutch that was spoken and transmitted by the Europeans (a more conservative force) and served as the superstrate of the Cape Colony and, on the other hand, the Dutch that the Khoi and the slaves learned 'imperfectly' and ended up switching to en masse (a more progressive force) (e.g. den Besten 1989; Van Coetsem 1988: 129–144). This process resulted not only in morphological simplification (similar to what happened to English, French and Continental North Germanic) but also in some 'complexification'. The varieties of the Khoi and the slaves were probably heavily influenced by the languages that they initially spoke – in fact, the three main dialects of present-day Afrikaans still reflect the varying degrees of influence from Khoisan (Orange River Afrikaans), Malay (Cape Afrikaans) and Settler Dutch (Eastern Cape Afrikaans) (van Rensburg 1983) – and the origin of particular complexities of Afrikaans has been a matter of considerable discussion among scholars (e.g. den Besten 1986 and Bernini and Ramat 1996: 51–81 on the Dutch, Khoisan and/or Creole Portuguese basis of the double negation with the clause-final marker *nie*). Note, finally, that the contact between Afrikaans and Bantu has also given rise to new varieties (e.g. *Flaaitaal* 'Fly Language', a township argot primarily used by black men in urban areas: Makhudu 2002).

9.5 Conclusion

Studying the areal linguistics of Germanic has a good side to it as well as a bad side. The good side is that both linguistic and extralinguistic phenomena are reasonably well documented, at least in comparison with most other language families. The bad side to the study of Germanic areality is that many Germanic languages as well as the non-Germanic ones that they have been in contact with have been standardized, and standardization inhibits contact influence. For this reason the more interesting areality effects are to be found in either the period before these languages were standardized or in the non-standard varieties usually found in border regions, including the borders of linguistic enclaves. These two situations are also what we have focused on in this chapter. A further focus has been on the areality of grammar, the reason being that grammar is taken to be fairly stable, as compared to the lexicon. In this respect the Germanic languages are quite special: 'the Germanic group is only with some difficulty and chiefly historically kept together from the point of view of their grammars' (O'Neil 1978: 281), and this divergence is arguably due to contact, at least in part. This is most strongly arguable for the morphosyntactic simplification of English due to contact with North Germanic (and perhaps Celtic too) as well as for the morphosyntactic simplification of Continental North Germanic due to contact with Low German. For both West and North Germanic languages it is also argued that the intensity of the contact resulted in east–west clines, from English to Dutch (and Frisian) and then German, and from Icelandic to Faroese and then Continental North Germanic. Further parallels are the simplification of Afrikaans relative to Dutch, arguably due to contact with Khoi and other languages, and that of French, arguably due to contact with Frankish. In each of these four cases the process would primarily involve language shift and imperfect learning, factors that are also claimed to have resulted in at least three 'mixed languages', that is, Angloromani, Scandoromani and *Stadsfries*. In some cases these areal convergences feature as elements in the argumentation for linguistic areas. Thus the Hanseatic separation of the Continental North Germanic languages happened in the Circum-Baltic linguistic area, the 'Germanization' of French in the Standard Average European linguistic area, and the Celticization of English in a British Isles linguistic area.

References

Arhammer, Nils, 2007. Das Nordfriesische, eine bedrohte Minderheitssprache in zehr Dialekten: Eine Bestandsaufnahme. In Horst Haider Munske (ed.), *Sterben die Dialekte aus? Vorträge am interdisziplinären Zentrum für Dialektforschung an der Friedrich-Alexander-Universität Erlangen-Nürnberg, 22.10 – 10.12 2007*. www.dialektforschung.phil.uni-erlangen.de/publikationen/sterben-die-dialekte-aus.shtml

Bandle, Oskar, Kurt Braunmüller, Ernst Håkon Jahr, Allan Karker, Hans-Peter Naumann and Ulf Teleman (eds), 2002/2004. *The Nordic Languages: An International Handbook of the History of the North Germanic Languages*, two volumes. Berlin: de Gruyter.

Barnes, Michael P., 1998. *The Norn Language of Orkney and Shetland*. Lerwick: The Shetland Times.

Berend, Nina, 1998. *Sprachliche Anpassung: Eine sociolinguistische-dialektologische Untersuchung zum Rußlanddeutschen*. Tübingen: Narr.

Berend, Nina, 2009. Vom Sprachinseldialekt zur Migrantensprache: Anmerkungen zum Sprachwandel der Einwanderungsgeneration. In Wolf-Andreas Liebert and Horst Schwinn (eds), *Mit Bezug auf Sprache: Festschrift für Rainer Wimmer*, pp. 361–381. Tübingen: Narr.

Berend, Nina and Hugo Jedig, 1991. *Deutsche Mundarten in der Sowjetunion: Geschichte der Forschung und Bibliographie*. Marburg: Elwert.

Bergsland, Knut, 1992. Language contacts between Southern Sami and Scandinavian. In Ernst Håkon Jahr (ed.), *Language Contact: Theoretical and Empirical Studies*, pp. 5–15. Berlin: Mouton de Gruyter.

Bernini, Giuliano and Paolo Ramat, 1996. *Negative Sentences in the Languages of Europe: A Typological Approach*. Berlin: Mouton de Gruyter.

Biberauer, Teresa, 2009. Afrikaans. In Keith Brown and Sarah Ogilvie (eds), *Concise Encyclopedia of Languages of the World*, pp. 7–11. Oxford: Elsevier.

Bidese, Ermenegildo, James R. Dow and Thomas Stolz (eds), 2005. *Das Zimbrische zwischen Germanisch und Romanisch*. Bochum: Brockmeyer.

Boas, Hans C., 2009. *The Life and Death of Texas German*. Durham: Duke University Press.

Boberg, Charles, 2012. English as a minority language in Quebec. *World Englishes* 31: 493–502.

Bomhard, Allan R. and John C. Kerns, 1994. *The Nostratic Macrofamily: A Study in Distant Linguistic Relationship*. Berlin: Mouton de Gruyter.

Bowerman, Sean, 2004. White South African English: Morphology and Syntax. In Bernd Kortmann, Kate Burridge, Rajend Mesthrie,

Edgar W. Schneider and Clive Upton (eds), *A Handbook of Varieties of English*, vol. 2: *Morphology and Syntax*, pp. 948–961. Berlin: Mouton de Gruyter.

Brattegard, Olav, 1945. *Die mittelniederdeutsche Geschäftssprache des hansischen Kaufmanns zu Bergen*, two volumes. Bergen: A. S. John Griegs Boktrykkeri.

Braunmüller, Kurt, 1991. *Die skandinavischen Sprachen im Überblick*. Stuttgart: UTB.

Braunmüller, Kurt and Juliane House (eds), 2009. *Convergence and Divergence in Language Contact Situations*. Amsterdam: John Benjamins.

Campbell, Lyle, 2006. Areal linguistics: A closer scrutiny. In Matras, McMahon and Vincent (eds), pp. 1–31.

Carlie, Johan, 1925. *Studium über die mittelniederdeutsche Urkundensprache der dänischen Königskanzlei von 1330–1430 nebst einer Übersicht über die Kanzleiverhältnisse*. Lund: Gleerupska Universitetsbokhandeln.

Colleman, Timothy, 2013. 'n Germaanse toebroodjie: Three cases of English influence on the grammar of Afrikaans. Paper at the Germanic Sandwich conference held at the University of Leuven in January 2013.

Dahl, Östen, 2001. The origin of the Scandinavian languages. In Dahl and Koptjevskaja-Tamm (eds), vol. 1, pp. 215–235.

Dahl, Östen, 2009. Issues in complexity as a result of language contact. In Braunmüller and House (eds), pp. 41–52.

Dahl, Östen and Maria Koptjevskaja-Tamm (eds), 2001. *The Circum-Baltic Languages*, two volumes. Amsterdam: John Benjamins.

Dalton-Puffer, Christiane, 1996. *The French Influence on Middle English Morphology: A Corpus-based Study of Derivation*. Berlin: Mouton de Gruyter.

den Besten, Hans, 1986. Double negation and the genesis of Afrikaans. In Pieter Muysken and Norval Smith (eds), *Substrata and Universals in Creole Genesis*, pp. 185–230. Amsterdam: John Benjamins.

den Besten, Hans, 1989. From Khoekhoe foreignertalk via hottentot Dutch to Afrikaans: The creation of a novel grammar. In Martin Piitz and René Dirven (eds), *Wheels within Wheels: Papers of the Duisburg Symposium on Pidgin and Creole Languages*, pp. 207–250. Frankfurt: Peter Lang.

Diercks, Willy, 1993. Zur Verwendung prä- und postmodifizierender Morpheme in Mittelniederdeutschen und in den skandinavischen Sprachen. In Kurt Braunmüller and Willy Diercks (eds), *Niederdeutsch und die skandinavischen Sprachen*, vol. I: pp. 161–194. Heidelberg: Universitätsverlag C. Winter.

Donaldson, Bruce C., 1991. *The Influence of English in Afrikaans: A Case Study of Linguistic Change in a Language Contact Situation*. Pretoria: Van Schaik.

Drinka, Bridget, 2013. Sources of auxiliation in the perfects of Europe. *Studies in Language* 37: 599–644.

Durkin, Philip, 2014. *Borrowed Words: A History of Loanwords in English*. Oxford: Oxford University Press.

Eggers, Eckhard, 1998. *Sprachwandel und Sprachmischung im Jiddischen*. Frankfurt: Lang.

Emonds, Joseph, 2011. English as a North Germanic language: From the Norman Conquest to the present. In Roman Trušnik, Katarína Nemčoková and Gregory Jason Bell (eds), *Theories and Practice: Proceedings of the Second International Conference on English and American Studies*, pp. 13–26. Zlín: Univerzita Tomáše Bati.

Emonds, Joseph Embley and Jan Terje Faarlund, 2014. *English: The Language of the Vikings*. Olomouc: Palacký University.

Faatz, Jan Patrick, 2009. *Uwer unse Sprak is nich gut un warn klok ut . . . : Eine Untersuchung zum Gebrauch des Petuhtantendeutsch in der heutigen flensburger Alltagssprache*. Norderstedt: Grin.

Filppula, Markku, 2002. More on the English progressive and the Celtic connection. In Hildegard L. C. Tristram (ed.), *The Celtic Englishes III*: pp. 150–168. Heidelberg: Winter.

Filppula, Markku, Juhani Klemola and Heli Paulasto, 2008. *English and Celtic in Contact*. London: Routledge.

Filppula, Markku, Juhani Klemola and Heli Pitkänen (eds), 2002. *The Celtic roots of English*. Joensuu: Joensuu Yliopistopaino.

Fischer, Olga, 2013. The role of contact in English syntactic change in Old and Middle English periods. In Schreier and Hundt (eds), pp. 18–40.

Gadeanu, Sorin, 1998. *Sprache auf der Suche: Zur Identitätsfrage des Deutschen in Rumänian am Beispiel der Temerwarer Stadtsprache*. Regenburg: Roderer.

Gamillscheg, Ernst, 1934–1936. *Romania Germanica: Sprach- und Siedlungsgeschichte der Germanen auf dem Boden des alten Römerreichs*, three volumes. Berlin: Walter de Gruyter.

Gold, David L., 1985. Jewish English. In Joshua A. Fishman (ed.), *Readings in the Sociology of the Jewish Languages*, pp. 280–298. Leiden: Brill.

Hancock, Ian, 1992. Roots of inequity: Romani cultural rights in their historical and social context. *Immigrants and Minorities* 2 (1): 3–20.

Hancock, Ian, 2010. Romani and Angloromani. In Schreier, Trudgill, Schneider and Williams (eds), pp. 367–383.

Hansen, Björn, 2000. The German modal verb *müssen* and the Slavonic languages: The reconstruction of a success story. *Scando-Slavica* 46: 77–93.

Haspelmath, Martin, 1998. How young is Standard Average European? *Language Sciences* 20: 271–287.

Haspelmath, Martin, 2001. The European linguistic area: Standard Average European. In Martin Haspelmath, Ekkehard König, Wolfgang Oesterreicher and Wolfgang Raible (eds), *Language Typology and Language Universals: An International Handbook / Sprachtypologie und sprachliche Universalien: Ein internationales Handbuch / La typologie des langues et les universaux linguistiques: Manuel international*, pp. 1492–1510. Berlin: Walter de Gruyter.

Haugen, Einar, 1976. *The Scandinavian Languages: An Introduction to their History*. London: Faber and Faber.

Hawkins, John A., 1987. The Germanic languages. In Bernard Comrie (ed.), *The World's Major Languages*, pp. 68–76. London: Routledge.

Heine, Bernd and Tania Kuteva, 2006. *The Changing Languages of Europe*. Oxford: Oxford University Press.

Helgason, Pétur, Catherine Ringen and Kari Suomi, 2013. Swedish quantity: Central Standard Swedish and Fenno-Swedish. *Journal of Phonetics* 41 (6): 534–545.

Hélix, Laurence, 2011. *Histoire de la langue française*. Paris: Ellipses.

Hesseling, Dirk C., 1923. *Het Afrikaans*. Leiden: Brill.

Hickey, Raymond, 1999. Ireland as a linguistic area. In James P. Mallory (ed.), *Language in Ulster*, pp. 36–53. Special issue of *Ulster Folklife* 45. Holywood, Co. Down, Northern Ireland: Ulster Folk and Transport Museum.

Hickey, Raymond, 2007. *Irish English: History and Present-day Forms*. Cambridge: Cambridge University Press.

Hickey, Raymond (ed.), 2012a. *Areal Features of the Anglophone World*. Berlin: Mouton de Gruyter.

Hickey, Raymond, 2012b. Early English and the Celtic hypothesis. In Terttu Nevalainen and Elizabeth Closs Traugott (eds), *The Oxford Handbook of the History of English*, pp. 497–507. Oxford: Oxford University Press.

Hilty, G., 1968. Westfränkische Superstrateinflüsse auf die galloromanische Syntax. In K. Baldinger (ed.), *Festschrift W. v. Wartburg zum 80. Geburtstag*, vol. 1, pp. 493–510. Tübingen: Niemeyer.

Hofmann, Dietrich, 1955. *Nordisch–englische Lehnbeziehungen der Wikingerzeit*. Kopenhagen: Munksgaard.

Ingham, Richard (ed.), 2010. *The Anglo-Norman Language and its Contexts*. Woodbridge: Boydell.

Ingham, Richard, 2012. *The Transmission of Anglo-Norman: Language History and Language Acquisition*. Amsterdam: John Benjamins.

Jacobs, Neil G., 2001. Yiddish in the Baltic region. In Dahl and Koptjevskaja-Tamm (eds), vol. 1, pp. 285–311.

Jacobs, Neil G., Ellen F. Prince and Johan van der Auwera, 1994. Yiddish. In Ekkehard König and Johan van der Auwera (eds), *The Germanic Languages*, pp. 388–419. London: Routledge.

Jahr, Ernst Håkon, 2004. The special case of Norway in the twentieth century: language conflict and language planning. In Bandle et al. (eds), vol. 2, pp. 1635–1647.

Jespersen, Otto, 1905. *Growth and Structure of the English Language*. Leipzig: Teubner.

Jespersen, Otto, 1922. *Language: Its Nature, Development and Origin*. London: Allen & Unwin.

Jones, Mari C., 2010. Channel Island English. In Schreier, Trudgill, Schneider and Williams (eds), pp. 35–56.

Jones, Morris, 1973. The present condition of the Welsh language. In Meic Stephens (ed.), *The Welsh Language Today*, pp. 110–126. Llanddysul: Gomer Press.

Jordan, Sabine, 1995. *Niederdeutsches im Lettischen: Untersuchungen zu den mittelniederdeutschen Lehnwörter im Lettischen*. Bielefeld: Verlag für Regionalgeschichte.

Kaiser, Georg A. and Lenka Scholze, 2009. Verbstellung im Sprachkontakt: Das Obersorbische und Bündnerromanische im Kontakt mit dem Deutschen. In Lenka Scholze and Björn Wiemer (eds), *Von Zuständen, Dynamik und Veränderung bei Pygmäen und Giganten: Festschrift für Walter Breu zu seinem 60. Geburtstag*, pp. 305–330. Bochum: Brockmeyer.

Kaufmann, Götz, 2011. Looking for order in chaos: Standard convergence and divergence in Mennonite Low German. In Putnam (ed.), pp. 189–230.

Kiefer, Ferenc, 2010. Areal-typological aspects of word-formation: The case of aktionsart-formation in German, Hungarian, Slavic, Baltic, Romani and Yiddish. In Franz Rainer, Wolfgang Y. Dressler, Dieter Kastovsky and Hans Christian Luschützky (eds), *Variation and Change in Morphology: Selected Papers from the 13th International Morphology Meeting, Vienna 2008*, pp. 129–148. Amsterdam: John Benjamins.

King, Ruth, 2000. *The Lexical Basis of Grammatical Borrowing: A Prince Edward Island French Case study*. Amsterdam: John Benjamins.

Klemola, Juhani, 2013. English as a contact language in the British Isles. In Schreier and Hundt (eds), pp. 75–87.

Knipf-Komlósi, Elisabeth, 2006. Sprachliche Muster bei Sprachinselsprechern am Beispiel der Ungarndeutschen. In Nina Berend and Elisabeth Knipf-Komlósi (eds), *Sprachinselwelten: Entwicklung und Beschreibung der deutschen Sprachinseln am Anfang des 21. Jahrhunderts / The World of Language Islands: The Developmental Stages and the Description of German Languages Islands at the Beginning of the Twenty-First Century*, pp. 39–56. Frankfurt am Main: Lang.

Koivulehto, Jorma, 2002. Contact with non-Germanic languages II: Relations to the East. In Bandle et al. (eds), vol. 1, pp. 583–594.

Kontzi, Reinhold, 1982. Einleitung. In Reinhold Kontzi (ed.), *Substrate und Superstrate in den romanischen Sprachen*, pp. 1–27. Darmstadt: Wissenschaftliche Buchgesellschaft.

Koptjevskaja-Tamm, Maria and Bernhard Wälchli, 2001. The Circum-Baltic languages: An areal-typological approach. In Dahl and Koptjevskaja-Tamm (eds), vol. 2, pp. 615–750.

Kortmann, Bernd, 1998. Adverbial subordinators in the languages of Europe. In van der Auwera (ed.), pp. 457–561.

Kortmann, Bernd and Johan van der Auwera (eds), 2011. *The Languages and Linguistics of Europe: A Comprehensive Guide*. Berlin: de Gruyter Mouton.

Kühl, Karoline H. and Hjalmar P. Petersen, 2009. Converging verbal phrases in related languages: A case study from Faro-Danish and Danish–German language contact situations. In Braunmüller and House (eds), pp. 101–124.

Lagman, Herbert, 1971. *Svensk–Estnisk Språkkontakt: Studier över estniskans inflytande på de estlandssvenska dialekterna*. Stockholm: Almqvist & Wiksell.

Lagman, Svante, Stig Örjan Ohlsson and Viivika Voodla (eds), 2002. *Svenska språkets historia i Östsjöområdet*. Tartu: Tartu Ülikooli Kirjastus.

Lamiroy, Béatrice, 2011. Degrés de grammaticalisation à travers les langues de même famille. In *L'évolution grammaticale à travers les langues romanes*, pp. 167–192. Mémoires de la Société de Linguistique de Paris, vol. 19. Peeters.

Lass, Roger and Susan Wright, 1986. Endogeny vs. contact: 'Afrikaans influence' on South African English. *English World-Wide* 7: 201–223.

Le Coultre, Jean-Jules, 1875. De l'ordre des mots dans Crestien de Troyes. In Ernst Ziel (ed.), *XIV. Programm des Vitzhumschen Gymnasiums, als Einladung zu dem 17. 18 und 19. März 1875 stattfindenden öffentlichen Examen und Redeactus*, pp. 5–88. Dresden: Teubner.

Lenz, Alexandra N., Charlotte Gooskens and Siemon Reker (eds), 2009. *Low Saxon Dialects Across Borders / Niedersächsische Dialekte über Grenze hinweg*. Stuttgart: Steiner.

Lindell, Lenny and Kenth Thorbjörnsson-Djerf, 2008. *Ordbok över svensk romani: Resandefolkets språk och sånger. Inledning, grammatik och bearnetning av Gerd Carling*. Stockholm: Podium.

Lutz, Angelika, 2002. When did English begin? In Teresa Fanego, Belén Méndez-Naya and Elena Seoane (eds), *Sounds, Words, Texts and Change: Selected Papers from 11 ICEHL, Santiago de Compostela, 7–11 September 2000*, pp. 145–171. Amsterdam: John Benjamins.

Makhudu, K. Dennis Papi, 2002. An introduction to Flaaitaal (or Tsotsitaal). In Rajend Mesthrie (ed.), *Language in South Africa*, pp. 398–406. Cambridge: Cambridge University Press.

Manherz, Károly and Katalin Wild, 1987. *Zur Sprache und Volkskultur der Ungarndeutschen*. Budapest: Tankönyvkiadó.

Marchello-Nizia, Christiane, 1995. *L'évolution du français: Ordre des mots, démonstratifs, accent tonique*. Paris: Armand Colin.

Markey, Thomas L., 1969. *The Verbs Varda and Bliva in Scandinavian, with Special Emphasis on Swedish*. Stockholm: Almqvist & Wiksell.

Markey, Thomas L., 1982. Afrikaans: Creole or non-creole? *Zeitschrift für Dialektologie und Linguistik* 49: 169–207.

Matisoff, James A., 1991. Sino-Tibetan linguistics: Present state and future prospects. *Annual Review of Anthropology* 20: 469–504.

Matras, Yaron, 2009. *Language Contact*. Cambridge: Cambridge University Press.

Matras, Yaron and Peter Bakker (eds), 2003. *The Mixed Language Debate: Theoretical and Empirical Advances*. Berlin: Mouton de Gruyter.

Matras, Yaron, April McMahon and Nigel Vincent (eds), 2006. *Linguistic Areas: Convergence in Historical and Typological Perspective*. Basingstoke, UK: Palgrave.

Matras, Yaron and Jeannette Sakel, 2007. Investigating the mechanisms of pattern replication in language convergence. *Studies in Language* 31: 829–865.

McWhorter, John H., 2002. What happened to English? *Diachronica* 19: 217–272.

McWhorter, John H., 2008. *Our Magnificent Bastard Tongue: The Untold Story of English*. New York: Gotham Books.

Meister Ferré, Barbara, 1994. *Stability and Change in the Pennsylvania German Dialect of an Old Order Amish Community in Lancaster County*. Stuttgart: Steiner.

Melchers, Gunnel and Peter Sundkvist, 2010. Orkney and Shetland. In Schreier, Trudgill, Schneider and Williams (eds), pp. 17–34.

Messner, Dieter, 1997. *Einführung in die Geschichte des französischen Wortschatzes*. Darmstadt: Wissenschaftliche Buchgesellschaft.

Mesthrie, Rajend, 2002. Endogeny versus contact revisited: Aspectual *busy* in South African English. *Language Sciences* 24: 345–358.

Miller, D. Gary, 2012. *External Influences on English: From its Beginnings to the Renaissance*. Oxford: Oxford University Press.

Mitterand, Henri, 1968. *Les mots français*. Paris: Presses Universitaires de France.

Mossé, Fernand, 1952. *A Handbook of Middle English*. Baltimore, MD: The Johns Hopkins Press.

Moulin, Claudine and Damaris Nübling (eds), 2006. *Perspektiven einer linguistischen Luxemburgistik*. Heidelberg: Winter.

Munske, Horst Haider with Nils Arhammer, Volkert F. Faltings, Jarich F. Hoekstra, Oebele Vries, Alastair G. H. Walker and Ommo Wilds (eds), 2001. *Handbuch des Friesischen / Handbook of Frisian Studies*. Tübingen: Niemeyer.

Murelli, Adriano and Bernd Kortmann, 2011. Non-standard varieties in the areal typology of Europe. In Kortmann and van der Auwera (eds), pp. 525–544.

Nielsen, Hans Frede, 1985. *Old English and the Continental Germanic Languages*. Innsbruck: Innsbruck University Press.

Ohlsson, Stig Örjan, 2004. Language contact in the sixteenth, seventeenth and eighteenth centuries: The Kingdom of Sweden. In Bandle et al. (eds), vol. 2, pp. 1361–1368.

O'Neil, Wayne, 1978. The evolution of the Germanic inflectional systems: A study in the causes of language change. *Orbis* 28: 248–286.

Östman, Jan-Ola, 2011. Language contact in the North of Europe. In Kortmann and van der Auwera (eds), pp. 359–380.

Otheguy, Ricardo and Ana Celia Zentella, 2012. *Spanish in New York: Language Contact, Dialect Leveling, and Structural Contiguity*. Oxford: Oxford University Press.

Pawischitz, Sabine, 2009. Deutsche Lehnwörter in der burgenlandkroatischen Umgangssprache. In Lenka Scholze and Björn Wiemer (eds), *Von Zuständen, Dynamik und Veränderung bei Pygmäen und Giganten: Festschrift für Walter Breu zu seinem 60. Geburtstag*, pp. 331–346. Bochum: Brockmeyer.

Pedersen, Karen Margrethe, 2000. German as first language and minority second language in Denmark. In Gabrielle Hogan-Brun (ed.),

National Varieties of German outside Germany: A European Perspective, pp. 195–220. Oxford: Lang.

Pedersen, Karen Margrethe, 2009. South Schleswig Danish: A border-regional minority language. In Lenz, Gooskens and Reker (eds), pp. 297–316.

Picoche, Jacqueline and Christiane Marchello-Nizia, 1994. *Histoire de la langue française*. Paris: Nathan.

Polanska, Ineta, 2002. *Zum Einfluss des Lettischen auf das Deutsche im Baltikum*. Inaugural dissertation, Otto-Friedrich-Universität, Bamberg.

Polomé, Edgar C., 1972. Germanic and the other Indo-European languages. In Frans Van Coetsem and Herbert L. Kufner (eds), *Toward a Grammar of Proto-Germanic*, pp. 43–69. Tübingen: Niemeyer.

Poplack, Shana, 2008. Quebec English. *Anglistik* 19: 189–200.

Putnam, Michael T. (ed.), 2011. *Studies on German-Language Islands*. Amsterdam: John Benjamins.

Raidt, Edith H., 1983. *Einführung in Geschichte und Struktur des Afrikaans*. Darmstadt: Wissenschaftliche Buchgesellschaft.

Rainsford, T. M., Céline Guillot, Alexei Lavrentiev and Sophie Prévost, 2012. La zone préverbale en ancien français: apport des corpus annotés. In Franck Neveu, Valelia Muni Toke, Peter Bluenthal et al. (eds), *Congrès mondial de linguistique française*, pp. 159–176. www.shs-conferences.org/arti cles/shsconf/abs/2012/01/shsconf_cmlf12_000246/shsconf_cmlf12_000246 .html

Reershemius, Gertrud, 2007. Reste des Westjiddischen in niederdeutschen Sprachgebiet. In Christian Fandrych and Reinier Salverda (eds), *Standard, Variation und Sprachwandel in germanischen Sprachen*, pp. 241–264. Tübingen: Narr.

Roberge, Paul, 2010. Contact and the history of Germanic languages. In Raymond Hickey (ed.), *The Handbook of Language Contact*, pp. 406–431. Malden, MA: Wiley-Blackwell.

Roca, Ana and John M. Lipski (eds), 1993. *Spanish in the United States: Linguistic Contact and Diversity*. Berlin: Mouton de Gruyter.

Scheler, Manfred, 1977. *Der englische Wortschatz*. Berlin: Schmidt.

Scholze, Lenka, 2008. *Das grammatische System der obersorbischen Umgangssprache im Sprachkontakt*. Bautzen: Sorbisches Institut.

Schreier, Daniel and Marianne Hundt (eds), 2013. *English as a Contact Language*. Cambridge: Cambridge University Press.

Schreier, Daniel, Peter Trudgill, Edgard W. Schneider and Jeffrey P. Williams (eds), 2010. *The Lesser-known Varieties of English: An Introduction*. Cambridge: Cambridge University Press.

Seip, Didrik Arup, 1931. Hvad norsk språk gav, og hvad det fikk i middelalderen. In *Norge og Europa i middelalderen*, pp. 88–103. Oslo: Ashehaug.

Smith, Johannes J., 1952. *Theories about the Origin of Afrikaans*. Johannesburg: Witwatersrand University Press.

Smits, Ton F. H., 2009. Prinzipien der Dialektresistenz: Zur Bestimmung einer dialektalen Abbauhierarchie. In Lenz, Gooskens and Reker (eds), pp. 297–338.

Spence, N. C. W., 1984. Channel Island French. In Trudgill (ed.), pp. 345–351.

Stenson, Nancy, 1993. English influence on Irish: The last 100 years. *Journal of Celtic Linguistics* 2: 107–128.

Stolz, Thomas, 2006. All or nothing. In Matras, McMahon and Vincent (eds), pp. 32–50.

Talmy, Leonard, 1972. Yiddish verb prefixes between Germanic and Slavic. In *Proceedings of the Eighth Annual Meeting of the Berkeley Linguistics Society*, pp. 231–250.

Thomason, Sarah G. and Terrence Kaufman, 1988. *Language Contact, Creolization, and Genetic Linguistics*. Berkeley, CA: University of California Press.

Townend, Matthew, 2012. Contacts and conflicts: Latin, Norse and French. In Lynda Mugglestone (ed.), *The Oxford History of English*, updated edition, pp. 75–105. Oxford: Oxford University Press.

Tristram, Hildegard L. C., 1999. *How Celtic is Standard English?* St Petersburg: Russian Academy of Sciences.

Tristram, Hildegard L. C., 2002. Attrition of inflections in English and Welsh. In Filppula, Klemola and Pitkänen (eds), pp. 111–149.

Trubetzkoy, Nicolai S., 1930. Proposition 16. In *Actes du premier congrès international des linguistes à la Haye, du 10–15 avril 1928*, pp. 17–18. Leiden: A.W. Sijthoff.

Trudgill, Peter (ed.), 1984. *Languages in the British Isles*. Cambridge: Cambridge University Press.

van Bree, Cor and Arjen P. Versloot with Rolf H. Bremmer Jr, 2008. *Oorsprongen van het Stadsfries: With an extensive summary*. Ljouwert: Fryske Akademy.

Van Coetsem, Frans, 1988. *Loan Phonology and the Two Transfer Types in Language Contact*. Dordrecht: Foris.

van der Auwera, Johan, 1998a. Phasal adverbials in the languages of Europe. In van der Auwera (ed.), pp. 25–145.

van der Auwera, Johan, 1998b. Conclusion. In van der Auwera (ed.), pp. 813–836.

van der Auwera, Johan (ed.) with Dónall P. Ó Baoill (ed.), 1998c. *Adverbial Constructions in the Languages of Europe*. Berlin: Mouton de Gruyter.

van der Auwera, Johan, 2011. Standard Average European. In Kortmann and van der Auwera (eds), pp. 291–306.

van der Auwera, Johan and Inge Genee, 2002. English *do*: On the convergence of languages and linguists. *English Language and Linguistics* 6: 283–307.

van der Auwera, Johan, Ewa Schalley and Jan Nuyts, 2005. Epistemic possibility in a Slavonic parallel corpus: A pilot study. In Björn Hansen and Petr Karlík (eds), *Modality in Slavonic Languages*, pp. 201–217. Munich: Otto Sagner.

Van Ness, Silke, 1990. *Changes in an Obsolescing Language: Pennsylvania German in West Virginia*. Tübingen: Narr.

van Rensburg, M. C. J., 1983. Nie-standaardvorme, variasiepatrone en Afrikaans uit de vorige eeu. In G. N. Claassen and M. C. J. van Rensburg (eds), *Taalverskeidenheid: 'n Blik op die Spektrum van taalvariasie in Afrikaans*, pp. 134–161. Pretoria: Academica.

van Rensburg, Christo, 2012. *So Kry Ons Afrikaans*. Pretoria: Lapa.

Vennemann, Theo, *gen.* Nierfeld, 2003. *Europa Vasconica – Europa Semitica*, edited by Patrizia Noel Aziz Hanna. Berlin: Mouton de Gruyter.

Vennemann, Theo, *gen.* Nierfeld, 2012. *Germania Semitica*, edited by Patrizia Noel Aziz Hanna. Berlin: de Gruyter Mouton.

von Wartburg, Walther, 1946. *Problèmes et méthodes de la linguistique*. Paris: Presses Universitaires de France.

von Wartburg, Walther, 1967. *La fragmentation linguistique de la Romania*. Paris: Klincksieck. Translation of 1950, *Die Ausgliederung der Romanischen Sprachräume*, Bern: Francke.

Wälchli, Bernhard, 2011. The Circum-Baltic languages. In Kortmann and van der Auwera (eds), pp. 325–340.

Walker, Alistair H., 2001. Extent and position of North Frisian. In Munske (ed.), pp. 263–284.

Walter, Henriette, 1994. *L'Aventure des langues en Occident: Leur origine, leur histoire, leur géographie*. Paris: Laffont.

Weerman, Fred, 2006. It's the economy, stupid! Een vergelijkende blik op *men* en *man*. In Matthias Hüning, Ulrike Vogel, Ton van der Wouden and Arie Verhagen (eds), *Nederlands tussen Duits en Engels*, pp. 19–47. Leiden: Stichting Neerlandistiek Leiden.

Wehr, Barbara, 2001. Ein west-atlantischer Sprachbund: Irish, Französisch, Portugiesisch. In Heiner Eichner, Peter-Arnold Mumm, Oswald Panagl and Eberhard Winkler (eds), *Fremd und Eigen: Untersuchungen zu Grammatik und Wortschatz des Uralischen und Indogermanischen in memoriam Hartmut Katz*, pp. 253–278. Vienna: Edition Praesens.

Weinreich, Uriel, 1958a. Yiddish and colonial German in Eastern Europe: The differential impact of Slavic. In *American Contributions to the Fourth International Congress of Slavicists, Moscow, September 1958*, pp. 369–421. The Hague: Mouton.

Weinreich, U., 1958b. On the compatibility of genetic relationship and convergent development. *Word* 14: 374–379.

Wessén, Elias, 1929. Om det tyska inflytandet på svenskt språk under medeltiden. *Nordisk tidskrift för vetenskap, konst och industri utgiven af Letterstedtska föreningen* 5: 265–280.

Wexler, Paul, 2002. *Two-tiered Relexification in Yiddish*. Berlin: Walter de Gruyter.

White, David L., 2002. Explaining the innovations of Middle English: What, where and why. In Filppula, Klemola and Pitkänen (eds), pp. 153–174.

Wiik, Kalevi, 1997. The Uralic and Finno-Ugric phonetic substratum in Proto-Germanic. *Linguistica Uralica* 33: 258–280.

Wogan-Browne, Jocelyn with Carolyn Collette, Maryanne Kowalski, Linne Mooney, Ann Putter and David Trotter (eds), 2009. *Language and Culture in Medieval Britain: The French of England c. 1100 – c. 1500*. Woodbridge, UK: York Medieval Press and Boydell Press.

Worren, Dagfinn, 2004. Interscandinavian language contact II: Linguistic influence. In Bandle et al. (eds), vol. 2, pp. 2032–2048.

10

Britain and Ireland[1]

Raymond Hickey

10.1 Delimiting Geographical Areas

Discussions of areality and linguistic areas generally assume a circumscribed spatial dimension to the topic: candidates for such areas are all geographically delimited in some particular way. This delimitation can be realized by a topographical feature such as a mountain range or a major river which can often act as an obstacle to population movements, or at the very least such a topographical feature may induce a perception among the members of a population that it represents a dividing line between them and others. The delimitation issue might seem less controversial if the area being considered consists of an island separated from a larger mainland. But there is nothing *per se* which makes an island a linguistically separate area from any nearby mainland. It is the behaviour of populations and various political and cultural events in history which may increase the linguistic separateness of islands. Relative geographical isolation does lead to linguistic conservatism, as can be seen, for example, with Newfoundland vis-à-vis mainland Canada or Iceland vis-à-vis mainland Scandinavia. The larger the islands in question and the larger and more heterogeneous their populations, the more linguistically complex they are and the less they can simply be regarded as relic areas. When it comes to islands with the size and population of Britain, the relationship to a nearby mainland is more or less irrelevant. There are a few linguistic traits which the south of England shares with the Low Countries of Europe, for instance initial fricative voicing (in Dutch), but the European continent does not now have any linguistic influence on language in England.

[1] The terminology surrounding references to the two large islands off the northwest coast of Europe is fraught with political and cultural sensitivities, and the older geographical term 'The British Isles' is viewed with disfavour in the Republic of Ireland and is increasingly avoided in Britain as well (see Davies 1999). After considerable reflection the names of the two islands were chosen for this chapter as they imply two separate entities, but the conjunction 'and' (intentionally) highlights their relatedness, including their linguistic connections.

The islands of Britain and Ireland are roughly comparable in size: Britain at 209,000 square kilometres is more than twice as large as Ireland at 84,000 square kilometres. The remaining islands of the archipelago, above all the Isle of Man between England and Ireland, the Hebrides off the northwest coast of Scotland and the Shetland and Orkney Islands off the northeast coast of Scotland are, in size, only a fraction of the two main islands. The present-day political division of the islands is as follows: Britain consists of three political entities, England, Wales and Scotland, each constituent parts of the United Kingdom of Great Britain and Northern Ireland. The island of Ireland is divided in two politically: the Republic of Ireland consists of the southern two-thirds of the island with Northern Ireland, the fourth constituent part of the United Kingdom, occupying the remaining third of Ireland in the northeast of the island.

10.1.1   Areality in Britain and Ireland: Some Caveats

When dealing with the areality of language in Britain and Ireland, no claim is made about whether Britain or Ireland are linguistic areas in the classical sense (see Campbell, Chapter 2, this volume; Hickey 2012a). But the issues discussed, specifically the factors promoting or demoting areality in Britain and Ireland, are concerns shared with the other studies in this volume.

When considering areality in Britain and Ireland some caveats apply which are not pertinent to similar considerations in, say, native South America or Africa. In both islands English has a long-documented presence going back to the late sixth century and the early fourteenth century for Britain and Ireland respectively. This gives us a time depth which is not normally found in parts of the world outside Europe. For nearly all the language scenarios considered in this volume the treatments are present-day snapshots of developments which reach far back into the past but for which there is no documentation. In the case of English one cannot ignore the large textual record of the language which relativizes many features which one finds in the present-day language.

The second major caveat is that the effects of supraregionalization and the standardization of English cannot be ignored, as these processes serve to mask feature distributions which existed before both supraregionalization (Hickey 2013a) and standardization (Hickey 2012f) set in, essentially leading to a levelling of strongly local features.[2]

Supraregionalization is a process by which vernacular features are removed from local varieties and more general features take their place. Consider the case of the FOOT/STRUT split, a reference to the split of Early Modern English /u/ into [ʊ] and [ʌ] (Britain 2012: 26). This occurred in the

---

[2] An approach which examines vernacular features but without considerations of areality is found in discussions of putative vernacular universals; see Szmrecsanyi and Kortmann (2008) for a typical discussion.

seventeenth century in southern England (but not in the north) with the general unrounding and lowering of /u/, e.g. in *cut* [kʊt] > [kʌt] (Dobson 1968: 585–593). The high vowel was retained in rounded environments, e.g. before [ʃ], before a velarized [ɫ] and sometimes after a labial stop, which is why *push, pull* and *put* still have [ʊ].[3] Given that the FOOT/STRUT split originated in the south of England and affected speech in London and the Home Counties, later standard varieties of English incorporated this shift, leaving the north of England as a region which contrasted with Standard English in this respect. Furthermore, in local Dublin English the [ʊ] > [ʌ] shift did not take place either, as seventeenth century southern English had no influence on this vernacular, and so it did not experience the FOOT/STRUT split. However, an [ʌ]-pronunciation was introduced for STRUT-like words (*cut, cud, done, dove*, etc.) through supraregionalization, that is, the local pronunciation without a split was abandoned with the rise of an educated middle class in Ireland, probably in the early nineteenth century, and the English pronunciation of STRUT-like words with [ʌ] was adopted. Hence the split is found in all non-vernacular forms of English in Ireland, not because of an internal change but due to the adoption of a pronunciation from England.

Standardization processes are closely connected to prescriptive notions of language. Such notions came to the fore in eighteenth century England with such figures as Robert Lowth, John Walker and Thomas Sheridan (Hickey 2010). This led to the removal of certain features from non-vernacular usage. For instance, the use of demonstratives as personal pronouns in the third person plural is a feature of many traditional dialects of England and Ireland, e.g. *Them boys out on the street, Them shoes are too big for me*. This feature was also found in official registers before the eighteenth century in England (Claridge and Kytö 2010: 30–32) but did not become part of the later standard. The same is true for certain verbs which previously had two forms but now have three in non-vernacular varieties, for example *see* (*see – seen – seen*), *I seen him*, and *do* (*do – done – done*), *I done the work* (Anderwald 2009).

10.1.2   The Textual Record of English

The documentation and orthography of English can help one recognize previous instances of change which have been completed, e.g. the loss of initial /kn-/ and /gn-/ clusters, where only the orthography betrays the pre-change situation; cf. *know* and *gnaw* respectively. Despite the considerable historical documentation of mainland English it is sometimes necessary to look to lesser-known sources to determine the time depth of certain

---

[3] In the word *foot* Middle English /oː/ was shifted to /uː/ as part of the Great Vowel Shift and then shortened to [ʊ], but because the shortening took place after the [ʊ] > [ʌ] shift, the word was not affected (contrast *blood* [blʌd] in this respect).

changes. An example is TH-fronting, the realization of /θ, ð/ as /f, v/, a stereotypical feature of Cockney which has been and is still spreading to urban vernacular varieties throughout Britain (Foulkes and Docherty 1999: 11). Certain peripheral documents, such as the glossaries of the archaic and now extinct dialect of Forth and Bargy in southeast Wexford, Ireland have instances such as *brover* 'brother', *aulaveer* 'altogether' (Hickey 2007: 77) which indicate that TH-fronting has a considerable vintage in English. Another instance is the LAUGH-shift, the historical shift of /x/ to /f/ (Hickey 1984a), compare English *laugh* and German *lachen* with /-x-/, or southern English *dough* with northern *duff* 'steamed pudding'. This shift appears to have survived at least into the seventeenth century and to have been found in the south and east of England because it appears in the documents of the Salem Witch Trials, court petitions and depositions from Massachusetts, New England in 1692 and 1693 (Rosenthal et al. 2009), for example *dafter* (*daufter*) for *daughter* and *thof* for *though*.

10.1.3 The Historical Sociolinguistics of Language Contact

The information one has about societies throughout history can be useful in accounting for how contact arose and the effects it had on the languages involved (Hickey 2012d). Indeed one and the same language can have different contact effects in differing sociolinguistic scenarios. An example of this is provided by Anglo-Norman in medieval Britain and Ireland. Forms of northern French were taken to England in the second half of the eleventh century as a result of the Norman invasion of 1066. Over a century later, in 1169, Norman warlords from the Welsh marches (present-day southwest Wales) started a large-scale military campaign in Ireland, thus introducing their forms of Anglo-Norman to Ireland in the late twelfth century. But the social situation of Anglo-Norman in Britain and in Ireland in the Middle Ages was different. In Britain the French took over leading positions in English society at the time, at the court, in the administration, the military and in the higher clergy. The representation of French in upper levels of English society meant that the borrowings into English were part of more formal registers, and to this day the split of English vocabulary can be seen in words pairs like *freedom* and *liberty, work* and *labour*, etc. In Ireland the situation of the Anglo-Normans was different. Their primary concern was gaining land, and to this end they built fortified castles in the countryside, so-called keeps, and settled down there, interacting with the surrounding Irish population in the process. The linguistic result of this is that many loans from Anglo-Norman appear in Irish, and not a few of them are 'core' vocabulary items like the words for 'boy' (*garsún* < Anglo-Norman *garçon*) and 'child' (*páiste* < Anglo-Norman *page*). Given that Anglo-Norman was the superstrate in the medieval Irish society, why should the Irish have borrowed such core vocabulary items as 'boy' or 'child'? The answer would seem to lie in the manner in which these words entered Irish. Consider that the Anglo-Normans used such words in their variety of Irish. It is a historical fact that the Anglo-Normans lived in the countryside among the Irish and gradually shifted to their language. During the shift period an intermediate variety was spoken by the Anglo-Normans in which they used words from their own language like *garçon* and *page*. Because of the status the Anglo-Normans enjoyed in Irish society, the native Irish adopted core vocabulary items of their variety of Irish and, for example, the negation structure *Níl puinn Gaeilge agam* [is-not point Irish at-me] 'I cannot speak Irish', which shows the negative use of French *point* (Rockel 1989: 59). The likelihood of this scenario can be strengthened by considering that the Anglo-Norman loans in Irish did not necessarily replace the native Irish words. For instance, the Anglo-Norman loan *páiste* exists side by side with the original Irish word *leanbh* [lʲænəv] 'child'; for 'boy' Irish has two words: *garsún* (with the later form *gasúr*) and the original *buachaill* [buəxɪlʲ], but without the stylistic distinction similar word pairs have in English. To use a metaphorical term, the Anglo-Normans 'imposed' elements of their second language variety of the Irish language onto those who surrounded them in late medieval rural Irish society. The conclusion to be drawn from these considerations is that the results of contact depend crucially on varying sociolinguistic scenarios, which must be taken into account where historical information about them is available.

10.1.4   Remnants of Former Distributions

When viewed areally, Britain and Ireland show geographically discontinuous attestations of features, suggesting that previously there was a much wider occurrence of features which has been reduced to a few disconnected locations. For instance, the T-to-R rule, which allows the realization of /t/ as /r/ intervocalically or between prosodically linked words, as in *bottom* [bɒɹəm] or *get up* [gɛ-ɹ-ʊp] is found in the north of England (Buchstaller et al. 2013) and in local Dublin English (Hickey 2005: 41). Another instance is the uvular *r*, which was common in Northumbria in the northeast of England (called the Northumbrian *burr*). In Ireland uvular *r* was very common, in both Irish (Hickey 2011: 162–166) and English, and is still found in the town of Drogheda (north of Dublin) and in many vernaculars of the east and south (Hickey 2004: 78–79) as well as occasionally among speakers of Irish.

The NURSE/TERM distinction, a continuation of the Middle English distinction between /ʊ/ and /ɛ/ before tautosyllabic /r/, falls into this category. This is now only found in traditional dialects of the British Isles, especially in Scotland and Ireland. Elsewhere the sounds in these words have merged, usually to a central schwa-type vowel. However, it is not restricted to specifiable locations as would be the case with the vestiges of second person singular pronouns (Hickey 2003; Raumolin-Brunberg 2005). For example, in rural Yorkshire as well as on Orkney and Shetland, the original second person singular pronoun *thou*, with the oblique form *thee*, is still available. In the West Midlands and in the southwest, *thee* serves as a nominative form (Upton and Widdowson 2006: 66–67).[4]

The lowering of /e/ to /a/ before /r/ is widely attested in the history of English and can be termed SERVE-lowering, as it occurred in this common word (Hickey 2014: 279–280). In some cases there has been an orthographic adjustment so that certain instances, like *barn* (< ME *bern*), *dark* (< ME *derk*), *harken* (< ME *herken*) or *marsh* (< ME *mersh*), are no longer obvious. In England such lowering is recognizable from county names, such as *Derbyshire, Berkshire, Hertfordshire* (Ekwall 1975: 27). With common nouns, those instances which were not adjusted in spelling have been reversed, with the exception of *clerk* /klɑːk/ (Lass 1987: 277). Dialects in England retain this lowering in conservative pronunciations to the present day, for example in East Anglia: cf. hɑr (= *her*), *garl* (= *girl*), etc. (Trudgill 2002: 37; 2008: 183). Historically, there is evidence of a much wider distribution of the lowering before /r/, for example in the southwest (Wakelin 1988: 628). There are a few cases of this lowering in Standard English where the original and the lowered form are found, e.g. *thresh* and *thrash*, *wreck* and *rack* in the phrase *to rack and ruin* (in these cases the lowering is after /r/). This type of lowering in Irish English has practically disappeared though it used to be very widespread (Hickey 2008), but it may still be found occasionally in rural forms of English in Ulster, e.g. *nerves* [narvz].

Vowel epenthesis in heavy syllable codas, i.e. those consisting of two sonorants, is generally associated with Irish English, which shows it in enregistered instances such as *film* [fɪləm]. But there is textual evidence that this feature was widespread in England in previous centuries. Shakespeare, an author from the west of England, has in his plays no fewer than 114 instances of *alarm* (from Old French *alarme*), all written *alarum* [əˈlarəm], showing schwa epenthesis in the sonorant coda /rm/.

Grammatical gender has long ceased to exist in English, though masculine and feminine pronouns can be used for reference to inanimate objects, for example *She's a beaut, the new car*. Occasionally, there are dialect forms which are derived historically from gender-distinctive pronouns, for example /(ə)n/ for 'him/it' in southwest England deriving from the Old English masculine accusative *hine* (Wakelin 1984: 81), e.g. *Tom saw un* (= 'him'). Also in this area one can find gendered pronouns used for inanimate objects, e.g. *Pass the loaf – he's over there* (Ihalainen 1994; Wagner 2012).

10.1.5   Diagnostic Value of Features

The diagnostic value of vernacular features for considerations of areality depends on their relative unusualness. If a feature is statistically uncommon and nonetheless occurs in geographically adjacent languages or varieties, then there is a greater likelihood that this arose

---

[4] This situation is different in principle from the passive knowledge of *thou/thee*, present with many speakers from religious contexts.

through the influence of one language on the other. For instance, in colloquial forms of English the number of consonants is reduced in word-final position, for example *task* [tæs], *best* [bɛs] (Schreier 2005: 126–197). Such deletions are normally sensitive to style, with the greatest amount evident in informal registers. There are frequently specific conditions for deletion, for example in post-nasal, or more generally in post-sonorant, positions, e.g. *pound* [paʊn], *field* [fiːl], *hard* [haːr]. This may also occur word-internally, e.g. *twenty* [tweni], *plenty* [pleni]. The deletion may apply only to voiced consonants, e.g. *bold* [boʊl] but *bolt* [boʊlt]. Clusters consisting of three elements are commonly reduced to two, e.g. *facts* [fæks], or to a single long consonant if a cluster has two similar elements separated by a third, e.g. *tests* [tesː]. But these developments are very common and are of little or no assistance in determining feature areality.

10.2   Language Change in Britain and Ireland

The extensive documentation of English shows that some changes, which have occurred in the last century or so and which are, in some locations, still taking place at present, form part of long-term developments which have roots deep in the history of the language. For instance, the loss of a voice distinction for approximants (Hickey 1984b) due to the voicing of the labio-velar [ʍ] <wh> is of late modern origin (Jespersen 1940 [1909]: 374–375). Historically, word pairs such as *which* [ʍɪtʃ] and *witch* [wɪtʃ] were distinguished consistently. This is just the final stage in the loss of voiceless sonorants in the history of English: cf. the voiceless nasals and liquids of Old English which were lost in Middle English, e.g. *hnutu* > *nut(u)* 'nut', *hlaf* > *laf* 'loaf', *Hrothgar* > *Roger*.

The increasing urbanization of Britain in the past two centuries or so has led to different patterns of language change which need to be borne in mind for areal studies. The main one is cascade diffusion, which takes place by going from one urban centre to another without necessarily encompassing the intervening countryside. An instance is the spread of TH-fronting to urban centres around Britain which are far from London, without the rural areas in between being affected.[5]

10.2.1   Internally Motivated Change
Areal features generally arise as a result of language contact and are instances of externally motivated change (Hickey 2012b). But there are also instances of internally motivated change that can arise and then

---

[5] The second type of diffusion is counterhierarchical and involves the spread of features from a rural to an urban setting. It is labelled 'counterhierarchical' because this is the opposite of what usually happens. A few cases exist such as the spread of rural *fixin' to* into urban areas of Oklahoma.

spread areally, in which case they would be relevant to the present study. An example would be analogical change where one element changes to another on the basis of a similar pattern that already exists, the latter providing the model for the change, for example a plural *fishes* on the basis of *dish: dishes*. Another instance would be the vernacular plural *youse* /juːz/ formed by adding the plural morpheme {S} to *you*. The similarity in such cases is usually phonetic. There are also instances of analogy from syntax, for instance where a regular structural pattern provides a model. In Irish English positive epistemic *must* provided the model for the negative by the addition of a negator, that is, *mustn't* means 'it cannot be the case', as in *He mustn't be Welsh* 'He can't be Welsh'. Analogical change may have the effect of masking earlier changes in a language and must always be considered when reconstructing historical forms.

The alternation of two or more forms in a variety to render their distribution more regular is another type of internally motivated change, for instance the use of *were* for the entire past of *be*, or the distribution of *was* for positive statements and *were* for negative ones. Anderwald (2002: 17) offers a cognitive explanation for the remorphologization according to polarity, that is, it offers marking of negation via the verb form, in addition to the negator *not*.

10.2.2   Differing Degrees of Manifestation

Areality may be characterized not only by the presence or absence of features but by the degree to which a feature is present. Consider the widespread phenomenon of lenition, the weakening of consonants under certain phonetic conditions.

Lenition is a weakening in articulation, usually leading to a change in a consonant from voiceless to voiced, from stop to fricative, from oral to glottal stop, or to the vocalization of a consonant entirely (see Table 10.1). The following are two types of lenition attested in different parts of Britain and Ireland.

(a)   T-glottalization, a feature of many vernaculars in Britain, whereby /t/, outside word-initial position, is preferentially realized as [ʔ], e.g. *putty* [pʌʔɪ], *put* [pʊʔ]. There may be phonotactic conditioning, e.g. [ʔ] may occur post-vocalically/ pre-pausally but not intervocalically, e.g. *putty*

Table 10.1 *Types of consonant lenition*

Degemination	V CC [voiceless] V,#	>	V C [voiceless] V,#
Fricativization	V C [voiceless] V,#	>	V F [voiceless] V,#
Tapping	V C [voiceless] V,#	>	V [ɾ] V
Debuccalization	V C [alveolar] V,#	>	V C [glottal] V,#
Voicing	V C [voiceless] V,#	>	V C [voiced] V,#
Deletion	V C V,#	>	V Ø V,#

[pʌti], *put* [pʊʔ]. This distribution is typical of colloquial varieties intermediate between Received Pronunciation and Cockney. T-glottalization is also found in Scots, Ulster Scots and local Dublin English. Given that the process of debuccalization, i.e. the removal of the oral gesture for stops, is common, the diagnostic value of T-glottalization in areal studies is very slight.

(b)   Stop fricativization is a type of lenition which leads to a change in articulation but with retention of the oral gesture. In traditional Liverpool English lenition is widespread with voiceless stops /p, t, k/ realized as corresponding fricatives, i.e. [f, t̞, x] (Honeybone 2007; Watson and Clark 2016). This kind of lenition, although only for alveolars, is also typical of Irish English (Hickey 2009).

In its manifestation type (b) is quite different from type (a), and so its appearance in three locations in Britain and Ireland, which are historically connected with each other, would suggest a contact explanation. It is known that in the nineteenth century there was considerable Irish input to both Liverpool and Middlesbrough, so it would appear to be no coincidence that vernacular speech in these cities should show this type of lenition given that it has existed in Ireland for centuries (Hickey 2009). However likely it is that the Irish input was responsible for lenition in Liverpool and Middlesbrough, this only provided an impetus for a development which later continued on a trajectory somewhat different from Irish English with the generalization of lenition from /t/ to all voiceless stops, hence the occurrence with /p/ and /k/ (in Liverpool).

10.2.3   Constraint Hierarchies

A well-researched feature of non-standard English syntax is the 'Northern Subject Rule'. Basically this is a co-occurrence pattern involving verbs and preceding subjects: -*s* is absent when the verb is immediately preceded by a pronoun, but not otherwise. An illustration would be *We meet and talks together.* The occurrence of -*s* is also favoured by preceding nouns, as in *The workers gets extra time off at Christmas*, possibly a priming effect due to the plural -*s* on the noun. This agreement pattern is well attested in northern Middle English and Middle Scots. In middle and southern England the distribution is uneven (Klemola 2000: 336). East Anglia favours zero marking on all persons, while other southern dialects tend to show a freer use of -*s* with adjacent pronominal subjects than in the north.

The areal distribution of a feature or construction can be determined by a variety of factors. One of these is the hierarchy which specifies the order in which certain forms are likely to occur. Consider in this context the use of suffixal -*s* outside the third person singular, a prominent characteristic of many vernacular varieties of English. These vary in the extent to which the -*s* occurs. At least three determining factors can be recognized and placed in a hierarchy: (i) person and number of verb, (ii) relative weight of subject (pronoun, noun, noun phrase), (iii) syntactic distance of subject from verb. The ordering in terms of likelihood of occurrence varies, and parallels in a constraint hierarchy have been used (Poplack and Tagliamonte 2001) to demonstrate the historical relatedness of varieties. In some varieties the factors just listed do not seem to cause different inflectional behaviour; for example, in Tyneside singular concord is found with third person plurals, irrespective of the factors (i)–(iii) (see Beal 1993: 194). This also applies to forms of southern Irish English, particularly on the east coast, but in the north the bare plural pronoun does not use inflectional -*s* (Harris 1993: 155). Lack of concord can also apply to the past in the case of the auxiliaries *have* and *be: They was going to buy the house.*

Various proposals have been put forward concerning the origin of non-standard verbal concord. Klemola (2000) considered the possibility of influence on English dialects from northern forms of Brythonic, the language spoken in England by the Celtic population at the time of the Germanic invasions and also spoken in Cumbria, Westmorland and other parts of the far north. In his opinion this would have led to the distribution of verbal -*s* just outlined. Such agreement rules are rare cross-linguistically (Klemola 2000: 337). However, in P-Celtic languages, notably in Welsh (but not in Irish), there is an agreement rule whereby plural forms of the present are only used with verbs when the pronoun *nhw* 'they' follows immediately. In all other cases the singular is found (Klemola 2000: 337; Williams 1980: 94–95). In essence this is the Northern Subject Rule: the plural forms of Welsh (*maen* 'is'-PL) correspond to the *s*-less forms of English, the Welsh verbal singular (*mae* 'is'-SG) is the equivalent to the *s*-full forms: *Maen nhw'n dysgu Cymraeg* 'They are learning Welsh', *Mae Trevor a Sian yn dysgu Cymraeg* 'Trevor and Sian are learning Welsh'. Klemola stresses that the Northern Subject Rule is most widespread in regions of northern Britain which were bilingual with Brythonic and Anglian in the Old English period.

Internal arguments for the Northern Subject Rule are also possible: the decline in inflectional morphology, which had probably set in during late Old English (masked by the West Saxon koiné), meant that language learners in the Middle English period were faced with difficulties analysing the remaining inflections in some systemic way and must have hit on alternative interpretations. In the northern areas, either close to Brythonic-speaking districts or indeed bilingual, there would probably have been an embryonic Northern Subject Rule which could then have spread to monolingual English speakers and hence become entrenched. However, the standard wisdom on the matter is that it was originally a feature of Scots which spread into the north of England. Further south, different situations may obtain, e.g. generalized -*s* may be found as in the southwest (Ihalainen 1994: 214), or there may be no -*s* at all as in East

Anglia, a situation which may be the result of contact with Dutch speakers in this area in previous centuries (Trudgill 1998).

10.3   The Historical Dimension

The areality of the English language can be examined with considerable time depth. From the time of the first settlements of Germanic tribes in England there is evidence of contact influence from Celtic given that a large proportion of the Celts switched to English in ensuing generations. This led to certain features spreading from Brythonic and appearing in the textual record of late Old English (Hickey 2012c). The scholarly opinion that Brythonic had a significant effect on the development of English is known as the 'Celtic hypothesis' (Filppula and Klemola 2009, 2012). Supporters of this hypothesis criticize the view that because there are only a few loanwords from Celtic there was no other influence on English (Filppula, Klemola and Paulasto 2008: 25). However, if contact persists over many generations, then the substrate can have a gradual and imperceptible influence on the superstrate, leading in some cases to grammatical change at a later time. This can be termed 'delayed effect contact' (Hickey 2010), and may well be the source of syntactic features in English which the latter has in common with Celtic (Hickey 1995; Poussa 1990; Vennemann 2002). If speakers of two languages live in close proximity then child language learners in one group can pick up features from the other group, irrespective of which group is superstrate relative to the other.[6] This type of infection through contact applies to speech habits, such as phonetic realizations, prosodic patterns, alternative exponents of identical grammatical categories alongside the use of lexical items from the other group.

Consider that in the fifth and sixth centuries in England the Germanic invaders probably shared the same environment with most of the Celts they had subjugated, at least in the south of England. Several facts point to this. There is no record of a single battle in which the Germanic invaders were victorious over the Celts. The notion that they banished the latter into highland areas in the north and west of England and down to the remoter parts of the southwest is an assumption based on the later distribution of P-Celtic languages in England – Welsh and Cornish (descendants of Brythonic). In addition, Old English *wealh* meant 'foreigner' but also 'Celt'. The word came to be used for 'servant, slave' (cf. *wielen/wíln* 'female servant, slave' with the same root, Holthausen 1974: 393), which apparently indicates the status of the Celts vis-à-vis the Germanic settlers. Lutz (2009:

---

[6]   These issues are discussed in detail in Trudgill (2010), where the concern is primarily to account for grammatical simplification which is apparent in the later Old English period. Trudgill refers (2010: 29) to features traced to contact by other authors (many of the features are discussed in the present chapter) but returns (2010: 30–35) to the issue of simplification. He sees the contact between Old English and Brythonic speakers as having been most intense and prolonged in the north and that, along with the contact with Old Norse, it may have combined to make northern English of the Middle Ages the most innovative form in England.

239–240), drawing on work by the historian David Pelteret, emphasizes that the meaning of 'servant, slave' was predominantly used in West Saxon, although there were other words with a similar meaning. This would suggest that the subjugation of the Celts was most marked in the south of England where the concentration of the Germanic settlers, and hence language contact, was greatest. Furthermore, the view that the Celts, left in the south and east of England, would have had to shift to English is subscribed to by scholars investigating the Celtic hypothesis (Lutz 2009: 228). Earlier scholars of English highlighted this fact, for example Chadwick (1963) and Tolkien (1963), but their work was regarded as peripheral and was not given consideration in 'mainstream' works such as Campbell (1959) or Mitchell and Robinson (2007).

That the majority of the West Saxon population of the sixth and seventh centuries consisted of Celts who had shifted to English is evident from the numerical relationship of the Celts to the Germanic tribes in the early Old English period. Estimates vary here: the number of Germanic settlers during the fifth century has been put at anything between 10,000 and 200,000 (Filppula, Klemola and Paulasto 2008: 15). But given a population of Britain just before the Germanic arrivals of approximately one million then the relationship would have been anything from 1:100 to 1:5. The latter ratio is hardly likely as it would have implied a huge movement from the continental North Sea rim to England. A figure somewhere in the middle, say 1:20, would still imply that the Celts greatly outnumbered the Germanic settlers, assumed to be about 50,000 with this ratio. In the generations following the initial Germanic settlements, most Celts in contact with the new settlers would have given up their native Brythonic, speaking shift varieties of the newcomers' dialects during the transition.

10.3.1   The Rise of the Internal Possessor Construction

English is the only Germanic language which categorically uses possessive pronouns with instances of inalienable possession, e.g. *My head is sore* (contrast with German *Mir tut der Kopf weh* lit. 'me.DATIVE does the head hurt'). Structures like *The head is sore to me* are not possible in present-day English.[7] In Old English the dative of a personal pronoun was found with the head of the noun phrase accompanied by a determiner. In the Old English *Poem of Judith* one can see this use:

(1)   *þæt him þæt heafod wand*
      forð on ða flore
      lit: 'that him-DATIVE that head . . .'
      'that his head rolled forth on the floor'

---

[7] A very small set of verbs expressing physical contact still allow the external possessor, e.g. *He hit him in the face, She patted the child on the head.* All such verbs take two objects, the first animate and the second prepositional referring to a part of the body.

Such structures are labelled 'external possessor' constructions because possession is expressed by an oblique case pronoun which is outside the semantically related noun phrase. Nowadays the possessive element is internal to the noun phrase – a determiner modifying the head noun – hence the expression 'internal possessor construction'.

Why did English develop this construction? Consider that external possessor constructions apply in most European languages. Usually they involve a dative-like case for the possessor (in function and commonly in form as well, Haspelmath 1999: 110–111). This is an areal feature in Europe (Haspelmath 1999: 116–117) for, while most languages with this feature are Indo-European, some of these are from outside this family, such as Basque, Hungarian and Maltese.

Remarkably, English, Welsh and Irish have NP-internal possessors as the norm. Put in areal terms, one has internal possessor constructions in Britain and Ireland and generally external possessor constructions in continental Europe. Only in the extreme south-east are internal possessor constructions found widely again, in Turkish and Lezgian, a Caucasian language.

A contact explanation would assume that the use of possessive pronouns in instances like (1) diffused from language shift varieties of the Germanic dialects into inherited varieties and became established there. This transfer did not affect the existence of a possessor construction, but it changed the exponence of the category, a frequent effect of language contact, especially in language shift situations (Hickey 2007: 133–137).

10.3.2   The Twofold Paradigm of 'to be'

West Saxon is known to have had a twofold paradigm of 'to be'. One paradigm began with a vowel in the singular and with *s-* in the plural, and a further paradigm existed with forms in *b-* (see Table 10.2). Both paradigms were inherited from Indo-European.

The Germanic languages, apart from English, have combined the two paradigms to yield just one, for example German *ich bin, du bist, er ist, wir sind*, etc. The West Saxon double paradigm is thus remarkable in the Germanic context, but not when considering Brythonic, with which it co-existed in the early Old English period. Here one also finds two paradigms with a similar syntax and semantics (see Table 10.3).

Table 10.2 *West Saxon present-tense forms of 'to be' (after Campbell 1959: 349)*

Existential present tense	
Singular	Plural
1. *eom*, 2. *eart*, 3. *is*	*sindon, sint*
Habitual present tense	
Singular	Plural
1. *bēo*, 2. *bist*, 3. *biþ*	*bēoþ*

Table 10.3 *Middle Welsh present-tense forms of 'to be'*
(Evans 1976: 136)

Existential present tense

Singular	Plural
1. *wyf, oef*	*ym*
2. *wyt*	*ywch*
3. *yw, (y) mae, (y) taw, oes*	*ynt, (y) maent, y maen*

Habitual present tense

Singular	Plural
1. *bydaf*	*bydwn*
2. *bydy*	*bydwch*
3. *byd, bit*	*bydawnt, bwyant, bint*

The Old English double paradigm is attested from the eighth century which, as Lutz (2009: 233) rightly highlights, was almost three centuries after the coming of the Germanic settlers. This suggests that both 'be' paradigms were entrenched in Old English from earlier transfer, probably by Celtic speakers shifting to the language of the invaders.

10.3.3   The Development of the Progressive

There are basically three views on the development of the progressive in English: (i) it developed independently (Visser 1963–1973), (ii) it arose under Latin influence,[8] perhaps via French (Mossé 1938), and (iii) it resulted from contact with Celtic (Braaten 1967; Dal 1952; Keller 1925; Preußler 1938; Wagner 1959).

A type of progressive structure in which a gerund was governed by a preposition existed sporadically in Old English: *ic wæs on huntunge* 'I was hunting' (Braaten 1967: 173). This also occurs in vernacular German, with an infinitive, as in *Ich bin am Schreiben* [I am at write.INFINITIVE] 'I am writing' and in Dutch *Hij was aan het schrijven* [he was on the write. INFINITIVE].

In this context a further, typological consideration is necessary (Mittendorf and Poppe 2000: 120–122). Progressive aspect is frequently expressed – in many unrelated languages – via a locative structure meaning to be 'at' or 'in' an activity. Furthermore, the step from structures like *ic wæs on huntunge* to *I was hunting* is small, involving only the deletion of the preposition and the shift of gerund to non-finite verb form. The fully developed progressive appears in Middle English, but the apparent time delay between contact with Brythonic and the later progressive can be attributed to the strong written tradition in Old English (Dal 1952: 113).

The progressive is found in all Celtic languages and can be seen in a Modern Welsh sentence like *Mae John yn torri coed* [is John in cut-VERBAL

---

[8] The influence of Latin on languages in the British Isles has been treated variously in the literature: see Genee (2005) for possible influence of Latin on Old Irish.

NOUN wood] 'John is cutting wood' (Jones and Thomas 1977: 63). This shows a prepositional expression for the progressive aspect and is structurally parallel to Old English *ic wæs on huntunge*.

In summary one can say that in both Old English and Brythonic the category of progressive existed. Both languages maintained this; English lost the locative preposition, increasing the syntactic flexibility and range of the structure, perhaps under the supportive influence of Celtic contact. A further point is that with habitual and progressive verb forms both English and Brythonic had aspect structures of a process-oriented nature in contrast to the goal-oriented nature of aspect types in other Germanic languages, such as German, which are largely telic in nature. This general orientation of aspect can be viewed as an areal feature of languages in Britain and Ireland.

10.3.4   The Rise of Periphrastic *do*

The syntax and semantics of the verb *do* is one of the most researched matters in the history of English and there are several opinions concerning why its development took the course it did (Garrett 1998; Klemola 2002). The consensus among the different views is that English developed a causative use of *do* involving a direct object followed by an infinitive and that this structure was not inherited from earlier forms of (West) Germanic.

(2)   *Þe biscop of Wincestre . . . did heom cumen þider.*
       'The bishop of Winchester . . . had them come thither.'

In the course of the Middle English period variants of this structure developed which had no direct object. There is some dispute about whether the object-less structure was causative or not (van der Auwera and Genee 2002: 293) but agreement exists about the resulting periphrastic construction involving *do* + lexical verb, a developmental path also found in German and Dutch.

Contact was already appealed to by those supporting the above development, e.g. Ellegård (1953) and Denison (1985), but it is contact with Latin and possibly with French *faire*. For other accounts geography plays a role. While causative uses of *do* are common in eastern texts, periphrastic uses were first observed in western texts. In the east (and southeast) of England French survived longest, and in the west (and southwest) Celtic was spoken most widely (Welsh and Cornish, both from Brythonic).

Although it is difficult to provide a cast-iron case for a Celtic origin of English periphrastic *do*, one can mention the line of argument which claims that contact situations *per se* tend to give rise to auxiliaries, and so high-contact areas of England (west/southwest) would be where periphrastic *do* would be expected to surface first (Poussa 1990: 412; Tristram 1997:

415). Furthermore, *do* can be used with nouns and so does not require that speakers know sets of corresponding lexical verbs. In a language contact situation, consisting in its early stages of adults shifting from Celtic, this device would improve communication despite being inflectionally less complex. Furthermore, this use of *do* + noun as equivalent to a lexical verb is an established feature of Celtic, for example Modern Irish *Rinne sí iarracht é a sheachaint*, lit. 'did she try.NOUN him to avoid'. In addition, using *do* for emphasis may well have been part of the pragmatic mode of adult Celtic second language learners. With the removal of stress from *do* the periphrastic use would have remained.

The Celtic–English contact situation involves the issue of directionality. It is not certain that Celtic first had periphrastic *do* and thus supplied the model for English. So the question of which direction the transfer went is open. Tristram (1997) assumes mutual influence, and views contact as an areal phenomenon with bidirectional transfer. There are other structures in Celtic and English which are now areal features, for instance the internal possessor construction (see above), and the progressive and habitual aspect (in vernacular varieties of English). However, the use of *do* as a type of auxiliary is found in other West Germanic languages, so there could well have been language-internal input involved in the rise of periphrastic *do*.

Bearing all such factors in mind can help avoid monocausal contact assumptions such as that by McWhorter, who has recently suggested that periphrastic *do* came from Cornish (McWhorter 2009: 168). This single-view approach ignores the frequent cases in West Germanic languages where *do* is a tense carrier used with a lexical verb in non-finite form, for instance in West Germanic and Low German dialects (van der Auwera and Genee 2002: 286–288), e.g. *Ich tue dir das morgen bringen*, lit. 'I do you.DATIVE that tomorrow bring'. The inherent semantics of *do* as a verb denoting direct action also makes it a likely candidate to be employed as tense carrier or aspect marker.

10.3.6 Dental Fricatives in the History of English

A central part of the Germanic Sound Shift is the change of a strongly aspirated /tʰ/ into a dental fricative /θ/, e.g. *thin* /θɪn/ from an earlier **tʰin*, in stressed onsets (not preceded by /s/). The individual Germanic languages all lost this fricative later, except Gothic, Icelandic and English.[9] Gothic did not survive long enough to be relevant here. However, both present-day Icelandic and English have dental fricatives from Germanic. But apparently for different reasons: Icelandic has changed little over time. English, however, has experienced great phonological change over the centuries; for example, it has lost consonantal length, has

---

[9] Danish developed a voiced dental fricative through the lenition of /d/ seen in *mad* [ð] 'food', for instance.

acquired phonemic voiced fricatives and has developed contrastive word stress under Romance influence. So why does a language with so much phonological change still show dental fricatives? These are relatively rare cross-linguistically: the friction of dental fricatives is acoustically much less prominent than with /s/, for instance.

A contributory factor could be the existence of dental fricatives in Brythonic (still found in Welsh). Assuming that much of the later Old English population consisted of Celts who had shifted from Brythonic, dental fricatives would have been natural to them. This could be one of the reasons why Welsh, English and Scots still have dental fricatives. Contact as a contributory factor can also be appealed to when considering the loss of front rounded vowels in English. The Celts who shifted to English would not have had front rounded vowels from Brythonic and would in all likelihood not have used rounded realizations of Old English rounded vowels (which arose through i-umlaut), much as say Slavic speakers of German today do not have rounded realizations of /y, ø/.

10.3.7   Assessment of Early Contact with Celtic

The contact between speakers of Brythonic and those of Germanic dialects taken from the continent to England as of the fifth century may well have led to the transfer of features from the former to the latter (Ahlqvist 2010). In addition, such contact may have played a supportive role in the maintenance of features in the input Germanic dialects as these gradually evolved into forms of later Old English. Without wishing to overstate the case for contact, one can list seven features whose existence in English may possibly be related to the contact with British Celts and to the language shift which large numbers of this section of the population underwent in the generations following the initial Germanic settlement (see Table 10.4).

These features vary in the extent and the timing of their documentation, and listing them in a single table does not imply that they have an equal

Table 10.4 *Possible transfer features from Celtic (Brythonic) to English*

Morphosyntactic
1. Internal possessor construction
2. Twofold paradigm of *to be*
3. Progressive verb forms
4. Periphrastic *do*
5. Northern Subject Rule
Phonological
6. Retention of dental fricatives
7. Loss of front rounded vowels

status as transfer features. Furthermore, for features 3–5 there are cogent internal arguments for their development, so it is possible that contact provided support for their development but it can hardly have been the sole origin.

Paradoxically, the consideration of internal factors may strengthen the case for contact accounts, as the operation of two factors in principle provides more evidence for the genesis of specific features. So while contact alone may, in an instance like the Northern Subject Rule, be viewed by scholars as too weak a source, the additional reinterpretation of decaying present-tense verbal inflections in medieval English by language learners offers, in tandem with possible transfer from Brythonic, a more plausible scenario for the rise of this feature.

10.4 Historical Remnants in Low-contact Areas

The regions of Britain and Ireland can be characterized according to the amount of language contact they have experienced in history (Kortmann and Schröter, Chapter 11, this volume; Klemola 2013). The low-contact areas of England are typically those of central and southern England, along with the north of England after the Viking era. The east of England is generally a low-contact area, but East Anglia did experience considerable contact with Low Country inhabitants in Norwich in previous centuries (Goose et al. 2005; Trudgill 1998). In the north of Britain, Scotland presents a mixed picture. The Lowlands and the Borders region have been low-contact areas since the Viking period, much as northern England. The north of Scotland and the islands off the west coast (the Hebrides) as well as those off the northeast coast (Orkney and Shetland) have had sustained contact, mostly with Scottish Gaelic for the former and Old Norse (later in the form of Norn, the variety spoken on Orkney and Shetland) in the latter case.

The central lowland region of Scotland is the core area of Scots, and shows many historical developments not shared with varieties of English to the south. The morphology of Scots, e.g. that of modals[10] and negators, has developed from northern forms of the Anglian dialect of Old English. In its phonology, Scots is noted for an absence of phonemic vowel length, unusual in the context of first language varieties of English. In varieties of Scots (McClure 1994: 50–51), Scottish English (McClure 1994: 80–81) or Ulster Scots (Harris 1984: 119–123), vowel length may be similar in word pairs like *full* and *fool*, both [fʉˑl]. Despite the absence of contrastive vowel length in word pairs such as that just cited, the varieties in question do have long and short vowels. However, their occurrence is determined by

---

[10] For a general treatment of this complex in England, see Kortmann, Herrmann, Pietsch and Wagner (2005) or Hernández, Kolbe and Schulz (2011).

the nature of the syllable-coda consonant. The constraints in question are known collectively as the *Scottish Vowel Length Rule* (Maguire 2012: 59). The rule specifies that in stressed syllables all vowels before /r, v, ð, z, ʒ/, before another vowel and before a morpheme boundary are long. In other environments the vowels are generally short. Diphthongs also vary in their quality according to the rule, for example *sight* has a raised onset while *size* has a lowered and lengthened one.[11]

Archaic features of morphology are also found in Scotland (and rural Ulster). For instance, there are remnants of a nasal plural, the older weak plural in *-n*, above all in Scots and Ulster Scots (Montgomery and Gregg 1997), for example with *eyen* < *eyes* (Burchfield 1994a: 9) or /ʃin, ʃøn/ for *shoes* in Scots (McClure 1994: 69).

Moving south to northern England one finds such features as definite article reduction (DAR: Britain 2012: 26; Jones 2002; Rupp and Page-Verhoeff 2005) in which the schwa in *the* /ðə/ is lost, leaving either (i) the initial interdental fricative, (ii) a glottalized fricative or (iii) a glottal stop. There is historical evidence that this was also typical of West Country accents further south again; for example, Shakespeare displays the feature abundantly. It is indicated in writing as *th'* or *t'* (Hickey 2015: 12).

In the south of England a prominent phonological feature is initial fricative voicing, the change of a voiceless fricative at the beginning of a word to a voiced one. This happened in the early history of southern English dialects, yielding pronunciations such as *say* [zeɪ] *shilling* [ʒɪlɪŋ], *father* [vɑːðər] (Wakelin 1986, 1988).

The south and southeast of England are known for the widespread occurrence of zero pronouns with subject reference. While this is found with object reference in Standard English, e.g. *The woman ___ he knows has come*, it is legal in the south/southeast of England when the referent is the subject, as in *The woman ___ lives here has come, That's the woman ___ taught me.* This is a feature of London and Home County English (Edwards 1993: 228–229).

In the southwest of England pre-nasal Z-stopping is found whereby /z/ is realized as [d] when it occurs before /n/, typically in the contracted verb forms *isn't* [ɪdn̩t] and *wasn't* [wɒdn̩t], but possibly also in nouns like *business* [bɪdnəs]. This feature also occurs in southeast Irish English and some varieties of southern American English (Thomas 2008: 109), and in both cases it would appear to be due to contact by emigration. Although the southwest of England has a Celtic contact past, the origin of pre-nasal Z-stopping does not seem traceable to transfer from Cornish.

Southwestern dialects of English also evince the rare phenomenon of pronoun exchange which involves the use of a subject pronoun in object position or that which would demand the oblique case, e.g. *Well, if I didn't*

---

[11] This is sometimes called *Aitken's Law* in honour of the Scottish linguist A. J. Aitken, who was the first to describe the rule in detail. See Aitken (1981).

know they, they knowed I (Wagner 2012). This feature is generally thought to stem from an emphatic usage of the pronouns. The varieties which show this usage (Devon, part of Cornwall and a small part of west Somerset) can also have object pronouns in subject position, though this is less common, *Him isn't coming today*. Pronoun exchange is found to a limited extent in other vernaculars, for instance in northern English for the first person plural, e.g. *You can come with we to that as well; Us'll do it* (Beal 2008: 377). The use of *us* together with a subject noun is more common colloquially, e.g. *Us Irish often work abroad*.

10.5   Possible Celtic Areality

The features discussed in Section 10.4 are, so to speak, a negative image of contact-induced areality given that they arose in situations of little or no contact and so must have been internal to the relevant speech community. For the present section a number of features are to be discussed which show noticeable occurrence patterns in the Celtic regions of Britain and Ireland.[12] These can be possibly traced to structural transfer (Winford 2005) from the source Celtic language to target English during the historical language shift. This shift applies[13] to both that in Ireland and that in the west of Scotland, especially the Hebrides where a shift from Scottish Gaelic to English took place and is still taking place in a manner similar to that in Ireland from Irish to English.[14]

10.5.1   Over-use of Definite Article

In varieties of English which historically have been in contact with Celtic languages, the definite article is found in generic senses. This usage may be extended to those varieties which in turn have been in contact with Celtic varieties of English (Harris 1993: 144–145).[15] The following is a brief list of contexts in which the definite article appears contrary to more standard usage: (i) Generic statements: *The life there is hard.* (ii) Institutions: *She's gone to the hospital. The young ones are going to the school already.* (iii) Diseases: *The child has got the measles.* (iv) Seasons: *We left in the spring.* Additionally,

---

[12] For a consideration of shared features among different forms of Insular Celtic and their areal significance, see Matasović (2007).

[13] For reasons of space the influence of Welsh, and possibly Cornish, on English over the centuries has not been considered in this chapter. These influences have been slight by comparison with those in Ireland and western Scotland; see Penhallurick (2008a, 2008b).

[14] General literature on contact forms of Scottish English, essentially Hebridean English, is difficult to come by, but see Sabban (1982, 1985) and Shuken (1984). Not infrequently the variety is simply not recognized, for example in the comprehensive overview volume by Kortmann and Lunkenheimer (2012), where all varieties of English in Scotland are treated together and classified as 'low-contact' (Kortmann and Lunkenheimer 2012: 2) and hence end up in cluster 1a and not cluster 1c in their NeighborNet diagram (Kortmann and Lunkenheimer 2012: 921).

[15] The definite article in forms of American English has been viewed as a legacy of Irish influence (Butters 2001: 337; Montgomery 2001: 133).

there are further contexts in which the definite article is found in highly vernacular varieties, above all in Ireland: (v) Quantifiers: *He asked the both of them.* (vi) Abstract nouns, including languages and objects of study: *Well, I think she likes the languages.* (vii) Parts of the body, afflictions: *There's nothing done by the hand anymore. It nearly broke the leg on me. I always had problems with the ol' back.* (viii) Relatives, spouses, in-laws: *Go in now to see the mother.* (ix) Days of the week, months, seasons, occasions: *So we went into town on the Saturday. Well, how did the Christmas go for you?* Wagner (2008: 418–419) suggests that the over-use of the definite article in the southwest of England could be due to Celtic influence.

10.5.2   Cleft Sentences

These sentences are used for topicalization purposes and involve moving an element to the left and placing it in a dummy main clause with *it* as subject, e.g. *It's tomorrow we're leaving for Spain.* Such sentences occur with moderate frequency in Standard English but in some varieties, such as Scottish and Irish English (Harris 1993: 175–176) they are much more common. In both Irish and Scottish English the number and kind of topicalized elements is greater than in other forms of English (*It's to Dublin he's gone today. It's her brother who rang up this morning*).

10.5.3   Subordinating *and*

This is a syntactic feature of Irish English[16] in which a subordinate clause (usually concessive or restrictive in nature) is introduced by *and* plus a continuous form of a verb, e.g. *They went for a walk and it pouring rain.* The structure is probably a calque on Irish, e.g. *Chuaigh siad ar siúlóid agus é ag cur báistí*, lit. 'Went they on walk and it at putting rain' (Hickey 2007: 261–265). This structure is also found in Hebridean English, e.g. *But many's a time I was along with my auntie on the loom, and her weaving* (Filppula 1997: 950).

10.5.4   Extended *now*

The structure being referred to by this label (Filppula 1999: 90, 122–128) can be seen in a sentence like *I know Brian and Sheila for many years now.* Essentially, the present tense is used in contexts where the time-span is from some point in the past to the present. In these situations, Standard English uses the present perfect, that is, the sentence just quoted would be *I have known Brian and Sheila for many years.* The use of the simple present in contexts which conceptually stretch back into the past is a widespread

---

[16] Klemola and Filppula (1992) examined the occurrence of the structure in non-Celtic Englishes and found it to be very rare or non-existent.

feature of English in the entire island of Ireland and in contact varieties of English in western Scotland (Filppula 1997; Sabban 1985: 128).

The question of origin is difficult to answer conclusively, as Filppula (1999: 123–124) rightly notes. The use of the present in English has a long history and is probably the older Germanic type, still seen in present-day German, e.g. *Ich kenne ihn seit mehreren Jahren*, lit. 'I know him since many years'. This type may have continued well into the early modern period and so been present in the input varieties of English during the language shift in Ireland. On the other hand, auxiliary *have* did not, and does not, have a formal equivalent in Irish or Scottish Gaelic, and so it is more than likely that Celtic speakers in a language shift situation would have ignored this form. The Irish equivalent to the present perfect is expressed quite differently:

(3)   *Tá aithne agam ar Bhrian agus ar Shíle le blianta anuas anois.*
        [is knowledge at-me on Brian and on Sheila with years down now]

The acceptance of extended *now* in present-day Irish English was tested in *A Survey of Irish English Usage* (Hickey 2007: 144–145) and the rates were consistently high. There was a bias towards the south of Ireland, with Wexford in the southeast scoring the highest value, considerably higher than the Ulster Scots core areas of Antrim and Down in the northeast of the country. This may be due to the very early settlement of the east coast before the present perfect had become established in English.

10.5.5   Aspectual Categories in Celtic Englishes

Both varieties of English and the Celtic languages are known for the aspectual distinctions which they evince. For a discussion of these, at least three types of aspect need to be recognized: (i) perfective, which signals that an action is completed, (ii) *progressive*, which indicates that an action is on-going, and (iii) *habitual*, which highlights the repeated occurrence of an action. Creoles are noted for having complex aspectual distinctions (Singler 1990), and those which have developed from English have a more nuanced aspectual system than the original input. Second in line, in terms of aspectual complexity, are language-shift varieties of English (Hickey 1997; Mesthrie 1992), followed by low-contact varieties, which generally show the aspectual distinctions known from Standard English today. Table 10.5 offers a classification of aspectual types with appropriate subdivisions for varieties of English (see also Kortmann and Schröter, Chapter 11, this volume).

The progressive is established in all varieties of English, e.g. *She was singing when he arrived home*, and is currently expanding (Leech et al. 2009: 118–143), encompassing verbs like *want*, e.g. *I'm wanting to leave that matter be*. Perfective aspect is widespread in the world's languages and in some, such as the Slavic languages, pairs of perfective and imperfective verbs are found.

Table 10.5 *Aspectual distinctions for varieties of English*

Information about action	Aspect
duration	progressive
repetition	habitual
completion	perfective
Subdivision of perfective	**Types**
very recent completion	immediate perfective
completion of planned action	resultative perfective
Subdivision of habitual	**Types**
repeated shorter action	iterative
repeated longer action	durative

10.5.5.1   Immediate Perfective

In Celtic Englishes a distinction is common between an immediate perfective and a resultative perfective. The immediate perfective with *after* is a calque on Irish *tar éis* (Harris 1993: 141), which is used for the same purpose.[17] A similar structure exists in Hebridean English (Filppula 1997; Sabban 1982: 155–168; Sabban 1985: 134–135). The position in Gaelic is considered by Sabban (1982: 162), and she notes that Gaelic has a construction with *air* 'after, behind', as in *tha e air bualadh* [is he after striking] 'he is after striking' (Adger 2010). The form *air* used to exist in this function in Irish (*iar*) but was later replaced by *tar éis/i ndiaidh* (both meaning 'after') a long time after the transportation of Irish to Scotland (Hickey 2013b).

10.5.5.2   Resultative Perfective

The resultative perfective indicates that something planned is now completed. In Irish English the word order 'object + past participle' is used (Harris 1993: 160; Hickey 2007: 208–213), e.g. *I've the book read* 'I am finished reading the book', which contrasts with *I've read the book* 'I read it once' (the O+PP word order has a precedent in the history of English, but also an equivalent in Irish in which the past participle always follows the object: *Tá an leabhar léite agam* lit. 'Is the book read at-me').

10.5.5.3   Habitual Aspect

The habitual exists in English by contrast with the progressive, e.g. *He's meeting the students (now)* (progressive) versus *He meets the students (every Thursday morning)* (habitual). In addition, many traditional dialects of English have explicit marking of the habitual, with the verb *do*, by using *be* + inflectional *-s* or combinations of these, e.g. *He does be drinking a lot, He*

---

[17] In Kortmann and Lunkenheimer (2012: 915) this perfective is classified as 'present in' Irish, Scottish English and Newfoundland English along with occasional occurrences in Sri Lankan English and Palmerston Island English. Szmrecsanyi in the same volume lists the *after* perfective under 'Features rare or very rare in L1 varieties' (2012: 828–829). A similar distribution pattern across varieties of English worldwide is found for the resultative perfective, classified in Kortmann and Lunkenheimer (2012) and elsewhere as the 'Medial-Object Perfect'. The classification of both perfectives in the present chapter derives from their function and not their form.

Table 10.6 *Classification of English habitual aspect in Britain and Ireland*

Structure	Example	Comment
Suffixal -*s* on lexical verb stem	*I meets my sister on a Friday afternoon.*	Denotes the iterative habitual in the south and southeast of Ireland.
Suffixal -*s* on *be* or uninflected *be*	*The men bees at home at the week-ends.*	Expression of the durative habitual in Northern Irish English.
Suffixal -*s* on *do* or uninflected *do* plus *be*, with the lexical verb in the progressive form	*He does/do* [də] *be buying and selling old cars.*	Uninflected, unstressed *do* is found in southern and southeastern Irish English for the durative habitual.

bees drinking a lot, He does drink a lot (with unstressed *does*). The dialects with an explicit habitual usually occur in Celtic areas, for instance Ireland or southwest England (former Cornish area), and by extension Newfoundland, a fact which strongly suggests that language contact has played a role in its genesis. There are two types of habitual, one indicating a repeated brief action and one referring to a repeated but longer action. In Irish English, especially of the southeast, an inflectional -*s* expresses the iterative habitual, e.g. *They calls this place City Square*, while *does be* / *duh* [də] *be* is found for the durative habitual, e.g. *She does be worrying about the children* (Hickey 2007, Chapter 4).

10.5.5.4 Category and Exponence

When shifting to another language, temporarily or permanently, adults initially expect to find in the target language the grammatical distinctions which they know from their native language. To this end they search in the target for equivalents to categories they are familiar with (Hickey 2013b). This process is an unconscious one, and persists even with speakers who have considerable target language proficiency. If the categories of the outset language are semantically motivated, then the search to find an equivalent in the target is all the more obvious. Apart from restructuring elements in the target, speakers can transfer elements from their native language. This transfer of grammatical categories is favoured if the following conditions apply:

(a) The target language has a formal means of expressing this category.
(b) There is little variation in the expression of this category.
(c) The expression of this category is not homophonous with another one.
(d) The category marker, in the outset language, can be identified and easily extracted from source contexts.

Table 10.7 illustrates the formal correspondence of the habitual in Irish and Irish English. In this instance the match is poor and the exponence of this aspectual type is different in both languages (except perhaps type 2 in

Table 10.7 *Category and exponence in Irish and Irish English*

Category	Exponence in Irish English	Exponence in Irish
Habitual	1. *do(es) be* + V-*ing* They *do be* fighting a lot.	*bíonn* + non-finite verb form *Bíonn siad ag troid go minic.* [is-HAB they at fighting often]
	2. *bees* (northern) The lads *bees* out a lot.	
	3. verbal -*s* (first person) I *gets* tired of waiting for things to change.	

the left-hand column). However, the syntactic means which early modern English provided – unstressed *do* + verb and/or verbal inflection – were sufficiently transparent semantically for speakers across the community to grasp the usage and adopt it themselves.

Such structures go through a period of mixture and fluidity – much as in New Dialect Formation scenarios – and only gain a clear linguistic profile somewhat later. This means that some features present in the early stages of a language-shift variety are not continued by later generations of speakers. Furthermore, a particular feature may itself undergo a development in the shift variety after the latter has become independent of the original source language, which may or may not be still extant. It would appear that only those features which have a fairly good structural match between outset and target language, and which are semantically transparent, have a chance of survival in a later focused form of the transfer variety. Take, for instance, the autonomous in Irish. This is a finite verb form – but without a personal pronoun – where relevance is expressed via a preposition, e.g. *Rugadh mac di* 'She gave birth to a son' [born-PAST son to-her]. This structure is (and was) never transferred to Irish English, probably because of the difficulty of mapping it onto English syntactically.

10.5.6   Assessment of Later Contact with Celtic

Present-day varieties of English in Ireland and Scotland, which have arisen through language shift from Irish and Scottish Gaelic respectively, still show significant syntactic features which are probably derived from the Celtic source language in question. The large degree of agreement in transfer features between Ireland and the Hebrides in Scotland testifies to the considerable degree of syntactic areality between Ireland and the west of Scotland (Sabban 1982: 99–116), as can be seen from Table 10.8.[18]

---

[18] There are a few more features common to Ireland and Western Scotland in this respect, e.g. focus constructions such as those formed with an unbound reflexive pronoun as verbal subject, seen in a sentence like (Irish) *Himself and his wife were buried . . . himself was buried twelve months ago* and (Scottish) *And himself and his brother was up in the Orkney Isles* (Filppula 1997: 951).

Table 10.8 *Suggested areal features in the regions of Celtic Englishes*

Feature	Comment
Habitual aspect	Convergence with southwest English input on east coast, possibly with influence from Scots via Ulster. Otherwise transfer of category from Irish.
Immediate perfective aspect with *after*	Transfer from Irish, Scottish Gaelic
Resultative perfective with OV word order	Possible convergence with English input, primarily from Irish/Scottish Gaelic
Subordinating *and*	Transfer from Irish/Scottish Gaelic
Variant use of suffixal -s in present	Southwest input to Ireland in first period on east coast
Clefting for topicalization	Transfer from Irish/Scottish Gaelic, with some possible convergence
Greater range of the present tense	Transfer from Irish/Scottish Gaelic, with some possible convergence

One significant feature which does not appear in Hebridean English is an explicitly expressed habitual via *do* + verb or via a verbal inflection, as in forms of Irish English (see Table 10.7 above). This was noted by Filppula (1997: 952–953), who quotes an explanation by Bliss (1972) concerning a putative relationship between dependent verb forms in Irish and the appearance of *do* in Irish English. Bliss's suggestion does not bear linguistic scrutiny and is not capable of accounting for the complexities of habitual aspect exponence in varieties of Irish English. It is more likely that during the language shift in Scotland, unstressed periphrastic *do* was not available to speakers to anything like the degree that this was true for Irish speakers, and so its use as an exponent of a formally marked habitual in contact English in Scotland never reached a sufficiently high level for it to become established in the speech community of the time.

10.6   Overall Assessment and Conclusion

Areality in Britain and Ireland presents a complex and shifting picture throughout the attested history of languages in these islands. The internal interaction of speakers, and the linguistic results this engendered, is separate for both islands until the late twelfth century, after which the political, social and linguistic fate of Ireland became inextricably linked with Britain. The influence exerted since the late Middle Ages has been almost exclusively from Britain to Ireland, bar nineteenth century emigration from Ireland to parts of England and Scotland – Liverpool, Middlesbrough, Glasgow, to mention the most obvious cases – which resulted in some diffusion of Irish features into English in these cities or at least triggered developments which continued after immigration from Ireland ceased, as in the case of Liverpool (Honeybone 2007).

Those features which can be labelled as areal in Britain and Ireland need to be classified at least in terms of the time during which they occurred and the manner in which they arose. The earliest features are those which appeared in later Old English and which were probably the result of shift varieties of English arising among the descendants of speakers of Celtic in the south of England. This interpretation requires a revision of the standard view that the Celts were banished to the highland areas of the west and north of England (Hickey 2012c; Trudgill 2010). Strong features, such as the rise of the internal possessor construction (essentially the use of possessive pronouns in cases of inalienable possession), testify to the areality of Celtic and early English. The later influence of Celtic on English is largely confined to shift varieties of English in Ireland and Scotland (Hickey 2013b). There are significant parallels between later Irish English and Hebridean English in the transfer features from Irish and Scottish Gaelic respectively. These testify to the similar outcome of contact and shift along the western seaboard of Britain and Ireland suggesting an areal spread from the northwest of Scotland to the southwest of Ireland, a high-contact zone contrasting with a low-contact zone in recent centuries reaching from central Scotland down to the south of England.

References

Adger, David, 2010. Gaelic syntax. In Moray Watson and Michelle Macleod (eds), *The Edinburgh Companion to the Gaelic Language*, pp. 304–351. Edinburgh: Edinburgh University Press.

Ahlqvist, Anders, 2010. Early Celtic and English. *Australian Celtic Journal* 9: 43–73.

Aitken, A. J., 1981. The Scottish vowel-length rule. In Michael Benskin and Michael Samuels (eds), *So Meny People, Longages and Tonges: Philological Essays in Scots and Medieval English Presented to Angus McIntosh*, pp. 131–157. Edinburgh: Edinburgh University Press.

Anderwald, Lieselotte, 2002. *Negation in Non-standard British English: Gaps, Regularizations and Asymmetries*. London: Routledge.

Anderwald, Lieselotte, 2009. *The Morphology of English Dialects: Verb-formation in Non-standard English*. Cambridge: Cambridge University Press.

van der Auwera, Johan and Inge Genee, 2002. English *do*: On the convergence of languages and linguists. *English Language and Linguistics* 6: 283–307.

Beal, Joan C., 1993. The grammar of Tyneside and Northumbrian English. In Milroy and Milroy (eds), pp. 187–213.

Beal, Joan C., 2008. English dialects in the North of England: Phonology. In Kortmann and Upton (eds), pp. 122–144.

Bliss, Alan J., 1972. Languages in contact: Some problems of Hiberno-English. *Proceedings of the Royal Irish Academy*, Section C, 72: 63–82.

Braaten, Björn, 1967. Notes on continuous tenses in English. *Norsk Tidskrift for Sprogvidenskap* 21: 167–180.

Britain, David, 2012. English in England. In Hickey (ed.), *Areal Features of the Anglophone World*, pp. 23–52.

Buchstaller, Isabelle, Karen Corrigan, Anders Holmberg, Patrick Honeybone and Warren Maguire, 2013. T-to-R and the Northern Subject Rule: Questionnaire-based spatial, social and structural linguistics. *English Language and Linguistics* 17 (1): 85–128.

Burchfield, Robert W., 1994a. Introduction. In Burchfield (ed.), pp. 1–19.

Burchfield, Robert W. (ed.), 1994b. *English in Britain and Overseas: Origins and Development*. The Cambridge History of the English Language, vol. 5. Cambridge: Cambridge University Press.

Butters, Ronald R., 2001. Grammatical structure. In John Algeo (ed.), *English in North America*, pp. 325–339. The Cambridge History of the English Language, vol. 6. Cambridge: Cambridge University Press.

Campbell, Alistair, 1959. *Old English Grammar*. Oxford: Clarendon Press.

Chadwick, Nora, 1963. The British or Celtic part in the population of England. In *Angles and Britons* (The O'Donnell Lectures), pp. 111–147. Cardiff: University of Wales Press.

Claridge, Claudia and Merja Kytö, 2010. Non-standard language in earlier English. In Raymond Hickey (ed.), *Varieties of English in Writing: The Written Word as Linguistic Evidence*, pp. 15–42. Amsterdam: John Benjamins.

Clarke, Sandra, 2004. The legacy of British and Irish English in Newfoundland. In Raymond Hickey (ed.), *Legacies of Colonial English: Studies in Transported Dialects*, pp. 242–261. Cambridge: Cambridge University Press.

Dal, Ingerid, 1952. Zur Entstehung des Englischen Participium Praesentis auf -ing. *Norsk Tidskrift for Sprogvidenskap* 16: 5–116.

Davies, Norman, 1999. *The Isles: A History*. Oxford: Oxford University Press.

Denison, David, 1985. The origins of periphrastic *do*: Ellegård and Visser reconsidered. In Roger Eaton et al. (eds), *Papers from the 4th International Conference of English Historical Linguistics*, pp. 44–60. Amsterdam: John Benjamins.

Dobson, E. J., 1968. *English Pronunciation 1500–1700,* vol. 1: *Survey of the Sources,* vol. 2: *Phonology*, second edition. Oxford: Oxford University Press.

Edwards, Viv, 1993. The grammar of Southern British English. In Milroy and Milroy (eds), pp. 214–238.

Ekwall, Eilert, 1975. *A History of Modern English Sounds and Morphology* translated by A. Ward. Oxford: Blackwell.

Ellegård, Alvar, 1953. *The Auxiliary Do: The Establishment and Regulation of its Use in English*. Gothenburg Studies in English, vol. 2. Stockholm: Almqvist and Wiksell.

Evans, D. Simon, 1976. *A Grammar of Middle Welsh*. Dublin: Dublin Institute for Advanced Studies.

Filppula, Markku, 1997. Cross-dialectal parallels and language contacts: Evidence from Celtic Englishes. In Raymond Hickey and Stanisław Puppel (eds), *Language History and Linguistic Modelling: A Festschrift for Jacek Fisiak on his 60th Birthday*, pp. 943–957. Berlin: Mouton de Gruyter.

Filppula, Markku, 1999. *The Grammar of Irish English: Language in Hibernian Style*. London: Routledge.

Filppula, Markku and Juhani Klemola (eds), 2009. *Re-evaluating the Celtic Hypothesis. Special issue of* English Language and Linguistics 13 (2).

Filppula, Markku and Juhani Klemola, 2012. Celtic and Celtic Englishes. In Alexander Bergs and Laurel Brinton (eds), *English Historical Linguistics: An International Handbook*, pp. 1687–1703. Berlin: Mouton de Gruyter.

Filppula, Markku, Juhani Klemola and Heli Paulasto, 2008. *English and Celtic in Contact*. London: Routledge.

Foulkes, Paul and Gerry Docherty (eds), 1999. Urban voices: Overview. In Paul Foulkes and Gerry Docherty (eds), *Urban Voices*, pp. 1–24. London: Edward Arnold.

Garrett, Andrew, 1998. On the origin of auxiliary *do*. *English Language and Linguistics* 2: 283–330.

Genee, Inge, 2005. Latin influence on Old Irish? Contact linguistics and the study of medieval language contact. *Journal of Celtic Linguistics* 9: 33–72.

Goose, Nigel et al. (eds), 2005. *Immigrants in Tudor and Early Stuart England*. Brighton: Sussex Academic Press.

Harris, John, 1984. English in the North of Ireland. In Trudgill (ed.), pp. 115–134.

Harris, John, 1993. The grammar of Irish English. In Milroy and Milroy (eds), pp. 139–186.

Haspelmath, Martin, 1999. External possession in a European areal perspective. In Doris Wayne and Immanuel Barshi (eds), *External Possession*, pp. 109–135. Amsterdam: John Benjamins.

Hernández, Nuria, Daniela Kolbe and Monika Edith Schulz, 2011. *A Comparative Grammar of British English Dialects,* vol. 2: *Modals, Pronouns and Complement Clauses*. Berlin: de Gruyter Mouton.

Hickey, Raymond, 1984a. On the nature of labial velar shift. *Journal of Phonetics* 12: 345–354.

Hickey, Raymond, 1984b. Syllable onsets in Irish English. *Word* 35: 67–74.

Hickey, Raymond, 1995. Early contact and parallels between English and Celtic. *Vienna English Working Papers* 4 (2): 87–119.

Hickey, Raymond, 1997. Arguments for creolisation in Irish English. In Raymond Hickey and Stanisław Puppel (eds), *Language History and Linguistic Modelling: A Festschrift for Jacek Fisiak on his 60th Birthday*, pp. 969–1038. Berlin: Mouton de Gruyter.

Hickey, Raymond, 2003. Rectifying a standard deficiency: Pronominal distinctions in varieties of English. In Irma Taavitsainen and Andreas H. Jucker (eds), *Diachronic Perspectives on Address Term Systems*, pp. 345–374. Pragmatics and Beyond, New Series, vol. 107. Amsterdam: John Benjamins.

Hickey, Raymond, 2004. *A Sound Atlas of Irish English*. Berlin: Mouton de Gruyter.

Hickey, Raymond, 2005. *Dublin English: Evolution and Change*. Amsterdam: John Benjamins.

Hickey, Raymond, 2007. *Irish English: History and Present-day Forms*. Cambridge: Cambridge University Press.

Hickey, Raymond, 2008. Feature loss in 19th century Irish English. In Terttu Nevalainen, Irma Taavitsainen, Päivi Pahta and Minna Korhonen (eds), *The Dynamics of Linguistic Variation: Corpus Evidence on English Past and Present*, pp. 229–243. Amsterdam: John Benjamins.

Hickey, Raymond, 2009. Weak segments in Irish English. In Donka Minkova (ed.), *Phonological Weakness in English: From Old to Present-day English*, pp. 116–129. Basingstoke, UK: Palgrave Macmillan.

Hickey, Raymond, 2010. Attitudes and concerns in eighteenth-century English. In Raymond Hickey (ed.), *Eighteenth-century English: Ideology and Change*, pp. 1–20. Cambridge: Cambridge University Press.

Hickey, Raymond, 2011. *The Dialects of Irish, Study of a Changing Landscape*. Berlin: de Gruyter Mouton.

Hickey, Raymond, 2012a. English in Ireland. In Hickey (ed.), *Areal Features of the Anglophone World*, pp. 79–107. Berlin: de Gruyter Mouton.

Hickey, Raymond, 2012b. Internally and externally motivated language change. In Juan Manuel Hernández-Campoy and Juan Camilo Conde-Silvestre (eds), *The Handbook of Historical Sociolinguistics*, pp. 401–421. Malden, MA: Wiley-Blackwell.

Hickey, Raymond, 2012c. Early English and the Celtic hypothesis. In Terttu Nevalainen and Elizabeth Closs Traugott (eds), *The Oxford Handbook of the History of English*, pp. 497–507. Oxford: Oxford University Press.

Hickey, Raymond, 2012d. Assessing the role of contact in the history of English. In Terttu Nevalainen and Elizabeth Closs Traugott (eds), *The Oxford Handbook of the History of English*, pp. 485–496. Oxford: Oxford University Press.

Hickey, Raymond (ed.), 2012e. *Areal Features of the Anglophone World*. Berlin: de Gruyter Mouton.

Hickey, Raymond (ed.), 2012f. *Standards of English: Codified Varieties around the World*. Cambridge: Cambridge University Press.

Hickey, Raymond, 2013a. Supraregionalisation and dissociation. In J. K. Chambers and Natalie Schilling (eds), *The Handbook of Language Variation and Change*, second edition, pp. 537–554. Wiley-Blackwell.

Hickey, Raymond, 2013b. English as a contact language in Ireland and Scotland. In Daniel Schreier and Marianne Hundt (eds), *English as a Contact Language*, pp. 88–105. Cambridge: Cambridge University Press.

Hickey, Raymond, 2014. *A Dictionary of Varieties of English.* Malden, MA: Wiley- Blackwell.

Hickey, Raymond, 2015. The North of England and Northern English. In Raymond Hickey (ed.), *Researching Northern English*, pp. 1–24. Amsterdam: John Benjamins.

Holthausen, Friedrich, 1974. *Altenglisches etymologisches Wörterbuch*, second edition. Heidelberg: Winter.

Honeybone, Patrick, 2007. New-dialect formation in nineteenth century Liverpool: A brief history of Scouse. In Anthony Grant and Clive Grey (eds), *The Mersey Sound: Liverpool's Language, People and Places*, pp. 106–140. Liverpool: Open House Press.

Ihalainen, Ossi, 1994. The dialects of England since 1776. In Burchfield (ed.), pp. 197–274.

Jespersen, Otto, 1940 [1909]. *A Modern English Grammar on Historical Principles.* 6 vols. Copenhagen: Munksgaard.

Jones, Mark J., 2002. The origin of Definite Article Reduction in northern English dialects: Evidence from dialect allomorphy. *English Language and Linguistics* 6: 325–345.

Jones, Morris and Alan R. Thomas, 1977. *The Welsh Language: Studies in its Syntax and Semantics.* Cardiff: University of Wales Press.

Keller, Wolfgang, 1925. Keltisches im englischen Verbum. In *Anglica: Untersuchungen zur englischen Philologie,* vol. 1: *Sprache und Kulturgeschichte.* Leipzig: Mayer und Müller, pp. 55–66.

King, Gareth, 1993. *Modern Welsh: A comprehensive grammar.* London: Routledge.

Klemola, Juhani, 2000. The origins of the Northern Subject Rule: A case of early contact? In Hildegard L. C. Tristram (ed.), *The Celtic Englishes II*, pp. 329–346. Heidelberg: Carl Winter.

Klemola, Juhani, 2002. Periphrastic DO: Dialectal distributions and origins. In Markku Filppula, Juhani Klemola and Heli Pitkänen (eds), *The Celtic Roots of English*, pp. 199–210. Joensuu: University of Joensuu: Faculty of Humanities.

Klemola, Juhani, 2013. English as a contact language in the British Isles. In Daniel Schreier and Marianne Hundt (eds), *English as a Contact Language*, pp. 75–87. Cambridge: Cambridge University Press.

Klemola, Juhani and Markku Filppula, 1992. Subordinating uses of 'and' in the history of English. In Matti Rissaneni, Ossi Ihalainen and Irma Taavitsainen (eds), *History of Englishes: New Methods and Interpretations in Historical Linguistics*, pp. 310–318. Berlin: Mouton de Gruyter.

Kortmann, Bernd and Kerstin Lunkenheimer (eds), 2012. *The Mouton Atlas of Variation in English.* Berlin: de Gruyter Mouton.

Kortmann, Bernd, Tanja Herrmann, Lukas Pietsch and Susanne Wagner, 2005. A Comparative Grammar of British English Dialects, vol. 1: *Agreement, Gender, Relative Clauses.* Berlin: Mouton de Gruyter.

Kortmann, Bernd and Clive Upton (eds), 2008. Varieties of English, vol. 1: *The British Isles*. Berlin: Mouton de Gruyter.

Lass, Roger, 1987. *The Shape of English: Structure and History*. London: Dent.

Leech, Geoffrey, Marianne Hundt, Christian Mair and Nicholas Smith. 2009. *Change in Contemporary English: A Grammatical Study*. Cambridge: Cambridge University Press.

Lutz, Angelika, 2009. Celtic influence on Old English and West Germanic. In Filppula and Klemola (eds), pp. 227–249.

Maguire, Warren, 2012. English and Scots in Scotland. In Hickey (ed.), *Areal Features of the Anglophone World*, pp. 53–77.

Matasović, Ratko, 2007. Insular Celtic as a language area. In Hildegard L. C. Tristram (ed.), *The Celtic Languages in Contact*, pp. 93–112. Potsdam: Potsdam University Press.

McClure, J. Derrick, 1994. English in Scotland. In Burchfield (ed.), pp. 23–93.

McWhorter, John H., 2009. What else happened to English? A brief for the Celtic hypothesis. In Filppula and Klemola (eds), pp. 163–191.

Mesthrie, Rajend, 1992. *English in Language Shift: The History, Structure and Sociolinguistics of South African Indian English*. Cambridge: Cambridge University Press.

Milroy, James and Lesley Milroy (eds), 1993. *Real English: The Grammar of the English Dialects in the British Isles*. London: Longman.

Mitchell, Bruce and Fred Robinson, 2007. *A Guide to Old English*, seventh edition. Oxford: Blackwell.

Mittendorf, Ingo and Erich Poppe, 2000. Celtic contacts of the English progressive? In Hildegard L. C. Tristram (ed.), *The Celtic Englishes II*, pp. 117–145. Heidelberg: Carl Winter.

Montgomery, Michael, 2001. British and Irish antecedents. In John Algeo (ed.), *English in North America*, pp. 86–153. The Cambridge History of the English Language, vol. 6. Cambridge: Cambridge University Press.

Montgomery, Michael and Robert Gregg, 1997. The Scots language in Ulster. In Charles Jones (ed.), *The Edinburgh History of the Scots Language*, pp. 569–622. Edinburgh: Edinburgh University Press.

Mossé, Ferdinand, 1938. *Histoire de la Forme Périphrastique Être + Participe Présent en Germanique,* part 2: *Moyen-Anglais et Anglais Moderne*. Paris: Librairie C. Klincksieck.

Penhallurick, Robert, 2008a. Welsh English: Phonology. In Kortmann and Upton (eds), pp. 105–121.

Penhallurick, Robert, 2008b. Welsh English: Morphology and syntax. In Kortmann and Upton (eds), pp. 360–372.

Poplack, Shana and Sali Tagliamonte, 2001. *African American English in the Diaspora*. Malden, MA: Blackwell.

Poussa, Patricia, 1990. A contact-universals origin for periphrastic do, with special consideration of OE–Celtic contact. In Sylvia Adamson, Vivien Law, Nigel Vincent and Susan Wright (eds), *Papers from the Fifth*

International Conference on English Historical Linguistics, pp. 407–434. Amsterdam: John Benjamins.

Preußler, Walter, 1938. Keltischer Einfluß im Englischen. *Indogermanische Forschungen* 56: 178–191.

Raumolin-Brunberg, Helena, 2005. The diffusion of subject YOU: A case study in historical sociolinguistics. *Language Variation and Change* 17: 55–73.

Rockel, Martin, 1989. *Grundzüge einer Geschichte der irischen Sprache [Outline of a History of the Irish Language]*. Vienna: Verlag der Österreichischen Akademie der Wissenschaften.

Rosenthal, Bernard et al. (eds), 2009. *Records of the Salem Witch-Hunt*. Cambridge: Cambridge University Press.

Rupp, Laura and Hanne Page-Verhoeff, 2005. Pragmatic and historical aspects of Definite Article Reduction in northern English dialects. *English World-Wide* 26 (3): 325–346.

Sabban, Annette, 1982. *Gälisch–Englischer Sprachkontakt [Gaelic–English Language Contact]*. Heidelberg: Groos.

Sabban, Annette, 1985. On the variability of Hebridean English syntax: The verbal group. In Manfred Görlach (ed.), *Focus on Scotland*, pp. 125–144. Amsterdam: John Benjamins.

Schreier, Daniel, 2005. *Consonant Change in English Worldwide: Synchrony Meets Diachrony*. Basingstoke, UK: Palgrave Macmillan.

Shuken, Cynthia, 1984. Highland and Island English. In Trudgill (ed.), pp. 152–166.

Singler, John (ed.), 1990. *Pidgin and Creole Tense-Mood-Aspect Systems*. Amsterdam: John Benjamins.

Szmrecsanyi, Benedikt, 2012. Typological profile: L1 varieties. In Kortmann and Lunkenheimer (eds), pp. 827–842.

Szmrecsanyi, Benedikt and Bernd Kortmann, 2008. Vernacular universals and Angloversals in a typological perspective. In Markku Filppula and Juhani Klemola (eds), *Vernacular Universals and Language Contacts*, pp. 33–53. New York and London: Routledge.

Thomas, Erik, 2008. Rural southern white accents. In Edgar W. Schneider (eds), *Varieties of English*, vol. 2: *The Americas and the Caribbean*, pp. 87–114. Berlin: Mouton de Gruyter.

Tolkien, John R. R., 1963. English and Welsh. In *Angles and Britons* (The O'Donnell Lectures), pp. 1–41. Cardiff: University of Wales Press.

Tristram, Hildegard L. C., 1997. Do-periphrasis in contact? In Heinrich Ramisch and Kenneth J. Wynne (eds), *Language in Time and Space: Studies in Honour of Wolfgang Viereck on the Occasion of his 60th Birthday*, pp. 401–417. Stuttgart: Franz Steiner.

Trudgill, Peter (ed.), 1984. *Language in the British Isles*. Cambridge: Cambridge University Press.

Trudgill, Peter, 1998. Third-person singular zero: African American Vernacular English, East Anglian dialects and Spanish persecution in the Low Countries. *Folia Linguistica Historica* 18 (1/2): 139–148.

Trudgill, Peter, 2002. *Sociolinguistic Variation and Change*. Edinburgh: Edinburgh University Press.

Trudgill, Peter, 2008. The dialect of East Anglia. In Kortmann and Upton (eds), pp. 178–193.

Trudgill, Peter, 2009. Sociolinguistic typology and complexification. In Geoffrey Sampson, David Gil and Peter Trudgill (eds), *Language Complexity as an Evolving Variable*, pp. 98–109. Oxford: Oxford University Press.

Trudgill, Peter, 2010. What really happened to Old English? In Peter Trudgill, *Investigations in Sociohistorical Linguistics: Stories of Colonisation and Contact*, pp. 1–35. Cambridge: Cambridge University Press.

Upton, Clive and John D. A. Widdowson, 2006. *An Atlas of English Dialects*, second edition. Oxford: Oxford University Press.

Vennemann, Theo, 2002. On the rise of 'Celtic' syntax in Middle English. In Peter Lucas and Angela Lucas (eds), *From Tongue to Text: Papers from the Third International Conference on Middle English: University College Dublin, 1–4 July 1999*, pp. 203–234. Frankfurt: Peter Lang.

Visser, Federicus T., 1963–1973. *An Historical Syntax of the English Language*, four volumes. Leiden: E. J. Brill.

Wagner, Heinrich, 1959. *Das Verbum in den Sprachen der britischen Inseln [The Verb in the Languages of the British Isles]*. Tübingen: Niemeyer.

Wagner, Susanne, 2008. English dialects in the South-West: Morphology and syntax. In Kortmann and Upton (eds), pp. 417–439.

Wagner, Susanne, 2012. Pronominal systems. In Hickey (ed.), *Areal Features of the Anglophone World*, pp. 379–408.

Wakelin, Martyn, 1984. Rural dialects in England. In Trudgill (ed.), pp. 70–93.

Wakelin, Martyn, 1986. *The Southwest of England*. Varieties of English Around the World, Text Series, vol. 5. Amsterdam: John Benjamins.

Wakelin, Martyn, 1988. The phonology of South-Western English 1500–1700. In Jacek Fisiak (ed.), *Historical Dialectology: Regional and Social*, pp. 609–644. Berlin: Mouton de Gruyter.

Watson, Kevin and Lynn Clark, 2016. The origins of Liverpool English. In Raymond Hickey (ed.), *Listening to the Past: Audio Records of Accents of English*, pp. 113–141. Cambridge: Cambridge University Press.

Williams, Stephen, 1980. *A Welsh Grammar*. Cardiff: University of Wales Press.

Winford, Donald, 2005. Contact-induced changes: Classification and processes. *Diachronica* 22 (2): 373–427.

11

Varieties of English

Bernd Kortmann and Verena Schröter

11.1 Introduction

This chapter is solely concerned with areal patterns in the domain of morphosyntax in varieties of English around the world. Thus it tries to discern areality on that structural level of language where it is notoriously hardest to find; moreover, its focus is on areality, that is, 'the areal concentration of linguistic features' (Hickey 2012a: 2), on a global (world region) scale, not on a more delimited regional scale as is usual in dialectology or dialectometry. It adds to the line of research pursued in, for example, Anderwald (2012), Lunkenheimer (2012), Brato and Huber (2012), Kortmann and Wolk (2012), Kortmann (2013), and various chapters offering synopses of individual world regions published in the *Mouton World Atlas of Varieties of English* (WAVE: Kortmann and Lunkenheimer 2012a). The dataset used here is the one in eWAVE 2.0 (www.ewave-atlas .org), which includes ratings, examples and interactive maps for 235 morphosyntactic features in 50 L1 and L2 varieties of English as well as 26 English-based pidgins and creoles (see Table 11.1). The only major difference between the datasets in eWAVE 2.0 and WAVE is that for the former (launched in November 2013) Philippine English and Cape Flats English have been added. For more information on the varieties, their classification into different variety types, the complete feature set, methodology, rating system, informants, etc., see Kortmann and Lunkenheimer (2012b: 1–6) or http://ewave-atlas.org/introduction.

The Anglophone world regions considered in this chapter are, in alphabetical order, Africa, America, Asia (South and Southeast), Australia, the British Isles, the Caribbean and the Pacific. (Given the extreme geographical dispersal and isolation of the relevant varieties – Falkland English, St Helena English and Tristan da Cunha English – it would not make sense to also include in our discussion the eighth world region in WAVE, South Atlantic.) As argued in a range of previous

Table 11.1 Seventy-six L1 and L2 varieties, pidgins and creoles represented in eWAVE 2.0

	L1 (31)		L2 (19)	P (7) & C (19)
	low-contact L1 (10)	high-contact L1 (21)		
British Isles (11)	Orkney and Shetland E (O&SE), north of England (North), SW of England (SW), SE of England (SE), East Anglia (EA), Scottish E (ScE)	Irish E (IrE), Welsh E (WelE), Manx E (ManxE), Channel Islands E (ChIsE)	Maltese E (MltE)	British Creole (BrC)
Africa (17)	Liberian Settler E (LibSE), White South African E (WhSAfE), White Zimbabwean E (WhZimE)		Ghanaian E (GhE), Nigerian E (NigE), Cameroon E (CamE), Kenyan E (KenE), Tanzanian E (TznE), Ugandan E (UgE), Black South African E (BlSAfE), Indian South African E (InSAfE), Cape Flats English (CFE)	Ghanaian Pidgin (GhP), Nigerian Pidgin (NigP), Cameroon Pidgin (CamP), Krio, Vernacular Liberian E (VLibE)
America (10)	Newfoundland E (NfldE), Appalachian E (AppE), Ozark E (OzE), Southeast American Enclave dialects (SEAmE)	Colloquial American E (CollAmE), Urban African American Vernacular E (UAAVE), Rural African American Vernacular E (RAAVE), Earlier African American Vernacular E (EAAVE)	Chicano E (ChcE)	Gullah
Caribbean (13)		Bahamian E (BahE)	Jamaican E (JamE)	Jamaican C (JamC), Bahamian C (BahC), Barbadian C (Bajan), Belizean C (BelC), Trinidadian C (TrinC), Eastern Maroon C (EMarC), Sranan, Saramaccan (Saram), Guyanese C (GuyC), San Andrés C (SanAC), Vincentian C (VinC)

Table 11.1 (cont.)

	L1 (31)		L2 (19)	P (7) & C (19)
	low-contact L1 (10)	high-contact L1 (21)		
South and Southeast Asia (8)		Colloquial Singapore E (CollSgE), Philippine E (PhilE)	Indian E (IndE), Pakistan E (PakE), Sri Lanka E (SlkE), Hong Kong E (HKE), Malaysian E (MalE)	Butler E (ButlE)
Australia (5)		Aboriginal E (AbE), Australian E (AusE), Australian Vernacular E (AusVE)		Torres Strait C (TorSC), Roper River C (RRC [Kriol])
Pacific (8)		New Zealand E (NZE)	Colloquial Fiji E (CollFijiE), Acrolectal Fiji E (FijiE)	Hawai'ian C (HawC), Bislama (Bisl), Norfolk Island/Pitcairn E (Norf'k), Palmerston E (PalmE), Tok Pisin (TP)
South Atlantic (3)	St. Helena E (StHE), Tristan da Cunha E (TdCE), Falkland Islands E (FlkE)			

publications by the first author, most recently in Kortmann and Wolk (2012: 920–927), the overall morphosyntactic (or typological) profiles of varieties of English and English-based pidgins and creoles primarily pattern according to variety type (high-/low-contact L1, L2, pidgin, creole) and not according to the relevant world region where they are spoken. In other words, the sociohistorical conditions in which a given variety emerged have a far stronger impact than geography on the morphosyntactic feature set constituting the typological profile of that variety. This does not mean that geographical (or, alternatively, areal) clusterings cannot be observed, but they are only secondary to the primary patterning of morphosyntactic profiles according to variety type. This is shown very clearly in Figure 11.1, which offers a NeighborNet diagram (or phenogram) allowing us to visualize the degree of typological similarity and distance between any pair of the 76 varieties/pidgins/creoles considered here, similarity/distance being determined by the number of co-presences and co-absences of morpho-syntactic features for any two varieties in the WAVE dataset that are compared (for details of the method see Kortmann and Wolk 2012: 919–920). As can be seen, the NeighborNet diagram falls into four main clusters, that is, the members of each of these four clusters share more morphosyntactic properties with each other than with any member of any of the other three clusters. Most importantly, these clusters pattern rather neatly according to variety type: cluster 1 is the L1 cluster (notably including all low-contact, or traditional, L1s), cluster 2 is the L2 cluster, cluster 4 is the pidgin and creole cluster, and even the three main sub-clusters of the more diffuse cluster 3 are fairly coherent as regards variety type: creoles, high-contact L1s and so-called creoloids.

However – and this is the starting point for the present chapter – there are also some areal patterns which can be identified in Figure 11.1, though they can only be determined within each of the four major, variety-type-driven clusters: for example, there are sub-clusters of American varieties to be found in clusters 1 (Am1) and 3 (Am2), sub-clusters of African varieties in clusters 2 (Af1, Af2) and 4 (Af3), and sub-clusters of Caribbean varieties and creoles in clusters 3 (Car1) and 4 (Car2, Car3). What is even more welcome for a chapter focusing on areality in a large-scale comparison of the morphosyntactic properties covering most of the variation and vari-eties in the Anglophone world is the following observation: quite a number of these areal sub-clusters really are formed by varieties spoken in geographically contiguous areas of the relevant world region. Just take the L2 cluster 2, where the sub-cluster As1 is formed rather neatly by Southeast Asian Englishes; or consider the pidgin/creole cluster 4, where sub-cluster Af3 consists exclusively of the four West African pidgins/creoles (Ghanaian Pidgin, Nigerian Pidgin, Cameroon Pidgin plus Krio, the only West African creole) and where its immediate neighbour branch, sub-cluster Car3, is formed by the three radical creoles spoken in Surinam

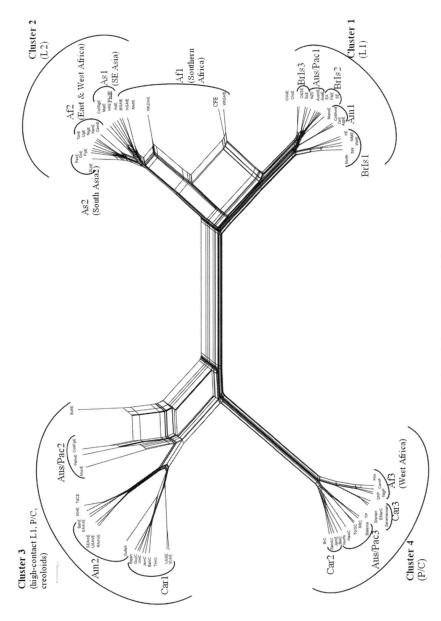

Figure 11.1 NeighborNet diagram: typological and areal clusters of 76 varieties, pidgins and creoles in eWAVE 2.0

Table 11.2 *Domains of grammar covered in WAVE (235 features in all)*

Grammatical domain	Feature totals	% of 235
Pronouns	47	20.0%
Noun phrase	40	17.0%
Tense and aspect	33	14.0%
Modal verbs	7	3.0%
Verb morphology	26	11.0%
Negation	16	6.8%
Agreement	15	6.4%
Relativization	15	6.4%
Complementation	11	4.7%
Adverbial subordination	5	2.1%
Adverbs and prepositions	7	3.0%
Discourse organization and word order	13	5.5%

(Sranan, Eastern Maroon Creole, Saramaccan).[1] But yet again a cautionary note needs to be struck: not all sub-clusters are to be (exclusively) interpreted areally. They may instead document historical links, such as in subcluster BrIs1 between Irish English and the English southwest as donor varieties of Newfoundland English, in sub-cluster BrIs2 between the southeastern dialects of England and Falkland English, or in sub-cluster Am2 between Earlier AAVE and its modern descendants (Rural and Urban) AAVE. Alternatively, such clusters may at least foster the hypothesis that historical links and directions of influence may have existed between certain varieties (e.g. between Earlier AAVE and Bahamian English). A recent example of this line of research into historical language contact is the paper by Eberle and Schreier (2013), who, based on the WAVE dataset and their own morphosyntactic survey following the WAVE feature catalogue, explore the 'Caribbean connection' for African Bermudian English and selected Caribbean varieties and creoles.

Hence the major aim of the present chapter is to make areality an even stronger factor in the interpretation of the WAVE data, focusing *not* on the overall typological profiles of the 76 varieties/pidgins/creoles, but on the individual features. The central task will be to identify features, and in some cases feature sets, that are highly distinctive of, possibly even diagnostic for, a given Anglophone world region. In this feature-based approach, it is in Section 11.2 that we will explore each of the twelve domains of grammar from which the 235 WAVE features are taken. The internal structure of that section will follow the order in which the relevant grammar domains are listed in Table 11.2.

Whereas in Section 11.2 we will only be interested in areality by grammar domain, in the synoptic Section 11.3 the seven Anglophone world regions will take centre stage. More exactly, it will offer generalizations, and possible

---

[1] For a discussion of areal patterns among the three major Anglophone pidgin and creole regions (West Africa, Caribbean, Pacific/Australia) see Kortmann (2013: 177–184).

explanations, for the areal patterns identified in this chapter. Section 11.4 will briefly address the issue of areality within individual world regions, for example between the varieties of the North and South of the British Isles and between the varieties of English in South and Southeast Asia. The concluding Section 11.5 will put the findings from the preceding sections in perspective and make suggestions for future research with the promise of a further strengthening of areality as a factor influencing and shaping not only morphosyntactic usage but, ultimately, morphosyntactic systems, typological profiles and, not least, local norms in World Englishes.

11.2   Top Diagnostic Features in Morphosyntax for Individual Anglophone World Regions

11.2.1   Defining the Thresholds for Areally Distinctive and Diagnostic Features

Most of the findings in this section will be presented in the form of tables, all of which are cut to the same pattern and fairly self-explanatory. For each of the features in a given grammar domain it was determined whether its geographical distribution across the seven world regions shows a certain bias, i.e. whether it is over-represented in one given world region compared with all others. As thresholds for features finding their way into the following tables we defined (a) the 50 per cent mark, i.e. all of the features must be attested in at least 50 per cent of all the L1/L2 varieties, pidgins or creoles in the relevant world region, and (b) the 30 per cent mark, i.e. only those features are listed in Section 11.2 whose attestation rate (AR) in one (and only one) world region exceeds the AR of this feature in the rest of the world (RoW) by at least 30 per cent (calculus: AR region minus AR RoW). As diagnostic for a given world region we consider features where this AR difference reaches or exceeds the 60 per cent mark. The relevant features are marked in bold print. The major ordering principle for each of the tables in this section is by region (alphabetical order), and within the individual world region in decreasing order by the rightmost column 'AR diff(erence) region – RoW'. Thus in Table 11.3a it turns out that WAVE feature F9 (Benefactive 'personal dative' construction), as in *I got me a new car* (Urban AAVE), is a diagnostic feature of America (i.e. in the WAVE dataset: USA and Newfoundland).[2] Note that for reasons of space no maps will be used in order to show geographical distribution and, especially, bias. For many of the features discussed below maps will be found in Kortmann and Lunkenheimer 2012 (see especially pp. xv–xx for the map survey ordered by feature numbers). In general, maps for every single feature can easily be produced with a few clicks by means of eWAVE (www.ewave-atlas.org).

---

[2] Since F9 is attested in 10/10 North American varieties (AR region 100 per cent) and in 23/66 varieties outside this region (AR RoW 34.85 per cent), this results in a difference in attestation rate (AR diff.) of 65.15 per cent.

Table 11.3a *Pronouns: top diagnostic features for individual world regions (AR difference region – rest of world* ≥ *30%; bold for* ≥ *60%)*

Feature		Region	AR region	AR RoW	AR diff. region –RoW
F9	**Benefactive 'personal dative' construction**	**Am**	**100.00%**	**34.85%**	**65.15%**
F39	Plural forms of interrogative pronouns: using additional elements	Am	70.00%	27.27%	42.73%
F13	Subject pronoun forms serving as base for reflexives	Am, Car	56.52%	20.75%	35.77%
F43	Subject pronoun drop: referential pronouns	As	100.00%	45.59%	54.41%
F40	Plural forms of interrogative pronouns: reduplication	As	50.00%	4.41%	45.59%
F37	**More number distinctions in personal pronouns than simply singular vs plural**	**Aus, Pac**	**61.54%**	**0.00%**	**61.54%**
F36	Distinct forms for inclusive/ exclusive first person non-singular	Aus, Pac	61.54%	1.59%	59.95%
F22	***You* as (modifying) possessive pronoun**	**Car**	**92.31%**	**22.22%**	**70.09%**
F19	**Subject pronoun forms as (modifying) possessive pronouns: first person plural**	**Car**	**76.92%**	**14.92%**	**62.64%**
F23	**Second person pronoun forms other than *you* as (modifying) possessive pronoun**	**Car**	**84.62%**	**22.22%**	**62.40%**
F17	Creation of possessive pronouns with prefix *fi-* + personal pronoun	Car	61.54%	3.18%	58.36%
F18	Subject pronoun forms as (modifying) possessive pronouns: first person singular	Car	69.23%	17.86%	51.37%
F21	Subject pronoun forms as (modifying) possessive pronouns: third person plural	Car	76.92%	31.75%	45.18%
F46	Deletion of *it* in referential *it is-* constructions	Car	76.92%	31.74%	45.18%
F10	No gender distinction in third person singular	Car	76.92%	39.68%	37.24%
F20	Subject pronoun forms as (modifying) possessive pronouns: third person singular	Car	53.85%	20.63%	33.21%
F32	Distinction between emphatic vs non-emphatic forms of pronouns	Car	53.85%	22.22%	31.63%

Table 11.3b *Pronouns: top diagnostic feature sets for individual world regions*

Feature		Region	AR region	AR RoW	AR diff. region – RoW
F42–F44	**Pronoun drop: object, referential subject, dummy subject**	**As**	**95.83%**	**34.80%**	**61.03%**
F18–F27	Alternative forms as (modifying) possessive pronouns: subject and object forms, first, second, third person	Car	63.08%	19.77%	43.31%
F1, F2	*She/her; he/him* used for inanimate referents	Brls	63.64%	33.08%	30.56%

While the attestation rates are based on the mere presence versus absence of features, the regional pervasiveness (rp-score) of a feature is captured by integrating its relative frequency in a given region based on the WAVE rating system. The rp-score of individual features is calculated as follows: a numerical value is assigned to the WAVE ratings A (pervasive/obligatory) = 1, B (neither pervasive nor rare) = 0.6, C (attested but rare) = 0.3, D (not attested), X (not applicable), ? (unknown) = 0. The sum of these is divided by the number of varieties in the respective region. With an rp score of 0.73, F9 is not only a diagnostic, but also a pervasive feature of the North American varieties.[3]

11.2.2   Areality in a Dozen Domains of Grammar

Let us begin with that grammar domain represented by the largest number of features (47) in WAVE, namely pronouns. As shown in Tables 11.3a and 11.3b, about half of the pronominal features have a pronounced geographical signal. This is especially strong for the Caribbean (for 11 of the 17 features in Table 11.3a), but also very noticeable for the Australian/Pacific region: F36 and F37 are found in more than 60 per cent of the Australian/Pacific varieties, but either nowhere else (!) in the Anglophone world (F37, as in Palmerston English *We two is going*) or in only one other variety of English (F36, as in Aboriginal English ***mela*** *new teacher gotta come* 'our [exclusive] new teacher will come'). Feature 13 (Subject pronoun forms serving as base for reflexives), as in *She say it for sheself* (Trinidadian Creole), is characteristic of the entire American and Caribbean area. There are also two areoversals to be observed in Table 11.3a: F9 (Benefactive 'personal dative' construction) is found in all 10 WAVE varieties of America, and F43 (Subject pronoun drop: referential pronouns, rp-score 0.76) is strongly attested in all eight WAVE

---

[3] For example in the 10 American varieties, F9 receives 4 A, 5 B and 1 C rating. $(4 \times 1 + 5 \times 0.6 + 1 \times 0.3)/10 =$ rp-score F9 = 0.73.

varieties of South and Southeast Asia, as in *When I come back from my work___ just travel back to my home* (Indian English).

What is also worth noting is the smaller or larger sets of pronominal features which exhibit a clear regional bias. Consider the three feature sets in Table 11.3b, which vary considerably in the strength of their geographical signal, with 'AR region' representing the average attestation rate for all features in the relevant set taken together.

Let us comment only on the first and areally most striking feature set. It is formed by the three pronoun-deleting features F42 (Object pronoun drop), as in *Do you say to Paul? Yes, I told Ø already* (Hong Kong English), F43 (see the Indian English example above) and F44 (Dummy subject drop), as in *Ø Raining so no tennis* (Sri Lankan English). The concentration of these three deletion features in Asia is of course reminiscent of Mesthrie and Bhatt's (2008) hypothesis of a broad dichotomy among World Englishes of 'deleters' versus 'preservers', with the Southeast Asian varieties allegedly representing the 'deleting' type and African varieties like Black South African English representing the 'preserving' type. The strong limitations of this dichotomy in an aggregate approach have been discussed elsewhere, for example in Lunkenheimer (2012: 865–869) and Kortmann (2013: 174–177). At the same time it must be acknowledged that there are individual deletion features, such as pronoun dropping/deletion, which send a very pronounced Asian signal. What we can also see, though, is that F42–F44 are not only extremely characteristic of Englishes in Southeast Asia, but of South Asian Englishes too.

Asia also plays a prominent role in the second-largest grammar domain in WAVE, namely noun phrase features.

Out of the 15 NP features in Table 11.4, almost half are characteristic of Asia. In light of the immediately preceding discussion on 'deletion' features, it is noteworthy that the only two true areoversals in Table 11.4, i.e. features attested in every single variety of the relevant world region, concern the deletion of definite (F62) and indefinite articles (F63) in Asia. Consider examples like Malaysian English *Vocabulary is very important at Ø elementary level* (F62) or Indian English *We decided to rent Ø apartment* (F63). Moreover, both features are attested pervasively in the respective varieties; with rp-scores of 0.8 and 0.75, zero articles are more prevalent than either definite or indefinite articles in the Asian Englishes. To these two, we may add a third deletion feature in the NP which exhibits an areal clustering in Asia, namely F86 (Zero marking of degree), as in Hong Kong English *Chemistry is one of the Ø interesting subjects when I was in secondary school*. A near-areoversal (95.65 per cent) of the widest reach in Table 11.4, namely for America and the Caribbean, is F70 (Proximal and distal demonstratives with *here* and *there*), as in *this here car* (Chicano English), *Knock that there spoon back* (Earlier AAVE), or *Don't touch this here, use that there* (Bajan, or Barbadian Creole). Two features deserve special mention because they are so rare outside the relevant Anglophone world region, where they are attested in

Table 11.4 *Noun phrase: top diagnostic features for individual world regions (AR difference region – rest of world ≥ 30%; bold for ≥ 60%)*

Feature		Region	AR region	AR RoW	AR diff. region – RoW
F59	Double determiners	Af	64.71%	20.34%	44.37%
F71	No number distinction in demonstratives	Af	76.47%	33.90%	42.57%
F83	Comparatives and superlatives of participles	Am	60.00%	9.09%	50.91%
F70	Proximal and distal demonstratives with *here* and *there*	Am, Car	95.65%	37.74%	57.92%
F63	Use of zero article where StE has indefinite article	As	100.00%	47.06%	52.94%
F81	*Much* as comparative marker	As	62.50%	14.71%	47.79%
F62	Use of zero article where StE has definite article	As	100.00%	52.94%	47.06%
F82	*As/to* as comparative markers	As	50.00%	14.71%	35.29%
F64	Use of definite article where StE favours zero	As	75.00%	42.65%	32.35%
F86	Zero marking of degree	As	50.00%	17.65%	32.35%
F61	Use of indefinite article where StE has definite article	As	50.00%	19.12%	30.88%
F76	Postnominal phrases with *bilong/ blong/long/blo* to express possession	Aus	60.00%	7.05%	52.95%
F51	Plural marking via postposed elements	Car	69.23%	23.81%	45.42%
F77	Omission of genitive suffix; possession expressed through bare juxtaposition of nouns	Car	92.31%	49.21%	43.10%
F66	Indefinite article *one/wan*	Car	92.31%	57.14%	35.17%

the majority of varieties. These are F76 (Postnominal phrases with *bilong/ blong/long/blo* to express possession), as in Aboriginal English *woman belong friend* 'the woman's friend', and F83 (Comparatives and superlatives of participles), as in Appalachian English *Daddy said he was the fightingest little rascal he ever hunted* or *He was the singingest man this side of Turnpike* (Montgomery 2008: 452).

Let us now turn to features of the verb phrase, more exactly to the domains of tense and aspect (Table 11.5), modal verbs (Table 11.6) and verb morphology (Table 11.7). We will see that almost all WAVE features in the domain of modal verbs exhibit striking areal distributions. In the domain of tense and aspect it is again Asia that is represented by the largest number of areally distinctive features, closely followed by the varieties spoken in America. Consider Table 11.5.

Three tense and aspect features turn out to be true areoversals. In terms of areal distinctiveness, the weakest of these is F113 (Loosening of sequence of tenses rule), which is found in all Asian varieties (e.g. in Pakistan English, as in *Even though I lost, I was happy that I participated in it*), but in about 62 per cent of the varieties elsewhere in the Anglophone

Table 11.5 *Tense and aspect: top diagnostic features for individual world regions (AR difference region – rest of world ≥ 30%; bold for ≥ 60%)*

Feature		Region	AR region	AR RoW	AR diff. region – RoW
F116	*Come*-based future/ingressive markers	Af	58.82%	13.56%	45.26%
F105	**Completive/perfect *have/be* + *done* + past participle**	**Am**	**70.00%**	**7.58%**	**62.42%**
F90	Invariant *be* as habitual marker	Am	60.00%	16.67%	43.33%
F92	Other non-standard habitual markers: synthetic	Am	50.00%	19.70%	30.30%
F104	**Completive/perfect *done***	**Am, Car**	**78.26%**	**13.20%**	**65.06%**
F100	**Levelling of the difference between present perfect and simple past: present perfect for StE simple past**	**As**	**100.00%**	**36.76%**	**63.24%**
F109	Perfect marker *already*	As	75.00%	26.47%	48.53%
F89	Wider range of uses of progressive *be* + V-*ing* than in StE: extension to habitual contexts	As	87.50%	44.12%	43.38%
F119	*Would* for (distant) future in contrast to *will* (immediate future)	As	62.50%	22.06%	40.44%
F113	Loosening of sequence of tenses rule	As	100.00%	61.76%	38.24%
F95	*Be sat/stood* with progressive meaning	Brls	63.64%	6.15%	57.49%
F102	*Be* as perfect auxiliary	Brls	54.55%	23.07%	31.48%
F114	***Go*-based future markers**	**Car**	**100.00%**	**36.51%**	**63.49%**

Table 11.6 *Modal verbs: top diagnostic features for individual world regions (AR difference region – rest of world ≥ 30%; bold for ≥ 60%)*

Feature		Region	AR region	AR RoW	AR diff. region – RoW
F125	**New quasi-modals: core modal meanings**	**Am**	**80.00%**	**15.15%**	**64.85%**
F121	Double modals	Am	80.00%	22.73%	57.27%
F122	Epistemic *mustn't*	Am	50.00%	19.70%	30.30%
F126	New quasi-modals: aspectual meanings	Am, Car	69.57%	11.32%	58.24%
F127	**Non-standard use of modals for politeness reasons**	**As**	**87.50%**	**17.65%**	**69.85%**
F123	Present tense forms of modals used where StE has past tense forms	As	87.50%	33.82%	53.68%

Table 11.7 *Verb morphology: top diagnostic features for individual world regions (AR difference region – rest of world ≥ 30%; bold for ≥ 60%)*

Feature		Region	AR region	AR RoW	AR diff. region – RoW
F135	a-prefixing on elements other than *ing*-forms	Am	70.00%	12.12%	57.88%
F144	Use of *gotten* and *got* with distinct meanings (dynamic vs static)	Am	60.00%	13.24%	46.76%
F128	Levelling of past tense/past participle verb forms: regularization of irregular verb paradigms	Am	90.00%	57.58%	32.42%
F133	Double marking of past tense	As	75.00%	24.24%	50.76%
F143	Transitive verb suffix -*em*/-*im*/-*um*	Aus	60.00%	5.63%	54.37%
F129	Levelling of past tense/past participle verb forms: unmarked forms	Brls	90.91%	60.00%	30.91%
F141	**Other forms/phrases for copula *be*: before locatives**	**Car**	**84.62%**	**14.29%**	**70.33%**
F150	**Serial verbs: *come* = 'movement towards'**	**Car**	**76.92%**	**15.88%**	**61.04%**
F149	Serial verbs: *go* = 'movement away from'	Car	76.92%	17.46%	59.46%
F151	Serial verbs: constructions with three verbs	Car	76.92%	17.46%	59.46%
F148	Serial verbs: *give* = 'to, for'	Car	61.54%	11.11%	50.43%
F140	Other forms/phrases for copula *be*: before NPs	Car	69.23%	19.05%	50.18%

world as well. A much more forceful Asian areoversal is F100 (Present perfect for StE simple past), as in Sri Lankan English *We've been there last year* or Hong Kong English *I have learned to play piano but now I forget*. This feature even crosses the 60 per cent threshold in the rightmost column, which makes it truly diagnostic of the South and Southeast Asian varieties. In the same league we find the Caribbean areoversal F114 (*Go*-based future markers, rp-score 0.83), as in Barbadian Creole *I gun go town tomorrow* or Trinidadian Creole *We go do that next week*. Two more areally diagnostic features are those involving *done* in the coding of the completive/perfect category: while the simpler construction F104 (Completive/perfect *done*), as in Appalachian English *Uncle Mingus was done dead*, Gullah *Uh done eat dat one already*, or Jamaican Creole *Sharon don riid di buk* is diagnostic of both America and the Caribbean, the more complex feature F105 (Completive/perfect *have/be* + *done* + past participle), as in *He is done gone* or *Ah fin' dat somebody has done talk about me*, is diagnostic only for the American varieties. At the same time F105 is found very rarely outside America, a property that it shares with only one more tense and aspect feature, namely F95 (*Be sat/stood* with progressive meaning). This feature is highly distinctive of the British Isles. Consider examples like *I was sat at the bus stop for ages* (North) or *He was stood on the corner* (East Anglia). However, even in their home regions, these two features are encountered rather sporadically (rp-score F105, 0.39; F95, 0.25).

There are only seven features in WAVE relating to modal verbs, but six of them clearly display an areal clustering in one particular part of the English-speaking world, with America figuring prominently in this respect. Consider Table 11.6.

The emergence of new quasi-modals such as 'counterfactual' *like to/liketa* ('almost', 'nearly'), *supposeta/sposeta, useta* (F125) or the aspectual *finna/fixin to* ('prepare, get ready/be about to', F126) is highly characteristic of varieties in America and additionally, but only for aspectual meanings (F126), of the Caribbean. Here are some examples from Appalachian English (Montgomery 2008: 437): *The measles like to kill me, I like to never in the world got away, I'm fixin' to leave now.* Another prominent modal feature of America is F121 (Double modals), as in Chicano English *We might could do that*, which is a well-known feature especially of Texas and Appalachian English. The areally most diagnostic feature in Table 11.6 is F127 (Non-standard use of modals for politeness reasons), which, apart from Malaysian English, is found in all Asian varieties and can be exemplified as follows: *I would be visiting your place tomorrow* ('I will visit your place tomorrow', Indian English), *Shall I use your phone?* ('May I use your phone?', Sri Lankan English), or *Must I give you some water?* ('Should / may I give you some water?', Hong Kong English).

The third and last VP-related domain concerns verb morphology. A cursory glance at Table 11.7 suffices to show the dominance of the Caribbean, which is due to the very widespread use of serial verbs in this world region, on the one hand (F148–F151), and other forms or phrases that Caribbean varieties and creoles use for the copula *be* (F140, F141), on the other hand.

Here are some examples for serial verb constructions from the Caribbean: F148 (*give* = 'to, for') *They fry fowl egg, many cake give* ['for'] *him* (Bahamian Creole), F149 (*go* = 'movement away from') *go a St Mary go* ['to'] *look pon di children dem* (Jamaican Creole), F150 (*come* = 'movement towards') *Him say him was guwane come look for mi dis morning* (Jamaican English), and F151 (Serial verbs: constructions with three verbs) *Come here go see if Olga home* (Bahamian Creole). The most diagnostic verb morphology feature of the Caribbean is F141 (Other forms/phrases for copula *be*: before locatives), as in *me deh a mi yard a wait pon him* (Jamaican Creole), *I de here every night* (Bahamian English), or *Mi pikni de a skuul* (Vincentian Creole). But in fact it is not only before locatives (F141) that Caribbean varieties and creoles use alternative forms for copula *be*; this is also true for the position before NPs (F140), as in *Evride a krismuhs* (Vincentian Creole). The rarity of F135 (*a*-prefixing on elements other than *ing*-forms) outside America makes it highly distinctive of this region, in spite of its low rp-score in the respective

Table 11.8 *Negation: top diagnostic features for individual world regions (AR difference region – rest of world ≥ 30%; bold for ≥ 60%)*

Feature		Region	AR region	AR RoW	AR diff. region – RoW
F156	*Ain't* as negated form of *have*	Am	90.00%	34.85%	55.15%
F158	Invariant *don't* for all persons in the present tense	Am	100.00%	63.64%	36.36%
F157	*Ain't* as generic negator before a main verb	Am, Car	53.08%	7.69%	45.39%
F162	*No more/nomo* as negative existential marker	Aus	60.00%	7.05%	52.95%
F163	*Was/weren't* split	Brls	54.55%	12.31%	42.24%
F161	*Not* as a pre-verbal negator	Pac	50.00%	19.12%	30.88%
F155–F157	*Ain't* as negated form of *be; have;* before main verb	Am	83.33%	28.28%	55.05%

varieties (0.27). Appalachian English is likely unrivalled in its range of options, including *he comes a-nigh me, a pass a-toward him, go back down a-Sunday, I didn't do it a-purpose, ride a-horseback, he was a-just tearing that window open* (all from Montgomery 2008: 440–441). One other feature in Table 11.7 worth mentioning is F143 (Transitive verb suffix *-em/-im/-um*), as in *Mi baiim kaikai* (Torres Strait Creole), *faksim* 'to fax', *imelim* 'email (someone)', since it is extremely rare outside Australia.

In the domain of negation (see Table 11.8), America is prominently represented with a true 100 per cent, highly pervasive areoversal (F158: Invariant *don't* for all persons in the present tense, rp-score 0.88) and the *ain't* cluster F155–F157, *ain't* as negated form of *be* (as in earlier AAVE but *I aint 'bleevin in nothin but de good Lawd*), *have* (as in Gullah *You ain fuh go* 'you don't have to go'), and *do*, i.e. before main verbs (as in Gullah *You ain like um?*). The latter use of *ain't* is distinctive of both America and the Caribbean and, at the same time, very rare elsewhere in the Anglophone world. The latter is also true of the only negation feature distinctive of Australia, namely F162 (*No more/nomo* as negative existential marker), as in Aboriginal English *Nomo nating insai dea* 'There isn't anything in there'.

The tables for the following domains of grammar are so short that they hardly warrant special comment. For agreement (Table 11.9), the Caribbean (recall F140 and F141 in Table 11.7 above) is again noticeable for two features relating to copula *be* (F177 and F178). This time what is striking for this world region is that the vast majority of Caribbean varieties and creoles delete copula *be* altogether: before adjective phrases (F177), as in Jamaican Creole *wen tings slow di man lazy* 'When things are slow the man is lazy', and before locatives (F178), as in Jamaican English *Mary in the garden*. With an rp-score of 0.86, zero copula before adjective phrases can be considered an almost categorical feature of Caribbean Englishes. Examples illustrating the other two features are as follows:

Table 11.9 *Agreement: top diagnostic features for individual world regions (AR difference region – rest of world ≥ 30%; bold for ≥ 60%)*

Feature		Region	AR region	AR RoW	AR diff. region – RoW
F173	Variant forms of dummy subject *there* in existential uses, e.g. *they, it* or zero	Am	80.00%	43.94%	36.06%
F180	*Was/were* generalization	Brls	90.91%	46.15%	44.76%
F177	Deletion of copula *be*: before AdjPs	Car	92.31%	42.86%	49.45%
F178	Deletion of copula *be*: before locatives	Car	76.92%	37.77%	39.15%

Table 11.10 *Relativization: top diagnostic features for individual world regions (AR difference region – rest of world ≥ 30%; bold for ≥ 60%)*

Feature		Region	AR region	AR RoW	AR diff. region – RoW
F186	*Which* for 'who'	Am	80.00%	27.27%	52.73%
F193	Gapping/zero-relativization in subject position	Am	90.00%	56.06%	33.94%
F198	Deletion of stranded prepositions in relative clauses ('preposition chopping')	Am	60.00%	28.79%	31.21%

F173   *They were saying that they had a lot of problems at Garner because <u>it</u> was a lot of fights and stuff.* (Chicano English)

F180   *When you come home fae your honeymoon if you had one, you <u>was</u> 'kirkit'.* (Scottish English)

Interestingly, the only three WAVE features in the domain of relative clauses exhibiting areality, at all, cluster in the same world region, namely America (see Table 11.10). The strongest areal signal of all is found with F186 (*Which* for 'who'), as in *With* (last name), *which is my relatives also* (Newfoundland English). Examples of F193 and F198 are as follows:

F193   *There's some people come here to look at water* (Newfoundland English)

F198   *T's only ting weh covetin happier* ('It's [the] only thing that coveting is happier than.' Gullah)

The Caribbean dominates Table 11.11, which offers the areally most distinctive features in the domain of complementation. The following features qualify as diagnostic of the Caribbean: F206 (Existentials with forms of *have*), as in Bahamian Creole *(Turtle, is there much turtle now?) No, don't have turtle round*, and F201 (*For*-based complementizers), as in Barbadian Creole *It hard fo /fi get ova wha he do*.

Table 11.11 *Complementation: top diagnostic features for individual world regions (AR difference region – rest of world ≥ 30%; bold for ≥ 60%)*

Feature		Region	AR region	AR RoW	AR diff. region – RoW
F203	*For (to)* as infinitive marker	Am	90.00%	36.36%	53.64%
F207	Substitution of *that*-clause for infinitival subclause	As	50.00%	17.65%	32.35%
F206	**Existentials with forms of *have***	**Car**	**76.92%**	**12.69%**	**64.23%**
F201	***For*-based complementizers**	**Car**	**84.62%**	**23.81%**	**60.81%**
F210	Non-finite clause complements with bare root form rather than *-ing* form	Car	61.54%	26.98%	34.56%

Table 11.12 *Adverbial subordination: top diagnostic features for individual world regions (AR difference region – rest of world ≥ 30%)*

Feature		Region	AR region	AR RoW	AR diff. region – RoW
F214	Conjunction doubling: clause + conj. + conj. + clause	Af	70.59%	25.42%	45.17%
F211	Clause-final *but* = 'though'	Aus	60.00%	21.12%	38.88%
F213	No subordination; chaining construction linking two main verbs (motion and activity)	Car	69.23%	38.09%	31.14%

The attentive reader may have noticed that Africa has hardly figured in any of the tables so far, appearing only in Table 11.4 on NP structure, with F59 (Double determiners) and F71 (No number distinction in demonstratives). In the domain of adverbial subordination, however, Africa is the Anglophone world region where the feature with the highest degree of areality is found (see Table 11.12). This is F214 (Conjunction doubling: clause + conj. + conj. + clause), as in White Zimbabwean English: *I'm happy here <u>but still</u> I'm homesick*. Characteristic of Australia is F211 (Clause-final *but* = 'though'), as in Aboriginal English *Yeah ... a few smashes but* 'Yes [we had] a few fights though', while chaining constructions linking two main verbs (F213) are slightly (by 31.14 per cent) over-represented in the Caribbean. Consider, for example, *dis man tel dem gwain du dat* 'this man told them (he was) going to do that' (Jamaican Creole).

Africa figures again in the domain of adverbs and prepositions, or rather postpositions (F217), as for example in *He came to office yesterday before* (Ugandan English), *We can do it in morning time* (Nigerian English), or *He lives Gwanda way* (White Zimbabwean English).

The top diagnostic feature in Table 11.13, however, is F218 (Affirmative *anymore* 'nowadays'), as in *Anymore they have had a hard time protecting things like that* (Appalachian English: Montgomery 2008: 455). This is one of the

Table 11.13 *Adverbs and prepositions: top diagnostic features for individual world regions (AR difference region – rest of world ≥ 30%; bold for ≥ 60%)*

Feature		Region	AR region	AR RoW	AR diff. region – RoW
F217	Use of postpositions	Af	58.82%	28.81%	30.01%
F218	**Affirmative *anymore* 'nowadays'**	**Am**	**70.00%**	**3.03%**	**66.97%**

Table 11.14 *Discourse and word order: top diagnostic features for individual world regions (AR difference region – rest of world ≥ 30%; bold for ≥ 60%)*

Feature		Region	AR region	AR RoW	AR diff. region – RoW
F226	**'Negative inversion'**	**Am**	**90.00%**	**12.12%**	**77.88%**
F231	Superlative marker *most* occurring before head noun	Am	50.00%	18.18%	31.82%
F223	Other options for clefting than StE	Am, Car	65.22%	28.30%	36.92%
F232	Either order of objects in double object constructions (if both objects are pronominal)	BrIs	72.73%	13.85%	58.88%
F225	Sentence-initial focus marker	Car	76.92%	22.22%	54.70%
F228	No inversion/no auxiliaries in *wh*-questions	Car	100.00%	65.46%	34.54%
F233	Presence of subject in imperatives	Pac	75.00%	38.24%	36.76%

most strongly US-affiliated features in WAVE (i.e. excluding Newfoundland English; see also Hickey 2012a: 8). This is also the feature which gives away Gullah as a distinctively US American creole.

The last domain of grammar to be checked for areal features is that of discourse and word order (Table 11.14). From an areal perspective, this domain is dominated again by America and the Caribbean.

Clearly the strongest American feature of all in Table 11.14 is F226 ('Negative inversion'), as in the following examples: *Didn't nobody show up* (Colloquial American English), *Ain nobody ga worry wid you* 'Nobody will worry with you' (Gullah), *There's an old house up here, but don't nobody live in it, Hain't nobody never set* [the trap] *for any bears since* (Appalachian English; Montgomery 2008: 444). The strongest Caribbean feature is F225 (Sentence-initial focus marker), as in *Is now where you does find we corn coming* (Bahamian Creole), *Is she love me* (Trinidadian Creole), or *Da uman him de luk* (San Andrés Creole). While Caribbean areoversal F228 is also rather common in other regions, the rp-score for this feature is remarkable: 0.94 means it is an obligatory feature in almost all Caribbean varieties. The British Isles are represented by only one feature (F232: Either order

Table 11.15 *Overview: diagnostic areal features per grammatical domain (sorted by proportion of areal features per domain)*

Domain	Number of diagnostic areal features (total: 93)	Proportion	Total number of WAVE features per domain (total: 235)
Modal verbs	6	85.71%	7
Adverbial subordination	3	60.00%	5
Discourse organization and word order	7	53.85%	13
Verb morphology	12	46.15%	26
Complementation	5	45.45%	11
Tense and aspect	13	39.39%	33
Noun phrase	15	37.50%	40
Negation	6	37.50%	16
Pronouns	17	36.17%	47
Adverbs and prepositions	2	28.57%	7
Agreement	4	26.66%	15
Relativization	3	20.00%	15

in double object constructions for two pronominal objects), as in *Give it me/ Give me it* (north of England), *He couldna gae him it* (Orkney and Shetland English), or *She'd give us it* (southwest England), but this feature nearly reaches the 60 per cent threshold necessary for qualifying as a truly diagnostic feature in areal terms.

Before reviewing and perspectivizing the main observations in this section from an areal perspective (see Section 11.3), let us briefly look at the preceding tables from the point of view of areality per grammatical domain (Table 11.15).

Table 11.15 is ordered by the column 'Proportion' of WAVE features per grammatical domain which have been found to be distinctive or even truly diagnostic of one particular Anglophone world region. This ordering is meant to relativize the no doubt correct observation that the largest number of features exhibiting areal concentrations (some 60 per cent) fall into the domains of the usual suspects, namely, pronouns (17 features), NP structure (15 features), tense and aspect (13 features), and verb morphology (12 features). Judged against the total of WAVE features for each of the twelve grammatical domains, however, it emerges that domains represented by far fewer features may exhibit a much stronger areal clustering. This is particularly pronounced for modal verbs (recall Table 11.6 above).

11.3   Synopsis: Areality in Morphosyntax Across the Anglophone World

What are the major lessons to be learnt concerning areal clusterings in each of the seven world regions across the 76 varieties, pidgins and creoles investigated here? Table 11.16, which lists by world region the most

Table 11.16 *Overview: list of most distinctive areal features per world region (AR difference region – rest of world $\geq$ 30%; bold for $\geq$ 60%; * for rp-score $\geq$ 0.5, ** for $\geq$ 0.75)*

Region	Feature total	Attested in 100% of all varieties per world region	Attested in 0–5 varieties in RoW	All other areal features with AR difference region – RoW $\geq$ 30%
America	22	9*, 158**	**218** (2 varieties)	39*, 83, 90, 92, **105**, 121*, 122, **125***, 128*, 135, 144, 156**, 173*, 186, 193*, 198, 203, **226***, 231
Caribbean	28	**114****, **228****	17 (2 varieties)	10*, 18*, 19*, 20, 21*, **22***, **23***, 32, 46*, 51*, 66**, 77**, 140*, **141***, 148, 149*, **150***, 151, 177**, 178*, **201***, **206***, 210, 213, 225*
America + Caribbean	6		157 (4 varieties)	13, 70*, **104***, 126*, 223
Asia	18	43**, 62**, 63**, **100***, 113*	40 (3 varieties)	61, 64*, 81, 82, 86, 89, 109, 119, 123, **127***, 133, 207
British Isles	6		95 (4 varieties)	102, 129*, 163, 180*, 232
Africa	5			59, 71*, 116, 214, 217
Australia	4		76 (5 varieties) 143 (4 varieties) 162 (5 varieties)	211
Pacific	2			161, 233*
Australia + Pacific	2		36 (1 variety) **37 (0 varieties)**	
	93/235 (39.57%)			

distinctive areal features in the tables of the previous section, helps us to answer this question.

The strongest geographical signals we receive are for America, the Caribbean and (South and Southeast) Asia. About 80 per cent of the 93 morphosyntactic features listed in Table 11.16 fall into one of these three Anglophone world regions, with the Caribbean clearly taking the lead (34), followed by America (28) and, at some distance, Asia (18). The Caribbean also exhibits the highest rp-scores overall, 21 of 28 exclusively Caribbean features are rated pervasive or even highly pervasive. Among the top diagnostic features for the Caribbean and America, there are six which are diagnostic of the entire American and Caribbean area. It does not appear to be a coincidence that these three belong to those Anglophone world regions which are clearly dominated by one variety type, and thus qualify as (fairly) homogeneous world regions: America is dominated by L1 varieties (8 out of 10), Asia by L2 varieties (6 out of 8), and the Caribbean by creoles (11 out of 13). At the same time it is noticeable that for the only other homogeneous Anglophone world region, namely the British Isles (10 out of 11 varieties are L1 varieties), only six features exhibit a high degree of areality. Additionally, the distinctively British features are overwhelmingly rated optional or rare. This may be interpreted as a reflex of (a) the British Isles as the historical homeland of English and the origin of its spread across the world from the seventeenth century onwards, which left few distinct British Isles features, or (b) the varieties in the British Isles having developed few morphosyntactic properties in the last 100–150 years or so which have not developed elsewhere in the Anglophone world as well. For South and Southeast Asia it is remarkable that five of its 18 areally distinctive features are found in all eight varieties, i.e. 100 per cent. This is the highest percentage of true areoversals for any Anglophone world region. For Australia and the Pacific it is striking that five out of eight features – a high proportion – are virtually unknown elsewhere in the Anglophone world, and that the two most important instances, F36 (Distinct forms for inclusive/exclusive first person non-singular) and F37 (More number distinctions in personal pronouns than simply singular versus plural), are diagnostic for the entire Australian and Pacific region. Such features, found rarely or not at all in other parts of the Anglophone world, in turn, send out an extra-strong geographical signal, most likely to be explained by very strong substrate influence. A last point worth noting is that Africa, that world region represented by the largest number (17) of varieties, pidgins and creoles in WAVE, has only five areally distinctive features, none of which (see the fourth column in Table 11.16) would qualify as a *rarum* in the rest of the Anglophone world (found in at most 10 per cent in RoW), let alone *rarissimum* (found in at most 5 per cent in RoW).

Even though the aggregate approach to morphosyntactic variation on a global scale, as underlying the NeighborNet diagram in Figure 11.1, leads to the conclusion that areality can be attributed only secondary importance compared with the explanatory potential of variety type, the approach adopted in this chapter has shown that the factor 'areality', i.e. the geographical signal, can indeed be strengthened. The overall typological profile of a given variety of English may not be determined by geography, i.e. by the part of the world where it is spoken, but this does not prevent a large number of morphosyntactic features from exhibiting distinct areal biases. In fact, it is highly astonishing that 40 per cent of all 235 features in the WAVE dataset (93, i.e. the sum total of all features listed in Tables 11.3–11.15) exhibit a noticeable areality in the sense that they are over-represented by at least a 30 per cent margin in one of the Anglophone world regions compared with the rest of the world. For 16 of these 93 features (marked in bold in Table 11.16) the attestation rate (AR) difference between the relevant Anglophone world region and all others is higher than 60 per cent. For example, F201 (*For*-based complementizers) is attested in 84.62 per cent of all 13 WAVE varieties in the Caribbean whereas its

Table 11.17 *Diagnostic morphosyntactic features per Anglophone world region (AR difference region – rest of world ≥ 60%; * for rp-score ≥ 0.5, ** for ≥ 0.75)*

Feature		Region	Example from world region
F9*	Benefactive 'personal dative' construction	Am	*They found them an apartment* (ChcE)
F105	Completive/perfect *have/be* + *done* + past participle	Am	*He is done gone* (EAAVE)
F125*	New quasi-modals: core modal meanings	Am	*He belongs to come here today 'he ought to come...'* (AppE)
F218	Affirmative *anymore* 'nowadays'	Am	*Anymore they have a hard time protecting things like that* (AppE)
F226*	'Negative inversion'	Am	*Ain nobody ga worry wid you* (Gullah)
F104*	Completive/perfect *done*	Am, Car	*He done gone* (Bajan)
F22*	*You* as (modifying) possessive pronoun	Car	*Tuck in you shirt* (TrinC)
F23*	Second person pronoun forms other than *you* as (modifying) possessive pronoun	Car	*Tek out unu buk!* (SanAC)
F114**	*Go*-based future markers	Car	*Mi go pik dem uhp* (VinC)
F141*	Other forms/phrases for copula *be*: before locatives	Car	*Mi de na mi mama oso.* (Sranan)
F150*	Serial verbs: *come* = 'movement towards'	Car	*Run come quick* (TrinC)
F201*	*For*-based complementizers	Car	*I haad fi kraas di riba* (JamC)
F206*	Existentials with forms of *have*	Car	*You have people that own big piece a land* (BelC)
F100	Levelling of the difference between present perfect and simple past: present perfect for StE simple past	As	*Ben has return back the product yesterday.* (MalE)
F127*	Non-standard use of modals for politeness reasons	As	*Must I give you some water?* (HKE)
F37*	More number distinctions in personal pronouns than simply singular vs plural	Aus, Pac	*We two is going ...* (PalmE)

attestation rate in all other 63 varieties, pidgins and creoles in the WAVE dataset is 23.81 per cent. These are the 16 features listed in Table 11.17.

Figure 11.2 illustrates the different layers of areal distinctiveness. The strength of the geographical signal increases towards the centre. Circles I and II represent the 16 core areal features that surpass a 60 per cent difference in attestation rate (see Table 11.17); the five features in circle I are additionally either areoversals or exceedingly rare in the rest of the world (see Table 11.16, columns 3 and 4). Areoversals and *rara* with an AR difference of 30–60 per cent are found in circle III. In the two more peripheral layers, areally distinctive features (Table 11.16, column 5) are distinguished according to their regional pervasiveness (circle IV, rp-score ≥ 0.5; circle V, rp-score < 0.5).

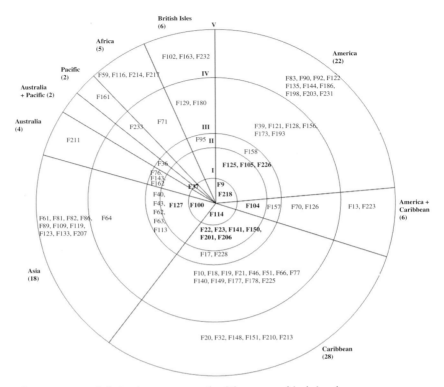

Figure 11.2 Areal distinctiveness: strength of the geographical signal

Taken together, this clearly shows that North America, i.e. in WAVE the US varieties joined by Newfoundland English, the Caribbean and Asia, are the Anglophone regions exhibiting the highest degree of areality (i.e. the largest number of features with a strong 'local' signal). Of these regions, the Caribbean is most distinctively marked by both diagnostic and highly pervasive features, whereas the majority of American and Asian features are found in the peripheral layer.

11.4 Smaller-scale Areal Patterns within Selected World Regions

Could the geographical signal for morphosyntactic variation be strengthened even more on the basis of the WAVE data? Yes it could, but only to a limited extent. Reasons of space prevent us from presenting the results of our relevant studies in detail here, but the following can be said. Zooming in from the set of Anglophone world regions on subregions within each of them, one can try to determine, for example, whether it is possible to find (bundles of) morphosyntactic features separating, for example, the north from the south in the British Isles, South Asia from Southeast Asia, or West

Africa from East and South(ern) Africa. It is indeed possible to do that. For the British Isles (see, for example, Kortmann 2012: 697–698) it turns out, for instance, that there are more distinctively northern features (the north being constituted by Orkney and Shetland English, the dialects of the north of England, Scottish English, Irish English and Manx English) than there are distinctively southern features (the south comprising the dialects of the southwest and southeast of England, East Anglia, Channel Island English and Welsh English). The only two features which are found exclusively in the north and not at all in the south are F69 (*Yon/yonder* indicating remoteness, attested in all five northern varieties), as in *yon oil company* (Orkney and Shetland English) or *it's allus light in yandhar place* (Manx English), and F124 (*Want/need* + past participle), as in *That shirt wants washed* (northern England dialects), *It needs cleaned out* (Northern Irish English), or *Does your floor need hoovered?* (Scottish English). F124 is only attested in exactly these three of the five varieties of the north, however. There are no such exclusively southern British Isles features. Zooming in even further into the south of England, though, one receives a pronounced geographical signal for British Creole, which, sociohistorically and typologically, is the obvious outlier in the British Isles since it is the only creole in an otherwise exclusively L1 world region. It can be taken as a crucial piece of evidence of areal impact on a given variety (or pidgin, creole, language for that matter) where the feature pool of this variety includes one or more morphosyntactic features characteristic of its (part of a) world region, but not documented at all for the typologically most closely related varieties/pidgins/ creoles in other parts of the world. For British Creole the most important test is, of course, Jamaican Creole, from which it derives historically. It turns out that British Creole has F155 (*Ain't* for negated *be*) and F 156 (*Ain't* for negated *have*), both of which are typical of East Anglia and the dialects of the Southeast of England, but neither of which is attested in Jamaican Creole (or in Jamaican English). A similar 'areal case' for certain morphosyntactic properties as for British Creole can, for example, be made for the West African pidgins, i.e. for Cameroon Pidgin, Ghanaian Pidgin, Nigerian Pidgin and Vernacular Liberian English. Thus F59 (Double determiners) and F116 (*Come*-based FUT/INGRESS markers) are documented in all four West African pidgins as well as in Krio (the only West African creole), but virtually unattested in pidgins and creoles elsewhere in the world. Moreover, it is important to note that exactly these two features are (with only one exception for each feature) also found in the West African L1 and L2 Englishes, only rarely in the East African L2s and not at all in the South African varieties.

F 59   double determiners (elsewhere: only in Saramaccan)
    Dí   *Yò*   *tú*   *bóy*   *pìkín dèm*   *chóp.* (NigP)
    This   2SG   POSS two   boy   child 3PL   eat
    These your two boys ate.

F 116   *come*-based FUT/INGRESS markers (elsewhere: only in Bislama and
         Butler English)

Ìm	kóm	yélo	wélwél. (NigP)
3sg.SJ	become	be.pale	thoroughly

He/she/it became very pale.

What the areal clusters for individual Anglophone world regions – especially
for the dominantly or exclusively non-L1 world regions, as well as the areal
sub-clusters briefly addressed above – are taken to indicate is the importance of language contact and thus substrate influence. The substrate
argument can, and has been, forcefully made for a range of properties of
West African pidgins, for example by Faraclas (2012) for Nigerian Pidgin,
which he sees as clearly influenced by the structural properties of the
languages of Southern Nigeria. The argument can also be made for deletion features in the varieties of English spoken in Asia (recall our discussion concerning Tables 11.3 and 11.4 on pronoun and article deletion), and
for features like F36 (Distinct forms for inclusive/exclusive first person
non-singular), F37 (More number distinctions in personal pronouns than
simply singular versus plural) and F143 (Transitive verb suffix *-em/-im/-um*),
all of which are almost uniquely found in Australia and the Pacific region,
thus constituting a powerful reflex of the structural properties of the local
languages.

11.5 Conclusion

We are convinced that future studies are bound to reveal more, and possibly
more powerful, cases of substrate impact on the morphosyntax of varieties
of English and English-based pidgins and creoles, thus at the same time
identifying more – and possibly stronger – geographical, even downright
local, signals in the observable variation worldwide. In order for this to
happen, though, different data from those compiled in WAVE are necessary;
for a full account of this line of argument see Kortmann (2013: 185–190).
WAVE offers a typologically informed survey at a macro-level. It cannot
zoom in on the entire range of specific (free or bound) markers used for
the coding of individual grammatical categories, for example, or the entire
range of specific constructions such as certain verb- or adjective-specific
complementation patterns found in the extremely complex lexis–syntax
interface. Least of all does WAVE take into consideration local usage (including pragmatic and stylistic) preferences and constraints, which are known to
play an important role, however, in the formation and stabilization of
Postcolonial Englishes (see Schneider 2007: 87). For the exploration of
morphosyntactic variation at such a micro-level, other research tools and
datasets need to be exploited (or to be compiled in the first place).
The available corpora of many varieties of English are certainly a good

starting point. However, the WAVE-based areal features identified in this chapter (see Tables 11.16 and especially 11.17) are a powerful indicator of the path the Englishes in the different Anglophone world regions are going to take in the development of distinctly pan-continental (or world-regional) Englishes – for example in the development of distinctly Asian, African or Pacific forms of English.

References

Anderwald, Lieselotte, 2012. Negation in varieties of English. In Hickey (ed.), pp. 299–328.

Brato, Thorsten and Magnus Huber, 2012. Areal features of English in Africa. In Hickey (ed.), pp. 161–185.

Eberle, Nicole and Daniel Schreier, 2013. African Bermudian English and the Caribbean connection. *English World-Wide* 34: 279–304.

Faraclas, Nicholas, 2012. Nigerian Pidgin. In Kortmann and Lunkenheimer (eds), pp. 407–432.

Hackert, Stephanie, 2012. The Caribbean. In Kortmann and Lunkenheimer (eds), pp. 704–732.

Hickey, Raymond, 2012a. Introduction: Areal features of the anglophone world. In Hickey (ed.), pp. 1–19.

Hickey, Raymond (ed.), 2012b. *Areal Features of the Anglophone World*. Berlin and New York: de Gruyter Mouton.

Huber, Magnus, 2012. Africa. In Kortmann and Lunkenheimer (eds), pp. 806–823.

Kortmann, Bernd, 2012. The British Isles. In Kortmann and Lunkenheimer (eds), pp. 679–702.

Kortmann, Bernd, 2013. How powerful is geography as an explanatory factor of variation? Areal features in the Anglophone world. In Peter Auer, Martin Hilpert, Anja Stukenbrock and Benedikt Szmrecsanyi (eds), *Space in Language and Linguistics: Geographical, Interactional, and Cognitive Perspectives*, pp. 165–194. Berlin and New York: Walter de Gruyter.

Kortmann, Bernd and Kerstin Lunkenheimer (eds), 2012a. *The Mouton World Atlas of Variation in English*. Berlin and Boston: de Gruyter Mouton.

Kortmann, Bernd and Kerstin Lunkenheimer, 2012b. Introduction. In Kortmann and Lunkenheimer (eds), pp. 1–11.

Kortmann, Bernd and Christoph Wolk, 2012. Morphosyntactic variation in the anglophone world: A global perspective. In Kortmann and Lunkenheimer (eds), pp. 906–936.

Lunkenheimer, Kerstin, 2012. Tense and aspect. In Hickey (ed.), pp. 329–353.

Mesthrie, Rajend, 2012. Asia. In Kortmann and Lunkenheimer (eds), pp. 784–805.

Mesthrie, Rajend and Rakesh M. Bhatt, 2008. *World Englishes: The Study of New Linguistic Varieties*. Cambridge: Cambridge University Press.

Montgomery, Michael B., 2008. Appalachian English: Morphology and syntax. In Edgar Schneider (ed.), *Handbook of Varieties of English*, vol. 2: *The Americas and the Caribbean*, pp. 428–467. Berlin and Boston: de Gruyter Mouton.

Schneider, Edgar, 2007. *Postcolonial English: Varieties around the World*. Cambridge: Cambridge University Press.

Schneider, Edgar W., 2012. North America. In Kortmann and Lunkenheimer (eds), pp. 734–762.

Siegel, Jeff, 2012. Australia Pacific region. In Kortmann and Lunkenheimer (eds), pp. 764–782.

Szmrecsanyi, Benedikt, 2013. *Grammatical Variation in British English Dialects: A Study in Corpus-Based Dialectometry*. Cambridge: Cambridge University Press.

Wagner, Susanne, 2012. Pronominal systems. In Hickey (ed.), pp. 379–408.

Wolk, Christoph, 2013. *Integrating Aggregational and Probabilistic Approaches to Dialectology and Language Variation*. PhD thesis, University of Freiburg, Germany.

12

Slavic Languages

Alan Timberlake

A concrete question: how and when, and in what context, did those languages contiguous with Eurasian territory acquire or develop or preserve an opposition in consonants of soft [palatalized] vs hard [unpalatalized]?

Roman Jakobson (1931: 185)

12.1 Introduction

The precipitous expansion and subsequent history of the Slavs brought them into linguistic encounters with other peoples and languages, including some that might qualify as linguistic areas, in the sense of areas of intense convergence among typologically diverse languages. The discussion below examines encounters of Slavs with others to determine not only what the results of convergence are but also 'in what context' convergence occurred: the modes of convergence and the communicative situations in which people and their languages interacted.[1]

12.2 The Southeastern Frontier

In an area we might call the Ukrainian Mesopotamia – from the Dnestr River over to the Dnepr, and from the southern edge of the basin of the Pripjat River down to the littoral of the Black Sea – culture complexes of pottery shaped like a tulip bulb, subterranean dwellings, and burial by cremation were continuous from 1500 BCE to the beginning of the common era. Because the same traits show up later among people we know to

---

[1] The approach here resonates with Bickel and Nichols (2006), who would define language areas 'based on a theory of population and language spread'.

be Slavs (in Bohemia, Danube basin, Greece), we can identify the people with this culture as Slavs.

From 500 BCE on, various peoples intruded on this Slavic homeland: Iranians (Scythians c. 500 BCE, then Sarmatians c. 200 BCE), Greeks on the Black Sea, Romans on the Lower Danube. Goths arrived in 166 CE but were chased out by the nomadic, westward-bound Huns in 376. During the Gothic interlude Slavs apparently moved to the periphery of their homeland, establishing settlements in the west on the upper Dnestr, in the centre in the Pripjat basin (previously inhabited by Balts), and in the east on the far side of the Dnepr (Barford 2001: maps II, III). It was from these newer outposts on the periphery of the ancient homeland that Slavs then moved to other areas (Gimbutas 1971: 80).

During the period from 500 BCE to 500 CE, Slavs had contact with others and borrowed lexicon: from Goths, the lexicon of technology and household (*xlěbъ [2] < Gothic *hlaifs* 'loaf', *kotьlъ < Germanic *katil(u)s* 'kettle', *dъlgъ < Gothic *dulgs* 'debt' [Gimbutas 1971: 77]) and from Iranians, possibly the lexicon of religion (*bogъ 'bestower of bounty, god' and *bogatъ 'blessed by beneficence, rich', akin to Avestan *baɣa* 'lord', Sanskrit *bhagas* 'donor'). Aside from lexical borrowings there is no evidence of areal convergence between Slavs and either Goths or Iranians.

12.3 Western Frontier

From the periphery of their homeland in the Ukrainian Mesopotamia, Slavs moved in at least three streams: south and west along the Danube and over to the Adriatic, around the Carpathians into Bohemia, and up the Dnepr north to the Baltic region.

Along the western frontier Slavs came into contact with other peoples with developed political structures, commerce and confession. In the south of the western frontier, Slavs came into unsurprising contact with Romans and their descendants who colonized the Adriatic coast. In the middle section of the western frontier, in Slovenia, Moravia, Bohemia and Sorbia, Slavs were subject to pressure to convert from new sees in Regensburg, Salzburg and Freising. Confessional conversion went hand-in-hand with the declaration of political fealty – as in the 890s when Bohemians adopted Roman Christianity and made an alliance with Bavaria. Such dual conversion brought in its wake colonization by western peoples and led to language contact and, not infrequently, to a shift in language from Slavic to German.

Possible contact effects of the first 500 years of contact between Czech and German have been reviewed by Berger (2014). Czech lost palatalization

---

[2] It is usual to cite Slavic etyma in the form they had in Late Common Slavic (c. 800 CE), using some idiosyncratic symbols: Roman ⟨y ě⟩ [i æ], ⟨c š ž č⟩ [ʦ ʃ ʒ ʧ] and the Cyrillic 'jer' letters ⟨ъ⟩ [ʊ], ⟨ь⟩ [ɪ].

as a binary phonological opposition. Czech diphthongized non-front high long vowels, as in *mu:čny:* [mou̯čnei̯] 'of flour', *dlu:hy:* [dlou̯hei̯] 'long'. Such diphthongizations, atypical of Slavic, are reminiscent of German.

Middle High German *durfen* and *müezen* were borrowed into Czech directly (as *drbiti* and *musiti*), enriching the class of modal verbs. Native *míti* 'have' extended its range of usage as a modal and as the means of expressing predicative possession. Originally Czech expressed predicate possession using the dative (Vulgate *et huic erat soror* > Dresden Bible (1360) *A tej bieše sestra* 'and to her there was a sister' [Lk 10: 39]) but under German influence switched to *míti* 'have' (Greek καί τῇδε ἦν ἀδελφὴ > Kralice Bible (1579–1596) *A ta měla sestru* 'and she had a sister' [Lk 10: 39]) (McAnallen 2011: 27–32).

In syntax, Czech reduced certain uses of cases, probably under German influence: the instrumental case for predicative nouns and adjectives and adverbial genitives with verbs like *pozorovati* 'observe', *ždáti* 'await', *přáti* 'wish for', *brániti* 'defend'. In Russian, the preposition *v* 'into' with an illative sense of entrance into a domain is vastly more frequent than the allative preposition *do* 'up to, into the vicinity of' (84 per cent *v* versus 16 per cent *do*). The preference is reversed in Czech (85 per cent *do* versus 15 per cent *v*), under influence of German *nach*. The Czech construction in (1) – in which the patient of an infinitive is the subject and agrees with the copula and adjective – is likely calqued from German constructions like (2):

(1) *Práce*$_{fem.sg}$ *jest* *krásna*$_{fem.sg}$ *hlédati*
     work   is   beautiful   to.observe
     'the work$_{fem.sg}$ is beautiful$_{fem.sg}$ to observe'

(2) *Emotionsgeladene Erinnerungen sind schwer zu vergessen.*
     'Emotional memories are difficult to forget.'

12.4 Northern Frontier

From the Elbe to the Oder the Slavic population was trapped between Germans on the west and Poles on the east. The Liutici, a confederation of Slavic tribes, attempted to fend off the outsiders (983 to the middle of the 1100s), but were ultimately subdued (Brüske 1955), leaving the Slavic population exposed to settlement from the west and language shift to German. The last Slavic speaker on the Slavic island of Rugen, Frau Gulitzin, died in 1404.[3] The shift from Slavic to German is substantiated by names like *Ivan von Belaw* – both first and last names of Slavic origin (1411, Witte 1906: 158) – and lexemes recorded in the Stralsund glossary (1460s): *iuche* 'soup', *stupe* 'pillory', *bruche* 'belly', *seze* 'trawl' (Damme 1987). Such lexical relics imply that during language shift there was a period of

---

[3] According to the ducal chronicler Thomas Kantzow writing in the 1530s (1816: 436–437).

bilingualism when speakers of the indigenous language, and then speakers of the intrusive language, used and preserved lexicon (and syntactic constructions) of the receding language.

The teleological process of colonization in Mecklenburg-Vorpommern was continued to the east by two institutions. The Hanseatic league of cities developed out of the practice of trade and marauding of the Vikings in the Baltic region (first centred in Visby on Gotland off the coast of Sweden and later in Lübeck). The Teutonic Knights, formed from the residue of the failed Third Crusade of 1190–1191, engaged in the sacred task of converting the heathens (Slavs, Balts, Finnic peoples), from the Oder across Pomerania through West and East Prussia all the way to Livonia. The commercial and confessional intrusion was supplemented by populating the newly converted lands with settlers.

The language of the Hanse is usually said to have been the Low German of Lübeck, but more important than the specific origin is the fact that Low German functioned as a lingua franca for the Baltic region.[4] This lingua franca was receptive to the influence of other languages, Scandinavian (especially Danish) and Livonian; it accepted borrowings in lexical fields such as goods (fur, clothing), currency, transport and shipbuilding, administration (Otsmaa 1975: 107) – that is, the terminology of trade, which after all was the primary communicative function of this lingua franca. Writing (correspondence or records) was originally in Latin. Latin was superseded by Low German by 1400, which in turn yielded to High German by 1600. All the way from the Elbe to East Prussia, the indigenous rural population on the littoral largely adopted Low German. When a Slavic pocket did survive, the grammar converged with German; Slovincian developed new perfects using auxiliaries 'have' and 'be' (Lorentz 1903: 11). In contrast to Pomerania and Prussia, indigenous languages survived in Lithuania, Latvia and Estonia.

In the Livonian cities of Riga and Reval, locals provided services for the German elite and staffed their households; to do so, they learned Low German to some extent (Johansen and von zur Mühlen 1973: 372). After 1494 (when Ivan III closed the Hanse outpost in Novgorod) Russian trade had to go overland through Riga and Reval, making these cities intermediaries in the lucrative trade between the Hanse and Russia. Inhabitants included Danes, Swedes and Finns. The cities were multilingual; there was an 'accommodationist'[5] disposition to multilingualism – an acceptance, even an embrace, of linguistic pluralism.

The vernaculars of Riga and Reval were influenced by the Hanse lingua franca. Latvian lost final syllables and introduced a 'broken' tone with a glottal catch, features reminiscent of Danish. Estonian experienced Low German influences such as: verbal prefixes (*ära-* 'through', *ümber-* 'around',

---

[4] See Dahl (2001) on the role of Danish as an early Baltic lingua franca.
[5] Substituting a different term for what Hill (2001) calls 'distributive'.

üle- 'over') – atypical of Finnic languages; the demonstrative *see* used as an article and borrowing of the conjunction *und* – two core grammatical functions considered resistant to borrowing; and borrowing of *doch* 'indeed', *trotz* 'notwithstanding' – dialogic discourse operators which tell the interlocutor how to evaluate information (Johansen and von zur Mühlen 1973: 370–371). These features presuppose a complex linguistic dynamic: speakers of the recipient language imitate Low German as they attempt to speak it, but more than that, they internalize patterns from the donor language and extend those patterns to innovations in their own language. Livonia continued to be an area of multilingualism, when, later in history, it was subjected to the Russian imperial language and circum-Baltic areal developments.

The easternmost outpost of the Hanse was Novgorod. The relation between the Hanse merchants and Novgorod was unique in the Hanse. Merchants did not colonize the foreign city. Because Hanse and Russian merchants did not learn each other's language, the conduct of trade required translators, trained in Novgorod or later in Reval.

In contrast to Livonian languages, Novgorodian Russian was subjected to only modest influence from Low German. Lexical borrowings are not extensive (Koškins 1996: 87). Some calquing did occur. A bilingual agreement from 1392 guarantees access to Novgorod with its flat landscape *goroju i vodoju* 'by hill and by water' (pp. 94–95). The phrase evidently calques Low German *to lande und to water* (itself based on Latin *per aquam aut per terram*). Novgorod commerce used two phrases for complex arithmetic calculations. One is diminution of a round number, for which Low German used *min* (*minn, myn*), glossed by Lübben (1888: s.v. *min*) as 'weniger, geringer, minder'; from correspondence, note *128 mark myn 1 fr* ('128 marks less one franc'). Novgorod has (3):

(3) *o: nъžъka*   *dova dъsjatь*   *bъrkovъsko*   *bъz ъrkovъska*
     from N   twenty   bushels   less bushel
     'from N [I took] twenty [10-lb.] bushels less one' (Zaliznjak 2004: B13)

Another calque may be the expression of intermediate quantity, as in *polc trъtija dъsjatino* 'half of the third decade' = '25' (Zaliznjak 2004: §4.11), parallel to Low German *achtehalf dusent rynsche Guldene* 'eight half thousand [= 7500] Rhine guilders'.

The history of the Baltic region shows the power of a supra-regional lingua franca – initially developed for trade but invigorated by confessional conversion and outright colonization – to spread norms of language. In the west and centre the indigenous languages were simply replaced by Low German. In Livonia the norms of the lingua franca were internalized by the local languages, Latvian and Estonian, and, more broadly, the lingua franca fostered a linguistic disposition of multilingualism and convergence that persisted. In Novgorod there was minimal convergence with the lingua franca or areal trends.[6] The importance of linguae francae will reappear in the Balkan linguistic area below (Sections 12.8–12.9).

12.5   Eastern Baltic Region, I

The eastern Baltic region, broadly understood, has been and continues to be an area rich in language encounters. The encounters are of different ages and of different kinds.

The oldest layer is a pair of uses of case shared by Baltic, Slavic and Finnic. These languages use a case other than accusative – genitive in Baltic and Slavic, partitive (distinct from accusative or genitive) in Finnic – for objects of predicates expressing restricted effect, including a portion of a mass (traditional partitive meaning), static relations with no agency (emotions, perceptions), partial but incomplete activity, and negated predicates (both transitive verbs and existential verbs). In Slavic the genitive of negation with intransitive existential verbs is well preserved, while the object genitive of negation is not equally attested in Slavic languages. It has declined in Czech, somewhat in East Slavic, not at all in Polish, and it is gone from southwestern Slavic (Willis 2013).

In Indo-European the use of the genitive for objects of negated verbs is unique to Baltic and Slavic (and Gothic). In Finnic languages (including Finnish) the partitive is used widely, even more than the genitive in Baltic and Slavic; thus the partitive can be used with a single definite patient when the event is incomplete. Also, it is not usual for linguistic features originating in Baltic or Slavic to penetrate Finnish. This suggests that the genitive (/partitive) of negation was indigenous to Finnic and was borrowed by Baltic and Slavic. When is unclear.

The second instance is the use of cases other than nominative – essive and translative – for predicatives. In Finnish, with the copula and a predicative noun ('s/he is/was a teacher'), the nominative is used overwhelmingly in the present tense (93 per cent) and predominantly in the past (66 per cent).[7] In its local sense, the essive case in {-na} expresses location within a container; with a predicative noun, the essive indicates a relationship contained within a time interval, as for example Artturi Laitinen's teaching post (4):

(4)   *hän oli   opettajana*ₑₛₛ *Utajärven kirkonkylän kansakoulussa 1914–43*
he was teacher   Utajärvi parish   school   1914–43
'he was a teacherₑₛₛ in the Utajärvi parish school from 1914 to 1943'

---

[6] The oldest Russkaja Pravda might have arisen to adjudicate conflicts between Novgorodians and Jaroslav's unruly Varengian (Scandinavian) entourage around 1015. (If so, it would date to the pre-Hanse period.) Because the code is formulated from the perspective of Novgorodians, it is generally assumed that the Russkaja Pravda (law code) is the codification of an autochthonous oral tradition. Yet it shows similarity to Western law codes, specifically that of Saxony (Feldbrugge 2009: 53–54, with references).

[7] Google searches conducted 24 September 2014.

The translative (in {-ksi}) marks a temporal boundary: *maanantaiksi*_{trnsl} 'by Monday'. With a predicative, it indicates a state with an (initial) boundary – 'the state into which anyone or anything passes' (Eliot 1890: 157); it is used with verbs that signify transformation, as in *Hän tuli*_{pst} *opettajaksi*_{trnsl} 'S/he became a teacher' (439 of 2571, or 17 per cent).

In Lithuanian, the instrumental indicates transformation. In Russian it indicates temporal or modal limitation on the state. The case has been productive in Polish. It is not well developed in South Slavic, suggesting only partial development in Slavic. In fact, the instrumental was rare in early East Slavic texts (twelfth century Kievan Chronicle) even with verbs of transformation. Thus the development of non-nominative case is restricted in Baltic and partial and late in Slavic, while in Finnic non-nominative predicative cases developed organically and autochthonously from local senses of the cases.

These cases uses – genitive (/partitive) of negation and non-nominative predicative – might seem to be areal, but Czech, which lies outside the Baltic area, has both; they must be due to contact convergence with Finnic. When is unclear. One might think of an encounter deep in prehistory (Thomason and Kaufman 1988: 238–251), except that both cases are inconsistent and recent in Slavic. Another hypothesis (Andersen 1996, followed below) is suggested by a phonological feature shared by Baltic and Slavic. A number of Slavic etyma begin with the reflex of a short non-high vowel (*j*)*e* or *o*. Examples are: 'lake', Russian *ozero*, Czech *jezero*; 'deer', Russian *olen′*, Czech *jelen*; 'alder', Russian *ol′xa*, Czech *olše*, Polish *olcha*, Slovincian *jelša*, Slovenian *jelša* (dial. *olša*), Serbo-Croatian *joxa*, Bulgarian *elxa*. The *e* is original (and *j* is a prothetic glide); there must have been a change of **#ĕ > *#ă > #o*. To judge by these examples, the change was frequent in East Slavic, less so in central Slavic (Czech, Slovenian), and infrequent on the peripheries (southeast Bulgarian, northwest Slovincian-Kashubian). The challenge is to account for the variation.

Internal accounts (Ablaut variants or some version of **je > jo*) do not work. It turns out that there is an analogous change of **#ĕ > *#ă* in Baltic, and this change also shows variation: 'ice-hole', Lithuanian *eketė* || *aketė*; 'bass', Lithuanian *ežegys* || *ažegys*; 'lake', Lithuanian *ažeras* || *ežeras*, Latvian *ezars*, Old Prussian *Assaran*. Slavic borrowed this change and variation from Baltic.

When and how? Modern Slavic has preserved etymologically Baltic hydronyms from the southern edge of the Pripjat basin (51°N) up to the western Dvina (Daugava) River (55°N). The fact that such Baltic hydronyms emerge in Slavic implies a specific historical scenario. Balts once inhabited that area; Slavs moved in and absorbed the Baltic population. During a transitional phase of asymmetric bilingualism (as is characteristic of a substratum), hydronyms and other features were absorbed by Slavic. The geographical gradation in reflexes of **#ĕ > *#ă > #o* – most in East Slavic, fewer in Czech, least on the peripheries – suggests the need for a more articulated model of migration than simply an all-or-nothing event: instead, scouts explore and set up outposts; subsequent migrants strengthen outposts and fill in gaps; return to the origin is possible (Anthony 1990). In such a model, the innovation *#ē > *#ā > #o could take place in the centre at the beginning of migration and then reach the mid-zones in weakened form and appear minimally on the peripheries. This model could also be used to explain the gradation in case usage if we posit two layers of substrata: case uses (genitive of negation, predicatives) were adopted by Baltic in Belarus from a prior Finnic substratum; then Slavs took these case uses from Balts, not directly from Fenns.[8] The geographical gradations are due to substratum plus migration, not areal spread.

12.6   Eastern Baltic Region, II

A slightly younger development which spread throughout the eastern Baltic area (Lithuanian, Latvian, Estonian, Finnish, North Russian dialects) is the construction called the nominative patient (or object) with infinitive. We illustrate with North Russian.[9] Patients of personal verbs – finite personal verbs (5) and infinitives dependent on finite personal verbs (6) – are accusative:

(5)   Ikonu$_{acc}$ pogrebli bjaxu   sъ   mertvecemь
      icon   had.buried   with   deceased
      'an icon$_{acc}$ they had buried with the deceased.' (VoprKir 37)

(6)   I   povelĕlъ   dati   opitemьju$_{acc}$
      And   he.ordered   do   penance
      'And he ordered [him] to do penance$_{acc}$' (VoprKir 59)

In contrast to the banal use of the accusative with personal verbs, patients of 'impersonal infinitives' – independent infinitives with modal force not dependent on any matrix predicate (7) and infinitives dependent on impersonal matrix verbs (8) – are nominative:

(7)   Kako   dъržati   imъ   opitemьja$_{nom}$?
      How   observe   them   penance
      'how it is [necessary] for them to observe penance$_{nom}$?' (VoprKir 59)

---

[8] Gimbutas (1971: 93, 97) insists that there is no archaeological record of Slavs in northern Belarus (Dvina basin) before the ninth century, which would be too late for these innovations to have spread. The transfer must have occurred earlier and then in the south, in Polesia and the Pripjat basin. For the distribution of Baltic hydronyms, see Toporov and Trubačev (1962: maps 16, 18).

[9] Examples cited from the oldest manuscript. In fact, the use of the nominative patient is predominant but not exclusive; it is used on 14 of 19 occasions. It is unclear whether this mixed usage represents originally optional usage or reversion to accusative in copying. Later manuscripts are known to preserve more archaic morphology (Gippius 1996), which use the nominative consistently.

(8)   *Dostoitъ*   *li*   *popu*   *svojei*   *ženě*   *molitva*$_{nom}$ *tvoriti*   *vsjakaja?*
      fitting   Q   priest   own   wife   prayer   make   any
      'is it fitting for a priest to say any sort of prayer$_{nom}$ for his own wife?' (VoprKir 29)

Impersonal infinitive constructions often include a dative, which is both the goal of modal force and the tacit agent of the infinitival action – *popu* 'priest' in (8). In the same context, animate nouns (which substitute genitive for accusative) take the accusative, as in (9):

(9)   *Ne*   *luče*   *Boga*$_{anm.acc}$ *moliti*
      not   better   God   beseech
      'Is it not better to beseech God$_{anm.acc}$' (VoprKir 53)

Lithuanian dialects use nominative for patients of impersonal infinitives, accusative for other patients. Latvian has a reflex of the nominative patient construction in its debitive:

(10)   *man*   {*Baumanis*$_{nom}$ / *viņš*$_{nom}$ / *tevi*$_{acc}$ }   *jā*$_{dbtv}$-*dzird!*
       to.me   {Baumanis / he / you }   listen-to
       'it is necessary for me to listen to$_{dbtv}$ {Baumanis$_{nom}$ / him$_{nom}$ / you$_{acc}$ }!'

The debitive, derived from an independent infinitive (Endzelin 1901), is an impersonal verb whose patient is nominative unless it is a first or second person pronoun (10).

The nominative patient with infinitive (or debitive) is unusual from the perspective of Indo-European languages, so much so that some investigators are inclined to derive it from a more palatable construction like that of Czech (1) above. But unlike the Czech construction, in which the patient really is the matrix subject and triggers agreement in the predicative adjective ('the work is beautiful to look at'), the nominative patient is not the subject but an object, as various syntactic properties show:[10] (a) a matrix predicate (adjective, copula) does not agree with the noun; (b) the patient is genitive under negation, whereas the subject of copular sentences like Czech (1) could never be genitive; (c) some patients with infinitives – pronouns or animates – are accusative and not subjects; by parallelism, neither are the nominative nouns. One could say that the nominative was subject at some prehistoric stage, but that would lead to positing a change from nominative subject to nominative object – in other words, a change towards the very construction deemed anomalous.

In truth, the construction does seem anomalous from an Indo-European perspective. But rather than denying the construction, we might rather look for its origin in convergence; convergence can lead to results uncharacteristic of the borrowing language (such as German-style prefixes in Estonian). In East Slavic territory, north of the belt of Baltic place names, there is a belt of hydronyms with Finnic etymology. This belt starts above

---

[10]   Arguments are presented in Timberlake (1974: chapter 2).

the Valdai Hills at 55°N, the dividing line between watersheds and between northern and central dialects of East Slavic. The non-native (from the point of view of Slavic) hydronyms show the existence of a substratum here. Indeed, considerable literature has pointed to the existence of a Finnic substratum for northern dialects of Russian (notably Veenker 1967). Such evidence includes *cokan´e* (non-distinction of affricates *c* [ts] and *č* [ʧ]); absence of atonic vowel reduction (prominent in former Baltic areas of Belarus); existential-possessive sentences using the adessive case or pre-position (McAnallen 2011). On the adessive in Finnish, Eliot (1890: 151) says it is used (of a person) to 'signify with, near, or in the house of'; he even glosses his example with French *chez: poika on meillä* 'le garçon est chez nous'. He goes on to say, 'from an extension of this use [the adessive] comes to denote possession', citing the example *on-ko teillä saksia?* 'have you scissors?' Both meanings of the adessive – sphere of influence, possession – are expressed by the preposition *u* plus genitive in modern Russian: *v gostjax **u** Ivanovyx* '. . . as guests *chez* the Ivanovs', ***u** Ivanovyx est´ kvartira v Kaliningrade* 'the Ivanovs have an apartment in Kaliningrad'. In Slavic the extended use of the adessive preposition *u* appeared earliest in Novgorod and subsequently spread to Moscow and the south, but not beyond Russian; its original locus was North Russian.

Against this background we might consider patients in Finnish (only singular nouns below, since nominative and accusative are not distinguished in the plural). The accusative is used for patients in structures headed by a personal verb (one with a subject), either a finite verb itself (11) or an infinitive dependent on a personal finite verb (12):

(11) *[traktori],*   *jolla*   *hän*   *keväisin*   *kynti*   *maan*$_{acc.}$
      [tractor]   by-which   he   in-spring   ploughed   land
      '[tractor], by means of which he ploughed the land$_{acc}$ in the spring'

(12) *Hän*   *haluaa*   *kyntää*$_{inf}$ *maan*$_{acc}$
      he   wants   to.plough   land
      'He wants to plough the land$_{acc}$'

But the patient of an infinitive dependent on an impersonal verb is nominative (13):

(13) *(Minun)*   *täytyy*   *kyntää*$_{inf}$ *maa*$_{nom}$
      me   necessary   to.plough   land
      'It is necessary for me to plough$_{inf}$ the land$_{nom}$'

Pronouns in Finnish (third as well as first and second person) have a distinct accusative form (distinct from the genitive), which is used even for patients of impersonal infinitives. Compare (14) with (13) above.

(14) *Minun*   *täytyy*   *kutsua*   {*sinut*$_{acc}$ / *hänet*$_{acc}$ / *teidät*$_{acc}$}
      to.me   necessary   to.invite   {you   / her   / you.all }
      'For me it is necessary to invite {you$_{acc}$ / her$_{acc}$ / you all$_{acc}$ }'

The nominative patient is a layered form of differential object marking: the accusative is used except when transitivity is reduced (Hopper and Thompson 1980) by the necessary absence of a subject in systematically impersonal contexts (Timberlake 1974). But as a subrule, normal (accusative) case marking is invoked even in impersonal contexts if the object is highly individuated (pronominal or, in Russian, animate). The nominative is also used in Finnic for the object of an imperative, when the subject is predictable from the verb form itself and the predicate is thereby of lower transitivity.

There is every reason, then, to believe that the nominative with infinitive in North Russian, Lithuanian and Latvian derives from Finnic substrata, not broad areal influence. Given that the construction is geographically limited in Slavic, the convergence must have come directly from the Finnic population in the very north of Russia, not from the intermediate Balts.

12.7 Eastern Baltic Region, III

Other, more recent, contact in the eastern Baltic region looks more like areal spread. Lithuania was able to deflect the pressure of western colonization. It defeated the Teutonic Knights in 1238, then joined Poland in a dynastic alliance (Grand Duchy of Lithuania), which became the Polish–Lithuanian Commonwealth in 1569, including Belarus and Ukraine. This alliance defeated the Knights at the Battle of Tannenberg in 1410, setting the Knights on a downward spiral. The Commonwealth was broken up in the partitions of Poland in the 1790s, when much of the region came under tsarist control.

The Grand Duchy, then Commonwealth, became a small linguistic area in its own right. Notable is the development of an impersonal passive of transitive verbs, impersonal in the sense that the patient remains in an object case: accusative in Polish, nominative in (older) Lithuanian. The competing personal passive reports a change of state in an independently established patient, while the impersonal presents a holistic view of the occurrence of an event including the patient. Thus in Lithuanian, (15) describes what is proper treatment as measured in terms of a specific type of horse; the passive participle agrees with 'horse':

(15) *Arklys*$_{\text{nom.msc.sg}}$ *gali būti jojamas*$_{\text{nom.msc.sg}}$ *trumpais periodais*
      horse   may be ridden   short   periods
      the horse$_{\text{nom.msc.sg}}$ may be ridden$_{\text{nom.msc.sg}}$ for short periods'

(16) *Žiūriu –   jo   arklys*$_{\text{nom.msc.sg}}$ *jojama*$_{\text{ntr.sg}}$ *į ganyklą.*
      I.look   by.him   horse   ridden   into pasture
      'I look –by him there's horse$_{\text{nom.msc.sg}}$-riding$_{\text{ntr.sg}}$ into the pasture'
      (Jablonskis 1922: §176D)

In (16) the focus is on the speaker's observing an event, not on the horse. The patient is nominative, but the participle does not agree with the nominative noun.

Polish and Lithuanian form impersonal passives from intransitive verbs as well. Passives of intransitives are frequent in Lithuanian (Jablonskis 1922: §177D), with the agent in the genitive; they have the overtone of evidentiality, as in (17), where tracks in the dirt invite an inference:

(17)   Jo$_{gen.sg}$ čia   per griovą   šokta$_{pass.ntr.sg}$
       him   here   over ditch   jumped$_{pass.ntr.sg}$
       'by him$_{gen.sg}$ it was apparently jumped$_{pass.ntr.sg}$ over the ditch here'

As an exuberant extension (18), a passive of copular 'be' (būta) can be formed:

(18)   Bilieto$_{msc.gen.sg.}$ būta$_{pass.ntr.sg.}$ laimingo$_{msc.gen.sg.}$
       Ticket   be   happy
       'The ticket evidently turned-out-to-be happy'
       (Eugenijus Ališanka, 21 January 2015)

The impersonal passive (of transitive verbs) is seen in northwestern Russian dialects (Pskov, Novgorod and its outposts), as in the idealized example in (19) (inspired by Kuz´mina and Nemčenko 1971: 27, 35, 38, 85). The patient is expressed in the nominative in areas with the 'nominative with infinitive' construction but in the accusative elsewhere. The participle and copula (if present) are neuter singular with either case marking; in this sense the construction is impersonal:

(19)   (U nas) {kartoška$_{fem.nom.sg}$ / kartošku$_{acc.sg}$}   zakopano$_{ntr.sg}$ bylo$_{ntr.sg}$
       (chez nous) potato   planted   was
       '(by us/among us) there was potato-planting'

Finnic languages have a morphologically invariant verb form expressing unspecified agency whose patient is nominative. It is difficult to say if this Finnic impersonal passive is responsible for the construction in the Commonwealth area; the counter-indication is that the impersonal passive skips Latvian (normally included in areal innovations of the Baltic region) but includes Ukrainian (not normally part of Baltic areal innovations). Apparently it was a feature not of the larger eastern Baltic region but specifically of the Commonwealth.

A shared development of the eastern Baltic region is the expression of mediated epistemology of events (quotation or sometimes inference based on evidence) by means of participles that are not attached to finite verbs. This *modus relativus* occurs in the two Baltic languages (it is used repetitively in Latvian folktales) and in Estonian and Finnish. Its origin is hard to date, but it does seem to be a genuinely areal phenomenon.

A possibly related Russian development is the use of (morphologically invariant) participles as autonomous predicates without a finite verb:

(20) *Prišli   bumagi,   čto   ubivši*ptcp *ego*
      arrived   papers   that   killed   him
      'documents have arrived, [saying] that [they] had killedptcp him'
      (Kuz′mina and Nemčenko 1971: 128)

(21) *Kotorye   byli   ušotči*ptcp *v Ščepcy   tye   pogibši*ptcp
      whoever   had   gone   to-Ščepcy   those perished
      'whoever had goneptcp to Ščepcy, those have perishedptcp'
      (Kuz′mina and Nemčenko 1971: 116)

While (20) might qualify as quotative (it reports the content of the papers), this construction seems rather to have a perfect or resultative sense (21). It is found most intensively in Russian dialects from latitude 56° up to 60°N and from longitude 28° to 36°E (Kuz′mina and Nemčenko 1971: karta-sxema 1). It appears to be a Baltic areal phenomenon spread into adjacent areas of Russia.

Numerous developments are shared by Belarus dialects with adjacent areas, at least local convergences, conceivably areal convergences (Wiemer, Seržant and Erker 2014).

12.8 Southwestern Slavdom, I

The Balkans, or southeastern Europe, or the southwest corner of Slavdom, has taken from Eurasia the title of language area par excellence. It covers more continuous area; it is more uniform not just in single features like consonant palatalization or evidentiality but in a whole range of features. Joseph (2010) gives a list, including reduction of case, conversion of infinitives to finite complements, future tense formed with 'want', definite article, analytic comparative adjective, adnominal possession by clitic dative pronouns evidentiality, pleonastic (doubled) object clitic pronouns. All of these seven features have to do with creating a particular typology of syntax organized as phrases. These are shared by all but two peripheral members of the area. The breadth and number of features and the degree of uniformity are remarkable.

The list of uniformly spread features gives the impression of timelessness and inevitability. Correlated with this, it is tacitly assumed that the spread of Balkan features was omnidirectional; indeed, it is sometimes asserted that the search for a source is futile (Tomić 2004). The danger here is that the emphasis on the synchronic results of convergence might obscure the processes and interactions that have given rise to the current situation. The discussion below attempts to develop a more articulated history.

At least two Balkanisms arose earlier in Greek than elsewhere: the analytic substitute for infinitives (Joseph 1983) and the ancient article, native to Greek. The fact that the article is pre-prepositional in Greek and post-positional in Slavic is minor. As the Slavic post-positive demonstrative gradually acquired the functions of an article, there was no reason to change the order.

Let us consider pleonasm. Balkan languages (using Bulgarian as example) can express a direct object in three ways. First, as clitic pronoun without a noun – twice in (22):

(22) *Sled kato go dovărša šte   go pousna pod   drugo   zaglavie*
      After   it finish   want   it release under   another   title
      'After I finish it I will release it under a different title'[11]

The second and third options are a noun with or without a clitic pronoun. In examples adapted from Schick (2000), a clitic pronoun is not used if the referent is indefinite non-specific (23). The pronoun is 'optional' with specific indefinite and definite readings of the noun (24–25) and obligatory with a preposed (and unique in reference) noun (26):

(23) *Tărsjax   (edin)   lekar*
      look.1sg   (one, a)   doctor
      'I am looking for [any person who fits the description of being] a doctor'

(24) *Rada   {go$_{ecl}$ / 0}   tărsi   edno   pismo*
      Rada   {it / 0}   look.3sg   a certain letter
      'Rada is looking for a (certain) letter'

(25) *Rada   {go$_{ecl}$ / 0}   tarsi   pismoto*
      Rada   {it / 0}   look.3sg   letter.def
      'Rada is looking for the letter'

(26) *Ivo   {go$_{ecl}$ / *0}   običa   Rada*
      Ivo   {him / *0}   love.3sg   Rada
      'Ivo, Rada loves him'

Abstracting from these specific examples, it is possible to say (in the spirit of Friedman 2008) that pleonasm is favoured in proportion to discourse prominence (topicalized > non-topicalized), referential autonomy of the noun (definite > indefinite specific > indefinite), and predicate-internal prominence (objects of impersonal experiential verbs > ordinary transitives). These principles can be subsumed under a general rubric of referential autonomy (Laca 2006); they are also relevant to pleonasm in medieval (Laca 2006) and contemporary Spanish (Bull and Carmen 2004: §11.6).

As always, it is instructive to find a moment when a construction is just coming into being. For pleonasm the Bulgarian damaskini are useful.

---

[11] За истинските фенове на Токио Хотел! (25 January 2015).

Orzechowska (1973) examined usage in the Koprištenski and Trojanski damaskini, manuscripts from the early seventeenth century that go back to a common ancestor perhaps a century before. Orzechowska focused on the stylistic value of pleonasm – pleonasm is informal and oral while absence of pleonasm has overtones of formal and written – and did not analyse the distribution of pleonasm in terms of syntax or discourse. Nevertheless she did cite ten examples of the total of 23 tokens of pleonasm from the Koprištenski damaskin. If these ten are representative of the whole text, then it is telling that, in nine of these ten sentences with pleonasm, the noun is preposed, and six of those nine have the conjunction *da* – at this time a major boundary between the noun and the verb. See (27):

(27)   *němu*   *sъ*   *straxъ*   *i*   *sъs*   *radost da*   *mu*   *vъzdraduvame*
      to-him   with   fear   and   with   joy   that   him   rejoice
      'to him, it is with fear and with joy that we rejoice to him'

To judge by Orzechowska's examples, the locus of diffusion for pleonasm was topicalized arguments. This suspicion finds confirmation in Greek (de Boel 2008). Pleonasm was found in personal correspondence on papyrus up through the seventh century CE, when the supply of papyrus was interrupted (p. 94). Pleonasm shows up again in texts in the twelfth century in a new tradition of writing courtly poetry in the vernacular (Alexiou 2002: 100), notably in the twelfth century Ptochoprodromic Poems (=PtP) and Digenis Akritis, Escorial manuscript (=DA/E). The two examples in (28, 29) are cited by de Boel (pp. 97, 96):

(28)   *Τὴν θάλασσαν*   *τὴν*   *μὲ*   *ἔφερες,*   *γνωρίζεις. ἔπαρέ*   *την*
      the   red-petticoat   it   me   you-brought   you-know   take   it
      'the red petticoat you brought me it, you know, take it' (PtP I.58)

(29)   *Τὴν*   *δὲ*   *προῖκα*   *μου*   *τὴν*   *πολλὴν*   *ἄς*   *τὴν*   *ἔχουν*   *οἱ*   *γυναικάδελφοί*   *μου*
      the   but   dowry   my   the   rich   let   it   have   the   wife-brothers   my
      'the dowry of mine, the rich one, let my brothers-in-law have that' (DA/E 1007)

On the basis of Orzechowska and de Boel, we can hypothesize that pleonasm began as a resumptive pronoun associated initially with a syntactically and intonationally detached topic. That is to say, pleonasm has its origins in actual speech activity, not in an abstract change of grammar; moreover, it is striking that many of the examples cited by de Boel involve imperatives, the ultimate dialogic form. Preposing the object to guarantee clarity and comprehension is an adaptation speakers make when speaker or addressee does not have full and equal command over the same language. On that reasoning, pleonasm is linked to a specific kind of interlingual communicative situation. This link to interlingual speech is reminiscent of the adaptations of Estonian to Low German (demonstrative as article, discourse particles), which imitate the speech of the interlocutor.

Following that logic, we would now want to identify situations of inter-lingual communication involving Greeks and Slavs. There were many, and they stretched over a long time. Slavs appeared in the sixth century in the Danube valley raiding forts south of the Danube and eventually settling south of the Danube, to judge by characteristic Slavic pottery and subter-ranean houses (Văžarova 1965). The Avars captured Sirmium in 582 and then enlisted the Slavs as allies or vassals for further conquest; together they laid siege to Thessaloniki using sophisticated siege techniques (in 597, according to Vryonis 1981). Subsequently – especially in the interval of 610 to 626 – Slavs conducted raids throughout Greece, all the way to the Peloponnesus south of the Gulf of Corinth.

The Slavs not only raided, but to judge by Slavic pottery and burial by cremation (Vryonis 1981: 379), they settled. Settlement is also indicated by numerous Slavic place names preserved in Greek (Vasmer 1941), among them names invoking land-clearing (Τερπίτσα < *terbica 'clearing' [p. 76]) and cultivation (Σβάρνα < *borna 'harrow' [p. 289]) (Curta 2011: 211–212). The oldest place names fix a stage of Slavic earlier than any written source; for example, liquid diphthongs like Τερπίτσα and Σβάρνα still have the Common Slavic shape of *CVRC with the vowel before the liquid, whereas the rest of Slavic modifies that order. The mere fact that Slavic place names could be preserved in Greek implies a process analogous to the process discussed above for Mecklenburg-Vorpommern (Section 12.4): the newer settlers (here Greeks) interacted with the sedentary population (Slavs); the new settlers and the resulting mixed community adopted linguistic relics of the disappearing ethnos.

In response to Slavic settlement, Byzantine authorities initiated a programme of reclaiming territory by setting up administrative units ('themes') and converting the pagan Slavs. Civil administration, con-ducted in Greek, was rationalized. Some themes were established at the end of the seventh century, others thereafter. As Obolensky (1971: 78) summarized,

> Thus, by the end of the ninth century, the Byzantines had succeeded in establishing administrative control over a string of themes which formed an almost continuous edging around the Balkan peninsula. In some of these districts, notably in Thrace and in Southern Macedonia, Byzantine power extended far inland.

The military and administrative aspects of this policy of 'reconquest' were accompanied by a renewal of Byzantine Christianity and of the importance of the Greek language (Obolensky 1971: 80):

> In the Slavonic lands now reintegrated into the framework of the Byzantine provincial administration, Greek was not only the idiom of the church but the language of civil service, of the armed forces, of polite society; a knowledge of Byzantine Greek became henceforth the necessary key to social status and a successful career.

The combination of forces is strikingly similar to the combination of military, political, confessional and linguistic pressures observed in Mecklenburg-Vorpommern and Pomerania.

Thus there was extended linguistic interaction between Slavs and Greeks, and it was not unidirectional: Slavs invaded and inhabited Greek territory but then under pressure Slavs learned Greek, learning enough (or switching entirely) to participate in the up-and-coming prestige life of Greeks. (One is reminded of Constantine and Methodius who were said to know Slavic and whose father was a *drangarios* – could their parents have been assimilated Slavs?) Recall that, in Livonia, ethnic Estonians learned the Hanseatic lingua franca to some degree and allowed this language to influence patterns in their own language (prefixes, particles, word-level prosody). Conceivably the same thing happened here in the ninth or tenth century, when Slavs learning some Greek incorporated Greek patterns into their Slavic and Greeks dealing with imperfect speakers modified their language.

12.9   Southwestern Slavdom, II

The question then becomes how pleonasm, and all the other features attributed to the Balkan Sprachbund (Friedman and Joseph, Chapter 4, this volume), were spread so extensively in southeastern Europe. One possibility is a variation of wave theory, which, applied to this case, might attribute the overall uniformity to recursive processes of convergence from one village to the next, all throughout the Balkans. There are certainly micro-instances of micro-contact and convergence, which continue to this day. Yet it is fair to ask, is that how it happened? Would recurrent micro-convergences have been sufficient to produce the uniformity and geographical reach of Balkan features? In the case of Western Romance, there was a lingua franca that was responsible for spreading relatively uniform norms throughout Western Romance; similarly, in the Baltic area, from 1150 to at least 1550, some variety of Low German served as a lingua franca.

These parallels invite us to consider the possibility that, in southeastern Europe as well, there was a lingua franca (or linguae francae) used across the Balkans. It is well known that the Balkan area was an extremely fertile area for trade, as is discussed in the classic study by Stoianovich (1960). Trade grew especially in the interval from the fifteenth century to the seventeenth century, in concert with territorial expansion of the Ottoman Empire, which continued until the Treaty of Carlowitz (1699).

Trade moved towards the capital of Constantinople, especially from the eastern provinces, but also in the other direction, from Constantinople towards Vienna, even reaching the Netherlands. Trade was controlled by the state. A patent was required to engage in trade: 'Fur traders, salt farmers, purveyors of beef and mutton, and buyers and exporters of silk, wool, cotton, coffee, rice, oil, grains, wax, copper, lead, and saltpeter were all required to purchase government patents authorizing them to engage in the commerce of their choice' (Stoianovich 1960: 241).

Evidently the merchants interacted with peasants and (in cities) with artisans. Stoianovich comments (1960: 241), 'Merchants charged with satisfying the needs of the capital and state at first made their purchases in the port towns. Soon, however, they extended their operations into the interior.' A debt economy developed, whereby peasants would agree to low prices for future crops in order to have money to live on (1960: 303). There was a route of seasonal fairs at least in Thessaly. This is all to say that the itinerant merchants interacted directly with the sedentary population.

We cannot be sure what language merchants and their clients used. There is more than one possibility. It is certainly possible that there were regional Slavic or Romanian trade languages. But for all the diversity of ethnicities involved in trade, the one constant throughout the whole Balkan region was Greek traders. It is plausible that merchants, on the whole, used Greek or a simplified form of Greek. 'Trade Greek' would have had compromise syntactic structure, which is to say, it was highly phrasal.

Such a lingua franca of trade would have provided the region with (informal) norms to imitate. If so, the Sprachbund of the Balkans would look more like Livonia, where the resident urban population was multilingual and, if only for economic reasons, had an 'accommodationist' disposition to imitate, internalize and use the norms of the lingua franca. Unlike Western Romance, this attitude did not come at the expense of abandoning the indigenous languages.[12]

12.10 Eurasian Linguistic Area?

All study of areal linguistics harks back to Roman Jakobson's study (1931) of the Eurasian Sprachbund [Evrazijskij jazykovoj sojuz]. In this study he focused on phonemic palatalization of consonants (as in Russian); yet at points he seems to include more banal palatalizations like $ki > ji > t\!fi$ (ts) or $ti > t\!fi$ (ts) and, further, palatalization is subsumed under synharmony (agreement of frontness and backness of vowels and consonants).

Jakobson had two broader concerns. He announces early on (1931: 146) the importance of 'correspondence – the tight principled connection among phenomena of different spheres'. In his poetic studies, he blurred the boundary between ancient and modern culture (Merrill 2012); he does

---

[12] There is a parallel in early Scandinavian. Dahl (2001) argues that the uniformity of Scandinavian languages cannot be explained by preservation of original uniformity from an Ursprache, and also not by an extended down-the-line convergence from village to village throughout Scandinavia (which would create difference). Rather, a more powerful mechanism is needed: a koiné (lingua franca) that developed in tandem with regional economic activity which spread norms. The situation is analogous in the Balkans: it is uncertain whether recursive down-the-line convergence could produce the kind of structural homogeneity we see over the enormous space of the Balkan Sprachbund.

the same here with geographical boundaries. Secondly, it is no accident that the language union discussed here is Eurasia; Eurasianism – the belief that Russia represents a unique synthesis of Orient and Occident – was in vogue among émigrés after the Russian Revolution (N. S. Trubetzkoy, D. S. Mirsky, P. N. Savicky). The quest for connectedness and the investment in Eurasianism may have influenced Jakobson's analysis.

Jakobson begins with the clear case of Slavic. Leaving aside banal palatalizations (velars before front vowels or *j, dentals before *j), dentals and labials were palatalized before front vowels. Palatalization became contrastive as a result of apocope of final high lax vowels seen in pairs such as *plotъ [plotʊ] 'raft' > Russian /plot/ versus *plotь [plotʲɪ] 'flesh' > Russian /plotʲ/. Distinctive palatalization occurs in many environments in Russian (less in Ukrainian and Bulgarian); in other Slavic languages palatalization has either disappeared (Czech, Serbo-Croatian) or has been transformed into affrication (Polish).

Jakobson then moves around the Eurasian landmass noting languages with palatalization. In Finno-Ugric, Permic languages and Mordva have palatalization (Jakobson 1931: 171–172). (A recent study says Mordva has both allophonic palatalization of labials and velars in position before front vowels and a distinctive series of palatal consonants contrasting with dentals, namely /tʲ, dʲ, sʲ, zʲ, cʲ, lʲ, rʲ, nʲ/ opposed to /t, d/, etc., Zaicz 1997: 185–186.) Even Samoyed has palatalization. But Hungarian was evidently too far to the west and Lapp too far to the north to participate in Eurasian trends.

Jakobson cites Lithuanian and Latvian as border languages which have developed palatalization under Russian influence (1931: 181). Estonian fits into this category. Estonian (Viitso 1997: 123) has extensive palatalization, more in the south than in the north; it has become phonemic through apocope: *hullu > [hull] 'crazy' versus *kulli > [kulʲlʲ] 'hawk'. How old the distinctive palatalization is in Estonian is not clear. It might reflect a historically deep Finno-Ugric disposition (a possibility considered by Abondolo 1997b). Or Eurasian influence. Or, just as likely, more immediate contiguity and convergence with Russian.

Jakobson devotes much attention to Turkic languages, replacing palatalization with syllable synharmony: consonants and vowels harmonize as high tonality (= front) or low tonality (= back). The earliest Turkic writing, from the Orkhon and Yenesei valleys, does indeed distinguish two kinds of syllables (Jakobson 1931: 187). He notes distinctive palatalization in Mongolian proper (Khalkha) and certain other Mongolic languages (Buryat, Kalmyk); his geography and chronology of 'XIII–XIVth' centuries are consistent with contemporary work (Svantesson et al. 2005). Jakobson goes a step further and projects synharmony back to Proto-Altaic and talks of Altaic languages realizing their Altaic destiny step-by-step. Here he slips in an aside that the southern neighbour of Altaic – Chinese (= Ch.) – developed an opposition of palatalization (Jakobson 1931: 181). Evidently

Jakobson has in mind developments between Early Middle Chinese (=EMCh., Qieyun rime tables, 601 CE) and Late Middle Chinese (=LMCh., mid-twelfth century), when labials were palatalized by a medial *j and then bifurcated depending on the following vowel (Baxter 1992: 203): front vowels absorbed the palatalizing agent: OCh. *pjin 'guest' > EMCh. pjin > LMCh. pjin > bīn (賓); in contrast, before back vowels, the palatalized labial became a labio-dental: OCh. *pjang 'region' > EMCh. pjang > LMCh. fang > Ch. fāng (方). Jakobson's mention of geographical contiguity suggests that he thought Mongolian was responsible. But unless the Orkhon writing is meant, that would not fit chronologically, since Chinese labial palatalization occurred well before Mongolian palatalization.

These concerns registered, it is still true that it is hard to not be daunted by Jakobson's documentation of palatalization or synharmony spread over an enormous area. The difficulty of pinning down interlingual relatedness and chronologies fits with modern understanding of linguistic areas as a force operating with less immediate and less visible contact than ordinary contact. It may also be that some features are easier (or require less contact) to transfer than others – classifiers, tone (Emeneau 1956), discourse particles, and phonetic biases like synharmony; these can all be noticed and imitated by non-native speakers.

12.11   Slavic Linguistic Areas?

Above we examined encounters of Slavs with others on the edges of Slavic territory, some of which look like areal phenomena. The interest was both typological – to see how these encounters fit in the spectrum of possible encounters – and genetic – to see how linguistic areas evolve out of other encounters.

In some instances examined above, encounters where features are distributed over multiple languages turn out to be better analysed as substrata (Baltic, Slavic and Finnic interaction). Other encounters involved a lingua franca, which can indeed leave an imprint on multiple languages, but it is not necessarily a linguistic area. Both instances of linguae francae above are unusual, if not quite singular. The Baltic lingua franca occurred during dramatic growth of commerce, confessional conversion and colonization. The Balkan lingua franca likewise was driven by commerce. These linguae francae evolved in the direction of becoming linguistic areas. In the Baltic region that development was partial. In the Balkans the development, promoted by centuries of shifts in language allegiance between Greek and Slavic, was complete. In the mature stage, the lingua franca recedes, multiple languages participate, and grammar is so homogenized it appears to have no origin.

In these encounters, all participant languages were affected to some extent, reflecting a dialogic quality to language contact and convergence.

Superstratal languages seem to involve a power asymmetry, but even there, the receding language leaves a mark, implying accommodation of superstratum to substratum. Linguae francae not only absorb lexicon from local vernaculars but often (usually?) become compromise codes – speakers adjust to the imperfections of their interlocutors. The compromise code is obvious in the Balkans and Western Romance; Low German looks stripped down at earliest attestation. The compromise character of linguae francae arises from accommodations made in speech, such as the pleonastic – resumptive – pronouns at a distance and periphrastic futures; these accommodations become conventionalized features of the language and get extended.

References

Abondolo, Daniel (ed.), 1997a. *The Uralic Languages*. London and New York: Routledge.

Abondolo, Daniel, 1997b. Introduction. In Abondolo (ed.), pp. 1–42.

Alexiou, Margaret, 2002. *After Antiquity: Greek Language, Myth, and Metaphor*. Ithaca, NY: Cornell University Press.

Andersen, Henning, 1996. *Reconstructing Prehistorical Dialects: Initial Vowels in Slavic and Baltic*. Trends in Linguistics, vol. 91. Berlin and New York: Mouton de Gruyter.

Anthony, David, 1990. Migration in archeology: The baby and the bathwater. *American Anthropologist* 92: 895–914.

Barford, P. M., 2001. *The Early Slavs: Culture and Society in Early Medieval Eastern Europe*. Ithaca, NY: Cornell University Press.

Baxter, William H., 1992. *A Handbook of Old Chinese Phonology*. Berlin and New York: Mouton de Gruyter.

Berger, Tilman, 2014. The convergence of Czech and German between the years 900 and 1500. In Besters-Dilger et al. (eds), pp. 189–198.

Besters-Dilger, Juliane, Cynthia Dermarkar, Stefan Pfänder and Achim Rabus (eds), 2014. *Congruence in Contact-induced Language Change: Language Families, Typological Resemblance, and Perceived Similarity*. Freiburg Institute for Advanced Studies, School of Language and Literature, *Linguae & Litterae*, vol. 27. Berlin and Boston: Walter de Gruyter.

Bickell, Balthasar and Johanna Nichols, 2006. Oceania, the Pacific Rim, and the theory of linguistic areas. In *Proceedings of the Annual Meeting of the Berkeley Linguistics Society*, vol. 32. Berkeley, CA: Berkeley Linguistics Society.

de Boel, Gunnar, 2008. The genesis of clitic doubling from Ancient to Medieval Greek. In Kallulli and Tasmowski (eds), pp. 89–103.

Brüske, Wolfgang, 1955. *Untersuchungen zur Geschichte des Lutizenbundes: Deutsch-wendische Beziehungen des 10.–12. Jahrhunderts*. Mitteldeutsche Forschungen, vol. 3. Münster: Böhlau.

Butt, John and Carmen Benjamin, 2004. *A New Reference Grammar of Modern Spanish*, fourth edition. New York: McGraw Hill.

Curta, Florin, 2011. *The Edinburgh History of the Greeks, c. 500 to 1050: the Early Middle Ages*. Edinburgh: Edinburgh University Press.

Dahl, Östen, 2001. The origin of the Scandinavian languages. In Östen Dahl and Maria Koptjevskaja-Tamm (eds), *The Circum-Baltic Languages*, vol. 1: *Past and Present: Typology and Contact*, pp. 215–236. Amsterdam and Philadelphia: John Benjamins.

Damme, Robert, 1987. Westslavische Reliktwörter in Stralsunder Vokabular. In P. Sture Ureland (ed.), *Sprachkontakt in der Hanse: Aspekte des Sprachausgleichs im Ostsee- und Nordseeraum. Akten der 7. Internationalen Symposions über Sprachkontakt in Europa, Lübeck 1986*, pp. 163–178. Tübingen: Niemeyer.

Eliot, C. N. E., 1890. *A Finnish Grammar*. Oxford: Clarendon Press.

Emeneau, M. B., 1956. India as a linguistic area. *Language* 32: 3–16.

Endzelin, J., 1901. Ursprung und Gebrauch des lettischen Debitivs. *Beiträge zur Kunde der indogermanischen Sprachen (Bezzenbergers Beiträge)* 26: 66–74.

Feldbrugge, F. J. M., 2009. *Law in Medieval Russia*. Leiden and Boston: M. Nijhoff.

Friedman, Victor, 2008. Balkan object reduplication in areal and dialectological perspective. In Kallulli and Tasmowski (eds), pp. 33–64.

Gebauer, Jan, 1929. *Historická mluvnice českého jazyka*, vol. 4: *Skladba [Historical Grammar of Czech: Syntax]*. Prague: Česká Akademie Věd a Umění.

Gimbutas, Marija, 1971. *The Slavs*. New York: Praeger.

Gippius, A. A., 1996. 'Russkaja Pravda' i 'Voprošanie Kirika' v Novgorodskoj Kormčej 1282 g. (k xarakteristike jazykovoj situacii drevnego Novgoroda) ['Russian Law Code' and 'Kirik's Questions' in the Novgorod Nomocanon of 1282 (toward a characterization of the language situation of Old Novgorod)]. *Slavjanovedenie* 1996.1: 48–62.

Hill, Jane, 2001. Languages on the ground: Toward an anthropological dialectology. In John Edward Terrell (ed.), *Archeology, Language, and History: Essays on Culture and Ethnicity*, pp. 257–282. Westport, CT and London: Bergin & Garvey.

Hopper, Paul and Sandra A. Thompson, 1980. Transitivity in grammar and discourse. *Language* 56 (2): 251–299.

Jablonskis, Jonas, 1922. *Lietuvių kalbos gramatika. Etimologija: Vidurinėms mokslo įstaigoms [Grammar of Lithuanian Etymology: For Institutions of Secondary Education]*, second edition. Kaunas: Švyturio bendrovės leidinys.

Jakobson, Roman, 1931. *K xarakteristike evrazijskogo jazykovogo sojuza [Toward the Characterization of the Eurasian Linguistic Area]*. Paris: Izd. Evraziitsev. Reprinted in 1962, *Selected Writings*, vol. 1: *Phonological Studies*, pp. 144–201, The Hague and Paris: Mouton.

Johansen, Paul and Heinz von zur Mühlen, 1973. *Deutsch und Undeutsch im mittelalterlichen und frühneuzeitlichen Reval*. Ostmitteleuropa in Vergangenheit und Gegenwart, vol. 15. Köln: Böhlau, 1973.

Joseph, Brian D., 1983. *The Synchrony and Diachrony of the Balkan Infinitive: A Study in Areal, General, and Historical Linguistics*. Cambridge: Cambridge University Press.

Joseph, Brian D., 2010. Language contact in the Balkans. In Raymond Hickey (ed.), *The Handbook of Language Contact*, pp. 619–633. Malden, MA: Wiley-Blackwell.

Kallulli, Dalina and Liliane Tasmowski, 2008. *Clitic Doubling in the Balkan Languages*. Linguistik aktuell, vol. 130. Amsterdam; Philadelphia: John Benjamins.

Kantzow, Thomas, 1816. *Pomerania, oder, Ursprunck, Altheit und Geschicht der Völcker und Lande Pomern, Cassuben, Wenden, Stettin, Rhügen in vierzehn Büchern*, edited by Hans Gottfried Ludwig Rosengarten, vol. 1 Greifswald: Mauritins.

Koškins, Igors, 1996. Deutsches Lehngut in den altrussischen Novgoroder Urkunden. In Gisela Brandt (ed.), *Beiträge zur Geschichte der deutschen Sprache im Baltikum*, pp. 87–98. Stuttgart: Hans Dieter Heinz.

Kuz'mina, I. B. and E. V. Nemčenko, 1971. *Sintaksis pričastnyx form v russkix govorax [The Syntax of Participial Forms in Russian Dialects]*. Moscow: Nauka.

Laca, Brenda, 2006. El objeto directo: La marcación preposicional [The direct object: Prepositional marking]. In Concepción Company Company (ed.), *Sintaxis histórica de la lengua española*, part 1: *La frase verbal [Historical Syntax of Spanish: The Verb Phrase]*, pp. 423–478. México: Universidad Nacional Autónoma de México.

Lorentz, Friedrich, 1903. *Slovinzische Grammatik*. St Petersburg: Vtoroe Otdelenie Imperatorskoj Akademii Nauk.

Lübben, August, 1888. *Mittelniederdeutsches Handwörterbuch. Nach dem Tode des Verfassers vollendet von Christoph Walther*. Norden: D. Soltau.

McAnallen, Julia, 2011. *The History of Predicative Possession in Slavic: Internal Development vs. Language Contact*. PhD dissertation, University of California, Berkeley.

Merrill, Jessica, 2012. *The Role of Folklore Study in the Rise of Russian Formalist and Czech Structuralist Literary Theory*. PhD dissertation, University of California, Berkeley.

Obolensky, Dimitri, 1971. *The Byzantine Commonwealth: Eastern Europe, 500–1453*. New York: Praeger.

Orzechowska, Hanna, 1973. Podwajanie dopełnień w historii bułgarskiego języka literackiego [Object doubling in the history of the Bulgarian literary language]. Warsaw: Państwowe Wydawnictwo Naukowe.

Otsmaa, Lilia, 1975. O russkix zaimstvovanijax v baltijskom nižnenemeckom jazyke [On Russian borrowings in Baltic Low German]. *Linguistica* 6: 86–113.

Schick, Ivanka, 2000. Clitic doubling constructions in Balkan–Slavic languages. In Frits Beukema and Marcel den Dikken (eds), *Clitic Phenomena in European Languages*, pp. 259–292. Amsterdam: John Benjamins.

Stoianovich, Traian, 1960. The conquering Balkan Orthodox merchant. *The Journal of Economic History* 20: 234–313.

Svantesson, Jan-Olof, Anna Tsendina, Anastasia Karlsson and Vivan Franzén, 2005. *The Phonology of Mongolian*. Oxford: Oxford University Press.

Thomason, Sarah Grey and Terrence Kaufman, 1988. *Language Contact, Creolization, and Genetic Linguistics*. Berkeley, CA: University of California Press.

Timberlake, Alan, 1974. *The Nominative Object in Slavic, Baltic, and West Finnic*. Munich: Otto Sagner.

Tomić, Olga, 2004. The Balkan Sprachbund: Introduction. In Olga Tomić (ed.), *Balkan Syntax and Semantics*, pp. 1–55. Amsterdam: John Benjamins.

Toporov, V. N. and O. N. Trubačev, 1962. *Lingvističeskij analiz gidronimov Verxnego Podneprov´ja [Linguistic Analysis of Hydronyms of the Upper Dnepr Region]*. Moscow: Akademija Nauk SSSR.

Vasmer, Max, 1941. *Die Slaven in Griechenland*. Berlin: Akademie der Wissenschaften.

Văžarova, Živka N., 1965. *Slavjanski i slavjanobălgarski selišta v bălgarskite zemi VI–XI vek [Slavic and Slavobulgarian Settlements on Bulgarian Territory from the Sixth through the Eleventh Century]*. Sofia: Bălgarska Akademija na Naukite.

Veenker, Wolfgang, 1967. *Die Frage des finnougrischen Substrats in der russischen Sprache*. Indiana University Publications, Uralic and Altaic Series, vol. 82. Bloomington, IN: Indiana University Press.

Viitso, Tiit-Rein, 1997. Estonian. In Abondolo (ed.), pp. 115–148.

VoprKir, 1888. *Voprosy Kirika, Savvy i Il´i, s otvetami Nifonta, episkopa Novgorodskogo, i drugix ierarxičeskix lic*, no. 2: *Pamjatniki drevne-russkogo kanoničeskogo prava*, pt. 1. *Russkaja istoričeskaja biblioteka, izdavaemaja Arxeografičeskoj Kommissiej*, vol. 6. [*The Questions of Kirik, Savva, and Ilja, with Answers of Nifont, Bishop of Novgorod, and of Other Clerics. Monuments of Old Russian Canon Law. Russian Historical Library, published by the Archaeographic Commission*]. St Petersburg.

Vryonis, Spiros, 1981. The evolution of Slavic society and the Slavic invasions in Greece: The first major Slavic attack on Thessaloniki, A.D. 597. *Hesperia* 50: 378–390.

Wiemer, Björn, Ilja Seržant and Aksana Erker, 2014. Convergence in the Baltic–Slavic contact zone: Triangulation approach. In Besters-Dilger et al. (eds), pp. 15–42.

Willis, David, 2013. Negation in the history of the Slavonic languages. In David Willis, Christopher Lucas and Anne Breitbarth (eds), *The History of Negation in the Languages of Europe and the Mediterranean*, vol. 1: *Case Studies*, pp. 341–398. Oxford: Oxford University Press.

Witte, Hans, 1906. Wendische Zu- und Familiennamen aus mecklenburgischen Urkunden und Akten gesammelt und mit Unterstützung des Herrn Prof. Dr. Ernst Mucke zu Freiberg (Sachsen) bearbeitet.

Mecklenburgischer Jahrbücher, Verein für Mecklenburgische Geschichte und Altertumskunde 71: 153–290.

Zaicz, Gábor, 1997. Mordva. In Abondolo (ed.), pp. 184–218.

Zaliznjak, Andrej A., 2004. *Drevnenovgorodskij dialekt*, 2-e izd., pererabotannoe s učetom materiala naxodok 1995–2003 gg. [*Old Novgorod Dialect*, second edition, revised with consideration of finds 1995–2003]. Moscow: Jazyki russkoj kul´tury.

13

The Caucasus

Sven Grawunder

This chapter seeks to describe the area of the Caucasus Mountains as a linguistic contact area, as has been suggested by a number of authors (e.g. Catford 1977; Chirikba 2008a; Comrie 2008). After sketching the migration history, historical contacts and contact scenarios, including multilingualism, I will primarily focus on the occurrence and co-occurrence of contrastive sound features in language varieties described in the area so far (e.g. Alekseev et al. 1999; Harris 1991; Hewitt 1989; Job 2004; Kibrik and Kodzasov 1990; Smeets 1994). Additionally, the chapter attempts to demonstrate how the frequency of these occurrences as well as cross-linguistic comparison of the phonetic realization of features can improve our understanding of the areal characteristics of phonological contrasts.

13.1 Defining the Linguistic Area: The Caucasus as an Area of Contact

A necessary condition for a linguistic area is the existence of similarities, for example in terms of shared linguistic features. Since these similarities can result either from common descent, from contact-induced assimilation, or simply from chance and the general make-up of human languages (universalities), the emphasis lies on similarities that can only be explained by contact. By using areality as a vehicle for explaining higher or lower degrees of similarity, we should be able to infer degrees of contact with some caution.

Like the Himalayas, the Caucasus, too, is categorized as a Eurasian enclave, i.e. an area of accretion (Nichols 1997), which is surrounded by areas of migration. This means that '(i)ntrusive languages ... do not replace other languages or families but are added to them. Thus the Caucasus tends to increase in genetic and typological diversity over time' (Nichols 1992: 16). From this perspective, the high mountainous areas work as barriers against migration and cause a difference in population shift and mobility between highlands and lowlands; therefore, different depths of contact can be proposed. Linguistically, the Caucasus area today contains a fair amount of genealogical diversity, with at least five different language families (Nakh-Dagestanian, Adyghe-Abkhaz, Kartvelian, Altaic and Indo-European) comprising over 150 described varieties of around 45 languages. At least for the three inner Caucasian language families (Kartvelian = South Caucasian, Nakh-Dagestanian = Northeast Caucasian, and Adyghe-Abkhaz = Northwest Caucasian) along the Great Northern Crest – a mountain ridge across the borders of Russia, Georgia, Armenia and Azerbaijan – a very long period of contact can be assumed, which allowed the development of wide-ranging structural similarities. Northeast Caucasian (NEC) languages and Northwest Caucasian (NWC) languages are often grouped together as North Caucasian languages for reasons of typological similarity. The Transcaucasus area at the southern edge leads from the South Caucasian (SC) languages into a transitional area of its own (cf. the ARAXES area proposed by Stilo 1994) that carries traits from the compact Caucasus area of the north into the adjacent areas in Turkey, Armenia, Azerbaijan and Iran. With Semitic Aysor (Neo-Aramaic, Assyrian) a sixth language family comes into play (see Table 13.1) for this southern Caucasian area. And for the northern plains, the Mongolian language Kalmyk-Oirat could also be added, representing another branch of Altaic.

13.1.1 Divergence versus Convergence, Homogeneity versus Diversity

More or less independently of the now rejected hypothesis of a common Caucasian language family (e.g. the Ibero-Caucasian hypothesis by Yavakhishvili 1937: see Tuite 2008), a Caucasian sprachbund had been suggested by Dirr (1928) and Klimov (1994) but was rejected by Tuite (1999) and Comrie (2008) and recently reinforced by Chirikba (2008a). Given the long-standing contact, which in a number of cases lasted more than two millennia, such a sprachbund would imply a range of commonalities, similarities and overlaps. So one might end up arguing for contact in a circular fashion based on (structural) similarities to be found in today's language setup, whereas linguistic similarities are explained by possible contact, without considering shared innovations or even homologies, that is, independent changes with an equal outcome. Therefore a clear picture of the genealogy of the Caucasian families is needed to circumvent arguments about contact-based similarities instead of genealogical traits. Contact-induced changes occur more or less 'naturally' due to mechanisms of reanalysis, reinterpretation, grammaticalization and accommodation (Aikhenvald and Dixon 2001), and were found already at the beginning of language research in the Caucasus in the nineteenth century. Klimov (1994) refers here, for example, to Baudouin de Courtenay (1963), who had found 'common traits irrespective of original relatedness'. Despite the fruitful typological perspective, one that is more abstract and comparatively oriented, Klimov (1994) also predicts that if provided with an area-

Table 13.1 *Languages of the wider Caucasus, combined from Hewitt (1981) and Koryakov (2006). Italic terms are either dialects or reflect a non-established division. Note that the depths of the branches may not be the same in all places*

Family	Subfamily	Branch	Subgroup	Language
South Caucasian (Kartvelian)		East Kartvelian		Georgian
		West Kartvelian		Mingrelian, Laz
		Svan		Balian, Svan
Northwest Caucasian (Adyghe-Abkhaz)			Abkhaz	Abkhaz, Abaza
			Circassian	Kabardian, Adyghe
			Ubykh	Ubykh
Northeast Caucasian (Nakh-Dagestanian)	(North)	Nakh	Veynakh	Chechen, Ingush
				Bats
		Avar-Andic-Tsezic	Avar	Avar, *Zakhatli*
			Andic	Andi, Akhvakh, Tindi, Bagvalal, Chamalal, Godoberi, Karata
			Tsezic	Tsez, Bezhta, Hinukh, Khvarshi, Inkhokhvari, Hunzib
		Lak		Lak
	(Central)	Dargwic	North Dargwa	*Megeb, North Dargwa, Kadar, Muira Kaitak, Sirhwa, Kunki, Lower Vurqni*
			South Dargwa	*Kubachi-Ashti, Chiraq-Amuq*
	(South)	Lezgic		Lezgi, Tabasaran, Aghul, Rutul, Tsakhur, Udi, Kryz, Budukh
		Khinalug		Khinalug
		Archi		Archi
Indo-European	Iranian	Northeastern		Ossetic (Digor, Iron)
		Northwestern		Talysh, Kurdish, Zazaki
		Southwestern		Tat, Persian
	Armenian			Armenian
	Slavic	East Slavic		Russian
	Greek		Northern	Pontic Greek
Altaic	Turkic		Northwestern (Kypchak)	Nogai, Kumyk, Karachay-Balkarian
			Southwestern (Oghuz)	Turkic, Azerbaijani
Afroasiatic	Semitic	(Central)	West-central	Neo-Aramaic (Aysor)

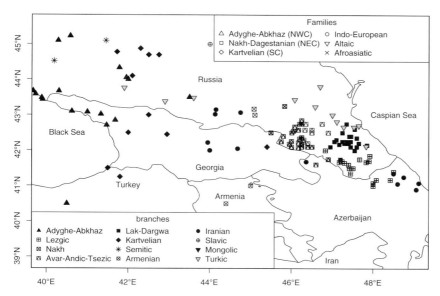

Map 13.1 The language families of the Caucasus, showing the main branches

linguistic perspective, one might gain a better understanding of the convergence processes under circumstances of language contact. The idea of also integrating dialectology (see Bisang 2004) needs to be taken into account since it will allow one to attain a more fine-grained mesh of contrasts on the one hand and to gain a better understanding of the particular changes that may spread through the entire language continua or be retained and lead to higher inner diversity on the other hand. Comrie (2008) locates the languages of the Caucasus at a middle position on a diversity scale, compared with Papua New Guinea, for example, but he proposes a zone of convergence with regard to certain grammatical structures. From their general typological profile, agglutinative, mainly prefixing, morphology and marking of the syntactic agents, as well as a three-way phonation contrast in the obstruent systems (see Comrie 2008) can be of value here. Klimov (1994) relegates, in terms of their lexical properties, a rich layer of 'internationalisms' of the Muslim world, that is, loanwords from Arabic, Persian or Turkic which are shared by all groups of Caucasian languages. But even beyond that, Klimov (1994), suggesting a sprachbund, talks of a possible core vocabulary of the Inner Caucasus languages – containing terms like those for 'cherry', 'chicken', 'sister/ daughter-in-law' or 'plough' – that seems to be similar enough in all three Inner Caucasian families (see Chirikba 2008a).

Also for reasons of structural similarities one can even argue for a wider conglomeration of languages that comprise especially the southern edges. The latter would concur with the notion of a Transcaucasian cultural and linguistic contact zone spanning along and around the Araxes river from Turkey to the Caspian sea, as in Stilo (2004), who actually describes a much greater spreading of linguistic features, with Iran as a buffer zone. Stilo (2006) finds here, for example, a north–south transition in the use of morphological marking from prepositions via circumpositions into postpositions. For the Caucasus, Chirikba (2008a) suggested a division into core languages (comprising NWC, NEC and SC languages), peripheral languages (Ossetic, Armenian languages), marginal (Karachay-Balkar, Kumyk, Azeri, Nogay, some varieties of Anatolian Turkish and Iranian Tat) and contiguous languages (Kurdish, Talysh, historically Persian, Pontic Greek, Trukhmen Turkic, etc.), which are spoken in adjoining areas. Nonetheless one wants to find at least continua of structural similarities if there are no total overlaps, so that feature spread would cover the entire linguistic area in question and allow for adjacent linguistic areas to touch and overlap.

13.1.2   Contact scenarios: Conditions for Processes of Convergence

13.1.2.1   Historical Spheres of Influence

Over the centuries a number of non-Caucasian languages played major roles in those periods when certain empires gave rise to a particular dominance and prestige of a speech community and their language. Similarly connected is a chronology of foreign invasions into the area that was already inhabited by the different Caucasian peoples, of which only the more 'recent' part can be sketched here (following mostly Wixman 1980 and Coene 2009, which readers should consult for more extensive historical portraits).

Iranian nomads (Scythians, Sarmatians), ancestors of the Ossetians, settled in the fifth century in the foothills of the central North Caucasus. Other Iranian languages, such as Persian, became more important due to the relations with the Kartvelian (Georgian) and Armenian empires. A Jewish Tat-(Iranian) speaking military colony south of Derbent was founded in the sixth century. The invasions of Hunnic tribes in the sixth and those of the Khazars in the seventh to ninth centuries could exemplify the very early and long standing influence of Turkic languages on the northern bounds of the Caucasus. The Khazar Empire was established in the eighth century in the northeastern steppes, and their people are regarded as ancestors of the Kumyks. The invasion from the east in the ninth to tenth century by the Pechenegs, likewise Turkic, was followed by an invasion of the Kypchak (Kypchaks, Kumans, Polovtsy) tribes in the eleventh to thirteenth centuries. Remnant groups of these remain in the North Caucasus (especially Karachay). After that, Oghuz Turks, the ancestors of today's Azerbaijanis, occupied the coastal plain of Dagestan as far as the city of Derbent. Hereafter, the Turkic Nogai established themselves in the area of the Lower Volga in the fifteenth century and were pushed southwards into northern Dagestan by the Mongolic Kalmyks and the Turkic Turkmen (Trukhmen) in the seventeenth century. Some Nogai

(Lesser Nogai) occupied the Kuban region in the Northwest Caucasus and were pushed further into the Caucasus by Crimean Tatars. Finally, the Ottoman Turks began to settle along the eastern Black Sea coast in the seventeenth to eighteenth centuries (see Johanson 2006). During the flourishing of the kingdoms (seventh to ninth centuries) of Orthodox Christian Georgia and Armenia, these languages became important as those of local powers. The Armenians seem to have been in the area for at least 2,500 years. Around the end of the fifth century, Armenia was incorporated into the (Persian) Sassanid Empire. Schulze (2005) and Nichols (2013) also mention a ruler situation, particularly in the sixth or seventh century, when Christian Caucasian Albania came into power with what is today called Caucasian Albanian (Alwan/Old Udi) as its dominant language; this presumably motivated many speakers to shift their language or to become bilingual.

In the ninth century, the incoming troops of the Umayyads and Abbasids introduced Islam and, at this point, brought some Arabic from the south into the area of Dagestan. Friedman (2009) assumes that, finally, after the spread of Islam in the seventeenth century, Arabic would serve as a written lingua franca. This adds another aspect to language influence, namely writing, which at least for North Caucasian had been to a small degree in Arabic script since it was part of religious life and also found use in other contexts (Dobrushina 2013). The southern Caucasus with Georgian and Armenian writing traditions are comparably ancient but not necessarily as pervasive due to the religious borders. The first Russian settlements were presumably those of the Cossacks (Terek and Grebenskoy armies) in the steppes of the east-central North. A later settlement was started by the Ukrainian Kuban Cossacks in the western Caucasus. With the expansion of the Russian empire in the eighteenth and nineteenth centuries, those Russian populations also grew larger and certainly made Russian a useful language for trade and commerce. Wixman (1980) points out that since the 1930s Soviet Union language politics was mainly oriented towards the complete dominance of Russian. Before that it was official policy to support the smaller languages and to develop a standard of literacy with Russian as a role model. After a very brief flourishing of alphabets in Latin scripts, local conventions of writing in Cyrillic were established in the 1930s and 1940s.

This means that there was presumably no single lingua franca for the entire Caucasus area at any time except in very recent history, the second half of the twentieth century particularly, when Russian became a major language of the area, serving not only as the language of administration, education and research but also slowly replacing the traditional regional lingua francas. Avar in the northwest of Dagestan, and Lak and Lezgi served this purpose in the central part. Among the Northwest Caucasus languages, the Western Circassian Adyghe and some Turkic languages (Karachay, Nogay, Ottoman) served as a lingua franca, whereas for

Kartvelian, Georgian was used in this respect (see Chirikba 2008a: 31 for a more extensive list).

13.1.2.2 Population Genetics, Migrations and Language Contacts

In general, human-genetic research corroborates the view of relative immobility in the centre of the Caucasus and suggests low genetic diversity with drift in the male population of isolated populations, and otherwise recently acquired similarity with Turkic and Iranian populations of Western Asia (Nasidze et al. 2004). Yunusbayev et al. (2012) characterize the 'Caucasus as an asymmetric semipermeable barrier to ancient human migrations', and this is the overall picture that emerges from studies of Y-chromosomal DNA. They state 'signals of regional Y chromosome founder effects distinguish the eastern from western North Caucasians. Genetic discontinuity between the North Caucasus and the East European Plain contrasts with continuity through Anatolia and the Balkans, suggesting major routes of ancient gene flows and admixture' (Yunusbayev et al. 2012: 359). The authors conclude that 'irrespective of the Early Upper Palaeolithic presence of anatomically modern humans both south and north of the Caucasus ... the combined autosomal and gender-specific genetic variation of the Caucasian populations testifies to their predominantly southern, Near/ Middle Eastern descent. Y-chromosomal variants under strong founder events, seen in particular among populations inhabiting the northern flank of the High Caucasus Mountain Range, appear to never have expanded to the East European Plain, while the nomadic people of the latter, once settled down predominantly on the northern slopes of the Caucasus, have likely preserved, to a different extent, some of their earlier genetic heritage.' With regard to the population-specific profiles, Balanovsky et al. (2011: 2918) found that each 'linguistic group ... ended up with one major haplogroup from the original Caucasus genetic package, whereas other haplogroups became rare or absent in it. The small isolated population of the Kubachi (Dargwa), in which haplogroup J1*-M267(xP58) became virtually fixed ... exemplifies the influence of genetic drift there.' Genetic drift is the frequency change of an allele due to random variation vis-à-vis natural selection. 'During population differentiation, haplotype clusters within haplogroups emerged and expanded, often becoming population specific. The older clusters became characteristic of groups of populations. Many younger clusters were specific to individual populations (typically speaking different languages)' (Balanovsky et al. 2011: 2918). All in all, population genetic research corroborates the general characterization of Caucasian societies as predominantly endogamic (e.g. Coene 2009: 64; Tuite 1999), which allows only slow drift in L1 and only small influence by direct contact through exogamy (L2 speakers). This is then reversed in those 'moments' of invasion and/or larger language shift.

The situation prior to the Russo-Circassian war (1830–1864) can, especially for the smaller communities with no writing tradition, only be reconstructed by means of reports from outsiders like Jacob Reineggs (1744–1793) or Johann Anton Güldenstädt (1745–1781), in addition to the long-spanning Georgian, Armenian and Persian sources and other deeper historical research by means of archaeology and the like. On the other hand, there are a number of recent historical events precisely known, such as invasions and conquests of the Russian or Ottoman Empire, for example, or other detrimental shifts which eventually led to deportations and other forced migrations of populations, like those of the Ubykhs in 1864 and other speaker populations like the Circassians and the Abkhazians in the 1860s, or like those of the Armenians in Anatolia in 1915/1916 and earlier. The majority of these languages have been maintained until today but have undergone structural changes due to the inevitably strong influence of Turkish (see Höhlig 1997) or other languages of contact. When analysing the historical geographical spread of particular features, it will often be necessary to leave out most of the current diaspora varieties. In cases like Ubykh, extinct since 1992, where the entire population shifted to Turkey, one will need to 'replace' the language in its native territory at the Black Sea around Sochi in order to account for areal effects.

In a number of studies, individual contacts between groups of languages in the Caucasus were focused upon, where the Dagestanian languages have often been taken as a whole. This makes sense because here particular words or structures may have been 'copied' several times (cf. Johanson 2006). Khalidova (2006) studied Avar-Andi contacts with mainly Avar as the donor to the smaller languages. Of those investigating non-Caucasian–Caucasian contacts, the study of Zabitov and Efendiev (2001) on Arab and Persian lexemes in Lezgian or Dzhidalaev (2010) on particular traits of Azerbaijani in Lak can be taken as examples of studies focusing on lexical borrowings and loanword adaptation strategies (e.g. Khalilov 2004). The perspective of Caucasian languages moving out of the area (e.g. Höhlig 1997) can also be turned around: Johanson (2006) points out that the speakers of Western Armenian were, for approximately seven centuries, in contact with Turkish, so that those structures could be copied. To what degree, for example, Kurds, Greeks and other smaller ethnicities, like the Assyrians, were also involved in this interwoven multilingual-net of the past centuries reaching from Anatolia and Kurdistan north to the Caucasus seems to be fairly hard to estimate accurately.

13.1.2.3 'Isolated' Communities, Multilingualism and the 'Vertical Archipelago' Phenomenon

Obviously there are a number of cases that allow one to study at least relatively recent contact influence, as it would take effect in situations where a small community is surrounded by speakers of a distantly related language or languages. These situations may have arisen due to migration of the community itself or due to remnant settlements (enclaves) of a former larger territory. Of this kind we find, for example, the Zakatly Avar dialect in Azerbaijan, the (long-documented) Kisti Chechen dialect in Eastern Georgia, or the Udi dialects of the villages Nizh and Vartashen (today Oguz) in Azerbaijan (Schulze 2005; Gippert 2008). The variety of Udi spoken in Zinobiani in Georgia should be close to that of Vartashen since this settlement was established and populated by Vartashen inhabitants in 1988/1989 during the secession of the Mountain Karabakh region as part of the Armenian–Azerbaijani conflict (see Schulze 2005). The frequency with which these situations led to multilingual settings can be illustrated by further examples given in Chirikba (2008a: 31). According to the author, the Megeb Dargwas, who live in the predominantly Avar-inhabited Gunib district, speak Dargwa, and also Avar, Lak and Russian. Many Abazas:

> in the Karachay-Cherkes Republic, speak, beside Abaza and Russian, also the distantly related Kabardian, and some also Turkic Karachay, the languages of their more numerous neighbours. The Ubykhs, who were numerically smaller than neighbouring Circassians and Abkhazians, were either bilingual with Circassian or Abkhaz as a second language, or trilingual Ubykh–Circassian–Abkhaz. In the Muslim Georgian area of Adzharia in the southern Caucasus adjacent to Turkey, Turkish has traditionally been the second language . . .; besides, nearly all Adzharians speak Russian . . . The very small Laz and Abkhaz communities in Adzharia, are to some degree quadrilingual since they speak . . . also Georgian, Russian, and Turkish . . . Avar was often used in the past by various Dagestanian communities as a lingua franca, and even a special form of Avar called *bolmac* ('public language') had developed . . . To some extent Turkic Kumyk was also used in some North Caucasian communities as a kind of lingua franca, a role now overwhelmingly taken over by Russian.
>
> *(Chirikba 2008a: 31)*

In terms of descriptions of exile varieties we also find examples in Vaux (1998) of Armenian in Yerevan, Tbilisi or Julfa, and in Chirikba (2008b) of Armenian spoken in Abkhazia, illustrating the influence of various linguistic contexts. Finally, as mentioned above, there are a number of communities with a great number of speakers of Caucasian languages scattered all over Central Turkey (see Koryakov 2006), some of them already having lived there for more than one-and-a-half centuries. Here we find limited descriptive data, mostly only for languages of Northwest Caucasian, like Turkish Kabardian (Gordon and Applebaum 2006) or Turkish Adyghe (Höhlig 1997) in Turkey. In particular, the two Circassian languages, whose speakers are usually found under the name *Cherkess*, are spread all over the Middle East, including Jordan, Syria and Israel but also Eastern Europe (Kosovo) and the USA.

Social factors, such as religious, ethnic, historical and political groupings, also limit or facilitate potential intermarriages or closer interaction. The major religious groups in the area today are Sunni Muslims and the Georgian and Armenian Orthodox Christian groups. Historically, the situation was presumably more heterogeneous, since local traditional beliefs, habits and folklores point to Zoroastrian, Mithraic and other substrates (Coene 2009). It is also assumed that Judaism spread as result of the Khazar settlement from the seventh or eighth century into northeastern Dagestan but disappeared by the thirteenth century (see Wixman 1980: 68). Smaller groups built their own enclaves, such as the Mountain Jews in Georgia and Azerbaijan, who speak Juhuri, a variety of Tat (see Authier 2012).

The physical geography of the main two mountain crests in terms of inhabitable valleys, migration-blocking mountain ridges, glaciers, water sheds, etc., certainly plays a major role in explorative migration, usage of pastures, settlement sizes and trading relations. In this way geography will have a regulating influence on the degrees of freedom of possible contact and interactions. With respect to the topographical situations in a populated high mountain area, Nichols (2013) used the term 'vertical archipelago'. In particular Dagestan is characterized by a high degree of multilingualism, especially among the male speakers and among those of smaller languages. Here – as a vertical component – the highland villagers usually know the languages that the lowlanders speak but not vice versa. The male population would spend a major part of their working life in the lowlands trading and working part-time, especially during the summer. A more recent sociolinguistic study of Dobrushina (2013) can provide support for Nichols' idea. Based on fieldwork surveys aiming at the acquired multilingualism of informants and similar to that of their parents, grandparents and great-grandparents, Dobrushina (2013) was able to sketch a picture of multilingualism that spans several generations back into the nineteenth century. Furthermore, Dobrushina describes a network of hosts (Archi: *xeˤle*), a social network which can at least be ascribed to the southeast outer boundaries, i.e. today's southern Dagestan and Azerbaijan, but which can certainly be verified for and extended to other areas of the Caucasus. These host relations comprise people who travel from the highlands down to market places and seasonal working places, trading their local goods. Such social networks would also include a form of exchange where the labour of young adult men is in part reciprocated by the transfer of a more widespread, useful and prestigious language of the lowlands. Dobrushina undertook the survey in three neighbouring villages with a different L1 (Archi, Lak and Avar) language each, differing in the size of the total speaker population and in prestige. L1-speakers of languages of higher prestige showed lower degrees of multilingualism and vice versa. Nichols (2013) and Gippert (2008) draw attention to the fact that in recent decades vertical relations have been disrupted, multilingualism is fading out, and parental language transmission of these small languages is on the decline, which all leads rapidly to endangerment. The predominant language shifts of these younger generations follow the borders of the major national languages (Russian, Georgian, Armenian, Azerbaijani, Turkish).

For a wider picture of the historical sociolinguistic situation, uncertainties remain concerning the number of speakers and semi-speakers, that is, L2/L3-speakers, which is to some degree more important in order to account for overlaps and language-specific contact phenomena. The use of lingua francas and interethnic contacts, within religious or ethnic boundaries, relates to a mechanism that was proposed as one of the most potent sources of contact-induced language change, as observable in unsupervised L2/L3/… acquisition, and which leads in most cases to incomplete acquisition (Lupyan and Dale 2010). Subsequently, larger groups of L2/L3 speakers are more easily facilitating the mechanism of misinterpretation, reanalysis, overgeneralization and fossilization, that is, the establishment of structural errors. Linguistic concepts (sound categories, morphological categories, semantic categories) are more or less consciously projected onto the L2 in analogy to the L1. As a consequence, languages used as a lingua franca and other more widely used 'bigger' languages tend to be simplified. Accommodated speech plays a significant role here; acquisition of this type of speech results in a number of structural parallelisms (including phonetic similarity and functional calques) as well as semantic transparency.

13.2   Phonological and Phonetic Areal Typology of the Caucasus

13.2.1   Phonological and Phonetic Areal Typology

A phonological areal typology aims at a distribution of attributes and characteristic features (see Hyman 2009 for an excellent discussion). A phonetically oriented areal typology considers the diversity and variability that occurs with the phonetic implementation of a phonemic contrast. If we take the voicing contrast of stops for example, we find in languages like Spanish or Russian that a /b/ in word-initial position is pronounced with an early voice onset, i.e. vocal fold vibration starts before the release of the bilabial closure. The voiceless counterpart /p/ would have a voice onset that starts slightly after the lip opening. In contrast other languages like German would have a 'voiced' bilabial stop /b/ starting about the same time as the /p/ in Spanish. The voice onset time (Lisker and Abramson 1964), that is, the distance in time of closure release and voice onset, serves here as a function of the abstract (phonemic) two-way contrast. From this perspective, it makes the most sense to adopt an understanding of phonetics and phonology as inseparable entities as, for example, argued for by Ohala (1990) and Blevins (2006). Such a view allows one to talk about the phonetic implementation of abstract contrasts in different phonetic domains (segmental, intersegmental, suprasegmental) as well as about diachronic processes and universals at the same time. From this viewpoint, most sound change relevant for phonemic distinctions would be driven by the listener's misinterpretation of articulatory variations on the part of the speaker. These variations can be caused by a number of (external) mostly speaker-related factors (see Hickey 2012b). Such could be the influence of the actual L1 or L2, L3 and LX in terms of competing systems, which all interfere and compete (see e.g. Blevins and Wedel 2009; Flege et al. 2003). With respect to articulatory and auditory capabilities, physical factors such as denture, vocal tract morphology and hearing (loss), etc., also need to be accommodated by a speaker/listener and create peculiar means of compensation. These processes add to redundancy in phonetic substance, that is, the way the contrast is expressed in the language and finally the way it is realized by the speaker, especially in fast speech. Regular speaker variations can also reflect social group norms and thus social barriers (Hickey 2012a). The tendencies towards regularity and systematicity driven by analogy and accommodation within a population of subgroups would then still lead to an areally homogeneous pattern, but presumably only when these subgroups are in contact. Trudgill (1996: 13) states that 'dense multiplex networks typical of relatively closed, stable, non-fluid communities are more likely to lead to conformity in linguistic behaviour and to the maintenance of group norms as well as the successful carrying through of ongoing linguistic change.'

However, we are looking here at the level of forms, in particular, sounds. What would the phonological and phonetic level tell us vis-à-vis the other linguistic levels? A number of authors point out (Hickey 2012a; McMahon 1994; Trudgill 2011: 2) that with regard to time depth, phonetic and phonological changes happen rapidly. Therefore we would also need to consider other mechanisms such as accommodation, where, especially in mutual bilingual situations, a convergence of L2 varieties, i.e. the varieties spoken by bilinguals, has been observed (see e.g. Flege and Port 1981 for Arabic to English). Most of the changes are fairly subtle for a particular point in time but accumulative given that, on the one hand, a number of speakers are experiencing similar influences within the community and, on the other hand, certainly repetitive input occurs. Eventually such phonetic variation can result in phonological changes which involve one or two speaker generations. Nonetheless, a basic assumption for sound change (Blevins 2006; Ohala 1990) would include the misinterpretation of a sound by a listener as one of the key mechanisms. Social hierarchies, concepts of prestige, traditions of loanword adaptation and the like can reinforce this perception-driven process. Lexical borrowing may enforce the borrowing of segments and other characteristics such as alternative patterns of word prosody. The notion of frequency or reoccurrence of words or functional structures seems to predict the subsequent changes in phonetic forms (Bybee 2003) so that frequency also emerges as the major factor for markedness (Haspelmath 2006). Thomason and Kaufman (1988) already noted that marked features are harder to acquire in a contact situation with late acquisition patterns. Other more production-driven changes, which involve continuous biases, for example, of biomechanical couplings of articulators and thus preferences of temporal coordination, lead only to slow changes within the population of speakers (see e.g. Lancia and Grawunder 2014). Given the longstanding presence of the three Caucasian families and the persistent contact of non-Caucasian in the area, stabilization and enhancing of local features can be assumed. In fact, similar to other major languages within a large multilingual environment such as, for example, English in India or French on the African West Coast, Daniel et al. (2011) demonstrate that Russian has also undergone some changes in Dagestan.

13.2.2   Phonological Features: Structure and Occurrence

A 'feature' in this context is used as a more familiar term as it is often met in the literature (Russ. признак). With respect to the recent discussion of the nature of features by Ladd (2014), the term 'attributive features' is used here in order to account for this wider view. The number of occurrences in a given phonological inventory, which reflects how often a particular attributive feature is applied, needs to be combined with the actual degrees of freedom that are used in the inventories of contrasts and that are thus much more revealing. Amongst the most challenging issues when accounting for the occurrence of features are the individual approaches of different authors towards the phonemic status of particular contrasts (Maddieson 1984: 4) – a general problem in typological approaches but also in other areal-linguistic research (see e.g. Gilles and Siebenhaar 2010; Maddieson 1984). For the languages of the Caucasus, this concerns in particular the status of contrasts involving secondary articulation such as labialization, gemination, palatalization, pharyngealization of consonants, as well the status of nasalized, long, pharyngealized vowels, and in general the status of vowel combinations.

13.2.2.1   Inventories and Sub-inventory Sizes

Caucasian languages are well-known for their large phoneme inventories with 50 or more phonemes, especially consonants. This is true in the case of the NWC languages and to some degree also for some of the northern NEC languages. Indeed, before the description of many Khoisan languages, Ubykh, with over 80, was considered the language with the highest number of contrasts, that is, the biggest phoneme inventory in the world's languages (see Catford 1983). Among the SC languages, Georgian, the biggest Caucasian language in terms of speakers, uses a relatively low number of consonant and vowel contrasts (see Figure 13.1).

However, Mingrelian and Laz also have more medium inventories, as well as Svan, with the only exception being its northern dialects. The vowel inventories of neighbouring Nakh and Dagestanian languages

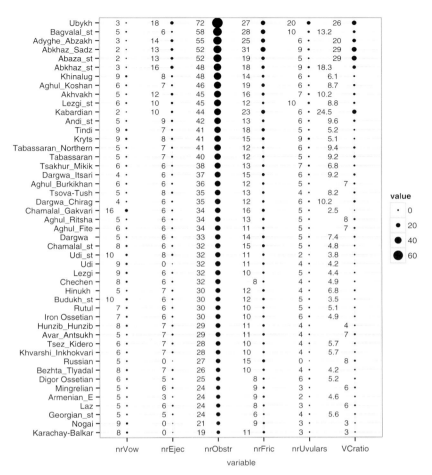

Figure 13.1 Sub-inventory sizes and vowel/consonant ratio. Numbers are based on descriptions in Alekseev et al. (1999), Harris (1991), Kibrik and Kodzasov (1990), Smeets (1994), Job (2004), Hewitt (1989), Testen (1997), Vaux (1998), Tolstoj (1997)[1]

appear to be comparably large and larger. The vowel systems of Bezhta (Kibrik and Kodzasov 1990), Lower Chechen (Comrie 1981) and Upper Bal, a dialect of Svan (Gippert 2008; see Figure 2) serve as examples of languages with long and umlauted vowels. The NWC family form is the opposite, with very low vocalism but high consonantism. Trubetzkoy (1958) suggested the number of vowel contrasts in relation to the number of consonant contrasts as a means of assessing the linguistic profile of a language as a basis for comparison. Maddieson (1984) links this consonant-to-vowel ratio to a general typological perspective. For the Caucasus, however (see Figure 13.1), a vowel/consonant ratio of a sample of 47

---

[1] Abbreviations: nrVow = number of vowels; nrEjec = number of ejectives; nrObstr = number of obstruents; nrFric = number of fricatives; nrUvulars = number of uvulars; VCratio = vowel/consonant ratio.

doculects, one would expect a stable figure if there is anything like a homogeneous setup, but the ratio seems to correlate with consonant inventory size (r^2 = 0.57, r = 0.76, t = 7.88, d.f. = 45, p < 0.00001). Furthermore, there appears to be a growing complexity of smaller languages that are closer to the main Caucasus crest, where we can describe a 'stacking' of contrasts in terms of feature combination. This generally involves consonants in the NWC languages, where we see labialization, palatalization and pharyngealization (see Section 13.2.2.3), and appending of a retroflex (/ʈʂ, ɖʐ, ʂ, ʐ/) and alveolo-palatal (/tɕ, dʑ, ɕ, ʑ/) fricative series and also, in some cases, the development of an (unaspirated voiceless) 'tensed' stop series. NWC and some of the adjacent Andic languages of the NEC also include fricatives in the glottalic contrast. For the NEC languages, the contrasts extend to the vowels, where nasalization, pharyngealization, length and diphthongization (vowel + vowel or vowel + glide combinations) are employed. In addition, a geminated series of stops and fricatives come into play for the northwestern part of Nakh-Dagestanian, and a 'tensed' stop series in the central and southeastern part – similar to NWC.

Trudgill (2004) reintroduced a discussion with regard to a relationship between inventory size and speaker population (community) size, given the various expected effects of social network density, contact intensity, adult L2 speaker proportion, etc. This question was also addressed in relation to the Caucasus by Nichols (2013), who applied her own measure of inventory size, including additional morphosyntactic features as well. Similar to her results, for a sample of 74 doculects, only a weak relationship can be presumed here at all for log-transformed population size (numbers taken from ASJP,[2] Brown et al. 2013) and consonant inventory size (r = −0.31, r^2 = 0.098; t = −2.81, d.f. = 72, p = 0.006). Thus population size could only explain 10 per cent of the trend in the consonant inventory size. Arguably, the average speech community size and its correspondence to social network size and density and again the L2 user proportion would, in contrast, need to be taken into account, although these are harder to assess.

Vowel inventories On the other hand, we can take the vowel system of Bezhta (see Map 13.2), another NEC language from the Avar-Andi-Tsezic branch that is also described as having umlauted vowels, length contrast and nasalized vowels. If we add these contrasts into the vowel scheme, it appears even bigger than the Chechen system of monophthongs (even when adding the six diphthongs). This is similar to the closely related language Hunzib, which Isakov and Khalilov (2012) describe as having at least 24 vowel phonemes, based on eight

---

[2] This is the Automated Similarity Judgment Program by Søren Wichmann and his colleagues: see asjp.clld.org.

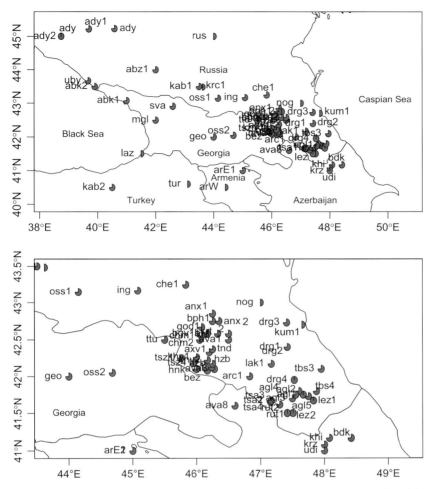

Map 13.2 Types of phonation contrasts in obstruent series (*N* = 85). The quartiles of the circles correspond to the number of types of contrast (two-, three-, four-way contrasts shown as black quartiles of circles)[3]

basic vowel qualities (/i, e, ɨ, ə, a, u, o, ɒ/) (see van den Berg 2005) with the addition of long (/iː, eː, ɨː, əː, aː, uː, oː, ɒː/) and nasalized vowels (/ĩ, ẽ, ɨ̃, ə̃, ã, ũ, õ, ɒ̃/). For Bezhta the combined nasal and long vowels also come into play, adding another series of contrasts. However, most descriptions comprise only the 'basic' vowel system and add those

---

[3] Abbreviations used in Maps 13.2–13.6: abz, Abaza; abk, Abkhaz; ady, Adyghe; ag, Aghul; axv, Akhvakh; ani/anx, Andi; arc, Archi; arE, Armenian East; arW, Armenian West; ava, Avar; aze, Azeri; bgv, Bagvalal; bez, Bezhta; bph, Botlikh; bdk, Budukh; chm, Chamalal; che, Chechen; drg, Dargwa; geo, Georgian; god, Godoberi; hnk, Hinukh; hzb, Hunzib; ing, Ingush; kab, Kabardian; kmk, Kalmyk; kcr, Karachay-Balkar; krt, Karata; khi, Khinalug; khv, Khvarshi; krz, Kryz; kum, Kumyk; kku, Kurdish; lak, Lak; laz, Laz; lez, Lezgi; mgl, Mingrelian; nog, Nogai; oss, Ossetian; rus, Russian; rut, Rutul; sva, Svan; tbs, Tabassaran; tat, Tat; tnd, Tindi; tsa, Tsakhur; tsz, Tsez; ttu, Tsova-Tush; tur, Turkish; uby, Ubykh; udi, Udi; zza, Zazaki.

with contrasts of secondary articulation (nasalization, pharyngealization) or length separately. Umlauted vowels would be considered
basic too, whereas in their formant structure, these only seem to
group for Lezgi and Khinalug with front rounded vowels (see
Catford 1994). Other samples for Lak (Catford 1994) and Bezhta
(Grawunder 2015) seem to suggest that umlauted vowels and front
rounded vowels as in Azerbaijani cannot easily be equated since they
show different formant characteristics.

Often not all possible vowel contrasts are analysed in the surveyed
descriptions, which is especially true for contrastive vowel length.
Although there is still discussion about the vowel inventories of some
NWC languages, these vowel systems can, with Catford (1992) and others
before, be characterized as vertical since these systems seem to mainly
contrast in vowel height. Most descriptions (Colarusso 1988; Hewitt 2005)
suggest two vowel qualities /ə, a/ for Ubykh, Abaza and Abkhaz as well as
two vowels /ə, a/ with an additional length contrast /aː/ (Höhlig 1997)
sometimes for the varieties of Adyghe (Western Circassian) and a three-
vowel system (/ə, e, a/ or /i, ə, ɐ/) for Kabardian (Eastern Circassian) (Catford
1994; Gordon and Applebaum 2006). From a phonetic standpoint, however, one can clearly observe cardinal vowel qualities (like [i, a, u]), and the
contextual predictability of such vowels may not be that transparent for
a second language learner.

Klimov (1994) and Catford (1994) also state that Caucasian vowel systems
employ no diphthongs, with Chechen and Ingush (Nichols 1994: 1) as the
only exceptions, where the sequences that correspond to the long vowels
are analysed as having a long initial vowel portion instead of a glide, like
those of the short vowels (/e > je/ versus /eː > ie/; /ü > ɥö/ versus /üː > üö~üe/;
/u > wo/ versus /uː > uo~uə/). Here one would need to argue against all
similar monophonemic analyses in favour of a biphonemic contrast of
glide plus vowel or vowel plus glide (/V+w/; /V+j/; /V+ɥ/), e.g. in Svan
(Gippert 2008) or Tsez (Job 2004) or recently Tabasaran (Vadzhibov 2012).
Kodzasov (1999) argues that the Andic language Godoberi is the only one
with diphthongs.

13.2.2.2   Commonalities and Overlapping of Attributive Features in the Caucasus

For the following discussion of the Caucasus, those attributive features are
taken that span across the Caucasian families in the core area (Maps 13.2
and 13.3).

Number of initiation (phonation) contrasts As already pointed out
above, all languages of the three (Inner) Caucasian language families
employ at least a three-way contrast in the obstruent system. Therefore,
we find as default contrasts in all three Caucasian families: ejective

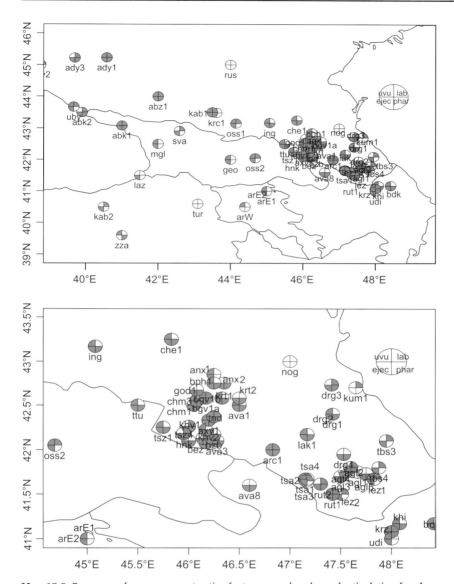

Map 13.3 Presence of common contrastive features: uvular place of articulation [uvu], labialization [lab], glottalic initiation (ejectives) [ejec], pharyngealization [phar]. Number of features shown as black quartiles of circles

(glottalic) versus aspirated/non-aspirated (pulmonic) versus voiced (pulmonic) obstruents. These ternary contrasts are additionally found in non-Caucasian peripheral Ossetic (Iron and Digor) and varieties of Eastern Armenian. A ternary contrast with voiced, voiceless unaspirated and voiceless aspirated stops is also found in the Transcaucasian periphery with Kurmanji Kurdish, Zazaki and some Assyrian (Neo-Aramaic) dialects (e.g. Barwar, Khan 2008: 29). Binary (two-way) systems with (voiced versus voiceless) pulmonic obstruents are otherwise found in Altaic languages (Turkic: Nogai, Kumyk; Mongolic: Kalmyk) and Indo-European (Russian) (see Map 13.2).

Especially for languages of the Lezgian group (Lezgi proper, Tabasaran) and for Lak but apparently also for Chechen (Nichols 1994), we find analyses of so-called 'tensed' stops, unaspirated pulmonic stops with a long closure. However, in Lezgi (Haspelmath 1993), Lak (Anderson 1997) and varieties of Dargwa (e.g. Itsari: Sumbatova and Mutalov 2003), these (voiceless unaspirated) 'tensed' stops do also occur word-initially and build, for a number of authors, a fourth series of non-aspirated voiceless stops. Among the NWC languages, this is the case for the Adyghe dialects of Shapsugh (Shapsegh), Armavir (Temirgoy) and Bzhedukh (Colarusso 1988). In these languages, aspiration would then need to be counted as a contrastive feature, whereas in other ternary (three-way) contrasts, including glottalic obstruents, aspiration is just an additional (redundant) attribute. Hence, for a number of NEC languages, like Chechen, Tsova-Tush, Bezhta or Hinukh, these long segments seem only to occur in word-medial position. But since these involve pulmonic and glottalic obstruents, including affricates and fricatives but also nasals and liquids, an analysis as geminates is certainly justified. The involvement of glottalic stops in this gemination seems to occur mainly among the Avar-Andi-Tsezic languages.

Ejectives (glottalic initiation) Tuite (1999: 217) pointed out that a quest for common traits in all three Caucasian families would result presumably in only one shared feature, the ejectives. Other authors (Catford 1977; Chirikba 2008a; Klimov 1994) saw more overlap of other non-phonological features such as complex agglutinative morphology, the marking of the agent (ergative and ergative-like constructions), or verbal conjoining and relativization.

However since the occurrence of glottalic stops (ejectives) has also been described for non-Caucasian languages of the Caucasus area such as Ossetic (Testen 1997), Eastern Armenian (Vaux 1998) and Kurmanji Kurdish (Jastrow 1977) and, according to Chirikba (2008a: 45), even for varieties of Turkish and for Neo-Aramaic in Urmia, Van and Mosul (Iraq), and since this feature seems to be phonetically well definable (Grawunder 2013; Grawunder et al. 2010), it is taken here as one of the core features of the Caucasus area.

The occurrence of the glottalic initiation feature, mainly in the form of ejective stops and affricates, ends outside the geographical area in the realm of peripheral languages and can therefore also serve best for deli-miting the linguistic area (see Map 13.3). Contrastive ejective fricatives are only found in NWC languages. However, phonetically there often seems to be more of a 'fade-out' in the periphery in terms of a faint phonetic realization of ejective stops, as is observed for varieties of Udi (Nidzh variety: Schulze-Fürhoff 1994), some coastal varieties of Georgian (Authier, personal communication), and Laz (Lacroix 2009). Simultaneously, there are also regular sound changes in the form of deglottalization taking place (see Fallon 2001: 217).

On the other hand, even such varieties of non-related Indo-European languages as Ossetic Iron and Digor (IE, Iranian: Testen 1997), Eastern Armenian (IE, Armenian: Vaux 1998) and Kurmanji Kurdish (IE, Iranian: Jastrow 1977) were described as employing ejectives or at least having ejective-like characteristics, the presumed results of contact. These slight categorical shifts lead only to small deviances within a category but not to a new contrast, i.e. a new phonemic category. Most likely we see here the influence of L2 speakers (re)introducing another contrast (glottalic/non-glottalic). Such a process would leave the aspirated stop as 'marked' because it is phonetically marked. Aspiration of stops was shown to be one of the most easily 'transferable' features in speaker contact (see e.g. Babel 2009). Chirikba (2008a: 43) states that for the non-Caucasian languages, glottalization in the Caucasus is attested in Ossetic, the Eastern Armenian dialects (e.g. Tiflis, Artvin), in dialects of Kumyk (e.g. Kaytag), northern Azeri (e.g. Zakatala-Kakh) and Karachay-Balkar (e.g. Malkar). Ossetic has glottalization not only in words borrowed from the Caucasian languages but also in the native IE vocabulary (e.g. *st'aly* 'star'). The same is claimed for the Malkar dialect of Karachay-Balkar (e.g. *k'ordum* 'I saw'). In the Kumyk dialects, glottalization is explained by the NEC substrate. Chirikba (2008a) also mentions that the population of several Kumyk villages, whose ancestors are known to be speakers of Avar originally, represents a separate Kumyk dialect, displaying such non-Turkic traits as the presence of glottalized consonants and the violation of the vowel harmony rules, etc.

Places of articulation Generally we find five places of articulation: bilabial, alveolar, velar, uvular and laryngeal. Additionally, pharyngeals and laterals would come into play as two other places that are employed across families, but these are only employed in NWC and NEC languages. The laterals comprise a series of obstruents that occur in the order of lateral fricative /ɬ/ > lateral affricate /tɬ/ > lateral affricate ejective /tɬ'/ in addition to the lateral approximant /l/. To be precise, this distinction actually concerns the direction of airstream in the oral cavity (lateral versus central). The actual place of articulation varies, both contextually and speaker specifically, especially with regard to tongue contact in the stop part of the affricates between (coronal) alveolar [tɬ] or postalveolar [ʈɬ] and (dorsal) palatal [cʎ̥] or even velar [kʟ̥] position. However, the coronal realization [tɬ] is the one most commonly observed.

The SC and NEC languages typically show no labio-dentals (/f, v/) but do show labio-velars [w] in native vocabulary, with a few exceptions for /f/ described for Laz (Holisky 1991), Rutul and Budukh (Alekseev 1994a, 1994b). On the other hand, all NWC languages seem to additionally employ voiced and voiceless labio-dentals. Kabardian, Abaza and Abkhaz also have a glottalic fricative [f'] (Hewitt 2005). The lack of labio-dentals is also seen in Turkic but not in Armenian and the Iranian languages.

A phonemic glottal stop occurs in most of the SC and NEC languages. For the inventory of Lak by Alekseev et al. (1999) a glottal stop is not analysed as phonemic, although other authors such as Kibrik and Kodzasov (1990) or Anderson (1997) included it. For the NWC languages, most authors agree with Colarusso (1988) that the glottal stop is sub-phonemic in Abaza and not phonemic in Abkhaz and Ubykh either.

Uvulars There is an almost ubiquitous occurrence of uvular stops (affricates) and fricatives in the languages of the Caucasus (see Map 13.3), which was considered as another commonality by Klimov (1994) and Chirikba (2008a). Catford (1977: 288) states: '[i]f there is only one type of dorsal fricative it is always uvular, not velar'. This seems to hold for Ossetic (/q, qw/: Testen 1997), Kurmanji Kurdish (/q/: Jastrow 1977) and Armenian (/χ, ʁ/: Vaux 1998). The use of the uvular place of articulation follows the following implicational scale: uvular fricative > uvular stop > labialized uvular fricative > labialized uvular stop. For the Avar-Andi-Tsezic branch but also other NEC languages, the uvular stops are often realized as affricates, for example in Chamalal (Magomedova 2004), Tsez (Alekseev and Radjabov 2004), Hinukh (Isakov and Khalilov 2004), Tsakhur (Talibov 2004). In the Turkish language Nogai, the uvular stop maintains at least a subphonemic status, whereas for Karachay-Balkar and Kumyk (Tolstoj 1997), the uvular stops are described as phonemic, which is not uncommon for Turkic in general. Furthermore, if we look at Kumyk near the Caspian Sea in the northeast, we observe that uvular articulation can also be easily perceived as slightly glottalized (ejective), especially in contexts where a final back vowel+/q/ is adjacent to a velar or uvular stop onset. However, the occurrence of uvulars fades out in the contiguous languages on the outer periphery, where uvulars are not described as being unconditionally contrastive for the standard languages Azerbaijani/Azeri (Schönig 1998: 249), Kalmyk (Bläsing 2003) and Turkish (Kornfilt 1997) but where they seem to occur as allophonic variants, for example of /k/ in the context of back vowels.

The voiced uvular stop [ɢ] is, according to Kibrik and Kodzasov (1990), found only in such NEC languages as Andi, Dübek Tabasaran, Rutul, Tsakhur, Kryz, Budukh and Khinalug, 'though it is reconstructed for both NC groups and for Proto-NC' (Chirikba 2008a: 48). However, since the voiced uvular does not occur unanimously in all languages (going by the descriptions in the literature), for example, not in Andi and Rutul in Alekseev et al. (1999), and not in all Dargwa dialects (Kibrik and Kodzasov 1990), it seems to keep its 'typologically rare character' across the Caucasus area.

Pharyngeals Chirikba (2008a) extends the 'uvular argument' to a generalization of a 'rich postvelar consonant system', a notion that might serve as an additional 'pan-Caucasian' characteristic. This postvelar attribute would involve the occurrence of uvulars, pharyngeals and laryngeals. Pharyngeals, in terms of voiced and voiceless fricatives, can be found in most of the NWC and NEC languages but not in SC languages (see Map 13.3). In fact they are not described in Andi and Botlikh (Alekseev et al. 1999: 228) and not in NWC Ubykh (Colarusso 1988; Hewitt 2005). Furthermore, they are also not found in Ossetic and Armenian but are found in Iranian Zazaki, Kurmanji Kurdish and Neo-Aramaic (see Map 13.5). Although the fricatives are transcribed as 'pharyngeal' (voiced) [ʕ] and voiceless [ħ], their articulation is characterized as involving epiglottal constriction (Kodzasov 1990; Ladefoged and Maddieson 1996). Kibrik and Kodzasov (1990) also analysed two additional 'epiglottal' fricatives [ʜ] and [ʢ] for Agul. However, it seems that these occur conditionally and thus count more as allophonic variants (see also Ladefoged and Maddieson 1996: 168).

Secondary articulation is usually referred to as modifying the primary articulation of a segment. Here one can expect the most varying points in the descriptions, since a decision about a segmental or intersegmental or suprasegmental secondary articulation entails a number of attributes that again are meaningful for the number of contrasts in the segmental inventory. It turns out to be more useful to assign the attributive feature to a word or syllable instead of just a particular segment, since these suprasegmental features have a larger domain, often spanning over the adjacent syllables. Nonetheless, this typological survey can only reflect the way it is laid out in the descriptions.

Labialization Labialization is seen here as an alteration of a C(C)V sequence achieved by inserting an intersegmental labial element (> C(C)WV), most typically a labio-dental [v] or labio-velar [w] but also a labio-palatal [ɥ] and bilabial [β, ɸ]. Although such consonant alteration can be seen as cross-linguistically widespread, it appears to occur consistently throughout the inventories of the Caucasus (see Map 13.3), even including labial consonants for some languages. In the SC languages and a number of northern NEC languages (Tsez, Hunzib, Hinukh), this is analysed as a separate segment that can follow a stop, e.g. /k'u, qw, ɡv, t͡ɬw/, or fricative, /ʁw/ (see e.g. Alekseev et al. 1999). Other languages, especially in the NWC and NEC languages to some degree, are described as using labialization extensively as a secondary feature, which would usually mean that there is a contrastive bilabial glide component at the burst phase of the stop (see Grawunder et al. 2010), typically transcribed with [ʷ] in IPA or [°] in traditional Caucasianist studies (see Klimov 1994). In the grammar of the standard literary variety of Western Circassian Adyghe (Rogava and Kerasheva 1966) we even find /pʷ/, /mʷ/ or /ʔʷ/

along with other labialized stops or fricatives of their plain, i.e. aspirated, ejective or voiced series. In the table for consonantal phonemes for Literary Eastern Circassian (Kabardian) by Hewitt (2005), only one series of labialized velar stops (voiced, aspirated, ejective) occurs vis-à-vis a uvular series of non-labialized and labialized stops. Similarly, in Hewitt's presentation of the phonemes in Ubykh, the non-labialized velar stop series seems to only have allophonic status. Hence, this feature alternates on the descriptive level between a secondary and primary feature. Hewitt (2004) illustrates the resulting inventories for the two different approaches for the Andi language Bagvalal as provided by Gudava (1964) and by Kibrik (2001: 41). Whereas the articulatory and acoustic outcome may only shift gradually from a fricative to an approximant [v ~ ʋ ~ β ~ β̞ ~ w] and finally to a partial rounding of a following vowel, the analysis again results in a different number of segments and thus a different inventory profile. The strongest structural argument for the monophonemic analysis appears to be the existence of labialized obstruents in word-final position, like Bagvalal /kitw/ 'cat', /ʁandʷ/ 'crow' or /haʃʷ/ 'voice' (Kibrik 2001: 38). A similar example is given by Tsakhur (Hewitt 2004: 52). Apart from Caucasian languages, Armenian also employs contrasts involving an obstruent + labial element, but these are of low frequency. Also, Testen (1997) decided on Iron and Digor Ossetian for a secondary articulation, i.e. monophonemic analysis, of the labialized uvular stops.

13.2.2.3   Areal Pockets

Some of the attributive features seem to occur only in circumscribable subareas, sometimes crossing the genealogical lines defined by the three families (Map 13.4).

Nasalization Properties such as nasalization or pharyngealization, which can occur sub-phonemically or only in a restricted set of the lexicon or in particular speech registers, may be easily overlooked, and we can therefore assume that the current list is still incomplete. Nasalization appears contrastively in a number of NEC languages, especially in the Avar-Andic-Tsezic branch, such as Bezhta (Kibrik and Kodzasov 1990), Hunzib (van den Berg 1995), Khwarshi (Khalilova 2009) and Inkhokhvari (Kibrik and Kodzasov 1990), but also the southern Andi languages (Akhvakh, Chamalal, Tindi, Karata) (see Catford 1994). Nasal vowels are also described for the Gjunej dialect of Lezgi (Mejlanova 1970). Furthermore, Kibrik and Kodzasov (1990) describe conditional nasalization occurring between 'emphatics' (e.g. [нãн] 'stool, chair'; [ʕuʕra] 'struma') in the Antsukh dialect of Avar. It appears sporadically in the NEC Nakh branch; Nichols (1997) describes nasalization for Chechen as conditionally occurring, for example at the coda of infinitives in /-an/, and similarly for Ingush (Nichols 2011). Otherwise, nasalization seems to

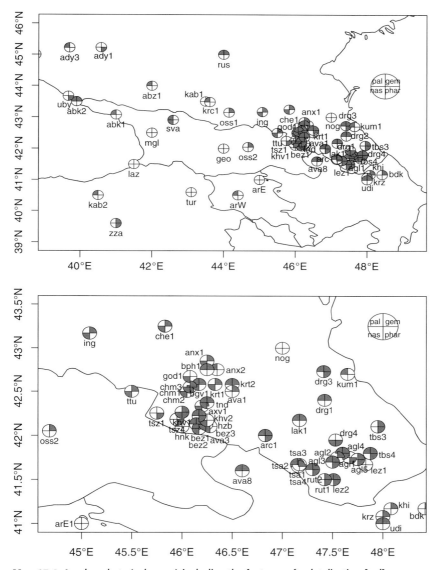

Map 13.4 Areal pockets (subareas) including the features of palatalization [pal], nasalization [nas], gemination [gem], pharyngealization [phar]. Doculect labels correspond to isocodes. Number of features shown as black quartiles of circles

be absent from the rest of the central and eastern NEC languages as well as from the NWC and SC languages (see Catford 1994).

Laterals The main area for the occurrence of lateral fricatives and affricates can be described for an area in the North Caucasus including only members of the Northeast Caucasian and Northwest Caucasian families. For Northeast Caucasian, only languages of the Andi-Avar-Tsezic group are involved. One exception here is Archi, a small one-village language belonging to the Lezgian branch but in geographical adjacency to villages with Avar and with Lak as a first language. From ethnographic work (Dobrushina 2013) it becomes clear that Archi speakers are very likely to also speak at least the major language Avar, which has frequently occurring lateral fricatives (/ɬ/) and affricates (/tɬ/, /tɬ'/). As van den Berg (2005) observes, Akhvakh shows the complete set of seven laterals /tɬ, tɬ:, tɬ', tɬ':, ɬ, ɬ:, l/, whereas Andi and Avar are in between – Andi lacking /tɬ:, tɬ':/ and Avar lacking the opposition for gemination (traditionally called 'intensity' in the Russian literature: see Section 13.2.2.1) in the lateral affricates; the singleton voiceless affricate occurs only in some Avar dialects.

Sibilants The NWC languages in particular employ a large number of fricatives, especially sibilants. This enlargement of the fricative inventory is brought about by involvement in contrasts of secondary articulation labialization, pharyngealization and palatalization, but also by the inclusion of gemination and glottalic initiation (ejection). On the one hand, the palatalized and labialized series in NWC languages have 'developed' into two additional series of sibilants, a retroflex (apico-palato-alveolar) and a lamino-palato-alveolar series (see Colarusso 1988). On the other hand, we can see that the sibilants, in an area that comprises both NWC languages and the geographically close Andi sub-branch of the NEC languages, take part in the pulmonic versus glottalic contrast. In the Andi languages, in addition, the sibilant inventory is enlarged by their geminated (intense) counterparts so that we find, for example, in Bagvalal (Kibrik 2001) these segments: /s, s', s:, z, ʃ, ʃ', ʃ:, ʒ/, labialized versions /sʷ, s:ʷ, sʷ', zʷ, ʃʷ, ʃ:ʷ, ʃʷ', ʒʷ/ plus most of the corresponding affricates /ts, tsʷ, ts', tsʷ', tʃ, tʃʷ, dʒ, tʃ'/. Some of the Lezgic languages of Nakh-Dagestanian also employ palatalized versions so that Kibrik and Testelec (1999: 16) identify /tsʲ, tsʲ', sʲ, s:ʲ, zʲ/ for Tsakhur.

Pharyngealization Pharyngealization is characterized by an epiglottal constriction, which is auditorily accompanied by a kind of vowel fronting (see Catford 1977, 1983). Pharyngealization as a contrastive feature is described for NEC languages in Tsez (Maddieson et al. 1996), Rutul (Kibrik and Kodzasov 1990), Lak (Anderson 1997) and Udi (Schulze-Fürhoff 1994: 447). Phonetically, it is primarily realized via vowels, and a phonemic contrast would imply that pharyngealized vowels occur unconditionally, i.e. not adjacent to pharyngeals. Although Kibrik and Kodzasov (1990) call pharyngealization a suprasegmental feature, they (and others) assign it to a particular segment, which follows the traditional custom in the grammars. Depending on the predictability by consonantal context, the feature is described as secondary articulation, attached to either a vowel or the particular consonant it occurs with.

Among the NWC languages, pharyngealization is attested phonemically in Ubykh and Bzhedukh Adyghe (Colarusso 1988; Hewitt 2005). It is remarkable that there are, unlike the other NWC languages, no attested pharyngeals in Ubykh. As a non-contrastive feature, pharyngealization can be found, for example, in Bezhta (Khalilov, personal communication), Hinukh (Forker 2013) and other NEC languages such as Chechen (Kingston and Nichols 1986). Though pharyngealization acts in a similar way to labialization, i.e. influencing the transition from the given obstruent into the following vowel (see Grawunder et al. 2010), both secondary articulations can occur together, as in the uvular series of Ubykh (see Map 13.6). But we can also find oppositions like /ʁwˤak'u/ 'hook' and /ʁwank'i/ 'deer without antlers' in Tsez. Comrie (2003) and others before have pointed out the correspondence of umlauted vowels with pharyngealized vowels in Tsez (cf. Tsez: /ʕatɬ/ Bezhta: /ätɬ/ 'village'). Similarity in formant structure and articulatory posture on a small-scale basis (Grawunder 2015) seems to support this hypothesis. Although some pharyngealized lexemes without uvulars can be identified as Arabic loanwords, it can in general be ruled out that this is the main source of this contrast rather than resulting from the loss of a previous pharyngeal. Furthermore, there seems to be a related process of vowel fronting in certain parts of the lexicon; this applies mostly to loanwords from Arabic, which are presumably brought in by non-native speakers of Arabic. Low front vowels ([æ~a]) occur in these loanwords in a number of Nakh-Dagestanian languages such as Tsez, Bezhta, Lezgi or Udi. Finally, we can also observe pharyngealization, manifested as 'emphatic' obstruents, in non-Caucasian languages of the area, as in Kurmanji Kurdish (Jastrow 1977) and Zazaki (Keskin 2008) and Neo-Aramaic (C'ereteli 1976).

Palatalization Palatalization is understood here as a secondary articulation of obstruents involving a palatal glide-offset and/or tongue body fronting. Among the NEC languages it is mainly described for languages of the Lezgi group such as Tsakhur (Kibrik and Testelec 1999: 16), Agul and Rutul, but also for dialects of Dargwa and Lak (Kibrik and Kodzasov 1990). And besides a palatalized lateral approximant [lʲ] in Khwarshi (Khalilova 2009) and Khinalug (Smeets 1994: 370), palatalization seems not to appear further as a contrastive feature in the other Dagestanian languages.

Among the NWC languages, palatalized series of velar and uvular stops and fricatives occur in the inventories of Abzhywa Abkhaz and T'ap'anta Abaza and Ubykh (Hewitt 2005), and likewise in the Shapsegh and Hakuchi dialects of Western Circassian (Colarusso 1988). The non-palatalized velar stop series in Ubykh is actually considered to be non-phonemic (Hewitt 2005). Outside the core area, this feature is found in Western Armenian (Vaux 1998), Kumyk (Berta 1998: 302) and, of course, Russian.

Clusters Phonotactics allow, for example, Georgian monomorphemic and monosyllabic clusters with up to eight segments. This is one extreme, whereas other languages in the Caucasus usually allow only two segments. In general, the clusters are classified into 'decessive' clusters, with places of articulation going from more front to more back (e.g. /bd, dg, px, t'k'/) and, the other way round, 'accessive' clusters, from more back to more front (e.g. /db, gd, xp, k't'/). On the whole, harmonic clusters consist of consonants with identical manner of phonation (voiced, aspirated, glottalized), e.g. /dg, tx, t'q'/ (Boeder 2005; Chitoran 2002; Klimov 1994). Harmonic and decessive clusters with a post-dorsal second component (pχ, tsx, p'k') seem to be preferred. With regard to legal initial obstruent clusters of the decessive type, one can observe that these apply to a number of NEC languages; see for example Chechen (Nichols 1994), Batsbi (Holisky and Gagua 1994), Lezgi (Haspelmath 1993), and similarly for the NWC languages Kabardian, Abkhaz (Hewitt 2005) and Abaza (Colarusso 1988). In NWC languages these clusters have the same distribution as single consonants (Hewitt 2005; Klimov 1994), that is, they occur in all positions. In Vaux's underlying phonological analysis (Vaux 1998) Armenian is considered as having clusters of up to ten segments, with an epenthetic vowel [ə] in the surface realizations.

For language contacts between Georgian and the Dagestanian languages, mainly those of the northwest of the Andi-Avar-Tsezic group, Khalilov (2004) illustrates how phonotactic constraints can be influenced by loanword incorporation via accumulation of unmarked clusters around (new) morpheme-boundaries.

13.2.3   Frequency of Occurrence

Although attributive features occur in Caucasian languages, their productivity is still unknown, which leaves an uncertainty about the likelihood of spread (disregarding here sociolinguistic and extra-linguistic factors). According to Testen (1997), obstruents of the glottalic ejective series (/p', t', ts', k'/ and Iron /tʃ'/) occur with lower frequency in Ossetic than in neighbouring Caucasian languages and the majority of the forms in which they occur are Caucasian loanwords. He gives Iron *k'utær*, Digor *k'otær* 'bush' from Chechen *k'otær*, *dʒit'ri* 'cucumber' from Georgian *k'it'ri* as examples. Glottalic stops also occur in Russian loanwords, where they reflect Russian voiceless (unaspirated) stops, as in *bulk'on* 'colonel' < *polkovnik*, *bap'iroz* 'cigarette' < *papiros* (Testen 1997). While one cannot find out about the actual realization by looking at the frequency of occurrence in texts, for example, one can still gain an insight into the degree of systemic usage and the degree of embedding of particular contrasts in lexical and functional morphology. Due to the apparent scarcity of large corpora for the area, I propose here an admittedly skewed shorthand in looking at the type frequency, gained from occurrences in a wordlist. Though this needs to be validated by token frequencies, type frequencies give an impression of how often a particular structure is employed in the make-up of lexical forms for a given variety.

The data used here mainly for (NEC) Nakh-Dagestanian are taken from Comrie and Khalilov (2010), and frequencies extracted for the use of a particular contrast and its related features are approximated by graphemes. With respect to the prevalent uvular place of articulation in the systems on the one hand and the relation of frequency and markedness on the other, one can approach some questions with respect to the general markedness of uvulars cross-linguistically. Do uvular stops occur more frequently in the lexicon? It turns out that for the given sample of 76 doculects of Nakh-Dagestanian languages, uvular glottalic stops occur more often than velar glottalic stops ($t = 3.9$, d.f. $= 75$, $p = 0.0002$), whereas the relative frequency (words with feature occurrence/words in sample) of velar pulmonic stops is still higher than that of uvular stops ($t = -2.6$, d.f. $= 85$, $p = 0.0103$). With respect to the distribution of these relative frequencies across the area of their spoken varieties, one can observe that we gain here a pattern that supports the idea of a core versus periphery distinction, even within the Nakh-Dagestanian languages. On a south-to-north axis, along lines of latitude, we observe an increase in relative frequency for uvular glottalic stops (Map 13.5). In a simplistic analysis applying a Poisson error distribution, one can test the z-transformed latitudinal coordinates (X1) against the frequency distribution (p-values for frequencies $\sim$ X1, X1, $p = 0.0008$, and frequencies $\sim$ X1 $+$ X1^2, X1, $p < 0.0001$, X1^2, $p < 0.001$). These results would primarily allow one to support a hypothesis of a non-random distribution of these type frequencies. More advanced statistical methods of geographically weighted regression seem to be more promising, as demonstrated by Kirby and Brunelle (Chapter 26, this volume).

13.2.4   Expression of Features: Phonetic Realization

The acoustic parameters found in phonetic descriptions, which cover durational measure, spectral measures of vowel formants, or fricative noise characteristics, need to be generalized for the entire speaker population and to be compared with measures of the same sort for other populations or other areas with different varieties. This implies that the significance of the measure for describing a particular contrast is reasonably established.

Nonetheless, linguistic phonetic analysis focuses on common physical properties and characteristics within a variety and uses methods to generalize over speakers/listeners. Sociolinguistic variation, of course, needs to be monitored as well and certainly adds to the pool of co-factors to be

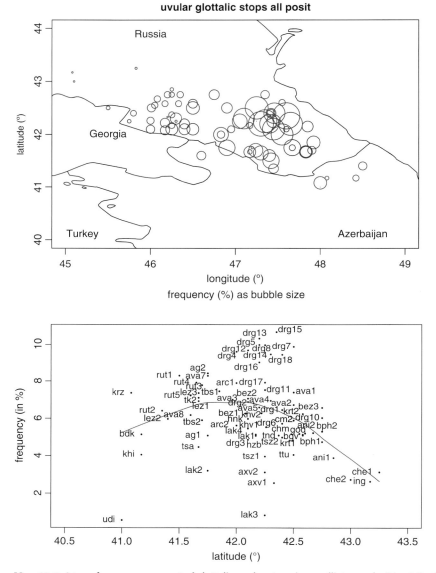

Map 13.5 A type frequency account of glottalic uvular stops in wordlist sample (*N* = 86) of Nakh-Dagestanian languages. Plot with frequency (as per cent per doculect)

controlled for. According to the H&H theory of Lindblom (1990), we may expect, depending on the communicative situation, a range of realizations across different phonetic dimensions.

A comparison across varieties requires comparable datasets. Whereas natural speech data collections are valuable in their own right, these are also much harder to assess in terms of validity (representativeness). Moreover, we face a data situation for comparable audio material that only allows for small samples, i.e. a handful of speakers per language, which makes it all the more necessary to focus on such measures or indices that are not speaker-dependent. With a small-scale sample of ten languages, the differences in phonetic expressions of the same phonological contrast can already be illustrated, namely that of pulmonic versus ejective (glottalic) stops. However, the relativeness of the measure has to be defined for each phonetic attribute. Two possible measures are suggested that should allow the initiation (phonation) contrasts of stops in the area to be characterized: (1) F0 (fundamental frequency) of the following vowel with discrete attributes like 'higher', 'lower' and 'equal' (see Warner 1996 for Ingush) with respect to (pulmonic) contrasts in the same position, and (2) VOT (voice onset time), which is the time from stop release (burst start) to the onset of the following vowel (voicing onset) (Abramson and Lisker 1964 in general; Catford 1992 for Caucasian stops). Especially for VOT, a vast amount of literature exists on conditional effects such as place of articulation, position in the word and phrase, and speaking rate (see Cho and Ladefoged 1999). Likewise, due to the possible effect of intrinsic F0 for the suggested F0 measure, the following vowel (fronting) may actually play a role. These are conditions that need to be controlled for in the sample. Other measures, like the closure duration, the total duration (= duration of closure plus VOT), or the recently developed intensity slope (Grawunder 2013), may also work here to differentiate stops and, specifically, phonation/initiation contrasts. Although these may eventually serve as diagnostics as well, we measure here pre-established categories arising from descriptions and grammars. In this preliminary dataset, we can already observe for VOT a split behaviour of languages that exhibit VOT in aspirated stops that is higher than ejective stops, or the other way round (see Map 13.6). This is incongruent to the compared VOT as observed by Catford (1992), since he averaged over place of articulation and suggested a uniform behaviour in terms of aspirated stops being longer than ejectives. We can in turn presume that this split results from a difference in the way the contrasts are 'organized' in the language, perhaps with respect to the way aspiration as a marker is implemented for the voiceless pulmonic stops on the one hand and of the gemination contrast ('intense' versus 'weak') in these languages. F0 of the following vowel does not, on the other hand, follow the split above, but more importantly, it exhibits another split, which is not immediately predicted but which points to another dimension of the pulmonic/glottalic contrast implementation.

Grawunder et al. (2010) observed that aspiration in voiceless aspirated stops in Georgian overlaps onto the beginning of the following vowel. This implies a subsequent lowering of F0 with respect to unaspirated stops. The F0 difference that Grawunder et al. (2010) observed for the

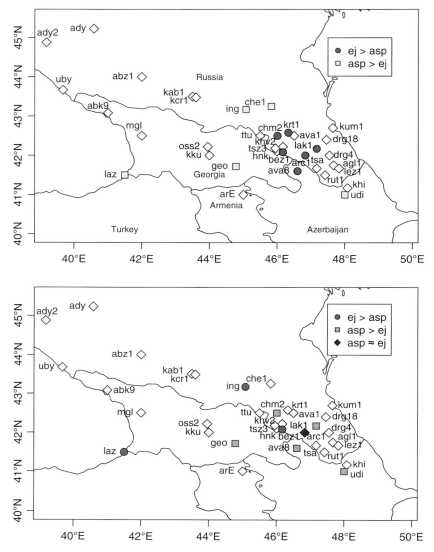

Map 13.6 Relative measures for F0 of the following vowel of a stop (lower panel); relative measures for voice onset time with pulmonic, i.e. aspirated [asp], versus ejective [ej] stops (upper panel)

Ingush female speaker was around one to two semitones, and therefore has to be counted as a potential 'signal' that is presumably also picked up by a listener. Nonetheless, the described F0-parameter and its general trend for an entire speaker population must be called into question since Grawunder et al. (2010) (eight speakers) and Vicenik (2010) (five speakers) found no clear tendencies.

13.3 Conclusion

It has been argued here that the Caucasus is a clear linguistic area and an area of contact – one that can be circumscribed by means of phonetic/phonological attributes, which appear to occur more often within the area and fade out towards its periphery. These attributes mostly concern feature density in both the sound system and across the area. The latter is driven by medium linguistic diversity and long-standing contact, slow intertwining migration patterns and prevalent exogamy. Supporting areality, various forms of functional multilingualism with incomplete L2/L3 acquisition come into play. The core of phonological features in the Caucasus area is built around a minimum three-way phonation/initiation contrast that includes ejective (glottalic) stops, which in addition are most likely to involve the uvular place of articulation. These obstruents often contrast with the presence or absence of segments that may involve subphonemic or phonemic labialization. In addition, one finds pharyngeal/epiglottal articulation either as a pharyngeal stop or as a fricative, along with possible suprasegmental processes. Another trait is seen in the process whereby the density of otherwise common features in the obstruent system of contrasts, such as labialization, palatalization and gemination, leads to higher complexity in terms of feature embeddings per possible slot in the system. From an areal perspective, this includes the combination and stacking of features, a process which represents a consistent expansion of (feature) components that are already in place. Nonetheless, linear feature combination, i.e. the clustering of consonants, forms an integral part of the areal profile of the Caucasus.

The genealogical borders of the three main Caucasus families overlap with different 'front lines', which can often be drawn showing particular groupings for individual features like nasalization or umlauted vowels. In other words, we do not see a process of complete assimilation. There is no vast area with completely the same setting. However, a number of structural components remain typical for the core area. The proposed area can and needs to be tested against its periphery (see Bickel 2008 and Bickel, Chapter 3, this volume), whereas, given the availability of data for a particular area, those frequency distributions are more suitable for fine-grained mapping and for demonstrating particular areal shifts. In order to enable solid quantitative hypothesis testing, more data are necessary, especially for those languages of the wider contact pool such as Tat (Muslim/Judeo) and Talysh, but also for dialectal and sub-varieties of languages that are otherwise often treated as homogeneous, such as Georgian, Kurdish, Armenian and Azerbaijani. This relates to the known problem of density of data points, which relates directly to population density (number of settlements, homogeneity of varieties, etc.).

Apart from the historical and sociodemographic situation and apart from general trends observable through phonemic systems today, it seems possible to enhance our understanding of areal feature distributions by means of type frequencies, as they are found in dictionaries. The other suggested shift in the typological approach focuses on the sound level, and emphasizes phonetic realizations rather than higher systemic levels. Feature expression seems far more appropriate (in the Caucasus area) as we often find similar phenomena, or transitional and gradual phenomena, that can surface as different features via interaction with other levels (syntax, prosody, lexicon). The underlying (phonetic) mechanisms need to be understood beforehand so that appropriate analytical measures can be chosen and clear predictions can be made with regard to feature expression. This phonetic approach opens up wider possibilities for substantiated hypotheses about historical sound change, whether it is induced through contact on the one hand or through 'internal' mechanisms of analogical expansion and optimization of sound systems on the other.

Acknowledgements

I wish to express my gratitude to the editor Raymond Hickey for his infinite patience and assistance during the genesis of this chapter in its manifold versions. Furthermore, I would like to thank Bernard Comrie and Brent Reed for their very helpful and valuable comments. My thanks also go to Hans Jörg-Bibiko, Lisa and Natalie.

References

Aikhenvald, Alexandra and Robert M. W. Dixon, 2001. *Areal Diffusion and Genetic Inheritance: Problems in Comparative Linguistics*. Oxford: Oxford University Press.

Alekseev, Mikhail E., 1994a. Budukh. In Smeets (ed.), pp. 259–296.

Alekseev, Mikhail E., 1994b. Rutul. In Smeets (ed.), pp. 213–258.

Alekseev, Mikhail E., Georgij A. Klimov, Sergei A. Starostin and Yakov G. Testelets (eds), 1999. *Jazyki Mira: Kavkazskie Jazyki [Languages of the World: Caucasian Languages]*. Moscow: Academia.

Alekseev, Mikhail E. and Ramazan Radjabov, 2004. Tsez. In Job (ed.), pp. 115–163.

Anderson, Gregory, 1997. Lak phonology. In Kaye and Daniels (eds), pp. 973–997.

Authier, Gilles, 2012. *Grammaire juhuri, ou judeo-tat, langue iranienne des Juifs du Caucase de l'est*. Beiträge zur Iranistik, vol. 36. Wiesbaden: Reichert.

Babel, Molly E., 2009. *Phonetic and Social Selectivity in Speech Accommodation*. PhD thesis, University of California, Berkeley.

Balanovsky, Oleg, et al. and The Genographic Consortium, 2011. Parallel evolution of genes and languages in the Caucasus region. *Molecular Biology and Evolution* 28 (10): 2905–2920.

Baudouin de Courtenay, Jan Ignacy Niecisław, 1963. *Izbrannyye trudy po obshchemu yazykoznaniyu [Selected Works on General Linguistics]*, vol. 2. Moscow: Izdatel'stvo Akademii Nauk SSSR.

van den Berg, Helma, 1995. *A Grammar of Hunzib*. Munich: LINCOM Europa.

van den Berg, Helma, 2005. The East Caucasian language family. *Lingua* 115 (1): 147–190.

Berta, Árpád, 1998. West Kipchak languages. In Johanson and Csató (eds), pp. 301–317.

Bickel, Baltasar, 2008. A general method for the statistical evaluation of typological distributions. Manuscript, University of Leipzig. www.uni-leipzig.de/~bickel/research/projects/publ.html

Bisang, Walter, 2004. Dialectology and typology: An integrative perspective. In Bernd Kortmann (ed.), *Dialectology Meets Typology: Dialect Grammar from a Cross-linguistic Perspective*, pp. 11–46. Berlin: Mouton de Gruyter.

Bläsing, Uwe, 2003. Kalmuck. In Juha Janhunen (ed.), *The Mongolic Languages*, pp. 229–247. New York: Routledge.

Blevins, Juliette, 2006. A theoretical synopsis of Evolutionary Phonology. *Theoretical Linguistics* 32 (2): 117–166.

Blevins, Juliette and Andrew Wedel, 2009. Inhibited sound change: An evolutionary approach to lexical competition. *Diachronica* 26 (2): 143–183.

Boeder, Winfried, 2005. The South Caucasian languages. *Lingua* 115 (1): 5–89.

Brown, Cecil, Eric Holman and Søren Wichmann, 2013. Sound correspondences in the world's languages. *Language* 89 (1): 4–29.

Bybee, Joan, 2003. Word frequency and context of use in the lexical diffusion of phonetically conditioned sound change. *Language Variation and Change* 14 (3): 261–290.

Catford, John C., 1977. Mountain of tongues: The languages of the Caucasus. *Annual Review of Anthropology*, 6: 283–314.

Catford, John C., 1983. Pharyngeal and laryngeal sounds in Caucasian languages. In Diane Bless and James Abbs (eds), *Vocal Fold Physiology: Contemporary Research and Clinical Issues*, pp. 344–350. San Diego: College-Hill.

Catford, John C., 1992. Caucasian phonetics and general phonetics. In Catherine Paris (ed.), *Caucasologie et mythologie comparée: Actes du Colloque International CNRS IVe Colloque de Caucasologie*, pp. 193–216, Paris: Peeters.

Catford, John C., 1994. Vowel systems of Caucasian languages. In Howard Isaac Aronson (ed.), *Non-Slavic Languages of the USSR: Papers from the Fourth Conference*, pp. 44–60. Bloomington, IN: Slavica Publishers.

C'ereteli, Grigol, 1976. K voprosu o klassifikacii novoaramejskix dialektov [On the question of classification of Neo-Aramaic dialects]. In *Philologia Orientalis*, vol. IV, Tbilisi: Mecniereba, pp. 224–232.

Chirikba, Viacheslav, 2008a. The problem of the Caucasian Sprachbund. In Pieter Muysken (ed.), *From Linguistic Areas to Areal Linguistics*, pp. 25–93. Studies in Language Companion Series, vol. 25. Amsterdam: John Benjamins.

Chirikba, Viacheslav, 2008b. Armenians and their dialects in Abkhazia. In Alexander Lubotsky, Jos Schaeken and Jeroen Wiedenhof (eds), *Balto-Slavic and Indo-European Linguistics*, pp. 51–67. Amsterdam: Rodopi.

Chitoran, Ioana, 2002. Georgian harmonic clusters: Phonetic cues to phonological representation. *Phonology* 15 (2): 121–141.

Cho, Taehong and Peter Ladefoged, 1999. Variation and universals in VOT: evidence from 18 languages. *Journal of Phonetics* 27 (2): 207–229.

Coene, Frederik, 2009. *The Caucasus: An Introduction*. London: Routledge.

Colarusso, John, 1988. *The Northwest Caucasian Languages: A Phonological Survey*. New York and London: Garland Publishing.

Comrie, Bernard (ed.), 1981. *The Languages of the Soviet Union*. Cambridge: Cambridge University Press.

Comrie, Bernard, 2003. A note on pharyngealization and umlaut in two Tsezic languages. In Winfried Boeder (ed.), *Kaukasische Sprachprobleme: Beiträge zu den Kaukasistentagungen in Oldenburg 1995–2001*, pp. 105–109. Bibliotheks- und Informationssystem der Universität Oldenburg.

Comrie, Bernard, 2008. Linguistic diversity in the Caucasus. *Annual Review of Anthropology* 37 (1): 131–143.

Comrie, Bernard and Madzhid Khalilov, 2010. *The Dictionary of Languages and Dialects of the Peoples of the Northern Caucasus: Comparison of the Basic Lexicon; Languages and Dialects of the Peoples of Republic of Daghestan, Ingush Republic, Republic of North Ossetia-Alania, Chechen Republic and of the Nakh-Daghestanian Peoples of Azerbaijan and Georgia*. Makhachkala, and Leipzig: Max Planck Institute for Evolutionary Anthropology.

Daniel, Mikhail, Nina Dobrushina and Sergey Knyazev, 2011. Highlanders' Russian: Case study in bilingualism and language interference in central Daghestan. In Arto Mustajoki, Ekaterina Protassova and Nikolai Vakhtin (eds), *Instrumentarium of Linguistics: Sociolinguistic Approach to Non-Standard Russian*, pp. 65–93. Slavica Helsingiensia, vol. 40. University of Helsinki.

Dirr, Adolf, 1928. *Einführung in das Studium der kaukasischen Sprachen: mit einer Sprachenkarte*. Leipzig: Asia Major.

Dobrushina, Nina, 2013. How to study multilingualism of the past: Investigating traditional contact situations in Daghestan. *Journal of Sociolinguistics* 17 (3): 376–393.

Dzhidalaev, Nurislam S., 2010. Tjurksko-dagestanskie jazykovye kontakty (na primere lakskogo jazyka) [Turkic-Dagestanian language contacts (on the example of Lak)]. Makhachkala: Russian Academy of Science in Dagestan.

Fallon, Paul D., 2001. *The Synchronic and Diachronic Phonology of Ejectives*. New York and London: Routledge.

Flege, James E., Carlo Schirru and Ian R. A. MacKay, 2003. Interaction between the native and second language phonetic subsystems. *Speech Communication*, 40: 467–491.

Flege, James E. and Robert Port, 1981. Cross-language phonetic interference: Arabic to English. *Language and Speech*, 24: 125–146.

Forker, Diana, 2013. *A Grammar of Hinuq*. Berlin: de Gruyter Mouton.

Friedman, Victor A., 2009. Sociolinguistics in the Caucasus. In Martin J. Ball (ed.), *The Routledge Handbook of Sociolinguistics Around the World*, pp. 127–138. London and New York: Routledge.

Gilles, Peter and Beat Siebenhaar, 2010. Areal variation in segmental phonetics and phonology. In Peter Auer and Jürgen Erich Schmidt (eds), *Language and Space*, pp. 760–786. Berlin: de Gruyter Mouton.

Gippert, Jost, 2008. Endangered Caucasian languages in Georgia: Linguistic parameters of language endangerment. In K. David Harrison, David S. Rood and Arienne Dwyer (eds), *Lessons from Documented Endangered Languages*, pp. 159–193. Amsterdam: John Benjamins.

Gordon, Matthew and Ayla Applebaum, 2006. Turkish Kabardian. *Journal of the International Phonetic Association* 36 (2): 255–264.

Grawunder, Sven, 2013. Intensity slopes as robust measure for distinguishing glottalic vs pulmonic stop initiation. *Journal of the Acoustical Society of America* 134 (5): 4069.

Grawunder, Sven, 2015. Foneticheskie kharakteristiki (nenazalizovannykh) glaznykh v bezhtinskom yazyke [Phonetic characteristics of (non-nasalized) vowels in Bezhta]. In Bernard Comrie (ed.), *Grammatika bezhtinskogo yazyka [A Grammar of Bezhta]*, pp. 52–62. Leipzig and Makhachkala: ALEPH.

Grawunder, Sven, Adrian P. Simpson and Madzhid S. Khalilov, 2010. Phonetic characteristics of ejectives: Samples from Caucasian languages. In Susanne Fuchs, Martine Toda and Marzena Żygis (eds), *Turbulent Sounds: An Interdisciplinary Guide*, pp. 209–244. Berlin: Mouton de Gruyter.

Gudava, Togo E., 1964. *Konsonantizm andijxskix yazykov [The Consonantism of the Andic Languages]*. Tbilisi: Izdatel'stvo Akademii Nauk Gruzinskoj SSR.

Harris, Alice C., 1991. *The Indigenous Languages of the Caucasus*, vol. I: *The Kartvelian Languages*. Delmar, NY: Caravan Books.

Haspelmath, Martin, 1993. *A Grammar of Lezgian*. Berlin: Mouton de Gruyter.

Haspelmath, Martin, 2006. Against markedness (and what to replace it with). *Journal of Linguistics* 42 (1): 25–70.

Hewitt, B. George, 1981. Caucasian languages. In Comrie (ed.), pp. 196–237.

Hewitt, B. George, 1989. *The Indigenous Languages of the Caucasus*, vol. 2: *The North West Caucasian Languages*. Delmar, NY: Caravan Books.

Hewitt, B. George, 2004. *Introduction to the Study of the Languages of the Caucasus*. Munich: LINCOM.

Hewitt, B. George, 2005. North West Caucasian. *Lingua* 115 (1): 91–145.

Hickey, Raymond, 2012a Areal features of the Anglophone world. In Raymond Hickey (ed.), *Areal Features of the Anglophone World*, pp. 1–19. Berlin: de Gruyter Mouton.

Hickey, Raymond, 2012b. Internally and externally motivated language change. In Juan Manuel Hernández-Campoy and Juan Camilo Conde-Silvestre (eds), *The Handbook of Historical Sociolinguistics*, pp. 387–407. Malden, MA: Wiley.

Höhlig, Monika, 1997. *Kontaktbedingter Sprachwandel in der adygeischen Umgangssprache im Kaukasus und in der Türkei: Vergleichende Analyse des russischen und türkischen Einflusses in mündlichen adygeischen Texten.* LINCOM Studies in Caucasian Linguistics, vol. 3. Munich: LINCOM Europa.

Holisky, Dee Ann, 1991. Laz. In Harris (ed.), pp. 395–472.

Holisky, Dee Ann and Rasudan Gagua, 1994. Tsova-Tush (Batsbi). In Smeets (ed.), pp. 147–212.

Hyman, Larry M., 2009. How (not) to do phonological typology: The case of pitch-accent. *Language Sciences* 31 (2): 213–238.

Isakov, Isak Abdulvakhidovich and Madzhid S. Khalilov, 2004. Hinukh. In Job (ed.), pp. 167–214.

Isakov, Isak Abdulvakhidovich and Madzhid S. Khalilov, 2012. *Gunzibskij jazyk (Fonetika Morfologija. Slovoobrazovanie. Leksika. Teksty) [The Hunzib Language]*. Makhachkala: Russian Academy of the Sciences.

Jastrow, Otto, 1977. Zur Phonologie des Kurdischen in der Türkei. *Studien zur Indologie und Iranistik*, 3: 84–106.

Job, Michael (ed.), 2004. *The Indigenous Languages of the Caucasus*, vol. 3: *The North East Caucasian Languages*, part 1. Delmar, NY: Caravan Books.

Johanson, Lars, 2006. On the roles of Turkic in the Caucasus area. In Yaron Matras, April McMahon and Nigel Vincent (eds), *Linguistic Areas*, pp. 160–181. Basingstoke, UK: Palgrave Macmillan.

Johanson, Lars and Éva Csató (eds), 1998. *The Turkic Languages*. London and New York: Routledge.

Kaye, Alan S. and Peter T. Daniels (eds), 1997. *Phonologies of Asia and Africa (including the Caucasus)*, vol. 1. Winona Lake, IN: Eisenbrauns.

Keskin, Mesut, 2008. *Zur dialektalen Gliederung des Zazaki*. Unpublished MA thesis, Johann-Wolfgang-von-Goethe-Universität Frankfurt, Institut für Vergleichende indogermanische Sprachwissenschaft.

Khalidova, Rasidat Sachrudinovna, 2006. *Avarsko-andijskie jazykovye kontakty [Avar-Andic Language Contacts]*. Makhachkala: Russian Academy of the Sciences.

Khalilov, Madzhid Sharipovic, 2004. *Gruzinsko-dagestanskie jazykovye kontakty [Georgian–Dagestanian Language Contacts]*. Moskva: Nauka.

Khalilova, Zaira, 2009. *A Grammar of Kwarshi*. PhD thesis, University of Leiden.

Khan, Geoffrey, 2008. *The Neo-Aramaic Dialect of Barwar. Handbook of Oriental Studies*, Section 1: *The Near and Middle East*, vol. 96. Leiden: Brill.

Kibrik, Alexander E., 2001. *Bagvalinskij jazyk: Grammatika, teksty, slovari [The Bagvalal Language: Grammar, Texts, Dictionary]*. Moscow: Russian Academy of the Sciences.

Kibrik, Alexander E. and Sandro V. Kodzasov, 1990. *Sopostavitel'noe izucenie dagestanskix jazykov: Imja, Fonetika [A Comparative Study of Dagestanian Languages: Nouns, Phonetics]*. Moscow: Izdatel'stvo Moskovskogo Universitet.

Kibrik, Alexander E. and Yakuv G. Testelec (eds), 1999. *Elementy tsakhurskogo yazyka v tipologicheskom osveshchenii [Elements of the Tsakhur Language in a typological light]*. Moscow: Nasledie.

Kingston, John and Johanna Nichols, 1986. Pharyngealization in Chechen. *Journal of the Acoustical Society of America* 80: 62.

Klimov, Georgij A., 1994. *Einführung in die kaukasische Sprachwissenschaft*, translated and revised by Jost Gippert. Hamburg: Helmut Buske.

Kodzasov, Sandro V., 1999. Caucasian: Daghestanian languages. In Harry van der Hulst (ed.), *Word Prosodic Systems in the Languages of Europe*, pp. 995–1020. Berlin and New York: Walter de Gruyter.

Kornfilt, Jaklin, 1997. *Turkish*. London: Routledge.

Koryakov, Yuri B., 2006. *Atlas kavkazkikh yazykov [Atlas of the Caucasian Languages]*. Moscow: RAN.

Lacroix, René, 2009. *Description du Dialecte Laze d'Arhavi (Caucasique du Sud, Turquie): Grammaire et Textes*. PhD thesis, Université Lumière Lyon 2, Lyon.

Ladd, D. Robert, 2014. *Simultaneous Structure in Phonology*. Oxford: Oxford University Press.

Ladefoged, Peter and Ian Maddieson, 1996. *The Sounds of the World's Languages*. Blackwell.

Lancia, Leonardo and Sven Grawunder, 2014. Tongue–larynx interactions in the production of word initial laryngealization over different prosodic contexts: a repeated speech experiment. In Susanne Fuchs et al. (eds), *Proceedings of the 10th International Seminar on Speech Production (ISSP), Cologne*, pp. 245–248.

Lindblom, Björn, 1990. Explaining phonetic variation: A sketch of the H&H theory. In William Hardcastle and Alain Marchal (eds), *Speech Production and Speech Modeling*, pp. 403–439. Dordrecht: Kluwer.

Lisker, Leigh and Arthur Abramson, 1964. A cross-language study of voicing in initial stops: Acoustical measurements. *Word* 20 (3): 384–422.

Lupyan, Gary and Rick Dale, 2010. Language structure is partly determined by social structure. *PLoS ONE* 5 (1): e8559.

Maddieson, Ian, 1984. *Patterns of Sounds*. Cambridge: Cambridge University Press.

Maddieson, Ian, Ramasan Rajabov and Aaron Sonnenschein, 1996. The main features of Tsez phonetics. *UCLA Working Papers In Phonetics*: 94–110.

Magomedova, Patimat, 2004. Chamalal. In Job (ed.), pp. 5–65.

McMahon, April M. S., 1994. *Understanding Language Change*. Cambridge: Cambridge University Press.

Mejlanova, Udeizat A., 1970. *Gjunejskij dialekt: osnova lezginskogo literaturnogo jazyka [The Gunei Dialect: Basis of the Lezgian Literary Language]*. Makhachkala: Inst. Istorii, Yazyka i Literatury im. G Cadasy.

Nasidze, Ivan et al., 2004. Mitochondrial DNA and Y-chromosome variation in the Caucasus. *Annals of Human Genetics* 68 (3): 205–221.

Nichols, Johanna, 1992. *Linguistic Diversity in Space and Time*. Chicago: University of Chicago Press.

Nichols, Johanna, 1994. Chechen. In Smeets (ed.), pp. 1–78.

Nichols, Johanna, 1997. Chechen phonology. In Kaye and Daniels (eds), pp. 941–971.

Nichols, Johanna, 2011. *Ingush Grammar*. Berkeley, CA: University of California Press.

Nichols, Johanna, 2013. The vertical archipelago: Adding the third dimension to linguistic geography. In Peter Auer, Martin Hilpert, Anja Stukenbrock and Benedikt Szmrecsanyi (eds), *Space in Language and Linguistics: Geographical, Interactional, and Cognitive Perspectives*, pp. 38–60. Berlin: Walter de Gruyter.

Ohala, John J., 1990. There is no interface between phonology and phonetics: A personal view. *Journal of Phonetics*, 18: 153–171.

Rogava, Georgij Vissarionovic and Zajnab Ibragimovna Kerasheva, 1966. *Adygabzem igrammatik – Grammatika adygejskogo jazyka [Grammar of the Adyghe Language]*. Maykop, Krasnodar: Krasnodarske Thylq Tedzapi [Krasnodar Publishing House].

Schönig, Claus, 1998. Azerbaijanian. In Johanson and Csató (eds), pp. 248–260.

Schulze, Wolfgang, 2005. Towards a history of Udi. *International Journal of Diachronic Linguistics*, 1: 55–91.

Schulze-Fürhoff, Wolfgang, 1994. Udi. In Smeets (ed.), pp. 447–514.

Smeets, Rieks (ed.), 1994. *The Indigenous Languages of the Caucasus*, vol. 4: *North East Caucasian Languages*, part 2. Delmar, NY: Caravan Books.

Stilo, Donald L., 1994. Phonological systems in contact in Iran and Transcaucasia. In Mehdi Marashi (ed.), *Persian Studies in North America: Studies in Honor of Mohammad Ali Jazayery*, pp. 75–94. Bethesda, MD: Iranbooks.

Stilo, Donald L., 2004. Iranian as buffer zone between the universal typologies of Turkic and Semitic. In Éva Ágnes Csató, Bo Isaksson and Carina Jahani (eds), *Linguistic Convergence and Areal Diffusion: Case Studies from Iranian, Semitic and Turkic*, pp. 35–63. London and New York: Routledge.

Stilo, Donald L., 2006. Circumpositions as an areal response: The case study of the Iranian zone. In Lars Johanson and Christiane Bulut (eds), *Turkic–Iranian Contact-Areas*, pp. 310–333. Wiesbaden: Harrassowitz.

Sumbatova, Nina R. and Rasul O. Mutalov, 2003. *A Grammar of Icari Dargwa*. Munich: LINCOM Europa.

Talibov, Bukar B., 2004. Tsakhur. In Job (ed.), pp. 347–419.

Testen, David, 1997. Ossetic phonology. In Kaye and Daniels (eds), pp. 707–731.

Thomason, Sarah G. and Terrence Kaufman, 1988. *Language Contact, Creolization, and Genetic Linguistics*. Berkeley, CA: University of California Press.

Tolstoj, Nikita I., 1997. *Tyurkskie Yazyki [Turkic Languages]*. Yazyki Mira, Moscow: Indrik, RAN.

Trubetzkoy, Nikolai Sergeevich, 1958 [1939]. *Grundzüge der Phonologie*, seventh edition. Göttingen: Vandenhoeck & Ruprecht.

Trudgill, Peter, 2011. *Sociolinguistic Typology: Social Determinants of Linguistic Complexity*. Oxford: Oxford University Press.

Trudgill, Peter, 1996. Dialect typology: Isolation, social network and phonological structure. In Gregory R. Guy, Crawford Feagin, Deborah Schiffrin and John Baugh (eds), *Towards a Social Science of Language: Papers in Honour of William Labov*, vol. 1, pp. 3–21. Amsterdam: John Benjamins.

Trudgill, Peter, 2004. Linguistic and social typology: The Austronesian migrations and phoneme inventories. *Linguistic Typology* 8 (3): 305–320.

Trudgill, Peter, 2011. *Sociolinguistic Typology: Social Determinants of Linguistic Complexity*. Oxford: Oxford University Press.

Tuite, Kevin, 1999. The myth of the Caucasian Sprachbund: The case of ergativity. *Lingua* 108 (1): 1–29.

Tuite, Kevin, 2008. The rise and fall and revival of the Ibero-Caucasian hypothesis. *Historiographia Linguistica* 35 (1–2): 23–82.

Vadzhibov, Malik, 2012. *Fonetika tabasaranskogo jazyka – sravitel'noe opisanie zvukovykh sistem literaturnogo jazyka i mezhgiul'skogo govora [Phonetics of the Tabasaran Language]*. Saarbrücken: Lambert Academic Publishing.

Vaux, Bert, 1998. *The Phonology of Armenian*. Oxford: Clarendon Press.

Vicenik, Chad, 2010. An acoustic study of Georgian stop consonants. *Journal of the International Phonetic Association* 40 (1): 59–92.

Warner, Natasha, 1996. Acoustic characteristics of ejectives in Ingush. In *Proceedings of the Fourth International Conference on Spoken Language Processing, ICSLP 96, 3, Philadelphia, PA*.

Wixman, Ronald, 1980. *Language Aspects of Ethnic Patterns and Processes in the North Caucasus*. Chicago: University of Chicago, Department of Geography.

Yunusbayev, Bayazit, et al., 2012. The Caucasus as an asymmetric semipermeable barrier to ancient human migrations. *Molecular Biology and Evolution* 29 (1): 359–365.

Zabitov, S. M. and I. I. Efendiev, 2001. *Slovar' arabskikh i persidskikh leksicheskikh zaimstvovanij v lezginskom jazyke [Dictionary of Arab and Persian Lexical Loans in the Lezgian Language]*. Makhachkala: Dagestan State University.

14

Western Asia: East Anatolia as a Transition Zone

Geoffrey Haig

14.1 Introduction

What is loosely referred to here as 'East Anatolia' covers the region of Turkey eastward of the town of Sivas (see Map 14.1). However, the cultural and linguistic traits that characterize the region do not cease at the borders of the Turkish state, but permeate outwards in all directions: into western Anatolia, Armenia and the Caucasus, West Iran, North Iraq and Syria. For this reason alone, attempts to define an East Anatolian 'linguistic area' are generally not compelling – if indeed the concept of 'linguistic area' has any intrinsic value at all (see Campbell 2006); this discussion is taken up in Section 14.5 below. Topographically, the region encompasses the upper catchment region of the Tigris and Euphrates rivers; it is ruggedly mountainous in the north and east, descending gradually towards the lower elevation of the plains of Mosul in North Iraq.

The earliest attempt at characterizing language contact across the region, Haig (2001), was based on data from just four languages, and the conclusions were correspondingly tentative. Since then, the amount of available data has increased dramatically: for North Eastern Neo-Aramaic (NENA), Geoffrey Khan and his associates have produced rich documentations for at least six varieties, and for Laz we now have the monumental grammar of the Arhavi variety (Lacroix 2009); several Arabic dialects of the region have been documented (see Talay 2011 for an overview), and material on Homshetsma (Western Armenian) is now more accessible (Vaux 2007), likewise on Domari of Aleppo (Herin 2012). For Kurmanji Kurdish, see Haig and Öpengin (2014) and Öpengin and Haig (2014). Furthermore, conditions for field work in the region have vastly improved since 2000 and a number of local academic initiatives have been established in eastern Turkey, in particular at Artuklu University in Mardin. These are, of course, exceedingly welcome developments, but they also mean that an overview chapter such as this cannot achieve anything like comprehensive coverage.

In what follows, I will present what I consider to be the most salient indicators of language contact across the region, and assess their relevance against what is known from language history and from related languages. In doing so, it will become evident that the notion of Anatolia as a coherent areal unit is probably not tenable.

The chapter is organized as follows: in Section 14.2, the notion of Anatolia as a transitional zone is outlined, and the varieties discussed in this chapter are introduced. Section 14.3 takes up selected structural features and discusses their distribution across the region, beginning with phonology. In Section 14.4, word order and adpositions are discussed, while Section 14.5 critically assesses attempts at defining an Anatolian linguistic area, and proposes an alternative view involving two subregions. Section 14.6 sums up the main points of the chapter.

14.2   East Anatolia as a Transitional Zone

To appreciate the dynamics of language contact in the region, it is worthwhile beginning with a macro-linguistic perspective. East Anatolia straddles the intersection of several major linguistic macro-areas: to the south, Anatolia fades into the Arabian peninsula and North Africa, dominated by VO, prepositional Afroasiatic languages; westwards it blends into the Mediterranean / Western European region, with their specific peculiarities (see Zeldes 2013); eastward we move into the Central Asian region of OV and postpositional languages (Turkic, Eastern Iranian, Indo-Aryan, etc.). Finally, the northeastern fringe of Anatolia borders on the Caucasus, and outlier Caucasian languages are also found in Anatolia (e.g. Laz, Kartvelian). The impact of all these regions is evident in various ways, which are discussed below.

As a consequence, what characterizes East Anatolia as a region is not the bundling of unique features emanating from a discernible geographic core, but the presence of multiple overlaps from the neighbouring regions. Nichols (1992) introduced the dichotomy between 'spread zones' and 'residual zones' to account for global patterns of feature distribution. Spread zones are large areas, with a low density of genetic variation among the languages of the region. Such zones are created through the expansion of a dominant group that imposes its language(s) over a large region, typically a region with few geographic obstacles that would inhibit the expansion of the dominant group. By contrast, a residual zone is characterized by high genetic density, which typically arises in geographically isolated and often inaccessible regions. A prototypical residual zone is the Caucasus, characterized by three indigenous (and probably unrelated) language families.

East Anatolia, however, is neither a spread zone nor a residual zone: it is a transitional or overlap zone. The relatively high degree of linguistic diversity in the region (see below), while typical of a residual zone, is not the result of a gradual accumulation of linguistic diversity through long-standing geographic isolation (the hallmark of Nichols' residual zones), but arises from the fact that East Anatolia is at the cusp of a number of distinct macro-regions. All the languages of East Anatolia have close relatives in neighbouring regions; its linguistic diversity is thus not indigenous, but a secondary product of its transitional status. Nevertheless, East Anatolia is more than just the sum of its contributing regions. It can be argued that some of the linguistic features characterizing the languages of the region cannot be explained in terms of diffusion from neighbouring regions, but are specific compromise responses to the conflicting typological profiles of the neighbouring languages (see Stilo 2005, 2012). This is particularly true in the realm of word order and adpositions, discussed in Section 14.4 below.

Finally, a brief note on the sociolinguistic situation. Over the last two millennia, the region has been at the intersection of two imperial epicentres: the Byzantine and Ottoman empires centred at Istanbul, and successive empires of Iran, e.g. the Achaemenid and Sassanid. Although different parts of the region nominally belonged to one or other of the dominant empires at various times, it is important to realize that up until the twentieth century, there was no single dominant 'official' language across the region, no compulsory mass education in that language, and no pressing reason, or indeed any particular advantage, for speakers to abandon their own language in favour of another. Although Islam was spreading throughout the region from the tenth century, numerous non-Muslim groups remained *in situ* and continued practising their religions. It was not until the upheavals of the early twentieth century that their situation deteriorated dramatically, unleashing an exodus that continues to the present day. But prior to this period, language was an emblematic feature of group identity, often coupled with membership of religious groups or tribal affiliation. And while some languages enjoyed more prestige than others, the vernacular Turkish of Anatolia and West Iran was notably not among them (see Bulut 2002: 55). Thus the general pattern that can be assumed over most of the period is the acquisition of neighbouring languages if required for trade and other purposes, coupled with retention of one's own.

With the founding of the Turkish Republic in 1923, a policy of wholesale Turkification was imposed on the entire country, leading to what can only be described as a catastrophic rupture in the delicate multilingual ecology of East Anatolia. In fact, the destruction of Anatolia's linguistic diversity had begun prior to the founding of the Republic, with the wholesale eradication of the Armenian minority and the forced resettlements of thousands of Neo-Aramaic speaking Jews and Christians. Over subsequent decades, Turkey's 'One State One Language' policy has resulted in massive language shifts towards the official language, Turkish, so that now, only the largest minority language communities have retained any degree of viability; see Skutnabb-Kangas and Bucak (1995), Haig (2004) and Öpengin (2012), among others, on Turkey's policies towards its minority languages.

In principle, then, it is important to distinguish the results of (probable) gradual convergence among the languages of East Anatolia over centuries of multilingual co-existence, with each group maintaining its own language (see Noorlander 2014), from the situation after the founding of the Turkish Republic, where Turkish has been imposed as the dominant language, and the speech of minority groups is characterized by imperfect first language acquisition (or complete shift to Turkish) and the code-switching practices evident in many of the growing urban centres of the region.

14.2.1   Overview of Varieties

The following list introduces the twelve varieties to which reference is made in this chapter. The numbering is reflected in Map 14.1, which indicates the respective locations.

1. Hemshinli (also called Homshetsma), a dialect assigned to Western Armenian and spoken in the Artvin province of northeastern Turkey on the Georgian border (Vaux 2007). The speakers converted to Sunni Islam at least two centuries ago.
2. Laz, a Kartvelian language spoken on the Black Sea coast of Turkey in a few towns and villages just short of the Georgian border; data here are taken from the Arhavi variety described in Lacroix (2009).
3. Northern Kurdish or Kurmanji Kurdish. Northwest Iranian, Indo-European. The most widely spoken minority language in East Anatolia. It is also spoken in the Urmiye region of Iran, in northeastern Syria and North Iraq.
4. Central Kurdish (Sorani), Northwest Iranian, Indo-European, is spoken southwards of Kurmanji and in the southeast towards Mahabad in Iran.
5. The so-called Şêxbizinî dialects of Kurdish, the language of the descendants of southern Kurdish tribes resettled in various parts of Anatolia in the sixteenth century. With the exception of a short description in Lewendî (1997), further data on these varieties are currently unavailable (data here from the Haymana variety).
6. Domari, the language of the Romani communities of much of the Middle East (Indo-Aryan). There are Dom communities scattered throughout much of East Anatolia, reputedly several thousand speakers in the Diyarbakir region. However, reliable information is extremely difficult to obtain; the most relevant recent source is Herin (2012) on the Aleppo variety (Syria); see Matras (2012) for an overview of Domari.

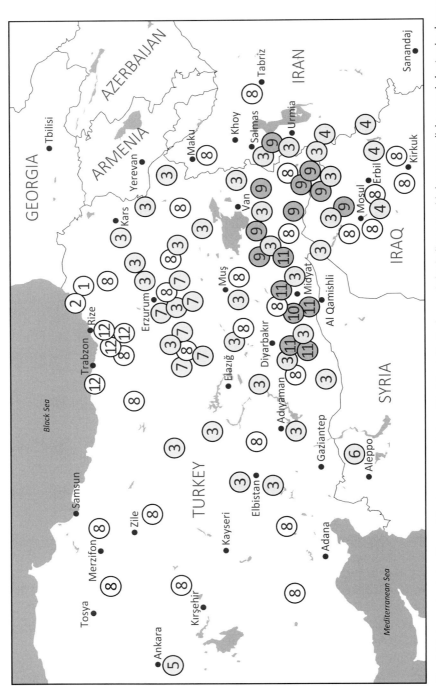

Map 14.1 Approximate locations of the language varieties of East Anatolia. Dark grey circles indicate Semitic languages, light grey circles Iranian languages, and white circles are other language families. Numbers refer to the language numbering in Section 14.2.1. Placement of circles provides only approximate indication of geographical distribution

7. Zazaki, Northwest Iranian, and culturally often considered part of 'Kurdish', is considered by Iranian philologists to be a distinct language; see Paul (1998).

8. Turkish, Turkic. The sole official language of the Turkish state since 1923 and the basis for Ottoman Turkish, the language of the Ottoman Empire. There is a chain of dialects across Anatolia spreading into present-day Azerbaijan and Iran (Bulut 2002, 2006), but Turkish influence in the far southeast (south of Lake Van) was not particularly strong prior to the twentieth century. Material for this chapter is from Tabriz (Kıral 2001), Erzurum (Gemalmaz 1995) and Turkmen of Iraq (Bulut 2007).

9. North Eastern Neo-Aramaic (NENA). A divergent group of dialects spoken by Christian and Jewish communities east of the Tigris river in Turkey, West Iran and North Iraq. NENA belongs to the West Semitic languages. The varieties included here are Jewish Urmi (Khan 2008b), Bohtan (Fox 2009), Ashitha (Borghero 2005), Barwar (Khan 2008c).

10. Central Neo-Aramaic, spoken further west but closely related to NENA, represented here by the variety of Ṭuroyo (Jastrow 1992).

11. Arabic dialects: the *qəltu*-dialects of Anatolia (Jastrow 1980; Talay 2011).

12. Romeyka. A Greek dialect spoken in a few villages between Rize and Trabzon on the Black Sea coast. It is currently being investigated in a project at the University of Cambridge: see www.romeyka.org.

14.3   Selected Structural Features

14.3.1   **Phonology**

The vowel systems of the Iranian and Semitic languages of eastern Anatolia are strikingly similar. They typically involve seven to nine vowel phonemes, of which five are long vowels and two or three are short. However, vowel length by itself is not a distinctive feature, and most vowels can be distinguished phonemically through vowel quality (short vowels are invariably more centralized than the long vowels). Table 14.1 shows the vowel phonemes of four varieties; the transcriptions of the sources have been normalized.

Turkic languages of the region likewise typically exhibit approximately eight vowel phonemes, and length is also generally not distinctive. However, Turkic varieties also include the front rounded vowels [y] and [œ]. In some varieties of Northern Kurdish, these vowels may occur as allophonic variants of the long vowels [uː] and [oː], and in loanwords. In the southeastern dialects (Hakkari (Kurd. Colemerg), Šemdinli (Kurd. Šemzinan)), [uː] tends to deround and front towards [iː], and [y] is often an intermediate stage in this process.

Table 14.1 *Typical vowel systems in Iranian and Semitic languages of Anatolia*

| | Semitic | | Iranian | |
	NENA (Bohtan) (Fox 2009: 10–14)	Mesop. Arab. (Jastrow 1980: 140–141; Talay 2011: 913)	Northern Kurd. (Öpengin and Haig 2014)	Zazaki (Paul 1998)
Long	[i]	[iː]	[iː]	[iː]
	[e]	[eː ~ ɛː]	[eː]	[eː]
	[a ~ æ]	[aː]	[aː]	[aː]
	[o]	[oː ~ ɔː]	[oː]	[oː]
	[u]	[uː]	[uː]	[uː]
Short	[ə] [a] [ʊ]	[ə] [a]	[æ] [ʊ] [ɨ]	[æ ~ ɛ] [ʊ][ɨ]

Table 14.2 *Three-way VOT distinction on bilabial, alveolar and dental stops, and affricates in Northern Kurdish*

Articulation	Bilabial + velar	Alveolar + affricates
Voiceless aspirated	[pʰoːr] 'hair'	[tʰæv] 'together'
Voiceless, unaspirated	[poːz] 'nose'	[tævɨr] 'hoe, mattock'
Voiced	[boːz] 'grey-white (of horses)'	[dæv] 'mouth'
Voiceless aspirated	[kʰaːr] 'work, matter, concern'	[tʃʰimaː] 'why'
Voiceless, unaspirated	[kaːl̩] 'old man'	[tʃæm] 'stream, brook'
Voiced	[gaːv] 'step, time'	[dʒæm] 'by, beside'

Turning to the consonants, a striking feature in both Zazaki and Northern Kurdish is a three-way distinction on the stops and affricates with regard to voice onset time (VOT). Table 14.2 shows a fairly typical system for Northern Kurdish.

The nature of the phonetic distinction between the two voiceless series has been the subject of some controversy. What are termed here 'unaspirated' have been claimed to possess an ejective quality, and in some dialects there is an undeniable perceptual similarity with (weak) ejectives, particularly with the unaspirated affricate [tʃ]. However, it is also the case that there is a significant difference in VOT, and most phonetic investigations have focused on this feature (Grawunder et al. 2013) while not excluding the possibility of an additional pharyngeal articulatory gesture. There is no plausible historical source for the additional series within Iranian, and it seems therefore most likely that they result from contact, most probably with Eastern Armenian (see Gippert 2007/2008 for discussion), though Neo-Aramaic has also been suggested as a possible influence (Kahn 1976). The additional series is also possibly preserved in the Armenian loanwords in the Erzurum dialect of Turkish, though the interpretation of the material is difficult (Menz 2010). However, the additional series is completely absent from Central Kurdish in Iraq, and our impression is that the frequency and saliency of the effects diminish across Anatolia towards the southeast, reflecting a diminishing Eastern Armenian influence.

All varieties of Kurdish have adopted pharyngealized consonants in some measure from neighbouring Semitic languages. However, the adoption of loan Semitic consonants in Kurmanji is subject to certain constraints: interdental consonants are never borrowed and geminate consonants in loanwords are generally de-geminated (see Kahn 1976: 80). In the only detailed study of loan phonology in Kurmanji, Kahn (1976: 89) notes a tendency for the over-generalization of pharyngealization in Arabic loans in Kurmanji. Thus Iraqi Arabic [dʒaːhil] is rendered [dʒaːħel] 'young', [zulal] as [zˤælaˤ] '(clear) water'. In the Kurmanji investigated by Kahn, pharyngealization in loanwords thus becomes a general signal of 'Arabic origin', rather than the actual rendering of the source phonology. It can, however, spread to items of the inherited lexicon; in Kurmanji Kurdish of the Iran/Turkey border region, Kahn (1976: 34) notes characteristic 'pharyngeal formant bending' for the first vowels in [sæd] '100' and [zawa] 'bridegroom', indicative of the pharyngeal quality of the initial consonants. Similarly, [ħ] is found in native words such as [ħæft] 'seven' or [mæħin] 'mare'.

The Semitic languages of the region are not just the donors of loan consonants, but have also undergone considerable phonological restructuring themselves under contact influence. For the Mesopotamian dialects of Arabic, Talay (2011: 912) notes the addition of /č/ (=[tʃ]), /g/, /p/ and /v/ to the native phoneme systems, clearly through the contact influence of Turkic and Iranian. Similarly, most of NENA have adopted /č/ (=[tʃ]) and /dʒ/, and sporadically /ʒ/ (Kapeliuk 2011). Talay (2006/2007: 181) also notes that some Anatolian Arabian dialects (e.g. Hasköy) have lost pharyngealization on some consonants, e.g. *tare* < **ṭarīq* 'way' and *sēbī* <**ṣabīy* 'boy'. Furthermore, in the Kozluk/Sason dialects, the characteristic Semitic interdental fricatives /θ/ and /ð/ (and their pharyngealized counterparts) may be realized either as sibilants or as stops. The latter are also lost in most varieties of NENA. Kapeliuk (2011) also notes the shift of interdental fricatives to dark-l in Jewish NENA of Azerbaijan, a development that has clear parallels in the Iranian languages of the region. The net result of these changes is to align the phoneme system of the local varieties of NENA and Arabic quite closely with those of their long-standing Kurdish neighbours.

14.3.2   Morphosyntax

14.3.2.1   Comparatives
All languages of Anatolia express the standard of comparison through a 'source' adposition or case marker (lit. 'he is bigger **from-me**'), either an ablative case suffix as in Turkish (-*den*/-*dan*/-*ten*/-*tan*) or in Laz (-*šen*:

Lacroix 2009: 93), or a preposition with a local meaning 'from', e.g. *ji* in Kurmanji, or *mən* (or variants thereof) in NENA and Arabic. This appears to be a universal feature across Anatolia.

The languages differ, however, as to how the adjective itself is marked as expressing the comparative degree. Three options are available: (i) there may be a particle preceding the adjective, as in Turkish *daha* or NENA *biš* (Khan 2008b: 229); (ii) the adjective may be left unmarked (Laz: Lacroix 2009: 93; this is also an option for Turkish); (iii) the Iranian languages have an inherited comparative suffix with most adjectives, as in Kurmanji *drêj-tir* 'long-er'. However, some Kurmanji speakers use the Turkish particle *daha* to express the comparative degree of an adjective. Conversely, the Kurdish comparative suffix *-tir* (or variants thereof) has been borrowed into Domari (Herin 2012: 23) and into Ṭuroyo Neo-Aramaic (Noorlander 2014). The cognate comparative suffix in Persian has also been borrowed into the Azeri Turkish of Tabriz in Iran (Kıral 2001: 19). The Turkish superlative particle *en* (*en güzel* 'most beautiful') is sometimes heard in Kurmanji Kurdish, and is reported for Domari (Herin 2012), Laz and Zazaki (Paul 1998: 58). In general, the morphosyntax of comparison is highly susceptible to contact influence, as noted for other contact regions (e.g. the Circum-Baltic languages: see Koptjevskaja-Tamm and Wälchli 2001: 684).

14.3.2.2   Copular Constructions

Most (all?) of the languages of Anatolia have a common pattern of expressing identity, or feature attribution, in copular clauses. The construction has been mentioned as a pan-Anatolian feature in Matras (2009: 270), and it is worth looking at in more detail. It involves a (usually) clitic copular element that follows the nominal predicate, yielding the pattern illustrated schematically in (1) (see Table 14.3 for examples):

(1)   this man   clever=is   'this man is clever'

There are two important commonalities here: first, an overt copula in the third person singular, indicative present, is *obligatory*, or at least extremely frequent. Second, its position in pragmatically neutral clauses is *clause-final*. However, we can only meaningfully assess the plausibility of a contact scenario by considering the histories of the different languages individually.

Turning first to the Iranian languages, the two features (clause-final position and obligatoriness) are inherited, and have characterized West Iranian throughout its attested history. Thus contact has not necessarily played a role in the copulas of these languages. For Turkic of the region, the presence of an obligatory third person copular in the indicative present can plausibly be attributed to Armenian and Iranian influence. In vernacular standard Turkish, there is no 'overt marking of the third person singular on predicates' (Göksel and Kerslake 2005: 128), thus to say 'my mother is tired', the two words 'mother-my' and 'tired' are simply juxtaposed, with no overt copular element: *Anne-m yorgun*. Spoken

Table 14.3 *Copular constructions, third person singular, present indicative*

Language	Non-verbal pred.		Copular, 3sg
Turkish of East Anatolia	*güzel*	'beautiful'	=*di(r)*
Northern Kurdish	*jwan*	'beautiful'	=*e*
Ṭuroyo Aramaic (Talay 2006/2007: 183)	*şefir*	'beautiful'	=*o*
Arab. (Kinderib) (Talay 2006/2007: 183)	*malīḥ*	'beautiful'	=*we*
Neo-Aramaic, Khabur dialect (Talay 2008: 201)	*xamte*	'beautiful'	=*la*
NENA (Urmi: Khan 2008b)	*jwān*	'beautiful'	=*ile*
Laz (Lacroix 2009: 148)	*genci*	'young'	*yen*
Domari of Aleppo (Herin 2012: 8)	*girān*	'heavy'	=*e*
Şêx Bizinî, Haymana dialect (Lewendî 1997)	*rind*	'good'	=*e*

standard Turkish does have a clitic element =*dir* (with vowel-harmonic variants), which may occur with third person nominal predicates, but it has specific pragmatic and modal functions, and is considered to be 'nowadays largely confined to formal language' (Göksel and Kerslake 2005: 341). What we observe in spoken Turkish from East Anatolia is a perceptible increase in the frequency of =*dir*, though this has not been noted in the literature nor systematically investigated. In the Azeri dialect of Tabriz (Kıral 2001) and in the Turkmen dialects of North Iraq (Bulut 2007), both under heavy Iranian influence, the use of an overt copula for the 3sg, -*di*, appears to be obligatory. Thus Turkish has moved closer to the pattern of Table 14.3 through a decrease in pragmatic markedness of an available option (=*dir*) and its consequent increase in frequency, rather than by any obvious restructuring.

Moving to the Semitic languages, it is here we find the most radical restructuring of inherited copular constructions. Historically, present-tense indicative clauses with non-verbal predicates lack an overt copular element: subject and predicate nominal are simply juxtaposed, and where overt copulas are found (e.g. in perfective aspect), they are not clause-final. This situation is maintained in most modern Arabic dialects outside Anatolia (Jastrow 1980: 148). Thus in colloquial Arabic of the Gulf and Saudi Arabia, we have the following in the present tense:

(2) *iš-šarīka*   *kabīra*
     DEF-company.FEM   big.FEM
     'The company (is) big' (Holes 1992: 41)

In Arabic dialects of Anatolia, however, an overt copula has become obligatory, though its position varies; in the Siirt dialect we find the order (subject) – cop – non-verbal predicate (Jastrow 1980: 148), which appears to be the only counter-example to the general Anatolian pattern of clause-final copulas (but see below):

(3) *āvi* *l-bənt*   *iye*   *bōš*   *malīḥa*
     this   DEF-girl   COP.3SG   very   good.F
     'This girl is very good'

In the other *qəltu*-dialects of East Anatolia, we find the clause-final type of Table 14.3, illustrated here for the Mardin dialect:

(4) *hāḏi*   *l-bənt*   *kṭīr*   *malēḥa=ye*
     this   DEF-girl   very   good.F=COP.3S

Example (5) would match word-for-word with the translational equivalent in neighbouring dialects of Kurmanji:

(5) *ev*   *keč*   *gelek*   *jwan=e*

Most varieties of NENA also have enclitic clause-final copulas, as in the Bohtan variety (Fox 2009: 62):

(6) *awa*   *ṭowé=le*
     this   good=COP.3M.SG   'This is good'

In the area of copular constructions then, the Semitic languages of Anatolia have undergone major internal restructuring of their inherited Semitic constructions to bring them in line with the general Anatolian pattern of obligatory clause-final copulas, presumably due primarily to Iranian influence. However, in southeast Anatolia a couple of wrinkles disturb the overall pattern, and these are worth pointing out briefly. They suggest that the Siirt pattern of medial copula, illustrated in (3) above, is not completely isolated.

A number of NENA dialects have an additional copular construction with a particular pragmatic force, described in Borghero (2005: 167) as being used to 'draw attention to a specific situation or to a non-permanent property of the subject'. This kind of copula is clause-medial, and in the Ashitha dialect it may also occur together with non-finite full verbs to express present continuous action. Similar forms are noted for several varieties of NENA including Bohtan (Fox 2009: 63) and Hertevin (Jastrow 1988: 27), who refers to the 'aktuelle Kopula'. In the Kurmanji dialects of southeast Anatolia and North Iraq, there is also a medial copula, based on the *ezafe* particle. It is formed by an *ezafe* particle which agrees in number and gender with its antecedent, but rather than link an adnominal modifier to the head, it introduces the predicate, in particular a non-verbal predicate (Haig 2011). The following example has a prepositional phrase as predicate (Kurmanji of Amadiye, North Iraq: Blau 1975: 106):

(7) *Xatûn=a*   *min*   **ya**   *l*   *hîvî=ya*   *te*
     lady=EZ.FEM   my   **EZ.FEM**   at   expectation=EZ.FEM   your
     'My lady is waiting for you (right now)' (lit. My lady which at your-waiting)

Another typical example is found in the name of a song, sung by a singer from Zakho, North Iraq (the Roman alphabet transcription in the original is *tuyal bîra min*, which is revealing from the point of view of speakers' perceptions of word boundaries, but which obscures the underlying morphology; in the glossed example I have added the morphological segmentation). Note that the noun *bīr* is feminine, hence the feminine form of the final *ezafe*, which is thus simply coincidentally identical to the first *ezafe*:

(8) tu   **ya**   l   bīr=a   min
     2SG   **EZ.FEM**   in   memory=EZ.FEM   my
     'you (fem.) are on my mind' (lit. you which on my mind)

As in the Ashitha NENA case mentioned above, the use of these clause-medial copular elements with non-verbal predicates typically expresses 'immediacy', and non-permanent attribution. Again like the NENA medial copulars, the Kurmanji particles may occur with full verbs to express the immediacy and continuity of the event. This is illustrated for the Bohtan dialect of NENA (Fox 2009: 63):

(9) duwəd   d-aw   oġa   **hawlala**   dməxta
     mother of   Agha   **COP.FEM.SG**   is.sleeping
     'The Agha's mother is sleeping'

Example (9) would translate word-for-word into the southeastern dialects of Kurmanji. For example the Šemzinan dialect of Kurmanji (Ergin Öpengin, personal communication) likewise uses a clause-medial *ezafe* particle combined with a verb to indicate immediacy:

(10) dayk-a   axê   **ya**   dnûvī-t
      mother-EZ.FEM   Agha.OBL   **EZ.FEM**   sleep.PRS-3SG

The Kurmanji case is in fact considerably more complex than the brief discussion here might suggest; see MacKenzie (1961: 205–208) and Haig (2011) for details. But the presence of a medial copular form, inflecting for gender, and etymologically derived from a pronominal form (the demonstrative/relative *ezafe*), with a clear semantic connection to immediacy, appears to be a unique development within Kurdish, and restricted to just those varieties that have been in close contact with NENA.[1] It certainly seems reasonable to assume mutual influence in the developments sketched here, which illustrate rather nicely how within Anatolia, subregions may develop quite divergent phenomena, which do not necessarily diffuse across the entire region.

14.3.2.3 The Clitic Additive or 'Recalled Topic' Marker

All languages known to me in the region possess an enclitic particle with a pragmatic function signalling some notion of contrast, addition or the reintroduction of a previously topical element. It has no exact correspondence in English; according to context, it could be translated with 'and X',

---

[1] The use of gender-sensitive particles following the subjects of copular constructions in dialects of Kurmanji spoken around Maraş in Turkey is quite similar, but these occur together with the normal clause-final copula (see Öpengin and Haig 2014).

'X too' or 'as for X'. It may also follow a predicate, in which case it has the entire event in its scope. The relevant marker is =žī in Kurmanji and Zazaki, =ti in Laz, =da/de in Turkish and =se in NENA of Bohtan (Fox 2009: 103). An example of typical usage from Zazaki is shown in (11), where the preceding context describes how the friends of a young boy used to call him by the nickname of Gukulah (Paul 1998: 232):

(11) *Lājikī=žī* *enā* *leqāmdā*   *xwi-rā*   *zāf* *xūy*   *kerdīnī*
      boy=**ADD** this nickname.of   his=ABL   very annoyance did
      'As for the boy, he was very annoyed about this nickname of his'

See Haig (2001: 208) for further exemplification of Kurmanji, Laz and Turkish. In Central Kurdish, the same function is expressed through =(i)š, which has been borrowed directly into Domari of Aleppo (Herin 2012: 47) and some dialects of Neo-Aramaic, for example in the dialect of Sulemaniyya and Ḥalabja (see Khan (2004: 399–408) for extensive discussion), and Urmi (West Iran):

(12) *anà=š*   *m-Urmí*   *ədyén*   *láxxa*
      1sg=ADD   from-Urmi   come.PST.1SG   here
      'I also have come from Urmi' (Khan 2008b: 332)

However, Iranian languages further east such as Persian, or Hawrami to the southeast, also have similar particles, as do some languages of the Caucasus and indeed from much further afield. Thus although this appears to be a feature of (possibly all?) languages of East Anatolia, it is also cross-linguistically quite common.

14.4 Word Order: Verbs and Objects, and Adpositions

For Standard Turkish, Laz and Eastern Armenian, both direct and indirect objects generally precede the verb, though the relative ordering of the two objects (if both are present) may vary according to their information status (for example, indefinite direct objects tend to immediately precede the predicate). Objects are flagged via case-suffixes or enclitics, though the presence of an overt case-marker may be mediated by differential object marking. This is given schematically in (13); the term 'Goal' here refers to recipients, addressees as well as local goals, and is intended to refer only to full NPs, rather than pronominal objects (Haig 2014b). The symbol '~' links two elements whose ordering may be reversed:

(13) goal-case ~ object-case verb

The following examples illustrate the pre-verbal position of direct object and goal for Eastern Armenian (14) and Laz (15), with glosses adapted and simplified:

(14) *dasaxos-ĕ*   *nor*   *girk-ĕ*   *mi*   *usanoł-i*   *talis*   *ē*
      lecturer-DEF new   book-DEF INDEF student-DAT give.PTCP.PRS COP.3S
      'The lecturer gives the new book to a student' (Dum-Tragut 2009: 566)

(15) *ar*   *orç'ay*   *k'oçi-k*   *oxorca-muşi-s*   *yali*   *muğudoren*
      INDEF of.Orçu man-ERG woman-POSS.3SG-DAT mirror he.brought.her
      'A man of Orçu brought his wife a mirror' (Lacroix 2009: 697)

For the Semitic languages, on the other hand, it can reasonably be assumed that historically, in pragmatically neutral clauses, both kinds of object follow the verb, and if flagged at all, then via prepositions, yielding:

(16) verb (prep-)object ~ prep-goal

This is illustrated for NENA, the dialect of Barwar (17) and of Hertevin (18):

(17) *ʾu-máxa*   *xa-məšxa*   *gu-be-ʾéne*   *dìye*
      and-they.put INDEF-oil on-forehead of.him
      'and they put oil on his forehead' (Khan 2008c: 882)

(18) *drélele*   *ḥalwe-hen*   *l=maška*
      they.poured   milk-POSS.3PL   into-butter.churn
      'they poured their milk into the goatskin butter churn' (Jastrow 1988: 108)

The two word order profiles illustrated in (13) and (16) represent diametrically opposed types, and it is of considerable interest to observe the various accommodation strategies that have emerged through contact between them. Two changes can be observed in the languages of the region.

First, among some of the Semitic languages we find a shift from VO to OV, notably in the Bohtan dialect of Christian NENA speakers and in the Urmi variety of NENA (Jewish speakers: Khan 2008b). Examples (19–20) are from Bohtan:

(19) *brota*   **axəst-aw**   *yawó-la*   *l-jambali*
      girl   ring-POSS.3SG.FEM give.PST-3SG.FEM to-Jambali
      'The girl gave **her ring** to Jambali' (Fox 2009: 101)

(20) **danw-i**   *nəmmun*   *qtəlax-le*
      tail-POSS.1SG why   cut_off.PST.2SG.FEM-OBJ
      'Why did you cut off **my tail**?'

However, OV word order in Bohtan is not the only option, and Fox provides several examples with post-predicate objects. Thus OV word order of the Bohtan dialect, unlike the OV order of neighbouring Kurdish dialects, is not a categorical rule, but rather a preference, 'the most common order' of verb and object (Fox 2009: 107).

Example (19) also illustrates the second point: the goal argument (*l-jambali*) is post-verbal, yielding the order OVG. This kind of word order is typologically

Table 14.4 *Word orders for direct object and goals in Anatolia*

Examples	Type	Order of verb, object and goal				
(14), (15)	original Turkic	object	~ goal	verb		
(19), (21)	Mesop. OVG		object	verb	goal	
(17), (18)	original Semitic			verb	object ~	goal

unusual and has received very little attention in the literature on word order.[2] It has a clear areal distribution, characterizing those dialects of NENA that have shifted to OV (e.g. Bohtan, or Urmi: Khan 2008b: 332) and all varieties of Kurdish spoken in southeast Anatolia and North Iraq, that is, precisely those varieties where contact with Semitic must have been most prolonged and intense. An example of Kurmanji from Amadiye (north Iraq) is the following:

(21) *to*   *vī*   *qaṭ'ā*   *'ard-ī*   *nā-da-ya*   *min*
       2SG   this.OBL   piece   land-OBL   NEG-give.PRS-DRCT   1SG.OBL
      'Won't you sell me this piece of land?' (MacKenzie 1962: 340)

I refer to the order illustrated in (19) and (21) as the Mesopotamian OVG word order.[3] It can be seen as a specific areal response to the conflicting demands of the two types illustrated in (13) and (16) above, and appears to be characteristic of all OV languages of North Iraq and southeastern Anatolia, including for example Iraqi Turkmen, a Turkic language under heavy Kurdish influence (Bulut 2007). Schematically, this is displayed in Table 14.4, whereby the respective ordering of goal and object is not rigidly fixed when both are on the same side of the verb.

It seems reasonable to seek the source of the post-predicate goals of the otherwise OV languages in the Semitic languages, which generally position their goals after the verb. Northern Kurdish is particularly instructive for investigating the areal distribution of post-verbal goals because it is spoken across a large area and subject to the influence of different contact languages. In the Mesopotamian region, it has been subject to heavy Semitic influence, while Semitic influence progressively diminishes as one moves northwards and westwards into Anatolia. The differences turn out to be at the level of differences in textual frequency (see Haig and Thiele 2014 or Haig 2014b for details), but there is one type of goal which shows a more categorical change in position and flagging type, depending on the location of the dialect. This is the addressee of verbs of speech. There are three options for marking addressees, involving different positions relative to the predicate and different kinds of flagging.

---

[2] One of the few typological contributions is Hawkins (2008), who considers the relative ordering of direct object and 'obliques'. However, Hawkins' notion of 'oblique' is not co-extensive with 'goal', as used here. Hawkins' obliques do not include Recipients, and do not extend to the local goals of intransitive verbs.

[3] Note that OVG refers to full NP objects; ordering of pronominal objects may differ.

(i) Post-predicate, with a preposition (or a directive (DRCT) particle on the verb, which is etymologically derived from a preposition). This possibility is illustrated in (22), from the Midyat region of southeastern Turkey (Haig 2014b):

(22)   *gōt-a*   ***Ūsufšá,***   *xatûn-ē*   *gō* . . .
        say.PST-DRCT   Usufsha,   lady-OBL.FEM   say.PST
        '(she) said to Usufsha, the lady said . . .'

(ii) Pre-predicate, introduced with a circumposition in (23):

(23)   *Wezîr*   ***ji***   ***jin-a***   ***xwe***   *ra*   *got-î-ye*
        Vizier   ADP   wife-ez.f   REFL   ADP   say.PST-PTCP-COP.3SG
        'The Vizier said to his wife'
                         (Muş dialect of Northern Kurdish, central Anatolia)

(iii) Pre-predicate, addressee flagged with a postpositional particle:

(24)   *mi*   *xewn-ek*   *dît-î-ye*   *ez=ê*
        1SG.OBL   dream-INDF   see.PST-PTCP-COP.3SG   1SG=FUT
        xewn-a   *xu*   ***te-ra***   *bêj-im*
        dream-EZ.FEM   REFL   2SG.OBL-to   say.PRS.SUBJ-1SG
        'I had a dream, I will tell **you** my dream'
                  (Northern Kurdish of Armenia: Djelil and Djelil
                  1978: 294; also typical of Tunceli: see Haig 2006)

The same pattern is also found in Zazaki, central Anatolia:

(25)   *šofir-dē-xo=rē*   *vano*
        driver-EZ-REFL=to   say.PRS.3SG
        '(He) says **to his driver**' (Paul 1998: 218)

This is essentially identical to the Turkic/Laz/Armenian pattern of pre-verbal addressees, marked with case suffixes or postpositions, illustrated for Laz in (26):

(26)   *tuti-s*   *ut'sumeski*
        bear-DAT   she.said
        'She said to the bear' (Lacroix 2009: 846)

What we see in Northern Kurdish is a progressive shift from a post-verbal, prepositional type of addressee, to a pre-verbal, postpositional one, roughly following a north/south cline through Anatolia. The patterns are illustrated schematically in Table 14.5.

    To conclude, Anatolia can be viewed as the region in which opposing word order tendencies overlap, a southern region of prepositional, VO Semitic languages and a northern/eastern region of postpositional, OV languages, in the spirit of Stilo (2005). When we look at the most well-known parameters of word order typology, we can discern certain accommodation strategies in the languages in this transitional zone. The first is

Table 14.5 *Marking the addressee of verbs of speech: areal changes across Northern Kurdish*

Region	Examples	Position/flagging of addressee		
Mesopotamian	(22)		Verb	PREP address.
Central Anatolia	(23)	ADP address. ADP	Verb	
North/west Anatolia	(24)	address.-CASE/ADP	Verb	

the shift from VO to OV in some varieties of NENA. The second is the extensive presence of post-predicate goals in all OV languages of the area, yielding an areally typical OVG word order. The third is the shifting use of adpositions, with postpositions and circumpositions dominant in the north and prepositions dominant in the south. While the presentation here is greatly simplified (see Haig 2014a, 2014b for more details), the overall outcome of these developments is undeniable: a specific areal profile resulting from the varied input of the region's languages.

14.5   East Anatolia as a Linguistic Area?

Haig (2001) initially tackled the question of whether East Anatolia would qualify as a 'linguistic area', concluding that a yes/no answer was premature at that stage. However, since then a good deal more data has become available, so that a reassessment appears to be overdue. In fact, the main problem is not lack of data, but the notion of linguistic area itself. On the whole I share the view of Campbell (2006) that linguistic areas are not particularly meaningful entities; at best they are secondary inferences derived from an investigation of individual contact phenomena (see Haig 2014a). Nor is East Anatolia clearly delineated as a geographic region, and depending on the extension of the definition, rather different results emerge. For example, Haig (2001) and Matras (2009: 270) both include the Kartvelian language Laz in their notion of East Anatolian linguistic area, but as will be seen below, such a pan-Anatolian approach in fact misses several important generalizations. In what follows, I will assess attempts to defend a pan-Anatolian linguistic area, before presenting a more fine-grained alternative solution below.

14.5.1   The Indicative/Progressive Prefix

Matras (2010) refers to an East Anatolian 'linguistic area', citing as one major diagnostic the presence of a 'progressive-indicative aspectual prefix' (2010: 75) in a number of the languages of the region: Kurdish, Levantine Arabic, Persian and Armenian; see also Matras (2007: 45) and (2009: 260) for similar claims. The proposed template for the 'present tense finite verb in languages of East Anatolia' (Matras 2009: 260) is provided in (27):

(27) ASPECT – PRESENT.STEM – PERSON.AGREEMENT
  e.g. Kurmanji *di-bêj-im*   'I say/am saying'

The claim is potentially interesting because it is concerned with bound verbal morphology, on most accounts the grammatical domain least susceptible to contact influence. But precisely because of its intrinsic interest, it requires careful assessment (see Haig 2014a for details). The first problem with this feature – at least as a diagnostic for an Anatolian linguistic area – is the absence of a progressive indicative prefix in a number of languages of the area, notably all varieties of Turkic, in Zazaki, in the Aleppo variety of Domari (Herin 2012) and in Laz.[4] Turning to those languages which do exhibit such a prefix, they are either Semitic or Iranian. With regard to the Iranian languages, a present indicative prefix is a feature of West Iranian generally, found in Iranian languages outside Anatolia including Hawrami, Vafsi, Balochi and the Central Plateau languages. The presence of this feature in Kurdish, then, is hardly the result of shared areal distribution, but simply of genetic inheritance.

Turning now to the Semitic languages, for the *qəltu* Arabic dialects of Kurdistan and Anatolia contact influence appears to be likely. They have innovated a present tense prefix *ku-* attached to the imperfect stem; similar formations are found in dialects throughout North Iraq, and it seems highly probable that Kurdish was influential in this development. For NENA, however, the facts are far from clear. Where such a prefix is found, it is not always just a general present indicative marker, but may contribute additional aspectual (e.g. progressive or habitual) nuances. For example, in the Hertevin dialect of NENA, the present tense generally lacks a prefix: *me ʔāmiton* what say.you.PRS.INDIC 'what do you think (say)?' (Jastrow 1988: 54), but a prefixed form is available for future or habitual senses. Or a prefixed present tense indicative is available, but only for a restricted number of lexical verbs (e.g. vowel-initial stems in Bohtan: Fox 2009: 55), or it may be entirely absent, as in Ashitha Neo-Aramaic, spoken in the village of Lower Ṭiyare in southeastern Turkey on the Iraqi border, squarely within East Anatolia. All this is quite different to the Kurdish case, where the prefix is present (in various forms) in all dialects, but lacks any aspectual value whatsoever; it is simply the default indicative present marker.

In sum, it is quite probable that the verbal system of the Semitic languages of southeast Anatolia (Arabic dialects and NENA) was strongly influenced by neighbouring Iranian languages, most significantly by Kurdish. The parallels

---

[4] Homshetsma, the sole surviving dialect of Western Armenian in Anatolia, has an indicative prefix in the present tense, but only with vowel-initial verb stems (Vaux 2007: 263). Eastern Armenian lacks an indicative prefix in the present entirely. Just where 'Western Armenian' should be geographically located is not a simple question, so assessing the specific areal relevance of the Western Armenian data is difficult; Matras (2010) does not include a source for the Western Armenian data.

are deep, and have led to developments in NENA that set it apart from all other Semitic languages. In particular, the development of ergative alignment based on participial forms of past-tense verbs, and the use of clitic pronouns to index the agent, are matched exactly by the developments in Middle Persian and Parthian, and in today's central Kurdish, and few scholars now doubt that the development of ergative structures with past transitives in NENA was in part the result of influence from Iranian (Kapeliuk 2011; Khan 2008a; Noorlander 2014). Against this backdrop, it would not be surprising if Iranian patterns of mood/aspect marking were also replicated in NENA and local varieties of Arabic, yielding the shared template given in (27). But viewed in this light, we have a straightforward case of contact influence of one language (or group of languages), Kurdish, on neighbouring groups, NENA and Arabic. But this is not a feature that has diffused in Anatolia as such, as other languages of Anatolia (e.g. Zazaki and Turkish) are totally unaffected by it. Thus the relevance of this feature as a diagnostic for an Anatolian linguistic area is questionable.

14.5.2   Finite Subjunctive Modal Complements after want

Another feature mentioned by Matras (2009: 270) as characteristic of East Anatolia is 'final subjunctives in modal complements'. Table 14.6 shows an example of the pattern concerned, illustrated by Neo-Aramaic and Kurmanji (Noorlander 2014) with the complement of want.

Superficially, NENA and Kurmanji appear to show close parallels.[5] But to what extent the parallelism evident in Table 14.6 is contact-induced, and to what degree it diffuses beyond the specific NENA/Kurdish contact situation across Anatolia as a whole, needs to be investigated.

Let us consider first the probable initial states of Kurmanji and NENA respectively by investigating related languages outside the region. We know that the pattern shown in Table 14.6 is also widespread across West Iranian and is not restricted to East Anatolia. Its presence in Kurmanji is thus predictable, regardless of any areal influence. Turning

Table 14.6 *Patterns of* WANT-*complementization*

	'I'	Present indicative			Present subjunctive			'home'
		ind-prog	base	pam	subj	base	pam	
Kurmanji	*Ez*	*di-*	*xwaz*	*-im*	Ø-	*her*	*-im*	*malê*
Ṭuroyo	*ʔono*	*k-*	*əbʕ*	*-ono*	(*d-*)	*əzz*	*-i(no)*	*l-ú=bayθo*

---

[5] Note that the form given in Table 14.6 for 'Kurmanji' is actually not found in those Kurmanji dialects spoken in the southeast of the Kurmanji region, in particular North Iraq (e.g. Zakho). Here the translational equivalent of Table 14.6 has a non-canonical subject (oblique) form for the 'wanter' (i.e. *min dvêt biçime mal* 'to-me is desirous I-go home'). Thus the common template suggested by Table 14.6 applies to a subset of Kurmanji dialects only.

to Semitic, we find that Semitic languages outside Anatolia also exhibit a pattern of WANT-complementization quite similar to Table 14.6, with a person-marked verb occurring after the modal. Example (28) is from Gulf Arabic; see also Brustad (2000: 234) on Egyptian and Moroccan Arabic:

(28) *aḥibb*   *aruuḥ*   *is-síinema*
      I.want   I.go   DEF-cinema
      'I like going to the cinema, I would like to go to the cinema'
      (Holes 1992: 231)

Thus although we can reasonably assume that Kurdish supplied the model for Table 14.6, NENA did not actually have to accommodate very drastically to arrive at the common form: from the Semitic predecessors of NENA we can assume that the linear order of WANT and its complement was already aligned with the Iranian model, and having person-marked verbs in the complement clause is also a feature widespread in Semitic. Another language of the region that shares this feature is Domari of Aleppo (Herin 2012: ex. 9). In other words, the common pattern shown in Table 14.6 is largely attributable to the genetic inheritances of Semitic and Iranian respectively, with contact influence achieving some fine-tuning, but little more.

However, the pattern found in Table 14.6 is also found in those varieties of Turkic under Iranian influence. It is generally assumed that historically in Turkic, complements of WANT are (i) non-finite, and (ii) placed before WANT. Thus standard Turkish for (28) is:

(29) *[sinema-ya*   *git-mek]*   *isti-yor-um*
      cinema-DAT   go-INF   want-PROG-1SG

The complement of WANT is preposed and non-finite. Turkic varieties under Iranian influence, however, develop postposed complement clauses containing a finite (optative) verb-form, as in the following example from Azeri Turkish from Tabriz, Iran:

(30) *vä*   *män*   *istird-im*   *[ǧïšǧïr-am]*
      and   1SG   want.PST-1SG   scream.OPT-1SG
      'and I wanted to scream'   (Kıral 2001: 82)

What we are seeing, then, is the spread of this pattern wherever Iranian influence is strong. For Semitic languages, such as NENA, synchronizing with the Iranian pattern does not involve major restructuring, whereas for Turkic it does. On the whole, the facts can be rather simply accounted for in terms of Iranian influence on neighbouring languages. Thus we have a case of bilateral contact influence, rather than the result of multilingual, pan-Anatolian diffusion. In the north of Anatolia, for example, this pattern is not prevalent. In Laz, the complement of WANT is non-finite and generally preposed:

(31) *yahudi-s*   *[k'inçi-şi*   *oçk'omo]*   *unt'u*
      Jew-DAT   bird-GEN   eat.NONFIN   want.PST.3SG
      'The Jew wanted to eat the bird'   (Lacroix 2009: 516)

Eastern Armenian has non-finite modal complements, but like Iranian, they are post-verbal. This in fact looks like a compromise solution between the Iranian and Turkic strategies, with Turkic providing the non-finite form of the complement and Iranian the post-verbal position:

(32) *Anuš-ĕ*   *uz-um*   *ĕ*   *[ašxat-el*   *gradaran-um]*
      Anuš-DEF   want-PTCP.PRES   COP.3SG   work-INF   library-LOC
      'Anuš wants to work in the library'

Finally, the remnant dialects of Romeyka, Greek dialects spoken near Trabzon, have actually *retained* non-finite complements of WANT despite the general drift in Greek to abandon them in favour of finite, subjunctive complements. In short, the shared pattern of subjunctive modal complements largely reduces to a matter of Iranian influence on neighbouring languages, with quite a clear directionality, and can be more cogently analysed in those terms, rather than in terms of a multidirectional diffusion.

14.5.3 An Alternative Solution: Two Spheres and an Intermediate Zone

From the preceding it follows that there are good grounds to take a more differentiated view of Anatolia. Essentially, we can identify two areas of denser contact, with an overlap zone between them.

14.5.3.1 The Mesopotamian Region

This centres on North Iraq and Turkey south of Lake Van and is historically dominated by Central and Northern Kurdish, interspersed by a series of NENA and Arabic-speaking speech communities. Across this region we find massive parallels at all levels: in the lexicon, for example, Khan (2008a: 209) gives the following figures for Kurdish borrowings in the lexicon of the Sulemaniyya NENA of North Iraq: nouns, 67 per cent; adjectives, 48 per cent; particles, 53 per cent; verbs, 15 per cent. We have already noted the parallels in the vowel system (see Section 14.3.1 above), shared word order patterns (OVG), shared morphology (the aspectual suffix *-awa* (and phonetic variants), not discussed here), the remarkable tolerance of complex syllable onsets in Central Kurdish and the southeastern dialects of Northern Kurdish (not discussed here), as well as similar complementation strategies, and a shared present-tense morphological template, to name but a few.

14.5.3.2 Caspian/Caucasian Region

Northeast Anatolia, north of Lake Van, is dominated by Turkic, dialects of Eastern Armenian and dialects of Northern Kurdish. Extending westward along the Black Sea coast, this region includes languages such as Laz and Romeyka. The languages of this region exhibit diametrically opposed values on a number of features when compared to those of the Mesopotamian region.

Between these two regions there is a large area that shows affinities with both. The languages spoken here include the central Anatolian and north-western varieties of Kurmanji Kurdish (generally referred to as Serhad dialects), Zazaki, dialects of Turkish and various varieties of Armenian.

An impression of the differences between the Mesopotamian and the Caucasian/Caspian spheres emerges when we plot a selection of morpho-syntactic features across the languages, as shown in Table 14.7. It will be seen that NENA, Central Kurdish and Arabic line up closely (barring two features of Central Kurdish), and that Turkish, Eastern Aramaic, Laz and Homshetsma likewise exhibit close similarities. But assigning Northern Kurdish, Domari of Aleppo or Zazaki to either type is problematic. For Northern Kurdish, the problem is simply the size and geographical spread of the speech community: the southeastern dialects align with the languages of Mesopotamia, the northern dialects show greater affinities with the Caspian/Caucasian languages. The position of Domari is rather special, and reflects both the Indo-Aryan origins of the language as well as traces of the speakers' movements prior to their current location.

Table 14.7 *Morphosyntactic features in languages of Anatolia*[6]

	CK	Ar.	NENA	Dom	NK	Za	Tu	Hom	Laz	EA
1	+	+	+	+?	+/−	+/−	−	−	−	−/+
2	+	+	+	+	−	−	−	−	−	−
3	+	+	+	−	+	+	−	−	−	−
4	+	+	+	+?	+	+	(+)	(+)	(+)	(+)
5	+	+	+	+?	+/−	−	−	−	−	−
6	+	+	+/−	−	+	−	−	+/−	−	−
7	−	+	+	−	+	+	−	−	−	−
8	−	+	+/−	+?	−	−	−	−	−	(+)
9	+	+	+	+	+	+	+/−	?	−	−

Features listed in the table
1 Local relations (*in, at, from* etc.) expressed through prepositions
2 Same set of clitic pronouns attaching both to verbs as object indices and to nouns as possessors
3 Noun–Possessor, Noun–Adjective word order in the NP
4 Post-predicate recipients of GIVE
5 Lack of postpositional marking of addressees of verbs of speech
6 Indicative/aspectual prefix on present-tense verb forms
7 Grammatical gender
8 VO word order
9 Finite complement of WANT

[6] Abbreviations: Dom, Domari of Aleppo, EA, Eastern Armenian, Hom, Homshetsma; +/−, varies according to local varieties; (+), not the unmarked option, but available as a pragmatically marked variant in all varieties; +?, feature attested, but insufficient data on frequency of occurrence; ?, source unavailable.

Table 14.8 *Possible shared features of a pan-Anatolian region*

(i)   the enclitic recalled-topic marker (cf. Section 14.3.2.3 above)
(ii)   an obligatory clause-final copula (cf. Section 14.3.2.2 above)
(iii) 'either-or' constructions based on *ya(n)* . . . *ya(n)* (Haig 2001)
(iv)   a grammaticalized indefinite article, accompanying indefinite singular NPs (not investigated here, but potentially of some interest)
(v)   echoic reduplication (Haig 2001; Matras 2009)
(vi)   the use of a general complementizer *ki* (with variant vowel values, Haig 2001)

The data thus generally support the assumption of two areal epicentres, with an intermediate zone, rather than a pan-Anatolian linguistic area. Nevertheless, a few candidates remain that could be considered shared features of a pan-Anatolian region. Table 14.8 gives a list of possible shared features, taken from morphosyntax, to which a number of shared discourse markers and (probably) the obligation particle *lazim* (in various phonetic variants, originally from Arabic) could be added.

Whether the features listed in Table 14.8 constitute grounds for assuming a linguistic area depends on how one defines 'Anatolia' (many of the features are geographically distributed far beyond the conventional boundaries of Anatolia, for example (i) and (v)), and the concept of 'linguistic area' itself. One could obviously tweak both definitions until they match the data, but that does not seem a particularly meaningful endeavour. What can be said with some degree of certainty is that two subregions of conspicuous structural parallels can be identified: the southeastern Kurdish/NENA/Arabic 'Mesopotamian' region and the northern Turkic/Kartvelian/Armenian 'Caspian/Caucasian' region. Much of Anatolia lies between the two, and disentangling the respective contact influences is correspondingly difficult.

14.6   Conclusions

East Anatolia lies at the overlap of several major macro-linguistic areas. It is thus neither a spread zone nor a residual zone, but a transition zone. Its linguistic diversity results from the overlay from its neighbouring areas, rather than through gradual accumulation of indigenous variation. Because different parts of the region show affinities to different neighbouring regions, it is extremely difficult to identify significant shared features covering the entire region. I suggest that it is more meaningful to identify the subregions, rather than simply assume the existence of an Anatolian linguistic area. The most prominent subregion is in the southeast (south of Lake Van into North Iraq), which I refer to as the Mesopotamian region; most of the shared features here can be relatively straightforwardly attributed to Kurdish influence on local Semitic languages (NENA and Arabic), but Kurdish itself has also been affected (pharyngeal consonants, medial copula in some varieties, the greater tolerance of complex syllables in Central Kurdish when compared to the northernmost dialects of Northern Kurdish). Languages of the northern part of Anatolia are only marginally implicated and in fact show quite different values on a number of features. I refer to them as the Caspian/Caucasian region; here, it seems that Turkish is the dominant language, and much of what can be found in languages like Laz can reasonably be attributed to Turkic influence.

A small number of pan-Anatolian features can nevertheless be identified, but their significance is not fully clear; they are either typologically commonplace, hence possibly coincidental, or represent inroads of larger shared areal patterns, extending well beyond the geographical boundaries of East Anatolia. On balance, the assumption of an Anatolian linguistic area now appears doubtful, though this in no way detracts from the overall interest of the region as characterized by multiple contexts of long-standing language contact among genetically unrelated languages, which has left its impact on all levels of language structure.

References

Blau, Joyce, 1975. *Le Kurde de 'Amādiya et de Djabal Sindjār: Analyse Linguistique, Textes Folkloriques, Glossaires*. Paris: Klincksieck.

Borghero, Roberta, 2005. *The Neo-Aramaic Dialect of Ashitha*. Unpublished PhD thesis, University of Cambridge.

Brustad, Kristen, 2000. *The Syntax of Spoken Arabic: A Comparative Study of Moroccan, Egyptian, Syrian, and Kuwaiti Dialects*. Washington, DC: Georgetown University Press.

Bulut, Christiane, 2002. Evliya Çelebi as a linguist and dialectologist: Seventeenth century East Anatolian and Azeri Turkic dialects. In Nuran Tezcan and Kadir Atlansoy (eds), *Evliya Çelebi ve Seyahatname*, pp. 49–64. Doğu Akdeniz Üniversitesi Yayınları.

Bulut, Christiane, 2006. Turkish elements in spoken Kurmanji. In Hans Boeschoten and Lars Johanson (eds), *Turkic Languages in Contact: Proceedings of the Wassenaar Meeting, Feb. 1996*, pp. 95–121. Wiesbaden: Harrassowitz.

Bulut, Christiane, 2007. Iraqi Turkman. In John Postgate (ed.), *Languages of Iraq, Ancient and Modern*, pp. 159–187. Cambridge: British School of Archaeology in Iraq.

Campbell, Lyle, 2006. Areal linguistics: A closer scrutiny. In Yaron Matras, April McMahon and Nigel Vincent (eds), *Linguistic Areas: Convergence in Historical and Typological Perspective*, pp. 1–31. Basingstoke, UK: Palgrave Macmillan.

Djelil, Ordixane and Celile Djelil, 1978. *Zargotina K'urda [The Oral Tradition of the Kurds]*. Moscow: Nauk.

Dum-Tragut, Jasmine, 2009. *Armenian*. Amsterdam: John Benjamins.

Fox, Samuel Ethan, 2009. *The Neo-Aramaic Dialect of Bohtan*. Piscataway, NJ: Gorgias Press.

Gemalmaz, Efrasiyap, 1995. *Erzurum ili Ağızları: İnceleme, Metinler, Sözlük ve Dizinler [The Spoken Varieties (of Turkish) in Erzurum: Analysis, Texts, Lexicon, Glossaries]*. Ankara: Türk Dil Kurumu.

Gippert, Jost, 2007/2008. Zur dialektalen Stellung des Zazaki. *Die Sprache* 47 (1): 77–107.

Göksel, Aslı and Celia Kerslake, 2005. *Turkish: A Comprehensive Grammar*. London: Routledge.

Grawunder, Sven, Anja Geumann, Geoffrey Haig, Cemile Celebi and Donald Stilo, 2013. Stop contrasts in Kurmanji Kurdish: Testing the ejectives hypothesis. Paper held at the Fifth International Conference on Iranian Linguistics (ICIL5), University of Bamberg, August 2013.

Haig, Geoffrey, 2001. Linguistic diffusion in present-day east Anatolia: From top to bottom. In Robert Dixon and Alexandra Aikhenvald (eds), *Areal Diffusion and Genetic Inheritance: Problems in Comparative Linguistics*, pp. 195–224. Oxford: Oxford University Press.

Haig, Geoffrey, 2004. The invisibilization of Kurdish. The other side of language planning in Turkey. In Stephan Conermann and Geoffrey Haig (eds), *Die Kurden: Studien zu ihrer Sprache, Geschichte und Kultur*, pp. 121–150. Hamburg: Schenefeld.

Haig, Geoffrey, 2006. Turkish influence on Kurmanji: Evidence from the Tunceli dialect. In Lars Johanson and Christiane Bulut (eds), *Turkic–Iranian Contact Areas: Historical and Linguistic Aspects*, pp. 283–299. Wiesbaden: Harrassowitz.

Haig, Geoffrey, 2011. Linker, relativizer, nominalizer, tense-particle: On the Ezafe in West Iranian. In Foong Ha Yap, Karen Grunow-Hårsta and Janick Wrona (eds), *Nominalization in Asian Languages: Diachronic and Typological Perspectives,* vol. 1: *Sino-Tibetan and Iranian Languages*, pp. 363–390. Amsterdam: John Benjamins.

Haig, Geoffrey, 2014a. East Anatolia as a linguistic area? Conceptual and empirical issues. In Lale Behzadi et al. (eds), *Bamberger Orientstudien*, pp. 13–35. Bamberg: Bamberg University Press.

Haig, Geoffrey, 2014b. Verb-goal (VG) word order in Kurdish and Neo-Aramaic: Typological and areal considerations. In Geoffrey Khan and Lidia Napiorkowska (eds), *Neo-Aramaic and its Linguistic Context*, pp. 407–425. New York: Gorgias Press.

Haig, Geoffrey and Ergin Öpengin, 2014. Kurdish: A critical research overview. *Kurdish Studies* 2 (2): 99–122.

Haig, Geoffrey and Hannah Thiele, 2014. Post-predicate goals in Northern Kurdish and neighbouring languages: A pilot study in quantitative areal linguistics. Paper held at the Second International Conference on

Variation and Change in Kurdish, Mardin Artuklu University, 8–9 October 2014.

Hawkins, J. A., 2008. An asymmetry between VO and OV languages: The ordering of obliques. In Greville Corbett and Michael Noonan (eds), *Case and Grammatical Relations: Essays in Honour of Bernard Comrie*, pp. 167–190. Amsterdam: John Benjamins.

Herin, Bruno, 2012. The Domari language of Aleppo (Syria). *Linguistic Discovery* 10: 1–52.

Holes, Clive, 1992. *Colloquial Arabic of the Gulf and Saudi Arabia*. London: Routledge.

Jastrow, Otto, 1980. Das mesopotamische Arabische. In Wolfdietrich Fischer and Otto Jastrow (eds), *Handbuch der Arabischen Dialekte*, pp. 140–154. Wiesbaden: Harrassowitz.

Jastrow, Otto, 1988. *Der Neuaramäische Dialekt von Hertevin (Provinz Siirt)*. Wiesbaden: Harrassowitz.

Jastrow, Otto, 1992. *Lehrbuch der Ṭuroyo-Sprache*. Wiesbaden: Harrassowitz.

Kahn, Margaret, 1976. *Borrowing and Regional Variation in a Phonological Description of Kurdish*. Ann Arbor, MI: Phonetics Laboratory of the University of Michigan.

Kapeliuk, Olga, 2011. Language contact between Aramaic dialects and Iranian. In Stefan Weninger (ed.), *The Semitic Languages: An International Handbook*, pp. 738–747. Berlin: de Gruyter.

Khan, Geoffrey, 2004. *The Jewish Neo-Aramaic Dialect of Sulemaniyya and Ḥalabja*. Brill: Leiden.

Khan, Geoffrey, 2008a. *Arabic Documents from Early Islamic Khurasan*. London: Nour Foundation.

Khan, Geoffrey, 2008b. *The Jewish Neo-Aramaic Dialect of Urmi*. Piscataway, NJ: Gorgias Press.

Khan, Geoffrey, 2008c. *The Neo-Aramaic Dialect of Barwar*, vol. 1: *Grammar*. Brill: Leiden.

Kıral, Filiz, 2001. *Das gesprochene Aserbaidschanisch von Iran: Eine Studie zu den syntaktischen Einflüssen des Persischen*. Wiesbaden: Harrassowitz.

Koptjevskaja-Tamm, Maria and Bernhard Wälchli, 2001. The Circum-Baltic languages: An areal-typological approach. In Östen Dahl and Maria Koptjevskaja-Tamm (eds), *Circum-Baltic Languages: Typology and Contact*, pp. 615–750. Amsterdam: John Benjamins.

Lacroix, René, 2009. *Description du Dialecte Laze d'Arhavi (Caucasique du Sud, Turquie): Grammaire et Textes*. Unpublished PhD thesis, Université Lumière Lyon 2.

Lewendî, Mahmûd, 1997. Kurdên Şêxbizinî [The Şêxbizinî Kurds]. *Bîrnebûn* 3: 78–98.

MacKenzie, David, 1961. *Kurdish Dialect Studies*, vol. 1. Oxford: Oxford University Press.

MacKenzie, David, 1962. *Kurdish Dialect Studies*, vol. II. Oxford: Oxford University Press.

Matras, Yaron, 2007. The borrowability of structural categories. In Yaron Matras and Jeanette Sakel (eds), *Grammatical Borrowing in Cross-Linguistic Perspective*, pp. 31–73. Berlin: Mouton.

Matras, Yaron, 2009. *Language Contact*. Cambridge: Cambridge University Press.

Matras, Yaron, 2010. Contact, convergence, and typology. In Raymond Hickey (ed.), *The Handbook of Contact Linguistics*, pp. 66–85. Malden, MA: Blackwell.

Matras, Yaron, 2012. *A Grammar of Domari*. Berlin: de Gruyter.

Menz, Astrid, 2010. Klusile und Affikaten im Anlaut armenischer Globalkopien im Dialektmaterial von Erzurum. In Hendrik Boeschoten and Julian Rentzsch (eds), *Turcology in Mainz*, pp. 173–190. Wiesbaden: Harrassowitz.

Nichols, Johanna, 1992. *Linguistic Diversity in Space and Time*. Chicago: University of Chicago Press.

Noorlander, Paul, 2014. Diversity in convergence: Kurdish and Aramaic variation entangled. *Journal of Kurdish Studies* 2 (2): 201–224.

Öpengin, Ergin, 2012. Sociolinguistic situation of Kurdish in Turkey: Sociopolitical factors and language use patterns. *International Journal of the Sociology of Language* 217: 151–180.

Öpengin, Ergin, 2013. *Clitic/Affix Interactions: A Corpus-Based Study of Person Marking in the Mukri Variety of Central Kurdish*. Unpublished PhD thesis. Paris Sorbonne/University of Bamberg.

Öpengin, Ergin and Geoffrey Haig, 2014. Variation in Kurmanji. A preliminary classification of dialects. *Journal of Kurdish Studies* 2 (2): 143–176.

Paul, Ludwig, 1998. *Zazaki: Grammatik und Versuch einer Dialektologie*. Wiesbaden: Reichert.

Skutnabb-Kangas, Tove and Sertaç Bucak, 1995. Killing a mother tongue: How the Kurds are deprived of linguistic human rights. In Tove Skutnabb-Kangas and Robert Phillipson (eds), *Linguistic Human Rights: Overcoming Linguistic Discrimination*, pp. 347–370. Berlin: Mouton.

Stilo, Donald, 2005. Iranian as buffer zone between the universal typologies of Turkic and Semitic. In Éva Ágnes Csató, Bo Isaksson and Carina Jahani (eds), *Linguistic Convergence and Areal Diffusion: Case Studies from Iranian, Semitic and Turkic*, pp. 35–63. London: Routledge.

Stilo, Donald, 2012. Intersection zones, overlapping isoglosses, and 'Fade-out/Fade-in' phenomena in Central Iran. In Behrad Aghaei and M. R. Ghanoonparvar (eds), *Iranian Languages and Culture: Essays in Honor of Gernot Ludwig Windfuhr*, pp. 3–33. Costa Mesa: Mazda Publishers.

Talay, Shabo, 2006/2007. The influence of Turkish, Kurdish and other neighbouring languages on Anatolian Arabic. In *Romano-Arabica VI-VII (2006–2007)*, pp. 179–188. University of Bucharest, Center for Arab Studies.

Talay, Shabo, 2008. *Die Neuaramäischen Dialekte der Khabur-Assyrer in Nordostsyrien: Einführung, Phonologie und Morphologie*. Wiesbaden: Harrassowitz.

Talay, Shabo, 2011. Arabic dialects of Mesopotamia. In Stefan Weninger (ed.), *The Semitic Languages: An International Handbook*, pp. 909–920. Berlin: de Gruyter.

Vaux, Bert, 2007. Homshetsma: The language of the Armenians of Hamshen. In Hoann Simonian (ed.), *The Hemshin*, pp. 255–278. New York: Routledge.

Zeldes, Amir, 2013. Is Modern Hebrew Standard Average European? The view from European. *Linguistic Typology* 17 (3): 439–470.

15

An Areal View of Africa

Bernd Heine and Anne-Maria Fehn

15.1 Introduction

Comparative work on African languages in the past has focused on the genetic relationship patterns among these languages. But there is now a growing interest in areal relationships, and some of the language groupings that were earlier proposed to be genetic units have more recently been redefined as contact-induced, areal groupings: see the contributions in Heine and Nurse (2008) and Hieda et al. (2011).

The present chapter provides an overview of major achievements that have been made in the areal classification of African languages. On the one hand, it will be concerned with smaller groups of areally related languages and the major regions of the continent. On the other hand, it will look at Africa as a possible macro-area. The main interest of the chapter will be with what, following Weinreich (1953), is referred to as replication, that is, the contact-induced diffusion of structures and/or meanings rather than that of phonetic/phonological or morphological material.

The questions that are our main concern in this chapter are the following.

 (i) Are there any geographically defined language groupings in Africa?
(ii) Can the African continent be set off from the rest of the world as a linguistic area of some kind?

Question (i) will be the subject of Section 15.2, while Sections 15.3 and 15.4 are devoted to question (ii). In line with Heine and Kuteva (2005: 182–187) and Heine (2011), it will be argued in Section 15.5 that the study of areas of grammaticalization offers a promising perspective of the diffusion of contact-induced phenomena in both linguistic micro- and macro-settings of language contact. In the final Section 15.6, some conclusions are drawn.

15.2 Areal Groupings within Africa

Two main types of areal classifications can be distinguished in African linguistics. On the one hand they are based on a single property or domain of language structure that is argued to be diagnostic of an areal relationship; we will refer to them as single-feature classifications. On the other hand they are feature-bundle classifications, involving a combination of several properties.

One of the properties that students of African languages recruited to arrive at generalizations on the areal patterning of languages is word order. Based on a survey of the order of meaningful elements in African languages, Heine (1975, 1976) concludes that there are a number of linguistically defined areas cutting across boundaries of language families. One such area consists of a large part of West Africa where Mande, Gur (Voltaic) and western Kwa languages are spoken. In addition to these languages, which are traditionally classified as Niger-Congo, this area also includes Songhai, a language usually classified as belonging to the Nilo-Saharan phylum (Greenberg 1963).[1] What characterizes this area most of all is the presence of a possessor-possessee word order syntax which is not restricted to the noun phrase but has also affected the structure of the clause (see Claudi 1993). Another area, called the Rift Valley convergence area, is defined by the presence of verb-initial (VSO) syntax, very rarely encountered elsewhere in Africa.[2] The languages of this East African area belong to Greenberg's (1963) Nilo-Saharan (Surma, Kuliak, Eastern Nilotic and Southern Nilotic) and Khoisan phyla (Hadza).[3]

Word order is also the subject of a more recent attempt by Dryer (2011) to look for areal features shared by African languages across the continent. Based on a worldwide survey of the word order arrangement of nouns and their modifiers in over 1,600 languages, Dryer concludes that languages in Africa exhibit a greater tendency to place modifiers *after* the noun than languages in other parts of the world; we will return to this work in Section 15.4.

Another property figuring in classifications on areal grouping concerns phonology: Can Africa be divided into significant, geographically defined phonological zones? This question is answered in the affirmative by Clements and Rialland (2008): the authors propose dividing the continent

---

[1] With the term *phyla* (singular *phylum*) we refer to the four African 'families' proposed by Greenberg (1963), namely Afroasiatic, Nilo-Saharan, Niger-Congo (i.e. his Kongo-Kordofanian) and Khoisan. In doing so, we follow a widespread convention in African linguistics. Not all of these phyla are now generally recognized as valid linguistic units. Nilo-Saharan and Khoisan in particular have so far not been satisfactorily established as genetically defined groupings.

[2] The only other clear cases of VSO languages reported so far are the Berber languages of northwestern Africa, a few Chadic languages, and Krongo, a Kordofan language nowadays considered to belong to the Kadu branch of Nilo-Saharan (Heine 1976).

[3] Whether the Khoisan languages of southern and eastern Africa do in fact form a linguistic family, as claimed by Greenberg (1963), is now a matter of much dispute. Hence we are using the term 'Khoisan' in a loose sense. See the contribution by Güldemann and Fehn, Chapter 18, this volume.

Table 15.1 *Linguistic zones in Africa*

North Africa
Its phonological properties coincide largely with those of Arabic and the Berber languages.
East Africa
It encompasses Ethiopia, Eritrea, Djibouti and Somalia. Nearly all of its languages are usually classed in the Afroasiatic phylum.
Sudanic Belt
It includes the vast savannah that extends across Sub-Saharan Africa bounded by the Sahel on the north, the Atlantic Ocean on the west and southwest, Lake Albert on the southeast and the Ethiopian–Eritrean Highlands on the east.
Central Africa
It is almost exclusively Bantu-speaking and is characterized by the linguistic features typical of Bantu languages.
South Africa
It includes semi-desert, savannah and temperate coastal regions. Its phonological characteristics derive from those of the Khoisan and Bantu languages spoken within it. This zone contains some of the richest consonant and vowel inventories of the world's languages.
Rift Valley
It includes much of the eastern branch of the Great Rift Valley in northern Tanzania and southwestern Kenya. In this region, languages of all four of Greenberg's phyla (or super-families) are found.

Map 15.1 Phonological zones in Africa according to Clements and Rialland (2008)

into zones on the basis of phonological distinctions, as shown in Table 15.1.

These zones are primarily geographic and only secondarily linguistic in nature; they must be viewed as a first approximation to areal phonology, where each zone stands for a prototype, or an ideal type. For example, a number of the languages of the Southern Africa zone have more phonological features in common with languages of Central Africa, and many features of the Rift Valley zone can also be observed in other zones.

The declared or implicit goal underlying feature-bundle classifications is to search for sprachbund-like linguistic areas (or convergence areas). The most frequently mentioned and most widely recognized linguistic area is Northeastern Africa, frequently called the Ethiopian language area (or Ethio-Eritrean sprachbund). Within roughly the last two millennia, the highlands of Ethiopia appear to have favoured cultural and linguistic exchange on a massive scale, with the effect that the languages of this region now share a number of linguistic properties (Crass and Meyer 2008; Ferguson 1976). The languages included in this area are mostly genetically interrelated, belonging to the Cushitic, Omotic and Semitic branches of the Afroasiatic family, but some languages of the Nilo-Saharan phylum are also included. First proposed by Ferguson (1970, 1976), the notion of an Ethiopian language area has not gone unchallenged (Tosco 2000), but Crass and Meyer (2008) find further support for it, adding more properties characterizing the area, which is not restricted to the nation state of Ethiopia but also includes languages spoken in Djibouti, Somalia, Kenya and Sudan.

While Ferguson (1976) proposed eight phonological and eighteen grammatical features to define the Ethiopian area, Crass and Meyer (2008) add another twelve criteria in support of the grouping, most of which are morphosyntactic in nature. Half of these criteria concern processes of grammaticalization shared by the languages of the area and, hence, are suggestive of grammaticalization areas (see Section 15.4).

Another grouping that qualifies as a linguistic area is the Tanzanian Rift Valley area (Kießling, Mous and Nurse 2008). It includes languages of all African families (or phyla) that have been identified by Greenberg (1963), namely Southern Cushitic languages of Afroasiatic, Southern Nilotic of Nilo-Saharan, some Bantu languages of Niger-Congo, and Sandawe and Hadza of Greenberg's Khoisan phylum. The authors adduce a range of altogether fifteen features to substantiate their sprachbund hypothesis. Five of the features are phonological: they include presence versus absence of a lateral fricative /ɬ/, of ejective obstruents, or of a seven-vowel system. The largest number of features are morphological, being either structural (presence versus absence of a pre-verbal clitic complex, of categories such as verbal plurality, applicatives, ventives, or the number of past and future tense distinctions) or formal (presence of subjunctive *-ee* or irrealis *laa*). Further criteria are syntactic, concerning the linear arrangement of constituents, or conceptual, involving polysemy and semantic transfer strategies (see Kießling et al. 2008, Table 6.5).

In more recent research on linguistic relationships in Africa there appears to be a gradual shift of interest from genetic to areal linguistics. It may therefore not be surprising that some language groupings that were analysed by earlier authors as genetic units are now reanalysed in terms of contact-induced change and areal relationships. Roughly a century ago, Westermann (1911) proposed an essentially genetically defined stock, namely the Sudanic languages (*Sudansprachen*).[4] As Güldemann (2008) argues convincingly, however, many of the *Sudansprachen* of Westermann are more plausibly re-classified as forming an areal grouping, referred to by him as the Macro-Sudan Belt, which is similar to, but should not be confused with, the Sudanic Belt of Clements and Rialland (2008; see above). Defining properties of this grouping are presence of (a) logophoric markers, (b) labial–velar consonants, (c) vowel harmony of the ATR (advanced tongue root position) type, (d) a word order pattern S (Aux) OV-X, where the object (O) precedes the verb, (e) another word order pattern V-O-NEG, where the negation marker (NEG) is placed clause-finally, and (f) labial flap consonants.[5] Not all the features are found in all languages of the belt, but there is a massive clustering of the features that appears to be distinctive.

The Kalahari Basin of southern Africa also forms some kind of linguistic area; it provides an instance of a refuge area where people have been living over centuries and probably millennia without much interference from outside. It is the homeland of traditional hunter–gatherer populations speaking languages belonging to the 'Khoisan' phylum of Southern Africa. Güldemann (1998) argues that the Kalahari Basin convergence area is not confined to languages conventionally classified as belonging to the Khoisan cluster but also includes a Bantu language, namely Tswana, but more evidence is required on this issue (see Güldemann and Fehn, Chapter 18, this volume).

A number of additional groupings, suggestive of contact-induced relationships, have been proposed, but have so far not received wider recognition as linguistic areas.

15.3 The Search for 'Africanisms'

In an attempt to isolate areal within Africa and separating Africa from other regions of the world, Greenberg (1959) proposed a number of what he called 'special' features of African languages. The properties listed by

---

[4] With the adverb 'essentially' we remind readers that at that time, no clear distinction between genetic and other kinds of linguistic relationship was made.

[5] Labial–dental flaps begin with the lower lip placed behind the upper teeth. The lower lip is then flipped outward, striking the upper teeth in passing. Its occurrence outside Africa is extremely rare, while in Africa it is found in more than a hundred languages in the Chadic family (Margi, Tera), Ubangian (Ngbaka, Ma'bo, Sera), Central Sudanic (Mangbetu, Kresh) and Bantoid (Ngwe, some Shona dialects).

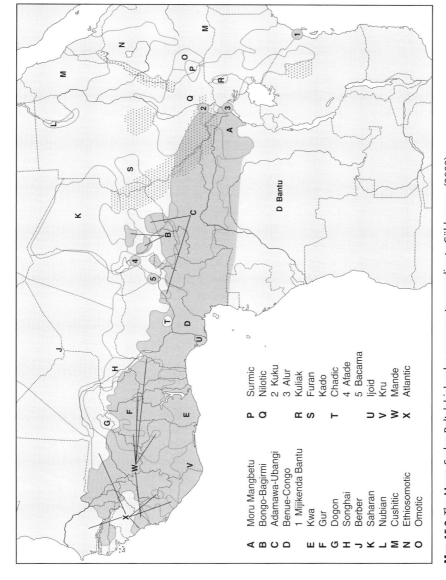

Map 15.2 The Macro-Sudan Belt: labial–velar consonants according to Güldemann (2008)

A	Moru Mangbetu	P	Surmic	
B	Bongo-Bagirmi	Q	Nilotic	
C	Adamawa-Ubangi		2 Kuku	
D	Benue-Congo		3 Alur	
	1 Mijikenda Bantu	R	Kuliak	
E	Kwa	S	Furan	
F	Gur		Kado	
G	Dogon	T	Chadic	
H	Songhai		4 Afade	
J	Berber		5 Bacama	
K	Saharan	U	Ijoid	
L	Nubian	V	Kru	
M	Cushitic	W	Mande	
N	Ethiosomotic	X	Atlantic	
O	Omotic			

him include in particular a number of lexical polysemies, such as the use of the same term for 'meat' and 'wild animal', of the same term for 'eat', 'conquer', 'capture a piece in a game' and 'have sexual intercourse', and the use of a noun for 'child' as a diminutive or of 'child of tree' to denote 'fruit of tree'.

Around this time, students of African languages began to search for what – following Meeussen (1975) – tends to be called 'Africanisms' (Greenberg 1983: 3; Heine and Leyew 2008), referring to properties that satisfy the following set of criteria.[6]

(a)   They are common in Africa but clearly less common elsewhere.
(b)   They are found, at least to some extent, in all major geographical regions of Africa south of the Sahara.
(c)   They are found in two or more of the four African language phyla.

Larochette (1959) presented a catalogue of linguistic properties characteristic of Congolese Bantu (Kikongo, Luba, Mongo), an Ubangian language (Zande) and a Central Sudanic language (Mangbetu), but a number of the properties proposed can also be found in other regions and genetic groupings of Africa. Building on this work, Meeussen (1975) proposed an impressive list of Africanisms, that is, phonological, morphological, syntactic and lexical properties widely found in African languages across genetic boundaries. Another range of properties characterizing many African languages was proposed by Welmers (1973, 1977).

In 1983, Greenberg proposed distinguishing between areal properties that are exclusive to Africa though not found everywhere within it, and properties that are especially common in Africa although not confined to the continent (Greenberg 1983: 3; see (a)–(c) above). As an example of the former he mentioned clicks; as instances of the latter he discussed in some detail the following 'characteristics' (Greenberg 1983: 4): (i) coarticulated labial–velar (or labio-velar) stops, (ii) labial–dental (or labio-dental) flaps, (iii) the use of a verb meaning 'to surpass' to express comparison, and (iv) a single term meaning both 'meat' and 'animal'. He demonstrated that these four properties occur across genetic boundaries and, hence, are suggestive of pan-African traits, especially since they are rarely found outside Africa.

Search for areal properties across Africa is associated to some extent with creole linguistics (see e.g. Boretzky 1983). In an attempt to establish whether, or to what extent, the European-based pidgins and creoles on both sides of the Atlantic Ocean have been shaped by African languages, researchers of creoles have pointed out a number of properties more widely found in Africa and/or a set of characteristics of African languages.

---

[6] 'Africanisms' correspond to what Greenberg (1983: 3) called African areal properties, that is, properties 'which are either exclusive to Africa, though not found everywhere within it, or those which are especially common in Africa although not confined to that continent'.

Perhaps the most detailed study is that by Gilman (1986). Gilman proposed a larger catalogue of pan-African areal properties, arguing that a large number of African-like structures in Atlantic and other pidgins and creoles are best explained by the influence of those areal properties which are widely distributed among the languages of Africa.

A number of the properties that are clearly more widespread in Africa than elsewhere are not considered here, for the following reasons. First, because they appear to be genetically determined. The presence of gender or noun class systems is a case in point. Most instances of such systems to be found in Africa are presumably genetically inherited. This can be assumed to apply on the one hand to the nature-based noun class systems found in Niger-Congo and the non-Khoe languages of the Khoisan unit, and on the other hand to the sex-based gender systems of Afroasiatic and Khoe (Central Khoisan) languages.[7]

Perhaps surprisingly, we will also not consider presence or absence of click types as distinct phonemic units to be a relevant property, although it appears to be the only property that is confined exclusively to Africa and although it satisfies most of the criteria proposed above. The reason for doing so is as follows. The main goal of this section is to find out whether African languages resemble one another more than they resemble other languages and what factors can be held responsible for such resemblances. To be sure, clicks occur in three of the four African language phyla, not only in all Khoisan languages. Rather, they are also found in Southern African Bantu (Niger-Congo) languages such as Zulu, Xhosa, Gciriku (Dciriku) or Yeyi (for more details see Maddieson 2003: 31–37, or Bostoen and Sands 2012) and in the Cushitic (Afroasiatic) language Dahalo (Tosco 1991: 4). Still, their occurrence is geographically restricted to southern Africa and three East African languages, that is, it is not representative of areal relationship in Africa as a whole.

Furthermore, although Khoisan languages are among the phonologically most complex languages in the world, some of them distinguishing more than 110 distinct phonemes (e.g. Heine and König, 2015; Traill 1994), this fact is ignored here since it does not appear to be a characteristic of Africa as a linguistic area. Furthermore, such complex sound inventories are restricted to a few Kx'a (Northern Khoisan) and Tuu (Southern Khoisan) languages.

In the following we will discuss a catalogue of properties that have been proposed to be characteristic of Africa as a linguistic area – especially by Greenberg (1959, 1983), Larochette (1959), Meeussen (1975) and Gilman (1986). Our selection is to some extent arbitrary in that we will ignore some properties that have been mentioned by other authors but where we are not entirely convinced that they are possible candidates for the status of

---

[7] It is possible that the presence of gender systems in the Eastern Nilotic languages (Maa, Teso-Turkana, Lotuxo, Bari) is the result of language contact with Cushitic languages, but the evidence for this is not conclusive.

'Africanisms'. Note that we restricted ourselves to properties that are suggestive of areal relationships, that is, that are not confined to genetically defined language groupings.

A general phonological property that has been pointed out by a number of researchers of African languages is the preponderance of open syllables and an avoidance of consonant clusters and diphthongs (Gilman 1986: 41; Meeussen 1975: 2). Furthermore, tone as a distinctive unit is characteristic of the majority of African languages, in many cases on both lexical and grammatical levels.

Ignoring click consonants, there are a number of consonant types that are widespread in Africa but uncommon elsewhere (see Clements and Rialland 2008 for detailed treatment). Prime examples, among others, are coarticulated labial–velar (or labio-velar) stops such as *kp* and *gb* (Gilman 1986: 41; Greenberg 1983: 4; Meeussen 1975: 2). There are also corresponding nasals and/or fricatives, but they do not show the wide distribution of stops, and their occurrence is largely predictable on the basis of stops (Greenberg 1983: 4). The distribution of this property is clearly areally constrained: Labial–velar stops occur in a broad geographical belt from the western Atlantic to the Nile–Congo divide, and they are also occasionally found outside this belt, for example in Katla and Giryama (see Welmers 1973: 47–48). Still, they are found in three of the four African phyla: only Khoisan languages have no labial–velar stops. Also, in the Afroasiatic and Nilo-Saharan phyla, their occurrence is restricted essentially to one branch each, namely Chadic and Central Sudanic, respectively (Greenberg 1983: 7; Güldemann 2008).

Perhaps even more characteristic are labial–dental (or labio-dental) flaps, where the teeth touch well below the outer section of the lip, which is flapped quickly outwards and downwards. They have been found in all African phyla except Khoisan, for example in Chadic of Afroasiatic (Margi, Tera), Niger-Congo (Ngwe, Ngbaka, Ngbaka Mabo, Ndogo-Sere, some Shona dialects) and Nilo-Saharan (Kresh, Mangbetu) (Clements and Rialland 2008; Greenberg 1983: 4, 11; Gregersen 1977: 31; Güldemann 2008). Still, their occurrence is confined to a relatively small number of languages, and even there they show restrictions in their use as phonemic units; not infrequently, these sounds are found only in special vocabulary such as ideophones. In their survey of 250 African and 345 non-African languages, Clements and Rialland (2008) did not find a single non-African language with such flaps, but at least 70 African languages did.

A third type of consonant that is widespread in Africa can be seen in implosives, which – following Clements and Rialland (2008) – we define as non-obstruent stops. To be sure, these exist in some non-African languages, such as the Indonesian language Auye (Mike Cahill, personal communication), but these languages are rare. Furthermore, word-initial prenasalized consonants, for the most part voiced stops, are widely found in Africa (Gilman 1986: 41; Meeussen 1975: 2), although they occur most of all in Niger-Congo languages.

An outstanding property relating to the vowel system can be seen in the presence of cross-height vowel harmony based on distinctions of the tongue root position, commonly known as ATR (advanced tongue root) vowel harmony. It is widespread in Niger-Congo and Nilo-Saharan languages across the continent but appears to be rare outside Africa; for discussion see Clements and Rialland (2008) or Güldemann (2008).

Morphological properties that have been mentioned as areal characteristics of African languages include reduplication of nouns and adjectives, used to express a distributive function (e.g. Swahili *tano tano* 'five each, in fives'; Gilman 1986: 40). Within the verbal word, many African languages are characterized by a wide range of derivational suffixes for functions such as reflexive, reciprocal, causative, passive, stative, andative (itive) and venitive (ventive), and these suffixes can be combined in sequence (Gilman 1986: 43; Meeussen 1975: 2). However, both these properties can also be observed widely in non-African languages.

A conspicuous feature of nominal morphology is the paucity of languages having case inflections. Those African languages that do distinguish grammatical case are mostly marked nominative, that is, in such languages it is the accusative rather than the nominative case that is unmarked (marked nominative languages are cross-linguistically exceptional). And a perhaps unique property of case systems is the presence of cases marked exclusively by tonal inflection, which so far has been found only in African marked nominative languages but apparently nowhere else in the world (König 2006, 2008).

With regard to word classes, African languages have been said to be characterized by a paucity of adjectives, and in a number of languages adjectives are claimed to be absent altogether. Those contents typically expressed in non-African languages by adjectives are likely to appear as verbs of state in Africa (see Gilman 1986: 40). On the other hand there is a word class of ideophones that appears to be remarkably salient in many African languages (Meeussen 1975: 3). While languages in other parts of the world have ideophones as well, African languages have been found to have them in distinctly larger numbers. Furthermore, ideophones expressing colour distinctions have so far only been found in Africa (Kilian-Hatz 2001; Voeltz and Kilian-Hatz 2001).

In their arrangement of words, African languages of all four phyla exhibit a number of general characteristics, such as the following: while on a worldwide level languages with verb-final syntax (SOV) appear to be the most numerous, in Africa there is a preponderance of languages with subject-verb-object (SVO) as their basic order: Roughly 71 per cent of all African languages exhibit this order (Heine 1975; 1976: 23; see also Gilman 1986: 37). Furthermore, the placement of nominal modifiers after the head noun appears to be more widespread in Africa than in most other parts of the world. Thus, in Heine's (1976: 23) sample of 300 African languages, demonstrative attributes are placed after the noun in 85 per cent, adjectives in 88 per cent and numerals in 91 per cent of all languages. Another characteristic in the arrangement of meaningful elements relates to verbal structures: in most African languages, pronominal subject clitics or affixes precede the tense markers (93 per cent), which again precede the verb (83 per cent), while adverbs follow the verb 93 per cent (Heine 1976: 24).

An arrangement of basic word order that occurs in a number of languages across the continent but which is fairly uncommon outside Africa concerns what now tends to be referred to as 'SOVX' order. In languages having this order, the direct object precedes the verb but the indirect object and adjuncts follow the verb. SOVX languages are likely to have postpositions and to place the genitival modifier before its head while other nominal modifiers follow the head noun (cf. the type B of Heine 1976).

With reference to information structure, front-focusing of nouns by means of some kind of cleft-construction has been mentioned, frequently used obligatorily in word questions, for example *who went?* is expressed by *who is it who went?* (Gilman 1986: 39; Gregersen 1977: 50–51). In addition to noun phrase focusing there is also front-focusing by means of verb-copying, where the verb appears first in the focus position and is repeated in the main clause (Gilman 1986: 39); the exact distribution of this phenomenon across Africa, however, is unknown. A striking characteristic of African languages can be seen in the widespread change of verb form, or the use of special auxiliaries, to express focus distinctions (Creissels et al. 2008: 138).

In addition, there are construction types that are said to be found in a number of African languages but to be rare outside Africa. One of them is called anastasis by Meeussen (1975: 4), consisting of the swapping of subject and complement participants within the clause, for example the possibility of expressing 'Worms enter the corpse' by 'The corpse enters worms'.[8] It is unknown how widespread anastasis is in Africa, and it would seem that it is not all that uncommon in other parts of the world (Felix Ameka, personal communication).

Logophoric marking constitutes another construction type that has been claimed to be specifically African. Logophoric pronouns indicate co-reference of a nominal in the non-direct quote to the speaker encoded in the accompanying quotative construction, as opposed to its non-co-reference indicated by an unmarked pronominal device (Güldemann 2008). Thus, whereas (1a) illustrates logophoric marking, (1b) is a plain, non-logophoric structure:

---

[8] Unlike, for example, an English medio-passive *get*-sentence like 'The thieves got arrested by the police', anastasis is not formally marked in any way.

(1)   Ewe (Kwa, Niger-Congo; data of authors)
       a. *é   gblɔ   bé   ye-   dzó*
          3.SG say   that LOG-   leave
          'She$_i$ said that she$_i$ left.'
       b. *é-   gblɔ   bé   é-   dzó*
          3.SG- say   that 3.SG- leave
          'She$_i$ said that she$_j$ left.'

Logophoric structures are with very few exceptions concentrated in a large belt extending from the southeastern corner of Ethiopia to the east up to the Niger River in the west and are found in three of the four language phyla (Güldemann 2008; see Section 15.2).

Finally, there are a number of conceptualization strategies that might qualify as Africanisms. This applies in particular to what is called the goose-file model of spatial orientation (Heine 1997: 12–14), to be found in at least three of the four African language phyla, described by Meeussen in the following way:[9]

> Imagine a place from which a house can be seen, and further away a small hill. In such a situation the hill will be referred to in African terms as being 'in front of the house', and the house as being 'behind the hill', whereas in European languages the reverse expressions will be used. *(Meeussen 1975: 3)*

The following example from the Kuliak language may illustrate the goose-file model, where an item to be located is conceptualized not as facing the speaker but rather as facing the same direction as the speaker:

(2)   So (Kuliak, Nilo-Saharan; own data)
       nɛ́kɛ   yóG   sú-   o   sóG
       be.at   people behind- ABL   hill
       'There are people in front of the hill.'

There is another conceptualization strategy that has been proposed as an Africanism (Meeussen 1975), being one manifestation of what is usually called the inclusive or inclusory construction, which is used in reference to a plural that refers to a set of individuals and includes two explicit constituents. The form the construction typically takes in African languages is illustrated as follows:

(3)   Swahili (Bantu, Niger-Congo; own data)
       sisi   na   wewe
       we   and   you
       'I and you'

It is unknown how widespread this construction type is; it is by no means restricted to Africa, being found in various other parts of the world (Moravcsik 2003: 479; Singer 1999).

---

[9] According to the 'goose-file' model, speakers and hearers are somehow conceived as following one another like in a goose file, rather than facing one another when talking.

Table 15.2 *Marking of terms for 'meat' and 'animal'*

Language	'Meat'	'Animal'
Hausa (Chadic, Afroasiatic)	*namà*	*namàn dajì* 'wild animal' ('meat of the bush')
!Xun (Kxʼa)	*ǀʼha*	*ǀʼha-mà* ('animal-DIM')

Another strategy which is not restricted to Africa but is perhaps more widespread in Africa than elsewhere and which can be found in all four language phyla, can be seen in affirmative answers to negative questions where the speaker wants to know if the propositional content of the question is correct or not, for example 'Didn't you sleep?' – 'Yes, I didn't' or 'No, I did' (Felix Ameka, personal communication; Gregersen 1977: 44; Meeussen 1975: 4).

Perhaps the most conspicuous domain where one might expect to find Africanisms involves lexical and grammatical polysemies. The following are a few examples that have been pointed out by researchers of African languages.

Within the domain of nominal polysemy, a paradigm case is where the same noun is used for 'meat' and 'animal' or, alternatively, that there are different but etymologically related nouns for 'meat' and 'animal' (Greenberg 1959; 1983: 4) – a case described by Lichtenberk (1991) more appropriately as heterosemy. Perhaps remarkably, if one of the two meanings is derived from the other, then it goes from 'meat' to 'animal' rather than vice versa.[10] This is suggested at least by the fact that whenever the two are distinguished by means of some derivational, compounding or other mechanism then it is the item for 'meat' that is likely to be unmarked and 'animal' to be marked; see the examples in Table 15.2 (for an example from the Bantu language Tonga, see Greenberg 1983: 16).

To be sure, such polysemy can also be observed in other parts of the world, but it appears to be much more frequent in Africa than elsewhere.

Another nominal polysemy that has been claimed to be 'pan-African' is that of nouns denoting both 'hand' and 'arm' or nouns denoting both 'foot' and 'leg' (and 'wheel') (Gilman 1986: 43). Note, however, that these polysemies are also widespread outside Africa; a worldwide survey shows that 50 out of the 109 languages analysed have a 'hand'/'arm' polysemy and 42 out of 109 languages a 'foot'/'leg' polysemy (see Heine 1997: 136).

Examples of polysemies involving activities include verbs for 'eat', which are said to also denote 'conquer', 'capture a piece in a game' and

---

[10] Greenberg (1983:16), however, says that this is not always so: 'The most conspicuous exception is the Grasslands languages where the form *bep* or the like is found in many languages with the meaning "meat" while the *nama* root survives as "animal"'. It would seem that this fact does not invalidate the hypothesis of a directionality 'meat' > 'animal'; rather, it might suggest that – for whatever reasons – an earlier meaning 'meat' received a new form of expression.

'have sexual intercourse' (Greenberg 1959), verbs for 'die', which tend to have many non-literal meanings in African languages such as 'be in a painful condition', 'break down' (see Meeussen 1975: 4), verbs for 'lie (down)' also meaning 'sleep', or verbs for 'hear' (to a lesser extent also 'see') also denoting other kinds of perception, such as 'smell', 'feel', 'taste', 'understand' (Meeussen 1975: 4–5). Meeussen (1975: 4) furthermore notes that the use of words for 'good' also tend to express 'nice', 'beautiful' and 'fine' in African languages. The status of some of these polysemies as cases of Africanisms, however, is far from clear. For example, meaning ranges expressed by verbs for 'die' in African languages may also be found in Australia or the Americas (Felix Ameka, personal communication), and much the same applies to polysemies involving 'hear' (see e.g. Evans and Wilkins 2000 for evidence on Australian languages).

15.4   Africa as a Linguistic Area

In much of the work examined in Section 15.3 there is an implicit assumption to the effect that the African continent can somehow be distinguished as a linguistic unit from other regions in the world. This is the topic of a study by Heine and Leyew (2008). On the one hand, they observe that the following generalization proposed by Greenberg (1983: 27) is in fact correct: 'Ideally, if what is meant by an African areal characteristic is one which is found everywhere in Africa but nowhere else, then clearly none exists' (Greenberg 1983: 27). On the other hand, they argue that it is possible to set the African continent off from the rest of the world at least by means of quantitative generalizations.

Using a sample of 99 African languages from all four language phyla and all major geographical regions of the continent plus fifty non-African control languages, Heine and Leyew (2008) analyse eleven properties that were used by previous authors to isolate 'Africanisms'.[11] On the basis of quantitative data such as those presented in Table 15.3 they suggest that it is possible to predict with a high degree of probability that if there is a language that possesses more than five of the eleven properties then this must be an African language. Furthermore, arguing that three of the eleven properties, namely labial–velar stops, implosive stops and ATR-based vowel harmony, have a higher diagnostic value than other properties, they conclude that if there is a language anywhere in the world that has two of these three properties then this must be an African language.

---

[11] These properties are: (a) labial–velar stops, (b) implosive stops, (c) lexical and/or grammatical tones, (d) ATR-based vowel harmony, (e) verbal derivational suffixes, (f) nominal modifiers follow the noun, (g) semantic polysemy of 'drink' or 'pull' for 'smoke', (h) semantic polysemy 'hear' or 'see' for 'understand', (i) semantic polysemy of 'animal' and 'meat', (j) comparative constructions based on the schema [X is big defeats/surpasses/passes Y], and (k) noun 'chi d' used productively to express diminutive meaning.

Table 15.3 *Quantitative distribution of 11 typological properties according to major world regions (sample: 99 African and 50 non-African languages; Heine and Leyew 2008: 30)*

Region	Total of languages	Average number of properties per language
Europe	10	1.1
Asia	8	2.6
Australia/Oceania	12	3.0
The Americas	14	3.4
Africa	99	6.8
Pidgins and creoles[12]	6	2.3
All regions	149	

That the generalizations proposed by Heine and Leyew (2008) raise some problems is argued by Dryer (2011). In particular, he draws attention to the possibility that quantitative distributions such as those presented in Table 15.3 may be due to coincidence and that future work should aim at a more balanced sample of languages, especially of non-African languages. Dryer (2011: 310) finds only two of the properties included by Heine and Leyew (2008) that argue for Sub-Saharan Africa as a linguistic area, namely postnominal modifiers and presence of tone systems.

15.5 Grammaticalization Areas

Another domain where Africa provides a wide range of common properties concerns grammaticalization processes, whereby the same conceptual schemas and constructions are employed to develop grammatical categories, and in situations of language contact these processes can be transferred from one language to another.

The notion of linguistic area or sprachbund has not gone unchallenged over the last few decades (e.g. Stolz 2002), and rather than looking for compact linguistic areas, a number of scholars working on language contact prefer to adopt an areal perspective where linguistic areas are only of marginal concern, if at all; see Muysken (2008: 4) and to a certain extent Hickey (2010; Chapter 1, this volume). As has been argued by Heine and Kuteva (2005: 182–187), most linguistic areas that have been identified so far can be analysed, at least to some extent, as consisting of grammaticalization areas.[13] With this term, they refer to groups of geographically contiguous languages that have undergone the same process of grammaticalization as

---

[12] Three of the six pidgin and creole languages are spoken in Africa and the rest in the Americas and in New Guinea.

[13] Grammaticalization is defined as the development from lexical to grammatical forms, and from grammatical to even more grammatical forms. Since the development of grammatical forms is not independent of the constructions to which they belong, the study of grammaticalization is in the same way concerned with constructions, and with even larger discourse segments; see e.g. Traugott and Heine (1991), Heine, Claudi and Hünnemeyer (1991), Hopper and Traugott (2003) and Bybee, Perkins and Pagliuca (1994).

a result of language contact (Heine 1994; Kuteva 1998, 2000; Stolz and Stolz 2001: 1549).

The following example may illustrate the process concerned. With few exceptions, Slavic languages are known for their lack of definite and indefinite articles. Now, in situations of language contact where speakers of Slavic minority languages were exposed for centuries to intense contact with dominant languages having articles, these minority languages developed article-like constructions. In some cases, these developments gave rise to fully fledged articles similar to those of the respective model language German or Italian. These contact-induced developments involved canonical processes of grammaticalization, whereby, for example, a minority language such as Upper Sorbian in Eastern Germany grammaticalized a demonstrative attribute to a definite article and their numeral for 'one' to an indefinite article on the model of German (Breu 2003, 2004). The result is that the Slavic minority language Upper Sorbian now shares with German the same grammaticalization area of articles.

Contact-induced grammaticalization processes of this kind must have happened in Africa on a massive scale. While we lack appropriate historical records for reconstruction, grammaticalization theory allows us to reconstruct at least an outline of some of these processes (Heine 1994, 2011; Leyew and Heine 2003).

Perhaps the most widely discussed example is that of comparative constructions, more precisely of comparatives of inequality, based on what Heine (1997) calls the action schema, taking either of the forms 'X is big defeats/passes Y' or 'X defeats/passes Y in size', that is, the use of a verb meaning either 'defeat', 'surpass' or 'pass' to express comparison (Gilman 1986: 39; Greenberg 1983: 4; Meeussen 1975: 4), as seen in the following example:

(4)   !Xun (W2 dialect, Khoisan: Heine and König 2015)[14]

   | !xō | má | nǁā̀ 'à | ! 'ālā̄ | gùmì. |
   | elephant | TOP | be.big | pass | cow |

   'An elephant is bigger than a cow.'

The grammaticalization from either of these verbs to a grammatical marker denoting the standard of comparison (cf. English *than*) must have taken place in some form or other in many African languages across genetic boundaries. To be sure, this grammaticalization has also been observed in some other parts of the world. Especially in Mainland Southeast Asian languages (Sinitic languages, Thai, Vietnamese and Hmong-Khmer languages) verbs for 'to cross' have given rise to standard markers of comparison (Ansaldo 2004: 490–493), but outside Africa it is extremely rare, while at least two-thirds of the African languages that have been

---

[14] The graphs ! and ǁ stand for an alveolar and a lateral click type, respectively.

documented in some detail appear to have undergone this process in some form or other (Heine 1997: 126–129; Heine and Leyew 2008; Leyew and Heine 2003).

Other possible pan-African grammaticalization areas are provided by processes leading from nominal to spatial concepts. Body part terms used metaphorically for deictic spatial distinctions are found throughout the world; for example, nouns for the body part 'back' are the conceptual source for spatial terms for 'behind' in many languages. But there are some developments that are likely in Africa but unlikely to happen elsewhere (Gilman 1986: 42; Meeussen 1975: 3). Such developments include, but are not restricted to, the grammaticalization of body parts for 'stomach/belly' to spatial concepts for 'in(side)', or of 'buttocks' or 'anus' to 'below' and/or 'behind' (Heine 1997: 37).

A number of other grammaticalizations that were proposed are less convincing as Africa-specific processes of areally defined diffusion. This applies on the one hand to sex distinctions used for the grammaticalization of the deictic spatial concepts 'right(side)' (> 'male, strong hand') and 'left(side)' (< 'female, weak hand') (Gilman 1986: 42). On the other hand, this also applies to the grammaticalization process leading from verbs for 'say' to quotative markers, complementizers, purpose clause markers, etc. (Gilman 1986: 44; Larochette 1959; Meeussen 1975: 3). But such processes appear to be also fairly common outside Africa (see Heine and Kuteva 2002) and hence do not appear to have a pronounced areal dimension.

15.6 Conclusions

Discussion in the present chapter has been severely limited in scope and raises a number of problems that have had to be ignored in this bird's-eye view of linguistic areality in Africa. In particular, we have not been able to do justice to the wide range of studies that have been or are being presently carried out on the dynamics of language contact and its areal implications in various parts of the continent. And we were also not able to do justice to the wide range of topics that researchers in areal linguistics are concerned with in Africa.

One major problem we have been confronted with concerns diachronic reconstruction. There are hardly any historical documents to support the reconstruction of historical events in Africa. Accordingly, the study of areal diffusion processes must rely on other means for reconstruction. To this end, we applied findings of grammaticalization theory to reconstruct areas of grammaticalization (Section 15.4). The theory draws on observations on regularities made in languages that are historically well documented to study languages for which there are no or hardly any earlier historical records. But it goes without saying that this theory is limited in scope; it works well when applied to morphosyntactic phenomena but is hard pressed when it comes to phonological, lexical or semantic processes.

The processes discussed in the chapter are all hypothesized to be due to language contact, that is, to have been externally induced. At the same time, many of them can also be described as involving language-internal developments. That external and internal linguistic changes are by no means mutually exclusive is not really new (see e.g. Heine and Kuteva 2005; Hickey 2012; Thomason 2001, 2003), but what exactly that means with reference to our understanding of linguistic change and of language structure is an issue that would seem to need much further attention in future research.

Abbreviations

ABL	ablative
DIM	diminutive
LOG	logophoric marker
SG	singular
TOP	topic marker
3	third person

References

Ansaldo, Umberto, 2004. The correlation between exceed comparatives and verby languages. In *Proceedings of the 11th Conference of the South East Asian Linguistic Society*. Program for Southeast Asian Studies, Arizona State University.

Boretzky, Norbert, 1983. *Kreolsprachen, Substrate und Sprachwandel*. Wiesbaden: Harrassowitz.

Bostoen, Koen and Bonny Sands, 2012. Clicks in south-western Bantu languages: Contact-induced vs. language-internal lexical change. In Matthias Brenzinger and Anne-Maria Fehn (eds), *Proceedings of the 6th World Congress of African Linguistics, WOCAL6, Cologne*, pp. 129–140. Cologne: Köppe.

Breu, Walter, 2003. Der indefinite Artikel in slavischen Mikrosprachen: Grammatikalisierung im totalen Sprachkontakt. In Holger Kuße (ed.), *Slavistische Linguistik 2001*, pp. 27–68. Munich: Sagner.

Breu, Walter, 2004. Der definite Artikel in der obersorbischen Umgangssprache. In Marion Krause and Christian Sappok (eds), *Slavistische Linguistik 2002*, pp. 9–57. Munich: Sagner.

Bybee, Joan L., Revere D. Perkins and William Pagliuca, 1994. *The Evolution of Grammar: Tense, Aspect, and Modality in the Languages of the World*. Chicago: University of Chicago Press.

Claudi, Ulrike, 1993. *Die Stellung von Verb und Objekt in Niger-Kongo-Sprachen: Ein Beitrag zur Rekonstruktion historischer Syntax.* Afrikanistische Monographien, vol. 1. Cologne: Institut für Afrikanistik, Universität zu Köln.

Clements, G. N. and Annie Rialland, 2008. Africa as a phonological area. In Heine and Nurse (eds), pp. 36–85.

Crass, Joachim and Ronny Meyer, 2008. Ethiopia. In Heine and Nurse (eds), pp. 228–250.

Creissels, Denis, Gerrit J. Dimmendaal, Zygmunt Frajzyngier and Christa König, 2008. Africa as a morphosyntactic area. In Heine and Nurse (eds), pp. 86–150.

Dryer, Matthew S., 2011. Noun-modifier order in Africa. In Hieda, König and Nakagawa (eds), pp. 287–311.

Evans, N. R. D. and D. P. Wilkins, 2000. In the mind's ear: The semantic extensions of perception verbs in Australian languages. *Language* 76 (3): 546–592.

Ferguson, Charles, 1970. The Ethiopian Language Area. *The Journal of Ethiopian Studies* 8 (2): 67–80.

Ferguson, Charles A., 1976. The Ethiopian language area. In Marvin L. Bender, J. D. Bowen, R. L. Cooper and Charles A. Ferguson (eds), *Language in Ethiopia*, pp. 63–76. London: Oxford University Press.

Gilman, Charles, 1986. African areal characteristics: Sprachbund, not substrate? *Journal of Pidgin and Creole Languages* 1 (1): 33–50.

Greenberg, Joseph H., 1959. Africa as a linguistic area. In W. R. Bascom and M. J. Herskovits (eds), *Continuity and Change in African Cultures*, pp. 15–27. Chicago: University of Chicago Press.

Greenberg, Joseph H., 1963. *The Languages of Africa.* The Hague: Mouton.

Greenberg, Joseph H., 1983. Some areal characteristics of African languages. In Ivan R. Dihoff (ed.), *Current Approaches to African Linguistics*, vol. 1, pp. 3–21. Dordrecht: Foris.

Gregersen Edgar A., 1977. *Language in Africa: An Introductory Survey.* New York, Paris and London: Gordon and Breach.

Güldemann, Tom, 1998. The Kalahari Basin as an object of areal typology: A first approach. In Mathias Schladt (ed.), *Language, Identity, and Conceptualization among the Khoisan*, pp. 137–196. Cologne: Köppe.

Güldemann, Tom, 2008. The Macro-Sudan Belt. In Heine and Nurse (eds), pp. 151–185.

Heine, Bernd, 1975. The study of word order in African languages. In R. K. Herbert (ed.), *Proceedings of the Sixth Conference on African Linguistics, Ohio State University, Columbus, April 12–13, 1975*, pp. 161–183. Columbus, OH: The Ohio State University.

Heine, Bernd, 1976. *A Typology of African Languages, Based on the Order of Meaningful Elements.* Berlin: Dietrich Reimer.

Heine, Bernd, 1994. Areal influence on grammaticalization. In Martin Pütz (ed.), *Language Contact and Language Conflict*, pp. 56–68. Amsterdam: John Benjamins.

Heine, Bernd, 1997. *Cognitive Foundations of Grammar*. Oxford and New York: Oxford University Press.

Heine, Bernd, 2011. Areas of grammaticalization and geographical typology. In Hieda, König and Nakagawa (eds), pp. 41–66.

Heine, Bernd, Ulrike Claudi and Friederike Hünnemeyer, 1991. *Grammaticalization: A Conceptual Framework*. Chicago: University of Chicago Press.

Heine, Bernd and Christa König, 2015. *The !Xun Language: A Dialect Grammar*. Quellen zur Khoisan-Forschung. Cologne: Köppe.

Heine, Bernd and Tania Kuteva, 2002. *World Lexicon of Grammaticalization*. Cambridge: Cambridge University Press.

Heine, Bernd and Tania Kuteva, 2005. *Language Contact and Grammatical Change*. Cambridge: Cambridge University Press.

Heine, Bernd and Zelealem Leyew, 2008. Is Africa a linguistic area? In Heine and Nurse (eds), pp. 15–35.

Heine, Bernd and Derek Nurse (eds), 2008. *A Linguistic Geography of Africa*. Cambridge: Cambridge University Press.

Hickey, Raymond, 2010. Language contact: Reassessment and reconsideration. In Raymond Hickey (ed.), *The Handbook of Language Contact*, pp. 1–28. Malden, MA: Wiley-Blackwell.

Hickey, Raymond, 2012. Internally and externally motivated language change. In Juan Manuel Hernández-Campoy and Juan Camilo Conde-Silvestre (eds), *The Handbook of Historical Sociolinguistics*, pp. 401–421. Malden, MA: Wiley-Blackwell.

Hieda, Osamu, Christa König and Hirosi Nakagawa (eds), 2011. *Geographical Typology and Linguistic Areas, With Special Reference to Africa*. Tokyo University of Foreign Studies (TUFS), *Studies in Linguistics*. Amsterdam and Philadelphia: John Benjamins.

Hopper, Paul J. and Elizabeth C. Traugott, 2003. *Grammaticalization*. Cambridge: Cambridge University Press.

Kießling, Roland, Maarten Mous and Derek Nurse, 2008. The Tanzanian Rift Valley area. In Heine and Nurse (eds), pp. 186–227.

Kilian-Hatz, Christa, 2001. *Ideophone: Eine typologische Untersuchung unter besonderer Berücksichtigung afrikanischer Sprachen*. Habilitationsschrift, University of Cologne.

König, Christa, 2006. *Case in Africa*. Oxford: Oxford University Press.

König, Christa, 2008. The marked-nominative languages of Eastern Africa. In Heine and Nurse (eds), pp. 251–271.

Kuteva, Tania, 1998. Large linguistic areas in grammaticalization: Auxiliation in Europe. *Language Sciences* 20 (3): 289–311.

Kuteva, Tania, 2000. Areal grammaticalization: The case of the Bantu–Nilotic borderland. *Folia Linguistica* 34 (3–4): 267–283.

Larochette, J., 1959. Overeenkomst tussen Mangbetu, Zande, en Bantu-talen. In *Handelingen van het XXIIIe Vlaams Filologencongres, Brussels*, pp. 247–248.

Leyew, Zelealem and Bernd Heine, 2003. Comparative constructions in Africa: An areal dimension. *Annual Publication in African Linguistics (APAL)* 1: 47–68.

Lichtenberk, Frantisek, 1991. Semantic change and heterosemy in grammaticalization. *Language* 67 (3): 475–509.

Maddieson, Ian, 2003. The sounds of the Bantu languages. In Derek Nurse and Gérard Philippson (eds), *The Bantu Languages*. London and New York: Routledge.

Meeussen, A. E., 1975. *Possible Linguistic Africanisms* (Fifth Hans Wolff Memorial Lecture). Language Sciences, vol. 35. Bloomington, IN: Indiana University.

Moravcsik, Edith, 2003. A semantic analysis of associative plurals. *Studies in Language* 27 (3): 469–503.

Muysken, Pieter (ed.), 2008. Introduction: Conceptual and methodological issues in areal linguistics. In Pieter Muysken (ed.), *From Linguistic Areas to Areal Linguistics*, pp. 1–23. Amsterdam: John Benjamins.

Singer, Ruth, 1999. The inclusory construction in Australian languages. *Melbourne Papers in Linguistics and Applied Linguistics* 18: 81–96.

Stolz, Christel and Thomas Stolz, 2001. Mesoamerica as a linguistic area. In Martin Haspelmath, Ekkehard König, Wulf Oesterreicher and Wolfgang Raible (eds), *Language Typology and Language Universals: An International Handbook*, vol. 2, pp. 1542–1553. Handbücher zur Sprach- und Kommunikationswissenschaft, vol. 20.2. New York: Walter de Gruyter.

Stolz, Thomas, 2002. No sprachbund beyond this line! On the age-old discussion of how to define a linguistic area. In Paolo Ramat and Thomas Stolz (eds), *Mediterranean Languages: Papers from the MEDTYP Workshop, Tirrenia, June 2000*, pp. 259–281. Bochum: Brockmeyer.

Thomason, Sarah Grey, 2001. *Language Contact: An Introduction*. Edinburgh: Edinburgh University Press.

Thomason, Sarah Grey, 2003. Contact as a source of language change. In Brian D. Joseph and Richard D. Janda (eds), *The Handbook of Historical Linguistics*, pp. 687–712. Oxford: Blackwell.

Tosco, Mauro, 1991. *A Grammatical Sketch of Dahalo*. Cushitic Language Studies, vol. 8. Cologne: Köppe.

Tosco, Mauro, 2000. Is there an 'Ethiopian language area'? *Anthropological Linguistics* 42 (3): 329–365.

Traill, Anthony, 1994. *A !Xóõ Dictionary*. Quellen zur Khoisan-Forschung, vol. 9. Cologne: Köppe.

Traugott, Elizabeth C. and Bernd Heine (eds), 1991. *Approaches to Grammaticalization*, vol. 1. Typological Studies in Language, vol. 19.1. Amsterdam and Philadelphia: John Benjamins.

Voeltz, F. K. Erhard and Christa Kilian-Hatz (eds), 2001. *Ideophones*. Typological Studies in Language, vol. 44. Amsterdam and Philadelphia: John Benjamins.

Weinreich, Uriel, 1953. *Languages in Contact: Findings and Problems.* New York: Linguistic Circle of New York. Reprinted 1963, The Hague: Mouton.

Welmers, William E., 1973. *African Language Structures.* Berkeley, CA: University of California Press.

Welmers, William E., 1977. *The Major Indigenous Languages of Africa.* Berkeley: University of California Press.

Westermann, Diedrich, 1911. *Die Sudansprachen.* Hamburg: L. Friederichsen.

16

Areal Contact in Nilo-Saharan

Gerrit J. Dimmendaal

16.1 Introduction

The phylum referred to today by the name Nilo-Saharan is spread over a vast area mainly south of the Afroasiatic phylum and north of the Niger-Congo phylum. The core of Nilo-Saharan was established more than fifty years ago by Joseph H. Greenberg. In his earliest genetic classification of African languages, Greenberg (1955) proposed a Macro-Sudanic family (renamed Chari-Nile in subsequent studies), consisting of a Central Sudanic and an Eastern Sudanic branch plus two isolated members, Berta and Kunama. This family formed the core of the Nilo-Saharan phylum as hypothesized in Greenberg (1963), where a number of groups were added which had been treated as isolated units in his 1955 classification, namely Songhay, Saharan, Maban and Mimi, Nyangian, Temainian, Koman and Gumuz. The present author, however, prefers to treat Songhay (spoken mainly in Mali) as well as Koman plus Gumuz (in the border area between Ethiopia and Sudan) as independent families (Dimmendaal 2011). This also applies to the Kadu languages spoken along the southern range of the Nuba Mountains, Sudan, which had been classified as Kordofanian, i.e. as members of the Niger-Congo phylum by Greenberg (1963), but which have been argued by Bender (1996) to be part of the Nilo-Saharan phylum.

Whereas there is little disagreement on the genetic unity of lower-level units of Nilo-Saharan, scholars like Bender (1996) and Ehret (2001) disagree on the subgrouping at deeper historical levels. The present author has defended the following subgrouping in a number of publications, e.g. Dimmendaal (2010a), where it is argued that Northeastern Nilo-Saharan languages innovated a case-marking system as well as other typological properties; Dimmendaal (in press) provides further evidence for the sub-grouping presented in Figure 16.1. This classification will also form the basis for a survey of areal phenomena below, since the subgrouping corresponds to important typological differences between its extant members.

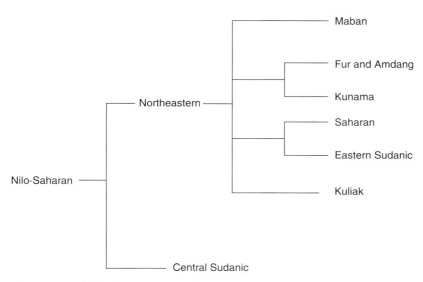

Figure 16.1 Subclassification of Nilo-Saharan languages

The approximately sixty Central Sudanic and 100 Northeastern Nilo-Saharan languages cover an area stretching from Eritrea and Ethiopia in the east across Northeastern Africa towards Niger with a southward extension into Eastern and Central Africa. The present typological survey is based on a summary of the existing literature on areal contacts in Nilo-Saharan with neighbouring groups, but some new perspectives are added too, for example on areal features shared between Central Sudanic and neighbouring Ubangian languages as well as on the areal distribution of (split) ergativity.

Convergence as a manifestation of areal contact has to do with multi-lingualism and its linguistic reflexes, shift-induced interference and metatypy. A second purpose of the present contribution is therefore the identification of areal sources for these phenomena. A third and final aim is to show that typological similarities between languages are not necessarily the result of areal contact, since self-organizing principles may also result in parallel developments. As argued below, these latter principles rather than areal contact probably help to explain the presence of so-called marked nominative case systems in Afroasiatic as well as Nilo-Saharan languages.

16.2 Central Sudanic

Within the Nilo-Saharan phylum, there is a relatively sharp typological cut between Central Sudanic languages on the one hand and Northeastern Nilo-Saharan languages on the other. Whereas most languages involved share widespread prosodic features of African languages south of the

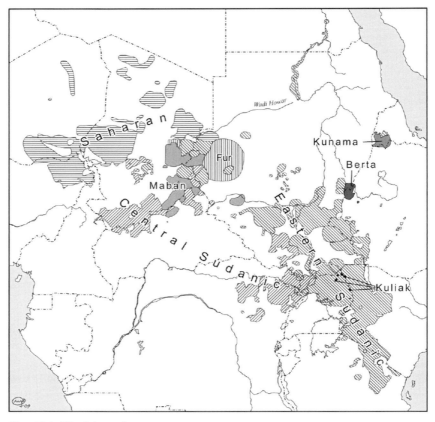

Map 16.1 Nilo-Saharan languages

Sahara such as advanced tongue root harmony and tone, these two primary branches of Nilo-Saharan differ in their morphosyntactic and pragmatic structures. Whereas Central Sudanic languages have a basic
constituent order SAuxOV or SVO, Northeastern Nilo-Saharan languages
tend to be verb-final, with the exception of a group of Eastern Sudanic
languages, which are verb-initial or verb-second, as shown below. This
dichotomy between the two primary branches of Nilo-Saharan coincides
with a number of other typological differences, such as the extensive number-marking system, the use of case, converbs, and coverb plus light verb
constructions in Northeastern Nilo-Saharan. Whereas converbs refer to
dependent (subordinate) verb forms with a reduced inflectional morphology, coverbs are complements of 'say'/'do' verbs belonging to different
syntactic categories like noun, adjective or adverb. These properties are
essentially absent in Central Sudanic languages, where we find properties
shared with neighbouring languages belonging to the Ubangian language
family, such as a reduced derivational morphology and word structure, and
the frequent use of discourse particles in post-verbal position. This latter
typological zone is discussed first below.

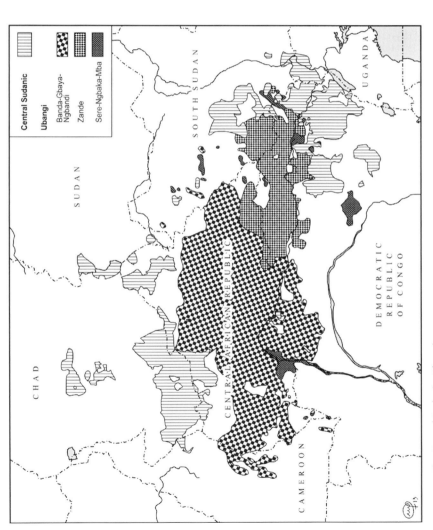

Map 16.2 The Central Sudanic–Ubangi contact zone

Greenberg (1966: 87) and Houis (1970: 59–66) made reference to a language type which is particularly common in West Africa and which is characterized by genitives preceding the governing noun, postpositions, and SAuxOV constituent order.

This type of constituent order is common, for example, in Gur, Kru, Kwa, Mande and Songhay. Heine (1976: 41–42) uses these properties as definitional features for his type B languages (as against type A or SVO, C or VSO, and D or SOV languages). Type B languages are further characterized by a VAdvP constituent order and an SVO word order, sometimes alternating with SOV, according to the same author. Heine (1976: 42) further points out that type B languages are also common in Central Sudanic. This well-defined branch of Nilo-Saharan is usually divided into two primary branches: a western (or Bongo-Bagirmi) branch and an eastern (or Moru-Mangbetu) branch (Boyeldieu and Nougayrol 2008; Tucker and Bryan 1966). The western branch consists of (Sara-)Bongo-Bagirmi plus Kresh, whereas the eastern branch consists of Moru-Madi, Mangbutu-Efe, Mangbetu and Lendu-Ngiti. S(Aux)VO constituent order, prepositions and possessed/possessor order are common in the western branch. The common constituent order in the eastern branch is SAuxOV alternating with SVO, with postpositions rather than prepositions, and the possessor preceding the possessed in genitive constructions. As shown by Andersen (1984), the alternation itself depends on aspectual marking in a clause; if the position after the subject is filled by an auxiliary (marking aspect), the main verb occurs after the object. The following examples from Moru (interlinear glossing added by the present author) illustrate the SVO/SAuxOV alternation:

(1)   mí-zī̄   ŋgàgà
      2SG-call   boys
      'You (sg) called the boys'

(2)   ɲ-á   ŋgàgà   ù-zī̄
      2SG-AUX boys   NF-call
      'You (sg) are calling the boys'

Similar constituent order patterns occur in neighbouring Ubangi languages. Greenberg (1963) refers to the Ubangi languages by the name Eastern and argues that it forms a subgroup with Adamawa within Niger-Congo. Boyd (1989: 192) arrives at the following subgrouping:

1. Gbaya
2. A. Gbanda
   B. Ngbandi
   C. I. Sere
      II. a. Ngbaka
          b. Mba

3. Zande

Dimmendaal (2011: 89–90) prefers to treat Ubangi as an isolated language family instead. It has been argued by Moñino (2012) that Ubangi does not even form a genetic unit in and by itself. However, whether Ubangi constitutes an areal rather than a genetic grouping is irrelevant for the present study, since areal features of Central Sudanic are at stake. And the genetic unity of eastern and western Central Sudanic is beyond any doubt (Boyeldieu and Nougayrol 2008: 11).

In the Mba group within Ubangi, the genitive order is possessor-possessed, whereas postpositions (though rare) occur as well (Tucker and Bryan 1966: 123, 126, 131). In at least one member of the Mba cluster, Ndongo, SAuxOV constituent order alternates with SVO, depending on aspect, as in neighbouring Central Sudanic languages:

(3) *á-mba   ŋgàràgʋ   mὲ*
     1SG-AUX   child   beat
     'I had beaten the child'

Constituent order in other Ubangi members (the Zande cluster, Gbaya, Gbanda, Ngbandi, Sere, Ngbaka) is similar to that in western members of Central Sudanic, in that S(Aux)OV is the common constituent order, as are prepositions, whereas in genitive constructions the possessor follows the possessed. Hence, they are classified as type A languages by Heine (1976). Gbaya, Gbanda, Ngbandi and Zande constitute expansion zones (in the sense of Nichols 1992), as shown in Map 16.2. The current distribution of Sere, Ngbaka and Mba at the periphery north, east and south of these two expansion zones on the other hand suggests that their ancestral communities were either engulfed by expanding Zande communities or their ancestral communities were expelled from areas now occupied by Zande speakers. Typologically, these peripheral Ubangi groups pattern along with the western branch of Central Sudanic.

Of course, the similarities in terms of constituent order, the position of adpositions and the order in genitive constructions could all be a coincidence. But a number of other common typological properties of languages in this area suggest that contact played a role too, even though the direction of areal diffusion is not clear. For example, Central Sudanic languages are characterized by a restricted system of derivational morphology (with only a few affixes; Dimmendaal 2014a) compared to the other primary branch, Northeastern Nilo-Saharan; instead, compounding is commonly used as a lexical strategy in the former. Also, nominal and verbal roots tend to be monosyllabic in Central Sudanic, with a preference for open syllables ((V)CV) and up to four tonal registers. This again parallels the system in neighbouring Ubangi languages; see Tucker and Bryan (1966: 26–166) for examples.

A further typologically interesting areal feature shared between Central Sudanic and Ubangian languages, first described by Tucker (1967: 247–262, 408–412), is the presence of up to three discourse markers usually occurring sentence-finally or post-verbally.[1] These particles, expressing how the speaker views the state of affairs being described in an utterance or how (s)he wishes it to be seen by the hearer, tend to be monosyllabic elements which form a phonological word with verbs when these precede; when more than one such marker occurs, these particles tend to form a phonological word together.[2] Tucker (1967: 166–176, 247–262, 408–412) gives examples from a range of eastern members of Central Sudanic, e.g. from Logo:

(4)   ma-nɔ   mi   'bɛ
       1SG-see   2SG   PART
       'I can see you'

(5)   ma-si-wa
       1SG-enter-PART
       'Shall I come in?'

The clitic nature of these particles is evident from their variable syntactic position, as shown for Logo (Tucker 1967: 247):

(6)   ma-fu   le'bi   dre
       1SG-kill water-buck   PART
       'I killed a water-buck'

(7)   ma-fu-dre   le'bi
       1SG-kill-PART   water-buck
       'I killed a water-buck'

The position of these particles within a sentence presumably depends on their scope, which may involve the verb or a verbal phrase, as in the examples above. Blackings and Fabb (2003) discuss such particles for the Central Sudanic language Madi, which belongs to the same cluster as Logo, under the heading 'modals' (pp. 451–466) and 'adverbials with a discourse function' (pp. 532–536). The modal ra, for example, expresses epistemic modal force:

(8)   a. kò-mū
          3:DIR-go
          'She should go'
       b. kò-mū   rá
          3:DIR   PART
          'She should definitely go (ensure that she goes)'

Santandrea (1970: 62–63, 75, 123) discusses these discourse particles for Yulu-Kara (which belong to the western branch of Central Sudanic)

---

[1] Tucker (1967) refers to these languages with the name 'Eastern Sudanic', as they constitute the easternmost representatives of the ancient grouping 'Sudanic'. His use of the term should not be confused with the term Eastern Sudanic in Greenberg's classification, which refers to a different branch of Nilo-Saharan.

[2] Such markers, which have also been referred to as discourse markers, attitude markers, or social-expressive and emotive elements, have been studied in detail for various Indo-European languages, but far less so in an African context.

and points out (p. 62) that '[s]ome (e.g. Tucker) have called [these] postpositions, but I think the rather vague term, particles, [is] quite suitable for the
purpose.' The author further points out (p. 127) that these particles 'are so
closely jointed to the preceding word that in pronunciation, they form
a single word with it', as in the following example from Yulu:

(9)　　*ake*　　　*luu'bo-lee*
　　　3PL.AUX　　find-PART
　　　'They will find it/him/her'

Similar particles, again usually occurring post-verbally or sentence-finally
and also behaving prosodically as clitical elements, have been reported in
studies of neighbouring Ubangi languages. Within the Zande cluster, this
phenomenon is restricted to one language, Barambu-Pambia, according to
Tucker and Bryan (1966: 153), which borders on Central Sudanic languages
such as Mangbetu:

(10)　　*nye-nzí*　　　*túngúà*
　　　1SG-AUX work PART
　　　'I have done work'

Tucker and Bryan (1966: 83) further observe: 'These languages are
characterized by a great number of words and/or Particles which are ...
postpositional to Verbs ... Many of these ... correspond to the
Postpositions of MORU-MANGBETU' (Tucker and Bryan 1966: 83).

　Cloarec-Heis (1986: 62–67) describes this phenomenon for the Banda-
Gbaya-Ngbandi languages and contrasts these syntactic elements with
'obligatory phrases' ('syntagmes nécessaires'). In his analysis of the
Ubangian language Yakoma, a member of the Ngbandi cluster, Boyeldieu
(1995: 130) discusses this phenomenon of post-verbal particles under the
heading of 'modalité de proposition', as in the following example, where
the particle expresses a kind of counter-expectation:

(11)　　*à*　　*hwὲ*　　　*wὲ*
　　　it　　be.finished PART
　　　'It has already been done'

16.3　Northeastern Nilo-Saharan and (Former) Contact Zones

In his typological survey of African languages, Heine (1976) pointed
out that features associated with Afroasiatic languages in the 'Ethiopian
convergence area'[3] extend into Nilo-Saharan languages spoken to the west

---

[3] This has been proposed by different authors, e.g. Leslau (1945), or Ferguson (1970). The notion has also been partly
criticized by Tosco (2000).

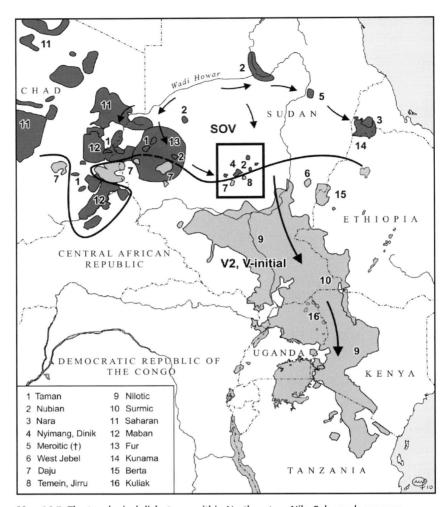

Map 16.3 The typological dichotomy within Northeastern Nilo-Saharan languages

of this area. These common features involve a verb-final constituent order and extensive case marking, which are also features of Nilo-Saharan subgroups such as Maban, Fur, or northern members of the Eastern Sudanic branch as well as Kunama; see Map 16.3 for the distribution of these language groups.

There is also no historical-comparative evidence that case marking was lost in Central Sudanic languages (as far as present knowledge goes). Boyeldieu (2013) shows that one language, Sinyar, a language in Chad bordering on Northeastern Nilo-Saharan languages with case systems (all of which have a system of differential object marking) has a marked nominative case system, a phenomenon which is also attested in a group of Eastern Sudanic languages, Nilotic and Surmic, discussed in Section 16.4 below.[4]

(12) *ngàar-rí*   *wéññí*
      stew-NOM:SG   3:be.nice
      'The stew is nice'

(13) *sùdáàn-nè*   *ùññàbí*   *ìngìltáràa*
      Sudan-NOM:SG   3:be.hot.pass   England:ACC:SG
      'Sudan is hotter than England'

However, as pointed out by Boyeldieu (2013) it is not at all clear that Sinyar is a member of the Central Sudanic family; Dimmendaal treats this language as a linguistic isolate.

Additional typological features supporting the claim by Heine (1976) that the Ethiopian convergence area extends into Sudan and Chad have been listed more recently by Dimmendaal (e.g. 2007, 2008). These properties include a tripartite number marking system, converbs as a discourse strategy, and coverb plus light verb constructions, which are illustrated briefly below.

Most Northeastern Nilo-Saharan languages have rich number-marking systems of a type which is also attested in Afroasiatic languages in Ethiopia and Semitic languages in the Middle East. Prototypically, such languages have a tripartite number-marking system, whereby either the plural or collective form is morphologically unmarked (with corresponding singulative marking), or the singular (with corresponding plural marking on the non-basic form); alternatively, both the singular and plural are inflected for number. The examples below stem from Dimmendaal (2000):

(14) Syrian Arabic (Semitic, Afroasiatic)
      tərk-i   'a Turk'
      tərk   'Turks (collective)'
      ʔatrāk   'Turks (plural)'

(15) Masalit (Maban, Nilo-Saharan)
      anyiŋ-gi 'fly'   *anyiŋ*   'flies'
      mama   'maternal uncle'   *mama-te*   'maternal uncles'
      mal-ko   'chattel'   *mal-ta*   'chattels'

Central Sudanic languages on the other hand, have a restricted system of plural marking (mainly on nouns referring to animate or human entities); again, there is no historical evidence that these languages lost the tripartite system of number inflection.

---

[4] Given the geographical distance between Sinyar on the one hand and Nilotic or Surmic on the other hand but also the dramatic typological differences between Sinyar and Nilotic plus Surmic in terms of other morphosyntactic strategies or constituent order, there is no reason to assume that these systems have a common historical origin. Similar variation between languages with differential object marking as against marked nominative case systems are found, for example, in Cushitic (Afroasiatic). Hence, such parallel systems are more likely to have come about independently through autogenetic (language-internal) processes, i.e. through self-organization.

Converbs constitute another common strategy, characteristic in particular of narrative discourse in Afroasiatic languages in Ethiopia and Nilo-Saharan languages spoken in a zone ranging from Ethiopia and Eritrea across northern and central Sudan into Chad, as shown by Amha and Dimmendaal (2006). The authors further point out that these constructions have often been referred to by such labels as 'gerunds', 'participles', 'consecutives' and other names in the past. This is one reason why this areal strategy has gone largely unnoticed in the general typological literature on converbs.[5]

One of the most detailed analyses of converbs in a Northeastern Nilo-Saharan language is to be found in Jakobi and Crass (2004: 165–176) on the Saharan language Beria. In this language, spoken in Chad and western Sudan, both converbs and main verbs take pronominal subject and object marking. With converbs, however, mood is not expressed, whereas plurality marking and aspect marking can be omitted. The first type of converb in Beria expresses mainly successive actions or events (apart from a number of other functions):

(16) béí   tine=e-n-e   sέ-nɔ́gɔ́
      goats thief-AUX-sSG:SU-CONV₁ eat-IMP:NEG
      'Don't steal goats and don't eat them'

The second type of converb construction is used in clauses expressing a purpose or a volitional act:

(17) έkɔ́l-dò   gèrì=έ-gέ   ɟú-g-í
      school-ADV   read-AUX-1SG:SU-CONV₂ go-1SG:SU-AFF-PERF
      'I went in order to study in/at school'

Such dependent verb forms are deeply rooted in the structure of the Omotic branch within Afroasiatic, for example. Based on two alternative morphological strategies for verbs, Rapold (2008) distinguishes between converbs and medial verbs in the Omotic language Bench. Both involve finite verbs in dependent clauses, but medial verbs involve co-subordination rather than subordination, as with converbs. This is reflected in the use of different pronominal anaphors as well as tense–aspect marking on these two types of dependent verbs. Converbs in Bench are less finite than medial verbs, for example, in that they carry no person-sensitive markers (Rapold 2008: 179). The following is an example with a medial verb whose interpretation in terms of tense or mood depends on the clause-final verb (Rapold 2008: 176–177):

(18) cɛ'ăɛt-í   ʃăl-n̄d
      clap-M   sing-PL
      'Clap and sing (Pl)!'

---

[5] Additional instances of convergence may be found at the lexical level. Hayward (1991) presents various examples with respect to Semitic, Cushitic, Omotic. Whether at least some of these extend into Northeastern Nilo-Saharan has not been investigated yet.

Whether there are also Northeastern Nilo-Saharan languages which distinguish between converbs and medial verbs is not known. Omotic languages also manifest switch reference between pronominal subjects in clause chaining. Again, such a system has also been identified for the Nubian (Nilo-Saharan) language Taglenaa by Gulfan (2013).[6]

A further typological property shared by Afroasiatic languages in Ethiopia and Northeastern Nilo-Saharan groups is the frequent use of coverb plus light verb ('do/say') constructions, as in the following examples from Tama, a member of the Eastern Sudanic branch (data with the author), where they commonly express positions of the body:

(19) *wut* nV- 'fall down'
      wii nV- 'return'
      salla nV- 'pray, prostrate'

In many Northeastern Nilo-Saharan languages in the Chad–Sudan area, such light verbs (e.g. nV- in the case of Tama) also tend to be used to accommodate verbs borrowed from Arabic. These languages differ as to the number of coverb plus light verb constructions they have. In Saharan languages like Kanuri, more than 90 per cent of the verbal predications are built with the verb 'say' (Hutchison 1981). The degree of productivity of this lexical strategy also varies between different Afroasiatic languages (where these light verbs are particularly common in combination with ideophonic words: see Amha 2001 for a detailed analysis of this phenomenon in the Omotic language Wolaitta).

Dixon (2002: 184 *passim*) describes a similar variation in terms of productivity of coverb constructions for languages in Australia, and argues that these languages appear to go through cycles in this respect. Whereas in some Australian languages, verbal predications are formed mainly through coverbs plus light verb constructions, other languages use this strategy next to a set of basic verbs, and in still others coverbs are absent. This corresponds to the situation in Northeastern Nilo-Saharan, where converbs are extremely common in the Saharan branch; in Eastern Sudanic groups like Taman, they are used next to a set of underived verbs, whereas in Nilotic or Surmic they are absent as main predictions.

Given the roughly west-to-east areal distribution of these typological features in Northeastern Nilo-Saharan, and given the former presence of a major riverine system in this area, it has been suggested by Rilly (e.g. 2007) and Dimmendaal (e.g. 2007, 2008) that this former tributary of the Nile, the Yellow Nile or Wadi Howar, most likely functioned as an important diffusion zone between Afroasiatic languages (or languages with typological features similar to Afroasiatic languages in Ethiopia today) and Northeastern Nilo-Saharan. This former river (shown in Map 16.1) connected the Ennedi

---

[6] Cyffer (2002) argues that there is a typological break within the Saharan branch of Nilo-Saharan in that languages like Kanuri match up typologically with Chadic (Afroasiatic) and other language groups in West Africa.

Mountains in Chad with the White Nile between the third and fourth cataract roughly between 10,000 BP and 3000 BP. As family-internal evidence in Nilo-Saharan suggests that Northeastern Nilo-Saharan acquired these features, and as these properties appear to be deeply rooted in Afroasiatic languages in Ethiopia (and beyond, in the case of number marking), they probably entered the former through areal contact.

Until recently, this scenario had to remain somewhat speculative. But these claims on population movements and areal influence through language contact have found independent support from archaeological research and genetics (DNA research and osteology), as shown by Becker (2011). Archaeological findings suggest that a 'pre-Leiterband' population of hunters and gatherers entered the Wadi Howar area in what is now Sudan from the east around 10,000 BP when wetter periods set in on the African continent. (Before that, human populations were restricted for thousands of years to zones along major rivers like the White Nile or higher elevations.) These hunter–gatherers spread across the Wadi Howar riverine system within a relatively short period and lived in semi-permanent settlements. Some 2,000 years later, pastoralists representing the Leiterband culture (after the pottery tradition associated with their cultures) and originating west of the Wadi Howar in Chad moved eastwards and absorbed many of these pre-Leiterband populations. This scenario is supported by osteological as well as DNA research (Becker 2011). If the pre-Leiterband populations indeed spoke Afroasiatic languages, they would have transferred features such as extensive case marking, converbs and other typological features onto their new primary languages, which belonged to the Nilo-Saharan phylum.[7]

16.4   The Typological Break within Eastern Sudanic

The desertification of the Wadi Howar area over the past 4,000 years must have forced people to migrate into wetter or higher elevations west, south and east of this zone, as archaeological research in the area indeed has confirmed (see, for example, Becker 2011). This is also reflected in the geographical distribution of Northeastern Nilo-Saharan languages, in particular of the largest subgroup, Eastern Sudanic, consisting of a northern branch and a southern branch. Whereas the northern members are scattered over a vast area in Chad, northern and central Sudan plus Eritrea, the southern members are in the Nuba Mountains (in Sudan) as well as in areas west, east and south of this area with an extension into Central Tanzania (see Map 16.3).

[7] Thomason and Kaufman (1988) have shown that shift-induced interference and heavy borrowing in a language shift situation are common causes for the kind of dramatic typological changes illustrated above.

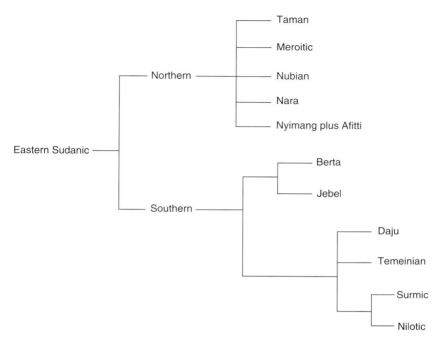

Figure 16.2 Subclassification of Eastern Sudanic languages

The northern members of the Eastern Sudanic branch share the set of typological properties described for other members of Northeastern Nilo-Saharan above.[8] But the southern members differ rather dramatically from the former. Whereas most languages belonging to the southern branch of Eastern Sudanic have retained the extensive number marking system as a lexical phenomenon, their morphosyntactic structures differ in several respects from those found in the northern sub-branch. Instead of a verb-final constituent order, a verb-second or verb-initial order is common in Nilotic and Surmic as well as Gaahmg (the only Jebel language still spoken today) and Berta. This change in constituent order is also accompanied by a different case system, namely marking of post-verbal subjects (A-roles), and absence of case marking on objects in these southern Eastern Sudanic languages; in addition, these groups manifest a reduced case-marking system compared to northern Eastern Sudanic, with only remnants of peripheral case marking (Dimmendaal 2005). The common system elsewhere in Northeastern Nilo-Saharan is one whereby the subject occurs pre-verbally and is not marked for case, whereby objects are subject to a differential object marking system (Dimmendaal 2010a).

The dramatic change in constituent order and case-marking strategies in languages belonging to the southern branch of Eastern Sudanic – all spoken east and south of the Nuba Mountains – was probably triggered

---

[8] Cases discussed here involve contact phenomena in situations with more or less stable patterns of bilingualism. Alternatively of course, language loss may occur. Whereas Nubian languages influenced Sudanese Arabic in various respects (something which cannot be discussed here for reasons of space), the latter is now gradually replacing Nubian languages in Sudan.

through areal contact.[9] The Kadu languages, spoken along the southern ranch of the Nuba Mountains in Sudan, which constitute an independent family according to the present author, are all verb-initial. A verb-initial constituent order with case marking on post-verbal subjects is also found in the Kuliak languages, which are spoken in northeastern Uganda (see Map 16.3). Andersen (1995) characterizes Berta (which is spoken northeast of the Nuba Mountains in Sudan) as a language with topic-verb-subject-object-adverbial constituent order, and shows that this language has a case system, whereby both S (the subject of intransitive predications) and A (the subject of transitive predications) are inflected for case in post-verbal (but not in pre-verbal) position:

(20)   a. *bùuŋú   ɓìid-óo   gálì*
          hyena   bite-PAST   dog:NOM
          'The dog bit the hyena'
       b. *gàlì   ɓìid-óo   búuŋù*
          dog   bite-PAST   hyena:NOM
          'The hyena bit the dog'
       c. *qól-á-láa   gálì*
          eat-PERF-NTS   dog:NOM
          'The dog has eaten it'

Exactly the same system, with case inflection for post-verbal subjects (S and A), usually referred to as a marked nominative case system (König 2008), is found in a range of Nilotic and Surmic languages. The case system of the Kuliak languages in northeastern Uganda is more complex (see Schrock 2013), but verb-initial predications are also common in this family. Nominative case may be expressed through segmental inflection, tonal inflection or a combination of these, sometimes in one and the same language.

Apart from Nilotic and Surmic languages with marked nominative case systems, we find languages belonging to the same subgroups which only allow subjects of transitive predications to occur post-verbally. Hence, only (post-verbal) A is marked for case, whereas S occurs pre-verbally and is not marked for case. Such split ergative systems are attested in Western Nilotic languages like Anywa, Päri and Shilluk, in Surmic languages like Majang or Tennet as well as in Gaahmg (Jebel group); see Map 16.4. The following examples illustrate these phenomena for Gaahmg, which is spoken east of the Nuba Mountains in Sudan (example adapted from Stirtz 2013):

---

[9] Two other branches of southern Eastern Sudanic, the Daju and Temeinian group, which are spoken in the Nuba Mountains and west of this area (extending into Chad) again have retained the number-marking system, but there are no traces of case marking (as far as present knowledge goes); moreover, SVO is the common constituent order, although languages like Sila and Njangulgule also allow for a verb-final constituent order, as in other Northeastern Nilo-Saharan languages in the area.

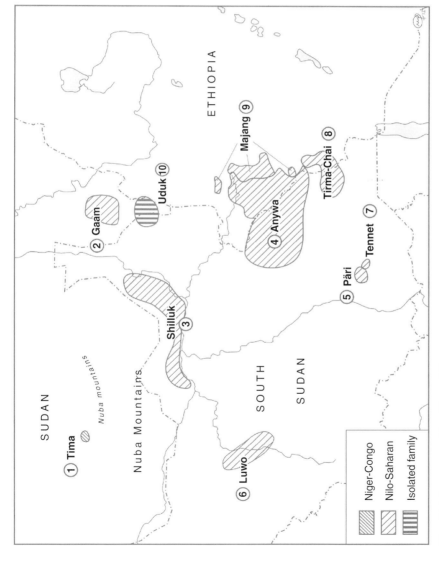

Map 16.4 Languages with split ergativity

(21)   ɲɔ́m-ɔ̄n-s-ɨ̄   aggaàr(-ὲ)
       break.CAUS-AP-COMP-PASS.A   hunter.GEN-ERG
       'Something was broken by a hunter making someone break it'

The system of post-verbal case marking for southern Eastern Sudanic languages probably constitutes a shared innovation of this subgroup, as the actual (ergative) case morphemes are cognate. Whereas in Gaahmg (Jebel) and in Western Nilotic Anywa plus Päri, the alternation between -ɛ/-e and -ɪ/-i is phonologically conditioned, the Surmic language Tennet uses -ɪ/-i with proper names, whereas -ɛ/-e occurs with other types of post-verbal subjects. What is more, Tennet has a marked nominative system for main clauses, that is, both A and S can occur post-verbally and are therefore inflected for case, whereas in subordinate clauses only A can occur in this position, giving rise to a split ergative system:

(22)   órôŋ   Lowór-i   kákát   Lohám-i   áríz
       want   Lowor-NOM   spear:SUBJ   Loham-NOM   bull:ABS
       'Lowor wants Loham to spear the bull'

(23)   órôŋ   Lowór-i   Lohám   kíkíya
       want   Lowor-NOM   Loham:ABS   come:SUBJ
       'Lowor wants Loham to come'

The post-verbal agent (ergative) marker -ɛ/-e in these southern members of Eastern Sudanic is cognate, presumably with an instrumental case marker with the same form in northern Eastern Sudanic, whereas the case marker -ɪ/-i is probably cognate with a genitive case marker in the northern branch of Eastern Sudanic, as argued in Dimmendaal (2014b).[10] According to the same author, the marked nominative system, that is, the case-marking strategy whereby both S and A are inflected for case in Nilotic and Surmic, results from an extension of post-verbal subject marking from A to S roles, that is, from transitive towards intransitive predications; this is still the situation for subordinate as opposed to main clauses in Tennet, as discussed above.

The fact that Nilotic and Surmic languages are spread over a huge area across South Sudan and extending into the Democratic Republic of the Congo, Uganda, Kenya, Tanzania and Ethiopia, and the fact that they are relatively closely related genetically, suggests that we are dealing with expansion zones in the sense of Nichols (1992). East of this expansion zone in the border area between Sudan, South Sudan and Ethiopia, and west of this zone in the Nuba Mountains, we find accretion or residual zones, i.e. areas characterized by genetic as well as typological diversity. Many of the languages in these areas are poorly studied. But initial evidence is now emerging that properties such as verb-second structures, split ergativity

---

[10] Western Nilotic Shilluk uses an alternative strategy, namely a proclitic marker, in combination with agent nouns or noun phrases (Miller and Gilley 2007). The same prenominal strategy is found in the Niger-Congo language Tima, spoken in the Nuba Mountains.

and the post-verbal marking of subjects are in fact found in a number of languages in these residual zones. Uduk, a member of the Koman family (treated as an independent language family in Dimmendaal 2011) has been reported to have OVS (or OVA) order with formal marking of the post-verbal subject (Don Kilian, personal communication). There is at least one Niger-Congo language in the Nuba Mountains, Tima, with split ergativity (Dimmendaal 2010b), but there may be other languages in this linguistically heterogeneous area manifesting the same type of syntactic alignment.

Surmic languages bordering on Omotic (i.e. Afroasiatic) languages in Ethiopia show some initial typological convergence with the latter through the presence of ejective consonants. These of course are common in Afroasiatic languages in Ethiopia, but within the Eastern Sudanic branch of Nilo-Saharan they are confined to southeastern Surmic languages bordering on Omotic, in Berta (bordering on Koman languages), and in the Kuliak languages in northeastern Uganda.

Nilotic languages belonging to the southern Lwoo cluster and bordering on Niger-Congo languages in South Sudan and Uganda also manifest clear evidence of areal contact with their distant relatives Central Sudanic as well as with Ubangi. In her monograph on the noun morphology of Western Nilotic languages, Storch (2005) identifies several layers of chronologically organized stages of historical influence, amongst others resulting in the formal reduction of nominal number marking in southern Lwoo. As shown by the same author (Storch 2005: 216–379), these languages also have various paired prefixes stemming from derivative morphemes (some of which go back to lexical roots). In Thuri, for example, one finds a deverbal stem *ŋàt-dwáár* (singular) / *jò-dwáár* (plural) 'hunter' (Storch 2005: 201). This latter system formed the basis for an even more elaborate system of number marking by way of prefixation in the southern Lwoo language Luo, as shown in the following.

16.5   The Nilotic Borderland

The southernmost member of the Lwoo cluster within Western Nilotic, Luo, is spoken in Kenya, Tanzania and Uganda, where its speakers have been in contact with speakers of Bantu languages for more than a century. The sociohistorical context in which these contacts between essentially pastoral speakers of Nilotic languages and mainly agricultural speakers of Bantu languages occurred, probably over several centuries, is summarized in Dimmendaal (2001). In the case of Luo, language shift among speakers of Bantu languages towards this Nilotic language was accompanied by heavy unadapted borrowing, for example by taking over the corresponding noun class alternation from the source language, sometimes combined with number suffixation, as in *mısomba* (sg) / *wa-sumb-ní* (pl) 'bachelor(s)'.

Additional noun-class prefixes emerged through a reinterpretation of specific lexical roots as prefixes, as with the irregular singular/plural root for 'guest' *ja- / jo-* from **jal- / *jol-* (Dimmendaal 2001):

(24)   Singular   Plural
        jà-lúô   jò-lúô   'Luo person'

Luo has several such prefixes, parallel to the noun class system of neighbouring Bantu languages. The actual prefixes are not cognate with those found in Bantu (except in borrowed nouns), but their formal as well as semantic structure is similar. Thus, the prefix *ra-* is used in Luo to express instruments (*ra-ŋî(y)* 'mirror' < *ŋıyɔ* 'recognize') as well as in referring to a person with a handicap (*ra-ŋɔl* 'lame person'). This parallels the use of the noun-class prefix *ki-* covering exactly the same semantic domains in neighbouring Bantu languages.

A further grammatical domain with a clear Bantu influence is found in the verbal system of Luo, where a four-way distinction for past tense is found.[11] A similar tense-marking system (with three distinctions for past tense) is also found in Kalenjin, a language cluster whose speakers have also been in close contact with Bantu speakers.[12] See Table 16.1.

However, whereas the Nilotic languages Luo (Western Nilotic) and Kalenjin (Southern Nilotic) both show influence from neighbouring Bantu languages in their verb systems, there are also interesting differences between the two. Kalenjin retained the rich, archaic tripartite system of number marking by way of suffixes of Northeastern Nilo-Saharan (discussed in Section 16.3 above), and there is no sign of convergence towards Bantu in this grammatical domain. In other words, convergence towards Bantu at the nominal level in Luo was 'pre-conditioned' by the already highly reduced system of number-marking suffixes in Luo. These divergent patterns of replication in Western Nilotic Luo and Southern

Table 16.1 *Past tense markers in Luo and Kalenjin*

Luo		Kalenjin	
ne-	'earlier today, recently'	*ka-, kä-*	'today in the past'
nyo-	'yesterday'	*kɔ-, ko-*	'yesterday'
yand(e)-	'a few days ago'	*kɪɪ-, kii-*	'before yesterday'
ne-	'long ago' (tonal difference on verb stem from 'earlier today')		

---

[11] See Nurse (2008) for a description of this widespread system in Bantu languages.

[12] Language shift from a Bantu language towards Kalenjin and corresponding shift-induced interference from the primary language lies at the heart of this convergence process, as argued in Dimmendaal (2001). The same process presumably occurred when hunter–gatherers speaking Afroasiatic (or typologically similar) languages in the Wadi Howar area shifted towards Nilo-Saharan, thereby causing replication of grammatical features in the newly acquired primary languages.

Nilotic Kalenjin show that the typological distance between languages is another factor affecting the (short term) outcome of language contact.

In the case of the Datooga cluster within Southern Nilotic, there is evidence for areal contact with neighbouring Bantu and Cushitic languages. Kießling, Mous and Nurse (2008) have described the complex linguistic situation in the Tanzanian Rift Valley area, where West Rift Cushitic languages are spoken next to Bantu, the linguistic isolate Hadza, as well as Sandawe (which is either a linguistic isolate or a language which is genetically related to Central Khoisan), Eastern Nilotic Maasai and Southern Nilotic Datooga. The authors also point towards 'a progressive trend away from postpositional marking of spatial relations … towards prepositional marking. This kind of reinforcement of prepositions is symptomatic of a more general trend in West Rift towards head-initial order … Syntactic position and conceptual models must be viewed as reflecting a Datooga substrate, probably originating in a large number of Datooga speakers shifting to pre-Iraqw and imposing Datooga syntactic and semantic structures onto pre-Iraqw' (Kießling, Mous and Nurse 2008: 215). Datooga has incipient pre-verbal clitic clustering (comprising four structural slots in front of the verb). This is atypical for (Southern) Nilotic, but characteristic of neighbouring West Rift Cushitic languages, where this complex expresses tense, subordination, sequentiality and focus:

(25) ák-àjà   gábá síisí   gùurs-á   òorjéedàa-ɲi
      SEQ:AFF-FUT   every person call:APPL-3   son-POSS.3SG
      'Then everyone will call his son'

The typological convergence described for different Nilo-Saharan groups above contrasts dramatically with the typological diversity observable for languages in the Nuba Mountains in Sudan. In this accretion zone, we find over 40 languages belonging to Nilo-Saharan, Niger-Congo as well as Kadu, which differ rather dramatically from a typological point of view in almost every respect. Nilo-Saharan languages in this area differ amongst each other and from unrelated languages in the area in terms of their prosodic structures, varying between pitch-accent systems and tonal systems with two or three registers. Moreover, some languages have a verb-final structure whereas others are verb-initial, using either case or head marking on the verb as grammatical strategies. The question why virtually no convergence or 'language union' (as Trubetzkoy called this phenomenon) is found in the Nuba Mountains cannot be addressed here for reasons of space, but is discussed in detail in Dimmendaal (2015: 25–63).

16.6   Some Conclusions

The Nilo-Saharan phylum covers a vast area across Eastern and Central Africa. The extant languages are spoken both in expansion zones and in residual zones, as shown above. Much of what one observes in terms of language contact today probably played a role in the development of this phylum over the past millennia.

The areal source for some of the dramatic changes is not always obvious. Within the northern branch of Eastern Sudanic, there are two closely related languages, Nyimang plus Afitti, which deviate rather dramatically from close relatives such as the Nubian languages. Hill Nubian languages, for example, are spoken in the same area in the Nuba Mountains, and are characterized by rich number-marking systems of the type discussed above in Section 16.3. This extensive number-marking system has disappeared from Nyimang and Afitti, where number marking on nouns is restricted to plural marking for nouns referring to human beings.

Data from the Nilo-Saharan area further show that replication of grammatical features in contact situations is facilitated by the proximity of grammatical systems. This can be observed when comparing historical processes in Nilotic languages like Luo or the Kalenjin cluster, whose speakers were, or are, in close contact with speakers of Bantu languages.

Marked nominative case systems are attested in Nilo-Saharan subgroups such as Nilotic, Surmic and Berta. In all three branches, this property is associated with post-verbal subjects (A-roles). As shown by König (2008), such case systems are also attested in Omotic (Afroasiatic) languages in Ethiopia, where subjects inflected for case precede the verb. Given the geographical distance between most of these languages, and the fact that there is no other lexical or grammatical evidence for convergence between these Afroasiatic and Nilo-Saharan groups otherwise, it seems more likely that these systems developed independently of each other. These latter 'autogenetic' processes may also form the ultimate explanation for the presence of marked nominative case systems in the Afroasiatic branch Omotic on the one hand and in the Eastern Sudanic branch within Nilo-Saharan on the other. Most of their extant members are not spoken in adjacent areas. Moreover, they differ in virtually every other typologically relevant respect: constituent order (verb-final versus verb-initial or verb-second), the presence versus absence of converbs, the extensive versus restricted use of case, to mention but a few features. The alternation with ergative systems, sometimes in the same language (as in Tennet) in Eastern Sudanic, suggests that marked nominative systems derive from the former. The frequently observed formal morphological link between nominative case and genitive case in Omotic (Afroasiatic) languages suggests a historical link between these two case forms. Genitive case constitutes one of the etymological sources of ergative constructions cross-linguistically (primarily for nominalized constructions). However, to date, no Omotic language has been reported to have a split ergative case system. The question why (split) ergative systems are so rare and presumably unstable remains one of the future challenges for areal linguistics in an African context.

Abbreviations

A	agent
ABS	absolutive
ADV	adverbial
AFF	affirmative
AP	antipassive
APPL	applicative
AUX	auxiliary
CAUS	causative
COMP	completive
CONV	converb
DIR	directive
ERG	ergative
GEN	genitive
M	medial verb marker
NF	non-finite verb marker
NOM	nominative
NTS	followed by a non-topical subject
PART	particle
PASS	passive
PERF	perfect
SEQ	sequential
SG	singular
SU	subject
SUB	subjunctive

References

Amha, Azeb, 2001. Ideophones and compound verbs in Wolaitta. In F. K. Erhard Voeltz and Christa Kilian-Hatz (eds), *Ideophones*, pp. 49–62. Amsterdam and Philadelphia: John Benjamins.

Amha, Azeb and Gerrit J. Dimmendaal, 2006. Converbs from an African perspective. In Felix Ameka, Alan Dench and Nick Evans, *Catching Language: Issues in Grammar Writing*, pp. 393–440. Berlin: Mouton de Gruyter.

Andersen, Torben, 1984. Aspect and word order in Moru. *Journal of African Languages and Linguistics* 6: 19–34.

Andersen, Torben, 1995. Absolutive and Nominative in Berta. In Robert Nicolaï and Franz Rottland (eds), *Proceedings of the Fifth Nilo-Saharan Linguistics Colloquium*, pp. 36–49. Cologne: Rüdiger Köppe.

Becker, E., 2011. *The Prehistoric Inhabitants of the Wadi Howar: An Anthropological Study of Human Skeletal Remains from the Sudanese Part of the*

Eastern Sahara. Doctoral Dissertation, Johannes-Gutenberg-Universität, Mainz.

Bender, Marvin Lionel, 1996. *Kunama*. Munich: LINCOM Europa.

Bickel, Balthasar, 2007. Typology in the twenty-first century: Major current developments. *Linguistic Typology* 11: 239–251.

Blackings, Mairi and Nigel Fabb, 2003. *A Grammar of Ma'di*. Berlin: Mouton de Gruyter.

Boyd, Raymond, 1989. Adamawa-Ubangi. In John Bendor-Samuel (ed.), *The Niger-Congo Languages*, pp. 178–215. Lanham: University Press of America.

Boyeldieu, Pascal, 1995. Le yakoma. In Raymond Boyd (ed.), *Le système verbal dans les langues oubangiennes*, pp. 113–139. Munich: LINCOM Europa.

Boyeldieu, Pascal, 2013. Case alignment(s) in Sinyar. Paper presented at the 11th Nilo-Saharan Linguistics Colloquium, University of Cologne.

Boyeldieu, Pascal and Pierre Nougayrol, 2008. Les langues soudaniques centrales: Essai d'évaluation. In Dymitr Ibriszimow (ed.), *Problems of Linguistic-Historical Reconstruction in Africa*, pp. 9–29. Cologne: Rüdiger Köppe.

Cloarec-Heiss, France, 1986. *Dynamique et équilibre d'une syntaxe: le banda-linda de Centrafrique*. Paris and Cambridge: Peeters-SELAF and Cambridge University Press.

Corbett, Greville G., 2000. *Number*. Cambridge: Cambridge University Press.

Cyffer, Norbert, 2002. The Lake Chad: A new Sprachbund boundary? In Robert Nicolai and Peter Zima (eds), *Lexical and Structural Diffusion*, pp. 27–43. *Corpus, Les Cahiers* 1.

Dimmendaal, Gerrit J., 2001. Language shift and morphological convergence in the Nilotic area. *Sprache und Geschichte in Afrika* 16/17: 83–124.

Dimmendaal, Gerrit J., 2005. Head marking, dependent marking and constituent order in the Nilotic area. In F. K. Erhard Voeltz (ed.), *Studies in African Linguistic Typology*, pp. 71–92. Amsterdam: John Benjamins.

Dimmendaal, Gerrit J., 2007. Eastern Sudanic and the Wadi Howar and Wadi El Milk diaspora. *Sprache und Geschichte in Afrika* 18: 37–67.

Dimmendaal, Gerrit J., 2008. Africa's verb-final languages. In Heine and Nurse (eds), pp. 271–307.

Dimmendaal, Gerrit J., 2010a. Differential Object Marking in Nilo-Saharan. *Journal of African Languages and Linguistics* 31: 13–46.

Dimmendaal, Gerrit J., 2010b. On the origin of ergativity in Tima. In Franck Floricic (ed.), *Essais de typologie et de linguistique générale: Mélanges offerts à Denis Creissels*, pp. 233–239. Paris: Presses Universitaires de l'École Normale Supérieure.

Dimmendaal, Gerrit J., 2011. *Historical Linguistics and the Comparative Study of African Languages*. Amsterdam and Philadelphia: John Benjamins.

Dimmendaal, Gerrit J., 2014a. Nilo-Saharan. In Rochelle Lieber and Pavol Štekauer (eds), *The Oxford Handbook of Derivational Morphology*, pp. 591–608. Oxford: Oxford University Press.

Dimmendaal, Gerrit J., 2014b. Marked nominative systems in Eastern Sudanic and their historical origin. *Afrikanistik Online* 11.

Dimmendaal, Gerrit J., 2015. *The Leopard's Spots: Essays on Language, Cognition and Culture*. Leiden: Brill.

Dimmendaal, Gerrit J., in press. Nilo-Saharan. In Rainer Vossen and Gerrit J. Dimmendaal (eds), *The Handbook of African Languages*. Oxford: Oxford University Press.

Dixon, R. M. W., 2002. *Australian Languages: Their Nature and Development*. Cambridge: Cambridge University Press.

Ehret, Christopher, 2001. *A Historical-Comparative Reconstruction of Nilo-Saharan*. Cologne: Rüdiger Köppe.

Fabb, Mairi and Nigel Fabb, 2003. *A Grammar of Ma'di*. Berlin and New York: Mouton de Gruyter.

Ferguson, Charles A., 1970. The Ethiopian language area. *Journal of Ethiopian Studies* 8 (2): 67–80.

Greenberg, Joseph H., 1955. *Studies in African Linguistic Classification*. New Haven, CT: Compass Publishing Co.

Greenberg, Joseph H., 1963. *The Languages of Africa*. Bloomington and The Hague: Indiana University Press, Research Center in Anthropology, Folklore and Linguistics and Mouton.

Greenberg, Joseph H., 1966. Some universals of grammar with particular reference to the order of meaningful elements. In Joseph H. Greenberg (ed.), *Universals of Language*, pp. 73–113. Cambridge MA: The MIT Press.

Gulfan, Gumma Ibrahim, 2013. Converbs in Taglennaa (Kordofan Nubian). In Thilo C. Schadeberg and Roger Blench (eds), *Nuba Mountain Language Studies*, pp. 371–379. Cologne: Rüdiger Köppe.

Hayward, Richard J., 1991. À propos patterns of lexicalization in the Ethiopian language area. In Ulrike Claudi and Daniela Mendel (eds), *Ägypten im afro-orientalischen Kontext*, pp. 139–156. Special issue of *Afrikanistische Arbeitspapiere (AAP)*.

Heine, Bernd, 1976. *A Typology of African Languages Based on the Order of Meaningful Elements*. Berlin: Dietrich Reimer.

Heine, Bernd and Zelealem Leyew, 2003. Comparative constructions in Africa: An areal dimension. *Annual Publications in African Linguistics* 1: 47–68.

Heine, Bernd and Derek Nurse (eds), 2008. *A Linguistic Geography of Africa*. Cambridge: Cambridge University Press.

Houis, Maurice, 1970. Réflexion sur une double corrélation typologique. *The Journal of West African Languages* 7 (2): 59–68.

Hutchison, John, 1981. *The Kanuri Language: A Reference Grammar*. Madison: African Studies Program.

Jakobi, Angelika and Joachim Crass, 2004. *Grammaire du beria (langue saharienne)*. Cologne: Rüdiger Köppe.

Kießling, Roland, Maarten Mous and Derek Nurse, 2008. The Tanzanian Rift Valley area. In Heine and Nurse (eds), pp. 186–227.

König, Christa, 2008. *Case in Africa*. Oxford and New York: Oxford University Press.

Kutsch Lojenga, Constance, 1994. *Ngiti: A Central Sudanic Language of Zaire*. Cologne: Rüdiger Köppe.

Leslau, Wolf, 1945. The influence of Cushitic on the Semitic languages of Ethiopia: A problem of substratum. *Word* 1: 59–82.

Miller, Cynthia L. and Leoma G. Gilley, 2007. Evidence for ergativity in Shilluk. *Journal of African Languages and Linguistics* 22: 33–68.

Moñino, Yves, 2012. Is [the] Ubangian branch a family among Niger-Congo languages? Paper presented at the Niger-Congo International Congress. Paris, 18–21 September 2012.

Nichols, Johanna, 1992. *Language Diversity in Space and Time*. Chicago: University of Chicago Press.

Nurse, Derek, 2008. *Tense and Aspect in Bantu*. Oxford: Oxford University Press.

Rapold, Christian H., 2008. Medial verbs in Benchnon. In Karen H. Ebert, Johanna Mattissen and Rafael Suter (eds), *From Siberia to Ethiopia: Converbs from a Cross-linguistic Perspective*, pp. 155–183. Zürich: Seminar für Allgemeine Sprachwissenschaft, Universität Zürich.

Rilly, Claude, 2007. *La langue du royaume de Méroé: Un panorama de la plus ancienne culture écrite d'Afrique subsaharienne*. Paris: Champion.

Santandrea, Stefano, 1970. *Brief Grammar Outlines of the Yulu and Kara Languages*. Bologna: Nigrizia.

Schrock, Terrill B., 2013. *A Grammar of Ik (Icé-tód), Northeast Uganda's Last Thriving Kuliak Language*. Utrecht: LOT.

Storch, Anne, 2005. Dynamics of interacting populations: Language contact in the Lwoo languages of Bahr el-Ghazal. *Studies in African Linguistics* 32 (1): 65–93.

Thomason, Sarah Grey and Terrence Kaufman, 1988. *Language Contact, Creolization, and Genetic Linguistics*. Berkeley, CA: University of California Press.

Tosco, Mauro, 2000. Is there an Ethiopian language area? *Anthropological Linguistics* 42 (3): 329–365.

Tucker, A. N., 1967. *The Eastern Sudanic Languages 1*. London: Dawsons.

Tucker, A. N. and Margaret A. Bryan, 1966. *Linguistic Analyses: The Non-Bantu Languages of North-Eastern Africa*. London: Oxford University Press for the International African Institute.

17

Niger-Congo Languages

Jeff Good

17.1 Niger-Congo: A Stock Spanning Many Areas

Niger-Congo is one of the largest language families in the world – perhaps even the largest – spanning an enormous area of Africa from the southern edge of the Sahara desert at the north of its extent to the very south of the continent itself. It further spreads across a diverse range of ecological environments, from rainforest to desert, as well as a number of apparent linguistic areas. Its internal genealogical diversity is similarly remarkable, as well as controversial in some key respects. Any discussion of the areal linguistics of the family can only begin to scratch the surface, especially if sociocultural dimensions of its language dynamics are to be taken into account. The goal of this chapter is, therefore, merely to give some general sense of the 'flavour' of the areal patterns of the family's languages and highlight select topics for the study of areal linguistics generally that these patterns raise.

The discussion begins with an overview of the geographic distribution of the family and the state of the art with respect to the genealogical classification of its languages in Section 17.2. A brief summary is then given regarding salient features that most Niger-Congo languages have in common in order to set a 'baseline' for discussion of areal patterns within the family, which is the subject of Section 17.3. The chapter then shifts in Section 17.4 from a more geographic-centred view of areality to consider the relatively underexplored issue of how an appreciation of the social dynamics of speakers of Niger-Congo languages is likely to play a crucial role in coming to a fuller understanding of the family's areal patterns. In Section 17.5, the chapter concludes with a brief discussion of possible future directions for the study of Niger-Congo areal linguistics.

17.2   Genealogical and Geographic Overview

17.2.1   Genealogical Overview

Niger-Congo, in the broadest sense, is the largest referential (if not genealogical) language group in world (Williamson and Blench 2000: 11), dominating Sub-Saharan Africa geographically. The extent to which the 'traditional' group of Niger-Congo languages forms a true genealogical unit is not clear, however, and this obviously complicates any examination of the areal linguistics of the family. Overviews of Niger-Congo can be found in the chapters of Bendor-Samuel (1989) and in Williamson and Blench (2000), with a more up-to-date discussion of the state of scholarship on the comparative linguistics of the family to be found in Dimmendaal (2011: 85–92). Only a brief summary is given here, and Dimmendaal's (2011) treatment is given the most serious consideration as an especially recent statement on the composition of the family, though it should be stressed that not all specialists would agree with the full range of his conclusions. For purposes of reference, Map 17.1 presents a map of the

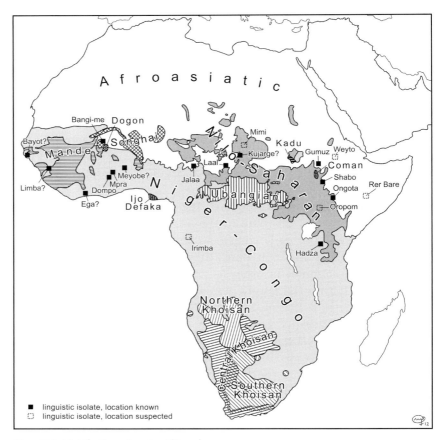

Map 17.1 Distribution of major African language groups

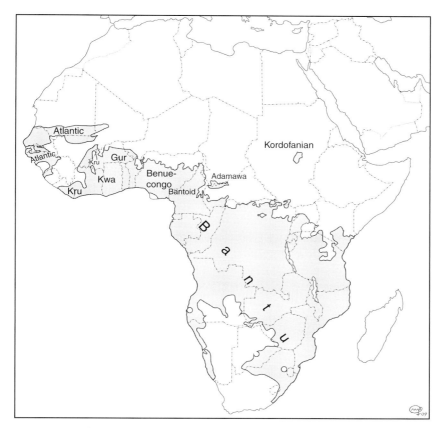

Map 17.2 Distribution of Niger-Congo languages

major African language groups and Map 17.2 presents a map of the sub-groups of Niger-Congo, as assumed in the discussion here.[1]

There is a relatively uncontroversial 'core' to Niger-Congo comprising the following subgroups: Benue-Congo, which includes many languages of southern Nigeria, the Bantu languages, and much in between; Kwa, found in southern West Africa from Côte d'Ivoire to the Nigerian border in a contiguous band along the Atlantic coast moving substantially inland; Gur, found in an inland region of West Africa, including the bulk of Burkina Faso, southern parts of Mali, northern parts of Côte d'Ivoire,

---

[1] Map 17.1 represents something closer to a 'splitting' approach to African language classification than the more familiar four-family 'lumping' approach that has dominated much of the work on African languages since Greenberg's influential proposals, and the interested reader can consider the evidence for each approach by comparing the overview references given above. As will be clear from the discussion below, Map 17.2 represents something along the lines of 'core' Niger-Congo, and language groups (e.g., Mande, Ijo, Dogon) which are treated as part of Niger-Congo in other sources are not necessarily indicated in Map 17.2 but, rather, Map 17.1. These maps essentially follow the treatment of Dimmendaal (2011), though they have been updated somewhat to make them more in line with the current state of the comparative evidence. Maps 17.1 and 17.2 were produced by Monika Feinen, cartographer at the Institut für Afrikanistik, University of Cologne, and I am grateful to her for making them available to me for inclusion in this chapter and to Gerrit Dimmendaal for helping me get in touch with her.

Ghana, Togo and Benin, as well as a small portion of western Nigeria, and whose southern and eastern borders are with Kwa and Benue-Congo languages respectively; Adamawa, also an inland group, found in scattered areas of Nigeria, Cameroon, Chad and the Central African Republic; Kru, mostly found in a strip along the West African coast directly to the west of Kwa, including the southwestern part of Côte d'Ivoire and much of Liberia; the so-called Atlantic group of languages found along and near the Atlantic coast, in an area detached from the other groups given above, in parts of Senegal, the Gambia, Guinea and Sierra Leone; and some languages commonly referred to as Kordofanian found in the Nuba mountains of Sudan, a region quite distant from the rest of the family.

Even if the membership of the languages of these groups as part of Niger-Congo is considered uncontroversial, there are still numerous questions concerning their subgrouping. To pick just one example, the validity of the languages grouped under the label 'Atlantic' as a coherent subgroup of Niger-Congo has never been properly established, with some even suggesting it has not been abandoned merely due to 'scholarly inertia' (Childs 2003: 47).

In addition to the above, various other groups have also been placed under the Niger-Congo umbrella, but their genealogical status with respect to the family remains controversial. Perhaps the most significant of these from an areal perspective is the Mande group, which occupies a large portion of western West Africa. While the inclusion of Mande within Niger-Congo has been part of textbook presentations of the family for decades (see e.g. Williamson and Blench 2000: 18), the evidence for its inclusion in Niger-Congo is comparatively weak, in large part because languages of the group neither exhibit functioning noun class systems nor clear-cut remnants of them (Williamson 1989b: 36; Williamson and Blench 2000: 19). If Mande is not part of Niger-Congo, then some of its noteworthy features which appear to show up in less robust form in other Niger-Congo languages would be good candidates for treatment as resulting from contact-induced change, affecting languages found in an area of historical Mande influence (see Section 17.3.4). For example, Mande languages are known for their rigid S-Aux-OV-Other clausal syntax; see Gensler (1994, 1997) for discussion in a comparative context. If they are not part of Niger-Congo, then cases of other Niger-Congo languages showing Mande-like word order patterns, of the sort documented in Güldemann (2007) – see also Heine (1975: 35–36), Heine (1976: 41–42) and Creissels (2006) – would be candidates for having undergone syntactic change due to Mande influence. On the other hand, if Mande is part of Niger-Congo, then one must also consider the possibility of shared inheritance. Problems like these do not prevent us from describing contemporary areal patterns in the family, though they do suggest that one must avoid over-interpreting the evidence at hand with respect to specific historical scenarios.

Where relevant, further aspects of Niger-Congo genealogical classification will be discussed below. Since it can be daunting for an outsider to keep track of the details of a family of this size, the key points to bear in mind are that (i) there is an uncontroversial core to the family, (ii) a number of other groups have been proposed to be part of the family but the evidence is less clear, and (iii) even within the 'core', significant aspects of subgrouping remain obscure.

17.2.2   Geographic Overview

There is one aspect of the geographic spread of Niger-Congo whose significance in terms of the areal patterns of the family seems hard to overstate: The family traverses an enormous north–south distance of around 5,000 kilometres, ranging from the south of the Sahara down to the Kalahari and the southeast coast of the continent. Across this distance, one finds a wide range of ecological environments, from rainforest to savannah to even Mediterranean climates in parts of South Africa. Moreover, differences in altitude can produce distinctive ecologies even in regions that are nearby to each other, thus highland areas such as the Cameroonian Grassfields can be markedly cooler than nearby lowland regions, with concomitant impacts on food production, presence of tropical disease, etc.

The north–south distribution of the family should not be viewed merely as an interesting curiosity. As discussed by Diamond (1997: 183–189) (see also Diamond and Bellwood 2003: 599), the relative consistency of patterns of daylight and seasons across an east–west axis facilitates spread of domesticated plants and animals, and, by extension, people and languages. Clearly, Niger-Congo patterns of language spread, especially the Bantu spread (see Section 17.3 for further discussion) managed to overcome this bias, but the dominating pattern of areality in the family, associated with what Güldemann (2008) has termed the Macro-Sudan Belt, does seem to fit within this pattern, capturing a number of branches of Niger-Congo across an east–west axis, not a north–south one. In addition, if we exclude the Bantu languages from consideration due to their relatively recent expansion and their status as a subgroup of Benue-Congo (see Schadeberg 2003: 155), rather than a primary branch of the family, Niger-Congo's overall pattern of geographic spread is much more strongly east–west than north–south.

A key concern for understanding the areal linguistics of Niger-Congo, then, is establishing the extent to which its areal patterns may have been shaped by ecological factors and determining what factors allowed Bantu to exceptionally spread from a point around the Cameroon-Nigeria borderland to contemporary South Africa. Aspects of these issues will be taken up below, though the present state of our knowledge in these regards is largely incomplete.

17.3 The Areal Patterns of the Family

17.3.1 Niger-Congo and 'African' Features

Any consideration of the areal linguistics of Niger-Congo must start with some sense of the features that are found throughout the family, bearing in mind the complications surrounding its precise composition discussed in Section 17.2.1. For instance, SVO word order predominates in the family, as it does in Sub-Saharan Africa generally (Dryer 2013b), though there are exceptional subgroups such as Mande, which, as mentioned in Section 17.2.1, exhibits an unusual type of SOV word order where only a single argument is permitted before the verb and other arguments after. Similarly, languages of the Ijoid group of the Niger Delta region of Nigeria, which is, at best, questionably Niger-Congo (Dimmendaal 2011: 92), exhibit a more canonical SOV syntax, where the verb tends to be final in the clause (Williamson and Blench 2000: 23), as do languages of the Dogon group (see e.g. Heath 2008: 17), though Dogon's status as a Niger-Congo language is also not proven (Dimmendaal 2011: 90). If we exclude these groups from Niger-Congo (as is done in Maps 17.1 and 17.2), SVO word order would dominate it much more than otherwise. If we were to include these groups, then, perhaps, SVO would be considered more areal in nature, prominent in the western and southern parts of the family but not as much so in the 'central' ones.

By contrast, another noteworthy feature of Niger-Congo, which is general to the family, is the presence of tone. Like SVO word order, this is also a general African feature (see Maddieson 2013b), but, while there are Niger-Congo languages lacking in tone, such as Wolof and Swahili, these are relatively restricted in their distribution rather than characterizing an entire major subgroup.

Not surprisingly, given Niger-Congo's expansive range over Sub-Saharan Africa and the ancient origins of its spread, it is difficult to find typological characteristics that would uniquely characterize Niger-Congo in opposition to the other major language families of Africa that it is in contact with.[2] Thus, in the summary of 'African' morphosyntactic features given in Creissels et al. (2008: 149–150), which lists around twenty different properties that seem especially common in African languages, many (if not all) of the points would apply just as well to Niger-Congo alone, such as, for instance, the relative lack of case (see e.g. Creissels et al. 2008: 87–91), or the presence of applicatives (Polinsky 2013).[3] This overlap between 'Niger-Congo' and 'African' features could be due, in principle, to

---

[2] Heine and Leyew (2008) suggest that Africa, in its entirety, may even form a linguistic area (see also Greenberg 1983 for earlier discussion along these lines). This conclusion would seem to require a relatively weak sense of the notion 'linguistic area', however, which is why the focus here is on possible areas within Africa *en route* to understanding Niger-Congo patterns. Güldemann (2010: 576) presents a view of the areal profile of the continent, dividing it into three 'areas' and two 'spread zones' in the sense of Nichols (1992, 1997).

[3] König (2008) provides a monograph-level overview of reported instances of case marking in African languages.

a contact situation where Niger-Congo features were spread to the rest of Africa with the family itself or where Niger-Congo 'absorbed' features common to much of Africa during its expansion, with the most likely possibility, of course, being some mix of the two.

From a historical-comparative perspective, the most significant features of Niger-Congo languages are probably their noun class systems (Heine 1980: 99) and verbal extensions, the latter of which constitute a class of suffixes involved in marking valency alternations, certain kinds of aspects, and other derivational or quasi-derivational functions (Hyman 2007a). The presence of each of these features has been reconstructed for Proto-Niger-Congo (see Williamson 1989a: 37–40 for noun classes and Voeltz 1977 for extensions), and noun class systems, in particular, have been used as a key diagnostic for family membership (see e.g. Schadeberg 1981: 122–124). However, while these are important historical features for the family, patterns of change, in many cases connected to areal influences (see Section 17.3.2), have dismantled these systems in even some 'core' Niger-Congo languages (Good 2012; Hyman 2004). Thus, these can only be considered to be Niger-Congo features from a diachronic perspective rather than a synchronic one.

17.3.2   The Macro-Sudan Belt Set Against the Periphery

Almost certainly, the most significant areal patterns of Niger-Congo are found in a region which Güldemann (2008, 2011) has recently termed the 'Macro-Sudan Belt', but which has long been known to be linguistically distinctive (see e.g. Westermann 1911 or Wallis 1978), even if the role of areality as the central factor in explaining this was not recognized (Güldemann 2008: 170–174).[4] This large region runs roughly from the Atlantic Ocean in the west to the Ethiopian Highlands in the east, and is bounded in the north by the Sahara and Sahel and in the south by the Central African rainforest. It contains Afroasiatic and Nilo-Saharan languages, as well as languages from essentially every major subgroup of Niger-Congo. The Bantu languages on the whole fall outside the region, while the other members of its parent subgroup, Benue-Congo, lie within it, allowing divergence between Bantu and its closest relatives to serve as a useful indicator of areality, though – as we will see – other 'peripheral' groups, such as Atlantic, are also relevant to establishing certain patterns as areal.

Perhaps the most salient linguistic feature of this region is the presence of labial–velar stops, such as *kp* and *gb*. Consonants of this kind are uncommon in almost the entire world except for within the Macro-Sudan Belt. And, as Maddieson (2013b) writes, 'The pattern is clearly

---

[4] Like this chapter, Dimmendaal (2001a: 365–387) also considers how features connected to the Macro-Sudan Belt relate to areal patterns in Niger-Congo.

strongly areal, as it is compact and crosses the boundaries of language families.' For present purposes, what is additionally significant is that it does not just cross the boundaries of language families but also subgroups of Niger-Congo. Thus, if we look at Benue-Congo, there is a clear divide between the Bantu languages and the rest of the subgroup: Bantu languages generally lack labial–velars while other Benue-Congo languages generally have them. Moreover, on the whole, those Bantu languages which do show labial–velar consonants are found at or near the southern edge of the Macro-Sudan Belt (Güldemann 2008: 157).

Other features which can be associated with the Macro-Sudan Belt are: the presence of ATR harmony (Clements and Rialland 2008: 50–53; Güldemann 2008: 158–159); the presence of labial flaps (Clements and Rialland 2008: 41–42; Güldemann 2008: 165–166; Olson and Hajek 2003); the presence of nasal vowels and the lack of contrastive nasal consonants (Clements and Rialland 2008: 45–49; Hajek 2013); implosive consonants (Clements and Rialland 2008: 55–60; Maddieson 2013a); the presence of three or more tone levels (Clements and Rialland 2008: 70–74; Maddieson 2013c; Wedekind 1985: 109); special 'lax' prosody for marking yes/no questions other than via final rising pitch (Clements and Rialland 2008: 75–80); the presence of logophoric markers (Güldemann 2003); S-Aux-OV-Other word order (see Section 17.2.1 and Güldemann 2008: 159–163); VO-Neg word order (Dryer 2009; Güldemann 2008: 163–164); and the presence of serial verb constructions (Dimmendaal 2001a: 382–387). On a macro-level, the relative typological similarity of languages within the belt can be seen in the treatment of African language typology in Cysouw and Comrie (2009: 202) which shows that, when looking at a number of typological features in aggregate, there is a pattern of east–west influence within the Macro-Sudan Belt not seen strongly elsewhere on the continent.

To these general Macro-Sudan patterns, which cross-cut major language families, one can add a more specific set of changes that have been discussed specifically for Niger-Congo languages in the centre of the Macro-Sudan Belt. These changes are most strongly associated with languages of the Kwa subgroup, and involve what one might broadly characterize as morphological reduction. This occurs both in the noun and noun phrase, where noun classes can show significant attrition, to the point of being lost entirely in synchronic terms (Good 2012), and in the verb and verb phrase, where, for instance, verbal derivational suffixes are lost, with serialization strategies often taking their place (Hyman 2004); see also Nurse (2007) for relevant comparative discussion of the Niger-Congo verb complex. There is a phonological aspect to this reduction as well, wherein roots tend to be reduced to CV, possibly with additional relic prefixes in nouns (Williamson 1985). This set of characteristics has been grouped together as comprising key features of the Kwa 'type', which encompasses not only Kwa languages but also many Benue-Congo

languages, especially in parts of Nigeria. At the same time, not all genealogical Kwa languages are good instances of the Kwa type. For instance,
Ghana-Togo Mountain languages do not show the noun class attrition
associated with the Kwa type (Heine 1968: 112–130; Schuh 1995). Thus,
this seems to be a good example of a properly areal pattern within Niger-
Congo.

The characteristics listed above do not, in fact, uniformly characterize
the entire Macro-Sudan Belt. For instance, the labial flap is isolated to
a central area of the region moving roughly southeast from Nigeria to
the border of Uganda. Other features spread past it, such as 'surpass'
comparatives, which are also found in eastern Bantu languages to the
south of the belt. And, while Kwa-type languages are found within the
Macro-Sudan Belt (Stassen 2013), they are restricted to a central area
within it, as just mentioned. Moreover, in some cases, categories like
those listed above mask significant variation. For example, while the
presence of more than three tone levels is, indeed, characteristic of the
Macro-Sudan Belt, this blanket classification leaves out the fact that there
are pockets within the region of higher tonal complexity. One finds languages with four or five tone levels in places such as southern Côte
d'Ivoire, where this is found for languages of the Kru, Kwa and Mande
groups, the first two of which are uncontroversially considered Niger-
Congo and the last questionably so (see Section 17.2.1).

At the same time, on the whole, the array of features found more or less
within the belt is striking, covering both phonological and syntactic features with no obvious coherence, some of which are also otherwise cross-
linguistically rare (e.g. labial–velar stops, ATR vowel harmony, VO-Neg
word order), strongly suggesting areality is at play. The region's vast geographic spread and the fluidity of the locations of its characteristic features
indicate that, rather than viewing this in terms of long-term convergence
due to multilingualism of the sort associated with prototypical sprachbunds (Thomason and Kaufman 1988: 95–97), it is better conceptualized as
a 'zone', generalizing from the sense of the word in the terms spread zone
and accretion zone of Nichols (1992, 1997). That is, what makes it an 'area'
is not the specific dynamics holding among its speaker communities at
any given moment but, rather, the fact that the region is conducive to the
spread of features within its borders but not across them. As discussed in
Section 17.2.2, the fact that the Macro-Sudan Belt is primarily oriented
along an east–west axis is probably not a coincidence here but, rather, is
connected to the tendency for subsistence strategies to generally spread
more effectively from east to west than north to south; see also
Güldemann (2010: 580).

In this regard, the region resembles a spread zone in the sense of Nichols
(1992, 1997), though one where features spread rather than whole languages, which is quite different from the more canonical case of a spread
zone, the Eurasian steppe, where features have spread more directly with

languages themselves (Nichols 1997: 369). Indeed, a striking feature of the Macro-Sudan Belt is the extent of its linguistic diversity since it overlaps notably with the Sub-Saharan Fragmentation Belt of Dalby (1970: 163), characterized by a greater density of distinctive languages and language groups than other parts of the continent, and stretching from Senegal to the East African highlands across a width averaging 700 miles to south of the Sahara (Good 2013). This pattern of feature convergence within a region of linguistic fragmentation is likely connected, at least partly, to a distinctive language ideology that characterizes the Niger-Congo area: see Section 17.4 below.

17.3.3 'Peripheral' Niger-Congo

The Macro-Sudan Belt, just discussed, encompasses the 'centre' of the Niger-Congo family, and it is largely by comparing Niger-Congo – or salient sub-parts of it, such as the region occupied by Kwa-type languages – within and outside the Belt that the areal features of Niger-Congo languages found within it can be established at all. One of the 'peripheral' groups used for such comparison, in particular, has long had a special place in Niger-Congo linguistics. These are the Bantu languages. In strict geographic terms, they hardly seem peripheral, occupying the greater part of the southern half of the African continent, ranging from Cameroon in the west to Kenya in the east to South Africa in the south. However, their current distribution is the result of a relatively late expansion in Niger-Congo terms, though its beginnings are not necessarily particularly recent, with Nurse and Philippson (2003a: 5) suggesting it commenced around 5,000 years ago. More important than the precise timing is the consensus that treats Bantu as a relatively minor offshoot of Benue-Congo in genealogical terms (Schadeberg 2003: 155), a conclusion first explicitly reached by Greenberg (1949).

Bantu languages are generally believed to be relatively conservative in a Niger-Congo context, especially in the morphological domain. This is quite clear, for example, when they are set against many of their closest relatives in Benue-Congo and Kwa, which have been affected by the Kwa-type changes described in Section 17.3.2. In all likelihood this is due to Bantu's status as a geographic 'offshoot', which protected it from waves of change within the Macro-Sudan Belt. There are still many open questions regarding the dynamics of the Bantu expansion; see, for example, Vansina (1995) for a significant, relatively recent proposal and Pakendorf et al. (2011) for an up-to-date synthesis bringing data from genetic investigations into the picture. However, the end result from an areal perspective is clear: a vast region of Sub-Saharan Africa has become much more linguistically homogeneous than its neighbouring regions, creating a distinctive linguistic area in its own right. Here, however, the overall consistency is primarily due to language spread, rather than convergence, though ongoing contact among Bantu languages has been extensive (Schadeberg 2003: 158), which presumably has served to reinforce spread-induced homogeneity.[5]

Nevertheless, one should be wary of overemphasizing the homogeneity of Bantu languages. Bantu languages of the 'canonical' type showing, for instance, well-developed noun class systems (Katamba 2003) and significant prefixing and suffixing verb morphology (Hyman 2011: 4) are not found throughout the Bantu spread area. In the northwest region of the Bantu area, in particular, one finds languages with highly reduced noun class systems, including one language, Komo, which is reported to have no noun classes (Harries 1958: 269; Maho 1999: 127–142 provides a general overview). Some of the explanation for such reduced systems may be due to the effects of contact with non-Bantu languages. Komo, for instance, is spoken in a region of the Democratic Republic of the Congo where Ubangian and Central Sudanic languages are found.[6] Moreover, the presence of labial–velars in the language (Harries 1958: 265–266; Thomas 2011: 11) suggests an affinity with the Macro-Sudan Belt (see Section 17.3.2) unlike most of Bantu. Similarly, a language like Ewondo, found at the northwest extreme of the Bantu area in Cameroon, shows a comparatively high degree of analyticity with respect to the marking of tense-mood-aspect, as evidenced by the ability of pronominal objects to appear between verbal auxiliaries and the main verb (Redden 1979: 166). This is presumably connected to contact with closely related Bantoid languages to the north that have been partly affected by the changes associated with the Kwa type discussed in Section 17.3.2.

To pick another, less extreme case, the so-called interlacustrine languages seem to represent a distinctive area within the larger Bantu region (Bastin 2003). These are languages found 'between the lakes', roughly to the west of Lake Victoria around southern Uganda, Rwanda and Burundi. By contrast, the Bantu languages found in the equatorial forest, another region that can be defined via physical features, are much more heterogeneous, suggesting that, despite common ecology, there has not yet been noteworthy areal convergence (Grégoire 2003). As a final example, Güldemann (1999a) discusses some unusual patterns of suffixation on nouns in Bantu languages found in disjoint areas in the eastern and southern portions of the Bantu zone. However, even if Bantu is not as homogeneous as often implicitly portrayed, it still is the case that the region is much more homogeneous than the rest of the Niger-Congo area, especially in terms of lexicon. The shorter time depth of the subgroup is clearly part

---

[5] In the present context, it is worth pointing out that, before the arrival of Bantu, there is evidence for the presence of an older (non-Niger-Congo) linguistic area which has been referred to as the Kalahari Basin. See Güldemann (2010: 572–573).

[6] Current consensus would seem to place the Ubangian languages outside Niger-Congo despite a common previous classification linking them to Adamawa languages (Dimmendaal 2008: 842). Central Sudanic languages have been classified within the Nilo-Saharan phylum.

of the explanation for this, but sociocultural factors have presumably also played a role, as will be discussed briefly in Section 17.4.4.

Another peripheral language group of Niger-Congo that should be considered here is Atlantic.[7] As mentioned in Section 17.2.1, the languages subsumed under Atlantic are not clearly a genealogical grouping, but this does not prevent them from being examined from an areal perspective. Found at the northwest edge of the Niger-Congo area, languages in this group are, like Bantu, not part of the core of the Macro-Sudan area (Güldemann 2008: 152). From a Niger-Congo perspective, what is striking about some languages of this group is their relatively elaborated morphology, for instance in the domain of noun class systems (Corbett 2013) and verb extensions (Hyman 2007a). For instance, some varieties of Fula have exceptionally large numbers of noun classes, numbering twenty or more (Arnott 1970: 67–109; Breedveld 1995: 295–460), making them much more 'Bantu-like' than 'Kwa-like', despite the fact that Kwa-type languages intervene between Atlantic and Bantu (Good 2012; Hyman 2004). Indeed, the parallels between the verbal structure attributed to Proto-Bantu (Meeussen 1967: 108–111) and that of the Atlantic language Bijogo, spoken on islands off the coast of mainland Guinea-Bissau (Segerer 2000: 369; 2002: 369), are particularly striking, especially given the geographic distance separating Bantu from Bijogo.

The historical interpretation for the similarities between Bantu and Atlantic is controversial, with the central question being the extent to which their similarities represent Niger-Congo archaisms as opposed to parallel developments, presumably facilitated by both groups' marginal status with respect to the Macro-Sudan Belt (Güldemann 2011; Hyman 2011; Nurse 2007). Nevertheless, from a synchronic areal perspective, this does not prevent us from speaking of a comparatively morphologically elaborated Niger-Congo 'periphery' against a more morphologically reduced Niger-Congo 'core', with extensive clinal variation in between as evidenced by, for instance, Gur languages (see the papers in Miehe and Winkelmann 2007).

17.3.4   Contact Among Language Groups and Families

The discussion to this point has largely focused on high-level areal-linguistic patterns within Niger-Congo, but, of course, there is also the issue of the role of more conventional kinds of language contact in shaping Niger-Congo grammars (see Childs 2010a for an overview and discussion of language contact in Africa). Probably the most well-known such case involves the presence of clicks in southwestern

---

[7] Due to its relative lack of study, I leave out detailed discussion of the most 'peripheral' Niger-Congo group, Kordofanian, which is markedly detached from the rest of the family. However, based on what we know of the family, its languages show reasonably robust noun classes and verbal extensions (Good 2012: 303, note 7; Hyman 2007b: 154), bringing them roughly in line with the other peripheral groups.

Bantu languages (Bostoen and Sands 2012; Herbert 1990). The presence of these in Bantu languages is universally attributed to contact with Khoisan languages (Güldemann and Stoneking 2008: 99), though it is not the case that clicks appear simply due to the borrowing of words with these sounds, since clicks can be found in words that are not borrowed from Khoisan languages, as in the form |*umáte* 'tomato' in Manyo (Gciriku) (Bostoen and Sands 2012: 125), a clear European loanword. The phonological category of click may have entered Bantu languages via Khoisan, but this has not prevented expansion in their range of use.

While clicks in some Bantu languages are the most salient outcome of contact between Bantu and Khoisan, other influences are reported as well, though these have not seen the same level of attention. Louw (1986: 152–153), for instance, discusses apparent cases of morphological borrowing from Khoe into the southern Bantu language Xhosa, such as a form that derives adjectives from other adjectives and nouns with a meaning comparable to English *-ish*; see also Louw (2013: 443) and Güldemann (1999b). However, Vossen (1997: 361) indicates that such effects were unusual in Bantu–Khoisan contact situations. Moreover, the presence of clicks has been attributed, at least in some cases, to the presence of avoidance registers in Bantu societies. This may have prompted the borrowing of clicks as a means to create lexical items fulfilling requirements of these registers, wherein words containing the same syllables as a specific set of names had to be avoided. Since clicks would not have originally been found in native Bantu words, any syllable in which they appeared would have automatically met the restrictions of such registers (see Herbert 1990: 304). This may have motivated their borrowing even in the absence of especially intimate language contact. All told, the observed patterns suggest relatively limited language contact between Bantu speakers and Khoisan speakers without, for example, the presence of long-term stable bilingualism (Vossen 1997: 362).

Less generally well-known contact situations are found in the northern parts of the Niger-Congo area, though these have had more significant grammatical effects than the Bantu–Khoisan case (even if the actual grammatical impact is less salient than the borrowing of clicks). One such contact situation is found between Benue-Congo and Chadic languages in central Nigeria, where there is evidence for lexical, phonological, morphological and syntactic convergence without a clear general pattern of the directionality of the changes as emanating from one group or the other (Gerhardt 1983; Wolff and Gerhardt 1977; see also Storch 2009: 301–303 for more recent discussion). For instance, one finds the relatively uncommon intransitive copy pronoun construction in languages of both groups – without a clear original source – wherein a copy of a subject pronoun appears after the verb in intransitive clause; see Atindogbé et al. (2011) for an overview.

Another significant region of contact influence in the northern Niger-Congo area involves the impact of Mande languages on various branches of the family. As discussed in Section 17.2.1, there is no consensus at present regarding Mande's genealogical affiliation, and it is variously classified within Niger-Congo or as an isolate family. Nevertheless, even among those who would place it within Niger-Congo, it is considered to represent an early branch from the rest of the family (Williamson and Blench 2000: 18), and it is grammatically and lexically distinctive enough to make contact between it and the rest of Niger-Congo more comparable to contact between distinct families than, say, contact among varieties in a dialect continuum, which is characteristic of other parts of Niger-Congo, especially the Bantu area.

The most salient apparent contact effect of Mande on other Niger-Congo languages involves impacts on word order. While there is no consensus on all historical details, Heine (1976: 57–58) identifies a region of West Africa that he terms the 'Mande nucleus', defined by the word order properties of its languages, for instance showing genitive-noun and SOV word order (which can be seen in recent surveys such as Dryer 2013a, 2013b). The special 'Mande' SOV pattern, characterizable as S-Aux-OV-Other (see Sections 17.2.1 and 17.3.2) is even more widespread as a contact effect than surveys indicate, since it often appears as a common variant word order in languages otherwise characterizable as SVO (Güldemann 2007; Heine 1976: 41). Childs (2003: 195–203; 2010a: 699–704; 2010b) discusses Mande influence on Atlantic and provides historical background accounting for why the influence appears to have mostly involved imposition of Mande patterns on other languages rather than the reverse.[8] However, this is not to say that Mande languages were not affected at all by contact. Bird (1970), for instance, suggests that some degree of simplification affected the Mande language Manding due to widespread second language acquisition.

The discussion here has emphasized cases where Niger-Congo languages were impacted by contact with other language families (or divergent members of their own family) but, of course, Niger-Congo languages have also significantly impacted languages in other families. Dimmendaal (2001b) describes cases where Nilotic languages have been affected by contact with Bantu languages, for instance with respect to the development of a set of tense markers in languages of the Kalenjin cluster which are functionally parallel to tense prefixes in nearby Bantu languages (Dimmendaal, this volume and 2001b: 89–93; Heine and Kuteva 2005: 144–147). A more striking example is found in the mixed language Ma'á (Mous 1994, 2003a, 2003b; Thomason 1997). Ma'á grammar is 'more or less identical to that of Mbugu', a Bantu language closely related to Pare (Mous 2003a:

---

[8] See Dombrowsky-Hahn (1999) for a detailed study of a contact situation between a Mande language and a language from the Gur subgroup which shows a similar asymmetry.

209–210). The difference between Ma'á and Mbugu is in the lexicon. Ma'á makes use of a 'parallel lexicon' containing morphological forms with generally the same syntax and semantics as corresponding forms in Mbugu, but differing in phonology. This parallel lexicon consists of a number of words of Cushitic origin, assumed to be elements retained from an earlier East Cushitic language spoken by the ancestors of the Ma'á speakers, making it another apparent case of Niger-Congo impact on a language of another family – in this case, almost to the point of complete language shift.

17.4   Sociocultural Dynamics and Language Ideologies

17.4.1   From Areal States to Areal Processes

The discussion up to this point has focused on what one might call areal 'states' rather than areal 'processes', extending ideas of Greenberg (1978, 1995) to areal patterns. However, it is clear that, if we want to fully understand the areal patterns of a family like Niger-Congo, we should be aiming to not only document them as they are now but also to understand the dynamics holding among the languages of the family that were the driving factor behind the development of those areal patterns in the first place.

At least in a Niger-Congo context, this issue has not received extensive investigation in the context of family-wide patterns of areality. However, there is work on the language dynamics of specific communities of clear relevance and which appears to be broadly consistent with observed family-wide patterns. In Section 17.4.2 I will discuss some cases of language contact in urban situations, which are comparatively well studied and in Section 17.4.3 I will compare these cases with selected work on the linguistic and cultural dynamics of rural regions. In Section 17.4.4 I will then sketch out the implications of the dynamics found in these two domains for our understanding of Niger-Congo areal linguistics.

17.4.2   The Formation of Urban Varieties in Niger-Congo

Language use in urban Africa has been the subject of comparatively extensive research, especially when set against non-urban areas of the continent: see the collected papers of Mc Laughlin (2009a) and the detailed sociolinguistic investigation of Accra in Kropp Dakubu (1997). While the languages of urban regions are, of course, not limited to those of the Niger-Congo group, including not only other languages of Africa but also colonial languages, the family's domination of the continent means that they are an integral part of the urban linguistic environment across the Sub-Saharan region.

One of the better studied cases of a Niger-Congo urban language variety is that of Urban Wolof in Senegal (Mc Laughlin 2008, 2009b); see also Irvine and Gal (2000: 47–59) for the broad historical context. Urban Wolof is a prestige variety, functioning as an informal national language (despite French being the official language of the country) and is most saliently distinct from rural varieties by virtue of extensive borrowing from French. It has further become associated with urbanization in Senegal in general, rather than being the variety of a specific city (Mc Laughlin 2009b: 84) and with a distinctive urban-oriented identity (Mc Laughlin 2008: 155–156). The significance of Urban Wolof in the present context relates to something that failed to happen in Senegal: rather than French or 'regular' Wolof becoming the language of the new urban populations, a new linguistic variety emerged, based on a Niger-Congo variety that was already present but with significant intermixing of 'foreign' elements. This urban variety, moreover, has not replaced rural varieties but, rather, is 'additive' in its sociolinguistic effect.

While each case of language contact has its own history, the particular result of contact in the Wolof case, the creation of a new variety, does not appear to be at all unusual in a Sub-Saharan African context. Kießling and Mous (2004), for instance, discuss a number of recently formed urban youth languages in Sub-Saharan African areas dominated by Niger-Congo languages. Not all of these are primarily based on Niger-Congo varieties. For instance, Camfranglais, a youth language of Cameroon, is primarily French-derived, but with significant influence from Cameroonian Pidgin and several other Cameroonian languages (Kießling and Mous 2004: 306). In other cases, such as that of Isicamtho (Childs 1997, 2003: 212–216; Kießling and Mous 2004: 310), the new language is primarily based on a Niger-Congo variety (in this case, Zulu). However, less important than the particular linguistic mixture is the fact that urban social contexts of this part of the world seem especially prone to the formation of youth varieties, and, as Kießling and Mous (2004: 305) point out, a notable feature of them is the fact that they do not merely arise but are also named, enhancing their visibility as lexicogrammatical codes.

Thus, as with Urban Wolof, urban youth languages again point to a pattern characteristic of Sub-Saharan Africa where language contact leads to the development of recognized new linguistic varieties. I am not aware of any work which suggests this is specifically a Niger-Congo pattern, as opposed to encompassing Sub-Saharan Africa more generally, but it certainly is the case that this linguistic culture implicates much, and in all likelihood most, of the Niger-Congo area. Of course, it is difficult in general to ever specifically separate out any 'Niger-Congo' pattern from a 'Sub-Saharan' one given Niger-Congo's spread on the continent.

Other examples of such new variety formation are not hard to find: see Childs (2003: 214–215) and Kießling and Mous (2004). A relatively well-studied case is that of Sheng, originating in Nairobi and which is described as involving a mixture of elements of Swahili, English and other languages of Kenya (Mazrui 1995; Rudd 2008). A less well-studied parallel variety has also arisen in Nairobi known as Engsh, which is more heavily English-based than the Swahili-dominated Sheng (Abdulaziz and Osinde 1997). While the general interpretation of the development of these varieties is that they are connected to the construction of new identities in urban contexts, as will be discussed in Section 17.4.3, there is reason to believe that the processes that underlie their development are not specifically 'urban' in nature but, rather, have their roots in patterns of language use also found in more traditional contexts.

Alongside varieties specifically associated with urban environments, the development of various contact varieties of Niger-Congo languages, some of which have been treated as partially pidginized or creolized, also bears mentioning at present as providing additional cases where new language formation has taken place as new social contexts emerge. Mufwene (2003) presents an overview of significant issues with respect to contact languages of the Bantu area, which are comparatively well studied in this regard.

17.4.3   The Continuity of Urban and Rural Language Dynamics

It is clear that many urban contexts dominated by Niger-Congo languages have proved to be fertile ground for the formation of new language varieties. A question that arises from this is whether there is something special about urban contexts in Africa that causes them to not merely be multilingual but to also promote the creation of new languages on top of indigenous and colonial ones, or whether this urban pattern may represent simply a new instantiation of processes that characterized the Niger-Congo area long before modern patterns of urban living.

In fact, there is a fair amount of evidence that what we see in urban environments is not particularly distinctive in historical terms. For instance, urban youth vernaculars, such as those discussed in Section 17.4.2, are typically seen as having developed, at least partly, out of a desire for secrecy. This is suggested, for example, by Isicamtho's origins in the milieu of criminals (Childs 1997: 345) and Sheng's purported origins as a variety for groups of teenagers seeking special in-group communication (Abdulaziz and Osinde 1997: 49). Such varieties show immediate parallels to secret languages used for ritual purposes, such as what is described in Storch (2004: 344–345) and Lüpke and Storch (2013: 81–82) for Jukun languages of the Benue-Congo subgroup. As Dimmendaal (2011: 252) describes it, 'modern youth languages constitute a continuation or extension of ancient traditions of language manipulation'. He thus draws an explicit link between urban and rural language dynamics. More generally, there is rich documentation of what one might call a tendency towards language 'inventiveness' found throughout Sub-Saharan Africa, where new varieties emerge to serve specific social functions, often via what appears to be deliberate linguistic manipulation (Lüpke and Storch 2013: 77–122; Storch 2011).[9]

It is instructive here to return to the case of Wolof given Irvine's (1978) study of variation in the language in a rural context. In this case, variability in the use of noun classes was associated with a speaker's social position. Wolof thus provides us with an instance where variation is tied to social status in both urban and rural contexts (see Section 17.4.2), but where the locus of variation is different in each environment. Urban Wolof is most saliently distinct by virtue of its French borrowings, while rural varieties construct distinctiveness using the 'native' material of noun classes. In both cases, one can observe a creative and active pattern of variety formation to serve social ends.

Di Carlo and Good (2014), on the basis of a case study of a small, linguistically diverse and rural Bantoid-speaking region of Cameroon known as Lower Fungom, have argued for the prominence of a language ideology in Sub-Saharan Africa that is primarily indexical rather than essentialist in orientation.[10] That is, languages are not treated as markers of 'essential' and immutable ethnicities, as is typical of Western language ideologies in the form of the so-called Herderian equation of language, culture and nation (see e.g. Foley 2005; Hymes 1968, 1972). Rather, their primary function is to index a speaker's association with a particular sociopolitical group (in the Lower Fungom case, a specific village), comparable to the notion of a 'community of practice' as developed in the sociolinguistic literature; see, for example, Bucholtz (1999) or Eckert (2000).

Di Carlo and Good (2014) further suggest that this ideology can be correlated with patterns of change that do not align well with standard models of language diversification as involving tree-like or wave-like patterns, but, rather, are more likely to involve language mixing as a means to rapidly create new identities. This would be a clear rural parallel to the formation of a variety like Sheng, discussed in Section 17.4.2, with the major difference that, in the rural Lower Fungom case, the apparent mixing is only among languages of the Bantoid subgroup of Niger-Congo, rather than taking place between a Niger-Congo language and an Indo-European one. It seems important to bear in mind, in this regard, that language mixing is most visible when involving distantly related languages. This means that there might be many cases of mixing among closely related Niger-Congo languages that have yet to be detected (if even detectable).

It is useful here to consider ethnographic work like that of Kopytoff (1987), which tries to identify general cultural patterns in Sub-Saharan Africa and, by extension, Niger-Congo (see also Zeitlyn and Connell 2003).

---

[9] Avoidance registers fall into this class as well and, as discussed in Section 17.3.4, an avoidance register is likely to have been one of the routes through which clicks entered southern Bantu languages.

[10] Good (2013) considers this region from an areal perspective.

Kopytoff (1987: 24) specifically characterizes societies in this part of the world as being built around groups of solidarity, ranging from the kin group to the village to the kingdom. A given individual would be attached to several such groups as a means to ensure personal security. Following Di Carlo and Good (2014), one of the most salient means to signal such group affiliation would be through the use of the linguistic varieties associated with these groups. While this is an emerging, rather than established, area of research, it suggests that a distinctive underlying cultural pattern may be responsible for noteworthy aspects of language use and diversification both in contemporary urban and traditional rural Sub-Saharan Africa. In particular, in this part of the world, new social contexts may be especially prone to the development of new linguistic varieties.

When this idea is linked to complex patterns of multilingualism observable in the Niger-Congo area (Lüpke and Storch 2013: 13–48), it suggests that one of the defining areal features of Niger-Congo may be the way a particular language ideology produces language dynamics associated with the frequent emergence (and, necessarily, loss) of language varieties to fulfil different social functions. These dynamics can involve creative use of ambient grammatical material, either through manipulation or mixing, to construct new varieties and are led by speaker communities where individual mastery of multilingual repertoires is the normal state of affairs. To the extent that this sketch may be correct, it has consequences for long-term patterns of historical change in Niger-Congo, and this is briefly explored in the next section.

17.4.4   From Local Dynamics to Areal Patterns

If we take seriously the idea that patterns such as those described in Sections 17.4.2 and 17.4.3 are not merely isolated cases of new variety formation but, rather, represent instantiations of a more general Niger-Congo pattern, then this has clear consequences for our understanding of the areal dynamics of the family. In particular, it seems clear that repeated instances of the formation of new varieties involving creative mixing and manipulation of ambient grammatical material would be unlikely to result in the tree-like and wave-like patterns of diversification that have long been considered to be the normal state of affairs for language change and are still frequently applied to Bantu data (see e.g. Holden and Gray 2006).

This is not to say that Niger-Congo diversification would never have involved such types of change. For instance, the genealogical division between some groups in contact, such as Gur and Kwa, has been viewed as completely unambiguous, indicating that tree-like diversification must have taken place at some (distant) point in Niger-Congo's history. But, at the same time, one is confronted with long-standing problems, such as the fact that clear criteria for distinguishing Bantu languages from their closest relatives have never been devised despite the general impression that there is something coherent about the group (Nurse and Philippson 2003a: 5–7). More strikingly, despite success in reconstructing Proto-Bantu elements, it has not been possible to arrive at a consensus on Bantu-internal subgrouping (Schadeberg 2003).

It seems worth considering that this may not be due to a failure on the part of comparative linguists to find the 'right' grammatical and lexical features for such tasks but may rather be due to the historical forces shaping language change in the family itself. Perhaps millennia of new variety formation, following the patterns outlined above, have obscured tree-like patterns of divergence, or even prevented them from developing in the first place in many cases.[11] If so, this suggests that the future of Niger-Congo areal studies may need to consider much more closely the special role that the cultural configurations of Niger-Congo societies and, in particular, their language ideologies, may have played in shaping the current areal patterns of the family. This would require moving away from models that simply treat language change as resulting from 'natural' processes of diversification and, instead, view it as inherently culturally embedded (Heggarty et al. 2010: 3830).

Adopting this perspective may also play a role in understanding why the Macro-Sudan Belt shows grammatical convergence in a manner reminiscent of what is found in spread zones, despite showing extreme linguistic diversity (see Section 17.3.2). Multilingual communities in this region may have required the active presence of outwardly distinct languages for social purposes while frequently exchanging grammatical features among them. The end result would be typological convergence without large-scale language shift.

17.5 Moving Forward in Niger-Congo Areal Studies

As obvious as it may be, it bears repeating that the present state of our knowledge of the areal linguistics of Niger-Congo is severely limited. The vastness of the family, in terms of numbers of languages, speakers and geographic spread presents daunting challenges for synthesizing the data required to come to a full understanding of its areal patterns. And, we are also confronted with a lack of consensus regarding the composition of the family and its internal subgrouping (see Section 17.2.1).

The usual response to such a situation – that we need more data – of course applies, to some extent. However, simply adding more data on

---

[11] One can, of course, attempt to fit a tree onto any comparative linguistic data, as Holden and Gray (2006) do with Bantu lexical data, but this sort of work begins with the assumption that the basic nature of divergence will result in tree-like patterns and cannot, therefore, test the validity of the model in the first place.

top of the already considerable amount of unsynthesized data already available will not suddenly reveal a clear picture where there was, previously, a murky one. Instead, we would seem to need new models for understanding the nature of language contact and language change in the Niger-Congo area, which build the observed realities of widespread multilingualism and rapid formation of new varieties into their foundations. Only by arriving at an improved understanding of how Niger-Congo cultures have impacted Niger-Congo languages will we be able to seriously explore salient linguistic questions such as what has allowed labial–velars to spread widely within the Macro-Sudan Belt but not beyond it, why the striking and 'marked' Khoisan feature of clicks was able to be integrated into Bantu languages without significant grammatical change, or why it has been so difficult to find clear linguistic dividing lines for many subgroups despite linguists' intuitions that they should exist – just to pick three of the many important areal questions posed by the family.

References

Abdulaziz, Mohamed H. and Ken Osinde, 1997. Sheng and Engsh Development of mixed codes among the urban youth in Kenya. *International Journal of the Sociology of Language* 125: 43–63.

Arnott, D. W., 1970. *The Nominal and Verbal Systems of Fula*. Oxford: Oxford University Press.

Atindogbé, Gratien G., Anne Storch and Roger M. Blench, 2011. Introduction. In Anne Storch, Gratien G. Atindogbé and Roger M. Blench (eds), *Copy Pronouns: Case Studies from African Languages*. Cologne: Rüdiger Köppe.

Bastin, Yvonne, 2003. The interlacustrine zone (zone J). In Nurse and Philippson (eds), pp. 501–528.

Bendor-Samuel, John (ed.), 1989. *The Niger-Congo Languages: A Classification and Description of Africa's Largest Language Family*. Lanham, MD: University Press of America.

Bird, Charles S., 1970. The development of Mandekan (Manding): A study of the role of extra-linguistic factors in linguistic change. In David Dalby (ed.), *Language and History in Africa*, pp. 146–159. New York: Africana Publishing Company.

Bostoen, Koen and Bonny Sands, 2012. Clicks in south-western Bantu languages: Contact-induced vs. language-internal lexical change. In Matthias Brenzinger and Anne-Maria Fehn (eds), *Proceedings of the 6th World Congress of African Linguistics (WOCAL 6)*, pp. 121–132. Cologne: Rüdiger Köppe.

Breedveld, J. O., 1995. *Form and Meaning in Fulfulde: A Morphophonological Study of Maasinankoore*. Leiden: Research School CNWS.

Bucholtz, Mary, 1999. 'Why be normal?' Language and identity practices in a community of nerd girls. *Language in Society* 28: 203–223.

Childs, G. Tucker, 1997. The status of Isicamtho, an Nguni-based urban variety of Soweto. In Arthur K. Spears and Donald Winford (eds), *The Structure and Status of Pidgins and Creoles*, pp. 341–367. Amsterdam: John Benjamins.

Childs, G. Tucker, 2003. *An Introduction to African Languages*. Amsterdam: John Benjamins.

Childs, G. Tucker, 2010a. Language contact in Africa: A selected review. In Raymond Hickey (ed.), *The Handbook of Language Contact*, pp. 695–713. Chichester, UK: Wiley-Blackwell.

Childs, G. Tucker, 2010b. The Mande and Atlantic groups of Niger-Congo: Prolonged contact with asymmetrical consequences. *Journal of Language Contact, Thema* 3: 15–46.

Clements, George N. and Annie Rialland, 2008. Africa as a phonological area. In Heine and Nurse (eds), pp. 36–85.

Corbett, Greville G., 2013. Number of genders. In Dryer and Haspelmath (eds), *The World Atlas of Language Structures Online*.

Creissels, Denis, 2006. S-O-V-X constituent order and constituent order alternations in West African languages. In Rebecca T. Cover and Yuni Kim (eds), *Proceedings of the Thirty-First Annual Meeting of the Berkeley Linguistics Society*, pp. 37–51. Berkeley, CA: Berkeley Linguistics Society.

Creissels, Denis, Gerrit J. Dimmendaal, Zygmunt Frajzyngier and Christa König, 2008. Africa as a morphosyntactic area. In Heine and Nurse (eds), pp. 86–150.

Cysouw, Michael and Bernard Comrie, 2009. How varied typologically are the languages of Africa?. In Rudolf Botha and Chris Knight (eds), *The Cradle of Language*, pp. 189–203. Oxford: Oxford University Press.

Dalby, David, 1970. Reflections on the classification of African languages: With special reference to the work of Sigismund Wilhelm Koelle and Malcolm Guthrie. *African Language Studies* 11: 147–171.

Di Carlo, Pierpaolo and Jeff Good, 2014. What are we trying to preserve? Diversity, change, and ideology at the edge of the Cameroonian Grassfields. In Peter K. Austin and Julia Sallabank (eds), *Endangered Languages: Beliefs and Ideologies in Language Documentation and Revitalization*, pp. 229–262. Oxford: Oxford University Press.

Diamond, Jared, 1997. *Guns, Germs, and Steel*. London: Vintage.

Diamond, Jared and Peter Bellwood, 2003. Farmers and their languages: The first expansions. *Science* 300: 597–603.

Dimmendaal, Gerrit J., 2001a. Areal diffusion versus genetic inheritance: An African perspective. In Alexandra Y. Aikhenvald and Robert M. W. Dixon (eds), *Areal Diffusion and Genetic Inheritance: Problems in Comparative Linguistics*, pp. 359–392. Oxford: Oxford University Press.

Dimmendaal, Gerrit J., 2001b. Language shift and morphological convergence in the Nilotic area. In Derek Nurse (ed.), *Historical Language Contact in Africa*, pp. 83–124. Sprache und Geschichte in Afrika, vol. 16/17. Cologne: Rüdiger Köppe.

Dimmendaal, Gerrit J., 2008. Language ecology and linguistic diversity on the African continent. *Language and Linguistics Compass* 2: 840–858.

Dimmendaal, Gerrit J., 2011. *Historical Linguistics and the Comparative Study of African Languages*. Amsterdam: John Benjamins.

Dombrowsky-Hahn, Klaudia, 1999. *Phénomènes de contact entre les langues minyanka et bambara (sud du Mali)*. Cologne: Rüdiger Köppe.

Dryer, Matthew S., 2009. Verb-object-negative order in central Africa. In Norbert Cyffer, Erwin Ebermann and Georg Ziegelmeyer (eds), *Negation Patterns in West African Languages and Beyond*, pp. 307–362. Amsterdam: John Benjamins.

Dryer, Matthew S., 2013a. Order of genitive and noun. In Dryer and Haspelmath (eds), *The World Atlas of Language Structures Online*.

Dryer, Matthew S., 2013b. Order of subject, object and verb. In Dryer and Haspelmath (eds), *The World Atlas of Language Structures Online*.

Dryer, Matthew S. and Martin Haspelmath (eds), 2013c. *The World Atlas of Language Structures Online*. Munich: Max Planck Digital Library.

Eckert, Penelope, 2000. *Linguistic Variation as Social Practice: The Linguistic Construction of Identity in Belten High*. Oxford: Blackwell.

Foley, William A., 2005. Personhood and linguistic identity, purism and variation. In Peter K. Austin (ed.), *Language Documentation and Description*, vol. 3, pp. 157–180. London: Hans Rausing Endangered Languages Project.

Gensler, Orin D., 1994. On reconstructing the syntagm S-Aux-O-V-Other to Proto-Niger-Congo. In Kevin E. Moore, David A. Peterson and Comfort Wentum (eds), *Proceedings of the Twentieth Annual Meeting of the Berkeley Linguistics Society, Special Session on Historical Issues in African Linguistics*, pp. 1–20. Berkeley, CA: Berkeley Linguistics Society.

Gensler, Orin D., 1997. Grammaticalization, typology, and Niger-Congo word order: Progress on a still-unsolved problem. *Journal of African Languages and Linguistics* 18: 57–93.

Gerhardt, Ludwig, 1983. Lexical interferences in the Chadic/Benue-Congo border-area. In Ekkehard Wolff and Hilke Meyer-Bahlberg (eds), *Studies in Chadic and Afroasiatic Linguistics*, pp. 301–310. Hamburg: Helmut Buske.

Good, Jeff, 2012. How to become a 'Kwa' noun. *Morphology* 22: 293–335.

Good, Jeff, 2013. A (micro-)accretion zone in a remnant zone? Lower Fungom in areal-historical perspective. In Balthasar Bickel, Lenore A. Grenoble, David A. Peterson and Alan Timberlake (eds), *Language Typology and Historical Contingency: In Honor of Johanna Nichols*, pp. 265–282. Amsterdam: John Benjamins.

Greenberg, Joseph H., 1949. Studies in African linguistic classification III: The position of Bantu. *Southwestern Journal of Anthropology* 5: 309–317.

Greenberg, Joseph H., 1978. Diachrony, synchrony, and language universals. In Joseph H. Greenberg (ed.), *Universals of Human Language*, pp. 61–91. Stanford, CA: Stanford University Press.

Greenberg, Joseph H., 1983. Some areal characteristics of African languages. In Ivan R. Dihoff (ed.), *Current Approaches to African Linguistics*, vol. 1, pp. 3–21. Dordrecht: Foris.

Greenberg, Joseph H., 1995. The diachronic typological approach to language. In Masayoshi Shibatani and Theodora Bynon (eds), *Approaches to Language Typology*, pp. 145–166. Oxford: Oxford University Press.

Grégoire, Claire, 2003. The Bantu languages of the forest. In Nurse and Philippson (eds), pp. 349–370.

Güldemann, Tom, 1999a. The genesis of verbal negation in Bantu and its dependency on functional features of clause types. In Jean-Marie Hombert and Larry M. Hyman (eds), *Bantu Historical Linguistics: Theoretical and Empirical Perspectives*, pp. 545–587. Stanford, CA: CSLI.

Güldemann, Tom, 1999b. Head-initial meets head-final: Nominal suffixes in eastern and southern Bantu from a historical perspective. *Studies in African Linguistics* 28: 49–91.

Güldemann, Tom, 2003. Logophoricity in Africa: An attempt to explain and evaluate the significance of its modern distribution. *Sprachtypologie und Universalienforschung* 56: 366–387.

Güldemann, Tom, 2007. Preverbal objects and information structure in Benue-Congo. In Enoch O. Aboh, Katharina Harmann and Malte Zimmerman (eds), *Focus Strategies in African Languages: The Interaction of Focus and Grammar in Niger-Congo and Afro-Asiatic*, pp. 83–112. Berlin: Mouton de Gruyter.

Güldemann, Tom, 2008. The Macro-Sudan Belt: Towards identifying a linguistic area in northern Sub-Saharan Africa. In Heine and Nurse (eds), pp. 151–185.

Güldemann, Tom, 2010. Sprachraum and geography: Linguistic macro-areas in Africa. In Alfred Lameli, Roland Kehrein and Stefan Rabanus (eds), *Language and Space: An International Handbook of Linguistic Variation*, vol. 2: *Language Mapping*, pp. 561–585. Berlin: de Gruyter Mouton.

Güldemann, Tom, 2011. Proto-Bantu and Proto-Niger-Congo: Macro-areal typology and linguistic reconstruction. In Osamu Hieda, Christa König and Hirosi Nakagawa (eds), *Geographical Typology and Linguistic Areas: With Special Reference to Africa*, pp. 109–141. Amsterdam: John Benjamins.

Güldemann, Tom and Mark Stoneking, 2008. A historical appraisal of clicks: A linguistic and genetic population perspective. *Annual Review of Anthropology* 37: 93–109.

Hajek, John, 2013. Vowel nasalization. In Dryer and Haspelmath (eds), *The World Atlas of Language Structures Online*.

Harries, Lyndon, 1958. Kᶷmu: A sub-Bantu language. *Kongo-Overzee* 265–296.

Heath, Jeffrey, 2008. *A Grammar of Jamsay*. Berlin: Mouton.

Heggarty, Paul, Warren Maguire and April McMahon, 2010. Splits or waves? Trees or webs? How divergence measures and network analysis can unravel language histories. *Philosophical Transactions of the Royal Society B: Biological Sciences* 365: 3829–3843.

Heine, Bernd, 1968. *Die Verbreitung und Gliederung der Togorestsprachen* Berlin: Dietrich Reimer.

Heine, Bernd, 1975. Language typology and convergence areas in Africa *Linguistics* 144: 27–47.

Heine, Bernd, 1976. *A Typology of African Languages: Based on the Order of Meaningful Elements*. Berlin: D. Riemer.

Heine, Bernd, 1980. Methods in comparative Bantu linguistics (the problem of Bantu linguistic classification). In Luc Bouquiaux (ed.). *L'Expansion Bantoue: Actes du colloque international du CNRS, Viviers (France) 4–16 avril 1977*, vol. II, pp. 295–308. Paris: SELAF.

Heine, Bernd and Tania Kuteva, 2005. *Language Contact and Grammatical Change*. Cambridge: Cambridge University Press.

Heine, Bernd and Zelealem Leyew, 2008. Is Africa a linguistic area? In Heine and Nurse (eds), pp. 15–35.

Heine, Bernd and Derek Nurse (eds), 2008. *A Linguistic Geography of Africa*, pp. 151–185. Cambridge: Cambridge University Press.

Herbert, Robert K., 1990. The sociohistory of clicks in southern Bantu. *Anthropological Linguistics* 3/4: 295–315.

Holden, Clare J. and Russell D. Gray, 2006. Rapid radiation, borrowing and dialect continua in the Bantu languages. In Peter Forster and Colin Renfrew (eds), *Phylogenetic Methods and the Prehistory of Languages*, pp. 19–31. Cambridge: McDonald Institute for Archaeological Research.

Hyman, Larry M., 2004. How to become a 'Kwa' verb. *Journal of West African Languages* 30: 69–88.

Hyman, Larry M., 2007a. Niger-Congo verb extensions: Overview and discussion. In Doris L. Payne and Jaime Peña (eds), *Selected Proceedings of the 37th Annual Conference on African Linguistics*, pp. 149–163. Somerville, MA: Cascadilla.

Hyman, Larry M., 2007b. Reconstructing the Proto-Bantu verbal unit: Internal evidence. In Nancy C. Kula and Lutz Marten (eds), *SOAS Working Papers in Linguistics*, vol. 15, pp. 201–211. London: SOAS.

Hyman, Larry M., 2011. The Macro-Sudan Belt and Niger-Congo reconstruction. *Language Dynamics and Change* 1: 3–49.

Hymes, Dell H., 1968. Linguistic problems in defining the concept of 'tribe'. In June Helm (ed.), *Essays on the Problem of Tribe: Proceedings of the 1967 Annual Spring Meeting of the American Ethnological Society*, pp. 65–90. Seattle: University of Washington Press.

Hymes, Dell H., 1972. Linguistic aspects of comparative political research. In Robert T. Holt and John E. Turner (eds), *The Methodology of Comparative Research*, pp. 295–341. New York: Free Press.

Irvine, Judith T., 1978. Wolof noun classification: The social setting of divergent change. *Language in Society* 7: 37–64.

Irvine, Judith T. and Susan Gal, 2000. Language ideology and linguistic differentiation. In Paul V. Kroskrity (ed.), *Regimes of Language: Ideologies, Polities, and Identities*, pp. 35–83. Santa Fe, NM: School of American Research Press.

Katamba, Francis, 2003. Bantu nominal morphology. In Nurse and Philippson (eds), pp. 103–120.

Kießling, Roland and Maarten Mous, 2004. Urban youth languages in Africa. *Anthropological Linguistics* 46: 303–341.

König, Christa, 2008. *Case in Africa*. Oxford: Oxford University Press.

Kopytoff, Igor, 1987. The internal African frontier: The making of African political culture. In Igor Kopytoff (ed.), *The African Frontier: The Reproduction of Traditional African Societies*, pp. 3–84. Bloomington, IN: Indiana University Press.

Kropp Dakubu, M. E., 1997. *Korle Meets the Sea: A Sociolinguistic History of Accra*. Oxford: Oxford University Press.

Louw, J. A., 1986. Some linguistic influence of Khoi and San in the pre-history of the Nguni. In Rainer Vossen and Klaus Keuthmann (eds), *Contemporary Studies on Khoisan: In Honour of Oswin Köhler on the Occasion of his 75th Birthday*, pp. 141–168. Hamburg: Helmut Buske.

Louw, J. A., 2013. The impact of Khoesan on Southern Bantu. In Rainer Vossen (ed.), *The Khoesan Languages*, pp. 435–444. Abingdon, UK: Routledge.

Lüpke, Friederike and Anne Storch, 2013. *Repertoires and Choices in African Languages*. Berlin: de Gruyter Mouton.

Maddieson, Ian, 2013a. Glottalized consonants. In Dryer and Haspelmath (eds), *The World Atlas of Language Structures Online*.

Maddieson, Ian, 2013b. Presence of uncommon consonants. In Dryer and Haspelmath (eds), *The World Atlas of Language Structures Online*.

Maddieson, Ian, 2013c. Tone. In Dryer and Haspelmath (eds), *The World Atlas of Language Structures Online*.

Maho, Jouni, 1999. *A Comparative Study of Bantu Noun Classes*. Göteburg: Acta Universitatis Gothoburgensis.

Mazrui, Alamin M., 1995. Slang and code-switching: The case of Sheng in Kenya. *Afrikanistische Arbeitspapiere* 42: 168–179.

Mc Laughlin, Fiona, 2008. The ascent of Wolof as an urban vernacular and national lingua franca in Senegal. In Cécile B. Vigouroux and Salikoko S. Mufwene (eds), *Globalization and Language Vitality: Perspectives from Africa*, pp. 142–170. London: Continuum.

Mc Laughlin, Fiona (ed.), 2009a. *The Languages of Urban Africa*. London: Continuum.

Mc Laughlin, Fiona, 2009b. Senegal's early cities and the making of an urban language. In Fiona Mc Laughlin (ed.), *The Languages of Urban Africa*, pp. 71–85. London: Continuum.

Meeussen, A. E., 1967. Bantu grammatical reconstructions. *Africana Linguistica* 3: 79–121.

Miehe, Gudrun and Kerstin Winkelmann (eds), 2007. *Noun Class Systems in Gur Languages*, vol. 1: *Southwestern Gur Languages (without Gurunsi)*. Cologne: Rüdiger Köppe.

Mous, Maarten, 1994. Ma'a or Mbugu. In Peter Bakker and Maarten Mous (eds), *Mixed Languages: 15 Case Studies in Language Intertwining*, pp. 175–200. Amsterdam: IFOTT.

Mous, Maarten, 2003a. The linguistic properties of lexical manipulation and its relevance for Ma'á. In Yaron Matras and Peter Bakker (eds), *The Mixed Language Debate: Theoretical and Empirical Advances*, pp. 209–235. Berlin: Mouton.

Mous, Maarten, 2003b. *The Making of a Mixed Language: The Case of Ma'a/ Mbugu*. Amsterdam: John Benjamins.

Mufwene, Salikoko S., 2003. Contact languages in the Bantu area. In Nurse and Philippson (eds), pp. 195–208.

Nichols, Johanna, 1992. *Linguistic Diversity in Space and Time*. Chicago: University of Chicago Press.

Nichols, Johanna, 1997. Modeling ancient population structures and movement in linguistics. *Annual Review of Anthropology* 26: 359–384.

Nurse, Derek, 2007. Did the Proto-Bantu verb have a synthetic or an analytic structure? In Nancy C. Kula and Lutz Marten (eds), *SOAS Working Papers in Linguistics*, vol. 15, pp. 239–256. London: SOAS.

Nurse, Derek and Gérard Philippson, 2003a. Introduction. In Nurse and Philippson (eds), pp. 1–12.

Nurse, Derek and Gérard Philippson (eds), 2003b. *The Bantu Languages*. London: Routledge.

Olson, Kenneth S. and John Hajek, 2003. Cross-linguistic insights on the labial flap. *Linguistic Typology* 7: 157–186.

Pakendorf, Brigitte, Koen Bostoen and Cesare de Filippo, 2011. Molecular perspectives on the Bantu expansion: A synthesis. *Language Dynamics and Change* 1: 50–88.

Polinsky, Maria, 2013. Applicative constructions. In Dryer and Haspelmath (eds), *The World Atlas of Language Structures Online*.

Redden, James E., 1979. *A Descriptive Grammar of Ewondo*. Carbondale, IL: Department of Linguistics, Southern Illinois University.

Rudd, Philip W., 2008. *Sheng: The Mixed Language of Nairobi*. PhD dissertation, Ball State University, Muncie, IN, USA.

Schadeberg, Thilo, 1981. Das Kordofanische. In Bernd Heine, Thilo C. Schadeberg and Ekkehard Wolff (eds), *Die Sprachen Afrikas*, pp. 117–128. Hamburg: Helmut Buske.

Schadeberg, Thilo C., 2003. Historical linguistics. In Nurse and Philippson (eds), pp. 143–163.

Schuh, Russell G., 1995. Avatime noun classes and concord. *Studies in African Linguistics* 24: 123–149.

Segerer, Guillaume, 2000. *Description de la langue bijogo (Guinée Bissau)*. PhD thesis, Université de la Sorbonne Nouvelle, Paris III, Paris.

Segerer, Guillaume, 2002. *La langue bijogo de Babaque (Guinée Bissau)*. Louvain and Paris: Peeters.

Stassen, Leon, 2013. Comparative constructions. In Dryer and Haspelmath (eds), *The World Atlas of Language Structures Online*.

Storch, Anne, 2004. Traces of a secret language: Circumfixes in Hone (Jukun) plurals. In Akinbiyi Akinlabi and Oluseye Adesola (eds), *Proceedings of the Fourth World Congress of African Linguistics*, pp. 337–349. Cologne: Rüdiger Köppe.

Storch, Anne, 2009. Cultured contact: Ritualisation and semantics in Jukun. In Wilhelm J. G. Möhlig, Frank Seidel and Marc Seifert (eds), *Language Contact, Language Change and History Based on Language Sources in Africa*, pp. 297–319. Sprache und Geschichte in Africa, vol. 20. Cologne: Rüdiger Köppe.

Storch, Anne, 2011. *Secret Manipulations: Language and Context in Africa*. Oxford: Oxford University Press.

Thomas, John Paul, 2011. *A Morphophonology of Komo: Non-tonal Phenomena. SIL Electronic Working Papers*, 2011–006. Dallas, TX: SIL International.

Thomason, Sarah G., 1997. Ma'a (Mbugu). In Sarah G. Thomason (ed.), *Contact Languages: A Wider Perspective*, pp. 469–487. Amsterdam: John Benjamins.

Thomason, Sarah G. and Terrence Kaufman, 1988. *Language Contact, Creolization, and Genetic Linguistics*. Berkeley, CA: University of California Press.

Vansina, Jan, 1995. New linguistic evidence and 'the Bantu expansion'. *Journal of African History* 36: 173–195.

Voeltz, Erhard Friedrich Karl, 1977. *Proto Niger-Congo Verb Extensions*. PhD dissertation, UCLA, Los Angeles.

Vossen, Rainer, 1997. What click sounds got to do in Bantu: Reconstructing the history of language contacts in southern Africa. In Birgit Smieja and Meike Tasch (eds), *Human Contact through Language and Linguistics*, pp. 353–366. Frankfurt: Peter Lang.

Wallis, Barry M., 1978. *Diedrich Westermann's Die westlichen Sudansprachen and the Classification of the Languages of West Africa*. PhD dissertation, Northwestern University, Evanston, IL, USA.

Wedekind, Klaus, 1985. Thoughts when drawing a map of tone languages. *Afrikanistische Arbeitspapiere* 1: 105–124.

Westermann, Diedrich, 1911. *Die Sudansprachen: Eine Sprachvergleichende Studie*. Hamburg: L. Friedrichsen.

Williamson, Kay, 1985. How to become a Kwa language. In Adam Makkai and Alan K. Melby (eds), *Linguistics and Philosophy: Essays in Honor of Rulon S. Wells*, pp. 427–443. Amsterdam: John Benjamins.

Williamson, Kay, 1989a. Benue-Congo overview. In Bendor-Samuel (ed.), pp. 247–274.

Williamson, Kay, 1989b. Niger-Congo overview. In Bendor-Samuel (ed.), pp. 3–45.

Williamson, Kay and Roger M. Blench, 2000. Niger-Congo. In Bernd Heine and Derek Nurse (eds), *African Languages: An Introduction*, pp. 11–42. Cambridge: Cambridge University Press.

Wolff, Ekkehard and Ludwig Gerhardt, 1977. Interferenzen zwischen Benue-Kongo- und Tschad-Sprachen. In Wolfgang Voigt (ed.), *XIX. Deutscher Orientalistentag*, pp. 1518–1543. Wiesbaden: F. Steiner.

Zeitlyn, David and Bruce Connell, 2003. Ethnogenesis and fractal history on an African frontier: Mambila-Njerep-Mandulu. *Journal of African History* 44: 117–138.

18

The Kalahari Basin Area as a 'Sprachbund' before the Bantu Expansion

Tom Güldemann and Anne-Maria Fehn

18.1 Introduction

Güldemann (1998 and following publications) not only challenged the 'Khoisan' family hypothesis established by Greenberg (1950, 1963) and popular among non-specialists ever since, but also proposed the areal concept 'Kalahari Basin' comprising the indigenous non-Bantu languages of southern Africa. If the linguistic isoglosses shared by these languages are compatible with a historical assessment in terms of multiple and partly long-standing contact, the areal approach is a viable explanation for the emergence of the modern linguistic panorama, as opposed to the genealogical hypothesis. Since the areal approach was proposed more than a decade ago, research on linguistic isoglosses and contact-induced convergence across the Kalahari Basin has increased considerably. This article summarizes the earlier results, supplements them with new findings, thus giving more substance to the 'Kalahari Basin' concept, and embeds it in the general discussion about linguistic areas.

18.1.1 The Three Independent 'Khoisan' Families of Southern Africa

The classification of the non-Bantu languages of southern Africa has been controversial since the first linguistic data were scrutinized from a historical perspective. By the second half of the last century linguists and non-linguists alike (but not necessarily language specialists) had largely settled on Greenberg's (1950, 1963) lumping proposal of a 'Khoisan'

This chapter greatly benefited from research undertaken within the EuroBABEL project 'The Kalahari Basin area: a "Sprachbund" on the verge of extinction'. We are grateful for the funding provided by the Deutsche Forschungsgemeinschaft (DFG). Anne-Maria Fehn would further like to thank the a.r.t.e.s. Graduate School at the University of Cologne and the German Academic Exchange Service (DAAD) for supporting research and fieldwork on Ts'ixa. We are also indebted to Hirosi Nakagawa and Christfried Naumann for valuable comments on an earlier version of this chapter, and to Falko Berthold and Linda Gerlach for sharing their data on N!aqriaxe with us.

language family, which even includes two isolated languages in eastern Africa – Sandawe and Hadza. Before embarking on the following discussion, it is important to recognize that this genealogical classification can no longer be followed, first of all because Greenberg's evidence was insufficient and no progress has been made in more than 60 years in substantiating his claim by means of standard historical-comparative methodology (Güldemann 2008b; Güldemann and Vossen 2000; Sands 1998; Westphal 1971).

The opinion of specialists is converging on the recognition of three independent lineages in southern Africa, as shown in Table 18.1; the evidence for the assumed affiliation of Kwadi and ǂ'Amkoe, on which our knowledge is still incomplete, with Khoe and Ju respectively, still needs to be extended; see Güldemann (2014a) for the most recent survey on classification and terminology. While Kwadi is crucial for an understanding of

Table 18.1 *The three lineages commonly subsumed under Southern African 'Khoisan'*

Lineages and (sub)branches	Languages (L) or language complexes (LC) and selected dialects or dialect groups	
Khoe-Kwadi		
Kwadi	single L†	
Khoe		
Kalahari Khoe		
East	Shua:	Cara, Deti, ǀXaise, Danisi, etc.
	Tshwa:	Kua, Cua, Tsua, etc.
West	ʔTsʼixa	
	Khwe:	ǀXom, ǀXo, Buga, ǁAni, etc.
	Gǀana:	Gǀana, Gǀui, etc.
	Naro:	Naro, Tsʼao, etc.
Khoekhoe	(Cape Khoekhoe)† LC	
	(ǃOra-Xiri) LC	
	(Eini)† LC	
	Nama-Damara LC	
	Haiǁom	
	ǂAakhoe	
Kxʼa		
Ju	single LC:	North: Angolan ǃXuun varieties
		North Central: Ekoka ǃXuun, etc.
		Central: Grootfontein ǃXuun, etc.
		Southeast: Tsumkwe Juǀʼhoan, Epukiro Juǀʼhoan, etc.
ǂAmkoe	single LC:	ǂHoan, Nǃaqriaxe, Sasi
Tuu		
Taa-Lower Nossob		
Taa	single LC:	West: West ǃXoon, (Nǀuǀʼen)
		East: East ǃXoon, ʼNǀoha, (Nǀamani), (Kakia), etc.
Lower Nossob	(ǀʼAuni)†	
	(ǀHaasi)†	
ǃUi	Nǁng:	Nǀuu = (ǂKhomani) = (Nǀhuki), Langeberg, etc.
	(ǀXam)†:	Strandberg, Katkop, Achterveld, etc.
	(ǂUngkue)†	
	(ǁXegwi)†	

Note: † = extinct, (...) = older data sources

the area's history, the following discussion excludes it, because the data on this extinct language are largely insufficient. This situation also holds for the Lower Nossob group of the Tuu family.

The three lineages, Tuu, Kx'a and Khoe(–Kwadi), are intended here to constitute the Kalahari Basin area and are referred to accordingly – this despite the fact that later colonizers like Bantu languages and Afrikaans may have come to share one or another local feature through language contact (see Section 18.3).

18.1.2 Previous Areal and Contact-Oriented Research

While Greenberg (1950, 1963) is responsible for the heretofore popular but spurious 'Khoisan' concept, he was probably also the first to entertain contact-induced convergence in the major relevant area, here called the Kalahari Basin (Greenberg 1959: 24). Since he did not give any data and discussion, one can only speculate about the exact evidence he had in mind. Heine's (1976: 56) research on word order patterns in Africa yielded more concrete indications of areal convergence. It is clear, however, that any areal concept for the relevant languages must remain highly problematic from a methodological perspective as long as they are simultaneously considered to be genealogically related.

Such a problem ceases to exist under a non-genealogical approach. Inspired by Nichols (1992), this was pursued for the first time by Güldemann (1998), who introduced the present areal concept. Although prefiguring the idea of a linguistic area before the Bantu expansion, the aim of this initial study was not to show any homogeneity across the area but rather its overall diversity compared to other parts of the continent and its potential nature as a 'residual/accretion zone', which would cast doubt on the 'Khoisan' hypothesis. In this article, the area also had a narrower geographical extension, excluding languages which are viewed here as belonging to its northern and eastern periphery.

Güldemann (1998: 152–154) did, however, identify several isoglosses across a subset of Kalahari Basin languages, thus establishing a typological group called since then 'non-Khoe'. In the present terminology, this entity comprises two of the three Kalahari Basin lineages, namely Tuu and Kx'a. Studies such as Güldemann and Vossen (2000) and Güldemann (2000, 2013e) reiterate and elaborate this finding, observing a basic typological split between this group on the one hand and Khoe-Kwadi on the other. The following list summarizes the non-Khoe isoglosses proposed in the four aforementioned studies, all written but not published around the same time.

Non-Khoe isoglosses
- low complexity (in terms of Nichols 1992)
- little bound morphology, phonological word often the same as lexical root

- neutral alignment
- clusivity
- verb-medial clause order
- very few or even no ditransitive verbs
- verb serialization
- head-initial noun phrase order with exceptional head-final genitive
- inalienable possession
- head of juxtapositional genitive conveys nominal derivation and locative flagging
- multi-purpose oblique (MPO) preposition (possibly leading to circumpositional flagging)
- noun categorization by means of a special type of gender system
- irregular number marking, including nominal and verbal root suppletion

The shared and often quirky properties of the sound structure of Kalahari Basin languages (see e.g. Güldemann 2001 for a more recent treatment of consonant systems) have long been known and mostly considered to be inherited from an assumed Proto-Khoisan. Under a non-genealogical approach these would be obvious signals of convergence.

Within the somewhat different context of historical research on Bantu languages, the areal homogeneity detected by Heine (1976) regarding the morphosyntax of genitives was discussed in more detail by Güldemann (1999); an additional finding of this study was that historically derived structures of nominal flagging and derivation are also widely shared across the Kalahari Basin.

Around the same time and later, research explicitly focusing on language contact started to identify non-phonological isoglosses that bridged the dichotomy of non-Khoe versus Khoe-Kwadi also on a more local scale. As will become clearer below, these are important for modelling the linguistic history of the Kalahari Basin as a whole.

Traill and Nakagawa (2000) treated a contact zone in the central Kalahari between G|ui from the Kalahari Khoe group of Khoe-Kwadi and the East !Xoon variety of the Tuu language Taa, and also indicated the involvement of western ǂ'Amkoe of the Kx'a family. Their discussion focused largely on lexical isoglosses. However, looking at Traill's (1980) phonological survey of the wider area, it becomes clear that the analysis of sound structure yields a similar picture, for example the languages' sharing of exceptionally large consonant inventories and a high frequency of clicks against non-clicks.

Güldemann (2002, 2006) focused on another zone where Khoe languages share a number of features with non-Khoe neighbours, namely the Cape area in South Africa, where Khoekhoe languages from Khoe-Kwadi and !Ui languages from Tuu were spoken. The studies did not focus on shared lexicon but on structural similarities in phonology and morphosyntax, which are listed below.

Structural similarities between Khoe and non-Khoe languages
- relatively small consonant inventories
- high click frequency compared to non-clicks
- fricativization of complex egressive stops (in the north)
- complex pronouns and clusivity
- lexically fixed gender, unusual association of feminine sex/gender and large size
- nominal derivation on non-canonical verbal, adjectival and pronominal hosts
- inclusory pronouns in 'recapitulative' coordination
- high load of verbal reduplication
- particular distribution pattern of temporal predicate operators
- lexically complex predicates
- clause-second marking for sentence type and information structure
- low semantic sensitivity of certain participant flagging
- similar tagging of reported discourse and proposition (a.k.a. 'complement') clauses

In Section 18.2 we recapitulate Kalahari Basin isoglosses from earlier research and entertain some new ones, the minimal requirements being that a feature is recurrent in the area and involves at least one language in each family, and the relevant languages are not all in contact today. Another important criterion is that a feature is sufficiently marked, locally or even better globally, so that multiple independent origins are less likely. The following isogloss list is not considered to be complete, nor is every feature thought to be an established areal trait, because some isoglosses are not distributed evenly geographically and/or within families and are not even rigorously defined yet, so their status as areal features requires more research.

18.2   Isoglosses across Kalahari Basin Languages

18.2.1   Phonetics and Phonology

Beach's (1938) ground-breaking work on the phonetics and phonology of Khoekhoe provided the first scientific basis for describing and comparing Kalahari Basin languages in terms of complex sound systems, in particular, typologically quirky clicks, as well as highly skewed root phonotactics. An equally important achievement was made later by Snyman (1975) and Traill (1985) with respect to the treatment of complex consonants, both clicks and non-clicks, and of vocalic phonation types comprising nasalization, pharyngealization, glottalization, breathiness and stridency.

Phonetic/phonological commonalities across the Kalahari Basin languages have been taken for granted because they were commonly thought to reflect common descent, even by Greenberg (1963: 67), who generally sought to exclude purely typological features as genealogical evidence. Later studies relying on a much better database and more fine-grained analyses found a considerable amount of diversity between languages (Güldemann 2001, 2013e; Traill 1980).

Nevertheless, the features shared across the three families are numerous enough, largely absent in Bantu outside the area (Hyman 2003; Kisseberth and Odden 2003; Maddieson 2003), and often so quirky, that they represent an unmistakable signal of linguistic convergence. Moreover, the isoglosses affect different domains of sound structure such as consonant types, suprasegmental features and phonotactics.

Segments shared across the Kalahari Basin are lingual ingressives a.k.a. clicks, glottalic egressives a.k.a. ejectives, uvular stops, aspirated obstruents and tautosyllabic obstruent-obstruent clusters.[1] Their possible co-occurrence and a strong tendency to series formation are the most important factors for the emergence of some of the largest consonant inventories in the world's languages.

Of the relevant suprasegmental features, nasalization is universal (though overlooked entirely by Hajek 2005) and pharyngealization is attested in all three families; glottalization and breathy voice are so far restricted to the non-Khoe lineages Tuu and Kx'a. In terms of pitch prosody, all Kalahari Basin languages share the feature of register tone systems largely relevant for lexical distinctions (*pace* Clements 2000: 157–158); the number of tone levels, still controversial for some languages, ranges between two and four. This picture is different from Bantu, where tone has a strong grammatical import, with predominantly two tone levels, H and L, often with 'significant asymmetries between H and L suggesting privative analysis of H versus toneless' (Kisseberth and Odden 2003: 59).

Another important isogloss is characteristic bimoraic patterns of lexical roots, namely basic C(C)VCV and derivative C(C)VV and C(C)VN, which in addition involve a very skewed phoneme distribution. For details, the reader is referred to Beach (1938), who discovered the phenomenon, and Nakagawa (2010), an innovative recent account. (In view of data provided by Chebanne (2000) and Snyman (2000), it remains to be determined whether all East Kalahari Khoe languages fully comply with these patterns).

18.2.2   Lexicon

Shared lexicon across the Kalahari Basin has always been assumed, commonly invoked as evidence for 'Khoisan'. While Greenberg (1950, 1963) and similar studies by non-specialists lacked comparative rigour, Köhler

---

[1] There is an alternative analysis according to which the relevant complex consonants are not clusters (see Miller 201˙). This approach does not alter the segments' status as shared and rare.

(1975: 312–313) and Traill (1986) also discussed substantial lexical iso-glosses crossing the major family boundaries, being arguably due to inheritance.

However, such isoglosses are far more extensive in bilateral compar-isons (cf. Köhler (1973/1974: 185–189) for Ju|'hoan~Caprivi Khwe, Snyman (1974: 40–42) for Ju|'hoan~Namibian Khoekhoe, and Traill and Nakagawa (2000) for East !Xoon~G|ui; see also Sands (2001: 201)); these would have resulted largely from language contact. Sands (2001) and Honken (2006) also recognized the possibility of extensive borrowing across the entire area. This hypothesis was studied more systematically by Güldemann and Loughnane (2012) for one specific lexical domain, namely body parts and related terms. Starting from a bottom-up recon-struction within the three secure lineages, many purported 'Macro-Khoisan' lexemes can be argued to have emanated from a single family and entered the others by way of language contact. Dense lexical distri-butions in the Kalahari Basin can thus be explained alternatively by linguistic convergence, whereby at least three different patterns should be distinguished regarding their geographical scope and time depth. They are illustrated in Table 18.2 with examples proposed by Honken (2006: 77–78, 81).

As indicated above, borrowing pattern (I) is a multitude of localized contact situations, some of them more recent, illustrated in Table 18.2 by a borrowing from Namibian Khoekhoe into Ju|'hoan. Pattern (II) is cross-areal lexical transfer from prestigious Khoekhoe varieties spoken by pastoralists into a large number of forager (i.e. 'San') languages from all three families, i.e. virtually all Tuu languages, southern Ju varieties from Kx'a, and Naro and possibly other West Kalahari Khoe languages. This is a phenomenon with

Table 18.2 *Examples of three major patterns of lexical borrowing in the Kalahari Basin*

		Tuu	Kx'a		Khoe-Kwadi	
Pattern	Meaning	Taa	ǂ'Amkoe	Ju	KK	KalK
(I)	stupid, insane	-	-	Ju|'hoan **!xúmó**	Namibian !XÒM-POÒ	-
(II)	tin, box, pot	E. !Xoon **tōʰo**	-	Ju|'hoan **tōʰò**	Namibian TÖÖ-p/s	Naro **tòó**
(III)	dirt(y)		Proto-Kx'a *!KX'URI		Proto-KK	Naro
			ǂHoan |x'órĩ	Owambo !Xuun g|x'úrĩ	***|kx'uri-** >	**|x'arĩ**
				Ju|'hoan |x'úrí	Namibian |'ÚRĨ-XÀ	
				|'ùrí-hä		

Note: here items in bold italics are **loans**, those in capital italics are the *SOURCE ITEM OF BORROWING*

a time depth of several centuries in Namibia and even longer in South Africa. The example in Table 18.2 shows that Namibian Khoekhoe *töö-s/p* 'tin, can', ultimately from Afrikaans *doos* and/or German *Dose*, is the source of borrowings in at least three genealogically unrelated San languages. As proposed by Güldemann (2006, 2008a), one can posit a third pattern, (III), in the form of substrate influence in various stages of Khoe-Kwadi, notably Kx'a influence on (Pre)-Khoe and Tuu influence on (Pre)-Khoekhoe. The relevant comparative series in Table 18.2 suggests a likely reconstruction *|kx'uri 'dirt' for Proto-Kx'a, which would have been the source of borrowings into Naro and Proto-Khoekhoe. The root regularly changed to ǀ'uri in northern Khoekhoe, which expanded from South Africa into Namibia, providing there the possibility for Juǀ'hoan to borrow the changed root together with a Khoekhoe adjective suffix -*xa*, leading to a double reflex.[2]

Word borrowing aside, there are also other shared lexical patterns across the Kalahari Basin. One such feature is restricted numeral systems, contrasting with Bantu in and outside the area for which numerals higher than three/four are normal, and such systems can be partly reconstructed (see e.g. Hoffmann 1953). For Tuu and Kx'a, the few items above 'three' are descriptive forms or borrowings, and even 'three' may sometimes not be a cardinal numeral but mean 'more than two': see Güldemann (in press) for the Tuu family, Honken (2013: 253) for ǂ'Amkoe, and Heine and König (2013: 310) for Ju. For Proto-Khoe, Vossen (1997) only reconstructs simplex numerals for 'one' to 'four'; some modern Kalahari Khoe languages no longer even attest reconstructed *haka* 'four'. The only Kalahari Basin languages with higher numerals are pastoral Khoekhoe varieties such as Nama and !Ora, as well as Naro (see Visser 2001), which is said to have borrowed numerals above 'three' from Khoekhoe in connection with a traditional game (Barnard, personal communication; Visser 2013: 190). Hahn (1881: 10–16) discusses the possibility that the forms exclusive to Khoekhoe have emerged more recently, as some are morphologically complex and/or show suggestive relations to other lexemes.

Another example is perception verbs. Recent studies in the wake of Viberg (1984), such as Brenzinger and Fehn (2013), Güldemann (2011) and Nakagawa (2012), demonstrate that languages in the Kalahari Basin show an increased incidence of lexical polysemy. Following Viberg's classification into SIGHT, HEARING, TOUCH, TASTE and SMELL, Table 18.3 shows different polysemy patterns in the

---

[2] This comparative series is actually more complex than suggested by Honken's discussion. On the one hand, the existence of forms in Kalahari Khoe, e.g. Danisi ǀ'ùrí (Fehn, field notes), indicates early borrowing on the part of Khoe and multiple independent reduction of velar ejectives to glottal stops. On the other hand, !Ui forms like ǀXam *ǀkʼʼwarri* (Bleek 1956: 340) and Nǀng *ǀkʼʼɔrre* (Bleek 1956: 608, presumably with mistranscribed click) are likely loans from Khoekhoe, either from southern varieties such as !Ora, which did not undergo the relevant sound change, or from early Khoekhoe before the change.

Table 18.3 *Polysemy in 'experience' perception verbs across the Kalahari Basin*[3]

	SIGHT	HEARING	TOUCH	TASTE	SMELL	Languages
1		▓				Ekoka !Xun (Ju, Kx'a); Shona, Ndonga (Bantu)
2					▓	Juǀ'hoan (Ju, Kx'a)
3			▓	▓	▓	Shua (Khoe)
4		▓	▓	▓	▓	Gǁana-Gǀui (Khoe); East !Xoon (Taa, Tuu); ǂ'Amkoe (Kx'a); Venda, Tswana, Zulu (Bantu)
5			▓	▓		Caprivi Khwe, Ts'ixa, Naro (Khoe)
6			▓	▓	▓	Namibian Khoekhoe, !Ora (Khoe)

'experience'[4] class of perception verbs. All Kalahari Basin languages except Ekoka !Xun, Namibian Khoekhoe and !Ora display polysemies covering at least three sense modalities, and all but Ekoka !Xun and Juǀ'hoan conflate specifically TOUCH and TASTE. The 'maximal' pattern where polysemy covers all non-SIGHT modalities is found today in the Central Kalahari area affecting languages of all three families. The reason for proposing this as a specific Kalahari Basin trend is as follows: while such Bantu languages close to/within the area as Venda, Tswana and Zulu also show this pattern, the overall trend in the family is different, namely towards less polysemy, and if any, rather conflating TOUCH and HEARING. This situation can be observed in Bantu languages at the areal periphery like Ndonga and Shona, and seems to have even affected peripheral Kalahari Basin languages such as Ekoka !Xun.

A distinct word class of ideophones was long thought to be absent in 'Khoisan' (Childs 1994: 179; Samarin 1971: 160–161). Given the salience of ideophones in Bantu, this might be viewed as an areal feature of pre-Bantu southern Africa. However, ideophones do feature in such languages as ǀXam (Bleek 1928–1930: 171; Bleek 1956), Taa (Traill 1994), Ju (Dickens 1994; König and Heine 2008) and Namibian Khoekhoe (Haacke and Eiseb 2002). This finding and studies dedicated to the topic, such as those of Kilian-Hatz (2001) for Caprivi Khwe, Nakagawa (2011, 2012) for Gǀui, and Brenzinger and Fehn (2013) for West Kalahari Khoe in general, call for a re-evaluation of the earlier claim (see also Childs 2003: 120). The apparent lower frequency

---

[3] Table 18.3 reflects the maximal meaning range of individual polysemous lexemes; it is possible that a language has a more specific verb in a certain domain in addition to the polysemous item. The list of languages (sources) is as follows: East !Xoon (Traill 1994), Ekoka !Xun (König and Heine 2008), Gǁana-Gǀui (Nakagawa 2012), Juǀ'hoan (Dickens 1994), Khwe and Ts'ixa (Brenzinger and Fehn 2013), Namibian Khoekhoe (Haacke and Eiseb 2002), Naro (Visser 2001), Ndonga (ELCIN Church Council Special Committees 1996), Shona (Dale 1975), Shua (Fehn, field notes), Tswana (Viberg 1984), Venda (van Warmelo 1989), Zulu (Doke et al. 1990), !Ora (Meinhof 1930), ǂ'Amkoe (Berthold and Gerlach, personal communication).

[4] This class was chosen from Viberg's (1984) three-way distinction – activity, experience, copulative – because it provided relatively complete and reliable data across the area.

of ideophones compared to Bantu aside, there might still be areal traits in the Kalahari Basin concerning the semantic profile of this class, offering an interesting field for future research. In particular, the more recent studies report a notable richness and salience of taste and food texture ideophones; this is not typical in Bantu and possibly even remarkable cross-linguistically, because these are low on implicational hierarchies entertained for ideophones (cf. Dingemanse 2012: 663, where they are merely subsumed under a more generic category 'other sensory perception').

Since lexical isoglosses beyond borrowing represent a largely untapped topic, future research on additional domains such as metaphors or lexical taboos, for example, is likely to yield new insights into the contact history of the Kalahari Basin.

18.2.3 Morphosyntax

As mentioned earlier, Heine (1976) noted the universal presence of head-final genitives in Kalahari Basin languages irrespective of word orders elsewhere, and Güldemann (1999) treated the fact that such juxtaposed genitives are widely employed to convey notions of location, natural sex and diminutives, which also results in host-final nominal flagging and derivation from the grammaticalization of compounds. This phenomenon even extends to the marking of number and gender, because former nominal heads could have encoded these categories and bequeathed them to grammaticalized structures, as illustrated in (1) and (2).

(1) Common Taa   West !Xoon
    qáé   *qáé-**tû*** (< **tuu* 'people')   > *qá**rú***
    mother.3   mother-ASS.P.4   mothers.4
    'mother'   'motherfolk, mothers'   (field notes)

(2) Juǀ'hoan
    *!xó-**mà***   *!xó-**mhɩ́***
    elephant-DIM.S   elephant-DIM.P
    'little elephant, e. calf' 'little elephants, e. calfs' (Dickens 2005: 27)

An exclusive/inclusive distinction in pronouns is also widespread in the Kalahari Basin; an early assessment is contained in Güldemann (1998). The feature has not been reconstructed for Proto-Khoe (Vossen 1997); Güldemann (2002; 2006: 111–112) gives concrete evidence that the opposition in Khoekhoe is due to contact with Tuu languages. This indicates that clusivity entered Khoe languages only after contact with local non-Khoe languages. Since clusivity has been attested in a few more languages, including the Gǁana-Gǀui group of Kalahari Khoe (Ono 2010), the East Kalahari Khoe sub-group is now the only one without any language known to have the feature.

After Güldemann and Vossen (2000: 109) identified verb serialization as a universal feature in non-Khoe, Güldemann (2006: 117–119) observed that 'lexically complex predicates' (comprising serial and compound verbs) are also found in Khoekhoe, and proposed that this is related to contact interference with Tuu. The short treatment suffered from an imprecise characterization of the relevant multi-verb construction(s) (henceforth MVC), which partly spurred the studies by Haacke (2014) and Rapold (2014). They rightly point out that MVCs in Kalahari Khoe employing the 'verb juncture' take care of functions very similar to those conveyed by MVCs without a segmental linker in Khoekhoe (and non-Khoe); Rapold provides convincing evidence that juncture verb constructions were a feature of Proto-Khoekhoe, contributing crucially to the emergence of the link-less constructions.

Against this background, and in contrast with neighbouring Bantu languages, MVCs can be regarded as a prominent feature of the Kalahari Basin, straddling all major lineages in the area. The following sources contain relevant data on this topic: Güldemann (2013d) on |Xam, Güldemann (2013c, 2013f) and Kießling (2014) on Taa, Collins (2002, 2003) on ǂ'Amkoe, Collins (2003), Dickens (2005) and König (2010) on Ju, Haacke (1999, 2014) and Rapold (2014) on Khoekhoe, Visser (2010) on Naro, and Kilian-Hatz (2008) on Caprivi Khwe. In addition, field notes were consulted from Berthold and Gerlach on the N!aqriaxe variety of ǂ'Amkoe, from Nakagawa on G|ui, and from Fehn on Ts'ixa and Shua. Note that the language-specific characterization of relevant structures as serial verbs, compounds, etc., does not always follow identical criteria.

Six different types of MVCs (mostly 'asymmetrical' in the terms of Aikhenvald 2006), which are attested in virtually all major subgroups of the three families, are presented in (3) (a lineage is also considered to possess a MVC type if it is synchronically more grammaticalized). Each example features the N!aqriaxe dialect of the non-Khoe language ǂ'Amkoe (a), and the Kalahari Khoe language Ts'ixa (b) employing the juncture. This array does not attempt to be complete but only illustrates the extent of shared types across the area.[5]

(3)   Sequential cause/effect
       a. *mā   ēn*   ***!'áú́   'n|áá́***   (ǂ'Amkoe)
          1S   TAM   fall   sit
          'I fell into a sitting position'
       b. *nóxá=ḿ*   *ín=mà*   *tí*   *kò*   ***muùn-à   'aàn*** (Ts'ixa)
          snake=M.S   DEM.REF=M.S   1S   IPFV   see-JUNCT   know
          'I recognize this snake'

(4)   Accompanying manner
       a. *mā   nà*   ***ǁqx'áā́   tsáá́***   (ǂ'Amkoe)
          1S   TAM   sing   come
          'I am coming while singing'

[5] It goes without saying that there exist other more localized MVC types which may also involve contact transfer. Thus, Güldemann (2006: 118–119) discusses the non-causative variant of the 'switch-function' type (see Aikhenvald 2006); this has a western distribution in the Kalahari Basin occurring in |Xam and various Khoekhoe varieties (see Haacke 2014 for new extensive data) as well as in Ju dialects (see e.g. König 2010).

   b. *tí* *kò* **pere**   **g‖ài**   (Ts'ixa)
      1S IPFV flee:JUNCT run
      'I run like a fugitive'

(5) Accompanying posture ('sit', 'stand', 'lie' etc.+V2)
   a. *mā* *!úí*   **!ōā**   **n∣ubō**   (ǂ'Amkoe)
      1S raise stand talk
      'I talk standing'
   b. *tí* *kò* **nyúun-a** **‖'àm̀** *katsí=sà* *'à*   (Ts'ixa)
      1S IPFV sit-JUNCT beat   cat=F.S OBJ
      'I beat the cat sitting'

(6) Path (V1+'enter', 'descend' etc.)
   a. *mā* *yā* **!hhōōn** *∣''òò* *bōksī* *kì* *!ōà*   *nā* (ǂ'Amkoe)
      1S IPFV push   insert box MPO house LOC
      'I am pushing the box into the house'
   b. *nguú=m̀*   *'à* *tí* *kò* **g‖ai-a**   **ky'oà**   (Ts'ixa)
      house=M.S LOC 1S IPFV run-JUNCT   exit
      'I run out of the house'

(7) Dative/benefactive (V1+'give')
   a. *mā* *yā* **n∣ūbō** **súú** *ām̀*   *sì*   *n!áā*   (ǂ'Amkoe)
      1S IPFV talk   give 1S.POSS POSS friend
      'I talk for my friend'
   b. *'ém̀* *tí* *'à* *k'oxú* *ká* **ǂuùn-à-mà**   (ma < 'give') (Ts'ixa)
      3M.S 1S OBJ meat MPO buy-JUNCT-BEN
      '(I asked him) to buy meat for me'

(8) Perfect/current relevance (V1+'exist')
   a. *tyàm̀à* **'n∣āā ā**   *kì*   *kātàbòksì n!āqrè*   (ā < 'exist)' (ǂ'Amkoe)
      dog   sit   RELV MPO box   bottom
      'The dog sits at the bottom of the box'
   b. *tí* **tsxaan-hàn**   (hàn < 'exist') (Ts'ixa)
      1S become.tired:JUNCT-STAT
      'I am tired'

In some languages the last MVC type is an essential ingredient for a special pattern of TAM encoding discussed briefly by Güldemann (2006: 116–117): perfect~stative~relevance is marked exceptionally *after* the verb or the entire clause. This directly relates to the general TAM morphotactics argued to be shared between !Ui and Khoekhoe in the Cape, namely that this post-verbal marker is part of a core system that also involves a pre-verbal imperfective opposed to a perfective zero. Modern data from ǂ'Amkoe (Berthold and Gerlach, personal communication), G∣ui (Nakagawa 2014; Ono 2014) as well as Ts'ixa and possibly even some eastern Kalahari Khoe languages (Fehn, field notes) indicate that such a system is to a large extent a wider isogloss of the Kalahari Basin.

Table 18.4 *Clause-second elements in declarative clauses in Kalahari Basin languages*

Dialect or language	Family, branch	Form	Label	Source
Ekoka !Xun	Kx'a, Ju	*má*	topic	König (2006)
North Juǀ'hoan	Kx'a, Ju	*m*	verb particle	Dickens (1994: 234; 2005: 44)
N!aqriaxe	Kx'a, ǂ'Amkoe	*ki*	–	Berthold and Gerlach (field notes)
East !Xoon	Tuu, Taa	*n*	indicative	Traill (1994: 193)
ǀXam	Tuu, !Ui	=ŋ	emphatic nominative	Bleek (1928–1930: 87–88)
Nǁng	Tuu, !Ui	*ke*	declarative	Collins and Namaseb (2011: 9)
Standard Khoekhoe	Khoe-Kwadi, KK	*ke*	(indicative) declarative	Haacke (2013: 335), Hagman (1977)
!Ora	Khoe-Kwadi, KK	*tje*	subject-determinative	Meinhof (1930: 49–50)

Another relevant feature initially identified by Güldemann (2006: 119–122) only for the Cape area concerns markers for sentence type and information structure. These bisect the clause into a pragmatically specific pre-field and a post-field containing the rest of the clause. While they are mostly particles, in ǀXam the relevant element, whose several allomorphs are represented here as an underlying velar nasal = ŋ, is transcribed as being attached to the subject topic (see Güldemann 2013d: 421), as illustrated in the following example:

(9) *au*   *too=**gnn***   *nǀe*   *!ii-ya*
     CONN   red.ochre=?   IPFV   be.red-STAT
     'But/and ochre is red.' (Güldemann 2013d: 428)

This feature, too, turns out to have a wider western Kalahari Basin distribution straddling all three families. Table 18.4 lists languages with such elements in declarative sentences; the diverse terminology in the fourth column reveals that their functional analysis is still far from conclusive.

Güldemann (2010b) discusses these elements in Tuu languages more extensively and presents data to the effect that ǀXam and Taa possess even younger bisected constructions whose clause-second elements encode term focus and entity-central theticity. A similar analysis can be applied to other languages: see Güldemann and Witzlack-Makarevich (2013) for Nama Khoekhoe and Nǁng and Güldemann and Pratchett (2014) for South Juǀ'hoan. This provides a new perspective on the possible emergence and early function of clause-second elements. In some languages, the markers in declarative clauses are in complementary distribution with other particles marking questions, such as ǀXam *ba/xa*, Nǁng *xa(e)*, Khoekhoe *kha*, and the different reflexes of the interrogative particle in Ju reconstructed as **re* by

Heine and König (2013: 319). Visser's (2013) data on Naro seem to indicate that syntactic phenomena revolving around a clause-second syntactic pivot do not necessarily depend on a segmental marker of the kind described above but can be rendered by subject-referring PGN (person-gender-number) markers alone.[6] More in-depth morphosyntactic and discourse-oriented research on all relevant languages is required to clarify whether the different phenomena referred to here are indeed related to each other, and if yes, what their underlying common denominator is/was.

Another intriguing feature, originally identified by Güldemann and Vossen (2000: 110) for non-Khoe, has also turned out to be of wider relevance: Tuu and Kx'a languages display an extremely versatile preposition, called here the multipurpose oblique (MPO) marker,[7] which is virtually void of semantic content; it flags any post-verbal term beyond the valency of a single transitive verb and thus marks a templatic syntactic clause slot rather than specifying the term with respect to its semantic relation to the predicate (see Güldemann 2004). Low semantic sensitivity of basic participant flagging also turns up in Khoekhoe in the form of the nominal suffix -*a*, which marks both subjects and objects as long as they occur after the clause-second pivot (see Güldemann 2006: 122–123).

The limited import of semantics in certain participant flagging is related to yet another factor, namely the strong tendency that animacy often ranks higher than semantics for the assignment of a more central grammatical clause relation. This is one reason why in the Kalahari Basin, as opposed to neighbouring Bantu, transitive patient and ditransitive recipient are frequently marked alike and the ditransitive theme follows the MPO (= 'secundative' alignment in the terms of Malchukov, Haspelmath and Comrie 2010), as illustrated by (10) from Ju|'hoan:

(10) *dà'áma jàn*   *|'àn*   *ha*   *bá*   *kò*   *màrì*
      child good   give   3S   father   MPO money
      'The good child gave his father money.' (Dickens 2005: 40)

It is noteworthy in this respect that some Kalahari Khoe languages tend to use their postposition *ka* with a wide functional spectrum and that in ‖Ani and Ts'ixa (cf. (7b) above) precisely this MPO-like marker flags the ditransitive theme, as in (10) of Ju|'hoan.

Another typologically remarkable feature in various unrelated Kalahari Basin languages is that relative(-like) constructions render nominal modification that is cross-linguistically conveyed by simple attributive numerals, other quantifiers, interrogatives and even possessors. Ju varieties, as the most extreme case, show this entire range: the earliest such case

---

[6] Note that subject PGNs in Khoekhoe also occur in clause-second position immediately before the markers discussed here.

[7] Other terms are 'linker' (Collins 2004), 'transitive particle' (Dickens 2005: 38–39) and 'transitive preposition' (Heine and König 2013: 313).

recorded by Dickens (1997) is the verbal nature of deictics in Ju|'hoan, which Heine and König (2013) and Lionnet (2014) show to hold for the entire group; for the other categories see Dickens (2005) and Heine and König (2013). A similar situation holds in Taa, notably for deictics involving (earlier) motion verbs (cf. *tV('VV)-jà kV* (proximate) and *tV('VV)-sà kV* (remote); Traill 1994: 154), quantifiers (Güldemann 2014b, in press) and attributive 'which' (Güldemann 2013c: 411). As shown in (11), the West Kalahari Khoe language G|ui uses its clausal attributive construction for a very similar functional range:

(11)   [[Noun$_x$ *kà* MODIFIER] PGN$_x$]
        a. *g∥àēkò*   *kà*   *ʔà-m̀*   *kì*   *mûũ*   *sì*
           woman$_x$ REL   PRO-3M.S   HOD.PST   see   3F.S$_x$
           'the woman who he saw today'
        b. *ŋ!úū*   *kà*   *ŋ|ìn*   *mà*
           house$_x$ REL   this   3M.S$_x$
           'this house'
        c. *ɟúù*   *kà*   *ŋ!ūnā*   *dzì*
           eland$_x$ REL   three   3F.P$_x$
           'three elands'   (Nakagawa, personal communication)

This cross-linguistically remarkable phenomenon, which may involve several underlying factors, deserves more attention regarding its language-specific profile as well as its areal distribution.

Yet another feature attested in all three families is reduplicative causatives. In non-Khoe it only occurs sporadically as in |Xam (Bleek 1928–1930: 171) and Ju|'hoan (Miller-Ockhuizen 2001). It can be reconstructed, however, for Proto-Khoe (Vossen 1997: 350), so that the feature may have emanated from this family.

As a final example, dedicated/unique markers of associative plural, which typically though not exclusively combine with personal names and kinship terms, are also found in all three families. Both better-known Tuu languages display such a marker, namely *-tu* in Taa (Güldemann 2013a: 238–239; see (1) above), whose status as an associative plural became evident only in later fieldwork, and *-gu* in |Xam (Güldemann 2006: 131; 2013b: 243). In Kx'a, the situation is not fully clear. In ǂ'Amkoe, no such marker has been found according to Berthold (personal communication). For Ju, Heine and König (2013: 304–305) report potentially relevant distinct plural markers, reconstructed as **sì* and **sin*, but do not comment on any semantic difference between them. However, Dickens' (1994: 263) information on *-sín* in Ju|'hoan, a reflex of **sin*, clearly suggests that at least in some dialects this marker is an associative plural. A unique associative plural can be identified in Khoekhoe: see Hagman's (1977: 29) description of so-called '*hàá* compounds'. Some Kalahari Khoe languages also possess such a marker, like G|ui (Nakagawa, personal communication) and Ts'ixa (Fehn, field notes):

(12)   *thòò*   *ǀuùn-**xà**=dzì*   *nǀgè*   *ǁʔáàn-kù*   *ǁʔáàn-kù*   *ʔé.sì* *ǀxòà*
        DS   parent-**ASS.P**=3F.P SEQ fight-RCPR fight-RCPR 3F.S COM
        'The mother folk fought and fought with it.' (Fehn, field notes)

Comparing this distribution with Daniel and Moravcsik's (2005) world-wide survey, the feature may qualify as an areal trait of the Kalahari Basin, because all Bantu languages close to the area and recorded by these scholars, namely Zulu, Sotho and Luvale, only have an associative plural which is the same as the normal additive plural. For the record, as opposed to Bantu, Afrikaans has innovated such a marker in the areal context of the Cape, although its origin might not (exclusively) be due to contact with Kalahari Basin languages (den Besten 1996; Nienaber 1994).

18.2.4 Summary

Table 18.5 summarizes the (potential) isoglosses of Sections 18.2.1–18.2.3. The feature values are as follows:

X	frequent or even universal in relevant group
(X)	common but with linguistic restrictions
language/dialect	so far only attestation(s)
–	absent
?	insufficient/lacking data

The last case holds in particular for East Kalahari Khoe, which is the least-known group among the languages still spoken. A similar, yet different situation applies to Khoekhoe of Khoe-Kwadi and !Ui of Tuu: here most languages spoken previously in South Africa became extinct before they could be documented sufficiently. Accordingly, X or a language name only refers here to the subset of documented varieties; these are ǀXam and Nǁng for !Ui, and !Ora, Nama and other Namibian varieties for Khoekhoe.

18.3 Discussion

From a continental perspective, the Kalahari Basin is one of several macro-areas in Africa. Given the results by Clements and Rialland (2008) and Güldemann (2010a), it must be distinguished first of all from the neighbouring Bantu spread zone. This entails a certain risk of invoking features for the Kalahari Basin that define it only negatively in opposition to its neighbour, which is genealogically homogeneous and has a specific linguistic signature with numerous shared features. Many such features are likely to be absent in any non-Bantu language and may thus give a strong signal of difference on an areal scale, which indeed holds for the Kalahari Basin.

     For example, Kalahari Basin languages predominantly possess a gender system but lack the specific Bantu type. However, this fact is not an areal trait, because the Kalahari Basin is diverse internally in possessing two other distinct types along the basic split of non-Khoe versus Khoe-Kwadi

Table 18.5 *Linguistic features shared across the Kalahari Basin*

Feature	Tuu			Kx'a		KK	Khoe-Kwadi	
	!Ui	Taa	‡'Amkoe	Ju			WKalK	EKalK
Phonetics/phonology								
1 Lingual ingressives = clicks	X	X	X	X		X	X	X
2 Glottalic egressives = ejectives	X	X	X	X		X	X	X
3 Uvular stops	Nǀng	X	X	–		–	X	Kua
4 Aspirated obstruents	X	X	X	X		X	X	X
5 Obstruent-obstruent clusters	X	X	X	X		X	X	X
6 Nasalization	X	X	X	X		X	X	X
7 Pharyngealization	X	X	X	X		–	Naro, Gǀui	S. Kua
8 Register tone system	X	X	X	X		X	X	X
9 Specific lexical root phonotactics	X	X	X	X		X	X	X
Lexical structures								
10 Restricted numeral system	X	X	X	X		–	X	X
11 Specific perception verb conflation	?	X	X	Juǀ'hoan		(X)	X	Shua
Morphosyntax								
12 Head-final genitive	X	X	X	X		X	X	X
13 Host-final locative flagging	X	X	X	X		X	X	X
14 Host-final derivation	X	X	X	X		X	X	X
15 Clusivity	X	X	X	X		X	Gǀui, Gǁana	?
16 MVC: V1 cause+V2 sequential effect	X	X	X	X		X	X	X
17 MVC: V1 manner+V2	X	X	X	X		X	X	?
18 MVC: V1 posture+V2	X	X	X	X		X	X	?
19 MVC: V1+V2 motion > path	X	X	X	X		X	X	?
20 MVC: V1+'give' > dative/benefactive	X	X	X	X		X	X	X
21 MVC: V1+'exist' > current relevance	X	X	X	X		X	X	X
22 MVC: non-causative switch-function	ǀXam	–	–	X		northern	–	–
23 TAM morphotactics	X	X	X	–		X	Gǀui, Ts'ixa	?
24 Clause-second pivot	X	X	X	X		X	?Naro	–
25 Non-semantic participant flagging	X	X	X	X		X	(ǀAni, Ts'ixa)	?
26 Non-canonical clausal noun modifiers	(X)	X	(X)	X		–	Gǀui	?
27 Reduplicative causative	ǀXam	–	–	Juǀ'hoan		X	X	X
28 Dedicated associative plural	ǀXam	X	–	Juǀ'hoan		northern	Gǀui, Ts'ixa	?

Note: EKalK = East Kalahari Khoe, KK = Khoekhoe, WKalK = West Kalahari Khoe (see Güldemann 2000). Another case in point is participant indexing on the verb. As opposed to Bantu, no Kalahari Basin language has subject cross-reference but Taa, Khoekhoe, ǁAni and possibly Deti have verbal object marking in addition to nominal objects – this is cross-linguistically marked. Pace Güldemann (2010a: 573–574), this should not be viewed as an areal feature either: the lack of subject indexing is typologically common, and only a negative criterion with respect to the Bantu spread zone, while exclusive object indexing, though rare, is not really common in the entire Kalahari Basin. Clearly, areal isoglosses must not be negatively defined absences but rather substantial positive features; this is indeed the case for all those proposed in Section 18.2.

The homogeneous Bantu spread zone does, however, play an indirect role for the profile of the Kalahari Basin: the former has so-to-speak 'sealed off' the latter from other similar areas in Africa, namely those hosting more diverse non-Bantu languages. It is important in this respect that the Kalahari Basin displays non-trivial linguistic affinities to eastern Africa in nominal morphosyntax and phonetics-phonology; these are arguably diagnostic for a hypothesis according to which the Kalahari Basin prior to the Bantu expansion was part of an earlier, far larger linguistic area that coincided with what is called in geography 'High Africa', and which would have been largely submerged by Bantu (Güldemann 1999; Güldemann 2010a: 578–579).

A history of 'decay' also concerns the Kalahari Basin itself. Recall that so far we have spoken of it as a linguistic area before the Bantu expansion. This raises the question of what happened after the advent of Bantu (and yet other colonizers) to the Kalahari Basin languages on the one hand and to these colonizing languages on the other.

With respect to the first issue, the answer is straightforward, when looking at the history and current sociolinguistic status of the relevant languages: virtually all languages in South Africa and southern Namibia have become extinct, and most surviving ones in these and other countries are marginalized, endangered or even moribund. That is, the Kalahari Basin in the present sense has been in a long process of dissolution through widespread language change and language loss induced by later population events. In fact, the data in Table 18.5 no longer reflect a situation in the present but rather a reconstructed approximation to the past, and the Kalahari Basin's likely prospects are that its former linguistic profile will vanish as a compact areal signal.

Nevertheless – and this relates to the second issue – it is far from disappearing completely, because it had a noticeable impact on later colonizing languages. We have not attempted here to systematically record whether or not a feature is also found in local Bantu languages and Afrikaans, but only mentioned such cases to the extent that they explain the establishment of the Kalahari Basin in the narrower sense. A detailed treatment of this wider topic is a project in its own right. Here we only give a first assessment of three important languages of the area

Table 18.6 *Kalahari Basin features shared by other local languages*

Language	1	2	3	4	5	6	7	8	9	10	11	12	13	14	15	16–22	23	24	25	26	27	28
Nguni	X	X	–	X	–	–	–	–	–	–	X	–	X	X	–	–	–	–	–	X	–	–
Tswana	(X)	(X)	–	X	–	–	–	–	–	–	X	–	X	X	–	–	–	–	–	X	–	–
Afrikaans	(X)	–	–	–	–	–	–	–	–	–	–	–	X	X	X	–	(X)	–	(X)	–	–	X

with respect to the features in Table 18.5. They are, followed by sources used, Nguni (Doke 1992; Poulos 1998), Tswana (Cole 1955; Krüger 2006) and Afrikaans (Donaldson 1993). In addition to language-specific material, there is also considerable literature dedicated to language contact between these and Kalahari Basin languages. The sources most relevant here for Nguni and Tswana are Meinhof (1905), Lanham (1962), Louw (1986), Herbert (1987, 1990), Vossen (1997) and Güldemann (1999). The contact-induced formation of Afrikaans, whose regional, non-standard varieties are especially relevant and partly taken into account here, has also been studied increasingly (e.g. Luijks 2001; Mesthrie and Roberge 2001/2002).

The results, given in Table 18.6, justify the conclusion that substrate interference contributed repeatedly to creating linguistic similarities with Kalahari Basin languages (or at least maintaining existing ones) but has not been strong enough to make the newcomers 'full' members of the area.

The following can be observed about the internal profile of the Kalahari Basin in the narrow sense. The best evidence for it are features with a homogeneous geographical and genealogical spread, which are indeed numerous: clicks, ejectives, aspirated obstruents, tautosyllabic obstruent-obstruent clusters, nasalization, register tone system, lexical root phonotactics, restricted numeral system (with the exception of Khoekhoe), head-final genitive, host-final flagging and derivation, and several types of multi-verb constructions.

At the same time, a number of features are not evenly distributed across the area and the three families. Only rarely is a feature found throughout the Khoe family while being sporadic in non-Khoe, for example the reduplicative causative. These are candidates for a scenario in which the feature spread from Khoe into various non-Khoe languages. The predominant situation is that a feature is well entrenched in the non-Khoe families while Khoe languages partake in it only incompletely. This situation holds for clusivity, TAM morphotactics, clause-second pivot, non-semantic participant flagging, non-canonical clausal noun modifiers, and dedicated associative plural.

If one conceptualizes a linguistic area in terms of centre versus periphery, the distributions of the last type can be seen as a variation on a more general theme. Khoe displays a geographical cline from the north and east towards the south and west, whereby the more its languages have encroached onto the Kalahari Basin the more pronounced is their change towards non-Khoe patterns (see Güldemann 2006: 105). One can tentatively establish the following Khoe-internal group hierarchy of increasing Kalahari Basin character (with the caveat that missing data on East Kalahari Khoe may yet change this picture): Shua+Tshwa+Khwe >

Ts'ixa+Gǁana+Naro > Khoekhoe. Güldemann (2008a) has proposed a concrete historical scenario for how this situation would have come about, the main idea being that Khoe-Kwadi is also a colonizing lineage associated with the spread of pastoralism into southern Africa.

The non-Khoe families Tuu and Kx'a represent the structural core of the Kalahari Basin, to whose profile the many isoglosses restricted to them can be added. As long as the two families are treated as genealogically independent, this finding reflects a yet earlier areality before the advent of Khoe-Kwadi – an idea reminiscent of Westphal's (1980: 77) concept of a '"Bush" language province'. Non-Khoe can thus be conceived of as having produced a kind of linguistic founder effect. The resulting areal profile has so-to-speak 'percolated up' into a later sequence of colonizing linguistic layers (in chronological order Khoe-Kwadi, Bantu, Dutch-Afrikaans) by means of multiple direct and indirect substrate interference. However, non-Khoe itself has been receding increasingly due to large-scale language shift.

Abbreviations

ASS	associative
BEN	benefactive
CLCO	clause connective
COM	comitative
DEM	demonstrative
DIM	diminutive
DS	different subject
F	feminine
HOD	hodiernal
IPFV	imperfective
JUNCT	juncture
LOC	locative
M	masculine
MPO	multipurpose oblique
MVC	multi-verb construction
OBJ	(direct) object
P	plural
PGN	person-gender-number (marker)
POSS	possessive
PRO	pronoun
PROX	proximative
PST	past
RCPR	reciprocal
RELV	current relevance
S	singular
SEQ	sequential
STAT	stative
TAM	tense-aspect-modality

References

Aikhenvald, Alexandra Y., 2006. Serial verb constructions in a typological perspective. In Alexandra Y. Aikhenvald, and Robert M. W. Dixon (eds), *Serial Verb Constructions: A Cross-linguistic Typology*, pp. 1–68. Explorations in Linguistic Typology, vol. 2. Oxford: Oxford University Press.

Batibo, Herman M. and Joe Tsonope (eds), 2000. *The State of Khoesan Languages in Botswana*. Gaborone: Basarwa Languages Project.

Beach, Douglas M., 1938. *The Phonetics of the Hottentot Language*. Cambridge: Heffer and Sons.

Bell, Arthur and Paul Washburn (eds), 2001. *Khoisan: Syntax, Phonetics, Phonology, and Contact*. Ithaca, NY: Cornell University.

Bleek, Dorothea F., 1928–1930. Bushman grammar: A grammatical sketch of the language of the |xam-ka-!k'e, *Zeitschrift für Eingeborenen-Sprachen* 19: 81–98; 20: 161–174.

Bleek, Dorothea F., 1956. *A Bushman Dictionary*. New Haven, CT: American Oriental Society.

Brenzinger, Matthias and Anne-Maria Fehn, 2013. From body to knowledge: Perception and cognition in Khwe-‖Ani and Ts'ixa. In Alexandra Y. Aikhenvald and Anne Storch (eds), *Perception and Cognition in Language and Culture*, pp. 161–191. Leiden: Brill.

Brenzinger, Matthias and Christa König (eds), 2010. *Khoisan Languages and Linguistics: Proceedings of the First International Symposium January 4–8, 2003, Riezlern/Kleinwalsertal*. Cologne: Köppe.

Chebanne, Anders M., 2000. The phonological system of the Cuaa language. In Batibo and Tsonope (eds), pp. 18–32.

Childs, G. Tucker, 1994. African ideophones. In Leanne Hinton, Johanna Nichols and John J. Ohala (eds), *Sound Symbolism*, pp. 178–204. Cambridge University Press.

Childs, G. Tucker, 2003. *An Introduction to African Languages*. Amsterdam: John Benjamins.

Clements, George N., 2000. Phonology. In Heine and Nurse (eds), pp. 123–160.

Clements, George N. and Annie Rialland, 2008. Africa as a phonological area. In Bernd Heine and Derek Nurse (eds), *A Linguistic Geography of Africa*, pp. 36–87. Cambridge University Press.

Cole, Desmond T., 1955. *An Introduction to Tswana Grammar*. Cape Town: Longman.

Collins, Chris, 2002. Multiple verb movement in ǂHoan. *Linguistic Inquiry* 33 (1): 1–29.

Collins, Chris, 2003. The internal structure of the verb phrase in Ju|'hoansi and ǂHoan. *Studia Linguistica* 57 (1): 1–25.

Collins, Chris, 2004. The absence of the linker in double object constructions in N|uu. *Studies in African Linguistics* 33 (2): 163–198.

Collins, Chris and Levi Namaseb, 2011. *A Grammatical Sketch of N|uuki with Stories*. Cologne: Köppe.

Dale, Desmond, 1975. *A Basic English–Shona Dictionary*. Gwelo: Mambo Press.

Daniel, Michael and Edith A. Moravcsik, 2005. The associative plural. In Haspelmath et al. (eds), pp. 150–153.

den Besten, Hans, 1996. Associative DP. In Crit Cremers and Marcel den Dikken (eds), *Linguistics in the Netherlands 1996*, pp. 13–24. Amsterdam: John Benjamins.

Dickens, Patrick J., 1994. *English–Ju/'hoan/Ju/'hoan–English Dictionary*. Cologne: Köppe.

Dickens, Patrick J., 1997. Relative clauses in Ju/'hoan. In Wilfrid H. G. Haacke and Edward D. Elderkin (eds), *Namibian Languages: Reports and Papers*, pp. 107–116. Cologne: Köppe.

Dickens, Patrick J., 2005. *A Concise Grammar of Ju/'hoan with a Ju/'hoan–English Glossary and a Subject Index*. Cologne: Köppe.

Dingemanse, Mark, 2012. Advances in the cross-linguistic study of ideophones. *Language and Linguistics Compass* 6: 654–672.

Doke, Clement M., 1992 [1927]. *Textbook of Zulu Grammar*. Cape Town: Longman.

Doke, Clement M. et al., 1990. *English–Zulu/Zulu–English Dictionary*. Johannesburg: Witwatersrand University Press.

Donaldson, Bruce C., 1993. *Afrikaans Grammar*. Berlin and New York: Mouton de Gruyter.

ELCIN Church Council Special Committees, 1996. *English–Ndonga Dictionary*. Oniipa: ELCIN Printing Press.

Greenberg, Joseph H., 1950. Studies in African linguistic classification VI: The click languages. *Southwestern Journal of Anthropology* 6 (3): 223–237.

Greenberg, Joseph H., 1959. Africa as a linguistic area. In William R. Bascom and Melville J. Herskovitz (eds), *Continuity and Change in African Cultures*, pp. 15–27. Chicago: University of Chicago Press.

Greenberg, Joseph H., 1963. *The Languages of Africa*. Bloomington, IN: Research Center in Anthropology, Folklore, and Linguistics, Indiana University.

Güldemann, Tom, 1998. The Kalahari Basin as an object of areal typology: A first approach. In Mathias Schladt (ed.), *Language, Identity, and Conceptualization among the Khoisan*, pp. 137–196. Cologne: Köppe.

Güldemann, Tom, 1999. Head-initial meets head-final: Nominal suffixes in eastern and southern Bantu from a historical perspective. *Studies in African Linguistics* 28 (1): 49–91.

Güldemann, Tom, 2000. Noun categorization in non-Khoe lineages of Khoisan. *Afrikanistische Arbeitspapiere* 63: 5–33.

Güldemann, Tom, 2001. *Phonological Regularities of Consonant Systems across Khoisan Lineages*. Leipzig: Institut für Afrikanistik, Universität Leipzig.

Güldemann, Tom, 2002. Die Entlehnung pronominaler Elemente des Khoekhoe aus dem !Ui-Taa. In Theda Schumann et al. (eds), *Aktuelle Forschungen zu Afrikanischen Sprachen: Sprachwissenschaftliche Beiträge zum 14. Afrikanistentag, Hamburg, 11.–14. Oktober 2000*, pp. 43–61. Cologne: Köppe.

Güldemann, Tom, 2004. Linear order as a basic morphosyntactic factor in non-Khoe Khoisan. Paper presented at the International Conference

'Syntax of the World's Languages', Leipzig, 5–8 August, 2004. www
.iaaw.hu-berlin.de/afrika/linguistik-und-sprachen/mitarbeiter/1683070/
dokumente/LinearWorldSyntaxH.pdf

Güldemann, Tom, 2006. Structural isoglosses between Khoekhoe and Tuu:
The Cape as a linguistic area. In Yaron Matras, April McMahon and
Nigel Vincent (eds), *Linguistic Areas: Convergence in Historical and
Typological Perspective*, pp. 99–134. Basingstoke, UK: Palgrave Macmillan.

Güldemann, Tom, 2008a. A linguist's view: Khoe-Kwadi speakers as the
earliest food-producers of southern Africa. *Southern African Humanities* 20:
93–132.

Güldemann, Tom, 2008b. Greenberg's 'case' for Khoisan: The morphological
evidence. In Dymitr Ibriszimow (ed.), *Problems of Linguistic-Historical
Reconstruction in Africa*, pp. 123–153. Cologne: Köppe.

Güldemann, Tom, 2010a. Sprachraum and geography: Linguistic macro-
areas in Africa. In Alfred Lameli, Roland Kehrein and Stefan Rabanus
(eds), *Language and Space: An International Handbook of Linguistic Variation*,
vol. 2: *Language Mapping*, pp. 561–585. Berlin: Mouton de Gruyter.

Güldemann, Tom, 2010b. The relation between focus and theticity in the
Tuu family. In Ines Fiedler and Anne Schwarz (eds), *The Expression of
Information Structure: A Documentation of its Diversity across Africa*,
pp. 69–93. Amsterdam: John Benjamins.

Güldemann, Tom, 2011. Perception verbs in N‖ng (!Ui, Tuu) and beyond.
Paper presented at the third KBA workshop, Somlószőlős, Hungary, 7–9
January 2011. http://www2.hu-berlin.de/kba/events/hungary/perception-
verbs.pdf

Güldemann, Tom, 2013a. Morphology: Taa (East !Xoon dialect). In Vossen
(ed.), pp. 234–241.

Güldemann, Tom, 2013b. Morphology: |Xam. In Vossen (ed.), pp. 241–249.

Güldemann, Tom, 2013c. Syntax: Taa (East !Xoon dialect). In Vossen (ed.),
pp. 408–419.

Güldemann, Tom, 2013d. Syntax: |Xam. In Vossen (ed.), pp. 419–431.

Güldemann, Tom, 2013e. Typology. In Vossen (ed.), pp. 25–37.

Güldemann, Tom, 2013f. Using minority languages to inform the
historical analysis of major written languages: A Tuu perspective on
the 'give' ~ object marker polysemy in Sinitic. *Journal of Asian and
African Studies* 85: 41–59.

Güldemann, Tom, 2014a. Introduction: 'Khoisan' linguistic classification
today. In Güldemann and Fehn (eds), pp. 1–41.

Güldemann, Tom, 2014b. The Lower Nossob varieties of Tuu: !Ui, Taa or
neither? In Güldemann and Fehn (eds), pp. 257–282.

Güldemann, Tom, in press. Did Proto-Tuu have a paradigm of cardinal
numerals? In Klaus Beyer et al. (eds), *New Perspectives on African
Languages*. Cologne: Rüdiger Köppe.

Güldemann, Tom and Anne-Maria Fehn (eds), 2014. *Beyond 'Khoisan':
Historical Relations in the Kalahari Basin*. Amsterdam: John Benjamins.

Güldemann, Tom and Robyn Loughnane, 2012. Are there 'Khoisan' roots in body-part vocabulary? On linguistic inheritance and contact in the Kalahari Basin. *Language Dynamics and Change* 2 (2): 215–258.

Güldemann, Tom and Lee J. Pratchett, 2014. KoMmenting on ǂKx'aoǁ'ae. Paper presented at the 5th International Symposium on Khoisan Languages and Linguistics, Riezlern, 14–16 July 2014.

Güldemann, Tom and Rainer Vossen, 2000. Khoisan. In Heine and Nurse (eds), pp. 99–122.

Güldemann, Tom and Alena Witzlack-Makarevich, 2013. The risks of analysis without spoken language corpora: Clause-second *ke* in Richtersveld Nama and Nǁng. Paper presented at the International Conference 'Information Structure in Spoken Language Corpora (ISSLaC)', Bielefeld, June 10–12, 2013. www.uni-bielefeld.de/lili/tagung/ISSLaC/files/Gueldemann_Witzlack_ISSLaC_handout.pdf

Haacke, Wilfrid H. G., 1999. *The Tonology of Khoekhoe (Nama/Damara)*. Cologne: Köppe.

Haacke, Wilfrid H. G., 2013. Namibian Khoekhoe (Nama/Damara): Syntax. In Vossen (ed.), pp. 325–240.

Haacke, Wilfrid H. G., 2014. Verb serialisation in northern dialects of Khoekhoegowab: convergence or divergence? In Güldemann and Fehn (eds), pp. 125–151.

Haacke, Wilfrid H. G. and Eliphas Eiseb, 2002. *A Khoekhoegowab Dictionary with an English–Khoekhoegowab Index*. Windhoek: Gamsberg Macmillan.

Hagman, Roy S., 1977. *Nama Hottentot Grammar*. Bloomington, IN: Indiana University Publications.

Hahn, Theophilus, 1881. *Tsuni-ǁGoam: The Supreme Being of the Khoi-Khoi*. London: Trübner.

Hajek, John, 2005. Vowel nasalization. In Haspelmath et al. (eds), pp. 46–49.

Haspelmath, Martin, et al. (eds), 2005. *The World Atlas of Language Structures*. Oxford University Press.

Heine, Bernd, 1976. *A Typology of African Languages Based on the Order of Meaningful Elements*. Berlin: Dietrich Reimer.

Heine, Bernd and Christa König, 2013. Syntax: Northern Khoesan: !Xun. In Vossen (ed.), pp. 293–325.

Heine, Bernd and Derek Nurse (eds), 2000. *African Languages: An Introduction*. Cambridge: Cambridge University Press.

Herbert, Robert K., 1987. Articulatory modes and typological universals: The puzzle of Bantu ejectives and aspirates. In L. Shockey and R. Channon (eds), *Festschrift for Ilse Lehiste*, pp. 401–413. Dordrecht: Foris.

Herbert, Robert K., 1990. The relative markedness of click sounds: Evidence from language change, acquisition, and avoidance. *Anthropological Linguistics* 32 (1/2): 120–138.

Hoffmann, Carl F., 1953. Zur Verbreitung der Zahlwortstämme in Bantusprachen, *Afrika und Übersee* 37: 65–80.

Honken, Henry, 2006. Fused loans in Khoesan. *Pula* 20 (1): 75–85.

Honken, Henry, 2013. Eastern ǂHoan: Morphology. In Vossen (ed.), pp. 249–261.

Hyman, Larry M., 2003. Segmental phonology. In Nurse and Philippson (eds), pp. 42–58.

Kießling, Roland, 2014. Verbal serialisation in Taa (Southern Khoisan). In Alena Witzlack-Makarevich and Martina Ernszt (eds), *Khoisan Languages and Linguistics: Proceedings of the Second International Symposium July 6–10, 2008*, pp. 33–60. Riezlern/Kleinwalsertal. Cologne: Köppe.

Kilian-Hatz, Christa, 2001. Universality and diversity: Ideophones from Baka and Kxoe. In F. K. Erhard Voeltz and Christa Kilian-Hatz (eds), *Ideophones*, pp. 155–163. Amsterdam: John Benjamins.

Kilian-Hatz, Christa, 2008. *A Grammar of Modern Khwe (Central Khoisan)*. Cologne: Köppe.

Kisseberth, Charles W. and David Odden, 2003. Tone. In Nurse and Philippson (eds), pp. 59–70.

Köhler, Oswin, 1973/1974. Neuere Ergebnisse und Hypothesen der Sprachforschung in ihrer Bedeutung für die Geschichte Afrikas. *Paideuma* 19/20: 162–199.

Köhler, Oswin, 1975. Geschichte und Probleme der Gliederung der Sprachen Afrikas: Von den Anfängen bis zur Gegenwart. In Hermann Baumann (ed.), *Die Völker Afrikas und ihre Traditionellen Kulturen*, part 1: *Allgemeiner Teil und Südliches Afrika*, pp. 135–373. Wiesbaden: Franz Steiner.

König, Christa, 2006. Focus in !Xun. In Sonja Ermisch (ed.), *Focus and Topic in African Languages*, pp. 249–263. Cologne: Köppe.

König, Christa, 2010. Serial verb constructions in !Xun. In Brenzinger and König (eds), pp. 144–175.

König, Christa and Bernd Heine, 2008. *A Concise Dictionary of Northwestern !Xun*. Cologne: Köppe.

Krüger, Caspar J. H., 2006. *Introduction to the Morphology of Setswana*. Munich: LINCOM Europa.

Lanham, Leonard W., 1962. The proliferation and extension of Bantu phonemic systems influenced by Bushman and Hottentot. In Horace G. Lunt (ed.), *Proceedings of the Ninth International Congress of Linguistics, Cambridge, Mass., August 27–31, 1962*, pp. 382–391. Janua Linguarum, Series Maior 12. The Hague: Mouton.

Lionnet, Florian, 2014. Demonstrative and relative constructions in Ju: A diachronic account. In Güldemann and Fehn (eds), pp. 181–207.

Louw, Johan A., 1986. Some linguistic influence of Khoi and San in the prehistory of the Nguni. In Rainer Voßen and Klaus Keuthmann (eds), *Contemporary Studies on Khoisan*, vol. 2, pp. 141–168. Quellen zur Khoisan-Forschung 5. Hamburg: Helmut Buske.

Luijks, Carla, 2001. The Khoekhoe and/or the San: Gathering the Afrikaans substrate languages. In Bell and Washburn (eds), pp. 184–199.

Maddieson, Ian, 2003. The sounds of the Bantu languages. In Nurse and Philippson (eds), pp. 15–41.

Malchukov, Andrej L., Martin Haspelmath and Bernard Comrie 2010. Ditransitive constructions: A typological overview. In Andrej L. Malchukov, Martin Haspelmath and Bernard Comrie (eds), *Studies in Ditransitive Constructions: A Comparative Handbook*, pp. 1–64. Berlin: Mouton de Gruyter.

Meinhof, Carl, 1905. Hottentottische Laute und Lehnworte im Kafir. *Zeitschrift der Deutschen Morgenländischen Gesellschaft* 58: 727–769, 59: 36–89.

Meinhof, Carl, 1930. *Der Koranadialekt des Hottentottischen*. Berlin: Reimer.

Mesthrie, Rajend and Paul T. Roberge (eds), 2001/2002. *Focus on Afrikaans Sociohistorical Linguistics*, two volumes. Special issues of *Journal of Germanic Linguistics* 13 (4), 14 (1).

Miller, Amanda L., 2011. The representation of clicks. In Marc van Oostendorp et al. (eds), *The Blackwell Companion to Phonology*, pp. 416–439. Oxford and Chichester, UK: Wiley-Blackwell.

Miller-Ockhuizen, Amanda L., 2001. Two kinds of reduplication in Ju|'hoansi. *Afrikanistische Arbeitspapiere* 66: 107–118.

Nakagawa, Hirosi, 2010. Phonotactics of disyllabic lexical morphemes in G|ui. *Working Papers in Corpus-based Linguistics and Language Education* 5: 23–31. Tokyo University of Foreign Studies.

Nakagawa, Hirosi, 2011. A first report on G|ui ideophones. In Osamu Hieda, Christa König and Hirosi Nakagawa (eds), *Geographical Typology and Linguistic Areas, With Special Reference to Africa*, pp. 279–286. Tokyo University of Foreign Studies, Studies in Linguistics 2. Amsterdam: John Benjamins.

Nakagawa, Hirosi, 2012. The importance of TASTE verbs in some Khoe languages. *Linguistics* 50 (3): 395–420.

Nakagawa, Hirosi, 2014. The aspect system and posture verbs in G|ui. Paper presented at the 5th International Symposium on Khoisan Languages and Linguistics, Riezlern, 14–16 July 2014.

Nichols, Johanna, 1992. *Linguistic Diversity in Space and Time*. Chicago: University of Chicago Press.

Nienaber, Gabriël S., 1994. Pa-hulle is kreools [Pa-hulle is creole]. *Khoekhoe en Afrikaans in gesprek [Khoekhoe and Afrikaans in Dialogue]. Suid-Afrikaanse Tydskrif vir Taalkunde*, Supplement 21: 14–67.

Nurse, Derek and Gérard Philippson (eds), 2003. *The Bantu Languages*. London: Routledge.

Ono, Hitomi, 2010. Personal pronouns. In Jiro Tanaka and Kazuyoshi Sugawara (eds), *An Encyclopedia of |Gui and ‖Gana Culture and Society*, pp. 91–92. Kyoto: Laboratory of Cultural Anthropology, Kyoto University.

Ono, Hitomi, 2014. Temporal expressions in G|ui. Paper presented at the 5th International Symposium on Khoisan Languages and Linguistics, Riezlern, 14–16 July 2014.

Poulos, George (with Christian T. Msimang), 1998. *A Linguistic Analysis of Zulu*. Cape Town: VIA Afrika.

Rapold, Christian, 2014. Areal and inherited aspects of compound verbs in Khoekhoe. In Güldemann and Fehn (eds), pp. 153–177.

Samarin, William J., 1971. Survey of Bantu ideophones. *African Language Studies* 12: 130–168.

Sands, Bonny E., 1998. *Eastern and Southern African Khoisan: Evaluating Claims of Distant Linguistic Relationships*. Cologne: Köppe.

Sands, Bonny E., 2001. Borrowing and diffusion as a source of lexical similarities in Khoesan. In Bell and Washburn (eds), pp. 200–224.

Snyman, Jan W., 1974. The Bushman and Hottentot languages of Southern Africa. *Limi* 2 (2): 28–44.

Snyman, Jan W., 1975. *Žu/'hõasi Fonologie and Woordeboek [Žu/'hõasi Phonology and Dictionary]*. Cape Town: Balkema.

Snyman, Jan W. (ed.), 1980. *Bushman and Hottentot Linguistic Studies (Papers of Seminar Held on 27 July 1979)*. Pretoria: University of South Africa.

Snyman, Jan W., 2000. Palatalisation in the Tsowaa and Gǀana languages of central Botswana. In Batibo and Tsonope (eds), pp. 33–43.

Traill, Anthony, 1980. Phonetic diversity in the Khoisan languages. In Snyman (ed.), pp. 167–189.

Traill, Anthony, 1985. *Phonetic and Phonological Studies of !Xóõ Bushman*. Hamburg: Buske.

Traill, Anthony, 1986. Do the Khoi have a place in the San? New data on Khoisan linguistic relationships. *Sprache und Geschichte in Afrika* 7 (1): 407–430.

Traill, Anthony, 1994. *A !Xóõ Dictionary*. Cologne: Köppe.

Traill, Anthony and Hirosi Nakagawa, 2000. A historical !Xóõ-ǀGui contact zone: Linguistic and other relations. In Batibo and Tsonope (eds), pp. 1–17.

Viberg, Ake, 1984. The verbs of perception: A typological study. *Linguistics* 21 (1): 123–162.

Visser, Hessel, 2001. *Naro Dictionary: Naro–English, English–Naro*. D'Kar: Naro Language Project.

Visser, Hessel, 2010. Verbal compounds in Naro. In Brenzinger and König (eds), pp. 176–200.

Visser, Hessel, 2013. Naro: Morphology. In Vossen (ed.), pp. 179–206.

Vossen, Rainer, 1997. *Die Khoe-Sprachen: Ein Beitrag zur Erforschung der Sprachgeschichte Afrikas*. Cologne: Köppe.

Vossen, Rainer (ed.), 2013. *The Khoesan Languages*. London: Routledge.

van Warmelo, Nicolaas Jacobus, 1989. *Venda Dictionary: Tshivenda–English*. Pretoria: J. L. van Schaik.

Westphal, Ernst O. J., 1971. The click languages of Southern and Eastern Africa. In Jack Berry and Joseph H. Greenberg (eds), *Linguistics in Sub-Saharan Africa*, pp. 367–420. The Hague and Paris: Mouton.

Westphal, Ernst O. J., 1980. The age of 'Bushman' languages in Southern African pre-history. In Snyman (ed.), pp. 59–79.

19

South Africa and Areal Linguistics

Rajend Mesthrie

19.1 Introduction

As far as language contact is concerned, South Africa has been reasonably well studied, though previous studies have focused on pairwise comparisons, rather than the broad sociohistorical overview with layered multiple comparisons attempted here. Languages of several major families have co-existed in South Africa since colonial times beginning in the mid-seventeenth century: chiefly Khoisan languages (which are not all related), Bantu (the majority languages) and Germanic (Dutch-Afrikaans and English). To these may be added regionally significant languages no longer spoken – e.g. those of Cape slaves (Malay, Malagasy, etc.) – or in decline – e.g. those of Natal indentured workers (Hindi, Tamil, etc.). Although South Africa is often characterized by the notorious practice of apartheid, which aimed to keep ethnic groups apart, a large amount of contact between groups of people and their languages nevertheless did occur. This chapter will provide an overview of the extent to which there has been convergence in South Africa across languages. The current language demographics in South Africa are given in Table 19.1 for home language speakers of the 11 official languages and Sign Language as returned in the 2011 census. While the census question did not aim to uncover speakers' full repertoires, it does give a first impression of L1 usage. Unfortunately, the census reports do not give figures for second language usage, crucial in any characterization of areal tendencies.

Table 19.1 shows the robustness of nine Bantu languages and English and Afrikaans. What the present day census misses is the presence of endangered Khoisan languages like |Nu, Gri and !Ora (see the overview in Güldemann and Fehn, Chapter 18, this volume). Yet two thousand years ago Khoisan languages would have filled the entire southern African landscape. Bantu languages arrived later – most likely from about the first four

Table 19.1 *Official languages of South Africa as first languages (Census 2011)*

Language	Speaker numbers	Proportion of population
IsiZulu	11,587,374	22.70%
IsiXhosa	8,154,258	16.00%
Afrikaans	6,855,082	13.50%
English	4,892,623	9.60%
Sepedi	4,618,576	9.10%
Setswana	4,067,248	8.00%
Sesotho	3,849,563	7.60%
Xitsonga	2,277,148	4.50%
SiSwati	1,297,046	2.50%
Tshivenda	1,209,388	2.40%
IsiNdebele	1,090,223	2.10%
Other	828,258	1.60%[1]
Sign language	234,655	0.50%
Total	50,961,442	

centuries CE, though the ancestors of present-day groups followed somewhat later (Herbert and Bailey 2002: 59). Khoisan languages gave way eventually, first to Bantu languages and later Dutch. In the process they affected Bantu languages like Xhosa, Tswana and Zulu significantly. They also contributed significantly to the social dialect of Dutch or Afrikaans that their own speakers eventually shifted to.

19.2 Phonetic and Vocabulary Influences of Khoisan on Other South African Languages

The greatest influence of Khoisan upon Bantu is in the area of phonology. Unlike Bantu languages outside southern Africa, several of their South African counterparts have clicks as an essential part of their phoneme inventories. Thus clicks relate to contact and synthesis between Khoisan and Bantu in precolonial times. The number of clicks in Khoisan languages varies from as few as 20 to as many as 85, though current research suggests an even higher upper limit (Bonny Sands, personal communication). These numbers encompass different places of articulation from bilabial, dental, alveolar, retroflex, lateral and palatal combined with options for voicing, pre-nasalization, aspiration and so forth. Of the Bantu languages of South Africa, Xhosa has the most phonemic clicks, then in turn Zulu, Swati and South Sotho (Herbert 1990). Khoisan influence in the phonologies of Xhosa and Zulu is extensive: Lanham (1964),

---

[1] The 1.60 per cent listed as 'Other' stems from respondents giving 'n/a' for the language question, presumably indicating a first language different from the twelve languages enumerated in the census (eleven official languages, plus sign language). It is a pity that the census did not analyse languages other than the official ones.

cited by Herbert (1990: 122), calculated that between 21 and 25 of the consonants of Xhosa are of Khoisan origin and occur in borrowed vocabulary. He also estimated that between one-seventh to one-sixth of Zulu words contain clicks. Scholars of Bantu languages assume that Xhosa clicks were borrowed from a Khoi language, possibly !Ora, while those of Swati and Sotho have a San language as their source (Herbert 1990, citing Lanham 1964 and sources therein). No definitive account exists of the nature of the bilingualism that promoted this large-scale phonological borrowing. Herbert (2002) suggested that the cultural practice called *hlonipha* (respect) in which married Xhosa and Zulu women had to consistently avoid the initial syllables of the names of their in-laws led to a search for alternative ways of expressing the tabooed syllable, including borrowed elements like clicks (see Finlayson 1984). Support for the theory comes from (a) the practice of hlonipha correlating strongly with the inventory of clicks in individual Bantu languages, and (b) the inconsistent way in which clicks are borrowed across languages. The weakness in the argument is how clicks were generalized to unmarked rather than taboo usage and transmitted to all speakers, not just resourceful young women. Language shift might prove a more transparent explanation, with speakers of both sexes who slowly shifted from a Khoisan to a Bantu language like Xhosa retaining traces of their earlier phonology and gradually influencing other Xhosa speakers. Such an explanation has parallels in ancient India (Emeneau 1956) and medieval England and Ireland (see Hickey 2010, who terms this an imposition scenario). That this is not a matter pertaining only to the distant past can be seen in the way clicks have survived shift in a small way in one contemporary case: Tony Links (1989) reports on the social dialect of Namaqualand, where descendants of Khoisan people retain clicks in a subset of words pertaining to plant and other traditional names in the language they have shifted to – Afrikaans. Current bilingual speech involving a Bantu language and English are also relevant to the theme of language convergence. Bilingual speakers of Xhosa and Zulu retain clicks when speaking English, though essentially in proper names of people, places and cultural concepts. Insistence on this practice has led to many South Africans using at least the word *Xhosa* ([|||^{h}osa], a widely spoken language) with a click, though not all L1 English speakers necessarily produce the correct (aspirated lateral) one. In at least one instance, young people of different language backgrounds that do not necessarily include a Bantu language use the now English slang term *(m)nca* ([(m)n|a]) 'cool, nice', getting the dental click [||] right. In my own interviews of the L2 English of Xhosa speakers there are sporadic instances of clicks being transferred to English. Only four instances of these were noted in about 20 hours of speech data: *do* (twice by the same speaker) and *twenty*, by another two speakers, all with an initial alveopalatal click [!] in place of [t] or [d]. While these were 'one-off' instances, they do suggest how bilingualism and later shift could have caused such large-scale areal convergence in a less prescriptive and literate past.

Regarding vocabulary, some basic terms for 'sheep', 'cow', 'grass' and 'milk' have been borrowed from Khoisan into Xhosa and Zulu (see Harinck 1969). Branford and Claughton (2002: 202) cite verbs of probable Khoisan origin in Xhosa like -*cela* 'to ask', -*qala* 'to begin' and -*nceda* 'to help'. And as is to be expected, several South African toponyms are of Khoisan origin, even if in diluted colonial form: *Karoo desert, Tsitsikamma forest, Gariep river/dam* etc. The lexical give and take between Bantu languages and English and Afrikaans is enormous. Everyday terms arising out of colonial contact in Zulu include words from English like *ingadi* 'garden', *imoto* 'car', *ilondolo* 'laundry', *imakede* 'market', and words from Afrikaans like *ijazi* 'overcoat' (Afrikaans *jas*), *iphulazi* 'farm' (Afrikaans *plaas*), *ubontshisi* 'beans' (Afrikaans *boontjie*), etc. Today as a result of the technological revolution and globalization, English (rather than Afrikaans) words continue to enter the Zulu lexicon.

Large-scale borrowing has led to the incorporation of new phonemes into African languages. For example, the traditional form of the English loanword 'rice' in Zulu is *i-layisi*; but this form that turns an /r/ into an /l/ is now considered old fashioned and rural, with younger speakers giving the form *i-rayisi*, with the newly introduced phoneme /r/. In Section 19.7 I discuss changes in the practice of choosing an appropriate noun class into which to place loanwords.

South African English vocabulary is a monument to language contact, not just in the numerous second language varieties in the country, but in 'superstrate' or L1 'Anglo' varieties. South African English has borrowed extensively from Afrikaans, giving new words to international English in the process (*trek, veld, apartheid*) and many terms that are less known internationally (*braai* 'barbecue', *rondavel* 'small circular building', *padkos* 'food taken for a journey', lit. 'roadfood'). The terms cited here are used even in parts of the country where Afrikaans is not widely used (for example parts of KwaZulu-Natal). In areas where English–Afrikaans bilingualism is widespread, the number of words used is even greater: hence *erf* 'plot of land', *vlei* 'seasonally intermittent lake area' and *water-blommetjie* (an edible water plant) in the Western Cape. Conversely, despite attempts to weed out Anglicisms in Afrikaans, the influence of English is unavoidable. Donaldson's (1988: 169–233) discussion of loanwords, neologisms, calques, hybrids, proverbial and similar expressions ranges over 60 pages – this from an era before the multitude of terms brought by the technological explosion of computers and cellphones. The lexical influence of Bantu languages on English is also notable. In the post-apartheid era, some new terms associated with politics may be noted: *lekgotla* 'a meeting of village or political leaders', *batho pela* 'people first' (in relations to politics). On the whole, new words adopted from the African languages into English of the general populace tend to be informal and associated with youth culture:

eish (an expression of hardship or dismay), *kasi* 'Black township or section of township' (a clipping from Afrikaans *lokasie*), *loxion* 'Black area of residence' (a rehabilitation of the apartheid term *location*), *kwaito* (high energy youthful musical style) etc. Thus *kasi* and *loxion* are etymologically related, both creative adoptions of the Afrikaans/English pair *lokasie/location*. Advertisers are trying to broaden their appeal by using such informal terms, even if they are unknown to non-African users of English: *mahala* 'free of charge', *ringa* 'make a call, speak to someone on the phone', *diski* 'football', etc. When English words are incorporated into an African language they tend to be less informal or interpersonal: dealing rather with technological and educational developments. Thus, although there is large-scale mutual lexical influence across languages, it tends to be asymmetrically structured according to domain.

19.3 Afrikaans and Contact

As we shall see, Afrikaans plays a pivotal role in the diffusion of features into different South African languages. Most analysts would accept the view of Afrikaans as at least a partially restructured variety of early modern Dutch, under pressure of contact with indigenous languages of the Cape and – more importantly – languages brought to the Cape by slaves in the period from the sixteenth to the eighteenth century. Features that became part of Standard Afrikaans that are attributable to such sources include the following:

- loss of all traces of ablaut and the distinction between strong and weak verbs
- loss of all regular verb endings of person, number and tense
- replacement of the past tense by perfective aspect, marked by prefixed *ge-*
- loss of gender in the article system.

Although this appears to be a set of fairly far-reaching structural changes, it must be noted that other prototypically Germanic features persist in Afrikaans (V2 order in main clauses; verb-final clause order if V2 is filled by an auxiliary; formal distinction between present and past modal auxiliaries). The features outlined above are of an attritional nature, detailing the loss of important structural distinctions in Dutch. They are not part of a sprachbund, attributable to large-scale and sustained bilingualism. In the early contact ecology of the Cape, Afrikaans survived and expanded its territory and number of speakers, while the indigenous Khoisan languages and languages of slaves (Bengali, Malay, Buganese, etc.) did not. On the other hand there are 'positive' adaptations in Afrikaans grammar, showing the addition of structural features under the influence of other languages.

19.3.1   Double Negation

Double negation is fairly complex in Afrikaans, distinguishing it from other Germanic languages. Combrink (1978: 79–85) provides an accessible discussion. He notes that with simple monoclausal sentences single negation is the rule when the VP is made up of only a verb (unlike French):

(1)   *Sy   eet   nie*
      she eat NEG
      'She does not eat/ She is not eating.'

If the VP contains an object, then negation is doubly marked:

(2)   *Sy   eet   nie   pap   nie*
      She eat NEG porridge NEG
      'She does not eat porridge.'

This rule would apply to adjectival and adverbial complements of verbs as well. In main clauses with the auxiliary in V2 position and the main verb in clause-final position, double negation is mandatory:

(3)   *Sy   sal   nie   eet   nie*
      She will NEG eat NEG
      'She won't eat.'

Combrink (1978: 82) notes that whereas Afrikaans inherited the first *nie* from seventeenth century Dutch, the second *nie* is 'the strange bird in the flock'. Double negation is notable for four characteristics:

 (i) It is never a stylistic variant of single *nie* negation, apart from poetic use.
 (ii) It is mandatory in many structures but inadmissible in root sentences with single verb and no object or verb complement.
(iii) The same particle is used twice (unlike, say, French *ne . . . pas*).
(iv) The second *nie* is always clause-final.

Although some scholars, notably Pauwels (1958, cited by Combrink 1978), had noted sporadic similarities in Flemish dialects in the Belgian province of Brabant, Combrink finds it implausible on demographic grounds that this should be the source of Afrikaans double negation. He suggests that Khoekhoe influence is more likely 'from below', citing the work of Nienaber (1965), who examined the use of negatives in Afrikaans sources between 1830 and 1844. Whereas colonists of Dutch descent use double negation 13 per cent of the time, people of Khoekhoe origins who had shifted to Afrikaans by then show higher usage at 40 per cent. Nienaber (1965) noted that Nama has three negative particles used in different moods. The negative particle for imperatives precedes the verb, but the particles for indicative and subjunctive follow it. Combrink (1978) and den Besten (2012: 243–245) accept that while Nama and presumably other Khoekhoe languages do not have double negation, the second *nie* of Afrikaans shows the influence of post-verbal negation in non-imperatives of Khoe. Double negation was in Combrink's analysis one of the features that was initially stigmatized in Cape Dutch, the forerunner of Afrikaans, but later accepted and 'ennobled' (1978: 85) when the promoters of Afrikaans as a new language emphasized its local innovations to mark it off as independent of Dutch.

19.3.2 Associative Plurals

Afrikaans has evolved a construction in which a third person plural pronoun *hulle* is adjoined to an NP that is typically human or at least animate, to form an associative plural carrying the sense 'X and others, X and friends, X and such'):

(4)   *Pa-hulle*
       father-3P
       'Father and others, father and friends'

In a detailed survey den Besten (2012: 31) proposes the influence of Khoekhoe and Eastern Indonesian languages here. From Khoekhoe he cites usage in Nama, which has 'X + *hã* + PGN', where PGN denotes a person-gender-number suffix (in this construction it would be a [-sg] suffix). He gives the following example:

(5)   *saru-hã-n*
       cigarette-ASS-3C.P
       'Cigarettes and stuff – smoking things.'

Den Besten argued that in transferring to Afrikaans the *hã* element would have been lost and an Afrikaans morpheme like *hulle* (third person plural pronoun) or *goed* 'stuff' taking the function of the PGN marker. Likewise, although standard Malay does not have associative plurals, eastern parts of the Indonesian archipelago (from which a majority of slaves originated) does: for example, Ambon Malay has an associative plural formed by noun + third person plural pronoun (den Besten 2012: 32). Hence *Anis dong* 'Anis and others' (where *dong* is a third person plural pronoun). Güldemann (2007) concurs with den Besten that contact with Khoekhoe and Asian slaves was the main source of this construction. However, he points to associative plurals in the San languages of the Tuu group: example (6) is from |Xam, the extinct San language once spoken in the areas closest to Cape Town:

(6)   *mama-gu²*
       mother-ASS.P
       'mother and others, mothers'

---

² Güldemann notes that *gu* is cognate with !Ui *gu-(ken)* 'stuff, things, creatures'.

The |Xam example, in fact, comes close to the form from the present day Orange River dialect of Afrikaans in semantics and phonetic similarity; see (7) below. *Goed* denotes 'stuff' in Afrikaans and is cognate with English *goods*, but the similarity of the initial syllable with Tuu *gu* 'stuff, things, creatures' might have played a reinforcing role:

(7)   *pa-goed*
      father-ASS.P
      'father and others, father and company'

19.3.3 Reduplication

This is a pervasive feature of Afrikaans, relevant to a number of word-classes. For some verbs reduplication serves to emphasize continuation and duration, as in (8) below taken from Botha's (1988: 24) full-length study of Afrikaans reduplication:

(8)   *Die donder   rammel-rammel   in   die   verte.*   (Botha 1988: 24).
      the   thunder   rumble-rumble   in   the   distance
      'The thunder rumbles continuously in the distance.'

Reduplication of other verbs of a temporally bound nature (e.g. *lek* 'lick') denote iteration or repetition. Some verbs of a non-punctual nature (e.g. *skop* 'kick'), however, carry an attenuative semantics when reduplicated. Punctual, experiential and stative verbs do not generally allow reduplication, unless some contextual material allowing an attenuative reading is present. Hence sentence (9) from Combrink (1978: 78):

(9)   *Sy   voel-voel   met   haar   voet   hoe   warm   die   water   is.*
      she   feel-feel   with   her   foot   how   warm   the   water   is
      'She hesitantly/carefully puts her foot into the water to feel how warm it is.'

In the other categories reduplication abounds with intensive or distributive meanings:

  (i) adverbs, e.g. *dronk-dronk* 'drunkenly';
 (ii) adjectives, e.g. *diep-diep* 'very deep';
(iii) numerals, e.g. *drie-drie* 'three at a time, groups of three';
(iv) nouns, e.g. *sakke-sakke* 'sacks and sacks'.

Auxiliaries and prepositions are less commonly reduplicated: den Besten (2012) cites an example of the reduplication of *wil* 'want' in the sense of 'about to, on the verge of'. Prepositions like *aan* 'on' may be reduplicated to form a noun for the children's game *on-on* (a game of tag or touch). In respect of origins den Besten (2012: 219) summarizes the position as follows:

> Reduplication in Afrikaans is essentially iconic in nature. The pertinent reduplication patterns almost exclusively derive from languages other

than Dutch and were selected on the basis of what one might call an iconicity principle. This explains why Khoekhoe contributed relatively little to reduplication in Afrikaans. The main influences came from Malay and Asian Creole Portuguese, with a small but important contribution from Khoekhoe, while the majority of the Malagasy slaves came too late to contribute something specifically Malagasy.

For details of the likely influences from Malay and Asian Creole Portuguese the reader is referred to den Besten, Luiks and Roberge (2003: 278–285).

19.3.4 Diminutives

Although Standard Dutch uses diminutives, Afrikaans shows a greater affinity for this structure. Firstly, Afrikaans seems to attach the diminutive suffix *-tjie* to a greater range of nouns and new meanings than is possible in ordinary Dutch. Valkhoff (1966: 231) cites examples like *dogtertjie* 'girl', in addition to the Dutch literal meaning of 'little daughter'. Secondly, Afrikaans has occasional double diminutives, which are not possible in Dutch and which hint at contact-induced restructuring: e.g. *baadjie-tjie* 'little coat'; *boontjie-tjie* 'little bean' (den Besten 2012: 281).

19.3.5 The Tag *nè*

Afrikaans has an invariant negative tag *nè*, equivalent to 'isn't it/ isn't that so, don't you know', etc.:

(10)   *Ek sien jou   môre,   nè?*
       I   see you tomorrow, TAG
       'I'll see you tomorrow, right?'

Although European sources of *nè* are sometimes cited (Dutch *nicht waar*, French *non*, West German colloquial *ne* [nə]); it seems to me that an Asian source is also possible – Sri Lankan Tamil has exactly the same form (*nè*), Bengali has *na*, and so has Kristang (Malacca Malayo-Portuguese Creole). The particular frequency of this tag among Indian and Coloured speakers of Afrikaans would appear to strengthen the case for an Asian origin, or at least a convergent effect from a variety of oriental and occidental languages.

19.4 Afrikaans Contact Effects in Relation to Other Languages

Of particular interest is the fact that a large number of these neologistic Afrikaans forms, arising in a high contact situation, have passed into English. I discuss the features covered in Section 19.3 in the same order here.

19.4.1   Double Negation

Of the above contact features of Afrikaans only double negation has not passed into general South African English. Where double negation occurs it is usually among L2 speakers following a common international pattern (*I didn't see no snakes*) rather than a specifically Afrikaans template. Although Afrikaans double negation has not generally influenced other languages, there is evidence that at one stage it had incipient influence on Urban Zulu of the Transvaal. In a comprehensive and carefully documented article, detailing the development of Xhosa and Zulu, Louw (1983) gives an example of *nie* from Afrikaans being adopted to form a triple negative as follows:[3]

(11) *A-ngi-hamb-i*   *ni*
      NEG-I-go-NEG   NEG
      'I do not go.'

The first two negatives in (11) are standard circumfixes of Zulu (double in form but single in the semantics of negation), to which speakers add an extra *ni* for emphasis (what Louw describes as a 'greater negative force'). This third negative is clearly the strange bird of the Afrikaans flock, i.e. the second *nie* of Afrikaans discussed above. It is a free form that rather goes against the agglutinating tendencies of standard Zulu syntax. (Urban Zulu draws upon other salient free forms like *why* and *never* from English, as (variably) expressive of a more modern and young way of speaking.) To my knowledge the use of this borrowed *ni* has not stabilized, and we may well conceive of it as sporadic switching that did not catch on. Even so, it is impressive that the contact features of Afrikaans should continue to prove so attractive to speakers of other South African languages. Louw's discussion makes it clear that he attributes this usage to Urban Zulu, and not its slang register for special effects (Tsotsitaal).[4]

19.4.2   Associative Plurals

Associative plurals are also common in South African English, as a sort of hypercorrect form in SAE *Johnny-and-them*. As Branford (1991: 11) notes, these forms are used for a group of people given in the discourse or known to the hearer. The direct calque is also found in South African Indian English and South African Coloured English: *Johnny-them* for 'Johnny and friends'.

19.4.3   Reduplication

This phenomenon is now part of general South African English, though not as prominently as in Afrikaans. Occasional examples can be found in several word classes:

---

[3] The article is dated 16 April 1978 by the author.
[4] Pierre Aycard (personal communication, December 2013) informs me that this usage does not occur in his present day database of urban Zulu and slang registers of African languages in Soweto.

(a) nouns, e.g. *Doctor-doctor, school-school* in children's games;
(b) prepositions, e.g. *on-on* which is a direct calque of the Afrikaans children's game *aan-aan* cited above, resulting in a compound noun;
(c) adverbs, e.g. *quick-quick* 'quickly', *now-now* 'shortly' (which has a more urgent triplicated form *now-now-now*).

There is also semantic but not lexical reduplication in South African English phrases like *a small little book*. Bantu languages show reduplication independently of Afrikaans. Afrikaans reduplication has not influenced African languages, since for the most part it would clash with the attenuative semantics associated with reduplication in languages like Zulu. Hence Zulu *hamba* 'to go, to travel', but *hamba-hamba* 'to saunter'.

19.4.4 Diminutives

The Afrikaans predilection for diminutives has also influenced South African English, which has an informal diminutive *boy-kie* 'young men, boys' (based on an English root and Afrikaans suffix *-kie*). The term *book-ie* 'a little book' (not the informal betting term, which is also possible) is also pertinent here. However, the role of Afrikaans might be reinforcive rather than primary in this example, since British English has colloquial endearments like *duckie* and *lovey*.

19.4.5 The Tag *nè*

This tag (equivalent to 'not so?, isn't it' – see Section 19.3.5 above) has proved very mobile in South Africa, and has passed into the colloquial English of mainly Coloured and Indian speakers in many parts of the country:

(12)   Take for instance the story of the ark. You know about Noah's Ark, nè? (D. Maclennan, cited in Branford 1991: 214).

The tag also occurs in colloquial Xhosa, among speakers influenced by Afrikaans. Although this usage is not recorded in conventional textbooks, it can occasionally be found in oral teaching materials for courses on colloquial Xhosa. It also occurs more generally in the informal street varieties of African languages, in which code-switching is prized. Aycard (2014) notes its occurrence in Urban Zulu of Soweto, where *nè* appears to have replaced the very similar standard Zulu particle *na*, which is also a tag, with negative interrogative interactive force equivalent to 'aren't you'.

19.5 The Story of *busy* as a Case of Weak Convergence

Proving that Afrikaans is the source for the English innovations is usually taken as unnecessary. Yet one should be cautious in attributing all

parallelisms to contact: historical linguists know that independent innovations are possible, or that careful historical work can show what is
assumed to be a (convergent) innovation could have older roots than
expected. The use of aspectual *busy* in South African English as a semi-
grammaticalized marker of ongoing activity has been studied in this vein
by Lass and Wright (1986) and further by Mesthrie (2002a). Two examples
showing how South African English has lifted the restriction of *busy* to
activity verbs are given in Branford and Branford's *Dictionary of South African
English* (1991: 56):

(13)   I rushed in and found two infants busy having convulsions – as
       though there were not enough troubles. (K. McMagh 1968, *Dinner
       of Herbs*)
(14)   There was a sign on the kitchen door saying 'Do not disturb me, am
       busy praying.' (*Sunday Times*, 28 October 1990)

South Africans can say without any trace of humour or irony things like
the following attested examples:

(15)   I'm busy relaxing.
(16)   You're busy losing weight!
(17)   His girlfriend is busy having a baby.
(18)   His jeans were busy being worn.

As these examples show, the construction denotes particularly intense
states or actions rather than 'merely busy' activities. The existence of
a parallel structure in Afrikaans as the usual way of marking ongoing
activity (i.e. progressive aspect) makes it relevant to a study of linguistic
convergence. Branford and Branford (1991: 56) consider South African
English *busy* to be calqued on Afrikaans *besig (om te)*, made up of the
Afrikaans for 'busy' followed by the infinitive. While they generally argued
against Afrikaans influence on South African English, Lass and Wright
concluded that Afrikaans may have played a minor role in lifting the
semantic restriction on *busy* to occur with verbs of conscious activity.
Mesthrie (2002a) notes that stylistic considerations also come into play,
since the collocation of *busy* with 'NON-BUSY' verbs does occur in British
and American English, but is usually consciously humorous, ironic or
poetic.[5] Thus Agatha Christie can have one of her characters say, 'This
isn't exactly a statement you're asking me to make, is it? No, it couldn't be,
because your Sergeant is busy upsetting the domestic staff' (*A Pocket Full of
Rye*, 1973 [1953]: 29). Mesthrie (2002a: 354) also gives examples from
American cartoons, and folk-rock music including Bob Dylan's 'It's all
right I'm only bleeding', a song steeped in irony. At one level then, the

---

[5] Lifting of the stylistic constraint may even have been incipient in the UK, judging from a sentence in Agatha Christie's
Curtain: Poirot's Last Case (1975: 71): 'I was so busy staring at him that I did not hear a footfall nearer at hand, and
turned with a start when Miss Cole spoke to me.'

South African usage is a continuation of endogenous developments of the kind found in British English, and direct influence from Afrikaans is probably not very strong. Further evidence for this comes from the observation that when some Afrikaans speakers use the construction in their L2 English they follow it with an infinitive. Thus a sentence like 'A theory was busy to develop in the eighties' may be found in occasional academic writing of people with Afrikaans L1, rather than 'A theory was being developed/ was busy developing in the eighties'. However, South Africa might be more advanced in respect of the bleaching of *busy* than US and UK varieties, as suggested by the decline of constructions like *so/very/ever busy* + V *-ing* and of *busily* + V, all of which occur fairly commonly in the British National Corpus. There is also the related South Africanism *busy with* (as in 'He's busy with another patient right now'). Branford (1991: 56) proposes that this is calqued on Afrikaans *besig met.* Some role for contact in the use of South African English *busy* therefore cannot be ruled out altogether. The influence of Afrikaans is therefore likely to be quantitative more than qualitative: bilingual speakers may have contributed to the frequency of the construction, turning it from a marked to unmarked construction for intense activities.

This salient lexico-grammatical item has been borrowed into Urban Zulu of Johannesburg, as the following example from Soweto Zulu shows (Aycard 2014: 169):

(19) *A-wu-bon-i*   *si-bhizi*   *si-ya-dla?*
      NEG-2SG-see-NEG   1PL.SC-busy   1PL.SC-PRES-eat
      'Don't you see we are busy eating?' (see note 8 for abbreviations)

19.6 English Influence on Afrikaans Syntax

The influence of Afrikaans on English syntax is mostly of an informal nature. By contrast – and not surprisingly given the status of English as H (prestige) language and language of higher education – Afrikaans syntax has changed in the direction of what counts in English as greater formality. This can be seen generally in Donaldson's (1988) book-length treatment of the influence of English on Afrikaans at all linguistic levels. Donaldson concedes that not all scholars of Afrikaans linguistics are in agreement with his claims of the syntactic influence of English, the investigation of *Anglicismes* being an ideologically controversial area in Afrikaans studies. The main features showing likely English influence are summarized below.

(a) The Anglicism *wees* 'was' co-varying with Afrikaans *word* in passive constructions (Donaldson 1988: 215–218).
(b) Use of *een* 'one' as an indefinite pronoun ('*n bloue,* covarying with the Anglicism '*n blou een* – indefinite usage for 'a blue one' where Dutch uses an adjective as substantive).

(c) Use of *een* as an anaphoric pronoun *'n dom seun en 'n slim een* 'a stupid boy and a smart one' with the anaphoric *een* a likely Anglicism (p. 277).

(d) Occasional non-final position of verbs in subordinate clauses as in (19), where Donaldson (1988: 278) argues that this treatment of *van haar* as a heavy PP postposed after the verb is inappropriate, since 'it is too short an utterance for final positioning'. He detects the influence of English SVO order instead.

(20) *Ek het   ge-hoor   van haar.*
　　　 I   have   PERF-hear of   her.
　　　 'I have heard of her.'

(e) Use of COMP element *dat* or Ø for 'that', followed by SVO order of the subordinate clause, as in (21):[6]

(21) *Dan   moet   ons   sê   dat   hierdie is net   die eerste stap.*
　　　 then must   we   say   that this   is only   the first   step
　　　 'Then we must say that this is only the first step.'

Donaldson (1988: 279) acknowledges that examples like (21) are not very common in Afrikaans and possibly have Dutch precedents in any case. However, after certain verbs like *beweer* 'maintain, claim, assert', *dink* 'think', *glo* 'believe, trust, think' and *hoop* 'hope', the omission of COMP and use of SVO order in the subordinate clause 'can be said to be the general rule', even though *dat* + SOV is still an option.

(f) Preposition-stranding leading to non-SOV in subordinate clauses. Donaldson cites Ponelis (1985) in connection with the likelihood of English influence in preposition-stranding in Afrikaans. Leaving a preposition stranded in final position obviously entails a non-final position for a subordinate clause verb as in (22):

(22) *drie   akker wat   hulle boer   in*
　　　 three acre   RELATIVE   they   farm   in
　　　 'three acres on which they farm . . .'

(g) Donaldson notes that although the inversion of subject and verb is still the rule in Afrikaans after adverbs (the V2 rule), there are frequent transgressions after *so* (an *ingeburgerde anglicisme* or naturalized Anglicism). Hence (23) shows the order *jy* + *kan* 'you can', rather than the inverted *kan* + *jy*:

(23) *So jy   kan   vergeet wat   ek ge-sê   het*
　　　 so you   can   forget   what I   PERF-say have
　　　 'So, you can forget what I've said.'

It seems to me that an alternative explanation – given the rarity of the putative feature – is that *so* is treated as a discourse marker here, rather

---

[6] However, Donaldson (1988: 279) notes that *dat* omission was common in Middle Dutch, without a change of SOV order in the subordinate clause.

than a true adverb of sequencing. The following subject plus verb is
then exempted from the V2 rule.

(h) Reduced adverbial phrases functioning as prenominal compounds: *'n
drie maande lank kursus* 'a three-month-long course' rather than *'n kursus
wat drie maande lank is* 'a course that is three months long'.

19.7 English and SLA

The examples of convergence in Sections 19.4 and 19.5 have shown the
influence of Afrikaans on L1 and L2 varieties of South African English.
However, South Africa is well known for the diversity of its English social
dialects, mainly along ethnic lines. Cross-linguistic influence from other
languages can be seen even more strikingly in the characteristic features of
these ethnic varieties. For reasons of space I shall focus on the majority dialect
of English in the country – that of Black South Africans (henceforth BSAE).
The English of Coloured people will be discussed under code-switching in
Section 19.8; for South African Indian English, see Mesthrie (1992).

Black South African English has now bifurcated into two: (a) a traditional
L2 variety and (b) crossover varieties showing considerable overlaps with
White SAE (see Mesthrie 2010). Given the social and geographical segregation of South Africa's race groups in the past it is not surprising that
traditional BSAE shows considerable influence from Bantu languages in its
phonetics and syntax. It may even be uncontroversial to suggest that traditional BSAE is in many ways phonetically closer to a Bantu language than to
White SAE. The characteristics of this basilectal variety may be summarized
briefly as follows, based on the work of Hundleby (1964), Wissing (2002) and
van Rooy (2004). It is well known that vowel length tends not to be differentiated in BSAE, and that schwa is rare (mainly occurring in words with
more than three syllables). Where vowels are lengthened it is often
a phonological effect, the penultimate syllable being lengthened by convention, unless the final syllable is super-heavy (van Rooy 2004: 951). However,
it appears to me that in many instances in my data, lengthening itself is
a secondary effect based on high tone realizations. Thus *seventy* is often
realized as [sevé:nti]. Tone as a phonological effect is thus present in the
basilectal BSAE feature pool. Final devoicing of consonants is common, and
combined with other rules can produce forms that differ radically from L1
patterns: in the interviews a word like *cards* ([kʰats]) sounded identical to *cuts*
([kʰats]), and is only disambiguated by context. There is a potential four-way
ambiguity between wordlist sets like *seed, Sid, seat* and *sit* (as [sid] or [sit], with
'half-long' vowels). Regarding the basic five-vowel system, unlike other
parts of L2 English in Africa BSAE tends to split TRAP into two. With
monosyllables (*trap, have, act, maths, that, thanks*) the most common realization is [e], but in polysyllables [a] is often used as in *salary* [salari], *advanced*

[advanst], *adamant* [adamant] etc. It is possible that the [e] realizations within this set are based on front vowel raising from broader varieties of White SAE (on which see Lass and Wright 1986).

The syntactic features of BSAE have been studied at length by de Klerk (2006) and Botha (2013), with shorter accounts by Gough (1996), Mesthrie (2006) and van Rooy (2006), among others. These accounts leave little room for doubting the enormous influence of Bantu languages on traditional BSAE syntax, though some effects may well come from more general second language acquisition processes. Thus Mesthrie (2014) speaks of a robust living substratum for traditional BSAE. This variety contains a number of features, many of which are attested in other parts of Africa, and in second language varieties of English the world over.

(a) Generalized modal form *can be able*:

> (24) I had to go with a bowl in the street and ask for porridge, so that my mother **can be able** to cook.

(b) A tendency to use *be* + *-ing* progressives where Standard English usually disallows it (van Rooy 2006):

> (25) The one I**'m** hav**ing** presently is a temporary post.

(c) Resumptive pronouns in relative clauses (de Klerk 2006: 150; Mesthrie 2008):

> (26) Students discovered that the type of education they are trying to give **it** to us . . .

(d) Appositional pronouns with topicalized NPs (Mesthrie 1997):

> (27) Most of my friends that I grew up with, **they** are working at garages . . .

(e) A tendency towards tense neutralization in subordinate clauses:

> (28) She made it a point that she **fend** for us . . . (= 'always fended for us')

(f) A general tendency not to delete structural elements like infinitive *to* (Mesthrie 2006):

> (29) Even my friends were asking me, 'Why do you let your child **to** speak Zulu?'

(g) The possibility of inserting elements like *that* which are disallowed in the standard:

> (30) As you know **that,** times were very hard then.

Mesthrie (2006) points to a general 'anti-deletion' tendency in mesolectal BSAE which has three subtypes, showing the following general predilections.

(a) 'Undeleting' elements like *to* as in sentence (29) above.
(b) Not deleting elements (e.g. very little pro-drop or copula deletion).
(c) Adding elements not found in Standard English like *but* in the second clause after a conjunction like *although* in the first clause:

(31)   Although he was so young, **but** he did not fear the authorities.

This cluster of properties covers a very large portion of the miscellaneous lists of features found in previous studies, e.g. Gough (1996). It brings about a broad typological property which might be stated as follows: 'have as few empty nodes on the surface as possible'. I believe that this is a valid characterization of the agglutinating Bantu languages like Xhosa and Zulu and hence suggests a great deal of syntactic convergence, at least making the L2 English like the substrate.

The reverse phenomenon – influence of English over Bantu language syntax – is perhaps too recent to be prominent, though code-switching effects are treated briefly in Section 19.8. One feature of ongoing convergence relates to English influence over the placement of loanwords into a particular word class in, for example, Zulu. In previous times loanwords were put into a Zulu grammatical class on the basis of their semantics or phonetics. Thus *isi-Ngisi* 'English' is assigned to class 7 with prefix *isi-* on the basis of its semantics ('language'). And *u-tisha* 'teacher' is assigned to class 1a for 'human beings'. Class 5 (with prefix *i-*) is a particularly common class into which loanwords are placed since it denotes inanimates: hence *i-shalofu* 'shelf'. In contrast *um-shini* 'machine', is assigned to class 3 on the basis of the initial consonant 'm', which is given a vowel to bring it in line with Zulu phonological and morphological patterns. The noun is treated as a regular member of class 3 inanimates and assigned a plural (in class 4) hence *imi-shini* 'machines'. Thus the English word has been resegmented with *m* treated as part of the noun class prefix and *-achine* or *-chine* as part of the stem. Ngcobo (2013: 32) shows how such resegmentation of new loanwords is currently avoided (or resisted) by younger educated speakers, who prefer to maintain the phonological structure of the English root. Thus a common new borrowing like *iselulafoni* 'cell phone' is put into class 7 by some speakers, who treat the prefix as *is(i)-*. Young educated speakers put this loanword in class 9, with prefix *i-* and keeping *se-* as part of the stem (as in English).[7] This ideological practice (signifying a need to follow the segmentation of the prestige language) increases the degree of convergence between the borrowing and donor languages.

---

[7] Ngcobo (2013: 27) calls this class 9a, a sub-class of 9, which involves loanwords without a nasal in the prefix.

19.8   Phase Three: Code-switching and Mixing

The development of fluent bilingualism in urban centres worldwide often results in code-switching and mixing, and South Africa has proved no exception. Urbanization resulting from colonization and rapid industrialization after the discovery of gold and diamonds in the late nineteenth century has brought together many languages which would have been previously socially and regionally distinct. Two case studies below will show that code-switching is not just a 'performance' phenomenon that juxtaposes two or more codes temporarily. Rather it leaves its mark on those codes when used in subsequent monolingual contexts, leading to restructuring and convergence. The first study continues the theme of convergence between the two closely related languages, English and Afrikaans – this time among mainly 'Coloured' people in District Six, Cape Town as studied by McCormick (2002). Convergence between Afrikaans and English reaches its zenith amongst people placed on the wrong side of South Africa's apartheid divide, who consequently had little need of heavy investment in the standard varieties of the two languages. At the time of McCormick's research in the 1980s and 1990s, using standard Afrikaans would have been inappropriate as it was associated with the very officialdom that promoted racial segregation, inequality and a disavowal of the Coloured people, despite their part-European heritage. At the same time, using too standard a variety of English would have signalled disloyalty to the community and its solidarity ethic. English was stiff and starchy, standing for king, country and empire rather than the give-and-take of ordinary community life. Given this ideology, there was an openness to code-switching and mixing, with the mixed code being used not just in the home and street, but in public domains like meetings. McCormick (2002: 230) lists two types of convergence between the two codes. The first shows Afrikaans being influenced by English. Although colloquial and standard Afrikaans of White speakers has been shown in Section 19.5 to undergo word order and other changes vis-à-vis English, McCormick documents a further degree of changes in the variety spoken by Coloured people in District Six, Cape Town.

(a) A tendency to use auxiliary and verb together in main clauses with VO order, rather than a clause-final verb.
(b) Occasional use of non-final verbs in subordinate clauses introduced by *wat* 'which/ who/what.'
(c) Use of demonstrative adjective *daai* 'that' (from standard form *daardie*) as demonstrative pronoun 'that'.

More often, it is the Afrikaans substrate that influences the English L2 among Coloured speakers:

(a) Use of an invariant tag *nè* for 'isn't it, not so, don't you', etc.
(b) Frequent use of zero in place of third person singular -*s*.

(c) Frequent use of singular auxiliary *is* for *are* with third person plural subjects.

(d) Use of unstressed *do* in past tense, making it somewhat parallel to Afrikaans past tense usage with *het* + *ge*-V stem.

(e) Deletion of future auxiliary *will*, e.g. 'I take it later', in line with one option in Afrikaans *Ek vat haar later*.

(f) Tendency to delete *-ly* as an adverbial suffix.

(g) Placement of adverbials before object, e.g. 'My mommy don't make everyday cake.'

(h) Placement of time adverbials before place adverbials, e.g. 'I'm going now home.'

(i) A tendency to use singular demonstrative forms in place of plurals, e.g. 'That is other people's constitutions.'

(j) Use of English prepositions with influence from Afrikaans semantics, e.g. 'He cry by the doctor.'

(k) Calques based on Afrikaans compounding or phrasal verb patterns. e.g. *to scold someone out* (Afrikaans *skel uit* 'scold out'), *to throw someone wet* 'to spray, splash water on someone' (Afrikaans *nat te spat/gooi*).

(l) Use of *for* with objects after verbs like *tell*, e.g. 'I did tell for him that . . .'

As McCormick acknowledges, it is hard to be sure whether it is substrate influence at work or general simplification in second language acquisition, as many of the above syncretisms are widely reported in research into World Englishes. Of the above only (e), (g), (h), (k) and (l) can unambiguously be related to Afrikaans influence. Nevertheless the differences between the set (a) to (l) and Standard English do make the local variety of English closer to the local variety of Afrikaans. A more convincing case for substrate influence is that – apart from feature (i) above – almost none of the features cited above occur in the second language variety, Black South African English, as summarized in Section 19.6. A few other features from this set occur in Black South African English but only if speakers are in frequent contact with Coloured speakers, especially (a) and (d). Here the pathway of influence is Afrikaans > Afrikaans–English of Coloured bilinguals > Xhosa–English of Black bilinguals.

The second illustration of the convergence fostered by code-switching comes from contact between Bantu languages and English. Once again the pervasive use of English in the education system has had an impact upon the everyday speech of young bilinguals. Thipa (1989: 108) gives an example of code-switching in an urban Xhosa educational context:

(32) *Loo*   **lecturer**   *i-***clear**   *kuba*   *i-ya-***read**-*a.*
      DEM   lecturer   he-be clear   because   he-PROG-read-FV[8]
      'This lecturer is clear-headed because he reads.'

---

[8] Abbreviations: AUX, auxiliary; DEM, demonstrative; PERS, persistative; PROG, progressive; FV, final vowel; PL, plural; INF, infinitive; INSTR, instrumental; SC, subject concord; SG, singular; OC, object concord.

One of the outcomes of code-switching is a partial restructuring of the African languages to include not just lexical elements as in (32) above but structural elements as well. In particular, the use of logical connectors and discourse markers like *and, but, if, even if, I mean, so, because, even though* is very salient amongst students speaking Xhosa in Cape Town (see Deumert et al. 2006). Also salient is the use of the free negative form *never* and the question word *why*. Interestingly, even *busy* as an adjective (e.g. (33)) or as a semi-auxiliary denoting 'in the process of' (e.g. (19), repeated as (34) below) has to be included here, as shown by the following two examples from Urban Zulu and its mixed slang register Isicamtho:

(33)   ... *be-se-ba-ya-ku-hleka*   *nga-le*   **taal**   *ma*
        ... PAST-PERS-3PL-PROG-2.OC-laugh   INSTR-this   language   when
        u-loko   *u-**busy***
        2SG.SC-AUX2   SG. SC-busy
        '... they would be laughing at you in this language when you're busy.' (Slabbert and Finlayson 2000: 125)

(34)   *A-wu-bon-i*   *si-**bhizi***   *si-ya-dla?*
        NEG-2SG-see-NEG   1PL.SC-busy   1PL.SC-PROG-eat
        'Don't you see we are busy eating?' (Aycard 2014: 169)

These stand out in contrast to other bound grammatical categories which do not easily admit English grammatical intrusions: noun class prefixes, concord markers on adjectives and demonstratives, auxiliaries and verb endings, copulatives,[9] etc.

Finally, intimate bilingualism between African languages in Soweto and neighbouring areas has resulted in give-and-take between Sotho and Zulu especially. Gunnink (2012) records the interchangeability of the Zulu and Sotho locatives amongst fluent urban bilinguals: Zulu *e* + noun stem + *-ini* and Sotho *ko/mo/φ* + noun stem + *-eng*. While this interchangeability does not occur outside this highly multilingual area, Aycard (2014) suggests that in informal youth language registers of Soweto this kind of language crossing is exploited to the full. He proposes that this mixture is in the process of becoming conventionalized and even stabilizing as a new language outside the special context of male youth informal street speech. Some English structural elements (the logical connectors cited above and elements like *never, why* and *busy*) play a key role in this new conventionalization.

19.9   Conclusion: Overall Areal Convergence

Several generalizations can be made from the kinds of borrowing illustrated in this chapter. All layers of language are amenable to convergence

---

[9] Copulatives are prefixes whose equivalent in English are forms of copular *be*.

with other languages in a multilingual milieu. Vocabulary diffusion is as old as language contact in South Africa and continues to be an active force, with a vengeance in the age of code-switching. As far as phonology is concerned, processes of second language acquisition and language shift can result in the transfer of salient sounds from one language to another, the large-scale incorporation of clicks into Bantu languages being a particularly striking case in point. The phonology of Black South African English shows how far vowel systems can be influenced by speakers' mother tongues. Syntactic features are also shared in the modern South African linguistic area, via robust processes of calquing, i.e. relexification of selected salient syntactic patterns of the L1 in a speaker's L2. The influence of English on the syntax of Afrikaans and Bantu languages has been a theme running through this chapter. Educated bilinguals seem to be dancing to an English tune in respect of changes in word order in Afrikaans and the use of English logical connectors in languages like Xhosa.

We might ask what areas of language are impermeable to contact. Morphological influence is perhaps less noticeable and bound morphemes are rarely transferred: the only examples cited in the literature are forms like -*rha* (an adjective-forming suffix, equivalent to English '-ish': Branford and Claughton 2002: 202), -*s, -she* (a feminine suffix in generalized use), and -*sholo* 'bad, coarse' (Herbert 2002: 302) from Khoe-San languages into Bantu languages. In this chapter the use of the Afrikaans diminutive -*kie* in colloquial English words was noted.

Herbert (2002: 311) noted that 'the stability of the Bantu noun classes and, especially, the system of concordial agreement in language contact situations and in Bantu languages used as *lingue franche*, is remarkable'. It appears to me that the VP is particularly robust in resisting the incursions of code-switching (of both lexical and morphological forms).

Finally, the development of an incipient South African sprachbund can be seen from the way in which some features occur in different bilingual layers and may even survive not one but two language shifts. Thus reduplication from Malay survived the shift to Afrikaans, and in some communities is surviving a subsequent shift from Afrikaans to English.

References

Aycard, Pierre, 2014. *The Use of Iscamtho by Children in White City-Jabavu, Soweto: Slang and Language Contact in an African Urban Context.* Unpublished PhD thesis, University of Cape Town.

Botha, Rudolf P., 1988. *Form and Meaning in Word Formation: A Study of Afrikaans Reduplication.* Cambridge: Cambridge University Press.

Botha, Yolande, 2013. Corpus evidence of anti-deletion in Black South African English noun phrases. *English Today* 29 (1): 16–21.

Branford, Jean, with William Branford, 1991. *A Dictionary of South African English*, fourth edition. Cape Town: Oxford University Press.

Branford, William and John Claughton, 2002. Mutual lexical borrowings among some languages of southern Africa: Xhosa, Afrikaans and English. In Mesthrie (ed.), pp. 199–215.

Calteaux, Karen, 1996. *Standard and Non-standard African Language Varieties in the Urban Areas of South Africa: Main Report for the STANON Research Programme*. Pretoria: HSRC Publishers.

Childs, G. Tucker, 1997. The status of Isicamtho, an Nguni-based urban variety of Soweto. In Arthur K. Spears and Donald Winford (eds), *The Structure and Status of Pidgins and Creoles*, pp. 341–370. Amsterdam: John Benjamins.

Christie, Agatha, 1973. *A Pocket Full of Rye*. London: Fontana. First edition 1953.

Christie, Agatha, 1976. *Curtain: Poirot's Last Case*. London: Book Club Associates. First edition 1975.

Combrink, J. G. H., 1978. Afrikaans: Its origin and development. In Len W. Lanham and K. P. Prinsloo (eds), *Language and Communication Studies in South Africa*, pp. 69–95. Cape Town: Oxford University Press.

de Klerk, Vivian, 2006. *Corpus Linguistics and World Englishes: A Study of Xhosa English*. London: Continuum.

den Besten, Hans, 2012. *Roots of Afrikaans: Selected Writings of Hans den Besten*, edited by Ton van der Wouden. Amsterdam: John Benjamins.

den Besten, Hans, Carla Luiks and Paul Roberge, 2003. Reduplication in Afrikaans. In Silvia Kouwenberg (ed.), *Twice as Meaningful: Reduplication in Pidgins, Creoles and Other Contact Languages*, pp. 271–287. London: Battlebridge.

Deumert, Ana, Ellen Hurst, Oscar Masinyana and Rajend Mesthrie, 2006. Logical connectors and discourse markers in Urban Xhosa. Paper presented at the Linguistics Society of Southern Africa conference, University of KwaZulu-Natal, South Africa.

Donaldson, Bruce C., 1988. *The Influence of English on Afrikaans*. Pretoria: Serva.

Emeneau, Murray B., 1956. India as a linguistic area. *Language* 33: 3–16.

Finlayson, Rosalie, 1984. The changing nature of isihlonipho sabafazi. *African Studies* 43 (2): 137–146.

Gough, David, 1996. Black English in South Africa. In Vivian de Klerk (ed.), *Focus on South Africa*. John Benjamins: Amsterdam.

Güldemann, Tom, 2006. A forgotten heritage? Southern African Khoisan and its importance for modern linguistic research. Keynote address to the Linguistics Society of Southern Africa, University of Pretoria.

Güldemann, Tom, 2007. Preverbal objects and information structure in Benue-Congo. In Enoch O. Aboh, Katharina Harmann and

Malte Zimmerman (eds), *Focus Strategies in African Languages: The Interaction of Focus and Grammar in Niger-Congo and Afro-Asiatic*, pp. 83–112. Berlin: Mouton de Gruyter.

Gunnink, Hilde, 2012. *A Linguistic Analysis of Sowetan Zulu and Sowetan Tsotsi.* Unpublished MA thesis, University of Leiden.

Harinck, G., 1969. Interaction between Xhosa and Khoe: Emphasis on the period 1620–1750. In Leonard Thompson (ed.), *African Societies in Southern Africa*, pp. 145–170. London: Heinemann.

Herbert, Robert, 1990. 'Hlonipha' and the ambiguous woman. *Anthropos* 85: 455–473.

Herbert, Robert, 2002. The sociohistory of clicks in Southern Bantu. In Mesthrie (ed.), pp. 297–315.

Herbert, Robert and Richard Bailey, 2002. The Bantu languages: Sociohistorical perspectives. In Mesthrie (ed.), pp. 50–78.

Hickey, Raymond, 2010. Language contact: Reconsideration and reassessment. In Raymond Hickey (ed.), *The Handbook of Language Contact*, pp. 1–28. Oxford: Blackwell.

Hundleby, Charles E., 1964. *Xhosa–English Pronunciation in the South-East Cape.* Unpublished PhD thesis, Rhodes University, Grahamstown.

Lanham, Leonard, 1964. The proliferation and extension of Bantu phonemic systems influenced by Bushman and Hottentot. In H. G. Lund (ed.), *Proceedings of the Ninth International Congress of Linguists*, pp. 382–391. The Hague: Mouton.

Lanham, Leonard and Carol Macdonald, 1979. *The Standard in South African History and its Social History*. Heidelberg: Julius Groos.

Lass, Roger, 1995. South African English. In Rajend Mesthrie (ed.), *Language and Social History: Studies in South African Sociolinguistics*, pp. 89–106. Cape Town: David Philip.

Lass, Roger and Susan Wright, 1986. Endogeny vs. contact: Afrikaans influence on South African English. *English World-Wide* 7: 201–223.

Links, Tony, 1989. *So Praat ons Namaqualanders*. Cape Town: Tafelberg.

Louw, J. A., 1983. The development of Xhosa and Zulu as languages In Istvan Fodor and Claude Hagège (eds), *Language Reform: History and Future*. Hamburg: Buske.

McCormick, Kay, 2002. Code-switching, meaning and convergence in Cape Town. In Mesthrie (ed.), pp. 216–234.

Mesthrie, Rajend, 1992. *English in Language Shift: The History, Structure and Sociolinguistics of South African Indian English*. Cambridge: Cambridge University Press.

Mesthrie, Rajend, 1997. A sociolinguistic study of topicalisation phenomena in South African Black English. In Edgar Schneider (ed.), *New Englishes: Studies in Honour of Manfred Gorlach*, vol. 2, pp. 119–140. Amsterdam: John Benjamins.

Mesthrie, Rajend, 2002a. Endogeny versus contact revisited: Aspectual *busy* in South African English. In Raymond Hickey (ed.), *Collecting Views on*

Language Change: A Donation to Roger Lass on his Sixty-Fifth Birthday, pp. 345–358. Special issue of *Language Sciences* 24 (2–4).

Mesthrie, Rajend (ed.), 2002b. *Language in South Africa*. Cambridge: Cambridge University Press.

Mesthrie, Rajend, 2006. Anti-deletions in an L2 grammar: A study of Black South African English mesolect. *English World-Wide* 27 (2): 111–145.

Mesthrie, Rajend, 2008. Black South African English: Morphology and syntax. In Rajend Mesthrie (ed.), *Varieties of English*, vol. 4: *Africa, South and Southeast Asia*, pp. 488–500. Berlin: Mouton de Gruyter.

Mesthrie, Rajend, 2010. Socio-phonetics and social change: Deracialisation of the GOOSE vowel in South African English. *Journal of Sociolinguistics* 14 (1): 3–33.

Mesthrie, Rajend, 2014. The sociophonetic effects of Event X: Post-apartheid Black South African English in multicultural contact with other South African Englishes. In Sarah Buschfeld, Thomas Hoffmann, Magnus Huber and Alexander Kautzsch (eds), *The Evolution of Englishes: The Dynamic Model and Beyond*, pp. 58–69. Amsterdam: John Benjamins.

Mesthrie, Rajend and Ellen Hurst, 2013. Slang registers, code-switching and restructured urban varieties in South Africa: An analytic overview of tsotsitaals with special reference to the Cape Town variety. *Journal of Pidgin and Creole Languages* 28 (1): 103–130.

Ngcobo, Mtholeni, 2013. Loan words *(sic)* classification in isiZulu: The need for a sociolinguistic approach. *Language Matters* 44 (1): 21–38.

Nienaber, P. J. (ed.), 1965. *Taalkundige opstelle*. Cape Town: A. A. Balkema.

Pauwels, Jan Lodewijk, 1958. *Het dialect van Aarschot en omstreken*. Tongeren: Michiels.

Ponelis, F. A., 1985. Setselskeiding in Afrikaans. *Tydskrif vir Geestes-wetenskappe* 25 (2): 106–127.

Roberge, Paul, 2002. Afrikaans: Considering origins. In Mesthrie (ed.), pp. 79–103.

van Rooy, Bertus, 2004. Black South African English: Phonology. In Edgar Schneider, Kate Burridge, Bernd Kortmann, Rajend Mesthrie and Clive Upton (eds), *A Handbook of Varieties of English*, vol. 1: *Phonology*, pp. 943–952. Berlin: Mouton de Gruyter.

van Rooy, Bertus, 2006. The extension of the progressive aspect in Black South African English. *World Englishes* 25 (1): 37–64.

Slabbert, Sarah and Rosalie Finlayson, 2000. 'I'm a cleva!': The linguistic makeup of identity in a South African urban environment. *International Journal of the Sociology of Language* 144: 119–135.

Thipa, Henry, 1989. *The Difference between Rural and Urban Xhosa Varieties*. Unpublished PhD thesis, University of Natal, Pietermaritzburg.

Valkhoff, Marius, 1966. *Studies in Portuguese and Creole, with Special Reference to South Africa*. Johannesburg: Witwatersrand University Press.

Wissing, Daan, 2002. Black South African English: A new English? Observations from a phonetic viewpoint. *World Englishes* 21 (1): 129–144.

20

Jharkhand as a 'Linguistic Area': Language Contact Between Indo-Aryan and Munda in Eastern-Central South Asia

20.1   Introduction

This study presents an overview of linguistic convergences between the Munda and Indo-Aryan languages of eastern-central India and Nepal, with special reference to the Indian state of Jharkhand, which can be considered the 'centroid' of a rather loosely defined area of language convergence stretching eastward into Bangladesh, northward through the state of Bihar into Nepal, and southward into the state of Orissa. The convergences to be discussed here encompass both large-scale lexical borrowing from Indo-Aryan into Munda but also a number of convergences of a grammatical nature whose origin is not always known.

20.2   The Languages of Jharkhand and Beyond

The state of Jharkhand is home to languages from three families – Indo-Aryan (henceforth 'IA', Indo-European), Munda (Austroasiatic) and

The present study summarizes and expands upon an earlier study (Peterson 2010) and is largely based on data obtained during several visits to Jharkhand. I would like to thank the German Research Foundation (*Deutsche Forschungsgemeinschaft*) for generous grants which made three of these trips possible (PE 872/4–1, PE 872/1–1, PE 872/1–2). I would also like to thank the Department of Tribal and Regional Languages at Ranchi University, and especially Dr Ganesh Murmu, for their unwavering support over the years. Thanks also go to Ramawatar Yadav for his invaluable insights into Maithili grammar and to both him and Alena Witzlack-Makarevich for their comments on an earlier version of this article. Of course, I alone am responsible for any oversights and errors.

Map 20.1 Jharkhand and its neighbours[1]

Dravidian. The present study focuses on contact between Indo-Aryan and Munda, as these have been in contact with one another for many centuries, if not millennia, whereas the Dravidian languages of the region, Kurukh and Malto, appear to be relatively new to this region. Hence we will only refer to these latter two languages on occasion. Since many of the languages of this region still await adequate documentation, we focus our attention on the larger, better described IA and Munda languages of the region, drawing upon published works and data collected during several research trips to Jharkhand. Map 20.1 shows our area of study.

The following gives a brief overview of the major IA and Munda languages native to the region. All figures for numbers of speakers are from Lewis et al. (2013) and, where applicable, refer to the total number of speakers or at least to those of India and Nepal combined.

Indo-Aryan
– **Sadri** – the lingua franca for much of Jharkhand, especially central and western Jharkhand, by speakers of various Munda and Dravidian languages. Spoken by 3,290,490 people. A number of other, smaller languages, such as **Kurmali** and **Panch Parganiya**, are also spoken in Jharkhand and are closely related to Sadri, but unfortunately little work has been conducted on these since Grierson (1903), hence they will only play a marginal role in this study.
– **Maithili**, spoken in Bihar and southern and eastern Nepal by an estimated 32,000,000 people, and the closely related **Magahi**, spoken to the south in Bihar by an estimated 14,000,000 people.

---

[1] The original map, which has been modified here and in Map 20.2 somewhat, is copyrighted by PlaneMad/Wikipedia and can be downloaded at the following site: de.wikipedia.org/w/index.php?title=Datei:India_Jharkhand_locator_map .svg&filetimestamp=20081229064837

I am grateful to Arun Ganesh for granting permission to use these maps without the terms of the Creative Commons ShareAlike License.

- **Oriya**, the state language of Orissa (32,137,290 speakers).
- **Bhojpuri**, spoken primarily in Uttar Pradesh, western Bihar and northward into Nepal, with c. 39,510,000 speakers.
- **Bengali**, spoken in eastern Jharkhand but especially in West Bengal and Bangladesh (193,263,700 speakers).

Munda

The approximately two dozen Munda languages, which form the western branch of the Austroasiatic phylum, belong to one of two groups, which are not mutually intelligible.

- The *northern group* includes the three largest Munda languages, **Santali**, with 6,218,900 speakers, **Mundari**, with 1,120,280 speakers, and **Ho**, with 1,040,000 speakers. A number of other, much smaller languages belonging to this group are also spoken in or near Jharkhand, such as **Asuri, Birhor, Korwa, Mahali** and **Turi**. As the languages of this group are largely mutually intelligible and as these smaller languages await documentation, we concentrate here on the three larger languages, on which there is considerable published data.
- The only member of the *southern group* spoken in Jharkhand is **Kharia**, with an estimated 241,580 speakers. Further languages from this group include **Juang**, spoken in central Orissa, as well as a number of other languages spoken in southern Orissa and further to the south in Andhra Pradesh, such as **Sora, Gadaba, Gorum, Remo**, etc. As most of these languages await serious documentation and are outside our area of study, we concentrate on Kharia from this group.

Map 20.2 provides an overview of the regions where the larger languages mentioned above are traditionally spoken. As these languages are spoken over extensive areas – for example, through migrations mainly in the nineteenth century, Mundari, Santali, Ho, Kharia and Sadri are now also spoken in eastern Nepal and further to the east – Map 20.2 provides only a very general indication of the core areas of the respective languages.

Given the number of languages in the region and the fact that many of these have not yet received adequate documentation, the present study lays no claim to being exhaustive. Instead, it builds upon three earlier studies (Abbi 1997; Osada 1991; Peterson 2010) and draws attention to a number of convergences which have so far been noted.

20.3   Convergence between Indo-Aryan and Munda

In the present section we examine evidence for linguistic convergence in the region of study, beginning in Section 20.3.1 with phenomena which are typical of much or even most of South Asia, before dealing in

Map 20.2 The major Indo-Aryan and Munda languages of eastern-central South Asia and their general relative positions[2]

Section 20.3.2 with instances of convergence which set this region off from its neighbours.

20.3.1   Eastern-central South Asia in the Larger Context

Since Emeneau's (1956) seminal study, which first brought the topic of linguistic convergence in South Asia to the attention of general linguists, a considerable amount of work has been conducted on the topic of South Asia as a 'linguistic area' or 'sprachbund', and a number of defining criteria have been suggested.[3] In fact, many of the criteria which have been suggested as typical of South Asia are also found in our area. These include, among others, the following.

(i)   Predicate-final word order (SOV). This is of special interest as it is generally assumed that Proto-Munda had a basic SVO order, whereas the Munda languages are all SOV.[4]

(ii)   Closely related to this last point is a strong head-final tendency in general.

(iii)   Predominantly agglutinative structure or grammatical marking expressed through enclitics.

[2] See note 1.
[3] The standard work on this topic is Masica (1976). A more recent overview (in German) is provided by Ebert (2001).
[4] See Donegan and Stampe (2004) for an account of the process which may have led to these changes in Munda.

(iv) The presence of morphologically marked causatives and, at least in some languages (e.g. Sadri, Kharia, etc.) double causatives.

 (v) The presence of sequential converbs ('conjunctive participles'), which appear to have been 'borrowed' into Munda from IA (Abbi 1997: 140–141; Peterson 2010: 61).

(vi) The so-called 'explicator compound verbs', in which a lexeme denoting the event is followed by one of a small number of 'explicator verbs' which derive from lexical verbs and which carry all grammatical marking (see e.g. Kharia *rema? ɖoɽho?* in (8) or Sadri *raih gelʌk* in (10)). These 'explicator verbs' generally denote aktionsart.

(vii) The 'dative-subject' construction, in which the experiencer appears in a non-nominative case (generally the dative, as the name implies) and the verb agrees in person and number with the stimulus, which appears in the nominative.

There are also a number of traits shared by most languages of this region which are typical of larger portions of eastern South Asia.

Accusative alignment. In all languages of this region we find a nominative/accusative alignment pattern with respect to case marking, and predicates in all these languages mark for the person/number/honorific status of the subject (S/A). In some languages, the predicate also marks for the object (P) and certain non-arguments as well (e.g. possessors), such as Maithili and North Munda in general. We find no signs of morphological ergativity in this region, unlike in the IA languages to the west, or in Nepali and the Tibeto-Burman languages to the north, which are either ergative or split-ergative languages.

Lack of grammatical gender as a productive category. In contrast, the IA languages to the west and southwest possess either two (e.g. Hindi) or three genders (e.g. Marathi). Other IA languages, such as Nepali to the north of our area, do possess two genders (which I consider 'feminine' and 'non-feminine') but generally only in formal registers, whereas less formal registers tend to have no gender distinction (Genetti 1999).

Numeral classifiers (Abbi 1997: 142; Osada 1991: 106–108). In addition to their use with numerals, these classifiers also attach in some languages to other units, such as demonstratives. However, the use of classifiers varies considerably throughout the region: in many of the IA languages of the region, classifiers may be placed after the noun to denote specificity (Neukom and Patnaik 2003: 24–34). See example (1) from Sadri, where *lʌɽki=go* refers to a girl who has already been mentioned in the preceding story:

(1)   Sadri
        *u=kʌr   bad   dhan=mʌn=ke   **lʌɽki=go**   bʌrka-l-ʌk*
        that=GEN   after   paddy=PL=OBL   girl=CLASS   boil-PST-3SG

sijh-ʌl-ʌk   *sukha-l-ʌk* …
boil-PST-3SG   dry(TR)-PST-3SG
'After that, **the girl** boiled the rice paddy, dried [it] …'

(BCB.0071)[5]

This is not possible in many languages of the region such as Maithili (Ramawatar Yadav, personal communication) or Kharia: although both of these languages do have classifiers, some of which are homophonous with those of Sadri, these have different distributions. In Kharia they attach only to numerals and a few other quantifiers but not to nouns as in (1), whereas in Maithili one classifier, =ʈa, can attach to nouns, but only if the noun is followed by an enclitic focus marker, such as =e in *(u) ram=e=ʈa* [(that) Ram=FOC=CLASS] 'that Ram'. Hence the presence of classifiers as a defining trait of a supposed sprachbund is only valid to the extent that we do not take their distribution into account. Nevertheless, the presence of often homophonous classifiers throughout this region does testify to *convergence* between these languages, even if there is no one-to-one correspondence.

20.3.2 Eastern-central South Asia as a Convergence Area

Of more interest here are those convergences which set this area off from neighbouring regions. The following presents a number of such tentative convergences.

20.3.2.1 The Lexicon

To begin with, there has been massive borrowing between the languages of our region, primarily from IA, to which the politically and economically dominant languages belong, into Munda. In fact, as Abbi (1997) notes, the Munda languages have incorporated large numbers of borrowings from IA into their lexica from virtually all areas, including core areas such as numerals, kinship terms, body parts, etc. This has also led to the incorporation of phonemes from IA into the respective inventories. However, as this is virtually always found in situations of prolonged intense contact, we concentrate in the following on other, less typical types of convergence between the two families. Unless otherwise noted, the processes by which these traits have spread cannot be reconstructed at present, but their presence in both language families clearly testifies to this prolonged contact.

20.3.2.2 Alienable versus Inalienable Possession

Many IA and Munda languages of the region distinguish between inalienable possession (e.g. with body parts and kinship relations), indicated by

---

[5] Examples given with sources of this type are from my own texts. The plural marker =mʌn in (1) denotes a large amount of paddy.

enclitic marking for the possessor on the possessum itself, and alienable possession, in which the possessor appears in the genitive and precedes the possessum:

(2) Kharia
     Inalienable   Alienable
     aba=ɲ   *iɲ=aʔ*   *khoɽi*
     father=1SG   1SG=GEN   village
     'my father'   'my village'

                                        (Peterson 2011: 164)

(3) Santali[6]
     hɔpɔn=me   *am=ak'*   *oɽak'*
     son=2SG   2SG=GEN   house
     'your son'   'your house'

                                   (adapted from Neukom 2001: 32)

(4) Sadri
     bhʌuji=har=mʌn   *u=mʌn=ʌk*   *jʌmin*
     sister.in.law=3POSS=PL   3=PL=GEN   land
     'his/her sisters-in-law'   'their land'

                                        (author's own data)

As the IA languages of central India do not otherwise seem to have this distinction, which is found in virtually all Munda languages, it is argued in Peterson (2010: 63–64) that the use of *=har* as a marker of inalienable possession in Sadri, which has this distinction only with third person possessors, is the result of the contact-induced reanalysis of the original postnominal use of *=har* as a marker of specificity, like *=go* in example (1), to denote inalienable possession. Thus, the category of inalienable possession in Sadri has most likely been 'borrowed' from Munda, although it is expressed by native IA morphology.[7]

20.3.2.3 'Start' versus 'keep on'

In many IA and Munda languages of the region, one and the same morpheme can have both an inceptive interpretation and either a durative interpretation ('keep on') or that of general imperfectivity.[8] For example, the morpheme *laʔ* in Kharia, which derives from Sadri *lag-* 'begin', can denote the inception of an action or event (5a), but much more commonly it denotes general imperfectivity (5b):

---

[6] Glosses and translations from other sources have occasionally been adapted to the conventions of this study. These modifications do not directly affect our discussion and only serve to unify the presentation of the data.

[7] That not only such categories but also the markers themselves can be 'borrowed' is shown by the following example, from Peterson (2010: 64): compare Sadri *ke* 'who?' and its alternative form *ke=har* [who=3POSS] 'who?' (with no apparent semantic difference) with Kharia *ber* 'who?' and its alternative form *behar* < **ber=har* 'who?' (also with no apparent semantic difference). Whatever the exact semantics of these complex forms may have been, which cannot be reconstructed at present, the Kharia form is clearly motivated by the Sadri form.

[8] This ambiguity does not depend on the aktionsart of the predicate, at least in those languages for which I have been able to check this.

(5) Kharia

    a. *hobne=te=ga*   *ubar kole? kundu?*   *jal=te*

       that.much=OBL=FOC   two parrot child   net=OBL

      ajhe=kon   *'ṭãy ṭãy'*   *toro?ḍ=na la?=ki=kiyar.*

      get.trapped=SEQ   'tay, tay!'   cry=INF 'IPFV'=MID.PST=3DU

      'Meanwhile (= in that much), two baby parrots got caught in the net and began <u>crying</u> "Tay! Tay!".'

                                                (BB, 2:33)

    b. ... *khaṛiya*   *lebu=ki*   *pujapaṭh*   <u>*karay=na*</u>   *la?=ki=may,* ...

      Kharia   man=PL   sacrifice   do=INF   IPFV=MID.PST=3PL

      'the Kharia men <u>used to perform</u> sacrifices'

                                                  (AK, 2:6)

Similar comments hold for Mundari, where the morpheme *-jan* depicts an event as having been started and/or as ongoing (see the discussion in Hoffmann 1905 [2001]: 183). Preliminary evidence also suggests that this category once existed in Santali but has since been lost (Peterson 2010: 65, note 11). Now consider example (6) from Sadri:

(6) Sadri

    rait   *bhe-l-ʌk.*   *ʌb*   *buḍha*   *buḍhiya*   *bicar*

    night become-PST-3SG   now   old.man old.woman   thought

    <u>*kʌr-ek*</u>   *hel-l-ʌẽ*   *ki* ...

    do-INF   'begin'-PST-3PL   CMPL

    'It became night. Now the old man and the old woman <u>began thinking</u> ...'

                            (adapted from Jordan-Horstmann 1969: 129)

Speakers I consulted confirmed that without the first sentence in (6) and without ʌb 'now', (6) could also have the meaning 'The old man and the old woman <u>kept on thinking</u>'. Similarly, in Bengali the auxiliary verb *lag-* can mean both 'begin' and 'go on / continue to' in combination with an infinitive (Radice 1994: 240, note 16).

20.3.2.4 'from' and 'to'

In many IA and Munda languages of this region we find similarities between markers with an ablative and an allative meaning. Where exactly the same marker is used for both meanings, I refer to this as the 'extensional' function, as it refers to the distance extending to or from an event or location. Examples include Bengali ⟨abadhi⟩ [ɔbodhi] 'since, until, n. limit' and Sadri *le* in (7):

(7) Sadri

    se=khʌn   <u>*le*</u>   *hʌmre=mʌn=ke*   *cik*   *bʌṛaik*   *kʌh-ʌl*

    that=time   EXT   1NSG=PL=OBL   Chik   Baraik   say-PTCP

ja-t=he.   *aij le.*
PASS-IPFV=PRS.3SG   today EXT
'Since that time we are called "Chik Baraik". Until today.'

In Munda languages of the region, although the ablative and allative
are different, they nevertheless often have strong formal similarities:
examples include Kharia *tay* 'from' and the allative postposition *khoʔtay*
'up to' (< **khoʔ tay* [place ABL] 'from the place'), Santali *həbic'* 'up to, until'
and *həbic' khɔn* 'from, since', with the postposition *khɔn*, which can
also mark the ablative alone, and the cognate Mundari forms *həbiʔ*
'up to, until' and *həbiʔkhɔn* 'from, since' (Ganesh Murmu, personal
communication).

20.3.2.5   Anticipatory Categories

Many languages of the region possess an 'anticipatory' predicative category denoting that one event is directly followed by another. This is shown
for Kharia in (8), where the 'explicator verb' (see Section 20.3.1) *ḍoṭh/ḍoḍ*,
which derives from the homophonous form with the meaning 'take',
denotes that this action is obligatorily followed by another action. The
following action is typically introduced by *ro* 'and'.

(8)   Kharia
       tay   raja   jhaṛi...   ḍoklóʔ   remaʔ ḍoṭh=oʔ   ro   ho=ki=te
       Then king all   meeting call   ANTIC=ACT.PST and that=PL=OBL
       'masih=te   ate jorme=na ayiʔj.'   *gam=oʔ   ro   jʊŋ=oʔ.*
       Messiah=OBL where be.born=INF PRS.COP   say=ACT.PST and ask=ACT.PST
       'Then the king called all ... to a meeting and asked (= said and asked) them
       "Where is the Messiah to be born?"'
                                                      (Kullū 1992: 2 = Luke, 2:4)

North Munda languages possess a similar category, expressed by non-
cognate forms. These are generally referred to as 'pluperfect', 'irrealis',
etc. in the respective studies. Consider (9) for Santali, adapted from
Neukom (2001: 80–81). Similar categories are also found in Mundari
(Osada 2008: 126) and Ho (Deeney 1975: 39–40):

(9)   Santali
       jɛmɔn=e   bɔlɔ gɔt'-len=a,   *tɛmɔn=ge=kin   kiləp*
       as=3SG.SUBJ enter TEL-ANTIC:[MID]=IND then=FOC=3DU.SUBJ close
       ɛsɛt   gɔt'-ked=e=a.
       close   TEL-ACT.PST=3SG.OBJ=IND
       'The moment he got in, they closed and shut him up.'
                                                (adapted from Neukom 2001: 80f.)

Many IA languages of the region, such as Sadri (10), have a similar category,
generally referred to as the 'conditional participle/converb':

(10)   Sadri
    . . . *jolha*   *u=ke*   <u>*poṛa-le*</u>   ʌ*ur* *ghoṛa* *upʌr* <u>*bʌiṭh-le*</u>
    Muslim   that=OBL grab-ANTIC and horse above sit.down-ANTIC
    rʌ⟨i⟩h   *ge-l-ʌk.*
    remain⟨LNK⟩ TEL-PST-3SG
    '. . . the Muslim <u>grabbed it and</u> remained seated (= <u>sat down [and]</u>
    remained) on top of the horse.'

                                         (Nowrangi 1956: 165)

Similar forms are found in Bengali (Thompson 2012: 77) and Oriya (Neukom and Patnaik 2003: 251–252). In addition to their use in the protasis of conditional constructions, these forms typically also fulfil a number of other functions, such as habitual situations where one event/situation precedes another; cf. the 'temporal *when*-conditionals' in Bengali (Thompson 2012: 178) and Neukom and Patnaik (2003: 251–252) on Oriya, especially their examples (89), (90) and (95).

Finally, the North Dravidian language Kurukh possesses a similar category, expressed by *xacc-*, which as a free morpheme has the meaning 'rip', and *liŋgh-* (meaning as an independent morpheme unknown) (Masato Kobayashi, personal communication; Grignard 1924: 147).

As argued in Peterson (2010: 68), this category probably originated in one language (family) in the region and then spread to others, although the details of this process remain obscure. The anticipatory form *-le* found in IA languages originally derives from the past participle marker *-l* followed by the locative marker *-e* (Chatterji 1926: 1004, §736) but is homophonous in most IA languages with the verb stem *le-* 'take', which is often used as a 'vector verb' to denote aktionsart. This is important since, as we noted above, the anticipatory marker in Kharia, *ḍoʔḍ/ḍoṭh*, is homophonous with and derives from the lexeme *ḍoʔḍ* 'take'. Finally, the fact that in many North Munda languages the form is homophonous with the 'conditional converbs' of IA suggests the possibility that the North Munda forms are borrowings from IA.

However, there are problems with this analysis, since there is considerable evidence that *-le* was not borrowed from IA into North Munda, as *-l* is found in many Munda languages to denote the 'anterior' or 'cislocative' (e.g. Anderson 2007, §§4.1–4.2; Pinnow 1966: 141, §3.2.12.1.2), suggesting that it derives from Proto-Munda.

In view of the semantic similarities between these categories in the individual languages, the historical development in Kharia, the phonological similarities between the North Munda and IA forms, and the presence of a semantically similar category with entirely unrelated forms in Kurukh, I suggest that at the very least the languages of this region mutually influenced one another such that forms which may have already been present and which were already semantically similar became

Table 20.1 *Sadri-L1/L2 and Kharia forms of the first persons*
(=**mʌn** 'PL')

	Number		
	Singular	Dual	Plural
Sadri-L1	*mõe*	-	*hʌmre*
Sadri-L2	*mõe*	*hʌmre dui=jhʌn*	*hʌmre(=mʌn)*
(= Kharia-L1)		*hʌmre duiy=o*	
Kharia	*iɲ*	*anaŋ* (INCL)	*aniŋ* (INCL)
		iɲjar (EXCL)	*ele* (EXCL)

semantically even more similar, while at least Kharia and Kurukh developed this category predominantly through contact with neighbouring languages.

20.3.2.6   A New Dual Category

In Peterson (2010: 68–70) the emergence of a new number distinction in the Sadri pronominal system due to Munda influence is noted: in Sadri we normally find a singular/plural opposition throughout the entire nominal system, whereas the Munda languages of this region have a singular/dual/plural number distinction. Interestingly, a Kharia-L1 speaker of Sadri (c. 50 years old), who has been an active speaker of Sadri most of her life, cited in interviews Sadri forms for singular, dual and plural pronouns. Table 20.1 provides by way of example an overview for the first persons of the 'traditional', L1-Sadri forms, the Sadri forms as indicated by this L1-Kharia speaker, and the corresponding Kharia forms. Note that the Kharia L1-system has an obligatory dual category not found in the Sadri-L1 system. This category has in effect been 'transferred' by this speaker into Sadri by the use of the numeral *dui(y)* 'two' and a classifier, either =*jhʌn* or =*o*, =*jhʌn* being restricted to humans, whereas =*o* is unmarked in this respect. These dual forms do not violate any principles of Sadri and simply mean 'we both', but crucially the Kharia-L1 speaker views them as obligatory, whereas Sadri-L1 speakers readily accepted them as correct but not obligatory.

There is evidence that a similar process is also taking place elsewhere: Ramawatar Yadav (personal communication) informs me of a similar, non-obligatory dual construction in Maithili. As there is at present no further information on this construction – that is, how and when it entered the language, the speakers who use it, and to what extent various speakers consider it obligatory – this issue requires further study.

20.3.2.7   The Genitive

The genitive provides an especially interesting field for the study of convergences between Munda and IA. To begin with, the genitive markers in most languages of this area have very similar forms, regardless of genetic affiliation, with the unmarked form =(ʌ)k/=(ə)k in IA or =(a)ʔ in North Munda and Kharia (for underlying /ak/ or /ag/).[9]

This formal similarity may be coincidental: In most IA languages, not just those of this region, the genitive marker derives from the verb 'do', which generally has the form kʌr-. For example, in Sadri the genitive can take any of the following forms: =kʌr/=ʌk/=k, largely depending on the last segment of the unit they attach to (for details see Jordan-Horstmann 1969: 45) or Maithili, where the form =ək/=k is found with all nouns.[10] Other forms are found, although these too derive from the same source, e.g. =(e)r in Bengali (Chatterji 1926: §503), which is also found in Sadri and Maithili with certain pronominals (Jordan-Horstmann 1969: 65–66, §4.4.2; Yadav 1996: 90–92, 108–114).

A similar form (allowing for language-specific phonotactic rules) is found in the North Munda languages and Kharia:[11]

(11)   Santali =ak' (= [aʔ]),   Mundari =aʔ,   Kharia: =aʔ

It is unclear whether this form goes back to Proto-Munda or whether this similarity is the result of contact. Note that Sora and Juang (both South Munda) mark the genitive by /=a/ (Anderson and Harrison 2008: 310–311; Patnaik 2008: 515–516), although all other South Munda languages make use of forms beginning with a nasal and followed by a vowel, which differs in the various languages (e.g. the data in the contributions in Anderson 2008). While the forms in North Munda, Sora, Juang and Kharia suggest that the form /=ak/ derives from Proto-Munda, the similarity to IA cannot be denied and the forms in other South Munda languages call this analysis into question. Further research is necessary.[12]

In the present study we assume that this similarity is coincidental and will not pursue the topic further, but whatever its origin, the genitive marker has assumed further functions in both IA and Munda, to which we now turn.

In many languages of the region, we find a marker which is homophonous with the genitive used to mark person, generally the third person singular in various predicative categories. For example, in Sadri a form deriving from the genitive marks the third person singular of the past tense, which

---

[9] There are a number of alternative forms in North Munda and Kharia, e.g. Santali =reak' [reaʔ], used with an inanimate possessum, =ʔ, =naʔ, =yaʔ and =waʔ in Kharia, and others, but as these are generally based on the underlying form /=ak/, we take this to be the basic form in Kharia and North Munda.

[10] However, Chatterji (1926: 756) questions this etymology for =k in the 'Magadhan' languages, including Sadri and Maithili.

[11] In native morphemes in Kharia an underlying /k/ or /g/ in the coda is realized as [ʔ]. A similar situation holds in Mundari (Osada 2008: 101) and Santali (Ghosh 2008: 26, 30).

[12] In view of the fact that Kharia also has a variant of the genitive beginning with /n/, i.e. =naʔ (see note 9), found with demonstratives, it is possible that the North Munda, Kharia, Juang and Sora forms are indeed cognate with the remaining South Munda forms and that the /ʔ/, to be discussed in the following main text, has been added to this unit in Kharia and North Munda through contact with IA, and that the initial /n/ of this marker has been lost in these languages, at least in most environments. This topic will be taken up in a future study.

Table 20.2 *The past tense in Sadri:* kha- *'eat' (Nowrangi 1956: 93)*

Person	Singular	Plural
1	*kha-l-ò*	*kha-l-i*
2	*kha-l-e*	*kha-l-a*
3	*kha-l-ʌk*	*kha-l-ʌē*

in earlier periods was unmarked for person (i.e. 'zero-marking'). Table 20.2 presents the conjugation of *kha-* 'eat' in the past tense by way of example; /k/ also marks the third person singular and plural of the subjunctive in Sadri, which functions as a kind of third person imperative.

Other IA languages of the region in which forms deriving from the genitive mark the third person singular include Kurmali (Grierson 1903: 149), Sadri Kol (Grierson 1903: 159) and Panch Pargarniya (cf. the texts in Grierson 1903: 168–172). To the north as well, for example in Magahi, /k/ forms part of the marking for virtually all forms of transitive verb marking involving the third person singular non-honorific in the composite present, past and future (Verma 1991), and a similar situation holds for Maithili (Yadav 1996: 174, 177), although /k/ is often omitted in the spoken language (see Bickel et al. 1999: 486–487).

In Bengali, /k/ is found in many forms: in addition to the standard language, where it is found in the imperative of the third person, e.g. *kor-uk* [do-IMP.3] 'let him/her do', Chatterji (1926: 989–990, §721) notes that this 'pleonastic affix' also occurs in the second, middle-grade honorific past and future and non-honorific third person past and future, dialectally in the third person past habitual, and occasionally in the second person imperative, noting that it is considered archaic except in the case of the third person imperative. According to him this element is documented for Bengali at least since the Middle Bengali period, being found in the Śrī-Kṛṣṇa-Kīrttana, whose date he gives as 'before 1400' (Chatterji 1926: 132).

Finally, Chatterji (1926: 990–992, §722) notes that this form was also found earlier in Oriya in the third person – but not in the third person imperative – although it is not found in the modern language, and also in languages further to the east, such as Early Assamese (to the northeast of the region under study here), where it is still found in the third person imperative in the modern language. As no forms are cited for *-k* in the verbal paradigms of Bhojpuri to the northwest of Jharkhand, this phenomenon appears to have western Bihar and Jharkhand as its western boundary, while its eastern boundary currently extends into West Bengal/Bangladesh (and further into Assam) and southward approximately to Jharkhand's border with Orissa.

Table 20.3 *Mundari enclitic person/number markers (based on Osada 2008: 120)*

	Singular	Dual	Plural
1INCL	=ɲ	=laŋ	=bu
1EXCL		=liŋ	=le
2	=m	=ben	=pe
3	=e/=i/=eʔ/=iʔ	=kin	=ko

In North Munda languages, forms deriving from the genitive marker =(a)ʔ can also mark the third person singular on predicative forms. For example, the third person singular in Mundari is marked on the predicate by the enclitic forms =e/=i, which are the 'original' markers for this person, although these can be followed by the glottal stop in some environments, i.e. =eʔ/=iʔ (Osada 1992: 64–65). See the data in Table 20.3.

As argued in Peterson (2010: 75–76) there appears to be a preference to use the enclitic subject marker with the glottal stop in Mundari, while the predicate-internal object marker is marked by the form without the glottal stop:

(12)   Mundari
   biŋ   coke=ʔ   jom-ja-ʔ=i=a.
   snake   frog=3SG.SUBJ   eat-INGR-TR[13]=3SG.OBJ=IND
   'The snake is eating the frog.'

(Osada 2008: 106)

This tendency in Mundari has been generalized in Ho, where the form =eʔ marks third person animate subjects in general while -ī, that is, the form without the glottal stop, marks animate third person objects (Deeney 1975: 1 and especially 20). In Santali the glottal stop marks the third person singular inanimate object in the imperfective and non-past applicative (Neukom 2001: 121–122). With that, the use of the genitive to mark various predicative forms, while recessive in many languages, is still found throughout Jharkhand (with the exception of Kharia), to the east into West Bengal and Bangladesh and beyond into Assam, and as far north as Nepal.

The genitive also marks focus in various languages of the region, e.g. Sadri in (13), adapted from Jordan-Horstmann (1969; 107), who glosses it as 'Ø'.

(13)   Sadri
   sob bhai   kʌh-l-ʌẽ: 'hã, cʌl-a!   aij   huã=e=kʌr
   all   brother say-PST-3PL yes go-IMP.2PL today there=FOC=FOC
   ja-b!
   go-FUT.1PL
   'All the brothers said: "Yes, let's go! Today we will go there (i.e., nowhere else)!"'

---

[13] The transitive marker has two allomorphs, -d and -ʔ (Osada 2008: 119). This -ʔ does not appear to derive from the genitive marker -k.

Speakers I consulted all confirmed that =kʌr in (13) highlights *huã* 'there', although they unanimously considered it non-standard, unlike the focal marker =*e*.[14] A similar situation is found in Kharia, where the genitive can also mark focus, although here as well speakers consider it non-standard or even incorrect in interviews.

(14)   Kharia

    ... ginir, amkul,   *banari ro*   *choʔɖɖ=aʔ*[15]   *beʔʈ=ɖom=aʔ*
    Ginir   Amkul   Banari and small=FOC son=3POSS=GEN
    ɲimi   *aw=ki*   *baroya.*
    name   COP=MID.PST Baroya
    '... Ginir, Amkul, Banari and the name of his <u>youngest</u> son was Baroya.'

                                 (Peterson 2011: 441, ln. 8)

This use of the genitive as a focus marker may also be related to the so-called 'genitive subjects' in Oriya (Neukom and Patnaik 2003: 59–61). These are complex subjects consisting of two or more coordinated NPs which appear in the genitive. Despite the genitive marking, these units trigger verb agreement just like nominative subjects. Further research is necessary to determine any possible pragmatic differences compared to nominative subjects.

(15)   Oriya

    <u>*mo=rɔ*</u>   <u>*ta-nkɔ=rɔ*</u>   *e*   *kamɔ=ʈa*   *kɔ-l-u.*
    1SG=GEN   3SG-OBL=GEN this work-CLASS do-PST-1PL.INCL
    '<u>He and I</u> did this work.'

                        (adapted from Neukom and Patnaik 2003: 59)

It is unclear if forms deriving from the genitive can be used to mark focus in other languages, perhaps due to the non-standard status of this construction. There is one possible case in Bengali: Chatterji (1926: 992, §723) writes that the use of /k/ is 'very popular' with certain words, such as *ekʈu(-k)* 'a little', the plural marker =*gula(-k)*, and dialectally with *kintu(-k)* 'but'. Chatterji (1926: 990, §721) also writes that *-k* may be used with negatives in all persons and tenses in Bengali. Considering the connection in many languages between negation and focus marking,[16] this fits in well with the Sadri and Kharia (and possibly also Oriya) data. Finally, Santali has a focus marker which Neukom (2001: 126–127) refers to as the 'intensive' infix *-k'-* [ʔ]. Although this would seem to be the same phenomenon at first glance, this form is an infix, hence it is not clear if it is related to the other forms and if so, how it became an infix in this language. Further research is necessary.

---

[14] =*kʌr* seems to reinforce =*e* in (13). It is possible that the two have slightly differing semantics, although this requires further research.

[15] NPs in Kharia are marked only once for case, hence =*aʔ* on *choʔɖɖ=aʔ* in (14) is not case agreement.

[16] For example, the neutralization with negation in English of the categories 'simple present' *I go* and 'emphatic present' *I do go*, both of which are negated by the negative form of the 'emphatic' construction, i.e. *I don't go*.

Table 20.4 *The Santali existential/locative copula (non-negated) (adapted from Neukom 2001: 168)*

	Singular	Dual	Plural
1 INCL	mena=ɲ=a	mena-ʔ=laŋ=a	mena-ʔ=bon=a
1 EXCL		mena-ʔ=liŋ=a	mena-ʔ=le=a
2	mena=m=a	mena-ʔ=ben=a	mena-ʔ=pe=a
3 ANIMATE	mena=e=a	mena-ʔ=kin=a	mena-ʔ=ko=a
3 INANIMATE	mena-ʔ=a		

An especially interesting convergence is found in the copular paradigms, which often contain a /k/~/ʔ/ which is homophonous with the genitive. Table 20.4 presents by way of example the paradigm of the non-negated existential/locative copula in Santali, whose stem *mena* is homophonous with the lexeme denoting 'remain'. Boxes containing forms with [ʔ] are shaded. Similar forms are found in Mundari and Ho, where however the glottal stop has spread to *all* persons, including the first and second persons, singular, so that /ʔ/ is now part of the stem of the copula in these two languages (Deeney 1975: 47–48; Osada 1992: 118).

In Peterson (2010) it is suggested that /ʔ/ in all three languages has spread throughout the respective paradigm via analogical levelling from the third person singular inanimate to these other positions, whereas in Santali the first, second and the third person singular animate have resisted this change, perhaps due to a higher frequency of these three forms. We assume that this /ʔ/ derives from the genitive and that its original function was to mark the third person singular, probably as a nominalizer.[17] This can be explained as follows.

Simplifying somewhat, in Santali, as in North Munda in general, the enclitic subject of a transitive predicate (A) attaches either to the last element preceding the predicate or, if the predicate is the only word in the clause, to the predicate itself, and the marking of the object (P) is marked predicate-internally, before the indicative marking, which precedes the marking for A, as in (16):

(16)   Santali
        dal=iɲ=a=e
        beat=1SG.OBJ=IND=3SG.SUBJ
        'he will hit me'

The subject of an intransitive predicate (S) is normally marked similarly to that of A, as in (17):

---

[17] Note that =*ak'* [aʔ] also functions as a nominalizer in Santali, e.g. *rɔhɔr-en=ak'* [dry-PST:MID−NML:INAN] 'what has become dry' (adapted from Neukom 2001: 58), from which the other functions such as person and focus marking undoubtedly originated. These will be dealt with in detail in a future study.

(17)   Santali

       hij-oʔ=a=e

       come-MID=IND=3SG.SUBJ

       'he will come'

However, there are a small number of intransitive predicates (the 'unaccusatives') which mark S at the 'object' position.

(18)   Santali

       rɛŋɛc=iɲ=a

       hungry=1SG.OBJ=IND

       'I'm hungry'

In light of this, I argue in Peterson (2010: 76–78) that the paradigm for Santali *mena* 'exist; COP; remain' was originally that of the class illustrated in (18). Recall from the discussion in the preceding pages that the genitive often marks the third person on verb forms in the languages of the area, so that we would expect it to appear at the object position if used with predicates which have the same marking pattern as *rɛŋɛc* in (18). This would result in the form *mena=ʔ=a* [remain=3SG.OBJ=IND], which is indeed the form we find in the third person singular inanimate in Table 20.4.

This analysis is supported by the suppletive negative paradigm of this copula, shown in Table 20.5. Here the stem *bən-* is followed by the marker of the middle voice *-uʔ/-ug*, but crucially the third person singular animate is marked by the nominalizer *=icʔ*, used exclusively for animate beings, instead of the usual animate marker of the third person singular, *-e* (Neukom 2001: 170, note 72). Note that here as well, subject marking is found in the 'object' position.

This strongly suggests that /ʔ/ in the non-negative paradigm derives from the genitive/nominalizer, originally to mark the third person singular inanimate, which then spread via analogical levelling to other forms – to all forms except the first, second and third, animate, singular in Santali, and to all forms in Mundari and Ho, so that it now forms part of the stem in these two languages.

This marking pattern has spread to a number of IA languages of the area, for example Sadri. Consider the four suppletive present-tense copulas in Sadri given in Tables 20.6 and 20.7. Boxes containing a form with /k/ are shaded.

Table 20.5 *The Santali existential/locative copula (negated) (adapted from Neukom 2001: 170)*

	Singular	Dual	Plural
1 INCL	*bən-ug=iɲ=a*	*bən-uʔ=laŋ=a*	*bən-uʔ=bon=a*
1 EXCL		*bən-uʔ=liɲ=a*	*bən-uʔ=le=a*
2	*bən-uʔ=me=a*	*bən-uʔ=ben=a*	*bən-uʔ=pe=a*
3 ANIMATE	*bən-ug=icʔ=a*	*bən-uʔ=kin=a*	*bən-uʔ=ko=a*
3 INANIMATE	*bən-uʔ=a*		

Table 20.6 *The identificational copula in Sadri*

Person	Affirmative		Negative	
	Singular	Plural	Singular	Plural
1	*he⟨k⟩ō*	*he⟨k⟩i*	*nʌlagō*	*nʌlagi*
2	*he⟨k⟩is*	*he⟨k⟩a*	*nʌlagis*	*nʌlaga*
3	*he⟨k⟩e*	*he⟨k⟩ʌẽ*	*nʌlage*	*nʌlagʌẽ*

Table 20.7 *The existential/locative copula in Sadri*

Person	Affirmative		Negative	
	Singular	Plural	Singular	Plural
1	*Ahō*	*ahi*	*nʌ⟨k⟩hō*	*nʌ⟨k⟩hi*
2	*Ahis*	*aha*	*nʌ⟨k⟩his*	*nʌ⟨k⟩ha*
3	*Ahe*	*ahʌẽ*	*nʌ⟨k⟩he*	*nʌ⟨k⟩hʌẽ*

The copular forms with the internal /k/ have long puzzled researchers, but in light of the patterns found in North Munda, it is argued in Peterson (2010: 80–81) that the /k/ in these forms, which fulfils no grammatical function, is motivated by the North Munda paradigms and derives from multilingual speakers of Sadri and North Munda. As there is no 'object position' in the Sadri verb which this /k/ could occupy, unlike North Munda, this is the most likely explanation. Finally, one form of the Sadri copula, *heke*, has been borrowed into Kharia, where it is entirely productive, so that a form with an internal /k/ has now found its way from North Munda via IA into South Munda.

This /k/ is also very common in copular forms of other IA languages of the area. For example, Tiwari (1960: 178) lists the forms *ho-*/*hokh-* (affirmative) and *naikhe* (negative) for Standard Bhojpuri. However, as Shukla (1981), describing northern varieties of Bhojpuri, cites no forms of the copula with an internal /k/, these forms appear to be restricted to southern Bhojpuri varieties. Chatterji (1926: 683, §431) also includes a number of relevant forms such as Bengali (in modern transliteration) *hoibe-k* 'it will be', *nahi-k* 'is not', and *thak-*, the latter, like the Santali form *mena*, also meaning 'remain, stay', but also Early Assamese *nahi-k-ɔntɔ* 'they are not', Magahi √*hī-k*, and Maithili *chi-k*[18] and √*thik*. In another section, he also mentions √*ha* / √*ha-k* 'to be' for Magahi, among others (Chatterji 1926: 991, §722).

---

[18] The accuracy of this form was questioned by Ramawatar Yadav (personal communication), a native speaker who is also a scholar of Old Maithili. Further research is required.

20.4   Summary and Outlook

The IA–Munda contact area provides evidence for a number of convergences between the languages of these two families, although due to the lack of historical data on most languages of the region it is often unclear which phenomena have originated in which family and how they have spread to other languages. Some of these traits are typical of most of South Asia, others are typical of larger areas of eastern South Asia, while still others appear to be restricted to eastern-central South Asia, our area of study.

In addition to massive lexical borrowings from IA into Munda, numerous convergences in the morphosyntax were also found, of which many are restricted to this region. These are summarized in Map 20.3.[19]

The map does not include all of the phenomena discussed in Section 20.3. For example, the use of the genitive to mark focus is not

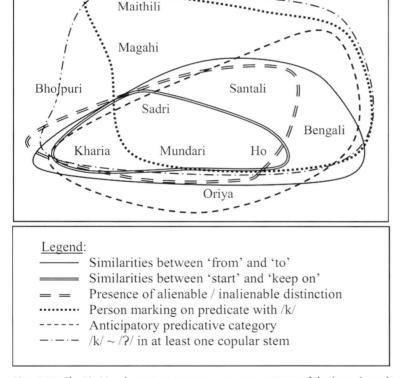

Map 20.3 The IA–Munda contact area: convergence patterns of the investigated traits

---

[19] Ho has been included in the group of languages possessing similarities between 'from' and 'to' due its otherwise close similarities to Mundari and Santali, although I have not been able to confirm this. Also, Bhojpuri is only half-included among the languages with a /k/~/ʔ/ in at least one copular form, as this trait is limited to the southern varieties of this language.

indicated in Map 20.3, as we only have positive data for Sadri and Kharia but no unambiguous data for other languages of the region. Similarly, for lack of data, Map 20.3 does not contain information on the presence of the dual, which is found throughout Munda but for which we only have very preliminary data on the informal varieties of the IA languages of the region. This is important, since the dual is not found in the standard varieties of these languages, so that data from other registers are required to ascertain to what extent it has spread in this group.

Despite these problems, the data discussed in the previous pages show that it is not possible to demarcate a well-defined 'linguistic area' or 'sprachbund' for this region, as no two 'isoforms' are identical. Not surprisingly, Sadri, the lingua franca for much of this region, clearly possesses all of the traits discussed here, but the distribution of these traits in the other languages of the region can vary considerably. Furthermore, we saw evidence that other languages further afield once shared some of the traits investigated here but have since lost them: for example, person marking deriving from the genitive has disappeared entirely from Oriya and seems to be gradually disappearing from North Munda and Maithili as well.

The various phenomena are also not uniform in the languages in which they are found. For example, it was mentioned above (see Section 20.3.1) that virtually all languages of the region possess numeral classifiers, although their distribution can differ considerably in the individual languages. Similar comments hold for the other phenomena discussed in the preceding pages as well. In other words, although the languages of our region often possess similar grammatical categories, these categories are just that – similar – and no two languages possess exactly the same category with exactly the same distribution. Nevertheless, the fact that similar categories are found in so many languages makes it clear that speakers of these languages have long been in close contact, even if there is no one-to-one correspondence between the languages.

Thus, instead of a monolithic, uniform sprachbund, the traits discussed here combine to define a rather diffuse and constantly changing area of language convergence in eastern-central India and Nepal, which itself is part of an even more diffuse South Asian convergence area; that is, the notion of South Asia as a homogeneous linguistic area or sprachbund is far too simplistic and is not supported by the data. Instead, we find a number of convergence areas which partially overlap, so that one area gradually fades into those around it. In our case, it would seem most promising at present to turn our search for further convergences to the north, to the Kiranti (Tibeto-Burman) languages of eastern Nepal. Ebert (1999) notes a number of interesting convergences between these languages and North Munda which require further study, above all with respect to subordination, although she notes the presence of the 'pleonastic k', discussed above in Section 20.3.2.7, in Kiranti as well (Ebert 1999: 397, note 19).

There is still much work to be done on the linguistic convergences of this region, and as our knowledge of these languages increases, it is almost certain that some of the phenomena discussed in the preceding pages will eventually have to be removed from the list of convergences but also that others will have be added. To cite just one example, there is a type of reduplication in Kharia in which one or more of the vowels of the stem is replaced by /i/ in the reduplicated form, e.g. *gupa* 'tend (cattle)' versus *gupa gupi* 'finish tending' or *kayom* 'talk' versus *kayom kiyim* 'talk something out' (Peterson 2011: 131). Similar forms are found in Bengali (Thompson 2012: 214), Oriya (Neukom and Patnaik 2003: 132–133) and Sadri (my own data), but to what extent this reduplication is typical of the rest of this area, and to what extent its semantics are similar in the different languages, awaits further study. In the light of evidence such as this, it is highly likely that the number of convergences for this area will increase as research on these languages progresses.

Abbreviations

1, 2, 3	person	L1	first/native language
ABL	ablative	L2	second language
ACT	active	LNK	linker
ADD	additive focus	MID	middle voice
ANTIC	anticipatory	NEG	negation
AUX	auxiliary	NMLZR	nominalizer
CLASS	classifier	NSG	non-singular
CMPL	complementizer	OBJ	object
COP	copula	OBL	oblique case
DU	dual	PASS	passive
EXT	extensional (case)	PERF	perfect
FOC	focus	PL	plural
FUT	future	POSS	possessive
GEN	genitive	PRS	present
IA	Indo-Aryan	PST	past
IMP	imperative	PTCP	participle
INCL	inclusive	SEQ	sequential converb
IND	indicative	SG	singular
INF	infinitive	SUBJ	subject
INGR	ingressive	TEL	telicizer
INST	instrumental	TR	transitive
IPFV	imperfective	VOC	vocative

References

Abbi, Anvita, 1997. Languages in contact in Jharkhand. In Anvita Abbi (ed.), *Languages of Tribal and Indigenous Peoples of India: The Ethnic Space*, pp. 131–148. Delhi: Motilal Banarsidass.

Anderson, Gregory D. S., 2007. *The Munda Verb: Typological Perspectives*. Trends in Linguistics, Studies and Monographs, vol. 174. Berlin and New York: Mouton de Gruyter.

Anderson, Gregory D. S. (ed.), 2008. *The Munda Languages*. London and New York: Routledge.

Anderson, Gregory D. S. and K. David Harrison, 2008. Sora. In Anderson (ed.), pp. 299–380.

Bickel, Balthasar, Walter Bisang and Yogendra P. Yādava, 1999. Face vs. empathy: The social foundation of Maithili verb agreement. *Linguistics* 37 (3): 481–518.

Chatterji, Suniti Kumar, 1926. *The Origin and Development of the Bengali Language: With a Foreword by Sir George Abraham Grierson*. Third impression, 2002, New Delhi: Rupa.

Deeney, John J., S.J., 1975. *Ho Grammar and Vocabulary*. Chaibasa: Xavier Ho Publications, St. Xavier's High School.

Donegan, Patricia and David Stampe, 2004. Rhythm and the synthetic drift of Munda. In Rajendra Singh (ed.), *The Yearbook of South Asian Languages and Linguistics, 2004*, pp. 3–36. Berlin and New York: Mouton de Gruyter.

Ebert, Karen, 1999. Nonfinite verbs in Kiranti languages: An areal perspective. In Yogendra P. Yadava and Warren W. Glover (eds), *Topics in Nepalese Linguistics*, pp. 371–400. Kathmandu: Royal Nepal Academy.

Ebert, Karen, 2001. Südasien als Sprachbund. In Martin Haspelmath, Ekkhard König, Wulf Oesterreicher and Wolfgang Raible (eds), *Sprachtypologie und sprachliche Universalien: Ein internationales Handbuch*. Handbücher zur Sprach- und Kommunikationswissenschaft, vol. 20.2.

Emeneau, Murray B., 1956. India as a linguistic area. *Language* 32: 3–16.

Genetti, Carol, 1999. Variation in agreement in the Nepali finite verb. In Yogendra P. Yadava and Warren W. Glover (eds), *Topics in Nepalese Linguistics*, pp. 542–555. Kathmandu: Royal Nepal Academy.

Ghosh, Arun, 2008. Santali. In Anderson (ed.), pp. 11–98.

Grierson, Sir George Abraham, 1903. *Linguistic Survey of India*, vol. V: *Indo-Aryan Family, Eastern Group*, part II: *Specimens of the Bihari and Oriya Languages*. Calcutta.

Grignard, A., 1924. *A Grammar of the Oraon Language and Study in Oraon Idiom*. Calcutta: Catholic Orphan Press.

Hoffmann, Revd Johann, S.J., 1905/1909. *Mundari Grammar and Exercises*, parts I and II. Reprint 2001, New Delhi: Gyan Publishing House.

Jordan-Horstmann, Monika, 1969. *Sadani: A Bhojpuri Dialect Spoken in Chotanagpur*. Indologia Berolinensis, vol. 1. Wiesbaden: Harrassowitz.

Kullū, Paulus, 1992. *Tonme kol-āṅgre [The New Testament]*. Ranchi: Catholic Press.

Lewis, M. Paul, Gary F. Simons and Charles D. Fennig (eds), 2013. *Ethnologue: Languages of the World*, seventeenth edition. Dallas, TX: SIL International. www.ethnologue.com

Masica, Colin P., 1976. *Defining a Linguistic Area: South Asia*. Chicago and London: University of Chicago Press.

Neukom, Lukas, 2001. *Santali*. Languages of the World/Materials, vol. 323. Munich: LINCOM Europa.

Neukom, Lukas and Manideepa Patnaik, 2003. *A Grammar of Oriya*. Zürich: Universität Zürich.

Nowrangi, Peter Shanti, 1956. *A Simple Sadāni Grammar*. Ranchi: D.S.S. Book Depot.

Osada, Toshiki, 1991. Linguistic convergence in the Chotanagpur area. In S. Bosu Mullick (ed.), *Cultural Chotanagpur: Unity in Diversity*, pp. 99–119. New Delhi: Uppal Publishing House.

Osada, Toshiki, 1992. *A Reference Grammar of Mundari*. Tokyo: Tokyo University of Foreign Studies.

Osada, Toshiki, 2008. Mundari. In Anderson (ed.), pp. 99–164.

Patnaik, Manideepa, 2008. Juang. In Anderson (ed.), pp. 508–556.

Peterson, John, 2010. Language contact in Jharkhand: Linguistic convergence between Munda and Indo-Aryan in eastern-central India. *Himalayan Linguistics* 9 (2): 56–86. escholarship.org/uc/item/489929c1

Peterson, John, 2011. *A Grammar of Kharia: A South Munda Language*. Brill Studies in South and Southwestern Asian Languages, vol. 1. Leiden and Boston: Brill.

Pinnow, Heinz-Jürgen, 1966. A comparative study of the verb in the Munda languages. In Norman H. Zide (ed.), *Studies in Comparative Austroasiatic Linguistics*. Indo-Iranian Monographs, vol. V. London, The Hague and Paris: Mouton and Co.

Radice, William, 1994. *Bengali: A Complete Course for Beginners*. Teach Yourself series. London: Hodder, and Chicago: NTC.

Shukla, Shaligram, 1981. *Bhojpuri Grammar*. Washington, DC: Georgetown University Press.

Thompson, Hanne-Ruth, 2012. *Bengali*. London Oriental and African Language Library, vol. 18. Amsterdam and Philadelphia: John Benjamins.

Tiwari, Udai Narain, 1960. *The Origin and Development of Bhojpuri*. The Asiatic Society, Monograph Series, vol. X. Calcutta: The Asiatic Society.

Verma, Manindra K., 1991. Exploring the parameters of agreement. *Language Sciences* 13 (2): 125–143.

Yadav, Ramawatar, 1996. *A Reference Grammar of Maithili*. Trends in Linguistics, Documentation, vol. 11. Berlin and New York: Mouton de Gruyter.

21

Sri Lanka and South India

Umberto Ansaldo

21.1 Background

The Indian subcontinent, including Sri Lanka, shows traces of three different populations: Austroasiatic, Dravidian and Indo-Aryan (Cavalli-Sforza et al. 1994). Austroasiatic is found today in the form of Munda languages, spoken in Central and Eastern India by several million speakers. Dravidian varieties today occupy the South of India as well as areas of Sri Lanka. Historically, however, Dravidian populations occupied the whole of the Indian subcontinent; it is likely that they arrived after Austroasiatic and before Indo-Aryan populations (Cavalli-Sforza et al. 1994). Linguistic analysis also seems to suggest that Dravidian populations occupied the area before Indo-Aryan people. Substantial presence of features of the Dravidian type can be found in Old Indo-Aryan, a fact that has prompted scholars to suggest that a language shift took place for speakers of Dravidian languages towards Indo-Aryan varieties (Erdosy 1995; Thomason and Kaufman 1988). This could be explained as a shift prompted by cultural assimilation with a more prestigious neighbour, or it could indicate that differential waves of migration took place. We return to this in Section 21.2.

Indo-Aryan languages are not predominant in South India but they constitute the dominant variety of Sri Lanka in the form of Sinhala. Similarly to South India, Sri Lanka shows traces of three different populations. Besides the Indo-Aryan we find Vedda, aboriginal populations of unclear genetic origins by now extinct, and Dravidian, in the form of Lankan Tamil.

Genetically, one cannot distinguish Dravidians from Indo-Aryans, which points to a deep and prolonged admixture between the two populations. According to Reich et al. (2009), the admixture of northern and southern

I would like to thank Kofi Yapko for valuable comments on this chapter.

Indian genetic traits could go back as far as 3,500 years. Lankan people are likewise extremely mixed. A study by Kshatria (1995) shows that present-day Sinhalese and Tamils of Sri Lanka are closer to Indian Tamils and South Indian Muslims than they are to Gujaratis and Punjabis of northwest India, Bengalis of northeast India, and Veddas. A genetic tree of 28 South Asian populations published by Cavalli-Sforza et al. (1994: 239) groups South Dravidian, Sinhala and Lambada within the same subgroup, testifying to the close relationship between these otherwise unrelated languages.

21.2   The Influence of Dravidian

It is well known that Emeneau defined a linguistic area as one which includes languages of different families with shared traits that set them apart from other members of those same families. He identified India as such an area, a place where Indo-Aryan and Dravidian resemble each other more than Indo-Aryan resembles other Indo-European languages (Emeneau 1956). Emeneau compiled a rich inventory of features that display 'Indianization', i.e. traits that are definitely not Proto-Indo-European but are mostly Dravidian in origin. These include the following.

– *Phonology*. Retroflex and coronal consonants in contrast with a dental series. The earliest Sanskrit records already display phonemes of this class, which are definitely not Proto-Indo-European and generally not found in other Indo-European languages. In Dravidian, retroflex consonants, which contrast with dentals, are Proto-Dravidian in origin. This led Emeneau to conclude that pre-Indo-Aryan and pre-Dravidian bilingualism might have provided the conditions under which pre-Indo-Aryan allophones became redistributed as retroflex phonemes.
– *Grammar* (based on earlier work by Bloch). (a) Loss of dual: starting from Sanskrit, then parallelled by the rest of the Indo-European domain. (b) Loss of infixation. (c) Disuse of verbal prefixes, starting in Modern Indo-Aryan and 'tied up with the general shift of accent to initial syllables'. (d) Absence of prepositions. (e) Two themes of personal pronouns, i.e. double stems in personal pronouns in Indo-European languages and the same phenomenon found in some Dravidian languages. (f) Constructions in which verb stems or non-finite verb forms are strung together in series which are closed by a finite verb form (or other predicate ending). This is a prominent feature in Dravidian and Munda languages, but a feature that makes Sanskrit stand out from other Indo-European languages. (g) Past participle constructions based on a nominalized form of a verb (or rather of a predication ending in a verb) followed by a postposition. These are common in Dravidian languages, Buddhist Hybrid Sanskrit, Pali and Asian languages outside India, but

not available in Munda languages: e.g. [Marathi] *tujhī āī vārlyā-pāsūn* [your mother died-since] for 'since your mother died, since the death of your mother'. (h) Echo-word construction, in which a basic word formulated as CVX is followed by an echo-word in which CV is replaced by a morpheme *gi-* or *u-* or the like (or C is replaced by *m-* or the like), and X echoes the X (or VX echoes the VX) of the basic word. The meaning of the echo-word is 'and the like'. (i) Classifiers or quantifiers, a shared feature among all the three families, which spread from Indo-Aryan but which are not an Indo-European phenomenon.

It is clear that Dravidian influence in Indo-Aryan is much stronger than Indo-Aryan influence in Dravidian (Sjoberg 1992). While Dravidian, especially South Dravidian, borrowed heavily in terms of lexicon, it shows little structural influence from Indo-Aryan. On the other hand Dravidian has had a deep structural impact on Indo-Aryan (Krishnamurti 1969). An explanation of this situation was first put forward by Krishnamurti (1969), who suggests that large numbers of Dravidians were responsible for a deep restructuring of Sanskrit – their 'lingua franca' – and ended up developing middle Indic. This would suggest that at some point a majority of Indo-Aryan speakers would have been of Dravidian origin. Acquiring varieties of Sanskrit as L2 led to the incorporation of substrate features, thus resulting in substantial language change. This analysis is corroborated by Emeneau's observation that Sanskrit really shows a Dravidian substratum. If this is correct, the evolution of North Indian vernaculars is actually through contact-induced change rather than internal processes of grammaticalization.

The Dravidian family today extends predominantly to the states of Karnataka, Tamil Nadu and Kerala (South Dravidian), Andhra Pradesh and the southern regions of Madhya Pradesh and Orissa (South-Central Dravidian) in the south. We also find pockets of Dravidian in Bihar and Nepal (Central Dravidian) and in Pakistan (North Dravidian).

21.3 Sri Lanka

Within the large linguistic area of India, Gair (1994) proposes a further, southern subarea, the South-South Asia (SSA) area. This area includes the southern states of India characterized by Dravidian varieties as well as Sri Lanka. The latter houses a number of interesting languages. Besides Lankan Tamil (South Dravidian) and the Indo-Aryan languages Sinhala and Maldivian (Dhivehi), we find Sri Lanka Malay (SLM) and Sri Lanka Portuguese (SLP), both contact languages developed during Portuguese, Dutch and British colonial rule.

Sinhala is somewhat unique among the Indo-Aryan languages as it detached itself before a number of major changes affecting its related varieties in the north (Gair 1998). It is reasonable to believe that it reached its current location around the sixth century BCE. A number of factors contribute to its uniqueness. First of all, Sinhala still retains a strong Indo-Aryan feel, despite having undergone multiple contacts (Gair 1998). Second, it shows influence of indigenous Vedda languages in the lexicon. Though still predominantly Indo-Aryan, the lexicon also shows strong Dravidian influences even in very basic terms and in the kinship system (Gair 1998). Sinhala–Tamil compounds are found, as are independent innovations in grammar not found in other neighbouring languages. In the gender system, for example, Sinhala has lost the neuter, present in both Indo-Aryan and Dravidian. Instead it has developed a system that distinguishes between animate and inanimate, a distinction also found in SLM (see below). Within animate Sinhala distinguishes between human and animal, and within these two a further distinction between general and feminine is made (Gair 1998: 9).

SLM and SLP are of great historical interest as they are contact languages that developed through the same processes that typically characterize linguistic areas. The original speakers of SLP were either Portuguese or Portuguese slaves from African colonies, as testified for example by the Kaffir population still found in parts of Sri Lanka, who are descendants of African slaves who arrived during the Portuguese colonial rule of Sri Lanka. When the Dutch took over Sri Lanka from the Portuguese, these groups started becoming more marginal. The ancestors of SLM, who were Indonesians and Malays deported from the Dutch colonies of Indonesia, grew in number as Dutch power increased. Today there are only a few pockets of SLP left, notably on the east coast around Batticaloa, in Puttalam (the 'Kaffirs') and in the northern area of Trincomalee. SLP is severely endangered. More vital is the situation of SLM communities, both in numbers and in linguistic vitality. Major communities are found in the capital Colombo, Kandy (Central Province) and Kirinda (Southern Province).

In both cases these contact languages have evolved away from their original structural type, to display strong typological affinities of SSA type. They are verb-final, morphologically agglutinative/fusional, phonologically 'Indian' and only retain traces of their European/Malay heritage in the lexicon. The list below, selected from Gair (2013) as the more convincing cases of areal features, shows common traits between Dravidian, Sinhala and SLM.[1]

(a) Post-verbal sentence-final question marker when ummarked, question-internal when focused. This feature is found in Sinhala, SLM as well as some Dravidian languages, though not in Tamil (Gair 2013: 171). In Sinhala, for example, (1) is neutral while (2) would be more focused.

---

[1] Scarcity of recent material on SLP only allows us a partial inclusion of SLP in the discussion that follows.

(1) *ee minihaa iiye gunapaala-ṭa salli dunnaa=da?* (Sinhala)
   That man yesterday G-DAT money gave=INTERR

(2) *ee minihaa=da iiye gunapaala-ta salli dunn-e?*   (Sinhala)
   That man+INTERR yesterday G-DAT money gave-FOC
   'Was it that man that gave Gunapala money yesterday?'

(b) Subordinate clause marking in the form of final verbal affixes or conjunctive forms (Gair 2013: 172). This is an areal feature of South Asia as a whole but it is distinct in SSA in that rather than placing the marker at the left margin, it displays it on the right one. In addition in SSA these markers tend to be multifunctional.

(3) *siri koeoema kaalaa gedara giyaa*   (Sinhala)
   S food eat-CP home went
   'Siri ate and went home'

(c) Preposed relative clauses occur in Sinhala, Tamil and SLM as the main form.

(d) Sentence-final quotative markers 'say' are used in all SSA varieties to mark indirect speech.

(e) Nominalization without genitivization via verbal affixes is found in all varieties, e.g. Sinhala (Gair 2013: 178):

(4) *Silva mahattaya ma-ta eeka kiww-a-eka oetta*   (Sinhala)
   Silva gentleman I-DAT that say\PAST-ADJ-EKA truth
   'It is true that Mister Silva said that to me'

Here the subject is in the nominative in an independent sentence. The only difference is in the relativizing verbal affix and the pronoun *eka*.

(f) A variety of complex negative forms including verbal, equational, existential and subordinate negative verbs are found in Sinhala, Tamil and SLM.

(g) Sentence-final hearsay particles function as evidential clitics.

In addition to these, it has also been noted that the nature of the case system shows metatypic effects that render Sinhala, SL Tamil, SLM and SLP comparable (Ansaldo 2009, 2011; Bakker and Mous 1994). Most striking is the fact that all varieties make use of 'dative subjects', i.e. they use dative marking for agents who are perceived as not being particularly in control of an action. As Table 21.1 illustrates, the dative case is used to mark experiential roles as well as goal, beneficiary and possessive in SLM, SL Tamil and Sinhala.

It is interesting to note that typological convergence deeply affects even recent contact languages, as summarized in Table 21.2 (based on Bakker 2006: 141–144). Most striking is the fact that both SLM and SLP have

Table 21.1 *Case in Sri Lanka Malay, Sinhala and Lankan Tamil*[2]

Case	Function SLM	Sinhala	Tamil
Dative	experiential, goal, beneficiary, possessive	experiential, goal, beneficiary, possessive	experiential, goal, beneficiary, possessive
Nominative	agent	agent	agent
Accusative	patient	patient	patient
Genitive	possession	temporary possession, locative	temporary possession, locative
Instrumental	instrumental, source	instrumental, source	source
Comitative	association	association	association

Table 21.2 *Lankan features of recent contact languages in Sri Lanka*

	SLP	SLM	Lankan
Nominal case marking	mostly suffixes (as case markers and postpositions)	all suffixes (as cases and postpositions)	all suffixes (all as cases)
Discourse particles	often enclitics, sentence-final, or attached to the verb		
Verbal categories	suffixes only	pre-verbal, suffixes	pre-verbal

developed morphological complexity in the nominal and verbal domain, as well as shifted to a verb-final, right-headed typology.

21.4   Multilingualism and Language Contact

It is clear that prolonged contact between unrelated languages has promoted a number of significant common developments in the region. The scenario advocated for the emergence of a South Asian linguistic area, namely restructuring through second language acquisition, can also be applied to the South-South Asian area. In fact, we need to factor in more than one type of shift and assume different phases of shift to reconstruct what happened in India and Sri Lanka.

The earliest type of contact in Sri Lanka, not considering the aboriginal Vedda languages, was that which occurred between South Dravidian and Sinhala. It seems plausible to assume prolonged contact between these two populations as well as a high degree of bilingualism. This explains why Sinhala looks deeply South Dravidian for an Indo-Aryan language. There is corroboration in genetic findings. The study of genetic admixture in Sri

---

[2] Based on the variety of SLM spoken in Kirinda, in the south of Sri Lanka. For a more detailed account of case in the upcountry variety of SLM (Kandy), see Nordhoff (2009: 583).

Lankan populations reveals that the Sinhalese of Sri Lanka have a higher contribution from Tamils of southern India (69.86 per cent +/– 0.61) compared with the Bengalis of northeast India (25.41 per cent +/– 0.51), whereas the Tamils of Sri Lanka have received a higher contribution from the Sinhalese of Sri Lanka (55.20 per cent +/– 9.47) compared with the Tamils of India (16.63 per cent +/– 8.73) (Kshatriya 1995). The difference between Sri Lanka and India is that here we are most likely looking at a more balanced ratio of populations. While for India the suggestion is of an Indo-Aryan elite whose language was restructured by large Dravidian populations acquiring it as an L2, in Sri Lanka the Dravidian population would have been equal or even inferior in numbers to the Sinhalese.

Just as the Tamils of Sri Lanka are closer to the Sinhalese because they were always in close proximity to each other historically, linguistically and culturally, the Malay and Portuguese of Sri Lanka, despite being more recent arrivals, have undergone convergence to Lankan language and culture. In the last 400 years, speakers of European (Portuguese) and Austronesian (Malay) varieties came into contact with Lankan languages. Here two processes of second language acquisition need to be invoked for the strong typological shift that these languages have undergone. As we saw, though lexically still related to its Malay lexifier, SLM today is clearly a Lankan language in its OV constituent order, its noun phrase and large parts of the VP domain (see Ansaldo 2009). In SLP we also note basic OV structure, postpositions, sentence-final particles to mark quotatives, as well as clear Lankan influences in the case system (Smith 1979a, 1979b).

In his analysis of SLM as a product of metatypy (see Ross 2006), Ansaldo (2011) offers a scenario in which bilinguals lead the way in the restructuring process, modelling the vernacular grammar on L2 models. In many multilingual communities around the world, and especially where multilingualism is not institutionally supported through school, education, etc., multilingual individuals may experience shifts within their multilingual competence. As pointed out in Matras (2010: 66), bilingual individuals can be seen as possessing an enriched linguistic system which they are capable of appropriately adapting to the context in which they function. In this sense, language contact phenomena can be seen as function-driven interferences that speakers are subject to in goal-oriented communicative interaction. Convergence thus emerges as a process that 'offers speakers the opportunity to accommodate and generalize and yet still hold on to a mental demarcation between subsets of word forms within their repertoire' (Matras 2010: 76).

This often goes hand in hand with a process of attrition of the heritage language. Following Thomason and Kaufman (1988), a gradual abandonment of ancestral languages (AL) happens in the transition from monolingualism in AL to multilingualism in L2/L3. This can occur typically in

(a) minority groups, (b) colonization scenarios, and (c) nation-expansion processes. In this transition process L2/3-dominant individuals lead the change through intense code-mixing, and structural and lexical transfer. As noted in Haugen (1971: 37), the speaker 'dismantles and reorders the language he already knows'. One common motivation is the AL speakers' increasing accommodation to L2/3 under strong social and structural pressure through increased multilingual competence (Ansaldo and Lim 2006; Ansaldo and Matthews 2007). In rare contexts where the AL is vital, a partial maintenance is indeed possible (e.g. Anglo-Romani: Thomason and Kaufman 1988), typically in cases where the change is gradual.

The type of contact-induced change that we see in this region leads to the emergence of complex structures rather than simplification. While this may be related to a substantial role of young learners in the restructuring, it is impossible not to note the role of the typological ecology in which this contact takes place. In typical creole scenarios we often note simplification effects, as exemplified by the fact that the inflectional morphology of the lexifier is typically absent in the restructured vernacular, the creole. This, according to Trudgill (2011), can be explained by the fact that adults were mostly responsible for the restructuring, and adults are allegedly prone to simplification. On the other hand, had children been more involved, complexification might have taken place. Following this line, we might be led to suggest that the varieties discussed in this chapter would have been more influenced by young bilingual/multilingual acquisition than adult acquisition, hence the morphological complexification observed.

I think there is a problem here. As has been noted more than once, it is difficult to imagine a scenario where only children, or only adults, affect the process of language change in a population. While adults and children can be separated in the artificial confines of a linguistic study and we can speak of adult versus child acquisition, in the real world this separation is impossible. I take it that both adults and children must have been communicating with each other while the restructuring was taking place. I therefore find it extremely difficult to imagine that, 'naturally', adults would be gifted with simplification tendencies while children would be gifted with the opposite, complexification tendency. An alternative possibility emerges here to explain what we perceive as simplification and complexification processes.

21.5 The Power of Typology

By and large in the region under discussion we observe conflation of non-analytic languages. The type of morphological shift we observe in Indo-

India
          Majority populations: + INFL (rich morphology)
                                                                    → Outcome: + INFL
          Minority populations: – INFL (modest morphology)
Caribbean
          Majority populations: 0 INFL (close to zero morphology)
                                                                    → Outcome: 0 INFL
          Minority populations: – INFL

Figure 21.1 Typological ecology and contact output

Aryan and Dravidian languages is from agglutinative to inflectional. This is a robust feature of the ecology in which language change takes place. When foreign linguistic constructs enter the picture, they are drawn towards this type of morphology. Malay, basically analytic, becomes morphologically more complex and turns into Sri Lanka Malay, an agglutinative language with incipient fusional tendencies (Ansaldo and Nordhoff 2008). The same happens in the case of SLP where, most likely, a somewhat creolized Atlantic Portuguese acquires elaborate morphology. This clearly shows the role that typology plays in contact-induced change. In a different part of the world, the Atlantic, a different ecology is in place. Here large numbers of speakers of strongly isolating languages had to absorb Standard Average European (van der Auwera 2011; Haspelmath 1998, 2001) with mildly fusional features. And this they did, by conforming them to their own, robust isolating types. Thus were born the Atlantic creoles. Figure 21.1 is an attempt to visualize these two ecologies (albeit with an unavoidable degree of simplification).

We can see what is happening in both cases: the dominant typological profile wins. It is a matter of type and token frequency, as already argued in Ansaldo (2009), that guides the restructuring. There is no doubt about this in the case of the SSA described above. On the other hand, while Atlantic creoles can be seen as sociohistorical continuations of their lexifiers, recent typological work (e.g. Lefebvre 2011) has shown that creole varieties can be structurally aligned with their substrate languages. In other words, we do not need to invoke the classical tenets of creole exceptionalism for the emergence of Atlantic creoles, just as we do not need to invoke other exceptional explanations for how India is a concentric series of linguistic areas (see Peterson, Chapter 20, this volume). Nor do we need to pitch adults versus children in terms of agency on the restructuring process, which does not make much sense in a naturalistic transmission scenario anyway. It is the interaction of typology and the acquisition of L2 in a rich multilingual environment, in which speakers restructure the new grammar based on their own fundamental competence, which is central. Where morphology is abundant morphology remains, where morphology is scarce morphology recedes.

References

Ansaldo, Umberto, 2009. *Contact Languages: Ecology and evolution in Asia*. Cambridge: Cambridge University Press.

Ansaldo, Umberto, 2011. Metatypy in Sri Lanka Malay. *Annual Review of South Asian Languages and Linguistics* 2011: 3–16.

Ansaldo, Umberto and Lisa Lim, 2006. Globalisation, empowerment and the periphery: The Malays of Sri Lanka. In R. Elangaiyan, R. McKenna Brown, N. D. M. Ostler and M. K. Verma (eds), *Vital Voices: Endangered Languages and Multilingualism*, pp. 39–46. Proceedings of the FEL X Conference. Bath: Foundation for Endangered Languages; Mysore: Central Institute of Indian Languages.

Ansaldo, Umberto and Stephen Matthews, 2007. Deconstructing creole: The rationale. In Umberto Ansaldo, Stephen Matthews and Lisa Lim (eds), *Deconstructing Creole*. Amsterdam: John Benjamins.

Ansaldo, Umberto and Sebastian Nordhoff, 2008. Complexity and the age of languages. In Enoch O. Aboh and Norval S. Smith (eds), *Complex Processes in New Languages*, pp. 345–363. Amsterdam and Philadelphia: John Benjamins.

van der Auwera, Johan, 2011. Standard Average European. In Bernd Kortmann and Johan van der Auwera (eds), *The Languages and Linguistics of Europe: A Comprehensive Guide*, pp. 291–306. Berlin: de Gruyter Mouton.

Bakker, Peter, 2006. The Sri Lanka Sprachbund: The newcomers Portuguese and Malay. In Yaron Matras, April McMahon and Nigel Vincent (eds), *Linguistic Areas: Convergence in Historical and Typological Perspective*, pp. 135–159. Houndmills, Basingstoke, UK and New York: Palgrave Macmillan.

Bakker, Peter and Maarten Mous, 1994. *Mixed Languages: 15 Case Studies in Language Intertwining*. Amsterdam: IFOTT.

Cavalli-Sforza, Luigi L., 2000. *Genes, Peoples, and Languages*. New York: North Point Press.

Cavalli-Sforza, Luigi L., Paolo Menozzi and Alberto Piazza, 1994. *The History and Geography of Human Genes*. Princeton: Princeton University Press.

Emeneau, Murray B., 1956. India as a linguistic area. *Language* 32 (1): 3–16.

Erdosy, George, 1995. *The Indo-Aryans of Ancient South Asia: Language, Material Culture and Ethnicity*. Berlin: de Gruyter.

Gair, James W., 1994. Universals and the South-South Asian language area. Keynote Address, 1994 SALA meeting, Philadelphia.

Gair, James W., 1998. *Studies in South Asian Linguistics: Sinhala and Other Languages*. New York: Oxford University Press.

Gair, James W., 2013. Sri Lankan languages in the South-South Asia linguistic area: Sinhala and Sri Lanka Malay. In Sebastian Nordhoff (ed.), *The Genesis of Sri Lanka Malay*, pp. 165–194. Leiden: Brill.

Haspelmath, M., 1998. How young is Standard Average European? *Language Sciences* 20: 271–287.

Haspelmath, Martin, 2001. The European Linguistic Area: Standard Average European. In Martin Haspelmath (ed.), *Language Typology and Language Universals*, vol. 2, pp. 1492–1551. Berlin: Mouton de Gruyter.

Haugen, Einar, 1971. The ecology of language. *Linguistic Reporter* 13 (1): 19–26.

Krishnamurti, B., 1969. *Comparative Dravidian Linguistics*, pp. 309–330. Current Trends in Linguistics, vol. 5. The Hague: Mouton.

Krishnamurti, B., 2003. *The Dravidian Languages*. Cambridge: Cambridge University Press.

Kshatriya, Gautam K., 1995. Genetic affinities of Sri Lankan populations. *Human Biology* 67 (6): 843–866.

Lefebvre, Claire (ed.), 2011. *Creoles, their Substrates and Language Typology*. Amsterdam and Philadelphia: John Benjamins.

Matras, Yaron, 2010. Contact, convergence and typology. In Raymond Hickey (ed.), *Handbook of Language Contact*, pp. 66–85. Oxford: Blackwell.

Nordhoff, Sebastian, 2009. *A Grammar of Upcountry Sri Lanka Malay*. PhD thesis, University of Amsterdam.

Reich, David, Thangaraj Kumarasamy, Nick Patterson, Alkes L. Price and Lalji Singh, 2009. Reconstructing Indian population history. *Nature* 461 (7263): 489–494.

Ross, Malcolm D., 2006. Metatypy. In Keith Brown (ed.), *Encyclopedia of Language and Linguistics*. Oxford: Elsevier.

Sjoberg, Andree, 1992. *The Impact of Dravidian on Indo-Aryan: An Overview. Reconstructing Languages and Cultures*. Trends in Linguistics, Studies and Monographs, vol 58. Berlin: Mouton de Gruyter.

Smith, Ian R., 1979a. Convergence in South Asia: A creole example. *Lingua* 48: 193–222.

Smith, Ian R., 1979b. Substrata versus universals in the formation of Sri Lanka Portuguese. *Papers in Pidgin and Creole Linguistics* 2: 183–200.

Thomason, Sarah G. and Terrence Kaufman, 1988. *Language Contact, Creolization, and Genetic Linguistics*. Berkeley, CA: University of California Press.

Trudgill, Peter, 2011. *Sociolinguistic Typology: Social Determinants of Linguistic Complexity*. Oxford: Oxford University Press.

22

The Transeurasian Languages

Martine Robbeets

22.1 Introduction

The present contribution is concerned with the areal concentration of a number of linguistic features in the Transeurasian languages and its historical motivation. The label 'Transeurasian' was coined by Johanson and Robbeets (2010: 1–2) with reference to a large group of geographically adjacent languages, traditionally known as 'Altaic', that share a significant number of linguistic properties and include up to five different linguistic families: Japonic, Koreanic, Tungusic, Mongolic and Turkic. The question whether all similarities between the Transeurasian languages should be accounted for by language contact or whether some are the residue of a common ancestor is one of the most debated issues of historical comparative linguistics (see Robbeets 2005 for an overview of the debate). Since the term 'linguistic area' implies that the shared properties are the result of borrowing, I will refrain from *a priori* attaching it to the Transeurasian region and rely on the concept of 'areality' instead, that is, the geographical concentration of linguistic features, independent of how these features developed historically. Only after evaluating 27 structural features shared across the Transeurasian languages will I consider how the insights from the data are relevant to historical statements about the way the languages may have come to share these features, considering diffusion, genealogical relationship or an interaction of both factors as possible explanations.

In spite of the strong polarization in the Transeurasian field between so-called 'retentionists', who view the similarities as arising from common descent, and 'diffusionists', who view them as arising from areal interaction, detailed characterizations of Transeurasian as a linguistic area are surprisingly rare in the linguistic literature. Poppe (1964) analysed Altaic as a 'language type' on the basis of a list of structural parallels shared between Korean, Tungusic, Mongolic and Turkic languages, and Rickmeyer (1989) elaborated on this research, adding data from Japanese. Even if these contributions provide an impressive list of shared features, they do not strictly identify Transeurasian as a language area because they do not (i) delimit the language type in relation to its neighbours, (ii) list deviations from the prototypical type in the peripheries, (iii) consider the extent to which the features in question are common or rare across the world as a whole, or (iv) attempt to distinguish contact-induced from genealogically motivated features.

In this chapter I attempt a partial answer to these concerns by providing a typological profile of selected Transeurasian languages, along with their oldest linguistically reliable historical varieties, and by comparing this profile with the behaviour of languages immediately outside the Transeurasian region. In order to examine external boundaries, I have included adjacent languages to the east (Ainu and Nivkh in the northeast and Rukai in the southeast), to the south (Mandarin Chinese) and to the north (Kolyma Yukaghir, Ket and Eastern Khanty).[1] These languages are taken as horizontal comparative points representative of surrounding areas such as the Siberian area (Nivkh, Kolyma Yukaghir, Ket, Eastern Khanty) or the Mainland Southeast Asia area (Mandarin) and neighbouring families such as Austronesian (Mantauran Rukai), Sino-Tibetan (Mandarin), Yukaghiric (Kolyma Yukaghir), Yeniseic (Ket), Uralic/Ob-Ugric (Eastern Khanty) or Ainuic (isolate Ainu). Although Eastern Khanty can be taken as a representative of the Uralic languages, the main boundary to the west, I have paid less attention to additional western boundaries, excluding sample languages from the Caucasus region or from the Indo-European languages because of the limited space available here.

The vertical comparison points in my analysis consist of a list of 27 features, denoted F1–F27, chosen to maximize positive (+) values for Transeurasian as opposed to neighbouring languages. Although all features reflect a certain internal coherence, about half of them (i.e. 13) display deviations from the prototypical type in the peripheries. Where possible, I add an estimation of the degree to which the feature under discussion is common or rare across the world's languages, relying on the counts in *The World Atlas of Language Structures* (Haspelmath et al. 2005) or on other typological research to be specified below.

Given the controversy between diffusionists and retentionists, we cannot simply amass a number of shared features among the Transeurasian languages and allow geographical adjacency to imply the probability of diffusion, without requiring any linguistic support for this. Therefore, historical evidence suggesting the diffusion or the retention of traits may be particularly telling in this particular case. For representatives of the contemporary varieties of the five families belonging to the Transeurasian continuum,

---

[1] The following sources were consulted for retrieving linguistic data underlying the feature values in neighbouring languages: Gruzdeva (1998) for Nivkh; Maslova (2003a) for Kolyma Yukaghir; Werner (1997), Vajda (2004) and Georg (2007) for Ket; Filchenko (2007) for Eastern Khanty; Li and Thompson (1989) for Mandarin; Zeitoun (2007) for Mantauran Rukai; Shibatani (1990) and Tamura (2000) for Ainu.

I have chosen Turkish (Turkic), Khalkha Mongolian (Mongolic), Evenki (Tungusic), Korean (Koreanic) and Japanese (Japonic) as horizontal comparison points.[2] However, in order to allow a diachronic perspective, their profile will be supplemented by values from the oldest linguistically reliable historical varieties of the individual families, namely Old Turkic (eighth to fourteenth centuries), Middle Mongolian (thirteenth to seventeenth centuries) and/or Written Mongolian, Manchu (seventeenth to nineteenth centuries), Middle Korean (fifteenth to sixteenth centuries) and Old Japanese (eighth century).[3] If a diachronic variety does not openly or productively reflect a certain feature but nevertheless preserves a trace of it, indicating that the value was positive in an earlier stage of the language, the historical variety will be marked with a plus. In this way, we can obtain a glimpse of the unrecorded typological past of the language in question.

The organization of this chapter is as follows. In Section 22.2 I will set up a typological profile of the Transeurasian languages in relation to that of the selected languages immediately outside the continuum. The linguistic levels discussed will include phonology, lexicon and semantics, morphology and syntax. I intend to treat grammaticalization patterns as a distinct level of analysis because, rather than representing a static feature value, they are concerned with a dynamic force, leading languages to change from a less to a more grammatical status. I will close Section 22.2 with a tabular overview, summarizing the presence of the 27 examined features in the selected languages by way of plus (+) and minus (−) values. In Section 22.3, I will consider how the insights from these data are relevant for general statements about areality, paying attention to the delimitation of areality, peripheral deviations from the prototype, changes in areality and the distinction between diffused and inherited features. In Section 22.4, I will conclude the chapter.

22.2   Typological Profile of the Transeurasian Languages

22.2.1   Phonology

F1 Predominantly polysyllabic root structure   The Transeurasian languages, together with their historical varieties, display a preponderance of polysyllabic roots, as do most languages in North Asia. Contemporary and Old Japanese possess a relatively great number of monosyllabic roots, many of which are attributed to root-internal consonant loss and subsequent

---

[2] The following sources were consulted for retrieving linguistic data underlying the feature values in contemporary Transeurasian languages: Göksel and Kerslake (2005) for Turkish; Janhunen (2012) for Khalkha Mongolian; Bulatova and Grenoble (1999) and Nedjalkov (1997) for Evenki; Martin (1992) and Sohn (1994) for Korean; Martin (1988) and Kaiser et al. (2001) for Japanese.

[3] The following sources were consulted for retrieving linguistic data underlying the feature values in historical Transeurasian languages: Erdal (2004) for Old Turkic; Street (1957), Weiers (1966) and Rybatzki (2003) for Middle Mongolian; Poppe (1954) for Written Mongolian; Gorelova (2002) for Manchu; Martin (1992) and Lee and Ramsey (2011) for Middle Korean; Vovin (2005, 2009) and Frellesvig (2010) for Old Japanese.

vowel contraction (Whitman 1990). These phonological reductions argue against Janhunen's (1997) suggestion that Japanese derives from an originally monosyllabic language. Austronesian languages such as Rukai are typically polysyllabic as well. Mandarin is the only language in the tables that is marked with a negative value. Similar to the languages of Mainland Southeast Asia it is predominantly monosyllabic, but, in comparison to Classical Chinese, it has developed a greater number of polysyllabic roots through compounding (Norman 1988: 86). As such, Japanese and Chinese occupy an intermediate position between the languages of North and Southeast Asia.

F2 Absence of complex tonal distinctions None of the Transeurasian languages is tonal in the sense that each syllable is characterized by a distinctive pitch pattern. This is also true for Austronesian languages, such as Rukai. With the exception of Ket, which has been attributed a tone system with five oppositions in recent descriptions by Vajda (2004) and Georg (2007), the neighbouring languages of North Asia are typically non-tonal as well. However, Nivkh, Japanese and some varieties of Korean have suprasegmental systems which can be seen as transitional between tonal and non-tonal languages. Nivkh makes distinctive use of two types of tones, whereas Middle Japanese and Middle Korean use a system of pitch-accent that differentiates words according to the position of one prominent syllable after which the pitch drops. This system survives in Contemporary Japanese, but it has been lost in Contemporary Standard Korean, where it developed into a vowel length distinction. The two-way tone distinction and the pitch-accent system are highly restricted in comparison to complex tonal systems such as in Ket and Mandarin, where each syllable is marked with one out of five distinctive tones. Tonal languages are not only extremely widespread throughout Southeast Asia, but also 42 per cent of languages in Maddieson's (2005: 58–61) sample of 526 languages across the world are tonal.

F3 Presence of vowel harmony Vowel harmony can be defined as a phenomenon whereby vowels within a domain agree with each other in terms of one or more features (Ko 2012: 7). It is a characteristic feature of the Transeurasian languages, except Japanese, but it is also present in most Uralic languages, including Khanty, and in many other languages in North Asia such as in Yukaghir, Nivkh and Ainu. Ket lacks vowel harmony and so do Rukai and Mandarin, as such reflecting prototypical Austronesian and Mainland Southeast Asian behaviour, respectively. In Old Japanese, however, there is a restriction on the shape of root morphemes, whereby the vowel o_2 cannot occur in a root together with the vowels u, o_1 or a. This phenomenon, known as Arisaka's law, has been taken as a kind of vowel harmony, but it has been rejected from comparisons with other Transeurasian languages because it applies to roots rather than to suffixes and because it does not reflect palatal harmony, the type of harmony which was attributed to the Transeurasian languages until recently (e.g. Frellesvig 2010: 44). However, in lexicalized verb stems incorporating derivational suffixes, as well as in the noun inflectional suffixes such as the plural suffix and the genitive suffix, there are traces of $a \sim o_2$ vowel alternation according to the quality of the vowels in the preceding root, e.g. OJ no_2 genitive versus OJ -*na*- petrified in compounds such as OJ mi_1-*na-moto* [< water-GEN-base] 'source, the headwaters' (Rickmeyer 1989: 316; Robbeets 2015).

F4 Presence of tongue root vowel harmony Among the various types of vowel harmony, the most frequently attested ones across the languages of the world are palatal harmony, labial harmony, height harmony and tongue-root harmony. Palatal harmony requires all vowels within a domain to be exclusively front or back. It can be found in most Uralic languages such as in Khanty as well as in the Turkic languages (e.g. Tk. *ip-ler* [rope-PL] 'ropes' versus *pul-lar* [stamp-PL] 'stamps'). Since the western Mongolic languages Oirat and Kalmuck display palatal harmony as well, it has been proposed that the original system of Mongolic harmony was palatal (Poppe 1955; Svantesson 1985). However, Ko (2012) demonstrated that the original vowel harmony in Mongolic was in fact based on opposition between the advanced versus retracted position of the tongue root, rather than on a palatal contrast. He argued that the tongue root retraction system in Khalkha (e.g. *od-o:s* [feather-ABL] versus *ɔd-ɔ:s* [star-ABL]) represents retention rather than innovation. Furthermore, he supported the view that Tungusic vowel harmony is retracted tongue root (RTR) based, as it is in Manchu and Evenki, and that the reduced vowel harmony in Contemporary Korean derives from a tongue root based system in Middle Korean. As far as the harmony-like opposition between o_2 and u, o_1 or a in Old Japanese is concerned, the recent reconstruction of a seven-vowel system in Proto-Japonic by Frellesvig and Whitman (2008) implies an underlying opposition between pJ *ɨ, *ə and *u, *o, *a, which does not exclude an original RTR-based contrast. Whereas Vovin (1993: 50–51) and Bugaeva (2015: 26–28) reconstruct palatal harmony in Ainu, Shibatani (1990: 15) speculates that the Ainu opposition between *o* and *u, a* might have its origin in tongue root harmony, but here the indications are even weaker than in the Japanese case. According to Maslova (2003a: 35), Yukaghir might be more appropriately described as having tongue root harmony than palatal harmony. Chukchi also displays tongue root harmony. Although Gruzdeva (1998: 10) suggests that Nivkh leaves traces of height harmony, Janhunen (1981) and Ko, Whitman and Joseph (2014) interpret the system in terms of tongue root harmony. Cross-linguistically, tongue root harmony seems to be concentrated in Niger-Congo and Nilo-Saharan languages. Outside Africa and the Northeast Asian region the phenomenon seems to be rather rare: only Native American languages such as Nez Perce and Coeur d'Alene Salishan are known to have the feature (Ko 2012: 11–12). A rough estimate would be that less than 10 per cent of the world's languages have a tongue root vowel harmony system.

F5 Absence of initial velar nasal In most Turkic languages as well as in Mongolic languages and Korean, the velar nasal ŋ- cannot appear in word-initial position. Japanese lacks a velar nasal phoneme. In the Tungusic languages, with the exception of Manchu, however, ŋ- can appear word-initially, but generally restricted to a specific phonological environment, notably when it is followed by the sonorants *n, r, l, m, y*, e.g. Evk. *ŋene-* 'to go', Ma. *genu-* 'to go together', Evk. *ŋe:le-*, Ma. *gele-* 'to fear', etc. According to Poppe (1964: 4) the initial velar nasal in Tungusic is the result of secondary assimilation of pTg. **g-*, which implies that originally *ŋ- was absent in Tungusic as well. The assimilation was probably triggered by influence from languages in the Siberian area, such as Nivkh, which allow initial velar nasals (Anderson 2006). It is under the same influence that initial ŋ became allowed in Dolgan (Turkic), e.g. *ŋassa* 'pipe'. In Khanty, Ket, Kolyma Yukaghir, Ainu and Mandarin, ŋ- does not occur in word-initial position. Rukai allows an initial velar nasal, e.g. *ŋaɭai* 'saliva'. In Anderson's (2005: 42) sample of 468 languages, 69 per cent lack an initial velar nasal. Among the languages of the world that have a velar nasal phoneme, as is the case for most Transeurasian languages, only 35 per cent do not use it in word-initial position.

F6 Absence of initial *r-* Throughout the Transeurasian languages, the consonant *r-* is not allowed to occur word-initially, except in borrowings (e.g. J *rajio*, K *latiwo*, Even *radio*, Khal. *radio*, Tk. *radyo* 'radio'). This is also true for Kolyma Yukaghir. Ket lacks a phoneme /r/ altogether. Although initial **r-* is not reconstructed for Proto-Uralic, Khanty is atypical in this sense, e.g. *raɣta* 'to drop, slide' and *räɣ* 'garbage'. Nivkh, Ainu, Mandarin and Rukai also have native words in initial *r-*.

F7 Absence of initial consonant clusters None of the Transeurasian languages tolerate initial consonant clusters, although medial clusters are tolerated in Turkic, Mongolic, Tungusic and Korean but, on the face of it, not in Japanese. On the basis of morphological, etymological, dialectal and textual evidence, however, it is safe to assume that the Old Japanese obstruents OJ *b, d, g, z* resulted from the rephonologization of nasal obstruent clusters pJ *np, pJ *nt, pJ *nk, pJ *ns (Robbeets 2008). Reminiscent of how the Transeurasian languages do not allow for consonant clusters in initial position, Old Japanese did not permit word-initial voiced obstruents except in mimetic adverbs. From the ninth century onwards, as loans from Chinese began to have a major impact, the restriction was relaxed and initial voiced obstruents began to appear in borrowings and in contracted native forms. The avoidance of consonant clusters is further characteristic of Uralic languages, such as Khanty. Similarly, Yukaghir, Ket, Ainu and Rukai tolerate only single consonants in word-initial position. Word-initial clusters may comprise at most two consonants in Nivkh, e.g. *mra* 'fault' and *ksynz* 'witch'. Although Mandarin lacks consonant clusters, there is strong evidence that in Old Chinese (first millennium BCE) a variety of consonant clusters could occur at the beginning of the syllable as well (Norman 1988:

9–10). The simplification and eventual loss of consonant clusters appears to be a tendency affecting most of the Mainland Southeast Asia area. It is possible that early contacts between Chinese and Transeurasian, that has never tolerated initial clusters, have triggered the development along these lines.

F8 Presence of voice distinction for stops Turkic, Mongolic and Tungusic languages share a voiced–voiceless opposition for stops. In Contemporary and Middle Korean, stops display an opposition between lax (p), aspirated (ph) and tensed (p'). Even if the lax stops become lightly voiced between voiced sounds, there is no phonemic voicing distinction. The Japanese voicing distinction for stops is a secondary development. As mentioned in the previous paragraph, voiced stops derive from prenasalized voiceless stops, so originally Japanese lacked a voicing distinction. Khanty lacks a voicing distinction for stops, a feature characteristic of Proto-Uralic, although many contemporary Uralic languages have developed an original singleton–geminate contrast into a voicing distinction. For example, although the contrast between /p/ and /pp/ in Proto-Uralic *lapa 'flat surface, leaf' and *tappa- 'to stamp with feet, to hit, knock' is maintained in the Finnish reflexes *lapa* 'shoulderblade, leaf surface' and *tappa-* 'to beat to death, kill', it has usually developed into a distinction between /b/ and /p/ such as in Estonian *laba* 'surface' and *tapa-* 'kill, slaughter'. Ket and Yukaghir display a voicing distinction, but languages to the extreme northeast such as Ainu, Nivkh and Chukchi do not. Mandarin, like Nivkh, has a distinction between aspirated and unaspirated stops, but lacks a voiced–voiceless opposition. Characteristic of most Austronesian languages, Rukai also displays voice distinction for stops.

22.2.2 Lexicon and Semantics

F9 Preference for a non-verbal strategy with (extra-family) verbal borrowing As far as the mechanisms of loan verb accommodation are concerned, most recipient languages can be categorized into two distinct groups: borrowed verbs either arrive as verbs, needing no formal accommodation, or they arrive as non-verbs and need formal accommodation. In Wohlgemuth's (2009) terminology, the first group represents *direct insertion*, while the second group represents either *indirect insertion*, when the formal accommodation involves a verbalizer, or *light verb strategy*, when the borrowed verb is integrated into a complex predicate. Turkic, Mongolic, Korean and Japanese can be assigned to the second group because they display a clear preference for the non-verbal strategy (Wohlgemuth 2009: 159, 161); for instance, Tk. *klik-le-* and *klik et-* << English *click*; Khal. *zee-l-* << Mandarin *zhài* 'borrow, lend'; K *coking ha-*, J *zyogingu suru* 'to jog' << English *jog*; J *demo-r-* << English *demonstrate*. Whereas the Northern Tungusic languages prefer to borrow verbs through direct insertion, e.g. Evk. *vypolńaj-* << Russian *vypolnja-t'* 'to fulfil, carry out', the Southern Tungusic languages use verbalizers, e.g. Ud. *tancewa-la-* << Russian *tancewa-t'* 'to dance' and Na. *voprosa-la-* << Russian *voproša-t'* 'to enquire, question'. In contrast to the Transeurasian languages, Uralic languages such as Khanty and Austronesian languages such as Rukai, Ainu and Mandarin show a strong preference for direct insertion (Tamura 2000: 267; Wohlgemuth 2009: 158, 161). Yukaghir and Nivkh did not integrate any recognizable verbal borrowings from Russian or from other foreign languages into their lexicons (Fubito Endo, personal communication; Ekaterina Gruzdeva, personal communication). In Wohlgemuth's (2009: 157) sample, 55 per cent of languages worldwide are found to use direct insertion, while the remainder prefer non-verbal strategies such as indirect insertion and the light verb strategy.

F10 Presence of a two-way proximal/distal distinction in demonstrative pronouns Although Old Turkic displays a two-way distinction in its demonstratives, i.e. OT *bo | bun-* 'this' versus *ol | an-* 'that', many contemporary Turkic languages such as Turkish make a three-way distinction, e.g. Tk. *bu* 'this', *şu* 'that', *o* 'that (over there)'. Demonstrative pronouns in earlier and contemporary varieties of Mongolic and Tungusic exhibit a proximal/distal distinction: MMo. *ene* 'this' versus *tere* 'that', Khal. *e-* 'this' versus *te-* 'that', Ma. *ere* 'this' versus *tere* 'that' and Evk. *er(i)* 'this' versus *tar(i)* 'that'. Demonstrative pronouns in Contemporary and Middle Korean, however, show a proximal/mesial/distal opposition: K *i* 'this', *ku* 'that', *ce* 'that over there' and MK *i* 'this', *ku* 'that', *tye* 'that over there'. This is also true for Contemporary Japanese: J *ko-* 'this', *so-* 'that', *a-* 'that over there'. In contrast to most accounts of Old Japanese demonstratives, which posit a three-way contrast between OJ ko_2 'this', so_2 'that' and *ka* 'that over there', Frellesvig (2010: 139–142) argued that OJ *ka* was not a productive member of the demonstrative system and that pre-Old Japanese had a simple proximal/distal distinction. While Khanty distinguishes between proximal *timi* 'this (here)' and distal *tomi* 'that (there)', Yukaghir, Ket and Ainu have a three-way opposition, each demonstrative pronoun denoting a different degree of proximity: Yukaghir *tiŋ* 'this' (proximal), *adiŋ ~ ediŋ* 'that' (mesial), *taŋ* 'that' (distal); Ket *tu-* 'this, that' (neutral), *ki-* 'this, that' (proximal); *qa-* 'this, that' (distal) and Ainu *ta an* 'this' (distal), *ne an* 'that' (mesial), *to an okai* 'that over there' (distal). Nivkh makes as many as five distinctions: *tyd'* 'this' (near and visible), *hyd'* 'this, that' (distant), *ad'* 'that' (more distant and visible), *aixnt* 'that' (most distant), *kud'* 'that' (absent).[4] Rukai distinguishes four demonstrative pronouns in terms of visibility and distance: *'ina* 'this' (proximal), *ana* 'that' (mesial), *ona* 'that over there' (distal but visible), *dhona* 'that over there' (distal and invisible). Mandarin has a two-way distinction between proximal *zhè(ge)* 'this' and distal *nà(ge)* 'that', which developed from a three-way distinction in Classical Chinese between neutral, proximal and distal. In Diessel's (2005: 170–173) sample

---

[4] Note that this analysis deviates from the feature values given for distance contrasts in demonstratives by Diessel (2005: 170–173), since he marks Ainu, Nivkh, Yukaghir and Turkish as having a two-way contrast.

of 234 languages, 54 per cent exhibit a two-way distance contrast in demonstratives, while 38 per cent exhibit a three-way contrast.

F11 Inclusive/exclusive distinction in first person plural pronouns Among the Turkic languages, there are no unique pronominal forms that distinguish inclusive from exclusive person forms. Although Old Turkic and most presently spoken varieties of Turkic distinguish between a first person plural (Tk./OT *biz* 'we') and an augmented plural form (Tk. / OT *biz-ler* 'we (as a group)'), Nevskaya (2010: 124) argues for a collective interpretation of the augmented plural, denoting 'an isolated group of people who want to oppose themselves to the others', rather than an inclusive interpretation as suggested by Grönbech (1936: 81). The Middle Mongolian distinction between exclusive *ba* and inclusive *bida* is formally preserved in the Khalkha oblique paradigm in the variation between formally exclusive *man-* and formally inclusive *bidn-*, but the functional distinction has been lost. In the Tungusic languages, however, the inclusive/exclusive opposition is generally well preserved, e.g. exclusive Ma. *be*, Evk. *bu* versus inclusive Ma. *muse*, Evk. *mut ~ mit*. Similar to the Turkic languages, Middle and Contemporary Korean distinguish between a first person plural (K/MK *wuli* 'we') and an augmented plural form (K *wuli-tul*, MK *wuli-tolh* 'we (as a group)') in which K *tul*, MK ·*tolh* is a collective marker. Contemporary Japanese lacks an inclusive/exclusive distinction and cannot derive an augmented plural from the first person plural *watasi-tati* [I-PL] 'we'. Old Japanese also lacks the distinction, but the stem OJ *wa-* 'I, we' can be used as a first person plural in the possessive case form, but it can also be augmented with a collective marker *-ra ~ -re* to OJ *ware* 'we', a form which in its turn has been augmented into *ware-ra* 'we' later in Japanese. As is the case for many Uralic languages, Khanty marks a dual distinction but not an inclusive/exclusive distinction on its personal pronouns. While Ket and Yukaghir lack the distinction, Nivkh distinguishes between exclusive *n'yŋ* and inclusive *mer ~ mir*. Although Ainu personal affixes on the verb have an inclusive/exclusive distinction, the first personal pronoun *aoka(i)* only has a single form.[5] The distinction found in the first person plural pronouns between exclusive *wǒmen* and inclusive *zánmen* 'we' of Beijing and certain other northern Chinese dialects may be due to Transeurasian influence. Such a distinction was not found in Old Chinese, and it began to appear in North China during the period of Altaic rule. It is significant in this regard that both Middle Mongolian, spoken under the Yuan dynasty, and Manchu distinguish exclusive and inclusive forms. Rukai distinguishes exclusive *-nai ~ nai-* [NOM] from inclusive *-mita ~ ta-* [NOM], a feature characteristic of Austronesian languages. In Cysouw's (2005: 166–167) sample of 200 languages, 31 per cent distinguish between inclusive and exclusive with independent pronouns.

---

[5] Note that my evaluation differs from Cysouw's (2005: 166–167) analysis, which marks Ainu as having an inclusive/exclusive distinction with independent pronouns.

F12 Property words may be verbally or nominally encoded Cross-linguistically adjectives have no prototypical encoding strategy of their own: they will align themselves either with verbs or with nominals (Stassen 1997: 30). Across the Transeurasian languages, the encoding of property words appears to be mixed because, at least in the earlier stages, both the nominal and the verbal strategy is used (Robbeets 2015). Generally, this mixed encoding is split in the sense that most property words have only a single encoding option, with the exception of some instances of switched encoding mentioned under feature value 13. In Old Turkic, most property words are nominally encoded, but there seems to be a tendency to apply the verbal strategy to words expressing time-unstable properties such as OTk. *bädü-* 'to be(come) big, great', OTk. *isi-* 'to be hot', OTk. *kat-* 'to be hard, firm, tough', OTk. *kïz-* 'to be red', OTk. *tumlï-* 'to be cold', OTk. *us-* 'to be thirsty', OTk. *tïgra-* 'to be tough', etc. Contemporary Turkic languages maintain only few reflexes of these verbal property words, e.g. Tk. *büyü-* 'to be(come) large', but in the majority of cases, the earlier verbal property word has been derived through a deverbal noun suffix into a nominal adjective (e.g. Tk. *büyük* 'big'). Similarly, most property words are nominally encoded in Mongolic, but there is a tendency to apply the verbal strategy to less permanent properties in Middle Mongolian such as MMo. *ayu-* 'to be(come) afraid', MMo. *čat-* 'to be ripe, be(come) saturated', MMo. *hiče-* 'to be ashamed', WMo. *qala-* 'to be(come) warm', MMo. *sohta-* 'to be drunk', etc. Contemporary Mongolic languages such as Khalkha maintain only a few reflexes of these verbal property words, e.g. Khal. *ayu:-* 'be afraid'. The same is true for Tungusic, where contemporary languages such as Manchu (e.g. Ma. *aka-* 'to be sad', Ma. *bere-* 'to be lame', Ma. *ebi-* 'to be satiated') and Evenki (e.g. Evk. *ukti-* 'to be hungry', Evk. *uwi-* 'to be satiated', Evk. *buli:-* 'to be sad') may occasionally exhibit verbal encoding.[6] In Korean, there are property words such as K *kanan ha-* 'to be poor' and *phikon ha-* 'to be tired' that consist of a nominal root and the auxiliary *ha-* 'to be in the state of' and whose bases are called 'adjectival nouns' (Martin 1992: 189, 190; Sohn 1994: 219–220). However, the majority of property words are inflected in essentially the same way as verbs, e.g. K *kwut-*, MK *kwut-* 'to be(come) hard', K *noph-*, MK *nwoph-* 'to be high', etc. Some Japanese property words, such as J *sizuka*, OJ *siduka* 'quiet', J/OJ *tasika* 'trustworthy' are encoded exclusively nominally, while others such as J/OJ *taka-* 'to be high', J/OJ *kata-* 'to be hard, tough' are essentially inflected in a similar way to verbs. In line with most Uralic languages, property words in Khanty are exclusively nominally encoded. This is also true for Ket. In Yukaghir, Ainu and Nivkh, however, property words are exclusively verbally encoded. As is the case with most Transeurasian languages, Ainu property verbs express both the property and the process leading to the property, e.g. *pirka* 'to be(come) good'. In line

---

[6] Note that my analysis deviates from the feature values inserted for predicative adjectives by Stassen (2005b: 480–481), in which Evenki and Manchu are marked as exclusively verbal encoding, in line with the traditional view.

with Mainland Southeast Asian and Austronesian languages, Mandarin and Rukai use verbal encodings for property words. In Stassen's (2005b: 478–481) sample of 386 languages, 27 per cent have mixed encoding in predicative adjectives.

F13 Some property words exhibit switched encoding Some property words in the Transeurasian languages, especially in the earlier varieties, further exhibit traces of switching, whereby the same property word can have both nominal and verbal encoding: e.g. OT *ač* 'hungry' / *ač-* 'to be hungry', OT *keč* 'late, slow'/ *keč-* 'to be late, slow'; MMo. *bulqa* 'hostile; hostility' / *bulqa-* 'to be hostile'; Ma. *jalu* 'full'/ *jalu-* 'to be full', Ma. *sula* 'loose, free'/ *sula-* 'to be loose, be free'; MK *toso-* versus MK *toso ho-* 'to be warm'; OJ *taka* 'high' / *taka-* 'to be high', OJ *opo* 'big' / OJ *opo-* 'to be big', etc. None of the neighbouring languages, except Tundra Yukaghir, exhibits such behaviour. There, two property words, i.e. *juku* 'small' and *t'ama* 'big', occur as noun modifiers without overt adnominalizers, e.g. *t'ama-d'ohoje* (big-sword) 'sabre', in addition to having a verbal encoding, for example, in the deverbal inchoative *t'ama-mu-* (be.big-INCH) 'to grow, become big' (Maslova 2003b: 14). Logically, the proportion of languages exhibiting mixed and switched encoding will be lower than 27 per cent, i.e. the proportion of languages with mixed encoding in general.

F14 Partial emphatic reduplication of nominal property words Partial emphatic reduplication is a phenomenon whereby the first consonant (if present) and vowel of a nominal property word are repeated with the addition of another consonant to indicate the presence of the property to the utmost degree. Whaley and Li (2000) found that it is widespread in Turkic, Mongolic and Tungusic, e.g. Tk. *bem-beyaz* 'snow white', OT *kap-kara* 'quite black', Kal. *xob-xoldu:* 'frozen through', WMo. *ub-ulaɣan* 'completely red', Evk. *ab-aya* 'very good'. I have not been able to find examples in Manchu, but the phenomenon is present in Sibe, a presently spoken variety of Manchu, e.g. *fak-farxun* 'extremely dark'. In Tungusic, emphatic reduplication is restricted to Sibe, Kile-Nanai, Solon Evenki and Oroqen, i.e. the languages spoken on Chinese soil, which have been under strong influence from the Mongolic languages Khalkha and Dagur. On the basis of this distribution and because the greatest flexibility, in terms of both the number of reduplicated words and the type of concepts they denote, is found in Turkic, Whaley and Li (2000: 358) argued for a diffusion of the feature from Turkic to Mongolic to Tungusic. Japanese, Korean and the neighbouring languages under examination do not display partial emphatic reduplication. In Rukai, however, descriptive verbs are partially reduplicated in comparative constructions (see feature 23).

22.2.3 Morphology
F15 Morphology is agglutinative Agglutinative languages connect morphemes linearly such that there is a one-to-one relationship between

a morpheme and its meaning. The Transeurasian languages belong to a North Asian and European belt of agglutinative languages together with the Uralic languages, including Khanty and other languages of the Siberian area such as Ket, Yukaghir, Chukchi and Nivkh. Ainu has agglutinative morphology and so do the Austronesian languages, including Rukai. Chinese, the only analytic language under examination, has triggered a decrease of agglutinating features in Tungusic as one moves from north to east and further south. Manchu is the most analytic among the Transeurasian languages; it treats case forms, for instance, as particles rather than suffixes.

F16 Inflectional morphology is predominantly suffixing Across the strongly suffixing Transeurasian languages, prefixation is rare and restricted to derivational morphology, such as the partial emphatic reduplication (see feature 14 above) and some derivational prefixes in Korean (e.g. K *yel-* 'young, new' in *yel-cwungi* 'a chick out of its shell') and in Japanese (e.g. J *ma-* intensive in *ma-siro* 'snow white'). As is the case for most Uralic languages, Khanty is strongly suffixing and so is Yukaghir. Nivkh is considered to be weakly suffixing. In Ket, nominal inflectional morphology is strongly suffixing, whereas verb inflection is predominantly prefixing. In Ainu and Rukai, inflection makes use of both prefixes and suffixes. Probably due to Transeurasian influence, Mandarin is hard to assign unequivocally to either the isolating or weakly suffixing type, but Sinitic varieties in general tend towards the isolating pole. In Dryer's (2005a: 110–113) sample of 894 languages, 43 per cent are strongly suffixing.

F17 Absence of obligatory numeral classifiers Although in Turkic and Mongolic some nouns of low countability may be accompanied by a unit of measure by means of which they can be counted, e.g. Tk. *sekiz bardak su* [eight glass water] 'eight glasses of water', OT *yeti tutum talkan* [seven handful parched.grain] 'seven handfuls of parched grain', Khal. *gourben debter nom* [three volume book] 'three volumes of books', etc., these languages do not make obligatory use of sortal numeral classifiers. Similar to the use of collective suffixes for counting people in Old Turkic (OT *-(A)gU* in e.g. *üčägü* 'three together') and Middle Mongolian (MMo. *-'UlA ~ AlA* in e.g. *qoya'ula* 'two together'), the Tungusic languages use a variety of collective suffixes following numerals from 'two' to 'ten' such as Evk. *-kt(e)* and *-ni* for counting people (e.g. *d'u-kte* 'two (people together), (we, you, they) two'), Evk. *-gdA/ -ngnA* for counting objects, Evk. *-llA* for counting the number of days (e.g. *nada-lla* 'seven days, a week'), Evk. *-nu / -pu* for counting the number of tents (e.g. *ilan-nu* 'three tents') and Evk. *-musa* denoting the number of places or directions. However, only Manchu has developed about 70 sortal numeral classifiers, which divide the inventory of count nouns into semantic classes, each of which is associated with a different classifier, such as *fesin* which is used for objects equipped with a handle, e.g. *ilan fesin loho* [three CLAS sword] 'three swords'. These words have original lexical meanings, e.g. *fesin* 'haft, shaft, handle', but under Chinese influence they have grammaticalized into classifiers, which are not obligatory in Manchu. *Loho ilan* [sword three] 'three swords', for instance, is equally possible. Whereas the standard pattern in Middle Korean was to modify a noun with a preposed numeral, e.g. *twu kalh* [two knife] 'two knives', the most common pattern in Contemporary Korean makes use of a classifier, e.g. *pus se:k calwu* [writing.brush three CLAS] in which *calwu* denotes long objects with handles. However, the original pattern surfaces in expressions such as K *twu nala* 'two countries' and the use of classifiers remains optional in Korean, e.g. *kalh hana-ka issta* [knife one-NOM be.present] 'there is one knife'.[7] With Chinese influence inundating the language from Middle Korean times onwards, the classifiers developed from native words under Chinese influence or were borrowed as such from Chinese. Note that Middle Korean leaves traces of specialized suffixes to count days, e.g. **-(o/u)l* in *saol* 'three days', *naol* 'four days' etc. and that some Korean dialects use a suffix *-i* to count persons, e.g. *se:-i* 'three people', *ne:-i* 'four people', which recalls the use of collective suffixes in the other Transeurasian languages. While there is an extensive list of obligatory classifiers in Contemporary Japanese, e.g. *enpitu san-bon* [pencil three-CLASS] 'three pencils', the system of classifiers is much less developed in Old Japanese, where Chinese influence is restricted to a minimum. Numerals could be used with nouns, without intervening classifiers, e.g. OJ *nana se* [seven rapid] 'seven rapids' and the so-called 'classifiers' are restricted to roughly six suffixes, i.e. *-ka* for counting days starting from the numeral 'two', *-tu* / *-ti* for counting objects, *-ri* for persons, *-mo₂to₂* for grassy plants, *-pe₁* for layers and *-ka* for plants. It is not unlikely that these suffixes originate in collective suffixes. Numeral classifiers are absent in Uralic languages such as Khanty, as well as in Yukaghir and Ket. Ainu makes use of a small set of obligatory classifiers such as *-n* / *-iw* for persons, *-pe* / *-p* for animals and things, and *rerko* for counting days starting from the numeral 'two' (with irregular forms *tutko* 'two days' and *rerko* 'three days'). Nivkh distinguishes between 26 semantic classes with different numeral forms for each class. The obligatory use of classifiers is a widespread feature shared by Mandarin and the languages of Southeast Asia, but the use of classifiers in Classical Chinese was the exception rather than the rule. In Rukai the use of classifiers is optional in the sense that it uses a set of unaffixed numerals without classifiers, as well as a set of bound numerals which combine with five different sortal classifiers to form verbs. In Gil's (2005: 226–229) sample of 400 languages, 80 per cent lack obligatory numeral classifiers.

F18 Presence of *mi–Ti* opposition in first versus second person singular pronouns Nichols (2012) observes that *mi–Ti* pronominal

---

[7] Note that my evaluation differs from Gil's (2005: 228–229) interpretation that Korean has obligatory numeral classifiers.

paradigms with first person labial nasal *m* and second person apical or palatal obstruent *t, c, s,* etc. are much more common in northern Eurasia than elsewhere in the world. Janhunen (2013: 213) adds that there is a smaller group of *mi–Ti* languages extending from Uralic in the west, to Turkic, Mongolic and Tungusic in the east to Yukaghir in the north, in which not only the initial consonant but also the root vowel of the singular stems shows a basic similarity, in that it contains a non-low unrounded front vowel *i* or *e*. Although *m* is absent in the nominative first person singular in the Turkic, Mongolic and Tungusic languages, e.g. Tk. *ben*, OT *ben*, Khal. *bii*, MMo. *bi*, Ma. *bi*, Evk. *bi:*, it has developed in oblique forms through assimilation to the nasal oblique suffix *-n*, e.g. OT *min-*, Khal. *min-ii* (GEN), MMo. *mi-nu* (GEN), Ma. *min-*, Evk. *min-*. The second person singular forms all reflect a voiceless dental T, i.e. Tk. *sen*, OT *sen*, Khal. *cii*, MMo. *ci*, Ma. *si*, Evk. *si:*. The Korean pronouns are, among others, first singular K/MK *na* and second singular K/MK *ne*. In Japanese, J *watasi* and OJ *wa* are among others used in the first singular, while a variety of contemporary pronouns and OJ *na* are used in the second singular. Although the Proto-Uralic first and second singular pronouns **mun* and **tun* reflect a *mi–Ti* distinction (Janhunen 1982: 35), Khanty is deviant in having first singular *mä* and second singular *nöŋ*. In Yukaghir, however, the *mi–Ti* opposition is present in first singular *met* versus second singular *tet*. In Nivkh, the distinction is absent in the singular pronouns, first person *n'i* versus second person *či*, but it is present in the opposition between the first plural inclusive *mir/mer* and the second plural pronoun *čiŋ*. The opposition is not found in Ket, Ainu, Chinese and Rukai. In Nichols and Peterson's (2005: 546–551) sample of 230 languages, 13 per cent display a *mi–Ti* opposition in first versus second person pronouns. Logically, languages reflecting a *mi–Ti* opposition will represent an even smaller proportion.

F19 Formation of a secondary oblique stem of personal pronouns With the exception of Korean, the Transeurasian languages share a tendency to form a secondary oblique stem of the personal pronouns by means of a suffix which phonologically may be identified as the dental nasal *-n-*. In most contemporary Turkic languages, the nominative and oblique forms have merged, e.g. Tk. *ben* for the first singular nominative and oblique, but in Old Turkic the first singular nominative *bän* is distinguished from the oblique stem *min-*, which can be derived from an original pTk. **bi-n-* [1SG-OBL-]. Similarly, the Mongolic and Tungusic languages derive oblique pronominal stems from the nominative roots through a nasal suffix, for instance, in the first person plural pronouns MMo. *ba* [NOM] versus *man-* [OBL] and Khal. *bid* [NOM] versus *bidn-* [OBL] and in the first person singular pronouns Ma. *bi* [NOM] versus *min-* [OBL], Evk. *bi:* [NOM] versus *min-* [OBL]. There are no oblique pronominal stems in Contemporary Japanese, but Old Japanese leaves traces of an oblique nasal suffix in some case forms, for example in the eastern OJ first person singular dative *wa-nu-ni* in alternation with western OJ *wa-ni*. Vovin (2005: 229–230) further found that an original Japonic pronominal oblique **-n-* is well supported by Northern Ryukyuan dialects, where the first person pronoun uses *waa-* as the nominative and genitive base and extended *waN-* in the oblique cases. The erosion of the pronominal paradigm in Korean and Japanese may be due to the gradual de-pronominalization in the recorded history of these languages, whereby the system of personal pronouns became replaced by various terms of address and self-reference, probably under Chinese influence. The oblique nasal suffix is an important element in the Uralic pronominal paradigm as well, for example the Khanty first person pronoun *mä* [NOM] versus *män-* [OBL]. Ket, Yukaghir, Ainu and Mandarin, however, do not derive secondary oblique stems. The third person singular pronoun in Nivkh has both regular and suppletive case forms, e.g. *if-øn* [3SG-NOM] versus *if-toX ~ e-rx* [3SG-DAT/ADD], but here the oblique form is not derived from the nominative base. Rukai personal pronouns have different shapes for nominative, topic, genitive and oblique cases, e.g. the first person singular *-lrao* [NOM], *ilrae* [TOP], *-li* [GEN] versus *-iae* [OBL], in which the oblique seems to be formally derived from the nominative base by means of the same *i- . . .-e* marking as in the topic form.

22.2.4 Syntax

F20 SOV (Subject-Object-Verb) sentence order Syntactically, the Transeurasian languages pattern as typical SOV languages but the sentence order is not rigid. SOV is also among the characteristic features of the Uralic languages, here represented by Khanty. Languages to the north such as Yukaghir and Ket or to the northeast such as Ainu and Nivkh are almost all SOV languages, while those to the southeast are virtually all SVO languages. Mandarin, and in fact all major varieties of Chinese, corresponds with Southeast Asia with respect to verb-object order. Like most Austronesian languages, Rukai tends to be verb-initial, but the word order is non-rigid, switching freely between VSO and VOS. In Dryer's (2005b: 330–333) sample of 1228 languages, 40 per cent have SOV sentence order.

 F21 GAN (genitive-noun / adjective-noun) phrase order A modifier-before-headword word order in the sentence (SOV) is expected to correlate with a modifier-head order within the noun phrase (GAN), whereby adjectives, genitives and modifiers in general occur before the nouns to which they refer. This is the case for the Transeurasian languages, the Uralic languages including Khanty, and other languages of North Asia such as Yukaghir, Ket, Ainu and Nivkh. Mandarin, however, runs against the implicational expectation, since genitives and adjectives occur before the nouns to which they refer in spite of SVO sentence order. This combination of feature values is absent from almost all the other languages of Southeast Asia and has probably arisen under the influence of the Transeurasian languages. Rukai combines an adjective-noun order with a noun-genitive order (ANG). In Dryer's (2005c: 350–357) sample of 1105 languages, 55 per cent have genitive-noun order, while out of 1213 languages, 28 per cent have adjective-noun order.

F22 Extensive use of converbs Converbs, also known as gerunds or adverbial participles, can be defined as non-finite verb forms whose main function is to mark adverbial subordination (Haspelmath 1995: 3). Originally coined by the Altaic scholar Ramstedt, the term converb was adopted from Transeurasian linguistics to denote a cross-linguistic category. The Transeurasian languages are converb-prominent languages in the sense that they use converbs rather than adverbial subordinators as found in many European languages (Alpatov and Podlesskaya 1995; Bisang 1995, 1998; Johanson 1995; Malchukov 2012; Nedjalkov 1995; Sohn 2009):

(1)   Turkish
    Ali   gel-ince   *şaşır-d-ı*
    Ali   come-CONV   be.surprised-PST-3SG
    'When Ali came, he was surprised' (Johanson 1995: 314)

(2)   Khalkha
    Ger-ees-ee   *gar-aad*
    house-ABL-REFL   exit-PFV.CONV
    deuc-en   *jil-iin*   *daraa*   *ol-d-lao*
    forty-AND   year-GEN   after   find-PASS-FIN
    'She went away from home and was found forty years later'
    (Janhunen 2012: 280)

(3)   Even
    Dagam-mi,   *kunte-le*   *d'u-v*   *it-ti-n*
    approach-CONV   clearing-LOC   house-ACC   see-PST-3SG
    'When he came nearer, he saw a house on a clearing' (Malchukov 2012: 213)

(4)   Korean
    Kiho-nun   *nol-ko*   *ca-ss-eyo*
    Kiho-TOP   play-CONV   sleep-PST-POL
    'Kiho played and then slept' (Sohn 2009: 300)

(5)   Japanese
    Taroo-ga   *bangohan-o*   *tabe-te*   *furo-ni*   *hait-ta*
    Taroo-NOM   dinner-ACC   eat-CONV   bath-DAT   enter-PST
    'Taroo took a bath after he ate dinner' (Alpatov and Podlesskaya 1995: 473)

Although the Uralic languages are characterized by an extensive use of converbs, Khanty is rather atypical in this sense because it has only a single converb in *-min*, which is the least frequent non-finite verb form. Yukaghir and Nivkh also use a variety of converbs to link clauses. Ainu, however, employs subordinating conjunctions. Ket has no converbs or serial verb constructions of any kind. In Mandarin, verbs or verbal phrases are merely juxtaposed, the relation between the items being largely unmarked. Rukai marks adverbial subordination through a variety of means such as subordinating conjunctions, changes in word order and nominalized verb forms.

F23 Use of a locative existential construction to encode predicative possession The Transeurasian languages show a clear preference to express the concept 'X has Y' on the basis of an existential sentence, whereby the possessed noun phrase functions as the grammatical subject of the 'exist'-predicate, while the possessor noun phrase is in a dative/locative case form. Although locative possessive constructions were standard in Old Turkic, Turkish uses genitive existential sentences as well as locative existential sentences. 'I have a book', for instance, can be expressed by *Ben-de bir kitab var* [I-LOC a book exist] or by *Ben-im bir kitab-ïm var* [I-GEN a book-1SG.POSS exist]. Middle Mongolian and Khalkha make use of either a conjunctional possessive which construes the possessor noun phrase as the grammatical subject of the copula and marks the possessed with the comitative -*tai*, e.g. Khalkha *Bi nom-tai bai-n'* [I book-COM be-DUR], or a locative possessive, e.g. *Nad-ed nom bai-n'* [I-DAT book be-DUR]. As is the case for most Tungusic languages, Manchu and Evenki employ locative existential constructions, e.g. Evk. *Min-du: kniga bisi-n* [I-DAT book be-3SG], Ma. *Min-de bithe bi* [I-DAT book be]. Korean uses a locative existential construction, e.g. K *Na-hanthey chayk-i issta* [I-LOC book-NOM exist], but the possessor can also be construed as the topic of the noun phrase, e.g. *Na-nun chayk-i issta* [I-TOP book-NOM exist]. This is also true for Japanese, e.g. *Watashi-ni hon-ga aru* [I-DAT book-NOM exist] and *Watashi-wa hon-ga aru* [I-TOP book-NOM exist]. Topic possessives may have developed under the influence of Chinese, since they represent the standard strategy in Mandarin. Among the strategies used to encode predicative possession in the Uralic languages, we find locative possession such as in Finnish and Hungarian, genitive possession such as in Nenets, and possession encoded by a transitive verb 'to have' such as in Khanty. Whereas Yukaghir employs a conjunctional possessive and Ainu a *have*-possessive, Ket and Nivkh use locational possessives. Although many Austronesian languages employ topic possessives, Rukai makes use of locative and genitive possessive constructions. In Stassen's (2005a: 474–477) sample of 240 languages, 20 per cent use a locative existential construction to encode predicative possession.

F24 Use of the ablative case form to encode predicative comparison The Transeurasian languages all form comparative constructions in which the standard noun phrase is constructed in the ablative case form, e.g. Tk. *bu araba-dan daha büyük* [this car-ABL more big] 'bigger than this car', OT *barča-da üzä-räk* [everything-ABL high-COMP] 'higher than anything else', Khal. *ene xun-ees iluu* [this person-ABL good] 'better than this person', MMo. *qola-sa qola* [far-ABL far] 'farther than far', Evk. *oron-duk gugda-tmar* [deer-ABL tall-COMP] 'taller than a deer', Ma. *ere niyalma ci sain* [this person ABL good] 'better than this person', OJ *ware-yo₁ri mo₂ madusi-ki₁ pi₁to₂* [I-ABL PT be.poor-ADN person] 'people poorer than me' and J *chikyu:-yori omci* [globe-ABL be.heavy] 'heavier than the globe'. In literary Korean the ablative marker *eyse* 'from' can be used in comparative constructions, e.g. K *i eyse tɔ khu-n salang* [this ABL more be.big-ADN love] 'a greater love than this', but it is more common to use a comparative particle *pota* 'than', e.g. K *kicha pota ppaluta* [train PT be.fast] 'faster than a train', MK *nyey pwota thak.wel hota* [past PT superior be] 'superior to the past'. This particle has grammaticalized from the verb MK *pwo-* 'to see' and the transferentive *-ta·ka*, which signals the interruption of an event before its completion, i.e. 'when one looks at'. It replaced earlier particles for comparison in Middle Korean, such as MK *tukwo* 'than' and *lawa* 'than'. The Uralic languages differ from one another with regard to comparative constructions: languages to the west, such as Finnish and Hungarian, use particle comparatives as in European languages, and languages to the east, such as Nenets and Udmurt, mark the comparative standard with the ablative case ending, as in the Transeurasian languages. In Khanty, the marker of comparison is a postposition *niŋə* 'since, from', which has ablative-like semantics but differs from the standard ablative case ending *-oɣ* or the ablative–elative ending *-i*. Yukaghir and Ket mark the comparative standard with the ablative case ending. In Nivkh, the comparative suffix *-yk* is traditionally considered as a separate case form as there is no evidence to relate it to the formally similar locative/ablative suffix *-(u)ɣe*; *-(u)x* (Gruzdeva, personal communication). Ainu forms comparative constructions by means of the particle *kasuno* 'than'. In comparative constructions in Mandarin the standard noun phrase is constructed as the direct object of a verb 'to exceed'. In Rukai, a comparative construction is formed through partial reduplication (CVV) of the descriptive verb stem. In Stassen's (2005c: 490–493) sample of 167 languages, 47 per cent use locational comparatives, but the proportion of languages that specifically use the ablative case form to encode predicative comparison is logically expected to be lower.

22.2.5 Grammaticalization

F25 Direct insubordination One of the driving forces of morphosyntactic change in the Transeurasian languages is a recurrent tendency to grammaticalize non-finite suffixes to finite suffixes (Robbeets 2009, 2016). In line with Evans (2008: 367), I call this development 'insubordination', i.e. the conventionalized main clause use of what appear to be formally subordinate clauses, but it can be further specified as 'direct' insubordination because non-finite suffixes are directly reanalysed as finite ones, without the omission of a specific matrix predicate (Robbeets 2016). Deverbal noun suffixes such as OTK *-(A)r* in OTk. *tug-* 'to be born, to rise (of sun) (intr.)' > *tugar* 'sunrise, east'; MMo. *-m* in MMo. *quri-* 'to come together (intr.)' > *qurim* 'feast'; Ma. *-rA* in *mute-* 'to be able' > *mutere* 'ability'; MK *-(·u/o)m* in *yel-* 'to bear (fruit)' > *yelum* 'fruit' and OJ *-sa* in *naga-* 'to be long' > *nagasa* 'length' develop over intermediate stages of clausal nominalizers and relativizers into finite suffixes, as illustrated in the following examples:

(6)   Old Turkic
    Ölüm-tä   *oz-upan*   *ögir-ä*   *savin-ü*   *yorï-**r**.*
    death-ABL   escape-CONV   rejoice-CONV   be.happy-CONV   go.on-**FIN**
    'Having been saved from death it happily goes on with its life.'
                                                  (Erdal 2004: 325)

(7)   Middle Mongolian
    udurit-basu   *ber*   *ulu*   *busire-**m**.*
    guide-COND   PT   NEG   believe-**FIN**
    'Even if you guide them, they don't believe.'   (Weiers 1966: 144)

(8)   Manchu
    si   *nene-me*   *isinji-ci*   *uthai*   *sin-de*   *bu-**re***
    you   be.first-CONV   come-CONV   at.once   you-DAT   give-**FIN**
    'If you come first, I shall give [it] to you straight away.'
                                           (Gorelova 2002: 256)

(9)   Korean
    onul-un   *swuep-i*   *eps-**um**.*
    today-TOP   class-NOM   not.exist-**FIN**
    'No class today.'

(10)   Old Japanese
    punapi$_1$to$_2$-wo   *mi$_1$-ru-ga*   *to$_2$mo$_2$si-**sa***
    boat.people-ACC   see-NML-GEN   be.enviable-**FIN**
    'How enviable it is to see the boat-people!'   (Wrona 2008: 206)

The Uralic languages also display a recurrent tendency towards direct insubordination. Deverbal noun suffixes such as Proto-Uralic **-k*, **-pÄ*, **-mə* and **-śÄ* are thought to have developed into finite markers for present (**-k*, **-pÄ*) and past (**-mə*, **-śÄ*) tense, either in Proto-Uralic or after the separation of the daughter languages (Collinder 1965: 110–115; Janhunen 1982: 36–37). Eastern Khanty preserves only a faint trace of this development since the finite form of the negative verb can be marked with the perfective participle *-əm*, as illustrated in example (11). However, the phenomenon is well preserved in the Mansi cognate deverbal noun suffix *-əm* in *uul-* 'to sleep' > *uuləm* 'sleep', which has developed into the finite past, illustrated in example (12). Nikolaeva (1999) also observes the development in the Northern Khanty dialects.

(11)   Eastern Khanty
    məta   *wajaɣ*   *lök*   *ənt-im*
    some   animal   track   NEG-FIN
    'There is not a single animal track'   (Filchenko 2007: 429)

(12) Mansi
       am   joht-um-m
       I   come-FIN-1SG
       'I have come'   (Collinder 1965: 113)

In Nivkh, there is a single instance of direct insubordination, but the phenomenon does not seem to be recurrent. It concerns the deverbal action noun and infinitive suffix *-d'* which has developed over participial use into a finite form *-d'*:[8]

(13) Nivkh
       if   hum-d'   hyjm-d'
       he   live-NML   know-FIN
       'He knows the living one/ (his) life.'   (Malchukov 2013: 200)

The remaining neighbouring languages under discussion display strategies other than direct insubordination in grammaticalizing non-finite suffixes to finite suffixes. In Yukaghir and Mandarin, for instance, clausal nominalization in a construction with a copula is the main source for developing new finite constructions. Many Sinitic languages use focus constructions consisting of a nominalizer plus a copula verb; dropping the copula then paves the way for developing finite constructions. The Mandarin *shi . . . de* focus constructions, for instance, consist of a copula *shi* and a nominalizer *de*, whereas the finite stance construction appears without the copula (Yap and Matthews 2008: 20). Similar processes are found in the Siberian area, for instance in Yukaghir (Malchukov 2013: 192–195). In Kolyma Yukaghir, the deverbal action noun suffix *-l* in *pala:-* 'to escape' > *pala:l* '(a situation of) escaping' has developed into a finite form in subject focus constructions, as illustrated in (14). The intransitive subject 'I' takes a focus marker *-ek*, which is also used to mark nominal predicates, thus pointing to its origin as a copula-like form. As such, the example in (14) can be derived from a cleft-like construction 'It is me sitting'.

(14) Kolyma Yukaghir
       *Met-ek   moda-**l***
       I-FOC   sit-**FIN**
       'I sit'   (Malchukov 2013: 194)

Ket displays yet another strategy to develop finite markers, namely to reduce the matrix predicate to an affix on the former dependent verb. In example (15), for instance, the matrix verb *bimbata* 'it is audible' is reduced to a present suffix *-bɛta ~ -bata* on verbs expressing sound production (Malchukov 2013: 196–197):

(15) Ket
(15a) *tam   bis'ɛŋ   in'ŋɛj   **bi-mbata***
       PT   what   sound   **be.audible-FIN**
       'a certain sound is audible'   (Werner 1997: 170)

---

[8] Note that Kortlandt (2004: 4) identified the Nivkh suffix *-d'* with the Indo-Uralic participial suffix *-nt*, considering it as evidence of a common origin.

(15b) *p-kutəl'ej-**bɛta***
       1SG.POSS-whistle-**FIN**
       'I whistle'   (Werner 1997: 187)

In Ainu, deverbal noun suffixes appear to be functioning as both derivational suffixes and syntactic clausal nominalizers, but there is no indication that they have developed into finite endings. Ainu lacks other non-
finite markers such as participial or converb affixes that could be open to
developing into finite markers. Similarly, Rukai does not exhibit traces of
direct insubordination.

   The languages of the world use a variety of mechanisms for developing
finite function on formerly non-finite forms such as (i) verbalization of
nominal predicates plus finite copula with subsequent copula erosion;
(ii) reduction of a finite verb to affix; (iii) insubordination through ellipsis
of a matrix clause and (iv) direct insubordination.

F26 Grammaticalization from negative verb to verbal negator
The historical development of negation in the Transeurasian languages
involves a recurrent development of an independent negative verb into
a negative auxiliary verb, which may move from preposed to postposed
position and eventually assume suffix status (Robbeets 2014). All Tungusic
languages except Manchu have preserved evidence supporting the reconstruction of a negative verb pTg. **e-* 'not to be, not to exist'. There are some
instances of independent use of the negative verb, i.e. without a lexical
verb, where it means 'not to exist, not to live' as in the Evenki example in
(16a). In example (16b), the negative verb acts as a finite auxiliary to the
lexical verb, which assumes an invariant adnominal form. In spite of SOV
word order, the finite negative verb is preposed to the lexical verb.
In emotive sentences, such as in example (16c), the negative auxiliary
may move to a postposed position. The Nanai example in (17) represents
the final stage of the negative cycle, i.e. fusion, whereby the auxiliary
negative verb has assumed the status of derivational suffix on the lexical
verb and its phonological form is reduced to lengthening of the stem-final
vowel. Although its predecessor Jurchen preserves traces of pTg. **e-* 'not to
be, not to exist', Manchu does not, but a similar negative cycle can be
reconstructed for the verbal negator Ma. *aku:*.

(16)   Evenki
       a. *esile   e-dyeli-m   tadu-gla*
          now   NEG-FUT-1SG   there-ENCL
          'Now I will not be (live) there.'   (Nedjalkov 1994: 27)
       b. *nungan nekun-mi   e-ce-n   suru-v-re.*
          he   younger.brother-POSS.REFL NEG-PST-3SG go.away-CAUS-ADN
          'He did not lead his younger   (Nedjalkov 1994: 11)
          brother away.'
       c. *nungan   songo-ro   e-ce-n*
          he   cry-ADN   NEG-PST-3SG
          'He did not cry [– what's the use of crying?].'   (Nedjalkov 1994: 8)

(17)   Nanai
       xola:-ci-si
       read.NEG-PST-2SG
       'You didn't read.'

Like Old Turkic, Turkish has a verbal negative suffix -*mA*- that can be derived from an original negative verb pTk. *ma- 'not to exist'. The verbal origin is supported by the occurrence of a negative postposition *mar* in Chuvash, which contains a deverbal noun suffix *-*r* and can take a nominal argument such as the directive case in debitive constructions. The Middle Mongolian negative verb stem *ese*- 'not to be, not to exist' survived in a number of conjugated forms, such as with the past marker -*be*- in example (18a), but gradually the negative auxiliary became used as an invariant form, transferring its entire inflection to the lexical verb, i.e. the past marker -*be* is attached to *ire*- 'to come' in example (18b).

(18)   Written Mongolian
       a. *ükü-be-üü*   *ese-be-üü*
          die-PST-INTER   NEG-PST-INTER
          'Did [he] die or did [he] not?'   (Poppe 1954: 175)
       b. *manu baɣši   ese   ire-be*
          our   teacher   NEG   come-PST
          'Our teacher did not come.'   (Poppe 1954: 175)

The Middle and Contemporary Korean verbal negator MK *a·ni*, K *an(i)* can be derived from an original negative verb *an- and the suffix MK -*i* that derives both nouns and adverbs from verbs. Gradually, the negator *ani* is being replaced by an analytic construction consisting of *ani* augmented by the finite auxiliary MK *ho*-, K *ha*- 'to do, be', which usually contracts to *anh*- 'not to do' in Contemporary Korean. This seems to reflect the start of the next negative cycle, whereby the grammaticalized verbal negator is replaced by a new negative construction in which a negative verb is restored in its function as finite auxiliary to the lexical verb, which is nominalized with the suffix -*ci*.

(19)   Middle Korean
       ˝es·tyey   a·ni   wo-no-·-n-ywo
       why   NEG   come-PROC-ADN-INTER
       'Why is [he] not coming?'   (Martin 1992: 420)

(20)   Korean
       apenim   un   ka-ci   anh-usy-e
       father   TOP   go-NML   NEG-HON-FIN
       'Father is not going.'   (Robbeets 2015)

Old and Contemporary Japanese use an independent negative existential adjective *na*- 'to be non-existent, not to exist', illustrated in (21a), which is thought to derive from the same origin as the Old Japanese negative suffix -*(a)n*-, illustrated in (21b) (Martin 1988: 821). As such, an original negative verb pJ *ana- 'not to exist' seems to have developed into a negative suffix. Negative imperative constructions with na- preserve a trace of the originally preposed position of the negative auxiliary.

(21)   Old Japanese
        a. *s-uru*   *sube₁-no₂*   *na-sa*
           do-ADN   way-GEN   NEG-NML
           'Nothing can be done.'   (Vovin 2009: 483)

        b. *ki₁mi₁-ga*   *k-i₁-mas-an-u*
           lord-GEN   come-CONV-deign-NEG-ADN
           'You did not come, [my] lord.'   (Vovin 2009: 788)

Similar to the Transeurasian languages, one of the characteristics of the Uralic languages is the expression of negation by means of a construction, comprising a fully inflected negative auxiliary and a largely invariant lexical verb (Comrie 1981; Honti 1997; Janhunen 1982: 37; Payne 1985: 215–221; Suihkonen 2002: 173). The construction may develop in ways which result in a redistribution of inflectional categories between the negative verb and the lexical verb. Eventually, as is the case for the negative particles Khanty *əntə* or Estonian *ei*, the negative auxiliary may become totally free of inflections and turn into an invariant verbal negator, which recalls the situation in Mongolic in (18b). However, there are no examples in Uralic in which the negative auxiliary ultimately becomes a suffix, as it does in Turkic, Tungusic and Japanese. In Yukaghir, clausal negation is expressed by a proclitic *el-*, which usually precedes the verb, but in spite of the formal similarity with the Proto-Uralic negative auxiliary *e-*, there are no language-internal indications that it originated in a negative verb or auxiliary (Fubito Endo, personal communication). Clausal negation in Nivkh is expressed in three ways: (i) a construction with the negative verb *ķ'au-* 'not to be, not to have' preceded by the lexical verb in an invariant dative case form; (ii) an incorporation of the negative verb *ķavr-/gavr-* 'not to be, not to have' incorporated into the verbal form; (iii) a negative suffix *-rla / -tla*. Given the formal similarity between the negative verb *ķ'au-* and the negative affix *-ķavr-*, it is not unlikely that they go back to the same source (Ekaterina Gruzdeva, personal communication). Among the many negatives used in Mandarin, the most general and neutral negation is expressed by *bu*, whereas the existential negative *mei* 'there is not, has not' is used to negate the completion of an event 'not yet'. Both *mei* and *bu* originate as verbs (van Gelderen 2008: 225). Ainu uses a negative particle that precedes the verb (e.g. *somo ku-oman* [NEG 1SG-go] 'I do not go'). The non-verbal status of *somo* is indicated by the fact that it does not take any personal affix. There are also no indications that the Ket negative particle *bə:n* or the Rukai negative suffix *-ka* originate in a negative verb.

The expression of negation via negative auxiliaries is worldwide a minor type to begin with, found in only 40 (17 per cent) out of 240 languages in

Dahl's (1979) sample, which is areally biased towards Uralic and Altaic languages, in 45 (4 per cent) out of 1,011 languages in Dryer's (2005d) sample, and in 16 (5 per cent) out of the 297 languages in Miestamo's (2005) sample. As a consequence, the particular development of negative verbs to auxiliaries to particles or suffixes is hence even rarer.

F27 A morphologically simplex first person plural pronoun is complemented by the grammaticalization of the first person pronoun augmented with a collective-plural marker When dealing with the inclusive/exclusive distinction in first person plural pronouns in Section 22.2.2 (F11), it was mentioned that most Turkic languages and Korean complement their first person plural pronoun (Tk./OT *biz* 'we'; K/ MK *wuli* 'we') with an augmented collective-plural form (Tk./OT *biz-ler* 'we (as a group)'; K *wuli-tul*, MK *wuli-tolh* 'we (as a group)'). A similar tendency has been found in the history of Japanese, where the first person singular / plural OJ *wa-* 'I, we' coexists with the same form augmented by a collective marker OJ *wa-re* 'we', a form which in its turn was later augmented into *ware-ra* 'we' in the history of Japanese. Etymologically, the Middle Mongolian inclusive *bida*, reflected in the Khalkha formally inclusive oblique *bidn-*, derives from the first person singular MMo. *bi* 'I' and a plural suffix *-dA*, which also occurs in the plural demonstrative pronouns MMo. *e-de* 'these' versus *te-de* 'those' (Doerfer 1985: 2; Domii 2006; Nevskaya 2010: 119).[9] Domii argues that originally, **ba* and **bi-da* complemented each other as plural pronouns and that the distinction between exclusive and inclusive meaning was a secondary development. The Tungusic exclusives Evk. *bu* and Ma. *be* can be derived from the first person plural pTg. **bö* and an augmented plural **bö-(x)e*, respectively (Doerfer 1978: 81–83, 95–96; Janhunen 2013: 217), whereas the inclusive Evk. *mut ~ mit* may go back to pTg. **bö* plus the collective suffix pTg. **-ti* (Benzing 1955: 1020) and the inclusive Ma. *muse* may be an extension of this root with the collective suffix *-sA* (Benzing 1955: 1017–1018). This analysis suggests that successive cycles of plural augmentation on morphologically simplex (or simplified) plural pronouns have triggered the secondary development of an inclusive/exclusive distinction in Tungusic. As far as the Uralic languages are concerned, Khanty makes a commonly found distinction between pronouns in the first person singular (*mä* 'I'), dual (*min* 'both you and me') and plural (*mǝŋ ~ miŋ* 'we'), but it does not reflect any trace of plural augmentation on the first person plural pronoun. Similarly, no traces of plural augmentation on first person plural pronouns are found in Ket or Yukaghir. In Rukai, the first person plural inclusive *-mita* [NOM] is formally underivable from the exclusive *-nai ~ nai-* [NOM]. The personal pronouns in Ainu have all grammaticalized from person affixes followed by any one of

---

[9] An alternative analysis, deriving the inclusive MMo. *bida* from the first person singular pronoun **bi* 'I' plus the second plural pronoun **ta* 'you (many)' is proposed by Janhunen (2013: 215), but the voicing of the medial dental stop would represent an irregular development.

several existential verbs meaning 'exist'. The first person plural pronoun *aoka(i)*, for instance, consists of the first person plural inclusive transitive subject affix *a-* and the verb *oka* 'to exist'. In Nivkh, however, all plural personal pronouns can optionally be augmented with a plural suffix; the first person plural exclusive pronoun, for instance, appears either as *n'yŋ-ø* or as *n'yŋ-gu* [1PL-PL] 'we'. In Mandarin, two separate roots for the first person singular *wŏ* and *zán* pluralized, along with the suffix *-men*, into the derived exclusive *wŏmen* and inclusive *zánmen* 'we'. However, since in Classical Chinese *wŏ* 'I' could be used as a first person plural 'we' as well, the exclusive *wŏmen* can be regarded as an instance of plural augmentation.

22.2.6 Overview

In the body of this chapter, I have set up a list of 27 feature labels, chosen to maximize positive values for the Transeurasian languages. These features, inserted as vertical comparison points in the tables below, have been examined for selected representatives among the Transeurasian languages and their linguistic neighbours, which are inserted as horizontal comparative points. In the tables, I summarize the observations made above by introducing plus (+) and minus (–) values in the corresponding cells. This then leads to a quantification of the number of plus values in the last row.

As far as the feature values for the Transeurasian languages are concerned, Table 22.1 shows the following tendencies. First, the typological coherence seems to be greater for historical than for the contemporary stages of the languages investigated. This suggests that Transeurasian areality has decreased over the last millennium. Second, maximal coherence is found in the Mongolic and Tungusic languages, with minor deviations from the prototype in the Turkic languages in the west and somewhat more in the Japonic and Koreanic languages in the eastern periphery. Third, the deviation from the prototype in the east does not reflect a gradual loss as we proceed from Korean to Japanese, but rather an *en bloc* reduction of features or even a slight increase for Old Japanese.

As far as the feature values for representative neighbouring languages are concerned, Table 22.2 shows the following tendencies. First, the neighbouring languages show significantly stronger deviations from the prototype than do any of the investigated Transeurasian varieties. This suggests that it is meaningful to apply the concept of 'areality' to the Transeurasian languages in the sense that they reflect a geographical concentration of linguistic features that sets them apart from the selected neighbouring languages. Second, Khanty and Yukaghir show more typological similarity with the Transeurasian prototype than do other neighbouring languages. Note that for at least three of the examined features (i.e. F6, F18, F22), Khanty yields a minus value where the Uralic prototype would yield a plus value. This suggests that 'areality' may also apply in a wider, but less

Table 22.1 *Feature values for selected Transeurasian languages along with their historical stages*

	Tk.	(pre-)OT	Khal.	(pre-)MMo.	Evk.	(pre-)Ma.	K	(pre-)MK	J	(pre-)OJ
F1	+	+	+	+	+	+	+	+	+	+
F2	+	+	+	+	+	+	+	+	+	+
F3	+	+	+	+	+	+	+	+	−	?
F4	−	−	+	+	+	+	−	+	−	?
F5	+	+	+	+	−	+	+	+	+	+
F6	+	+	+	+	+	+	+	+	+	+
F7	+	+	+	+	+	+	+	+	+	+
F8	+	+	+	+	+	+	−	−	+	−
F9	+	?	+	?	−	?	+	?	+	?
F10	−	+	+	+	+	+	−	−	−	+
F11	−	−	−	+	+	+	−	+	−	−
F12	−	+	−	+	+	+	+	+	+	+
F13	−	+	−	+	−	+	−	−	−	−
F14	+	+	+	+	+	−	−	+	+	+
F15	+	+	+	+	+	+	+	+	+	+
F16	+	+	+	+	+	+	+	+	+	+
F17	+	+	+	+	+	+	+	+	−	+
F18	−	+	+	+	+	+	−	−	−	−
F19	−	+	+	+	+	+	−	−	−	−
F20	+	+	+	+	+	+	+	+	+	+
F21	+	+	+	+	+	+	+	+	+	+
F22	+	+	+	+	+	+	+	+	+	+
F23	+	+	+	+	+	+	+	+	+	+
F24	+	+	+	+	+	+	+	−	+	+
F25	+	+	+	+	+	+	+	+	+	+
F26	+	+	+	+	+	−	+	+	+	+
F27	+	+	+	+	+	+	+	+	+	+
	20	24	24	26	24	25	19	19	18	20

Table 22.2 *Feature values for representative neighbouring languages*

	Khan.	Ket	Yuk.	Niv.	Ain.	Ch.	Ruk.
F1	+	+	+	+	+	−	+
F2	+	−	+	+	+	−	+
F3	+	−	+	+	+	−	−
F4	−	−	+	?	?	−	−
F5	+	+	+	−	+	+	−
F6	−	+	+	−	−	−	−
F7	+	+	+	−	+	+	+
F8	−	+	+	−	−	−	+
F9	−	−	?	−	−	−	−
F10	+	−	−	−	−	+	−
F11	−	−	−	+	−	+	+
F12	−	−	−	−	−	−	−
F13	−	−	+	−	−	−	−
F14	−	−	−	−	−	−	−
F15	+	+	+	+	+	−	+
F16	+	−	+	−	−	−	−
F17	+	+	+	−	−	−	+
F18	−	−	+	−	−	−	−
F19	+	−	−	−	−	−	+
F20	+	+	+	+	+	−	−
F21	+	+	+	+	+	+	−
F22	−	−	+	+	−	−	−
F23	−	+	−	+	−	−	+
F24	−	+	+	−	−	−	+
F25	+	−	−	+	−	−	−
F26	+	−	−	+	−	+	−
F27	−	−	−	+	−	+	−
	14	11	17	12	8	7	8

coherent sense to the belt of Transeurasian-Yukaghiric-Uralic languages. Third, the investigated languages of North Asia have more typological features in common than those in Southeast Asia, i.e. Mandarin and Rukai. This suggests a third ring of areality that is the least uniform, involving the languages of North Asia.

22.3   Interpretation of the Observations

22.3.1   Delimitation of Areality

The Transeurasian continuum has clear boundaries which delimit the language type in relation to its neighbours both to the north (Yeniseic, Yukaghiric) and east (Nivkh, Ainu) as well as to the south (Sinitic, Austronesian). Although the observations above are in line with Janhunen's (2009: 61–62) findings about a certain internal uniformity in the larger Ural-Altaic belt, they also suggest including Yukaghir in this larger belt, and they indicate additional boundaries in areality between the Uralic and the Transeurasian languages as such. Among the features that enable us to delimit the Transeurasian languages in relation to their Uralic neighbours are: F4 tongue root harmony in Transeurasian (and Yukaghir) versus palatal harmony in Uralic; F8 voicing distinction for stops in Transeurasian (and Yukaghir) versus original singleton–geminate distinction in Uralic; F9 non-verbal strategy of verbal borrowing in Transeurasian versus direct insertion in Uralic; F11 inclusive/exclusive distinction in Transeurasian versus none in Uralic (and Yukaghir); F12/F13 mixed and switched encoding of property words in Transeurasian (and perhaps originally in Yukaghir) versus nominal encoding in Uralic; F14 partial emphatic reduplication in Transeurasian versus none in Uralic (and Yukaghir); F18 absence of initial *m* in the nominative first person singular versus presence in Uralic (and Yukaghir); F25 development of a negative verb into a suffix in Transeurasian versus none in Uralic (and Yukaghir); and F27 augmented first person plural pronoun in Transeurasian versus none in Uralic (and Yukaghir). For some features such as F23 and F24, Uralic makes use of a larger variety of strategies than the Transeurasian languages, where all languages uniformly use locative possession or ablative comparatives. It is remarkable that Yukaghir aligns with Uralic rather than with Transeurasian in more than half of the delimiting features (i.e. F9, F11, F14, F18, F25 and F27), although it is geographically adjacent to Transeurasian languages such as Yakut (Turkic) and some Northern Tungusic languages, but not to the Uralic languages. In my opinion, this observation is probably not coincidental, but it might reflect the alleged genetic relatedness between Uralic and Yukaghir proposed by, among others, Collinder (1965).

22.3.2 Deviations from the Prototype

Along the margins of the Transeurasian continuum, we can observe examples of gradual loss of Transeurasian features in the western and eastern peripheries, as well as gradual adoption of Transeurasian features, as in the case of Mandarin.

Examples of original Transeurasian features changing in the western periphery under Uralic influence are: F4 Transeurasian tongue root harmony, which aligns with the Uralic languages as palatal harmony in Turkic; F12 gradual loss of verbal encoding of property words – mirroring Uralic nominal encoding – as one proceeds from older to contemporary varieties and from Tungusic in the east to Turkic in the west; and F18 the secondary development of *m*-initials yielding a *mi–Ti* opposition in first versus second person singular pronouns in Turkic, Mongolic and Tungusic.

Changes in areality in the eastern peripheries may take place under the influence of the languages to the extreme northeast of the Siberian area or under Chinese influence. Examples of original Transeurasian features in Tungusic and Mongolic changing under Siberian influence are: F5 the secondary assimilation of pTg. **g-* into an initial velar nasal in Tungusic, in line with Nivkh; and F11/F27 the secondary development of an inclusive/exclusive distinction on augmented plural pronouns, mirroring the situation in Ainu and Nivkh. Examples of Korean and Japanese features aligning with the extreme northeast Siberian area are the lack of voicing distinction in Korean and Old Japanese, in line with Ainu, Nivkh and Chukchi, and F10 the development of a mesial demonstrative distinction in Japanese and its presence in Korean, similar to the situation in Yukaghir, Ainu and Nivkh.

Chinese features seem to have diffused into Manchu, Korean and Japanese, for instance: F1 the gradual increase of monosyllabic roots in Japanese; F2 the development of simple tone systems in Japanese and Korean; F3/F4 the alleged erosion of tongue root vowel harmony in Old Japanese; F12 the relatively strong proportion of verbally encoded property words in Japanese and Korean in comparison to the other Transeurasian languages; F15 the increase of analytic features in Manchu in comparison to the other Tungusic languages; F17 the increase of sortal numeral classifiers in Manchu vis-à-vis the other Tungusic languages and in Japanese and Korean vis-à-vis older varieties of the languages; F19 the gradual de-pronominalization, which has taken place in the recorded history of Japanese and Korean; and F23 the development of topic possessives in Korean and Japanese. Note that some Transeurasian languages to the centre of the continuum, such as several Turkic and Mongolic languages of the Amdo Qinghai region, have also lost prototypical Transeurasian features under the influence of Chinese and other languages of the area (Janhunen 2007).

However, the above observations support previous studies by Hashimoto (1986), Norman (1988: 10–12, 20) and Comrie (2008), arguing that the Transeurasian languages have also left a serious mark on the linguistic structure of Chinese. The following developments illustrate how Chinese may have changed some of its original Mainland Southeast Asian features under Transeurasian influence: F1 the development of a greater number of polysyllabic roots compared to Classical Chinese; F7 the simplification and loss of consonant clusters compared to Old Chinese; F10 the development of a two-way distinction in demonstratives compared to the three-way distinction in Classical Chinese; F11 the development of an inclusive/exclusive distinction in first person plural pronouns in Beijing and certain other northern Chinese dialects, which was not found in Old Chinese; F16 the weak suffixing tendency of Mandarin as opposed to other Sinitic languages; and F21 the rare combination of SVO sentence order and GAN noun phrase order in Mandarin, absent in almost all the other languages of Southeast Asia. Geographically, Chinese is located between the Transeurasian languages and the languages of Mainland Southeast Asia, an intermediate position, which it also occupies from the point of view of typology.

Finally, some features in the Siberian languages to the extreme northeast seem to have diffused directly from Southeast Asia, without a Transeurasian intermediary: F2 the occurrence of two distinctive tones in Nivkh in comparison to the relatively simple pitch-accent systems of Japanese and Korean; F12 the exclusively verbal encoding of property words in Yukaghir, Nivkh and Ainu, similar to Mandarin, but different from mixed encoding in Japanese and Korean; and F17 the obligatory use of an extensive list of classifiers in the Nivkh lexicon, and a smaller one in Ainu, recalling the widespread and archaic use of classifiers in Southeast Asia, as opposed to their relatively late development in Japanese and Korean. This observation may gain relevance in the light of theories that derive Ainu from the south (e.g. Bengston and Blažek 2009; Murayama 1992; Vovin 1993).

22.3.3   Diffused versus Inherited Features

A simplistic interpretation of the observations would be to assert that the properties of the Transeurasian language type are universally so common that their parallel occurrence in several adjacent language families is coincidental. This is certainly not the case, however, because the Transeurasian continuum has clear boundaries which delimit the language type in relation to its neighbours both to the west (Uralic), north (Yeniseic, Yukaghiric), east (Nivkh, Ainu) and to the south (Sinitic, Austronesian). Moreover, the relatively low frequency of some features indicates that the shared properties are not due to mere universal principles in linguistic structuring. Above I have provided an estimation of the frequency of 19 out of 27 features. Seven features are not very common (i.e. F5, F9, F10, F16, F20, F21, F23) in the sense that they occur in less than half (50 per cent) but more than a third (33 per cent) of the languages worldwide. Eight features are relatively uncommon in the sense that they occur in less than a third (33 per cent) of the languages worldwide (F4, F11, F12, F13, F18, F19, F23, F25). Phenomena that are relatively infrequent and randomly spread across the world's languages but frequent and geographically concentrated in a specific group of languages provide evidence of a historical connection – be it areal or genealogical – between the languages concerned (Croft 1990: 206–207). The strength of the argument increases when a number of features correlate in a particular part of the world, but not in the world as a whole.

It is important to note that the typological similarities among the Transeurasian languages are accompanied by a significant number of correspondences in the lexicon (see Robbeets 2005) as well as in verb morphology (see Robbeets 2007a, 2007b, 2010, 2012) in such a way that – in my own judgement – these languages are likely to be genealogically related. The most plausible family tree, representing the overall relationships, is given in Figure 22.1. The affiliation of the Transeurasian languages remains debated, but even critics such as Janhunen (1996: 220) would agree that before the first millennium BCE the homelands of the individual language families concerned were all located in a compact area in southern Manchuria, along with the homelands of Ainuic and Nivkh speakers.

Although some of the shared features discussed above, such as F11 inclusive/exclusive distinction in first person plural pronouns, F14 partial emphatic reduplication of nominal property words, or F18 *mi–Ti* opposition in first versus second person singular pronouns are almost certainly contact-induced, others appear to be the residue of common ancestral features, as suggested by the following six observations.

(i) Geography: isolated position of Japanese Although the Sea of Japan and the Tsushima Strait form a strong geographical boundary separating Japanese from the other Transeurasian languages, Japanese is typologically closer to the Transeurasian languages than geographically less isolated languages such as Ket, Yukaghir, Ainu and Nivkh. Even within a prehistoric contact scenario, this suggests that the Transeurasian characteristics in Japanese did not exclusively arise through diffusion because Nivkh was also present in southern Manchuria.

(ii) History: older varieties are more prototypically Transeurasian A comparison of typological uniformity between historical and contemporary stages of the languages investigated suggests that Transeurasian areality has decreased over the last millennium. While influences diffusing from adjacent areas such as Mainland Southeast Asia, Siberian and Uralic have demonstrably displaced earlier Transeurasian features in certain contact zones, I find no evidence of Transeurasian features having displaced earlier Chinese, Siberian or Uralic features inherent to the continuum from Japanese to Turkic. Among the examples of displacement of features in contact zones, for instance, we find that initial velar nasals have developed in Tungusic under Siberian influence (F5), simple tone systems and classifiers have developed in Japanese and Korean under Chinese influence (F2 and F17), and palatal harmony has developed in Turkic under Uralic influence (F4). We furthermore note that nominal encoding of property words has increased in Turkic, Mongolic and Tungusic under Uralic influence, while verbal encoding has increased in Japanese and Korean under Siberian and Southeast Asian influence (F12). However, we find no evidence of Transeurasian features entering, for instance, from the Turkic languages and diffusing all over the Transeurasian area, while displacing original and prototypical Sinitic features. This suggests that Transeurasian features are inherent to these languages.

(iii) Distribution: maximal coherence in Mongolic and Tungusic Maximal structural uniformity is found in the Mongolic and Tungusic languages. This distributional pattern conforms to the expectations for the Mongolic languages within a diffusional scenario, since they constitute the centre of the linguistic continuum, but it is not what one

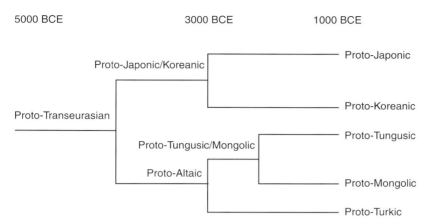

Figure 22.1 Family tree of the Transeurasian languages

would expect for the Tungusic languages, extending towards the north-eastern periphery. The structural coherence in Mongolic and Tungusic recalls the separation of Mongolo-Tungusic in Figure 22.1 as a distinct genealogical unit.

(iv) Distribution: en bloc reduction of features in Korean and Japanese Similarly, the collective rather than gradual reduction – if not slight increase – of features as we proceed from Korean to (Old) Japanese is not what we would expect within a scenario of gradual diffusion. It is furthermore difficult to explain how some Transeurasian features, such as F10 and F19, that show a gap in Korean, have diffused into Japanese without a Korean intermediary.

(v) Cyclicity: recurrent grammaticalization The features involving shared patterns of grammaticalization in Section 22.2.5 are particularly good candidates for genealogical motivation because they are recurrent in different forms and at various chronological stages of the same language. Aikhenvald (2013) characterized contact-induced grammaticalization as 'change against the grain' or atypical grammaticalization, while she regarded genealogically motivated grammaticalization as 'change that reinforces similarities' because it tends to maintain uniformity between related languages. Given that languages tend to renew their formal encodings in cyclic processes of grammaticalization while maintaining their inherited grammatical categories, new forms are thus expected to grammaticalize along shared conceptual pathways to restore old categories (Heath 1998: 729). Consequently, genealogically motivated grammaticalization is expected to recur on different formal encodings at various points in time, while contact-induced grammaticalization is expected to be restricted to a single formal encoding (or to a very limited number of encodings) during a certain period of contact. The repeated waves of grammaticalization and replacement involved in features F25–F27 imply that the parallel patterns are genealogically motivated.

(vi) Isomorphism: shared features combine with formal correspondences The observation that some structural features shared among the Transeurasian languages combine with a formal correspondence of the marker reflecting the particular feature is also indicative of genealogical retention. This is, for instance, the case for: F9 the non-verbal strategy of verbal borrowing employing a deverbal noun suffix of the common shape *-lA- (Tk. -lA-, Khal. -l-, Ud. -lA-, J -r(a)-) to accommodate for verbal borrowings; F19 the formation of a secondary oblique stem of personal pronouns through a common suffix *-n- in all Transeurasian languages, except Korean; F25 direct insubordination involving deverbal noun and finite suffixes of the common shape *-rA-, *-mA, *-n, *-xA ~ *-kA and *-sA (Robbeets 2009, 2015, 2016) across all Transeurasian languages; and F26 the grammaticalization from negative verb to verbal negator, involving common negative verbs of the common shape *ana-, *e- and *ma- across the Transeurasian languages (Robbeets 2014). In instances like these in which isostructuralism coincides with form–function isomorphism, the structural correspondence is likely to be genealogically motivated, especially when it concerns an instance of shared grammaticalization (Robbeets 2013). Note that the Uralic languages also display oblique personal pronouns in -n-, direct insubordination in *-k, *-mə and *-śÄ and grammaticalization of negative verbs in *e-, an observation which seems to point to remote genealogical ties between the Uralic and the Transeurasian languages.

22.4 Conclusion

In this chapter I have tried to show that the Transeurasian languages form an internally homogeneous linguistic continuum. For this purpose, I have examined the areal concentration of 27 features in the Transeurasian languages, providing a typological profile of some contemporary varieties in relation to historical stages of the languages involved and to selected languages immediately outside the continuum. Comparison with neighbours to the north (Yeniseic, Yukaghiric), south (Sinitic, Austronesian), east (Nivkh, Ainu) and west (Uralic) makes it possible to set up boundaries which delimit the Transeurasian prototype. Along the margins of the Transeurasian continuum, I have found examples of gradual loss of Transeurasian features in the western and eastern peripheries, as well as gradual adoption of Transeurasian features, as in the case of Mandarin. The data further suggest that the Transeurasian continuum in its turn is part of a larger Uralic-Yukaghiric-Transeurasian belt of languages, which again is part of a larger area of North Asian languages. Although it is meaningful to apply the concept of 'areality' to the Transeurasian languages in the sense of a historically motivated geographical concentration of linguistic features, I prefer avoiding the label 'area' with reference to these languages because this would imply that all shared properties are the result of diffusion. Observations relating to geography, history, distribution, cyclicity of grammaticalization and combined isomorphism indicate that this is not the case.

A fuller study would need to take more feature values into account and to insert a larger variety of Transeurasian languages as comparative points. Neighbouring languages should also be more diversified, and adjacent languages in the west such as Indo-European languages or languages of the Caucasus region should be included. One should also pay attention to structural dependencies between the features and to considering whether particular features can be more easily accounted for by diffusion or by genealogical retention. For the latter purpose, it would be particularly interesting to take common diachronic mechanisms, such as shared patterns of grammaticalization into fuller account. Although this chapter perhaps raises as many new questions as it answers, I hope to have contributed here to the understanding of areality among the Transeurasian languages.

Abbreviations

Linguistic forms

ABL	ablative
ACC	accusative
ADD	additive
ADN	adnominalizer
CAUS	causative
CLASS	classifier
COM	comitative
COMP	comparative
COND	conditional
CONV	converb
NEG	negative
NML	nominalizer
NOM	nominative
OBL	oblique
PFV	perfective
PL	plural
POL	polite
POSS	possessive
PROC	processive
PST	past
PT	particle
REFL	reflexive
SG	singular
TOP	topic

Languages

Ain.	Ainu
Ch.	Mandarin Chinese
Evk.	Evenki
J	Japanese
K	Korean
Ket	Ket
Khal.	Khalkha
Khan.	Khanty
Ma.	Manchu
MK	Middle Korean
MMo.	Middle Mongolian
Niv.	Nivkh
OJ	Old Japanese
OT	Old Turkic
pJ	Proto-Japonic
pK	Proto-Koreanic
pMo.	Proto-Mongolic
pTg.	Proto-Tungusic
pTk.	Proto-Turkic
Ruk.	Mantauran Rukai
WMo.	Written Mongolian
Yuk.	Yukaghir

Acknowledgement

The research leading to these results has further received funding from the European Research Council (ERC) under the European Union's Horizon 2020 research and innovation programme (grant agreement no. 646612) granted to Martine Robbeets. I thank Anna Bugaeva, Fubito Endo, Andrey Filchenko, Ekaterina Gruzdeva, Seongyeon Ko, Fukui Rei and Elisabeth Zeitoun as well as the editor, Raymond Hickey, for their helpful feedback.

References

Aikhenvald, Alexandra, 2013. Areal diffusion and parallelism in drift: Shared grammaticalization patterns. In Robbeets and Cuyckens (eds), pp. 23–42.

Alpatov, Vladimir and Vera Podlesskaya, 1995. Converbs in Japanese. In Haspelmath and König (eds), pp. 465–486.

Anderson, Gregory, 2005. The velar nasal (ŋ). In Haspelmath et al. (eds), pp. 42–45.

Anderson, Gregory, 2006. Towards a typology of the Siberian linguistic area. In Yaron Matras, April McMahon and Nigel Vincent (eds), *Linguistic Areas: Convergence in Historical and Typological Perspective*, pp. 266–300. Basingstoke, UK: Palgrave Macmillan.

Bengston, John D. and Václav Blažek, 2009. Ainu and Austric: Evidence of genetic relationship. *Journal of Language Relationship* 2: 1–24.

Benzing, Johannes, 1955. Die tungusischen Sprachen: Versuch einer vergleichenden Grammatik. *Abhandlungen der geistes- und sozialwissenschaftlichen Klasse* 11: 949–1099.

Bisang, Walter, 1995. Verb serialization and converbs: Differences and similarities. In Haspelmath and König (eds), pp. 137–188.

Bisang, Walter, 1998. Structural similarities of clause combining in Turkic, Mongolian, Manchu-Tungusic and Japanese: A typological alternative to the hypothesis of a genetic relationship. In Lars Johanson (ed.), *The Mainz Meeting: Proceedings of the Seventh International Conference on Turkish Linguistics*, pp. 199–223. Wiesbaden: Harrassowitz.

Bugaeva, Anna, 2015. Causative constructions in Ainu: A typological perspective with remarks on the diachrony. *STUF – Language Typology and Universals (Sprachtypologie und Universalienforschung)* 68 (4): 439–484.

Bulatova, Nadežda Ja. and Leonore A. Grenoble 1999. *Evenki*. Languages of the World/Materials, vol. 141. Munich: LINCOM.

Collinder, Björn, 1965. *An Introduction to the Uralic Languages*. Berkeley, CA: University of California Press.

Comrie, Bernard, 1981. Negation and other verb categories in the Uralic languages. In Osmo Ikola (ed.), *Congressus Quintis Internationalis Fenno-Ugristarum*, vol. VI, pp. 350–355. Turku: Suomen Kielen Seura.

Comrie, Bernard, 2008. The areal typology of Chinese: Between North and Southeast Asia. In Redouane Djamouri, Barbara Meisterernst and Rint Sybesma (eds), *Chinese Linguistics in Leipzig*, pp. 1–21. Collection des Cahiers de Linguistique Asie Orientale, vol. 12. Paris: École des Hautes Études en Sciences Sociales, Centre de Recherches Linguistiques sur l'Asie Orientale.

Croft, William, 1990. *Typology and Universals*. Cambridge: Cambridge University Press.

Cysouw, Michael, 2005. Inclusive/exclusive forms for 'we'. In Haspelmath et al. (eds), pp. 162–169.

Dahl, Östen, 1979. Typology of sentence negation. *Linguistics* 17: 79–106.

Diessel, Holger, 2005. Distance contrasts in demonstratives. In Haspelmath et al. (eds), pp. 170–173.

Doerfer, Gerhard, 1978. Urtungusisch ö. In Gerhard Doerfer and Michael Weiers (eds), *Beiträge zur nordasiatischen Kulturgeschichte*, pp. 66–116. Tungusica, vol. 1. Wiesbaden: Harrassowitz.

Doerfer, Gerhard, 1985. *Mongolo-Tungusica*. Wiesbaden: Steiner.

Domii, Tumurtogoo, 2006. The inclusive and the exclusive in Mongolian. In T. Shagdarsursen (ed.), *Mongol ulsin ix sürgüülijn: Erdem šinžilgeenij bičig*, pp. 77–78. Acta Mongolica, vol. 6.267. Ulanbaatar: National University of Mongolia.

Dryer, Matthew S., 2005a. Prefixing versus suffixing in inflectional morphology. In Haspelmath et al. (eds), pp. 110–113.

Dryer, Matthew S., 2005b. Order of subject, object, and verb. In Haspelmath et al. (eds), pp. 330–333.

Dryer, Matthew S., 2005c. Order of genitive and noun; Order of adjective and noun. In Haspelmath et al. (eds), pp. 350–357.

Dryer, Matthew, 2005d. Negative morphemes. In Haspelmath et al. (eds), pp. 454–457.

Erdal, Marcel, 2004. *A Grammar of Old Turkic*. Leiden: Brill.

Evans, Nicholas, 2008. Insubordination and its uses. In Irina Nikolaeva (ed.), *Finiteness: Theoretical and Empirical Foundations*, pp. 366–431. Oxford: Oxford University Press.

Filchenko, Andrey Yury, 2007. *A Grammar of Eastern Khanty*. PhD dissertation, Rice University, Houston.

Frellesvig, Bjarke, 2010. *A History of the Japanese Language*. Cambridge: Cambridge University Press.

Frellesvig, Bjarke and John Whitman, 2008. Evidence for seven vowels in Proto-Japanese. In Bjarke Frellesvig and John Whitman (eds), *Proto-Japanese: Issues and Prospects*, pp. 15–41. Current Issues in Linguistic Theory, vol. 294. Amsterdam: John Benjamins.

van Gelderen, Elly, 2008. Negative cycles. *Linguistic Typology* 12: 195–243.

Georg, Stefan, 2007. *A Descriptive Grammar of Ket (Yenisei-Ostyak)*, part 1: *Introduction, Phonology, Morphology*. Folkestone: Global Oriental.

Gil, David, 2005. Numeral classifiers. In Haspelmath et al. (eds), pp. 226–229.

Göksel, Aslï and Celia Kerslake, 2005. *Turkish: A Comprehensive Grammar*. London: Routledge.

Gorelova, Liliya, 2002. *Manchu Grammar*. Leiden: Brill.

Grönbech, Karl, 1936. *Der Türkische Sprachbau*. Copenhagen: Levin and Munksgaard.

Gruzdeva, Ekaterina, 1998. *Nivkh*. Languages of the World/Materials, vol. 111. Munich: LINCOM.

Hashimoto, Mantaro, 1986. The Altaicization of Northern Chinese. In John McCoy and Timothy Light (eds), *Contributions to Sino-Tibetan Studies*, pp. 76–97. Leiden: Brill.

Haspelmath, Martin, 1995. The converb as a cross-linguistically valid category. In Haspelmath and König (eds), pp. 1–56.

Haspelmath, Martin et al. (eds), 2005. *The World Atlas of Language Structures*. Oxford: Oxford University Press.

Haspelmath, Martin and Ekkehard König (eds), 1995. *Converbs in Cross-linguistic Perspective: Structure and Meaning of Adverbial Verb Forms – Adverbial Particles, Gerunds*. Berlin: Mouton de Gruyter.

Heath, Jeffrey, 1998. Hermit crabs: Formal renewal of morphology by phonologically mediated affix substitution. *Language* 74: 728–759.

Honti, László, 1997. Die Negation im Uralischen, parts I–III. *Linguistica Uralica* 2: 81–96, 161–176, 241–252.

Janhunen, Juha, 1981. Korean vowel system in North Asian perspective. *Hangeul* 172: 129–146.

Janhunen, Juha, 1982. On the structure of Proto-Uralic. *Finnisch-ugrische Forschungen* 44: 23–42.

Janhunen, Juha, 1996. *Manchuria: An Ethnic History*. Mémoires de la Société Finno-Ougrienne, vol. 222. Helsinki: Suomalais-Ugrilainen Seura.

Janhunen, Juha, 1997. Problems of primary root structure in pre-proto-Japanic. *International Journal of Central Asian Studies* 2: 14–30.

Janhunen, Juha, 2007. Typological interaction in the Qinghai Linguistic Complex. *Studia Orientalia* 101: 85–103.

Janhunen, Juha, 2009. Proto-Uralic: What, where, and when? *Mémoires de la Société Finno-Ougrienne* 258: 57–78.

Janhunen, Juha, 2012. *Mongolian*. Amsterdam: John Benjamins.

Janhunen, Juha, 2013. Personal pronouns in Core Altaic. In Robbeets and Cuyckens (eds), pp. 211–226.

Johanson, Lars, 1995. On Turkic converb clauses. In Haspelmath and König (eds), pp. 313–348.

Johanson, Lars and Martine Robbeets, 2010. Introduction. In Lars Johanson and Martine Robbeets (eds), *Transeurasian Verbal Morphology in a Comparative Perspective: Genealogy, Contact, Chance*, pp. 1–5. Turcologica, vol. 78. Wiesbaden: Harrassowitz.

Kaiser, Stefan, Yasuko Ichikawa, Noriko Kobayashi and Hirofumi Yamamoto, 2001. *Japanese: A Comprehensive Grammar*. London: Routledge.

Ko, Seongyeon, 2012. *Tongue Root Harmony and Vowel Contrast in Northeast Asian Languages*. PhD dissertation, Cornell University, New York.

Ko, Seongyeon, John Whitman and Andrew Joseph, 2014. Comparative consequences of the tongue root harmony analysis for proto-Tungusic, proto-Mongolic, and proto-Korean. In Martine Robbeets and Walter Bisang (eds), *Paradigm Change in the Transeurasian Languages and Beyond*, pp. 141–176. Amsterdam: John Benjamins.

Kortlandt, Frederik, 2004. Nivkh as a Uralo-Siberian language. In Adam Hyllested, Anders Richardt Jørgensen, Jenny Helena Larsson and Thomas Olander (eds), *Per aspera ad asteriscos: Festschrift in Honour of Jens E. Rasmussen*, pp. 285–289. Innsbruck: IBS.

Lee, Ki-Mun and Robert Ramsey, 2011. *A History of the Korean Language*. Cambridge: Cambridge University Press.

Li, Charles N. and Sandra A. Thompson 1989. *Mandarin Chinese: A Functional Reference Grammar*. Berkeley, CA: University of California Press.

Maddieson, Ian, 2005. Tone. In Haspelmath et al. (eds), pp. 58–61.

Malchukov, Andrej, 2012. Tungusic converbs and a typology of taxis. In Andrej Malchukov and Lindsay J. Whaley (eds), *Recent Advances in Tungusic Linguistics*, pp. 213–228. Turcologica, vol. 89. Wiesbaden: Harrassowitz.

Malchukov, Andrej, 2013. Verbalization and insubordination in Siberian languages. In Robbeets and Cuyckens (eds), pp. 177–208.

Martin, Samuel Elmo, 1988. *A Reference Grammar of Japanese*. Tokyo: Tuttle.

Martin, Samuel Elmo, 1992. *A Reference Grammar of Korean*. Tokyo: Tuttle.

Maslova, Elena, 2003a. *A Grammar of Kolyma Yukaghir*. Mouton Grammar Library, vol. 27. Berlin: Mouton de Gruyter.

Maslova, Elena, 2003b. *Tundra Yukaghir*. Languages of the World/Materials, vol. 372. Munich: LINCOM.

Miestamo, Matti, 2005. *Standard Negation: The Negation of Declarative Verbal Main Clauses in a Typological Perspective*. Empirical Approaches to Language Typology, vol. 31. Berlin: Mouton de Gruyter.

Murayama, Shichirō, 1992. *Ainugo no kigen [Origins of the Ainu Language]*. Tokyo: San'ichi Shobo.

Nedjalkov, Igor V., 1994. Negation in Evenki. In Peter Kahrel and René van den Berg (eds), *Typological Studies in Negation*, pp. 1–34. Amsterdam: John Benjamins.

Nedjalkov, Igor V., 1995. Converbs in Evenki. In Haspelmath and König (eds), pp. 441–464.

Nedjalkov, Igor V., 1997. *Evenki: Descriptive Grammar*. London: Routledge.

Nevskaya, Irina, 2010. Inclusive and Exclusive in Altaic Languages. In Lars Johanson and Martine Robbeets (eds), *Transeurasian Verbal Morphology in a Comparative Perspective: Genealogy, Contact, Chance*, pp. 115–128. Turcologica, vol. 78. Wiesbaden: Harrassowitz.

Nichols, Johanna, 2012. Selection for *M : T* pronominals in Eurasia. In Lars Johanson and Martine Robbeets (eds), *Copies versus Cognates in Bound Morphology*, pp. 47–70. Brill's Studies in Language, Cognition and Culture, vol. 2. Leiden: Brill.

Nichols, Johanna and David Peterson, 2005. Personal pronouns. In Haspelmath et al. (eds), pp. 546–553.

Nikolaeva, Irina, 1999. *Ostyak*. Languages of the World/Materials, vol. 305. Munich: LINCOM.

Norman, Jerry, 1988. *Chinese*. Cambridge Language Surveys. Cambridge: Cambridge University Press.

Payne, John R., 1985. Negation. In Timothy Shopen (ed.), *Language Typology and Syntactic Description*, vol. 1: *Clause Structure*, pp. 197–242. Cambridge: Cambridge University Press.

Poppe, Nicholas, 1954. *Grammar of Written Mongolian*. Wiesbaden: Harrassowitz.

Poppe, Nicholas, 1955. *Introduction to Mongolian Comparative Studies*. Mémoires de la Société Finno-Ougrienne, vol. 110. Helsinki: Suomalais-Ugrilainen Seura.

Poppe, Nicholas, 1964. Der altaische Sprachtyp. In B. Spuler et al. (eds), *Mongolistik*, pp. 1–16. Handbuch der Orientalistik, vol. 5.2. Leiden: Brill.

Rickmeyer, Jens, 1989. Japanisch und der altaische Sprachtyp. Eine Synopsis struktureller Entsprechungen. *Bochumer Jahrbuch zur Ostasienforschung* 12: 313–323.

Robbeets, Martine, 2005. *Is Japanese Related to Korean, Tungusic, Mongolic and Turkic?* Turcologica, vol. 64. Wiesbaden: Harrassowitz.

Robbeets, Martine, 2007a. How the actional suffix chain connects Japanese to Altaic. *Turkic Languages* 11 (1): 3–58.

Robbeets, Martine, 2007b. The causative-passive in the Trans-Eurasian languages. *Turkic Languages* 11 (2): 235–278.

Robbeets, Martine, 2008. If Japanese is Altaic, why is it so simple? In Alexander Lubotsky, Jos Schaeken and Jeroen Wiedenhof (eds), *Evidence and Counter-evidence: Essays in Honour of Frederik Kortlandt*, vol. 2: *General Linguistics*. Studies in Slavic and General Linguistics, vol. 33. Amsterdam: Rodopi.

Robbeets, Martine, 2009. Insubordination in Altaic. *Journal of Philology*, vol. 31. *Ural-Altaic Studies* 1: 61–79.

Robbeets, Martine, 2010. Transeurasian: Can verbal morphology end the controversy? In Lars Johanson and Martine Robbeets (eds), *Transeurasian Verbal Morphology in a Comparative Perspective: Genealogy, Contact, Chance*, pp. 81–114. Turcologica, vol. 78. Wiesbaden: Harrassowitz.

Robbeets, Martine, 2012. Shared verb morphology in the Transeurasian languages: Copy or cognate? In Lars Johanson and Martine Robbeets (eds), *Copies vs. Cognates in Bound Morphology*, pp. 427–446. Brill's Studies in Language, Cognition and Culture, vol. 3. Leiden: Brill.

Robbeets, Martine, 2013. Genealogically motivated grammaticalization. In Robbeets and Cuyckens (eds), pp. 147–175.

Robbeets, Martine, 2014. The development of negation in the Transeurasian languages. In Pirkko Suihkonen and Lindsay J. Whaley (eds), *On Diversity and Complexity of Languages Spoken in Europe and North and Central Asia*, pp. 401–420. Studies in Language Companion Series, vol. 164. Amsterdam: John Benjamins.

Robbeets, Martine, 2015. *Diachrony of Verb Morphology: Japanese and the Transeurasian Languages*. Trends in Linguistics, Studies and Monographs, vol. 291. Berlin: Mouton de Gruyter.

Robbeets, Martine, 2016. Insubordination and the establishment of genealogical relationship. In Nicholas Evans and Honore Watanabe (eds), *Insubordination*, pp. 209–246. Typological Studies in Language, vol. 115. Amsterdam: John Benjamins.

Robbeets, Martine and Hubert Cuyckens (eds), 2013. *Shared Grammaticalization: with Special Focus on the Transeurasian Languages*. Studies in Language Companion Series, vol. 132. Amsterdam: John Benjamins.

Rybatzki, Volker, 2003. Middle Mongol. In Juha Janhunen (ed.), *The Mongolic Languages*, pp. 57–82. London: Routledge.

Shibatani, Masayoshi, 1990. *The Languages of Japan*. Cambridge Language Surveys. Cambridge: Cambridge University Press.

Sohn, Ho-min, 1994. *Korean*. London: Routledge.

Sohn, Ho-min, 2009. The semantics of clause linking in Korean. In R. M. W. Dixon and Alexandra Aikhenvald (eds), *The Semantics of Clause Linking: A Cross-linguistic Typology*, pp. 285–317. Oxford: Oxford University Press.

Stassen, Leon, 1997. *Intransitive Predication*. Oxford: Clarendon Press.

Stassen, Leon, 2005a. Predicative possession. In Haspelmath et al. (eds), pp. 474–477.

Stassen, Leon, 2005b. Predicative adjectives. In Haspelmath et al. (eds), pp. 478–481.

Stassen, Leon, 2005c. Comparative constructions. In Haspelmath et al. (eds), pp. 490–493.

Street, John, 1957. *The Language of the Secret History of the Mongols*. New Haven, CT: American Oriental Society.

Suihkonen, Pirkko, 2002. The Uralic languages. *Fennia* 180 (1/2): 165–176.

Svantesson, Jan-Olof, 1985. Vowel harmony shift in Mongolian. *Lingua* 67 (4): 283–327.

Tamura, Suzuko, 2000. *The Ainu Language*. ICHEL Linguistic Studies, vol. 2. Tokyo: Sanseidō.

Vajda, Edward J., 2004. *Ket*. Languages of the World/Materials, vol. 204. Munich: LINCOM.

Vovin, Alexander, 1993. *A Reconstruction of Proto-Ainu*. Brill's Japanese Studies Library, vol. 4. Leiden: Brill.

Vovin, Alexander, 2005. *A Descriptive and Comparative Grammar of Western Old Japanese*, part 1: *Sources, Script and Phonology, Lexicon, Nominals*. Languages of Asia, vol. 3. Folkestone: Global Oriental.

Vovin, Alexander, 2009. *A Descriptive and Comparative Grammar of Western Old Japanese*, part 2: *Adjectives, Verbs, Adverbs, Conjunctions, Particles, Postpositions*. Languages of Asia, vol. 8. Folkestone: Global Oriental.

Weiers, Michael, 1966. *Untersuchungen zu einer Historischen Grammatik des Präklassischen Schriftmongolisch*. PhD dissertation, Rheinischen Friedrich-Wilhelms-Universität, Bonn.

Werner, Heinrich, 1997. *Die ketische Sprache*. Wiesbaden: Harrassowitz.

Whaley, Lindsay J. and Fengxiang Li, 2000. Emphatic reduplication in Oroqen and its Altaic context. *Linguistics* 38 (2): 355–372.

Whitman, John Bradford, 1990. A rule of medial *-r- loss in pre-Old Japanese. In Philip Baldi (ed.), *Linguistic Change and Reconstruction Methodology*, pp. 511–545. Trends in Linguistics: Studies and Monographs, vol. 45. Berlin: Mouton de Gruyter.

Wohlgemuth, Jan, 2009. *A Typology of Verbal Borrowings*. Berlin: Mouton de Gruyter.

Wrona, Janick, 2008. The nominal and adnominal forms in Old Japanese: Consequences for a reconstruction of pre-Old Japanese syntax. In Bjarke Frellesvig and John Whitman (eds), *Proto-Japanese: Issues and Prospects*, pp. 193–215. Current Issues in Linguistic Theory, vol. 294. Amsterdam: John Benjamins.

Yap, Foong Ha and Stephen Matthews, 2008. The development of nominalizers in East Asian and Tibeto-Burman languages. In María José López-Couso and Elena Seoane (eds), *Rethinking Grammaticalization: New Perspectives*, pp. 309–341. Amsterdam: John Benjamins.

Zeitoun, Elizabeth, 2007. *A Grammar of Mantauran (Rukai)*. Taipei: Institute of Linguistics, Academia Sinica.

23

The Changing Profile of Case Marking in the Northeastern Siberia Area

Gregory D. S. Anderson

23.1 Introduction

A range of phonological and morphosyntactic features can be found across various genetically unrelated Siberian languages that do not cluster in such manner outside the region, and so it has been argued that Siberia exhibits the core features of a linguistic area as conventionally understood (Anderson 2001, 2003, 2006). A closer inspection of the features discussed reveals that it is primarily the northeastern part of Siberia where the majority of the languages with the highest concentration of these features are found. In this chapter I examine several features found widely among the languages of Northeastern Siberia relating to case marking, and discuss possible developmental histories for certain of these. Like most linguistic areas there is no one source for the full set of features found. In individual instances, features may be characteristic of proto-languages of specific genetic units and not others, and thus diffusion, borrowing or interference through shift from one to another may explain their appearance, when the comparative data suggest such (a) feature(s) may be non-original. In particular, all of the features discussed in Anderson (2006) can be reconstructed to Proto-Northern Tungusic (and most to Proto-Tungusic) and as such, Northern Tungusic languages appear to be central to the development of the Northeastern Siberia linguistic area. Further, Northern Tungusic languages are by far the most widespread in the region, and bilingualism between Evenki – or Even – and other languages (e.g. Evenki/Even with Sakha/Yakut, Yukaghir, or Koryak, etc.) is or was common throughout the region, consistent with Northern Tungusic being the vector of diffusion in Siberia.[1] However, not all such case oppositions found in Northeastern

---

Siberia that are diagnostic of the area *per se* are of Tungusic origin; like most linguistic areas, the history of direct borrowing, calquing, diffusion and convergence is complex and varied, and in particular the role of Yukaghiric languages in the development of the linguistic area should not be downplayed. In this study I present four such features found in Northeastern Siberian languages with respect to case: (i) an instrumental versus comitative contrast, (ii) a prolative case form, (iii) a dative versus allative case contrast, and (iv) the use of particular case forms with semi-finite verb forms to create various functional types of subordinate clauses. Further, with respect to the use of case marking to encode subordination, the pre-Russian contact profile of Northeastern Siberian languages (and thus of the Northeastern Siberia linguistic area) differs from contemporary usage norms due to the fact that all Siberian languages have experienced intense language contact with Russian in the past two to five centuries. Russian influence is now pronounced across most indigenous Siberian languages, such that a new structural convergence type is emerging (Anderson 2005, 2015; Grenoble 2000, 2010, 2012a, 2012b, 2014; Oskolskaya and Stoynova 2013) that differs in obvious ways from the previous typological profile, specifically in the morphosyntax of complex sentences. This shift is briefly examined at the conclusion of this study.

23.1.1   Indigenous Languages of Siberia

Indigenous Siberian languages currently number slightly more than three dozen in total, though we know there were once more, as a number have not survived into the twenty-first century. Alas, it seems that most indigenous Siberian languages will not likely survive the twenty-first century. While numbering only a handful of languages, there is still a considerable amount of genetic-linguistic diversity attested within the ranks of indigenous Siberian languages. These are two of the reasons that (eastern) Siberia is considered to be a language hotspot (Anderson 2010, 2011). Indeed, no fewer than twelve independent genetic units and one genetically unclassifiable mixed language may be reckoned within Siberia, almost half of which only occur in this region.[2] A list of currently extant or recently extinct Siberian languages with their genetic affiliations is given in Table 23.1 (roughly structured in a west-to-east configuration).[3]

---

addresses similar genetic and linguistic interconnections between Turkic and Tungusic elements in the history of Sakha (Yakut).

[2] I take Siberia in this work to mean the entire Asian part of Russia east of the Ural mountains, and thus subsuming the Soviet and post-Soviet Federal Russian regions called Siberia and the Far East.

[3] Highly mobile and widespread, Evenki of the Tungusic genetic unit disrupts this distribution a bit, as does the enormous territory occupied by the Sakha. In addition to these still extant languages, the following now extinct languages have also been considered in this study: Sayan Samoyed[†] (Samoyedic), Arin[†], Assan[†], Kott[†], Pumpokol[†], Yugh[†] (Yeniseic), Chuvan[†], Omok[†] (Yukaghiric), Sireniki[†] (Eskimoic). There are conflicting reports on whether Kerek of the Chukotko-Kamchatkan genetic unit still has any living speakers, but given how recently it must have gone extinct if it has, there are quite likely to be semi-speakers remaining, so it is listed among the still extant languages in Table 23.1.

Table 23.1 *Languages of Native Siberia*

Language family	Languages
Samoyedic	Nenets, Enets, Nganasan, Sel'kup
Ob-Ugric[4]	Khanty, Mansi
Yeniseic	Ket
Turkic	Qumandy, Quu, Altai, Telengit, Teleut, Chulym, Dolgan, Shor, Tofa, Tuvan, Xakas, Tuba, Yakut (Sakha)
Mongolic	Buryat
Tungusic	Evenki, Even, Nanai, Negidal, Orochi, Orok, Udihe, Ul'cha
Yukaghiric	Wadul (Tundra), Odul (Kolyma)
Itelmenic	Itelmen
Chukotko-Kamchatkan	Al'utor, Chukchi, Kerek[(†)], Koryak
Eskimoic	Naukan, Siberian Yup'ik
Aleutic	Bering Aleut
Unclassifiable	Copper Island Aleut
Nivkh	Amur Nivkh, Sakhalin Nivkh

Traditionally, there were local connections and interactions between different groups such that chains of local bilingualism extend(ed) across almost the entire region.[5] Over the past 200 years or so, bilingualism in Russian has extended to be now nearly universal in indigenous Siberian communities.[5]

23.1.2   Case Systems of the Languages of Northeastern Siberia

Northeastern Siberian languages all make use of different nominal case forms, grammatical, locational/directional, instrumental, etc. Many have six to twelve case forms attested. Indeed, with respect to certain characteristic features of grammatical case marking, the languages of Northeastern Siberia have little in common, as, for example, northern Chukotko-Kamchatkan languages show ergative alignment and case marking, but Northern Tungusic and Turkic languages show accusative alignment and case marking, and Yukaghiric has a system of case marking based on the relative focal status or discourse-salience of arguments. However, three specific case functions and contrasts do typify the languages of Northeastern Siberia, and help to unite these groups in an areal cluster. Like all individual features in any putative linguistic area, any one feature may extend beyond this area, but it is the clustering of them that delineates Northeastern Siberian languages from adjacent areas. These three characteristic case phenomena include (i) the functional and formal contrast between instrumental and comitative, (ii) the presence of the prolative or prosecutive case, and (iii) a dative versus allative contrast.

---

[4] Khanty and Mansi each represent several languages or mutually unintelligible dialects. Some Mansi varieties and probably some Khanty ones too are currently extinct. Some eastern Ob-Ugric groups interacted with western Evenki.

[5] Studies on aspects of these interactions including lexical and structural interference can be found in such works as Tsyndendambaev (1981) or Pakendorf (2007).

[6] Tuva in southern Siberia just north of Mongolia stands out as the one area with extensive monolingualism in the indigenous language.

In general, one can observe a cline in number of contrastive case forms within a given Siberian language from lower to higher when moving from the southwest to the northeast.[7] The most reduced case inventories among indigenous Siberian languages are to be found outside the northeastern region that is the subject of the present study, in the south Siberian Turkic languages and various western Mansi and Khanty varieties. The most developed case systems, on the other hand, are to be found in the Northeastern Siberia region, in the Northern Tungusic languages Evenki and Even, and in various Koryak dialects.[8]

23.2   Instrumental versus Comitative Case in Northeastern Siberian Languages

Many different types of case functions can be rendered in English using the preposition 'with' (or 'by'), but two salient functions or roles, those of instrument and accompaniment, are generally kept formally distinct in Northeastern Siberian languages through the use of two separate case suffixes. Both an instrumental and a comitative case form are attested in the two Yukaghiric languages. Wadul (1) and Odul (2), have cognate elements, and this suggests that one should reconstruct this case opposition to Proto-Yukaghiric. Functionally the comitative encodes not only accompaniment but also possession, and further represents the default way of conjoining two nouns in Yukaghir.

(1)   Yukaghir (Wadul)
      a. *sa-lek*   *pajduk*
         stick-INS   hit
         'hit with a stick'
      b. *ile-ɲej*   *la:me*   *me-qaldej-ɲi*
         reindeer-COM   dog   PV-run.off-3PL
         'the dog ran off with the reindeer', 'the dog and the reindeer ran off'
                                             (Krejnovich 1982: 46, 49–50)

(2)   Yukaghir (Odul)
      a. *tʃoɣoje-le*   b. *núme-ɲej*
         knife-INS   dwelling-COM
         'with a knife'   'with a dwelling, he has a dwelling'
                                             (Krejnovich 1982: 45)

---

[7] Probable relatively recent newcomers Eskimoic (de Reuse 1994) and Aleut (Bergsland 1997) are exceptions to this.

[8] Formally speaking, what have been called case suffixes in Yeniseic (Anderson 2004; Georg 2007) should be analysed formally as postpositional clitics (Vajda 2008, 2012). Thus, this is more evidence that Yeniseic is anomalous within the Siberian area on numerous levels, and that shared features are often transparently distinct or different in realization, or probably calques on areal norms (see Fortescue 1998), with Tungusic or most often Sel'kup influence being the vector to explain such developments.

Only the most northeastern languages within the Turkic family, Dolgan and Yakut (Sakha), show such an opposition between instrumental and comitative cases. Two comitative case forms are actually attested in Dolgan (3)–(4), which contrasts with a single instrumental form (5). The second comitative appears to be cognate with elements in other Siberian Turkic languages that mark attributive or possessive adjectives.

(3)   Dolgan
      oɣo-luun   beye-liin   ooŋŋu-ur
      child-COM   self-COM   play-PRS
      'he is playing with the child'

                                                    (Ubrjatova 1985: 122)

(4)   Dolgan
      kiih-a   kihi-leek   olor-or
      daughter-3   person-COM.II   sit-PRS
      'his daughter is sitting with the person'

                                                    (Ubrjatova 1985: 122)

(5)   Dolgan
      munu   ikki   ilii-tinen   kus-put
      this.ACC   two   hand-3.INS   grab-PST.II
      'he grabbed this with both hands'

                                                    (Ubrjatova 1985: 121)

Sakha or Yakut (6)–(7) shows a similar opposition between comitative and instrumental case forms, although the form of the possessive comitative in Yakut appears to be cognate with the possessive instrumental in Dolgan. Note that Tenishev et al. (1988) reconstruct the contrast between instrumental and comitative for Proto-Turkic, but the older etymological instrumental -*In* is retained mainly only in lexicalized adverbials like Tofa *kuhuun* 'during the winter' or Turkish *gündüzün* 'during the day'. The earlier comitative, itself most likely a fused version of the postposition '(together) with', has shifted into the function of an *instrumental* case in languages such as Xakas (Anderson 1998a), where it is realized as -*naŋ*, and is also to be found in this function in Yakut as well.

(6)   Yakut (Sakha)
      a. *Alasov ije-tiniin   kel-le*
         Alasov mother-3.COM   come-PST
         'Alasov came with his mother'
      b. *Alasov   emeexsin-niin   kel-li-ler*
         Alasov   old.woman-COM   come-PST-3PL
         'Alasov came with the old woman'

                                                    (Ubrjatova 1985: 124, 123)

(7)   Yakut (Sakha)
      kini,   araaha,   eye-nen   tønn-ør   ete
      he   PRTCL   peace-INS   (re)turn-P/F   SBJV
      'he, by all appearance, would return peacefully'

                                                    (Petrov 1984: 49)

A formal and functional opposition between an instrumental and a comitative case was characteristic of Proto-Chukotko-Kamchatkan. As in Dolgan, there are actually two comitative forms, sometimes called the *first* and *second comitative*, at other times the *sociative* and the *comitative*. The instrumental in Chukotko-Kamchatkan is formally a suffix and in some languages functions as an ergative case as well, while the comitative/sociative forms are formally circumfixes. In Chukchi (8), this circumfix consists of a *ga-* prefix followed by the stem, followed by the instrumental suffix for the so-called first comitative or sociative, or by the suffix *-ma* for the so-called second or (plain) comitative. In Chukchi, the (second) comitative is formally a phrasal-type circumfix or prefix/enclitic, as seen in (8b).

(8)   Chukchi
　　　a. *ənpinatʃgərgəna-t qorat*　　　b. *ga-npənatʃgərgəna-qora-ma*
　　　　old.man-PL reindeer-PL　　　　　COM-old.men-reindeer-COM
　　　　'the old men's reindeers'　　　　'with the old men's reindeers'
　　　　　　　　　　　　　　　　　　　　　　　(Skorik 1986: 107)

When examining the broader comparative picture within Chukotko-Kamchatkan, one finds a variety of different prefixal elements used within the circumfix case marker (9), e.g. *(g)awun- ~ gA-* in the comitative and *gA- ~ gAyqə-* in the sociative in Koryak.

(9)   a.

	Chavchuven	Kamen	Palana	Chukchi	PNCK
INS	*-(t)A*	*-(t)a*	*-(t)A ~ -(t)a*	*-(t)A*	**-(t)A*
COM-1	*gA-..-(t)A*	*ga-..-(t)a*	*gA/a-..-(t)A/a*	*gA-. ..-(t)A*	**gA-. ...-(t)A*
COM-2	*gawun-..-ma*	*gawun-..-ma*	*awun-..-ma*	*ga-..-ma*	**ga-...-ma*

　　　　　　　　　　　　　　　　　　　　　(Stebnitskij 1994: 187)

　　　b.

	Koryak	Kerek	Chukchi	Al'utor	Itelmen
INS/ERG	*-te, -nek, yək*	*-ta, -nak, -yik*	*-k, -ne, -rək*	*-ta, -nak, -tək*	*-ɬ*
SOC	*g(e)-..-(t)e*	*g(a)-..-(t)a*	*g(e)–..-(t)e*	*g(a)–(t)a*	*k-/x-..-ɬ*
COM	*g(a)-..-ma*	*g(a)-..-ma*	*g(a)-..-ma*	*g(a)-..-ma*	*k-..-tʃam x-..tʃom*

　　　　　　　　　　　　　　　　　　　　　(Skorik 1986: 93)

The sociative in Koryak (Zhukova 1972: 120) is generally used with animate referents, while the comitative appears with inanimates, but this restriction is not rigid or absolute (10)–(11). Specifically, with inanimates the sociative is said to encode a greater degree of connectedness (12)–(13). Further, as (12)–(13) also demonstrate, the comitative and sociative belong to different harmonic classes in Koryak, the comitative belonging to the strong (roughly [+ATR]) class and the sociative to the weak harmonic class (roughly [–ATR]).

(10)   Koryak
　　　a. *ga-kajŋ-a ~ gayqə-kajŋ-a*　b. *geyqə-miml-e*　　c. *ga-ŋaviqqal'u-ta*
　　　　COM-bear-SOC　　　　　　　　COM-water-SOC　　COM-girl-SOC
　　　　'with the bear'　　　　　　　'with water'　　　'with (his) daughter'
　　　　　　　　　　　　　　　　　　　　　　　　　　(Zhukova 1972: 107)

(11) Koryak

a. **gawǝn**-*kajŋi*-**ma**   b.   **gawǝn**-*meml*-**ǝma**
   COM-bear-COM   COM-water-COM
   'with the bear'   'with water'

(Zhukova 1972: 120)

(12) Koryak

etʃgi   *ǝnno*   **gejqǝ**-*milgǝʕǝj*-**e**   *kuʕeqevǝŋ*   *nota*-*jtǝŋ*
today   he   COM-gun-SOC   went   tundra-ALL
'today he went to the tundra with his gun'

(Zhukova 1972: 121)

(13) Koryak

ǝnno   **gawǝn**-*melgǝʕǝy*-**ma**   *gapǝlqalin*
he   COM-gun-COM   drowned
'he drowned with his gun'

(Zhukova 1972: 121)

The instrumental appears to be the oldest of the forms since it has shifted into marking a grammatical function – as an ergative marker of an A argument – and thus it may be possible that the comitative forms were innovated secondarily. Note in this regard that in Koryak no comitative case forms of personal pronouns are used, but rather the postposition *omakaŋ* appears together with locative case marking.

(14) Koryak

a. *gǝm*-*ǝk omakaŋ*   b.   *muy*-*ǝk omakaŋ*
   I-LOC together.with   we-LOC together.with
   'with me'   'with us'

(Zhukova 1972: 45)

Northern Tungusic languages likewise exhibit an instrumental versus comitative opposition.[9] This contrast is likely reconstructible to the Proto-Tungusic stage. Note that as in Yukaghir, the comitative is the default means of conjoining NPs.

(15) Evenki

a. *si:*   *tara*   *bǝr*-*it*-*pi:*   *garpa*-*kal*
   you   that   gun-INS-REFL   shoot-FUT.IMPV.2SG
   'shoot that one with your gun'

b. *asi:*   *kiŋnǝ:*-*l*-*dʒi*   *ami:n*-*dula:*-*βi:*   *is*-*tʃa:*-*n*
   woman   ski-PL-INS   father-LOC-POSS   go-PST-3SG
   'the woman went up to her father on skis'

(Bulatova and Grenoble 1999: 9)

---

[9] Note that some researchers have questioned whether the comitative in Evenki formally belongs to the case system and is not rather some postpositional clitic or relator/relational noun, as it can also attach to an accusative form with conjoined definite direct object NPs (see Kilby 1980 for more on the general status of cases in Evenki). It is not clear that this really matters synchronically or diachronically, as other case forms in Evenki likely have their origin in clitics even if now integrated into the case system; see the discussion of the prolative below, as it appears to have historically included the dative case form within it.

(16) Evenki
  a. *ɲami:*   *əŋnekə:n-nu:n*   *bira-βa*   *daβ-dʒa-ra-Ø*
      female.deer   fawn-COM   river-ACC   cross-IMPV-AOR-3SG
      'the female deer crosses the river with the fawn'
  b. *bi:* *əkin-nu:n-mi:*   *təβlə:-m*
      I   sister-COM-REFL.SG   collect.berries-1SG
      'I went with my sister to gather berries'
                                              (Bulatova and Grenoble 1999: 12)

It is difficult to ascribe the opposition of an instrumental case with a comitative one in any of the Northeastern Siberian language families to (Northern) Tungusic influence – either directly or indirectly – as there is evidence for such an opposition in Turkic, Yukaghiric and Chukotko-Kamchatkan proto-languages as well, but it is certainly likely that the presence of the opposition in Tungusic may have helped maintain or expand it in the other groups in the region. The Proto-Yukaghiric form is of such shallow time depth as to reveal very little. The variation found in Chukotko-Kamchatkan suggests the feature is not a stable one in this genetic unit. Contact with Tungusic or indeed Yukaghiric might have played a role in one or another of the individual developments. Finally, it is only the northeasternmost Turkic language Yakut and Dolgan with heavy Tungusic adstratum or substratum (Pakendorf 2007; Stapert 2013) where the older ancestral Turkic instrumental versus comitative opposition has been maintained with separate, individual case forms, albeit in a reformed or non-etymological manner, and Tungusic influence in these instances has almost certainly played some role. So, in summary the feature is shared by languages of different genetic units throughout the northeast, but only with respect to the Turkic languages is direct influence from Tungusic likely to have had a role in maintaining or reconstituting an old featural opposition. However, given the age of the functional contrast in Turkic, even there Tungusic influence is not an absolutely certain explanation for the observed phenomena.

23.3 Prolative or Prosecutive Case in Northeastern Siberian Languages

The prolative or prosecutive case form (motion 'along' or 'through') is characteristic of most Northeastern Siberian language families. The prolative marked noun often indexes the semantic role of *route*.[10] A prolative case form can be safely reconstructed back to Proto-Yukaghiric and Proto-

---

[10] Among other roles; for more on the function of prolative and other case forms in Evenki, see Grenoble (2014). In literary Evenki there are two prolative type case forms. However, according to Grenoble (2000: 110), some of the more marginal case forms in the Evenki dialect she described, like the allative-prolative in *-kli:*, are recognized but not used by the speakers of that particular Evenki variety.

Tungusic. Correspondences are straightforward between Tundra (Wadul)
and Kolyma (Odul) Yukaghir:

(17)   a. Tundra (Wadul) Yukaghir
       *Ugurt'e-da-**han**   wa:j   ek-uo-j*
       legs-3-PROL   too   hole-STV-ITR(3)
       'there was also a hole along his feet'

(Maslova 2003a: 59)

       b. Wadul
       *enu-pul-ɣ**an**   jalɣi-pe-ɣ**an**   gorot-**qan***
       river-PL-PROL   lake-PL-PROL city-PROL
       'along rivers'   'along lakes'   'about town'

(Krejnovich 1958: 57)

(18)   a. Kolyma (Odul) Yukaghir
       *tʃuge-de-**gen**   qon-ŋi*
       trace-POSS-PROL   go-3PL:ITR
       'they went along his trace'

(Maslova 2003b: 113)

       b. Odul
       *Omolon-**gen***
       Omolon-PROL
       'along the Omolon (river)'

(Krejnovich 1958: 57)

The forms in Yukaghir appear to be built off the locative case form (Maslova
2003a: 56), and thus prolative, which Nikolaeva (2006: 80) reconstructs as
*-ŋkən, may well be a secondary development within the history of Yukaghir,
albeit one that occurred prior to the Proto-Yukaghir level.

Evenki generally uses the full or long form of the prolative, while in
Even, a clipped form in -*li* is used alongside the fuller form found also in
Evenki. Note that the prolative case appears to be derived from the dative
case marker in these Northern Tungusic languages.[11]

(19)   Evenki
       *oro-r   hoktoron-**duli**: hukti-dʒə-tʃə:-tin*
       deer-PL path-PROL   run-IMPF-PST-3PL
       'deer were running along the path'

(Bulatova and Grenoble 1999: 11)

(20)   Even
       *dʲuu-**li**   dʲuu-l-**duli***
       house-PROL   house-PL-PROL
       'along the house(s)'

(Malchukov 1995: 9)

---

[11]   Regardless of whether it originated in a postpositional or relational noun clitic in pre-Proto-Tungusic that governed and
       then subsequently included the dative case within it, as the data might suggest, the prolative does appear to be an old
       case form in Tungusic, and we can project it back to Proto-Tungusic most likely (Aleksander Vovin, personal
       communication, 2014), though Tsintsius (1948) does not reconstruct this explicitly.

Koryak of the Chukotko-Kamchatkan family (21) likewise follows the Northeastern Siberian areal pattern of having a prolative case marker. Note the different allomorphs of the prolative case marker found in the following Koryak forms. It is not possible at present to determine whether Tungusic or Yukaghiric is the likely source of diffusion of this case into Koryak (or both), but the prolative case feature is most likely not an old one in the history of Chukotko-Kamchatkan languages.

(21)   Koryak

a. *wajam-**gəpəŋ***	b. *ŋawətʃŋ-**epəŋ***	c. *jaja-**jpəŋ***
river-PROL	woman-PROL	house-PROL
'along the river'	'past the woman'	'past the house'
		(Skorik 1986: 95)

Note that Eskimoic language Siberian Yupik (22) has three prolative case forms, encoding singular, dual and plural (i.e. *-kun/-gnəkun/-txun* (SG/DL/PL)). Such portmanteau number+case marking is not found in other Northeastern Siberian languages, generally speaking.

(22)   Siberian Yupik

*juk   igləχta-quq   sna-**kun***
man   go.along-3   bank/coast/edge-PROL.SG
'the man is going along the edge, bank, coast'
(Menovshchikov and Vakhtin 1983: 92)

Outside the northeastern areal complex, prolative case can be found in a small number of other Siberian languages as well. Indeed, prolative case can be even reconstructed to Proto-(Northern-)Samoyedic.[12]

(23)

a. Nenets	b. Nganasan	c. Enets
*to-**wna***	*turku-**manu***	*Tau-**mone***
lake-PROL	lake-PROL	Nganasan-PROL
'along the lake'	'along the lake'	'along the Nganasan'
(Prokof'ev 1937a: 26)	(Prokof'ev 1937b: 62)	(Castrén 1854: 177)

A prolative case form is common among the case inventories of Siberian languages, and can even be reconstructed to various proto-languages, i.e. Proto-Tungusic or Proto-Yukaghiric (and Proto-Northern Samoyedic). In Proto-Yukaghiric the form appears to be secondarily created from the locative form. Southern Tungusic languages also use the prolative, but often the case marker itself is not cognate with the Northern Tungusic one, e.g. *-kii* in Ul'ch (Sunik 1997). With respect to other Siberian languages with prolative markers, Evenki influence is at least plausible for its development in Proto-Ket-Yugh, since the prolative does not appear to be old within Yeniseic *per se*. In Koryak and Al'utor on the other hand, where

---

[12] However, while non-adjacent at present, there is evidence for earlier Yukaghiric–Samoyedic contacts, and one can not exclude the possibility that the prolative case in Northern Samoyedic reflects this history. For more on the complex periodization of Uralic and Yukaghiric contacts, see Häkkinen (2012).

Tungusic influence is manifest in multiple ways, diffusion from Tungusic is quite likely, especially given the lack of the case in Chukchi and Itelmen. However, as mentioned above, Yukaghiric influence cannot be excluded in the development of the prolative in Koryak and Al'utor. On the other hand, Tungusic contact is extremely unlikely for the development of new prolative case semantics with a formally old case marker in southern Siberian Turkic Xakas (Anderson 1998a).

23.4 Dative versus Allative in Northeastern Siberian Languages

Northeastern Siberian languages frequently exhibit a formal contrast between dative case forms and allative case forms. Allative case canonically encodes the semantic role of the *goal* and thus generally indexes physical motion towards a location or an entity. Dative case on the other hand typically marks recipient arguments in ditransitive constructions, or with other roles typically associated with the syntactic relation of 'indirect object'.

Both a dative case form and an allative case form show cognate elements across the Tungusic languages of Siberia. It is thus relatively straightforward to reconstruct the contrast and the formal markers of this to Proto-Tungusic based on these correspondences. So one finds the contrast in such Siberian Tungusic languages as Nanai (24), Udihe (26), Oroch (25), Even (27), Negidal (28) and Evenki (29). Note that the opposition between dative and allative cases is lacking in certain Tungusic languages spoken outside the Siberian area, e.g. in Jurchen or Manchu, where Chinese influence is pronounced and Mandarin Chinese of course lacks such an opposition of case inflections. Also, unlike some other Siberian languages, in the Siberian Tungusic languages that do have the dative and allative contrast, addressees of verbs of speaking are typically encoded by the allative, not the dative, while recipients of 'give' (e.g. Udihe *bu-*, Evenki *ani-*) are encoded by the dative. Dative is typically used for both functions or roles in many other languages of the area, including Russian (which of course lacks a formal allative).[13]

(24) Nanai
    a. *ogda-**du**   b. *ogda-**tʃi***
       boat-DAT   boat-ALL
       'to the boat'   'toward the boat'

                                     (Sem 1997: 184)

(25) Oroch
    a. *ʊgda-**du**   b. *ʊgda-**ti***
       boat-DAT   boat-ALL
       'to the boat'   'towards the boat'

                               (Lebedeva 1997: 225)

---

[13] According to Grenoble (2000: 109), dative is increasingly replacing the allative for addressees of speech verbs in modern Evenki.

(26) Udihe
      a. *bi   sin-**du***   *xeleb-wa*   *bu-o:-mi*
         I   you-**DAT**   bread-ACC   give-PST-1
         'I gave you (some) bread'
                                      (Nikolaeva and Tolskaja 2001: 524)
      b. *zaŋä-ziga*   *Moskwa-**tigi***   *ŋene-zeŋe-ti*
         boss-PL   Moscow-**ALL**   go-FUT-3PL
         'the bosses will go to Moscow'
                                      (Nikolaeva and Tolskaja 2001: 517)

(27) Even
      a. *dʲuu-**du***   b. *dʲuu-**tki***
         house-DAT   house-ALL
         'to the house'   'towards the house'
                                                    (Malchukov 1995: 9)

(28) Negidal
      a. *min-**du**:*   b. *min-**tixi**:*
         I-DAT   I-ALL
         'to me'   'towards me'
                                              (Tsintsius 1997: 197)

(29) Evenki
      a. *nuŋartin*   *bəjətkə:n-**du**:*   *oron-mo*   *ani:-ra*
         they   boy-DAT   deer-ACC   give-AOR
         'they gave the boy a deer'
                                      (Bulatova and Grenoble 1999: 9)
      b. *tirgaka:kin*   *bira-**tki**:*   *ollo-mo:-sina-ß*
         noon   river-ALL   fish-go-INCP-1PL.EX
         'at noon we went to the river to fish'
                                      (Bulatova and Grenoble 1999: 10)

The presence of a fully developed opposition of allative versus dative cases that can freely attach to both pronouns and nouns in Proto-Northern Chukotko-Kamchatkan is not supported by the data. In Chukchi, the contrast is restricted to pronouns (30) and this likely reflects the earlier distribution found in the proto-language.

(30) Chukchi
      a. *gəmək-ə*   b. *gəmək-agtə*
         I-DAT   I-ALL
         'to me'   'towards me'
                                      (Kämpfe and Volodin 1995: 86)

Certain Koryak varieties, as well as Kerek, show a more fully developed opposition between dative and allative case forms (31). This more fully developed system may have been extended to all nouns in Koryak, which, like the use of a prolative case, might possibly reflect Northern Tungusic influence in this language. Note that both the dative and the allative in Koryak are dominant or strong suffixes and therefore trigger assimilation to dominant/strong vowel series in the stem, as seen in the examples below and in such forms as *mil'ut* 'hare' > *mel'otaŋ* [hare-DAT] as well.[14]

(31) Koryak
a. *wajam-əŋ*   b. *aɲpetʃe-nanaŋ*   c. *aɲpetʃe-najtəŋ*
[river-DAT]   [father-DAT]   [father-ALL]
'to the river'   'to (his) father'   'toward (his) father'
< *wejem* 'river'   < *eɲpitʃ* 'father'
(Stebnitskij 1994: 144; Skorik 1986: 93)

In Al'utor, the allative is lacking altogether, with functions of the Koryak allative marked by the dative.

(32) 'Palana Koryak'/Al'utor
a. *qlegi ʔənpəqlawol-əŋ*   b. *rara-ŋ bewweevlin*
drop.by old.man-DAT   house-DAT set.off.for.PST.3
'drop by and visit at the old man's'   'he set off for home'
(Zhukova 1980: 48–49)

The spread of a full dative versus allative contrast in Koryak may thus reflect Tungusic influence. Note that Itelmen lacks both allative and dative case forms.

In Yukaghiric the formal contrast is lacking *per se*, but there is an allative relational noun in Kolyma Yukaghir that has come to be grammaticalized in a referential or possessed form that functions as a type of third person singular allative pronominal form. In this manner, the development of a formal opposition between dative and allative may be being constituted in Yukaghir in third singular pronominals at least. Formally speaking, this new allative pronominal form is a relational noun marked in the dative case, and this type of development may reflect the same type of historical process that operated to give rise to case forms based on other case forms, which is seen throughout the Siberian region (and elsewhere).

(33) Kolyma (Odul) Yukaghir
qodo   al'-d-in   met   jaqa-te-m
how   ALL-POSS-DAT/DIR   I   arrive-FUT-ITR:1SG
'how shall I approach him?'
(Maslova 2003b: 268)

---

[14] This strong versus weak harmony system characterizes not only Chukotko-Kamchatkan languages but also Tungusic ones as well, with related phenomena found in other northern Siberian languages as well as velar height harmony in Sakha (Yakut); see Anderson (1998b). The phonetic or acoustical characteristics that distinguish the two series have been variably described for Even (and Tungusic more generally) as [±ATR] or [RTR] (Ko 2012) or [±pharyngealizec]. Aralova, Grawunder and Winter (2012) find that different Even dialects have different systems acoustically speaking, and that the systems mix properties associated with ATR harmony and pharyngealization.

(34)   Kolyma (Odul) Yukaghir
       tud-in   er-tʃuon   el+aː-ŋi-le-k   qamie-d'e-ŋi-k
       3-DAT   bad-SBNR   NEG+make-PL-PHB-2   help-DETR-PL-2
       'do not do anything bad to him, help him'

(Maslova 2003b: 177)

The spread of a dative versus allative case to Koryak may be the clearest example of the reflection of the influence of Northern Tungusic on the case system of a neighbouring language. The incipient opposition in third singular pronominals in Yukaghir likely reflects the same distributional restriction as is found in Chukchi, and may represent an instance of Chukchi influence in Yukaghir, possibly reinforced by the extensive contact of Kolyma Yukaghir with Tungusic Even as well.

23.5   Loss of Case-marked Clausal Subordination: The Role of Russian Contact

Syntactically, the basic constituent order SOV characterizes all the languages of the Siberian macro-area, though some languages exhibit stronger tendencies to verb-final order than others, and unsurprisingly other constituent orders are available to encode various types of information structure such as term focus. Further, many of the languages of the Northeastern Siberia linguistic area are highly endangered languages, and as such show pronounced influence from Russian morphosyntactically and syntactically. This has in part disrupted the relatively strict SOV structure in most discourse or informational structural configurations. Further, case usage norms are converging with those of Russian in many Siberian languages, so that according to Grenoble (2000: 109–110), agents of passives are now marked by instrumental typically in Evenki, not the original dative. Given the dismal state many Native Siberian languages find themselves in, this Russian influence is becoming quite widespread areally, such that a newly emerging structural type can be suggested. At least one such new feature deals with the system of case marking to encode various functional subtypes of complex sentences that once characterized the languages of the region. I exemplify this with some evidence from complex sentence structure where the languages of the area are showing shift from the original Siberian type, with non-finite subordinate clauses marked with various case forms that encode different functional sub-types of clausal subordination using non-finite predicates, to a new Russianized type or syntactic pattern involving adverbial subordinators, complementizers, etc., with finite verbs.

Pre-Russian contact varieties of Siberian languages signal(led) clausal subordination or dependency in complex sentences through a range of non-finite or semi-finite structures, which non-exhaustively includes various converbs and nominalized verb formations. Macro-areally, Siberian languages tend(ed) to use case morphology to encode specific functional types of subordinate clauses. Several formal sub-types of this type of case-marked clausal subordination are attested in Siberian languages; see Anderson (2004) for details on languages of central Siberia and Anderson (2005) for restructured and original formations in Xakas. In the most basic widespread and commonly attested type, the cases attach to some overtly nominalized form of the verb, variously called a participle, infinitive and so on.

One particularly common construction of this type is the use of a locative case element on a participial form of the verb to create temporally subordinate clauses. The person/number of the subject is often encoded by possessive morphology in these subordinate clauses. Individual languages vary as to the relative order that the case and possessive marker on these nominalized verbs occur in, e.g. person+case in Kolyma (Odul) Yukaghir (35), or case+person in Tungusic (36)–(38). In all instances these case and person markers follow a participial suffix.

(35) Kolyma (Odul) Yukaghir
    qa:qa:-pe-gi   *ajli-**de-ge***   *'el+qon-ŋi-lek'*   *mon-**de-ge***
    grandfather-PL-POSS forbid-3.**NF-LOC**   NEG-go-PL-PROHIB   say-**3.NF-LOC**
    tamun-gele   *uørpe-p-ki*   *el+med-o:l-ŋi*
    that-ACC   child-PL-POSS   NEG-listen-DES-3PL.ITR
    'their grandfather forbids (it), saying "don't go" but the children do not obey'
                                                                    (Maslova 2003b: 372)

Many different case forms can be found functioning to encode case-marked clausal subordination of various types throughout the languages of Siberia. Formally of the second type mentioned above, for example with the order participle+case+person, one finds both the dative (36) and ablative (37) cases used to mark different kinds of temporally subordinate clauses in Tungusic Evenki, while the prolative can be used to form dependent clauses with causal semantics (38).

(36) Evenki
    *bira   dagadun   o:-**ri-du-v***   *so:t   eduni-l-le-n*
    river   near   become-**PRTCPL-DAT-1**   very   blow.wind-INCH-NFUT-3
    'when I found myself near the river, a strong wind began to blow'
                                                                    (Nedjalkov 1997: 51)

(37) Evenki
    *min-duk pekture:vun-me ga-**na-duk-in***   *bega   itten-e-n*
    I-ABL   gun-ACC   take-**PRTCPL-ABL-3** month   PASS-NFUT-3
    'a month had passed since he took my gun from me'
                                                                    (Nedjalkov 1997: 51)

(38) Evenki
    *ajat   haval-**na-li-v**   min-du pekture:vun-me   bu-re*
    good   work-**PRTCPL-PROL-1** I-DAT gun-ACC   give-NFUT
    'they gave me a gun because I'd been working well'
                                                                    (Nedjalkov 1997: 53)

In Chukchi (39) at an earlier historical period pre-dating Russian penetra-
tion into the region, a formally different structure is found from that
which typifies Yukaghiric or Tungusic (or Turkic), albeit one that
appears to be calqued on these areal norms. Person marking is absent
on the verb in same-subject subordinate clauses in Chukchi, as is an
overt marker of nominalization, and thus the case marker that encodes
the specific functional type of subordinate clause attaches directly to an
otherwise unmarked verb stem. Like Evenki, different cases encode
different functional subtypes of subordination, for instance allative to
encode temporally preceding action, comitative to encode simultaneous action, etc. In each instance, the Chukchi case form attaches
directly to the verb stem, and not a nominalized form as in Tungusic,
Turkic or Yukaghiric.

(39)   Chukchi
       a. *yǝme-ɣtǝ*   *nelɣǝ-n*   *ɣǝm-nan*
          hang.up-**ALL**   pelt-**ABS**   I-**ERG**
          tǝ-ttʔǝ-ɣʔe-n   *ǝweyotʃɣǝn*
          1**SUBJ**-knock.over-**PRF**-3**OBJ**   vessel.**ABS**
          'when I hung up the pelt I knocked over the vessel'
                                         (Kämpfe and Volodin 1995: 106)

       b. *ŋewǝsqet*   *ga-gǝntow-ma*   *kulil'ǝrʔu-gʔi*
          woman   **COM**-run.away-**COM**   cry.out-**PRF**
          'the woman cried out while running away'
                                          (Kämpfe and Volodin 1995: 54)

Thus was the state of complex sentence formation in Siberian languages
in the pre-colonial or pre-contact period, and it is still true of the less
restructured speech of certain (often the most elderly) individuals within
contemporary communities. However, as alluded to above, Russia has
extended its territorial, cultural and linguistic hegemony to cover almost
every part of Siberia, and profound ethnolinguistic consequences have
been the result. In general it is true that, except possibly Sakha, all
indigenous Northeastern Siberian languages and communities are in
catastrophic decline. This can be seen when looking at census data over
the past half-century (1959–2010), where even in these highly charged
and politically sensitive accounts we can see the cumulative effects of
ethnic shame and language shift that almost all Native Siberian language
communities have been experiencing over this period (Anderson 2015).
Table 23.2 offers data on the self-reported ethnic group affiliation for
demographically small Native Siberian communities during the last four
Soviet censuses (1959, 1970, 1979 and 1989) and the first two Russian
Federation censuses (2002 and 2010) for communities found in
Northeastern Siberia.

Table 23.2 *Self-reported ethnic identity of Native Siberians 1959–2010*

	2010	2002	1989	1979	1970	1959
Evenki	38,396	35,527	30,163	27,294	25,471	24,151
Khanty	30,943	28,678	22,521	20,934	21,138	19,410
Even	21,830	19,071	17,199	12,523	12,029	9,121
Chukchi	15,098	15,767	15,184	14,000	13,597	11,727
Koryak	7,953	8,743	9,242	7,879	7,487	6,287
Dolgan	7,885	7,261	6,945	5,053	4,877	3,932
Itelmen	3,193	3,180	2,481	1,370	1,301	1,109
Yupik	1,738	1,750	1,719	1,510	1,308	1,118
Yukaghir	1,603	1,509	1,142	835	615	442
Aleut	482	540	702	546	450	421
Chuvan	1,002	1,087	1,511	–	–	–

One issue should be mentioned first in order to interpret these numbers correctly, and that is, all demographic factors being equal, population groups should be experiencing gradual increases; if the birth rate is lower than the death rate, the group is in demographic decline. Only four of the northernmost groups, Evenki, Even, Dolgan and Yukaghir, have shown increasing populations throughout the period 1959–2010. All of these communities occupy vast and sparsely populated regions, and one is inclined to believe that they reflect real demographic trends of gradual population increase. Ethnic shame plays a role in the decline of self-reported ethnic group membership, rather than actual demographic collapse, for example, in the reported decline of Koryak and Chukchi in 2010. Sometimes trends of this sort are reversed, as happened in the case of the Khanty when comparing the numbers of the 1970 and 1979 censuses, with that of 1989. The rise and fall in the reported numbers thus reflect sociological rather than demographic realities for the most part.

Self-reported language use also shows decline between 1959 and 2002, as seen in Table 23.3.[15] Here the cumulative effects of ethnic shame and actual language shift can be seen dramatically in the massive decline in percentages of self-reported language use across the tables right to left.

The cumulative effect of these trends is that a newly emerging type of area is being constituted, and there is Russian influence on virtually all levels of morphology and syntax to be observed in everyday use of most – if not all – Native Siberian languages, at least in the speech of younger speakers. As alluded to above, the diffusion of features across the languages from different genetic units within the Northeastern Siberian linguistic area occurred over numerous centuries or even millennia. However, in more recent times, a significant homogenizing force has operated over the indigenous languages of Siberia over a much shallower time depth, but has resulted in a new type of structural

---

[15] Sufficient 2010 census data have not yet been available to me.

Table 23.3 *Self-reported percentage of language use in censuses 1959–2002*[16]

	2002	1989	1979	1970	1959
Dolgan	67.0%	81.7%	90.0%	89.8%	93.9%
Chukchi	49.1%	70.3%	78.2%	82.6%	93.9%
Koryak	34.5%	52.4%	69.0%	81.1%	90.5%
Yupik	23.4%	51.6%	60.7%	60.0%	84.0%
Even	37.6%	43.9%	56.9%	56.0%	81.4%
Yukaghir	40.0%	32.8%	37.5%	46.8%	52.5%
Evenki	21.3%	30.4%	42.8%	51.3%	54.9%
Aleut	32.4%	28.3%	17.8%	21.8%	22.3%
Itelmen	12.1%	19.6%	24.4%	35.7%	36.0%
Yakut	102.8%!!	94.0%	95.3%	96.3%	97.6%

convergence. This is the establishment of Russian linguistic hegemony over the vast expanse of Native Siberia. Almost all Native Siberian people use Russian in the majority of communicative contexts, and norms of Russian that differ from those in the indigenous Siberian languages have begun to filter into the structures themselves of the Siberian languages. With respect to the structure of complex sentences one can begin to speak of a new areal type. In particular, Russian prefers finite subordinate and relative clauses introduced by complementizers and relativizers, instead of the non-finite, nominalized or case-marked clausal subordination patterns examined above.

Many speakers of Evenki show a partially calqued structure based on the Russian model along with frequent code-switching.[17] In examples (40)–(41) we find the borrowed subordinator *poka* and a finite verb, but no negative scope operator, as is found in Russian and in some heavily Russianized varieties of other Siberian languages.[18] Thus we find the insertion of calqued or borrowed subordinators and complementizers with finite verbs mimicking the structures found in Russian.

(40)   Evenki
       goro: **o:ki:n** *is-tʃana:-ß*   *tar* **poka do poselka**   *is-tʃana:-ß*
       far   when reach-FUT-1SG   there until <Russto village.GEN>
       reach-FUT-1SG

---

[16] Sources: Chislennost' i sostav naselenija SSSR po dannym Vsesojuznoj perepisi naselenija 1979 goda [Size and composition of the population of the USSR according to the All-Union population census of the year 1979], Finansy i statistika, Moskva (1984); Itogi vsesojuznoj perepisi naselenija 1959 goda (svodnyj tom) [Results of the All-Union census of 1959 (including a summary)], Tsentral'noe statistitsjeskoe upravlenie pri sovete ministrov SSSR, Moskva (1962); Itogi Vsesojuznoj perepisi naselenija 1970 goda [Results of the 1970 All-Union census], Statistika, Moskva (1970); Vestnik Statistiki [Statistical Bulletin] 10/1990, Finansy i statistika, Moskva (1989). Available from www.perepis2002.ru/, www.perepis-2010.ru/message-rosstat.php.

[17] For more on Russian interference in Evenki, see Grenoble (2000, 2010, 2012a, 2012b).

[18] Such as the Xakas spoken by younger Xakas speakers in Abakan (Anderson 2005) or in certain Ket varieties as well (Grishina 1977; Kostjakov 1976). Nivkh likewise reflects a host of morphosyntactic interference and syntactic calques from Russian (Gruzdeva 2000).

> **poka**　Ljuda-ßa　baka-dʒina-ːß
> until　Ljuda-ACC　find-FUT-1SG
> 'It was far until I would get there, until I would reach the village, until I would find Ljuda'
>
> (Grenoble 2012b: 104)

(41)　Evenki

> hunaːtkaːn-miː　ele　Doždalas'　**oːkiːn**　huru-ßruː
> girl-REFL　hardly　(Russ).waited　**when**　go-PRF
> 'His girlfriend could hardly wait until they would go'
>
> (Grenoble 2012b: 104)

Such influence from Russian has been recognized in Evenki syntax since at least the mid-1960s (Grenoble 2010, 2012a, 2012b, 2014; Kolesnikova 1966: 19).

23.6　Summary

The languages of Northeastern Siberia share a range of features in their case systems that distinguish them in this clustering from neighbouring languages. The one common language in each contact situation that defines the different genetic units found in Northeastern Siberia are the Northern Tungusic languages Evenki and Even, which are structurally very similar in their case systems. The case features discussed above include the opposition of an instrumental and a comitative case, the presence of a prolative or prosecutive case form, and an opposition between a dative and an allative case form, and finally the use of case-marking on nominalized verbs to create many functional subtypes of subordinate clauses. All features can be reconstructed to Proto-Tungusic, but not every one can be for the other genetic units of the area. In particular, for the first three features mentioned, in the languages with a higher degree of Tungusic contact, e.g. Koryak versus Chukchi within Chukotko-Kamchatkan or Dolgan and Yakut versus other Turkic languages, one finds a more Tungusic-looking profile with respect to these features, and thus diffusion from Tungusic seems plausible as at least a partial explanation for the appearance of the features involved. With respect to case-marked clausal subordination, regardless of whether the original system had cases attached to finite(-looking) verbs or nominalized ones, all indigenous languages of Northeastern Siberia have been undergoing profound influence from contact with Russian, and one may now begin to speak of the emergence of a new areal type that has replaced or is replacing the system of case-marked clausal subordination with a system of subordinate clauses introduced by adverbial subordinators and complementizers, with finite verbs, etc. Thus, linguistic areas are not static entities only unfolding and developing over millennia, but may be subject to newly introduced yet commonly shared homogenizing forces that can

alter the characteristic profile of the area with respect to individual specific features involved within a relatively short time frame, given proper
sociolinguistic contexts, as in the case of the rapid expansion of Russian
linguistic and cultural hegemony over the vast expanses of Siberia during
the past few centuries.

Abbreviations

1	first person	INV	inverse
2	second person	ITR	intransitive
3	third person	LOC	locative
ABL	ablative	N	noun
ABS	absolutive	NEG	negative
ACC	accusative	NF	non-finite
ALL	allative	NFUT	non-future
AOR	aorist	OBJ	object
AUX	auxiliary	OBV	obviative
CAUS	causative	PASS	passive
COM	comitative	P/E	prolative/equative
CV	converb	P/F	present/future
DAT	dative	PFV	perfective
DES	desiderative	PL	plural
DETR	detransitive	POSS	possessive
DIR	directional	PRED	predicat(iv)e
ERG	ergative	PRF	perfect
EX	exclusive	PROL	prolative
F[EM]	feminine	PRS	present
FIN	finite	PRTCL	particle
FUT	future	PRTCPL	participle
GEN	genitive	PST	past
GER	gerund	PV	preverb
HAB	habitual	PX	possessive
II	class-II	REFL	reflexive
IMP	imperative	SBJV	subjunctive
IMPF	imperfect	SBNR	subject nominalizer
IMPV	imperfective	SF	stem formant
INAN	inanimate	SG	singular
INCH	inchoative	STV	stative
INCMPL[TV]	incompletive	SUBJ	subject
INCP	inceptive	SUBORD	subordinator
INF	infinitive	TERM	terminative
INS	instrumental	VSF	verb stem formant
INT	intentional		

References

Anderson, Gregory D. S., 1998a. *Xakas*. Languages of the World/Materials, vol. 251. Munich: LINCOM Europa.

Anderson, Gregory D. S., 1998b. Historical aspects of Yakut (Sakha) phonology. *Turkic Languages* 2 (2): 1–32.

Anderson, Gregory D. S., 2001. Deaffrication in the Siberian area. In Howard I. Aronson (ed.), *Non-Slavic Languages,* vol. 9: *Linguistic Studies,* pp. 1–17. Columbus, OH: SLAVICA.

Anderson, Gregory D. S., 2003. Towards a phonological typology of native Siberia. In Dee Ann Holisky and Kevin Tuite (eds), *Current Trends in Caucasian, East European and Inner Asian Linguistics: Papers in Honor of Howard I. Aronson,* pp. 1–22. Amsterdam: John Benjamins.

Anderson, Gregory D. S., 2004. The languages of central Siberia: Introduction and overview. In Edward Vajda (ed.), *Languages and Prehistory of Central Siberia,* pp. 1–119. Amsterdam: John Benjamins.

Anderson, Gregory D. S., 2005. *Language Contact in South Central Siberia.* Turcologica, vol. 54. Wiesbaden: Harrassowitz.

Anderson, Gregory D. S., 2006. Towards a typology of the Siberian linguistic area. In Yaron Matras, April McMahon and Nigel Vincent (eds), *Linguistic Areas: Convergence in Historical and Typological Perspective,* pp. 266–300. Basingstoke, UK: Palgrave Macmillan.

Anderson, Gregory D. S., 2010. Perspectives on the global language extinction crisis: The Oklahoma and Eastern Siberia language hotspots. *Revue Roumaine de Linguistique* XLV: 129–142.

Anderson, Gregory D. S., 2011. Language hotspots: What (applied) linguistics and education should do about language endangerment in the twenty-first century. *Language and Education* 25 (4): 273–289.

Anderson, Gregory D. S., 2015. Russian colonialism and hegemony and Native Siberian languages. In Christel Stolz (ed.), *Language Empires in Comparative Perspective.* Colonial and Postcolonial Linguistics, vol. 6. Berlin: Mouton de Gruyter.

Aralova, Natalia, Sven Grawunder and Bodo Winter, 2012. The acoustic correlates of tongue root vowel harmony in Even (Tungusic). In *The 17th International Congress of Phonetic Sciences,* pp. 240–243. Hong Kong: City University.

Bergsland, Knut, 1997. *Aleut Grammar: Unangam Tunuganaan Achixaasix̂.* Fairbanks: Alaska Native Language Center.

Bulatova, N. J. and Leonore A. Grenoble, 1999. *Evenki.* Munich: LINCOM.

Castrén, M. A., 1854. *Grammatik der samojedischen Sprachen.* Reprinted in 1966 as Uralic and Altaic Series, vol. 53. Bloomington, IN: Indiana University.

Fortescue, Michael, 1998. *Language Relations across the Bering Strait: Reassessing the Archaeological and Linguistic Evidence.* London and Washington: Cassell.

Georg, Stefan, 2007. *Descriptive Grammar of Ket (Yenisei-Ostyak)*, part 1: *Introduction, Phonology, Morphology*. Leiden: Brill.

Gilbers, Dicky G., John Nerbonne and Jos Schaeken, 2000. *Languages in Contact*. Studies in Slavic and General Linguistics, vol. 28. Atlanta: Rodopi.

Grenoble, Lenore A., 2000. Morphosyntactic change: The influence of Russian on Evenki. In Gilbers et al. (eds), pp. 105–120.

Grenoble, Lenore A., 2010. Switch or shift: Code-mixing, contact-induced change and attrition in Russian-Evenki contacts. In Arto Mustajoki, Ekaterina Protassova and Nikolai Vakhtin (eds), *Sociolinguistic Approaches to Non-Standard Russian*, pp. 139–152. Slavica Helsingensia, vol. 40. Helsinki: Instrumentarium of Linguistics.

Grenoble, Lenore A., 2012a. Contact induced change and language shift: The impact of Russian and the creation of the Russian Language Empire. Paper presented at Language Empires conference, Bremen, Germany, March 2012.

Grenoble, Lenore A., 2012b. Areal typology and syntactic change. *Vestnik TGPU (TSPU Bulletin)* 116 (1): 101–105.

Grenoble, Lenore A., 2014. Spatial semantics, case and relator nouns in Evenki. In Pirkko Suihkonen and Lindsay J. Whaley (eds), *On Diversity and Complexity of Languages Spoken in Europe and North and Central Asia*, pp. 111–131. Studies in Language Companion Series, vol. 164. Amsterdam: John Benjamins.

Grishina, N. M., 1977. Upotreblenie slova bang v slozhnom predlozhenii ketskogo jazyka [Use of the word bang in complex sentences in Ket]. *Jazyki i Toponimija* 4: 102–107.

Gruzdeva, Ekaterina, 2000. Aspects of Russian–Nivkh grammatical interference: The Nivkh imperative. In Gilbers et al. (eds), pp. 121–134.

Häkkinen, Jaakko, 2012. Early contacts between Uralic and Yukaghir. *Mémoires de la Société Finno-Ougrienne* 264: 91–101.

Joki, A. J., 1977. Die Tungusen und ihre Kontakte mit anderen Völkern. *Studia Orientalia* 47: 109–118.

Kämpfe, H. R. and A. P. Volodin, 1995. *Abriss der Tschuktschischen Grammatik*. Wiesbaden: Harrassowitz.

Kilby, David, 1980. Universals and particulars of the Evenki case system. *International Review of Slavic Linguistics* 5: 45–74.

Ko, Seongyeon, 2012. *Tongue Root Harmony and Vowel Contrasts in Northeast Asian Languages*. PhD Dissertation, Cornell University, New York.

Kolesnikova, V. D., 1966. *Sintaksis èvenkijskogo jazyka [Evenki Syntax]*. Moscow and Leningrad: Nauka.

Kostjakov, M. M., 1976. Ketskie sootvetsvija russkomu slozhnopodchinennomu predlozheniju s pridatochnym vremeni [Ket correspondences to the Russian temporally subordinate clause]. *Jazyki i toponimija* 1: 56–63.

Krejnovich, E. A., 1958. *Jukagirskij jazyk [The Yukaghir Language]*. Moscow and Leningrad: Akademija Nauk SSSR.

Krejnovich, E. A., 1982. *Issledovanija i materialy po jukagirskomu jazyku [Research and Materials on Yukaghir]*. Leningrad: Nauka.

Lebedeva, E. P., 1997. Orochskij jazyk [The Orochi language]. In Romanova et al. (eds), pp. 215–226.

Mal'chukov, A., 1995. *Even*. Munich: LINCOM Europa.

Maslova, E., 2003a. *Tundra Yukaghir*. Munich: LINCOM Europa.

Maslova, E., 2003b. *A Grammar of Kolyma Yukaghir*. Berlin: Mouton de Gruyter.

Menovshchikov, G. A. and N. B. Vakhtin, 1983. *Èskimosskij jazyk [The Eskimo Language]*. Leningrad: Proveshchenie.

Nedjalkov, Igor V., 1997. *Evenki*. London: Routledge.

Nikolaeva, Irina, 2006. *A Historical Dictionary of Yukaghir*. Berlin: Mouton de Gruyter.

Nikolaeva, Irina and Maria Tolskaja, 2001. *A Grammar of Udihe*. Berlin: Mouton de Gruyter.

Oskolskaya, Sofia and Natasha Stoynova, 2013. The LA-form: Russian verbs in Nanai speech. *Eesti ja soome-ugri keeleteaduse ajakiri / The Journal of Estonian and Finno-Ugric Linguistics* 4 (2): 99–116.

Pakendorf, Brigitte, 2007. *Contact in the History of the Sakha (Yakuts): Linguistic and Genetic Perspectives*. Leiden: LOT.

Petrov, N. E., 1984. *Modal'nye slova v jakutskom jazyke [Modal Words in Yakut]*. Novosibirsk: Nauka.

Prokof'ev, G. N., 1937a. Sel'kupskij (ostjako-samoedskij) jazyk [The Sel'kup language]. In G. N. Prokof'ev (ed.), *Jazyki i pis'mennost' narodov severa*, part 1, pp. 91–124. Moscow and Leningrad: Uchpedgiz.

Prokof'ev, G. N., 1937b. Nganasanskij (tavgijskij) jazyk [The Nganasan language]. In G. N. Prokof'ev (ed.), *Jazyki i pis'mennost' narodov severa*, part 1, pp. 53–74. Moscow and Leningrad: Uchpedgiz.

de Reuse, W., 1994. *Siberian Yupik Eskimo: The Language and its Contacts with Chukchi*. Salt Lake City: University of Utah Press.

Romanova, O. et al. (eds), 1997. *Jazyki Mira: Mongol'skie jazyki, Tunguso-Man'chzhurskie jazyki, Japonskij jazyk, Korejskij jazyk*. Moscow: Indrik.

Sem, L. I., 1997. Nanajskij jazyk [The Nanai language]. In Romanova et al. (eds), pp. 173–188.

Skorik, P. J., 1986. Kategorii imeni sushchestvitel'nogo v chukotsko-kamchatskikh jazykakh [Categories of the noun in Chukotko-Kamchatkan languages]. In P. J. Skorik (ed.), *Paleoaziatskie jazyki*. Novosibirsk: Akademija Nauk SSSR.

Stapert, Eugénie, 2013. *Contact-Induced Change in Dolgan: An Investigation into the Role of Linguistic Data for the Reconstruction of a People's (Pre-)History*. PhD Dissertation, Leiden University.

Stebnitskij, S. N., 1994. *Ocherki po jazyku i fol'kloru korjakov [Studies on Koryak Language and Folklore]*. Moscow: Muzej antropologii i ètnografii RAN.

Sunik, O. P., 1997. Ul'chskij jazyk [The Ul'chi language]. In Romanova et al. (eds), pp. 248–260.

Tenishev, È. R. et al., 1988. *Sravnitel'no-istoricheskaja grammatika tjurkskikh jazykov: Morfologija [Comparative-historical Grammar of the Turk Languages: Morphology]*. Moscow: Nauka.

Tsintsius, V. I., 1948. *Problemy sravnitel'noj grammatiki tunguso-man'chdzhurskikh jazykov [Problems in the Comparative Grammar of the Manchu-Tungus Languages]*. Moscow: Nauka.

Tsintsius, V. I., 1997. Negidal'skij jazyk [Negidal language]. In Romanova et al. (eds), pp. 188–201.

Tsydendambaev, T. B., 1981. Zametki ob etnicheskikh i jazykovykh kontaktakh burjat i evenkov [Notes on the ethnic and linguistic contacts between Buryat and Evenki]. In E. I. Ubrjatova (ed.), *Jazyki i Fol'klor narodov severa [Languages and Folklore of the Peoples of the North]*, pp. 70–91 Novosibirsk: Nauka.

Ubrjatova, E. I., 1985. *Jazyk noril'skix dolgan [The Language of the Norilsk Dolgan]*. Novosibirsk: Nauka.

Vajda, Edward, 2008. Head-negating enclitics in Ket. In Edward Vajda (ed.), *Subordination and Coordination Strategies in North Asian Languages*, pp. 179–201. Amsterdam: John Benjamins.

Vajda, Edward, 2012. The Dene–Yeniseian connection: A reply to G. Starostin. *Journal of Language Relationship* 8: 138–152.

Zhukova, A. N., 1972. *Grammatika korjakskogo jazyka [Grammar of Koryak]*. Leningrad: Nauka.

Zhukova, A. N., 1980. *Jazyk palanskikh korjakov [The Language of the Palana Koryak]*. Leningrad: Nauka.

24

Languages of China in their East and Southeast Asian Context

Hilary Chappell

After describing the nature of the correspondence between demography and the principal language families or groups found in China, this chapter next outlines the main sets of features used to support the proposal of continental East and Southeast Asia as forming a single linguistic area.

Second, in light of these areal features, three case studies will be treated as the main part of this chapter, two located in frontier areas of China and one in its interior:

(i) Gansu-Qinghai in northwestern China where a variety of different Mandarin languages meets Mongolic, Tibetan and Turkic languages,

(ii) Guangxi in the south of China where Zhuang (Tai) languages intermingle with western dialects of Cantonese Yue and the little explored Pinghua Chinese,

(iii) Hunan in central China where Southwestern Mandarin and Xianghua, an unaffiliated Chinese language, are spoken alongside Hmong (Hmong-Mien) and Tujia (Tibeto-Burman).

The purpose will be to describe the clustering of shared features in these micro-areas, if not the degree of linguistic impact, given the protracted periods of contact between the communities in question. It is only in recent decades that studies on contact-induced linguistic change have begun to be examined in China from the point of view of transferral from non-Chinese languages into Sinitic. The first two case studies report on this recent research. The third is a case study of language contact between related Sinitic languages, a contact situation which is only at an early stage.

I would like to thank the editor, Raymond Hickey, Alain Peyraube and Laurent Sagart for their very useful comments on this chapter. This research has been supported by funding from the European Research Council under the European Community's Seventh Framework Programme (FP7/2007–2013) / ERC Advanced Grant Agreement n° 230388 for the 41/2-year project 'SINOTYPE' (2009–2013).

24.1   China and its Languages: A Linguistic Demography

The principal language families in continental East and Southeast Asia are the following six: Sino-Tibetan, Altaic, Tai-Kadai, Hmong-Mien, Austroasiatic and Austronesian, each of which is briefly discussed in turn below, with respect to China, the focus of this chapter.

While 91.5 per cent of China's population are of Han (汉) stock, that is, belong ethnically to the Chinese nationality according to the most recent 2010 census, the remaining 8.5 per cent comprise the so-called 'national minorities' including Zhuang, Uygur, Tibetan and Korean of which there are 55 recognized ethnic groups.[1]

24.1.1   Sino-Tibetan (Sinitic, Tibeto-Burman)

As the family name suggests, the Sino-Tibetan family comprises the two main branches of (i) Sinitic, the technical term for Chinese languages, and (ii) Tibeto-Burman, a family tree configuration which continues to be contested; for differing viewpoints, see Sagart (2005) on Sino-Austronesian and van Driem (2011) on the Trans-Himalayan linguistic phylum.

The heartland of Sinitic languages is found in China, where the ten subgroups are spread across the territory from Manchuria in the north-east, through central China to Guangdong in the south and Sichuan in the southwest. They have also made incursions into northwestern China (Section 24.1.7). The Tibeto-Burman languages, approximately 250 in number, complement this distribution by virtue of their principal locations in Tibet, the western province of Qinghai and in the southwestern corner of China in Sichuan and Yunnan provinces. From the larger Asian perspective, this branch of Sino-Tibetan is essentially centred in the Himalayas and Tibetan plateau, straddling several neighbouring polities including Myanmar (Burma), Bhutan, Nepal and Northeastern India.

The main subgroups of Tibeto-Burman found within the borders of China are the Yi (or Lolo-Burmese), mainly located in southwestern Yunnan, but also scattered across Guizhou and Sichuan provinces (Naxi, Lisu, Hani, Lahu, etc.), the Jingpho in Yunnan, the Qiangic and Gyalrongic in northern Sichuan, and Tibetan languages in Tibet, Sichuan, Qinghai and parts of Gansu. Its easternmost branch of Tujia is located in Xiangxi, northwestern Hunan (Section 24.3.3).

Excepting Karen (Thailand, Burma) and Bai (Yunnan), Tibeto-Burman languages are, in the main, SOV with postpositions and adjuncts preceding

---

[1] According to the Sixth National Census carried out on 1 November 2010, the population count yielded the figure of 1,339,724,852 inhabitants. This figure has probably increased to more than 1.4 billion at the time of writing. Facts and figures in this section are drawn from several sources, including the sixteenth edition of *Ethnologue* (Lewis 2009), as well as the eighteenth edition of *Ethnologue* (Lewis et al., 2015), Shearer and Sun (2002) for the non-Sinitic languages of China, and Xiong and Zhang (2008), Wurm and Li (1987) and Zhang (2012) for Sinitic.

the verb, but, unlike Sinitic, not all the subgroups are tonal, while some make use of register distinctions. The branches located to the southwest of China in Nepal and the Himalayan region, including Kiranti, may possess inflectional features such as person agreement.

24.1.2   Altaic

The Altaic phylum comprises three language families, some of whose members are located in the north and northwest of China and include principally Tungus-Manchu, Mongolic and Turkic. Note, however, that the existence and make-up of such an Altaic phylum or macro-family is the subject of much disagreement. The isolates of Korean and Japanese are also frequently included in this group by some scholars.

The Manchu language could be described as practically extinct within Manchuria (Dongbei), the northeastern provinces of China, if it were not for the related variety of Sibe (Sibo), spoken in Xinjiang. The fate of Manchu reveals an interesting case of language shift from a conquering nation to that of the conquered: the Manchus became gradually sinicized during the Qing dynasty (1644–1911) that they had founded, shifting to Mandarin by the end of the seventeenth century. There are nonetheless reports that some elderly speakers can still be found in two small communities in the northeastern province of Heilongjiang: Heihai 黑海 and Sanjiazi 三家子 (Beffa and Even 2011). Tungus is represented by two small communities of Oroqen and Evenki speakers in Inner Mongolia.

Mongolic languages are spoken widely not only in the Mongolian People's Republic to the north of China but also in the neighbouring Autonomous Region of Inner Mongolia (part of China) and in the western provinces of Gansu, Qinghai and Xinjiang. This family includes Bao'an, Dongxiang (Santa), Monguor and Eastern Yughur in Gansu and Qinghai.

The Turkic family is spread across Central Asia all the way to its westernmost branch in Turkey. In China, it is represented by the Uygur, Kazakh, Uzbek, Tatar and Kirghiz languages, spoken in the far northwestern Uygur Autonomous Region of Xinjiang (former Chinese or Eastern Turkestan), Western Yugur spoken in Gansu and Salar, spoken in Qinghai and Gansu. These historically peripheral regions of China have inevitably produced unusual scenarios of language contact between unrelated languages, including those with the more recent immigrant Mandarin varieties that belong to the Northern, Northwestern Lanyin and Central Plains subgroups (Section 24.3.1).

Altaic languages are well-known for their strictly SOV order, postpositions and agglutinative features, including the use of suffixed case-markers (see Robbeets, Chapter 22, this volume). Some show vowel harmony.

24.1.3   Tai-Kadai

The Tai-Kadai language stock, which has also become known as 'Kra-Dai' in western literature, has the different name in China of Zhuang-Dong 壮侗. While the heartland for the numerically dominant Zhuang languages is in the Guangxi Autonomous Region of the far south of China, this subgroup extends south into Vietnam and north into Guizhou, where members of the Kam-Sui branch are also found, likewise under a different name in China, that of Dong-Shui 侗水. This group includes Mulao (Mulam) and Maonan. Southwestern Tai languages, known as Dai 傣 in China, are located further to the west in Xishuangbanna in southern Yunnan and straddle the borders of Burma and Laos. This happens to be the subdivision to which Standard Bangkok Thai belongs. Another important branch within China is constituted by the Li or Hlai languages of Hainan Island; see also Diller et al. (2008).

   In terms of word order correlations, Tai-Kadai languages represent almost the ideal for SVO languages (Dryer 2003), conforming to the predictions of modified–modifier in most of their syntactic features, unlike Sinitic, which is head-final for its nominal syntax and for certain aspects of its predicate syntax (see Chappell, Li and Peyraube 2007).

   The ancestors of the Tai-Kadai, known from historical texts as the Bai Yue 百越 or 'Hundred Yue tribes', are believed to have had their homeland in a large area south of the Yangzi River, well before the arrival of the first Han military colonizers in the late third century BCE (Bauer 1996; Ouyang 1995; Yue-Hashimoto 1991). A very ancient Tai substratum in the Yue Cantonese languages has been well established (F.-K. Li 1977; Bauer 1996).

24.1.4   Hmong-Mien

This language family is known under the different name in China of Miao-Yao 苗瑶. The Hmong languages are found as far north as the province of Hunan in central China and extend southwards through Guizhou, Sichuan and Yunnan provinces into Vietnam, Laos and thence further into Thailand. Mien languages are found in scattered pockets across the highland areas of southern China. Historically, speakers of these languages migrated slowly southwards under pressure from the Han over many centuries and may have pre-dated the ancestors of the Austroasiatics and the Tai in southern China (Yue-Hashimoto 1991).

   The SVO Hmong languages are well known for their high number of lexical tones and large array of consonant initials, including prenasalized and preglottalized series (Niederer 2011; Sposato 2014).

24.1.5   Austronesian

Apart from Huihui 回辉语, an isolated Chamic language of Hainan, the island province located to the south of Guangdong, a large group of Austronesian languages is located in Taiwan, which are known as

Formosan, the most ancient members of this large family. While Formosan languages number approximately twenty, many are endangered, if not already extinct. Forming 2 per cent of the Taiwanese population, the aboriginal communities who speak languages such as Atayal, Bunun and Rukai are located in what have been, until comparatively recently, the more inaccessible mountainous areas of central and eastern Taiwan.

Formosan languages do not form a single branch within Austronesian. Nonetheless, they share many features such as VSO or VOS word order, focus systems, case marking and a well-developed verb morphology.

24.1.6 Austroasiatic

Austroasiatic languages are generally divided into two main branches: Munda languages spoken in central and eastern India, and Mon-Khmer spoken in Vietnam, Cambodia and parts of Laos and Thailand. It is claimed that the ancestral languages to the Mon-Khmer branch of the Austroasiatic language family were originally spoken in parts of eastern and southeastern China and that substratum effects identified in Southern Min dialects support this hypothesis (Diffloth 2011; Norman and Mei 1976).

Today, only a few languages from this group are present on China's soil, including small communities of Va (Wa), Khmu and Blang (Bulang) in Xishuangbanna, Yunnan province, and also Vietnamese in Guangxi, known as Gin, Kin or Jing in China.

In addition to these six large families of greater Southeast and East Asia, also present within the borders of China are:

(i) sizeable Korean communities in the northeast of China (in the three provinces formerly known collectively as Manchuria – Liaoning, Jilin, Heilongjiang),
(ii) Indo-European: Tajik (Iranian) and Russian (Slavic) in Xinjiang.

24.1.7 Sinitic Languages

The ten main divisions for Sinitic languages (or Chinese dialect groups) currently recognized are Northern Chinese (Mandarin), Xiang, Gan, Wu, Min, Kejia (or Hakka), Yue, Jin, Pinghua and Hui dialects (as, for example, in the *Language Atlas of China*, second edition, 2012). Some disagreement exists with respect to the status of Pinghua and Hui, as being independent from the Yue and the Wu dialect groups, respectively. The linguistic diversity of the Sinitic languages is immense and, as yet, is neither fully explored nor acknowledged. Lack of mutual intelligibility is regularly the case even within each of these large, often heterogeneous dialect groups. For example, Southwestern Mandarin is not immediately comprehensible to speakers of the various Northern Mandarin dialects, nor is Hokkien to Teochiu speakers, even though both the latter are classified as Southern

Min varieties. Sinitic or Chinese languages could be thus considered to be as diverse as the Indo-European family.

The somewhat artificially created language of Standard Mandarin was adopted as the official language of China in 1958 and is called *pǔtōnghuà*普通話 or literally 'the common language'. The use of *pǔtōnghuà* has since been very effectively implemented across China through the domains of education, government and media as the national lingua franca. It is modelled on the pronunciation of the Beijing dialect, the lexicon of Northern Mandarin dialects and the grammar of modern vernacular literature (Chen 1999: 124). However, every provincial city has tended to develop its own variety or registers of *pǔtōnghuà*, defined by the extent to which local elements and pronunciation are mixed in (e.g. plastic *pǔtōnghuà* of Changsha: Wu Yunji 2005).

Table 24.1 gives the most up-to-date figures on the ten main groups of Sinitic languages.[2] The enormous Mandarin branch is itself further classified into eight subgroups. The greatest linguistic diversity for Sinitic is concentrated in the southeast of China where eight of the non-Mandarin dialect groups are located (III–X). Only the northern Jin group is co-territorial with Mandarin.

Table 24.1 *The Sinitic branch of Sino-Tibetan*

	Language branch	Region of China	Population (millions)	Representative Varieties
I	Mandarin 北方話	North, Northeast, Southwest of China	799	Beijing, Tianjin Nanjing
II	Jin 晉	Shanxi, Inner Mongolia	63	Taiyuan, Huojia
III	Xiang 湘	Hunan	36	Changsha, Chengbu
IV	Gan 贛	Jiangxi	48	Nanchang
V	Hui 徽	Anhui	3.3	Jixi
VI	Wu 吳	Zhejiang, Southern Jiangsu	74	Shanghainese, Suzhou, Ningbo
VII	Min 閩	Fujian, NE Guangdong, Taiwan	75	Hokkien, Teochew
VIII	Kejia 客家	SW Fujian, NE Guangdong	42	Meixian Hakka
IX	Yue 粵	Guangdong and Guangxi	59	Cantonese
X	Pinghua 平話 & Tuhua 土话	Guangxi, Hunan and Guangdong	7.8	Nanning, Guilin
Total 1,207,100,000 (1.2 billion)				

[2] These figures are based on those given by Xiong Zhenghui 熊证辉 and Zhang Zhenxing 张振兴 (2008: 97) and the second edition of the *Language Atlas of China* (中国语言地图集 第二版 *Zhongguo Yuyan Dituji Di'er ban*, 2012) and have been rounded up. Xiong and Zhang explain that they have used the *2004 China Administrative Regions Yearbook* (中国行政区划简册 *Zhongguo Xingzhengqu Huajiance*) for the population figures. This compares with the sixteenth edition of *Ethnologue* (Lewis 2009) and also the online eighteenth edition (Lewis et al. 2015), which are both based on an extrapolation of the 2000 China census, the last census to pose questions on language and dialect use. Lewis (2009) and Lewis et al. (2015) estimate 840 millions of speakers for the different Mandarin dialects within China, rather than 799 million as above.

Next, in Section 24.2, we review some of the principal works on typological characteristics of East and Southeast Asia, concluding with recent research on linguistic areas in China.

24.2   Typological Features of Sinitic Languages in their Southeast Asian Context

The received wisdom is that, in particular, Sinitic, Tai-Kadai, Hmong-Mien and Mon-Khmer show isolating or analytic tendencies while Tibeto-Burman does so to a somewhat lesser extent, particularly its western branches. In general, East and Southeast Asian languages do not possess inflectional morphology, that is, they do not use special affixes on their verbs to code tense, nor to indicate person agreement. Nouns do not usually take markers for number (singular and plural), gender (masculine, feminine, neutral), nor for case (nominative, accusative, dative etc.). At word or morpheme level, there is claimed to be a preference for monosyllabicity.

However, typology is a relative matter. Sinitic languages do possess small inventories of affixes, predominantly making use of suffixes and clitics. Adpositions, mainly prepositions, are used to code case roles such as direct object, agent in the passive construction, or the comitative. These may be found to form portmanteau morphemes in many dialects when they fuse with following pronouns – one high-frequency counterexample to the isolating stereotype that lingers on with respect to Chinese, based largely on the typological profile of Standard Mandarin. In contrast to this, Central Plains and Jilu Mandarin dialects, also Jin dialects, may use changes to the syllable finals similar to ablaut or stem alternation to indicate aspectual functions such as the perfective (Lamarre 2015). Furthermore, the use of tone sandhi (tone change), vowel lengthening and reduplication with grammatical functions is widespread in Sinitic for closed classes such as pronouns and demonstratives to indicate, for example, the plural forms of pronouns or semantic distinctions in demonstrative paradigms (Chen 2015).

In addition to these important features, Marybeth Clark (1974, 1985, 1989), who worked extensively on Hmong, Vietnamese and other Southeast Asian languages, pinpointed the following features, which prove to be equally applicable to Sinitic languages:

(a) widespread use of tone (Tai, Hmong, Sinitic, some Tibeto-Burman languages),

(b) use of numeral classifiers as part of the nominal structure with quantified nouns,

(c) SVO or medial word order in the east and southeast (NB verb-final word order in the west for Tibeto-Burman),

(d) stative verbs to express qualities as opposed to adjectives,

(e) polar 'yes/no' questions formed with verbs and negative adverbs, either VERB-NEG or VERB-NEG-VERB,

(f) serial verb constructions (SVCs),

(g) adversative passive constructions,

(h) identity of existential and possessive verbs.

This has been elaborated upon by Enfield (2005) *inter alia* (see Chapter 25, this volume), who discusses further features such as:

(i) use of ellipsis and noun phrase movement,

(j) polyfunctionality of nouns and verbs,

(k) lack of explicit marking on complex clauses,

(l) use of rhyming expressions and reduplication.

Bisang has also contributed many studies on Mainland Southeast Asia, with his major areal study of different kinds of SVCs (1992), a typology of extended uses of classifiers (1996), and the notion of hidden complexity (2009) that accompanies the lack of explicit morphological coding.

24.2.1 Studies on Areal Diffusion in East and Southeast Asia

Some of the earliest pioneering work on the areal typology of Sinitic languages was carried out by Mantaro Hashimoto 桥本万太郎, who argued that due to centuries-long contact, Northern Sinitic languages have become substantially altaïcized while Southern Sinitic languages have similarly become taïcized. His evidence comes in the form of phonological, lexical and syntactic features (see Hashimoto 1974, 1976a, 1976b, 1986, 1987).[3] Some of these tendencies are listed in Table 24.2 for the Chinese languages found in the two zones. His treatment of the north/south opposition as a continuum can be clearly perceived in features such as the

Table 24.2 *Tendencies in Sinitic languages according to Hashimoto's north/south division*

Altaïcization (north)	Taïcization (south)
Stress-based and fewer tones	More tones
Higher proportion of polysyllabic words	Higher proportion of monosyllabic words
Smaller inventory of classifiers	Larger inventory of classifiers
Modifier-modified for NPs	Modified-modifier for NPs
Gender prefixes on certain animal terms	Gender suffixes on certain animal terms
IO-DO word order for prepositionless ditransitives	DO-IO word order for prepositionless ditransitives
Less complex syllable structure	More complex syllable structure
Pre-verbal adverbs	Possibility of clause-final adverbs
Passive markers < causative verbs	Passive markers < verbs of giving[4]
Comparative of inequality: marker(<COM- PARE 比)-standard-adjective	Comparative of inequality: adjective-marker (< SURPASS)-standard

---

[3] Hashimoto could well have usefully included Austroasiatic languages in this continuum, which, similarly to the Tai (or Kra-Dai) languages, lie in and to the south of China (see Section 24.1.6; also Norman and Mei 1976).

[4] This feature is only pertinent to Southern and Central Sinitic languages and not to mainland Southeast Asia where *give* verbs grammaticalize only as far as the causative verb stage.

increasing number of classifiers, tones and consonantal endings to syllables, not to mention the greater preference for monosyllabic morphemes as one moves southwards.

Hashimoto's dichotomy cannot be faulted in terms of general trends. However, are they all due to areal convergence? Indeed, for some of the features, further analysis unearths certain complications. For example, passive markers arising from causative verbs is not a purely Northern Sinitic feature in China, as he would claim: Chappell and Peyraube (2006) have argued that Southern Sinitic *give* verbs must pass through a causative verb stage before they develop into markers of the passive, and have also pointed out that the causative > passive grammaticalization was attested long before any intense contact with Altaic.

For prepositionless ditransitive constructions, known as 'double object' constructions in Chinese linguistics, counterexamples to this generalization are the fact that the Northern *recipient-theme* or IO-DO (*indirect object–direct object*) word order is also found in Pinghua Chinese (de Sousa 2015) and in Southern Min dialects, both Southern Sinitic. With respect to comparatives of inequality, Chappell and Peyraube (2015) have argued that the head-marking type of *adjective-marker-standard* found in Cantonese, Hakka and many other Southern Sinitic languages is in fact a native construction, attested in historical documents from as early as the Late Archaic period (fifth to third centuries BCE). Without further historical evidence from Tai languages, it would be imprudent to uphold any hypothesis of taicization in this case.

In another approach to Southeast Asian areal linguistics, Matisoff (1991a, 1991b) has proposed that Mainland Southeast Asia may be divided into the Sinospheric and the non-Sinospheric or Indospheric zones. The Sinospheric area includes Southern Sinitic languages located south of the Yangzi. In this study, he adduces that several common grammaticalization pathways basically involve the syntactic reanalysis of one of the main verbs in asymmetrical serial verb constructions (SVCs), as in cases (2)–(7):

(1) modal verbs > desiderative markers, 'be likely to',
(2) verbs meaning 'to dwell' > progressive aspect markers,
(3) verbs meaning 'to finish' > perfective aspect markers,
(4) verbs meaning 'to get, obtain' > 'manage to do', 'able to', 'have to',
(5) verbs of giving > causative and benefactive markers,
(6) verbs of saying > complementizers, topic and conditional markers,
(7) formation of resultative and directional compound verbs through verb concatenation.

As pointed out in Chappell (2001), nearly all of these pathways of grammaticalization apply to Northern Sinitic as well, apart from the limited use of 'give' with a causative meaning. Hence, they may be profitably added to the inventory of shared areal features for East and Southeast Asia.

Dryer (2003) has developed Hashimoto's areal classification further by providing a careful analysis of word order typology in Mainland Southeast Asia, setting up a continuum from west to east, or SOV to SVO and their principal correlations. He observes that GEN-N and REL-N are two common areal features, regardless of word order.[5] For Sinitic and Tibeto-Burman languages, he concludes that they are influenced by their closest neighbours.

24.2.2   Five Linguistic Areas of China

On the foundation of these earlier studies, particularly those of Hashimoto (cited above), Norman (1982, 1988) and Yue (2003), Chappell (2015b) argues the case for five linguistic areas in China for Sinitic languages on the basis of the distribution and intersection of five main types of grammatical constructions: differential object marking constructions, adversative passives and their related causative constructions, comparative constructions of inequality, and ditransitive constructions. It is shown that the parameters used in establishing linguistic areas for unrelated languages can also be clearly applied to related languages involving intralinguistic contact, such as in the case of the different divisions of Sinitic.

The five areas in question involve a refinement of the north/south divide proposed by Hashimoto, based on the clustering of major syntactic features, whereby the northern area continues to be opposed to a southern area, but this is itself composed of three smaller areas. A central transitional buffer zone, manifesting great linguistic turbulence in terms of linguistic features, is sandwiched in between the northern and southern linguistic areas.

(i)	Northern	Northern Mandarin dialect groups (Central Plains, Jilu, Jiaoliao, Northeastern Mandarin), Jin dialect group[6]
(ii)	Southwestern	Southwestern Mandarin dialects spoken in Hubei, Sichuan, Yunnan, Guizhou, NW Hunan
(iii)	Far Southern	Yue (Cantonese) and Hakka dialects in Guangdong and Guangxi[7]
(iv)	Southeastern	Min dialect group in Fujian province and Taiwan
(v)	Central Transitional zone	Wu, Hui, Gan, Xiang and Jianghuai Mandarin

Significant for the areal linguistics of Southeast Asia is the fact that the two Southern Sinitic linguistic areas share their use of SURPASS comparatives with Thai, Lao, Hmong, Vietnamese and Khmer, as well as SUFFER-

---

[5] Only Karen is the 'odd man out' here: it makes use of N-REL.

[6] The Lanyin or Northwestern Mandarin dialects are rather aberrant in many respects of their syntactic behaviour, due to contact influence from Altaic, and so are not included in this list of core Northern Mandarin dialects; see Section 24.3.1 for more information on their special features.

[7] The Pinghua dialects of Guangxi Autonomous Region prove to possess many Northern features, or if not, to be transitional between the Southwestern area and the Southern area; see de Sousa (2015), Section 24.3.2 below, and Chappell (2015b) for more details.

passives based on contact verbs, but this is in the case of Southwestern only. Note that the Southwestern province of Yunnan shares borders with Burma (Myanmar), Laos and Vietnam. The Far Southern zone shares its southern border just with Vietnam (Guangxi). The latter's preference for non-grammaticalized serial verb constructions where the first verb is TAKE is also found in several Southeast Asian languages according to Bisang (1996). These have not yet become fully fledged differential object markers (DOMs) as in the Northern area (see Chappell 2013).

24.3   Case Studies of Language Contact and its Outcomes in China

24.3.1   Northwestern China: The Gansu-Qinghai Linguistic Area and Contact between Altaic and Chinese

The northwest of China is historically a frontier area where Han Chinese have carried out trade along the Silk Route with many different ethnicities, or have engaged in warfare to occupy and re-occupy the same border territories, if not to be occupied in their turn. This part of China meets with and forms part of Central Asia, where languages of the Mongolic and Turkic families are found (Section 24.1.2), such as in the Xinjiang 新疆 Autonomous Uygur Region, former Chinese Turkestan.

To the southeast of Xinjiang, in Qinghai青海 province, speakers of Tibetan and Mongolic languages intermingle with smaller communities speaking Turkic languages, such as Salar. Lanyin (Northwestern Mandarin), Central Plains and Northern Mandarin are relative latecomers to this area bordering on a vast expanse of deserts such as the Qaidam and Taklimakan and also the Yellow River plateau.

Across the eastern border of Qinghai, the linguistic situation is similarly mixed in Gansu甘肃, with large communities composed of a variety of different Turkic and Mongolic languages. Two of the main Turkic languages in this area are Salar and Western Yughur, while the main Mongolic languages are Baonan, Monguor (Tu), Eastern Yughur and Dongxiang (Santa).

In this section, we will concentrate on a small sprachbund which straddles the border between Qinghai and Gansu and has been proposed on the basis of language contact between varieties of Chinese, Tibetan and Mongolian. Furthermore, the claim has been made that several of these languages are mixed, including Wutun 五屯话, Linxia 临夏话 (Hezhou) and Tangwang 唐汪话 in particular.

What is linguistically striking about the northwestern area is first of all the widespread development of case-marking systems in the Chinese languages located in this zone, undoubtedly the result of contact with the surrounding Altaic languages. Secondly, the Chinese languages in this area have undergone a general word order change to verb-final, SOV, that is, the same word order as in Altaic. Thirdly, the plural suffix, normally restricted to personal pronouns in Sinitic (and sometimes a handful of human, animate nouns), has been extended in use to the pluralization of non-human animate and inanimate common nouns, once more replicating the model of plural suffixes found in many Altaic languages. For example, it is common to find the application of the Mandarin plural suffix -men 们 in the Chinese languages in this sprachbund to any kind of common noun, producing forms such as HUAR**men**[8] 花儿们 'flowers', HONGQI**men** 红旗们 'red flags', YEZI**men** 叶子们 'leaves' and even to abstract nouns, yielding 'kindnesses' – ENQING**men** 恩情们 (see Li Keyou and Li Meiling 1998: 25–26), all unacceptable in Standard Mandarin. Further examples of these intriguing contact features are presented immediately in the following.

Gangou 甘沟话, Tangwang 唐汪话, Linxia 临夏话 and Wutun 五屯话 are all fundamentally Chinese or have a Chinese language-base.[9] Nonetheless, quite atypically for Sinitic, they use a mixture of suffixes and postpositions to mark a minimum of four or five different case roles, including a form that syncretizes the direct object with the dative and the benefactive, as well as an ablative/comparative marker, an allative marker and a syncretized form for comitative/instrumental/ manner.[10] The use of the accusative and dative postposition -ha or -xa can be seen in examples (1) and (2), which also clearly show the typical SOV word order in this micro-area.

(1)   Gangou Chinese, Qinghai
 Aijie-liar   *mian-ha*   *wa-shang,*   *you-ha*   *dao-shang-zhi*
 she-two   flour-ACC   take out-PERF,   oil-ACC   pour-out-CHAIN
 youbingzi   *zha-liao.*
 friedcake   fry-PERF
 'The two took out the flour, poured the oil into a cauldron and then they fried fried-cakes.'[11]

(Zhu et al. 1997 : 438–439)

(2)   Tangwang Chinese, Gansu
 nə   *nə*   *ɕʲɛ*   *kaxɔ̃-mu-xa-nə*   *wawa-mu-xa-nə*
 3SG   DEM   some   apricot-PL-ACC-LOG   child-PL-DAT-LOG
 ʦʰɻ̩-ki-xa-xa-lʲɔ
 eat-CAUS-RES-POT-PERF
 'He was able to get his children to eat those few apricots he had.'

(Djamouri 2015)

---

[8] I use the *pīnyīn* Romanization for standard Mandarin with small capitals wherever the IPA transcription is not available in the original source.

[9] Tangwang and Wutun are claimed to be mixed languages by some, including *Ethnologue* (2009, 2015) and Wurm and Li (1987). For a different conclusion, see Peyraube (2008, 2015) and Djamouri (2015) on Tangwang.

[10] Peyraube (2008, 2015) observes that the label 'case' for adpositions does not strictly speaking conform to the traditional notion of case. This is a controversial issue which we leave open for further discussion, while noting that the adpositions in these Northwestern Chinese languages fulfil a similar function to case inflections.

[11] This example (1) faithfully reproduces the text in Zhu et al. (1997). The grammatical abbreviations used in the glossing are as follows: ACC, accusative case; CHAIN, clause chaining marker; PERF, perfective. In example (2): CAUS, causative; DAT, dative; DEM, demonstrative; LOG, logophoric; PERF, perfective; PL, plural; POT, potential; RES, resultative.

The ablative marker may double up as a comparative marker, as in Gangou Chinese and in the neighbouring Mongolic language of Monguor, not to mention in Tangwang Chinese as well. It is a source frequently found cross-linguistically in comparatives of inequality (the 'separative' strategy of Stassen 1985) but is not attested elsewhere in Sinitic for synchronic data (Chappell 2015b).

(3) Gangou Chinese, Qinghai
    Zhi-ge   *huar*   *hao-mei,*   *zhi-ge-ha-**sha***   *han da-zhi*   *zhə-gei*
    this-CL   flower   good-NEG   this-CL-ACC-COMP   more big-GEN   pick-CAUS
    'This flower isn't good, I'll pick a bigger one than this.'

                                          (Zhu et al. 1997 : 445)

Finally, the instrumental/comitative case is a regional calque from Altaic languages, based on the morpheme for 'two' LIANG ~LIA in the Chinese languages of Linxia (Dwyer 1992: 165–168), Wutun (Janhunen et al. 2008: 60), Tangwang and Gangou (Peyraube 2015). While its syncretism with instrumental and manner roles is typical in European languages (Heine and Kuteva 2002; Stolz 1999), it is rare in Sinitic languages, in which the comitative regularly develops into an NP coordinative conjunction, but never into an instrumental marker. In certain languages, the comitative grammaticalizes into a differential object marker as well, via a benefactive/dative use (Chappell 2013, 2015b).

(4) Wutun
    gu   *agu*   *shetek-**liangge***   *zhaze*   *da-pe-lio*   *ze-li*
    that   girl   stone-SOC   window   hit-break-PRF   EXEC-OBJ
    'That girl broke the window with a rock.'[12] (instrumental)

                                          (Janhunen et al. 2008: 60)

(5) Wutun
    ngu   *ngu-de*   *tixang-**liangge***   *qhi-zhe*
    1P:SG   1P:SG   younger:brother-SOC   go-CONT
    'I will go together with my younger brother.' (comitative)

                                          (Janhunen et al. 2008: 60)

Dwyer (1992: 165) proposes that the source of the compound form *liaŋkə* 两个 'two together' in Linxia is a calque on a similar compound in Yellow River plateau Mongolic and that its reanalysis from a compound numeral [Numeral-CL] must have taken place in Mongolic at some time before the loan translation was adopted, since this phenomenon is not found in Sinitic at all.

24.3.2   Guangxi, Southern China: Tai and Sinitic Languages

The far south of China is the location of the Guangxi Zhuang Autonomous Region, which shares its southern border with Vietnam. As the name

---

[12] The grammatical abbreviations for the Wutun examples are: SOC, sociative (i.e. instrumental/comitative case); PRF perfective; EXEC, executive; OBJ, objective; 1P:SG, first person singular; CONT, continuative.

implies, the predominant linguistic group is composed of Zhuang speakers. The Zhuang languages 壮语 belong to the Tai branch of Tai-Kadai (or Kra-Dai) (Diller 2008).[13]

In this region, Sinitic is represented by the Western Yue dialects and Pinghua, in addition to Southwestern Mandarin and a small enclave of Xiang in the northeast. On the eastern side of Guangxi, next to Guangdong province, Yue (Cantonese) dialects predominate, intermingled with Hakka communities. In the area of Southern Guangxi, both Pinghua and Cantonese have come under influence from Zhuang languages, but notably to differing degrees (Huang 1997; Kwok 2010; de Sousa 2013, *inter alia*) while Zhuang languages, in their turn, have been similarly subject to contact-induced change from Sinitic languages (Wu Fuxiang 2013). In this section, we will observe the effects of language contact on the Southern Pinghua variety of Nanning.

While it is generally accepted that there is a Tai substratum present in the Yue or Cantonese dialect group, for example, identifiable in the presence of a contrasting series of long vowels and a sizeable number of ancient loanwords (see, in particular, F.-K. Li 1977, Yue-Hashimoto 1991, Bauer 1996), recent research on Tai–Yue linguistic interaction has turned up interesting grammatical phenomena such as changes to word order, including the non-Sinitic order of V-PP, as opposed to PP-V word order for benefactive NPs in Nanning Cantonese (see Kwok 2010), and the use of clause-final adverbs such as *sin* 先 'first' and *tim* 添 'too' in a variety of Yue dialects, including Hong Kong Cantonese, where these would normally precede the verb in pan-Sinitic. With respect to Nanning Cantonese, Ouyang (1995) has similarly identified the same clause-final position for intensifiers and also the use of a particular type of reduplication for verbs, both directly calqued from Zhuang.

In a comparison of Nanning Pinghua with Nanning Cantonese and Northern Zhuang, de Sousa (2015) has found that Nanning Pinghua is in fact far less influenced by Zhuang than is the local variety of Nanning Cantonese. At first blush, this may appear somewhat counter-intuitive since Pinghua speakers, as de Sousa explains, have been resident in the Guangxi area since the eleventh century, when military troops from the Northern province of Shandong were sent to quell the Zhuang during the Northern Song dynasty (960–1127). In contrast to this, the Cantonese speakers have only arrived relatively recently in the past 150 years, migrating westwards along the river routes from Guangdong province, from the time of the First Opium War onwards.

De Sousa shows that while Nanning Southern Pinghua follows expectations in revealing more Zhuang loans in its lexicon than does Nanning

[13] Zhuang is further classified into Northern and Southern branches in China. According to the traditional division into Northern, Central and Southwestern Tai made by F.-K. Li (1977), Northern Zhuang belongs to Northern Tai while Southern Zhuang belongs to Central Tai.

Cantonese, by way of contrast, in its morphology and grammar, Pinghua unexpectedly exhibits many important Northern Sinitic features including IO-DO word order (or *verb-recipient-theme*) as the unmarked word order in prepositionless ditransitives (also known as 'double object' constructions), gender prefixes on terms for domestic animals, the typical use of pre-verbal adverbs, and a strong dispreference for monosyllabic words (Section 24.2.1). The latter is evident in the higher incidence of suffixes, acting as markers of the noun class, which results in the creation of disyllabic words. In contrast to this, the Yue dialect of Nanning Cantonese displays the predictable DO-IO word order (or *verb-theme-recipient*) common to the Yue group of Sinitic with verbs of giving,[14] gender suffixes, the presence of clause-final adverbs, as remarked upon above, and no dispreference for monosyllabicity at word-level. Two of these features are selected in Table 24.3 for exemplification.

(6)   Nanning Pinghua *verb-recipient-theme* order in ditransitive
       constructions

系	佢	錢,	佢	就	抓	去	賭。
$hɐi^{25}$	$kəi^{13}$	$tʃin^{11}$	$kəi^{13}$	$tʃəu^{22}$	na^{53}	$həi^{25}$	tu^{33}.
give	3SG	money,	3SG	then	take	go	gamble

       'If you give him/her money, s/he will take it to gamble.'

Another set of features which link Yue dialects more closely with Northern Zhuang or Tai languages can be seen in the category of the nominal classifier. In a similar pattern to Tai languages, Nanning Cantonese displays a far greater polyfunctionality in its extended uses of the classifier than does Nanning Pinghua. The most striking difference is seen in the use of the appropriate classifier to code possession in preference to the general marker of subordination in Nanning Cantonese, 嘅 $kɛ^{33}$, which may also be employed. This preference is shared with Northern Zhuang (Milliken 1998), while the use of classifiers to mark the relation of possession is not possible in Nanning Pinghua. Nanning Pinghua, like Northern Sinitic languages in general, must use the general

Table 24.3 *Gender affixes in three languages spoken in Nanning, Guangxi (de Sousa 2015)*

Language	'Hen'	'Rooster'	Affix
Nanning Cantonese	kei^{55}-na^{25} 雞乸	kei^{55}-$kuŋ^{55}$雞公	gender suffix
Northern Zhuang	gaeq-meh	gaeq-boux	gender suffix
Nanning Pinghua	mu^{13}-kei^{53} 母雞	$kuŋ^{53}$-kei^{53}公雞	gender prefix

[14] As de Sousa (2015) observes, the *theme-recipient* word order with verbs of giving in Cantonese may well be an internal development. Furthermore, verbs of deprivation allow the *recipient-theme* order. Both word orders for ditransitives are possible in many Tai languages, which seems to vitiate the argument in favour of the hypothesis that borrowing took place in the direction from Zhuang, or Tai in general, into Southern Sinitic languages. See also on this topic, Xu and Peyraube (1997).

marker of modification (MOD), which is $kə^{55}$. Compare (7) with Northern Zhuang in (8) and Nanning Pinghua in (9) (data from de Sousa 2015).

(7)   Nanning Cantonese: N$_{POSSESSOR}$–CL–N$_{POSSESSUM}$
       佢   隻   崽
       k^hy^{13} $tʃɛk^3$ $tʃɐi^{25}$
       3SG   CL   son
       'His/her son'

(8)   Northern Zhuang: CL–N$_{POSSESSUM}$–N$_{POSSESSOR}$
       aen   *vanj*   *mwngz*
       CL   bowl   2SG
       'Your bowl'

(9)   Nanning Pinghua: N$_{POSSESSOR}$–MOD–N$_{POSSESSUM}$
       細   蘇   個   (*隻)   狗兒
       $lɐi^{55}$ $łɔ^{53}$ $kə^{55}$ (*$tʃət^3$) $kɐu^{33}$-$ɲi^{11}$
       Little   Sū   MOD   (*CL)   dog-DIM
       'Little Su's puppy/ puppies'

This is, however, a general feature that is also shared by Zhuang with Standard Cantonese.[15] Nanning Cantonese, however, goes one step further in allowing attributive adjectives to be linked by the appropriate classifier to the head noun, just as in Northern Zhuang (for details, see de Sousa 2015).

De Sousa (2013) argues that the less extensive impact of Zhuang on Nanning Southern Pinghua can above all be attributed to the very low rate of intermarriage that traditionally existed between the two groups before the mid-twentieth century and the 'social distance' maintained by the Pinghua communities towards the Zhuang, a situation which has not been applicable to the same degree at all for the Nanning Cantonese communities. In fact, since the arrival of the Cantonese in Nanning in the mid-nineteenth century, there has been large-scale language shift from Zhuang to Cantonese (Kwok 2010) which has tended, therefore, to reinforce the already existing Tai substratum in Cantonese Yue dialects.

24.3.3   Hunan, Central China: Southwestern Mandarin and Xianghua

Hunan province lies just to the south of the Yangzi River in central China. The main Sinitic languages spoken in Hunan belong to the central transitional Sinitic language group known as the Xiang 湘 group. There are also pockets of Gan speakers in the southwest, scattered Hakka communities and a group of largely undescribed patois or *tǔhuà* 土话 in the south of the province, an area bilingual with Southwestern Mandarin (for locations, see Wurm and Li 1987: Map B-11). The northwest of Hunan is the main target of this third case study in a linguistically diverse area known as Xiangxi 湘西, from which an autonomous Tujia and Hmong prefecture has been

---

[15]   Note that the use of classifiers to mark possession is also found in other Sinitic languages, such as the Wu dialects, for which there is no connection with Zhuang. It is not found in Northern Sinitic, however.

created: Southwestern Mandarin is the lingua franca in this area, rather than Standard Mandarin, reserved for formal and official domains, if not for communicating with people from outside this area. This being said, Standard Mandarin is very well understood due to its use in all the different types of media. The main languages are thus:

(i) Southwestern Mandarin,
(ii) Hmong,
(iii) Tujia,
(iv) Xianghua (also known as Waxiang).

According to Xiong and Zhang (2008), there are 260 million speakers of Southwestern Mandarin dialects, a subgroup of Mandarin which is not readily comprehensible with the standard language. It spreads from Hubei through northwestern Hunan to Sichuan, Guizhou and Yunnan provinces, and is itself made up of a large number of dialects. As the speakers of Southwestern Mandarin arrived fairly late in the Xiangxi region, during the Qing dynasty (1644–1911), their language has come to be known as *kèhuà* 客话 'guest language' by the local population. This is in fact the dominant language, particularly in the towns and cities.

The Hmong languages of Xiangxi belong to the northernmost group of western Hunan Hmong, which is itself further divided into western and eastern dialects and is spoken, in the main nowadays, in rural villages. The population is estimated at 770,000 of a total Hmong population of over five million (Wurm and Li 1987: Map C-9) and 900,000 in *Ethnologue* (Lewis et al. 2015). Urban speakers have already long ago undergone massive language shift to Southwestern Mandarin. The same situation applies for speakers of the easternmost Tibeto-Burman language of Tujia, whose localities overlap to some extent with the Hmong speakers in Xiangxi, although not entirely. According to Wurm and Li (1987: Map C-10), only approximately 170,000 speakers are left of an estimated 2.8 million (or even less – 71,500 – according to the eighteenth edition of *Ethnologue*).

Xianghua, by way of contrast, remains an unclassified, Sinitic language, whose speakers are estimated to number approximately 300,000–400,000 (Bao and Yan 1986). Xianghua can be divided up into at least four main dialects: those of Guzhang 古丈, Luxi 泸溪, Yuanling 沅陵 and Nanshan 南山. Apart from Nanshan, located near Chengbu in southwestern Hunan, the other three are located in Xiangxi. According to their family genealogies, they claim to have migrated into northwestern Hunan several hundred years ago from Jiangxi, the neighbouring province to the east. A subsequent, further migration south to Chengbu, in southern Hunan, saw the Xianghua speakers settling in and around the mountainous border areas on the frontier with Guangxi. The family histories of two of the communities – Guzhang and far-flung Chengbu, over 500 kilometres to the south – both independently confirm each other's stated origins, for which we at present do not have any documentary evidence.

The Xianghua dialects are similarly under threat of extinction, possibly within the next generation. It is interesting to compare their plight with the Hmong and Tujia population: a sociolinguistic survey carried out by Yunji Wu in 1998 showed overwhelming sinicization of language use for the Tujia and the Hmong – and this from an early stage, as far as records can tell us. Wu observes that even by the early twentieth century, Hmong and Tujia speakers had already undergone a massive swing to the monolingual use of Southwestern Mandarin, according to the gazetteer of Dong Hongxun (1907). In 1907, from the data that Dong collected in 282 villages in Xiangxi, 72 per cent of Tujia and Hmong speakers, were already L2 speakers of Mandarin. By way of contrast, for the Xianghua community, a mere 9 per cent were L2 speakers, while 13 per cent were monolingual having undergone complete shift to Mandarin. The remaining majority of 78 per cent were monolingual Xianghua speakers. Nearly 100 years later, Yunji Wu carried out her own survey in Guzhang county and was able to identify an increase in the shift to Southwestern Mandarin use to over 90 per cent for the Xianghua speakers (reported in Wu and Shen 2010).[16]

Before the mid-twentieth century, intermarriage was rare between different ethnic groups in Xiangxi and openly discouraged. In the rural Xianghua-speaking villages, the disappearance of this social ban has not really affected the linguistic situation greatly: intermarriage is not common, simply because the district village populations are fairly uniformly made up of Xianghua families, apart from the case of men who have moved outside the village at some stage to work and have brought back speakers of other Chinese languages as their wives.

Living in separate communities could partially explain why it is difficult to detect any linguistic influence on Xianghua from Hmong or Tujia. Instead, we find an increasing influence on Xianghua from Southwestern Mandarin, the local lingua franca. We also find that, unsurprisingly, this influence is more easy to observe with city speakers than with rural speakers, for example, Xianghua speakers in Guyang 古阳市, the town which is the seat of government for Guzhang county 古丈县, versus Xianghua speakers in Lijiadong 李家洞 village, in the remote mountainous district of Gaofeng 高峰乡.[17] This third case study thus outlines the outcome of interdialectal contact in a Southwestern Mandarin sprachbund, which includes this northwestern area of Hunan and neighbouring Sichuan and Guizhou provinces, whose borders it shares.

---

[16] According to our own fieldwork, this tendency is much more in evidence in the county towns of Xiangxi than in the rural villages. In Lijiadong village of Gaofeng district, where my fieldwork was conducted, more than 90 per cent of the village of over 1000 inhabitants speak Xianghua in the home and non-official domains, in addition to Southwestern Mandarin.

[17] Data have been collected during eight field trips carried out by the author since 2006 in the town of Guzhang and in the village of Lijiadong, Xiangxi.

Xianghua shows many archaic features in its lexicon, syntax and morphology, and so may represent a very early branch of Sinitic (Baxter and Sagart 2014). Nonetheless, borrowing of lexical items connected with domains such as politics, government and technical terms from Southwestern Mandarin is the norm for Xianghua.

In some respects, the syntax of Xianghua is also very conservative when compared with Mandarin dialects. For example, the comparative of inequality in Xianghua makes use of the polarity cognitive schema (Heine 1997) with a complex coordinate structure that combines antonyms. The stative verbs in the predicates of each clause represent antonyms of one another. The comparee occurs in the first clause, while the standard NP occurs in the second. Apart from structural considerations, the only overt marker is the use of the plural classifier sa^{55}些 'some' which acts as an adverbial quantifier in this construction. The construction is at an early stage of grammaticalization.

(10) Xianghua polarity comparative:

NP$_{COMPAREE}$	Verb$_x$	Q($<$CL$_{PL}$),	NP$_{STANDARD}$	Verb$_{\sim x}$	Q($<$CL$_{PL}$)
你	高	些,	我	矮	些。
ηi^{25}	kau^{55}	sa^{55},	wu^{25}	γa^{13}	sa^{55}.
2SG$_{COMPAREE}$	tall	some$_{DEG}$	1SG$_{STANDARD}$	short	some$_{DEG}$

Literally: 'You're a little tall; I'm a little short.' = 'You're taller than me.'

This structure has not been widely reported to date in the literature on comparatives in Southeast and East Asian languages, including the research on comparatives in Chinese linguistics. Nonetheless, in most Sinitic languages, we can also find the predicative use of a gradable stative verb followed by a quantifier which can be regarded as the coding of a non-conventionalized comparative that lacks its standard NP, for example Hong Kong Cantonese: *gāmyaht yiht dī* 今日熱啲 [lit. today hot a.bit] 'It's hotter today'. At present, it is not clear to what extent the complex type of conjoined comparative found in Xianghua with its polarity semantics can be identified in other Chinese languages in the form of a conventionalized comparative.

What is interesting for the present study is a kind of hybrid comparative that has arisen with the borrowing of the SW Mandarin 'compare' comparative into Xianghua. The hybridization leads to double marking, since the Mandarin comparative marker, pi^{25} 比 < 'compare' is accompanied by the quantifier sa^{55}些, the only morphological vestige of the polarity structure which remains, apart from the gradable predicative adjective. And this native marker is obligatory in the new comparative. The original complex sentence form with two clauses that coded the Xianghua comparative has been conflated into a monoclausal structure. This can be regarded as one piece of evidence attesting to intense contact, since the resultant structure largely reflects Mandarin syntax and morphology for this type of comparative (see Chappell and Peyraube 2015).

(11)   NP$_{COMPAREE}$ pi^{25} NP$_{STANDARD}$ Verb Q
      你   比   我   肥   些。
      ηi^{25} **pi^{25}** wu^{25} fi^{213} **sa^{55}**.
      2SG   CM   1SG   fat   some$_{DEG}$
      'You're fatter than me.'

A second example of borrowing concerns the differential object marking construction whose marker, kai^{55} 跟, has evolved from the unusual source of a comitative in Xianghua (Chappell, Peyraube and Wu 2011), exemplified by (12). It is being slowly replaced in the speech of more educated speakers by the Southwestern Mandarin marker pa^{41}把 (13). The tonal value of 41 for pa^{41}把 belies the fact that it is borrowed: The corresponding tone for the Xianghua native morpheme is a 25 contour.[18] Example (14) records the use of SW Mandarin pa^{41}把 in a Xianghua narrative.

(12)   Xianghua differential object marking construction:
      (NP$_{AGENT}$) – [kai^{55} – NP$_{DO}$] – VP
      跟履端来 !   跟门闭下。
      kai^{55} li^{25} to^{55} $z\epsilon^{13}$.   **kai^{55}** mai^{55} pi^{33} ka^{33}.
      GEN$_{OM}$ shoe   carry   come   GEN$_{OM}$ door   close   PRT
      'Bring the shoes over here!'   'Close the door!'

(13)   Southwestern Mandarin differential object marking construction:
      (NP$_{AGENT}$) – [pa^{41} – NP$_{DO}$] – VP
      酸肉它就是把它称起来,
      $suan^{55}zu^{13}$ t^ha^{55} $t\varphi i\partial u^{25}$ si^{25} **pa^{41}** t^ha^{55} $ts^h\partial\eta^{55}$ $t\varphi^hi^{41}lai^{13}$,
      sour.meat   3SG   then   be   BA$_{OM}$ 3SG   weigh-DIR

      买起来,   把肉买起来。
      mai^{41}-$t\varphi^hi^{41}lai^{13}$,   **pa^{41}** zu^{13} mai^{41}-$t\varphi^hi^{41}lai^{13}$.
      buy-DIR   BA$_{OM}$ meat   buy-DIR
      'As for sour pork, when (you've) purchased the meat, . . .' (literally: 'sour pork, when it's been weighed and bought, the meat's been bought.')

(14)   Xianghua narrative extract with SW Mandarin DOM: pa^{41}
      需要好多菜 ,   才能够把喜事办得来.
      $\epsilon y^{55}iau^{25}$ xau^{25} $ti\epsilon^{55}$ $ts^h\gamma^{33}$ $tsai^{13}$ $lin^{13}k\partial u^{25}$ **pa^{41}** $\epsilon i^{41}si^{25}$
      need   very   many   dish   only.then   can   DOM   wedding
      $pan^{25}.t\gamma^{13}$.$liau^{25}$.
      do.ABLE.complete
      '(She'll) need very many dishes in order to be able to successfully carry out the wedding.'

---

[18] This morpheme is natively used in Xianghua as a classifier for handfuls of substances.

Xianghua speakers mix the two DOMs in their speech. The frequency is determined to a large extent by the age and level of education of the speaker and the city/rural divide, as Wu and Cao (2008) have observed in a text study. Other features that have been modified are the aspectual and modal system with the borrowing from Southwestern Mandarin of aspectual suffixes to the verb such as *liau*[41] 了 < 'finish', the borrowing of a negative marker that brings with it an innovative polar question form VERB-NEG-VERB that may eventually replace the native one of CLAUSE-NEG. These additions create an asymmetry in Xianghua vis-à-vis its native paradigms.

The important role of geographical isolation and little intermarriage outside their own traditionally isolated communities suggests an explanation for the scant evidence of Hmong or Tujia linguistic influence, not to mention the high degree of sinicization for the two latter groups, already evident in the early twentieth century.

24.4 Conclusion

This chapter has considered the main language families present in China and the issues of areal linguistics from both the macro-perspective of East and Southeast Asia, with respect to Sinitic languages, and the micro-perspective of three small *Sprachbünde* within China. First, the influence of Altaic languages on Chinese languages in the Qinghai-Gansu area of Northwest China has been briefly examined to reveal major structural and morphological changes to the grammatical system. Second, features of a Tai substratum were described for Sinitic languages located in Guangxi, in the far south of China, namely Southern Pinghua and Nanning Cantonese, in the form of both ancient and more recent borrowings. Third, in the case of Xianghua, a conservative Sinitic language of Hunan in central China, we argued that Southwestern Mandarin has not ceased to impact on its linguistic structure from the mid-twentieth century onwards.

References

Bao Houxing and Yan Sen 鲍厚星, 颜森, 1986. Hunan fangyan de fenqu 湖南方言的分区 [The distribution of dialects in Hunan]. *Fangyan* 3: 273–276.

Bauer, Robert S., 1996. Identifying the Tai Substratum in Cantonese. In *Pan-Asiatic Linguistics: Proceedings of the Fourth International Symposium on Languages and Linguistics V*, pp. 1806–1844. Bangkok: Institute of Language and Culture for Rural Development, Mahidol University.

Baxter, William and Laurent Sagart, 2014. *Old Chinese: A New Reconstruction*. Oxford: Oxford University Press.

Beffa, Marie-Lise and Marie-Dominique Even, 2011. Le mandchou. In Bonvini et al. (eds), pp. 964–976.

Bisang, Walter, 1992. *Das Verb im Chinesischen, Hmong, Vietnamesischen, Thai und Khmer*. Tübingen: Narr.

Bisang, Walter, 1996. Areal typology and grammaticalization: Processes of grammaticalization based on nouns and verbs in East and mainland South East Asian languages. *Studies in Language* 20 (3): 519–597.

Bisang, Walter, 2009. On the evolution of complexity: Sometimes less is more in East and mainland Southeast Asia. In Geoffrey Sampson, David Gil and Peter Trudgill (eds), *Language Complexity as an Evolving Variable*, pp. 34–49. Oxford: Oxford University Press.

Bonvini, Emilio, Joëlle Busuttil and Alain Peyraube (eds), 2011. *Dictionnaire des langues*. Paris: Presses Universitaires de France.

Chappell, Hilary, 2001. Language contact and areal diffusion in Sinitic languages: Problems for typology and genetic affiliation. In Alexandra Aikhenvald and R. M. W. Dixon (eds), *Areal diffusion and Genetic Inheritance: Problems in Comparative Linguistics*, pp. 328–357. Oxford: Oxford University Press.

Chappell, Hilary, 2013. Pan-Sinitic object markers: morphology and syntax. In Cao Guangshun, Hilary Chappell, Redouane Djamouri and Thekla Wiebusch (eds), *Breaking Down the Barriers: Interdisciplinary Studies in Chinese Linguistics and Beyond*, two volumes, pp. 785–816. Taipei: Academia Sinica.

Chappell, Hilary (ed.), 2015a. *Diversity in Sinitic languages*. Oxford: Oxford University Press.

Chappell, Hilary, 2015b. Linguistic areas in China for differential object marking, passive and comparative constructions. In Chappell (ed.), pp. 13–52.

Chappell, Hilary, Li Ming and Alain Peyraube, 2007. Chinese linguistics and typology: The state of the art. *Linguistic Typology* 11 (1): 187–211.

Chappell, Hilary and Alain Peyraube, 2006. The analytic causatives of Early Modern Southern Min in diachronic perspective. In Dah-an Ho, H. S. Cheung, W. Pan and F. Wu (eds), *Shan gao shui chang: Linguistic Studies in Chinese and Neighboring Languages*, pp. 973–1011. Taipei: Academia Sinica.

Chappell, Hilary and Alain Peyraube, 2015. The comparative construction in Sinitic languages: Synchronic and diachronic variation. In Chappell (ed.), pp. 134–152.

Chappell, Hilary, Alain Peyraube and Yunji Wu, 2011. A comitative source for object markers in Sinitic languages: *kai*[55] in Waxiang and *kang*[7] in Southern Min. *Journal of East Asian Linguistics* 20 (4): 291–338.

Chen Ping, 1999. *Modern Chinese: History and Sociolinguistics*. Cambridge: Cambridge University Press.

Chen, Yujie, 2015. The semantic differentiation of demonstratives in Sinitic languages. In Chappell (ed.), pp. 89–109.

Clark, Marybeth, 1974. Submissive verbs as adversatives in some Asian languages. In Nguyen Dang Liem (ed.), *South-East Asian Linguistic Studies*, pp. 85–110. Pacific Linguistics, vol. C-31. Canberra: Australian National University.

Clark, Marybeth, 1985. Asking questions in Hmong and other South-East Asian languages. *Linguistics of the Tibeto-Burman Area* 8 (2): 60–67.

Clark, Marybeth, 1989. Hmong and areal Southeast Asia. In David Bradley (ed.), *Papers in Southeast Asian Linguistics,* vol. 11: *South-East Asian Syntax*, pp. 175–230. Pacific Linguistics, vol. A-77. Canberra: Research School of Pacific Studies, Australian National University.

Diffloth, Gérard, 2011. Les langues austroasiatiques. In Bonvini et al. (eds), pp. 1099–1101.

Diller, Anthony, 2008. Introduction. In A. Diller, J. Edmondson and Y. Luo (eds), *The Tai-Kadai Languages*, pp. 3–8. London and New York: Routledge.

Djamouri, Redouane, 2015. Object positioning in Tangwang. In Cao Guangshun, Redouane Djamouri and Alain Peyraube (eds), *Languages in Contact in Northwestern China*. Monograph series of the Cahiers de linguistique Asie orientale. Paris: CRLAO.

Dong Hongxun 董鸿勋, 1907. 《古丈坪厅志》 *Guzhangping Tingzhi [Guzhang Gazetteer]*. For more information, see parts reprinted in Wu and Shen 2010.

van Driem, George, 2011. The Trans-Himalayan phylum and its implications for population prehistory. *Communication on Contemporary Anthropology* 5: 135–142.

Dryer, Matthew, 2003. Word order in Sino-Tibetan languages from a typological and geographical perspective. In Graham Thurgood and Randy LaPolla (eds), *The Sino-Tibetan Languages*, pp. 43–55. London and New York: Routledge.

Dwyer, Arianne, 1992. Altaic elements in the Linxia dialect. *Journal of Chinese Linguistics* 20 (1): 160–178.

Enfield, Nicholas J., 2005. Areal linguistics and Mainland South-East Asia. *Annual Review of Anthropology* 34: 181–206.

Hashimoto, Mantaro, 1974. Aspect and tense in Asian languages. *Computational Analyses of Asian and African Languages* 1: 15–25.

Hashimoto, Mantaro, 1976a. Language diffusion on the Asian continent: Problems of typological diversity in Sino-Tibetan. *Computational Analyses of Asian and African Languages* 3: 49–65.

Hashimoto, Mantaro, 1976b. The double object construction in Chinese. *Computational Analyses of Asian and African Languages* 6: 33–42.

Hashimoto, Mantaro, 1986. The altaicization of Northern Chinese. In John McCoy and Timothy Light (eds), *Contributions to Sino-Tibetan Studies*, pp. 76–97. Leiden: E.J. Brill.

Hashimoto, Mantaro, 1987. Hanyu beidongshi de lishi, quyu fazhan [The history and areal development of the Chinese passive]. *Zhongguo Yuwen* 1: 36–49.

Heine, Bernd, 1997. *Cognitive Foundations of Grammar*. Oxford: Oxford University Press.

Heine, Bernd and Tania Kuteva, 2002. *Word Lexicon of Grammaticalization*. Cambridge: Cambridge University Press.

Hickey, Raymond, 2010. Language contact: Reconsideration and reassessment. In Raymond Hickey (ed.), *The Handbook of Language Contact*, pp. 1–28. Chichester, UK: Wiley-Blackwell.

Huang, Yuanwei, 1997. The interaction between Zhuang and the Yue (Cantonese) dialects. In Jerold A. Edmondson and David B. Solnit (eds), *Comparative Kadai: The Tai Branch*, pp. 57–76. Dallas, TX: Summer Institute of Linguistics and the University of Texas at Arlington.

Janhunen, Juha, Marja Peltomaa, Erika Sandman and Xiawu Dongzhou, 2008. *Wutun*. Munich: LINCOM Europa.

Kwok, Bit-Chee 郭必之, 2010. Yǔyán Jiēchù zhōng de Yǔfǎ Biànhuà: Lùn Nánníng Yùeyǔ 'Shúyǔ + Bīnyǔ + Bǔyǔ' Jiégòu de Láiyuán 語言接觸中的語法變化：論南寧粵語 「述語＋賓語＋補語」 結構的來源 [Grammatical change in language contact: on the origin of the 'verb + object + complement' construction in Nanning Yue]. In Hung-nin Samuel Cheung 張洪年 and Song Hing Chang 張雙慶 (eds), *Diachronic Change and Language Contact: Dialects in South East China* 歷時演變與語言接觸 – 中國東南方言, pp. 201–216. Journal of Chinese Linguistics Monograph, vol. 24.

Lamarre, Christine, 2015. The morphologization of verb suffixes in Northern Chinese. In Cao Guangshun, Redouane Djamouri and Alain Peyraube (eds), *Languages in Contact in Northwestern China*, pp. 275–307. Monograph series of the Cahiers de linguistique Asie orientale. Paris: CRLAO.

Lewis, Paul (ed.), 2009. *Ethnologue: Languages of the World*, 16th edition. Dallas, TX: SIL International. www.ethnologue.com

Lewis, M. Paul, Gary F. Simons and Charles D. Fennig (eds), 2015. *Ethnologue: Languages of the World*, 18th edition. Dallas, TX: SIL International. www.ethnologue.com

Li, Fang-kuei, 1939. Languages and dialects. In *The Chinese Yearbook (1938–1939)*, pp. 44–46. Shanghai: Commercial Press.

Li, Fang-Kuei, 1977. *A Handbook of Comparative Tai*. Honolulu: The University of Hawai'i Press.

Li Keyou 李克郁 and Li Meiling 李美玲, 1998. Hanyu Qinghaihua mingci de tedian. 汉语青海话名词的特点 [Features of nouns in the Chinese of Qinghai]. *Qinghai Minzu Yanjiu* 青海民族研究 3: 25–34.

Matisoff, James, 1991a. Grammatization in Lahu. In Elizabeth Closs Traugott and Bernd Heine (eds), *Approaches to Grammaticalization*, vol. 2, pp. 383–453. Amsterdam: John Benjamins.

Matisoff, James, 1991b. Sino-Tibetan linguistics: Present state and future prospects. *Annual Review of Anthropology* 20: 469–504.

Milliken, Margaret, 1998. The classifier Gij in northern Zhuang. In S. Burusphat (ed.), *The International Conference on Tai Studies*, pp. 173–200.

Institute of Language and Culture for Rural Development. Bangkok: Mahidol University.

Niederer, Barbara, 2011. Les langues hmong-mjen (miao-yao). In Bonvini et al. (eds), pp. 1283–1299.

Norman, Jerry, 1982. Four notes on Chinese-Altaic linguistic contacts. *Tsinghua Journal of Chinese Studies* 14 (1/2): 243–247.

Norman, Jerry, 1988. *Chinese*. Cambridge: Cambridge University Press.

Norman, Jerry and Tsu-Lin Mei, 1976. The Austroasiatics in Ancient South China: Some lexical evidence. *Monumenta Serica* 32: 274–301.

Ouyang, Jueya, 1995. Liangguang Yue fangyan yu Zhuangyu de zhong zhong guanxi 两广粤方言粤语与状语的种种关系 [Different kinds of relationships between the Yue dialects of Guangxi and Guangdong and Zhuangyu]. *Minzu Yuwen* 民族语文 6: 49–52.

Peyraube, Alain, 2008. Languages in contact in Northwestern China: Convergence, mixed languages or linguistic area? Paper delivered at the *16th Annual Conference of the International Association of Chinese Linguistics*, Beijing, 29 May to 2 June 2008.

Peyraube, Alain, 2015. A comparative analysis of the case system in some Northwestern Sinitic languages. In Cao Guangshun, Redouane Djamouri and Alain Peyraube (eds), *Languages in Contact in Northwestern China*. Monograph series of the Cahiers de linguistique Asie orientale. Paris: CRLAO.

Sagart, Laurent, 2005. Sino-Tibetan-Austronesian: An updated and improved argument. In L. Sagart, R. Blench and A. Sanchez-Mazas (eds), *The Peopling of East Asia: Putting together Archaeology, Linguistics and Genetics*, pp. 161–176. London: RoutledgeCurzon.

Shearer, Walter and Sun Hongkai, 2002. *Speakers of the Non-Han Languages and Dialects of China*. Lewiston: Edwin Mellen Press.

de Sousa, Hilário 蘇沙 2013. Nánníng Shàngyáo Pínghuà de Yīxiē Míngcí Duǎnyǔ Xiànxiàng Duìbǐ Yánjiū 南宁上尧平话的一些名词短语现象对比研究 [Comparative studies of some noun phrase phenomena in Nánníng Shàngyáo Pínghuà]. In Dānqīng Liú 刘丹青, Léi Zhōu 周磊 and Cáidé Xuē 薛才德 (eds), *Hànyǔ Fāngyán Yǔfǎ Yánjiū de Xīnshìjiǎo – Dì Wǔ Jiè Hànyǔ Fāngyán Yǔfǎ Guójì Xuéshù Yántǎohuì Lùnwénjí* 汉语方言法研究的新视角 – 第五届汉语方言语法国际学术研讨会论文集 [New Viewpoints in the Studies of Grammar of the Chinese Dialects: Proceedings of the Fifth International Conference on Syntax of Chinese Dialects], pp. 141–160. Shanghai: Shanghai Educational Publishing House 上海教育出版社.

de Sousa, Hilario, 2015. Language contact in Nanning: From the point of view of Nanning Pinghua and Nanning Cantonese. In Chappell (ed.), pp. 157–189.

Sposato, A., 2014. Word order in Miao-Yao (Hmong-Mien). *Linguistic Typology* 18 (1): 83–140.

Stassen, Leon, 1985. *Comparison and Universal Grammar*. Oxford: Blackwell.

Stolz, Thomas, 1999. Comitatives vs. instrumentals vs. agents. In Walter Bisang (ed.), *Aspects of Typology and Universals*, pp. 153–174. Studia Typologica, vol. 1. Berlin: Akademie Verlag.

Wu Fuxiang 吴福祥, 2013. Nanfang minzu yuyan bijiaoju yuxu de yanbian he bianyi 南方民族语言比较语序的演变和变异 [Development and variation in the word order of comparatives in the minority languages of Southern China]. In Cao Guangshun, Hilary Chappell, Redouane Djamouri and Thekla Wiebusch (eds), *Breaking Down the Barriers: Interdisciplinary Studies in Chinese Linguistics and Beyond*, two volumes, pp. 831–864. Taipei: Academia Sinica.

Wu Yunji, 2005. *A Synchronic and Diachronic Study of the Grammar of the Chinese Xiang Dialects*. Berlin: Mouton de Gruyter.

Wu Yunji and Cao Xilei, 2008. Xiangxi Waxianghua he Xinan guanhua biao chuzhishi de 'gen' suo yinfa de yiwen 湘西瓦乡话和西南官话表处置的'跟'所引发的疑问 [The unusual case of [gēn] 跟 used as a disposal marker in Waxiang and the Southwestern Mandarin of Western Hunan, China]. *Zhongguo Yuwen Yanjiu* 《中國語文研究》 [Chinese Language Studies]. 26 (2): 1–14.

Wu, Yunji and Ruiqing Shen, 2010. 湘西古丈瓦乡话调查报告 *Xiangxi Guzhang Waxianghua Diaocha Baogao [Research Report on the Waxiang Language of Guzhang, Western Hunan]*. Shanghai: Jiaoyu Chubanshe.

Wurm, Stephen and Li Rong (eds), 1987. *Language Atlas of China* 中国语言地图集. Zhongguo Yuyan Dituji. Hong Kong: Longman.

Xiong Zhenghui 熊证辉 and Zhang Zhenxing 张振兴, 2008. 汉语方言的分区 Hanyu fangyan de fenqu [The distribution of Chinese dialects]. 方言 *Fangyan* 2: 97–108.

Xu, Liejiong and Alain Peyraube, 1997. On the double-object construction and the oblique construction in Cantonese. *Studies in Language* 21 (1): 105–127.

Yue, Anne O., 2003. Chinese dialects: Grammar. In Graham Thurgood and Randy LaPolla (eds), *The Sino-Tibetan Languages*, pp. 84–125. London and New York: Routledge.

Yue-Hashimoto, Anne, 1991. The Yue dialects. In William S-Y. Wang (ed.), *Languages and Dialects of China*, pp. 294–324. Journal of Chinese Linguistics, Monograph Series, vol. 3. Berkeley: Project on Linguistic Analysis.

Zhang Zhenxing 张振兴 (ed.), 2012. *Zhongguo Yuyan Dituji Di'er ban* 中国语言地图集: 第二版 *[Language Atlas of China]*, second edition. Beijing: Commercial Press.

Zhu, Yongzhong, Ujiyediin Chuluu, Keith Slater and Kevin Stuart, 1997. Gangou Chinese dialect: A comparative study of a strongly altaicized Chinese dialect and its Mongolic neighbor. *Anthropos* 92: 433–450.

25

Language in the Mainland Southeast Asia Area

N. J. Enfield

25.1   Mainland Southeast Asia and its People

Mainland Southeast Asia (hereafter MSEA) can be broadly defined as the area occupied by present day Cambodia, Laos, Peninsular Malaysia, Thailand, Myanmar and Vietnam, along with areas of China south of the Yangzi River. Also sometimes included are the seven states of Northeast India, and – although here the term 'mainland' no longer applies – the islands from Indonesia and Malaysia running southeast to Australia and West Papua (see Map 25.1).

There are no exact borders around the MSEA area. Different scholars draw lines in different places. But there is nevertheless a core (Comrie 2007: 45). MSEA is always taken to include Indochina – Vietnam, Laos and Cambodia – together with Thailand, and usually Peninsular Malaysia and part or all of Myanmar (see Map 25.2). But there is often a broader scope of Greater MSEA, moving beyond the core area of Indochina and Thailand, in all directions; for recent work, see Vittrant (2015) and Jenny and Sidwell (2015) on Myanmar (cf. Bradley 1995; Watkins 2005), Post (2015) on Northeast India (cf. Hyslop, Morey and Post 2011, 2012, 2013; Morey and Post 2008, 2010), Gil (2015) on Insular Southeast Asia (cf. Adelaar and Himmelmann 2005; Blust 2013a, 2013b), and de Sousa (2015) on southern China (cf. Ansaldo and Matthews 2001; Bauer 1996; Chappell 2001).

MSEA is a tropical and sub-tropical area with rugged and well-forested hills and river systems running from higher altitudes in the northwest to the plains and deltas of the south. Among the biggest rivers are the Mekong, the Brahmaputra, the Red River in North Vietnam, the Salween and Irrawaddy rivers in Myanmar, the Pearl and Yangzi rivers in China, and the Chaophraya in central Thailand. The lower reaches of these river systems are well-fertilized plains, which have attracted people partly because of the mobility the environment affords, but also because of the suitability for paddy rice farming. Paddy farming, in which rice plants are

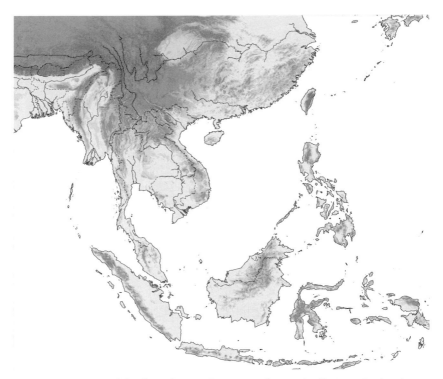

Map 25.1 Greater Mainland Southeast Asia: present-day Cambodia, Laos, Peninsular Malaysia, Thailand, Myanmar and Vietnam, along with China south of the Yangzi River, Northeast India and Insular Southeast Asia

kept continually flooded as they grow, requires management of water via systems of dikes and channels (Hartmann 1998). This method is significantly more productive than upland dry-field methods and can support larger populations (Bellwood 1992: 90). It also reduces biodiversity.

MSEA has seen a long and complex history of human movement, contact and diversification. Evidence from genetics and archaeology suggests that there has been human activity in the area since some 40,000 years ago, when conditions were very different from today. At around 20,000 years ago, global sea levels were 120 m lower than now (Chappell and Shackleton 1986; Tooley and Shennan 1987), implying different possibilities for human movement and livelihoods. Then, one could walk on dry land in a straight line from the site of present-day Ho Chi Minh City to Kuala Lumpur, and then in another straight line to Bali and again up to Brunei (Oppenheimer 2011; Voris 2000; White 2011). While a fair amount is known from bioarchaeological evidence about more recent human activity in the pre-agricultural period (Oxenham and Tayles 2006), the time horizon of comparative linguistics is limited to the last few thousand years (for recent reviews, see Enfield 2011b). Just behind that horizon are the beginnings of agriculture in MSEA some 4,000 or so years ago.

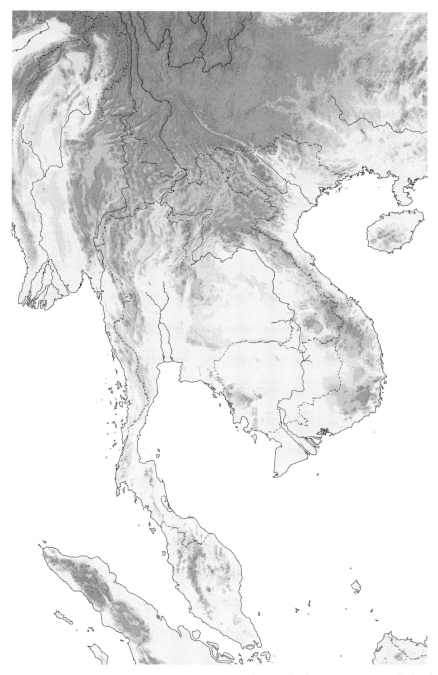

Map 25.2 Core Mainland Southeast Asia: present-day Cambodia, Laos, Vietnam, Thailand and neighbouring parts of China, Malaysia and Myanmar

A widely accepted view is that the people of MSEA once spoke Austroasiatic languages in a 'continuous distribution', and that this distribution was 'broken up by the historical expansions of the Chinese, Tai, Vietnamese, Burman and Austronesian (Malay and Cham) peoples' (Bellwood 1992: 109; cf. Sidwell and Blench 2011: 338 and *passim*; Post 2011). By what mechanism did this take place? Some have argued that modern ethnolinguistic diversification in MSEA was associated with demic diffusion (Bellwood 1992; Blust 1994; Edmondson and Gregerson 2007; Higham 2002). This implies the incoming migration of groups of people who rely on agriculture and who can thereby support large populations. The incomers replace less populous and less powerful existing forager populations (Ammerman and Cavalli-Sforza 1971; Cavalli-Sforza, Menozzi and Piazza 1993; Nichols 1992).[1] An alternative to demic diffusion is cultural diffusion, whereby resident populations remain in place, but adopt new practices and ways of speaking. According to O'Connor (1995: 987), 'there is no direct evidence that an actual influx of immigrants ever displaced earlier peoples' in MSEA. He argues instead that an 'agricultural paradigm' is what diffused, bringing with it a 'society-shaping complex' (see Jonsson 2011, 2014 for discussion). For other critiques of the application of a demic diffusion model in MSEA see White (2011) on the view that hunter–gatherer communities have played a central role in shaping modern MSEA ethnographic diversity, and Fix (2011) on the genetics of ethnolinguistic diversification, in which he presents an alternative to the standard account of demic diffusion in the Malay Peninsula, with a model he calls *trickle-effect colonization*.

Regardless of whether one thinks the historical process of peopling and ethnolinguistic diversification in MSEA was driven primarily by the spread of people or by the spread of ideas – here, more work is needed – the modern distribution of ethnolinguistic groups is clear. In lowland areas, populations are denser, more culturally and linguistically homogeneous, and more closely affiliated with state political power. In upland areas, populations are sparser, more culturally and linguistically diverse, and have limited if any access to infrastructure, education or power. The dominant lowland populations are clearly distinct from each other in terms of political identity ('the Thai' versus 'the Lao' versus 'the Khmer', etc.), but the upland minority populations that straddle these nations have something in common: they are politically and geographically marginalized.

The upland areas in which many MSEA minorities live are conjoined in a single, elongated area, crossing political borders and encompassing

---

[1] Demic diffusion is the spread of genes. It is usually associated with the outcomes of migration. In world history, this has often involved the movement of groups who have adopted agriculture, and who are therefore more populous and viable than those (e.g. hunter–gatherers) who are resident in the area being entered. Demic diffusion may be associated with population displacement or replacement, but this need not necessarily be the case. There may be genetic admixture between an incoming population and a resident population, such that some fraction of the genes of the resident population survives. Thanks to Mark Stoneking and Dan Dediu for clarification of these points.

'virtually all the lands at altitudes above roughly three hundred meters all the way from the Central Highlands of Vietnam to northeastern India' (Scott 2009: ix). This area has been referred to as *Zomia*, a term coined by van Schendel (2002) in making the point that arbitrary research areas can be constructed and reified by 'academic politics', as he puts it (cf. Michaud 2010). Van Schendel's proposal of a Zomia area is a conceptual exercise, useful because it counteracts the politically sanctioned alternatives. The term has gained some recognition (though ironically not without danger of creating the reification it was warning against: Jonsson 2011, 2014), particularly due to Scott (2009). According to Scott, it is not that the inhabitants of Zomia simply share the fate of having been marginalized by states. Instead, he argues, they share a cultural distaste for being governed: they have chosen to remain isolated from central government control.

We do not have space in this chapter for more on the detailed history of human activity – peopling and migration, social contact and cultural shift, state formation and avoidance, war and peace – in MSEA. For further information, see Tarling (1992), Scott (2009) and Enfield (2011b).

25.2   Mainland Southeast Asian Languages

The degree of linguistic diversity in MSEA (i.e. the number of languages per square km) is high (Enfield 2011c), and it is highest in upland areas. Lower language density in lowland areas is likely related in part to geographical factors and their implications for the nature of social networks (see Nettle 1999). In historical demographic processes of the kinds noted above, formerly diverse lowland communities in MSEA have become homogenized by a combination of two processes. One process was ethnolinguistic shift. Some groups stayed where they were but stopped passing on their languages and identities to their children, instead adopting the languages and identities of new dominant groups. This process can be observed all over MSEA today. Another process was out-migration, typically to more isolated hill areas (Scott 2009). Geographical isolation is a force that still promotes language diversity in the region, where former diversity of lowland areas is on its last legs. Many of the lowland languages are heavily endangered or extinct (Bradley 2007; Enfield 2006; Suwilai Premsrirat 2007). This is quickened by effects of the concentration of political power of modern nation states in the lowlands. In recent decades, processes of language standardization in MSEA nations (Simpson 2007) have helped to heavily reduce language diversity.

The languages of MSEA are from five major language families: Sino-Tibetan, Tai-Kadai, Hmong-Mien, Austroasiatic and Austronesian.[2] There

---

[2]   The Andamanese languages are located just outside MSEA as defined here, though we note with interest new work on these lesser-known languages: see Abbi's recent reference grammar (2013) and dictionary (2012) of Great Andamanese.

Table 25.1 *A breakdown of numbers of languages in MSEA, separated into language families*

	Core MSEA	Greater MSEA
Austroasiatic	122 (44%)	138 (24%)
Sino-Tibetan	74 (26%)	288 (49%)
Tai-Kadai	51 (18%)	93 (16%)
Austronesian	25 (9%)	26 (4%)
Hmong-Mien	8 (3%)	38 (7%)
Total	280	583

are nearly 600 distinct languages spoken in Greater MSEA.[3] If we exclude the China and India data, thus representing the Core MSEA area, the number of languages is about half this amount; see Table 25.1.

The very high linguistic diversity (i.e. the number of languages) in north-eastern India and southern/southwestern China adds dramatically to the number of languages included in the area. It also reverses the relative proportion of Sino-Tibetan and Austroasiatic languages.

The MSEA area is unusual in global terms in that there is good agreement among scholars as to the basic language family affiliation of known languages. There are unresolved issues about lower-level subgroupings and there are unresolved hypotheses about possible macro-groupings. But for every known language, scholars agree as to which of the five main language families it fits into. This is unusual, firstly because it means that each language's basic affiliation is apparently uncontroversial and secondly because it suggests that there are no language isolates (Blench 2011: 125–126).[4] For a survey of the historical-linguistic background, see Sidwell (2013).

Following is a list of some of the typological features that characterize MSEA languages (drawing mostly from Enfield 2005: 186–190, and 2011c: 69–70; see further references there).

Sound system features
– Large vowel systems. It is sometimes difficult to determine how many vowels a system has. There are alternative analyses of features such as diphthongs and phonation splits.

---

[3] Data are from glottolog.org, accessed in May 2014. Many thanks to Harald Hammarström for his input and assistance. Core MSEA was defined for this count as Cambodia, Laos, Myanmar, Thailand and Vietnam; Greater MSEA included this, along with Peninsular Malaysia, areas of India east of 90 degrees (i.e. the states of Arunachal Pradesh, Nagaland, Manipur, Mizoram, Assam, Meghalaya and Tripura) and China south of the Yangzi river (specifically, the provinces of Zhejiang, Jiangxi, Hunan, Guizhou, Yunnan, Guangxi, Guangdong, Fujian and Hainan).

[4] Not considered in this chapter are sign languages. The sign language used in Ban Khor, Thailand (Nonaka 2004) appears to be an isolate, and there are surely more of its kind. Among spoken languages in MSEA there is Kenaboi, now extinct, and known only from two early twentieth century word lists. Hajek (1998) refers to Kenaboi as 'unclassified' but does not call it an isolate. Benjamin (2006) summarizes and analyses the available data as far as is possible. His view is that Kenaboi is 'a specially-invented form of speech', a 'taboo-jargon' associated with forest collecting trade. Kenaboi had large proportions of both Austroasiatic and Austronesian vocabulary, along with some unexplained forms. The data are too tenuous to establish whether it was an isolate or not.

- Common underlying structure of vowel phoneme system, often 9-place, symmetrical, hi-mid-low by front-central-back.
- Long versus short vowel distinctions.
- Many more consonants are possible in initial position than in final position. Syllables have an initial-and-rhyme structure.
- Preference for one (major) syllable per word, with many languages featuring minor syllables or pre-syllables in an iambic pattern; see Pittayaporn (2015), Butler (2015), Post (2015) and Brunelle and Kirby (2015).
- Lexical contrast is marked by laryngeal features including pitch and phonation type, often in combination. Tone systems are complex: number of tones ranges from 4 to 15, with counts for a language differing depending on the analysis chosen. Phonation type systems usually distinguish two registers, e.g. 'clear' versus 'breathy'. Lexically contrastive pitch and phonation type are strongly correlated in functional and historical terms.
- Gap in voiced stop series at velar place of articulation (no voiced 'g').

Morphosyntax–semantics system features
- No inflectional morphology: no case, gender, number or definiteness marked on noun phrases, no agreement or tense-marking on verbs. Note that *derivational* morphology is widespread and sometimes highly productive in Austroasiatic languages of MSEA (see Alves 2015).
- Open class items – mostly nouns and verbs – serve functions that are expressed by dedicated functional morphemes (including bound morphology) in other languages, e.g., nominals as prepositions, verbs as aspect markers, comparative markers, adversative passive markers and valence-changing devices (Ansaldo 1999; Clark and Prasithrathsint 1985; Kölver 1991).
- Widespread use of verb serialization (meaning a range of different kinds of predicative structures that use combinations of verbs), with a rich array of types and functions in each language (Bisang 1991).
- Order of major constituents of the clause tends to be relatively flexible within languages, sensitive to pragmatic factors (though verb-object constituent order is dominant). Noun phrases tend to be left-headed and may have discontinuous constituents, especially when classifiers are involved.
- Zero anaphora: noun phrases may be ellipsed when their referents are contextually retrievable. This combined with flexibility in constituent order results in quite variable surface options; for a case study see Enfield (2007: 271–284).
- Extensive use of topic-comment structure in clauses.
- Large set of labile or ambitransitive verbs, especially of the causative/inchoative or unaccusative type (e.g. Lao *hak2* can mean transitive 'snap' or intransitive 'is/has been snapped').

- Rich inventories of sentence-final particles that make subtle distinctions in sentence type, stance, evidentiality and combinations thereof.
- Rich inventories of ideophones (or 'expressives') and other expressive forms, including rhyming four-syllable expressions and productive elaborative rhyming devices.
- Numeral classifiers and related systems of nominal classification (see Blench 2015).
- Complex pronominal systems, with multi-level social-deictic meanings.

Some of the most noteworthy commonalities among MSEA languages concern their *lack* of marking of certain semantico-grammatical categories. Most notably, as remarked upon in the list above, the languages almost entirely lack inflectional morphology in the usual sense of that term (i.e. including agreement, case, gender/number/definiteness on noun phrases, tense-marking on verbs). For an overview of selected national languages, see Comrie (1990), while Goddard (2005) presents a more topic-oriented approach; see also Vittrant and Watkins (in press).

25.3   Linguistics of MSEA: Resources and Developments

25.3.1   Conferences and Publications

The community of scholars working on MSEA linguistics is steadily growing. The South East Asia Linguistic Society (SEALS) – founded by Martha Ratliff and Eric Schiller at Wayne State University, Detroit, in 1990 – held its 25th annual meeting in 2015. Prior to 2009, proceedings of SEALS meetings were published in edited volumes. Since then they have appeared in the open-access *Journal of the Southeast Asian Linguistics Society* (for which, see www.jseals.org/). The SEAlang Projects website (www.sealang.net) is an invaluable resource that makes accessible a range of primary and secondary sources on MSEA languages. Other regular publishing venues for research on MSEA languages include the journals *Mon-Khmer Studies* (an open-access journal, see www.mksjournal .org/) and *Linguistics of the Tibeto-Burman Area* (see sealang.net/sala/ltba/ htm/index.htm). Some recent interdisciplinary explorations of ethnolinguistic diversification have focused on languages of MSEA and neighbouring places (e.g. Enfield 2011b; Sagart, Blench and Sanchez-Maras 2005). The last 10 years have seen the publication of multiple landmark overviews of MSEA language families, including Tai-Kadai (Diller, Edmondson and Luo 2008), Sino-Tibetan (Thurgood and LaPolla 2003; cf. Matisoff 2003a), Austroasiatic (Jenny and Sidwell 2015; cf. Shorto 2006), and the Austronesian languages of MSEA (Blust 2013b: 70–75; Grant and Sidwell 2005; Larish 2005; Thurgood 1999).

25.3.2 New Descriptive Work

A key measure of progress in an area is the production of reference materials based on new empirical research.[5] Full-sized descriptions of MSEA languages published since the turn of the century include grammars of Semelai (Kruspe 2004), Jahai (Burenhult 2005), Garo (Burling 2004), Deuri (Jacquesson 2004), Mongsen Ao (Coupe 2007), Lao (Enfield 2007), Anong (Sun and Liu 2009), Hainan Cham (Thurgood, Thurgood and Li 2014), Turung (Morey 2010), the Tai languages of Assam (Morey 2005), Lisu (Yu 2007), Thai (Higbie and Thinsan 2003; Iwasaki and Ingkaphirom Horie 2005) and Cambodian (Haiman 2011). Numerous grammars have been completed as PhD dissertations; just in the area of northeast India, for example, see grammars of Galo (Post 2007), Atong (van Breugel 2014) and Karbi (Konnerth 2014). Sketches or partial descriptions have appeared on languages including Pacoh (Alves 2006), Kri (Enfield and Diffloth 2009) and Arem (Ferlus 2014), and detailed descriptions have appeared of specific domains of grammar such as phonetics/phonology; see for example Watkins (2002) on Wa and Coupe (2003) on Ao. Major dictionaries of minority languages are less abundant; two notable examples are Watkins (2013) on Wa and Svantesson et al. (2013) on Kammu Yùan. An important preoccupation of descriptive linguistics globally is the documentation of endangered languages; for excellent examples of new empirical work with this orientation in the MSEA context, see Morey (2005, 2010; see also Suwilai Premsrirat 1998, 2008).

A significant amount of new data and analysis from MSEA languages has become available on most if not all domains of interest to linguists, and on most if not all language families and subareas of MSEA. As just one example, here we mention the Aslian languages of Peninsular Malaysia. In the last decade or so, we have seen the publication of typological overviews of the Aslian languages as a group (Matisoff 2003b), new reference grammars (Burenhult 2005; Kruspe 2004), other descriptive materials (Burenhult and Wegener 2009; Wnuk 2016), new interdisciplinary research on the history and diversification of ethnolinguistic subgroups (Bulbeck 2011; Burenhult, Kruspe and Dunn 2011; Dunn et al. 2011; Dunn, Kruspe and Burenhult 2013; Fix 2011; Oppenheimer 2011), and field research on the psychological implications of semantic systems that are indigenous to Aslian languages and world views (Burenhult and Majid 2011; Majid and Burenhult 2014; Wnuk and Majid 2014). Not only is this breadth and depth of new work improving our basic understanding of MSEA languages and their sociohistorical contexts, it is also helping to

---

[5] We mention here only a selection of those recent materials that have been published in English, though we note that a substantial descriptive literature on MSEA languages is being published in other languages, including Chinese, French, Indonesian, Thai and Vietnamese. For some examples, see Bo (2002), Bon (2014), Buakaw (2012), Chen (2005), Gai (2002), Giaphong (2004), Kosaka (2000), D. Li (2003, 2004), Y. Li (2003), Lidz (2010), Zongwu Mao and Yunbing Li (2002, 2007), Mayuree (2006), Ploykaew (2001), Samarina (2011), Seng Mai (2012), Shee (2008), Shintani (2008), Srisakorn (2008), Wayesha (2010).

balance our perspective on the MSEA area, with effects on our image of what a Southeast Asian language is typically like (see below). The availability of new descriptive materials means that we can progress in the field by testing existing proposals and by continuously expanding the scope of our work (see Pittayaporn 2009 for a good illustration of this point).

25.3.3   New Methods

As new methods in linguistic research are being developed and applied in linguistics globally, so they are being developed and applied in Mainland Southeast Asia. In phonetics and phonology, for example, new instrumental and computational technologies are rapidly transforming the realms of possibility in data collection and analysis, both by making new kinds of measurement possible and by making the equipment smaller and more portable for fieldwork; see Edmondson and Esling (2006: 172–175) for the use of laryngoscopy to study the phonetics of breathy vocal register in Jianchuan Bai (spoken in Yunnan), and Brunelle (2009) for the use of electroglottography to study register in Cham dialects in Vietnam (see also Brunelle, Nguyễn and Nguyễn 2010 on Northern Vietnamese). Newly developed statistical techniques are being applied with interesting results: in historical linguistics, probability-based bioinformatic techniques are being used for exploring cladistic representations of language relatedness (see for example Burenhult, Kruspe and Dunn 2011), and in areal typology, statistical modelling is being used to test dependencies among phonological features, language history and language contact (Brunelle and Kirby, Chapter 26, this volume). In lexical and grammatical work, new field methods are being applied in the exploration of semantic fields, in a range of functional and conceptual domains (see e.g. Burenhult 2006; Enfield 2015; Wnuk and Majid 2014). There is an increasing interest in combining methods in order to further our knowledge of the area's languages, for example in the interdisciplinary collaborations of historical work (van Driem 2007; Enfield 2011b; Sagart et al. 2005). And computational power is being exploited in building larger and better databases of, or including, MSEA languages (Donohue et al. 2013; Dryer and Haspelmath 2013).

25.3.4   Historical–comparative Linguistics

Research in historical–comparative linguistics continues apace in MSEA. At the level of subgrouping, advances are being made in all the major language families. Old hypotheses are being tested with new data and techniques, and new hypotheses are being put forward. The appearance of new data, in particular, has made an important difference, enabling, for example, Pittayaporn (2009) to propose a new reconstruction of

Proto-Southwestern Tai phonology, Sidwell (2009) to offer an improved account of vowels in Proto-Mon-Khmer, and Matisoff (2015; cf. Matisoff 2003a) to re-examine the place of the Jingpho language within Tibeto-Burman. In research on historical Hmong-Mien, Ratliff (2010) has recently provided an assessment of previous work and offers substantial new reconstructions, with consideration of their implications. Historical Austroasiatic has seen substantial developments, including a suspension of the assumption of a highest-level split between Munda and Mon-Khmer. It is no longer widely assumed that 'Mon-Khmer languages' represent descendants of a single ancestor language below Proto-Austroasiatic, although the term is still useful with the meaning 'non-Munda Austroasiatic languages'; for a range of perspectives on this, see discussion in Sidwell and Blench (2011), Diffloth (2011), Sagart (2011) and van Driem (2011). Similarly, in Sino-Tibetan linguistics, assumptions are being questioned. For example, recent reconsiderations of the position of Chinese in the family have assigned it to a lower-level subgroup rather than the standard placement as a high major branch; more subgroups of Sino-Tibetan are identified, and the time depth of reconstructed Proto-Sinitic is pushed back to well before Old Chinese (Blench and Post 2013; van Driem 2013).

25.3.5   Language in Social Life

Numerous lines of work in linguistics deal with the role of language in social life. An important theme in recent work in MSEA is the sociolinguistics of language endangerment, and associated issues including language protection and revitalization; for an example, see Phattharathanit (2012) on identity maintenance in Lanna (cf. Bradley 2007; Suwilai Premsrirat 2007). Research on linguistic politeness continues, mostly in relation to national languages, and with reference to the languages' elaborated systems of social deixis, for example in their systems of personal pronouns, and the pragmatic alternatives that effectively create open class systems for person reference (Cooke 1968; Enfield 2015: Ch. 5; Haas 1969; Luong 1990). The more complex documented systems of person reference are those belonging to the major literate languages of the area, including Thai, Cambodian, Vietnamese and Burmese (Cooke 1968). There has been recent work in this domain on languages including Lao (Enfield 2007: Ch. 5; 2015: Ch. 5). On Vietnamese, see Sophana (2008) on politeness strategies, and Sidnell and Shohet (2013) on avoidance strategies (see also Luong 1988). Linking social life to central concerns of historical linguistics and typology, there has been recent work on sociolinguistic conditions for borrowing (Alves 2009); for similar work see Thurgood (2010) comparing two varieties of Cham with the Tibeto-Burman language Anong. A new line of work in MSEA is conversation analysis: Enfield (2013) presents several case studies of Lao language in conversation; Hạ (2010, 2013) presents studies of

Vietnamese conversation with a focus on the role of prosody, for example in repair and backchannelling (see also Umaporn 2007 on backchannelling in Mon).

25.3.6   Changing Perceptions

Like in any area, linguistics in MSEA is subject to preconceptions. As soon as an idea becomes something of an orthodoxy it is right to revisit and question it. A trend in recent scholarship of MSEA languages has been to raise and sometimes challenge certain assumptions about the linguistics of this area.

25.3.6.1   The Idea of a Typical MSEA Language

Comrie (2007: 45) finds that, on measures taken using data from *The World Atlas of Language Structures* (Haspelmath et al. 2005), 'Thai turns out to be the most typical of the three major national languages of Mainland Southeast Asia considered here.'[6] This conclusion is shared by Dahl (2008). This of course does not mean that Thai is the most typical of all MSEA languages, although this is often assumed to be the case. The national languages of the area are the better-described and better-known languages, and they happen to share many typological features that characterize Thai, such as a tendency for monosyllabicity, a lack of productive affixation, and an elaborate numeral classifier system. But there are many MSEA languages whose properties differ from these and many other properties found in Thai and other national languages like Vietnamese. In fact, many languages of the area lack these features. Within MSEA linguistics one's view of what is typical may depend on one's academic background, and, especially, on which language one worked on first, or has worked on most, in one's research career. If, for example, one's earliest and most in-depth work on MSEA languages was on Lao (as is the case with the present author), then languages like Lao and Thai would seem typical. They are typologically very similar to other major languages like Vietnamese. Another researcher's background would suggest otherwise. The viewpoint professed by our colleague Gérard Diffloth is that a typical MSEA language lacks lexical tone, has complex phonotactics including syllable-initial consonant clusters, and has productive derivational morphology, quite a contrast from the oft-cited set of features of MSEA languages; see Henderson (1965), Capell (1979), Suwilai Premsrirat (1987) and Kruspe (2004); cf. Alves (2001, 2015). The problem with treating the area's major national languages as reference points is not only that they are a tiny sample but that they are known to be not like the rest, due to factors including (1) they are spoken by very large, often urbanized populations,

---

[6] The idea that a language may be 'typical' of an area seems to be an intuitive one, but the relevant sense in which a language can be said to be typical is seldom defined.

(2) they are spoken as second languages by large sections of the population, (3) they are official languages, used in major education systems, media and broadcasting, and legal documents.

25.3.6.2   Nominal Classification

MSEA is often cited in typologies of nominal classification as an area that has numeral classifiers (Aikhenvald 2000; Grinevald 2000). Recent research shows that systems of nominal classification in MSEA can be more complex than this. They not only contain the classic numeral classifier type, consisting of a large set of classificatory nominals that are used whenever something is being numerated, but also systems that resemble the *noun class* systems found widely in Africa and the Amazon, and ancillary systems that resemble numeral classifiers but which are involved in the use of more simple modifiers such as demonstratives and specifiers. Enfield (2007: 119–156) shows that in Lao there are in fact four distinct grammatical systems of nominal classification, of which numeral classifiers are one (see Blench 2015).

25.3.6.3   Sesquisyllables

Researchers of the sound structure of words in MSEA languages often refer to the idea of 'sesquisyllables' and even the property of 'sesquisyllabicity'. This term was introduced by Matisoff (1973) to refer to the 'one-and-a-half syllable' form of words found in many MSEA languages (Butler 2015; Henderson 1952; Pittayaporn 2015; Shorto 1960). The term has not always been applied in an exact or consistent way. In a narrow sense, it can refer specifically to a syllable with schwa epenthesis between elements of an initial consonant cluster; that is, a syllable whose onset is phonologically /CC/ but phonetically [CᵊC]. In a broad sense, it can refer to any word that has an iambic structure, with the main stressed syllable coming at the end. Consider the following three words in Kri (Enfield and Difflotth 2009): /cakaaŋ/ [caka:ŋ] 'to measure something by handspans', /ckaaŋ/ [cᵊka:ŋ] 'a hand span', and /caaŋ/ [ca:ŋ] 'buttress of a tree' (or /kaaŋʔ/ [ka:ŋʔ] 'chin/jaw'). In the broad sense, both /cakaaŋ/ [caka:ŋ] and /ckaaŋ/ [cᵊka:ŋ] are sesquisyllabic, while in the narrow sense, only /ckaaŋ/ [cᵊka:ŋ] is. Recent work – by Butler (2015) and Pittayaporn (2015) – has made a significant advance not only by insisting that we be consistent and precise in the use of such terms, but by turning to empirical and theoretical accounts in order to offer motivated solutions, making the intuitive idea of sesquisyllabicity accountable to current theory and data in theoretical phonology and articulatory phonetics. Butler (2015) calls for more thoughtful consideration of the terms, and seeks to make progress by holding certain phonological ideas of syllable structure accountable to phonetic behaviour that can be experimentally tested. Pittayaporn (2015) takes a broader comparative approach to the problem, offering a typology of sesquisyl-labic languages, defining the distinct meanings that this term can have.

25.3.6.4   Tone Phonetics and Phonology

An oft-cited feature of MSEA languages is that many of them are tone languages. When asked what this means, most linguists would agree with Yip (2002: 1): 'A language is a "tone language" if the pitch of the word can change the meaning of the word.' But as linguists of MSEA languages since Henderson (1952, 1965, 1967) have insisted, it is wrong to think that *pitch* is the sole or defining feature of a tone system in MSEA (see Brunelle and Kirby 2015 and Sidwell 2015; see also Abramson and L-Thongkum 2009): 'It is important to recognize that pitch is frequently only one of the phonetic components of "tone" as a phonological category ... A phonological tone is in our area very frequently a complex of other features besides pitch – such as intensity, duration, voice quality, final glottal constriction and so on' (Henderson 1967: 171). From this perspective, while tone and phonation type are sometimes considered to be distinct phonological organizations, they should instead be treated as instances of a single sound system property insofar as they each involve the use of laryngeal features for lexical contrast. Pitch contours, distinc-tions in phonation and other glottalic effects are all produced in the larynx, by the vocal folds, and are all articulatorily independent of seg-mental speech sounds produced with the lips, teeth and tongue (i.e. con-sonants). Tone and phonation are intimately bound and not essentially distinct. For this reason we recognize that the sound system of an MSEA 'tone' language, such as Vietnamese, is not of a different species from that of a classical MSEA 'register' or 'phonation type' language such as Kri (Enfield and Diffloth 2009). Most systems that are identified as one or the other (in phonological terms) actually display properties of both (in pho-netic terms).

25.3.6.5   MSEA as a Linguistic Area

In research on areal linguistics, a great deal of new empirical and concep-tual work from around the world has improved our understanding of historical processes of ethnolinguistic diversification, contact and conver-gence, while at the same time some of the basic tenets of areal linguistics have come under question (Muysken 2008; Stolz 2002). MSEA has been widely regarded as a classic linguistic area with close parallelism in struc-ture between neighbouring languages that have no demonstrable com-mon ancestor: see Henderson (1965), Capell (1979), Clark (1989), Matisoff (1991), Bisang (1991), Enfield (2005), Comrie (2007), Dahl (2008) and Vittrant and Watkins (in press). The cause of this parallelism is widely assumed to be language contact. While much work examines typological parallels across language families and interprets these as evidence of effects from language contact, recent work by Sidwell (2015), Ratliff

(2015) and Brunelle and Kirby (2015) calls for caution in jumping to that conclusion. If neighbouring but unrelated languages share typological features this can also be a result of parallel language-internal development (Enfield 2005; Thurgood 1998). That possibility is equally deserving of consideration, and so the idea that convergence is due to contact should not be assumed without question.

25.4 Summary

Languages in the Mainland Southeast Asia area are well known for their seemingly high degree of convergence in many – if not all – aspects of their grammar. Recent empirical and theoretical advances in the study of Mainland Southeast Asian languages are driving important developments in our understanding of the area. While much new work is confirming and enriching our understanding of known patterns of structure in the area, other contributions are challenging orthodoxy, including the idea of what a 'typical' Mainland Southeast Asian language is like, and even the very notion that the high degree of convergence in the area is a direct result of social contact among historical speech communities.

Acknowledgements

This chapter draws directly on sections of a chapter co-authored with Bernard Comrie that appeared as the introduction to our 2015 edited book *Languages of Mainland Southeast Asia: The State of the Art* (2015): I thank Bernard for allowing me to revise and submit this chapter, based on our earlier co-authored work. For financial support, I am grateful to the Max Planck Institute for Evolutionary Anthropology (Department of Linguistics), the Max Planck Institute for Psycholinguistics (Language and Cognition Department), and the European Research Council (through grant 240853 'Human Sociality and Systems of Language Use'). I would like to thank Maarten van den Heuvel for technical assistance in preparing the manuscript for publication, and Angela Terrill at Punctilious Editing (www.punctilious.net/) for copy-editing. For comments and suggestions on a draft, I thank Roger Blench, Jeremy Collins, Bernard Comrie, Mark Donohue, David Gil, Pittayawat Pittayaporn, Mark Post, Martha Ratliff and Paul Sidwell.

References

Abbi, Anvita, 2012. *Dictionary of the Great Andamanese Language: English–Great Andamanese–Hindi*. Delhi: Ratna Sagar.

Abbi, Anvita, 2013. *A Grammar of the Great Andamanese Language: An Ethnolinguistic Study*. Leiden: Brill Academic.

Abramson, Arthur S. and Theraphan L-Thongkum, 2009. A fuzzy boundary between tone languages and voice-register languages. In Gunnar Fant, Hiroya Fujisaki and Jiaxuen Shen (eds), *Frontiers in Phonetics and Speech Science*, pp. 149–155. Beijing: The Commercial Press.

Adelaar, Alexander and Nikolaus P. Himmelmann, 2005. *The Austronesian Languages of Asia and Madagascar*. London: Routledge Curzon.

Aikhenvald, Alexandra Y., 2000. *Classifiers: A Typology of Noun Categorization Devices*. Oxford: Oxford University Press.

Alves, Mark J., 2001. What's so Chinese about Vietnamese? In Graham W. Thurgood (ed.), *Papers from the Ninth Annual Meeting of the Southeast Asian Linguistics Society*, pp. 221–242. Phoenix: Arizona State University.

Alves, Mark J., 2006. *A Grammar of Pacoh: A Mon-Khmer Language of the Central Highlands of Vietnam (Shorter Grammars)*. Pacific Linguistics, vol. 580. Canberra: Australian National University.

Alves, Mark. J., 2009. Sino-Vietnamese grammatical vocabulary and socio-linguistic conditions for borrowing. *Journal of the Southeast Asian Linguistics Society* 1: 1–9.

Alves, Mark J., 2015. Morphological functions among Mon-Khmer languages: Beyond the basics. In Enfield and Comrie (eds), pp. 524–550.

Ammerman, Albert J. and Luigi L. Cavalli-Sforza, 1971. Measuring the rate of spread of early farming in Europe. *Man* 6 (4): 674–688.

Ansaldo, Umberto, 1999. *Comparative Constructions in Sinitic: Areal Typology and Patterns of Grammaticalisation*. Dissertation, Stockholm University, Stockholm.

Ansaldo, Umberto and Stephen J. Matthews, 2001. Typical creoles and simple languages: The case of Sinitic. *Linguistic Typology* 5 (2/3): 311–324.

Bauer, Robert S., 1996. Identifying the Tai substratum in Cantonese. In *Pan-Asiatic Linguistics: Proceedings of the Fourth International Symposium on Languages and Linguistics*, vol. V, pp. 1806–1844. Bangkok: Mahidol University.

Bellwood, Peter, 1992. Southeast Asia before prehistory. In Tarling (ed.), vol. 1, pp. 55–136.

Benjamin, Geoffrey, 2006. Hervey's 'Kenaboi': Lost Malayan language or forest-collecting taboo jargon? Paper presented at the 10th International Association of Historians of Asia Conference, Singapore, October 1986.

Bisang, Walter, 1991. Verb serialization, grammaticalization and attractor positions in Chinese, Hmong, Vietnamese, Thai and Khmer. In Hansjakob Seiler and Waldfried Premper (eds), *Partizipation: Das sprachliche Erfassen von Sachverhalten*, pp. 509–562. Tübingen: Narr.

Blench, Roger, 2011. The role of agriculture in the evolution of Mainland Southeast Asian language phyla. In Enfield (ed.), pp. 125–152.

Blench, Roger, 2015. The origins of nominal classification markers in MSEA languages: Convergence, contact and some African parallels. In Enfield and Comrie (eds), pp. 551–578.

Blench, Roger and Mark W. Post, 2013. Re-thinking Sino-Tibetan phylogeny from the perspective of North East Indian languages. In Nathan Hill and Thomas Owen-Smith (eds), *Trans-Himalayan Linguistics*, pp. 71–104. Berlin: Mouton de Gruyter.

Blust, Robert, 1994. The Austronesian settlement of Mainland Southeast Asia. In Karen L. Adams and Thomas John Hudak (eds), *Papers from the Second Annual Meeting of the Southeast Asian Linguistics Society*, pp. 25–83. Tempe, AZ: Arizona State University.

Blust, Robert, 2013a. Southeast Asian islands and Oceania: Austronesian linguistic history. In Peter Bellwood (ed.), *The Encyclopedia of Global Human Migration*, vol. 1: *Prehistory*. Oxford: Wiley-Blackwell.

Blust, Robert, 2013b. *The Austronesian Languages (revised edition)*. Canberra: Asia-Pacific Linguistics.

Bo, Wenze, 2002. *A Study of Mulao*. Beijing: The Nationalities Press.

Bon, Noëllie, 2014. *Une Grammaire de la Langue Stieng, Langue en Danger du Cambodge et du Vietnam*. Dissertation, Université Lumière Lyon 2, Lyon.

Bradley, David, 1995. *Papers in Southeast Asian Linguistics,* vol. 13: *Studies in Burmese Languages*. Pacific Linguistics, vol. A-83. Canberra: Research School of Pacific and Asian Studies, Australian National University.

Bradley, David, 2007. Language endangerment in China and Mainland Southeast Asia. In Matthias Brenzinger (ed.), *Language Diversity Endangered*, pp. 278–302. Trends in Linguistics: Studies and Monographs. Berlin: Mouton de Gruyter.

van Breugel, Seino, 2014. *A Grammar of Atong*. Leiden: Brill.

Brunelle, Marc, 2009. Contact-induced change? Register in three Cham dialects. *Journal of the Southeast Asian Linguistics Society* 2: 1–22.

Brunelle, Marc and James Kirby, 2015. Re-assessing tonal diversity and geographical convergence in Mainland Southeast Asia. In Enfield and Comrie (eds), pp. 80–108.

Brunelle, Marc, Nguyễn Duy Dương and Nguyễn Khắc Hùng, 2010. A laryngographic and laryngoscopic study of Northern Vietnamese tones. *Phonetica* 67: 147–169.

Buakaw, Supakit, 2012. *A Phonological Study of Palaung Dialects Spoken in Thailand and Myanmar, with Focuses on Vowels and Final Nasals*. Doctoral dissertation, Mahidol University, Bangkok.

Bulbeck, David, 2011. Biological and cultural evolution in the population and culture history of Homo sapiens in Malaya. In Enfield (ed.), pp. 207–255.

Burenhult, Niclas, 2005. *A Grammar of Jahai*. Pacific Linguistics, vol. 566. Canberra: Australian National University.

Burenhult, Niclas, 2006. Body part terms in Jahai. *Language Sciences* 28: 162–180.

Burenhult, Niclas, Nicole Kruspe and Michael Dunn, 2011. Language history and culture groups among Austroasiatic-speaking foragers of the Malay Peninsula. In Enfield (ed.), pp. 257–275.

Burenhult, Niclas and Asifa Majid, 2011. Olfaction in Aslian ideology and language. *The Senses and Society* 6 (1): 19–29.

Burenhult, Niclas and Claudia Wegener, 2009. Preliminary notes on the phonology, orthography and vocabulary of Semnam (Austroasiatic, Malay Peninsula). *Journal of the Southeast Asian Linguistics Society* 1: 283–312.

Burling, Robbins, 2004. *The Language of the Modhipur Mandi (Garo)*, vol. I: *Grammar*. New Delhi: Bibliophile South Asia.

Butler, Becky, 2015. Approaching a phonological understanding of the sesquisyllable with phonetic evidence from Khmer and Bunong. In Enfield and Comrie (eds), pp. 437–493.

Capell, Arthur, 1979. Further typological studies in southeast Asian languages. In Nguyen Dang Liem (ed.), *South-East Asian Linguistic Studies*, vol. 3, pp. 1–42. Canberra: Pacific Linguistics.

Cavalli-Sforza, Luigi, Paolo Menozzi and Alberto Piazza, 1993. Demic expansions and human evolution. *Science* 259 (5095): 639–646.

Chappell, Hilary, 2001. Language contact and areal diffusion in Sinitic languages. In Alexandra Y. Aikhenvald and R. M. W. Dixon (eds), *Areal Diffusion and Genetic Inheritance: Problems in Comparative Linguistics*, pp. 328–357. Oxford: Oxford University Press.

Chappell, John and N. J. Shackleton, 1986. Oxygen isotopes and sea level. *Nature* 324 (6093): 137–140.

Chen, Guoqing, 2005. *Kemieyu yanjiu* [A Study of Kemie]. Beijing: Minzu chubanshe.

Clark, Marybeth, 1989. Hmong and areal South-East Asia. In David Bradley (ed.), *Papers in Southeast Asian Linguistics,* vol. 11: *Southeast Asian Syntax*, pp. 175–230. Canberra: Pacific Linguistics.

Clark, Marybeth and Amara Prasithrathsint, 1985. Synchronic lexical derivation in Southeast Asian languages. In Suriya Ratanakul and Suwilai Premsrirat (eds), *Southeast Asian Linguistic Studies Presented to André-G. Haudricourt*, pp. 34–81. Bangkok: Mahidol University.

Comrie, Bernard (ed.), 1990. *The Major Languages of East and South-East Asia*. London: Routledge.

Comrie, Bernard, 2007. Areal typology of mainland Southeast Asia: What we learn from the WALS maps. In Pranee Kullavanijaya (ed.), *Trends in Thai Linguistics*, pp. 18–47. Special issue of *Manusya* 13. Bangkok: Chulalongkorn University.

Cooke, Joseph R., 1968. *Pronominal Reference in Thai, Burmese and Vietnamese*. Berkeley, CA: University of California Press.

Coupe, A. R., 2003. *A Phonetic and Phonological Description of Ao: A Tibeto-Burman Language of Nagaland, North-East India*. Canberra: Pacific Linguistics.

Coupe, A. R., 2007. *A Grammar of Mongsen Ao*. Mouton Grammar Library, vol. 39. Berlin: Mouton de Gruyter.

Dahl, Östen, 2008. An exercise in 'a posteriori' language sampling. *Sprachtypologie und Universalienforschung* 61 (3): 208–220.

Diffloth, Gérard, 2011. Austroasiatic word histories: Boat, husked rice and taro. In Enfield (ed.), pp. 295–313.

Diller, Anthony V. N., Jerold A. Edmondson and Yongxian Luo, 2008. *The Tai-Kadai Languages*. London: RoutledgeCurzon.

Donohue, Mark, Rebecca Hetherington, James McElvenny and Virginia Dawson, 2013. *World Phonotactics Database*. Canberra: Australian National University. http://phonotactics.anu.edu.au

van Driem, George, 2007. Austroasiatic phylogeny and the Austroasiatic homeland in light of recent population genetic studies. *Mon-Khmer Studies* 37: 1–14.

van Driem, George, 2011. Rice and the Austroasiatic and Hmong-Mien homelands. In Enfield (ed.), pp. 361–390.

van Driem, George, 2013. Trans-Himalayan. In Nathan Hill and Thomas Owen-Smith (eds), *Trans-Himalayan Linguistics*. Berlin: Mouton de Gruyter.

Dryer, Matthew S. and Martin Haspelmath (eds), 2013. *The World Atlas of Language Structures Online*. Leipzig: Max Planck Institute for Evolutionary Anthropology. http://wals.info

Dunn, Michael, Niclas Burenhult, Nicole Kruspe, Sylvia Tufvesson and Neele Becker, 2011. Aslian linguistic prehistory: A case study in computational phylogenetics. *Diachronica* 28 (3): 291–323.

Dunn, Michael, Nicole Kruspe and Niclas Burenhult, 2013. Time and place in the prehistory of the Aslian languages. *Human Biology* 85: 383–399.

Edmondson, Jerold A. and John H. Esling, 2006. The valves of the throat and their functioning in tone, vocal register and stress: laryngoscopic case studies. *Phonology* 23 (2): 157–191.

Edmondson, Jerold A. and Kenneth J. Gregerson, 2007. The languages of Vietnam: Mosaics and expansions. *Language and Linguistics Compass* 1 (6): 727–749.

Enfield, N. J., 2005. Areal linguistics and mainland Southeast Asia. *Annual Review of Anthropology* 34: 181–206.

Enfield, N. J., 2006. Languages as historical documents: The endangered archive in Laos. *South East Asia Research* 14 (3): 471–488.

Enfield, N. J., 2007. *A Grammar of Lao*. Mouton Grammar Library, vol. 38. Berlin: Mouton de Gruyter.

Enfield, N. J. (ed.), 2011a. *Dynamics of Human Diversity: The Case of Mainland Southeast Asia*. Canberra: Pacific Linguistics.

Enfield, N. J., 2011b. Introduction: Dynamics of Human Diversity in Mainland Southeast Asia. In Enfield (ed.) pp. 1–8.

Enfield, N. J., 2011c. Linguistic diversity in mainland Southeast Asia. In Enfield (ed.), pp. 63–80.

Enfield, N. J., 2013. *Relationship Thinking: Agency, Enchrony, and Human Sociality*. New York: Oxford University Press.

Enfield, N. J., 2015. *The Utility of Meaning: What Words Mean and Why*. Oxford: Oxford University Press.

Enfield, N. J. and Bernard Comrie (eds), 2015. *The Languages of Mainland Southeast Asia: The State of the Art*. Berlin and Boston: Mouton de Gruyter.

Enfield, N. J. and Gérard Diffloth, 2009. Phonology and sketch grammar of Kri, a Vietic language of Laos. *Cahiers de Linguistique – Asie Orientale* 38 (1): 3–69.

Ferlus, Michel, 2014. Arem, a Vietic Language. *Mon-Khmer Studies* 43 (1): 1–15.

Fix, Alan, 2011. Origin of genetic diversity among Malaysian Orang Asli: An alternative to the demic diffusion model. In Enfield (ed.), pp. 277–291.

Gai, Xingzhi, 2002. *A Study of Tanglang*. Beijing: The Nationalities Press.

Giaphong, Suchada, 2004. *Plang Grammar as Spoken in Huay Namkhun Village, Chiang Rai Province*. MA thesis, Mahidol University, Bangkok.

Gil, David, 2015. The Mekong-Mamberamo linguistic area. In Enfield and Comrie (eds), pp. 262–351.

Goddard, Cliff, 2005. *The Languages of East and Southeast Asia*. Oxford: Oxford University Press.

Grant, Anthony and Paul Sidwell, 2005. *Chamic and Beyond: Studies in Mainland Austronesian Languages*. Canberra: Pacific Linguistics.

Grinevald, Colette, 2000. A morphosyntactic typology of classifiers. In Gunter Senft (ed.), *Systems of Nominal Classification*, pp. 50–92.

Hạ, Kiều Phương, 2010. Prosody of Vietnamese from an interactional perspective: *ờ, ừ* and *vâng* in backchannels and requests for information. *Journal of the Southeast Asian Linguistics Society* 3 (1): 56–76.

Hạ, Kiều Phương, 2013. Prosodic means in repair initiation as an activity in Northern Vietnamese conversation. In Daniel Hole and Elisabeth Löbel (eds), *Linguistics of Vietnamese: An International Survey*, pp. 35–54. Berlin and New York: de Gruyter Mouton.

Haas, Mary Rosamond, 1969. Sibling terms as used by marriage partners. *Southwestern Journal of Anthropology* 25 (3): 228–235.

Haiman, John, 2011. *Cambodian: Khmer*. London Oriental and African Language Library, vol. 16. Amsterdam: John Benjamins.

Hajek, John, 1998. Kenaboi: An extinct unclassified language of the Malay Peninsula. *Mon-Khmer Studies* 28: 137–149.

Hartmann, John, 1998. A linguistic geography and history of Tai Meuang-Fai (Ditch-Dike) techno-culture. *Language and Linguistics* 16 (2): 67–101.

Haspelmath, Martin, Matthew S. Dryer, David Gil and Bernard Comrie (eds), 2005. *The World Atlas of Language Structures*. Oxford: Oxford University Press.

Henderson, Eugénie. J. A., 1952. The main features of Cambodian pronunciation. *Bulletin of the School of Oriental and African Studies* 14: 149–174.

Henderson, Eugénie J. A., 1965. The topography of certain phonetic and morphological characteristics of South East Asian languages. *Lingua* 15: 400–434.

Henderson, Eugénie J. A., 1967. Grammar and tone in South East Asian languages. *Wissenschaftliche Zeitschrift der Karl-Marx-Universität Leipzig* 16 (1/2): 171–178.

Higbie, James and Snea Thinsan, 2003. *Thai Reference Grammar: The Structure of Spoken Thai*. Bangkok: Orchid Press.

Higham, C., 2002. *Early Cultures of Mainland Southeast Asia*. Bangkok: River Books.

Hyslop, Gwendolyn, Stephen Morey and Mark W. Post (eds), 2011. *North East Indian Linguistics*, vol. 3. New Delhi: Cambridge University Press India.

Hyslop, Gwendolyn, Stephen Morey and Mark W. Post (eds), 2012. *North East Indian Linguistics*, vol. 4. New Delhi: Cambridge University Press India.

Hyslop, Gwendolyn, Stephen Morey and Mark W. Post (eds), 2013. *North East Indian Linguistics*, vol. 5. New Delhi: Cambridge University Press India.

Iwasaki, Shoichi and Preeya Ingkaphirom Horie, 2005. *A Reference Grammar of Thai*. Cambridge: Cambridge University Press.

Jacquesson, François, 2004. *Le Deuri: Langue Tibéto-Birmane d'Assam*. Leuven, Paris and Dudley, MA: Peeters.

Jenny, Mathias and Paul Sidwell (eds), 2015. *Handbook of the Austroasiatic Languages*. Leiden: Brill.

Jonsson, Hjorleifur, 2011. Ethnology and the issue of human diversity in Mainland Southeast Asia. In Enfield (ed.), pp. 109–122.

Jonsson, Hjorleifur, 2014. *Slow Anthropology: Negotiating Difference with the Iu Mien*. Ithaca, NY: Cornell Southeast Asia Program Publications.

Konnerth, Linda, 2014. *A Grammar of Karbi*. Dissertation, University of Oregon, Eugene, OR.

Kosaka, Ryuichi, 2000. *A Descriptive Study of the Lachi Language: Syntactic Description, Historical Reconstruction and Genetic Relation*. Doctoral dissertation, Tokyo University of Foreign Studies, Tokyo.

Kölver, Ulrike, 1991. Local prepositions and serial verb constructions in Thai. In Hansjakob Seiler and Waldfried Premper (eds), *Partizipation: Das sprachliche Erfassen von Sachverhalten*, pp. 485–508. Tübingen: Narr.

Kruspe, Nicole, 2004. *A Grammar of Semelai*. Cambridge: Cambridge University Press.

Larish, Michael D., 2005. Moken and Moklen. In Nikolaus P. Himmelmann and Alexander Adelaar (eds), *The Austronesian Languages of Asia and Madagascar*, pp. 513–533. London: RoutledgeCurzon.

Lebar, Frank, Gerald Hickey and John Musgrave, 1964. *Ethnic Groups of Mainland Southeast Asia*. New Haven, CT: HRAF Press.

Li, Daqin, 2003. *A Study of Geman*. Beijing: The Nationalities Press.

Li, Daqin, 2004. *Sulong Yu Yan Jiu [A Study of Sulong]*. Beijing: Minzu Chubanshe.

Li, Yongsui, 2003. *A Study of Sangkong*. Beijing: The Nationalities Press.

Lidz, Liberty A., 2010. *A Descriptive Grammar of Yongning Na (Mosuo)*. Doctoral dissertation, University of Texas at Austin.

Luong, H. V., 1988. Discursive practices and power structure: Person-referring forms and sociopolitical struggles in colonial Vietnam. *American Ethnologist* 15 (2): 239–253.

Luong, H. V., 1990. *Discursive Practices and Linguistic Meanings: The Vietnamese System of Person Reference*. Amsterdam: John Benjamins.

Majid, Asifa and Niclas Burenhult, 2014. Odors are expressible in language, as long as you speak the right language. *Cognition* 130 (2): 266–270.

Mao, Zongwu and Yunbing Li, 2002. *A Study of Jiongnai*. Beijing: Central Nationalities University Press.

Mao, Zongwu and Yunbing Li, 2007. *Younuoyu Yanjiu [A Study of Younuo]*. Beijing: Minzu University of China Publishing House.

Matisoff, James A., 1973. Tonogenesis in Southeast Asia. In Larry M. Hyman (ed.), *Southern California Occasional Papers in Linguistics*, no. 1, pp. 72–95. Los Angeles: University of Southern California.

Matisoff, James A., 1991. Areal and universal dimensions of grammatization in Lahu. In Elizabeth Closs Traugott and Bernd Heine (eds), *Approaches to Grammaticalization*, pp. 383–453. Amsterdam: John Benjamins.

Matisoff, James A., 2003a. *Handbook of Proto-Tibeto-Burman*. Berkeley, CA: University of California Press.

Matisoff, James A., 2003b. Aslian: Mon-Khmer of the Malay Peninsula. *Mon-Khmer Studies* 33: 1–58.

Matisoff, James A., 2015. Re-examining the genetic position of Jingpho: Putting flesh on the bones of the Jingpho/Luish relationship. In Enfield and Comrie (eds), pp. 109–150.

Mayuree, Thawornpat, 2006. *Gong: An Endangered Language of Thailand*. Doctoral dissertation, Mahidol University, Bangkok.

Michaud, Jean (ed.), 2010. Editorial: Zomia and beyond (Special Issue). *Journal of Global History* 5 (2): 187–214.

Morey, Stephen, 2005. *The Tai Languages of Assam: A Grammar and Texts*. Canberra: Pacific Linguistics.

Morey, Stephen, 2010. *Turung: A Variety of Singpho Language Spoken in Assam*. Canberra: Pacific Linguistics.

Morey, Stephen and Mark W. Post (eds), 2008. *North East Indian Linguistics*, vol. 1. New Delhi: Cambridge University Press India.

Morey, Stephen and Mark W. Post (eds), 2010. *North East Indian Linguistics*, vol. 2. New Delhi: Cambridge University Press India.

Muysken, Pieter (ed.), 2008. *From Linguistic Areas to Areal Linguistics*. Amsterdam: John Benjamins.

Nettle, Daniel, 1999. *Linguistic Diversity*. Oxford: Oxford University Press.

Nichols, Johanna, 1992. *Linguistic Diversity in Space and Time*. Chicago: University of Chicago Press.

Nonaka, Angela M., 2004. The forgotten endangered languages: Lessons on the importance of remembering from Thailand's Ban Khor sign language. *Language in Society* 33 (5): 737–767.

O'Connor, Richard A., 1995. Agricultural change and ethnic succession in Southeast Asian states: A case for regional anthropology. *The Journal of Asian Studies* 54 (4): 968–996.

Oppenheimer, Stephen, 2011. MtDNA variation and southward Holocene human dispersals within Mainland Southeast Asia. In Enfield (ed.), pp. 81–108.

Oxenham, Marc and Nancy Tayles, 2006. *Bioarchaeology of Southeast Asia*. New York: Cambridge University Press.

Phattharathanit Srichomthong, 2012. Identity maintenance in Lanna (Northern Thai). *Journal of the Southeast Asian Linguistics Society* 5: 67–84.

Pittayaporn, Pittayawat, 2009. Proto-Southwestern-Thai: A new reconstruction. *Journal of the Southeast Asian Linguistics Society* 2: 119–143.

Pittayaporn, Pittayawat, 2015. Typologizing sesquisyllabicity: The role of structural analysis in the study of linguistic diversity in Mainland Southeast Asia. In Enfield and Comrie (eds), pp. 494–523.

Ploykaew, Pornsawan, 2001. *Samre Grammar*. Doctoral dissertation, Mahidol University, Bangkok.

Post, Mark W., 2007. *A Grammar of Galo*. Dissertation, La Trobe University, Melbourne.

Post, Mark W., 2011. Prosody and typological drift in Austroasiatic and Tibeto-Burman: Against 'Indosphere' and 'Sinosphere'. In S. Srichampa, Paul Sidwell and K. J. Gregerson (eds), *Austroasiatic Studies: Papers from International Conference on Austroasiatic Linguistics (ICAAL4)*, pp. 198–211. Special issue of *Mon-Khmer Studies* 3. Canberra: Pacific Linguistics.

Post, Mark W. 2015. Morphosyntactic reconstruction in an areal-historical context: A pre-historical relationship between North East India and Mainland Southeast Asia? In Enfield and Comrie (eds), pp. 205–261.

Ratliff, Martha, 2010. *Hmong-Mien Language History*. Studies in Language Change, vol. 8. Canberra: Pacific Linguistics.

Ratliff, Martha, 2015. Word-initial prenasalization in Southeast Asia: A historical perspective. In Enfield and Comrie (eds), pp. 29–48.

Sagart, Laurent, 2011. The Austroasiatics: East to west or west to east? In Enfield (ed.), pp. 345–359.

Sagart, Laurent, Roger Blench and A. Sanchez-Mazas (eds), 2005. *The Peopling of East Asia: Putting Together Archaeology, Linguistics and Genetics*. New York: RoutledgeCurzon.

Samarina, Irina, 2011. *Jazyki gelao: Materialy k sopostavitel'nomu slovarju kadajskich jazykov [Gael Languages: Materials for a Comparative Dictionary of Kadai Languages]*. Moskva: Academia.

van Schendel, Willem, 2002. Geographies of knowing, geographies of ignorance: Jumping scale in Southeast Asia. *Environment and Planning D: Society and Space* 20 (6): 647–668.

Scott, James C., 2009. *The Art of Not Being Governed: An Anarchist History of Upland Southeast Asia.* New Haven, CT: Yale University Press.

Seng Mai, Ma, 2012. *A Descriptive Grammar of Wa.* MA thesis, Payap University, Chiang Mai, Thailand.

Shee, Naw Hsar, 2008. *A Descriptive Grammar of Geba Karen.* MA thesis, Payap University, Chiang Mai, Thailand.

Shintani, Tadahiko, 2008. *The Palaung Language: the Comparative Lexicon of its Southern Dialects.* Tokyo: Research Institute for Languages and Cultures of Asia and Africa (ILCCA).

Shorto, H. L., 1960. Word and syllable pattern in Palaung. *Bulletin of the School of Oriental and African Studies* 23 (3): 544–557.

Shorto, H. L., 2006. *A Mon-Khmer Comparative Dictionary*, edited by Paul Sidwell. Canberra: Pacific Linguistics.

Sidnell, Jack and Merav Shohet, 2013. The problem of peers in Vietnamese interaction. *Journal of the Royal Anthropological Institute* 19 (3): 618–638.

Sidwell, Paul, 2009. Proto-Mon-Khmer vocalism: Moving on from Shorto's 'alternances'. *Journal of the Southeast Asian Linguistics Society* 1: 205–214.

Sidwell, Paul, 2013. Southeast Asian Mainland: Linguistic history. In Peter Bellwood (ed.), *The Encyclopedia of Global Human Migration,* vol. 1: *Prehistory*, pp. 259–268. Oxford: Wiley-Blackwell.

Sidwell, Paul, 2015. Local drift and areal convergence in the restructuring of Mainland Southeast Asian languages. In Enfield and Comrie (eds), pp. 49–79.

Sidwell, Paul and Roger Blench, 2011. The Austroasiatic Urheimat: The southeastern riverine hypothesis. In Enfield (ed.), pp. 315–343.

Simpson, Andrew (ed.), 2007. *Language and National Identity in Asia.* Oxford: Oxford University Press.

Sophana Srichampa, 2008. Patterns of polite expressions in Vietnamese. *The Mon-Khmer Studies Journal* 38: 117–147.

de Sousa, Hilário, 2015. The Far Southern Sinitic languages as part of Mainland Southeast Asia. In Enfield and Comrie (eds), pp. 352–436.

Srisakorn, Preedaporn, 2008. *So (Thavung) Grammar.* Dissertation, Mahidol University, Bangkok.

Stolz, Thomas, 2002. No Sprachbund beyond this line! On the age-old discussion of how to define a linguistic area. In Paulo Ramat and Thomas Stolz (eds), *Mediterranean Languages: Paper from the MEDTYP Workshop, Tirrenia, June 2000*, pp. 259–281. Bochum: Brockmeyer.

Sun, Hongkai and Guangkun Liu, 2009. *A Grammar of Anong: Language Death under Intense Contact*, edited translation and annotation, with translation, editing, annotation and expansion by Graham Thurgood, Fengxiang Li and Ela Thurgood. *Languages of the Greater Himalayan Region.* Leiden: Brill.

Suwilai Premsrirat, 1987. *Khmu, a Minority Language of Thailand*. Canberra: Pacific Linguistics.

Suwilai Premsrirat, 1998. Language maintenance and language shift in minority languages of Thailand. In Kazuto Matsumura (ed.), *Studies in Endangered Languages*, pp. 191–211. Tokyo: Hituzi Syobo.

Suwilai Premsrirat, 2007. Endangered languages of Thailand. *International Journal of the Sociology of Language* 186: 75–93.

Suwilai Premsrirat, 2008. Orthography development: A tool for revitalizing and maintaining ethnic minority languages. *Journal of Language and Culture* 26: 18–34.

Svantesson, Jan-Olof, Raw Kam, Kristina Lindell and Håkan Lundstrom, 2013. *Dictionary of Kammu Yuan Language and Culture*. Honolulu: University of Hawai'i Press.

Tarling, Nicholas, 1992. *The Cambridge History of Southeast Asia: from Early Times to c. 1800*, vol. 1. Cambridge University Press.

Thurgood, Graham, 1998. The development of the Chamic vowel system: the interaction of inheritance and borrowing. In David Thomas (ed.), *Papers in Southeast Asian Linguistics, no. 15: Further Chamic Studies*, pp. 61–90. Canberra: Pacific Linguistics.

Thurgood, Graham, 1999. *From Ancient Cham to Modern Dialects: Two Thousand Years of Language Contact and Change*. Honolulu: University of Hawai'i Press.

Thurgood, Graham, 2010. Hainan Cham, Anong, and Eastern Cham: Three languages, three social contexts, three patterns of change. *Journal of Language Contact, Varia* 3: 39–61.

Thurgood, Graham and Randy J. La Polla, 2003. *The Sino-Tibetan Languages*. London: Routledge.

Thurgood, Graham, Ela Thurgood and Fengxiang Li, 2014. *A Grammatical Sketch of Hainan Cham: History, Contact, and Phonology*. Berlin: Mouton de Gruyter.

Tooley, M. J. and Ian Shennan (eds), 1987. *Sea Level Changes*. Oxford: Blackwell.

Umaporn, Sungkaman, 2007. Backchannel response in Mon conversation. *Mon-Khmer Studies* 37: 67–85.

Vittrant, Alice, 2015. Expressing motion: The contribution of Southeast Asian languages with reference to East Asian languages. In Enfield and Comrie (eds), pp. 579–625.

Vittrant, Alice and Justin Watkins (eds), in press. *Languages of Mainland Southeast Asia Linguistic Area: Grammatical Sketches*. Boston and Berlin: de Gruyter.

Voris, Harold K., 2000. Maps of Pleistocene sea levels in Southeast Asia: Shorelines, river systems and time durations. *Journal of Biogeography* 27 (5): 1153–1167.

Watkins, Justin, 2002. *The Phonetics of Wa: Experimental Phonetics, Phonology, Orthography and Sociolinguistics*. Canberra: Pacific Linguistics.

Watkins, Justin (ed.), 2005. *Studies in Burmese Linguistics*. Canberra: Pacific Linguistics.

Watkins, Justin, 2013. *Dictionary of Wa*, two volumes. Leiden: Brill.

Wayesha, Ahsi James, 2010. *A Phonological Description of Leinong Naga*. MA thesis, Payap University, Chiang Mai, Thailand.

White, Joyce C., 2011. Cultural diversity in Mainland Southeast Asia: A view from prehistory. In Enfield (ed.), pp. 9–46.

Wnuk, Ewelina, 2016. *Semantic Specificity of Perception Verbs in Maniq*. Nijmegen: Radboud University.

Wnuk, Ewelina and Asifa Majid, 2014. Revisiting the limits of language: The odor lexicon of Maniq. *Cognition* 131 (1): 125–138.

Yip, Moira, 2002. *Tone*. Cambridge: Cambridge University Press.

Yu, Defen, 2007. *Aspects of Lisu Phonology and Grammar, a Language of Southeast Asia*. Canberra: Pacific Linguistics.

26

Southeast Asian Tone in Areal Perspective

James Kirby and Marc Brunelle

26.1 Introduction

Tone is often presented as one of the quintessential features identifying Mainland Southeast Asia (MSEA)[1] as a linguistic area (Enfield 2011; Henderson 1965; Matisoff 2001). For Matisoff, the proliferation of tone languages is '[p]erhaps the most striking phonological feature of the South-East Asian linguistic area' (2001: 291), while the ubiquity of tone tops Henderson's list of 'features ... typologically characteristic of a South East Asian linguistic area' (1965: 401). The presence of tone in a large number of genetically unrelated languages has commonly been attributed to areal diffusion, with Chinese most commonly hypothesized as the ultimate source (Benedict 1996; Matisoff 1973; Pulleyblank 1986).

The reference to tone as a 'feature' in the preceding citations might suggest that there exists a simple typological dichotomy between languages with and without tone. Upon closer inspection, however, the phonetic, phonological and typological characteristics of MSEA tone systems differ in important ways. To the extent that this diversity reflects substantive differences between languages, it raises the question of precisely what role contact has played in the evolution of tone in MSEA. In this chapter, we address this question through an examination of the phonetic and phonological properties of MSEA tone systems as well as of proposals regarding their evolution. After briefly discussing tone systems in the broader typological perspective, we present an overview of the phonetic, phonological and genetic characteristics of MSEA tone systems, emphasizing the rich variability of tonal realization found in the region. Next, we discuss the ways in which languages can become tonal, reviewing evidence for the spread of tone through contact as well as for the idea that

---

[1] In this chapter, we use the term 'Mainland Southeast Asia' (MSEA) to refer to the Indochinese peninsula comprising the modern states of Vietnam, Laos, Cambodia, Thailand, Myanmar (Burma), Singapore and the mainland territory of Malaysia.

much of the observed tonality on the ground in modern MSEA might be traced to a small number of 'tonogenetic events' rather than a large number of borrowings. In light of this discussion, we consider whether a re-evaluation of the notion of tone as a canonical indicator of 'linguistic area' more generally is warranted. While our treatment is focused on a particular geographic region, we hope that this areal perspective on tone can also be of use to scholars working in other linguistic areas where large numbers of genetically unrelated tone languages are present.

26.2 Synchronic Typology of Tone in MSEA

26.2.1 On the Definition of 'Tone Language'

Before discussing the tonal properties of MSEA languages, it may be useful to briefly review some standard approaches to classifying and typologizing tone systems. As suggested above, the notion of a fundamental dichotomy between 'tone languages' on the one hand and 'non-tone languages' on the other has tempted researchers since the dawn of prosodic analysis (Lehiste 1970). Unlike (segmental) phonological features such as presence versus absence of voiceless nasals or final consonant clusters, the essential qualities of tone have proved harder to pin down, but definitions of 'tone language' almost always involve some reference to the paradigmatic use of pitch. For example, Pike (1948: 3) offers the following: 'A tone language may be defined as a language having lexically significant, contrastive, but relative pitch on each syllable.' Hyman (2009: 229) gives a similar definition: 'A language with tone is one in which an indication of pitch enters into the lexical realization of at least some morphemes.'

Setting aside the complications such definitions raise for the classification of languages such as Japanese or Swedish (so-called 'pitch-accent' languages), the primary role of pitch is also assumed by researchers who subdivide the set of tone languages into 'simple' and 'complex' based on the number and nature of the pitch movements. Pike himself distinguished between 'register-tone' and 'contour-tone' languages, with the former encompassing languages with a 'small, restricted number of tone contrasts between *level tonemes*' (1948: 5, emphasis ours), while the latter type comprises languages 'in which glides are basic to the system, with no level tonemes whatsoever' (1948: 8). Similarly, Maddieson (2011) makes a distinction between *simple* and *complex* tone languages, where *simple* languages are 'essentially those with only a two-way basic contrast, usually between high and low levels' and *complex* languages are everything else.

Such classifications likely stem from the observation that African- and New World-type tone systems often have phonetically less complex tone systems compared to those of East and Southeast Asia. However, the differences between these systems may rest less with aspects of phonetic realization and more with the fact that the tone systems of African and

New World languages tend to exhibit phonological properties such as decompositionality or spreading, as well as a tendency for tone to be employed for grammatical functions (inflection, derivation, etc.).[2] Conversely, tone may have less of a lexically contrastive function in Africa and the Americas, whereas purely tonal minimal pairs are extremely common in many MSEA languages. In any case, there is significant tonal variability in each of these areas, as we show for MSEA in the next section.

26.2.2 Variation in MSEA Tone Systems

In principle, a division between simple and complex tone languages could be useful for typologizing a given geographic region. At least in MSEA, however, the closer one stays to the phonetic ground, the less satisfying the simple/complex dichotomy becomes: not only is the boundary between tone and non-tone languages difficult to ascertain, but there is considerable variation in the properties of tone systems even between 'clearly' tonal languages (Abramson and L-Thongkum 2009). Here we consider several types of tone-related phenomena commonly encountered in MSEA: variation in pitch realization, phonation type, register, and the domain of tonal contrasts.

26.2.2.1 Variation in Pitch Realization

One reason that application of a simple/complex dichotomy to MSEA languages can be misleading is that there exists a large number of languages with just a two-tone system ('register-tone' languages in Pike's sense) but where one of the tones is phonetically realized as a contour, at least some of the time. One such example is Western Khmu (Kammu) (of the 'tone 1' variety given in Table 26.1), which contrasts a low and a falling tone – pitch apparently being the primary or sole phonetic parameter of relevance here. This contrasts with other Western dialects in which phonation type also plays a role.

It is not clear exactly how many MSEA languages have 'simple' (i.e. two- or three-tone) systems where one, or possibly both, of the tones are realized with rising, falling or more complex pitch movements, in part because tone systems are often described solely for their phonological (i.e. contrastive) rather than phonetic properties. At the same time, care must also be taken when designating surface pitch movements to be inherent tonal properties, as non-lexical factors may also influence surface tonal realization. For example, the Tibeto-Burman language Naxi has four surface tones (high,

---

[2] Note that languages with both of these properties exist in MSEA as well: the contour tones in several Naish languages have been argued to be properly analysed as sequences of level tones (Michaud and Xueguang 2007; cf. Clements et al. 2011), and tone is frequently deployed to grammatical ends in Hmongic (Ratliff 1992b) and Tibeto-Burman (Henderson 1967) languages, especially those of the Chin group (Hartmann-So 1989; Hyman 2010; Watkins 2013; see also Ratliff 1992a).

Table 26.1 *Tones in Khmu dialects (after Suwilai Premsrirat 2001). The initial voicing contrast maintained in (toneless) Eastern Khmu is transphonologized into a low versus falling contrast in one Western dialect ('tone 1'), a low versus high contrast in another ('tone 2'), and a breathy versus falling contrast in a third ('register')*

E. Khmu	W. Khmu (tone 1)	W. Khmu (tone 2)	W. Khmu (register)	Gloss
bùːc	pùːc	pʰùːc	pṳːc	'rice wine'
puːc	pûːc	pʰúːc	pûːc	'to take off clothes'
glaːŋ	klàːŋ	kʰlàːŋ	kla̤ːŋ	'stone'
klaːŋ	klâːŋ	kʰláːŋ	klâːŋ	'eagle'

mid, rising and falling), but the falling tone is an intonational allotone of the high and mid (level) tones, while the rising tone is often the result of a (phonological) process of tonal reassociation (Michaud 2006, 2013).

26.2.2.2   Phonation Types and Tone: Tone is Not (Only) Pitch

A second factor complicating the analysis of tone in MSEA is that *voice quality*, or phonation type, is a crucial aspect of tone in many languages of the region.[3] By this we mean that a voice quality setting (modal, breathy, creaky, tense, etc.) is canonically present as an (obligatory) phonetic cue to the tone category along with pitch (and potentially other features as well). Far from being unusual, tone systems involving different phonation types are a common feature of many widely spoken MSEA languages such as Vietnamese (Maspero 1912; Nguyễn and Edmondson 1997), Burmese (Gruber 2011; Watkins 2001) and Green Hmong (Andruski and Ratliff 2000); indeed, in an early survey Henderson remarked that '"tone" is seldom, if ever, a matter of pitch alone' (1965: 404). Such systems are sometimes termed 'phonation-prominent' (Matisoff 1973) or 'mixed pitch/phonation type' (Andruski and Ratliff 2000); for brevity, we will use the term 'mixed' to refer to this type of system throughout this article.

The canonical example of a mixed tone system is Northern Vietnamese, where at least two and possibly three of the language's six tones (low-falling *hỏi*, broken-rising *ngã* and falling-glottalized *nặng*) involve glottalization or laryngealization along with a distinctive pitch movement (Michaud 2004; Nguyễn and Edmondson 1997; Pham 2003),[4] and where the voice quality setting serves as a crucial perceptual cue for listeners (Brunelle 2009; Kirby 2010). While most mixed tone systems involve either breathy or creaky/laryngealized voice quality alongside modally voiced

---

[3] Following Abercrombie (1967), Laver (1980) and others, we use the term 'voice quality' as a general term referring to voice settings for a variety of purposes and 'phonation type' to refer to the phonetic realization of voice quality when employed for phonological purposes.

[4] The low-falling (*huyền*) tone in Northern Vietnamese is also optionally breathy (Nguyễn and Edmondson 1997).

Table 26.2 *Possible phonetic correlates of register. High register typically develops from proto-voiceless stops, low register from proto-voiced/ aspirated stops*

High register (voiceless stops, [*pa])	Low register (voiced stops, [*ba])
Higher pitch	Lower pitch
Tense/modal voice	Lax/breathy voice
Monophthongs/shorter vowels	Diphthongs/longer vowels
Raised F1/lower vowels/[+ATR]	Lowered F1/higher vowels/[−ATR]
Plain stops/shorter VOT	Aspirated stops/longer VOT

tones, many Hmongic languages have tone systems involving modal, breathy and creaky phonation types, and tone in dialects of the Tai-Kadai language Nùng is reported to involve both modal and glottalized phonation types along with either creaky or breathy voice (Nicolson 2000).

The widespread tendency of MSEA languages to involve phonation type as an integral part of tonal specification makes for a fuzzy boundary between mixed tone systems and so-called *register systems*, to which we now turn.

26.2.2.3   Register Systems

In many MSEA languages, especially those of Austroasiatic or Austronesian stock, lexical contrasts are signalled by a 'bundle' of (broadly suprasegmental) features, such as phonation type, pitch, vowel quality, intensity and vowel duration. Such languages have been termed *(voice-)register languages* in the Southeast Asian linguistic literature (Diffloth 1982; Ferlus 1979; Gregerson 1976; Henderson 1952). Here, register normally refers to a type of phonological contrast arising from the neutralization of voicing in onsets and subsequent phonologization of phonetic properties originally associated with voicing,[5] but in rarer cases, the loss of final laryngeals conspires with voicing neutralization to lead to the development of complex register systems, as in some Pearic and Vietic languages (DiCanio 2009; Enfield and Diffloth 2009; Ferlus 2004). Depending on the language in question, register may be a property of the onset, the rime or the entire syllable; phonetically, however, register systems involve a common set of acoustic correlates, listed in Table 26.2 (the low register derives from former voiced stops and the high register derives from former voiceless stops).

It is important to note that not all of the phonetic properties in Table 26.2 are found in all register languages. For example, despite evidence that many of these properties are present to some extent in Eastern Cham at a fine-grained phonetic level (Brunelle 2005, 2006), this language primarily contrasts registers through pitch and voice

---

[5] Note that this use of the term must be distinguished both from Pike's use of 'pitch registers' (referring to pitch levels) as well as from its use when referring to the sociolinguistically distinct speech styles associated with many Austronesian languages (Uhlenbeck 1964).

Table 26.3 *'Tone' in Burmese (examples and notation from Watkins 2001)*

Low	/ma/	[maː˩]	'hard'
High	/má/	[maː˥]	'towering'
Creaky	/ma̰/	[ma̰˩]	'female'
Killed	/maʔ/	[maʔ˩˥]	'March'

quality. In modern Standard Khmer, register is expressed exclusively through vowel quality, although historical evidence and the acoustic analysis of more conservative dialects suggest that it may have passed through a stage in which phonation type was a prominent cue (Jenner 1974; Wayland and Jongman 2001, 2002). Huffman (1976) and Ferlus (1979) provide good overviews of the range of variation in register systems among Mon-Khmer languages.

Since tone systems can also make use of phonation types, as we have just seen, this raises the question of how one decides whether one is dealing with a register system or a mixed tone system. Some researchers have suggested that register systems constitute a typological profile distinct from tone languages, including those of the 'mixed' variety. DiCanio (2009) provides a careful phonetic analysis of the Takhian Thong variety of Chong, which involves modal, breathy, tense and breathy-tense phonation types, accompanied by (marginal) pitch differences. This suggests to him a fundamental distinction between register languages and tone languages (DiCanio 2009: 162):

> a register language is distinct from a tone language because contrastive phonation type typifies the former, while contrastive pitch typifies the latter. Phonation type is to a register language what tones are to a tone language.

The problem with this definition is that it is not always (or even usually) clear which feature is dominant, acoustically, perceptually or phonologically. A classic example here is that of Burmese, which has been described both as a register system (e.g. Bradley 1982; Jones 1986) and as a (mixed) tone language (e.g. Gruber 2011; Watkins 2001). While the precise details are somewhat complicated, Burmese syllables can bear one of four registers/tones, shown in Table 26.3. However, Gruber (2011) has shown that glottalization, creakiness and the presence of a high pitch target are all important perceptual cues, thus demonstrating that Burmese cannot be analysed only in terms of pitch or voice quality.

Abramson and L-Thongkum (2009) also suggest a distinction between tone and register based on the prominence of the primary cue, with tone languages being primarily cued by pitch and voice-register languages primarily cued by phonation type. However, they acknowledge that this boundary can be fuzzy, and suggest that tradition and researcher degrees of freedom are likely to play a significant role in the assignment of languages to one category or the other. A similar sentiment is echoed by Watson (1996: 202) in an essay on Pacoh vowel phonology:

> [t]here tends to be a dichotomy in voice quality ranging from breathy to clear to creaky, in pitch ranging from high to mid to low, in voicing of initial consonants, in vowel height between close and open, in vowel gliding between onglided, plain or offglided, and tension from tense to lax. In some cases there has been a general movement from a distinction between voicing in initial consonants to a distinction in vowel quality and/or pitch.

Enfield (2011: 69) suggests treating tone and phonation

> as instances of a single sound system property because they each involve the use of laryngeal features for lexical contrast. While tone and phonation type are often considered to be fundamentally distinct phenomena, in fact most systems that are identified as one versus the other (in phonological terms) actually display properties of both (in phonetic terms: Henderson 1967: 171). Pitch contours, distinctions in phonation type, and glottalic effects are all produced in the larynx (specifically, by the vocal folds), and are all articulatorily independent of segmental speech sounds produced with the lips, teeth, and tongue (i.e., typical 'consonants'). Tone and phonation are intimately bound, not essentially distinct, and for this reason I do not regard the sound system of a classical MSEA tone language such as Vietnamese to be of a different species from that of a classical MSEA register language such as Kri (Enfield and Diffloth 2009).

While we are broadly in agreement with this position, it is worth noting that laryngeal and supralaryngeal features are at least weakly related via the connection of the tongue root to the larynx via the hyoid bone.

Additional evidence for the fluidity of laryngeal features in MSEA can be found in the comparison of related languages (or dialect continua) where the same set of segmental and suprasegmental properties seem to take on different degrees of prominence in different dialects. In other words, prominence is often *unstable*. The Khmu dialects described in Table 26.1 above constitute one such example; Lamet, a Palaungic Mon-Khmer language, is another. Narumol (1982) and Svantesson (1988) describe versions of the language with two contrastive voice registers, but no pitch (tone) distinction, while Conver (1999) describes a phonemic two-tone system realized as high and low pitch. Conversely, Lindell et al. (1978) indicate that none of the dialects they studied made use either of tone or of contrastive phonation type distinctions. The nascent tone contrast in some dialects of Khmer shows similar variation, ranging from dialects that maintain differences in voice quality, F0 and vowel quality (Wayland and Jongman 2001) to dialects that retain vowel quality distinctions only, such as modern Standard Khmer.

There are at least two ways one might begin to address the issue of phonetic prominence in tone/register systems. One is to look at the weighting of cues in production by conducting linear discriminant or factor analyses of acoustic data, for example (e.g. Andruski and Ratliff 2000 on Green Hmong, Abramson et al. 2004 on Suai, Abramson et al. 2007 on Khmu). Such studies may also reveal diachronic changes in progress. In their study of Khmu Rawk, for example, Abramson et al. (2007) found that male speakers no longer produce a measurable phonation type difference between voice registers, suggesting that F0 is becoming a more prominent cue for at least some speakers of this language.

The issue of establishing acoustic separability is in principle a separate undertaking from determining whether a given cue is used by native listeners in perception (see e.g. the previously cited work by Abramson and colleagues; Brunelle 2009; Brunelle and Finkeldey 2011; Gruber 2011; Hombert 1977; Kirby 2014; Mazaudon and Michaud 2008). This type of work involves experimental manipulation of acoustic properties of natural or resynthesized stimuli, using either an alternative forced-choice identification paradigm (and subsequent analysis of error rates and classification trees) or discrimination tasks (which facilitate analysis of reaction time data: see e.g. Gandour 1983; Kirby 2010). The interpretation of perceptual responses may be complicated by the existence of learned and/or inherent perceptual dependencies between cue dimensions (Brunelle 2012). Nevertheless, the available perceptual studies suggest that the relation between acoustic separability and perceptual weighting in MSEA tone and register systems is far from straightforward, and this remains an area of active research.

Even if a prominence hierarchy can be established, it is not clear that languages in which pitch is the most prominent aspect of the system are fundamentally different from languages in which voice quality, or vowel height, or even voicing are the most prominent aspects, or that any of these are different from languages in which no laryngeal cue is prominent. Indeed, given that redundancy is the default state of phonetic contrast (Lisker 1986), one might argue that clear instances of 'pure tone' or 'pure voice quality' languages are actually rather unusual from a functional perspective, and that register systems or systems in flux would be expected if perceptual robustness were somehow privileged. Thus, while there may be a descriptive utility to terms such as 'register language', 'mixed pitch/phonation type tone language', etc., it is important to bear in mind that the borders between them are likely to be extremely porous.

As a final note, it is worth pointing out that while pitch and phonation type often cross-cut one another in the prosodic systems of MSEA languages, there are also languages that have segmentally anchored phonation type distinctions in addition to fully developed tone systems. One such example is the endangered Tibeto-Burman language Mpi, spoken in northern Thailand (Ladefoged and Maddieson 1996). This language has a system of six tones, each of which may co-occur with a plain or laryngealized (tense or stiff-voiced) vowel, as shown in Table 26.4. While this type of

Table 26.4 *Contrasting tones and phonation types in Mpi (after Ladefoged and Maddieson 1996: 316)*

	Tone	Modal voice	Stiff voice
[1]si	low rising	'to be putrid'	'to be dried up'
[2]si	low	'blood'	'seven'
[3]si	mid rising	'to roll'	'to smoke'
[4]si	mid	(a colour)	(classifier)
[5]si	high rising	'to die'	(man's name)
[6]si	high	'four'	(man's name)

system seems to be relatively rare among MSEA languages, further examples may be found among the Sino-Tibetan languages spoken in China such as Yi and Bai (Edmondson et al. 2001), as well as in the Oto-Manguean languages of Central America such as Itsunyoso Trique (DiCanio 2012).

26.2.2.4 The Domain of Tonal Contrast

Another important aspect, implicit or explicit, in many definitions of 'tone language' is that the syllable is cast as the relevant domain over which relative differences in pitch are defined. The resulting problem of how to classify 'marginally' tonal languages such as Swedish or Japanese has led some prosodic typologists to propose a tripartite classification of 'tone', 'stress' and 'pitch-accent' languages (Ding 2006; van der Hulst 2011), although Hyman (2006, 2009) points out that the unique properties of pitch-accent can be difficult to separate from those of tone and stress.

Languages where lexical tones are associated to units larger than the syllable are hard to come by in MSEA, but one does not have to go too far to find such languages. Many Tibeto-Burman languages of the Bodish and Qiangic subgroups such as Tamang (Mazaudon and Michaud 2008), Naxi (Michaud and Xuegang 2007) and Prinmi (Ding 2001), spoken in nearby China, Tibet and Nepal, are characterized by 'cumulative' tone systems, where distinctive pitch patterns are defined over units determined both prosodically and morphologically (Evans 2001a; Hildebrandt 2007; Mazaudon 1973; Mazaudon and Michaud 2008). In the Tibeto-Burman language Lizu (Chirkova and Chen 2013), for example, monosyllabic words contrast low(-rising) and high(-falling) tones, e.g. /[R]ŋu/ 'silver' versus /[F]ŋu/ 'cow', while three pitch patterns are observed in disyllabic words: two mid-level pitch contours of equal prominence (/[EP]midzɹ̩/ 'hare'), a left-prominent falling contour (/[LP]midzɹ̩/ 'pepper') and a right-prominent rising contour (/[RP]mutsɹ̩/ 'cat').

Another way in which the 'domain' of tone can differ is in the extent to which it has diffused through the lexicon. Most tone languages of East and Southeast Asia have a restricted tonal inventory in syllables closed by an obstruent (often called 'checked' or 'dead' syllables). This impoverished inventory is usually attributed to the fact that these syllables preserved their segmental coda during the three-way split stage of tonogenesis (see Section 26.3.1) and therefore did not develop a contrastive tone. Tai-Kadai languages often have similar (though less systematic) restrictions between tones and onsets. In Central Thai, for instance, a high tone may not appear after a voiced onset. In some languages, these tone–consonant interactions are even more radical: tone is phonemically marginal, with pitch-based contrast restricted to certain words or phonological environments. In several varieties of Khmer, an incipient tone contrast has developed following the loss of /r/ in onset position, leading to a small number of minimal pairs distinguished solely by pitch (Kirby 2014; Wayland and Guion 2005; see also Section 26.3.2), while in the Tibeto-Burman language Kurtöp, tone is only contrastive following sonorants and the palatal fricative /ç/ (Hyslop 2009). It is also not uncommon to find tones that are restricted to certain lexical strata, such as loanwords. For example, although Mal (T'in), a Mon-Khmer language of Thailand, contrasts both a falling and a rising tone, the rising tone is largely (though not exclusively) used with Thai loanwords (L-Thongkum and Chommanad 2008).

26.2.3 Some Tonal Characteristics of the Individual Language Families

To give a different sense of the range of tonal diversity in MSEA, we include here a brief overview of the tonal properties of languages included in the database described in Brunelle and Kirby (2015). At the time of writing this database includes 186 Southeast Asian languages from five families. As noted by Matisoff (2001), migration patterns in Southeast Asia have traditionally been rather different from those in Europe; the result is that the branching-tree model of genetic relationships, already a simplification, is perhaps even less insightful in the MSEA case. For this and other reasons, subgroupings and sub-branches are often contested; as such, we restrict our classification to major language families only.

As the preceding discussion makes clear, it is difficult to place MSEA languages into a single category on the basis of their lexical treatment of prosodic properties. Thus, instead of insisting on labels, we describe the languages in terms of the number of contrastive prosodic units, the number of distinct pitch units and the number of voice quality dimensions they distinguish. In our database, we furthermore make note of properties such as consonant–tone restrictions, maximal canonical word shape (mono-, sesqui-,[6] or polysyllabic) and the complexity of codas. As we are relying largely on published sources, it is not always clear if descriptions should be

---

[6] A sesquisyllable (Matisoff 1973) is a disyllabic word composed of a main, stressed, final syllable that may contain the full range of phonological contrasts of a language, preceded by an unstressed reduced 'presyllable' that is subject to radical contrast neutralization.

interpreted phonetically or phonologically, but this approach has the advantage of allowing a more nuanced overview of the tonal properties of MSEA languages than would be gained by yet another arbitrary classification into a small number of sub-types.

26.2.3.1   Austroasiatic

Our sample contains 78 Austroasiatic languages (41.9 per cent), all of them Mon-Khmer.[7] The vast majority of the AA languages in our sample are sesquisyllabic. Around a third of these (24) are non-tonal, while another third (27) have systems of two tones or registers. This includes languages such as Riang (Luce undated), Conver's Lamet (Conver 1999), and T'in (Lua') (L-Thongkum and Chommanad 2008), which are described as having two pitches but no phonation type differences; languages like Western Bru (L-Thongkum 1979) or Narumol's Lamet (Narumol 1982), described as register systems distinguished by phonation type differences only; and (most commonly) languages like Mon (L-Thongkum 1988) or Suai (Abramson et al. 2004), for which both phonation type and pitch distinctions are described.

The remaining Austroasiatic languages in our sample have systems of three or more tones. These languages almost always employ a combination of pitch and phonation type distinctions to signal tone categories. This set includes Vietic languages such as Rục (Nguyễn Văn Lợi 1993), Chứt and Thavung (Ferlus 1998), and Northern Vietnamese (Nguyễn and Edmondson 1997; Vũ Thang Phương 1981), as well as Pearic languages such as Takhian Thong Chong (DiCanio 2009), where each of the four phonemic phonation types (modal, tense, breathy and breathy-tense) are consistently realized with a unique pitch. The notable exceptions here are Kháng (Edmondson 2010), a language with six tones but no reported phonation type distinctions, and Southern Vietnamese. Kháng has demonstrably had considerable recent contact with Tai-speaking groups, although the same cannot be said for Southern Vietnamese.

It is interesting to note that the tone sandhi phenomena that are so pervasive in the Sino-Tibetan and Hmong-Mien families are unknown in Austroasiatic languages, although complex tone spreading processes are attested in Kammu (Svantesson 1983). This could be due to a lack of thorough descriptions, but it is at least worth noting that tone sandhis are so far unattested in otherwise well-described Vietnamese dialects.

26.2.3.2   Austronesian

While the Austronesian family contains many thousands of languages spoken by hundreds of millions of people, they are relatively thin on the

---

[7] While often used interchangeably with Mon-Khmer, the Austroasiatic group is also thought to include the Munda languages, spoken in India and Bangladesh. The internal classification of Mon-Khmer languages is complicated; see Diffloth (2005) and Sidwell (2013) for overviews of the issues involved.

ground in MSEA. There are just 20 Austronesian varieties in our sample (10.8 per cent); of these, 11 are Chamic languages/dialects spoken in Vietnam and Cambodia, with the rest spoken in the Malay Peninsula and its vicinity. Austronesian languages of the Malay Peninsula tend to be disyllabic, while Chamic languages are mainly sesquisyllabic. Cham dialects proper show a tendency to monosyllabicity, the most extreme case being colloquial Eastern Cham, which has become almost entirely monosyllabic (Brunelle 2009).

The majority of these varieties are atonal, but three dialects of Cham (Eastern Cham, Vietnamese Western Cham and Cambodian Western Cham) and two dialects of Raglai (Cac Gia Raglai and Southern Raglai) have developed register systems combining pitch and voice quality to various degrees (Brunelle 2009; Lee 1966, 1998). Haroi, another coastal Chamic language, formerly had a register system that was restructured into a complex vowel system, in a manner reminiscent of Standard Khmer (Mundhenk and Goschnick 1977). Moken Dung, a Malayic language of the Andaman sea, is reported to have a two-tone system, although information about its source is scant at best (Naw Say Bay 1995). In short, some mainland Austronesian languages have undergone minor tonal developments, but this seems mostly limited to register.

Some other Austronesian languages spoken outside Mainland Southeast Asia, strictly construed, have also developed forms of tonality. Javanese has a register system normally described as a tense/lax stop contrast, but which is in practice almost identical to MSEA register systems (Adisasmito-Smith 2004; Brunelle 2010; Fagan 1988; Thurgood 2004); other Malayo-Polynesian languages of Indonesia, such as Sundanese and Madurese, have similar systems. Tsat, a Chamic language spoken in Hainan, has developed a five-tone contrast from laryngeal codas and onset voicing, just like Vietnamese or Chinese (Maddieson and Pang 1993).

26.2.3.3 Sino-Tibetan

Sino-Tibetan languages, including Chinese dialects, make up 19.9 per cent of our sample (37 languages). All of these languages are tonal to some degree, ranging from the two-tone systems of Bwe Karen (Henderson 1979) or Daai Chin (Hartmann-So 1989) to five- and six-toned Loloish languages such as Akha (Lewis 1973) or Lisu (La Maung Htay 2011). Roughly half of the Sino-Tibetan languages are purely pitch-based (e.g. many Chin languages, Pa'o Karen), while the other half are mixed pitch/phonation-type systems (e.g. Lisu, Sgaw Karen).

Most of the Sino-Tibetan languages spoken in MSEA are polysyllabic, largely because of a more or less opaque concatenation of monosyllabic roots and affixes. There are however many exceptions (sesquisyllabic

Burmese, [largely] monosyllabic Yue Chinese) and these languages rank among the most widely spoken.[8]

In addition to tone sandhi processes (where the surface tone realization is affected by tonal environment), which are especially common in Chinese dialects, the tone systems of many Sino-Tibetan languages display tonal alternations such as spreading, re-association, contour simplification and OCP effects more commonly associated with African tone systems (Evans 2008; Hyman 2010; Michaud 2008; Watkins 2013). Besides these strictly phonological processes, Tibeto-Burman languages often have morphophonological tonal process and grammatical tones (Henderson 1967; Hyman and Haokip 2004).

26.2.3.4 Tai-Kadai

Tai-Kadai (also Kra-Dai) languages make up another 23.1 per cent of our sample (43 languages). Tai-Kadai languages are mostly monosyllabic, although some languages have acquired sesqui- and polysyllables through borrowing from Khmer, Pali and Sanskrit and through occasional semantic bleaching of compounds. All Tai-Kadai languages in our database are tonal, with systems of four to seven tones. Seventeen of these languages (39.5 per cent) make no recorded use of voice quality, while the rest have mixed tone systems in which complex contour tones are combined with creakiness and/or glottalization. Interestingly, despite the complexity of Tai-Kadai tone inventories, no instances of tone sandhi have to our knowledge been reported in this language family.

26.2.3.5 Hmong-Mien

There are eight Hmong-Mien varieties in our sample (4.3 per cent), which reflects the fact that most of these languages are spoken in China rather than MSEA *per se*. All Hmong-Mien languages are highly tonal, having between six and eight tones. In nearly all documented cases, phonation type contrasts (modal, breathy and/or tense/creaky) are an integral part of the tone system. For example, two of the seven tones in Hmong Leng (the low checked -*m* tone and the mid-falling -*g* tone) are creaky and breathy voiced, respectively (Andruski and Ratliff 2000). The exception here appears to be Iu Mien (Bruhn 2007; L-Thongkum 1979), the only Mienic language in our sample to lack a phonation type contrast.

Tone sandhi processes are found in most Hmong-Mien languages, although they are reported to be highly variable and lexicalized (Ratliff 1987). However, tonal alternation is commonly employed for morphological purposes (word classes and compounding) as well as in ideophonic expressives such as *poob* [pɔ̰́ːŋ] 'to fall' versus *poog* [pɔ̰̀ːŋ] 'the sound of falling' (Ratliff 1987, 1992b).

---

[8] Note that Burmese also contains a large number of polysyllabic loanwords, and that Chinese languages, especially Mandarin, contain many disyllabic compounds.

Table 26.5 *Haudricourt's schematic view of Vietnamese tonogenesis. Following an initial three-way split into level, rising and falling, a subsequent two-way split, conditioned by the voicing of the initial obstruent, produced the modern six-tone system (the fourth column shows the diacritics used in Vietnamese orthography)*

BCE (no tone)	Sixth century (three tones)	Twelfth century (six tones)	Modern Vietnamese
pa	A	A1	ba
ba	(level)	A2	bà
pa?	B	B1	bá
ba?	(rising)	B2	bạ
pah	C	C1	bả
bah	(falling)	C2	bā

26.3 Tonogenesis

26.3.1 The Usual Path to Tone

For those tone languages that can be reconstructed as having a prior toneless state, it is broadly accepted that the origins of lexical tones (dubbed *tonogenesis* by Matisoff 1973) normally lie in earlier laryngeal contrasts. The now-standard tonogenetic scenario was proposed by Haudricourt (1954) in a convincing demonstration that Vietnamese is indeed an Austroasiatic language despite having a well-developed tone system (although since that time, tones have been found in a number of Austroasiatic languages). Haudricourt showed that Vietnamese underwent a two-step process of tonogenesis in which an initial three-way tone split (conditioned by laryngeal properties of the coda) was followed by a subsequent two-way split (conditioned by laryngeal properties of the onset), resulting in a system of six tones (Table 26.5). The precise phonetic outcome of the second split varies with language, but in general, voiceless onsets condition higher variants and voiced onsets lower variants; in the initial phase, final glottal stops give rise to rising tones while final aspirates have a pitch-lowering effect.

Haudricourt then applied this scenario to other languages (Haudricourt 1961) and today there is little doubt that similar two-way and/or three-way splits were involved in tonogenesis in Chinese, Tai-Kadai, Karen, Tibeto-Burman languages of Nepal (Mazaudon 2012), Tsat (Maddieson and Pang 1993) and possibly Hmong-Mien (Ratliff 2015). Furthermore, the two-way split proposed by Haudricourt seems to be the driving force in the development of register in a large number of Austroasiatic (Ferlus 1979) and Chamic (Lee 1966) languages.

Shortly after publishing his canonical scenario, Haudricourt suggested the possibility of an initial two-way split involving a crucial stage of voice quality contrast, where voiced initials induce breathiness

Table 26.6 *Examples of Hu tonogenesis from vowel length (after Svantesson 1989)*

	Hu	Lamet	
*short	jám	jąm	'to die'
	phíɲ	pi̯ɲ	'to shoot'
	θúk	khu̯k	'hair'
*long	jàm	jąam	'to cry'
	thàɲ	tąaɲ	'to weave'
	nasòk	jo̯ok	'ear'

on the following vowel, which then causes pitch lowering (Haudricourt 1965). This idea has regularly been revisited since (Diffloth 1989; Egerod 1971; Ferlus 2009; Mazaudon 2012; Pulleyblank 1978; Thurgood 2002), and while it is still unclear if breathiness is a compulsory stage in the two-way tone split, the available data certainly suggest that this is a common evolutionary trajectory. Since then, based on observations by Gage (1985), the possibility that creakiness or tenseness plays a role in the three-way split alongside the glottal stop has been proposed by Ferlus (1998) and Diffloth (1989); while the phonetic explanation to support these accounts has yet to be fully worked out, it is worth noting that a similar account has been proposed for the origin of tones in Athabaskan languages (Kingston 2005; Leer 1999).

26.3.2 Less Common Paths to Tone

Despite the prevalence of the canonical tonogenetic scenario, other types of tonogenetic mechanisms have been described for Southeast Asian languages. In the Palaungic languages U and Hu, tone is claimed to have developed from differences in vowel height and vowel length, respectively (Svantesson 1989, 1991). Table 26.6 gives examples of some Hu forms compared to those of related Lamet, demonstrating that the Hu tones are not related to the voicing of the initial consonant.

Segments other than stops and aspirates may also induce tonogenesis. In some dialects of Khmer, loss of /r/ in syllable onsets has led to an incipient tone contrast between words like /kru:/ > [kʰǔ:] 'teacher' and /kʰu:/ > [kʰu:] 'venerable' or /rien/ > [hǐen] 'to learn' and /hien/ > [hien] 'to dare' (Kirby 2014; Thạch 1999; Wayland and Guion 2005). While Thạch (1999) proposes a contact-based explanation and Wayland and Guion (2005) suggest that phonologization of F0 was conditioned by a combination of the high degree of airflow necessary for trilling and subsequent devoicing of the trill, Kirby (2014) argues that this sound change may have arisen via the perceptual reanalysis of changes in spectral balance, coupled with the coarticulatory influence of the dorsal gesture accompanying /r/.

Finally, suprasegmental contrasts may also serve as a source of lexical tone systems. Evans (2001a, 2001b) argues that certain Southern Qiang dialects developed tone systems after pitch-accent, developed from an earlier lexical stress system, was reanalysed in the wake of phonological reduction and heavy borrowing from Mandarin. While evidently uncommon in MSEA languages, this type of evolutionary trajectory is reminiscent of the probable path to tone in Germanic languages (e.g. Gussenhoven 2000).

26.4   Areality and Contact

26.4.1   Contact-induced Tonogenesis

The view that tone spread from Chinese to other languages of MSEA (Matisoff 1973; Pulleyblank 1986) is now so well-established that it is often considered as received knowledge (cf. the tonogenetic 'waves' posited by Ratliff 2002 and Mazaudon 2012). Unfortunately, in the absence of solid historical and sociophonetic data, claims about contact-induced tonogenesis, however likely they may seem, remain unproven. Even for the most likely cases of contact-induced tonogenesis in MSEA, it is difficult to decide if we are looking at accidentally parallel internal developments or at contact.

Thomason (2001: 59–60) suggests a number of conditions that should ideally be met when making a case for a contact-induced structural change. In addition to clear recipient and donor languages, a strong case will seek to establish that the feature(s) in question were present in the donor language but *not* present in the recipient language prior to contact. While these conditions may be straightforward to establish when looking at morphemes or even syntactic structures, they are surprisingly difficult to meet in the case of a phonological feature like tone. For instance, Vietnamese is often claimed (quite reasonably) to have acquired tone while under Chinese influence, but it is unclear if this development occurred as a result of this contact or simultaneously with it. The first Sino-Vietic contact probably took place in what is now northern Vietnam around the time of the Qin dynasty (second century BCE), with Chinese administrative control solidifying under the Han empire around 100 BCE (Gernet 1996; Phan 2013). Given estimates that (toneless) Old Chinese was spoken until the early centuries CE (Baxter 1992; Pulleyblank 1962, 1978; cf. Ferlus 2009) and evidence from conservative Vietic languages that maintain four-way laryngeal distinctions or tonal contour systems (Ferlus 1996), it is not implausible to assume that initial emergence of tone in Vietnamese was an internal development.

In fact, since most cases of tonogenesis in MSEA involve the same regular internal factors (i.e. loss of laryngeal codas and neutralization of onset voicing), it is in general difficult to determine if contact is really playing a role or if we are just looking at independent parallel processes (although as Thomason 2001 correctly points out, the fact that a change *can* occur through internal factors in another situation is not necessarily a valid argument for rejecting contact). In the end, as discussed by Ratliff (2002), there are only two possible scenarios for contact-induced tonogenesis (besides the adoption of loanwords with their tones): (1) two atonal languages can become tonal simultaneously as bilinguals transphonologize the same laryngeal contrasts in both languages, or (2) an atonal language can become tonal because its speakers, who are bilingual in a tonal language and thus 'tone-prone', phonologize previously allophonic pitch variation. Proving either of these scenarios after the fact is probably impossible, at least in the absence of detailed acoustic and perceptual data gathered over several generations, but this does suggest that substantive proposals of contact-induced tonogenesis would include evidence of a high level of bilingualism in at least part of the language community in question.

26.4.2   Tone as an Areal Feature

Given all this variation, then, why is tone upheld as an areal feature of MSEA languages? Put differently, what is the evidence for tone as an indicator of areality? Aikhenvald and Dixon (2001) describe a sprachbund as 'a geographically delimited area including languages from two or more language families, sharing significant traits (*which are not found in languages from these families spoken outside the area*)' (p. 11, emphasis ours). This description is not meant to be used for a single feature, but a quick look at the five MSEA language families suffices to note that tone does not bear the hallmarks of an especially 'areal' feature. While tonal Austroasiatic languages seem limited to MSEA, tonality in Austronesian languages is not limited to MSEA. Register is attested in Javanese, for example, and Tsat, a Chamic language of Hainan, is highly tonal. These languages could of course be included in a larger Southeast Asia area, but even then a number of Oceanic (Austronesian) languages of New Caledonia have also developed tone (Haudricourt 1971; Rivierre 1993). Hmong-Mien, Tai-Kadai and Sino-Tibetan are all spoken outside MSEA proper, and all of these families are highly tonal. All the Hmong-Mien languages of China have tones (and some of them are spoken so far north that it would be hard to regard them as Southeast Asian proper), as do all Tai-Kadai languages, be they spoken in southern China or in India, such as Aiton and Khamti (Morey 2005). As for Tibeto-Burman languages, many of their representatives in China, but also in the Himalayas, are tonal as well.

Of course, the criterion given by Aikhenvald and Dixon may be too restrictive for tone in MSEA. There could be areal convergence even if some of the language families were tonal before arriving in the region. However, in a recent study based on the same database of 186 languages as this chapter, we were unable to establish geographical proximity as a factor of tonal convergence independent of language family and word type (Brunelle and Kirby 2015). In the end, the real question that needs to be addressed is not why MSEA languages are so frequently tonal, but if the number of tonogenetic events in MSEA Austroasiatic and Austronesian languages in the past two millennia were higher than would have been the case if it had not been for contact.

That tone cannot unambiguously be shown to be a contact phenomenon (at least as measured by proximity) does not mean that MSEA is not a linguistic area full stop (Aikhenvald 2006; Haig 2001). Linguistic areas are not defined by any single feature, but by a cluster of features (Campbell, Chapter 2, this volume), with different features having different weights, and much of the evidence for an MSEA linguistic area is based on convergence of grammatical and lexico-semantic features. In these respects, the Austroasiatic and Austronesian languages of MSEA are rather different from their non-MSEA counterparts. Matisoff (2001) provides a lengthy, though by no means exhaustive, list of some of these shared features, as well as of phonological features other than tone relevant for the establishment of a linguistic area; see also Enfield (2005) and Donohue and Whiting (2011).

26.4.3 The Role of Word Shape in Tonogenesis

If the role of contact in tonogenesis is downplayed, however, how are we to account for the relatively high frequency of tone in MSEA? The chief alternative is to assume that multiple tonogenetic events took place more or less independently in different languages of the region. Mechanistically, this is not problematic; the universality of microprosody (intrinsic F0 or 'pitch skip'), thought to be the 'seeds' of tonogenesis, is well established (Gandour 1974; Hanson 2009; Hombert 1978; Hombert et al. 1979; House and Fairbanks 1953; Ohala 1973). This, however, raises the questions of (a) what types of pressures/conditions might cause languages to rely upon and ultimately enhance these microprosodic differences into tone systems, and (b) why the relevant conditions should have appeared in several languages at more or less the same time (like in the two-way split that seems to have occurred in Chinese, Vietnamese and Tai-Kadai around the tenth century).

It is here that contact may play a role, albeit an indirect one, in the spread of tone throughout the region. Matisoff (1973, 2001) has repeatedly emphasized the relationship between monosyllabicity and tone, a correlation that we also found in the statistical study of our database (Brunelle and Kirby 2015; cf. Donohue 2012). Is it possible that instead of a direct relationship between contact and tonality, there is a more complex causal chain in which contact with monosyllabic languages favours monosyllabization, which in turn favours tonality? In our database we find that there is a strong correlation between monosyllabicity and number of tones; as one moves to languages that retain presyllables, or morphology, one finds fewer or no tones, or word-level tones (as in many Tibeto-Burman languages). This is at least consistent with the idea that loss of segmental material makes a language increasingly 'tone-prone'.

While it seems unlikely that languages borrow the concept of monosyllabicity *per se* (much as it would be unusual to borrow a fully formed tone system), they surely borrow large numbers of lexical items. If language A is primarily sesquisyllabic and language B primarily monosyllabic, and if there exists an asymmetric prestige relationship between A and B such that A borrows more from B than vice versa, this would increase the number of monosyllabic forms in the lexicon of language A. This could have the effect of encouraging further loss of segmental material, driving the language towards a canonically monosyllabic template and increasing the likelihood of phonologizing prosodic properties such as pitch, length or voice quality. Such a trend would be even more likely if pre-existing structural factors favour monosyllabization (Brunelle and Pittayaporn 2012).

However, despite the empirical correlation between monosyllabization and tone, its mechanistic underpinnings remain unclear. One possible motivation could be driven by functional considerations. Consider the case of a sesquisyllabic language with a laryngeal contrast in final stops. If the presyllables were to reduce and eventually disappear, the burden of lexical contrast would now be borne entirely by the final laryngeal contrast, known to be perceptually fragile (Steriade 2001/2008). This fragility could increase the likelihood that previously redundant phonetic properties, such as differences in pitch or voice quality, could become enhanced (Kirby 2013), eventually transphonologizing if the cues to the segmental identity of the coda are subsequently lost (Hyman 1976). While perhaps intuitively plausible, the specifics of such an account remain to be worked out in sufficient detail to be tested experimentally.

26.5 Conclusions

In this chapter, we have reviewed the properties of tone and register systems of Mainland Southeast Asia (MSEA), describing both their synchronic diversity as well as a range of theories to account for their development. While MSEA may still earn the title of 'the ultimate Sprachbund' (Dahl 2008), the presence of 'tone' may not in and of itself constitute a particularly strong indicator of convergence. As we have seen, the tone systems of this region are extremely diverse, and it is difficult to establish unambiguous cases where tone (or register) has been spread via contact. More detailed acoustic and perceptual research on tone systems, together with longitudinal studies of speech communities, promise to enhance our understanding of the mechanisms underlying tonogenesis in MSEA and elsewhere.

References

Abercrombie, David, 1967. *Elements of General Phonetics*. Edinburgh: Edinburgh University Press.

Abramson, Arthur, Theraphan L-Thongkum and Patrick W. Nye, 2004. Voice register in Suai (Kuai): An analysis of perceptual and acoustic data. *Phonetica* 61: 147–171.

Abramson, Arthur and Theraphan L-Thongkum, 2009. A fuzzy boundary between tone languages and voice-register languages. In Gunnar Fant, Hiroya Fujisaki and Jiaxuen Shen (eds), *Frontiers in Phonetics and Speech Science*, pp. 149–155. Beijing: The Commercial Press.

Abramson, Arthur, Patrick Nye and Theraphan L-Thongkum, 2007. Voice register in Khmu': Experiments in production and perception. *Phonetica* 64: 80–104.

Adisasmito-Smith, Niken, 2004. *Phonetic Influences of Javanese on Indonesian*. PhD dissertation, Cornell University, New York.

Aikhenvald, Alexandra Y., 2006. Reflections on language contact, areal diffusion, and mechanisms of linguistic change. In Bernard Caron and Petr Zima (eds), *Sprachbund in the West African Sahel*, pp. 23–36. Louvain-Paris: Peeters.

Aikhenvald, Alexandra Y. and Robert M. W. Dixon, 2001. Introduction. In Alexandra Y. Aikhenvald and Robert M. W. Dixon (eds), *Areal Diffusion and Genetic Inheritance: Problems in Comparative Linguistics*, pp. 1–26. Oxford: Oxford University Press.

Andruski, Jean E. and Martha Ratliff, 2000. Phonation types in production of phonological tone: The case of Green Mong. *Journal of the International Phonetic Association* 30: 37–61.

Baxter, William H., 1992. *A Handbook of Old Chinese Phonology*. Berlin: Mouton de Gruyter.

Benedict, Paul, 1996. Interphyla flow in Southeast Asia. In *Pan-Asian Linguistics: Proceedings of the Fourth International Symposium on Language and Linguistics*, pp. 1579–1590. Institute of Language and Culture for Rural Development, Mahidol University.

Bradley, David, 1982. Register in Burmese. In David Bradley (ed.), *Papers in Southeast Asian Linguistics, no. 8: Tonation*, pp. 117–132. Canberra: Pacific Linguistics.

Bruhn, Daniel, 2007. The phonetic inventory of Iu-Mien. Manuscript, University of California, Berkeley. http://linguistics.berkeley.edu /~dwbruhn/dwbruhn_iu-mien.pdf

Brunelle, Marc, 2005. *Register in Eastern Cham: Phonetic, Phonological and Sociolinguistic Approaches*. PhD dissertation, Cornell University, New York.

Brunelle, Marc, 2006. A phonetic study of Eastern Cham register. In Paul Sidwell and Anthony Grant (eds), *Chamic and Beyond*, pp. 1–36. Canberra: Pacific Linguistics.

Brunelle, Marc, 2009. Tone perception in Northern and Southern Vietnamese. *Journal of Phonetics* 37 (1): 79–96.

Brunelle, Marc, 2010. The role of larynx height in the Javanese tense ~ lax stop contrast. In Raphael Mercado, Eric Potsdam and Lisa de Mena Travis (eds), *Austronesian and Theoretical Linguistics*, pp. 7–23. Amsterdam: John Benjamins.

Brunelle, Marc, 2012. Dialect experience and perceptual integrality in phonological registers: Fundamental frequency, voice quality and the first formant in Cham. *Journal of the Acoustical Society of America* 131 (4): 3088–3102.

Brunelle, Marc and Joshua Finkeldey, 2011. Tone perception in Sgaw Karen. In *Proceedings of the 16th International Congress of Phonetic Sciences*, pp. 372–375.

Brunelle, Marc and James Kirby, 2015. Re-assessing tonal diversity and geographical convergence in Mainland Southeast Asia In Bernard Comrie and Nick Enfield (eds), *Languages of Mainland Southeast Asia: The State of the Art*, pp. 82–110. Berlin: Mouton de Gruyter.

Brunelle, Marc and Pittayawat Pittayaporn, 2012. Phonologically-constrained change: The role of the foot in monosyllabization and rhythmic shifts in Mainland Southeast Asia. *Diachronica* 29 (4): 411–433.

Chirkova, Ekaterina and Yiya Chen, 2013. Lizu. *Journal of the International Phonetic Association* 43 (1): 75–86.

Clements, Nick, Alexis Michaud and Cédric Patin, 2011. Do we need tone features? In Elisabeth Hume, John Goldsmith and W. Leo Wetzels (eds), *Tones and Features*, pp. 3–24. Berlin: Mouton de Gruyter.

Conver, Lynn C., 1999. A sketch of the phonology of a Lamet dialect. *Mon-Khmer Studies*, 29: 35–56.

Dahl, Östen, 2008. An exercise in *a posteriori* language sampling. *Sprachtypologie und Universalienforschung* 61: 208–220.

DiCanio, Christian T., 2009. The phonetics of register in Takhian Thong Chong. *Journal of the International. Phonetic Association* 39 (2): 162–188.

DiCanio, Christian T., 2012. Coarticulation between tone and glottal consonants in Itunyoso Trique. *Journal of Phonetics* 40 (1): 162–176.

Diffloth, Gérard, 1982. Registres, dévoisement, timbre vocalique: Leur histoire en katouique. *Mon-Khmer Studies* 11: 47–82

Diffloth, Gérard, 1989. Proto-Austroasiatic creaky voice. *Mon-Khmer Studies* 15: 139–154.

Diffloth, Gérard, 2005. The contribution of linguistic palaeontology and Austro-Asiatic. In Laurent Sagart, Roger Blench and Alicia Sanchez-Mazas (eds), *The Peopling of East Asia: Putting Together Archaeology, Linguistics and Genetics*, pp. 77–80. London: Routledge Curzon.

Ding, Picus S., 2001. The pitch-accent system of Niuwozi Prinmi. *Linguistics of the Tibeto-Burman Area* 24 (2): 57–83.

Ding, Picus S., 2006. A typological study of tonal systems of Japan and Prinmi: Towards a definition of pitch-accent languages. *Journal of Language Universals* 7 (2): 1–35.

Donohue, Mark, 2012. The shape and spread of tone. In Cathryn Donohue, Shunichi Ishihara and William Steed (eds), *Quantitative Approaches to Problems in Linguistics: Studies in Honor of Phil Rose*, pp. 9–20. Munich: LINCOM Europa.

Donohue, Mark and Bronwen Whiting, 2011. Quantifying areality: A study of prenasalisation in Southeast Asia and New Guinea. *Linguistic Typology* 15 (1): 101–121.

Edmondson, Jerold A., 2010. The Kháng language of Vietnam in comparison to Ksingmul (Xinh-mun). In Kenneth A. McElhanon and Gerard P. Reesink (eds), *A Mosaic of Languages and Cultures: Studies Celebrating the Career of Karl J. Franklin*, pp. 138–154. Dallas, TX: SIL International.

Edmondson, Jerold A., John Esling, Jimmy G. Harris, Li Shaoni and Lama Ziwo, 2001. The aryepiglottic folds and voice quality in the Yi and Bai languages: Laryngoscopic case studies. *Mon-Khmer Studies* 31: 83–100.

Egerod, Søren C., 1971. Phonation types in Chinese and South East Asian languages. *Acta Linguistica Hafniensia* 13 (2): 159–172.

Enfield, Nicholas J., 2005. Areal linguistics and mainland Southeast Asia. *Annual Review of Anthropology* 34: 181–206.

Enfield, Nicholas J., 2011. Linguistic diversity in mainland Southeast Asia. In Nicholas J. Enfield (ed.), *Dynamics of Human Diversity*, pp. 63–79. Canberra: Pacific Linguistics.

Enfield, Nicholas J. and Gérard Diffloth, 2009. Phonology and sketch grammar of Kri, a Vietic language of Laos. *Cahiers de Linguistique – Asie Orientale* 38 (1): 3–69.

Evans, Jonathan P., 2001a. Contact-induced tonogenesis in Southern Qiang. *Language and Linguistics* 2 (2): 63–110.

Evans, Jonathan P., 2001b. *Introduction to Qiang Phonology and Lexicon: Synchrony and Diachrony*. Tokyo: ILCAA, Tokyo University of Foreign Studies.

Evans, Jonathan P., 2008. 'African' tone in the Sinosphere. *Language and Linguistics* 9 (3): 463–490.

Fagan, Joel L., 1988. Javanese intervocalic stop phonemes. *Studies in Austronesian Linguistics* 76: 173–202.

Ferlus, Michel, 1979. Formation des registres et mutations consonantiques dans les langues mon-khmer. *Mon-Khmer Studies* 8: 1–76.

Ferlus, Michel, 1996. Langues et peuples viet-muong. *Mon-Khmer Studies* 26: 7–28.

Ferlus, Michel, 1998. Les systèmes de tons dans les langues viet-muong. *Diachronica* 15 (1): 1–27.

Ferlus, Michel, 2004. The origin of tones in Viet-Muong. In Somsonge Burusphat (ed.), *Papers from the Eleventh Meeting of the Southeast Asian Linguistic Society*, pp. 297–313. Tempe, AZ: Arizona State University, Program for Southeast Asian Studies.

Ferlus, Michel, 2009. What were the four divisions of Middle Chinese? *Diachronica* 26 (2): 184–213.

Gage, William W., 1985. Glottal stops and Vietnamese tonogenesis. In Veneeta Z. Acson and Richard L. Leed (eds), *Oceanic Linguistics Special Publications*, no. 20: *For Gordon H. Fairbanks*, pp. 21–36. Honolulu: University of Hawai'i Press.

Gandour, Jack, 1974. Consonant types and tone in Siamese. *Journal of Phonetics* 2: 337–350.

Gandour, Jack, 1983. Tone perception in Far Eastern languages. *Journal of Phonetics* 11: 149–175.

Gernet, Jacques, 1996. *A History of Chinese Civilization*. Cambridge Cambridge University Press.

Gregerson, Kenneth J., 1976. Tongue-root and register in Mon-Khmer. In Philip N. Jenner, Laurence C. Thompson and Stanley Starosta (eds), *Austroasiatic Studies*, pp. 323–370. Honolulu: University of Hawai'i Press.

Gruber, James, 2011. *An Articulatory, Acoustic, and Auditory Study of Burmese Tone*. PhD thesis, Georgetown University, Washington, DC.

Gussenhoven, Carlos, 2000. On the origin and development of the Central Franconian tone contrast. In Aditi Lahiri (ed.), *Analogy, Leveling, and Markedness*, pp. 215–260. Berlin: Mouton de Gruyter.

Haig, Geoffrey, 2001. Linguistic diffusion in present-day Anatolia: From top to bottom. In Alexandra Y. Aikhenvald and Robert M. W. Dixon (eds), *Areal Diffusion and Genetic Inheritance: Problems in Comparative Linguistics*, pp. 195–224. Oxford: Oxford University Press.

Hanson, H. M., 2009. Effects of obstruent consonants on fundamental frequency at vowel onset in English. *Journal of the Acoustical Society of America* 125 (1): 425–441.

Hartmann-So, Helga, 1989. Morphophonemic changes in Daai Chin. *Linguistics of the Tibeto-Burman Area* 12 (2): 51–65.

Haudricourt, André-Georges, 1954. De l'origine des tons en viêtnamien. *Journal Asiatique* 242: 69–82.

Haudricourt, André-Georges, 1961. Bipartition et tripartition des systèmes de tons dans quelques langues d'Extrême-Orient. *Bulletin de la Société de Linguistique de Paris* 56 (1): 163–180.

Haudricourt, André-Georges, 1965. Les mutations consonantiques des occlusives initiales en mon-khmer. *Bulletin de la Société de Linguistique de Paris* 60 (1): 160–172.

Haudricourt, André-Georges, 1971. New Caledonia and the Loyalty Islands. In Thomas A. Sebeok (ed.), *Current Trends in Linguistics*, vol. 8: *Linguistics in Oceania*, pp. 359–396. The Hague: Mouton.

Henderson, Eugénie J. A., 1952. The main features of Cambodian pronunciation. *Bulletin of the School of Oriental Studies* 17: 140–174.

Henderson, Eugénie J. A., 1965. The topography of certain phonetic and morphological characteristics of South East Asian languages. *Lingua* 15: 400–434.

Henderson, Eugénie J. A., 1967. Grammar and tone in South-East Asian languages. *Wissenschaftliche Zeitschrift der Karl-Marx Universität Leipzig* 16 (1/2): 171–178.

Henderson, Eugénie J. A., 1979. Bwe Karen as a two-tone language? In Nguyen Dang Liem (ed.), *South-East Asian Linguistic Studies*, vol. 3, pp. 301–326. Canberra: Pacific Linguistics.

Hildebrandt, Kristine A., 2007. Tone in Tibeto-Burman languages: Typological and sociolinguistic approaches. In Matti Miestamo and Bernhard Wälchli (eds), *New Trends in Typology: Young Typologists' Contributions to Linguistic Theory*, pp. 67–90. Berlin: Mouton de Gruyter.

Hombert, Jean-Marie, 1977. Development of tones from vowel height? *Journal of Phonetics* 5: 9–16.

Hombert, Jean-Marie, 1978. Consonant types, vowel quality, and tone. In Victoria A. Fromkin (ed.), *Tone: A Linguistic Survey*, pp. 77–111. New York: Academic Press.

Hombert, Jean-Marie, John J. Ohala and William G. Ewan, 1979. Phonetic explanations for the development of tones. *Language* 55 (1): 37–58.

House, Arthur S. and Grant Fairbanks, 1953. The influence of consonant environment upon the secondary acoustical characteristics of vowels. *Journal of the Acoustical Society of America* 25: 105–113.

Huffman, Franklin E., 1976. The register problem in fifteen Mon-Khmer languages. In Philip N. Jenner, Laurence C. Thompson and Stanley Starosta (eds), *Austroasiatic Studies*, part I, pp. 575–589. Honolulu: University of Hawai'i Press.

van der Hulst, Harry, 2011. Pitch-accent systems. In Marc van Oostendorp, Colin J. Ewan, Elisabeth Hume and Keren Rice (eds), *The Blackwell Companion to Phonology*, vol. 2, pp. 1003–1027. Malden, MA: Wiley-Blackwell.

Hyman, Larry M., 1976. Phonologization. In Alphonse G. Julliand (ed.), *Linguistic Studies Offered to Joseph Greenberg on the Occasion of his Sixtieth Birthday*, vol. 2, pp. 407–418. Saratoga: Anma Libri.

Hyman, Larry M., 2006. Word prosodic typology. *Phonology* 23: 225–257.

Hyman, Larry M., 2009. How (not) to do phonological typology: The case of pitch-accent. *Language Sciences* 31: 213–238.

Hyman, Larry M., 2010. Kuki-Thaadow: An African tone system in Southeast Asia. In Franck Floricic (ed.), *Essais de typologie et de linguistique générale*, pp. 31–51. Lyon, France: Les Presses de l'Ecole Normale Supérieure.

Hyman, Larry M. and Thien Haokip, 2004. *Kuki-Thaadow Grammar* (draft). http://linguistics.berkeley.edu/person/19

Hyslop, Gwendolyn, 2009. Kurtöp tone: A tonogenetic case study. *Lingua* 119: 827–845.

Jenner, Philip N., 1974. The development of registers in Standard Khmer. In Nguyen Dang Liem (ed.), *South-East Asian Linguistic Studies*, vol. 1, pp. 47–60. Canberra: Pacific Linguistics.

Jones, Robert B., 1986. Pitch register languages. In John McCoy and Timothy Light (eds), *Contributions to Sino-Tibetan Studies*, pp. 135–143. Leiden: Brill.

Kingston, John, 2005. The phonetics of Athabaskan tonogenesis. In Sharon Hargus and Keren Rice (eds), *Athabaskan Prosody*, pp. 137–184. Amsterdam: John Benjamins.

Kirby, James, 2010. Dialect experience in Vietnamese tone perception. *Journal of the Acoustical Society of America* 127 (6): 3749–3757.

Kirby, James, 2013. The role of probabilistic enhancement in phonologization. In Alan C. L. Yu (ed.), *Origins of Sound Change: Approaches to Phonologization*, pp. 228–246. Oxford: Oxford University Press.

Kirby, James, 2014. Incipient tonogenesis in Phnom Penh Khmer: Acoustic and perceptual studies. *Journal of Phonetics* 43: 69–85.

L-Thongkum, Theraphan, 1979. The distribution of the sounds of Bruu. *Mon-Khmer Studies* 8: 221–293.

L-Thongkum, Theraphan, 1988. Another look at the register distinction in Mon. In Cholticha Bamroongraks, Wilaiwan Khanittanan and Laddawan Permch (eds), *The International Symposium on Language and Linguistics*, pp. 22–51. Bangkok: Thammasat University.

L-Thongkum, Theraphan and Intajamornrak Chommanad, 2008. Tonal evolution induced by language contact: A case study of the T'in (Lua') language of Nan province, northern Thailand. *Mon-Khmer Studies* 38: 57–68.

La Maung Htay, 2011. *A Sociolinguistic Survey of Three Lisu Dialects*. MA thesis, Payap University, Chiang Mai, Thailand.

Ladefoged, Peter, 1971. *Preliminaries to Linguistic Phonetics*. Chicago: University of Chicago Press.

Ladefoged, Peter and Ian Maddieson, 1996. *The Sounds of the World's Languages*. Oxford: Blackwell.

Laver, John, 1980. *Phonetic Description of Voice Quality*. Cambridge: Cambridge University Press.

Lee, Ernest W., 1966. *Proto-Chamic Phonological Word and Vocabulary*. PhD dissertation, Indiana University.

Lee, Ernest W., 1998. The contribution of Cat Gia Roglai to Chamic. In David Thomas (ed.), *Papers in Southeast Asian Linguistic Studies,* no. 15: *Further Chamic Studies*, pp. 31–54. Canberra: Pacific Linguistics.

Leer, Jeff, 1999. Tonogenesis in Athabaskan. In Shigeki Kaji (ed.), *Cross-linguistic Studies of Tonal Phenomena, Tonogenesis, Typology, and Related Topics*, pp. 37–66. Tokyo: Institute of the Study of the Languages and Cultures of Asia and Africa, Tokyo University of Foreign Studies.

Lehiste, Ilse, 1970. *Suprasegmentals*. Cambridge, MA: The MIT Press.

Lewis, Paul W., 1973. Tone in the Akha language. *Anthropological Linguistics* 15: 183–188.

Lindell, Kristina, Jan-Olof Svantesson and Damrong Tayanin, 1978. Two dialects of the Romeet (Lamet) language. *Cahiers de linguistique Asie Orientale* 4: 5–22.

Lisker, Leigh, 1986. 'Voicing' in English: A catalogue of acoustic features signaling /b/ versus /p/ in trochees. *Language and Speech* 29: 3–11.

Luce, Gordon H., undated. Draft letter, incomplete, addressee not indicated (to Henderson?), concerning analysis of Riang tones and grammar. Luce Collection, MS 6574-7, 050a-b. National Library of Australia.

Maddieson, Ian, 1978. Universals of tone. In Joseph H. Greenberg, Charles A. Ferguson and Edith A. Moravcsik (eds), *Universals of Human Language*, vol. 2: *Phonology*, pp. 335–363. Stanford, CA: Stanford University Press.

Maddieson, Ian, 2011. Tone. In Matthew S. Dryer and Martin Haspelmath (eds), *The World Atlas of Language Structures Online*, chapter 13. Munich: Max Planck Digital Library. http://wals.info/chapter/13

Maddieson, Ian and Keng-Fong Pang, 1993. Tone in Utsat. In Jerold A. Edmondson and Kenneth J. Gregerson (eds), *Tonality in Austronesian Languages*, pp. 91–106. Honolulu: University of Hawai'i Press.

Maspero, Henri, 1912. Etudes sur la phonétique historique de la langue annamite: Les initiales. *Bulletin de l'École française d'Extrême-Orient* 12: 1–124.

Matisoff, James, 1973. Tonogenesis in Southeast Asia. In Larry Hyman (ed.), *Consonant Types and Tone*, pp. 71–95. Los Angeles: Linguistics Program, University of Southern California.

Matisoff, James, 2001. Genetic versus contact relationship: Prosodic diffusability in South-East Asian languages. In Alexandra Y. Aikhenvald and Robert M. W. Dixon (eds), *Areal Diffusion and Genetic Inheritance: Problems in Comparative Linguistics*, pp. 291–327. Oxford: Oxford University Press.

Mazaudon, Martine, 1973. *Phonologie du Tamang*. Langues et Civilisations à Tradition Orale, vol. 4. Paris: SELAF.

Mazaudon, Martine, 2012. Paths to tone in the Tamang branch of Tibeto-Burman (Nepal). In Gunther de Vogalaer and Guido Seiler (eds), *The Dialect Laboratory: Dialects as a Testing Ground for Theories of Language Change*, pp. 139–177. Amsterdam and Philadelphia: John Benjamins.

Mazaudon, Martine and Alexis Michaud, 2008. Tonal contrasts and initial consonants: A case study of Tamang, a 'missing link' in tonogenesis. *Phonetica* 65: 231–256.

Michaud, Alexis, 2004. Final consonants and glottalization: New perspectives from Hanoi Vietnamese. *Phonetica* 61 (2/3): 119–146.

Michaud, Alexis, 2006. Tonal reassociation and rising tonal contours in Naxi. *Linguistics of the Tibeto-Burman Area* 29 (1): 61–94.

Michaud, Alexis, 2008. Phonemic and tonal analysis of Yongning Na. *Cahiers de Linguistique – Asie Orientale* 37 (2): 159–196.

Michaud, Alexis, 2013. Studying level-tone systems in Asia: The case of the Naish languages. Paper presented at the International Conference on Phonetics of the Languages in China (ICPLC-2013), City University of Hong Kong, 2–4 December 2013.

Michaud, Alexis and He Xueguang, 2007. Reassociated tones and coalescent syllables in Naxi (Tibeto-Burman). *Journal of the International Phonetic Association* 37 (3): 237–255.

Morey, Stephen, 2005. *The Tai Languages of Assam: A Grammar and Texts.* Canberra: Pacific Linguistics.

Mundhenk, Alice T. and Hella E. Goschnick, 1977. Haroi phonemes. In David Thomas (ed.), *Papers in Southeast Asian Linguistics,* no. 4: *Chamic Studies,* pp. 1–16. Canberra: Pacific Linguistics.

Narumol, Charoenma, 1982. The phonologies of a Lampang Lamet and Wiang Papao Lua. *Mon-Khmer Studies* 11: 35–45.

Naw Say Bay, 1995. The phonology of the Dung dialect of Moken. In David Bradley (ed.), *Papers in Southeast Asian Linguistics,* no. 13: *Studies in Burmese Languages*, pp. 193–205. Canberra: Pacific Linguistics.

Nguyễn Văn Lợi, 1993. *Tiếng Rục.* Hanoi: Nhà xuất bản Khoa học xã hội [Social Sciences Publishing House].

Nguyễn Văn Lợi and Jerold Edmondson, 1997. Tones and voice quality in modern northern Vietnamese: Instrumental case studies. *Mon-Khmer Studies* 28: 1–18.

Nicolson, Beth, 2000. The Nung An language of Vietnam: Stepchild or aberrant son? In *The Fifth International Symposium on Languages and Linguistics*, pp. 266–295. Vietnam National University, Ho Chi Minh City University of Social Sciences and Humanities.

Ohala, John J., 1973. The physiology of tone. In Larry M. Hyman (ed.), *Consonant Types and Tone*, pp. 1–14. Los Angeles: Linguistics Program, University of Southern California.

Pham, Andrea, 2003. *Vietnamese Tone: A New Analysis.* New York: Routledge.

Phan, John D., 2013. *Lacquered Words: The Evolution of Vietnamese under Sinitic Influences from the First Century BCE through the Seventeenth Century CE.* PhD dissertation, Cornell University, New York.

Pike, Kenneth L., 1948. *Tone Languages.* Ann Arbor, MI: The University of Michigan Press.

Premsrirat, Suwilai, 2001. Tonogenesis in Khmu dialects of SEA. *Mon-Khmer Studies* 31: 47–56.

Pulleyblank, Edwin G., 1962. The consonantal system of Old Chinese. *Asia Major, Series* 2 (9): 58–144, 206–265.

Pulleyblank, Edwin G., 1978. The nature of the Middle Chinese tones and their development to early Mandarin. *Journal of Chinese Linguistics* 6: 173–203.

Pulleyblank, Edwin G., 1986. Tonogenesis as an index of areal relationships in East Asia. *Linguistics of the Tibeto-Burman Area* 19 (1): 65–82.

Ratliff, Martha, 1987. Tone sandhi compounding in White Hmong. *Linguistics of the Tibeto-Burman Area* 10 (2): 71–105.

Ratliff, Martha, 1992a. Grammar and tone in Asian languages. In *The Third International Symposium on Language and Linguistics, Bangkok, Thailand*, pp. 1064–1078. Bangkok: Chulalongkorn University.

Ratliff, Martha, 1992b. *Meaningful Tone: A Study of Tonal Morphology in Compounds, Form Classes and Expressive Phrases in White Hmong*. Dekalb, IL: Northern Illinois University Press.

Ratliff, Martha, 2002. Timing tonogenesis: Evidence from borrowing. *Berkeley Linguistics Society* 28: 29–41.

Ratliff, Martha, 2015. Tonoexodus, tonogenesis, and tone change. In Patrick Honeybone and Joseph Salmons (eds), *The Oxford Handbook of Historical Phonology*, pp. 245–261. Oxford: Oxford University Press.

Rivierre, Jean-Claude, 1993. Tonogenesis in New Caledonia. In Jerold A. Edmondson and Kenneth J. Gregerson (eds), *Tonality in Austronesian Languages*, pp. 155–173. Honolulu: University of Hawai'i Press.

Sidwell, Paul, 2013. Issues in Austroasiatic classification. *Language and Linguistics Compass* 7 (8): 437–457.

Sidwell, Paul and Roger Blench, 2011. The Austroasiatic Urheimat: The Southeastern Riverine Hypothesis. In Nicholas J. Enfield (ed.), *Dynamics of Human Diversity*, pp. 1–30. Canberra: Pacific Linguistics.

Steriade, Donca, 2001/2008. The phonology of perceptibility effects: The P-map and its consequences for constraint organization. In Kristin Hanson and Sharon Inkelas (eds), *The Nature of the Word: Studies in Honor of Paul Kiparsky*, pp. 151–179. Cambridge, MA: The MIT Press.

Svantesson, Jan-Olof, 1983. *Kammu Phonology and Morphology*. Travaux de L'Institut de Linguistique de Lund, vol. 18. Malmö: CWK Gleerup.

Svantesson, Jan-Olof, 1988. U. *Linguistics of the Tibeto-Burman Area* 11: 64–133.

Svantesson, Jan-Olof, 1989. Tonogenetic mechanisms in Northern Mon-Khmer. *Phonetica* 46: 60–79.

Svantesson, Jan-Olof, 1991. Hu: A language with unorthodox tonogenesis. In Jeremy H. C. S. Davidson (ed.), *Austroasiatic Languages: Essays in Honour of H. L. Shorto*, pp. 67–79. London: SOAS.

Thạch Ngọc Minh, 1999. Monosyllabization in Kiengiang Khmer. *Mon-Khmer Studies* 29: 81–95.

Thomason, Sarah G., 2001. *Language Contact: An Introduction*. Edinburgh: University of Edinburgh Press.

Thurgood, Ela, 2004. Phonation types in Javanese. *Oceanic Linguistics* 43 (2): 277–295.

Thurgood, Graham, 2002. Vietnamese tone: Revising the model and the analysis. *Diachronica* 19 (2): 333–363.

Uhlenbeck, Eugenius M., 1964. *A Critical Survey of Studies on the Languages of Java and Madura*. The Hague: Nijhoff.

Vũ Thang Phương, 1981. *The Acoustic and Perceptual Nature of Tone in Vietnamese*. PhD dissertation, Australian National University.

Watkins, Justin, 2001. Burmese. *Journal of the International Phonetic Association* 31: 291–295.

Watkins, Justin, 2013. A first look at tone in Myebon Sumtu Chin. *SOAS Working Papers in Linguistics* 16: 79–104.

Watson, Richard L., 1996. Why three phonologies for Pacoh? *Mon-Khmer Studies* 26: 197–205.

Wayland, Ratree and Allard Jongman, 2001. Chanthaburi Khmer vowels: Phonetic and phonemic analyses. *Mon-Khmer Studies* 31: 65–82.

Wayland, Ratree and Allard Jongman, 2002. Registrogenesis in Khmer: A phonetic account. *Mon-Khmer Studies* 32: 101–115.

Wayland, Ratree and Susan A. Guion, 2005. Sound changes following the loss of /r/ in Khmer: A new tonogenetic mechanism? *Mon-Khmer Studies* 35: 55–82.

Yip, Moira, 2002. *Tone*. Cambridge: Cambridge University Press.

27

The Areal Linguistics of Australia

Luisa Miceli and Alan Dench

27.1 Introduction

Australian languages are particularly interesting from the point of view of areal linguistics as there is little consensus on which historical processes are responsible for the current distribution of shared features. The mainstream interpretation is that much of the similarity reflects genetic relationship – retentions of considerable time depth of widespread features, or more recent common innovations in a subgroup of languages when confined to a region (see Koch 2014 for a review). The picture is undeniably complex due to the large number of languages involved (at least 250 at the time of European colonization[1]) over a small population,[2] and also due to the fact that indigenous societies were often highly multilingual, with as many as four to six languages spoken within a group.

This chapter aims to present an overview of the difficulties involved in interpreting the history of these languages, whether on the wide or small scale. Section 27.2 deals with the macro-scale picture while Section 27.3 presents a regional case study. Section 27.4 argues that similar difficulties are in fact encountered at both levels of analysis, and that the same 'overall' comparative pattern emerges regardless of scope. This pattern is characterized by a 'mismatch' between structure and form, and is highly suggestive of unbroken transmission unfolding in a multilingual context – which is indeed the kind of sociolinguistic setting we can assume to have been in place for much of Australia. For language histories of this type, the internal/external distinction is problematic since the usual theoretical assumptions do not hold. In a speech community that is mostly bilingual, speaker-internal motivations for

---

[1] Research by Bowern suggests that this figure may be considerably higher, exceeding 360. Her updated language list can be accessed at pamanyungan.sites.yale.edu/master-list-australian-languages-v12.
[2] Koch and Nordlinger (2014b) cite an estimate of around one million.

change are not necessarily also language-internal. Current theory there-fore provides few answers on how to interpret language relationships in a historical context of this type, so it is not surprising that there is a lack of consensus among Australianists. The final paragraph of the chapter summarizes previous discussion and outlines possible directions for future research.

27.2 Macro-level Patterns

Australian languages show a number of recurrent similarities.[3] The degree of similarity in phonemic inventories is particularly remarkable (Busby 1980), as is a similarity in the constraints on permissible phonotactic patterns (Dixon 1980; Hamilton 1996) and of patterns of prosody (Baker 2014). We also find recurrence of similar patterns of semantic structure (Evans and Wilkins 2000; Dench 1997; see Gaby and Singer 2014 for a recent overview) and a number of short forms, both lexical and gramma-tical, that have widespread distribution. It is therefore not surprising that there is a longstanding assumption that Australian languages must all be ultimately related. Furthermore, a large subset of languages (about three-quarters of the total number) shares a more extensive set of similarities. There are widespread lexical forms for around 200 concepts confined to this group, these languages are of the suffixing type[4] and they lack num-ber-segmentable non-singular pronouns typical of northern languages. The received view is that they constitute a language family known as Pama-Nyungan (see Map 27.1) – though some treat it as a subgroup of the larger assumed Australian family/phylum. The remaining languages have been grouped into 24 separate language families, some of which are thought possibly to share a more recent common ancestor than the assumed Proto-Australian. Despite the existence of obvious similarities. it is surprisingly difficult to support most hypotheses of genetic relation-ship with the kind of evidence that is expected to emerge when languages are related as a family.

That the Australian comparative pattern is unusual was already being discussed at the time of publication of O'Grady, Voegelin and Voegelin's (1966) lexicostatistical study that provides the general classificatory schema still in general use today. The problem lies in the lack of phonolo-gical differentiation given the densities of cognates (in the lexicostatistical

---

[3] Dixon (2002) assumes areality for the majority of recurrent features. The reader is referred to this work for a detailed discussion of the geographical distribution of such features. For a more succinct overview see also Dixon (2001); his Table 1 (2001: 67–69) lists 23 of these recurrent features that have very widespread distribution – many of these being found in over 70 per cent of Australian languages.

[4] An important parameter of variation in Australia involves the position of morphological markers relative to the root/stem. Some languages use suffixes only (and all but one of the languages currently classified as Pama-Nyungan belong to this typological group), some use both prefixes and suffixes.

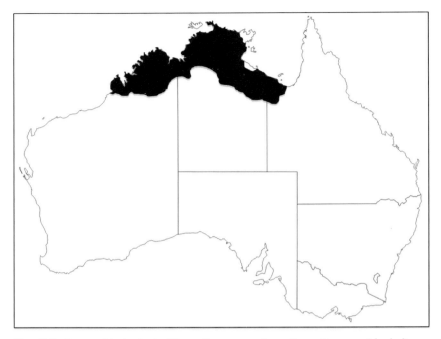

Map 27.1 Geographical extent of Pama-Nyungan and non-Pama-Nyungan (shaded) languages

sense) observed. Voegelin et al. (1963) explain that Pama-Nyungan, which they classify as the largest family in the Australian phylum, has a cognate density more like that of a phylum in other parts of the world, and that this is then inconsistent with the degree of phonological differentiation, which matches that of the least differentiated families in their worldwide sample. For this reason, and in order to avoid being 'misleading' (O'Grady et al. 1966: 11), they adapt the classificatory labels used in the Australian case: the Australian phylum is referred to as a macro-phylum, families like Pama-Nyungan are 'phylum-like language families', and the label 'family-like language' is used in those cases where dialects of the same language display similar cognate densities to a language family elsewhere. So, when looking at Australian data there is a constant feeling that a greater time depth must be involved than the near-identical form of potential cognate items implies.[5]

A potential explanation for the poverty of phonological diversity lies in the nature of the typical Australian segment inventory, which is cross-linguistically unusual; see Miceli (2015a: 718–720) for a summary. Going against global trends, Australian languages have twice as many sonorants

---

[5] Note here that we are careful to distinguish the use of the term 'cognate' as used in lexicostatistical studies (similar forms with similar meaning) from its more precise sense used in comparative reconstruction (forms derived from a single reconstructable ancestor form). The two senses – 'potential cognate' and 'cognate' – are, unfortunately, not always distinguished in the Australianist literature.

as obstruents. Butcher (2012) describes the system as 'long and thin' because, very often, five places of articulation are distinguished but there is no manner or voicing contrast. This over-reliance on place of articulation results in phonemic contrasts that are often acoustically subtle, with the most important spectral cues occurring in VC transitions. Butcher (2012) argues that this may inhibit speakers from partaking in cross-linguistically common connected speech processes such as anticipatory assimilation since such consonants are in prosodically strong positions; see also Butcher and Fletcher (2014) and Baker (2014). Furthermore, Round's (2013) investigation of dynamic features of Australian phonologies suggests that the most widespread morphophonological alternations occurring in Australian languages, such as those that involve the lenition of stops to glides or zero, actually imply changes that would have a stabilizing or reinforcing influence on the static phonological patterns described above (Miceli and Round 2014). Miceli and Round (2014) argue that, given their typical shape, Pama-Nyungan roots comprised segments not prone to the most typical Australian sound changes. It follows that the near-identical forms we see in the comparative data do not necessarily imply shallow time depth.

Nevertheless, this poverty of sound change remains problematic – regardless of whether or not an explanation can be provided. This is because demonstrations of cognacy, which allow us to identify those features that are shared as a result of inheritance, rely heavily on the presence of sound change. Although not usually explicitly specified, it is crucial that a significant number of the regular sound correspondences that we identify via application of the comparative method involve *non-identical* sounds (see Miceli and Round 2014). This is because only regular, non-identical sound correspondences demonstrate the persistence of a system – that the phonology, word forms (including any associated morphology) and semantics of the languages involved are linked and have been transmitted as a whole. Identical/near-identical correspondences can also arise between languages that have borrowed heavily from each other. The crucial importance of *non-identical* lexical correspondences is partly obscured by the fact that both types of correspondence occur in all language families. However, in well-established language families, the predominance of non-identical lexical correspondences makes it possible for the comparativist to be confident in assuming that identical lexical correspondences must also reflect inheritance. In cases where lexical correspondences are all (near)-identical, there is no subset of words that allows such an assumption to be made, and as a result arguments of proposed cognacy are considerably weaker. Miceli and Round (2014) present Pama-Nyungan as an extreme case of such a situation.

Due to the fact that morphemes/words are either very similar or completely different, many Australianists have proceeded to do comparisons of pronouns and other items in paradigmatic relationships, on the basis of formal and functional similarity, relying on the assumption that such morphology is more resistant to borrowing and that shared irregularities in paradigms must reflect inheritance (see papers in Evans 2003 for examples). Campbell and Poser (2008: 160) point out that Australian reconstructions are therefore not reconstructions in the traditional sense. They write: 'Australianists call what they see in common in this kind of superficial morphological comparison a "reconstruction", even though this notion of reconstruction is not what scholars outside the Australian field do in comparative reconstruction ... *such a procedure is unlikely to convince outsiders*' (emphasis ours). Furthermore, detailed studies such as that presented below give us an interesting insight into how different paradigms may have a life of their own, with different reconstructed paradigms suggesting alternative groupings of languages. We must therefore be cautious with genetic hypotheses that stand solely on the basis of this type of evidence.

Dixon has tried to resolve the problems encountered in doing comparative diachronic work on Australian languages by taking a very different approach. While in his first extensive study on the topic (Dixon 1980) he presented a number of reconstructions attributed to Proto-Australian, he has since written the following about his attempts at reconstruction (Dixon 2002: xvii–xviii):

> There was, we assumed, likely to have been an ancestor language, proto-Australian. LoA [Dixon 1980] was the first serious attempt to put forward a hypothesis concerning proto-Australian. But the procedure was flawed ... The method was selective; by comparing similar paradigms in a number of languages, I reconstructed proto-paradigms, which were certainly sound and valid with respect to the data employed. However, they did not justify the label proto-Australian.

He has proposed an alternative model to explain how languages are likely to be related. Passages such as the one just quoted, and further comments on the ease of applying the comparative method to Amazonian languages in comparison to work on Australian languages, reveal that the unusual comparative pattern is his main motivation for seeking an alternative model – and this motivation is quite justifiable. Unfortunately, this quite valid motivation has been overshadowed by the model itself.

Dixon (1997, 2001) explains what he sees as a lack of evidence for an articulated family tree in terms of an adapted version of the *punctuated equilibrium* model (Eldredge and Gould 1972). The main premise of this model is that for much of human history peoples and languages have been in a state of equilibrium, occasionally disrupted by punctuation events. Language splitting events, as modelled in family trees, are the outcome of periods of punctuation, when settlement patterns are disrupted and languages spread. During periods of equilibrium, there are no major changes to settlement patterns, neighbouring languages borrow back and forth from each other and converge, so that evidence of tree-like relationships is slowly erased. Dixon says that on the basis of the evidence available, Australia is best understood as a linguistic area of great time depth resulting from a long period of equilibrium. He argues that following the initial population dispersal at time of colonization, there would have been no other major punctuation events until the period of European colonization, making Australia the only part of the world where the effects of a long period of equilibrium are still evident.

We do not provide an in-depth assessment of Dixon's model here; see e.g. Kuteva (1999), papers in Aikhenvald and Dixon (2001), and Bowern (2003, 2006) for discussion. We simply identify a few of the problematic issues with Dixon's use of punctuated equilibrium as an explanatory model in the Australian context. Firstly, it is unclear whether it can be argued that an equilibrium state dominated the full 40,000 years (conservatively) of human occupation. The Australian archaeological record suggests that there were major demographic changes in the Holocene (the period following the last glacial maximum, i.e. the last 10,000 or so years) and these would have to be interpreted as punctuation events; see e.g. Ulm (2013) and Williams et al. (2015). Secondly, although Dixon is quite justified in concluding that the evidence in support of genetic relationships remains considerably weak, his alternative conclusion that the observed recurrent similarities are clearly diffusional is not based on strong evidence. As well as concluding that we will never know whether all Australian languages go back to a common ancestor due to the time depth he thinks is involved, Dixon also rejects the other hypothesized major genetic grouping; Pama-Nyungan. He argues against it on non-linguistic grounds by concluding that there is no punctuation event that could have caused its spread (others would link it to the Holocene demographic changes that were just mentioned: see e.g. Sutton and Koch 2008: 497–500). On linguistic grounds he points to the lack of clear isogloss bundling, which he says would be needed in order to identify Pama-Nyungan as a genetic group.[6] He writes that only one typological feature has an areal distribution that corresponds exactly to the full set of languages currently classified as Pama-Nyungan. They all lack number-segmentable non-singular pronouns. He dismisses the feature that many (see e.g. Evans 2005: 264–267) consider to be the most important innovation/form diagnostic of Pama-Nyungan, the first person dual pronoun *ngali*, by pointing out that although it does not occur in any non-Pama-Nyungan languages, it is also missing in about one-fifth of Pama-Nyungan languages, all on the geographical fringe. He argues that it is simpler to assume that the form diffused over a contiguous area than that it was independently lost in eight separate regions. Both Sutton and Koch (2008) as well as Evans (2005) take up this point in their reviews of Dixon (2002), and argue that while loss is to be

---

[6] As already mentioned, due to the widely held assumption that all Australian languages must be related, Pama-Nyungan has often been treated as a subgroup, and evidence in its favour has generally been presented in the form of a subgrouping argument (see Miceli 2004).

expected in all linguistic systems, Dixon's account does not explain why this proposed diffusional feature, like many of the other features that could be reconstructed for Proto-Pama-Nyungan, always stops at the Pama-Nyungan border. Evans (2005: 270) argues that Dixon is *literally* correct when he says that isoglosses do not coincide, but that considering the number of forms that never go beyond Pama-Nyungan, and that have quite wide distributions within it, 'we have a very significant clustering indeed'.

What emerges from this discussion is a tendency for scholars to have a 'default position'. Evans himself suggests that disagreements between Dixon and 'Pama-Nyunganists' are not really about data but rather about whether one considers a form 'diffused until proven inherited, or inherited until proven diffused' (2005: 264). However, holding a default position, whichever it may be, is not methodologically defensible. One should always be considering and comparing the likelihood of both hypotheses, and in some cases there will be no principled way of deciding which is the most likely scenario. We are then faced with and must accept possible indeterminacy. In the following section, we present a detailed regional study that shows that many of the problems found on the wider scale are just as evident at the lower level.

27.3   Regional Patterns: The Pilbara[7]

There are around 20 named languages recognized (by their speakers) in the larger Pilbara region.[8] The received view is that the languages fall into a number of named 'subgroups' of Pama-Nyungan. While the labelling of these groups is well established in the Australian literature, their status as genetic subgroups has not (yet) been strongly supported by detailed comparative reconstruction. It is reasonable to assume that the languages of the region are related, at some level, but there is a degree of typological and morphosyntactic variation across the region that might initially suggest some depth to these connections. Map 27.2 shows the approximate original location of the languages referred to in this summary survey and the received classification into the named Ngayarta, Kanyara, Mantharta and Kartu subgroups based on O'Grady et al.'s (1966) original

[7] We have chosen to present a single case study in order to provide a more detailed analysis. We consider this case study to be representative of the problems faced in unravelling the history of shared features in the Australian context, especially within Pama-Nyungan. For a detailed case study of areal features across the Pama-Nyungan/non-Pama-Nyungan boundary, see Heath's (1978) study of languages in Arnhem Land. For an overview of outcomes of language contact in Australia see also McConvell (2010).

[8] Named language varieties within the wider area that are not discussed here include Warriyangka, Pinikura, Thiin, Jurruru, Nhuwala and Kariyarra. The materials available for these languages are especially limited and do not illuminate the issues. Sources used for the languages are: Yingkarta (Dench 1998a); Wajarri (Marmion 1996); Thalanyji, Payungu, Purduna (Austin 1994b); Jiwarli and Tharrkari (Austin 1994a); Martuthunira (Dench 1995); Kurrama (Hill 2011); Panyjima (Dench 1991); Yinhawangka (Dench, fieldnotes); Ngarluma (Kohn 1994); Yindjibarndi (Wordick 1982); Ngarla (Westerlund 2007, 2013); Nyamal (Dench, fieldnotes); Nyiyaparli (Kohn, fieldnotes).

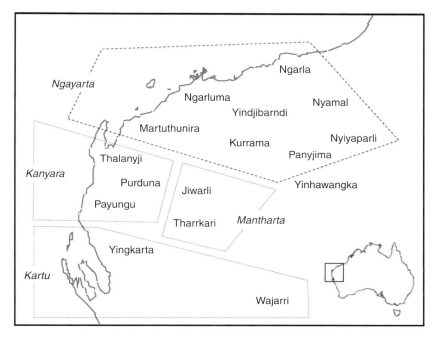

Map 27.2 The Pilbara: approximate locations of languages and classification following O'Grady et al. (1966)

lexicostatistical classification, reinforced by O'Grady (1966) and Austin (1988) (see Dench 2001 and Koch 2004 for reviews). More recent comparative work calls some aspects of this into question (Dench 1998b, 2001). Note that initial documentation of Yinhawangka postdates these classifications.

The languages of the southern Pilbara (including Jiwarli, Tharrkari, Thalanyji) and the northern Pilbara (Nyiyaparli, Nyamal, Ngarla) have an essentially ergative pattern of alignment with varying degrees of tripartite case marking within the nominal paradigm and some differentiation in case assignment by predicate type and clause type (Austin 1981c; Dench 2006, 2008). By contrast, languages in the central Pilbara (Panyjima, Yinhawangka, Kurrama, Yindjibarndi, Martuthunira, Ngarluma) have innovated a consistent accusative alignment and a productive passive voice (Dench 1982). While there is some similarity in nominal morphology across the region, the verbal inflectional paradigms show a high degree of diversity both in the number of categories represented and the inflectional forms employed (Stirling and Dench 2012). Languages in the southern Pilbara share patterns of switch-reference in subordinate clause with languages to the east (Austin 1981a), but these patterns are not diffused more generally within the Pilbara.

Despite this diversity and the relatively secure assumption of an ultimately shared origin, grouping the languages is problematic. The phonological changes that have occurred in a number of the languages (and the region is a little unusual in Australia in showing evidence of sound change) are restricted in extent and provide little basis for anything more than very low-level subgrouping (Austin 1981b; O'Grady 1966). At the same time, the phonetic bases of these changes are reflected in a range of languages in ways that suggest a tendency to genetic drift, or diffusion of phonetic traits (Dench 2001). The diachronic investigation of paradigms and forms confronts a not uncommon problem in the Australian context: the reconstructions arrived at differ little from those posited for the presumed highest order grouping of the languages – Pama-Nyungan.

The resulting picture is one of significant diversity arising from some deep differences (verbal systems) and a range of perhaps more shallow shared similarities with different regional distribution. For these latter cases especially, it is difficult to determine whether they have arisen from a shared inheritance or through processes of diffusion. As we have suggested above, the ultimate explanation must lie in particular patterns of multilingualism across the region (both in the past and in recent times), the relative salience for their speakers of particular linguistic features as markers of language difference, and associated with this the appetite for variation within the community of speakers of any identified linguistic variety.

What can we say then of patterns of cultural and social connection that might inform these questions? The traditional language communities of the region can be grouped by some broad cultural criteria, the most salient features of which include the westward extent of particular male initiation rites (their linguistic significance first being suggested by O'Grady 1958) and the patterning of kinship systems (first discussed by Radcliffe-Brown 1913). However, these traits do not pattern in a way that immediately suggests distinct cultural clusters, and there is no evidence that the different practices inhibited contact and extensive interaction between groups.

Some evidence of historical connections between particular communities of speakers can be gleaned from traditional narrative texts. For example, a set of traditional Martuthunira stories (Dench 1995) describes the introduction of the returning boomerang and hafted stone axe in a context of conflict between inland and coastal peoples. Interwoven stories also describe the establishment of coastal trading routes and the seemingly more peaceful introduction from the east of those patterns of male initiation mentioned above.[9] What emerges in these stories is a received understanding of a historical distinction between coastal people – who subsisted on

---

[9] Earliest dates for these artefacts is 12–15,000 BP, at a time of relatively fast-rising sea levels (Peter Veth, personal communication) and thus what was likely to have been a time of demographic pressure and social upheaval on the coast. If the stories do indeed date from that time, and if they do relate relatively local events, then it would assume an extreme degree of linguistic conservatism to expect linguistic patterns from those times to have survived into the modern languages. The introduction of initiation rites, woven into these same stories, is likely to be of more recent origin and is thus more likely to have linguistic correlates.

marine, mangrove estuarine coastal hinterland resources – and people who inhabited the inland river valleys and plateaus.

As in most other parts of Australia, multilingual contact was the norm (Sutton 1997). In the Pilbara, traditional marriage patterns were exogamous and this exogamy was encouraged by a system of promised marriage established through male initiation arrangements that brought with them extensive patterns of kin avoidance. There was thus some incentive to establish important relationships with people already at some social distance. Children naturally grew up speaking at least their mother's and their father's languages.

Colonial settlement in the 1870s severely and irrevocably disrupted historical social patterns. European contact and settlement resulted in the partial collapse of coastal populations from a range of introduced diseases (many likely preceding European settlement) and the ravages of an enforced labour programme in the early pearling industry. The more extended post-colonial period was characterized by the apportionment of much of the land into pastoral holdings on which introduced stock were tended by a primarily indigenous workforce, who thus mostly remained in their traditional country or were moved as largely intact extended family groups from traditional inland country to the by now less populous coastal regions. General labour strikes among the indigenous pastoral workers in the mid-twentieth century led to further forced displacements (from pastoral properties and traditional homelands) and generally greater daily contact between speaker groups in government 'ration camps' or town fringe camps. The changes have meant greater prolonged contact between the languages originally spoken in the inland ranges (Yindjibarndi, Kurrama, Panyjima) with those of the coast and southern Pilbara than was likely to have occurred prior to European settlement. Other than a few early wordlists dating from the late nineteenth century, there are no descriptions of the languages before O'Grady's initial short sketches based on data collected in 1958. In the absence of any substantial records of languages from the time of first settlement, it is now very difficult to determine to what extent patterns of similarity we see in the descriptions of Pilbara languages that may be due to contact reflect relatively recent conditions of social interaction rather than the longstanding traditional multilingualism engendered by exogamy.

Received traditions of linguistic integrity apply more to country[10] than to (communities of) speakers, in a similar way to that described by Merlan

---

[10] In the Australian context references to Aboriginal land generally use the term 'country' (rather than 'territory', 'land'), to describe areas of land with which there is some identified connection – proprietary, spiritual, etc. Thus common formal meeting protocols in Australia, including in the parliaments, often include a 'Welcome to country' and/or 'Acknowledgement of country' to respect the indigenous inhabitants of the particular area in which the meeting is taking place. In his speech as Australian of the Year for 2009, Mick Dodson describes its sphere of reference in the following way: '[f]or us, country is a word for all the values, places, resources, stories and cultural obligations associated with that area and its features.' His speech can be accessed from https://ncis.anu.edu.au/_lib/doc/MD_Press_Club_170209.pdf

(1981) and Sutton (1997). Languages belong to country, and speakers traditionally identified both with a language and with a country; see also descriptions in Koch and Nordlinger (2014b) and Harvey (2011). While language identity was perhaps primarily mediated by affiliation to country historically, in the modern context this is less clear, and an affiliation to language is often constructed as a claim to country. We see some contestation over which linguistic variety is properly associated with particular country, and also negotiated succession in cases of language loss. There is also some interrogation of what properly constitutes the named variety. It is difficult to know whether this has arisen as a result of more than three decades of legal struggle for rights to traditional land and the imperative to identify legitimate claimants, or whether this contestation has always occurred and has simply been exacerbated by modern circumstances. Argument about the legitimacy of association with country based on linguistic affiliation naturally brings with it a particular metalinguistic awareness.

Folk descriptions of dialect and language differentiation now very often cite lexical differences between varieties – sometimes with strong assertions as to the exclusive provenance of particular forms despite evidence that these have been common to a number of languages for at least a number of generations. Thirty years ago, linguists' questions about perceived differences between varieties often produced statements about phonological differences. Speakers described general impressions but also recognized the sometimes subtle phonotactic differences among languages with similar inventories, using particular (apparently cognate) forms for exemplification. Lexical differences were certainly recognized, usually simply taken for granted, often with reference to received shibboleths.[11]

The speakers Dench worked with in collecting materials in Panyjima, Kurrama, Martuthunira, Nyamal and Ngarla would generally seek to achieve linguistic purity in elicitation sessions – sometimes to the point of resorting to correspondence mimicry to construct a missing or forgotten word (Dench 2001). The use of alternative lexical items in freely offered narrative discourse was explained as stylistic effect or as generosity to protagonists with a different language background, but it was sometimes maintained that the alternatives were not 'true' native forms. At other times speakers described the use of a range of 'synonymous' forms (see Hansen 1984 for patterns of lexical use in the Western Desert).

We noted in Section 27.1 that the comparison and reconstruction of pronoun paradigms has been given particular significance in the

---

[11] The naming of varieties by reference to a particular lexical feature, or isogloss, is common across Australia and is perhaps most interestingly described for the Western Desert region (see Miller 1971). In the Western Desert, names may consist of the local variant of a nominalization of 'go', or a demonstrative form, followed by the proprietive or 'having' affix. Thus, *Pitjantja-tjara, Yankuntja- tjara, Ngaanja-tjarra*. Similar name constructions appear to exist in the Pilbara but are, interestingly, fossilized. Thus while the names *Nyiya+parli, Panyji+ma, Yinha-wangka* and *Yindji+barndi* are all apparently based on demonstrative forms, the names are either no longer morphologically transparent or the root (and/or suffix) does not (now) occur in the language bearing the name.

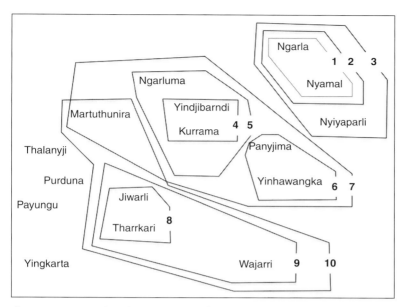

Figure 27.1 Innovations in pronoun paradigms most likely reflecting shared inheritance

Australian context. The discussion that follows focuses on patterns of innovation in pronoun and demonstrative paradigms in the Pilbara languages. Dench (1994) presents an initial reconstruction of pronominal paradigms in the Pilbara and argues that it is particularly difficult to decide for any innovation whether it is the result of shared inheritance or the result of contact. The most extensive restructuring of the pronoun paradigm has taken place in the accusative Pilbara languages – Panyjima, Yindjibarndi, Kurrama, Ngarluma, Martuthunira – and in Jiwarli and Tharrkari. The remaining languages are relatively conservative. General changes within the paradigm involve the replacement of forms through the analogical extension of paradigm mates. Only the 1du.inc, *ngali*, remains immune to analogical restructuring within the non-singular paradigm, and it often serves as the base for other forms. While the analogical levelling of the paradigms in the different languages produces similar results, the base forms selected and the morphological forms employed differ, and thus the languages remain very clearly distinct.

Nevertheless, it is possible to identify some low-level shared innovations that are the most likely to reflect a shared inheritance. These include the following features, illustrated in Figure 27.1.

1 Replacement innovation of 1pl.exc *ngana-rtu* (and *ngantu-rtu*) (Ngarla, Nyamal).
2 Replacement innovation of 1pl.inc *nganyju-la* (Ngarla, Nyamal).
3 Innovation of 3du *piyalu* (Ngarla, Nyamal, Nyiyaparli).

4 Compound oblique plurals with *karrangu* (Yindjibarndi, Kurrama).

5 Replacement of 2pl based on 2sg: *nyinta-kuru* / *nyinku-(ku)ru* (Yindjibarndi, Kurrama, Ngarluma).

6 The 3pl *thana* shifts to a restricted demonstrative function ('singular') (Panyjima, Yinhawangka).

7 Replacement of 1pl.inc based on 1du.inc: *ngali-kuru* (Yindjibarndi, Kurrama, Ngarluma, Martuthunira, Panyjima, Yinhawangka).

8 Shift of *2pl (*nhurra*) to 2sg (Tharrkari, Jiwarli).

9 Innovation of exclusive pronouns in *-ju* (-1sgDAT) (Tharrkari, Jiwarli, Wajarri).

10 Innovated 1sg.DAT/GEN *nganaju* (< *nganu-ju*) (Tharrkari, Jiwarli, Wajarri, Martuthunira).

The patterns shown here generally coincide with the received classifications, but with the following qualifications: Martuthunira is placed with the central Pilbara languages on feature 7, but with southern Pilbara languages on feature 10; Nyiyaparli (Palyku) is grouped with Ngarla and Nyamal rather than with Panyjima (the lexicostatistical studies treat Palyku as in a 'dialectal' relationship with Panyjima).

While these pronominal innovations are likely to have arisen through a shared inheritance, other innovations are more clearly diffusional. For example, there is widespread replacement of the original 1sgNOM pronoun form *ngayi* by *ngatha* (a reflex of an original 1sgERG), with just Martuthunira, Yindjibarndi, Kurrama, Ngarluma and Ngarla retaining reflexes of the original (feature 11 in Figure 27.2).

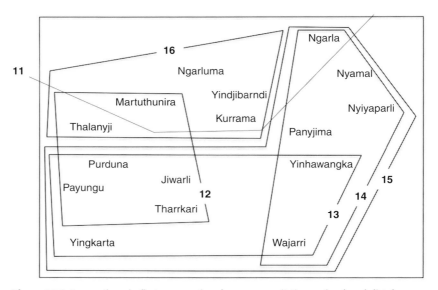

Figure 27.2 Innovations in first person singular pronoun (11), proximal and distal demonstratives (12–14), and the levelling of irregular verbs (15, 16)

Table 27.1 *Reconstructed demonstrative stems*

	Proximal	Mid-distal	Distal
Ergative	*nhulu	*palu	*ngulu
Nominative	*nhiya	*panha	*ngunha
Accusative	*nhinha	*panha	*ngunha
Dative/oblique	*nhurnu	*parnu	*ngurnu
Locative	*nhula	*pala	*ngula
Locational	*nhungu	–	*ngunthi

The diachronic development of demonstrative paradigms is complicated by the complex pragmatic functions of demonstrative systems. In the Australian context we see a range of innovations of category and form including the development and loss of adverbial forms, shifts from three-term to two-term systems, innovation of third person pronouns from demonstratives (and possibly vice versa), and the denaturing of paradigm sets into a small number of isolated non-inflecting particles (Koch 2009). Indeed, it is not necessarily the case that the demonstratives form a symmetrical or coherent system. In the Pilbara the reconstructed mid-distal ('near you') has a complex history that differs markedly from the proximal ('near me') and generally conservative distal. Table 27.1 lists demonstrative forms reconstructed from a comparison of Pilbara languages (note that no claim is made here about the deeper history of these forms within Pama-Nyungan).

The mapping of diachronic pathways for these demonstrative forms shows patterns of historical connection between languages that cut across other evidence. Thus, reconstruction of the proximal and distal demonstratives yields the following general patterns. In a set of southwestern languages including (at least) Jiwarli, Tharrkari, Thalanyji, Payungu and Purduna, an original accusative form *nhinha has become *yinha*. In Martuthunira, the direct reflex of *nhinha has been lost with the shift to an accusative alignment system, but the fuller paradigm reveals evidence of the earlier change (feature 12 in Figure 27.2). The original nominative proximal stem has been replaced by a reflex of the original accusative in a set of languages including Payungu, Purduna, Jiwarli, Tharrkari, Yingkarta, Wajarri and Yinhawangka. This change is not co-extensive with the aforementioned innovation. In particular it does not affect Thalanyji and Martuthunira (which thus remain conservative) and it extends to Yinhawangka, which by other criteria is closer to Panyjima (feature 13 in Figure 27.2). Both the proximal and distal paradigms have been levelled on the nominative stem in a set of eastern languages including Ngarla, Nyamal, Nyiyaparli, Panyjima, Yinhawangka and Wajarri. In the latter two languages the proximal nominative is a reflex of the original accusative, and thus this change follows the previously noted innovation (feature 13). In Wajarri, the distal nominative stem is a reflex of an original mid-distal accusative (feature 14 in Figure 27.2).

Table 27.2 *Paradigm reflexes of the* *pa- *mid-distal demonstrative (see Dench 2007)*

	*palu	*parnu	*panha	*pala
Ngarla, Nyamal	3sg		Ø	DEM
Ngarluma	3sg		Ø	Ø
Nyiyaparli	3sg	Ø	Ø	DEM
Panyjima	Ø	Ø	DEM	
Yindjibarndi, Kurrama	Ø	Ø	Ø	DEM
Martuthunira	Ø	Ø	Ø	PART
Thalanyji	Ø	Ø	Ø	3sg
Yingkarta, Payungu	Ø	Ø	3sg	
Jiwarli	Ø	3sg		Ø
Wajarri	3sg		DEM	DEM

The history of the mid-distal is much more elaborate and involves the splitting of the original paradigm (Dench 2007). The result is the development of distinct paradigms with different functions built from original paradigm mates.

The ergative mid-distal form occurs as a third person pronoun in Nyiyaparli, Nyamal, Ngarla, Ngarluma and Wajarri.[12] In Nyamal, Ngarla and Ngarluma the original genitive also survives in this paradigm, with the other forms being elaborations of the ergative. The original nominative occurs as a mid-distal demonstrative in Panyjima and Yinhawangka, with the locative surviving as a member of this paradigm. Yingkarta shares the same pattern but the paradigm is described as a third person pronoun. In Wajarri, the nominative and locative forms survive, and serve as the basis for separate demonstrative paradigms ('distal anaphoric' and 'distal' respectively: Marmion 1996). In Nyiyaparli, Nyamal, Yindjibarndi and Kurrama, the modern mid-distal is based on the original locative stem. In Thalanyji, the paradigm based on the old locative is a third person pronoun. In Martuthunira, only the locative form survives, as a non-inflecting 'definite' particle.

Table 27.2 maps the extent of surviving reflexes of the original paradigm and their functional alignment with the pronoun paradigm (3sg), demonstrative paradigm (DEM) or as a non-inflecting particle (PART). The innovations thus include paradigm splits and functional shifts, the creation of new forms to fill gaps in innovated paradigms, and varying degrees of analogical levelling – levelling which has proceeded differently depending on whether or not the bases for the analogy are inflected members of the pronoun paradigm or of the extant proximal and/or distal demonstrative paradigm.

The resulting picture is something of a patchwork of differences across the array of languages, in which the innovations shared and also *not* shared

---

[12] Western Desert languages also have paradigms based on the *palu* stem, for example the 'definite nominal' in Yankunytjatjara (Goddard 1985).

are changes that have arisen through analogy. The demonstrative forms are essentially transparent; they are unaffected by regular phonological change (though there are some sporadic changes). Given the general similarities of form and some degree of functional congruity, there is little to prevent analogy operating both within and between languages (where these languages are spoken by bilinguals).

A number of additional features can be added to the picture emerging here. The languages share a general reduction of an inherited conjugational complexity in the verb paradigm. The simplification has proceeded through the levelling of irregular verb forms on selected stems. In an arc of contiguous languages extending from the northern coast, across the inland ranges, to the southwestern coast of the region – in Ngarla, Nyamal, Nyiyaparli, Panyjima, Yinhawangka, Jiwarli, Purduna, Payungu, Yingkarta – the 'past' stem of a small set of originally irregular verbs serves as the new stem form (feature 15 in Figure 27.2). Within this arc – in Thalanyji, Martuthunira, Ngarluma, Kurrama and Yindjibarndi – the new forms are built on the 'purposive' stems, a pattern also found in the Western Desert languages (Dench 1998b) (feature 16 in Figure 27.2).

As noted earlier, there are interesting differences in morphosyntactic patterning across the Pilbara, including the innovation of an accusative alignment system and a productive active/passive voice alternation (features 17 and 18 in Figure 27.3 respectively), and the development of switch-reference in relative and purpose subordinate clauses (feature 19 in Figure 27.3).

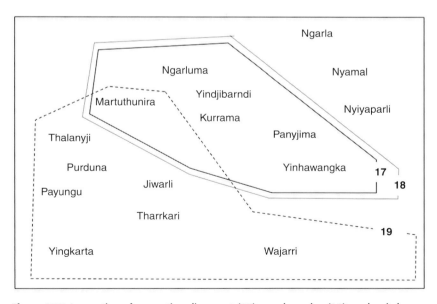

Figure 27.3 Innovation of accusative alignment (17), passive voice (18), and switch-reference in subordinate clauses (19)

The patterns in Figure 27.3 are most like those in Figure 27.1, perhaps suggesting that case marking and voice innovations are inherited innovations in a central Pilbara group. Martuthunira then presents a particularly intriguing case in that it shares quite marked typological features with Yindjibarndi, Kurrama, Panyjima, Yinhawangka and Ngarluma, and has participated in a number of pronominal innovations that align it with this set of languages, yet on the other hand other innovations in the pronoun and demonstrative paradigms and the presence of a switch-reference system suggest a strong connection to southern Pilbara languages, including both Thalanyji and Jiwarli. Martuthunira is unusual in having both a switch-reference system and an interacting voice system (Dench 1987, 1995), and this raises the question of how this level of syntactic complexity might have arisen.

Austin (1981a) demonstrates convincingly that switch-reference is a diffusional feature in Australia, and thus it might initially be assumed that Martuthunira developed its patterns under diffusional pressure from neighbouring languages to the south and east. That is, switch-reference emerged into a system that had already innovated accusative alignment and a passive voice. However, a number of factors argue against this. First, it is difficult to imagine what kind of pressure might have led to the innovation of switch-reference (same- or different-subject marking) in a consistently nominative–accusative language that has the resources (a passive voice) to place patient and theme arguments into the morphologically transparent nominative subject relation. Second, the Martuthunira subordinate clause verb morphology that marks switch-reference is formally quite similar to that of Thalanyji and Jiwarli, suggesting that either the switch-reference constructions were borrowed (supplanting existing subordinate clause inflections) or Martuthunira shares a history with these languages.[13] The latter seems more plausible, which might suggest instead that it is accusative alignment and the passive voice that are the later developments in Martuthunira.

The general alignment shift in this context is again an instance of levelling – the extension of a nominative–dative pattern for transitive verbs into contexts where such verbs originally selected an ergative–accusative/absolutive pattern of marking (see Dench 1982).[14] Case marking patterns – like patterns of general levelling in the verb paradigm or the analogical creation of new pronoun and demonstrative forms – are subject to indirect pattern diffusion, and we return to the essential Australian problem. In the absence of extensive regular sound change as a guide to the stratification of genetic relationships among languages, we are forced to consider instead altogether more

---

[13] Though determining this would depend on a detailed comparative reconstruction of verb morphology in the region, and that work remains in its infancy.

[14] The Martuthunira passive might then involve the borrowing of a construction (in the case of the derivational passive) or the reanalysis of existing morphology (in the case of inflectional passives).

psychologically salient features as potential evidence: lexical similarity and differentiation, shared innovations and irregularities within paradigms, and interacting morphosyntactic patterns.

What is still missing from this discussion is some measure of relative salience. Unless we know in more detail which aspects of a language variety are salient markers of language distinctiveness for the multilingual speakers themselves, we cannot develop a complete understanding of which features may be subject to (relatively unconscious) convergence and which may be subject to (a perhaps subconscious) divergence. Ideally, we would like to be able to approach situations like that presented by the Pilbara languages with some knowledge of individual speaker variation and levels of tolerance for the kind of calquing of pattern and possible diffusion of form that might be expected in this multilingual context. Unfortunately, many of the language descriptions we have are based on data mostly salvaged from a few remaining speakers.

27.4　Discussion and Concluding Remarks

The two previous sections reveal the same problematic issues. The comparative Australian pattern at both wide and regional levels is unusual, and detailed analysis fails to clarify the indeterminacy encountered when considering competing hypotheses. As already mentioned, the pattern can be described as a form/structure 'mismatch': we find much structural similarity – near-identical sound systems, recurring patterns in morphosyntax, recurring patterns of semantic structure – but cognate densities are often lower than expected, with a variety of quite different forms often associated with what are essentially the same semantics (whether lexical or grammatical categories are involved). The significant clustering of features that we often find, such as in the case of Pama-Nyungan, suggests that we are dealing with genetically related languages, but the overall pattern is not consistent with family-tree-like transmission.

Although the Australian situation is rendered more complex by the paucity of sound change, which usually provides essential clues on stratigraphy, comparative patterns that reveal a form/structure mismatch are not confined to Australia, and are not uncommon. They are commonly found in linguistic situations characterized by a high degree of multilingualism. One detailed study of languages that display this type of pattern is that of François (2011), who focuses on the Torres and Banks islands of Northern Vanuatu. Here a group of seventeen closely related Oceanic languages have developed morpheme-for-morpheme inter-translatability (or structural isomorphism), but where the actual phonological forms involved are often completely distinct. An example sentence from two of these languages, Lemerig and Koro, illustrating the very obvious mismatch (data from François 2011: Table 1) is given in Table 27.3.

Table 27.3 *Structural isomorphism in Lemerig and Koro*

Lemerig	tær	ɪ		yɒlɒl	ʔɒrmaʔ	ʔæ.kiʔis	n	tɛktɛk	mʊɣʊt
Koro	nɪr	tɪ		rɔŋ	taβul	wʊs.mɛlɛ	ɔ	βalβalaw	namɪɣɪn
	3pl	NOT.YET₁		know	properly	NOT.YET₂	ART	speech	POSS:1incl.pl
	'They don't know our language very well yet.'								

Abbreviations: 3pl = third person plural; ART = article; POSS:1incl.pl = possessive, first person inclusive plural

Ross (2001) describes the development of a similar mismatch in Takia, an Oceanic language whose speakers are currently bilingual in the Papuan language Waskia. The Takia lexicon has been semantically reorganized, along with the morphosyntax, so that it closely matches that of Waskia, but there has been little to no borrowing of forms. When comparing Takia to its Oceanic relatives we therefore find a mismatch that goes in the opposite direction to that typical of Australia: many forms are shared, but little else – there has been a general structural divergence. From these and other studies, we can draw the conclusion that structure and form may follow quite different historical paths.

Moreover, studies of highly multilingual contexts (see also Epps and Michael, Chapter 32, this volume), strongly suggest that phonological form is a more salient marker of language distinctiveness than semantic or grammatical structure. François (2011: 234) argues that '[i]n speakers' meta-discourse, the distinctive identity of each particular language is typically defined by the form of its words rather than by their structural properties, which appear to be less accessible to spontaneous representations.' It follows that structure is more likely to converge, while word forms are more likely to be either maintained as distinct or become distinct (in the case of related languages) due to this speaker bias. Most of these studies therefore explain the fate of word forms – whether they are maintained as distinct or are differentiated – by highlighting the emblematic role of languages in these multilingual contexts. Word forms, being highly salient, are then best at fulfilling this particular role. François (2011: 228–229) explains form differentiation in Northern Vanuatu in terms of a broader social bias for cultural differentiation in place in this part of Melanesia.

However, a recent study by Ellison and Miceli (in press) suggests that specific social factors giving languages a high emblematic function are not *necessary* for form differentiation to occur. The study investigates the lexical choices of Dutch–English bilinguals through the administration of a production task designed to identify any cognitive bias either for or against the selection of similar forms when language distinctive options are also available for the target meaning. Using the choices of monolingual speakers as a baseline, a statistically significant bias against similar forms is identified. Simulations of the diachronic effects of such a bias show that in communities with ongoing bilingualism and substantial numbers of bilinguals, forms will be replaced at much faster rate than they would be if those languages were to have no bilingual speakers. That is, there is an apparent tendency towards differentiation without any particular social biases favouring differentiation being in place (though these may, of course, amplify the effect of the bias if they do exist). Since we rarely know the exact sociolinguistic conditions prevailing in a given context prior to historical documentation – one of the criticisms often extended to explanations that rely on social factors – this result is particularly useful. It suggests that an assumption of ongoing active multilingualism is a sufficient basis for arguing that differentiation may have occurred.

Given the paucity of sound change in Australia and the likelihood that multilingualism extended well into the past, the presence of such a cognitive bias may help to explain why we might find the high replacement rates posited between certain pairs of neighbouring languages that are assumed both to be related and to have remained in close contact.[15] Since cognate word forms would not be differentiated much by sound change, the bias would affect a larger portion of the vocabulary and give rise to a higher replacement rate than in situations where sound change has a more prominent role.[16] Similarly, the bias is likely to have its strongest effect when languages that come into a relationship of bilingualism are closely related because there will be more cognate forms to be affected. The Australian pattern – at both the macro-level of Pama-Nyungan and micro-levels such as in the Pilbara – is therefore likely to reflect relatively long periods of unbroken transmission in a multilingual context.

It may be possible to do more with the findings of Ellison and Miceli's study than just providing general explanations. For example, an investigation of the patterns of form replacement in a group of languages may be useful in gaining insights into contact relationships within a region. A study focusing on the Pilbara is currently under way (Miceli 2015b), comparing the number of expected shared replacements between pairs of languages (calculated on the basis of individual rates of replacement) to the observed number of replacements. Initial results are suggestive of a weak bilingual differentiation bias between Martuthunira and Kurrama.

To conclude, Australian languages offer unique insights into the complex interaction between genetic relationship and language contact. They lead us to consider often ignored questions such as whether contact-induced change may actually proceed differently depending on whether languages are genetically related. They further establish the emerging picture that

---

[15] Harvey (2011) gives specific examples of such cases where as little as 8 per cent of the basic vocabulary is shared

[16] Avoidance of word forms due to social practices such as death-taboo is one example of a social factor that could have amplified the cognitive bias identified in Ellison and Miceli's study.

structure and form often have independent histories, which we see reflected in the history of paradigms as well as in the history of the lexicon. They highlight the problematic nature of the traditional assumption underlying comparative work that all speaker-internal change is also language-internal.[17] Although many difficulties are encountered in seeking to determine the historical processes that have given rise to the current distributions of shared features in Australia, there are valuable opportunities here. It is likely that ongoing detailed comparative study of Australian languages will continue to push traditional theoretical boundaries in interesting ways.

References

Aikhenvald, Alexandra Y. and R. M. W. Dixon (eds), 2001. *Areal Diffusion and Genetic Inheritance: Problems in Comparative Linguistics*. Oxford: Oxford University Press.

Austin, Peter, 1981a. Switch-reference in Australia. *Language* 57: 309–334.

Austin, Peter, 1981b. Proto-Kanyara and Proto-Mantharta historical phonology. *Lingua* 54: 295–333.

Austin, Peter, 1981c. Case-Marking in Southern Pilbara languages. *Australian Journal of Linguistics* 1: 211–226.

Austin, Peter, 1988. Classification of Southern Pilbara languages. Pacific Linguistics, Papers in Australian Linguistics, no. 17. Canberra: Australian National University.

Austin, Peter K., 1994a. A reference grammar of the Mantharta languages, Western Australia. Unpublished manuscript, La Trobe University.

Austin, Peter K., 1994b. A reference grammar of the Kanyara languages, Western Australia. Unpublished manuscript, La Trobe University.

Baker, Brett, 2014. Word structure in Australian languages. In Koch and Nordlinger (eds), pp. 139–214.

Bowern, Claire, 2003. Another look at Australia as a linguistic area. In *Proceedings of the Twenty-Ninth Annual Meeting of the Berkeley Linguistics Society* (General Session and Parasession on Phonetic Sources of Phonological Patterns: Synchronic and Diachronic Explanations).

Bowern, Claire, 2006. Another look at Australia as a linguistic area. In Yaron Matras, April McMahon and Nigel Vincent (eds), *Linguistic Areas*, pp. 244–265. Basingstoke, UK: Palgrave Macmillan.

Busby, Peter, 1980. The distribution of phonemes in Australian Aboriginal language. In Bruce E. Waters and Peter A. Busby (eds), *Papers in Australian*

---

[17] Usually no distinction is made between change that is due to causes within the language system and change that is due to language implementation in individual speakers (i.e. cognitively motivated change). This is because although the two causes are distinct they give rise to indistinguishable biases in monolingual speaker behaviour. Both types of change are therefore traditionally classified as 'internal'. However, this is a problematic working assumption when dealing with bilingual speakers or with languages spoken in a multilingual context.

Linguistics, vol. 14, pp. 73–139. Pacific Linguistics, vol. A-60. Canberra: Australian National University.

Butcher, Andrew, 2012. On the phonetics of long, thin phonologies. In Cathryn Donohue, Shunishi Ishihara and William Steed (eds), *Quantitative Approaches to Problems in Linguistics: Studies in Honour of Phil Rose*, pp. 133–154. Munich: LINCOM.

Butcher, Andrew and Janet Fletcher, 2014. Sound patterns of Australian languages. In Koch and Nordlinger (eds), pp. 89–132.

Campbell, Lyle and William J. Poser, 2008. *Language Classification: History and Method*. Cambridge: Cambridge University Press.

Dench, Alan, 1982. The development of an accusative case marking pattern in the Ngayarda languages of Western Australia. *Australian Journal of Linguistics* 2: 43–59.

Dench, Alan, 1987. Complex sentences in Martuthunira. In Peter Austin (ed.), *Complex Sentence Constructions in Australian Aboriginal Languages*, pp. 97–139. Typological Studies in Language, vol. 15. Amsterdam: John Benjamins.

Dench, Alan, 1991. Panyjima. In R. M. W. Dixon and Barry Blake (eds), *Handbook of Australian Languages*, vol. 4, pp. 124–243. Melbourne: Oxford University Press.

Dench, Alan, 1994. The historical development of pronoun paradigms in the Pilbara region of Western Australia. *Australian Journal of Linguistics* 14: 155–191.

Dench, Alan, 1995. *Martuthunira: A Language of the Pilbara Region of Western Australia*. Pacific Linguistics, vol. C-125. Canberra: Australian National University.

Dench, Alan, 1997. Where do complex kinterms come from? In Darryl Tryon and Michael Walsh (eds), *Boundary Rider: Essays in Honour of Geoffrey O'Grady*, pp. 107–132. Pacific Linguistics, vol. C-136. Canberra: Australian National University.

Dench, Alan, 1998a. *Yingkarta*. Munich: LINCOM Europa.

Dench, Alan, 1998b. What is a Ngayarta language? A reply to O'Grady and Laughren. *Australian Journal of Linguistics* 18: 91–107.

Dench, Alan, 2001. Descent and diffusion: The complexity of the Pilbara situation. In Aikhenvald and Dixon (eds), pp. 105–133.

Dench, Alan, 2006. Case marking strategies in subordinate clauses in Pilbara languages: Some diachronic speculations. *Australian Journal of Linguistics* 26 (1): 81–105.

Dench, Alan, 2007. Demonstrative paradigm splitting in the Pilbara languages of Western Australia. In Joseph Salmons and Shannon Dubenion-Smith (eds), *Historical Linguistics 2005*, pp. 224–237. Amsterdam: John Benjamins.

Dench, Alan, 2008. Case in an Australian language: Distribution of case and multiple case-marking in Nyamal. In Andrej Malchukov and Andrew Spencer (eds), *The Handbook of Case*, pp. 756–769. Oxford: Oxford University Press.

Dench, Alan. Field notes: Ngarla, Nyamal, Yinhawangka. Manuscript, University of Western Australia, 1995–1997.

Dixon, R. M. W., 1980. *Languages of Australia*. Cambridge: Cambridge University Press.

Dixon, R. M. W., 1997. *The Rise and Fall of Languages*. Cambridge: Cambridge University Press.

Dixon, R. M. W., 2001. The Australian linguistic area. In Aikhenvald and Dixon (eds), pp. 64–104.

Dixon, R. M. W., 2002. *The Australian Languages: Their Nature and Development*. Cambridge: Cambridge University Press.

Eldredge, Niles and Stephen Jay Gould, 1972. Punctuated equilibria: An alternative to phyletic gradualism. In T. J. M. Schopf (ed.), *Models in Palaeobiology*, pp. 82–115. San Francisco: Freeman Cooper and Co.

Ellison, T. Mark and Luisa Miceli, 2013. New perspectives on language change: L2 transmission and the cognitive basis for contact-induced differentiation of lexical forms. Paper presented at the 21st International Conference for Historical Linguistics, Oslo.

Ellison, T. Mark and Luisa Miceli, in press. Language monitoring in bilinguals as a mechanism for rapid lexical divergence. *Language* 93.

Evans, Nicholas (ed.), 2003. *The non-Pama-Nyungan Languages of Northern Australia: Comparative Studies of the Continent's Most Linguistically Complex Region*. Canberra: Pacific Linguistics.

Evans, Nicholas, 2005. Australian languages reconsidered: A review of Dixon (2002). *Oceanic Linguistics* 44 (1): 242–286.

Evans, Nicholas and David Wilkins, 2000. In the mind's ear: The semantic extensions of perception verbs in Australian languages. *Language* 76 (3): 546–592.

François, Alexandre, 2011. Social ecology and language history in the Northern Vanuatu linkage: A tale of divergence and convergence. *Journal of Historical Linguistics* 1 (2): 175–246.

Gaby, Alice and Ruth Singer, 2014. Semantics of Australian Aboriginal languages. In Koch and Nordlinger (eds), pp. 295–327.

Goddard, Clifford, 1985. *A Grammar of Yankunytjatjara*. Alice Springs: Institute for Aboriginal Development Press.

Hamilton, Philip, 1996. *Phonetic Constraints and Markedness in the Phonotactics of Australian Aboriginal Languages*. PhD thesis, University of Toronto.

Hansen, Kenneth C., 1984. Communicability of some Western Desert communalects. In Joyce Hudson and Noreen Pym (eds), *Language Survey*, pp. 1–112. Work Papers of SIL/AAB, vol. B-11. Darwin: SIL.

Harvey, Mark, 2011. Lexical change in pre-colonial Australia. *Diachronica* 28 (3): 345–381.

Heath, Jeffrey, 1978. *Linguistic Diffusion in Arnhem Land*. Canberra: Institute of Aboriginal Studies.

Hill, Peter, 2011. *Morphology and Sentence Construction in Kurrama: A Language of the Pilbara Region of Western Australia*. PhD thesis, University of Western Australia.

Koch, Harold, 2004. A methodological history of Australian linguistic classification. In Claire Bowern and Harold Koch (eds), *Australian Languages: Classification and the Comparative Method*, pp. 17–60. Amsterdam: John Benjamins.

Koch, Harold, 2009. On reconstructing pronominal proto-paradigms: Methodological considerations from the Pama-Nyungan language family of Australia. In Bethwyn Evans (ed.), *Discovering History Through Language: Papers in Honour of Malcolm Ross*, pp. 317–344. Canberra: Pacific Linguistics.

Koch, Harold, 2014. Historical relations among the Australian languages: Genetic classification and contact-based diffusion. In Koch and Nordlinger (ed.), pp. 23–89.

Koch, Harold and Rachel Nordlinger (eds), 2014a. *The Languages and Linguistics of Australia: A Comprehensive Guide*. The World of Linguistics, vol. 3. Berlin: Mouton de Gruyter.

Koch, Harold and Rachel Nordlinger, 2014b. The languages of Australia in linguistic research: Context and issues. In Koch and Nordlinger (eds), pp. 3–21.

Kohn, Allison, 1994. *A Morphological Description of Ngarluma*. BA (Hons) dissertation, University of Western Australia.

Kohn, Allison. Nyiyaparli field notes. Manuscript, University of Western Australia.

Kuteva, Tanja, 1999. Languages and societies: The 'punctuated equilibrium' model of language development. *Language and Communication* 19: 213–228.

Marmion, Douglas, 1996. *A Description of the Morphology of Wajarri*. BA (Hons) dissertation, University of New England.

McConvell, Patrick, 2010. Contact and indigenous languages in Australia. In Raymond Hickey (ed.), *The Handbook of Language Contact*, pp. 770–794. Malden, MA: Wiley-Blackwell.

Merlan, Francesca, 1981. Land, language and social identity in Aboriginal Australia. *Mankind* 13 (2): 133–148.

Miceli, Luisa, 2004. Pama-Nyungan as a genetic entity. In Claire Bowern and Harold Koch (eds), *Australian Languages: Classification and the Comparative Method*, pp. 61–68. Amsterdam: John Benjamins.

Miceli, Luisa, 2015a. Pama-Nyungan. In Claire Bowern and Bethwyn Evans (eds), *The Routledge Handbook of Historical Linguistics*, pp. 704–725. London and New York: Routledge.

Miceli, Luisa, 2015b. Looking for evidence of an anti-doppel bias in the Pilbara. Paper presented at *Workshop on Comparative Australian Linguistics*, Australian National University.

Miceli, Luisa and Erich R. Round, 2014. Sound change in Australia: Current knowledge and research priorities. Paper presented at *Third Biennial Workshop on Sound Change*, University of California, Berkeley, May 28–31 2014.

Miller, W. R., 1971. Dialect differentiation in the Western Desert Language. *Anthropological Forum* 3: 61–78.

O'Grady, Geoffrey, 1958. *The Significance of the Circumcision Boundary in Western Australia.* BA thesis, Sydney University.

O'Grady, Geoffrey, 1966. Proto-Ngayarda phonology. *Oceanic Linguistics* 5: 71–130.

O'Grady, Geoffrey, Carl F. Voegelin and Frances M. Voegelin, 1966. Languages of the World: Indo-Pacific Fascicle Six. *Anthropological Linguistics* 8 (2): 1–197.

Radcliffe-Brown, A., 1913. Three tribes of Western Australia. *Journal of the Royal Anthropological Institute* 43: 141–195.

Ross, Malcolm, 2001. Contact-induced change in Oceanic languages in North-East Melanesia. In Aikhenvald and Dixon (eds), pp. 134–166.

Round, Erich R., 2013. The phonologically exceptional continent: A large cross-linguistic survey reveals why Australia is, and is not, typologically unusual. Paper presented at the Association for Linguistic Typology 10th Biennial Conference, Leipzig.

Stirling, Lesley and Alan Dench, 2012. Tense, aspect, modality and evidentiality in Australian languages: Foreword. *Australian Journal of Linguistics* 32: 1–6.

Sutton, Peter, 1997. Materialism, sacred myth and pluralism: Competing theories of the origin of Australian languages. In Francesca Merlan, John Morton and Alan Rumsey (eds), *Scholar and Sceptic: Australian Aboriginal Studies in Honour of L. R. Hiatt*, pp. 211–242. Canberra: Aboriginal Studies Press.

Sutton, Peter and Harold Koch, 2008. Australian languages: A singular vision. *Journal of Linguistics* 44: 471–504.

Ulm, Sean, 2013. 'Complexity' and the Australian continental narrative: Themes in the archaeology of Holocene Australia. *Quaternary International* 285: 182–192.

Voegelin, C.F., F. M. Voegelin, Stephen Wurm, Geoffrey N. O'Grady and Tokuichiro Matsuda 1963. Obtaining an index of phonological differentiation from the construction of non-existent minimax systems. *International Journal of American Linguistics* 29 (1): 4–29.

Westerlund, Torbjörn, 2007. *A Grammatical Sketch of Ngarla: A Language of Western Australia.* Master's thesis, Uppsala University.

Westerlund, Torbjörn, 2013. *Finite Verbs in Ngarla (Pama-Nyungan, Ngayarta).* PhD thesis, Uppsala University.

Williams, Alan, Sean Ulm, Chris S. M. Turney, David Rohde, Gentry White, 2015. Holocene demographic changes and the emergence of complex societies in prehistoric Australia. *PLoS ONE* 10 (6) 1–17.

Wordick, Frank, 1982. *The Yindjibarndi Language*. Canberra: Pacific Linguistics.

28

Languages of the New Guinea Region

Malcolm Ross

28.1 Background: Geographical and Socioeconomic

The island of New Guinea is linguistically the most diverse area on earth. According to Nettle (1999: 117), New Guinea has 1,109 languages and 27 stocks in an area of 786,000 square kilometres. This is three times as many languages and stocks in proportion to area as any other continent-sized region in the world. Estimates of the number of languages in New Guinea range from 850 to 1,200, and of the number of its lineages from the low 20s to 60 or more. By any figures within these ranges New Guinea displays startling diversity.

In order to profile New Guinea's structural diversity, Comrie and Cysouw (2012) take a sample of 48 New Guinea languages from Haspelmath et. al. (2005) and compare it with the latter's worldwide sample. The diversity of the New Guinea sample turns out to be a microcosm of planet-wide structural diversity.

The topic of this chapter is areality among the languages of the New Guinea Region (henceforth NGR).[1] The NGR recognized by scholars (e.g. Comrie and Cysouw 2012; Foley 1986, 2000; Wurm 1975a) extends beyond the island of New Guinea itself to embrace islands to its west and its east (Map 28.1), and is defined as the region in which languages conventionally labelled 'Papuan' are found. It also contains numerous Austronesian languages. A count based on the *Ethnologue* (Lewis, Simons and Fennig 2014) gives 1,365 NGR languages.

Austronesian languages belong to a well researched language family (Blust 2013). Proto-Austronesian was located in Taiwan, and archaeology

I am indebted to Andrew Pawley and Ger Reesink for their comments on an earlier draft of this chapter and to Raymond Hickey for his careful editing work on a very complex text.

[1] Abbreviations for regional designations are ENus (East Nusantara), NGR (New Guinea Region), NWIM (northwest island Melanesia), NWNG (northwest mainland New Guinea); for linguistic lineages ENB (East New Britain), OMTK (Orya-Mawes-Tor-Kwerba), RLS (Ramu-Lower Sepik), TAP (Timor-Alor-Pantar), TNG (Trans New Guinea).

suggests that from about 2200 BCE its daughters spread out to occupy the Philippines, bits of Mainland Southeast Asia, most of the Indo-Malaysian archipelago, Madagascar, small mainly coastal enclaves on the island of New Guinea, and the Pacific islands of Melanesia, Micronesia and Polynesia (Bellwood et al. 2011). Austronesian speakers had reached the Bismarck Archipelago (New Britain, New Ireland and the Admiralty Islands) to the east of New Guinea by 1300 BCE.

Whereas Austronesian is a single lineage, 'Papuan' denotes a number of apparently unrelated lineages which share in common only that they are spoken in the NGR and are not known to be related to any lineage outside the NGR. The westernmost known Papuan language is Tambora, now extinct, on the Indonesian island of Sumbawa (Donohue 2007a). The easternmost is Savosavo of Savo Island in the middle of the Solomon Islands (Map 28.1). The islands of the NGR to the west of New Guinea have acquired the collective label East Nusantara (ENus). Exact definitions of ENus vary, but I follow Klamer and Ewing (2010: 1) by including in it Halmahera and the Bird's Head of New Guinea.[2] Politically they belong – with the exception of Timor Leste (East Timor) – to Indonesia. The island of New Guinea itself ('the mainland') is divided between Indonesia (its western half) and Papua New Guinea (its eastern half). The islands of the NGR to New Guinea's east and southeast as far as Bougainville also form part of Papua New Guinea, while those beyond Bougainville form the western half of the Solomon Islands. Just one Papuan language, Meryam Mir, is spoken on Australian territory in the Torres Strait Islands, just off the south coast of New Guinea, cheek by jowl with Western Torres Strait, an indigenous Australian language.

The western and northwestern boundary of the NGR not only marks the extent of Papuan languages, but also divides Austronesian languages of different structural types from one another. Beyond this boundary are morphosyntactically more conservative Austronesian languages. Within it are languages that share features with various Papuan lineages and with Austronesian languages throughout the western Pacific. The structural boundary coincides with the phylogenetic boundary drawn by Blust (1982, 1993, 2009) between Western Malayo-Polynesian languages and those of the Central Malayo-Polynesian subgroup of Austronesian. This correspondence of boundaries is surely not fortuitous, and its historical interpretation is discussed in Section 28.4.

From a Papuan perspective the NGR's Austronesian languages are very recent arrivals. It is reasonably well established that human beings had entered Australia during the last Ice Age by 50,000 years ago and New Guinea by 40,000, and recent archaeology suggests that human habitation in New Guinea is perhaps as ancient as in Australia (Summerhayes et al. 2010). Indeed, this is probable, as sea levels were lower than they are today,

---

[2] Hence the areas labelled 'East Nusantara' and '(New Guinea) mainland' overlap, as both include the Bird's Head.

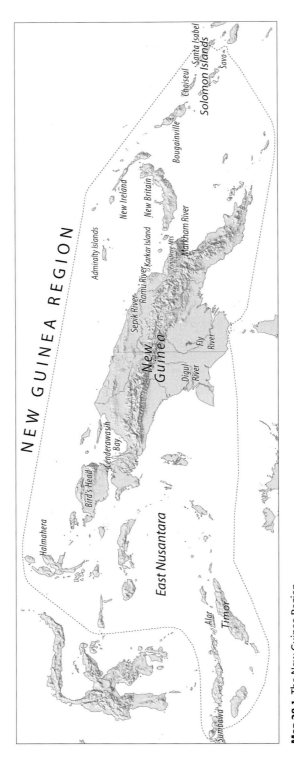

Map 28.1 The New Guinea Region

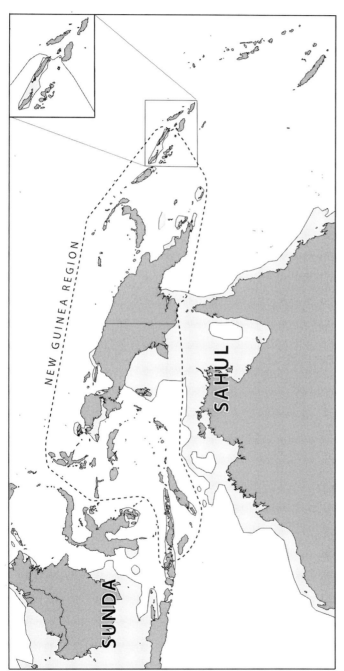

Map 28.2 Sunda and Sahul 40,000 years ago

and until just 8,500 years ago New Guinea and Australia formed a single continent, known as Sahul. Map 28.2 shows the coastline of Sahul 40,000 years ago when the sea level was 87 metres lower than it is today (Coller 2007). Nonetheless, even when the sea level was lowest, there was still a sea-crossing of some 70 kilometres between Sunda (a much extended Mainland Southeast Asia) and Sahul. The sea gap was enough to prevent the transfer of Sunda's placental mammals to Sahul or of Sahul's marsupials to Sunda, giving rise to the biogeographical boundary known today as the Wallace Line – and population genetics points to initial human settlement of Sahul between 50,000 and 25,000 years ago by a single population or a few already related populations, with no further genetic input until Austronesian speakers arrived (Friedlaender et al. 2007; Scheinfeldt et al. 2007). Once in Sahul, however, people could island-hop southeastwards from New Guinea to the southeastern extreme of the Solomon Islands by way of short sea-crossings, and had settled many of these islands by 30,000 years ago.[3] For much of this time, there was a land bridge linking the island combining Choiseul and Santa Isabel to the island of Guadalcanal. This bridge subsumed today's Savo Island, the location of the easternmost Papuan language.[4] The geography of Sahul partly explains the extent of today's Papuan languages. Tambora is close to the Wallace Line, and Savo is almost as far east as settlers from Sahul could travel.

If this initial settlement scenario is approximately correct, it provides a partial explanation for New Guinea's extraordinary linguistic diversity. Papuan lineages have been evolving more or less *in situ* for fifty millennia. Since it is usually reckoned that the comparative method detects relationship only to a time depth of ten millennia, it is small wonder that there appear to be so many unrelated Papuan lineages, and that none of these appear to be related to Australian lineages, which were, after all, on the same continent. Time depth cannot be the only cause of diversity, however. Other parts of the world have also been continuously inhabited for many millennia, and show nothing like New Guinea's phylogenetic diversity. Nettle (1999: 72–73) argues that economic interdependence between groups fosters social contact, hinders divergence and mediates the adoption of lingua francas. For example, pastoralists on the southern margins of the Sahara and in eastern central Asia developed social networks for mutual support in times of disaster, resulting in a single language or several closely related languages being spoken over a large area. But for perhaps forty millennia of their history Papuan speakers were foragers (hunter–gatherers). About 10,000 years ago agriculture appeared in at least

---

[3] New Britain and New Ireland by 35,000 years ago (Specht 2005; Spriggs 1997: 47), Buka-Bougainville by 32,000, Manus Island in the Admiralty Islands by 21,000 years ago (Kennedy 2002).

[4] Until Ross and Næss (2007) showed that the languages of the Reef and Santa Cruz Islands were Oceanic Austronesian, not Papuan, there was considerable discussion of how Papuan-speakers had found their way to these islands 390 kilometres beyond the Solomons. In fact, however, it was Oceanic speakers who reached them in their ocean-going outrigger canoes around 1100 BCE.

the Sepik-Ramu Basin in the northern lowlands (Swadling and Hide 2005: 291) and then in the highlands (Denham et al. 2003; Golson 1977). But these Neolithic farming communities, which continue today in much of the NGR, were and are small. Each extended family cultivated root crops on its own land and continued to hunt birds and mammals, remaining economically independent. In pre-contact times there were long-distance trading networks, but they tended to be single-purpose (e.g. the trading of shells from the coast to the highlands) and the links in the network were fairly short, so that encounters with people more than 20–30 kilometres away would have been rare. One relied on one's neighbours mainly for wife exchange, and there was little social motivation for larger speech communities (Sahlins 1963).

This history helps us to understand the three geolinguistic subregions into which the NGR naturally falls. Two of these have already been mentioned: mainland New Guinea and ENus to its west. The third subregion, to its east, is northwest island Melanesia (NWIM), comprising the Admiralties, New Britain, New Ireland, Bougainville and the Solomon Islands.

The mainland is the principal locus of Papuan languages, which fall into numerous lineages (Table 28.1). By the time Austronesian speakers arrived, agriculture was well established across much of its habitable territory, with a concomitant growth in population density. This evidently left little room for the newcomers, also Neolithic farmers. But there is almost certainly a second reason why incoming Austronesian speakers initially bypassed much of New Guinea, namely that they were not only farmers but also seafarers and traders, as well as reef foragers. This expressed itself in a preference for small offshore islands with fringing

Table 28.1 *A tentative listing of Papuan lineages*

East Nusantara and northwest mainland New Guinea		18	Sepik
		19	Ramu-Lower Sepik
1	West Papuan	20	Yuat
Northwest mainland New Guinea (NWNG)		21	Upper Yuat
2	East Bird's Head	**Fly-Digul Shelf and surrounds**	
3	Mairasi	22	Bulaka (alias Yelmek-Maklew)
4	East Cenderawasih Bay (ECB)	23	Yam (alias Morehead-Upper Maro)
5	Lakes Plain	24	Pahoturi
6	Orya-Mawes-Tor-Kwerba (OMTK)	25	Eastern Trans-Fly
7	Nimboran	26	Eleman
8	Sentani	**East Nusantara and mainland New Guinea**	
9	Skou		
10	Border	27	Trans New Guinea (TNG)
11	Pauwasi	**Northwest island Melanesia (NWIM)**	
12	Senagi	28	Anêm-Ata
13	Kwomtari	29	East New Britain (ENB)
14	Amto-Musan	30	North Bougainville
15	Leonhard Schultze	31	South Bougainville
16	Left May	32	Central Solomons
17	Torricelli		

reefs, which they found in the Bismarcks (Lepofsky 1988). Indeed, the reconstructable history of Austronesian languages spoken on the mainland indicates that all except those around the Bird's Head and Cenderawasih Bay resulted from later Oceanic back-migrations from the Bismarcks to the mainland (Ross 1988).

Whereas the mainland is largely occupied by Papuan speakers, the converse is true of ENus and NWIM, where Austronesian speakers predominate and Papuan languages are spoken only in small enclaves. This evidently points to important socioeconomic differences between the mainland on the one hand and ENus and NWIM on the other when Austronesian speakers arrived. Whereas the mainland was relatively densely populated by Papuan-speaking agricultural groups, it is tempting to infer that ENus and NWIM either lacked agriculture altogether or had much less of it, resulting in lower population densities that permitted incoming Austronesian speakers gradually to occupy the larger islands from their smaller offshore habitats. The issues here are controversial, however. Archaeology suggests that pre-Austronesian NWIM populations were at least sedentary arboriculturalists, not mobile foragers, but it is unclear whether agriculture was already present (Kennedy and Clarke 2004; Spriggs 1996, 1997: 31–34, 61). Linguistics points to contact-induced change in Austronesian languages, and here the arguments concern what contact processes occurred (Donohue and Denham 2010; Ross 2013). What is reasonably clear is that ENus and NWIM were not swamped by a large immigrating population of Austronesian speakers, but that Austronesian languages largely won out as their speakers achieved a degree of cultural dominance.

28.2   Background: Linguistic

A linguistic area is conventionally defined as one with 'three or more languages that share some structural features as a result of contact rather than as a result of accident or inheritance from a common ancestor' (Thomason 2001: 99). In the case of Papuan languages, however, it is often unclear whether two languages are related or not. Consequently, it is sometimes difficult to determine whether shared features result from contact or from inheritance.

28.2.1   Papuan Classification

The difficulty of deciding whether two Papuan languages are related has two causes. First, some possible relationships are so old that they lie at the very limit of the comparative method. Second, Papuan historical studies are in their infancy, and attempts to catalogue relationships and lineages vary greatly in their methods. There is thus no agreed list of Papuan lineages.

The first modern attempt was that of Wurm (1975b),[5] which included survey articles by Wurm's team members. They organized Papuan languages into eight lineages and a number of isolates (single-language lineages). They relied largely on wordlists – the collection of which was in itself a monumental achievement – to classify Papuan languages into numerous microgroups, i.e. groups of two to sometimes 30–40 languages that were obviously related. They employed lexicostatistical analysis, which, however, often failed them when they came to combine microgroups into larger groupings, because cognate percentages dropped to a level consistent with chance lexical similarities. Larger groups were then based on typological similarities, which meant that some groups (or parts of them) were based on areal features that might or might not reflect common inheritance. The largest of their groupings was the Trans New Guinea (TNG) phylum with 491 languages (Wurm, Voorhoeve and McElhanon 1975), a much smaller version of which had been proposed by McElhanon and Voorhoeve (1970). Wurm and McElhanon (1975) distinguished between (A) a 'main section' with 256 languages in 35 or so microgroups plus several isolates and (B) a further 20 or so microgroups and various isolates outside the main section with a TNG superstrate imposed on a non-TNG base.

Ross (2005a) used pronouns as a preliminary diagnostic for grouping Papuan languages, arriving at 23 possible lineages.[6] The goal was to set up hypotheses for future work, rather than an actual catalogue, and it is unfortunate that some writers have treated it as a catalogue (e.g. Lewis, Simons and Fennig 2014). Ross's listing retains within a 311-member TNG family all the microgroups of Wurm et al.'s main section except one (Sentani) and also includes a few microgroups external to the main section. The remaining microgroups are treated as distinct lineages.

Hammarström's (2010) Papuan classification has a different goal, as it forms part of a worldwide listing of language families based on a consistent criterion, namely that for each family there should be a published demonstration of its integrity 'by orthodox comparative methodology' and 'no convincing published attempts to demonstrate a wider affiliation'. The classification is thus far more conservative than Wurm et al.'s or Ross's, and has 65 lineages and 46 isolates.

The point of enumerating these classifications is not to debate their merits but to highlight the uncertain state of Papuan classification. The classification adopted here of 32 lineages and numerous isolates (see Table 28.1, Maps 28.3 and 28.4) is more conservative than Ross (2005a) but decidedly less conservative than Hammarström's. It is adopted more for the sake of manageability than out of a conviction of its correctness.

---

[5] Wurm (1975b) was summarized in more manageable form as Wurm (1982). It also formed the basis for the New Guinea area maps in Wurm and Hattori (1981).

[6] This methodology is criticized by Hammarström (2012).

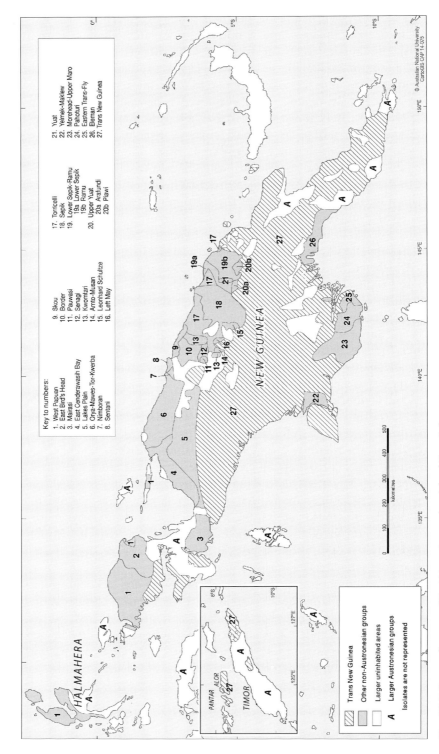

Map 28.3 Papuan lineages of East Nusantara and mainland New Guinea

Key to numbers:

1. West Papuan
2. East Bird's Head
3. Mairasi
4. East Cenderawasih Bay
5. Lakes Plain
6. Orya-Mawes-Tor-Kwerba
7. Nimboran
8. Sentani

9. Skou
10. Border
11. Pauwasi
12. Senagi
13. Kwomtari
14. Amto-Musan
15. Leonhard Schultze
16. Left May

17. Torricelli
18. Sepik
19. Lower Sepik-Ramu
    19a Lower Sepik
    19b Ramu
20. Upper Yuat
    20a Arafundi
    20b Piawi

21. Yuat
22. Yelmek-Maklew
23. Morehead-Upper Maro
24. Pahoturi
25. Eastern Trans-Fly
26. Eleman
27. Trans New Guinea

Trans New Guinea

Other non-Austronesian groups

Larger uninhabited areas

Larger Austronesian groups

A Isolates are not represented

© Australian National University
CartoGIS CAP 14-075

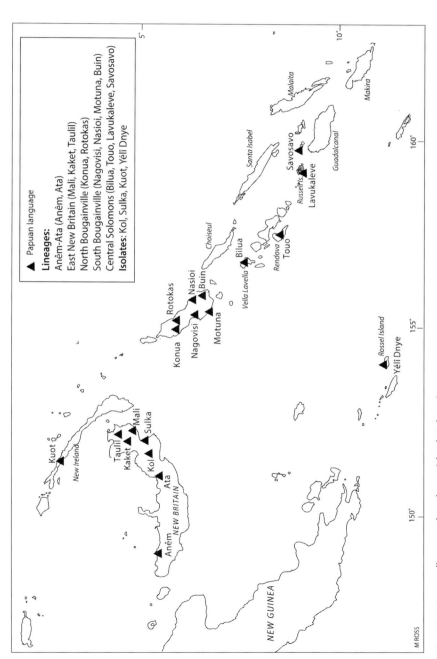

Map 28.4 Papuan lineages of northwest island Melanesia

All these classifications agree that one Papuan lineage, TNG, is much larger than any other. This means that the phylogenetic diversity is crammed into two smaller parts of the mainland. One is the northwest New Guinea (NWNG) area that stretches from the Bird's Head to the Sepik-Ramu Basin (the latter arguably the linguistically most diverse area on earth; Foley, in press). The other lies on and around the Fly-Digul Shelf in the south. This uneven distribution of lineages has a historical explanation. The NWNG and Fly-Digul areas reflect a diversity that covered a larger portion of the mainland before the spread of TNG, a diversity that resulted from forty millennia of pre-agricultural populations. This ancient period ended about 10,000 years ago, when taro- and banana-based agriculture began somewhere in the east-central highlands and spread across the valleys of the cordillera in both directions. These agriculturalists apparently spoke early TNG languages (Pawley 2005), and the spread of TNG is thus one of the agriculturally based spreads which Renfrew (2002) and Bellwood (2002) posit for a worldwide set of tropical and sub-tropical locations.

The history of TNG studies is tracked by Pawley (2005, 2007, 2012), while Pawley (2012) and Pawley and Hammarström (in press) summarize what we can reconstruct of early TNG. Regular sound correspondences, lexicon and bound morphology have been reconstructed for a few microgroups (Dutton 2010; Healey 1964, 1970; Loughnane and Fedden 2011; Smallhorn 2011; Usher and Suter 2015; Voorhoeve 2001), but regular sound correspondences across microgroups are elusive, partly because the number of apparent cognates is small. One of the most promising pieces of evidence for at least a portion of TNG is Suter's (2012) reconstruction of object prefixes on a small number of frequently used transitive verbs, a phenomenon first noted by Foley (1986: 259). Whether more detailed work will uncover sound correspondences or whether because of its antiquity TNG will remain on the list of what Nichols (2010) calls 'macrofamilies' – 'hypothetical or debated older groupings posited by comparing proven families' such as Afroasiatic – remains to be seen.

The second largest lineage posited in Wurm (1975b) is the Sepik-Ramu phylum, the largest occupant of the Sepik-Ramu Basin. Foley (2005a) shows that there is no serious evidence for the phylum as a whole, but a small but persuasive body of evidence for two relatively large lineages, Sepik and Ramu-Lower Sepik, with 49 and 32 members respectively (figures from Hammarström 2010).

28.2.2   Studies of Language Contact in the New Guinea Region

If shared inheritance is one side of the areality coin, contact is the other. A category of 'mixed' (Oceanic/Papuan) languages arising from contact has long been recognized by scholars working in the NGR, discussion of which has been dominated by the question 'Are they the outcomes of radical discontinuity – pidginization and creolization – or the results of more gradual change in bilingual communities?' The pidginization hypothesis remained on the table from the 1940s to the 1970s, but has faded from view in the light of more nuanced contact studies worldwide.

In 1911 Ray and Strong had both published papers on Maisin, an alleged mixed Oceanic/Papuan language of southeast Papua New Guinea. However, neither author imagined that two sets of ingredients had been thrown into a pot and stirred. Each thought that Maisin had a single origin – Oceanic according to Strong, Papuan according to Ray – but had acquired elements from the other source through contact,[7] prefiguring later work initiated by Weinreich (1953) on bilingually induced change.

Capell (1943, 1952), however, believed that the Austronesian languages of southeast mainland New Guinea were the outcomes of pidginizations by Papuan speakers, thereby contradicting the claim by Dempwolff (1937) and Milke (1958, 1961) that the Austronesian languages of the eastern three-quarters of the mainland belonged to the Oceanic subgroup of Austronesian, along with the languages of NWIM and the Pacific. A somewhat similar argument was made by Thurston (1982, 1987, 1989, 1992, 1994), who sought to show that Lusi, an Oceanic language on the northwest coast of New Britain, also reflected something akin to pidginization. However, a pidginized language is likely to display irregular sound correspondences with its alleged relatives and simpler morphology than they do. In the event, the Oceanic languages of the NGR display regular sound correspondences (Ross 1988), pointing instead to bilingually induced change. In comparative perspective Lusi shows no evidence of simplification but is perhaps the outcome of language shift over a number of generations (Ross 2014).

The histories of Maisin and another 'mixed' language, Takia, the Oceanic language of Karkar Island, off the north coast of New Guinea, were examined by Ross (1996). Several papers have sought to analyse the effects of contact on Takia and to relate them to the Neolithic social scenarios that brought them about (Ross 2001, 2003, 2013). The 1996 paper also coined the term 'metatypy' to label the change in morphosyntactic type, e.g. from VO to OV and from preposition to postposition, that appears quite often in Oceanic languages as the outcome of Papuan contact. Comparison across the Bel group of languages, to which Takia belongs, shows that Bel metatypy was a gradual process, not a sudden discontinuity (Ross 2008). Maisin (and to a lesser degree its Oceanic neighbours) and the Bel languages have progressively become more like local TNG languages, in some respects joining the core mainland linguistic area (Sections 28.3.5.2, 28.3.5.5).

As noted in Section 28.2.1, the controversy about mixed languages also affected Wurm and colleagues' Papuan classification. If (most of) the languages that they attributed to TNG on typological grounds but excluded

---

[7] In the event, Strong proved to be right (Lynch 1977; Ross 1996).

from its main section are languages of other lineages that have undergone metatypy as a result of speakers' bilingualism in a TNG language, then they are not, on today's criteria, members of the TNG family any more than Maisin and Takia are. They are in varying degrees members of the same linguistic area as their TNG neighbours.

28.2.3   Areal Studies Embracing the New Guinea Region

The first large-scale typological study of New Guinea's languages was Capell (1969). Earlier scholars had mapped and briefly described numerous languages,[8] and some also produced grammars (e.g. Dempwolff 1939, unpublished mimeograph; Drabbe 1952, 1953, 1955, 1959; Pilhofer 1933; Ray 1932).

In his 1969 volume Capell appropriated and organized the knowledge of his predecessors in the first work on the typology of languages of the NGR. So soon after Joseph Greenberg had laid the foundations of modern typology, this was a remarkable feat (Capell was inspired by Greenberg 1960), in contrast to his failed pidginization hypothesis (Section 28.2.2). Capell's major insight was to divide NGR languages into three types: event-dominated, object-dominated and dominationally neutral. The morphology of event-dominated languages displays complexity in the verb phrase, including argument indices and elaboration of tense, aspect and/or mood markings. Object-dominated languages have genders and/or noun classes that are reflected in the morphology of either the noun phrase, the verb or both. In dominationally neutral languages verb phrase and noun phrase are equally (un)complicated.

More recent NGR typology deconstructs Capell's types into their component constructions, as languages do not fall as neatly into types as his categories imply, a fact he himself recognized. But the features on which Capell focused continue to loom strikingly large in NGR typology. Some of the longer sections of Foley's (1986) Papuan languages textbook concern gender and nominal classification systems (1986: 77–91) and aspects of verbal morphology (1986 : 128–166), a pattern repeated in his 2000 update (2000: 370–382).

Although Capell does not major on areality, his map (1969: 129) of the distribution of domination types locates object-dominated languages in the NWNG and Fly-Digul areas, as well as in southern Bougainville, and event-dominated languages elsewhere. This prefigures the areality outlined in Section 28.3.3.

The very fact that Wurm et al.'s TNG included groups with a non-TNG substrate points to the copying of structural features across lineage boundaries that is the hallmark of areality. However, since Capell little attention

---

[8] They included, in British/Australian Papua, Sidney H. Ray (e.g. 1923, 1926, 1929, 1938); in Dutch/Indonesian New Guinea, Peter Drabbe (e.g. 1940/1941, 1949a, 1949b, 1950); and in German/Australian New Guinea, a number of missionary linguists (e.g. Kaspru 1945; Klaffl and Vormann 1905) and Arthur Capell himself (e.g. 1948, 1949, 1952).

Table 28.2 *WALS variables distinguishing Austronesian and West Papuan from the other non-Austronesian languages*

WALS variable		Value typical of Austronesian and West Papuan languages		Value typical of other Papuan languages	
69	Position of tense-aspect affixes	5	No tense-aspect inflection	2	Tense-aspect suffixes
81	Order of subject, object and verb	2	Subject-verb-object (SVO)	1	Subject-object-verb (SOV)
85	Order of adposition and noun phrase	2	Prepositions	1	Postpositions

has been paid to areality on the mainland or in the NGR as a whole. Only Comrie and Cysouw (2012) come close (Section 28.1). They find a basic typological division between (1) Austronesian and West Papuan languages (plus their one Torricelli language, Arapesh) and (2) the remaining Papuan languages in their 48-language sample. Given that it is possible to draw a line on the map around each of these divisions, this is effectively a statement about linguistic areas. However, their coverage is limited. It excludes Fly-Digul lineages and several NWNG lineages, and smaller lineages are represented by just a single language. They list the WALS values that are typical of languages in each of the two divisions in their sample, but provide contrasting values for only three variables, listed in Table 28.2.[9]

Nichols (1997) looks at the typological profiles of Sahul languages as evidence of their ancient history. A 'southeast interior' profile evidenced in the New Guinea highlands and in Australia's Pama-Nyungan languages is said to be associated with the initial settlement of Sahul, whilst a 'northwest coastal' profile, on the north coast of New Guinea, is the product of a migration occurring when the Pacific Rim, including the Americas, was colonized. However, whilst most of her northwest coastal features (presence of head-marking, low complexity, adpositions, exclusive/inclusive distinction, noun classes, numeral classifiers, tone, absence of ergativity) can be readily associated with some (not all) languages of NWNG, only a minority of her southeast interior features (presence of high complexity, absence of noun classes and numeral classifiers) are typical of New Guinea highlands (i.e. TNG) languages. The remaining features – presence of ergativity and absence of head-marking, adpositions and tones – are not features of highlands languages. TNG languages often use their instrumental postposition as a typically optional agent subject marker, and this is often labelled 'ergative', but the languages are in all other respects solidly accusative in alignment (Donohue 2005c). Tone, on the other hand, is now known also to be widely present in highlands languages (Donohue 2005a; Ross 2005b). An exclusive/inclusive distinction in

---

[9] Actually they list a fourth, order of object and verb, but this is entailed by order of subject, object and verb.

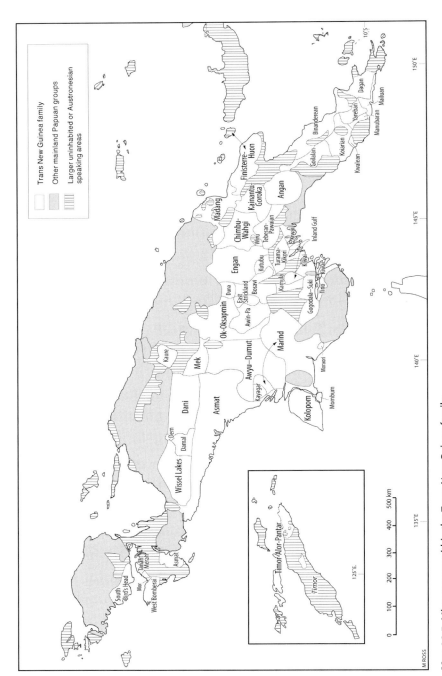

Map 28.5 Microgroups within the Trans New Guinea family

M ROSS

pronouns occurs sporadically all over New Guinea, though admittedly somewhat more densely in NWNG (Section 28.3.5.10).

Dunn et al. (2008) use the *Structure* algorithm to identify probabilistic clusters of NWIM languages based on structural features. Reesink, Singer and Dunn (2009) apply it to a more extensive sample of 121 languages, 81 of them in the NGR and 40 in adjacent areas (Borneo, the Philippines, Australia, Oceania beyond the Solomons), using 160 structural features.[10] Reesink and Dunn (2012) add a more detailed study of ENus (and western Indonesia). The algorithm organizes the languages into clusters, the number being determined by the user. Reesink et al. (2009) apply *Structure* iteratively, dividing their sample first into two clusters, then three, and so on up to fifteen. However, only the first nine iterations have respectable probability values. The main results for the latter, as they apply to NGR languages, are shown in Table 28.3, employing the nomenclature of Table 28.2. Numbers in the leftmost column indicate the number of groups assumed for that iteration (missing iterations only affect non-NGR languages). The table is read from top to bottom. Hence iteration 3 divides NGR languages into two clusters: A, consisting of Austronesian, West Papuan and the Timor-Alor-Pantar microgroup of TNG (Map 28.5), and B, all other Papuan languages – thus reflecting the two-way division of Comrie and Cysouw (2012). At iteration 5, B is divided into a 'rump TNG' (TNG minus the Timor-Alor-Pantar, Marind and Kiwai microgroups (Map 28.5), which each cluster with non-TNG neighbours: see Map 28.5) and a large cluster that includes all other Papuan lineages. At iteration 6 cluster A is divided into Austronesian and the Papuan languages of ENus. Iteration 8 divides the large cluster of Papuan lineages from iteration 5 into a NWNG cluster and a Fly-Digul/NWIM cluster, and iteration 9 divides the latter into NWIM and Fly-Digul clusters.

The table is a gross simplification of Reesink et al.'s (2009: 5) Map 3, as clusters often overlap. Many languages from the sample display minor participation(s) in clusters other than their principal membership, reflecting features shared with languages of another cluster. These cluster-overlap features are due either to contact or to chance. For example, Kobon, a TNG language, also shares features with NWNG languages, presumably due to its proximity to Sepik languages. Table 28.3 depicts one important overlap, however: the East New Britain lineage and neighbouring isolates Kol, Sulka and Kuot share features with the languages listed at each iteration in the cells to both their left and their right.

One cannot tell *a priori* from Reesink et al.'s analysis whether a given cluster is phylogenetic or contact-induced (or both). Some lineages are represented in their sample by only one language, which may be atypical of its lineage, and a number of lineages in Table 28.2 are not represented at all.

---

[10] Their sample contains one Andamanese language, 48 Austronesian languages (39 Oceanic, 9 western Austronesian), 55 Papuan languages (22 putative TNG, 33 putative non-TNG), 17 Australian (7 Pama-Nyungan, 10 non-Pama-Nyungan).

Table 28.3 *Typological clustering of NGR languages (after Reesink, Singer and Dunn 2009: 5)*

	A		ENB, Kol, Sulka, Kuot	B		
3	Austronesian, W Papuan, TNG-Timor-Alor-Pantar			all other Papuan		
5				**NWNG:** ECB, OMTK, Skou, Border, Sepik, Torricelli **Fly-Digul:** Yam, Trans-Fly, TNG-Kiwai, TNG-Marind **NWIM:** *Yélî Dnye*, N and S Bougainville, C Solomons		rump TNG
6	Austronesian	**E Nusantara:** W Papuan, TNG-TAP				
8				**NWNG:** W Torricelli **Fly-Digul:** Yam, Trans-Fly, TNG-Kiwai, TNG-Marind **NWIM:** *Yélî Dnye*, N and S Bougainville, C Solomons		**NWNG:** ECB, OMTK, Skou, Border, Sepik, E Torricelli
9				**NWIM:** N and S Bougainville, C Solomons	**NWIM:** *Yélî Dnye*, **Fly-Digul:** Yam, Trans-Fly, TNG-Kiwai, TNG-Marind	

Notes: Names in *italics* are isolates. The area between dashed vertical lines represents overlap between A and B.

Nonetheless, the analysis reveals quite strong areality with numerous local overlaps. The overall pattern, however, suggests that the areas identified in Table 28.3 have nothing like the homogeneity of better-known linguistic areas in the Balkans, India (Emeneau 1956, 1980) or Mainland Southeast Asia (Enfield 2003, 2005). Instead, the NGR is a patchwork of overlapping and somewhat heterogeneous areas. This is hardly surprising, given a pattern of small-group economic independence over a long history. Indeed, large-scale homogeneous areality is not expected in these circumstances.

The patterning that we do find perhaps calls into question the useful-ness of the concept of 'linguistic area', at any rate for the NGR, in agreement with the conclusion of Campbell (2006: 21–22):

> the concept 'linguistic area' is not significant in itself. Instead of pursuing definitions of linguistic areas, we should attempt to account for the history of individual borrowings and diffusion, together with language change in general, in order to answer the question, 'What happened?'

There is one respect in which one might take issue with Campbell, however. Although there is a qualitative difference between areality in, say, Mainland Southeast Asia and in the NGR, the concept of areality remains useful if one treats it as a continuum running from more to less homogeneous, placing NGR areas nearer to the 'less' end of the scale than perhaps areas in India and Mainland Southeast Asia.

28.3   The Northern Arc, the Fly-Digul Shelf and the Core Mainland Area

28.3.1   The Northern Arc

The remainder of this chapter evaluates claims about areality within the NGR, some of which are mentioned in Section 28.2.3. The one part of the NGR that has earned the label 'linguistic area' is ENus (Klamer and Ewing 2010: 12–13; Klamer, Reesink and van Staden 2008).[11] The features that have given rise to this are discussed in Sections 28.3.5.2–28.3.5.4, 28.3.5.7–28.3.5.9. The same features, however, also occur sporadically along the NWNG coast and into NWIM, and I label this discontinuous area the 'Northern Arc'. It embraces the following languages and lineages.

A In East Nusantara:

> (i) Austronesian languages,
> (ii) the West Papuan lineage,
> (iii) marginally, the Timor-Alor-Pantar languages of TNG (TNG-TAP).[12]

B In northwestern mainland New Guinea:

> (i) the East Bird's Head lineage,
> (ii) the Torricelli lineage,
> (iii) (perhaps the Skou lineage).

C In northwest island Melanesia:

> (i) most Oceanic Austronesian,
> (ii) the Anêm-Ata lineage,
> (iii) the East New Britain lineage,
> (iv) the isolates Kol, Sulka and Kuot.

The arc formed by these lineages was apparently an ancient voyaging corridor. It was certainly the route by which Austronesian speakers would later penetrate the NGR as far as the Bismarck Archipelago (Pawley 2008).[13] The fact that certain commonalities occur along this corridor, but do not occur in combination elsewhere in the NGR, suggests that this is not a chance constellation of features but reflects a historical circumstance. We will perhaps never know with any certainty whether this circumstance was a common origin in the ancient period, or contact among ancient ancestors, or – more probably – both.

The Northern Arc shows up in the literature in various ways. It bears an approximate resemblance to Nichols' (1997) northwest coastal area

---

[11] Gil's (2015) Mekong-Mamberamo linguistic area came to my notice after the NGR research was complete. It includes ENus, west Nusantara and Mainland SE Asia, thus overlapping with the NGR. As the features used in Gil's and the present work are almost mutually exclusive, the relationship between the two areas is unclear.

[12] Microgroups within the large TNG family are denoted as TNG-TAP, TNG-Madang, TNG-Marind and so on.

[13] There are today Oceanic languages in the southeast of the mainland, but they came somewhat later from the Bismarcks (David et al. 2011; Ross 1988: 211–212).

(Section 28.2.3). It is reflected in Comrie and Cysouw's (2012) Austronesian-West Papuan-Torricelli grouping, the more so when one recognizes that TNG-TAP, the East Bird's Head lineage, and the lineages and languages listed under C above are not represented in their sample. But in particular it resembles Reesink's (2003) 'North Papuan linkage', based on a set of variables that overlaps with the set considered below. Reesink's variables are gender encoding, noun classification, encoding of plurality in noun morphology, quinary numeral systems, clause-final negation and possessum/possessor order.

28.3.2 The Investigation

In order to gain a picture of NGR areality, data from 508 languages were collated. As complete coverage of NGR languages as possible was attempted, since some putative Papuan phylogenetic groups are very small, and vanish if a sampling procedure is used. As a statistical comparison with other regions of the world was not intended, sampling was unnecessary. Of the 508 languages, 321 are Papuan and 187 Austronesian, and of the latter 138 are Oceanic; 290 out of 508 are represented in WALS Online, but a number have values for phonological features only, which are not considered here. Due to descriptive gaps not all languages yielded a value for all variables. By way of comparison, Comrie and Cysouw (2012) use a sample of 48 languages, Reesink et al. use 81 NGR languages, and Nichols 36 NGR languages.

With just the 17 variables listed in Table 28.4, the scope of this investigation was less ambitious than two of those mentioned above.[14] Comrie and Cysouw (2012) use all the 140 WALS variables. Reesink, Singer and Dunn (2009) constructed a database of 160 variables.[15] Nichols (1997) has just eleven variables.

The list in Table 28.4 is divided into morphosyntactic ordering variables and semantic encoding variables. The latter concern how morphology partitions conceptual space. The division between the two sets of variables is discussed briefly in Section 28.3.3. Commentary on each variable is given in Sections 28.3.5.1–28.3.5.11.

Each of the 17 variables has two or three contrasting values common in the NGR, and on the basis of known collocations, the values are organized into two canonical language types A and B, somewhat in the style of Capell

---

[14] Values for variables 1–2, 5–6, 8–11, 14–15 and 17 were imported where available from *WALS online* (Dryer and Haspelmath 2013), supplemented by data from the online supplement to Reesink et al. (2009). The remaining data were culled from language descriptions. Data were also collected for three further variables: the encoding of elevation distinctions in the demonstrative paradigm (Schapper 2014), the position of phasal adverbs in the clause (Section 28.3.5.4), and gender in object indices. The first two were excluded from analysis because data were absent from language descriptions, the last because of the weight, alongside free pronoun and subject index gender (Section 28.3.5.10), that it would have placed on gender.

[15] There are considerable differences in the ways that *WALS* and Reesink et al. define variables, but this matter lies beyond the scope of this chapter.

Table 28.4 *Variables used to investigate NGR areality and their assignment to two types A and B (also a key to abbreviations used in Section 28.3.5 and in Tables 28.5 and 28.6)*

		Type A	Type B
Morphosyntactic ordering			
1	Verb/object order	**VO**	**OV**
2	Adposition/NP order	**Prep**	**Postp**
3	Actor/subject index on verbs	**sV**	**_Vs**
4	Undergoer/object index on verbs	**Vo**	**oV**
5	Possessor index on nouns	**Npr**	**prN**
6	clause-final negator in declarative realis clause	**ClNeg** (clause-final negator word)	**N**egation other than a clause-final negator word
7	clause sequences	**–Ch** (parataxis and coordination)	**+Ch** (clause-chaining)
8	noun/adjective order	**NA**	**AN**
9	noun/demonstrative order	**ND**	**DN**
10	possessum/possessor order	**PmPr**	**PrPm**
Semantic encoding			
11	alignment of verbal argument indices	**Spl**(it-S)	**Acc**(usative)
12	realis/irrealis distinction basic in verbal morphology	**+Irr** (realis vs irrealis basic)	**–Irr** (realis vs irrealis not basic)
13	at least one degree of past distinguished in verbal morphology	**–Past** (no past tense morphology)	**+Past** (present vs at least one degree of past)
14	clusivity in free first person pronouns	**+Inc** (inclusive/exclusive distinction)	**–Inc** (no inclusive/exclusive distinction)
15	masculine/feminine distinction in pronominals	**+Gnd** (gender encoded in at least 3SG)	**–Gnd** (No encoding of gender)
16	distinction between two or more non-SG numbers in free pronouns	**+Dual** (two or more non-singular numbers)	**–Dual** (one or no non-singular number)
17	distinction between inalienable and alienable possession constructions	**+Inal** (dedicated inalienable possession construction)	**–Inal** (no dedicated inalienable possession construction)

(1969). These represent the typological extremes found in the NGR and have no theoretical status beyond being a convenient presentational tool: a language is more A-like or more B-like.

Table 28.5 summarizes the values of the morphosyntactic ordering variables in the various lineages and in certain isolates for which sufficient data are available. Table 28.6 does the same for the semantic encoding variables.

The values shown in the tables are mostly the A and B values of Table 28.4. but for some variables an M, 'mixed', or Ø (zero) value appears. For example, variable 9, order of demonstrative and noun, has the value M when both orders appear in a single language. The zero value of variable 4 occurs when a language has no undergoer affix, and of variable 11 when the verb has no argument-indexing affixes.

Table 28.5 *Morphosyntactic ordering variables: dominant values by lineage*

M-rank	A-index, max=10	B-index, max=10	Type A / Type B	1 VO / OV	2 Prep / Postp	3 sV / Vs	4 Vo / oV	5 Npr / prN	6 ClNeg not ClNeg	7 −Ch / +Ch	8 NA / AN	9 ND / DN	10 PmPr / PrPm	Sem-rank, from Table 28.5
1.5	9	1	Anêm-Ata	A	A	A	A	A	A	A	A	A	B	2
1.5	8.5	1	Austronesian	A	A	A	AØ	A	AB	A	A	A	AB	6.5
3	8.5	1	Torricelli	A	A	A	A	Ø	AB	A	A	A	AB	6.5
—	:	:	Kol	A	A	A	Ø	B	...	A	A	A	A	—
4	7.5	2	E Bird's Head	A	A	A	AØ	B	A	A	A	A	B	3
5	7	2.5	W Papuan	A	A	A	BØ	B	A	A	A	A	B	11.5
6	6	3	Sulka	A	A	A	Ø	B	B	A	A	A	*B*	14
7	6.5	3	E New Britain	A	A	A	A	BØ	B	A	A	AB	B	9
8.5	5	2	*Kuot*	*A*	*A*	*M*	*M*	*Ø*	*B*	*A*	*A*	*B*	*A*	1
8.5	5	3.5	Skou	B	AB	A	AØ	Ø	A	A	A	B	B	9
10	4.5	4.5	OMTK	B	B	AB	AØ	AØ	B	A	A	A	B	20.5
—	:	:	Kwomtari	B	B	A	*ABØ*	Ø	*AB*	A	...	...	B	—
11.5	4	3	Eleman	B	B	Ø	Ø	Ø	A	A	A	A	B	20.5
—	:	:	*ECB (Bauzi)*	*B*	*B*	*Ø*	*Ø*	*A*	*A*	*...*	*...*	*A*	*M*	—
—	4	4	TNG-TAP	B	Ø	Ø	B	B	A	A	A	A	B	—
11.5	4	6	*Yélî Dnye*	*B*	*B*	*A*	*A*	*B*	*B*	*A*	*A*	*B*	*B*	20.5
13	3.5	5.5	Senagi	B	B	B	A	AØ	B	AB	AM	AM	B	17
15.5	3	4	*Lakes Plain (Iau)*	*B*	*B*	*Ø*	*Ø*	*Ø*	*A*	*B*	*A*	*A*	*B*	26
15.5	3	5	*Taiap*	*B*	*B*	*M*	*A*	*Ø*	*A*	*A*	*B*	*B*	*B*	9
15.5	3	5.5	Nimboran	B	B	B	AØ	Ø	B	A	A	AB	B	17
15.5	3	7	*Mairasi*	*B*	*B*	*B*	*B*	*B*	*B*	*A*	*A*	*A*	*B*	14
19.5	2.5	5	Sepik	B	B	Ø	Ø	AØ	AB	AB	AB	AB	B	20.5

19.5	2.5	RLS	B	B	Ø	Ø	AØ	AB	B	A	AB	B	26
19.5	2.5	Sentani	B	B	B	A	Ø	*AB*	B	A	B	B	26
19.5	2.5	S Bougainville	B	B	B	A	B	B	B	A	AB	B	11.5
23.5	2	Border	B	B	Ø	Ø	ABØ	B	AB	A	AB	B	29
23.5	2	C Solomons	B	B	AØ	M	BØ	B	AB	AB	AB	B	3.5
23.5	2	Trans New Guinea	B	B	B	BØ	BØ	B	B	A	A	B	23
—	2	*TNG-Kiwai*	*B*	*B*	*A*	*—*	*Ø*	*B*	*A*	*B*	*B*	*B*	*—*
23.5	2	*Yade*	*B*	*B*	*B*	*A*	*B*	*B*	*A*	*M*	*B*	*B*	*26*
—	2	*TNG-Marind*	*B*	*B*	*A*	*B*	*B*	*B*	*A*	*B*	*M*	*B*	*—*
26	1.5	*E Trans-Fly*	*B*	*B*	*BM*	*B*	*AØ*	*B*	*A*	*B*	*B*	*B*	*17*
—	:	*Bulaka*	*B*	*B*	*B*	*BØ*	*AØ*	*B*	*:*	*A*	*:*	*MB*	*—*
27	1	*Pauwasi (Karkar-Yuri)*	*B*	*B*	*Ø*	*Ø*	*Ø*	*A*	*B*	*M*	*B*	*B*	*14*
28.5	1	N Bougainville	B	B	B	Ø	A	B	B	B	B	B	5
28.5	1	Yam	B	B	BØ	B	BØ	A	A	B	MB	B	26

Table 28.6 Semantic encoding variables: dominant values by lineage

Sem-rank	A-index, max = 7	B-index, max = 7	Type A / Type B	11 Spl / Acc	12 −Past / +Past	13 +Irr / −Irr	14 +Inc / −Inc	15 +Gnd / −Gnd	16 +Dual / −Dual	17 +Inal / −Inal
1	7	0	*Kuot*	*A*	*A*	*A*	*A*	*A*	*A*	*A*
2	5.5	1.5	Anêm-Ata	*AB*	*A*	*AB*	*A*	*A*	*A*	*AB*
3.5	5	2	E Bird's Head	*AB*	*A*	*A*	*AB*	*B*	*A*	*A*
–	5	2	TNG-TAP	*A*	*A*	*B*	*A*	*B*	*A*	*A*
–	5	2	*Kol*	*A*	*A*	*B*	*A*	*A*	*B*	*A*
3.5	5	2	C Solomons	*AB*	*A*	*B*	*A*	*A*	*A*	*AB*
5	4.5	2.5	N Bougainville	*A*	*B*	*AB*	*A*	*A*	*A*	*B*
6.5	4.25	2.75	Austronesian	B(∧)	*A*	*AB*	*A*	*B*	*AB*	*A*
6.5	4.25	2.75	Torricelli	B(A)	*A*	*A*	*B*	*A*	*AB*	*AB*
9	4	3	*Taiap*	*A*	*A*	*A*	*B*	*A*	*B*	*B*
9	4	3	E New Britain	*AB*	*AB*	*B*	*B*	*A*	*A*	*A*
9	4	3	Skou	*B*	*A*	*A*	*B*	*A*	*A*	*B*
11.5	3.25	3.75	W Papuan	B(A)	*A*	*B*	*AB*	*A*	*B*	*AB*
11.5	3.25	3.75	S Bougainville	B(A)	*A*	*B*	*AB*	*A*	*B*	*AB*
14	3	4	*Mairasi*	*B*	*A*	*A*	*B*	*B*	*B*	*A*
14	3	4	Sulka	*B*	*B*	*A*	*B*	*B*	*A*	*A*
14	3	4	*Pauwasi (Karkar-Yuri)*	*B*	*A*	*B*	*A*	*B*	*B*	*A*
17	2.5	4.5	Senagi	*B*	*B*	*A*	*A*	*AB*	*B*	*B*
17	2.5	4	Nimboran	*BØ*	*AB*	*B*	*A*	*AB*	*AB*	*B*
17	2.5	4.5	E Trans-Fly	*B*	*B*	*AB*	*A*	*AB*	*AB*	*B*
–	2	4	*ECB (Bauzi)*	*Ø*	*A*	*A*	*B*	*B*	*B*	*B*
20.5	2	4	Eleman	*Ø*	*B*	*B*	*A*	*B*	*A*	*B*
20.5	2	5	OMTK	*B*	*B*	*B*	*AB*	*B*	*A*	*AB*

20.5	2	Sepik	B	B	B	B	A	B
20.5	2	*Yélî Dnye*	*B*	*B*	*B*	*B*	*A*	*A*
–	2	TNG-Marind	B	B	B	A	B	A
23	1.5	Trans New Guinea	B	B	B	AB	AB	AB
–	1.5	Kwomtari	B	B	A	B	B	*AB*
26	1	*Lakes Plain (Iau)*	*Ø*	*A*	*B*	*B*	*B*	*B*
–	1	TNG-Kiwai	Ø	B	B	B	A	B
26	1	Yam	*AB*	*B*	*B*	*B*	*B*	*AB*
26	1	Sentani	B	B	B	B	B	*B*
26	1	RLS	Ø	AB	B	B	AB	B
26	1	*Yade*	*B*	*B*	*B*	*B*	*B*	*A*
29	0.5	Border	BØ	B	AB	B	B	B
–	0	Bulaka	B	B	B	B	B	B

For each variable, Tables 28.5 and 28.6 show its dominant value in each lineage, where 'dominant' is defined as 'present in at least 75 per cent of the lineage's members'. Where there is no dominant value, two values are shown. If there is only one representative of a lineage for a given variable, or two representatives that disagree in value, then this is signalled by italics. Also shown in italics are all values of isolates and of the East Cenderawasih Bay and Lakes Plain lineages, each represented by a single language.

In both tables an A-ness index is created for each lineage by summing the row's values: A = 1; AB, AM or AØ = 0.5; any value not containing A = Ø. The B(A) value of variable 11 is weighted 0.25 (it is described in Section 28.3.5.8). A B-ness index was similarly calculated. Lineages are arranged in each table in rank index order with the most A-like at the top, the most B-like at the bottom. Kwomtari and Bulaka are excluded from the ranking as values are missing. The three TNG microgroups (TAP, Marind and Kiwai) that on Reesink et al.'s (2009) analysis did not cluster with TNG are also included in both tables, but are not ranked, as they are also included within the Trans New Guinea entry. The semantic encoding ranking is copied from Table 28.6 to Table 28.5 to facilitate comparison.

28.3.3   The Results

Table 28.5 allows us to distinguish three possible linguistic areas, although all three have a fuzzy boundary and a degree of internal heterogeneity. They are the Northern Arc, the Fly-Digul Shelf and surrounds, and the core area that occupies much of the mainland.

A dashed line across Table 28.5 below Skou marks the boundary between the more A-like Northern Arc lineages, where the A-index is higher than the B-index, and lineages with predominantly B values. Variables 8, 9 and 10 play little role in this difference, as they remain much the same for the lineages above and below the line.

The placing of a second dashed line above TNG-Kiwai is more arbitrary, but the lineages below it include all those of the Fly-Digul Shelf and surrounds (TNG-Kiwai, TNG-Marind, E Trans-Fly, Bulaka, Yam). With the exception of the Bulaka lineage, for which there are gaps in the data, the Fly-Digul lineages have B values for variables 8 and 9, unlike the lineages above the line. Whether the Fly-Digul Shelf represents a linguistic area is unclear because descriptions of these languages are only now emerging from ongoing research, but Evans (2012) points to possible areal features linking Nen, a Yam language, and Idi, a language of the Pahoturi lineage.[16]

The fact that the isolate Yade, the Pauwasi language Karkar-Yuri, and the North Bougainville lineage also occur here is perhaps due to chance (but Yade and Karkar-Yuri are located close to one another).

---

[16] The Pahoturi lineage is not included in Tables 28.5 and 28.6 because adequate data were not available to me.

The languages between the two dashed lines in Table 28.5 constitute the core mainland area. It consists of languages that are B-like on variables 1–7 but A-like on variables 8 and 9. One can infer that much of this area has developed in the past ten millennia through the spread of TNG and through metatypy on TNG models in languages around its periphery. But caution is needed: according to Table 28.5 the South Bougainville and Central Solomons lineages fall into this 'area', but because of their geographic separation from the mainland any phylogenetic relationship or contact between them and other members of the core area would be very ancient indeed, perhaps thirty millennia ago. It is likely therefore that their presence in this part of Table 28.5 is due to chance – and if their presence is due to chance, then so perhaps too is the presence of some mainland lineages.

The rank order in the leftmost column of Table 28.5 refers only to the dominant lineage values for the morphosyntactic ordering variables shown in the table. The rank order of Table 28.6, which shows dominant lineage values for the semantic encoding variables, is replicated in the rightmost column of Table 28.5. The differences between the two rank orders are striking, but the ten more A-like lineages of Table 28.5 (except for the isolate Sulka) are also found in the top 12 lineages of Table 28.6, whereas the next lineage (OMTK) in Table 28.5 is at rank 20.5 in Table 28.6. A difference in behaviour between the two sets of variables is not surprising, as bilingually induced grammatical calquing typically precedes metatypy (Ross 2007, 2013), so a language's semantic encodings will usually change before its linear orderings do. A language that is higher in rank in Table 28.6 than in Table 28.5 may be one that has undergone some grammatical calquing through contact with a neighbour but has yet to undergo metatypic change. This may explain the presence of the North Bougainville and Central Solomons lineages high in the rank order of Table 28.6 but low in Table 28.5. Both have been in contact with Oceanic languages with features of type A for perhaps 3,000 years (a relatively short period on a Papuan time scale). But this is an issue that needs targeted comparative research.

The results for a number of the variables in Tables 28.5 and 28.6 are shown in Maps 28.6–28.12 below, where each symbol represents a language. The lineage to which the language belongs is indicated by its symbol shape, to which Table 28.7 provides a key.

The shading of each symbol indicates the value(s) of the relevant variable(s) in that language, as indicated in the key that accompanies the map. Where two variables are mapped together, the symbol for a language in which both variables have A values is dark grey, and for one in which both have B values it is white. Where a symbol is split into two different shades, the values differ. In Map 28.6, for example, the left-hand part of each symbol indicates OV or VO order, and the right-hand part postpositions or prepositions. If a language has VO order and prepositions (both

Table 28.7 *Key to lineage symbols in Maps 28.6–28.12*

▷	Anêm-Ata	⊌	Orya-Mawes-Tor-Kwerba (OMTK)
○	Austronesian	⊹	Ramu-Lower Sepik
⬠	Border	⌢	Senagi
◇	Bulaka (alias Yelmek-Maklew)	▢	Sentani
◁	Central Solomons	▽	Sepik
☆	East Bird's Head	○	Skou
◇	Eastern Trans-Fly	☆	South Bougainville
☆	East New Britain (ENB)	◇	Torricelli
◯	Eleman	△	Trans New Guinea (TNG)
◯	Kwomtari	☐	West Papuan
◯	Nimboran	◊	Yam (alias Morehead-Upper Maro)
☆	North Bougainville	⊗	Other Papuan languages, including isolates

A values) its symbol is dark grey, but if it has OV order and postpositions it is white. (In this instance the adposition variable has two additional values, as indicated in the map key.)

These and other similar maps were created as a heuristic in the search for areality.[17] The islands at the western and eastern extremes of the NGR appear in insets, retaining their latitude and the scale of the rest of the map.

28.3.4 An Example of Contact-induced Change

Before discussing each variable, it may be useful to provide an example of the contact-induced change that is at least partly responsible for today's areality. Unlike many such changes, the example is one where fairly detailed inferences can be made about what has happened.

It is reasonably certain that TNG-TAP languages have undergone contact-induced structural change to join the Northern Arc (Table 28.5). Recall that Reesink et al. (2009) find that TNG-TAP belongs to their West Papuan and Austronesian cluster (Table 28.3). Yet it is as certain as it can be in the present state of TNG studies (Section 28.2.1) that this group is descended from a TNG language whose speakers migrated west from the mainland. The integrity of TNG-TAP is demonstrated by Schapper, Huber and van Engelenhoven (2014). Its languages maintain certain TNG features, as shown by comparison of the Teiwa (TNG-TAP) and Nggem (mainland) examples below: OV clause order (1a, 2a, 2b), object-indexing prefixes, some of them cognate with mainland counterparts (1a, 1b, 1c, 2a, 2b), and possessor prefixes on inalienably possessed nouns (1a, 2b). But other

---

[17] The maps were created with the mapping application *TileMill*, which reads a table of values and locations and interprets them in accordance with a script. The tables were produced from the typological database briefly described in Section 28.3.2.

TNG values have been replaced by values found in West Papuan and local Austronesian languages. TNG verbal suffixation is lost. This entails loss of subject indexing suffixes (2a, 2b), loss of a distinction between present and (often multiple) past tenses (2a, 2b), and loss of clause-chaining morphemes (see Section 28.3.5.5). Negation is encoded by a clause-final negator word (1b) instead of a pre-verbal or affixal negator (2c).[18]

(1)   Teiwa (TAP, TNG)
        a. *Nome   ha'an n-oqai   g-un-ba'?*
           Sir   you   1sP-child   3sO-APPL-fall
           'Sir, did you see/meet my child?'
        b. *Maan,   na   g-un-ba'   maan.*
           NEG 1sF   3sO-APPL-fall   NEG
           'No, I haven't seen/met him' (Klamer 2010: 275)
        c. *Ha   wa   ni-paxai!*
           2sF   come 1peO-divide
           'You divide us!' [e.g. in groups]. (Klamer 2010: 55)

(2)   Nggem (Dani, TNG)
        a. *Ap   andi   en   dirup   nini-t-as*
           man   that   AGT   syringe   1pO-hit-R.3sS.RPST
           'That man "syringe hit" (injected) us.' (Etherington 2002: 117)
        b. *Ap   ako   at   aninis   en   o-gwa   ako   at... w-at-igi.*
           man   DEM the 3sP.rage POSTP 3sP-wife   DEM the... 3sO-hit
           -R.FPST.3sS
           'That man hit his wife . . . in a rage.' (Etherington 2002: 117,
           edited)
        c. *Nit   yup   ya-g-atek*
           1pS   cry   plant-R-NEG
           'We did not cry.' (Etherington 2002: 110)

In some TNG-TAP languages, alignment of verbal argument indices has shifted from accusative to split-S, so that the erstwhile object prefixes like *ge-* '3s' in (3a) now also serve as subject prefixes (3b) with certain lexically specified intransitives.

(3)   Klon (TAP, TNG)
        a. *ge-uur*   'see him/her'
           ge-eek   'rebuke him/her'
           ge-moi   'help him/her'
        b. *ge-ampi*   's/he follows'
           ge-eten   'it's ripe'
           ge-wet   's/he urinates'
           (Baird 2008: 73)

---

[18] Abbreviations in interlinears follow the Leipzig Glossing Rules, plus DS (different subject), FPST (far past), R (realis), RPST (recent past), SS (same subject). Pronominal functions are A (actor), F (free), O (object), P (possessor), S (subject), U (undergoer).

Larike illustrates the split-S pattern present in certain ENus Austronesian languages.

(4)   Larike (Austronesian, ENus)
     a. *pese-ne*   'hold you (SG)'
     b. *hanahu-ne*   'you (SG) fell'
         lopo-ne   'you (SG) are wet'
         duarene-ne   'you (SG) are hungry'
         (Laidig and Laidig 1995)

It would be easy to assume that the new features in TAP reflect contact with Austronesian languages, but their history is probably more complex. It is a reasonable assumption that on their arrival in ENus, TNG-TAP languages were, like most TNG languages, accusative. At some point, however, they lost their subject suffixes, retained their object prefixes and become split-S. Split-S is a local areal feature of ENus, where it is fairly widespread in scattered Austronesian and West Papuan languages as well as TNG-TAP (Section 28.3.5.2), and it is very reasonable to infer that this is an outcome of contact. But if it is, where was the model from which speakers copied? Although split-S appears sporadically in western Austronesian languages, apparently ancestors of ENus Austronesian and Oceanic languages had accusative alignment. No Oceanic language has split-S verbal morphology and a number of ENus Austronesian languages that are conservative in other respects are also accusative. It is fairly safe to assume that ENus Austronesian and TNG-TAP languages both reorganized their alignment on an indigenous Papuan model, which may or may not have been related to the West Papuan lineage, where split-S alignment already occurred. Such a substrate is apparently also responsible for the innovation of clause-final negation (Section 28.3.5.4), the loss of inherited mood-prominence in many ENus Austronesian languages (Section 28.3.5.9), and the innovation of a distinction between alienable and inalienable possession constructions (Section 28.3.5.11).

28.3.5   The Variables

28.3.5.1   Variables 1 and 2: Verb/Object and Adposition/NP Orders

Map 28.6 shows that in the NGR, reflecting a worldwide trend (Dryer 2013c), there is a strong tendency for verb/object and adposition/NP in a given language to share a single head/complement order. Given the existence of a common grammaticalization path from verb to adposition, this is unsurprising. Most instances in Map 28.6 where head/complement order is not shared are languages that lack adpositions altogether. This is true of a few Sepik and western Torricelli languages and of a cluster of TNG-TAP languages on Alor and Pantar – OV languages that have evidently lost their postpositions, as their immediate relatives in Timor retain them.

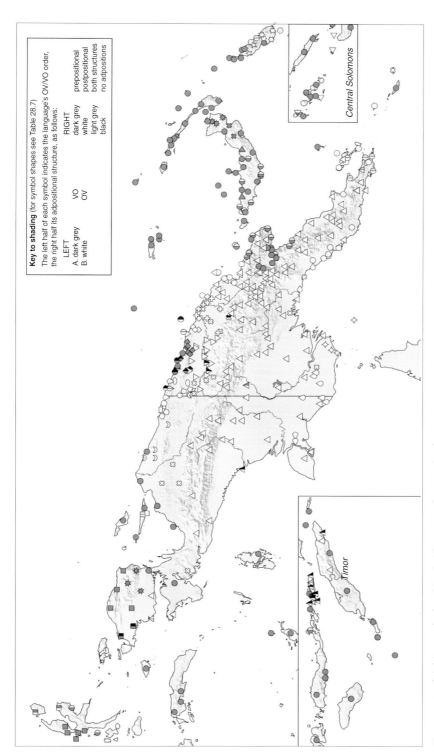

Key to shading (for symbol shapes see Table 28.7)

The left half of each symbol indicates the language's OV/VO order, the right half its adpositional structure, as follows:

LEFT		RIGHT	
A. dark grey	VO	dark grey	prepositional
B. white	OV	white	postpositional
		light grey	both structures
		black	no adpositions

Central Solomons

Timor

Map 28.6 Verb/object and adposition/NP in New Guinea Region languages

Map 28.6 also highlights the Northern Arc, as Austronesian, West Papuan, East Bird's Head, western Torricelli and the Papuan languages of New Britain and New Ireland all display VO&Prep,[19] in contrast with the OV&Postp pattern of the core mainland area and the Fly-Digul Shelf. The Skou languages are missing from the Northern Arc on this variable as they have OV order and display various values for adpositions. In fact, the map exaggerates the Northern Arc because one lineage, Austronesian, stretches its full length.

Within OV languages of the NGR there is a seemingly sharp difference between those that allow a post-verbal adjunct and those that do not, i.e. between OVX and OXV. Many TNG languages appear to insist on OXV, whereas many languages of the Sepik-Ramu Basin allow OVX (Foley, in press).

An important feature of Map 28.6 is that where Oceanic and eastern Torricelli languages are in close proximity to OV&Postp languages, they tend to replace inherited VO&Prep with OV&Postp. Because much more is known about the histories of Oceanic languages than of Papuan, recognizing these changes in Oceanic is fairly straightforward. We find clusters of OV&Postp Oceanic languages in two locations: on the coasts and offshore islands of the southeast mainland (Ross 1996) and on the north mainland coast, the latter including the Bel languages, whose history has been studied in some detail (Ross 2008). In both cases there has been intense contact with TNG languages, and Oceanic languages have been remodelled on TNG patterns. In central and southern Bougainville we find Oceanic languages that are headed in the same direction. Papapana and Mono-Alu vary between SVO and SOV and between pre- and postpositions, whilst Torau is now SOV but has mixed adpositions (Evans and Palmer 2011; Smith 2016). It is a reasonable inference that the eastern Torricelli languages, with OV&Postp, have undergone a similar set of changes thanks to their isolation from the more conservative (VO&Prep) western part of the lineage and to their interaction with neighbouring Sepik and RLS languages with an OV&Postp template.

Map 28.6 shows that the Oceanic languages around the Vitiaz Strait between the mainland and New Britain have VO clause order but a mixture of prepositions and postpositions – but no neighbouring Papuan language is an evident source of this value combination. One may reasonably infer, though, that the innovation of postpositions in these languages reflects contact with now extinct Papuan languages of New Britain. The languages of New Britain's south coast have other quite un-Austronesian features, among them pronominal gender, also a Northern Arc feature (Section 28.3.5.10) which can only be reasonably explained by contact (Ross 2013).

---

[19] Abbreviations for typological features follow those in Table 28.5.

28.3.5.2 Variables 3 and 4: Subject and Object Indices on Verbs

In many languages of the NGR the subject of a clause is indexed on the verb (Ewing 2010; Reesink 2010). In fewer languages, the object is also indexed, and in fewer still only the object is indexed (Map 28.7). An index is either an affix or a clitic, but sources often do not distinguish between them, and 'prefix' and 'suffix' should here respectively be read as including proclitics and enclitics.

'Subject' and 'object' imply accusative alignment, but a minority of NGR languages have split-S alignment (Section 28.3.5.8). For the purposes of variables 3 and 4, if there is split-S alignment the index of the actor argument of both transitive (A) and intransitive (S_A) verbs is treated as subject, and the index of the undergoer argument (U, S_U) as object.

An index has three possible values – prefix, suffix, absence – giving nine possibilities, listed below with their distributions (where {s,o} indicates a sequence of subject and object indices in either order).

Distribution of subject and object indices

sVo	Some ENus Austronesian, widespread Oceanic, one East Bird's Head, some Skou, some Torricelli, Anêm-Ata, East New Britain, Bilua (Central Solomons).
sV	Some W Papuan, East Bird's Head, some ENus Austronesian, some Oceanic, some Skou, some Torricelli.
Vo	Some Oceanic in New Britain and New Georgia (Solomons), Touo and Savosavo (Central Solomons).
{s,o}V	Some TNG-TAP, TNG-Marind, some West Papuan.
oVs	Scattered TNG.
oV	Some TNG-TAP.
Vs	Scattered TNG, North Bougainville.
V{s,o}	A few TNG, Nimboran, Sentani, Senagi, Kwomtari, some Sepik, South Bougainville.
V	TNG south of cordillera, Border, Sepik, LSR.

From this distribution, sVo emerges as a Northern Arc feature, although it is under-represented in ENus, where TNG-TAP and West Papuan languages have other configurations. Examples are as follows.

(5)   a. Allang (Austronesian, Ambon, ENus)
        *mane **me**=patina=**wa**.*
        3sF **3sA**=know=**2sU**
        'He knows you.' (Ewing 2010: 121)
    b. Manam (Oceanic, NWNG)
        ʔu-lele-ʔama.
        2sS-look.for-**1peO**
        'You looked for us.' (Lichtenberk 1983: 125)

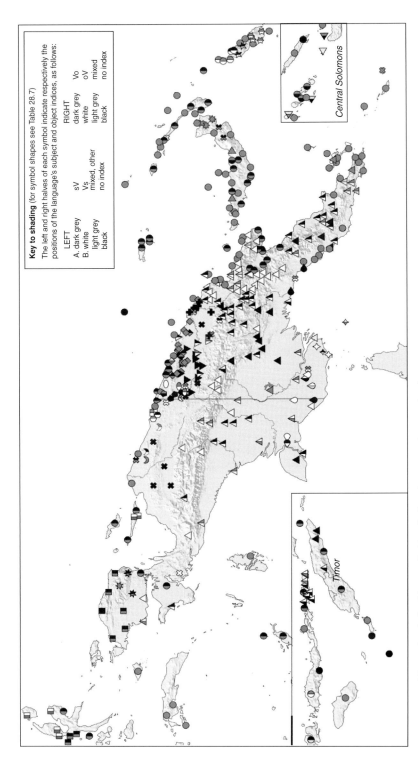

Map 28.7 Positions of verbal subject and object indices in New Guinea Region languages

Key to shading (for symbol shapes see Table 28.7)

The left and right halves of each symbol indicate respectively the positions of the language's subject and object indices, as follows:

LEFT		RIGHT	
A. dark grey	sV	dark grey	Vo
B. white	Vs	white	oV
light grey	mixed, other	light grey	mixed
black	no index	black	no index

Central Solomons

Timor

c. Meyah (East Bird's Head)
   Memef   ***me**-agob-**ir**.*
   1peF **1peA**-strike-**3pU**
   'We strike them.' (Gravelle 2002: 138)
d. Barupu (Skou, NWNG)
   /k-**opu**-jara-**ni**/ LH —> [kòpìljàrăní]
   R-**2pmS**-see-**1sfO**
   'You see me.' (Corris 2005: 77)
e. Bukiyip (Torricelli, NWNG)
   n**-a-hw-**ok
   3smS-R-hold-**3sfO**
   'He married her.' (Conrad and Wogiga 1991: 24)
f. Anêm (Anêm-Ata, NWIM)
   da**-b-**ur
   IRR.1sS-hit-**2sO**
   'I'll hit you.' (Thurston 1982: 48)

The Oceanic evidence indicates that sV often reflects earlier sVo, whilst Vo does so more occasionally. Apart from the Central Solomons languages Bilua, Touo and Savosavo, all the languages that manifest sVo, sV or Vo belong to the Northern Arc.

The order oV is found only in TNG languages, whilst oVs, {s,o}V, Vs, V{s, o} and V are found in TNG and other Papuan lineages. On the evidence of its distribution and of morphological reconstruction by Suter (2012) oVs was evidently a Proto-TNG feature, which has undergone a variety of erosions and transformations.

The common grammaticalization path *free pronoun* > *bound pronoun* gives rise to a prediction that sVo will occur in VO&Prep languages and oVs in OV&Postp languages, and this is confirmed for the NGR.

28.3.5.3   Variable 5: Possessor Index on Nouns

Possessor indices occur on possessum nouns in 296 of the 387 languages for which there is relevant information in the database. In the vast majority of these, indices occur only on inalienably possessed nouns, or they are obligatory on inalienably possessed nouns and optional elsewhere (see Section 28.3.5.11). There is a strong tendency throughout the NGR for possessor indices to complement subject indices in their placement. That is, if a language has both possessor indices on nouns and subject indices on verbs, either the possessor index is a prefix and the subject index a suffix, or vice versa. This is tantamount to saying that possessor indices usually match object indices in their position. This is true of languages that have both possessor and object indices, but there are enough languages that lack one or the other for the correlation not to be obvious.

Npr&sV(o) occurs in a good many ENus Austronesian languages, in many Oceanic languages, and in Anêm-Ata. The prN&oV(s) pattern is found in a good number of scattered TNG languages, and this was evidently the Proto-TNG pattern. It also occurs in South Bougainville.

However, there are also mismatches, i.e. prN&sV or Npr&Vs, a number of which are attributable to a historically reconstructable shift in the position of the possessor index. Thus in the Austronesian languages Tugun and Tulehu (ENus) and Waropen and Warembori (Cenderawasih Bay area, mainland) inherited Npr is replaced by prN, giving prN&sV. Since this pattern is also reflected in Kamang and Wersing of eastern Alor (TNG-TAP), and in the West Papuan and East Bird's Head lineages, one may infer that Papuan contact has played a role in the change. The usual Torricelli pattern is subject prefixes and no possessor affixes, but the eastern Torricelli languages Kamasau and Monumbo have apparently acquired possessor prefixes. The TNG-Marind microgroup also manifests prN&sV(o), but this reflects a shift from subject suffixes to subject prefixes (Section 28.3.5.2).

Apparently the converse change in possessor affixes, from prN to Npr, has occurred in a number of TNG microgroups, giving rise to Npr&Vs in the Gogodala-Suki, Koiari, Managalasi, Dagan, Finisterre-Huon and Chimbu-Wahgi microgroups, a distribution wide enough to imply that possessor suffixes occurred alongside prefixes in early TNG.

28.3.5.4   Variable 6: Negator Position in Declarative Realis Clause

Clause-final negation is commonly mentioned as an ENus areal feature (Klamer, Reesink and van Staden 2008; Reesink 2002),[20] and Reesink (2003) shows that it stretches from ENus along the north coast to New Britain and also occurs in the Oceanic languages of the Admiralties. Map 28.8 shows that negators occur clause-finally in declarative realis clauses in all the Northern Arc languages, other than some Torricelli languages and the East New Britain lineage. The languages in (6) have VO order, those in (7) OV.

(6)   a. Taba (Austronesian, ENus)
          *nik   calana   kuda-k   asfal   **te***
          my   trousers   be.black-APPL   asphalt   **NEG**
          'My trousers are not blacked with asphalt.' (Bowden 2001: 336)
       b. Arop-Lokep (Oceanic, mainland north coast)
          *i-yiri ookoo   **tiap**.*
          3sS-board canoe   **NEG**
          'I did not board (the) canoe.' (D'Jernes 1990)
       c. Maybrat (West Papuan, Bird's Head)
          *ana   m-amo   Kumurkek   **fe***
          they   3pS-go   Kumurkek   **NEG**
          'They do not go to Kumurkek.' (Reesink 2002: 246)

---

[20] For a slightly different view, see Lichtenberk (2013).

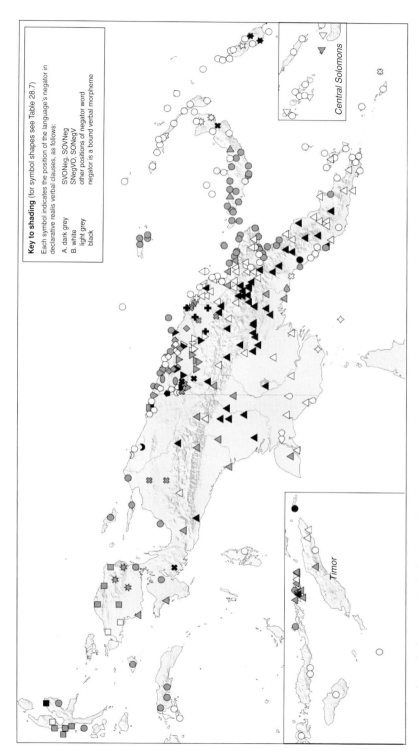

Key to shading (for symbol shapes see Table 28.7)

Each symbol indicates the position of the language's negator in declarative realis verbal clauses, as follows:

A. dark grey	SVONeg, SOVNeg
B. white	SNegVO, SONegV
light grey	other positions of negator word
black	negator is a bound verbal morpheme

Central Solomons

Timor

Map 28.8 Clause-final negators in declarative realis verbal clauses in New Guinea Region languages

d. Meyah (East Bird's Head)

me-en-et   *mat* **guru**
1peA-DUR-eat   food **NEG**
'We have not eaten food.' (Gravelle 2002: 168)

e. Bukiyip (Torricelli, NWNG)

… *m-u-wu_*   *kakwich*   **e**
2pS-IRR-plant   garden.food   **NEG.PAST**
'… we would not have planted garden food.' (Conrad and Wogiga 1991: 131)

f. Anêm (Anêm-Ata, NWIM)

Paulus   *u-tl-u*   *aba* **mantu**
Paulus   3sS-spear-3sO   pig   **NEG**
'Paulus didn't spear a pig.' (Thurston 1987: 75)

(7)   a. Bunaq (TNG-TAP, ENus)

hot   *baq*   *no*   *zapal*   *ga-sasi*   **niq**
sun   noon   OBL   folktale   U3-say   **NEG**
'During the day (we) don't tell folktales.' (Schapper 2009: 181)

b. I'saka (Skou, NWNG)

…   *tàu*   *d-ei*   **mi**
noise   1sS-do   **NEG**
'… I didn't make any noise.' (Donohue and San Roque 2004: 100)

There are two possible objections to a claim of areality, however. First, most languages with clause-final negation have VO order, but some (TNG-TAP, West Papuan, Skou) have OV order. Are these the same value of a single variable? VONeg is clause-final negation, but OVNeg could also be interpreted as post-verbal negation, corresponding with VNegO. Second, OVNeg crops up in places outside the Northern Arc: in scattered TNG languages – Mbaham (Bomberai Peninsula), Ekari (Wissel Lakes), Asmat (Asmat-Kamoro), Pisa (Awyu-Dumut), Kati and Tifal (Ok), Pawaian (Teberan-Pawaian), Koriki (Purari) – and in the Eleman languages (which may be phonologically unusual TNG languages) and Lavukaleve (Central Solomons). However, there are no cases of VONeg outside the Northern Arc. This suggests that OVNeg can develop fairly spontaneously, initially as an alternative to the morphological negation that is widespread in OV languages. It does so perhaps because the negator is adjacent to the verb.

Reesink (2002, 2003; Klamer et al. 2008) makes the well-supported proposal that clause-final negation, at least in ENus, has a Papuan origin. It appears more consistently in ENus Papuan (TNG-TAP, West Papuan) languages than in Austronesian. Indeed TNG-TAP's Austronesian neighbours do not have clause-final negation, so they are not the source of its presence in TAP languages. On the other hand, the Papuan languages of ENus (TNG-TAP and West Papuan) are OVNeg, so clause-final negation may well have developed in one or more Papuan groups, subsequently infecting their Austronesian neighbours.

Support for this comes from the worldwide distribution of SVONeg languages. They occur particularly in two areas, one centred around

Cameroon, the other around New Guinea and especially along its north coast (Dryer 2013e). This implies a contact-induced origin for VONeg and that clause-final negation is indeed an areal feature of the Northern Arc.

Reesink (2009) claims that clause-final phasal adverbs ('still', 'no longer', 'already', 'not yet') are also a feature of an area that roughly corresponds to the Northern Arc. It is difficult to check this claim in detail as so few language descriptions recognize the category, but a survey of languages where information is available suggests that these are usually also languages with clause-final negation.

28.3.5.5 Variable 7: Clause Sequences

One of the signature structures of Papuan languages is the clause chain (Foley 1986: 175–198; Longacre 1972). This consists of two or more OV clauses, of which only the final clause verb is independent, i.e. fully specified with suffixes for tense, aspect, mood and indexing the subject (see the suffixes of *toto-i-ʔa* 'they cut' in (8) below). Medial (= non-final) clauses are dependent, i.e. cannot normally end a sentence. If they have the same subject as the final verb, they may be morphologically simple. But a medial verb may also have morphological complexity, indicating a temporal or causal relationship (e.g. sequence, simultaneity, reason) with the following clause, and indicating whether the subject of the medial verb is the same as or different from that of the final verb. A morphological indication that their subjects are different is known in the literature as switch-reference, a very common feature of clause chains (Roberts 1997) but not an invariable one, and Map 28.9 distinguishes between clause-chaining with and without switch-reference. Foley and Van Valin (1984: 242) and Foley (1986: 177) characterize medial verbs as dependent but coordinate.[21]

In the Tauya example in (8), switch-reference is morphologically simple. If the next clause has the same subject (SS), the medial verb takes the suffix *-pa*. If it has a different subject, the suffix is *-te*. The morphology of the chain-final verb is italicized.

(8)   Tauya (TNG-Madang)

    nono   *Ø-imai-te-**pa***   *mai*   *mene-a-**te***   *pai* *aʔate-**pa*** *nono* *wi*
    child   3sO-carry-get-**SS**   come.up stay-3sS-**DS** pig hit-**SS** child show

    *nen-fe-**pa***   *yene* *wawi* *wi* *nen-fe-**pa***   *mene-**pa*** *pai*
    3pO-TR-**SS** sacred flute show 3pO-TR-**SS** stay-**SS** pig

    aʔate-ti   *tefe-**pa*** *ʔeʔeri-**pa*** *toto-i-ʔa*
    hit-CONJ put-**SS** dance-**SS** cut-*3pS-IND*
    'She carried the child, arrived and stayed, and they killed the pigs and showed them to the children, and showed them the sacred flutes and stayed, and killed the pigs and put them (down), and danced and cut (the pigs up).' (MacDonald 1990: 218)

---

[21] Foley (2010) offers a revision of this view.

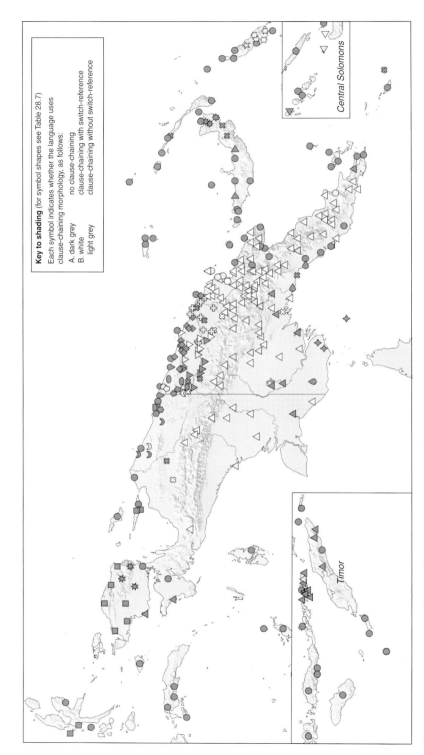

Key to shading (for symbol shapes see Table 28.7)

Each symbol indicates whether the language uses clause-chaining morphology, as follows:

A. dark grey   no clause-chaining

B. white   clause-chaining with switch-reference

light grey   clause-chaining without switch-reference

Central Solomons

Timor

Map 28.9 Clause-chaining with and without switch-reference in New Guinea Region languages

Clause-chaining is absent from languages of the Northern Arc and from the Fly-Digul Shelf and its surroundings. It is present in much of the rest of the NGR: in many TNG languages, in a number of Sepik and South Bougainville languages and in Savosavo (Central Solomons) and without switch-reference in Ramu-Lower Sepik and North Bougainville languages and in Lavukaleve (Central Solomons). Clause-chaining without switch-reference is also found in Oceanic languages that have intense contact with TNG languages: the Bel group on the north coast of the mainland (Ross 1987, 2008) and in Maisin in southeast mainland New Guinea (Ross 1984, 1996). These are clearly instances of metatypy.

28.3.5.6   Variables 8 and 9: Noun/Adjective Order and Noun/ Demonstrative Order

NA order is an areal feature of the NGR as a whole. Many linguists postulate headedness harmony, i.e. VO&NA or OV&AN, on the basis of Eurasian languages, but neither worldwide nor NGR data support it (Dryer 1988, 1992, 2013a, 2013b). In fact OV&NA is common among the world's languages. In Dryer's (2013a) sample there are 216 OV&AN languages and 332 OV&NA. He notes that New Guinea is a region where OV&NA is common, but that OV&AN intervenes in the Sepik lineage and the TNG-Kainantu-Goroka microgroup. It also occurs in the Fly-Digul lineages.

Almost all VO languages in the NGR have the pattern VO&NA. Only one, Bilua, a Papuan language surrounded by Oceanic, displays VO&AN, and this presumably reflects a contact-induced switch from OV to VO, as the other three scattered members of the putative Central Solomons lineage have OV order.

Throughout the NGR order of noun and demonstrative almost always matches order of noun and adjective. ND is thus also a NGR areal feature. The results of combining the two variables in WALS Online are: NA&ND = 476 languages; NA&DN = 25; AN&ND = 266; AN&DN = 184. There is thus a strong worldwide tendency for NA to be associated with ND (but not for AN to be associated with DN).

28.3.5.7   Variable 10: Possessum/Possessor Order

It is usually assumed that verb/object and possessum/possessor orders will agree in headedness direction, but, as Dryer (2013d) remarks, things are not that simple, as VO languages that are near to OV&PrPm languages are also likely to have PrPm order. This implies that PrPm order spreads through contact faster than OV order. This is relevant to the NGR, as it has often been observed (since Brandes 1884) that PrPm order is a widely distributed feature of NGR VO Austronesian languages, and a little less often asserted that this is due to contact with Papuan languages (Grimes 1991: 282; Klamer et al. 2008: 128). In light of Dryer's generalization, this is probably true.

Thus PrPm order is a NGR feature, regardless of whether a language has OV or VO order. However, as Map 28.10 shows, there are parts of the NGR

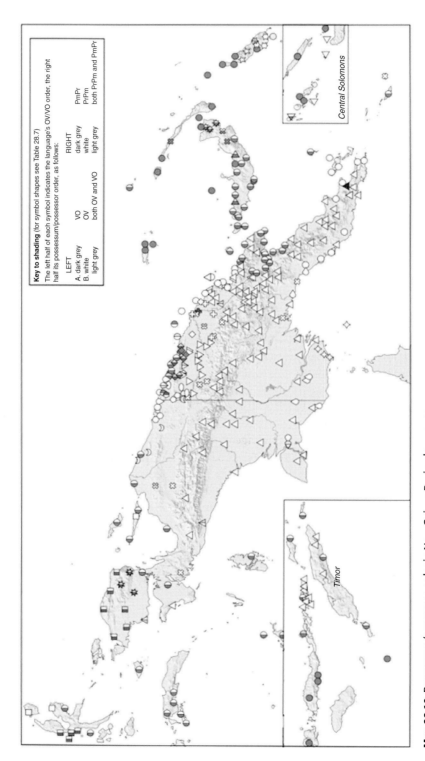

Map 28.10 Possessum/possessor order in New Guinea Region languages

where PmPr order occurs. The Austronesian languages of the extreme west of ENus (on Flores and Sumbawa) and of the Bismarcks, Bougainville and the western Solomons all have the inherited Austronesian PmPr order. Significantly, many of these languages are well away from Papuan languages, and the likelihood of contact-induced change is lower than elsewhere in the NGR. But Bougainville and the Solomons are an exceptional area in this regard: their Papuan languages have OV&PrPm, but only a few of their Oceanic neighbours (Papapana, Torau, Mono-Alu) have shifted to the Papuan pattern.

Combining the adposition/NP and possessum/possessor variables in WALS Online gives these results: Prep&PmPr = 351; Prep&PrPm = 54; Postp&PmPr = 13; Postp&PrPm = 442. In words, there is a strong likelihood worldwide that prepositional phrases will co-occur with postposed possessors, and postpositional phrases with preposed possessors. Again this is unsurprising, as adpositions are sometimes grammaticalized from possessum nouns ('inside of the house' becomes 'inside the house'). The VO&PrPm languages of the NGR are thus exceptional, displaying Prep&PrPm.

28.3.5.8 Variable 11: Alignment of Verbal Argument Indices

In a large majority of NGR languages subject and object indices are accusatively aligned. In the few that are not, there is a split-S pattern. In split-S alignment, if the single argument of an intransitive verb is semantically more actor-like than undergoer-like, then its index is identical to the transitive subject index. If, on the other hand, it is semantically more undergoer-like, then its index is the same as the transitive object index. Where the line is drawn between actor-like and undergoer-like arguments of intransitives differs from language to language (Foley 2005b), and there are even cases in ENus where the choice is lexically determined, with no obvious semantic basis (Holton 2010).

Klamer (2008) shows that split-S is an ENus areal feature embracing Austronesian and Papuan languages (also Ewing 2010 on Austronesian). Examples (1) and (3) illustrate split-S in the TNG-TAP microgroup, replacing the TNG accusative alignment of (2). However, the domain of split-S languages in the NGR extends beyond ENus along the Northern Arc. Split-S also turns up in the Fly-Digul lineages.

As Map 28.11 shows, in the Northern Arc split-S is found alongside accusative in West Papuan, the Torricelli language Mufian, Anêm-Ata and East New Britain (and in the isolate Taiap in the Sepik-Ramu Basin). Split-S also occurs in Lavukaleve in the Central Solomons. There are two possible explanations for this distribution. Either some languages in Northern Arc groups have shifted independently from accusative to split-S, or these languages reflect an ancient Northern Arc split-S pattern that has been masked by a general shift to accusative alignment. Only the latter possibility explains the distribution of split-S languages across the Northern Arc.

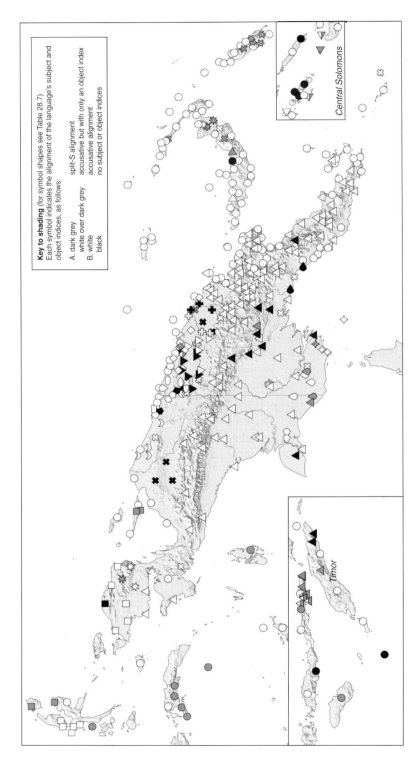

Key to shading (for symbol shapes see Table 28.7)
Each symbol indicates the alignment of the language's subject and object indices, as follows:

A. dark grey   split-S alignment
   white over dark grey   accusative but with only an object index
B. white   accusative alignment
   black   no subject or object indices

Central Solomons

Timor

Map 28.11 Alignment of argument indices in New Guinea Region languages

Further evidence for this hypothesis lies in languages that are accusatively aligned but have only object indices. They lack subject indices. Lineages that include such a language are notated B(A) in Table 28.6. Such languages are rare in the NGR, but they are located in the neighbourhoods of split-S languages. They are: a TNG-TAP cluster on Pantar, the Torricelli language Urim (near Mufian), the Oceanic language Nakanai (neighbouring Ata), Touo and Savosavo (putative sisters of Lavukaleve in the Central Solomons) and the Oceanic languages Hoava, Marovo and Roviana (adjacent to Touo). This distribution is too good to be coincidental. In accusative languages, the privileged argument (Van Valin and LaPolla 1997: 176) is the subject, i.e. A+S. The fact that the undergoer index survives, rather than the actor, goes back to a time when U+S was a privileged argument in either an ergatively aligned pattern or, in these instances, a split-S pattern.

28.3.5.9 Variables 12 and 13: Basic Tense/Mood Distinctions in Verbal Morphology

Among NGR languages that encode tense, aspect and/or mood, there are two contrasting types. In one the primary contrast is between present tense and past tense, often with two or three different past tenses (today, yesterday, remote). If one tense is morphologically unmarked, it is the present. In the other type the primary contrast is between realis and irrealis, where realis is understood to denote actual events, past or present (both often morphologically unmarked), and irrealis is understood to denote future events, expressions of ability or obligation, and hypothetical events present and past.[22] Exactly where a language draws the line between realis and irrealis varies (Bugenhagen 1994). For example, some of these languages mark an imperative as irrealis, and some don't.

If a language belongs to one of these two classes, this is usually plain from the description of its verbal morphology, as the first statement about its tense/aspect/mood morphology concerns one of these two basic distinctions. One might describe these two types as 'tense-prominent' and 'mood-prominent'. There is also a less common class of 'aspect-prominent' languages, but this variable awaits investigation.

Mood-prominence is a feature of the Northern Arc, represented in scattered ENus Austronesian and many Oceanic languages, in the East Bird's Head, Skou and Torricelli lineages, in Anêm (Anêm-Ata) and the isolates Sulka and Kuot. Apart from Skou, these are VO languages. Mood-prominence is illustrated in (9)–(13). The encoding of the realis/irrealis contrast is almost always pre-verbal, but the encoding patterns vary.

---

[22] It is important to differentiate between this usage of 'irrealis' and the much narrower usage in some Papuan language descriptions that excludes the encoding of future events.

In Larike there are distinct mood morphemes. In Manam and Anêm, there are different subject indexing prefixes. In I'saka irrealis is encoded by reduplication of a syllable consisting of the subject indexing prefix and the root-initial vowel. In Urat there is a pre-verbal irrealis morpheme and the verb stem itself undergoes change.

(9)   Larike (Austronesian, ENus)
       a. *arua-**i**-lena*   b. *arua-**na**-lena*
          1deA-**R**-walk   1deA-**IRR**-walk
          'we two are   'we two will walk' (Laidig and Laidig
          walking'   1995)

(10)   Manam (Oceanic, NWNG)
       a. *ŋau*   ***u**-pile*   b. *ŋau*   *masa*   ***m**-eno*
          1sF   1sS.**R**-speak   1sF   INDEF.IRR   1sS.**IRR**-sleep
          'I spoke'   'I will sleep' (Lichtenberk 1983: 112–113)

(11)   I'saka (Skou, NWNG)
       a. *k-elei*   b. ***ke**-k-elei*
          3smS-see   **IRR**-3smS-see
          'he sees'   'he will see' (Donohue and San Roque 2004: 25)

(12)   Urat (Torricelli, NWNG)
       a. *ŋam m-al*   b. *m-**a***   *m-il*
          1sF 1sS-R.go   1sS-**IRR**   1sS-IRR.go
          'I am going'   'I will go' (Barnes 1989)

(13)   Anêm (Anêm-Ata,NWIM)
       a. ***nu**-k*   b. ***na**-k*
          2sS.**R**-go   2sS.**IRR**-go
          'you are going/went'   'you will go' (Thurston 1982: 41)

Map 28.12 shows, however, that ENus languages are mostly exceptions to the Northern Arc pattern, being neither mood-prominent nor tense-prominent. Mood-prominence is an inherited Austronesian feature, so the scattered mood-prominent ENus Austronesian languages are conservative, while most have lost mood-prominence, bringing them into line with TNG-TAP and West Papuan.

TNG, OMTK, Border, Sepik, the Fly-Digul lineages, Eleman and North and South Bougainville are tense-prominent. They all have OV order and most index the subject with a suffix that simultaneously encodes tense, as in (14).

(14)   Kyaka Enga (TNG-Engan)
       a. *kande-**lyo***   b. *kanda-**pu***
          see-**PRS**.1sS   see-**PST**.1sS
          'I see/look'   'I saw/have seen'
       c. *kande-**yo***   d. *kanda-**lono***
          see-**FPST**.1sS   see-**RPST**.1sS
          'I saw'   'I have just seen'

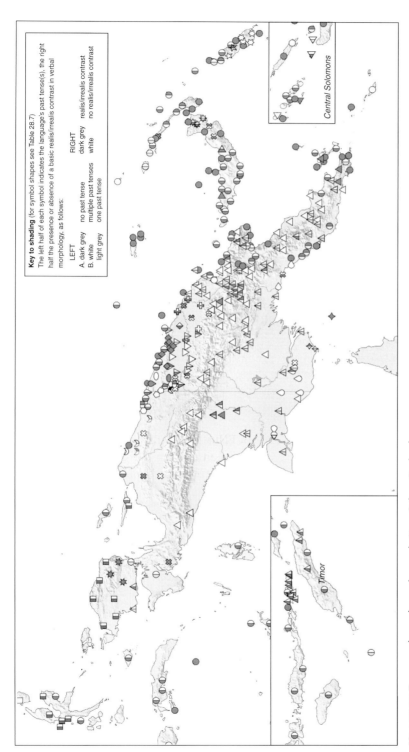

Key to shading (for symbol shapes see Table 28.7)

The left half of each symbol indicates the language's past tense(s), the right half the presence or absence of a basic realis/irrealis contrast in verbal morphology, as follows:

LEFT		RIGHT	
A. dark grey	no past tense	dark grey	realis/irrealis contrast
B. white	multiple past tenses	white	no realis/irrealis contrast
light grey	one past tense		

Central Solomons

Timor

Map 28.12 Tense- and mood-prominence in New Guinea Region languages

e. *kanda-**ro***   f. *kanda-**rono***
    see-**FUT**.1sS   see-**IMMEDIATE.FUT**.1sS
    'I shall see'   'I am about to see'
                               (Draper and Draper 2002: 28–31)

Generally tense- and mood-prominent languages are in complementary distribution in the NGR, but occasionally languages crop up that are both, like Sentani, Senagi and Kwomtari (the two last are contiguous) and the Oceanic languages of the southeast mainland coast. The latter are mood-prominent by inheritance, but have added a past tense through speakers' bilingualism in a TNG language.

28.3.5.10   Variables 14–16: Clusivity and Number in Free Pronouns and Gender in Pronominals

These three variables concern pronominals. Clusivity makes a distinction between first person exclusive ('we' = 'I' + '(s)he/they') and inclusive ('we' = 'I' + 'you') free pronouns. Number concerns whether free pronouns distinguish more than one non-singular number (i.e. dual, trial, quadral or paucal). Gender is defined as a masculine/feminine distinction in free pronouns and/or subject indices (a human/non-human distinction, quite common in ENus, is ignored). The three variables were selected because of an impression that they were typical of the Northern Arc. In the event, the impression proved wrong, as Table 28.6 shows.

Gender overlaps with noun class, which is important in various Papuan lineages other than TNG, but has so many variants that it lay beyond the scope of this investigation.

Inclusive forms that are otherwise atypical of their lineages appear in a broad scattering of TNG languages and in a few Sepik and Torricelli languages, implying perhaps that the distinction is quite easily innovated independently.

A cursory look at these distributions shows that they do not coincide. One can hardly argue that the patchy presence of these features is a Northern Arc characteristic, first because there are too many absences of each one from Northern Arc lineages, and secondly because there are numerous non-Northern Arc languages in which these features are present. There may come a time when some historical sense can be made of these distributions – for example when an account can be given of absences from the Northern Arc – but such an account is at present fragmentary. Thus one can argue that the presence of only one non-singular number in the free pronouns of various Oceanic microgroups is due to Papuan contact, but one then has to explain why gender has entered Oceanic languages through Papuan contact only in southwestern New Britain.

The way that these values are interleaved geographically, and across lineage boundaries in local areas, suggests that they are quite sensitive to contact-induced change and perhaps to spontaneous innovation. Interestingly, Oceanic languages of the southeast mainland have only one non-singular number, whilst many of their TNG neighbours have both dual and plural.

28.3.5.11   Variable 17: Distinction between Inalienable and Alienable Possession Constructions

A distinction between constructions encoding inalienable and alienable possession ('(in)alienability') is common in the NGR, but it is near-universal only in Oceanic languages of the NGR. In most languages with the distinction, the possessor is indicated by an obligatory affix on an inalienably possessed noun (Section 28.3.5.3), while possession of other nouns is marked either by the same affix, but optionally, or by some other means. The distinction is common but not always present in ENus (in Austronesian, TNG-TAP and West Papuan). It also occurs in East Bird's Head, East New Britain and South Bougainville languages. Its occurrence is sporadic in TNG languages, but seems to have been present in Proto-TNG, encoded by possessor prefixes. It is also sporadically present in the Sepik and Torricelli lineages. However, it is absent from Lakes Plain, Border, Skou, RLS, Bulaka, Eastern Trans-Fly, Eleman and from Lavukaleve and Savosavo of the Central Solomons lineage.

Whilst (in)alienability is present in all Northern Arc groups except Skou, the fact that in most lineages there are some languages with it and others without suggests that the inalienable construction is quite easily lost. Moreover, the fact that the distinction is not exclusive to the Northern Arc groups and is present in TNG means that it is not really diagnostic of areality.

Ross (2001: 138) suggested that (in)alienability had probably been copied into Proto-Oceanic or its immediate precursor from a Papuan language, and Donohue and Schapper (2008) show that its introduction into both ENus Austronesian and Oceanic can indeed be attributed to Papuan contact. As they note, it was the alienable construction that was innovated. The inalienable construction continues the inherited general possession construction.

28.4   Discussion

What emerges from the distributions of the A and B values of the variables discussed in Section 28.3.5 in each of the three areas of Table 28.5 above?

The Northern Arc, despite its somewhat chimerical appearance, stands up to scrutiny, and the various claims of such an area, especially Reesink's (2003) North Papuan linkage hypothesis, appear to be supported by the following features:

(a) VO&Prep (Section 28.3.5.1)
(b) sVo (Section 28.3.5.2)
(c) clause-final negation (Section 28.3.5.4)
(d) split-S (Section 28.3.5.8)
(e) mood-prominence (Section 28.3.5.9)
(f) (in)alienability (Section 28.3.5.11)

The only lineages that participate in all these values are Torricelli and Anêm-Ata, and even here definition is weakened by the fact that not all languages in each lineage display all values. Only one Torricelli language is known to have split-S alignment (Section 28.3.5.8) and only some display (in-) alienability. Of Anêm and Ata, only Anêm is mood-prominent and only Ata has split-S alignment and (in)alienability. Classifying their lineages as representing these values assumes that the values reflect history in some way.

Features (a)–(f) above are affected by contact in different ways. A number of Oceanic languages, by inheritance VO&Prep, have so to speak departed from the Northern Arc by copying OV&Postp from their Papuan neighbours, yet these same languages have retained sVo. That is, bound morphology is less readily affected by contact than is clause syntax. A similar history can probably be reconstructed for eastern Torricelli languages.

The predominance of B values, especially in the orders AN and DN, in the Fly-Digul Shelf area also suggests areality, but more data will be needed before this can be confirmed. The fact that the TNG microgroups Marind and Kiwai occur almost in a block with the Bulaka, Yam and Eastern Trans-Fly lineages in Table 28.5 also suggests areality.

The core 'area', however, is neither a geographic nor a typological area. The North and South Bougainville and Central Solomons lineages hardly form a typological area with the mainland, nor for that matter with each other. The non-Northern Arc languages of the mainland share OV&Postp, tense-prominence and accusativity, but lack consistency with regard to object indexing, pronominal gender and (in)alienability. Some core languages famously chain clauses (TNG, Sentani, some Border, Senagi, some Sepik, RLS, North and South Bougainville, and Lavukaleve in the Central Solomons), but others do not (OMTK, Nimboran, Kwomtari, Yam, Eastern Trans-Fly, Eleman). Areality here is weak yet complex, to put it mildly.

Because so many exceptions to core area tendencies are found among lineages in the area of extreme diversity towards the northern end of the border between Indonesia and Papua New Guinea, I have looked for signs of a separate areality embracing the Nimboran, Sentani, Border, Senagi and Kwomtari lineages. They agree on oV, on absence of both prN, Npr and inalienability, and except for Nimboran they are mood-prominent. However, the single members of lineages omitted from the investigation – Ama (Left May), Karkar Yuri (West Pauwasi) – do not share these features, and further data from the languages of the region are needed before one can discern its areality, if any.

Thus only the Northern Arc shows a constellation of values that point to areality, and this is fairly blurred. It does, however, display values that are distinct from those of much of the core mainland area, and its languages are arranged along what by Austronesian times was a maritime corridor. The lineages along the Arc are not related to each other at any time depth that the comparative method can detect. Some of the typological similarities among them may reflect ancient relationships. Others perhaps reflect ancient contact.

28.5   Concluding Thoughts

Scholars have often assumed that one can distinguish Austronesian from Papuan languages not just phylogenetically but also typologically, implying that there is a common Papuan type (Klamer and Ewing 2010: 11; Klamer, Reesink and van Staden 2008: 113–114; Reesink 2010: 71), but this is not well supported by the data.

In Section 28.1 I noted that the western and northwestern boundary of the NGR marks a typological boundary within the Austronesian lineage. NGR Austronesian languages are typologically more similar to their Papuan neighbours than to their Austronesian sisters to the west and northwest. As Donohue (2007b) argues, this is suggestive of contact – from an earlier time than the localized contact effects mentioned in Sections 28.3.5.1 and 28.3.5.5. It has long been inferred that PrPm order in NGR Austronesian languages is due to its presence in one or more substrate languages (Section 28.3.5.7). Clause-final negation (Section 28.3.5.4) and the (in)alienability (Section 28.3.5.11) are attributed to contact with a Papuan source. Donohue (2005b) justifiably questions the claim that languages of, for example, the East Bird's Head and Torricelli lineages have acquired their SVO order by contact with Austronesian languages when they display few other signs, if any, of Austronesian contact. Rather, as SVO was not the order inherited by ENus Austronesian and Oceanic languages from earlier verb-initial Austronesian, he suggests that they acquired it from one or more Papuan substrates, whilst Papuan SVO languages have either done the same or continue the substrate's SVO order. One can also argue that the presence of subject indexing prefixes on verbs in most NGR Austronesian languages and the presence of object indexing suffixes on many of them is an outcome of contact (Section 28.3.5.2). To be sure, the indexing morphemes had been present in Austronesian at earlier stages, but there was a change in distribution and function with the shift to SVO. In this scenario, Papuan languages did not change under Austronesian influence, but early Austronesian entrants to the NGR were recruited into the Northern Arc under Papuan influence.

However, PrPm, clause-final negation, (in)alienability, sVo and SVO have different distributions, and just what this tells us about the history of

Austronesian in the NGR remains to be worked out. It is, of course, tempting to look around for modern descendants of ancient substrates, but these may well have disappeared. Nonetheless, as the West Papuan lineage displays features common to ENus and in considerable measure to the Northern Arc, one can reasonably suggest that at least one ENus substrate was related to West Papuan. How closely related we will never know.

Occasionally one encounters mild scepticism about positing extinct substrates (e.g. Florey 2010), but with an area whose languages have been more or less in place for as long as in the NGR, they are a reasonable hypothesis.

It is just possible that a substrate might survive by accident. One such candidate is the isolate Taiap, spoken in the Sepik Basin. Its location happens to coincide with the one island in what 6,000 years ago was an inland sea (Ross 2005a), and one wonders if it is a relic from the deep past. However, Taiap's features group it with no known lineage. It displays OV&Postp, mixed sV and Vs, Vo, clause-final negation, no clause chaining, split-S alignment and mood-prominence, a combination which, but for OV&Postp, places it within the Northern Arc – yet prenominal modifiers put it with the Fly-Digul languages of the south!

One of the features claimed for the Northern Arc is sVo, a feature that entails bound morphology. There is, however, no clear sign that this morphology is cognate across lineages. The claim is rather that where an sVo pattern occurs in one of a bilingual community's languages it may be copied into their other language by cliticizing free pronominals to the verb. With that, clitics become affixes. Once an sVo pattern is established it tends to be maintained in the face of phonetic erosion by new cliticizations, a process that can readily be documented in Austronesian languages of ENus and Oceania that share sV but not the forms of subject prefixes.

A challenge of much work on areality is choice of variables. Bickel and Nichols (2006) propose defining areas on the basis of various approaches to population history and seeking statistically significant differences in the frequency of features inside versus outside the area. An obvious starting point is then variables known to be distinctive of or within the area, and this is where the investigation described in Section 28.3 began. There are, however, a number of almost equally distinctive variables that could have been chosen: the OVX versus OXV distinction (Section 28.3.5.1), phasal adverb position (Reesink 2009), relative clause position, noun classification (Foley 2000; Nichols 1997; Reesink 2003; Terrill 2002), numeral classifiers (Nichols 1997), encoding of plurality in noun morphology (Foley 2000; Reesink 2003), case-marking and alignment of noun phrases, aspect prominence (Section 28.3.5.9), gender in argument indices (Klamer et al. 2008), verbal morphology indexing the number but not the person of an argument, indirect object indices on verbs, and valency increasing morphology.

All 17 variables in Section 28.3.5 are morphosyntactic. Lexical and phonological variables could in theory also be collected. Since bilingually induced calquing gives rise to similar lexical polysemies and collocations, lexical variables would probably be revealing, but relevant data across enough NGR languages are not yet available. Comrie and Cysouw (2012) identify just one phonological variable as common in Papuan languages, an absence of lateral consonants in languages other than West Papuan. Yet a number of highlands TNG languages have laterals at more than one point of articulation (Ladefoged, Cochran and Disner 1977; Ladefoged and Maddieson 1996: 190). Also of phonological interest would be the distribution of tone systems across NGR languages, as tone plays a role especially in the TNG, Skou and Lakes Plain lineages (Donohue 1997, 2005a), and tonogenesis has also happened in some NGR Austronesian languages (Cahill 2011; Remijsen 2001, 2002; Ross 1993). However, so many descriptions of TNG languages omit mention of tone that this variable cannot yet be systematically evaluated.

What does the NGR have to teach us about areality? Perhaps that everywhere areas refuse to come into focus because the features that almost define them are not quite coterminous, it is possible to observe constellations of variable values that are unlikely to be due to chance and perhaps tell us something about deep history. We also need to understand better which features are more stable and which not, and why and under what circumstances some features change and others do not.

References

Baird, Louise, 2008. *A Grammar of Klon: A Non-Austronesian Language of Alor, Indonesia*. Pacific Linguistics, vol. 596. Canberra: Australian National University.

Barnes, Barney, 1989. Urat grammar essentials. Unpublished manuscript. Summer Institute of Linguistics Papua New Guinea Branch.

Bellwood, Peter, 2002. Farmers, foragers, languages, genes: The genesis of agricultural societies. In Bellwood and Renfrew (eds), pp. 17–28.

Bellwood, Peter and Colin Renfrew (eds), 2002. *Examining the Farming/Language Dispersal Hypothesis*. Cambridge: McDonald Institute of Archaeological Research.

Bellwood, Peter, Malcolm Ross, Geoff Chambers and Hsiao-chun Hung, 2011. Are 'cultures' inherited? Multidisciplinary perspectives on the origins and migrations of Austronesian-speaking peoples prior to 1000 BCE. In Ben Roberts and Marc Vander Linden (eds), *Investigating Archaeological Cultures: Material Culture, Variability and Transmission*, pp. 321–354. New York: Springer.

Bickel, Balthasar and Johanna Nichols, 2006. Oceania, the Pacific Rim, and the theory of linguistic areas. *Berkeley Linguistics Society* 32.

Blust, Robert A., 1982. The linguistic value of the Wallace Line. *Bijdragen tot de Taal-, Land- en Volkenkunde* 138: 231–250.

Blust, Robert A., 1993. Central and Central-Eastern Malayo-Polynesian. *Oceanic Linguistics* 32: 241–293.

Blust, Robert A., 2009. The position of the languages of Eastern Indonesia: A reply to Donohue and Grimes. *Oceanic Linguistics* 48: 36–77.

Blust, Robert, 2013. *The Austronesian Languages*, revised edition. *Asia-Pacific Linguistics Open Access Monographs*, vol. A-PL 008. Canberra: Australian National University. http://hdl.handle.net/1885/10191

Bowden, John, 2001. Taba: Description of a South Halmahera Language. Pacific Linguistics, vol. 521. Canberra: Australian National University.

Brandes, J. H. L., 1884. *Bijdragen tot de vergelijkende klankleer der westerse afdeling van de Maleisch-Polynesische taalfamilie.* PhD dissertation, Rijksuniversiteit te Leiden.

Bugenhagen, Robert D., 1994. The semantics of irrealis in the Austronesian languages of Papua New Guinea. In Ger P. Reesink (ed.), *Topics in Descriptive Austronesian Linguistics*, pp. 1–39. *Semaian*, vol. 11. Leiden: Vakgroep Talen en Culturen van Zuidoost-Azie en Oceanie, Rijksuniversiteit te Leiden.

Cahill, Michael, 2011. Tonal diversity in languages of Papua New Guinea. *SIL Electronic Working Papers* 2011:008.

Campbell, Lyle, 2006. Areal linguistics: A closer scrutiny. In Yaron Matras, April McMahon and Nigel Vincent (eds), *Linguistic Areas: Convergence in Historical and Typological Perspective*, pp. 1–31. Basingstoke, UK: Palgrave Macmillan.

Campbell, Lyle and William J. Poser, 2008. *Language Classification: History and Method.* Cambridge: Cambridge University Press.

Capell, Arthur, 1943. *The Linguistic Position of South-Eastern Papua.* Sydney: Australasian Medical Publishing Company.

Capell, Arthur, 1948. Distribution of languages in the Central Highlands of New Guinea. *Oceania* 19: 104–129, 234–253, 249–377.

Capell, Arthur, 1949. Two tonal languages of New Guinea. *Bulletin of the School of Oriental and African Studies* 13: 184–199.

Capell, Arthur, 1952. Languages of Bogia District, New Guinea. *Oceania* 22: 130–147, 178–207.

Capell, Arthur, 1969. *A Survey of New Guinea Languages.* Sydney: Sydney University Press.

Capell, Arthur, 1976. Austronesian and Papuan 'mixed' languages: General remarks. In S. A. Wurm (ed.), *New Guinea Area Languages and Language Study*, vol. 2: *Austronesian Languages*, pp. 527–579. Pacific Linguistics, vol. C-39. Canberra: Australian National University.

Coller, Matthew, 2007. *Sahul Time.* Melbourne: Monash University. http://sahultime.monash.edu.au

Comrie, Bernard and Michael Cysouw, 2012. New Guinea through the eyes of WALS. *Language and Linguistics in Melanesia* 30: 65–94.

Conrad, Robert J. and Kepas Wogiga, 1991. *An Outline of Bukiyip Grammar.* Pacific Linguistics, vol. C-113. Canberra: Australian National University.

Corbett, Greville G., 2013. Canonical morphosyntactic features. In Dunstan Brown, Marina Chumakina and Greville G. Corbett (eds), *Canonical Morphology and Syntax*, pp. 48–65. Oxford: Oxford University Press.

Corris, Miriam, 2005. *A Grammar of Barupu: A Language of Papua New Guinea*. PhD thesis, University of Sydney.

David, Bruno, Ian J. McNiven, Thomas Richards et al., 2011. Lapita sites in the Central Province of mainland Papua New Guinea. *World Archaeology* 43: 576–593.

Dempwolff, Otto, 1937. *Vergleichende Lautlehre des Austronesischen Wortschatzes*, vol. 2: *Deduktive Anwendung des Urindonesischen auf austronesische Einzelsprachen*. Beihefte zur Zeitschrift für Eingeborenen-Sprachen, vol. 17. Berlin: Dietrich Reimer.

Dempwolff, Otto, 1939. *Grammatik der Jabêm-Sprache auf Neuguinea*. Hamburg: Friederichsen, de Gruyter.

Dempwolff, Otto. Grammar of the Graged language. Unpublished mimeograph, Lutheran Mission, Narer, Karkar Island.

Denham, T. P., S. G. Haberle, C. Lentfer et al., 2003. Origins of agriculture at Kuk Swamp in the Highlands of New Guinea. *Science* 301: 189–193.

D'Jernes, Lucille, 1990. Arop-Lokep grammar. Unpublished manuscript, Summer Institute of Linguistics, Ukarumpa.

Donohue, Mark, 1997. Tone systems in New Guinea. *Linguistic Typology* 1: 347–386.

Donohue, Mark, 2005a. Tone and the Trans New Guinea languages. In Kaji (ed.), pp. 33–53.

Donohue, Mark, 2005b. Word order in New Guinea: Dispelling a myth. *Oceanic Linguistics* 44: 527–536.

Donohue, Mark, 2005c. Configurationality in the languages of New Guinea. *Australian Journal of Linguistics* 25: 181–218.

Donohue, Mark, 2007a. The Papuan language of Tambora. *Oceanic Linguistics* 46: 520–537.

Donohue, Mark, 2007b. Word order in Austronesian from north to south and west to east. *Linguistic Typology* 11: 349–391.

Donohue, Mark and Tim Denham, 2010. Farming and language in Island Southeast Asia: Reframing Austronesian history. *Current Anthropology* 51: 223–256.

Donohue, Mark and Lila San Roque, 2004. *I'saka*. Pacific Linguistics, vol. 554. Canberra: Australian National University.

Donohue, Mark and Antoinette Schapper, 2008. Whence the Austronesian possession construction? *Oceanic Linguistics* 47: 316–327.

Drabbe, Peter, 1940/1941. Beitrag zur Sprachgruppierung in Holländisch-Neuguinea. *Anthropos* 35/36: 355.

Drabbe, Peter, 1949a. Bijzonderheden uit de talen van Frederik-Hendrik-Eiland: Kimaghama, Ndom en Riantana. *Bijdragen tot de Taal-, Land- en Volkenkunde* 105: 1–24.

Drabbe, Peter, 1949b. Aantekeningen over twee talen in het centraal gebergte van Nederlands Nieuw-Guinea. *Bijdragen tot de Taal-, Land- en Volkenkunde* 105: 423–444.

Drabbe, Peter, 1950. Talen en dialecten van Zuid-West Nieuw-Guinea. *Anthropos* 45: 545–574.

Drabbe, Peter, 1952. *Spraakkunst can het Ekagi.* The Hague : Martinus Nijhoff.

Drabbe, Peter, 1953. *Spraakkunst van de Kamoro-taal.* The Hague: Martinus Nijhoff.

Drabbe, P., 1955. *Spraakkunst van het Marind, zuidkust Nederlands Nieuw-Guinea.* Studia Instituti Anthropos, vol. 11. Posieux and Fribourg: Instituut Anthropos.

Drabbe, P., 1959. *Kaeti en Wambon: Twee Awju Dialecten.* The Hague: Martinus Nijhoff.

Draper, Norm and Sheila Draper, 2002. *Dictionary of Kyaka Enga, Papua New Guinea.* Pacific Linguistics, vol. 532. Canberra: Australian National University.

Dryer, Matthew S., 1988. Object-verb order and adjective-noun order: Dispelling a myth. *Lingua* 74: 185–217.

Dryer, Matthew S., 1992. The Greenbergian word order correlations. *Language* 68: 81–138.

Dryer, Matthew S., 2013a. Order of adjective and noun. In Dryer and Haspelmath (eds), chapter 87. http://wals.info/chapter/87

Dryer, Matthew S., 2013b. Relationship between the order of object and verb and the order of adjective and noun. In Dryer and Haspelmath (eds), chapter 97. http://wals.info/chapter/97

Dryer, Matthew S., 2013c. Relationship between the order of object and verb and the order of adposition and noun phrase. In Dryer and Haspelmath (eds), chapter 95. http://wals.info/chapter/95

Dryer, Matthew S., 2013d. Order of genitive and noun. In Dryer and Haspelmath (eds), chapter 86. http://wals.info/chapter/86

Dryer, Matthew S., 2013e. Position of negative morpheme with respect to subject, object, and verb. In Dryer and Haspelmath (eds), chapter 144. http://wals.info/chapter/144

Dryer, Matthew S. and Martin Haspelmath (eds), 2013. *The World Atlas of Language Structures Online.* Leipzig: Max Planck Institute for Evolutionary Anthropology. http://wals.info

Dunn, Michael, Stephen C. Levinson, Eva Lindström, Ger Reesink and Angela Terrill, 2008. Structural phylogeny in historical linguistics: Methodological explorations applied in Island Melanesia. *Language* 84: 710–759.

Dutton, Tom, 2010. *Reconstructing Proto-Koiarian: The History of a Papuan Language Family.* Studies in Language Change, vol. 7. Canberra: Pacific Linguistics.

Emeneau, Murray B., 1956. India as a linguistic area. *Language* 32: 3–16.

Emeneau, Murray B., 1980. The Indian linguistic area revisited. In Murray B. Emeneau (ed.), *Language and Linguistic Area*, pp. 197–249. Stanford, CA: Stanford University Press.

Enfield, Nicholas J., 2003. *Linguistic Epidemiology: Semantics and Grammar of Language Contact in Mainland Southeast Asia*. London: RoutledgeCurzon.

Enfield, Nicholas J., 2005. Areal linguistics and mainland Southeast Asia. *Annual Review of Anthropology* 34: 181–206.

Etherington, Paul, 2002. *Nggem Morphology and Syntax*. MA thesis, Northern Territory University.

Evans, Bethwyn and Bill Palmer, 2011. Contact-induced change in southern Bougainville. *Oceanic Linguistics* 50: 483–523.

Evans, Nicholas, 2012. Even more diverse than we had thought: The multiplicity of Trans-Fly languages. In Nicholas Evans and Marian Klamer (eds), *Melanesian Languages on the Edge of Asia: Challenges for the Twenty-first Century*, pp. 109–149. *Language Documentation and Conservation Special Publication* 5. Honolulu: Language Documentation and Conservation.

Ewing, Michael C., 2010. Agentive alignment in Central Maluku languages. In Ewing and Klamer (eds), pp. 119–141.

Ewing, Michael and Marian Klamer (eds), 2010. *East Nusantara: Typological and Areal Analyses*. Pacific Linguistics, vol. 618. Canberra: Australian National University.

Florey, Margaret J., 2010. Negation in the Moluccan languages. In Ewing and Klamer (eds), pp. 227–250.

Foley, William A., 1986. *The Papuan Languages of New Guinea*. Cambridge: Cambridge University Press.

Foley, William A., 2000. The languages of New Guinea. *Annual Review of Anthropology* 29: 357–404.

Foley, William A., 2005a. Linguistic prehistory in the Sepik-Ramu basin. In Pawley et al. (eds), pp. 109–144.

Foley, William A., 2005b. Semantic parameters and the unaccusative split in the Austronesian language family. *Studies in Language* 29: 385–430.

Foley, William A., 2010. Clause linkage and nexus in Papuan languages. In Isabelle Bril (ed.), *Clause Linking and Clause Hierarchy: Syntax and Pragmatics*, pp. 27–50. Amsterdam: John Benjamins.

Foley, William A., in press. The languages of the Sepik-Ramu Basin and environs. In Bill Palmer (ed.), *The Languages and Linguistics of New Guinea: A Comprehensive Guide*. Berlin: de Gruyter Mouton.

Foley, William A. and Robert D. Van Valin, 1984. *Functional Syntax and Universal Grammar*. Cambridge: Cambridge University Press.

Friedlaender, Jonathan S. (ed.), 2007. *Genes, Language and Culture History in the Southwest Pacific*. Oxford: Oxford University Press.

Friedlaender, Jonathan S., F. R. Friedlaender, J. A. Hodgson et al., 2007. Mitochondrial DNA variation in Northern Island Melanesia. In Friedlaender (ed.), pp. 61–80.

Gil, David, 2015. The Mekong-Mamberamo linguistic area. In N. J. Enfield and Bernard Comrie (eds), *Mainland Southeast Asian Languages: The State of the Art*, pp. 261–350. Berlin: de Gruyter Mouton.

Golson, Jack, 1977. The making of the New Guinea Highlands. In J. H. Winslow (ed.), *The Melanesian Environment*, pp. 45–56. Canberra: Australian National University Press.

Gravelle, Gilles, 2002. Morphosyntactic properties of Meyah word classes. In Ger P. Reesink (ed.), *Languages of the Eastern Bird's Head*, pp. 109–180. Pacific Linguistics, vol. 524. Canberra: Australian National University.

Greenberg, Joseph H., 1960. A quantitative approach to the morphological study of language. *International Journal of American Linguistics* 26: 178–194. Originally published in Robert F. Spencer (ed.), 1954, *Method and Perspective in Anthropology: Papers in Honor of Wilson D. Wallis*, Minneapolis: University of Minnesota Press.

Grimes, Charles E., 1991. *The Buru Language of Eastern Indonesia*. PhD thesis, Australian National University.

Hammarström, Harald, 2010. Online appendix for 'A full-scale test of the language farming dispersal hypothesis' (*Diachronica* 27: 197–213).

Hammarström, Harald, 2012. Pronouns and the (preliminary) classification of Papuan languages. In Hammarström and van den Heuvel (eds), pp. 428–538.

Hammarström, Harald and Wilco van den Heuvel (eds), 2012. *History, Contact and Classification of Papuan Languages*, part 2. Special issue of *Language and Linguistics in Melanesia*. Port Moresby: Linguistic Society of Papua New Guinea.

Haspelmath, Martin, Matthew Dryer, David Gil and Bernard Comrie (eds), 2005. *The World Atlas of Language Structures*. Oxford: Oxford University Press.

Healey, Alan, 1964. *The Ok Family in New Guinea*. PhD dissertation, Australian National University.

Healey, Alan, 1970. Proto-Awyu-Dumut phonology. In S. A. Wurm and D. C. Laycock (eds), *Pacific Linguistic Studies in Honour of Arthur Capell*, pp. 997–1063. Pacific Linguistics, vol. C-13. Canberra: Australian National University.

Holton, Gary, 2010. Person-marking, verb classes, and and the notion of alignment in Western Pantar. In Ewing and Klamer (eds), pp. 97–117.

Kaji, Shigeki (ed.), 2005. *Crosslinguistic Studies of Tonal Phenomena: Historical Development, Tone-Syntax Interface, and Descriptive Studies*. Tokyo: Research Institute for Languages and Cultures of Asia and Africa, Tokyo University of Foreign Studies.

Kaspruś, Alois, 1945. The languages of the Mugil District, NE-New Guinea. *Anthropos* 37–40: 711–778.

Kennedy, Jean, 2002. Manus from the beginning: An archaeological overview. In Christian Kaufmann, C. Kocher Schmid and S. Ohnemus (eds), *Admiralty Islands: Art from the South Seas*, pp. 17–29. Zürich: Museum Rietberg.

Kennedy, Jean and William Clarke, 2004. *Cultivated Landscapes of the Southwest Pacific*. Resource Management in Asia-Pacific Working Paper, vol. 50. Canberra: Resource Management in Asia-Pacific Program, Research School of Pacific and Asian Studies, The Australian National University.

Klaffl, Johann and Friedrich Vormann, 1905. Die Sprachen des Berlinhafen-Bezirks in Deutsch-Neuguinea. *Mitteilungen des Seminars für Orientalische Sprachen* 8: 1–138.

Klamer, Marian, 2010. *A Grammar of Teiwa*. Berlin: de Gruyter Mouton.

Klamer, Marian and Michael Ewing, 2010. The languages of East Nusantara: An introduction. In Ewing and Klamer (eds), pp. 1–24.

Klamer, Marian, Ger P. Reesink and Mirjam van Staden, 2008. East Nusantara as a linguistic area. In Pieter Muysken (ed.), *From Linguistic Areas to Areal Linguistics*, pp. 95–149. Amsterdam: John Benjamins.

Ladefoged, Peter, Anne Cochran and Sandra Disner, 1977. Laterals and trills. *Journal of the International Phonetic Association* 7: 46–54.

Ladefoged, Peter and Ian Maddieson, 1996. *The Sounds of the World's Languages*. Oxford: Blackwell.

Laidig, Wyn D. and Carol J. Laidig, 1995. A synopsis of Larike morphology and syntax. *NUSA* 38: 18–42.

Lepofsky, Diane, 1988. The environmental context of Lapita settlement locations. In Patrick V. Kirch and T. L. Hunt (eds), *The Archaeology of the Lapita Cultural Complex: A Critical Review*, pp. 33–47. Thomas Burke Memorial Washington State Museum Monographs, vol. 5. Seattle: Burke Museum.

Lewis, M. Paul, Gary F. Simons and Charles D. Fennig (eds), 2014. *Ethnologue: Languages of the World*, 17th edition. Dallas, TX: SIL International. www.ethnologue.com

Lichtenberk, Frantisek, 1983. *A Grammar of Manam*. Honolulu: University of Hawai'i Press.

Lichtenberk, Frantisek, 2013. The rise and demise of possessive classifiers in Austronesian. In Ritsuko Kikusawa and Lawrence A. Reid (eds), *Historical Linguistics 2011: Selected Papers from the 20th International Conference on Historical Linguistics, Osaka, 25–30 July 2011*, pp. 199–225. Amsterdam: John Benjamins.

Longacre, Robert E., 1972. *Hierarchy and Universality of Discourse Constituents on New Guinea Languages: Discussion*. Washington, DC: Georgetown University Press.

Loughnane, Robyn and Sebastian Fedden, 2011. Is Oksapmin Ok? A study of the genetic relationship between Oksapmin and the Ok languages. *Australian Journal of Linguistics* 31: 1–42.

Lynch, John, 1977. Notes on Maisin: An Austronesian language of the Northern Province of Papua New Guinea. Paper presented to the Annual Congress of the Linguistic Society of Papua New Guinea.

MacDonald, Lorna, 1990. *A Grammar of Tauya*. Berlin: Mouton de Gruyter.

Maddieson, Ian, 2013. Lateral consonants. In Dryer and Haspelmath (eds), chapter 8. http://wals.info/chapter/8

McElhanon, Kenneth A. and C. L. Voorhoeve, 1970. *The Trans-New Guinea phylum: Explorations in Deep Level Genetic Relationships*. Pacific Linguistics, vol. B-16. Canberra: Australian National University.

Milke, Wilhelm, 1958. Zur inneren Gliederung und geschichtlichen Stellung der ozeanisch-austronesischen Sprachen. *Zeitschrift für Ethnologie* 83: 58–62.

Milke, Wilhelm, 1961. Beiträge zur ozeanischen Linguistik. *Zeitschrift für Ethnologie* 86: 162–182.

Nettle, Daniel, 1999. *Linguistic Diversity*. Oxford: Oxford University Press.

Nichols, Johanna, 1997. Sprung from two common sources: Sahul as a linguistic area. In Patrick McConvell and Nicholas Evans (eds), *Archaeology and Linguistics: Aboriginal Australia in Global Perspective*, pp. 135–168. Oxford: Oxford University Press.

Nichols, Johanna, 2010. Macrofamilies, macroareas and contact. In Raymond Hickey (ed.), *The Handbook of Language Contact*, pp. 361–379. Oxford: Wiley-Blackwell.

Pawley, Andrew, 2005. The chequered career of the Trans New Guinea hypothesis: Recent research and its implications. In Pawley et al. (eds), pp. 67–107.

Pawley, Andrew, 2007. Recent research on the historical relationships of the Papuan languages, or, what does linguistics say about the prehistory of Melanesia? In Jonathan Friedlaender (ed.), *Population Genetics, Linguistics, and Culture History in the Southwest Pacific: A Synthesis*, pp. 36–59. New York: Oxford University Press.

Pawley, Andrew, 2008. Where and when was Proto Oceanic spoken? Linguistic and archaeological evidence. In Yury A. Lander and Alexander K. Ogoblin (eds), *Language and Text in the Austronesian World: Studies in Honour of Ülo Sirk*, pp. 47–71. Munich: LINCOM Europa.

Pawley, Andrew, 2012. How reconstructable is Proto Trans New Guinea? Problems, progress, prospects. In Hammarström and van den Heuvel (eds), pp. 88–164.

Pawley, Andrew, Robert Attenborough, Jack Golson and Robin Hide (eds), 2005. *Papuan Pasts: Cultural, Linguistic and Biological Histories of Papuan-speaking Peoples*. Pacific Linguistics, vol. 572. Canberra: Australian National University.

Pawley, Andrew and Harald Hammarström, in press. The Trans New Guinea family. In Bill Palmer (ed.), *The Languages and Linguistics of New Guinea: A Comprehensive Guide*. Berlin: de Gruyter Mouton.

Pilhofer, G., 1933. *Grammatik der Kâte-Sprache in Neuguinea*. Berlin: Dietrich Reimer.

Ray, Sidney H., 1911. Comparative notes on Maisin and other languages of eastern Papua. *Journal of the Royal Anthropological Institute* 41: 397–405.

Ray, Sidney H., 1913. The languages of the Papuan Gulf District, Papua. *Zeitschrift für Kolonialsprachen* 4: 20–80.

Ray, Sidney H., 1923. The languages of the Western Division of Papua. *Journal of the Royal Anthropological Institute* 53: 332–360.

Ray, Sidney H., 1926. *A Comparative Study of the Melanesian Island Languages*. Cambridge: Cambridge University Press.

Ray, Sidney H., 1929. The languages of the Central Division of Papua. *Journal of the Royal Anthropological Institute* 59: 65–96.

Ray, Sidney H., 1932. *A Grammar of the Kiwai Language, Fly Delta, Papua, with a Kiwai Vocabulary by E. Baxter Riley*. Port Moresby: E.G. Baker, Government Printer.

Ray, Sidney H., 1938. The languages of the Eastern and South-Eastern Divisions of Papua. *Journal of the Royal Anthropological Institute* 68: 153–208.

Reesink, Ger, 2002. Clause-final negation: Structure and interpretation. *Functions of Language* 9: 239–268.

Reesink, Ger, 2003. The North Papuan Linkage: A hypothesis. Paper for the Workshop Pioneers of Island Melanesia, Cambridge, April 2003.

Reesink, Ger, 2009. A connection between Bird's Head and (Proto) Oceanic. In Bethwyn Evans (ed.), *Discovering History through Language: Papers in Honour of Malcolm Ross*, pp. 181–192. Pacific Linguistics, vol. 605. Canberra: Australian National University.

Reesink, Ger, 2010. Prefixation of arguments in West Papuan languages. In Ewing and Klamer (eds), pp. 71–95.

Reesink, Ger and Michael Dunn, 2012. Systematic typological comparison as a tool for investigating language history. In Nicholas Evans and Marian Klamer (eds), *Melanesian Languages on the Edge of Asia: Challenges for the Twenty-first Century*, pp. 34–71. *Language Documentation and Conservation Special Publication* 5. Honolulu: Language Documentation and Conservation.

Reesink, Ger, Ruth Singer and Michael Dunn, 2009. Explaining the linguistic diversity of Sahul using population models. *PLoS Biology* 7: e1000241.

Remijsen, Bert, 2001. *Word-prosodic Systems of Raja Ampat Languages*. PhD dissertation, University of Leiden.

Remijsen, Bert, 2002. Lexically contrastive stress accent and lexical tone in Ma'ya. In Carlos Gussenhoven and Natasha Warner (eds), *Laboratory Phonology*, vol. 7, pp. 585–614. Berlin: Mouton de Gruyter.

Renfrew, Colin, 2002. 'The emerging synthesis': The archaeogenetics of farming/language dispersals and other spread zones. In Bellwood and Renfrew (eds), pp. 3–16.

Roberts, John R., 1997. Switch-reference in Papua New Guinea: A preliminary survey. In Andrew Pawley (ed.), *Papers in Papuan Linguistics*, no. 3, pp. 101–241. Pacific Linguistics, vol. A-87. Canberra: Australian National University.

Ross, Malcolm, 1984. Maisin: A preliminary sketch. In *Papers in New Guinea Linguistics*, no. 23, pp. 1–82. Pacific Linguistics, vol. A-63. Canberra: Australian National University.

Ross, Malcolm, 1987. A contact-induced morphosyntactic change in the Bel languages of Papua New Guinea. In Donald C. Laycock and W. Winter (eds), *A World of Language: Papers Presented to Professor S. A. Wurm on his 65th Birthday*, pp. 583–601. Pacific Linguistics, vol. C-100. Canberra: Australian National University.

Ross, Malcolm, 1988. *Proto Oceanic and the Austronesian Languages of Western Melanesia*. Pacific Linguistics, vol. C-98. Canberra: Australian National University.

Ross, Malcolm, 1993. Tonogenesis in the North Huon Gulf chain. In Jerold A. Edmondson and Kenneth J. Gregerson (eds), *Tonality in Austronesian Languages*, pp. 133–153. Oceanic Linguistics Special Publications, vol. 24. Honolulu: University of Hawai'i Press.

Ross, Malcolm, 1994. Areal phonological features in north central New Ireland. In Tom Dutton and Darrell Tryon (eds), *Language Contact and Change in the Austronesian World*, pp. 551–572. Berlin: Mouton de Gruyter.

Ross, Malcolm, 1996. Contact-induced change and the comparative method: Cases from Papua New Guinea. In Mark Durie and Malcolm Ross (eds), *The Comparative Method Reviewed: Regularity and Irregularity in Language Change*, pp. 180–217. New York: Oxford University Press.

Ross, Malcolm, 2001. Contact-induced change in Oceanic languages in north-west Melanesia. In Alexandra Y. Aikhenvald and R. M. W. Dixon (eds), *Areal Diffusion and Genetic Inheritance: Problems in Comparative Linguistics*, pp. 134–166. Oxford: Oxford University Press.

Ross, Malcolm, 2003. Diagnosing prehistoric language contact. In Raymond Hickey (ed.), *Motives for Language Change*, pp. 174–198. Cambridge: Cambridge University Press.

Ross, Malcolm, 2005a. Pronouns as a preliminary diagnostic for grouping Papuan languages. In Pawley et al. (eds), pp. 15–66.

Ross, Malcolm, 2005b. Towards a reconstruction of the history of tone in the Trans New Guinea family. In Kaji (ed.), pp. 3–31.

Ross, Malcolm, 2007. Calquing and metatypy. *Journal of Language Contact, Thema* 1: 116–143.

Ross, Malcolm, 2008. A history of metatypy in the Bel languages. *Journal of Language Contact, Thema* 2 (1): 149–164.

Ross, Malcolm, 2013. Diagnosing contact processes from their outcomes: The importance of life stages. *Journal of Language Contact* 6: 5–47.

Ross, Malcolm, 2014. Reconstructing the history of languages in northwest New Britain: Inheritance and contact. *Journal of Historical Linguistics* 4: 84–132.

Ross, Malcolm and Åshild Næss, 2007. An Oceanic origin for Äiwoo, the language of the Reef Islands? *Oceanic Linguistics* 46: 456–498.

Sahlins, Marshall D., 1963. Poor man, rich man, big-man, chief: Political types in Melanesia and Polynesia. *Comparative Studies in Society and History* 5: 285–303.

Schapper, Antoinette, 2009. *Bunaq: A Papuan Language of Central Timor*. PhD thesis, The Australian National University.

Schapper, Antoinette, 2014. Elevation in the spatial deictic systems of Alor-Pantar languages. In Marian Klamer (ed.), *Alor-Pantar Languages: History and Typology*, pp. 247–284. Berlin: Language Science Press.

Schapper, Antoinette, Juliette Huber and Aone van Engelenhoven, 2014. The relatedness of Timor-Kisar and Alor-Pantar languages: A preliminary demonstration. In Marian Klamer (ed.), *Alor-Pantar Languages: History and Typology*, pp. 99–154. Berlin: Language Science Press.

Scheinfeldt, Laura B., F. R. Friedlaender, Jonathan S. Friedlaender et al., 2007. Y-chromosome variation in Northern Island Melanesia. In Friedlaender (ed.), pp. 81–95.

Smallhorn, Jacinta, 2011. *The Binanderean Languages of Papua New Guinea: Reconstruction and Subgrouping*. Studies in Language Change, vol. 9. Canberra: Pacific Linguistics.

Smith, Ellen, 2016. Contact-induced change in a highly endangered language of northern Bougainville. *Australian Journal of Linguistics* 36 (3): 369–405.

Specht, Jim, 2005. Revisiting the Bismarcks: Some alternative views. In Andrew Pawley, Robert Attenborough, Jack Golson and Robin Hide (eds), *Papuan Pasts: Cultural, Linguistic and Biological Histories of Papuan-Speaking Peoples*, pp. 235–288. Pacific Linguistics, vol. 572. Canberra: Australian National University.

Spriggs, Matthew, 1996. Chronology and colonisation in Island Southeast Asia and the Pacific: New data and an evaluation. In Janet Davidson, Geoffrey Irwin, Foss Leach, Andrew Pawley and Dorothy Brown (eds), *Oceanic Culture History: Essays in Honour of Roger Green*, pp. 33–50. Dunedin: New Zealand Journal of Archaeology.

Spriggs, Matthew J. T., 1997. *The Island Melanesians*. Oxford: Blackwell.

Strong, W. M., 1911. The Maisin language. *Journal of the Royal Anthropological Institute* 41: 381–396.

Summerhayes, Glenn R., Matthew Leavesley, Andrew Fairbairn et al., 2010. Human adaptation and plant use in highland New Guinea 49,000 to 44,000 years ago. *Science* 330: 78–81.

Suter, Edgar, 2012. Verbs with pronominal object prefixes in Finisterre-Huon languages. In Hammarström and van den Heuvel (eds), pp. 23–59.

Swadling, Pamela and Robin Hide, 2005. Changing landscape and social interaction: Looking at agricultural history from a Sepik-Ramu perspective. In Pawley et al. (eds), pp. 289–327.

Terrill, Angela, 2002. Systems of nominal classification in East Papuan languages. *Oceanic Linguistics* 41: 63–88.

Thomason, Sarah Grey, 2001. *Language Contact: An Introduction*. Edinburgh: Edinburgh University Press.

Thurston, William R., 1982. *A Comparative Study of Anêm and Lusi*. Pacific Linguistics, vol. B-83. Canberra: Australian National University.

Thurston, William R., 1987. *Processes of Change in the Languages of North-Western New Britain*. Pacific Linguistics, vol. B-99. Canberra: Australian National University.

Thurston, William R., 1989. How exoteric languages build a lexicon: Esoterogeny in West New Britain. In Ray Harlow and Robin Hooper (eds), *VICAL 1, Oceanic Languages: Papers from the Fifth International Conference on Austronesian Linguistics*, pp. 555–579. Auckland: Linguistic Society of New Zealand.

Thurston, William R., 1992. Sociolinguistic typology and other factors effecting change in northwestern New Britain, Papua New Guinea. In Tom Dutton (ed.), *Culture Change, Language Change: Case Studies from Melanesia*, pp. 123–139. Pacific Linguistics, vol. C-120. Canberra: Australian National University.

Thurston, William R., 1994. Renovation and innovation in the languages of north-western New Britain. In Tom Dutton and Darrell Tryon (eds), *Language Contact and Change in the Austronesian World*, pp. 573–609. Berlin: Mouton de Gruyter.

Usher, Timothy and Edgar Suter, 2015. The Anim languages of Southern New Guinea. *Oceanic Linguistics* 54 (1): 110–142.

Van Valin, Robert D. Jr and Randy J. LaPolla, 1997. *Syntax: Structure, Meaning and Function*. Cambridge: Cambridge University Press.

Voorhoeve, C. L., 2001. Proto Awyu-Dumut phonology II. In Andrew Pawley, Malcolm Ross and Darrell Tryon (eds), *The Boy from Bundaberg: Studies in Melanesian Linguistics in Honour of Tom Dutton*, pp. 361–381. Pacific Linguistics, vol. 514. Canberra: Australian National University.

Weinreich, Uriel, 1953. *Languages in Contact: Findings and Problems*. Publications of the Linguistic Circle of New York, vol. 1. New York: Linguistic Circle of New York.

Wurm, Stefan A., 1975a. Language distribution in the New Guinea area. In Wurm (ed.), pp. 3–38.

Wurm, Stefan A. (ed.), 1975b. *New Guinea Area Languages and Language Study*, vol. 1: *Papuan Languages and the New Guinea Linguistic Scene*. Pacific Linguistics, vol. C-38. Canberra: Australian National University.

Wurm, Stefan A., 1982. *The Papuan Languages of Oceania*. Tübingen: Narr.

Wurm, Stefan A. and Shirō Hattori (eds), 1981. *Language Atlas of the Pacific Area*, part 1. Pacific Linguistics, vol. C-66. Canberra: Australian National University.

Wurm, Stefan A. and K. A. McElhanon, 1975. Papuan language classification problems. In Wurm (ed.), pp. 145–164.

Wurm, Stefan A., C. L. Voorhoeve and K. A. McElhanon, 1975. The Trans-New Guinea phylum in general. In Wurm (ed.), pp. 299–322.

29

Languages of Eastern Melanesia

Paul Geraghty

Melanesia is, in effect, a 'linguistic area' in the classic sense that the Balkans, India, or mainland Southeast Asia are linguistic areas, because distinctive structural features are shared across major genetic boundaries. The difference is that in other linguistic areas, languages of all the interacting genetic groupings are present ... This condition is met in Western Melanesia, where Papuan and Austronesian languages are so closely associated that they may even be spoken in the same village (as Motu and Koita in Hanuabada). What is peculiar about Vanuatu and southern Melanesia is that they participate in this same linguistic area, but Papuan languages are curiously absent ... this absence is almost certainly a product of widespread language extinction, a conclusion that will force a major rethinking of Pacific prehistory, and possibly provide yet another reminder of the importance of linguistics to the enterprise of archaeology. (Blust 2005: 556)

29.1 Introduction

The purpose of this chapter is to review the history of the study of the languages of Eastern Melanesia, with a view to assessing the above controversial claim by Robert Blust, the doyen of Austronesian linguistics, in the light of support from Donohue and Denham (2008, 2012) and adverse reactions from Pawley (2006: 243–248), Ross and Næss (2007: 460–461) and others.

My thanks to Robert Early, Rod and Beverley Ewins, Alexandre François, Raymond Hickey, John Lynch, Peter Moore, Patrick Nunn, Bill Palmer, Elizabeth Pascal, Andrew Pawley and Jeff Siegel, who helped me in various ways while I was writing this chapter; the usual disclaimers apply.

Note that 'Melanesia' is a geographical term for the area of the Western South Pacific comprising Papua New Guinea, the Solomon Islands, Vanuatu, New Caledonia and (usually) Fiji. 'Melanesian' is not normally used as a linguistic term. Within Melanesia, there are two major language 'families'. 'Papuan'[1] languages are only found in Western Melanesia, that is, Papua New Guinea and the western Solomon Islands, while Austronesian languages, belonging to the Western Oceanic and the western part of the Eastern Oceanic subgroups, are found throughout the area. Blust (2008: 445–446) divides Eastern Melanesia further, using the term 'Remote Melanesia' for Vanuatu and New Caledonia, his main area of interest, and 'Southern Melanesia' for New Caledonia, including the Loyalty Islands.

'Eastern Oceania', on the other hand, is a linguistic term, referring to all Pacific islands where Eastern Oceanic languages are spoken. Eastern Oceanic is the easternmost subgroup of Oceanic, itself the easternmost subgroup of the Austronesian language family. Although its precise nature and membership are still being debated (Lynch, Ross and Crowley 2002: 108; Pawley 2009: 535), I use the term to cover all the languages of the Pacific islands excluding (1) those of Papua New Guinea and the western Solomon Islands, for which see Malcolm Ross's contribution to this volume (Chapter 28), and (2) those of the westernmost Micronesian islands of Belau (formerly Palau) and the Marianas, which are Western Austronesian (see chapter by Grant, Chapter 30, this volume). Hence Eastern Oceanic comprises all the languages of the eastern Solomon Islands (from Bugotu on Santa Isabel eastwards), the Santa Cruz group, Vanuatu, New Caledonia, Fiji (including Rotuma), Polynesia and most of Micronesia, encompassing a vast area from the Solomon Islands in the west to Easter Island (Rapanui) in the east, and from Hawai'i in the north to New Zealand (Aotearoa) in the south.

Eastern Oceanic was proposed as a subgroup by Biggs (1965), then defined more precisely by Pawley (1972) and modified by Lynch and Tryon (1985). It corresponds closely to what prehistorians have called Remote Oceania (Green 1991), being the islands that lie beyond Near Oceania – the chain of inter-visible islands that are believed to have been settled by speakers of Papuan (non-Austronesian) languages perhaps as many as 40,000 years ago. The current interpretation (e.g. Pawley 2009: 517) is that the speakers of Papuan languages did not have the maritime technology to expand further, so remained largely confined to Near Oceania. The earliest speakers of Oceanic languages, however, now

---

[1] Note that I follow the tradition (Ray 1926: 24) of using 'Papuan' as a term for all non-Austronesian languages of Oceania – though some authors prefer the term 'non-Austronesian', abbreviated to NAn or NAN. Papuan languages do not constitute a single language family, but belong to some twenty-odd families and isolates (Ross 2005). For the argument that typological comparison indicates that Papuan and Austronesian languages share a remote common ancestor, see Dunn et al. (2005, 2007) and the counter-argument from Donohue and Musgrave (2007), who attribute what there is in common, e.g. inclusive/exclusive pronouns, to areal diffusion.

known as the Lapita people and believed to have originated from Southeast Asia, were skilful canoe-builders, sailors and navigators, and sailed eastwards to become the first occupants of Remote Oceania over 3,000 years ago.

In this chapter, I will not be using the terms 'Western/Eastern Oceanic' or 'Remote/Southern Melanesia', since my main concern is to compare and contrast Western Melanesia – the islands of Melanesia where Papuan languages are still spoken – with Eastern Melanesia, where currently no Papuan languages are found.

By 'linguistic area' I mean an area where different languages share features as a result not of common inheritance but of borrowing (i.e. the spread or diffusion of 'areal features'), taken to be due to widespread bilingualism, indeed multilingualism. Classic examples of linguistic areas outside Oceania include the Balkans (see Friedman and Joseph, Chapter 4, this volume), where numerous features are shared exclusively by Albanian, Romanian, Bulgarian and Greek, languages that are only distantly related, as well as by unrelated Turkish dialects; and India, where languages of Indo-European and Dravidian ancestry have come to share features such as retroflex consonants, and in extreme cases appear to even share a common grammar, with only the lexicon being distinct. Closer to the Pacific, the Mainland Southeast Asian language area (Enfield, Chapter 25, this volume) includes a number of Austronesian languages spoken in Vietnam.[2]

I will introduce in this chapter the term 'post-linguistic area', meaning an area comprising languages that share exclusively features diffused from a common unrelated language (or group of similar languages) that has disappeared – in other words, that share a common substrate that is now extinct. Thus, for example, for those who believe that the French dialects have a common Gaulish substrate, France would be a 'post-linguistic area'.

There are four separate areas in Eastern Melanesia that have been considered possible post-linguistic areas, similar to the linguistic areas described by Ross (1996 and this volume) for northwest Melanesia, where seemingly aberrant features, from the standpoint of canonical Oceanic languages, have been attributed to contact with non-Austronesian languages that are no longer spoken there. These areas are: (1) the Reefs Santa Cruz group in the far eastern Solomon Islands, including Santa Cruz, Utupua and Vanikoro, where some linguists have claimed that the languages either are Papuan or have been influenced by a Papuan substrate; (2) the islands of Santo and Malakula (and perhaps others such as Ambrym and Efate) in northwestern and central Vanuatu, in which a former linguistic area comprising Oceanic and Papuan languages has

---

[2] Grace (1981) proposed a rather different use of the term 'linguistic area' to refer to a community of languages in New Caledonia that are clearly related and share a single grammatical system, but appear to have borrowed freely among themselves, even in core vocabulary, thus making reconstruction by the comparative method difficult if not impossible; see also discussion by Harrison (1981: 220–224).

been proposed; (3) southern Vanuatu, comprising the languages of Erromango, Tanna and Anejom, where a Papuan substrate has also been proposed; and (4) New Caledonia (including the Loyalty Islands), where the non-Oceanic component of the post-linguistic area has been proposed as Papuan or Australian.

A different type of linguistic area is found in those parts of Eastern Melanesia where Polynesians have settled, probably within the last 800 years or so, in some cases in close proximity to non-Polynesian communities, and retained their languages. I will attempt below to demonstrate that the study of the changes resulting from contact between these Polynesian 'outliers' and their Melanesian neighbours may provide indications of the results of language contact among Oceanic peoples, and hence clues as to what might have happened in such situations in the more distant past.

Further east, the distances between some of the islands of the Central Pacific subgroup of Eastern Oceania (comprising Fijian, Rotuman and Polynesian languages) may have inhibited the diffusion that is necessary for the development of linguistic areas; see Map 29.1. Indeed, Polynesia was until quite recently viewed by some historical linguists as a perfect 'laboratory' of language change, with each island or island group being almost totally isolated, so that borrowing or other external influence could almost be ruled out as factors in language change. However, this view has recently lost favour, as evidence from archaeology, linguistics, oral tradition, toponymy and other disciplines (see, for example, Geraghty 2004 and references therein) has painted a picture of long-distance voyaging across much of the Pacific, at least during certain periods of prehistory, so that perhaps only Easter Island appears to have been totally isolated since initial occupation – and even there a loanword or two from South America appears to have made it through, most notably *kumara/kumala* 'sweet potato, *Ipomoea batatas*'. Arguments have been made for the existence in the past of linguistic areas in Western Polynesia (Tonga, Samoa and adjacent islands) and in what is now French Polynesia, but I will neither relate nor pursue those arguments here.

29.2 The Problem of 'Aberrant' Oceanic Languages

It has long been recognized that there are major differences among the Oceanic languages of Melanesia with regard to their 'Oceanic-ness'.[3] While there are indeterminate cases, by and large the Oceanic languages of Melanesia can be classified into two groups: those that are similar to Proto-Oceanic (POc), usually labelled 'exemplary', and those that are very different from Proto-Oceanic, usually labelled 'aberrant'. There has been much

---

[3] For a summary of grammatical features of Proto-Oceanic, see Lynch, Ross and Crowley (2002: 54–91).

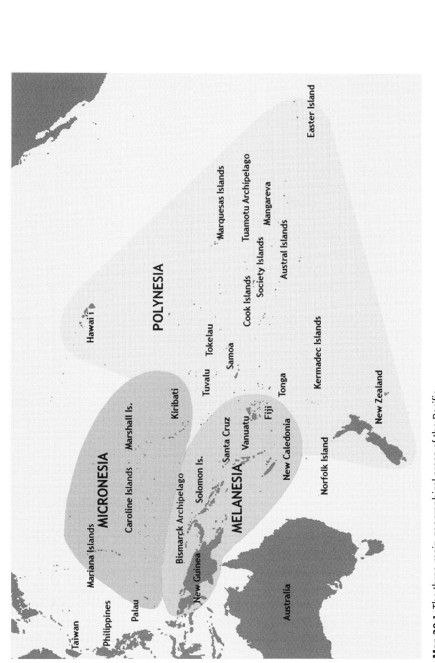

Map 29.1 The three main geographical areas of the Pacific

discussion regarding the cause of this aberrancy – in particular, whether it is due to internal factors or contact-induced change.

Aberrant languages are found in all subgroups of Oceanic except Micronesian and Central Pacific (which comprises the languages of Fiji, Rotuma and Polynesia). In particular, they are found in the western Solomon Islands, the Santa Cruz group, western and southern Vanuatu and New Caledonia and the Loyalties. Perhaps the first linguist to recognize this distribution was Ray (1926: 37, 594), who further pointed out that exemplary languages (in his terminology those with a large 'Indonesian' content) tend to be found on small, often off-shore islands, while aberrant languages tend to be found on large islands – a distribution paralleling that of Austronesian versus Papuan languages in Papua New Guinea and Western Melanesia.

The question of aberrant languages raises the broader question of the origins of the Melanesian people. As has been pointed out by anthropologists, the fact that the Melanesians are physically distinct from other speakers of Austronesian languages to the west (e.g. Indonesia) and north and east (Polynesia and Micronesia) requires an explanation. Hocart (1923) put it thus: 'There are other languages which are descended from the same original as Melanesian, namely, Polynesian, Malay, Malagasy. The people who use these languages are nearly all light in colour, straight-haired and somewhat Mongoloid, very unlike the Melanesian type … Either, therefore, the Melanesian type borrowed its speech from the Malayo-Polynesian or vice versa. The map most decidedly lends its support to the first view.'

Ray's (1926) monumental survey of Melanesian languages was, in part, a response to such observations. He viewed all the Melanesian languages as resulting from borrowing from an Austronesian language or languages, which he called 'Indonesian', spoken by colonizers from the west and adopted in varying degrees by speakers of Papuan languages.

The presence of such contact-induced change in Western Melanesia (Papua New Guinea and the western Solomon Islands) has never been in dispute, since Papuan languages are there in great numbers and there are linguistic areas where diffusion continues to take place in both directions. It is in Eastern Melanesia that the historical interpretation is disputed, with some attributing the changes from Proto-Oceanic seen in aberrant languages solely to internal factors, and others following Ray in attributing the changes at least in part to external factors, specifically features transferred from non-Oceanic languages that have since become extinct.

The more traditional view of Ray was espoused by Dempwolff (1937: 142, 160, 193), Capell (1943, 1962, 1971), Wurm (1954) and Cowan (1962) (see discussion in Pawley 2006: 224–227). As summarized by a more recent adherent (Thurston 1982: 77), the Austronesian languages of Melanesia are 'Austronesian languages with NAN substrate of various kinds and to varying degrees'. Siegel (2016) has also pointed out that one of the objections to this 'pidginization' hypothesis, as it is sometimes called – the relative lack of Papuan loans in aberrant languages – is not valid, since a high degree of lexical loans is not expected in pidgins and creoles of this nature. He further argues that 'some of the grammatical features they [Austronesian languages in Melanesia] display could have been the result of one of the processes involved in the development of pidgin and creole languages – i.e. language transfer. This could have been Papuan speakers transferring features into the Austronesian languages they were acquiring ... in most cases they were entirely absorbed into Austronesian communities, and their original languages no longer exist.'

Grace (1961; 1962: 409–410) was perhaps the first to seriously question the 'pidginization' hypothesis. He pointed out that there is a tendency to uniformity in the Austronesian vocabulary shown by aberrant languages, which one would not expect if people from different parts of Indonesia had settled different parts of Melanesia, as was, according to Grace, implicit in the 'pidginization' hypothesis. He added that no-one had demonstrated that any of the supposed Papuan words of aberrant languages could be sourced to any known Papuan language – to which, of course, the response is that the source languages are now all extinct, in Eastern Melanesia at any rate. As Capell (1962: 423) pointed out, such languages would have been very disparate, judging by those Papuan languages that remain in Western Melanesia. Nevertheless, Grace acknowledged that he was by no means certain that pidginization had played no role in the linguistic history of Melanesia.

The more recent orthodox view (Pawley 1981, 2006) concurs with Grace's doubts about pidginization, and holds that aberrant languages are so because of rapid internal change. It points to the fact that no Papuan language is found in Eastern Oceania, and therefore the hypothesis that such Papuan languages have become extinct is 'a pretty uneconomical hypothesis' (Pawley 2006: 226). This is despite the fact that, as Pawley acknowledges, non-Austronesian languages have become extinct in many parts of Western Melanesia, such as the Admiralties (Blust 2008: 456) and New Ireland (Pawley 2006: 246);[4] and Pawley has stated elsewhere (2009: 531) his belief that there were Papuan languages also in the eastern Solomon Islands, where there are none today, that have since become extinct.

In this chapter, I will argue with the former camp: that at least some of the features of aberrant languages of Eastern Melanesia can be attributed to the influence of non-Oceanic languages that were spoken previously but have since become extinct. The essential question which I will attempt to answer is: how can one demonstrate that an area is a post-linguistic area where substrate languages once existed and where features were transferred to the surviving languages when the donor languages were never recorded and are all now extinct?

---

[4] Note also the original languages of the Negritos of the Philippines, all now extinct and replaced by Austronesian languages (Reid 1994: 449).

29.3   Papua New Guinea and the Western Solomon Islands

It has never been disputed that Oceanic and Papuan languages have been in contact in Papua New Guinea and the western Solomons. As a result, linguistic areas have developed, for example, Papua Tip and the western Solomons, where both Oceanic and non-Oceanic languages show OV order and postpositions, presumably replacing the VO order and prepositions of the earlier Oceanic languages (Evans and Palmer 2011; Lynch, Ross and Crowley 2002: 15; see also Ross, Chapter 28, this volume). Ball (2007: 140) also claims that the Papua Tip language Hula may have picked up ergativity from contact. In other areas, Papuan languages have acquired SVO order and other features from their Oceanic neighbours,[5] and there has been considerable lexical replacement in both directions. A similar situation obtains in northwestern New Britain, for which Thurston (1994) has meticulously documented the results of areal diffusion among Austronesian and Papuan languages.[6]

It has also been claimed that the ancestral language, Proto-Oceanic, added a series of labio-velars (*bw, *pw and *mw) to its phonemic inventory as a result of extensive borrowing from Papuan languages (Blust 1981; Dempwolff 1920: 91–92; Lynch 2002: 320–322; Lynch, Ross and Crowley 2002: 65). It is possible too that the Oceanic innovation of indirect possessive classifiers (Lynch, Ross and Crowley 2002: 77–80) was the result of the influence of Papuan nominal classifier systems.[7] This would suggest that a linguistic area already existed, probably in the Bismarck archipelago, during the early development of Proto-Oceanic over 3,000 years ago.[8]

The addition of a final echo vowel in the western Solomons and Vanikoro, e.g. POc *onom 'six' > PWS *onomo, may also have resulted from substrate influence, to match the open syllabic structure of the Papuan languages.

In the western Solomons, where formerly there were many Papuan languages, only a small number of which survive, it is believed that these languages affected, and were affected by, the incoming Austronesian languages in many ways (Pawley 2009: 527, 536; Terrill 2011), notably through lexical replacement.[9] After demonstrating the relatively high

---

[5] But see Thurston (1994: 586–587), Donohue (2005) and others cited therein for the argument that SVO is itself an innovation in some Austronesian languages, which had previously been VSO, resulting from the substrate influence of some non-Austronesian languages, e.g. in Bird's Head. Lynch, Ross and Crowley (2002: 86–87) also believe that Proto Oceanic was verb-initial.

[6] While some have assumed that these linguistic areas involved Austronesian speakers acquiring fluency in Papuan languages, see Pawley (2007: 40) and Siegel (2016) for the argument that the reverse was the case. Undoubtedly diffusion occurred in both directions.

[7] Donohue and Schapper (2008) have pointed out that similar possessive constructions are found in languages of eastern Indonesia, and claim that they originate from contact with Papuan languages there.

[8] Indeed, Ross (2001: 312) has argued that the Papuan languages of this area may have earlier formed a linguistic area, as witnessed by the common feature of gender marking in the pronoun systems.

[9] Terrill (2011: 313) demonstrates, however, that in the Western Solomons 'long-term contact does not necessarily entail major structural borrowing, even over . . . thousands of years.'

rate of replacement of the Proto-Oceanic lexicon in the western Solomons, Pawley (2009: 531) comments that a 'reasonable inference is that … the speakers of incoming NW Solomonic languages encountered substantial populations of non-Austronesian languages and that sustained bilingualism, especially on Choiseul and Santa Isabel but also in the New Georgia group, led to many non-Austronesian loanwords entering the basic vocabulary of the NW Solomonic languages.'

29.4 Eastern Solomon Islands

In the eastern Solomons (Guadalcanal, Malaita, Makira and adjoining islands), by contrast, there are now no Papuan languages, though they were 'presumably … once spoken on all the main Solomon Islands at least as far east as Guadalcanal and possibly on Malaita and Makira as well' (Pawley 2009: 521). However, there is little evidence of any substrate influence from Papuan languages – for example, there are no quinary numeral systems – because the 'non-Austronesian speaking populations in this region were small and were easily absorbed or replaced' (Pawley 2009: 531), so that eastern Solomonic languages appear to be on the whole more conservative than their western counterparts (Pawley 2009: 530).

29.5 The Reefs Santa Cruz Group

The three main languages of the Reefs Santa Cruz area in Temotu Province, the most easterly province in the Solomon Islands, have caused problems in their classification ever since they were first described by Codrington (1885: 16). The more traditional view has been that they are essentially Papuan (Capell 1962: 371, 382, who writes that they have 'such a thin veneer of AN [Austronesian] as to be practically still NAN [non-Austronesian]'; Davenport 1962; Tryon and Hackman 1983: 41, 43–45; Wurm 1978, 1985). Tryon and Hackman (1983: 44) summarize their history thus: 'In view of the complexities of Reefs-Santa Cruz noun and verb morphology so central to the languages and typical of Papuan languages in general, it seems unlikely that such features would have been borrowed by Austronesian speakers, but would much more probably represent retentions from earlier forms of the Reefs-Santa Cruz languages which remained fully functional when their speakers took over many features of an Austronesian language.' Tryon (1994: 635–637) also stated that they 'have undergone contact-induced change to such an extent that they are difficult to classify … they appear to share a core structure with obvious Papuan affiliations, while sharing just as obvious Austronesian features', and pointed out specific links between these languages and the Papuan languages of the Solomons and Bougainville.

More recently, however, the pendulum has swung in the other direction, beginning with Lincoln (1978) arguing that they are Oceanic. Terrill (2002: 84) and Næss (2006: 288–290) have since demonstrated convincingly that at least one of the features that Wurm had attributed to Papuan influence, the multiple noun classes of Äiwoo, bears no similarity to Papuan structures, that many of the markers derive from Austronesian roots, and the system has parallels in some languages of Vanuatu. While Næss (2006: 293) has pointed out striking parallels between nominalizing affix systems of Reefs Santa Cruz and those of Nasioi and Buin, Papuan languages of Bougainville, and while there do remain questions about the large quantity of non-Oceanic vocabulary (Ross and Næss 2007: 466) and other features of these languages, such as their highly complex agglutinative verb structure and ergative verb phrase (Næss 2013), Ross and Næss (2007) nevertheless conclude that the Reefs Santa Cruz languages are Austronesian, probably constituting a first-order subgroup of Oceanic. This conclusion is supported on typological grounds by Dunn et al. (2007: 398–499).

François (2006) has also queried whether the languages of nearby Vanikoro are truly Austronesian, and demonstrated (2009) that the three languages share a common grammar with distinct lexicons – a typical outcome of prolonged contact and bilingualism in a linguistic area.[10]

29.6 Vanuatu

While it is generally accepted that there are no Papuan languages in Vanuatu, and archaeologists have so far failed to find traces of any pre-Lapita (Oceanic-speaking) population, a number of linguists have speculated that there may once have been. Codrington, the compiler of the first major work on the languages of Melanesia, while at pains to affirm that Melanesian languages were as Oceanic as Polynesian languages, nevertheless believed that Melanesians may have once spoken a non-Melanesian language which is no longer recoverable (1885: 14–15, 17, 30–33). Capell (1962: 394) was of the opinion that Vanuatu was 'probably … inhabited before the coming of the Austronesians', while Lynch (1981: 111, 119–120), Wurm (1982) and Tryon (1982: 245) have all raised the possibility of certain linguistic features being due to borrowing from now-extinct Papuan languages.[11]

More recently, Blust (2005: 551–556) has drawn attention to a number of features that are found in parts of Vanuatu, especially the westernmost

---

[10] However François (personal communication, July 2014) has now reassessed the evidence and believes that Vanikoro languages may well be Oceanic, but are remarkably aberrant, showing many lexical and morphological innovations.

[11] Lynch (personal communication, July 2014) no longer believes that Papuan languages were ever spoken in Vanuatu or New Caledonia, largely because of the absence of archaeological evidence for pre-Lapita occupation.

islands of Santo and Malakula (and, in some cases, New Caledonia) and in many Papuan languages, but not among Oceanic speakers elsewhere: (1) quinary[12] (five-based) numeral systems, (2) 'twenty' being represented by 'one man' in some languages, e.g. Paamese,[13] and (3) extensive verb serialization. He also pointed out a number of cultural traits that arguably reinforce the linguistic evidence: (1) penis sheaths (more correctly penis wrappers or nambas), (2) insertion of large ornaments into the pierced septum (these two features are elaborated on in Blust 2008: 453), and (3) physical resemblance: 'In Malakula and Espiritu Santo, the prominent noses and full beards of many men are strikingly similar to features common among New Guinea highlanders' (Blust 2005: 554).

Another physical trait, not mentioned by Blust, is short stature. Like the negritos of the Philippines, who are believed to have originally spoken a non-Austronesian language or languages (Reid 1994), some of the inland inhabitants of Santo and Malakula are significantly shorter than average (Speiser 1990: 54–55). There is, as observed by the anthropologist John Layard (1942: 9), a 'definite racial distinction between the coastal people . . . all of whom share certain physical characteristics, and the small, almost pygmoid inhabitants of the mountainous interior of South Malekula who represent the last remnants of an earlier racial stock similar to that found in the interior of certain other larger land-masses in the Western Pacific.'[14]

Later, Blust (2008: 453) added other cultural traits: 'wide girdles of rattan cane used by men in some highland New Guinea groups, and similarly wide waistbands of other materials among the Big Nambas of Malakula . . . [and] the thick, mop-like headdresses of red fibers worn by Big Nambas women . . . strikingly similar to those used by women in the eastern highlands of New Guinea.' Nevertheless, Blust (2008: 454) adds a note of caution: 'cultural comparison of such traits is difficult because little information is available about them, even in works that are otherwise fairly thorough'.

Another pertinent cultural trait – again, not mentioned by Blust – is tooth avulsion (also known as tooth ablation), specifically the removal of the upper incisors, found in parts of Santo and Malakula as part of girls' and women's initiation ceremonies (Muller 1972: 64–67; Speiser 1990: 162). This practice appears to be otherwise absent in Oceania, the sole exception being parts of Hawai'i (Pietresewsky and Douglas 1993) where it was a sign of mourning, but relatively common in Australia, at least in parts of northern South Australia, Victoria and New South Wales, where it was part of boys' maturity rites (Arthur and Morphy 2005: 96; Attenbrow 2010: 131; Horton 1994: 1086). Incidentally this custom may have given

---

[12] Following Blust (2008: 446), I use 'quinary' here to mean any system that uses additive numerals for 'six' to 'nine', regardless of whether the word for 'ten' is monomorphemic or not.

[13] Lynch (2009: 395) lists Southeast Ambrym and Lenakel in Vanuatu and Nemi and Xaracuu in New Caledonia as languages expressing twenty as a phrase incorporating the word for 'man', 'person' or 'fingers/toes/digits'.

[14] See also Deacon (1934: 8).

rise to the presence of labiolingual consonants replacing bilabials in south Santo and north Malakula (Lynch 2005: 403).

Donohue and Denham (2008: 435), encouraged by Blust's proposals, have added grist to the Papuan mill, largely with phonological arguments. First they point out the distribution of labio-velars in Oceania: they are largely confined to the north coast of New Guinea, close to where presumably they were first added to the phonemic inventory of Proto-Oceanic, and southeast Solomons, Vanuatu and New Caledonia. Elsewhere in Oceania they have largely disappeared. They suggest that 'the labiovelars found greater support in Vanuatu because of a stronger non-Austronesian substrate'. Similarly, rounded labial fricatives, while not reconstructed for Proto-Oceanic, are found only along the north New Guinea coast and in Vanuatu.

Donohue and Denham further point out (2008: 438) that the lack of /p/ in phoneme inventories is relatively rare, occurring in the Pacific only in a small group of languages in Papua New Guinea and in Proto-North-Central Vanuatu and Fiji. Of the 360 Oceanic languages the authors surveyed, only 11 per cent lack /p/, while in Vanuatu the figure is 27 per cent. Furthermore, languages lacking both /p/ and /c/ (voiceless palatal stop) are only found among Papuan languages of Papua New Guinea and in North-Central Vanuatu. They conclude that the 'appearance of a double gap in older Vanuatu is an enigma, unless we posit an earlier Papuan substrate in the area that influenced the development of the Austronesian languages that later arrived in Vanuatu'.

Another new strand of evidence introduced by Donohue and Denham (2008: 440) is genetic. They cite a number of recent works that show that 'the people of Vanuatu share most molecular markers with the Melanesians of northeast Papua New Guinea, and not with the peoples of insular Southeast Asia or Polynesia'.

Even though such arguments have been put forth for the former existence of linguistic areas in Eastern Melanesia, as in present-day Western Melanesia, involving Papuan and Austronesian languages, proponents of this theory accept that there is no archaeological evidence for any human occupation prior to the arrival of the Lapita culture approximately 3,000 years ago. As reported by Blust (2008: 454), Matthew Spriggs, a leading archaeologist of the region, has stated that, with regard to Vanuatu, 'archaeologically there is no evidence of pre-Lapita occupation despite a targeted campaign to look for such over the last 14 years'. So if the speakers of Papuan languages were not in Eastern Melanesia before the arrival of the Lapita culture, whose bearers were supposedly Austronesian speakers, what scenario can best explain the facts?

Donohue and Denham (2008: 440–441; 2012) argue that the bearers of Lapita pottery and its associated culture were not necessarily, as has been commonly assumed, only speakers of Proto-Oceanic: 'We suggest that it is just as likely that Papuan-speaking Melanesians, occupying the islands out to the end of the main Solomons chain for at least 30,000 years and having settled Manus by 20,000 years ago … would have participated in the maritime expansion that accompanied the spread of Lapita.' They then offer two possible historical scenarios that are compatible with the linguistic and culture-historical evidence. First, that the first settlers in Vanuatu were 'people whose ancestors had been resident in Melanesia for many millennia, and who adopted various aspects of a new immigrant culture, including an Austronesian language [which] exhibited a number of structural features inherited from pre-Austronesian language(s) in New Guinea, and these features were borne, more-or-less undiluted, to Vanuatu'. This is essentially the theory of Speiser (1946, cited in Schmitz 1962: 418).

The second scenario offered by Donohue and Denham (2008: 441) is that 'the settlers were Papuan-speaking peoples who arrived with Lapita pottery (and other technologies), but without an Austronesian language … who were later swamped by the expansion of Austronesian-language speaking groups and their languages … they were relatively quickly submerged in the developing Austronesian linguistic milieu, though not without leaving traces of their passing in the phonology and semantic organization of the languages … as well as preserving many aspects of their original ethnic identities.' They point out that this latter scenario is almost identical to the theory of Codrington (1885: 32–35), and deem it the more likely of the two because 'the "Papuan" traits that are found are not uniformly represented in the languages of Vanuatu. They are attested among other languages with a more typical Austronesian profile, suggesting either a linguistically complex initial settlement or a complex post-settlement linguistic ecology (or both).'

Donohue and Denham's hypothesis also includes (2008: 441–442) an explanation for some features in which southern Vanuatu differs from North-Central Vanuatu, claiming that 'the appearance of echo subject agreement mirrors the switch reference systems that proliferate in mainland New Guinea, especially in the east' and that verb-initial clause order is found 'only in the far south, indicating that a later spread of SVO order was less successful in the south than in the rest of Vanuatu'.

An opposite stance is taken by Blust (2008: 454–456), following Spriggs (1997: 158–159), offering a 'linguistic Melanesianization' theory, that is, the original inhabitants of Eastern Melanesia were indeed Proto-Oceanic speakers, of what we would now judge to be Polynesian appearance, and that a second, more numerous, wave of migrants speaking Papuan (or Papuan-influenced Austronesian) languages followed soon after, most likely spread over a long period (the 'trickle in' model), since they appear to have had no effect on material culture. However, Blust agrees with Donohue and Denham that, if the archaeological evidence is put to one side, a more likely scenario is one in which the '"melanesianisation" of Remote Melanesia was carried out by a population of largely PM [Papuan] physical type that had acquired certain aspects of material culture, including the outrigger canoe complex and pottery, from Proto-Oceanic speakers in Near [West] Melanesia, but that still spoke Papuan languages and retained some distinctively Papuan cultural traits when they arrived in Vanuatu'.

Regarding lexical replacement in Vanuatu, it was noted above with respect to the Solomon Islands that Pawley (2009) demonstrated that all western Solomonic languages in a sample he surveyed had a higher rate of lexical replacement than any eastern Solomonic language in the survey; from this he inferred that the speakers of Papuan languages were far more numerous in the west than in the east during the period of eastward expansion of Austronesian languages. In the same study, Pawley (2009: 531–532) extended the survey to a small number of languages beyond the Solomons to demonstrate that they 'probably had no direct contact with non-Austronesian languages after these islands were settled'. However, he reported that in Erromangan, a language of southern Vanuatu, the retention rate on the same list was 61 per cent, only 2 per cent higher than that of Roviana, a western Solomonic language, and lower than the lowest eastern Solomonic language (65 per cent). By this reasoning, then, the extent of lexical replacement in Erromangan could well indicate that it was in contact with a Papuan language. Note also that no language of Reefs Santa Cruz, Santo, Malakula or the Loyalties or New Caledonia was included in this survey. Had some of these been included, their retention rates would certainly have been found to be as low as, if not lower than, those of the western Solomonic languages.

29.7 New Caledonia

The languages of New Caledonia and the Loyalty Islands have also been viewed as difficult to classify in the past (Capell 1962: 377; Codrington 1885: 16; Ray 1926: 76), but the recent increase in the quantity and quality of descriptions has now persuaded most linguists that, as with Vanuatu, these languages are essentially Oceanic (Geraghty 1989), and archaeologists have failed so far to find convincing evidence of a pre-Lapita population. However, Lynch (1981: 119–120) suggested the possibility of a Papuan substrate (but see note 11 above). Blust (2005: 551–556) then pointed to the following features (some also found in Vanuatu) which also suggest a Papuan substrate: (1) quinary numeral systems, (2) twenty being formed by 'one man' in a number of languages in New Caledonia and the Loyalties (Iaai, Xaracuu, Paici, Nyelayu, Canala, Nengone etc.), and (3) some verb serialization. Blust (2008: 456) also noted – as have many before him – the physical resemblance of some New Caledonians to aboriginal Australians.

To this may be added a cultural trait not mentioned by Blust for New Caledonia, the use of penis sheaths or wrappers.[15]

The current standard account of the prehistory of New Caledonia (e.g. Kirch 1997: 72–73; Sand 1996: 46) holds that there is no evidence of any human occupation prior to the arrival of the 'Lapita people', making Lapita pottery and speaking Oceanic languages, some 3,000 years ago. Yet up until the 1980s, many authorities (e.g. Dubois 1976: 20; 1981: 5; 1982: 13; Howells 1973: 35, 168) agreed that there was evidence for a pre-Lapita population from various disciplines, including oral traditions, material culture and physical anthropology. Also pertinent is the fact that it would have been possible 20,000 years ago to walk from Australia to New Caledonia with no sea-crossing greater than 30 kilometres, raising the possibility that in the case of New Caledonia the substrate language may have been not Papuan but Australian.

Given the extreme difficulty of discovering anything about an Australian aboriginal language that may have been spoken in New Caledonia some 20,000 years ago, Geraghty and Nunn (2013) have proposed an innovative method of demonstrating, at least, that a substrate language may have existed. They argue that there is linguistic evidence for a non-Oceanic substratum, particularly in the names given to novel flora and fauna – that is, natural species that were found in New Caledonia but had not been present in the Vanuatu homeland of the Lapita colonizers. The evidence does not take the form of identifying borrowings from Australian languages since, given that the presumed donor languages are now long extinct, and in any case of uncertain relationship to contemporary Australian languages, such would be difficult to find. However, given that the usual response of Pacific colonizers of uninhabited lands was to create names for newly discovered flora and fauna by semantic expansion and compounding, as has been demonstrated for New Zealand Maori by Biggs (1991: 67–68), the fact that most of the reconstructed names for novel natural species in New Caledonia appear not to have been coined using these methods suggests that there was a now vanished language that served as a source of these new terms.[16]

Unusually for Oceanic languages, those of New Caledonia and the Loyalty Islands are largely ergative. Ball (2007: 141) has argued that the 'New Caledonian languages likely developed ergativity through some shared process ... The development of ergativity in New Caledonia was also likely not a direct inheritance from Proto-Oceanic ... the Loyalty Island languages, too, suggest that there is not a single Proto-Oceanic source of ergativity, because the distribution of and the form for marking

[15] Captain Cook noted in 1774 that they 'had no other covering than a little case to the Penis which was suffered to hang down' (Beaglehole 1969: 530).

[16] Note that this argument cannot be applied to Vanuatu, since the colonizers would have been familiar with most of the natural species there from their earlier home in the Solomon Islands. It is only in New Caledonia that many new species would have been encountered, some with close relatives in Australia.

ergative NPs does not match anything else in the Oceanic family.' Since ergativity is relatively common in both Papuan (Foley 1986) and Australian (Dixon 1980) languages, either of these could be sources of the unexpected ergativity of New Caledonia and the Loyalties.

As in Vanuatu, certain non-linguistic features of New Caledonia and the Loyalty Islands can be adduced to suggest the possibility of a non-Austronesian, in some cases specifically Australian, substrate. These include: oral traditions of a very different earlier population with no agriculture, chiefs, houses or mats (Dubois 1976: 20), presence of spear-throwers (Labillardière 1800: 424) and boomerangs (Dubois 1976; 1981: 10), and, as also pointed out by Blust and others, physical appearance (Howells 1973: 35, 168; Labillardière 1800: 388).

Finally, the presence in the Nengone language spoken on Mare in the Loyalty Islands of the typologically unusual change of bilabials to apicals (*b > d, *m > n), presumably by way of apicolabials (see Lynch 2005 for discussion of a similar phenomenon in Vanuatu), is possibly evidence of the former practice of tooth avulsion, which would provide a physiological motivation for such a marked change. As noted above, tooth avulsion was widely practised in Australian aboriginal society but practically non-existent in Oceania.

In the following sections, I will focus on certain linguistic features that may indicate Papuan substrate influence on Oceanic languages of the Reef Santa Cruz Islands, Vanuatu and New Caledonia: serial verb constructions and quinary numeral systems (as proposed by Blust), then toponyms and pot-and-handle borrowings.

29.8 Serial Verb Constructions

Extensive verb serialization is one of the typological features found in Eastern Melanesia that Blust (2005: 553) attributed to a Papuan substrate. This attracted a riposte from Pawley (2006: 247) to the effect that SVCs (serial verb constructions) are not particularly rare in Austronesian languages outside Oceania, and indeed must be reconstructed for Proto-Oceanic (Ross 2004). He added that the kinds of SVCs found in Vanuatu and Southern Melanesia are structurally unlike those found in the Papuan languages of New Guinea.

Blust (2008: 447) responds to this, first, with a novel method that I will call 'bibliostatistics'. He presents a statistical analysis of available grammars of a sample of Austronesian languages to determine what percentage of the text is devoted to verb serialization. Among the grammars of Austronesian languages in Melanesia, the percentage ranges from 2.4 to 12.1 per cent. Among the grammars of Austronesian languages outside Melanesia, 11 of the 14 selected have no discussion at all of verb serialization – the inference being that it does not exist – while the three that do discuss verb serialization are of languages, such as Tetun of East Timor, which have long been in contact with Papuan languages or, as in the case of Buru, where verb serialization appears to be of minor importance. Whilst there are scattered languages in Western Austronesia that show verb serialization to varying degrees, it is totally absent in the Philippines, Borneo, Sumatra, Sulawesi and most of Western Indonesia (Blust 2008: 449). Turning to Oceanic languages, Blust (2008: 448–449) points out that verb serialization is also absent in Micronesia, and further argues that the few recent descriptions of verb serialization in Polynesian languages are highly contrived, due to the fact that verb serialization was a linguistic fad of the 1990s, and such analyses can only be viewed as valid by 'diluting the definition of verb serialization to the point that it ceases to be distinctive'.

In response to Pawley's claim that verb serialization must be reconstructed for Proto-Oceanic, Blust (2008: 449–450) points out that such reasoning is invalid, since the currently accepted subgrouping of Oceanic is such that a feature can be reconstructed for POc if it is found only in certain languages of Western Melanesia – precisely the area where Papuan languages are found, or are believed to have formerly existed. Blust concludes that the data suggest strongly that 'the wide distribution of serial verbs in the AN languages of Melanesia is a product of recurrent acquisition after the breakup of POc'.

Finally, Blust rejects Pawley's assertion that 'the types of SVC found in Vanuatu and Southern Melanesia are structurally unlike those found in the Papuan languages of New Guinea', countering that there is no such thing as a typically Papuan serial verb construction, so without more detailed study it is premature to conclude that Papuan and Melanesian SVCs are different. He sums up (Blust 2008: 450) by making the simple observation that published grammars tell us that verb serialization is very common in most Papuan languages and many Austronesian languages of Melanesia, but absent in most other Austronesian languages.

29.9   Quinary Numeral Systems

The historical implications of the presence of quinary numeral systems in parts of Melanesia has been commented on since at least the ground-breaking survey of Codrington (1885: 220–251). He concluded that 'the oldest method is the quinary, and it is pretty certain that the decimal notation in Melanesia is comparatively recent there and introduced' (Codrington 1885: 222, see also 229–230, 246–247). This view has been challenged by Lynch (2009) who considers the quinary systems 'innovative'. These differing interpretations result from Codrington's view that the earliest languages of Vanuatu were not Austronesian, as opposed to Lynch's view that they were.

Blust (2005: 552–554) also views the quinary systems as innovative, but in the sense that they are an innovation in Oceanic languages. He argues that only a decimal system has been reconstructed for Proto-Oceanic, therefore the fact that quinary systems are found in many Oceanic languages in New Guinea, much of Vanuatu and New Caledonia and the Loyalty Islands, but nowhere else in Oceania, requires an explanation, and a plausible explanation is that the quinary systems of Eastern Melanesia were acquired from Papuan languages spoken there at an early date when all of Melanesia, according to Blust, was a chain of linguistic areas.

Pawley (2006: 247) countered that Papuan languages typically have 'one, two, many' systems, or systems based on body parts, and offered two alternative explanations: first, that quinary systems existed in POc along with decimal systems, and second, that quinary systems spread into parts of Vanuatu and Southern Melanesia some time after Lapita settlement of the region. This echoes in part the proposal of Lynch, Ross and Crowley (2002: 72), who reconstructed a decimal system for Proto-Oceanic, but commented, contrary to Codrington: 'to judge from today's traditional cultures, numerals above ten were not much used in parts of early Oceania. Indeed, so widespread are quinary systems (but with the term for 10 preserved) that one suspects that the numerals 6–9 were dropping out of use among some early Oceanic speakers'.

Blust (2008: 450) does not comment on Pawley's objection regarding typical Papuan counting systems, though he could have pointed out that none of the Papuan languages of the western Solomons has either of the systems Pawley mentions (Terrill 2011: 318; Tryon and Hackman 1983).[17] He rejects the first proposed explanation by stating that no quinary system has been reconstructed for Proto-Oceanic, the inference being that it is impossible to do so, the existing quinary systems being so morphologically and formally disparate. Regarding the second explanation, Blust responds that such a spread of counting systems is simply implausible. He then presents a synopsis of the quinary systems of Vanuatu by subgroup (Blust 2008: 451–452), demonstrating that, under the current subgrouping hypothesis, the data require us to posit at least fourteen historically distinct replacements of decimal by quinary systems in Vanuatu – something which has happened only twice in the history of all Austronesian languages outside Melanesia.

Lynch (2009) has also provided a response to Blust, in the form of a detailed study of how the current quinary systems of Vanuatu and New Caledonia can be derived by regular processes from previous decimal systems. Blust (2008: 452) accepts the mechanisms proposed by Lynch, but points out that the question of actuation remains, since Lynch's

---

[17] Lynch (2009: 406) cites this personal communication from Michael Dunn: 'All the Solomons Papuan languages have productive decimal systems, but there's internal evidence . . . that they developed out of a quinary system.'

explanation, as indeed Lynch (2009: 408) acknowledges, 'does not broach the question *why* the languages of this region have such atypically high rates of structural innovation in the numeral system as compared to Austronesian languages generally'.

29.10   Toponyms

Given that toponyms are an area of the lexicon in which traces of substrate languages are often found in post-linguistic areas – such as the Celtic *Avon* as a river name in England, or many Gaulish names of towns in France – it is surprising that no-one has ever, to my knowledge, attempted a serious study of the origin of place names in Melanesia. Codrington (1885: *passim*; 1891: 4–8) attempted to identify the indigenous names of the main islands of central Melanesia – cautioning that '[l]arge islands seldom have a name' – but was not concerned with their etymologies. Ray (1926: *passim*) similarly listed place names that had been recorded for the islands whose languages he studied, again largely without comment, and many dictionaries of Melanesian languages include at least some place names. Here, then, is an area where it might be possible to associate an island name with a cognate in a Papuan language, though the probability that the source language has become extinct does indeed reduce the likelihood of identifying a cognate. Obvious names to start with are Gera (Guadalcanal), Mala (Malaita), Ulawa, Ndeni (Santa Cruz), Mota, Malakula, Maewo, Raga, Oba, Efate, Erromanga and Anejom/Aneityum, since all of these appear to be genuine indigenous names, and none has an obvious Oceanic etymology. Here again, the contrast with Micronesia and the Central Pacific is striking: in these areas, with their relatively shallow linguistic history and perhaps lack of substrate languages, many island and archipelago names have obvious etymologies, such as Viti (Fiji) and Tahiti both meaning 'sunrise, east', Tonga 'south', Tokelau 'north', Futuna 'land of *Barringtonia* trees', Niua 'land of coconuts' (see Geraghty 2001 for more examples).

29.11   Pot-and-Handle Loanwords

To fill what is, I believe, a lexical gap in English, I will use the term 'pot-and-handle' loanword to refer to a loanword that is borrowed together with a minor morpheme with which it typically occurs, and reanalysed in the recipient language as a single morpheme.

In the spirit of Blust's survey of serial verb constructions in Oceanic grammars, as mentioned above, I now offer some bibliostatistics. Table 29.1 gives a sample of dictionaries of typical exemplary Oceanic

Table 29.1 *Oceanic languages with words beginning in /a/, /e/, /o/ and /n/*

Language	Source	Total pages	a/e/o	%	n	%
Tuvaluan	Jackson (2001)	278	16/2/5	6/1/2	5	2
Tongan	Churchward (1959)	574	15/2/4	3/1/1	9	2
Fijian	Capell (1941)	342	1/2/3	0/1/1	5	1
Nggela	Fox (1955)	265	9/1/2	3/1/1	6	2

Table 29.2 *Southern Vanuatu languages with words beginning in /a/, /e/, /o/ and /n/*

Language	Source	Total pages	a/e/o	%	n	%
Erromanga	Crowley (2000)	155	1/1/3	1/1/2	84	54
Kwamera	Lindstrom (1986)	137	26/5/5	20/4/4	23	17
Lenakel	Lynch (1977)	104	21/5/5	20/5/5	25	24
Anejom	Lynch and Tepahae (2001)	279	65/25/5	24/9/2	87	31

languages indicating the percentage of the dictionary containing words beginning with /a/, /e/, /o/ and /n/.

Now compare with Table 29.2, which gives figures from dictionaries of some aberrant languages of southern Vanuatu.

It is clear from the tables that exemplary languages have a very small proportion of words beginning with 'n', but some aberrant languages have considerably more, in the case of Erromanga over half. I do not have access to a dictionary of a Reefs Santa Cruz language, but a perusal of entries in Tryon and Hackman (1983) suggests that they also have a large number of words beginning with 'n'. It is also clear that words beginning with a non-high vowel are relatively common in Anejom, Kwamera and Lenakel, but not in exemplary languages.

The reason for the large number of words with initial 'n' is that common nouns in these languages have undergone a process of article fusion (or accretion), with the common article *na* becoming fused to the following noun. This process is described for southern Vanuatu by Lynch (2001: 109–114) but, as with the change to quinary numeral systems, no motivation for the change is offered. Other languages of Vanuatu that appear to have undergone article fusion, at least to some extent, are found in Efate, Nguna, Paama, Malakula, Santo and the Banks Islands (for the last, see François 2007: 315, 317–318). In Reefs Santa Cruz, languages of Utupua and Vanikolo also show some article fusion. On the basis of a cursory survey, there appears to be an implicational relationship between the phenomena of quinary systems and article fusion, in that all areas that show article fusion also show quinary systems, though not vice versa.

A possible motivation for article fusion is found in borrowing. When nouns are borrowed, it is not uncommon for them to be borrowed with the article they are typically accompanied by. Examples in the Pacific include Bislama from French (e.g. *lafet* 'celebration' < *la fête, loto* 'truck' < *l'auto, lae* 'garlic' < *l'ail*) (Crowley 1990), Fijian (e.g. *toa* 'Banaban canoe' < Rabe Banaban *te wā*), Fiji Hindi from Fijian (e.g. *nakai* 'freshwater mussel' < *na kai*) and some borrowings from Polynesian languages in Rotuman (*tarau* 'a hundred' < *ta lau*) (Churchward 1940), Pohnpeian (*sakau* 'kava' < *ta kawa*) (Geraghty 1994: 244) and Reefs Santa Cruz (e.g. Reefs *toponu* 'turtle' < *te fonu*, Santa Cruz *tækutu* 'louse' < *te kutu*) (Ray 1926: 449–451, 455–456, 462; Tryon 1994; Tryon and Hackman 1983). Of course, the fact that such article fusion is common in borrowing does not necessarily mean that this must have been the cause in the languages of Reefs Santa Cruz and Vanuatu in which it occurs, but it is perhaps significant that in Oceanic languages spoken where there is little likelihood of there having been any non-Austronesian languages – those of Micronesia, Rotuma, Fiji and Polynesia – there is no evidence for article fusion.

A similar phenomenon may underlie the preponderance of verbs beginning with non-high vowels in certain languages of Eastern Melanesia, illustrated above by Kwamera and Lenakel of Tanna. While not so common as article accretion, verbs can also be borrowed with a typically accompanying particle, as for example in Pidgin Fiji Hindi, where verbs are consistently borrowed from Fiji Hindi with the suffix *-o*, which marks the imperative, e.g. Pidgin Fiji Hindi *baito* 'sit, existential, copula' < Fiji Hindi *baith-o* 'sit!' [imperative]. Similarly, verbs in Pidgin Fijian recorded from the early nineteenth century often show fusion with the preposed aspect particle *sā*, e.g. Pidgin Fijian *salako* 'go' < Fijian *sā lako* 'has gone' (Geraghty 1977: 59–60). Lynch (2001: 144–145) argues that the accreted non-high vowel in languages of southern Vanuatu is the result of a process of denominalization of verbs that had earlier been nominalized and undergone article accretion parallel to the same process in nouns. Again there is no proposed motivation for this very unusual change. I would tentatively propose, without having explored the phonological evidence, that the source of the non-high vowel accreted to verbs in Vanuatu might have been *e*, the third person singular subject marker that can be reconstructed for Proto-Oceanic (Lynch, Ross and Crowley 2002: 68) and Proto-Eastern Oceanic.

My proposal, then, is that pot-and-handle borrowings provide evidence that early Oceanic languages were the lexifiers of contact languages that developed in linguistic areas in early Vanuatu (and elsewhere), with these nouns and verbs being borrowed *en masse* in the formation of new languages. These languages now appear to be undeniably Oceanic in their lexicon (and in some cases in other aspects, due to subsequent diffusion from more exclusively Oceanic languages) but in reality are of mixed origin, in much the same way as Melanesian pidgins appear to be Germanic in their lexicon but remain, arguably, Oceanic in their structure. This accords with the proposal of Donohue and Denham (2008: 441), cited above, that 'the settlers were Papuan-speaking peoples who arrived with Lapita pottery (and other technologies), but without an Austronesian language ... who were later swamped by the expansion of Austronesian-language speaking groups and their languages ... relatively quickly submerged in the developing Austronesian linguistic milieu, though not without leaving traces of their passing in the phonology and semantic organization of the languages ... as well as preserving many aspects of their original ethnic identities.' This in turn echoes the rather less prosaic analogy of Codrington (1885: 33): 'We may conceive of the peopling of Melanesia and the settlement of its languages as of the filling with the rising tide of one of the island reefs. It is not a single simultaneous advance of the flowing tide upon an open beach, but it comes in gradually and circuitously by sinuous channels and unseen passages among the coral, filling up one pool while another neighbouring one is dry, apparently running out and ebbing here and there while generally rising ...'

29.12 Polynesian Outliers in Melanesia

The Polynesian outliers in Melanesia present a relatively recent case of the establishment of linguistic areas in parts of Melanesia (Clark 1986, 1994).[18] They are colonies – eleven in Papua New Guinea and the Solomons, four in Vanuatu and one in New Caledonia – set up by Polynesians on small islands hundreds of years ago, and the resulting physical, cultural and linguistic diffusion has been largely a function of distance from the nearest Melanesian settlements. Codrington (1885: 8) noted this with regard to physical appearance, while Clark (1994: 113) similarly classed the outliers linguistically into two groups, those that have experienced only 'cultural borrowing' versus 'intimate borrowing', again largely a function of their relative proximity to Melanesian neighbours: cultural borrowers are remote (Takuu, Luangiua, Sikaiana, Tikopia, Anuta), while intimate borrowers are close to Melanesian communities (Rennell, Pileni and all those in Vanuatu and New Caledonia). Among the grammatical changes listed by Clark (1994: 119) as occurring in Polynesian languages as a result of this contact is the change to strict SVO order in Mele-Fila, an echo perhaps of similar changes in more remote times in Western Melanesia.

Clark has also observed that the extent of borrowing is not reciprocal, that is, while there are Polynesian outlier languages that have borrowed extensively from their Melanesian neighbours, all borrowing by

---

[18] There are also two Polynesian outliers in Micronesia, Kapingamarangi and Nukuoro.

Melanesian languages has been of the limited 'cultural' variety – similar to the situation in the western Solomons observed by Terrill (2011: 313), where long-term contact does not necessarily result in heavy borrowing. Clark (1994: 120–121) proposes a historical explanation based on the small numbers of founding settlers of outliers necessitating the taking of wives from Melanesian communities.

Remarkably, there is at least one relatively clear example of a post-linguistic area among the outliers: as Blust (1987) has demonstrated, the Melanesian language which was the source of two new phonemes and extensive vocabulary in Rennellese cannot be any of the extant languages of the Solomons, and is most plausibly explained as a Solomonese language that was spoken by an aboriginal population on Rennell, but is now extinct, an explanation that is supported by Rennellese oral traditions. This, then, is arguably a relatively modern example of the kind of language contact event that occurred 3,000 years ago in the Solomon Islands, and perhaps elsewhere in Melanesia, in which an aboriginal language and an immigrant language functioned as a linguistic area, followed by the extinction of the aboriginal language, but not before the immigrant language had acquired many features of the aboriginal language.[19]

Finally, the argument that the change from a decimal to a quinary system of numbers could be the result of calquing in a linguistic area is strengthened by evidence that precisely this has happened in Fagauvea, the sole outlier language of New Caledonia, which has abandoned the decimal system of Proto-Polynesian to adopt a quinary system modelled on that of its Melanesian neighbour Iaai (Clark 1994: 117–118).

29.13 Linguistic 'Necessity' and Historical Reality in Post-linguistic Areas

Ross and Næss (2007: 456) refute the notion of a non-Austronesian speaking population having lived in the Reefs Santa Cruz group by claiming that 'there is no need to posit a Papuan element' to understand the origin of the Reefs Santa Cruz languages. Indeed, but it is equally true that there is no need to posit a Celtic element to understand the history of the languages now spoken in England – but that does not alter the historical fact that Celtic languages were spoken throughout England 2,000 years ago, and have since become extinct.[20]

---

[19] It is of course possible that other Polynesian outlier communities existed in the past but have shifted to a Melanesian language.

[20] This is not to deny that certain features may be best understood with reference to a Celtic substrate: see Hickey (2012).

Of course in Eastern Melanesia we do not have the written records that would permit us to identify what languages, if any, were spoken there before the arrival of Austronesian speakers, but the arguments proposed by Blust, and others presented in this chapter, do offer some clues, and by not burying our heads in the golden sands of Melanesia, and by expanding our search, as Blust and others have done to some extent, to cultural and other non-linguistic traits, I believe we may arrive at a more correct account of the prehistory of these Melanesian islands.

29.14 Conclusion

In conclusion, I return to the question I posed above: how can one demonstrate that an area is a post-linguistic area – i.e. that substrate languages once existed there and that features were transferred to the surviving languages – when the donor languages were never recorded and are all now extinct? Clearly it is impossible to prove conclusively, and it is possible that the transfer of some features occurred in Western Melanesia before the settlement of Eastern Melanesia, but I tentatively propose the features listed in Table 29.3 as indicators of post-linguistic areas in Eastern Melanesia, and propose that the more of these features that are shown by a language now classed as Oceanic, the more likely it is that it was influenced by a Papuan (or Australian) language.

Table 29.3 *Indicators of post-linguistic areas in Eastern Melanesia*

Indeterminate	
Non-linguistic	Located on large islands, large ornaments in pierced septum, oral traditions of earlier population
Linguistic	Aberrant with respect to Proto-Oceanic, lexical replacement, ergativity, pot-and-handle borrowings (article fusion, accretion of verbal morphology)
Papuan	
Non-linguistic	Physical resemblance, short stature, genetic markers, penis wrappers, wide waistbands worn by men, red fibre headdresses worn by women
Linguistic	Echo vowels, labio-velars, rounded labial fricatives, lack of /p/, lack of /c/; 'quinary' numeral systems, 'twenty' expressed by 'one man/person', complex morphology (especially agglutinative verb phrases), certain nominalizing affixes, extensive verb serialization, verb-initial clause order, echo subject agreement
Australian	
Non-linguistic	Physical resemblance, tooth avulsion in initiation rites, spear-throwers, boomerangs
Linguistic	Bilabial > labiolingual (> dental) (resulting from tooth avulsion)

References

Arthur, Bill and Frances Morphy (eds), 2005. *Macquarie Atlas of Indigenous Australia*. New South Wales: Macquarie Library Pty.

Attenbrow, Val, 2010. *Sydney's Aboriginal Past: Investigating the Archaeological and Historical Records*. University of New South Wales Press.

Ball, Douglas, 2007. On ergativity and accusativity in Proto-Polynesian and Proto-Central Pacific. *Oceanic Linguistics* 46 (1): 128–153.

Beaglehole, J. C. (ed.), 1969. *The Journals of Captain James Cook: The Voyage of the Resolution and Adventure, 1772–1775*. Cambridge: Cambridge University Press for the Hakluyt Society.

Bedford, Stuart, Christophe Sand and Sean P. Connaughton (eds), 2007. *Oceanic Explorations: Lapita and Western Pacific Settlement*. Canberra: Australian National University Press.

Biggs, Bruce, 1965. Direct and indirect inheritance in Rotuma. *Lingua* 13: 373–405. Revised version in Geraghty and Tent (eds), pp. 1–32.

Biggs, Bruce, 1991. A linguist revisits the New Zealand bush. In Andrew K. Pawley (ed.), *Man and a Half: Essays in Pacific Anthropology and Ethnobiology in Honour of Ralph Bulmer*, pp. 67–72. Auckland: The Polynesian Society.

Blust, Robert A., 1981. Some remarks on labiovelar correspondences in Oceanic languages. In Hollyman and Pawley (eds), pp. 229–253.

Blust, Robert A., 1987. Rennell-Bellona /l/ and the 'Hiti' substratum. In Donald C. Laycock and Werner Winter (eds), *A World of Language: Papers Presented to Professor S. A. Wurm on his Sixty Fifth Birthday*, pp. 69–79. Pacific Linguistics, vol. C-100. Canberra: Australian National University.

Blust, Robert, 2005. Review of Lynch, Ross and Crowley 2002. *Oceanic Linguistics* 44 (2): 544–558.

Blust, Robert, 2008. Remote Melanesia: One history or two? An addendum to Donohue and Denham. *Oceanic Linguistics* 47 (2): 445–459.

Capell, Arthur, 1941. *A New Fijian Dictionary*. Sydney: Australian Medical Publishing Company.

Capell, Arthur, 1943. *The Linguistic Position of South-East Papua*. Sydney: The Australasian Medical Publishing Co.

Capell, Arthur, 1962. Oceanic linguistics today. *Current Anthropology* 3 (4): 371–428.

Capell, Arthur, 1971. The Austronesian languages of Australian New Guinea. In T. E. Sebeok (ed.), *Current Trends in Linguistics,* vol. 8: *Oceania*, pp. 240–340. The Hague: Mouton.

Churchward, C. Maxwell, 1940. *Rotuman Grammar and Dictionary*. Sydney: Australasian Medical Publishing Co.

Churchward, C. Maxwell, 1959. *Tongan Dictionary*. Government of Tonga.

Clark, Ross, 1986. Linguistic convergence in Central Vanuatu. In Paul Geraghty, Lois Carrington and Stephen A. Wurm (eds), *FOCAL II: Papers from the Fourth International Conference on Austronesian Linguistics*, pp. 333–342. Pacific Linguistics, vol. C-94. Canberra: Australian National University.

Clark, Ross, 1994. The Polynesian outliers as a locus of language contact. In Dutton and Tryon (eds), pp. 109–139.

Codrington, R. H., 1885. *The Melanesian Languages*. Oxford: Clarendon Press.

Codrington, R. H., 1891. *The Melanesians: Studies in their Anthropology and Folk Lore*. Oxford: Clarendon Press.

Cowan, H. K. J., 1962. Comments on Arthur Capell, 'Oceanic linguistics today'. *Current Anthropology* 3: 398–400.

Crowley, Terry, 1990. *An Illustrated Bislama–English and English–Bislama Dictionary*. Vila: Pacific Languages Unit, University of the South Pacific.

Crowley, Terry, 2000. *An Erromangan (Sye) Dictionary*. Pacific Linguistics, vol. 508. Canberra: Australian National University.

Davenport, William, 1962. Comments on Arthur Capell, 'Oceanic linguistics today'. *Current Anthropology* 3: 400–402.

Deacon, A. Bernard, 1934. *Malekula: A Vanishing People in the New Hebrides*. London: Routledge.

Dempwolff, Otto, 1920. Die Lautentsprechungen der indonesischen lippenlaute in einigen anderen austronesischen Südseesprachen. *Zeitschrift für Eingeborenen-Sprachen*, Supplement 2. Berlin: Dietrich Reimer.

Dempwolff, Otto, 1937. *Vergleichende Lautlehre des Austronesischen Wortschatzes*, vol. 2. Berlin: Dietrich Reimer.

Dixon, R. M. W., 1980. *The Languages of Australia*. Cambridge: Cambridge University Press.

Donohue, Mark, 2005. Word order in New Guinea: Dispelling a myth. *Oceanic Linguistics* 44 (2): 527–536.

Donohue, Mark and Tim Denham, 2008. The languages of Lapita: Vanuatu and an early Papuan presence in the Pacific. *Oceanic Linguistics* 47 (2): 433–444.

Donohue, Mark and Tim Denham, 2012. Lapita and Proto-Oceanic: Thinking outside the pot? *The Journal of Pacific History* 47 (4): 443–457.

Donohue, Mark and Simon Musgrave, 2007. Typology and the linguistic macrohistory of Island Melanesia. *Oceanic Linguistics* 46 (2): 348–387.

Donohue, Mark and Antoinette Schapper, 2008. Whence the Austronesian indirect possession construction? *Oceanic Linguistics* 47 (2): 316–327.

Dubois, M. J., 1976. Peuplement du Pacifique. *Bulletin de la Société d'Etudes Historiques de la Nouvelle-Calédonie* 28: 12–28.

Dubois, M. J., 1981. *Histoire résumée de Maré (Iles Loyauté)*. Publication 27. Nouméa: Société d'Etudes Historiques de la Nouvelle-Calédonie.

Dubois, M. J., 1982. *Kwênyii: l'Ile des Pins aux temps anciens*. Publication 30. Nouméa: Société d'Etudes Historiques de la Nouvelle-Calédonie.

Dunn, Michael, Robert Foley, Stephen Levinson, Ger Reesink and Angela Terrill, 2007. Statistical reasoning in the evaluation of typological diversity in Island Melanesia. *Oceanic Linguistics* 46 (2): 388–403.

Dunn, Michael, Angela Terrill, Ger Reesink, Robert A. Foley and Stephen C. Levinson, 2005. Structural phylogenetics and the reconstruction of ancient language history. *Science* 309 (5743): 2072–2075.

Dutton, Tom and Darrell T. Tryon (eds), 1994. *Language Contact and Change in the Austronesian World*. Berlin: Mouton de Gruyter.

Evans, Bethwyn (ed.), 2009. *Discovering History through Language: Papers in Honour of Malcolm Ross*. Pacific Linguistics, vol. 605. Canberra: Australian National University.

Evans, Bethwyn and Bill Palmer, 2011. Contact-induced change in southern Bougainville. *Oceanic Linguistics* 50 (2): 483–523.

Foley, William A., 1986. *The Papuan Languages of New Guinea*. Cambridge: Cambridge University Press.

Fox, C. E., 1955. *A Dictionary of the Nggela Language*. Auckland: Unity Press.

Fox, Charles E., 1978. *Arosi Dictionary*. Pacific Linguistics, vol. C-57. Canberra: Australian National University.

François, Alexandre, 2006. Are Vanikoro languages really Austronesian? Paper read at Second Conference on Austronesian Languages and Linguistics, Oxford.

François, Alexandre, 2007. Noun articles in Torres and Banks languages: Conservation and innovation. In Siegel, Lynch and Eades (eds), pp. 313–326.

François, Alexandre, 2009. The languages of Vanikoro: Three lexicons and one grammar. In Evans (ed.), pp. 103–126.

Geraghty, Paul A., 1977. Fijian dialect diversity and foreigner talk: The evidence of pre-missionary manuscripts. In Schütz (ed.), pp. 51–67.

Geraghty, Paul A., 1983. *The History of the Fijian Languages*. Oceanic Linguistics Special Publication 19. Honolulu: University of Hawai'i Press.

Geraghty, Paul, 1989. Proto Southern Oceanic and its relationships. In Ray Harlow and Robin Hooper (eds), *VICAL 1: Oceanic Languages: Papers from the Fifth International Conference on Austronesian Linguistics,* special publication: *Te Reo*. Auckland: Linguistic Society of New Zealand.

Geraghty, Paul, 1994. Linguistic evidence for the Tongan Empire. In Dutton and Tryon (eds), pp. 233–249.

Geraghty, Paul, 1996. Problems with Proto Central Pacific. In John Lynch and Fa'afo Pat (eds), *Oceanic Studies: Proceedings of the First International Conference on Oceanic Linguistics*, pp. 85–93. Pacific Linguistics, vol. C-133. Canberra: Australian National University.

Geraghty, Paul, 2001. Amazing -*a*: The suffix that named the Pacific world. *Rongorongo Studies* 11 (2): 63–74.

Geraghty, Paul, 2004. Borrowed plants in Fiji and Polynesia: Some linguistic evidence. In Geraghty and Tent (eds), pp. 65–98.

Geraghty, Paul and Patrick Nunn, 2013. Pre-European contact between Australia and New Caledonia: linguistic and other evidence. Paper presented at COOL9 [Ninth International Conference on Oceanic Linguistics], University of Newcastle, NSW, Australia.

Geraghty, Paul and Jan Tent, 2004. *Borrowing: A Pacific Perspective*. Canberra: Pacific Linguistics.

Grace, George W., 1961. Austronesian linguistics and culture history. *American Anthropologist* 63: 359–368.

Grace, George W., 1962. Comments on Arthur Capell, 'Oceanic linguistics today'. *Current Anthropology* 3: 408–410.

Grace, George W., 1981. *An Essay on Language*. Columbia, SC: Hornbeam.

Green, Roger, 1991. Near and remote Oceania: Disestablishing 'Melanesia' in culture history. In Andrew Pawley (ed.), *Man and a Half: Essays in Pacific Anthropology and Ethnobiology in Honour of Ralph Bulmer*, pp. 491–502. Auckland: The Polynesian Society.

Harrison, Sheldon P., 1981. Recent directions in Oceanic linguistics: A review of the contributions to Studies in Pacific Languages and Cultures. *Oceanic Linguistics* 20: 151–231.

Hickey, Raymond, 2012. Early English and the Celtic hypothesis. In Terttu Nevalainen and Elizabeth Closs Traugott (eds), *The Oxford Handbook of the History of English*, pp. 497–507. Oxford: Oxford University Press.

Hocart, A. M., 1923. Who are the Melanesians? *Journal of the Royal Anthropological Institute of Great Britain and Ireland* 53: 472.

Hollyman, Jim and Andrew Pawley (eds), 1981. *Studies in Pacific Languages and Cultures in Honour of Bruce Biggs*. Auckland: Linguistic Society of New Zealand.

Horton, David (ed.), 1994. *The Encyclopaedia of Aboriginal Australia*. Canberra: Aboriginal Studies Press.

Howells, William, 1973. *The Pacific Islanders*. New York: Scribners.

Jackson, Geoffrey W., 2001. *Tuvaluan Dictionary*. Suva: the author.

Kirch, Patrick Vinton, 1997. *The Lapita Peoples: Ancestors of the Oceanic World*. Oxford: Blackwell.

Labillardière, J., 1800. *An Account of a Voyage in Search of La Pérouse*. John Stockdale.

Layard, John, 1942. *Stone Men of Malekula*. London: Chatto and Windus.

Lincoln, Peter, 1978. Reef-Santa Cruz as Austronesian. In Stephen Wurm and Lois Carrington (eds), *Second International Conference on Austronesian Linguistics: Proceedings*, pp. 929–967. Pacific Linguistics, vol. C-61. Canberra: Australian National University.

Lindstrom, Lamont, 1986. *Kwamera Dictionary*. Pacific Linguistics, vol. C-95. Canberra: Australian National University.

Lynch, John, 1977. *Lenakel Dictionary*. Pacific Linguistics, vol. C-55. Canberra: Australian National University.

Lynch, John, 1981. Melanesian diversity and Polynesian homogeneity: The other side of the coin. *Oceanic Linguistics* 20: 95–129.

Lynch, John, 2001. *The Linguistic History of Southern Vanuatu*. Pacific Linguistics, vol. 509. Canberra: Australian National University.

Lynch, John, 2002. The Proto-Oceanic labiovelars: Some new observations. *Oceanic Linguistics* 41 (2): 310–362.

Lynch, John, 2005. The apicolabial shift in Nese. *Oceanic Linguistics* 44 (2): 389–403.

Lynch, John, 2009. At sixes and sevens: The development of numeral systems in Vanuatu and New Caledonia. In Evans (ed.), pp. 391–411.

Lynch, John, Malcolm Ross and Terry Crowley, 2002. *The Oceanic Languages*. Curzon Language Family Series. Richmond, UK: Curzon Press.

Lynch, John and Philip Tepahae, 2001. *Anejom Dictionary*. Pacific Linguistics, vol. 510. Canberra: Australian National University.

Lynch, John and D. T. Tryon, 1985. Central-Eastern Oceanic: A subgrouping hypothesis. In Andrew Pawley and Lois Carrington (eds), *Austronesian Linguistics at the Eleventh Pacific Science Congress*, pp. 31–52. Pacific Linguistics, vol. C-88. Canberra: Australian National University.

Muller, Kal, 1972. Taboos and magic rule Namba lives. *National Geographic* 141 (1): 56–83.

Næss, Ashild, 2006. Bound nominal elements in Äiwoo (Reefs): A reappraisal of the 'multiple noun class systems'. *Oceanic Linguistics* 45 (2): 269–296.

Næss, Ashild, 2013. From Austronesian voice to Oceanic transitivity: Äiwoo as the 'missing link'. Paper presented at COOL9 [Ninth International Conference on Oceanic Linguistics], University of Newcastle, NSW, Australia.

Pawley, Andrew, 1972. On the internal relationships of Eastern Oceanic languages. In Roger Green and M. Kelly (eds), *Studies in Oceanic Culture History*, vol. 3, pp. 1–142. Pacific Anthropological Records. Honolulu: Bishop Museum.

Pawley, Andrew, 1981. Melanesian diversity and Polynesian homogeneity: A unified explanation for language. In Hollyman and Pawley (eds), pp. 269–309.

Pawley, Andrew, 2006. Explaining the aberrant Austronesian languages of Southeast Melanesia: 150 years of debate. *Journal of the Polynesian Society* 115 (3): 215–258.

Pawley, Andrew, 2007. The origins of Early Lapita culture: The testimony of historical linguistics. In Bedford, Sand and Connaughton (eds), pp. 17–49.

Pawley, Andrew, 2009. The role of the Solomon Islands in the first settlement of Remote Oceania: Bringing linguistic evidence to an archaeological debate. In Alexander Adelaar and Andrew Pawley (eds), *Austronesian Historical Linguistics and Culture History: A Festschrift for Robert Blust*, pp. 515–540. Pacific Linguistics, vol. 601. Canberra: Australian National University.

Pietrusewsky, Michael and Michele T. Douglas, 1993. Tooth ablation in old Hawai'i. *Journal of the Polynesian Society* 102 (3): 255–272.

Ray, Sidney Herbert, 1926. *A Comparative Study of the Melanesian Island Languages*. Cambridge: Cambridge University Press.

Reid, Lawrence A., 1994. Unravelling the linguistic histories of Philippine Negritos. In Dutton and Tryon (eds), pp. 443–475.

Ross, Malcolm, 1996. Contact-induced change and the comparative method: Cases from Papua New Guinea. In Mark Durie and Malcolm Ross (eds), *The Comparative Method Reviewed: Regularity and Irregularity in Language Change*, pp. 180–217. New York: Oxford University Press.

Ross, Malcolm, 2001. Is there an East Papuan phylum? Evidence from pronouns. In Andrew Pawley, Malcolm Ross and Darrell Tryon (eds), *The Boy From Bundaberg: Studies in Melanesian Linguistics in Honour of Tom Dutton*, pp. 301–321. Pacific Linguistics, vol. 514. Canberra: Australian National University.

Ross, Malcolm, 2004. The grammaticalization of directional verbs in Oceanic languages. In Isabelle Bril and Françoise Ozanne-Rivierre (eds), *Complex Predicates in Oceanic Languages: Studies in the Dynamics of Binding and Boundness*, pp. 297–329. Berlin and New York: Mouton de Gruyter.

Ross, Malcolm, 2005. Pronouns as a preliminary diagnostic for grouping Papuan languages. In Andrew Pawley, Robert Attenborough, Jack Golson and Robin Hide (eds), *Papuan Pasts: Cultural, Linguistic and Biological Histories of the Papuan-Speaking Peoples*, pp. 15–65. Pacific Linguistics, vol. 572. Canberra: Australian National University.

Ross, Malcolm and Ashild Næss, 2007. An Oceanic origin for Äiwoo, the language of the Reef Islands? *Oceanic Linguistics* 46: 456–498.

Sand, Christophe, 1996. *Le début du peuplement austronésien de la Nouvelle-Calédonie: données archéologiques récentes*. Les cahiers de l'archéologie en Nouvelle-Calédonie, vol. 6. Nouméa: Département de l'archéologie, Service Territorial des Musées et du Patrimoine.

Schmitz, Carl A., 1962. Comments on Arthur Capell, 'Oceanic linguistics today'. *Current Anthropology* 3: 417–420.

Schütz, Albert (ed.), 1977. *Fijian Language Studies: Borrowing and Pidginization*. Bulletin of the Fiji Museum, vol. 4. Suva: Fiji Museum.

Siegel, Jeff, 2016. Contact-induced grammatical change in Melanesia: Who were the agents of change? *Australian Journal of Linguistics* 36 (3): 406–428.

Siegel, Jeff, John Lynch and Diana Eades (eds), 2007. *Language Description, History and Development: Linguistic Indulgence in Memory of Terry Crowley*. Creole Language Library, vol. 30. Amsterdam: John Benjamins.

Speiser, Felix, 1946. *Versuch einer Siedlungsgeschichte der Südsee*. Denkschriften der schweizerischen naturforschenden Gesellschaft, vol. 72:1.

Speiser, Felix, 1990. *Ethnology of Vanuatu: An Early Twentieth-Century Study*, translated by D. Q. Stephenson. Bathurst: Crawford House Press.

Spriggs, Matthew, 1997. *The Island Melanesians*. Oxford: Blackwell.

Terrill, Angela, 2002. Systems of nominal classification in East Papuan languages. *Oceanic Linguistics* 41: 63–88.

Terrill, Angela, 2011. Languages in contact: An exploration of stability and change in the Solomon Islands. *Oceanic Linguistics* 50 (2): 312–337.

Thurston, William R., 1982. *A Comparative Study in Anêm and Lusi*. Pacific Linguistics, vol. B-83. Canberra: Australian National University.

Thurston, William R., 1994. Renovation and innovation in the languages of north-western New Britain. In Dutton and Tryon (eds), pp. 573–609.

Tryon, Darrell T., 1982. The Solomons and Vanuatu: Varying responses to diversity. In R. J. May and Hank Nelson (eds), *Melanesia: Beyond Diversity*, pp. 241–248. Canberra: Research School of Pacific Studies, Australian National University.

Tryon, Darrell T., 1994. Language contact and contact-induced language change in the Eastern Outer Islands, Solomon Islands. In Dutton and Tryon (eds), pp. 611–648.

Tryon, Darrell T. and B. D. Hackman, 1983. *Solomon Islands Languages: An Internal Classification*. Pacific Linguistics, vol. C-72. Canberra: Australian National University.

Wurm, Stephen, 1954. The Indonesian element in Melanesia: A reply. *Journal of the Polynesian Society* 63: 266–273.

Wurm, Stephen, 1978. Reefs-Santa Cruz: Austronesian, but... In Stephen Wurm and Lois Carrington (eds), *Second International Conference on Austronesian Linguistics: Proceedings*, pp. 969–1010. Pacific Linguistics, vol. C-61. Canberra: Australian National University.

Wurm, Stephen A., 1982. *Papuan Languages of Oceania*. Ars Linguistica, vol. 7. Tübingen: Günter Narr.

Wurm, Stephen, 1985. Language contact and special lexical developments. In Ursula Pieper and Gerhard Stickel (eds), *Studia Linguistica Diachronica et Synchronica: Werner Winter sexagenario anno MCMLXXXIII*, pp. 961–971. Berlin: Mouton de Gruyter.

30

The Western Micronesian Sprachbund

Anthony P. Grant

30.1 Introduction

Thomason (2000) has written about the difficulties involved in proving that constellations of shared features, which are found among a number of languages spoken in the same region, means that the languages in question constitute a linguistic area. Such heuristic problems will be discussed here in regard to the potential sprachbund status of Western Micronesia in the northwest Pacific, an area which has been characterized by extensive and intensive networks of language contact.

The languages involved here are Trukic or Chuukic, especially western Trukic varieties,[1] Yapese of the island of Yap, now part of the Federated States of Micronesia, Palauan of Palau (now the Republic of Belau), and – peripherally – Chamorro of the Marianas. Mapian, a Trukic variety, was spoken a little north of Irian Jaya (see Map 30.1 for locations in Micronesia). Like Sonsorolese-Tobian and Pulo Annian, it was spoken considerably to the west even of Palauan and Yapese, so that the spread of Trukic languages is the greatest of that of all the languages discussed in this chapter. The westernmost and easternmost languages of Western Micronesia that are discussed here, Chuukese and Sonsorolese, are both Trukic.

Among the Trukic languages, Sonsorolese-Tobian, the westernmost one which is spoken several hundred kilometres away from the epicentre of Trukic languages, is especially archaic at the phonological level, such that Sonsorolese phonological forms are closer to the phonological shapes of cognate stems in other Nuclear Micronesian languages than other Trukic

I would like to thank the members of the NWCL, as well as Bob Blust, Francesco Goglia, the late Thomas Klein, Laurie Reid, Malcolm Ross and Sakiyama Osamu for various forms of help with this chapter.

[1] Sonsorolese-Tobian and Pulo Annian, Ulithian, Woleaian and varieties of Saipan Carolinian, a migrant language from the central Trukic belt; Puluwatese, Mortlockese and Lagoon Trukese or Chuukese are also Trukic languages, while the extinct language of Mapia is the westernmost Trukic language of all.

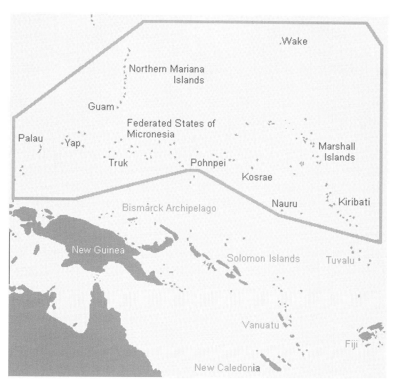

Map 30.1 Micronesia area of the Western Pacific[2]

forms are.[3] Like Woleaian (though more comprehensively) it preserves on stems the word-final voiceless vowels which manifest themselves only in inflected forms in other Trukic languages. Either Sonsorolese-Tobian is phonologically conservative because it has moved little from the first point of settlement of speakers of Trukic languages, or because, surrounded by speakers of Palauan (and Yapese), it has remained isolated from waves of phonological change which have spread throughout the rest of the Trukic continuum.

All of these languages belong to the Malayo-Polynesian branch of Austronesian, so they are ultimately related to one another, though at considerable time depths. Most of them are Oceanic: Trukic participates in Nuclear Micronesian, Yapese is possibly part of the Admiralties group of languages, originally from northeastern Papua New Guinea, and which constitute a primordial division of Oceanic; indeed Ross (1996) suggests that these languages were probably the first languages to break away from the rest of Oceanic.[4] Proto-Micronesian has been

---

[2] Map by courtesy of Holger Behr, licensed under Public Domain via Wikimedia Commons.

[3] Evidence for a Tobian-based pidgin from the 1830s is presented in Holden (1836) and discussed in Grant (2014).

[4] In more recent work, for instance in Lynch, Ross and Crowley (2002), Yapese is represented as the first division of Oceanic against all the other Oceanic languages, which are then divided into Admiralties languages versus all the others.

reconstructed by Bender et al. (2003), with due attention to loanwords and other contact features. But Palauan and Chamorro belong to the Western Malayo-Polynesian 'anti-group': that is, the residuum of languages which is left after the Central-Eastern Malayo-Polynesian group, which can be justified by the adduction of shared innovations, is separated off. They are not closely related to one another and have not successfully been subclassified further beyond the level of separate branches of Malayo-Polynesian (Blust 2000); the claims in Zobel (2002) that they belong, on the grounds of possessing shared morphological innovations, with many other languages in a 'Nuclear-Malayo-Polynesian' group, which is one rung down from Proto-Malayo-Polynesian in the Austronesian family tree, have been disproved in Reid (2002).

Thus two of the four groupings in this sprachbund are near-'isolates' (in relative terms, naturally) and Yapese is an Admiralties offshoot which is spoken several hundred miles away from (and which is completely out of contact with) its nearest genetic relatives and without close relatives in Micronesia. Only the Trukic languages are part of a linguistic group which has other members that are spoken in Micronesia. 'Western Micronesian' is therefore a geographical term.[5]

The part of Micronesia where Nuclear Micronesian languages are used is usually assumed to have been settled from east to west, with Kosrae as an early landfall (see Jackson 1983), though the centre of greatest linguistic diversity among Nuclear Micronesian languages is in the southeast, and according to Ross (1996), lexical evidence from the reconstruction of Nuclear Micronesian, naming geological and similar items, suggests that the proto-language was spoken on a high island such as Kosrae rather than an atoll such as Chuuk. Ross (1996) and Blust (2000) each suggest that the period of continued settlement of Nuclear Micronesia and the Marianas respectively took place between 3,000 and 3,500 years before the present, and Blust (personal communication to Anthony Grant, April 2002) has suggested that Palau may have been settled some millennia ago from the Talaud Islands off Sulawesi, where Sangiric languages (part of the Greater Central Philippine group of Austronesian languages) are now spoken, but that this does not imply that Palauan is Sangiric. We are less sure when Yap was first settled, but the overall picture is that most of the linguistic components of this potential sprachbund were in place a few millennia ago.

---

[5] For the record, the languages of Eastern Micronesia – the other Trukic languages, the Ponapean languages, Kosraean, Marshallese, Kiribatese – are mostly part of the deeply ramified Nuclear Micronesian subgroup of Oceanic, although Nukuoro and Kapingamarangi, spoken to the south of the eastern Trukic languages, are Polynesian outliers, and it appears that Nauruan is coordinately related to the Nuclear Micronesian languages as their closest genetic relative.

30.2 Some Intense 'Contact Languages' in Western Micronesia: Contact-induced Change in Nguluwan, Carolinian and Chamorro

Some languages in this area have been especially strongly shaped by the effects of language contact or contact-induced linguistic change, and as a result they seem at first hand to be ideal places to look for the bundling together of areal-linguistic features.

There is, first of all, the question of Nguluwan (Sakiyama 1982), a language which is spoken by a few score people living on Nglulu(w), an island included in Yap. This is a variety of Yapese used by a population which is (or was recently) bilingual in Ulithian (some older Nguluwanese apparently still know Ulithian but younger ones do not). It contains the same lexical elements from Palauan which Yapese contains (in addition to a few others unique to Nguluwan), but in addition to the western Trukic loans which are found in Yapese, it has an extra layer of both basic and non-basic loans from Ulithian which are not found elsewhere in Yapese. Furthermore, both typologically and phonologically it resembles Ulithian more and Yapese less; for instance, it has developed velarized labials out of inherited and pre-existing non-velarized forms, while shedding some of the distinctions which are characteristic of Yapese phonology. For example, the feature of glottalization has been shed from Nguluwan phonology and Yapese glottalized consonants are unglottalized consonants in Nguluwan, although eleven pairs of Yapese consonants, including some continuants, distinguish glottalized and unglottalized forms. Yapese is the only language among those of Western Micronesia which has any glottalized consonants apart from the simple glottal stop, which is widely distributed within Micronesia. This loss in Nguluwan is probably the result of language contact involving Ulithian, as Ulithian lacks these sounds.

Another language which deserves attention here is Carolinian (sometimes called 'Saipan Carolinian'), which is spoken in three dialects on Saipan in the Northern Marianas, dialects which have their origins on Satawal, Lamotrek and the Mortlocks respectively, all of them central or (in the case of Mortlockese) eastern Trukic lects which have been transported northwest to Saipan, where they have all been influenced by the same languages. In terms of historical and numerical precedence the major sources of loans into Carolinian are Chamorro, Japanese and English, with a handful of words also taken from German. It appears from my study of Fritz (1911) and Jackson and Marck (1991) that the bulk of Chamorro copies into Carolinian are themselves copies from Spanish, constituting a subset of the massive tranche of Spanish items which have been copied into Chamorro. It is furthermore clear that Chamorro is the source of most if not all Spanish elements in Carolinian, and that additionally most of these loans are 'acculturational' items inasmuch as they are phonologically Carolinianized versions of the names of introduced items from the various languages of the people who introduced these items to the Carolinians.

The degree of copying of elements from other languages into Chamorro itself deserves some analysis. The copying profile of Chamorro is interesting, since the Marianas had a different colonization pattern from the Carolines (which include the islands on which the other languages which we are concerned with here are spoken). In fact, Guam had a different pattern of settlement from that of the Northern Marianas, and this is instantiated linguistically. The important factors here are historical: contact with Spaniards since the 1520s and settlement by the Spanish of Guam from the 1660s onwards, the decimation of the Chamorros and the relocation of all Chamorros from Saipan and other northern islands onto Guam (apart from a maroon group which remained on Rota), the landing of the first boatload of Carolinians on Saipan in 1815, the resettling of some Chamorros on Saipan in 1817, and the occupation of Guam by the Americans in 1898 but the cession of the northern Marianas by Spain to Germany from 1899 to 1915, with their post-WWI cession to Japan, which based its regional headquarters on Saipan (Japan also occupied Guam during WWII), and the transfer of all these islands to the US in 1945. Salas Palomo and Stolz (2008) discuss the impact of Spanish on Chamorro and on attempts to 'reaustronesianize' the language. The book by Rodríguez-Ponga Salamanca (1995) is the largest study of the impact of Spanish on Chamorro, but Blust (2000) indicates that Tagalog or other Philippine languages, and also a Malayo-Polynesian language which has yet to be identified, have also shaped the language. This was noticed by Costenoble (1940). A few other forms of varied origins (Palauan, Chuukese, Pidgin English) are listed in Blust (2000).

Saipan Chamorro contains lexical elements deriving from Japanese, and these are not found in Guamanian or Rotanese forms of Chamorro, which have absorbed more forms from English (as has Saipan Chamorro). As we saw above, Saipan Chamorro has given many copies to Carolinian, many of these being of Spanish origin. Neither variety has copied much from German (there are a very few German loans in Carolinian and none in Chamorro). The reason for this is that the Chamorros had a greater and longer exposure to European cultural elements than any other Micronesians (including the Carolinians), and they had already adopted the acculturational lexicon which they felt they needed to have from Spanish. No other Micronesian language has copied more than a handful of (acculturational) loans from Chamorro. I do not know of any loans from Carolinian that occur in Saipan Chamorro, and given the disparity of the low status of the Carolinians and their language as against that of the Chamorros on Saipan in earlier days, we might be surprised to find any such loans.

30.3   Areal Features in Western Micronesia: Lexical and Structural Elements

These languages of Western Micronesia show partial convergence over time through the sharing and spread of many structural features, especially some highly marked phonotactic and morphosyntactic properties, which are absent in many of the languages spoken nearby. Additionally, they share further structural features (and these are mostly typological rather than morphological, transfers of pattern rather than transfers of fabric: Grant 2002a, 2003), which are presumably inherited from Proto-Malayo-Polynesian.

There is also a plentiful body of shared lexicon of various kinds, which can be stratified historically: there are many items of shared inherited Malayo-Polynesian lexicon, additional items originating in one language which passed to others in the group (with words flowing especially from Palauan and Trukic to Yapese: Ross 1996), and later shared cultural loans from Philippine languages, German, Spanish, Japanese and (in most cases) two layers of loans from English, one from the Pidgin English which was used by nineteenth century American whalers and traders who visited Micronesia, and the other as a result of the influence of post-1945 American administrators and educators. American missionaries who had previously established Protestant missions further east in Micronesia are also responsible for the loans from Mortlockese and Pohnpeian which one finds in some eastern Trukic lects.

Generally, the major direction for copying lexicon in Micronesia is from west to east. Loans, mostly labels for acculturational items, diffused from beyond Micronesia and from imperial administrative centres (e.g. Koror on Palau and Donguch/Colonia on Yap) to more easterly or less politically dominant locations. Most of these come from European languages but some are items from other 'Western Micronesian' languages – for instance the name of the mineral 'lime', which is often incorporated in betel chews (Palauan *chaus* /ʔaus/, from Proto-Malayo-Polynesian (PMP) **qapuʀ*; it also means 'white' in Yapese), diffused from Palau (which has the phonological reflex for this word which one would expect from the processes of Palauan historical phonology: Grant 2002a) into Yapese and Nuclear Micronesian languages as far east as Kosrae (Ross 1996).

A few other words are widely dispersed. 'Pig' is labelled as *vaviy* in Yapese, itself a copy from Tagalog *baboy* by way of Chamorro *babui* and then via Palauan *babii*. 'Rice' in Woleaian is *peraas*, probably from Palauan *beras*, which has taken it from Malay *beras* (Chamorro has the expected reflex of this word, namely *pugas*, cf. Bisayan *bugas*). The word for 'paper' in Chamorro is Spanish-derived *papet*, complete with the usual Chamorro reflex of syllable-final /-l/. But in Palauan it is *babier*, from German *Papier*, which has passed into Yapese as *babyoor* (it has clearly come into Yapese from Palauan since Yapese distinguishes between /p/ and /b/, though Palauan did not do so at this time), and thence into Woleaian as *babiyoor*. This is a form which indicates that some diffusion of European cultural items and their labels occurred from west to east into the era of German occupation. Palauan and Yapese speech communities had apparently not quite lost all contact and ability to influence one another by the time the Europeans began to exert substantive influence in the area at the start of the twentieth century.

A table of major sources of loans in the various languages is presented in the Appendix as Table 30A.1. It needs to be recognized that by no means all the lexical elements in any of these languages have been fully sourced. For instance, Blust (2000) argues for the existence of an extensive stratum of phonologically distinctive but as yet unsourced etyma in the Chamorro vocabulary, in addition to an under-explored stratum of words which have been taken from one or more Philippine languages, possibly with Spanish 'assistance' inasmuch as they relocated many Filipinos to Guam.[6] This stratum postdates the split of these languages from Proto-Malayo-Polynesian but is apparently pre-Spanish (and pre-Philippine contact?) in its dating.

Some common structural features, which are often cross-linguistically unusual but which are found in this area, are given in Table 30A.2 (phonological features) and Table 30A.3 (morphosyntactic features) in the Appendix. In this examination I have prioritized phonological features, which are easier to identify, though there are also many cross-linguistic parallels in morphosyntax. Not all these shared features are diffused. Some have simply been inherited from the proto-languages of the various languages under discussion, and thus may be shared with Admiralties languages in the case of Yapese or with other Nuclear Micronesian languages in the case of Trukic. Others may go back to Proto-Malayo-Polynesian.

Similarly the value of these features for proving Western Micronesia as a sprachbund varies intrinsically from feature to feature. Some features are simply stronger evidence, because the phenomenon which they instantiate is less frequent universally than others are. For instance, not all of the world's languages have both prefixes and suffixes, but all four groups surveyed here use both prefixes and suffixes, especially in the verb complex. Is this then a strong feature with which to prove the existence of this sprachbund? There again, what really is the probative power for the construction of a sprachbund (if it has any)? Is it the fact that all the languages in Western Micronesia (apart from Chamorro, which uses only Spanish loans) denote 'twelve' by expressions which translate as 'ten and two'? Or the fact that the pronominal systems in all four groups distinguish between inclusive and exclusive first person

---

[6] On the other hand some of the Philippine borrowings, for instance, Chamorro *bibengka*, a borrowing from Tagalog *bibingka* 'a kind of sweet cake', may date only from the widespread arrival of Filipinos as workers on Guam, a population move which was especially strong in the twentieth century.

plural, just as Proto-Malayo-Polynesian did? Or the fact that, like most Austronesian languages, they are all prepositional rather than postpositional languages?

Even when we have evidence of shared features which are cross-linguistically highly marked, they do not always present the uniform picture of origin, distribution and development which we may expect, and their various origins may be very different from language to language. For example, Palauan, Yapese and Trukic all permit word-initial geminate clusters. And yet these are infrequent in Palauan and are probably of recent origin there, though other initial CC-sequences involving different consonants are fairly common. Yapese has such clusters, but they are found only with sonorants and are also infrequent, while the only other CC-initial clusters in Yapese are infrequent dissimilated clusters such as that found in *bpiin* 'woman' (Jensen et al. 1977). On the other hand, while geminate initial consonant clusters are both basic and very frequent in Trukic languages, other CC-clusters, in which the first and second consonants are different, are not attested there. Meanwhile, Chamorro, which does not permit word-initial geminate consonant clusters (though these are common enough word-medially), still has a great proportion of CC-initial stems, but these were unknown before the impact of Spanish on Chamorro, and Spanish is the source of the vast majority of these forms.

30.4 On the Difficulties of Showing that Western Micronesia is a Sprachbund

In substantiating Western Micronesia as a potential sprachbund we may discuss probative issues which are raised by the fact that two of the four participatory stocks, namely Chamorro and Palauan, lack close relatives, while the genetic connection of Yapese to the Admiralties languages has been obscured on both sides by millennia of separate internal development (and in the case of Yapese, also hundreds of years of intimate contact with speakers of other Austronesian languages). We should try to separate diffused from inherited features among a group of ultimately related languages. We may further discuss the paradox that many typological and especially phonological features connecting these languages appear to run in the opposite direction from those features mediating lexical influence.

An important first stage when looking for possible sources of linguistic change is to start with lexical transfers and to list the sources of the lexical loan elements in the various languages: Trukic, Palauan, apparently Malay, Philippine languages, German, Spanish, Japanese, two layers of English loans (the first layer of which was introduced by nineteenth century American whalers and thus predating German and Japanese elements in these languages) as well as Chamorro. Some languages have acquired elements from further languages (there is a small Western

Malayo-Polynesian tranche of loans in Chamorro, Palauan and Yapese, and loans from other Trukic languages and Pohnpeian in Trukic languages), and there appears to have been some 'dialect mixture' among Trukic languages and beyond (there have been a few mission-actuated, post-European contact, acculturational borrowings from Pohnpeian and Mortlockese into Lagoon Trukese and Puluwatese, for instance, as the material in Goodenough and Sugita 1990 shows).

The effects of borrowing on each language should be noted, as it is not enough simply to count loans: with just under 600 recognized loans in a list of c. 3,000 discrete lexical stems, Yapese has proportionately slightly fewer borrowings than Lagoon Trukese (Goodenough and Sugita 1990 indicate that Lagoon Trukese has about 760 recognized loans as against c. 3,000 non-loan stems). But the impact of loan elements (especially from Austronesian languages) on Yapese is important out of all comparison to the impact of borrowing on Lagoon Trukese or on any other Trukic language. The everyday non-acculturational vocabulary of Chuukese (or for that matter Puluwatese) is unaffected by loans from Japanese or English, but the basic vocabulary of Yapese is full of loans (especially nouns) from Palauan and even more so from Ulithian. This has happened to such an extent that the ultimate affinities of Yapese were long in doubt; even Blust (1980: 152) assumed that Yapese was derived from a creole, of which a key component was Palauan while another was an unidentified Oceanic language.

There is also the issue of lexical and morphological elements which are independent innovations and which have not arisen as the result of contact-induced language change. Some 110 items on the Chamorro translation of the Blust list,[7] about 120 on the Palauan Blust list, and maybe two-thirds of the relevant elements on the Yapese Blust list, all fall into this category.

Indeed, Yapese shows a very great degree of independent innovation, as well as having received an inordinate number of lexical borrowings from neighbouring languages (and on the Blust list these almost exceed the number of elements retained from Proto-Malayo-Polynesian). One such innovation is the development of a separate set of glottalized consonants (both stops and continuants), which are found nowhere else in Micronesia (so they cannot have been introduced through the transfer of numerous loans from relevant languages) but which are quite frequent in Yapese. In Yapese they represent the end-result of a process of reduction of what were originally CVC-sequences. Another innovation, which appears to be fairly recent if we are to judge from the scant philological evidence, is the development of original Yapese voiced stops into voiced fricatives in most instances. This change is not found in other Western Micronesian languages.

---

[7] This is a modification of the Swadesh list which has proved useful in helping to sub-classify Austronesian languages because it is provided with reliable Proto-Malayo-Polynesian reconstructions.

There are historical reasons for bracketing these languages of Western Micronesia together as a linguistic area and for positing a history of cultural exchange between several of the islands and atolls, given the role of the maritime Yap empire in pre-modern times, the role of Ulithi as the major atoll group within this empire, and the Yap Empire's dependence upon pieces of stone money which could only be obtained from Palau. Yapese did not apparently influence Palauan, lexically or otherwise and at a very basic lexical level, but the reverse flow of influence did take place. Meanwhile Yapese borrowed much basic vocabulary from Ulithian and donated a certain amount of cultural vocabulary to it and to Woleaian.[8] We can additionally trace the patterns and directionality of influences, or at least explore some of the history of such influences, by doing philological work on some of these languages; this is especially feasible with Chamorro but it can also be done with Palauan, Yapese and Woleaian to a lesser extent, and there is a certain amount of older data on the dialects of Carolinian. In this light, a study of the Chamorro, Woleaian and Yapese vocabularies in Chamisso (1864), collected in 1817, shows that Yapese had already absorbed its Ulithian and Palauan elements but that Chamorro's inherited sets of numerals were still obtainable as artefacts from some Chamorro-speakers (the others having switched to using Spanish numerals only).

30.5   Common Phonological Developments which Cut across 'Genetic' Boundaries in Western Micronesia

Several important changes from the phonological system reconstructed for Proto-Malayo-Polynesian show parallel developments in more than one of the four branches in Western Micronesia:

PMP *p > /f/ (Chamorro, and possibly earlier in Palauan where it is now /w/),
        > /w/ (Palauan, Trukic when it occurs before back vowels, Yapese)
PMP *s > /t/ (Palauan, Woleaian),
        > /θ/ (Yapese, Nguluwan, Ulithian).
PMP *b > /p/ (Chamorro; Trukic and Oceanic languages generally where this merger occurs),
PMP *n > /l/ (Palauan; Ulithian, also in the Tanapag form of Carolinian, though it does not occur in all Trukic languages[9])
PMP *t > /ð/ (Palauan), /Ø/ (Trukic languages).
PMP *d > /r/ (Palauan, Trukic)

There are other important phonological trends which are distributed across genetic boundaries in Western Micronesia. A rhotic/sibilant

---

[8] This is alluded to in Walsh and Harui-Walsh 1979; see also the short list of loans from Yapese into Woleaian which is given in Sohn 1975.

[9] Some other Trukic languages merge original /l/ and /n/ as /n/; this is the case with Lagoon Trukese. Sonsorolese changes original /l/ to /r/.

interplay, manifested in several ways, is found in some Western Micronesian languages: PMP *R > /s/ in Palauan (and in earlier Palauan loans into Yapese it was represented as /c/, presumably close to the sound which it had in Palauan at the time). The same sound is represented by trilled and assibilated rhotics in some Trukic languages (it occurs thus in Satawalese and Puluwatese) and by a retroflex sibilant or other kinds of sibilant in some others, such as Woleaian (and by palatal stops or affricates in yet others, such as Lagoon Trukese and Ulithian).

There is also a tendency for major words (especially contentives) in surface forms in Western Micronesian languages (and some beyond) to be C-initial and C-final, e.g. in Palauan, Yapese and to a large extent also many Trukic languages (certainly Puluwatese). Chamorro and Palauan prefix epenthetic consonants to vowel-initial words (/gw, g/ in Chamorro and /ŋ/ in Palauan), while Yapese uses word-initial (and word-final) glottal stops to reinforce the use of the C-initial and C-final template, and Trukic languages prefix /w/ to word-initial back vowels and /y/ to front vowels. These principles are relaxed with regard to post-1885 loans in some of the languages, which permit loans that can be vowel-initial and vowel-final, although the rule had already been relaxed by the time Spanish loans flooded into Chamorro. Initial CC-clusters are only found in Chamorro (in loans only), in Palauan (where they are secondary and are usually broken up at the phonetic level by a svarabhakti schwa) and in a small number of stems in Yapese, such as *bpiin* 'woman', where it looks, on the basis of comparative evidence (cf. Proto-Polynesian *fafine* and modern Hawai'ian *wahine*), as though an intermediate vowel was recently deleted.

A third phonological tendency is for there to be essentially one stop series in these languages in terms of the lack of contrastive voicing, although allophonic conditioning through gemination (not a process present in Proto-Malayo-Polynesian phonology) and other changes can have their effect in phonetic realizations. Trukic languages have one stop series (as is the case with many other Oceanic languages), while Palauan has /b/ but no /p/ except in recent loans from Japanese and English, /t k/ but no /d g/, and a voiced interdental fricative /ð/ but no voiceless one, plus /s/ but no /z/ until that was introduced in recent Japanese loans. Yapese has two sets of voiceless consonants (glottalized and unglottalized) as well as a voiced set, which is usually realized as voiced fricatives. Chamorro turned the voiced stops into voiceless ones, turned /p/ into /f/ and earlier /k/ into /h/ (though /kk/, if it is inherited from forms occurring in Proto-Malayo-Polynesian – though this is a language lacking geminate consonants – remains intact in Chamorro). But Chamorro kept /t/ as /t/, and eventually turned PMP *R into /g/, as did many Western Austronesian languages, while PMP *Z became /c/. Blust (2000) points out that /b d k/ are indicative of loanwords in Chamorro, as is /r/. Not all these loans are Spanish or Philippine in origin, though many of them are; where the remainder come from has as yet not been ascertained.

Of course there are other Proto-Malayo-Polynesian sounds which have produced different reflexes in each of the four branches. PMP *R is the most notable of these: it goes to zero in Trukic, /r/ in Yapese, /s/ (formerly /c/) in Palauan and /g/ in Chamorro. It is also too easily forgotten that there are many more features which set these languages apart than which unite them. For instance, Chamorro has a 'Philippine-type' goal-focus system, part of which is also found in Palauan, and which can be reconstructed back to Proto-Austronesian. But this system is not found in either Yapese or Trukic. The structures of tense–mood–aspect systems are more complex in both Yapese and Trukic than in Chamorro, with Palauan standing between these poles in having a system of 'medium complexity'.

When looking for possible sprachbund features, we need to separate out universals and near-universals from features which were inherited from the proto-language, and distinguish these from further features which have been transmitted by diffusion and from yet other features which languages have evolved individually. The features which enable us to build a plausible sprachbund are 'shared diffusions' in typology, and these consist of innovations which arose in one language and which have spread by contact to others. As such they are analogous to the shared innovations whose presence enables us to subgroup clusters of related languages in genetic classifications.

30.6 How Did the Sprachbund Come About? Earlier Contact Patterns

The question is how these features diffused from one language to another. Instead of looking at the whole region as a massive sprachbund, we can usefully decompose the territory into smaller portions, in terms of the patterns of diffusion. The domain of the Yap Empire or at least a tributary system centred on Yap, with the interaction of speakers of western Trukic, Palauan and Yapese itself, is one such sub-area. Guam and the Marianas are home to Chamorro, which has had a much longer period of closer interaction with speakers of European languages than the other languages have had, which shows very different patterns of massive borrowing from those found elsewhere in Micronesia, and which is peripheral to many of the shared areal features.[10] A third factor enhancing the possibility of the geographical spread of changes is the superb knowledge of traditional techniques of navigation among

---

[10] Chamorro and Yapese-Nguluwan are by far the biggest and most profound 'borrowers' in this area, but the latter has not unambiguously borrowed free grammatical morphs, whereas Chamorro does this to a very great extent.

speakers of Trukic languages, which are still preserved to this day on the atoll of Satawal. This enabled them to make long voyages to many distant islands and helped linguistic innovations to diffuse very far – though some of these innovations never reached the far western Trukic languages.

We may mention here the presence of some possible Micronesian (Trukic and maybe Palauan) elements in Chamorro. Can we detect language shift from these languages to the more powerful Chamorro? This stratum of forms includes apparently Trukic (or at least Nuclear Micronesian) forms such as *pwengi* 'last night', *bwente* 'perhaps' (cf. Carolinian *bwete* 'although'), *yalibaw* 'to thrash', *gwatu* 'there', *sirek* 'to copulate'; and a couple of forms which may (according to Reid 2002) be from Palauan: *palau'an* 'woman', possibly once 'Palauan woman slave', and *un* (an oblique form for 'you plural'). The Micronesian-derived forms are common to all forms of Chamorro, including that of Guam; they are not recent loans into Saipan Chamorro from Carolinian. The possibility of the existence of a sizable Micronesian or Palauan component in Chamorro has never been clearly detected, let alone been explored *in extenso*, but the chance that some speakers of Guam Chamorro once had ancestors speaking Micronesian languages cannot quite be excluded. But even though Trukic substrate languages (or stray speakers of Trukic languages who were washed off course during their voyages) may have influenced Chamorro, there is no evidence that this happened to Palauan. There are some speakers of Sonsorolese-type dialects who live in Chechang Village on Palau, but they are relatively recent migrants there. The reduction of the consonant inventory of Palauan appears to have been an independently motivated phenomenon.

30.7 Conclusions

The arguments for the existence of a Western Micronesian sprachbund are largely phonological and lexical in nature, and it is anomalous that the language which has most closely approximated the Trukic phonological system (especially in regard to the abolition of voicing as a distinctive feature) is Palauan, which has had the least contact with, and which is the one least influenced by, Trukic languages. The morphosyntactic characteristics which mark these languages as being similar are (1) mostly typological rather than overtly morphological in nature, instances of similar patterns rather than similar fabric,[11] and (2) (probably) inherited rather than diffused.

---

[11] Which are therefore of no real use in relating these languages to one another genetically; the actual morphs used derive from the genetic component of these languages.

I use parentheses for the word 'probably' because we cannot always tell whether these features were diffused or inherited. There are two reasons for this uncertainty: (1) because our records of these languages are mostly too recent for us to be able to discern this, and (2) because Chamorro, Palauan and Yapese are each of them languages with no close relatives.[12] Many of the features which bind these languages together may have been inherited from earlier stages of Malayo-Polynesian. Syntactic influence of one language upon another is clearest where it is most discordant, thus it has clearly taken place in Nguluwan under Ulithian influence (for example in the way of handling alienable possession in nouns) and in Chamorro under Spanish influence (where it is manifested in the borrowing of many conjunctions and modal and temporal adverbs, which are sometimes semantically reinterpreted). But the unusual form of possession in Chamorro exemplified by *ga'-ña haguini* [ANIMAL.CLASSIFIER-3SG sandcrab] 'his sandcrab' (Topping and Ogo 1980: 289) is strongly reminiscent of the Trukic possessive constructions which are found in Nguluwan because of its Ulithian element.

We are dealing with several different kinds and degrees of influence and change here, a situation which has to be examined on a language-by-language basis. The impact of Spanish on Chamorro is a case of unidirectional language contact on a scale unprecedented elsewhere in Micronesia, although these do not impinge very heavily on the vocabulary of the Chamorro translation of the Blust list, where they constitute only 3–4 per cent (they are more prominent among the elements of the Swadesh list). A further 2 per cent of the items on the Blust Palauan list are acquired from other languages (Spanish words for 'salt' and 'root' and Japanese for 'dust' and one form for 'egg'), and even these are anomalous as instances of relexification (rather than extension) in the Palauan vocabulary; Palauan has mostly absorbed new labels for new items, and apart from possibly borrowing the Oceanic applicative *-akini* as *-akl* on some verb stems which cannot be analysed within Palauan morphology (Zobel 2002), there is no concrete evidence for transfer of fabric into Palauan from Oceanic languages, although the Palauan phonological system does read a bit like a parody of a Nuclear Micronesian phonological segment roster.

On the other hand, the impact of other languages upon Yapese is profound. In the lexicon alone, there are about 30 borrowings from Ulithian and Palauan on the Blust Yapese list, in addition to the form

---

[12] Yapese's fellow-members of the Admiralties group, even moderately well-described ones such as Loniu, are very different from Yapese in surface and substance, the number of shared innovations of any kind linking Yapese to Admiralties languages is probably not large, and it is unlikely that there has been much contact between speakers of Yapese and those of other Admiralties languages for some millennia.

giriin 'green' from English or just possibly German, and this impact continues to be found to a similarly high degree throughout the Yapese vocabulary. The richness of the Yapese vowel system is reminiscent in size and nature of the vowels found in that of Trukic languages such as Carolinian. Nonetheless, many of the features which make Yapese stand out from the other languages, such as the extensive glottalization in the form of numerous ejective consonants, come neither from Palauan nor Ulithian, nor, as far as I know, are they inherited from Proto-Admiralties (if that is Yapese's ancestor rather than its elder sister language): they are simply internal innovations. By contrast, the impact of other Western Micronesian languages (and this really means Chamorro) on Trukic languages is confined to a thin sliver of acculturational vocabulary which may predate strong Spanish contact (though Chamorro has had a stronger impact on Saipan Carolinian). This goes to show that in Western Micronesia some languages have been important donors, some have been major recipients, and some have been both.

Appendix

Statistics on the number and proportion of loan elements in some Micronesian languages

Chamorro
Approximately 38 per cent Spanish, 2.5 per cent Japanese and English, 0.5 per cent other (especially from Philippine languages), out of a total of c. 8,400 dictionary entries (Topping et al. 1973). *Note.* All these may be an underestimate, especially regarding the Spanish elements, which are found in all form classes in Chamorro. With the possible exception of a sole form from Pidgin English that also occurs in Tok Pisin (*puspus* 'to copulate'), all English loans are post-1898.[13]

Palauan
Loans comprise 33 words from German, 63 from Spanish and 4 from Tagalog; over 660 from Japanese, plus 205 elements from English out of a total of c. 5,000 entries in McManus (Josephs 1977) and the lists on http://tekinged .com/show_words.php. To the best of my knowledge, no loans originating in Chamorro, Trukic languages or Yapese have so far been identified in the Palauan lexicon. Palauan has been a donor but hardly a recipient language in Western Micronesia. Most English loans are post-WWII.

---

[13] An uncertain but considerable proportion of the remaining Chamorro lexicon can be shown on historical phonological grounds to be borrowed from as yet unidentified languages rather than to have been inherited from PMP.

Yapese

Out of a total of c. 2,900 entries in Jensen et al. (1977) which are not among the 147 personal or place names: 155+ items derive from a Nuclear Micronesian language, almost all from a Trukic language, probably Ulithian or Woleaian, 98 from Palauan, 15 from a lost language which was closely related to Palauan, 7 from an unidentified Oceanic language (possibly a Polynesian one), 102 from Japanese, 21 from German, 30 from Spanish, 157 from English, and there are a handful of early loans from Malay or Philippine languages which are often widely dispersed in other Western Micronesian languages. The same sources of elements are found in Nguluwan, which has sometimes made different loan choices from Yapese: Nguluwan *lapis* (< Spanish), Yapese *pensel* 'pencil' (< English). Many further loans from Palauan and Ulithian may actually be present and may be waiting to be spotted in the Yapese vocabulary. Most of the English loans in Yapese are post-WWII. Ross (1996) deals with much of this, and provides the insights on the Palauan-related language and the Oceanic language; other counts are the author's.

Woleaian

Out of some 4,000 entries in Sohn and Tawerilmang (1975), there are 300 words from Japanese, 100 from English, about 30 from Spanish, about 10 from German, a few others from other languages (*peraas* 'rice' from Malay, *kaarebaw* 'water buffalo, cattle' from Malay via Spanish or possibly Tagalog, and a few cultural loans from Yapese). Ulithian has a similar loan profile, maybe with fewer German loans but with more loans taken from Yapese (Walsh and Harui-Walsh 1979). Most of the English loans in Woleaian are post-WWII adoptions.

Puluwatese

Out of 6,300 entries and c. 4,000 stems in Elbert (1972), there are c. 18 stems from Spanish (some of them via Chamorro), c. 90 from Japanese, 7 from German, 5 from Pohnpeian, 2 from Mortlockese, also hundreds of loans from English.

Chuukese (Lagoon Trukese)

Out of c. 3,750 stem-level elements given in Goodenough and Sugita (1990), there are c. 310 from Japanese, c. 400 from English, 6 from Pidgin English, 5 from Latin, 4 from Chamorro, 1 each from Korean, Puluwatese and Samoan, 13 from German, 13 from Spanish, 6 from Mortlockese and 11 from Pohnpeian (statistics from Goodenough and Sugita 1990).

Table 30A.1 Sources of loans in the languages of Western Micronesia

	Chamorro	Palauan	Yapese	Trukic	Polynesian	Pohnpeian	Philippine languages	Spanish	Pidgin English	Japanese	German	US English
Chamorro	X	tiny?	no	tiny? a couple of items	no	no	yes	massive	tiny: 1 item	only on Saipan	no	increasing
Palauan	no	X	no	no?	no	no	a few	a few dozen	c. 8	large	a few	increasing
Yapese	no	sizeable and basic	X	sizeable and basic	a few	no	a handful	c. 35	a few	yes	a few	increasing
Nguluwan	no	no	X	no	no	no	a handful?	presumably	a few?	yes	a few?	increasing
Sonsorol.	no	maybe now	no?	X	no	no	no?	presumably	a few	yes, a few	?	increasing
Ulithian	no	no	many	X	no	no	no?	over a score	a few	yes	?	increasing
Woleaian	no	no	many	X	no	no	no?	c. 30	c. 300 in all	yes, c. 100	c. 10	increasing
Carolinian	large	maybe	no	X	no	no	not directly	dozens, many by way of Chamorro	some	yes	several	increasing
Puluwatese	no	no	no	X	no	yes	no	about a dozen	a few dozen	yes	a dozen?	increasing
Lagoon Trukese	tiny	no	no	X	no	yes	no	c. 12	c. 15	yes	c. 10	increasing, over 300

Sources of items employed in partial relexification (lexical replacement) in Western Micronesian languages

Chamorro	Spanish, minimally Philippine, Oceanic and (on Saipan) Japanese.
Palauan	Some Japanese, Spanish to a tiny extent.
Yapese	Palauan, western Trukic, other Oceanic.
Nguluwan	Palauan and especially Ulithian (at least four items on the 100- item Swadesh wordlist are Nguluwan loans from Ulithian which are not also found in the sizable Ulithian tranche of loans which have entered Yapese).
Sonsorolese	?none; maybe some nowadays from Palauan.
Ulithian	?none; some acculturational lexicon from Yapese.
Woleaian	?none; some acculturational lexicon from Yapese.
Carolinian	Some Chamorro.
Puluwatese	?none; the sizable borrowed lexicon is all acculturational.
Lagoon Trukese	?(there are plenty of loans in the lexicon but they are not relexificational in nature).

Table 30A.2 Some areal-typological phonological features in selected Western Micronesian languages

Feature/Language	Palauan	Yapese	Nguluwan	Sonsorol-Tobian	Woleaian/Ulithian	Carolinian	Chamorro
/n/ and /l/ are distinct phonemes	/n/ occurs only in loans	yes	yes	no	no	/n/ only in loans	yes
/f/ phonemic	no (but maybe yes once)	yes	yes	yes	yes	yes	yes
One stop series in native forms	yes	no	no	yes	yes	yes	yes, though voiced geminates are technically phonemic
Consonantal gemination is phonemic	yes but secondarily so	no	yes?	yes	yes	yes	yes
Interdental fricatives are phonemic	yes; voiced phonemic	yes, voiceless phonemic, voiced phonetic	voiceless only	yes, voiceless phonemic	not in W, which has substituted /t/, but the voiceless one is used in U	no	no
/h/ is present	only in recent loans	only in recent loans	no?	yes	yes	yes	yes, from original /k/
Voiceless velar fricatives	no, but in nineteenth century yes	no, though a voiced velar fricative has phonetic status as allophone of /g/	no	yes	yes	yes, as a single allophone of /k/	no
Glottal stop is present	yes	yes	no, lost under Ulithian influence	no	no	no	yes
Other glottalized consonants	no	yes; 11 such	no	no	no	no	no

Velarized labial consonants	no	yes	yes, in Ulithian loans and also in inherited forms	yes	yes	no
Long vowels are phonemic	no	yes	yes	yes	no	no
Complex vowel nuclei	yes?	no	no	no	no	no
Word-final voiceless vowels	no	yes	no	yes in W, no in U	no	no
Number of vowel phonemes	8 plus length for all 8	5	8	6 short and 7 long	9	6 (4 plus 2 loan phonemes)
Central vowels?	non-phonemic schwa	yes	yes	yes	yes	no
Parasitic initial glides?	no	yes	yes	yes	yes (though less frequent)	yes
Are there loan phones?	yes, 6	no?	yes, /bw mw/ from Ulithian replace older Yapese /b m/ in many cases	no?	very recent borrowing of some from Chamorro	yes, /r/
Loan phonological canons?	no? if so, recent	no	no	no	no	yes, CCV-

Proto-Malayo-Polynesian had four vowels, *e, *i, *a, *u and diphthongs *ay *aw *ey *iw. Proto-Oceanic (= Proto-Eastern Malayo-Polynesian) changed *e and *aw to *o and *ay to *e. This last appears to have been the Proto-Micronesian vowel system as well, though only Kiribatese and some forms of Pohnpeian appear to have kept the Proto-Micronesian system intact. By contrast Marshallese has three or four vowel phonemes while Kosraean has twelve.

Table 30A.3 Some structural parallels in Western Micronesian languages

Feature/Language	Palauan	Yapese	Nguluwan	Sonsorol.-Tobi.	Woleaian-Ulithian	Carolinian	Chamorro
Numeral classifiers?	no, but some special number sets	not now, but possibly formerly	no	yes	yes	yes	no, but there were formerly special numeral sets
Distinction between alienable versus inalienable possessions on nouns	yes	no	yes	yes	yes	yes	no
Decimal numeral system?	yes	no, modified quinary	no, modified quinary	yes	yes	yes	yes, both Austronesian original and modern Spanish
Ablaut in noun or verb stems	yes	yes	yes	yes	yes	yes	no
Definite article?	yes, preposed	no, though pre-Yapese apparently had one	no	yes, postposed	yes, postposed	yes, postposed	yes, preposed
Indefinite article?	no	no	no	no	no	no	yes, from Spanish
Possession by cliticization	yes, for inalienable nouns	yes, for inalienable nouns	yes, for inalienable nouns	yes, for inalienable nouns	yes, for inalienable nouns	yes, for inalienable nouns	yes
Possessive order	N-Poss	N-Poss	N-Poss (inalienable), Classifier-Poss Noun (alienable)	N-Poss (inalienable), Classifier-Poss Noun (alienable)	N-Poss (inalienable), Classifier-Poss Noun (alienable)	N-Poss (inalienable), Classifier-Poss Noun (alienable)	N-Poss, sometimes Classifier-Possessor Possessed-Noun

Numeral/Noun	Num-Classifier Noun	Num-Noun	Num-Noun	Classified num-Noun	Classified num-Noun	Classified num-Noun	Num-Noun
Genitive/Noun	Noun-possessive linker-Noun	N-Gen	N-Gen	N-Gen	N-Gen	N-Gen	Noun-possessive linker-Noun
Adjective/Noun	Adj-N	N-Adj	N-Adj	N-Adj	N-Adj	N-Adj	Adj-Lig-N
Adposition/Noun	Prep-N	Prep-N	Prep-N	Prep-N	Prep-N	Prep-N	Prep-N
Determiner/Noun	Det-N	Det-N	Det-N?	N-Det	N-Det	N-Det	N-Det
Negative/Verb	Neg-V	V-Neg	V-Neg	Neg-V	Neg-V	Neg-V	Neg-V
Basic constituent order	VSO	VSO	SVO	SVO	SVO	SVO	VSO
Is it ergative?	split ergative	no	no	no	no	no	split ergative

What is transferred in interlingual contact in Western Micronesia

- Acculturational lexicon of all kinds, including social borrowings such as greetings in Chamorro and some central and eastern Trukic languages (this is true of all languages surveyed here).
- Non-core lexicon (in some languages only: there is some borrowing from Japanese into Palauan and massive borrowing from Spanish into Chamorro, and extensive borrowing from Palauan and Trukic into Yapese, with further Trukic loans found in Nguluwan).
- Core lexicon (strongly in Chamorro, also Yapese and Nguluwan, marginally in Palauan).
- Verbs which are incorporated into pre-existing morphological paradigms (there are many examples of these being borrowed in Chamorro, Nguluwan and Yapese).
- Loan phonemes (marginally and only recently in Yapese and Palauan, more strongly in Chamorro).
- New loan phonological canons.*
- Phonological features at a phonemic level (mid-vowels).*
- Adjectival comparative markers.*
- Numerals.*
- Some personal and other pronouns.*
- Some conjunctions.*
- Some prepositions.*
- Some temporal, spatial and phasal adverbs.*
- Copula* (in part).
- Indefinite article.*
- Discourse markers (many in Chamorro and maybe some in Carolinian, also possibly a polite imperative marker in Nguluwan).
- Metatypy of constructions (copying of certain constructions from Ulithian to Nguluwan and from Spanish to Chamorro).

What remains undiffused from one language to another in these cases

- Bound morphs indicating either inflectional or derivational processes (the Spanish derivational affixes found in the Spanish-derived lexicon in Chamorro rarely spread to pre-Spanish forms in the language).
- Free grammatical morphs (except in Chamorro, where several of these have been borrowed; these largely derive from Spanish).

* These kinds of items are only transferred in Chamorro.

Relative degrees of retention of Proto-Malayo-Polynesian items on the modified Swadesh list used in Blust (1981) and Jackson (1983: 227)

Malay[14]	56 per cent
Chamorro	44 per cent
Pulo Annian	37.9 per cent
Chuukese	37.8 per cent
Kiribatese	32 per cent
Palauan	32 per cent
Pohnpeian	30.2 per cent
Marshallese	29.9 per cent
Kosraean	28.6 per cent
Yapese	18 per cent

References

Bender, Byron W., et al., 2003. Proto-Micronesian reconstructions, parts I, II. *Oceanic Linguistics* 42: 1–110, 271–358.

Blust, Robert, 1980. More on the origin of glottalic consonants. *Lingua* 52: 123–156.

Blust, Robert, 1981. Variation of retention rate among Austronesian languages. Paper presented at the Third International Conference on Austronesian Linguistics, Denpasar, Bali.

Blust, Robert, 2000. Chamorro historical phonology. *Oceanic Linguistics* 39: 83–123.

von Chamisso, Adelbert, 1864 [1836]. *Reise um die Welt*. Berlin: Weidmann.

Costenoble, Hermann, 1940. *Die Chamoro-Sprache*. The Hague: Martinus Nijhoff.

Elbert, Samuel H., 1972. *A Puluwat Dictionary*. Pacific Linguistics, vol. C-24. Canberra: Australian National University.

Fritz, Georg, 1911. *Die zentralkarolinische Sprache*. Berlin: Reimer.

Goodenough, Ward H., 1992. Gradual and quantum changes in the history of Chuukese (Trukese) phonology. *Oceanic Linguistics* 31: 93–114.

Goodenough, Ward H. and Hiroshi Sugita (eds), 1990. *Trukese–English Dictionary, Supplementary Volume: English–Trukese Finderlist*. Philadelphia: American Philosophical Society.

Grant, Anthony P., 2002a. Fabric, pattern, shift and diffusion: What change in Oregon Penutian languages can tell historical linguists. In Laura Buszard-Welcher (ed.), *Proceedings of the Meeting of the Hokan-Penutian Workshop, June 17–18, 2000, University of California at Berkeley,*

---

[14] Standard Malay is the Austronesian language with the highest rate of retention of PMP origin on the Blust list.

report 11: *Survey of California and Other Indian Languages*, pp. 33–56. Berkeley, CA: Department of Linguistics, University of California.

Grant, Anthony P., 2002b. Problems in placing Palauan within Malayo-Polynesian. Unpublished manuscript, University of Manchester.

Grant, Anthony P., 2003. Review of Ruth King, The Lexical Basis of Grammatical Borrowing: A Prince Edward Island Case Study (Amsterdam: John Benjamins, 2000). *Word* 54 (3): 251–256.

Grant, Anthony P., 2014. The 'language of Tobi' as presented in Horace Holden's *Narrative*: Evidence for restructuring and lexical mixture in a Nuclear Micronesian-based pidgin. In Isabelle Buchstaller, Anders Holmberg and Mohammad Almoaily (eds), *Pidgins and Creoles beyond Africa-Europe Encounters*, pp. 41–56. Amsterdam: John Benjamins.

Hall, Robert A. Jr, 1945. English loan-words in Micronesian languages. *Language* 21: 212–217.

Holden, Horace, 1836. *Narrative of the Shipwreck, Captivity and Sufferings of Horace Holden and Benj. H. Nute*. Boston: Russell, Shattuck and Co.

Izui, Hironasuke, 1965. The languages of Micronesia: Their origin and diversity. *Lingua* 15: 349–359.

Jackson, Frederick Henry, 1983. *The Internal and External Relationships of the Trukic Languages of Micronesia*. PhD dissertation, University of Hawai'i. Ann Arbor: University Microfilms International.

Jackson, Frederick H. and Jeffrey C. Marck, 1991. *Carolinian–English Dictionary*. Honolulu: University of Hawai'i Press.

Jensen, John Thayer, 1977. *Yapese Reference Grammar*. Honolulu: University of Hawai'i Press.

Jensen, John Thayer, Leo David Pugram and Raphael Defeg, 1977. *Yapese–English Dictionary*. Honolulu: University of Hawai'i Press.

Josephs, Lewis S., 1975. *Palauan Reference Grammar*. Honolulu: University of Hawai'i Press.

Josephs, Lewis S., 1977. *Handbook of Palauan Grammar*, two volumes. Koror: Bureau of Curriculum and Instruction, Ministry of Education.

Josephs, Lewis S., 1984. The impact of borrowing on Palauan. In Byron W. Bender (ed.), *Studies in Micronesian Linguistics*, pp. 81–123. Pacific Linguistics, vol. C-80. Canberra: Australian National University.

Lynch, John, Malcolm Ross and Terry Crowley, 2002. *The Oceanic Languages*. Curzon Language Family Series. Richmond, Surrey: Curzon Press.

McManus, Edwin, S.J., edited by Lewis S. Josephs, 1977. *Palauan–English Dictionary*. Honolulu: University of Hawai'i Press.

Reid, Lawrence A., 2002. Morphosyntactic evidence for the position of Chamorro in the Austronesian language family. In Robert S. Bauer (ed.), *Collected Papers on Southeast Asian and Pacific Linguistics*, pp. 63–94. Canberra: Australian National University.

Rodríguez-Ponga Salamanca, R., 1995. *El elemento español en la lengua chamorra (Islas Marianas)*. Madrid: Servicio de Publicaciones de la Universidad Complutense.

Ross, Malcolm, 1996. Is Yapese Oceanic? In Bernd Nothofer (ed.), *Reconstruction, Classification, Description: Festschrift in Honor of Isidore Dyen*, pp. 121–166. Hamburg: Abera.

Sakiyama, Osamu, 1982. The characteristics of Nguluwan from the viewpoint of language contact. In Machiko Aoyagi (ed.), *Islanders and their Outside World: A Report of the Cultural Anthropological Research in the Caroline Islands of Micronesia in the Years 1980–1981*, pp. 105–127. Tokyo: Committee for Micronesian Research, St Paul's (Rikkyo) University.

Salas Palomo, R. and Thomas Stolz, 2008. Pro or contra Hispanisms: Attitudes of native speakers of modern Chamoru. In Thomas Stolz, D. Bakker and R. Salas Palomo (eds), *Hispanisation: The Impact of Spanish on the Lexicon and Grammar of the Indigenous Languages of Austronesia and the Americas*, pp. 237–267. Berlin and New York: Mouton de Gruyter.

Sohn, Ho-Min 1975. *Woleaian Reference Grammar. PALI Language Texts*. Honolulu: University of Hawai'i Press.

Sohn, Ho-Min and Byron W. Bender, 1973. *A Ulithian Grammar*. Pacific Linguistics, vol. C-23. Canberra: Australian National University.

Sohn, Ho-Min and Anthony F. Tawerilmang, 1975. *Woleaian–English Dictionary*. Honolulu: University of Hawai'i Press.

Thomason, Sarah Grey, 2000. Linguistic areas and language history. In Dicky Gilbers, John Nerbonne and Jos Schaeken (eds), *Proceedings of the Groningen Conference on Languages in Contact*, pp. 311–327. Amsterdam: Rodopi.

Topping, Donald M. (with the assistance of Bernadita C. Dungca), 1973. *Chamorro Reference Grammar*. Honolulu: University of Hawai'i Press.

Topping, Donald M. and Pedro M. Ogo, 1980. *Spoken Chamorro*. Honolulu: University of Hawai'i Press.

Topping, Donald M., Pedro M. Ogo and Bernadita C. Dungca, 1975. *Chamorro-English Dictionary*. Honolulu: University of Hawai'i Press.

Walsh, John A. and Eulalia Harui-Walsh, 1979. Loan words in Ulithian. *Anthropological Linguistics* 21: 154–161.

Zobel, Erik, 2002. The position of Chamorro and Palauan in the Austronesian family tree: Evidence from verb morphosyntax. In Fay Wouk and Malcolm Ross (eds), *The History and Typology of Western Austronesian Voice Systems*, pp. 406–434. Pacific Linguistics, vol. 520. Canberra: Australian National University.

31

Native North American Languages

Marianne Mithun

The languages indigenous to North America provide an especially fruitful arena for investigating circumstances underlying areal phenomena. Nearly 300 different languages are known to have been spoken over this vast geographical region before the arrival of Europeans, and there were surely many more. They comprise well over 50 distinct genetic groups, some spread over great distances. There are recognized culture areas, but not all correspond to linguistic areas, raising questions about the geographical, social and linguistic factors behind the discrepancies. Intriguingly, most North American linguistic areas constitute exceptions to classical expectations about relative borrowability, the notion that vocabulary is copied first, then sounds, speech habits, sentence structure, and finally deeper grammar. In fact the strongest North American linguistic areas show surprisingly few loanwords, but often extensive parallelisms in grammatical categories and structures. Here social circumstances are described that can foster the emergence of such areas, and cognitive and communicative processes by which they might develop.

31.1 Contact Areas in North America

There are ten commonly recognized culture areas in North America, as shown in Map 31.1.

Culture areas of North America (Sturtevant 1988: ix)
- Arctic
- Subarctic
- Northwest Coast
- Plateau
- Great Basin

I am grateful to Wallace Chafe, Danny Hieber, Robert Rankin and David Rood for sharing their great expertise on various languages discussed here.

Map 31.1 Culture areas of North America (Sturtevant 1988: ix)

- California
- Southwest
- Great Plains
- Northeast
- Southeast

Both culture and linguistic areas result from interactions among peoples. But most cultural traits can be transferred more easily than linguistic ones. One can adopt pottery styles, for example, with less intense contact than auxiliaries. Intensity of contact is related to both the nature of interaction and its duration.

31.1.1 The Nature of the Contact
The intensity of contact varies widely over North American culture areas. Where communities were large and population density light, as in the Northeast, speakers often had relatively little contact with outsiders. Where density was greater and communities were small, as in Northern

California, exogamy and multilingualism were often the norm. In some areas there were differences in prestige, as in the Northwest and Southeast, but in others not, as in California and the Northeast. In some, language played a strong role in identity, as in the Southwest. In some areas contact is ancient, as along the Northwest Coast, while in others it is relatively recent, as on the Plains. The Southeast has long traditions of trade with neighbours, often via a lingua franca, either a pidgin such as Mobilian Jargon, or one of the languages spoken there, such as Creek in the Creek Confederacy. Still, there is much we cannot know about the social nature of prehistoric contacts, including patterns of language maintenance and shift.

31.1.2   Linguistic Profiles

The culture areas also vary in their linguistic heterogeneity. The Arctic was occupied by speakers of a single language family, Eskimo-Aleut. On the Plains, several large families are represented: Athabaskan, Algonquian, Siouan, Uto-Aztecan, Kiowa-Tanoan, Caddoan and the isolate Tonkawa, but most of the shared linguistic traits there are inherited. The Northwest Coast is home to languages from a dozen distinct genetic units, many of which vary in their structures, but they share numerous features. In California, twenty-two different families are represented, but, as in the Northwest, numerous traits cross genetic lines.

31.1.3   Areal Boundaries

Early large-scale investigation of North American linguistic areas was undertaken by Sherzer (1968, 1973, 1976). Observing that linguistic areas are rarely sharply delineated, he distinguished four trait types.

Areal traits (Sherzer 1973: **759)**

Whole areal trait	Found in most languages of a given culture area.
Central areal trait	Found in most languages of an area with locus of distribution in the centre of this area.
Regional areal trait	With a continuous or almost continuous distribution within one region of a given culture area.
Family trait	In language X retained from proto-language A.

The first three pertain to the complexity of contact situations. In the simplest situations, a linguistic area is delineated on all sides by borders which might hinder contact among groups, such as oceans, rivers or mountain ranges. Languages on the Northwest Coast and in California have the Pacific Ocean to their west. Languages in the Southeast have the Atlantic Ocean to their east and the Gulf of Mexico to their south. But people do travel by water.

Even with strong borders, contact is rarely homogeneous within an area, and features seldom pass through all languages uniformly. They might flow from a core outward, a central trait. The Southeast core cultural and linguistic areas contain the entire Muskogean family and isolates Atakapa, Chitimacha, Natchez and Tunica. As one moves outward, shared traits become progressively sparser. Ofo and Biloxi share many traits with the core; Dhegiha, Cherokee, Tutelo, Catawba and Caddo some; Nottoway, Shawnee and Timucua a few.

Traits may spread from several points, complicating the identification of basic-level areas. The Northwest Coast, stretching from the Subarctic to California, is a strong linguistic area, but some traits extend only over sub-areas. One is the Northern Northwest Coast, with Eyak and Tlingit, Haida (isolate), Tsimshianic, some Wakashan (Haisla, Heiltsuk, Kwak'wala), and some Salishan (Nuxalk = Bella Coola, Comox). Another extends from the Nass River in British Columbia to the Columbia between Washington and Oregon. Still others are the South Central Coast and Central Oregon. Many overlap, and some are included within others. California also contains identifiable sub-areas, such as Northwestern California (Wiyot, Yurok, Karuk), Clear Lake or Central California (Pomoan, Yuki, Lake Miwok, Wappo, Patwin), the South Coast Range (Esselen, Salinan, Chumashan), and perhaps Southern California–Western Arizona (Yuman, Takic Uto-Aztecan).

The distribution of traits is not necessarily continuous over even a well-defined area. Populations can move around, establishing relationships with different groups at different times, like the Apacheans (Athabaskan) in the Southwest. And the likelihood of transfer of a given trait depends on numerous other factors such as prestige, group identity, cultural practices and language structures.

Sherzer's final type, the family trait, plays a crucial role in the study of contact: traits shared by two languages but inherited from a common parent are not considered strong evidence of contact effects. To distinguish common inheritances, it is helpful if the languages within an area have relatives outside. A number of linguistic areas in North America present this situation. The Algic languages Wiyot and Yurok of Northwestern California have Algonquian relatives all across the continent, from Montana (Blackfoot, Cheyenne) to the Atlantic (Micmac, Maliseet, Passamaqoddy). The Pacific Athabaskan languages of Oregon and California have relatives in the Southwest, western Canada, and Alaska. The Siouan languages in the Southeast have relatives on the Plains.

31.1.4 Inheritance versus Contact

Genetic classification necessarily depends on the criteria admitted for evidence of relatedness. During the twentieth century, some remote relationships among families in North America were hypothesized on the assumption that structural similarities alone can be diagnostic of common origin. On the Northwest Coast, a 'Mosan' stock was proposed consisting of the Wakashan, Salishan and Chimakuan families. Various 'Hokan' proposals have grouped families and isolates from Northern California south into Mesoamerica and even South America, and from Baja California on the Pacific, into south Texas: Karuk, Chimariko, Shastan, Paliahnihan, Yana, Washo, Pomoan, Esselen, Salinan, Yuman, Cochimí, Seri, Tequistlatecan, Coahuiltecan, Jicaque, Subtiaba-Tlappanec, Coahuilteco, Comecrudan and Quechua. Some of these families may be very remotely related (perhaps at time depths greater than Indo-European), but many have been spoken in contiguous areas for so long that it is difficult to separate shared inheritances from ancient contact effects. The 'Penutian' hypothesis presents a similar picture, merging recognized families in California (Wintun, Maidun, Yokuts, Utian), Oregon (Takelma, Coosan, Siuslawan, Alsean, Kalapuyan, Chinookan), the Plateau of eastern Oregon, Washington and Idaho (Klamath-Modoc, Cayuse-Molala, Sahaptian), British Columbia (Tsimshianic), and Mexico (Mixe-Zoque, Huave). Again, some of these families may be very remotely related, but many observed similarities are likely the result of long-standing intensive contact. In the Southeast, a 'Gulf' stock was once proposed, uniting the Muskogean family and isolates Natchez, Tunica, Chitimacha and Atakapa. In the Southwest, an 'Aztec-Tanoan' stock was proposed uniting the Uto-Aztecan and Kiowa-Tanoan families. Further details on these proposals are in Campbell (1997) and Mithun (1999). As more has been learned about the kinds of structures that can emerge from contact, these hypotheses have been reconsidered.

Of course, related languages are not immune to areal effects (Epps et al. 2013). They tend to be typologically similar, facilitating bilingualism and convergence. It is easier to transfer substance when lexical, morphological and syntactic categories are similar (Mithun 2013). Learners often reanalyse structures in a second language on the model of counterparts in their first where possible. And bilinguals often extend the functions of elements and constructions within one language on the model of the other.

31.1.5   Linguistic Areas in North America

Not all of the culture areas listed in Section 31.1 (see also Map 31.1) are considered strong linguistic areas, for the kinds of reasons discussed above. The Arctic contains just one language family, Eskimo-Aleut. The Subarctic contains single branches of just two, Athabaskan and central Algonquian. The Plateau shows some genetic diversity, but most of its shared linguistic traits are also found on the Northwest Coast. The Great Basin contains just two genetic units: the Numic branch of Uto-Aztecan and the isolate Washo; most common traits are also shared with adjacent California languages. The Plains culture area was constituted recently, within the last several hundred years. Furthermore, the area was sparsely populated, so speakers of different languages were not generally in close contact. The Northeast contained branches of just three families: Siouan, Iroquoian and Algonquian. This area too was relatively sparsely populated, and so far there is little evidence of significant contact across family lines. Most shared traits can be reconstructed for their respective parent languages.

Some culture areas, however, are also strong linguistic areas, particularly the Northwest, California and the Southeast. All were densely populated before contact by small groups speaking a variety of genetically unrelated languages, a situation conducive to multilingualism. Contact was both intense and enduring. But none of the areas is crisply delineated or homogeneous. There are core areas and peripheral areas. There are sub-areas of varying strengths. And a number of traits extend beyond their outer boundaries. A fourth area, the Southwest, also exhibits some shared traits presumably due to contact, but fewer than the others and of slightly different types.

31.1.5.1 Northwest

The Northwest linguistic area stretches from the Subarctic to California, and, with the inclusion of the Plateau, east to the Rockies (Maps 31.2 and 31.3). Generally considered one of the strongest areas in the world, it is home to 20 genetic groups, 21 with Pacific Yupik. The most thorough descriptions are in Thompson and Kinkade (1990) for the Northwest Coast, and Kinkade, Elmendorf, Rigsby and Aoki (1998) for the Plateau.

Intensive contact including intermarriage extends back millennia throughout the Northwest. Suttles reports that 'There is evidence for gene flow throughout the area and beyond' (1990b: 1). 'The Tlingit, Haida, Tsimshian, and Haisla shared a system of matrilineal lineages … that could be equated for purposes of intergroup marriage' (1990b: 12). Texts from Boas (1921: 836–1277) indicate 'a network of intermarriage and ceremonial relations extending from the Oowekeno to the Comox (Northern Coast Salish)' (1990b: 13). Evidence from early explorers indicates that 'marriages, visiting, shared access to resources, and trade in food linked tribes on the coast from the Makah to the Alsea with the upriver Chinookans, Southwestern Coast Salish Cowlitz, and Tualatin' (1990b: 12, citing Hajda 1984: 123–132). There were similar networks in the adjacent Plateau, as noted by Kinkade et al.:

> Contacts and mutual inter-influences among the languages and language families of the Plateau are of long standing. It is clear that the majority of them participated in a common linguistic area. Plateau ethnographic studies have demonstrated mechanisms of group interaction that, projected into the past, would have produced these linguistic results. In this area intermarriage, trade, and joint participation in economic and ritual activities set up social relationships that frequently crossed linguistic boundaries … These patterns of bilingualism in certain parts of the region obscured linguistic boundaries, and at times led to language replacement.
> *(Kinkade et al. 1998: 69–70)*

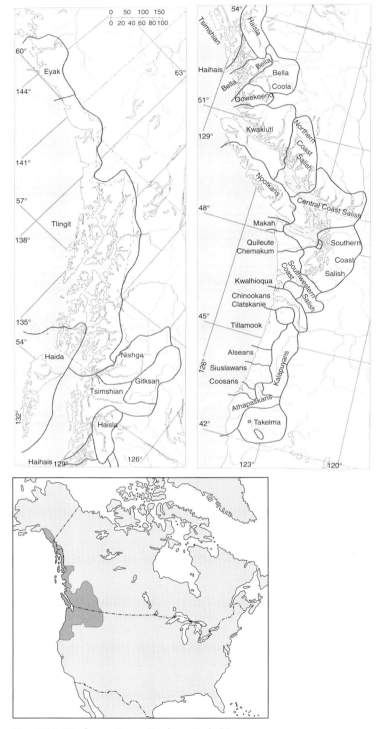

Map 31.2 Northwest Coast (Suttles 1990b: ix)

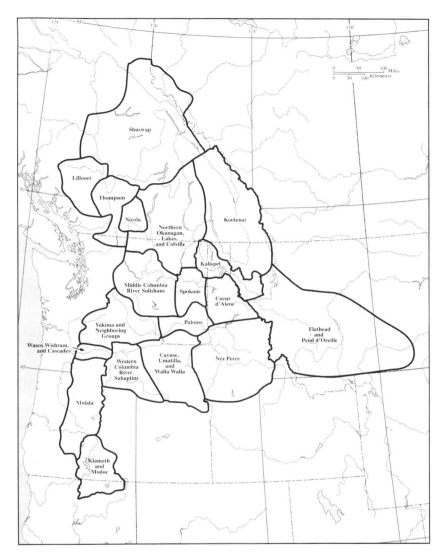

Map 31.3 Plateau (Walker 1998: iii)

Three families, Wakashan, Chimakuan and Salishan, constitute the core of the area. There is relatively little lexical borrowing, but contact is so ancient that many structural traits, otherwise rare cross-linguistically, can be reconstructed for the respective parent languages. There are large consonant inventories, contrasting plain and ejective obstruents and often resonants, velars and uvulars, multiple laterals, rounded and unrounded back obstruents, and distinctive glottal stops. Most of the languages have only three or four distinctive vowels but contrastive length. Consonant clusters can be complex, sometimes with four or more consonants; words in some languages can consist uniquely of

Map 31.4 Northern and Central California (Heizer 1978: ix)

consonants. There is extensive reduplication. Many languages have numeral classifiers, and many deictic systems distinguish visible and invisible referents. The languages are generally polysynthetic and primarily suffixing. Constituent order is basically predicate-initial. Particularly in the core languages, the noun/verb distinction is weak: most content words can be used to predicate.

31.1.5.2 Northern California

Northern California is home to a large number of typologically diverse languages (Map 31.4), generally spoken in small communities. Detailed discussions can be found in Jacobs (1954), Haas (1967, 1976), Conathan (2004), O'Neill (2008), Jany (2009) and Mithun (2012a).

Active trade, intermarriage and multilingualism were typical over at least a millennium. Languages differed little in prestige. There was no lingua franca or code-switching: it was polite to speak the language of the community one was in at the moment. Bilinguals thus exerted conscious efforts to keep their languages separate. O'Neill notes:

Intermarriage was common (see Waterman and Kroeber 1934), so growing up around speakers of several languages was not unusual if one's parents came from faraway places, as they often did. Generally, the wife moved to her husband's village after marriage, so females were often especially multilingual. As a consequence, children often grew up in the presence of bilingual mothers, often being exposed to a number of unrelated languages even from their earliest days.

(O'Neill 2008: 290)

There would have thus been both language maintenance and language shift.

Within California and even within subareas, there is considerable typological diversity. Some languages are quite polysynthetic, many are mildly synthetic, and some more analytic. Some are basically predicate-initial and others predicate-final. Some are head marking and others dependent marking. There are nominative/accusative, agent/patient and hierarchical alignment patterns. Numerous shared features have been observed, however. Many extend over just a small subarea, while others extend even beyond California. Among the traits noted are uvular stops, voiceless laterals, back apical or retroflex stops, a distinct voiced stop series, sound symbolism, pronominal dual, inclusive/exclusive first persons, nominal case, alienable/inalienable possession, verbal reduplication for distribution or repetition, means/manner prefixes, locative/directional suffixes, evidentials, and classificatory numeral systems.

31.1.5.3   The Southeast

The Southeast (Map 31.5) is home to all Muskogean languages (Choctaw, Chickasaw, Alabama, Koasati, Hitchiti, Mikasuki, Creek, Apalachee), some Siouan languages (Dhegiha, Biloxi, Ofo), isolates Natchez, Tunica, Chitimacha and Atakapa, and more peripherally Cherokee (Iroquoian), Shawnee (Algonquian), Yuchi, Tutelo (Siouan), Catawba (related to Siouan), Timucua and Caddo (Caddoan). Surveys are in Haas (1971, 1973, 1979), Crawford (1975), Booker (1991) and Martin (2004). Contact especially among the core groups has been intimate and long-standing.

Long-distance trade networks extended throughout the Southeast from late prehistoric to early historic times (Waselkov 2004: 686). Muskogean groups also maintained alliances and 'mechanisms for incorporating autonomous local groups into intricate political structures capable of concerted action' (Walker 2004: 375), but there was economic, political and social inequality (Brown 2004: 677). The Creek were particularly numerous and powerful: 'The larger, more powerful Muskogee [Creek] incorporated members from other groups, such as the Yuchi, Alabama, Hitchiti and Shawnee, during their tenure in the Southeast' (Innes 2004: 393). In the late seventeenth or early eighteenth century, the Creek Confederacy was formed, which included speakers not only of Creek, but also Alabama, Koasati, Apalachee, Natchez, Yuchi, Shawnee and probably

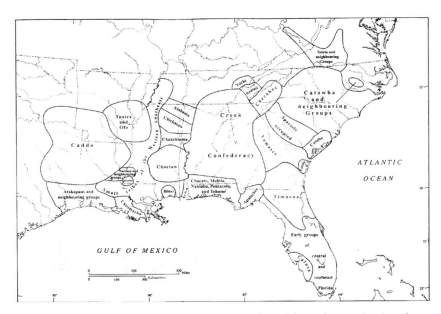

Map 31.5 The Southeast of North America, sixteenth to eighteenth centuries (Fogelson 2004a: ix)

more. Creek was used as a lingua franca. The Alabama and Koasati were closely linked, residing near each other over a long period and 'at various times, near the Choctaw, Pakana, Biloxi, Caddo, Pascagoula, Tunica, and Ofo' (May 2004: 413). There was also a Choctaw Confederacy, which 'may have included speakers of Natchez, Alabama, and other languages' (Galloway and Kidwell 2004: 499). Louisiana settlements composed of Choctaw, Tunica and Biloxi are described by Brain, Roth and de Reuse (2004: 589). The Natchez were also connected to the Tunica, having taken in a number as refugees, and with the Chitimacha through intermarriage (Galloway and Jackson 2004: 500). After their defeat by the French in 1731, the few Natchez survivors settled among the Creeks and Cherokees and intermarried (Kimball 2005: 385). The last speakers were trilingual in Natchez, Creek and Cherokee. The Cherokee also incorporated speakers of other languages into their communities via capture and intermarriage, and 'multilingualism was common and valued' (Fogelson 2004a: 337).

The languages of the Southeast are typologically more similar to each other than those of California. Most at the core are mildly synthetic, with basic SOV order and postpositions. Most contain pronominal affixes on verbs with agent/patient alignment. Among the linguistic traits listed in the literature for Southeastern languages are labial fricatives, voiceless laterals, retroflex sibilants, sound symbolism, independent possessive pronouns, alienable/inalienable possession, agent/patient pronominal affixes, pronominal duals and plurals, inclusive/exclusive first person,

Map 31.6 The Southwest culture area: Ortiz (1983: ix)

diminutive noun suffixes, verb reduplication for distribution or repetition, locative/directional verbal prefixes, tense/aspect verbal suffixes, pervasive postural distinctions, auxiliary constructions and quinary counting systems (Campbell 1997; Martin 2004; Sherzer 1973).

31.1.5.4 The Southwest

The Southwest (Map 31.6) is a strong culture area with some shared linguistic traits. Bereznak (1995) provides detailed discussion of these. Five genetic units are represented: Tanoan languages, Keresan languages, Hopi (Uto-Aztecan), Zuni (an isolate) and Apachean Athabaskan languages, particularly Navajo. The Pueblo communities have been neighbours for a long time, but the Apacheans are more recent arrivals. Population density was high, and groups were linked by trade relations, particularly in prehistoric times. There was later active trade between the Pueblos and the Navajo, in which Navajo was used as a trade language, spoken by many Arizona Tewas, Hopis and Zunis (Ford 1983: 720; Kroskrity 1982). Intermarriage among Pueblo groups (Hopi, Zuni, Keresan, Tanoan, shaded in Map 31.6) and between them and Navajos was common, as was bilingualism (Parsons 1939, cited in Bereznak 1995: 77). Bereznak notes that 'marriage partners from other villages introduced new songs, dances, and societies . . . Ceremonial dancers and ritualists commonly participated in ceremonies in other villages' (1995: 60).

Bereznak identifies 28 traits shared among various Southwestern languages, but considers just four to be reasonable areal indicators: glottalized consonants, tones, final devoicing and pronominal duals. Not surprisingly, more features are shared among Pueblo languages than with the more recent Apachean arrivals. These include distinctive voiced stops, an *s/š* opposition, labio-velars, alienable/inalienable possessive noun prefixes, plural and locative noun suffixes, tense/aspect verbal suffixes, noun incorporation, a three-way demonstrative system, classificatory verbs, distinctions in the kinship system, and some actual morphemes, including the evidential *ʔas*, directional marker *-mi*, and passive *-ti*. Many shared traits extend beyond the Pueblo area westward to Yuman languages, north to Great Basin languages, and eastward to Tonkawa and Caddo (Bereznak 1995: 159, 166).

Sherzer explains the fact that this strong culture area is not matched by an equally robust linguistic area in terms of attitudes:

> In other areas with dense populations (Northwest Coast, Plateau, California), many linguistic traits were found to have continuous distributions cutting across genetic linguistic boundaries. In the Southwest, traits tend to be more randomly distributed, suggesting that little mutual linguistic influencing has occurred. The explanation of this situation may be found in a sociolinguistic factor about which we rarely have data – attitude toward language. The Southwest is one area for which many observers have reported attitudes towards one's own language and that of others, perhaps because these attitudes are often quite explicit. Southwest Indians are very conservative with respect to language, taking pride in their own language and often refusing to learn that of others. When they do learn other languages, they seem consciously to avoid allowing alien linguistic traits to penetrate their own linguistic system.
>
> *(Sherzer 1973: 785–786)*

31.2   Evaluating Shared Linguistic Traits

Sherzer (1973, 1976) provides lists of shared traits for all of the culture areas. As he realizes, not all contribute equally to areal strength.

31.2.1   Feature Strength

An important consideration is the cross-linguistic frequency of the trait. The SOV order shared by Southeastern languages, for example, could be the result of contact: word order patterns spread easily. At the same time, it is characteristic of a majority of the languages of the world, so it could be due to internal development. A second consideration is the relationship among traits. Many Southeastern languages contain postpositions. But postpositions often develop out of SOV structures, so the two traits are not necessarily independent.

Conspicuous absence of a trait is sometimes cited as an areal feature. The significance of the absence also depends on its cross-linguistic frequency and its source. Among the features cited by Sherzer (1973: 768) as characteristic of the Northwest Coast and the adjacent Plateau are 'lack of one-stop-series languages'. But many languages in the world have multiple stop series. Sherzer also reports that languages of the Subarctic lack nominal reduplication, nominal case, and instrumental markers in verbs (1973: 765). Those of the Plains lack uvular q, labio-velar k^w, and nasals other than m and n. These traits do distinguish the languages from those in other areas, but all are inherited from their respective parent languages. In a sense they are a testament to the lack of areal effects. Still, in some cases gaps are significant. A group of neighbouring languages along the Northwest Coast lack n: Nitinaht and Makah (Wakashan), Quileute (Chimakuan), and Twana and marginally Island Comox and Upriver Halkomelem (Salishan). This gap can be traced to shifts of original nasals to prenasalized stops which ulti-mately lost their nasalization (*n > ^{n}d > d), habits of pronunciation transferred across genetic lines (Thompson 1972). Related languages outside the area still contain the nasals.

31.2.2 Levels of Structure

Different domains of language are known to show different propensities for replication in contact situations. A commonly cited scale is shown in Figure 31.1.

Interestingly, the strongest linguistic areas of North America do not show this pattern at all. Loanwords are strikingly rare, while structural parallelisms are often extensive. The distributions reflect both social circumstances and cognition.

The ranking in Figure 31.1 corresponds to decreasing degrees of con-sciousness and control on the part of speakers. Vocabulary is highly acces-sible to consciousness: speakers can easily incorporate foreign lexical items into their own speech if they wish, even with little mastery of the donor language. They can also consciously avoid doing so.[1] Morphological structure, by contrast, is routinized, generally below the level of conscious-ness and more difficult to manipulate intentionally.

---

[1] This is true of the lexicon as an open class. A similar influence on grammar but not vocabulary can be seen in Old English from Brythonic (forms of Celtic in Britain): see the discussion in Hickey (2012).

Levels most affected

Vocabulary (loanwords, phrases)
Sounds (present in loanwords)
Speech habits (general pronunciation, suprasegmentals [stress, intonation])
Sentence structure, word-order
Grammar (morphology: inflections)

Levels least affected

Figure 31.1 Borrowability[2]

The speech of second language speakers can reflect the hierarchy in reverse. Learners usually focus on using new vocabulary, but they may retain speech habits (a foreign accent) and syntactic patterns from their first language. They may also carry over more subtle features, such as the relative frequency of certain stylistic choices (passivization, topicalization) or attention to particular semantic distinctions (location, direction, manner of motion, shape).

But shift is not the whole story. Even more balanced bilinguals making a conscious effort to speak a particular language tend to be more conscious of vocabulary. Where their two languages contain comparable constructions, they might transfer the relative frequencies of semantic and stylistic choices. The longer intimate contact persists, the more deeply it can shape language structure, as such choices become entrenched and routinized. In what follows, some of the mechanisms behind this shaping are described and illustrated.

31.3 Lexicon

Because chance similarity is rarer between vocabulary items than abstract structures, it can be easier for analysts to identify loanwords than copied grammar. But lexical borrowing is strikingly rare in North America, though not completely unknown, and some undoubtedly remains undiscovered. The rarity of loanwords in the Northwest is often remarked on, though Kinkade (1991, cited in Beck 2000: 169) notes certain vocabulary in the Salishan language Nuxalk pertaining to maritime culture and certain flora and fauna, adopted from coastal Wakashan languages. For Northern California, Bright (1959) remarks on the paucity of loanwords, but notes terms for 'pelican', 'quail', 'white man', 'Wiyot Indian', 'dog', 'cow', 'dog', 'cherry' and 'hello'. For the Southeast, Rankin (1988: 643) notes the

---

[2] This scale is based on the relative openness of levels of language. The most open is most prone to code copying (borrowing). However, because open classes show a high degree of consciousness for speakers, they may well have the lowest degree of code copying if the speakers of the receiving community wish to distance themselves from the donor community (see Epps and Michael, Chapter 32, this volume) or if the former occupies a lower position than the latter within a society (see e.g. Hickey 2012).

conspicuous scarcity of loans between Dhegiha and Muskogean languages, though Martin (1994) discusses some loanwords among Southeastern languages, including 'money', 'black person', 'oyster', 'interpreter', 'peach', 'buzzard', 'turtle' and 'cedar'. Kimball observes that 'Natchez seems to have been extraordinarily resistant to borrowing from European languages and from other American Indian languages. Most of the borrowings are personal and tribal names' (2005: 436–437). He notes loans 'hackberry' and 'vulture' from Chitimacha, 'corn' and 'wild goose', from Tunica, and 'Creek Indian' and 'Alabama Indian' from Creek. For the Southwest, Kroskrity (1982) notes the general dearth of loanwords, though Bereznak (1995) mentions borrowed ceremonial vocabulary among the Pueblos in the Southwest, not surprising given that ceremonies, with songs and prayers, were diffused.

31.4   Phonology

Sounds and sound patterns are usually ranked immediately after vocabulary in borrowability, because they often ride into a language on loanwords, though often the sounds which appear in borrowed words already are incipiently present in the borrowing languages. If lexical borrowing is rare, we might expect fewer phonological areal traits as well.

31.4.1   Sounds

Sounds do show areality in North America. Overall, consonant inventories are more elaborate in the West than the East. Ejectives are common in the West, from the Western Subarctic, through the Northwest Coast and Plateau, California, the Southwest, and into the Plains, but they are generally absent in the East. The Algic language Yurok, for example, spoken in Northern California, has ejectives, while its Algonquian relatives to the East do not. In some cases, new sounds can be seen to have entered a language in loanwords. Lake Miwok, spoken in the Clear Lake area of California, contains plain, aspirated and ejective stops, while related languages, spoken elsewhere, contain just a plain series. These did enter the language via loanwords then spread to native forms (Callaghan 1964: 47; 1987; 1991: 52). This is not the only possible route for transfer, however. Two areal traits often cited for the Southeast are a voiceless labial fricative and voiceless lateral. Each tells a different story.

Labial fricatives are present in all Muskogean languages, in the isolates Atakapa, Tunica and Chitimacha, in the Siouan Ofo and Biloxi (marginally), in Yuchi, and in Timucua, but they are rare elsewhere in North America. One is reconstructed for Proto-Muskogean (Booker 2005: 254), where it was bilabial, though now in many languages it has become a labio-dental *f*. In the isolates, labial fricatives occur in only a few loanwords, such as Tunica *káfi* 'coffee' (< French *café*) (Haas 1941: 18) and Chitimacha *dotriv* '(Lake) D'Autre-Rive' (< French) (Swadesh 1939: 19–30), reflecting the expected pattern. In the Siouan language Ofo, however, *f* is pervasive, even in basic vocabulary. Robert Rankin (personal communication) reports that Ofo *f* is the result of a regular sound change: Proto-Siouan **s* > Ofo *fh*. Compare, for example, Biloxi *ịsu*, Ofo *ífha* 'tooth'; Biloxi *su*, Ofo *ífhu* 'seed'; Biloxi *sạ*, Ofo *afhą́* 'white'; Biloxi *sindi*, Ofo *fxį́te* 'tail' (Dorsey and Swanton 1912). Cognates in other branches of the family show *s* or *š*: Lakhota *sịté* 'tail'. The *f* was apparently not brought in via loanwords, but might have been heard as a prestigious variant of *s* by Ofo speakers, who then replicated it in their own language.

The voiceless lateral fricative *ł* appears in most Muskogean languages and is reconstructed for Proto-Muskogean (Booker 2005: 252). Voiceless laterals also occur in the neighbouring Cherokee (but not its Northern Iroquoian relatives), as well as in the isolates Natchez, Tunica and Atakapa. Scancarelli (2005: 360) explains their source in Cherokee. Cherokee resonants *n*, *l*, *y* and *w* are voiceless adjacent to *h* (as throughout Iroquoian). There is also metathesis of *lh* to *hl*; *hl* sequences are pronounced as voiceless lateral fricatives. The effects of both processes can be seen in the following example.

(1)   Cherokee
        ya:nahlsde:hldohda
        y-ani:-a<u>h</u>lsde:<u>l</u>-<u>h</u>dohd-a
        CTRF-3PL.AGT-help-INST.INF-INDIC
        'it would be a benefit to them'   Scancarelli (2005: 358)

The voiceless lateral developed within the language by a familiar process, assimilation of voicelessness adjacent to *h*. Phonetic spirantization to *ł* may have been stimulated by contact. Mid-sixteenth century explorers encountered Muskogean speakers in the Little Tennessee River area, but by the eighteenth century this was Cherokee territory (Fogelson 2004a: 338). Many Cherokee town names are earlier Muskogean forms (Booker, Hudson and Rankin 1992: 432). In the eighteenth and early nineteenth centuries Cherokee populations expanded into northern Georgia and northeastern Alabama, 'replacing, displacing, or assimilating previous populations' (Fogelson 2004a: 338). Muskogean speakers shifting to Cherokee could easily have substituted their native voiceless fricative lateral *ł* for the Cherokee lateral that was already voiceless, a minor pronunciation variant. Loanwords were not necessarily involved.

For Natchez, Kimball posits a series of voiceless resonants /M/, /N/, /L/, /W/ and /Y/, but he also notes that syllable-final, morpheme-final resonants are automatically devoiced before a consonant: *ʔe<u>L</u>-pa:-ta<u>N</u>-ni-l-ạ* 'May you two look at me!' (2005: 399). *M*, *W* and *Y* were later lenited to *h*. The Natchez voiceless *L* is actually not fricative, however. For Tunica, Haas (1941: 18) explains that *n, l* and *r* are automatically devoiced before voiceless consonants (except ʔ) and phrase-finally. She is careful to note that the Tunica voiceless lateral is also not fricative.

The voiceless lateral cited as an areal trait of the Southeast is thus more interesting than it first appears. It has varying phonetic status across the languages: a fricative in some, a simple voiceless liquid in others. It has varying phonemic status as well: a distinctive consonant in some, a predictable variant in others. Importantly, it did not enter the languages via loanwords. The devoicing of laterals adjacent to voiceless consonants could have occurred independently in each language, or it could have been stimulated by contact, as bilinguals transferred automatic habits of pronunciation from one of their languages to the other. Voiceless laterals are actually widespread in North America, also occurring in the Northwest, California and the eastern Subarctic. Identification of the mechanisms by which they may have been transferred adds weight to their value as an areal feature.

31.4.2 Sound Patterns

Another areal trait sometimes cited for the Southeast is fricative symbolism. Forms vary only in the point of articulation, with increasing backness corresponding to increasing intensity. Rankin (1987) cites numerous examples such as those in (2) from the 1915 Byington dictionary of Choctaw, a Muskogean language with f/s/š/č/ł/h alternations. Forms to the right are Rankin's hypothesized roots, in which S represents the ablauting fricative. (Some of these include additional derivation.) Rankin notes that the process was productive.

(2)   Choctaw
        fopa   'murmur'   *Sop-*
        chopa   'roar, as water'
        hompa   'whoop, bang'
        sihinka   'to neigh, whinny'   *Sin-*
        shinkachi   'whiz like musket ball, tingle'
        chinka   'to squeal'
        hinha   'to groan'
        ak   'noise made among dry leaves'   *SaS-*
        chasha   'to rattle'
        haḷa   'stamp, tread'
        shana   'to turn, twist'   *San-*
        chnaha   'round, coiled'
        hana nukichi   'be dizzy, cause dizziness'
                                    Byington (1915) cited in Rankin (1987)

Fricative symbolism occurs in other Muskogean languages as well, such as Koasati *wasíhlin* 'to itch', *wačíplin* 'to feel a stabbing pain' (Rankin from Kimball, personal communication) and Creek *fi:pki:* 'unravelled', *sí:pki:* 'torn, ripped' (Rankin from Booker, personal communication).

Fricative symbolism also occurs in the unrelated Quapaw, a neighbouring Dhegiha Siouan language: *šótte* 'smoky (air), muddy (water)', *xótte* 'grey'; *zi* 'yellow', *žihí* 'reddish yellow' (Rankin 2005: 468–469). Fricative ablaut is widespread in Siouan languages, where it involves the fricatives s/š/x and z/ž/γ (Matthews 1970; Rankin 1987).

(3) Dakota

zi	'yellow'	*sota* 'clear'	*sleča* 'sliced, of bread'
ži	'brown'	*šota* 'muddy, smoky'	*šleča* 'split, of logs'
γi	'dark brown'	*xota* 'grey'	*xleča* 'rent, of fabrics'

Boas and Deloria (1941: 16–17), cited in Rankin (1987)

(4) Winnebago

-*sox*	'frying sound'	-*zap* 'tear roughly'	-*riš* 'bend wide'
-*šox*	'bubbling sound'	-*žap* 'peel'	-*rix* 'coil'
-*xox*	'breaking sound'	-*γap* 'remove layer'	

Adapted from Lipkind (1945: 47–49), cited in Rankin (1987)

(5) Kansa

zi	'yellow'	*sabe* 'black'	*leze* 'striped'
ži	'orange'	*šabe* 'dark'	*leže* 'spotted'
γi	'brown'		

Rankin (1987)

It can be reconstructed for Proto-Siouan and was inherited in Quapaw, from where it apparently spread to Muskogean languages. It was not transferred via loanwords: the actual fricatives involved are not the same, nor are the lexical items. The items in which it appears in the various Muskogean languages are not necessarily cognate. The pattern indicates that bilinguals can exploit patterns from one of their languages, here Siouan, in creating new forms in the other, without necessarily copying actual forms.

Another kind of sound symbolism occurs over a wide area of the West. Diminutive sound symbolism was noted early by Sapir for Wishram Chinook (1911, 1929), by Haas for Northwestern California (1970) and by Langdon for Yuman (1971), and surveyed more widely by Nichols (1971). Sapir cites such examples as *i-č'iau* 'snake', *i-c'iau* 'small snake'. Nichols characterizes the process as 'the alteration, in point or manner of articulation, of consonants in verb or noun roots – expressing the diminutive category and, by extension, an attitude of endearment, affection, pity, or the like' (1971: 826). In some languages the shifts are productive, in others unproductive but lexically well preserved, and in still others vestigial.

Nichols distinguishes three basic types of sound alternation: (i) strengthening, (ii) tonality, and (iii) apical resonant shifts. Only some types occur in each language. Her strengthening involves shifts from lenis to fortis (s > ts; ɬ > λ), continuant to non-continuant (θ > č, s > č, w > b) and glottalization (C > C'). The processes may affect all points of articulation or only some. Her tonality involves such shifts as š > s, x > š and q > k. Dental, alveolar and palato-alveolar consonants alternate symbolically, as do velar, post-velar and palato-velar, but there is no interaction between the two groups. Her apical resonant shifts include l > r, r > n and l > n.

> Glottalization is a northern, typically Salish form of shift, concentrated particularly in the state of Washington and spread at least to neighboring Wishram. Shifts among dental resonants are centered farther south, spreading from Mexico to Oregon and central Idaho; the northernmost example, the Sahaptin and Nez Perce shift of n > l, is reversed in compar-ison to the more southern shifts, and its peripheral location may be partly responsible for its anomaly. No overlap in glottalizing and dental resonant shifts has been found. Tonality, however, is used in shifts throughout the area, either alone or together with any other shift.   *(Nichols 1971: 840)*

The distribution of the phenomenon is clearly areal, crossing genetic boundaries. Nichols suggests three possible origins for it. One is dialect borrowing, which could result in doublets within a language. The alter-nants could then be given symbolic value (Aoki 1962: 173; Jacobsen 1969: 150–151). This could underlie Sahaptian n > l shifts. A second source could be morphophonemic alternations of consonants, espe-cially when the conditioning factor has been lost. This could underlie Karok r > n shifts (Bright 1957: 39–40). A third source could be vowel alternations which in turn affected adjacent consonants. Rigsby and Silverstein (1969: 56) point to Sahaptian k ~ q and s ~ c alternations, which could have resulted from diminutive affixes, which triggered vowel harmony and then consonant shifts. Such events would have occurred in just a few languages, with subsequent extension of the patterns and spread through contact, as suggested by the geographical distribution of shift types. Again we find an unusual phonological pat-tern with a strong areal distribution not transferred via vocabulary. Bilingual speakers apparently replicated a pattern in one of their lan-guages for expressive purposes in the other.

31.5   Basic Replication of Grammar

The strongest linguistic areas of North America show shared grammatical distinctions, categories and structures, but the shared patterns are not generally attached to similar substance. In some cases, copying could occur relatively quickly.

31.5.1   Assembly From Native Components: Inclusive/Exclusive

Many languages in the world distinguish inclusive first person ('you and I')
from exclusive ('he/she/it/they and I'). Jacobsen (1980a) discusses the areal
distribution of the trait and various paths of development. It is sometimes
a family trait, but it often appears in just some members of a family;
it occurs in Choctaw alone in the Muskogean family in the Southeast
(Haas 1969: 5), in Yuki alone in Yuki-Wappo in California, and in
Shuswap alone in Salishan, and in Kwak'wala (Northern Wakashan) but
not Nuuchahnulth (Southern Wakashan) on the Northwest Coast. It also
goes beyond family boundaries. It is present in a continuous area including
all languages of the Great Basin (Washo, the Numic branch of Uto-Aztecan)
and adjacent California (Achumawi, Wintu, Miwok, Yokuts, Yuki), but it is
absent from California languages outside that area, west and south of
Yokuts, and from the Southwest. It is not found in languages in Central
California or Southern Oregon. It recurs, however, on the Oregon Coast
(Coos, Siuslawan and Alsea), and in Chinookan along the Columbia River
and contiguous Sahaptin, but not the related Nez Perce.

Jacobsen points out that the distinction is easily diffused, because it is
not bound to the syntactic structure of a language in the way that, for
example, case might be. He catalogues various structural means exploited
to replicate it. A new exclusive form might be built on a first person plus
third person marker, as in Siuslaw, narrowing the original first person
plural to an inclusive.

(6)   Siuslaw

		SG	DU	PL
1	(EXCL)		-aʷxûn	-nxan (innovation)
	(INCL)	-n	-ns	-nł
2	-nx	-ts	-tî	
3			-aʷx	-nx

Frachtenberg (1922: 468)

A new inclusive form may be based on a second person marker, as in
Yokuts, narrowing the original first person plural to an exclusive.

(7)   Yawelmani Yokuts pronouns

		SG	DU	PL
1	(EXCL)	na'	na'ak'	na'an
1	(INCL)		mak'	may (innovation)
2		ma'	ma'ak'	ma'an
3		ama'	amak'	Aman

Newman (1944: 231–232)

Other strategies can be found as well.

The inclusive/exclusive distinction is not uncommon cross-linguistically, but it is often the result of contact, as bilinguals replicate a distinction using native resources.

31.5.2 Stimulated Reanalysis: Agent/Patient Systems

Alignment patterns have been hypothesized to be stable over time (Nichols 1992: 181). Yet even the rarer patterns show areal distributions. Nichols found that in her sample of 172 languages, 65 per cent showed nominative/accusative or neutral systems, 19 per cent ergative systems, 14 per cent agent/patient or stative/active systems, and just 3 per cent hierarchical systems (1992: 187). These last two patterns show strong areal distributions in North America.

Agent/patient systems distinguish two (or three) core arguments. Grammatical agents are prototypically those who volitionally instigate and control events and states. Grammatical patients are those who are not in control but are significantly affected by the situation. Examples of such a system can be seen in Creek, a Muskogean language of the Southeast.

(8)   Creek (Muskogean)
       1SG AGENT *-éy-*   1SG PATIENT *(a)ca-*
       a:ł-éy-s   'I'm going about'   *ca-tkolí:s*   'I'm cold'
       homp-éy-s   'I'm eating'   *ca-nockilí:s*   'I'm sleeping'
       ta:sk-éy-s   'I'm jumping'   *ca-capákki:s*   'I'm mad'
                                                           Martin (2004: 138)

This is not an active/stative system: the distinction between events and states is not the determining factor. Creek grammatical agents occur with voluntary, controlled states, and grammatical patients with uncontrolled events.

(9)   Creek (Muskogean)
       1SG AGENT *-éy-*   1SG PATIENT *(a)ca-*
       lêyk-ey-s   'I'm sitting'   *ca-latêyks*   'I fell'
                                                    Martin (2004: 140, 139)

A few verbs allow either an agent or patient, depending on volitionality: *hosi:l-éy-s* 'I (AGENT) am urinating', *ca-hósi:lís* 'I (PATIENT) am urinating (unable to control it)'.

Both agent and patient forms occur in transitives. Third persons are unmarked.

(10)   Creek (Muskogean)
       a. *Ci-na:fk-éy-s*
          2SG.PATIENT-hit-1SG.AGENT-INDIC
          'I (AGENT) am hitting you (PATIENT).'
       b. *Ó:wa-n*   *ca-yá:c-i:-s.*
          water-ACC   1SG.PATIENT-want-DUR-INDIC
          'I (PATIENT) want water.'
       c. *Ó:wa-n*   *ca-hos-î:t-t*   *ó:-s.*
          water-ACC   1SG.PATIENT-want-SPONT-SS   be-INDIC
          'I (PATIENT) forgot water.'
                                                           Martin (2004: 140)

The system is thus neither 'split intransitive' (i.e. limited to intransitives) nor ergative.

Such systems are widespread across North America. They occur throughout the Southeast, in the Northeast, across the Plains, in the Southwest, in California, and along the Northwest Coast. Some are ancient. In the Southeast, they can be reconstructed for Proto-Muskogean, the ancestor of Creek. In the Northeast and the Plains they occur throughout three families, Siouan, Caddoan and Iroquoian, where they are all inherited. In the Southwest, they can be reconstructed for Proto-Kiowa-Tanoan. But the systems extend beyond these families. In the Southeast, they occur not only throughout Muskogean, the Siouan languages Quapaw, Ofo and Biloxi, the Iroquoian language Cherokee, and the Caddoan language Caddo, but also in isolates Chitimacha, Natchez, Tunica, Atakapa and Tonkawa, the western neighbour of Caddo. In Northern California they occur not only in all of the Pomoan languages, but also the adjacent Yuki, though not its relative Wappo. On the northern Northwest Coast they appear in the isolate Haida and its neighbour Tlingit, but not in its Eyak and Athabaskan relatives (Mithun 2008). The shapes of the markers in neighbouring languages are not the same, however.

In the Southeast, the isolate Chitimacha distinguishes agent and patient pronominal suffixes on verbs. Pronominal suffixes exist only for first person singular and plural; second and third persons are identified by independent pronouns where necessary. The grammatical agent suffixes (1 s G -ik(i)) appear with intransitives (ʔušt'iš-ik 'I am eating', nušmišu-k 'I shall work') and transitives (k'et-ik 'I beat (him)', ʔam-ik 'I see (him)'). Grammatical patient suffixes (1 s G -ki) similarly identify the single arguments of intransitives (nu:p-ki-ču:š 'if I die', t'at'iwa-ki-:k'i 'I felt cold') as well as the goals/recipients of transitives (k'et-ki '(He) beat me'). Swadesh states that patient forms occur with verbs denoting both events and states, with such meanings as 'die', 'forget', 'make a hoarse sound in the throat', 'get sprained', 'shiver', 'fall asleep, sleep', 'become wearied', 'be tired', 'be afraid', 'be greedy', 'suffer pain', 'feel itchy', 'be pleased', 'want'. This is thus not an active/stative system. Some verbs occur with either agents or patients (Swadesh 1939: 94, 119; Hieber, manuscript).

The isolate Atakapa also shows agent/patient pronominal affixes on verbs. Grammatical agent suffixes appear with intransitives (hîš-o 'I plant') and transitives (peni-o 'I have healed him'). They appear with events (pál-o 'I break it') and states (hatpéʔ-o 'I am ready'). Patient prefixes similarly appear with intransitives (hi-láwet 'I was burnt') and transitives (hi-lóišat '(he) helped me'). They appear with both events (hi-makaukit 'I fell') and states (hi-lak 'I am strong') (Gatschet and Swanton 1932). Second and third person singular agent affixes are unmarked, but independent pronouns are not infrequent.

The isolate Tonkawa, spoken immediately to the west of the Southeast area, also shows agent/patient patterning (Hoijer 1933). Arguments are identified by verbal prefixes and suffixes. Suffixes are used for agents. As in many such systems, third person singulars are unmarked.

(11)   Tonkawa

	Patients	Agents (Imm Present)
1	*ge-*	*-c'*
2	–	*-n'ei*
3	–	–
3PL		*-nik*

yagb-o'-c̱   'I̱ hit (him)'
ge̱-igab-o'   '(he) hits <u>me</u>'

Hoijer (1933: 68, 72)

Prefixes are used for both goals/recipients of transitives, as above, and the non-volitional arguments of intransitives (*-o'* = present declarative).

(12)   Tonkawa

hedjin-o'-c̱   'I̱ lie down'
g-e:djin-o'   'I̱ fall down, i.e. I lie down involuntarily, stumble and fall'
m'e:idj-o'-c̱   'I̱ urinate'
ge̱-m'eidj-o'   'I̱ urinate involuntarily'
ge̱-xadjlew-o'   'I̱ am angry'
ge̱-dic'abx-o'   'I̱ have been punctured; I bleed to death'
ge̱-xamdj-o'   'I̱ break my arm/legs'
ge̱-nc'ol-o'   'I̱ have sores, blisters'

Hoijer (1933: 70–71)

The isolate Natchez also shows some agent/patient patterning. Grammatical agents in Natchez appear in both intransitives (*ʔe:taku:š a̱-htik* 'I̱ will go to the house') and transitives (*cop-a̱-pkuk* 'I̱ will pluck you'). Grammatical patients also identify the single argument of intransitives (*ʔuNcnuš-iṉ-u:ʔa:* 'I̱ forget', *laW-ne̱-u:ʔa:* 'I̱ shiver', *šihi-ni̱-wa:* 'I̱ am full of food') and the goals/recipients of transitives (*ma:pa-ni̱-škʷ* 'you will eat <u>me</u>', *ca:-ya i:Mi-ni̱-wa* 'I am tired of deer meat'). Third person agents are unmarked. Kimball notes that verbs with patient forms 'refer to actions that are not controlled by their translation subjects. These verbs are uncommon, in contrast to the adjacent Muskogean languages' (2005: 439).

It is easy to see how agent/patient patterns could spread. Muskogean, Siouan and Caddoan languages in the Southeast, as well as the adjacent Chitimacha, Atakapa, Tonkawa and Natchez, share several other characteristics.

  i Intransitive and transitive verbs are not distinguished formally.
 ii Topical third persons are unmarked.
iii Basic word order is predicate-final.

These features would facilitate reanalysis of a nominative/accusative system as an agent/patient system, or vice versa.

(13) (SUBJECT) OBJECT   TRANSITIVE VERB   'It scared me (OBJECT)'
      (it)   *me*   *scared*   < >
                 PATIENT INTRANSITIVE   'I (PATIENT) was
                         VERB   scared'

Languages in other linguistic areas with agent/patient patterns show the same features: the Pomoan languages and adjacent Yuki of California, and Haida and the adjacent Tlingit in the Northwest. Yuki's only relative, Wappo, shows a nominative/accusative system, as do Tlingit's Eyak and Athabaskan relatives. We can catch a glimpse of reanalysis in the opposite direction in the speech of the last Wappo speaker. Her first language was (nominative/accusative) Wappo but she was bilingual in (agent/patient) Southern Pomo. When speaking Southern Pomo, she used the agent pronouns as subjects and the patient pronouns as objects.

This reanalysis is not the only mechanism by which agent/patient patterns can spread through contact. Still another Southeast isolate, Tunica, shows patterning that is quite similar. Documentation of the language comes from three sources. Gatschet collected vocabulary and texts in 1886. Swanton collected additional material between 1907 and 1910 and compiled a grammatical sketch in 1921 based on all sources. Haas worked with the last fluent speaker between 1933 and 1939 and published a grammar (1941), grammatical sketch (1946), text collection (1950) and dictionary from all sources (1953).

In Tunica, core arguments are identified by pronominal affixes on the verb or auxiliary. Prefixes identify transitive goals and recipients. Suffixes (fused with aspect markers) identify transitive and intransitive agents.

(14) Tunica pronominal affixes
      a. *Tánisarahč,*   *sáhkun,*   *ʔuhtákanʔákihč,*
         tá-nísara-hči   sáhku   ʔuhk-táka-n-áki-hč
         DET-young.person-F.SG one   3M.SG-chase-CAUS-3F.SG.
                                            PFV-when
         the girl   one   when <u>she</u> chased <u>him</u>
         'The girl chased one (of the puppies)
         ʔuhtápʔɛkɛ̀nì.
         ʔuhk-tápi-ʔáki-áni
         3M.SG-catch-3F.SG.PFV-HEARSAY
         <u>she</u> caught <u>him</u>
         and caught it.'
      b. *Tánisarahč,*   *ʔákʔamʔɛkɛ̀nì.*
         tá-nísara-hči   ʔáka-ʔámi-ʔáki-áni
         DET-young.person-F.SG enter-disappear-3F.SG.PFV-HEARSAY
         the girl   <u>she</u> went in and disappeared, it is said
         'The girl had gone down (into the water) and disappeared.'
                                                          Haas (1941: 135)

Prefixes are also used for the single arguments of intransitive verbs with meanings 'be excited/distraught', 'belch', 'be tired/fatigued', 'be lonesome', 'be withered/shrivelled/shrunken', 'be named', 'lack', 'be left or left over', 'be tipsy/slightly intoxicated/half-drunk', 'be pitiable/helpless/unfortunate/miserable', 'be angry/irate/enraged/wrathful', 'be hungry', 'be happy/glad/pleased/like', 'own/possess', 'remember/understand/know', know how', 'want/wish/be willing', 'feel cold/chilly', 'be dry/thirsty' and 'be old'.

(15)   Tunica pronominal prefix
  Tíhči tíyaši.
  tíhči <u>ti</u>-yáši
  she 3F.SG-be.angry
  '<u>She</u> is angry.'

                  Haas (1941: 60)

The system looks much like the agent/patient systems in the area, but closer examination shows that it is not exactly the same. All arguments are overtly marked. Furthermore, the suffixes that identify transitive and intransitive agents of events also identify participants who are not in control, in verbs with meanings such as 'fall', 'die', 'slip', 'yawn', 'snore', 'groan/moan in pain', 'mew/whimper/cry', 'cry/weep/bawl', 'vomit', 'topple over', 'break/snap in two (rope)', 'topple over' and 'start, jerk away as when startled'. The crucial distinction is not control, but events versus states. This is an active/stative or active/inactive system.

 But there is another layer to the Tunica system, likely a more recent result of contact with the agent/patient systems in the area. There is a set of verbs termed by Haas 'transimpersonal'. These are exactly the kinds of verbs that appear with patient forms in agent/patient systems: 'bleed', 'wake up', 'cough', 'gasp for breath, pant (dog)', '(eye) to twitch', 'get an erection', 'sneeze', 'belch', 'sweat/perspire', 'become lame/paralysed', 'have bad luck', 'choke', 'stink', 'get burned', 'get scalded', 'get pinched', 'get stung (as by a mosquito) or get a bump (from a bite)', 'get a cramp', 'be swollen', 'be sore', 'get a swelling', 'be constipated', 'get cured/ healed', 'get lost', 'lose in gambling', 'be born', 'have a fever', 'get hooked/caught/ trapped/snared', 'have diarrhoea' and 'itch' (Haas 1953). Arguments of these verbs, not in control, are identified with the same prefixes as the goals and recipients of transitives. These verbs also contain a pronominal suffix 'referring to a nameless entity which cannot be expressed by a substantival referee' (Haas 1941: 105). The same suffix is used in verbs Haas terms 'impersonals', such as *šíhtuna yá-ti-hč* 'when <u>it</u> became dark' [dark become-<u>3SG.SML</u>-SUBORDINATE 1941: 58], and in inchoatives based on statives, such as *ʔu-yáhpa-ti-hč* 'when he got hungry' [M.SG-be. hungry-<u>3SG.SML</u>-SUBORD 1941: 61]. This suffix is also used for feminine singulars.

Some of the stems used in transimpersonal constructions also occur in intransitives: *lé* transimpersonal 'lose in gambling', intransitive 'disappear'. Some also appear in impersonal constructions: *píra* transimpersonal 'become/turn into/revive/come to life/be born', impersonal 'appear'. Some also appear in basic transitives: *pála* transimpersonal 'get hooked/caught/trapped/snared', transitive 'catch/trap/snare'. But other stems appear only in transimpersonals. Haas notes, for example, that *híyu* 'wake up' never occurs as a transitive. This suggests that the transimpersonals were not simply basic transitives, but were developing into a new construction. More recently, reanalysis was apparently beginning to take them in a different direction. Haas noted that some of the transimpersonal verbs recorded by Gatschet in 1886 were inflected as intransitives in the 1930s by the last speaker: 'There is evidence that stems denoting involuntary action (e.g., 'to breathe', 'to cough') were formerly used as transimpersonals. The more usual procedure now is to treat such stems as intransitives' (1941: 59).

(16) Tunica remodelling
      Older transimpersonal   Newer Intransitive
      ʔihkʔówikatí   *ʔówikaní*
      ʔihk-ʔówi-katí   ʔówi-kaní
      1SG.PAT-sweat-UNSPECIFIED.AGT.PFV   sweat-1SG.PFV
      'I am sweating'   or   'I am sweating'
                                                             Haas (1941: 59)

This last speaker, Sesostrie Youchigant, was born around 1870 and had not spoken the language since 1915 or earlier. He also spoke French and English, so this later remodelling could have been stimulated by contact with those languages. Heaton (2013) points out that Sesostrie Youchigant was also apparently remodelling the shapes of pronominal prefixes. Where all of the verbal prefixes recorded by Gatschet matched those of alienable possessive prefixes on nouns, Sesostrie Youchigant used inalienable possessive forms in stative and transimpersonal constructions.

   In any case, Tunica provides an example of likely contact-induced replication of an agent/patient pattern through a second mechanism, with an overt unspecified/indefinite agent.

31.6 Gradual Replication of Grammar

We can see how bilinguals might replicate categories from native material (inclusive/exclusive) or reanalysis (nominative/accusative < > agent/patient). It is more difficult to imagine how speakers could replicate more abstract, tightly integrated grammatical structure, that at the bottom of the hierarchy in Figure 31.1. It is here that the length of contact can be key. Grammatical patterns need not be transferred in a single step.

31.6.1 Abstract Grammatical Structure

It is well known that word order spreads easily under contact. Mechanisms are clear. All languages allow some variation in order, though the frequency and pragmatic markedness of alternatives varies. Basic clause structure could be predicate-initial or predicate-final, for example, but constituents might appear before the nuclear clause in topicalization constructions or after it in antitopic constructions. Under bilingualism, what may be copied is the relative frequency of alternatives – Johanson's (2008) frequential copying. Over time, what was once a highly marked order can become progressively less marked, even ultimately a basic order. Many Northwest languages show predicate-initial clause structure: all of those in the core Wakashan, Chimakuan and Salishan families, the adjacent Tsimshianic and Chinookan families, and Alsea, Coosan, Siuslaw and Kutenai (strongly reflecting discourse status in some). Surrounding languages generally show predicate-final structure, more common cross-linguistically. The fact that predicate-initial order can be reconstructed for each family suggests that it spread early. It is also likely that it fostered further convergence.

31.6.1.1 Negation

Another feature often cited for Northwest languages involves negative constructions consisting of an initial negative predicate or auxiliary, followed by the negated clause. Describing Quileute (Chimakuan), Andrade says, 'the negative morphemes *wa* or *é:* or the two in succession ... function as the main verb, and the action negated is expressed by a subordinate verb' (1933: 268).

(17)   Quileute (Chimakuan)
     é: *wa-ł-litš*   *siyá'-a*
     NEG   NEG-INTENDED-2SG   see-SUBORD
     'You do not intend to see it.'

                                        Andrade (1933: 269)

For Coeur d'Alene (Salishan), Reichard comments, 'The negative is almost certainly a verb, for it has many verbal characteristics ... When used as an independent stem it means "refuse" ... In the intransitive *lutä-* takes the possessive affixes with an *s-* prefix which may be nominal' (1938: 664–665). Another nominalizer in Coeur d'Alene is *y-*.

(18)   Coeur d'Alene (Salishan)
  ämts   'he shared it'
  lutⁱ-y'-ämts 'he did not share it'
  lutä-s-xʷät'iš 'he did not get up'

                  Reichard (1938: 665)

Similar constructions appear in neighbouring unrelated languages.

(19)   Nuuchahnulth (Wakashan)
  Wik'aλ   *wiinapuλ*   *saayaa.*
  wik-'aλ   wi:nap-uλ   sayaa
  not-FINITE stopping-MOM far
  'They didn't stop for long distances.'

                 Nakayama (2003: 342)

(20)   Nisgha (Tsimshianic)
  Niindii   *Gipt*
  ni:-nə-ti: kíp-t
  be.not-1SG.ERG-INTS eat.SG-3
  'I did not eat it.'

                  Tarpent (1987: 357)

Complement constructions with an initial negative matrix are to be expected in predicate-initial languages, and could easily spread because of their fit within the existing systems. The propensity for spread is heightened by the fact that negative constructions typically cycle at a high rate, as speakers strive to restore the force of a crucial distinction which is especially susceptible to fading due to its frequency.

31.6.1.2 Lexical Suffixes

The languages at the core of the Northwest Coast area share another notable construction involving suffixes. In many ways the suffixes resemble roots, with their large inventories, often numbering in the hundreds, and their often concrete meanings. Technically, they are suffixes, however, never serving on their own as the bases of words. They appear in both predicates and referring expressions.

(21)   Coeur d'Alene (Salishan)
  a. *Tsan-ts'ul-ts'ulxʷ-áxe̲n-ts*
    under-RDP-claw-<u>arm</u>-3>3
    'He clawed it under the arms.'
  b. *tšu̲gw-tšu̲gw-áxʷe̲-s*
    RDP-feather-<u>arm</u>-3SG.POSS
    'his wing feathers'

                  Reichard (1938: 609)

The meanings of the suffixes seem at first surprisingly concrete and specific for affixes, but they are often more diffuse and abstract. The Coeur d'Alene suffix *tsin*, for example, is translated sometimes 'mouth', sometimes 'eat', 'edge', 'shore', etc.

(22) Coeur d'Alene (Salishan)
      a. *gwiy'-tsín-ilš*
         finish-<u>mouth</u>-3 P L
         'They finished eating.'
      b. *tšits-pänä'ä-yaR-tsí-stus-ilš*
         hither-as.far.as-be.at.edge-<u>mouth</u>-C U S T-3 P L
         'This way they brought it to shore.'

Reichard (1938: 611)

Other Coeur d'Alene suffixes are glossed 'attachment/handle/connection', 'back/ridge', 'billowy', 'body', 'bottom', 'breast', 'breath', 'bush/ plant/root/tree', 'camas', 'clothes', 'day/sky/atmosphere', 'ear', 'effort', 'end', 'eye/face/fire', 'feeling', 'fire/fuel', 'fish', 'foot/leg', 'food', 'forehead', 'foundation', 'ground', 'hand', 'head/tip/top', 'heart/stomach', 'hide/skin/mat/covering', 'hollow object/abdomen/canoe/wagon', 'horn', 'horse/stock', 'house', 'inside/from within', 'tree/log/sticklike object', 'mouth interior', 'neck', 'nose/beak/oral and nasal cavity/seat of taste', 'child/offspring', 'person/man', 'persons', 'pharynx', 'property', 'road', 'shoulder', 'rock/surface of round object', 'throat/nape', 'tongue', 'tooth', 'vegetation', 'voice/throat', 'water/liquid', 'weather', 'times', 'round object', 'source', and more. For the most part, the suffixes have no phonological relationships to roots with similar meanings.

Similar structures can be found in unrelated neighbours.

(23) Quileute (Chimakuan)
      Tsix̣   há't'šá:ƚowá'.
      tsix̣   ha'tš-**a:ƚ**-o-wa'
      very   be.good-**weather**-L I N K E R-away
      'It was very good weather.'

Andrade (1933: 279, 283)

Here too there is a large inventory of such suffixes, with such meanings as 'colour', 'wood', 'food', 'decorated blanket', 'tree/log', 'intestines/sinew', 'stone arrowhead', 'rock', 'flounder', 'navel', 'nose', 'point', 'beach', 'wall', 'sky', 'basket', 'bow/gun/weapon', 'plant/bush/tree', 'bow', 'leg/foot', 'fish tail', 'anus (male)', 'skin/hide', 'hat', 'tooth', 'forehead', 'elbow', 'day', 'gravel at bottom of sea', 'footprints', 'dress', 'fishing equipment', 'food for journey', 'bowstring', 'place where something is done', 'mind/heart', 'dwelling/indoors', 'breast/trunk/lungs', 'village', 'dead whale', 'door', 'breasts', 'eye', 'prairie', 'place', 'sick', 'sealing canoe', 'fishtrap', 'bed', 'spouse', 'hand/twig/branch', 'odour', 'tail of quadruped', 'head', 'shaman', 'vulva', 'extreme/end', 'eyebrow', 'knife', 'thigh', 'manner', 'territory', 'wife', 'river canoe', 'whale', 'fire', 'size/room/space', 'river', 'throat', 'salmon egg', 'body', 'heel', 'arrow', 'kelp', 'strand of rope', 'canoe/vehicle', 'hair', 'friend', 'canoe-mate', 'bunch/handful', 'custom', 'cave/box interior', 'tool', 'place/container/dish', 'side of canoe', 'sun', 'kind', 'neck', 'mussels', 'piece', 'hip', 'backpack', 'fur', 'meat/flesh', 'box', 'roof', 'body of water', 'human hair', 'load', 'guardian spirit', 'muscle', 'fire', 'remainder/waste', 'feather/wing/gill', 'penis', 'companion', 'language', 'occasion/turn/time', 'food', 'platform', 'shoulder', 'testicles', 'year', 'inside of mouth', 'nape', 'blanket/bed covers', 'stump', 'spear', 'trout/smelt/sucker', 'packstrap', 'water', 'rib', 'fishing line', 'female', 'side', 'top of bag', 'gillnet', 'leaf', 'village', 'bird egg', 'small basket', 'bait', 'arrowpoint', 'nose', 'riverbank', 'point/peak', 'noise', 'combustible wood', 'coast', 'ear', 'hill', 'face', 'grass/hay', 'offspring', 'cape', 'road', 'tongue', 'magic', 'child', 'hand', 'palm of hand', 'soil', etc. In rare cases there is slight overlap, as in *-tq, -á'lotq* 'sealing canoe', but it is not clear whether the free form originated as another root plus the same suffix.

The suffixes have free counterparts, but close scrutiny shows that the suffix is often more generic.

> There are several words for the different types of canoes, but *-qa* may refer to any of them, as well as to a wagon or an automobile. Also, there are free morphemes for bow and arrow, as well as for the modern gun … but all may be rendered by *-pa*.   *(Andrade 1933: 194)*

The Wakashan languages show similar large inventories of lexical suffixes. For Kwak'wala, Boas (1947) lists suffixes glossed 'head', 'face', 'cheek', 'forehead', 'ear', 'mouth/opening of a bag/vessel', 'tooth/sharp edge', 'throat', 'shoulder/forearm', 'hand', 'chest', 'back', 'front of body', 'calf', 'shin', 'knee', 'foot', 'mind', 'dried meat of', 'piece of remains of', 'country', 'receptacle', 'season', 'useless part', 'woman', 'effluvia of mouth and nose', 'fire', 'branches/leaves/body hair', 'inside hollow object', 'top of surface', 'down to beach', 'throat/under water', 'up from beach', 'out to sea', 'downriver/down inlet', 'into woods', 'on surface of water', 'along riverbank', 'on rock', 'on ground', 'open space/bottom of sea/world/beach/in body', 'canoe', 'floor of house', 'into house/inlet', 'mouth of river', 'top of hill/riverbank', 'outside front of house', 'roof', 'crotch of tree' and 'bow of canoe'.

Immediately to the north of this core area, the Tsimshianic languages also show similar suffixes, often with relatively concrete meanings, but they are fewer in number and more transparently related to independent roots. Sm'algyax, for example, contains the suffixes *-sk, -ks, kwsa, -aks, -üks* and *-iks*, which Dunn relates to the word *aks* 'water'. The suffixes *-gn, -gan, -xn*, he relates to the word *gan* 'tree/wood/stick'. The suffixes *-gyit* and *-git* he relates to *gyet* 'man'. The suffixes *-bn* and *-n* he links to *ban* 'belly'. And *-mx, -mk̲* and *-xi* are possibly related to *diilmx* 'respond'.

(24)   Sm'algyax (Tsimshianic)
    a. *Batsgn*
       batsk-gan
       arrive-tree
       'arrive in a canoe'
    b. *yel-gan*
       drill-stick
       'fire drill'

Dunn (1995: 36–37)

For all of the languages, the suffixes are necessarily translated with noun-like and verb-like English glosses, but the constructions do not specify a semantic or syntactic role.

The lexical suffix constructions of the Northwest are ancient, reconstructable for the various proto-languages. The suffix forms were not copied across family lines. But the constructions, unusual cross-linguistically, must have developed through contact, probably over an extended period. Rather than being grammaticalized gradually one at a time, they apparently originated in highly productive compounding comparable to the noun–noun and verb–noun (noun incorporation) constructions of other languages. A very few of the suffixes show resemblances to roots in the same language or a related one like -*ałqixʷ* 'breath/smell' and *qixʷ* 'breathe/smell' of Coeur d'Alene (Reichard 1938: 633). The initial -*ał* of this suffix actually matches the linker that appears in compounds in the language. A source in compounding explains the large inventory of suffixes and their relatively concrete and specific meanings: constituents of compounds are drawn from the full inventory of lexical roots. Like non-heads of compounds, the lexical suffixes do not serve specific syntactic roles. The suffixes can serve the same range of functions as incorporated nouns (Mithun 1997). They are used to create lexemes for nameworthy concepts, such as the Kwak'wala *da:xs* 'take aboard', with suffix -*xs* 'canoe' (Boas 1947: 239). They are used to manipulate argument structure, as in *'wəs'wədāā* 'have cold ears', with suffix -*ʔa* 'ear', a use which explains the large inventories of suffixes evoking body parts. They are used to shape the flow of information, representing established or incidental entities unobtrusively. Over time, via regular processes of grammaticalization, the second constituents of compounds apparently eroded into suffixes, sometimes losing phonetic substance, sometimes gaining new or more abstract meanings as were extended in new formations, like the Kwak'wala -*'sto* 'eye > door > round opening'. The grammaticalization of the compound constructions could have taken place individually in each language, but it was likely stimulated by ongoing contact.

This shared grammaticalization process is responsible for other areal features as well, such as numeral classifiers. These consist of lexical suffixes attached to number roots, as in Kwak'wala *okʷ* 'human beings', *me'ló:kʷ* 'two persons'; *-xsa* 'flat', *q'é:xsa* 'many (leaves)', *'né:mxa* 'one (day)' (Boas 1947: 240).

31.6.1.3 Means/Manner and Location/Direction

Many languages in California, Oregon, Washington, Idaho and Nevada also share certain abstract morphological structures: verbal prefixes indicating means or manner of motion and/or suffixes indicating location or direction (Mithun 2007a). Atsugewi, a Palaihnihan language of Northern California, contains prefixes with glosses such as 'pulling', 'pushing', 'sitting', 'stepping/kicking', 'biting', 'sucking', 'spitting', 'bodily', 'swinging/pounding/chopping', 'orally', 'poking/piercing/impaling', 'thrusting/digging/sewing/leaning/propping', 'scraping/whittling/hugging', 'slicing/sawing/driving/carting/getting run over', 'paddling/stirring', 'boring', 'dragging/suspending', 'binding/girding', 'cutting with knife edge', 'sailing/falling', 'blowing', 'flowing', 'raining', 'steady pressure', 'steady pulling', 'bearing down', 'by gravity', 'by heat/ fire', 'by light shining', 'visually', 'auditorily', 'touching', 'smelling', 'tasting'. They are actually semantically more abstract and diffuse than verbal or nominal translations suggest. Many could be described in terms of instruments ('with a pole', 'with the buttocks') just as well as manner of motion ('poking', 'sitting'). They may indicate only vague involvement: 'with the eye, involving an eye-shaped object such as a hailstone or button'. Talmy (1972) provides a detailed description.

(25)   Atsugewi affixes
    a. *C'waswálmic'.*
       ʔ-w-ca-swal-mic'
       3-FACTUAL-<u>blowing</u>-limp.material.move-<u>down.onto.ground</u>
       'The clothes blew down from the clothesline.'
    b. *W'oswalíc'ta.*
       ʔ-w-uh-swal-ic't-a
       3-FACTUAL-<u>thrusting</u>-limp.material.move-<u>into.liquid</u>-EFFECTIVE
       'She threw the clothes into the laundry tub.'

                            Talmy (1972: 432)

The pattern crosses genetic lines between families and even the most ambitious proposed superstocks. The prefixes occur in the Palaihnihan, Pomoan and Yuman families, and in Karuk, Yana and Washo, all once hypothesized to be 'Hokan', but not in Shasta, Esselen or Salinan also grouped as Hokan. They occur in the Maidun and Sahaptian families and in Klamath and Takelma, once grouped as 'Penutian', but not in Wintun, Utian, Yokuts, Coos, Siuslaw or Alsea, also grouped as Penutian. They occur in Chumashan and Wappo-Yuki, each agreed to be a distinct family. They occur in the Numic branch of Uto-Aztecan, spoken throughout the Great Basin in eastern California, adjacent Oregon, Idaho and into Utah and Wyoming, but not in Uto-Aztecan languages spoken further away.

Locative/directional suffixes show a similar but not identical distribution. They occur in the Palaihnihan and Pomoan families, in Karuk, Shasta and Yana, all once labelled Hokan, but not in Yuman or Washo, also included in Hokan. They appear in the Maidun and Sahaptian families and Klamath, once grouped as Penutian, but they are not mentioned in descriptions of Wintun, Utian, Yokuts, Takelma, Coos, Siuslaw or Alsea. They do not appear in Chumashan, Wappo-Yuki or Uto-Aztecan.

The shapes of markers are not similar across family lines. Such tightly integrated, abstract morphological structures would not seem amenable to simple replication by bilinguals. Many of the markers are quite small, often just a consonant and sometimes just preglottalization or preaspiration. It is difficult to imagine an Atsugewi speaker deciding to replicate the 'thrusting/digging/sewing/leaning/propping' prefix in (25b) above in another language. The affixes are derivational; speakers generally select full lexical items as they speak rather than assembling them online. Some languages at the edge of the area provide a clue to the mechanisms behind this areal distribution.

Both the means/manner and locative/directional constructions appear to be descended from compounds, as might be expected. We can still see the kinds of [NOUN+VERB]$_{VERB}$ and [VERB+VERB]$_{VERB}$ compounds that could give rise to means/manner prefixes at the eastern edge of the area, in the Numic languages. Tümpisa Shoshone still shows NOUN–VERB compounds in which the noun indicates an instrument, such as *ki-kuttih* 'elbow-shoot' = 'jab with the elbow' (Dayley 1989: 92). Tümpisa also contains a sizeable inventory of means/manner prefixes that Dayley traces to Proto-Uto-Aztecan noun and verb roots, among them *ku-* 'with heat or fire' < **kuh* 'fire', *kü-* 'with teeth or mouth' < **kü'i* 'bite', *ma-* 'with the hand' < **maa* 'hand', *mu-* 'with the nose' < **mupi* 'nose', *ni-* 'with words, talking' < **niya/niha* 'name', *pa-* 'involving water' < **paa* 'water', *pi-* 'with the butt or behind' < **pih* 'back', *sü-* 'from cold' < **süp* 'cold', *sun-* 'with the mind, by feelings, sensing' < **suuna* 'heart' or **suuwah* 'notice, believe', *ta-* 'with the foot' < **tannah* 'foot', and *tsa-* 'grasping in hand' < Numic **tsa'i* 'grasp, hold' (Dayley 1989: 95–96).

Examples of the kinds of compounds that could develop into locative/directional constructions can be seen at the northern edge of the area. Kathlamet Chinook of Oregon contains a kind of [VERB+VERB]$_{VERB}$ compounding in which the second root indicates motion in a particular direction, such as *-pa* 'motion out of', *-pq* 'motion into', *-pck* 'motion from open to cover, especially from water to shore or inland', *-ƛx* 'motion from cover to open, especially toward water', *-ti* 'motion, position down', *uulx̣* 'motion up': *ikux̣úni-pck* 'she drifted <u>ashore</u>' [*-x̣uni-pck* 'drift-from.water.to.shore']. These roots also occur independently: *txú-pck-a* 'Let us go inland' (Hymes 1955: 218).

Confirmation of the compounding origins of these prefix and suffix constructions can be seen in what Jacobsen (1980b) and DeLancey (1996) term 'bipartite stem' constructions: some of the languages contain verb stems which now appear to consist only of a prefix and a suffix. Maidu, for example, contains a means/manner prefix *wi-* 'with hands' and a suffix *-doj* 'upward': <u>*wi-dók-doj*</u> 'grasp with the hand and pull up' (Shipley 1963: 187). It also contains stems like *wi-dój* 'pull (something) up'. Such stems are likely descendants of lexicalized compounds.

While it is unlikely that bilinguals would replicate the small, abstract affixes seen in many of these languages directly, they could easily replicate compounding types, with initial means/manner roots or with final locative/directional roots. Over time, perhaps also stimulated by ongoing contact, frequently recurring elements of such compounds could easily erode into affixes. Various stages of development can be seen across the area, with affixes of varying productivity, varying degrees of abstraction and varying phonological size.

31.6.2 Alignment: Hierarchical Systems

The alignment type Nichols found to be the rarest cross-linguistically is hierarchical, where 'access to inflectional slots for subject and/or object is based on person, number, and/or animacy rather than (or no less than) on syntactic relations' (1992: 66). This type appeared in only 3 per cent of her sample. Hierarchical systems also show areal patterning in North America, and it is possible to discern mechanisms behind their geographical distribution (Mithun 2012b).

31.6.2.1 Northwest Coast

In Nuuchahnulth (Nootka), a Southern Wakashan language spoken on Vancouver Island, British Columbia, arguments are identified by first and second person enclitics to predicates. Third person is unmarked. The first person singular is =*s*.

(26)   Nuuchahnulth (Wakashan)
      wałši?ał=<u>*s*</u>   'I went home.'
      ?unaak=<u>*s*</u>*-i:š̌*   'I have a friend.'
      ʕiihši=<u>*s*</u>   'I cried.'
      ?uuyimłckʷi=<u>*s*</u> *c'u?ič.*   'I was born in winter.'
      waa?ałat=<u>*s*</u> *...*   'He said to <u>me</u>.'
                            Nakayama (2003: 195, 204, 166, 163, 192)

This pronominal enclitic is not simply a subject, object, absolutive, ergative, agent or patient. This is a hierarchical system, in which only one argument may be specified. If there is a first or second person, this referent takes precedence over a third person. If there is both a first and second person, the agent takes precedence over the patient (imperatives allow both). The system is thus 1, 2 > 3, agent > patient.

The hierarchy is maintained through the use of a suffix *-at*. Much like a passive in many languages, it functions to ensure that the discourse topic is cast as a core argument (overt or not). Speaker George Louie was describing how to make a canoe. One begins by looking for a cedar tree in the forest.

(27) Nuuchahnulth (Wakashan)

ɁuuwaɁat	*ḥumapt,*
Ɂu-wa-'at	ḥumapt
it-find-**SHIFT**	cedar.tree
'You find a cedar tree	
yacp'ičuɁat.	
yac-p'ič-u-'at.	
step-at.base.of.pole-MOM-**SHIFT**	
and then step up to the base of it.'	

HiistiɁat	*n'an'aan'ičat,*	*ɁustɁas*	*takqiinuɁat,*
hista-''iƛ-'at	n'an'a :n'ič-'at	Ɂust-'as	tak-qi :nu-'at
there-start.from-**SHIFT**	look-**SHIFT**	LOC-on.ground	facing-on.top.MOM-**SHIFT**
'You look it over from the ground to the top . . .'			

Nakayama (2003: 232–233)

The *-at* suffix was used here to indicate that though the cedar tree was a semantic goal, it was the discourse topic at this point in the discussion. The same suffix is used whenever a third person acts on a first or second.

(28) Nuuchahnulth shifter

waaɁaƛat-s . . .
wa :-'aƛ-'at=s
say-FINITE-SHIFT=1SG
'He said to **me** . . .' ('it was said to me')

Nakayama (2003: 192)

This suffix cannot be used if a first or second person acts on a third.

The two other Southern Wakashan languages, Nitinaht (Ditidat) and Makah, spoken to the south, also show hierarchical systems, maintained by suffixes cognate with the Nuuchahnulth *at*. Here the suffixes are also used pervasively to maintain topicality through discourse, as well as whenever a third person acts on a first or second. The hierarchical system has not penetrated quite as far as in Nuuchahnulth, however. When both first and second persons are present, both can be identified by clitics. The system is thus 1, 2 > 3.

There is only a hint of the hierarchy in the Wakashan language immediately to the north of Nuuchahnulth, Kwak'wala. Here subjects are identified by enclitics attached to the first element of the clause, and objects by suffixes on the predicate. The language does not show a hierarchical system like those of its Southern Wakashan relatives, but there is a significant gap in the pronominal object paradigm: there are no suffixes for first person objects. Periphrastic constructions are used in their place, built from a predicate 'come' for actions directed toward a first person, and 'go' for those directed toward a second or third. The other North Wakashan languages spoken still further to the north, Heiltsuk and Haisla, contain full sets of pronominal subject clitics and object suffixes, used in all combinations.

To the south of the Wakashan family is the Chimakuan language Quileute. Here, too, a hierarchical system can be seen, but it has not penetrated quite as deeply as in Wakashan, affecting only second persons: 2 > 3. If a third person acts on a second ('He saw you'), a passive suffix must be used, as in Wakashan ('you were seen'), though the forms of the markers are completely different.

To the east of the Wakashan and Chimakuan families is the Salishan family. Some Salishan languages also show hierarchical systems, those closest geographically to Nuuchahnulth. To the east along the Central Coast, Northern Straits and Klallam privilege first and second persons over third, again maintaining the hierarchy via obligatory passivization: 1, 2 > 3. Immediately to the north, Halkomelem and Squamish privilege just second persons over third: 2 > 3. Salishan languages beyond this area show no restrictions.

The distribution of the hierarchical systems of the Northwest is clearly areal. Nuuchahnulth is at the core, privileging first and second persons over third and, among first and second, agents over patients. Immediately adjacent languages privilege just first and second over third. Languages immediately beyond these privilege just second over third. The hierarchies in all of them are maintained by obligatory passivization, though the markers differ across family lines.

It is easy to see how this areal distribution could come about. In languages with subjects, various factors can enter into subject selection: person (first and second over third), humanness, animacy, givenness, identifiability, agency, etc., features associated with discourse topicality. A propensity to privilege first and second persons over third would be easily spread by bilinguals, becoming crystallized as a grammatical requirement to varying degrees (Mithun 2007b).

31.6.2.2   Northern California

Another hierarchical area occurs further south, but it developed in slightly different ways. The Chimariko, Yana, Yurok and Karuk languages of Northern California are genetically unrelated, but all exhibit hierarchical systems to some degree. The foundations of the pronominal systems differ from language to language, as do the forms of their markers. Chimariko shows basic agent/patient alignment, Yana and Yurok nominative/accusative alignment, and Karuk a mixture of the two.

In Chimariko, only one core argument is represented pronominally on any verb. First and second persons have priority over third; if both parties are speech act participants, the agent takes priority over the patient: 1, 2 > 3; agent > patient. The roles of first person arguments are distinguished by the shape of the pronominal affix: grammatical agents have one form and grammatical patients another. Thus 'I hit him' = 1SG.AGENT-hit, 'He hit me' = 1SG.PATIENT-hit and 'You hit me' = 2SG.AGENT-hit. Independent pronouns can be added for clarification.

In Yana, core arguments are represented by pronominal suffixes on verbs. Third persons are unmarked: 'I will eat it' = 'I will eat'. If a third person agent is involved in a transitive event, however, an element -*wa* appears in the pronominal suffix complex. Its source survives in modern Yana as a passive marker. The only way to say 'he hit me' is literally 'I was hit'; 'he hit you' is literally 'you were hit'. When both arguments are speech act participants (1/2, 2/1), the suffix includes -*wa:*- plus a patient subject pronominal. The verb meaning 'I love you' is essentially 'you are loved'. Such sentences are no longer necessarily interpreted as passives, however: they may contain overt lexical agents. (Other elements have since been added to the suffix complexes, so they are no longer identical with passive constructions.)

The Yurok language is spoken in the same area as Chimariko and Yana, but it is not related to either. It is Algic, remotely related to Algonquian. Yurok indicative verbs carry pronominal suffixes identifying their core arguments. The system appears to show a nominative/accusative basis. The same pronominal suffixes appear in intransitives ('go slowly', 'be in pain') and transitives ('hear someone'). Some of the transitive pronominals are still transparent combinations of an object marker followed by a subject marker.

But not all core arguments are represented overtly in all combinations. Third person transitive patients are often not expressed at all. The pronominal inflection of 'we hear them', for example, contains no object marker for 'them': the form is the same as that for 'we hear'. Third person transitive agents are also sometimes not overtly represented. The form for 'he meets me' contains no 'he'. Such verbs do, however, show an extra element -*y*-. Its source is clear: a passive marker. Together these observations suggest a hierarchical system based on person priorities. The hierarchy has not penetrated the entire transitive paradigm, however. For some transitive combinations, there are choices between a marker overtly specifying both arguments and a passive formation. Taken together, the endings reflect a hierarchy 1PL > 2 > 3SG > 3PL. The strategies apparently used to achieve the priorities in Yurok are reminiscent of those in Yana: omission of some third person transitive patients and passivization in certain contexts. The Yurok pronominal suffixes, like those in Yana, do not constitute a regular, synchronic system, however. They reflect earlier priorities whose traces have become frozen in the pronominal strings.

Karuk is spoken directly to the east of Yurok. Core arguments are identified by pronominal prefixes on verbs. First person prefixes distinguish subjects and objects, though Bright (1957: 59) notes that one set of intransitive verb stems allows object forms, suggesting an incipient agent/patient pattern: 'be hungry', 'be jealous', 'be afraid', 'bleed', 'be thin, lose weight', 'defecate', 'be cross-eyed', 'fall asleep', 'be tired', 'burn oneself', 'be hot', 'feel pain', 'thirst for', 'be sick', 'have good luck with', 'be unwilling, lazy, tired', 'be cross-eyed', 'be bald', 'be nervous, cranky, fretful', 'be late, be offended', etc. But only one argument can be expressed within a Karuk verb. The choice of argument depends on person and number. Traces of a person hierarchy similar to those in Chimariko, Yana and Yurok can be perceived. First and second persons are always chosen over third: 1, 2 > 3. When a first or second person acts on a third, the third person is omitted, as in the other languages. Second person plurals have priority over all other participants: 2PL > 1 > 2SG > 3.

When a third person acts on a second person (3/2), the prefix refers to the second person, but a suffix -*ap* appears on the verb. There is no passive construction in modern Karuk (Macaulay 1992; 2000: 475), but the distribution of the *ap* suffix suggests that it may have had a passive origin. The suffix appears in clauses describing transitive events in which the semantic agent would normally be viewed as less topical or lower on a person hierarchy than the semantic patient, such as 'A monster is going to eat you' or 'They do not like you'. Lexical agents in such constructions also carry a special postposition *ʔi:n*, labelled an agentive marker by Bright, suggestive of an earlier oblique marker for passive agents. The postposition occurs only in clauses describing semantically transitive events.

The four languages in this area of California thus share hierarchical alignment, but there is no shared substance, and the systems differ in detail and in entrenchment. As on the Northwest Coast, a propensity to privilege speech act participants over others was apparently spread across languages by bilinguals. What was transferred was not a grammatical structure, but rather a behaviour pertaining to preferred choices among constructions already available in the languages. Over time the stylistic tendencies became crystallized in grammar, in different constructions with similar effects.

31.6.3   From Posture to Aspect

Evidence of the gradual development of grammatical patterns stimulated by contact can be seen in another cluster of constructions in the Southeast. A striking areal trait is the propensity of speakers to specify the posture or position of entities, typically 'sitting', 'standing (vertical)', 'lying (horizontal)' and often 'moving'.

(29) Creek (Muskogean)
    Ci:pâ:na:t hî:cit á:leykatí:s.   'The boy was (<u>sitting</u>) there watching.'
    Afánna:kit <u>siho:katí:s</u>.   'They were (<u>standing</u>) looking around.'
    Ísti hámkit inókki:t <u>wâ:kkati:s</u>.   'A man was (<u>lying</u>) sick.'
    Icinɬapí:t <u>aɬi:ⁿpayeys</u> o:mí:s.   'I (<u>go about</u>) opposing you.'
                   Haas and Hill (2015: 39, 26, 685), Martin (2011: 354)

(30) Quapaw (Siouan)
    datą <u>mįkhé</u>   'I am (<u>sitting</u>) drinking'
    wákiwébdabdá <u>thą́he</u> mą́.   'I was (<u>standing</u>) working for him.'
    Áwittąwe ažątta <u>mįkhe</u>.   'I will be (<u>lying</u>) watching you.'
    Kóišǫ́ttą ekíži bdé <u>ttánihé</u>. 'So I am going to go (<u>moving</u>) somewhere else.'
                         Rankin (2005: 484, 459, 467, 458)

(31) Biloxi (Siouan)
    Kʰǫni naxé <u>nąki</u>.   'His mother was (<u>sitting</u>) listening.'
    Skákʰanadi naxé <u>nédi</u>. 'The opossum (<u>stood</u>) listening.'
    Te ǫ <u>mąkí</u>.   'He was (<u>lying</u>) dead.'
    Nkákitupé nka<u>dédi</u>.   'I was (<u>moving</u>) carrying it on my shoulder.'
                Dorsey and Swanton (1912: 28, 26, 275, 150)

(32) Natchez (isolate)
    O:ya sanaskuk <u>kaséNcik</u>.   'He was (<u>sitting</u>) eating persimmons.'
    Waskupe: sewetik <u>sucik</u>.   'The dog was (<u>lying</u>) dead.'
    ŠinakaY <u>suhtik</u>.   'He was (<u>going</u>) carrying it on his back.'
                              Mary Haas (p.c.)

(33) Tunica (isolate)
    Sáku-hk-ʔuná-ni.   'He was (<u>sitting</u>) eating.'
    Látīhč hέr-ʔunaná-ni. 'At night they kept watch (<u>sitting</u>).'
    Léhpi-<u>náuni</u>-hk-éni.   'They two (alligators) were (<u>lying</u>) blocking it.'
    ʔusólʔu<u>wáni</u>.   'He was (<u>going</u>) creeping up on it.'
                             Haas (1946: 50, 51)

(34) Chitimacha (isolate)
    Waʔaš his kečmi:k' <u>hiʔin</u>.   'He was (<u>sitting</u>) waiting for the others.'
    Him yaʔa ni wopmi:k' ʔap ču:k'š čikin
                        'I've come (<u>standing</u>) to ask for your daughter'
    Weʸ nekaš kap nu:pkš <u>pen</u>.   'That devil <u>lay</u> dead.'
    Ku:kš mi:pk <u>pentka</u>, . . .   'Although he <u>lay</u> drunk, [he wanted more].'
    Swadesh (1946: 332, 322), texts A35d, A49b from Daniel Hieber (p.c.)

(35) Atakapa (isolate)
    <u>Ké</u>-ukámškinto.   'I am (<u>seated</u>) paddling.'
    Náu <u>tá</u>-uwalwálekit. 'The feather is (<u>standing</u>) waving.'
    Iškalít-<u>núl</u>-wilwílhiento 'I rock a child (<u>lying down</u>).'
                      Gatschet and Swanton (1932: 64, 123, 94)

In most of the languages, the posture is indicated by an auxiliary construction.

(36) Quapaw (Siouan)
Wákiwébdabdá   *thą́he*   *mą́.*
o-wá-ki-wé-wa-da-wa-dá   wa-thą́-he   wa-ʔą́
V1–1SG.AGT-BEN-INDEF-1SG.AGT-work   1SG.AGT-<u>stand</u>.CONT
                                                   1SG.AGT-do.IMPF

'I was (<u>standing</u>) working for him.'
                                                        Rankin (2005: 459)

(37) Biloxi (Siouan)
Nkį́txa   *nkákitupé*   *nkadédi*
nkį-txa   nka-kitupe   nka-de-di
1SG.PAT-alone   1SG.AGT-carry.on.shoulder   1SG.AGT-<u>go</u>-M.DECL
'I carried it (<u>moving</u>) on my shoulder alone.'
                                             Dorsey and Swanton (1912: 150)

(38) Creek (Muskogean)
Łałó pasáti:pít   *akhoyłĩ:pin.*
łałó   pasát-i:p-í-t   ak-hoy-łĩ:p-i-n.
fish   kill-SPONT-I-SAME.SUBJECT   in.water-<u>stand</u>-SPONT-I-DIFF.
SUBJ
'He was <u>standing</u> there killing fish.'
                                                        Martin (2004: 279)

(39) Chitimacha (isolate)
Ni:ki:k'   *peken.*
nii:k-i:k'   pe-ke-n
sick-PARTICIPLE.SAME.SUBJECT   <u>lie</u>-1SG-CONT
'I am (<u>lying</u>) sick.'
                                                     Swadesh (1939: 238)

These constructions are not exactly equivalent. All contain a lexical verb followed by an inflected auxiliary. In the Siouan languages, the lexical verb is also inflected, in Muskogean it is not inflected but it ends in a same-subject linker, and in Chitimacha it is a same-subject participle. Swadesh notes that the Chitimacha neutral 'sit' auxiliary *hi(h)* had begun to contract: it 'often loses its initial *h* and amalgamates with a preceding participle when the latter ends in -*š* (an optional element in participles), e.g. *teyk'š hin* > *teyk'šin* "he is seated"' (1939: 25.47). In Atakapa the positionals are generally loosely attached verbal prefixes.

(40) Atakapa
<u>*Kéukámškinto.*</u>
ke-u-kam-š-kint-o
<u>sit</u>-HAB-paddle-be-CONT-1SG.AGT
'I am (<u>seated</u>) paddling.'

                                         Gatschet and Swanton (1932: 64)

In Tunica they are now an integral part of the verb word, which consists of a bare lexical root followed by the inflected positional.

(41)　Tunica
　　　Látīhč　　　　*hɛ́r-ʔunaná-ni.*
　　　at.night　　　watch-sit.M.DU-HEARSAY
　　　'At night they kept watch (sitting).'

Haas (1946: 50)

The auxiliaries do not necessarily match such independent lexical verbs as 'sit', 'stand', 'lie' in form. Specification of position is not unknown elsewhere in the world. Many of the examples above have English counterparts ('they sat waiting'). The pervasiveness of the postural auxiliaries across the Southeast suggests an areal trait, however. In a series of works, Rankin (1977, 1978, 2004, 2011) has demonstrated that it originated in the Siouan family. The positional roots 'sit', 'stand (animate)', 'stand (inanimate)', 'lie' and 'move' can be reconstructed for Proto-Siouan. In the modern Muskogean languages, positionals are used in similar ways, but they are not generally cognate across the family.

(42)　Muskogean positional verbs

'sit'	SINGULAR	DUAL	PLURAL
Choctaw-Chickasaw	*binili*	*chiiya*	*binoh-* (ANIMATE)
	talaya	*taloha*	*taloh-* (INANIMATE)
Creek-Seminole	*léykita*	*káákita*	*apóókita*
Hitchiti-Mikasuki	*čokooli-*	*wiik-*	*iił-*
Alabama-Koasati	*čokooka-*	*čikiika*	*čikka, iisa*
'stand'			
Choctaw-Chickasaw	*hikiya*	*hiili*	*(hi)yoh-*
Creek-Seminole	*hoyíłita*	*sihóókita*	*sapááklìta*
Hitchiti-Mikasuki	*hačaali-*	*lokooka-*	*lokooka-*
Alabama-Koasati	*hačaali-*	*hikiili-*	*lokooli-*
'lie'			
Choctaw-Chickasaw	*ittola*	*kaha*	*kah-*
Creek-Seminole	*wakkita*	*wakhokita*	*lomhita*
Hitchiti-Mikasuki	*talaaka-*	*šolka-*	*šolka-*
Alabama-Koasati	*balaaka*	*balka-*	

Rankin (1978)

The mismatches across the languages suggest that the distinction came into Muskogean after they had diverged. Positional distinctions were replicated from different native resources. Rankin provides detailed discussion of the formations. Choctaw and Chickasaw singular and plural *binili* and *binohli* 'sit' are derived from a noun denoting a type of abode: *bina(h)* 'lodge, tent, camp'. The Hitchiti-Mikasuki *čokoo(l)-* and Alabama-Koasati *čokoo(ka)-* 'dwell, sit' came from the Proto-Muskogean **čokk-* 'house'. Choctaw and Chickasaw contain verbs derived from this noun, but they mean 'enter' and are not part of the positional paradigm. The Choctaw-Chickasaw dual *čiiya* is the passive form of the verb *celi* 'to bear, bring forth young', so 'to enter' or 'to exist'. Rankin notes that the use of verbs meaning 'be born' as auxiliaries is also characteristic of the Alabama-Koasati 'sit' positionals. The Creek cognates of these forms mean 'enter', and are not positionals.

The modern Choctaw 'stand' plurals *hiyohli* and *hiyohmaáya* originated as duals containing the dual marker *-oh-*. The modern dual *hiili* is based on the same root *hi-* 'upright' with the active suffix *-li*. The Koasati singular, dual and plural positionals for 'stand' were formed from three different roots. All of the Hitchiti-Mikasuki and Alabama-Koasati non-singular positionals are based on a Common Muskogean root **lokoo-* 'be in a group'. Cognates in Creek, Choctaw and Chickasaw are not positional in meaning: Choctaw *lukoli* 'to collect, flock, cluster, huddle', Creek *loyétv* 'to fill (as a container)'. Rankin reconstructs the ancestor of the Creek plural 'stand' as **(i)si-apaak-lita* 'to have or hold together in a group'. Both the Choctaw inanimate 'sit' positionals and the Hitchiti-Mikasuki singular 'lie' are traced to a general locative verb 'remain, be fixed'.

The various 'lie' positionals developed from verbs of falling, crawling, placing and grouping. The Choctaw singular *ittol-* comes from the verb *ittola* 'fall, remain, lie'. Creek has a cognate *tóletv* 'fall'. The Choctaw dual and plural *kah-* are based on the root *kah-* 'lie, fall down'. Creek has cognates outside the auxiliary system, with the suppletive plural *kááyita* 'to lay eggs, have young'. Rankin reconstructs the common ancestor as 'put, place'. The Hitchiti-Mikasuki singular 'lie' positional *talaakom* is cognate with the Choctaw *talaya, taloha* 'sit', a more general locational. The Hitchiti dual and plural 'lie' positional *sol(k)-* is cognate with Creek *sulkii* 'many, much, a herd'. The Alabama-Koasati 'lie' positional *bal(a)-* matches the regular Choctaw and Chickasaw verbs *bala-li* 'crawl, creep'.

Positionals occur in other constructions as well. They appear in existential/presentative/locational constructions throughout the area: 'There is a house (sitting) over there', 'There is a stream (lying) over there', etc. They occur in possessive constructions. They also mark aspect. Already in Proto-Siouan, they had undergone grammaticalization to durative or continuative markers.

(43)   Osage Dhegiha (Siouan)

Awáachi	*ąhé.*	*awáachie*
a-waachi	ąðįhé	wa-waachi-ðe
1SG.AGT-dance	1SG.CONT.moving	1SG.AGT-dance-DECL
'I'm dancing.'		'I danced'.

Quintero (2004: 312)

Quintero notes that in Osage, all positionals can serve as basic continuatives distinguishing position, but individual forms have taken on specialized implications: 'moving' auxiliaries imply that the action has been

ongoing for some time, and the 'standing' continuative can convey immi-
nence, being on the verge of undertaking an activity (2004: 315).

The positional aspect markers now co-occur with lexical positional verbs.

(44) Biloxi (Siouan)
  a. *Xe   nǫki.*
     sit   sitting.CONT
     'She is sitting (sitting).'
  b. *Tox   mǫki.*
     lie   lying.CONT
     'He was lying (lying).'
  c. *Sįhįx ne.*
     stand stand.CONT
     'It was standing (standing).'

Einaudi (1976: 154)

Kaufman (2013: 298) notes that in Biloxi, certain positionals were coming
to be routinely associated with particular entities: the sun, forests, lakes
and villages sit; rain, hens and rivers lie; thunder moves.

Similar developments have occurred elsewhere in the Southeast to
varying degrees. In some languages, all of the positionals serve as durative/
continuative/progressive markers. In others, just one or two have become
specialized in this function.

(45) Creek (Muskogean)
  a. *Im-ititâ:k-aha:ni-t*   *apô:ki-t*   *ó:-s.*
     DAT.APPL-get.ready-going.   sit.PL-SAME.   be-INDIC
     to-SAME.SUBJECT   SUBJECT
     'They're [sitting waiting] going to get ready.'
  b. *Ahî:ci-t*   *leyk-icki-n*   *yéyc-al-i:-s*
     watch-SAME.SUBJECT   sit.SG-2SG.AGT   arrive.SG-FUT-DUR-INDIC
     'Keep [sit] looking, and they'll come.'
  c *Ahkopan-î:t-t*   *ał-ĭ:ⁿp-at-i:-s.*
     play-SPONT-SS   go.about.SG-SPONTANEOUS-ANT-DUR-INDIC
     'He kept on playing.'

Martin (2011: 304, 304, 443)

Martin notes that in their aspectual use, the forms based on 'sit' need not
involve actual sitting. The aspectual auxiliary in (46) based on *apô:k* 'sit PL'
could be translated as 'settled down'.

(46) Creek (Muskogean)
  Opán-ka-ta:t   *tâyi:*   *hĭ:ⁿi-n*   *opa:ni-t*
  dance.GER-FOC   be-DUR   very-DIFF.SUBJ   dance-SAME.SUBJ
  apô:ki-t   *ómho:yi-n ...*
  sit.PL-SAME.SUBJ   be-DIFF.SUBJ
  'And as they were really beginning to dance, [he sat down].'

Martin (2011: 304)

The Natchez aspectual use of auxiliaries is less developed, but beginnings can be seen. The motion verb 'be about' could be spatial in meaning or temporal below.

(47) Natchez (isolate)

ʔohoti:nuhc	cu:tahaw	pološaL	šupitine …
ʔohoti:nuh-c	cu:tahaw	polo-š-al-k	šu-piti-ne
wildcat-ERG	rail	split-HEARSAY-AUX-CONN	HEARSAY-be.about-WHEN

'When Wildcat was <u>around</u> splitting rails, so it is said, [Turkey arrived].'

Kimball (2005: 386)

The Tunica positionals 'sit' and 'lie' are also used as aspectual markers. With a basic verb they are stative or durative. With habitual aspect they function as progressives.

(48) Tunica (isolate)

kátăn, …	títihtʔɛ	hopíʔurahč
kátăn	títihtʔɛ	hopí-ʔúra-hč
where	river	get.out-M.SG.lie-SUBORD

'where a river came out'

Táwišīhč	híštaha	wíčihkʔaráni.
ta-wiši-hč-	híštahaki	wíči-hk-ʔara-áni
ART-water-F.SG	still	rise-HAB-F.SG.lie-HEARSAY

'The water <u>was</u> still <u>rising</u>.'

Haas (1941: 50)

The Chitimacha 'sit' (neutral), 'stand' (vertical) and 'lie' (horizontal) positionals are also exploited for aspectual meanings.

(49) Chitimacha

a.
ʔasi	nancʼipʼu	hikinakiš.
ʔasi	nahcʼipʼu	hi-ki=nk=i=š
man	small	sit-1SG.PAT-LOC=NZR-SUBORD

'When I was a boy'

b.
kʼihkite	hikin.
kʼiht-ki-te	hi-ki-n
want-1SG-PTCP	sit-1SG.AGT-CONT

'I am (<u>sitting</u>) wanting (it)'

c.
Teykʼiš	hiʔi.
tey-kʼiš	hi-ʔi
sit-PARTICIPLE.SAME	sit-3SG

'He just sat (<u>sitting</u>) there.'

d. *Nat'ik'iš pekin.*
nat'i-k'iš pe-kin
lie-PARTICIPLE.SAME lie-1SG
'I am (lying) lying down.'
Hieber (p.c.) from Swadesh texts A36d, A1b, A30d

The horizontal 'lie' auxiliary is often translated as an anterior.

(50) Chitimacha
a. Weʸ po: sek'is tapši:k' *či*
weʸ po: sekʔis tapši-k' Či
that plant among be.standing-PARTICIPIAL.SAME.SUBJECT stand
'She had stood among those plants.'
b. *Wetk kas tuhyt:k' peʔanki*
we-t-k ka tuhyte-:ik' pe-ʔe=nk=i
DEM-RFL-LOC back stoop-PARTICIPIAL lie-3SG=LOC-NZR
'When he had stooped down . . .'
Swadesh (1939: 234, 255, text A30e)

The co-occurrence of the auxiliary *hi-* 'sit' with the lexical verb *tey* 'sit', the auxiliary *či* 'stand' with the verb *tapši-* 'stand', and *pe-* with *nat'i-* 'lie' confirm their aspectual function.

The Chitimacha positionals have become still further grammaticalized as elements of the verbal continuative aspect suffix, which consists of a continuative element *-ʔiš-* plus a positional.

(51) Chitimacha continuative
Kow-ʔiš-čiʔi-í
call-CONT-standing-3SG
'He stood calling.'
Swadesh (1939: 239)

Swadesh (1933) notes that the vertical ('standing') positional has developed a refined or respectful connotation, and the horizontal ('lying') a derogatory or disrespectful one.

The distribution of postural/positional constructions through the Southeast raises intriguing questions about the mechanisms behind the development of such areal traits. Postural distinctions originated in the Siouan languages and were well-established in existential/locational, possessive, auxiliary, aspectual and demonstrative constructions in those languages in the Southeast. Speakers of other Southeastern languages apparently replicated the distinctions using native material. But without a philological record, the relative timing of developments can only be a matter of conjecture.

It is not uncommon cross-linguistically for postural verbs to develop into continuative/durative/progressive markers. Such developments have been noted for Ngambay, Diegueño, Alyawarra, Imonda, Kxoe,

Tatar, Tamil, Diola-Fogny, Mamvy, Nobiin, Tibetan and Kabyle, in addition to Siouan (Blansitt 1975; Bybee et al. 1994; Heine 1993; Kuteva 2001). Kuteva proposes a sit/stand/lie auxiliation chain, with examples from Swedish, Norwegian, Danish, Dutch and Bulgarian (2001: 43–74). The postural verbs are first used with human subjects to specify the orientation of the human body in space ('She is (sitting) over there'). Their meanings include inherent stative semantics, or temporal 'unboundedness'. They can also appear in coordinate bi-clausal structures with co-referential subjects ('She is sitting on the couch and writing a letter'). Next they are extended to express the canonical spatial position of physical objects ('The clothes are (sitting) in the corridor'). Finally the inherent temporal unboundedness becomes a focal feature, yielding continuative/durative/progressive markers (perhaps first with inanimates and then animates), and the bi-clausal structure is reanalysed as monoclausal.

Each of these stages persists in the Southeastern languages. Any of them could have occurred in any of the languages in isolation. Given the geographical distribution, however, it is more likely that each was stimulated and/or facilitated by contact. Bilinguals may have begun by simply increasing the frequency of postural specification, with constructions that already existed in the languages. Specification via auxiliary constructions was not a big step, since auxiliary constructions already existed in the languages at various stages of development (cf. Munro 1985 on Muskogean). The Atakapa positional prefixes may have been stimulated by contact with the neighbouring Caddo, which contains stem-initial sit/stand/lie postural elements, cognate with other Caddoan languages out of the area (Chafe 2005: 432; David Rood p.c.).

The result is what Heine and Kuteva (2005: 5.2.1) term a 'grammaticalization area': 'a group of geographically contiguous languages that have undergone the same grammaticalization process as a result of language contact.'

31.7 Conclusion

North America, with its vast territory, large numbers of languages and genetic units, and diversity of environmental, social, cultural and linguistic situations, provides an excellent arena for investigating the development of linguistic areas. The strongest areas have emerged out of long-term, intensive contact among small communities, in relatively densely populated areas with long-standing intermarriage practices and multilingualism. Significantly, the traits that characterize these areas go against many expectations about the relative ease of borrowing:

vocabulary > sounds > sound patterns > syntax > morphology. They generally show little lexical borrowing, but often extensive parallelisms in abstract structures that are deeply embedded in grammar. At least two kinds of factors might be responsible.

The first kind are social and cognitive. In many areas of North America, there was a marked absence of extensive code-switching: so far as is known, bilinguals worked hard to keep their languages apart, often for social reasons. In some cases language was viewed as a sign of identity, while in others it was simply socially appropriate to speak the language of the community one was in. In both cases, attention was paid to those aspects of language most accessible to consciousness, particularly vocabulary choice. Second language speakers tend to focus on vocabulary as well. Less attention was paid to tightly integrated grammatical constructions, particularly morphology, which tend to be less accessible to consciousness and less isomorphic across unrelated languages.

The second kind of factors involve the duration of contact. Some parallelisms can develop relatively rapidly. A bilingual may copy an inclusive/exclusive distinction in first person pronouns by simply combining existing first and second person forms to create a new inclusive form. Language learners may reanalyse a nominative/accusative system as agent/patient or vice versa. Other parallelisms can develop more gradually, often in layers. The early spread of predicate-initial order can set the stage for certain kinds of complement constructions, like the negation on the Northwest Coast. The early spread of predicate-final order could facilitate the parallel development of auxiliary constructions. Grammatical parallelism can also arise simply from recurring patterns of expression. Language communities differ not only in what speakers are required to specify, but in what they tend to express most often. Bilinguals might easily carry a propensity for elaboration of manner, location or posture from one to another, exploiting native lexical resources. They might carry over relative frequencies of stylistic alternatives like subject selection without violating grammatical norms. The recurring choices can become routinized and undergo further integration into the grammar. Such grammaticalization processes could occur in any of the languages in isolation, but they can also be stimulated by ongoing contact, as speakers extend the uses of constructions in one language on the model of the other, like specification of position to continuative aspect in the Southeast.

There is much we will never know about the circumstances underlying the emergence of linguistic areas, but we continue to discover routes by which they can develop.

References

Andrade, Manuel J., 1933. *Quileute*. In Franz Boas (ed.), 1933–1938, *Handbook of American Indian Languages*, part 3, pp. 149–292. Glückstadt, Hamburg and New York: J. J. Augustin.

Aoki, Haruo, 1962. Nez Perce and Northern Sahaptin: A binary comparison. *International Journal of American Linguistics* 28: 172–182.

Beck, David, 2000. Grammatical convergence and the genesis of diversity in the Northwest Coast Sprachbund. *Anthropological Linguistics* 42 (2): 147–213.

Bereznak, Catherine, 1995. *The Pueblo Region as a Linguistic Area: Diffusion among the Indigenous Languages of the Southwest United States*. Unpublished PhD thesis, Louisiana State University.

Blansitt, E. L., 1975. Progressive aspect. *Working Papers on Language Universals* 18: 1–34.

Boas, Franz, 1921. Ethnology of the Kwakiutl. *Bureau of American Ethnology Annual Report 35, for the Years 1913–1914*. Washington.

Boas, Franz, 1947. *Kwakiutl Grammar*, edited by Helene Boas Yampolsky. Transactions of the American Philosophical Society, vol. 37.2.

Boas, Franz and Ella Deloria, 1941. *Dakota Grammar*. Memoirs of the National Academy of Sciences, vol. XXIII.2. Washington, DC: Government Printing Office.

Booker, Karen M., 1980. *Comparative Muskogean: Aspects of Proto-Muskogean Verb Morphology*. Unpublished PhD thesis, University of Kansas.

Booker, Karen M., 1991. *Languages of the Aboriginal Southeast: An Annotated Bibliography*. Native American Bibliography Series, vol. 15. Metuchen, NJ: Scarecrow Press.

Booker, Karen M., 2005. Muskogean historical phonology. In Hardy and Scancarelli (eds), pp. 246–298.

Booker, Karen M., Charles Hudson and Robert Rankin, 1992. Place name identification and multilingualism in the sixteenth-century Southeast. *Ethnohistory* 39: 399–451.

Brain, Jeffrey P., George Roth and Willem J. de Reuse, 2004. Tunica, Biloxi, and Ofo. In Fogelson (ed.), pp. 586–597.

Bright, William, 1957. *The Karok Language*. University of California Publications in Linguistics, vol. 13.

Bright, William, 1959. Review of The Yurok language, by R. H. Robins. *Language* 35: 100–104.

Brown, James A., 2004. Exchange and interaction until 1500. In Fogelson (ed.), pp. 677–685.

Bybee, Joan, Revere Perkins and William Pagliuca, 1994. *The Evolution of Grammar: Tense, Aspect and Modality in the Languages of the World*. Chicago: University of Chicago Press.

Byington, Cyrus, 1915. *A Dictionary of the Choctaw Language*, edited by John R. Swanton and Henry Halbert. Washington, DC: Government Printing

Office. 1973 reprint, Oklahoma City, OK: Oklahoma City Indian Calendar, Inc.

Callaghan, Catherine, 1964. Phonemic borrowing in Lake Miwok. In William Bright (ed.), *Studies in Californian Linguistics*, pp. 46–53. University of California Publications in Linguistics, vol. 34. Berkeley, CA: University of California Press.

Callaghan, Catherine, 1987. Lake Miwok naturalization of borrowed phonemes. In Brian Joseph and Arnold Zwicky (eds), *A Festschrift for Ilse Lehiste*, pp. 84–93. Working Papers in Linguistics, vol. 35. Columbus, OH: Ohio State University Department of Linguistics.

Callaghan, Catherine, 1991. Climbing a low mountain. In Sandra Chung and Jorge Hankamer (eds), *A Festschrift for William F. Shipley*, pp. 47–59. Santa Cruz: Syntax Research Center, University of California.

Campbell, Lyle, 1997. *American Indian Languages: The Historical Linguistics of Native America*. Oxford: Oxford University Press.

Chafe, Wallace, 2005. Caddo. In Hardy and Scancarelli (eds), pp. 323–350.

Conathan, Lisa, 2004. *The Linguistic Ecology of Northwestern California: Contact, Functional Convergence and Dialectology*. PhD dissertation, University of California, Berkeley.

Crawford, James, 1975. Southeastern Indian languages. In James M. Crawford (ed.), *Studies in Southeastern Indian Languages*, pp. 1–120. Athens, GA: University of Georgia Press.

Dayley, Jon, 1989. *Tümpisa (Panamint) Shoshone Grammar*. University of California Publications in Linguistics, vol. 115. Berkeley, CA: University of California Press.

De Laguna, Frederica, 1990. Tlingit. In Suttles (ed.), pp. 203–228.

DeLancey, Scott, 1996. Penutian in the bipartite stem belt: Disentangling areal and genetic correspondences. In *Proceedings of the Twenty-Second Annual Meeting of the Berkeley Linguistics Society: Special Session on Historical Topics in Native American Languages*, pp. 37–54.

Dorsey, James Owen and John R. Swanton, 1912. *A Dictionary of the Biloxi and Ofo Languages, Accompanied with Thirty-one Biloxi Texts and Numerous Biloxi Phrases*. Bureau of American Ethnology Bulletin, vol. 47. Washington, DC: Smithsonian Institution.

Dunn, John, 1995. *Sm'algyax: A Reference Dictionary and Grammar for the Coast Tsimshian Language*. Seattle, WA: University of Washington/Sealaska Heritage Foundation.

Einaudi, Paula, 1976. *A Grammar of Biloxi*. New York: Garland

Elmendorf, William W. and A. L. Kroeber, 1960. The structure of Twana culture. Washington State University Research Studies 28.3: Monographic Supplement 2. Pullman. Reprinted 1992 in *Coast Salish and Western Washington Indians IV*, Seattle, WA: Washington State University Press.

Epps, Patience, Na'ama Pat-El and John Huehnergard (eds), 2013. *Contact among Genetically Related Languages*. Special issue of *Journal of Language Contact* 6 (2).

Fogelson, Raymond D., 2004a. Cherokee in the East. In Fogelson (ed.), pp. 337–353.

Fogelson, Raymond D. (ed.), 2004b. *Handbook of North American Indians,* vol. 14: *Southeast.* Washington, DC: Smithsonian Institution.

Ford, Richard, 1983. Inter-Indian exchange in the Southwest. In Ortiz (ed.), pp. 711–722.

Frachtenberg, Leo, 1922. Siuslawan (Lower Umpqua). In Franz Boas (ed.), *Handbook of American Indian Languages,* part 2, pp. 431–629. Washington, DC: Government Printing Office.

Galloway, Patricia and Jason Baird Jackson, 2004. Natchez and neighboring groups. In Fogelson (ed.), pp. 598–615.

Galloway, Patricia and Clara Sue Kidwell, 2004. Choctaw in the East. In Fogelson (ed.), pp. 499–519.

Gatschet, Albert S. and John R. Swanton, 1932. *A Dictionary of the Atakapa Language, Accompanied by Text Material.* Bureau of American Ethnology Bulletin, vol. 108. Washington, DC: Smithsonian Institution.

Haas, Mary R., 1941. Tunica. In Franz Boas (ed.), *Handbook of American Indian Languages,* pp. 159–204. Bureau of American Ethnology Bulletin, vol. 40.1. New York: J. J. Augustin.

Haas, Mary R., 1946. A grammatical sketch of Tunica. In *Linguistic Structures of Native America,* pp. 337–366. Viking Fund Publications in Anthropology, vol. 6. New York: Wenner-Gren.

Haas, Mary R., 1950. Tunica texts. *University of California Publications in Linguistics* 6 (1): 1–174.

Haas, Mary R., 1953. Tunica dictionary. *University of California Publications in Linguistics* 6 (2): 175–332.

Haas, Mary R., 1967. Language and taxonomy in northwestern California. *American Anthropologist* 96: 358–362.

Haas, Mary R., 1969. *The Prehistory of Languages.* The Hague: Mouton.

Haas, Mary R., 1970. Consonant symbolism in northwestern California: A problem in diffusion. In Earl H. Swanson Jr (ed.), *Languages and Cultures of Western North America: Essays in Honor of Sven S. Liljeblad,* pp. 86–89. Pocatello: Idaho State University Press.

Haas, Mary R., 1971. Southeastern Indian linguistics. In Charles Hudson (ed.), *Red, White, and Black: Symposium on Indians in the Old South.* Southern Anthropological Society Proceedings, vol. 5. Athens, GA: University of Georgia Press.

Haas, Mary R., 1973. The Southeast. In Thomas Sebeok (ed.), *Linguistics in North America,* pp. 1210–1249. Current Trends in Linguistics, vol. 10. The Hague: Mouton. Reprinted in 1976 in Thomas Sebeok (ed.), *Native Languages of the Americas,* pp. 121–152. The Hague: Mouton.

Haas, Mary R., 1976. The Northern California linguistic area. In Margaret Langdon and Shirley Silver (eds), *Hokan Studies: Papers from the First Conference on Hokan Languages,* pp. 347–359. The Hague: Mouton.

Haas, Mary R., 1979. Southeastern languages. In Lyle Campbell and Marianne Mithun (eds), *The Languages of Native North America*, pp. 299–326. Austin, TX: University of Texas Press.

Haas, Mary R. and James H. Hill, 2015. *Creek Texts*, edited and translated by Jack B. Martin, Margaret McKane Mauldin and Juanita McGirt. Berkeley, CA: University of California Press.

Hajda, Yvonne, 1984. Regional social organization in the Greater Lower Columbia. Paper read at the Annual Meeting of the American Anthropological Association, Chicago.

Hardy, Heather and Janine Scancarelli (eds), 2005. *Native Languages of the Southeastern United States*. Lincoln, NE: University of Nebraska Press.

Heaton, Raina, 2013. Active/stative agreement in Tunica. Manuscript, University of Hawai'i.

Heine, Bernd, 1993. *Auxiliaries: Cognitive Forces and Grammaticalization*. New York: Oxford University Press.

Heine, Bernd and Tania Kuteva, 2005. *Language Contact and Grammatical Change*. Cambridge: Cambridge University Press.

Heizer, Robert (ed.), 1978. *Handbook of North American Indians,* vol. 8: *California*. Washington: Smithsonian Institution.

Hickey, Raymond, 2010. Language contact: Reconsideration and reassessment. In Raymond Hickey (ed.), *The Handbook of Language Contact*, pp. 1–28. Oxford: Blackwell.

Hickey, Raymond, 2012. Early English and the Celtic hypothesis. In Terttu Nevalainen and Elizabeth Closs Traugott (eds), *The Oxford Handbook on the History of English*, pp. 497–507. Oxford: Oxford University Press.

Hoijer, Harry, 1933. Tonkawa: An Indian language of Texas. In Franz Boas (ed.), 1933–1938, *Handbook of American Indian Languages*, part 3, pp. 1–148. Glückstadt, Hamburg and New York: J. J. Augustin.

Hymes, Dell, 1955. *The Language of the Kathlamet Chinook*. Unpublished PhD thesis, Indiana University.

Innes, Pamela, 2004. Creek in the West. In Fogelson (ed.), pp. 393–403.

Jacobs, Melville, 1954. The areal spread of sound features in the languages north of California. In *Papers from the Symposium on American Indian Linguistics Held at Berkeley, July 7, 1951*. University of California Publications in Linguistics, vol. 10.

Jacobsen, William H., 1969. Origin of the Nootka pharyngeals. *International Journal of American Linguistics* 35: 125–153.

Jacobsen, William H., 1980a. Inclusive/exclusive: A diffused pronominal category in native western North America. In *Proceedings of the Chicago Linguistic Society, Papers from the Parasession on Pronouns and Anaphora*, pp. 204–227.

Jacobsen, William., 1980b. Washo bipartite verb stems. In Kathryn Klar, Margaret Langdon and Shirley Silver (eds), *American Indian and Indoeuropean Studies*, pp. 85–100. The Hague: Mouton.

Jany, Carmen, 2009. *Chimariko Grammar: Areal and Typological Perspective*. University of California Publications in Linguistics, vol. 142.

Johanson, Lars, 2008. Remodeling grammar: Copying, conventionalization, grammaticalization. In Peter Siemund and Noemi Kintana (eds), *Language Contact and Contact Languages*, pp. 61–79. Hamburg Studies on Multilingualism, vol. 7. Amsterdam: John Benjamins.

Kaufman, David, 2013. Positional auxiliaries in Biloxi 1. *International Journal of American Linguistics* 79 (2): 283–299.

Kimball, Geoffrey, 2005. Natchez. In Hardy and Scancarelli (eds), pp. 385–453.

Kinkade, M. Dale, 1991. Prehistory of the Native languages of the Northwest Coast. In *Great Ocean Conference: The North Pacific to 1600*, pp. 37–158. Portland: Oregon Historical Society Press.

Kinkade, M. Dale, William H. Elmendorf, Bruce Rigsby and Haruo Aoki, 1998. Languages. In Walker (ed.), 49–72.

Kroskrity, Paul, 1982. Language contact and linguistic diffusion: The Arizona Tewa speech community. In F. Barkin, E. Brandt and J. Ornstein-Galicia (eds), *Bilingualism and Language Contact: Spanish, English, and Native American Languages*, pp. 51–72. New York: Teachers College Press.

Kuteva, Tania, 2001. *Auxiliation: An Enquiry into the Nature of Grammaticalization*. Oxford: Oxford University Press.

Langdon, Margaret, 1971. Sound symbolism in Yuman languages. In Jesse Sawyer (ed.), *Studies in American Indian Languages*, pp. 149–174. University of California Publications in Linguistics, vol. 65.

Lipkind, William, 1945. *Winnebago Grammar*. New York: King's Crown Press.

Macaulay, Monica, 1992. Inverse marking in Karuk: The function of the suffix -*ap*. *International Journal of American Linguistics* 58: 182–210.

Macaulay, Monica, 2000. Obviative marking in ergative contexts: The case of Karuk '*iin*. *International Journal of American Linguistics* 66: 464–498.

Martin, Jack B., 1994. Modeling language contact in the prehistory of the southeastern U.S. In Patricia Kwachka (ed.), *Perspectives on the Southeast: Linguistics, Archaeology, and Ethnohistory*, pp. 14–24, 143–163. Southern Anthropological Society Proceedings, vol. 27. Athens, GA: University of Georgia Press.

Martin, Jack, 2004. Languages. In Fogelson (ed.), pp. 68–86.

Martin, Jack B., 2011. *A Grammar of Creek (Muskogee)*. Lincoln, NE: University of Nebraska Press.

Matthews, G. Hubert, 1970. Notes on the Proto-Siouan continuants. *International Journal of American Linguistics* 36: 98–109.

May, Stephanie, 2004. Alabama and Koasati. In Fogelson (ed.), pp. 407–414.

Mithun, Marianne, 1991. Active/agentive case marking and its motivations. *Language* 67: 510–546.

Mithun, Marianne, 1997. Lexical affixes and morphological typology. In John Haiman, Joan Bybee and Sandra Thompson (eds), *Essays on Language Function and Language Type*, pp. 357–372. Amsterdam: John Benjamins.

Mithun, Marianne, 1999. *The Languages of Native North America*. Cambridge: Cambridge University Press.

Mithun, Marianne, 2007a. Grammar, contact, and time. *Journal of Language Contact, Thema* 1: 133–155.

Mithun, Marianne, 2007b. Integrating approaches to diversity: Argument structure on the Northwest Coast. In Yoshiko Matsumoto, David Oshima, Orrin Robinson and Peter Sells (eds), *Diversity in Language*, pp. 9–36. Stanford, CA: CSLI (Center for the Study of Language and Information).

Mithun, Marianne, 2008. The emergence of agentive systems. In Mark Donohue and Søren Wichmann (eds), *The Typology of Semantic Alignment Systems*, pp. 297–333. Oxford University Press.

Mithun, Marianne, 2012a. Morphologies in contact: Form, meaning, and use in the grammar of reference. In Thomas Stolz, Martine Vanhove, Hitomi Otsuka and Anna Urdzu (eds), *Morphologies in Contact*, pp. 15–36. Studia Typologica, vol. 10. Berlin: Akademie Verlag.

Mithun, Marianne, 2012b. Core argument patterns and deep genetic relations: Hierarchical systems in Northern California. In Pirkko Suihkonen, Bernard Comrie and Valery Solovyev (eds), *Typology of Argument Structure and Grammatical Relations*, pp. 257–294. Amsterdam: John Benjamins.

Mithun, Marianne, 2013. Challenges and benefits of contact among relatives: Morphological copying. *Journal of Language Contact* 6: 243–270.

Munro, Pamela, 1985. Auxiliaries and auxiliarization in Western Muskogean. In Jacek Fisiak (ed.), *Historical Syntax*, pp. 333–362. Berlin: Mouton de Gruyter.

Nakayama, Toshihide (ed.), 2003. *George Louie's Nuu-chah-nulth (Ahousaht) Texts with Grammatical Analysis*. Endangered Languages of the Pacific Rim, vol. A2-028. Kyoto: Nakanish.

Newman, Stanley, 1944. *Yokuts Language of California*. Viking Fund Publications in Anthropology, vol. 2. New York: Wenner-Gren.

Nichols, Johanna, 1971. Diminutive consonant symbolism in Western North America. *Language* 47 (4): 826–848.

Nichols, Johanna, 1992. *Linguistic Diversity in Space and Time*. Chicago: University of Chicago Press.

O'Neill, Sean, 2008. *Cultural Contact and Linguistic Relativity among the Indians of Northwestern California*. Norman, OK: University of Oklahoma Press.

Ortiz, Alfonso (ed.), 1983. *Handbook of North American Indians*, vol. 10: *Southwest*. Washington: Smithsonian Institution.

Parsons, Elsie Clews, 1939. *Pueblo Indian Religion*. Chicago: University of Chicago Press.

Quintero, Carolyn, 2004. *Osage Grammar*. Lincoln, NE: University of Nebraska Press.

Rankin, Robert L., 1977. From verb to auxiliary to noun classifier and definite article. Grammaticalization of the Siouan verbs 'sit', 'stand', 'lie'. In R. L. Brown et al. (eds), *Proceedings of the 1976 Mid-America Linguistics Conference*, pp. 273–283. St Paul, MN: Department of Linguistics, University of Minnesota.

Rankin, Robert L., 1978. On the origin of the classificatory verbs in Muskogean. Paper presented at the Annual meeting of the American Anthropological Association, Los Angeles.

Rankin, Robert L., 1987. Fricative ablaut in Choctaw and Siouan. Paper presented at the Kentucky Foreign Language Conference Session on the Southeast, Lexington.

Rankin, Robert L., 1988. Quapaw: Genetic and areal affiliations. In William Shipley (ed.), *In Honor of Mary Haas*, pp. 629–650. Berlin: Mouton de Gruyter.

Rankin, Robert, 2004. The history and development of Siouan positionals with special attention to polygrammaticalization in Dhegiha. *Sprachtypologie und Universalienforschung (STUF)* 2/3: 202–227.

Rankin, Robert L., 2005. Quapaw. In Hardy and Scancarelli (eds), pp. 454–498.

Rankin, Robert L., 2011. The Siouan enclitics: A beginning. Paper prepared for the Comparative Linguistics Workshop, University of Michigan, Ann Arbor.

Reichard, Gladys, 1938. Coeur d'Alene. In Franz Boas (ed.), 1933–1938, *Handbook of American Indian Languages*, part 3, pp. 517–707. Glückstadt, Hamburg and New York: J. J. Augustin.

Rigsby, Bruce and Michael Silverstein, 1969. Nez Perce vowels and Proto-Sahaptian vowel harmony. *Language* 45: 45–59.

Sapir, Edward, 1911. Diminutive and augmentative consonantism in Wishram. In Franz Boas (ed.), *Handbook of American Indian Languages*, part 1, pp. 638–645. Washington, DC: Government Printing Office.

Sapir, Edward, 1929. A study in phonetic symbolism. *Journal of Experimental Psychology* 12: 225–239. Reprinted in 1949 in D. G. Mandelbaum (ed.), *Selected Writings of Edward Sapir*, pp. 61–72. Berkeley, CA: University of California Press.

Scancarelli, Janine, 2005. Cherokee. In Hardy and Scancarelli (eds), pp. 351–384.

Sherzer, Joel, 1968. *An Areal-Typological Study of the American Indian Languages North of Mexico*. PhD dissertation, University of Pennsylvania, Philadelphia.

Sherzer, Joel, 1973. Areal linguistics in North America. In Thomas A. Sebeok (ed.), *Linguistics in North America*, pp. 749–795. Current Trends in Linguistics, vol. 10. The Hague: Mouton.

Sherzer, Joel, 1976. *An Areal-Typological Study of American Indian Languages North of Mexico*. Amsterdam: North Holland.

Shipley, William, 1963. *Maidu Texts and Dictionary*. University of California Publications in Linguistics, vol. 33. Berkeley, CA: University of California Press.

Sturtevant, William (ed.), 1988. *Handbook of North American Indians*, vol. 4: *History of Indian–White Relations*. Washington, DC: Smithsonian Institution.

Suttles, Wayne (ed.), 1990a. *Handbook of North American Indians*, vol. 7: *Northwest Coast*. Washington, DC: Smithsonian Institution.

Suttles, Wayne, 1990b. Introduction. In Suttles (ed.), pp. 1–15.

Swadesh, Morris, 1933. Chitimacha verbs of derogatory or abusive connotation with parallels from European languages. *Language* 9: 192–201.

Swadesh, Morris, 1939. *Chitimacha Grammar*. Philadelphia, PA: American Philosophical Society Library.

Swadesh, Morris, 1946. Chitimacha. In *Linguistic Structures of Native America*, pp. 312–336. Viking Fund Publications in Anthropology, vol. 6. New York: Wenner-Gren.

Swanton, John R., 1921. The Tunica language. *International Journal of American Linguistics* 2: 1–39.

Swanton, John R., 1929. A sketch of the Atakapa language. *International Journal of American Linguistics* 5: 121–149.

Talmy, Leonard, 1972. *Semantic Structures in English and Atsugewi*. Unpublished PhD thesis, University of California, Berkeley.

Tarpent, Marie-Lucie, 1987. *A Grammar of the Nisgha Language*. Unpublished PhD thesis, University of Victoria, BC, Canada.

Thompson, Laurence D., 1972. Language universals, nasals, and the Northwest Coast. In Estelle Smith (ed.), *Studies in Linguistics in Honor of George L. Trager*, pp. 441–456. Janua Linguarum, Series Maior, vol. 52. The Hague: Mouton.

Thompson, Laurence D. and M. Dale Kinkade, 1990. Languages. In Suttles (ed.), pp. 30–51.

Walker, Deward E. Jr (ed.), 1998. *Handbook of North American Indians*, vol. 6: *Plateau*. Washington, DC: Smithsonian Institution.

Walker, Willard, 2004. Creek confederacy before removal. In Fogelson (ed.), pp. 373–392.

Waselkov, Gregory A., 2004. Exchange and interaction since 1500. In Fogelson (ed.), pp. 686–696.

Waterman, T. T. and A. L. Kroeber, 1934. Yurok marriages. *University of California Publications in American Archaeology and Ethnology* 35: 1–14.

32

The Areal Linguistics of Amazonia

Patience Epps and Lev Michael

32.1 Introduction

Amazonia is one of the most linguistically diverse regions of the world, with a density of distinct genetic groupings – some fifty families and isolates – rivalled only by New Guinea. We know very little about the historical processes that have shaped the Amazonian linguistic picture, or gave rise to its plethora of languages. However, despite common assumptions, the Amazon basin provides ample evidence that the maintenance of diversity does not entail a lack of contact among groups speaking different languages. In many areas of the lowlands, contact among Amazonian language communities has been intense and long-term. Such contact situations have themselves profoundly shaped the linguistic profile of Amazonia and neighbouring regions, giving rise to zones of typological similarity that cross-cut genetic-linguistic differences.

Working out a precise account of how contact has influenced the languages of lowland South America presents a 'vast and almost intractable' problem, as observed by Muysken (2012: 235). A significant aspect of this intractability lies in the paucity of descriptive and historical work that has been carried out on these languages. For many languages, it is already too late – they have been extinguished before they could be documented. However, the past few decades have seen an explosion of high-quality descriptive work on many surviving Amazonian languages, some of which are highly endangered, with new historical work building closely upon this foundation. We have thus entered an exciting new period of investigation into Amazonian language history, which is already yielding fresh insights into linguistic areality in the Amazon basin. In this chapter, we offer our assessment of the current state of the art in understanding linguistic areality in Amazonia.

Epps gratefully acknowledges support from the US National Science Foundation (HSD-0902114).

Amazonia, which we define loosely here as the lowland region drained by the Amazon and Orinoco Rivers and extending to the northern and eastern litorals of the continent (see Dixon and Aikhenvald 1999b: 4; Rodrigues 2000: 15), is bordered by the Andes mountains to the west, the Caribbean and Atlantic oceans in the north and east, and the drier regions of the Gran Chaco to the south. Most of this vast area is covered by tropical rainforest, with pockets of savannah on the margins. The majority of the linguistic diversity encountered within the Amazon region is concentrated on the western periphery, for reasons that are currently as mysterious as those behind the overall diversity itself. The major language families that do exist, most notably Arawak, Carib, Tupí and Macro-Jê, are characterized by predominantly non-contiguous distributions, with their members interspersed by many other smaller families and isolates; see e.g. O'Connor and Muysken (2014) or Campbell and Grondona (2012a) for further discussion. While this linguistic patchwork renders the task of investigating language contact complex, it also makes it to some degree more accessible, since contact-induced change tends to be easier to identify among unrelated languages.

While our focus here is on the linguistic effects of contact, we emphasize that contact necessarily takes place among speakers, and it is the dynamics of these speakers' interactions that produces the particular linguistic outcomes that we observe. The contact-motivated similarities that cross-cut language boundaries are evident not only in lexicon and grammar, but also in discourse and sociocultural practice more generally, and include the ways in which people tell stories, sing songs, prepare food, raise children, heal the sick, and so on. Speaker interactions are grounded in, and structured by, approaches to trade, intermarriage, and ritual and convivial practice. The extent of these interactions should not be underestimated; recent work has demonstrated that many areas of pre-Columbian Amazonia hosted large population densities and relatively complex societies (e.g. Heckenberger and Neves 2009). Documentation of long-distance trade networks (e.g. Nordenskiöld 1922; Vidal 2000; cf. Hornborg 2005) and of migrations over large distances (e.g. Clastres 1995) likewise indicates that many native Amazonians had ample opportunity to interact with other language groups.

Our discussion is primarily concerned with the effects of contact among indigenous languages, and most of the patterns we consider are undoubtedly rooted in pre-Columbian social dynamics. However, the displacement and restructuring of many Amazonian societies in the centuries following the European invasion have introduced profound changes into those dynamics, and it is in many cases unclear to what extent contemporary sociocultural practices represent continuity with pre-Columbian times, or how patterns of linguistic diffusion have been altered over the last 500 years. Moreover, contact with European languages, particularly Spanish and Portuguese, as well as with European-mediated languages such as

Quechua and Nheengatú (a Tupí-Guaraní language promoted by early Jesuit missionaries as a lingua franca), has profoundly affected many indigenous languages, in many instances culminating in language shift (see e.g. Muysken 2012). Interestingly, these contact scenarios are often characterized by a rather different mix of processes from those observed among indigenous Amazonian languages, with considerably more code-switching, lexical borrowing and language shift – in keeping with the different sorts of social relations that pertain among these groups. We will not address these differences in detail here, but will focus on the observable outcomes of contact in indigenous Amazonian contexts, which have tended toward grammatical diffusion and language maintenance.

This chapter is organized as follows. We begin in Section 32.2 with a discussion of the principal localized contact zones that have been investigated within Amazonia (the Vaupés, the Upper Xingu and other areas), where speakers of multiple languages live in close proximity and engage in frequent interaction. Section 32.3 provides a wider scope, with an assessment of evidence for larger areal diffusion zones within the lowlands. This section also addresses the possibility that the Amazon basin as a whole might represent a single large-scale diffusion zone, with substantive contrasts between it and other South American regions such as the Andes and the Southern Cone. Section 32.4 summarizes our current understanding of Amazonian areal linguistics and outlines directions for future research.

32.2 Localized Diffusion within Amazonia

Most historically recent situations of regular contact among speakers of different indigenous languages are found in localized zones within the South American lowlands, and it is in these contexts that areal diffusion is most easily identified. While all of these zones have been profoundly affected by the European-derived national society, they have maintained aspects of their traditional social structures and cultural practices, suggesting a degree of continuity with pre-Columbian dynamics. Many of these contemporary contact zones share some notable similarities: in particular, they are characterized by multiple groups speaking different languages, who maintain a relatively egalitarian relationship with respect to one another, and whose interaction is frequent, conventionalized and profound – a context that clearly favours areal diffusion. Within these 'regional systems', as they are sometimes termed, groups tend to be characterized by a striking degree of cultural homogeneity on one hand, but on the other by a set of locally salient differences, such that they function rather like a set of interlocking cogs in a single machine. Map 32.1 illustrates the location of the principal regions discussed here.

Map 32.1 Lowland South American contact zones

Language plays a recurrent role as an emblem of difference in these zones, and local ideologies of language tend to strictly constrain the mixing of codes, even where frequent interaction among groups fosters intensive multilingualism (Hill 1996). We widely encounter long-term language maintenance, limited code-switching, and low levels of lexical borrowing, often buttressed by explicit articulations of the quality and importance of linguistic difference. At the same time, particularly where individual multilingualism is high, there is considerable convergence among languages on a grammatical level. This combination of low lexical borrowing with substantial grammatical diffusion is in striking contrast with the outcomes of language contact in many other parts of the world, where lexical borrowing tends to precede and facilitate grammatical diffusion (e.g. Thomason and Kaufman 1988); nevertheless, it appears to be commonplace in Amazonia. This outcome is undoubtedly linked to speakers' conscious efforts to avoid language mixing – of which they are most aware on the level of lexical forms – and their frequent exposure to multiple codes, which fosters the convergence of grammatical structures and categories below speakers' 'limits of awareness', in Silverstein's terms (1981; see also Aikhenvald 2001a and Mithun, Chapter 31, this volume).

In many of these interactive zones, our assessment of the effects of contact on the languages themselves is facilitated by the presence of distinct language families, and by the possibility of comparison with related languages outside the region. These factors allow us to attribute similarities within the area to contact rather than to common inheritance, especially where the shared features are too numerous and/or too unusual to be easily explained as independent innovations (see Campbell et al. 1986; Epps et al. 2013). While this historically grounded approach yields relatively robust evidence of contact-induced change, cases where related languages are undocumented or do not occur outside the region require us to fall back on the identification of a set of features shared among languages within the area. Where these features cannot be shown to be significantly different from those that exist in the languages outside the area, the case for a regional contact zone is weakened (see Campbell and Grondona 2012a; Muysken 2012); however, solid comparative analysis can provide evidence for areal diffusion regardless of whether we can define a precise contrast between a particular region and the neighbouring areas.

32.2.1   The Vaupés Region

The Vaupés region of the northwest Amazon has received the most in-depth attention of any South American contact zone. The area of the Vaupés river basin is home to dozens of languages belonging to four distinct families, Tukanoan, Arawak, Nadahup and Kakua-Nukak (formerly lumped together with Nadahup to form the 'Makú' group).[1] The Vaupés region is a particularly intensive contact zone within the larger Upper Rio Negro basin, which itself appears to be a region of less profound areal diffusion (see Aikhenvald 1999a; Epps and Stenzel 2013). While most of the existing work concerning language contact in the Vaupés has focused on particular languages or on particular linguistic features, the following discussion offers a short synthesis of our current understanding of diffusion across the region as a whole, and situates it within the wider lowland South American context.

The Vaupés has been described as a regional 'system', in which distinct groups function together, and as a culture area, in that these groups share many features in common (see e.g. Bruzzi 1977; Epps and Stenzel 2013). Similarities include various aspects of material culture, such as house construction, manioc-processing technology and bodily adornment, and likewise many ritual practices. Discourse practices throughout the region

---

[1] The post-colonial arrival Nheengatú (Tupí-Guaraní) is also marginally represented in the region, but is not discussed here.

are also strikingly similar, despite their delivery in different languages, with shared song traditions, stories, incantations and conversational norms. On the other hand, certain salient differences underscore the systemic nature of the region, such that groups maintain an identity as distinct, interactive units. Among the most locally meaningful of these differences is language, which is emphasized in the context of linguistic exogamy – obligatory marriage across language groups – practised by most of the East Tukanoan and some Arawak groups in the region. Another salient difference is subsistence pattern, with an opposition between the Nadahup and Kakua-Nukak 'forest peoples', who prioritize hunting and gathering, and the East Tukanoan and Arawak 'river peoples', who focus on fishing and farming. These subsistence distinctions are accompanied by social asymmetries (such that the river peoples are 'ranked' more highly than the forest peoples). Interaction among regional units is also promoted by trade specializations (for example, the Nadahup people provide meat and baskets; the East Tukanoan Tuyukas the canoes, etc.).

The systemic nature of the region engenders widespread multilingualism, coupled with language maintenance. East Tukanoan peoples tend to speak several of each other's languages, as did Tariana (Arawak) speakers,[2] facilitated by the linguistic exogamy system. The forest peoples in the region have traditionally spoken at least one river-Indian language; in their case, however, bi- or multilingualism has been almost always uni-directional, due to the local social imbalance. The active maintenance of distinct languages, despite intense multilingualism and even social asymmetry, has been viewed as an outcome of linguistic exogamy, which explicitly links marriageability to linguistic difference (Aikhenvald 2001a; Jackson 1983; Sorensen 1967; Stenzel 2005, *inter alia*). However, Epps argues that the salience of the link between language and identity is probably as much a cause as an effect of linguistic exogamy, in light of broader trends across lowland South America (see below).

The Vaupés emphasis on language as an emblem of identity translates into tight constraints against the mixing of languages. Intrasentential code-switching is avoided and socially condemned: see e.g. Aikhenvald (2001a: 412), Chernela (2013: 213). East Tukanoan speakers explicitly characterize their awareness of linguistic differences, stating for example that some languages 'flow slowly and smoothly, "like waves of water" while others "sound like lightning" … with sharp angles, stops, and starts' (Chernela 2013: 216–217). In keeping with these maintenance practices, the region's languages have experienced remarkably low levels of lexical borrowing despite the intense long-term contact among them. A systematic lexical study of ten different Vaupés languages reveals only

---

[2] However, recent decades have seen Tariana and many other East Tukanoan speakers shifting to Tukano, which has gained a new, colonially mediated level of status (see Aikhenvald 1999a: 387; Stenzel 2005), and in some contexts to Portuguese.

2–4 per cent loans in basic vocabulary (Bowern et al. 2011, 2014; see also Epps 2009), with slightly higher levels in flora–fauna and material/ritual culture terms (around 10–12 per cent in Nadahup and Kakua-Nukak languages, lower in Tukanoan and Arawak). On the other hand, the existing loans include various *Wanderwörter* (see Haynie et al. 2014; Epps 2012), which offer the impression that *if* a lexical item is to be borrowed, it is likely to travel widely, possibly because it loses an association with a particular language in the process and thus becomes 'fair game' (see also Muysken 2012: 252).

Despite the low levels of lexical borrowing, the effects of contact in the region's languages have had significant effects on local lexicons, particularly involving the congruence of semantic categories and the calquing of lexical items across languages. Calquing is especially pervasive in place names and ethnonyms, binomial names for flora and fauna, and items of material and ritual culture (e.g. the name of a regional culture hero: Tukano *o'ã-kó* 'Bone-Son', Tariana *yapi-riku-ri* 'One on the Bone', Hup *g'ǽg tǽh* 'Bone Son'); see Aikhenvald (2002: 229), Epps (2013), Floyd (2013).

Grammatical structures and categories among the Vaupés languages have been profoundly affected by areal diffusion, giving rise to a significant degree of morpheme-to-morpheme and word-to-word inter-translatability (see Aikhenvald 2007a: 261). East Tukanoan languages have provided the model for many of these changes, but in some cases they too have converged to be more like their neighbours. The extent to which East Tukanoan languages have been shaped by contact with each other is not as easy to determine, but diffusion among these languages has also undoubtedly occurred (Chacon 2013; Gomez-Imbert 1993).

The heavy restructuring experienced by Tariana, the only Arawak language fully incorporated into the Vaupés linguistic exogamy system, has been explored in detail by Aikhenvald (1999a, 2001b, 2002, 2007a, *inter alia*). As Aikhenvald demonstrates through comparison with Baniwa, Tariana's closest Arawak sister outside the Vaupés region, Tukanoan influence has led to changes throughout Tariana grammar, including a realignment of morphemes and constituent order; the development of case-marking on nominal arguments (topical non-subject and oblique, as well as the reduction of multiple locative markers to one catch-all marker); the elaboration and restructuring of the nominal classifier system; the augmentation of the evidential system from two categories to five; the development of verb compounding, switch-reference, new complementation strategies, discourse marking, etc. Tariana also exhibits significant convergence in its phonological inventory towards the typical Tukanoan profile, diverging from typical Arawak profiles (Chang and Michael 2014: 1–2). Examples (1)–(3) (from Aikhenvald 2007a: 245–246) illustrate the near-isomorphism between Tariana and Tukano, in contrast to Tariana's sister Baniwa, as can be seen in the following examples.

(1)   Tariana (Arawak)
     nese   pa:ma   *di-na*
     then   one+NUM.CL.ANIMATE.FEM   3sgnf-OBJ
     du-yana-sita-pidana
     3sgf-cook-ALREADY-REM.PAST.REP
     'She had reportedly cooked him already.'

(2)   Tukano (East Tukanoan)
     tîita   ni'kó   *kĩĩ-re*
     then   one+NUM.CL.ANIMATE.FEM   he-OBJ
     do'á-toha-po'
     cook-ALREADY-REM.PAST.REP.3sg.fem
     'She had reportedly cooked him already.'

(3)   Baniwa (Arawak)
     hneʈe-pida   apa:ma   *ʒu-dzana-ni*   *ʒu-ʈaita*
     then-REP   one+CL.FEM   3sgf-cook-3sgnfO/So   3sgf-finish
     'Then she had reportedly finished cooking him.'

The Nadahup languages have also undergone significant restructuring through Tukanoan influence, facilitated by the one-way bilingualism that predominates among many Nadahup speakers in the Vaupés. Hup appears to have been most profoundly affected (see Epps 2005, 2007a, 2008, *inter alia*), having developed prosodic nasalization, verb compounding, nominal classification, evidentials (as with Tariana, a five-way distinction built atop an earlier two-way one), future and recent/distant past tense distinctions, and new strategies of number marking and case-marking (including an object/non-subject marker that is sensitive to animacy and definiteness, and a catch-all locative), among many other features (compare example (4) to those above). Hup's sister Yuhup, also spoken in the Vaupés, has likewise experienced significant Tukanoan influence (with diffusion-induced changes probably beginning in their common ancestor), while Dâw, located on the periphery of the Vaupés, has been less affected. Nadëb, their most distant sister, has been essentially unaffected by diffusion from Tukanoan (though it has almost certainly been influenced by Arawak) and its grammar is strikingly different from those of its sisters.

(4)   Hup (Nadahup)
     yɨt   yúp=ʔǎy   tíh-ăn   cɨw-yiʔ-cɨ̃wĩy=mah   *j'ám*
     then   that=FEM   3sg-OBJ   cook-TEL-ALREADY=REP   DST.PAST
     'Then she had reportedly cooked him already.'

Kakua (Kakua-Nukak) likewise shows evidence of diffusion, probably also from Tukanoan languages. As can be seen in example (5) (from Bolaños 2012: 3), Kakua resembles its neighbours with respect to characteristics such as evidentiality, verb compounding, a recent/distant past tense distinction, non-subject case marking and verb-final constituent order. Chang and Michael (2014) also find evidence of phonological convergence between Kakua and the Nadahup languages Hup and Yuhup.

(5)   Kakua (Kakua-Nukak)

    hiw   *kan-diʔ*   *ʔã-t-hěm-ep-wit-be*
    jaguar   3sgm-NON.SUBJ   3sgm-SECOND.HAND-eat-PAST-REP-REC.PST
    'The jaguar reportedly ate him.'

Arawak languages have also exerted influence on some East Tukanoan languages. Evidence for diffusion in this direction includes the development of aspirated stops in Kotiria (Wanano), possessive proclitics in Kotiria, Kubeo, Tatuyo and certain other languages, and the use of shape classifiers with non-human animates in Kubeo and (to a limited extent) in Kotiria (Gomez-Imbert 1996; Stenzel and Gomez-Imbert 2009).

A number of further studies have undertaken in-depth comparative investigations of particular grammatical features across Vaupés languages, noting their many similarities; these have explored serial verb constructions, including grammaticalization of the verbs *come/go* as directionals (Aikhenvald 1999b; Ospina and Gomez-Imbert 2013); the expression of spatial relations (Epps and Neely 2014; Stenzel 2013b); possessive constructions, including the development of a comparable alienable/inalienable distinction and similar marking strategies (Stenzel 2013a); differential object marking strategies (Stenzel 2008; Zuñiga 2007); and nominal classification (Aikhenvald 2007b; Epps 2007b).

The Vaupés languages provide intriguing insights into the mechanisms by which areal diffusion takes place. In many instances, these mechanisms have involved the grammaticalization of native material to create new categories and structures. The process can involve the calquing of whole constructions, as can be seen for example in the close parallels in event packaging via serial verb constructions. Rather than resulting in simplification, the development of new material through contact-driven grammaticalization often produces an overall *increase* in grammatical complexity by adding to existing repertoires of categories and structures, as in the case of Tariana's development of case-marking in addition to its earlier strategy of pronominal cross-referencing (see Aikhenvald 2003). Stenzel's (2013a) discussion of possession-marking strategies among Vaupés languages highlights the fact that even while distinct languages may converge on a common model through processes of diffusion, the language-internal dynamics of change give rise to fine-grained differences, such that the outcomes are not isomorphic. Epps (2012) shows that despite the constraints against the borrowing of form in this region, perceived formal similarities nevertheless can and do play a role in facilitating structural adaptations, as in the case of the development of an evidential form *ni* from an existential verb in Tukanoan and Hup, and in Tariana from a functionally distinct marker *nhi* 'anterior tense' (Aikhenvald 2002: 123).

Particular examples of diffusion-driven change in Vaupés languages also highlight the role of discourse in motivating these processes; compare also Aikhenvald's (2007a: 261) observation that 'the more pragmatically motivated, the more diffusable'. The development of evidentials provides a good example: norms of conversation, story-telling and other discourse forms, shared among speakers, foster an expectation that one's source of information will be explicitly stated (and that if it is not, one's reliability or responsibility may be in question). In Hup, this discursive expectation apparently led to an increase in the frequency of verb roots associated with information source appearing in verbal compounds encoding events, which in time grammaticalized into evidentials (see Epps 2005). Moreover, regional norms for narrating traditional stories may have given rise to a further change in Hup. In these stories, almost every clause is marked by the reported evidential =*mah*, followed directly by the distant past tense marker *j'ám* (itself a fairly recent addition to Hup grammar), as can be seen in (6) – although in other discourse contexts the past markers only appear when the temporal information is contrastive or particularly emphasized. Moreover, in one dialect of Hup, the reported evidential appears fused together with the distant past marker in traditional stories to produce =*máam* (example (7)). Given that Hup has almost no other portmanteau morphs, the parallel with the fused tense-evidential suffixes in Tukanoan languages is striking.

(6)   Hup, Middle Tiquié River
      yíníy=**mah**   **j'ám**   tíh   bí?-íh,
      SO=REPORTED   DIST.PAST   3sg   make-DECL
      húp=n'ăn   tíh   bí?-íh
      person=PL.OBJ   3sg   make-DECL
      'Thus (long ago, they say) he made (them), he made people.'
(7)   Hup, Lower Tiquié River
      j'ŭg-út=**maám**   tíh   wɔn-kot=máh-ah
      forest-OBL=REP.DIST.PAST   3sg   follow-go.in.circles=REP-DECL
      'In the forest (long ago, they say), he wandered following (the tapir).'

32.2.2   The Caquetá-Putumayo Region

The Caquetá-Putumayo area of southern Colombia and northern Peru is another local diffusion zone, though it is not nearly as well studied as its northern neighbour the Vaupés. In this region, speakers of languages belonging to the Bora and Witoto families, the Arawak language Resígaro and the isolate Andoke interact intensively through marriage, ritual contexts, etc., refer to themselves together as the 'People of the Centre', and are widely multilingual[3] (Echeverri 1997; Londoño Sulkin

---

[3] However, as in many of the other regions discussed in this chapter, recent decades have seen significant language loss as speakers shift to Spanish (or other colonially mediated languages).

2012; Seifart et al. 2009). Distinctive shared cultural practices include the ritual ingestion of powdered coca leaves and liquid tobacco, extensive song cycles and particular styles of warfare, personal hygiene, etc.; at the same time, the groups have maintained distinct languages, origin stories and certain other emblems of identity (Seifart 2011: 7–8; Whiffen 1915).

As in the Vaupés, the People of the Centre share an 'inhibition against lexical borrowing' (Seifart 2011: 88). Despite their close contact, Seifart (2011: 20) finds that only about 5 per cent of Resígaro lexical stems have been borrowed from Bora (gauged via an extensive set of core and non-core vocabulary), of which many are flora–fauna terms; similarly low loan rates between Bora, Resígaro and other languages of the region are identified in work by Bowern et al. (2011, 2014).[4] However, Resígaro has borrowed a striking number of bound morphological forms, including whole sets of nominal classifiers (over half of Resígaro's total), number markers, quantifiers and other forms, totalling over 50 distinct items (Seifart 2011, 2012). Further diffusion has affected grammatical structures and categories in Resígaro, with or without the mediation of directly borrowed morphemes. These features include the development of an inclusive/exclusive distinction, second-position tense–aspect–mood clitics, the loss of object cross-referencing suffixes, and the restructuring of verbal morphology (Aikhenvald 2001b: 189; Seifart 2011: 14). Resígaro phonology has also been affected, with the addition of new phonemes (/ɸ/, /dʒ/, /ʔ/), syllable structure restrictions and a two-tone contrast (Aikhenvald 2001b; Chang and Michael 2014; Seifart 2012). Indeed, Chang and Michael (2014) show that Boran and Witotoan languages, Resígaro and the isolate Andoke exhibit significant convergence in their phonological inventories, allowing us to pick out the People of the Centre as a well-defined phonological area.

The People of the Centre have been involved in longer-range processes of diffusion as well. They are in contact with the Arawak Yukuna to the north, which themselves are in close contact with the East Tukanoan Tanimuka (Retuarã: see Aikhenvald 2001b; Seifart 2007); the Caquetá-Putumayo groups share a number of characteristics with their northern neighbours in the Vaupés. These similarities are both cultural (e.g. large signal drums) and linguistic (e.g. the distributional and functional properties of nominal classifiers, nominative–accusative alignment, etc.; see Aikhenvald 2001b: 189; Seifart and Payne 2007).

Figure 32.1 models a subset of northwest Amazonian languages as a NeighborNet splitsgraph, with respect to 226 grammatical features (mostly morphosyntactic; see Epps 2015). The splitsgraph illustrates the extent to which areal diffusion has produced regional grammatical profiles among the Vaupés and Caquetá-Putumayo languages. The Vaupés cluster

---

[4] The figure of 24 per cent loans in Resígaro given by Aikhenvald (2001b: 182; see also Eriksen and Danielsen 2014: 188) was probably erroneously inflated by the inclusion of borrowed classifier forms.

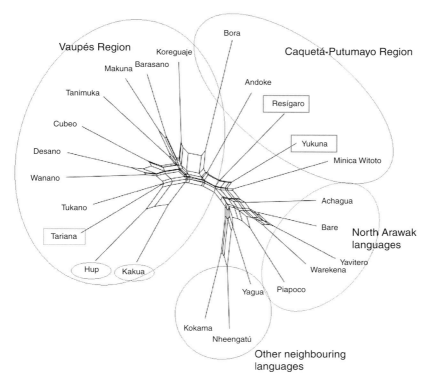

Vaupés region	Caquetá-Putumayo region	North Arawak languages	Other neighbouring languages
East Tukanoan family	**Boran family**	Achagua	**Peba-Yaguan family**
Koreguaje	Bora	Bare	Yagua
Barasano	**Witotoan family**	Yavitero	**Tupí-Guaraní family**
Makuna	Minica Witoto	Warekena	Nheengatú
Tanimuka	**Isolate**	Piapoco	Kokama
Cubeo	Andoke		
Desano	**Arawak family**		
Wanano (Kotiria)	Resígaro		
Tukano	Yukuna		
Arawak family			
Tariana			
Nadahup family			
Hup			
Kakua-Nukak family			
Kakua			

Figure 32.1 NeighborNet representation of grammatical structures in languages of the northwest Amazon, divided into four groups

includes East Tukanoan, Hup and Kakua, while the Arawak languages Tariana, Resígaro and Yukuna pattern more closely with their non-Arawak neighbours than they do with their closest northern Arawak relatives. Also included are Kokama and Nheengatú (both Tupí-Guaraní) and Yagua (Peba-Yaguan); the association between these three languages is undoubtedly indicative of areal diffusion in the region where Yagua and Kokama are spoken, just south of the Caquetá-Putumayo area.[5]

32.2.3 The Upper Xingu Region

Contact among the Upper Xingu peoples has been relatively well documented ethnographically, but its linguistic effects have only begun to be explored. This region is home to more than a dozen languages belonging to the Carib, Arawak, Jê and Tupí families, as well as the isolate Trumai, although several of these groups are relative newcomers (arriving between the sixteenth and twentieth centuries in response to colonial pressures). Like the Vaupés and other Amazonian regional systems, the Xingu is an area of intense interaction among groups, particularly through ritual contexts and trade. The groups share a distinctive 'cultural package' (Fausto et al. 2008: 137; see also Franchetto 2011), with particular rituals, hairstyles, house architecture, etc., to which newcomer groups have assimilated as they were absorbed into the Xingu system (see e.g. Guirardello-Damien's 2011 discussion of the Trumai).

As in the Vaupés, language plays an important role in the Xingu as a 'basic diacritic' of ethnic identity and place within the regional system (Fausto et al. 2008: 141). Speakers provide explicit characterizations of linguistic differences, observing for example that the Carib groups speak 'in the throat' or 'inwards', while the Arawak peoples of the region speak 'outwards', 'on the tip of the teeth' (Fausto et al. 2008: 143). These 'rigorous and active processes of differentiation' are realized via a monolingual everyday ethos (Ball 2011: 93; see also Seki 2011: 85), in contrast to the Vaupés; yet multilingualism is extensive in ritual contexts, and the frequency of interaction has led to characterizations of the region as a 'communications network' (Basso 1973: 5) or even a speech community (Ball 2011: 93). Little code-switching and relatively little lexical borrowing occur (though some loans exist; see Seki 1999, 2011).

Seki (1999, 2011) has characterized the Xingu as an 'incipient' linguistic area, primarily on the basis of lexical similarities and common features of myth and ceremonial discourse. She identifies several grammatical features that have diffused within the region, and it is likely that further linguistic exploration will reveal more; these include the loss of a masculine/feminine gender distinction in the Arawak languages of the region (in cross-referencing and in independent pronouns), the development of a phoneme /ɨ/ in Arawak, a p > h shift in Carib and Tupí-Guaraní, and a change to CV syllable structure in Carib. Chang and Michael (2014) clarify the multilateral nature of phonological borrowing in the Xingu

---

[5] We note that the tendency for grammars to change through areal diffusion while lexicons remain relatively conservative, as seen in these and other Amazonian languages, presents a challenge for the view that typological features will in general be more likely to retain a deep-time genetic signature (e.g. Dunn et al. 2005; Sicoli and Holman 2014).

area, confirming the diffusion of /ɨ/ into Xinguan Arawak languages from their Carib or Tupí-Guaraní neighbours, and adding the diffusion of /ts/ into the Xinguan Carib languages from their Arawak neighbours and the diffusion of nasal vowels into the Xinguan Arawak and Carib languages from their Tupí-Guaraní neighbours. Lexical restructuring and calquing have also taken place, including the development of comparable systems of post-nominal elements meaning 'big, supernatural, hyper', 'similar to', 'true/genuine' and 'bad/worthless/unsatisfying', which are used productively to create new complex nouns. For example, in Yawalapiti *úi* 'snake' + *kumã* 'hyper' yields *úi-tyumã* [*kumã*] 'snake-spirit' (Viveiros de Castro 2002), and in Trumai *fi* 'cigar, cigarette (tobacco)' + *yuraw* 'hyper' (itself a loan from Tupí-Guaraní Kamayurá) yields *fi yuraw* 'marijuana cigarette' (considered abnormal, dangerous; see Guirardello-Damien 2011: 120). The diffusion among the Xingu languages appears to be generally multidirectional.

32.2.4 The Guaporé-Mamoré Region

The Guaporé-Mamoré of southwest Brazil and northeast Bolivia is home to over fifty languages from a wide range of families (Arawak, Macro-Jê, Chapakuran, Tupí, Nambikwara, Pano, Takanan and many isolates). Ethnographic documentation indicates that many of these groups have engaged in extensive interethnic contact, intermarriage and exchange, yielding a regional culture area with commonalities in territorial subgroups, bodily adornment, mythological themes, etc. (Lévi-Strauss 1948; Maldi 1991).

The investigation of contact among the Guaporé-Mamoré languages has not yet been extensive, but work by Crevels and van der Voort (2008; see also van der Voort 2005) indicates that diffusion has certainly taken place and that this is a rich area to explore. As in the other regions considered here, levels of lexical borrowing among these languages appear to be quite low (estimated at around 5 per cent by van der Voort 2005: 395; see also Crevels and van der Voort 2008: 164); however, they share many structural similarities, including evidentials, an inclusive/exclusive distinction, a high incidence of prefixes and a strong preference for verbal number (i.e. alteration of the verb via suppletion, reduplication or affixation to express the number of the subject or object), accompanied by a general lack of nominal number (Crevels and van der Voort 2008: 167). Further similarities include verbal cross-reference systems with similar morpheme positions and rich systems of directional morphemes, such as Kwaza's 'movement in a circle', 'into fire', 'behind the house' (van der Voort 2005: 399; see also Guillaume, in press). Eriksen and Danielsen (2014: 175) also note areal influence in verbal morphology and personal pronominal distinctions in two Arawak languages of the region (Paunaka and Moxo).

Table 32.1 *Similar classifier forms in Guaporé-Mamoré languages (van der Voort 2005: 397)*

	'bark'	'fruit'	'bone'	'tooth'	'liquid'	'round'	'thorn'	'porridge'	'powder'
Kwaza (isolate)	-kalo	-ko	-su̱	-māi	-mũ	-tɛ	-n	-mɛ̃	-nũ
Kanoê (isolate)		-ko			-mũ	-tæ			-nũ
Aikana (isolate)			-zu	-mũj	-mũ	-ðāw			-nũ
Arikapú (Macro-Jê)							-n	-mrɛ̃	-nũ
Nambikwara (Namb.)	-kalo		-su³						-nũx³

A particularly interesting aspect of areal diffusion in the Guaporé-Mamoré involves the direct borrowing of morphological forms, particularly within nominal classifier systems (Crevels and van der Voort 2008: 167; van der Voort 2005: 397) – a striking parallel to the effects of contact in the Caquetá-Putumayo. Several of these forms are given in Table 32.1; none of the five languages listed are known to be related.

As Muysken et al. (2015) point out, the fact that so many of the Guaporé-Mamoré languages are small families or isolates located only within this region makes it difficult to test for contact by comparison with relatives outside. However, these authors apply quantitative measures to demonstrate that at least some features must have converged via diffusion in this region. Other features that are more widely attested may themselves be the outcome of more far-reaching contact networks that existed in the past, as discussed in Section 32.3 below.

32.2.5   Other Regional Diffusion Zones in Lowland South America

Several other localized diffusion zones exist in the Amazon basin and adjacent lowland regions, and still others probably remain undetected. One area that has had some documentation is the Southern Guiana region, where Carib, Arawak and Salivan groups exhibit notable cultural continuity resulting from 'constant interaction through marriage, trade, and migration' (Rivière 1984: 8; see also Arhem 1989; Carlin 2011: 226). Much like the other regions discussed here, linguistic distinctions are maintained as key markers of ethnic identity (Howard 2001: 341) and loanwords are relatively few (Bowern et al. 2011, 2014; Carlin 2007). Carlin (2007) discusses grammatical diffusion from Carib languages (principally Trio and Waiwai) into the Arawak language Mawayana, established in part via comparison with Mawayana's sister Wapishana. Contact-induced changes in Mawayana include the addition of a first person exclusive distinction (via borrowing of a Waiwai pronominal form), the development of nominal tense marking, affective marking on nouns or verbs to express 'pity' or 'recognition of unfortunate circumstance', a frustrative marker on verbs (indicating that the action was carried out 'in vain') and a 'similative' or 'as if' marker on nominals (see examples (8–9), from Carlin 2007: 329). Carlin notes that all of these categories are obligatory in the local Carib languages.

(8)   Mawayana (Arawak)
        waata-ni   *r-ayādīyā*
        opossum-SIMIL   3s-transform.PAST
        'He changed into an opossum.'
(9)   Trio (Carib)
        kaikui-me   *tëmetæ*
        jaguar-SIMIL   he.transformed
        'He transformed into a jaguar.'

The Southern Guiana region may itself be part of a much larger contact zone that includes parts of the Orinoco and northern Amazon watersheds (Migliazza 1985: 20; cf. Campbell 2012: 306). Further possible diffusion zones include the area of the Tocantins and Mearim Rivers in northeastern Brazil, home to Jê and Tupí-Guaraní languages (Braga et al. 2011), and the Venezuelan–Antillean area (Campbell 2012: 307; Constenla-Umaña 1991: 125–126).

Finally, the region of the Gran Chaco, located just to the south of the Amazon basin, bears striking similarities to the Amazonian regional 'systems' discussed here. The speakers of its six distinct language families share many cultural similarities (Braunstein and Miller 1999: 9–11), shun code-switching and lexical borrowing (Campbell and Grondona 2010, 2012a: 657; Vidal and Nercesian 2009: 1023), practise a form of linguistic exogamy, and identify strongly with a single language while understanding many (Campbell and Grondona 2010). The Chaco languages share many structural features, including animal classifier(s), active/inactive verb alignment, similar strategies of pronominal affixation, and rich demonstrative systems, many of which are undoubtedly due to diffusion (Campbell and Grondona 2012a).

We will probably never know the extent to which the dynamics of these regional diffusion zones applied more generally in the Amazon basin, across both space and time. However, the wide distribution of regional 'systems' and their notable social and linguistic parallels suggest that these are not isolated cases. If Eriksen and Danielsen (2014: 163) are correct in their assertion of 'a vast socio-religious and economic exchange system that affected the lives of all inhabitants of northern South America between 1000 BCE and 1000 CE', then longer-range diffusion would undoubtedly have linked these local zones within wider networks. We turn to this question below.

32.3 Long-range Language Contact and Macro-areality in Amazonia

The linguistic areas discussed in Section 32.2 generally arose through interactions between neighbouring peoples in networks that span relatively small geographical regions in comparison to Amazonia as a whole. There is clear evidence, however, that pre-Columbian Amazonian peoples were linked via large-scale social, ritual and trade networks that spanned considerable areas of the continent, raising the possibility that Amazonia may exhibit linguistic areality on a similarly large scale. The fact that many cultural features and practices, such as perspectivism in mythology (Viveiros do Castro 1998; 2012: 48–51), the use of sacred flutes (Hornborg and Hill 2011b: 17) and a variety of subsistence techniques (see e.g. Carneiro 2000 on manioc-processing technology), have diffused over large areas of Amazonia suggests that linguistic features may have diffused on a similar scale.

Although the full extent of pre-Columbian South American trade networks is impossible to recover at this point, ethnohistorical and archaeological evidence clearly indicates that such networks spanned large areas of Amazonia, and linked Amazonia to adjacent regions, such as the Andes and Chaco. The earliest accounts of the colonial period provide ample evidence of vast trade networks crisscrossing the continent. Citing Oviedo y Valdés (1851–1855[1535]), for example, Nordenskiöld (1922: 7) describes Arawak traders then living near the mouth of the Amazon making 1,500 kilometre trading journeys along the coast in groups of 50–60 canoes and 500–800 men. He similarly discusses evidence of trade between the Cariban peoples of the Guianas and the Cariban Carijona of the Putumayo, and further still to peoples on the Amazon proper (1922: 149–150). Trade links between the Amazon and the Guianas are echoed by Fritz (Edmundson 1922), who indicates that the Omaguas, who occupied much of the Amazon between the Japurá and Napo, formed a node in a trade network linked to the Guianas, and traded with peoples deeper into the Amazonian headwaters regions. Nordenskiöld presents evidence of similarly long-distance trade between the Guaranian peoples of the Paraná and Paraguay River Basins and the Andean Inca Empire (1922: 7–10, 133–134). Trade of specific rare products is similarly known to have extended over thousands of kilometres, as in the case of salt – mined by the Arawak Ashéninkas in the Perené River basin in the Andean foothills, and compellingly argued by Rydén (1962: 652) to have reached the Tupinambás who had resettled on the Amazon at Tupinambarana, downriver of the mouth of the Rio Negro. Eriksen and Danielsen (2014) cite ethnohistorical and archaeological evidence to argue for the existence of an extensive Arawak-dominated trade network spanning much of western Amazonia, extending the arguments of Vidal (2000), who provides evidence for a major Arawak-dominated pre-Columbian trade network in northwestern Amazonia.

Long-distance trade of this sort survived well into the modern period. Lathrap (1973), for example, describes the varied networks in which the Shipibo communities, located on the Ucayali River, participated. In some of these networks, raw materials for ceramic production circulated up to 240 kilometres from the communities studied. Other networks were even more expansive and interethnic, and included Yagua communities some 1,000 kilometres downriver, through which Shipibos obtained blowguns, as well as Tikuna communities, located a further 500 kilometres along the Amazon proper, from which they obtained blowgun darts. Roth (1924) similarly describes a network spanning the eastern Orinoco basin and the Guianas, characterized by circulation of rare materials and high degrees of craft specialization (see also Dumont 1991). This network linked the Tupí-Guaraní communities on the Oyapock, producers of valued grinding stones; the river-craft-producing Warao at the mouth of the Orinoco; the Cariban Waiwai, located along the hills separating the Guianas from the Amazon watershed, and who specialized in a number of palm products; and the Cariban Makiritare, located in the central Orinoco basin, who produced hammocks, cassava graters and ornamental products.

Whether far-flung networks of interaction like these have led to widespread grammatical borrowing and convergence, and to the emergence of linguistic macro-areas within Amazonia, has become a topic of increasing prominence in Amazonian linguistics, as has the question of whether Amazonia as a whole constitutes a linguistic area. One of the earliest macro-area proposals considered the region encompassing the Orinoco River Basin and the portion of the Amazon Basin containing the northern tributaries of the Rio Negro (Migliazza 1985). Features that Migliazza attributed to this area included ergative alignment, OV order, lack of a passive construction, and relative clauses formed by apposition and nominalization. Most Amazonianists would now recognize this list as including several features of broader Amazonian distribution, and indeed, the features that Derbyshire (1987: 311) tentatively proposed as defining an Amazonian linguistic area include most of these, and in addition, a preference for OS order, subject and object verb agreement, null free argument realization, head-modifier order and complex morphology. Derbyshire and Payne (1990) subsequently added noun classifiers to this list of tentative features.

Perhaps the most promising macro-area proposals have been based on typological divisions bisecting the east/west axis of the continent. In one of the earliest such proposals, Doris Payne (1990: 5) suggested the existence of a Western Amazonian area consisting of the lowland areas to the west of the Andes characterized phonologically by complex stress and 'pitch-accent' systems and morphosyntactically by a strong tendency towards polysynthesis and complex verbal morphology, directional, locational and positional morphemes, and a distinctive type of noun classification system. The validity of this proposal is somewhat difficult to evaluate because neither the precise limits of the area nor the distribution of indicated features inside and outside the proposed area are given; but as discussed below, recent quantitatively based work lends support to an east/west areal split in South America.

As descriptions of Amazonian languages increase in both number and quality, work identifying macro-areas on the basis of relatively fine-grained linguistic phenomena will probably become more common. A promising example of this type is Guillaume and Rose's (2010) suggestion that sociative causatives may be an areal feature of southwest Amazonia, with the distribution of sociative causatives outside this area attributed to the spread of Tupían languages from their southwestern homeland. A systematic examination of the distribution of such morphemes both within South America and beyond is an obvious target for future research.

The question of linguistic macro-areas within Amazonia naturally leads to an issue already raised in our discussion: whether Amazonia as a whole constitutes a linguistic area. Although this remains an open question, an emerging consensus points to Amazonia not forming a linguistic area *sensu strictu*. Dixon and Aikhenvald (1999b: 7–10) is perhaps one of the best-known and most explicit efforts to enumerate characteristics that define Amazonia as a linguistic area and as complementary to an Andean linguistic area. The grammatical features proposed to be 'shared by all (or most)' Amazonian languages range from polysynthesis and head-marking, to tense–aspect–mood categories being expressed as optional suffixes, to adverbs and adpositions being incorporable into verbs. As Birchall (2014) observes, however, the empirical basis for the claimed areality of these features is unclear (as, indeed, it is for Derbyshire's (1987), Migliazza's (1985) and Payne's (1990) proposals, discussed above), raising the need to move beyond impressionistic claims regarding areality to explicit quantitatively grounded methods that make use of suitably organized, sufficiently large and dense, and – ideally – publicly available datasets (Haspelmath 2004).

Steps towards databases of these types for South America include the *South American Indigenous Language Structures* (SAILS) database (Muysken et al. 2014) and the *South American Phonological Inventory* database (SAPhon; Michael et al. 2012), and quantitatively sophisticated work based on these resources has recently begun to appear. Significantly, these works support not an Andean/Amazonian areality split, that leaves Amazonia as a clearly defined area, but a different west/east split – where the western area corresponds roughly to the Andes, Southern Cone and Doris Payne's Western Amazonian region, while the other large linguistic area to the east consists of the remainder of the continent (see also van Gijn et al., Chapter 33, this volume).

One illustration of this east/west division can be seen in Birchall's (2014) study of argument marking features in 74 South American languages, in which he tests for a statistically significant concentration in each of seven South American geographical macro-areas. Echoing Krasnoukhova's (2012) qualitative results on noun phrase features in South America, Birchall's analysis suggests that the features he examined pattern similarly within an Eastern South American linguistic area (ESALA) on one hand, comprising northern and southern Amazonia and the Chaco-Planalto area, and within a Western South American linguistic area (WSALA) on the other, comprising the northern and central Andes, western Amazonia and the Southern Cone. For example, Birchall (2014: 203) finds that ergative alignment, suggested by Dixon and Aikhenvald (1999b) to be a general Amazonian feature, has a statistically significant association only with the southern Amazon region and ESALA, and not with northern or western Amazonia. Similarly, clusivity distinctions, proposed by Adelaar (2008: 29) to be an Andean feature, do not emerge as particularly Andean, but once again, as a WSALA feature (Birchall 2014: 205–206). In contrast, several features, such as the use of both indexation and case as argument marking strategies, and accusative alignment for NP and pronoun arguments, turn out to be not mainly Andean, as proposed by Dixon and Aikhenvald (1999b), but WSALA characteristics, providing further evidence for an E/WSALA areality split rather than an Andean/Amazonian one.

These results are broadly congruent with quantitative computational work on phonological areality in South America, which finds that lowland languages exhibiting phonological similarities to Andean ones – for example, uvular and ejective consonants, palatal laterals, multiple liquids and small vowel inventories – cluster near the central Andes and in the Southern Cone (Michael et al. 2014), forming a phonological area corresponding roughly to WSALA. Similarly, languages in the remainder of the continent, corresponding approximately to ESALA, exhibit larger vowel inventories that include mid and high central vowels, nasal vowels or supersegmental nasality, labial fricatives and a glottal stop, among other features.

Despite the lack of support for a general Amazonian linguistic area evident in these results, there are nevertheless phenomena that are found in many Amazonian languages, although these are not pervasive enough to be diagnostic of a linguistic area in the usual sense of the term. In recognition of this fact, Aikhenvald (2012: 68–71) has more recently introduced the term 'language region', in contrast to the more rigorously defined notion of 'linguistic area', to characterize Amazonia as a whole. The precise explanation for recurrent but sporadically attested 'Amazonian' features, such as antipassives and complex classifier systems (2012: 70), is unclear, but there is suggestive evidence that in some cases, linguistic items and features have diffused along long-range networks of the kind discussed earlier in this section. For example, Epps (2014; see also

Haynie et al. 2014) identifies several dozen *Wanderwörter* that indicate the widespread diffusion of terms associated with important animal and plant species and food items across much of northern Amazonia. Further work identifies a widespread tendency across Amazonia for numeral terms indicating '4' (and occasionally '3' and '5') to be formed using 'relational' nouns or verbs, usually meaning 'companion' or 'accompany', a strategy that appears to be rare outside Amazonia (Epps 2013; Epps et al. 2012). Epps suggests that Tupí-Guaraní languages in particular may have played an important role in the diffusion, but observes that the ultimate source of these apparently diffused items remains an open question. Regardless, the fact that items like these have circulated widely but sporadically across Amazonia suggests that borrowing may be mediated by sparse networks that link relatively distant languages without directly affecting closer neighbours.

Another line of research addressing Amazonian areality seeks to identify areal patterns not in grammatical structure, but in discourse practices and language ideologies. Beier et al. (2002), for example, argue that particular discourse practices, such as the dialogical discourse genres, ritual wailing and the pragmatically motivated use of evidentials, are common over large areas of Amazonia in a manner consonant with that of a language region. Bowern et al. (2011) similarly find that lexical borrowing is unusually low in Amazonia, in comparison with other global macro-regions (see also Section 32.2 above), a tendency that Epps attributes to a widely diffused language ideology that discourages language mixing.

32.4   Conclusion

Amazonia offers important insights into the dynamics of language contact and the development of areal-linguistic patterns. As this chapter has explored, striking similarities exist among regional contact zones throughout the Amazonian lowlands, in which intense interaction and a degree of cultural homogeneity tend to go hand in hand with high linguistic diversity. In these regions, language is afforded special salience as a marker of distinct social identities, and thus while individuals are often highly multilingual, there is a marked absence of phenomena that are commonly associated with multilingualism in other parts of the world – most notably code-switching and lexical borrowing. Similarly, linguae francae and clear examples of language shift (aside from those associated with the expansion of the European and Quechuan spheres), while common in many other regions of the world where multiple languages are represented, appear to be rare or even unattested in these Amazonian contact zones. At the same time, the diffusion of grammatical categories and structures across languages is ubiquitous in these regions, although for most of these contact zones these processes have only begun to be explored. In some cases, the grammatical borrowing even includes the transfer of bound morphology, most notably that associated with nominal classification. This prevalence of extensive grammatical diffusion coupled with restrained lexical borrowing is typologically significant, since current conceptions of language contact dynamics stress the importance of lexical mediation in the diffusion of grammatical material and particularly of bound morphology.

On a larger scale, Amazonian linguistic areality provides some intriguing glimpses into the dynamics of human interaction in prehistory, when extensive trade routes would have crisscrossed the Amazon basin and linked it with other parts of the continent. The broad east/west division outlined above suggests that social networks linking the Andes, the western lowlands and the Southern Cone on one hand, and the eastern and central lowlands on the other, would have been particularly active, whereas networks that set the Amazon basin apart from other regions may have been less significant or functioned in different ways.

The study of areality in Amazonia and South America more generally has entered an exciting new phase. The empirical basis for such studies has been greatly enriched by the recent surge in basic descriptive work, which in turn is feeding a number of databases that will facilitate systematic study. Likewise, new analytical and theoretical approaches to areality are being developed through the application of quantitative techniques and via holistic approaches that take geography, demographics and culture into account. We look forward to exciting findings in the coming decades, and to the new insights these will provide into South American prehistory and the mechanisms and processes involved in language contact.

References

Adelaar, Willem, 2008. Towards a typological profile of the Andean languages. In Alexander Lubotsky, Jos Schaeken and Jeroen Wiedenhoff (eds), *Evidence and Counter-Evidence: Essays in Honour of Frederik Kortlandt*, vol. 2: *General Linguistics*, pp. 23–33. Amsterdam: Rodopi.

Aikhenvald, Alexandra Y., 1999a. Areal diffusion and language contact in the Içana-Vaupés basin, north-west Amazonia. In Dixon and Aikhenvald (eds), pp. 384–416.

Aikhenvald, Alexandra Y., 1999b. Serial constructions and verb compounding: Evidence from Tariana (North Arawak). *Studies in Language* 23 (3): 469–498.

Aikhenvald, Alexandra Y., 2001a. Language awareness and correct speech among the Tariana of NW Amazonia. *Anthropological Linguistics* 43 (4): 411–430.

Aikhenvald, Alexandra Y., 2001b. Areal diffusion, genetic inheritance, and problems of subgrouping: A North Arawak case study. In Alexandra Y. Aikhenvald and Robert M. W. Dixon (eds), *Areal Diffusion and Genetic Inheritance: Problems in Comparative Linguistics*, pp. 167–194. Oxford: Oxford University Press.

Aikhenvald, Alexandra Y., 2002. *Language Contact in Amazonia*. Oxford and New York: Oxford University Press.

Aikhenvald, Alexandra Y., 2003. Mechanisms of change in areal diffusion: New morphology and language contact. *Journal of Linguistics* 39: 1–29.

Aikhenvald, Alexandra Y., 2007a. Semantics and pragmatics of grammatical relations in the Vaupés linguistic area. In Alexandra Y. Aikhenvald and Robert M. W. Dixon (eds), *Grammars in Contact: A Cross-linguistic Typology*, pp. 237–266. Oxford: Oxford University Press.

Aikhenvald, Alexandra Y., 2007b. Classifiers in multiple environments: Baniwa of Içana/Kurripako: A North Arawak perspective. *International Journal of American Linguistics* 73: 475–500.

Aikhenvald, Alexandra Y., 2012. *The Languages of the Amazon*. Oxford: Oxford University Press.

Arhem, Kaj, 1989. The Makú, the Makuna and the Guiana system: Transformations of social structure in northern lowland South America. *Ethnos* 54: 5–22.

Ball, Christopher, 2011. Pragmatic multilingualism in the Upper Xingu speech community. In Franchetto (ed.), pp. 87–112.

Basso, Ellen B., 1973. The use of Portuguese relationship terms in Kalapalo (Xingu Carib): Changes in a central Brazilian communicative network. *Language in Society* 2: 1–21.

Beier, Christine, Lev Michael and Joel Sherzer, 2002. Discourse forms and processes in indigenous lowland South America: An areal-typological perspective. *Annual Review of Anthropology* 31: 121–145.

Birchall, Joshua, 2014. *Argument Marking Patterns in South American Languages*. PhD dissertation, Radboud Universiteit, Nijmegen.

Bolaños Quinonez, Katherine, 2012. Contact induced categories: A case study of evidentiality in Kakua. Conference presentation, The Nature of Evidentiality. Leiden, 14 June 2014.

Bowern, Claire, Patience Epps, Russell Gray et al., 2011. Does lateral transmission obscure inheritance in hunter–gatherer languages? *PLoS ONE* 6 (9): e25195.

Bowern, Claire, Hannah Haynie, Catherine Sheard et al., 2014. Loan and inheritance patterns in hunter–gatherer ethnobiological nomenclature. *Journal of Ethnobiology* 34 (2): 195–227.

Braga, Alzerinda, Ana Suelly A. C. Cabral, Aryon Dall'Igna Rodrigues and Betty Mindlin, 2011. Línguas entrelaçadas: Uma situação sui generis de línguas em contato [Intertwined languages: A sui generis situation of languages in contact]. *Papia* 21 (2): 221–230.

Braunstein, José and Elmer S. Miller, 1999. Ethnohistorical introduction. In Elmer S. Miller (ed.), *Peoples of the Gran Chaco*, pp. 1–22. Westport, CT: Bergin & Garvey.

Bruzzi Alves da Silva, Alcionilio, 1977. *A Civilação Indígena do Vaupés [The Indigenous Civilization of the Vaupés]*. Rome: LAS.

Campbell, Lyle, 2012. Typological characteristics of South American Indian languages. In Campbell and Grondona (eds), pp. 259–330.

Campbell, Lyle and Verónica Grondona, 2010. Who speaks what to whom? Multilingualism and language choice in Misión La Paz. *Language in Society* 39: 617–646.

Campbell, Lyle and Verónica Grondona, 2012a. Languages of the Chaco and Southern Cone. In Campbell and Grondona (eds), pp. 625–668.

Campbell, Lyle and Verónica Grondona (eds), 2012b. *The Indigenous Languages of South America: A Comprehensive Guide*. Berlin: de Gruyter Mouton.

Campbell, Lyle, Terrence Kaufman and Thomas Smith-Stark, 1986. Mesoamerica as a linguistic area. *Language* 62: 530–570.

Carlin, Eithne, 2007. Feeling the need: The borrowing of Cariban functional categories into Mawayana (Arawak). In Alexandra Y. Aikhenvald and Robert M. W. Dixon (eds), *Grammars in Contact: A Cross-Linguistic Perspective*, pp. 313–332. Oxford: Oxford University Press.

Carlin, Eithne, 2011. Nested identities in the southern Guyana-Suriname corner. In Hornborg and Hill (eds), pp. 225–236.

Carneiro, Robert L., 2000. The evolution of the *tipiti*: A study in the process of invention. In Gary Feinman and Linda Manzanilla (eds), *Cultural Evolution: Contemporary Viewpoints*, pp. 61–91. New York: Kluwer Academic Publishers.

Chacon, Thiago, 2013. Kubeo: Linguistic and cultural interactions in the Upper Rio Negro. In Epps and Stenzel (eds), pp. 403–440.

Chang, William and Lev Michael, 2014. A relaxed admixture model of language contact. *Language Dynamics and Change* 4 (1): 1–26.

Chernela, Janet, 2013. Toward an East Tukano ethnolinguistics: Metadiscursive practices, identity, and sustained linguistic diversity in the Vaupés basin of Brazil and Colombia. In Epps and Stenzel (eds), pp. 197–244.

Clastres, Hélène, 1995. *The Land-without-Evil: Tupí-Guaraní Prophetism*. Urbana and Chicago: University of Illinois Press.

Constenla-Umaña, Adolfo, 1991. *Las lenguas del área intermedia: introducción a su estudo areal [The Languages of the Intermediate Area: Introduction to their Areal Study]*. San José: Editorial de la Universidad de Costa Rica.

Crevels, Mily and Hein van der Voort, 2008. The Guaporé-Mamoré region as a linguistic area. In Pieter Muysken (ed.), *From Linguistic Areas To Areal Linguistics*, pp. 151–179. Amsterdam: John Benjamins.

Derbyshire, Desmond, 1987. Morphosyntactic areal characteristics of Amazonian languages. *International Journal of American Linguistics* 53: 311–326.

Derbyshire, Desmond and Doris Payne, 1990. Noun classification systems of Amazonian languages. In Doris Payne (ed.), *Amazonian Linguistics: Studies in Lowland South American Languages*, pp. 243–271. Austin, TX: University of Texas Press.

Dixon, Robert M. W. and Alexandra Y. Aikhenvald (eds), 1999a. *The Amazonian Languages*. Cambridge: Cambridge University Press.

Dixon, Robert M. W. and Alexandra Y. Aikhenvald, 1999b. Introduction. In Dixon and Aikhenvald (eds), pp. 1–22.

Dumont, Jean-Paul, 1991. *The Headman and I: Ambiguity and Ambivalence in the Fieldworking Experience*. Prospect Heights, IL: Waveland Press.

Dunn, Michael, Angela Terrill, Ger Reesink, Robert Foley and Stephen Levinson, 2005. Structural phylogenetics and the reconstruction of ancient language history. *Science* 309: 2072–2075.

Echeverri, Juan Alvaro, 1997. *The People of the Center of the World: A Study in Culture, History, and Orality in the Colombian Amazon*. PhD dissertation, New School for Social Research, New York.

Edmundson, George, 1904. The Dutch on the Amazon and Negro in the seventeenth century, part II: Dutch trade in the basin of the Rio Negro. *The English Historical Review* 19 (73): 1–25.

Edmundson, George, 1922. Introduction. *Journal of the Travels and Labours of Father Samuel Fritz in the River of the Amazons Between 1686 and 1723*, pp. 3–31. London: Hakluyt Society.

Epps, Patience, 2005. Areal diffusion and the development of evidentiality: Evidence from Hup. *Studies in Language* 29 (3): 617–650.

Epps, Patience, 2007a. The Vaupés melting pot: Tukanoan influence on Hup. In Alexandra Y. Aikhenvald and Robert M. W. Dixon (eds), *Grammars in Contact: A Cross-linguistic Typology*, pp. 267–289. Oxford: Oxford University Press.

Epps, Patience, 2007b. Birth of a noun classification system: The case of Hup. In W. Leo Wetzels (ed.), *Language Endangerment And Endangered Languages: Linguistic and Anthropological Studies with Special Emphasis on the Languages and Cultures of the Andean–Amazonian Border Area*, pp. 107–128. The Netherlands: Leiden University.

Epps, Patience, 2008. Grammatical borrowing in Hup. In Yaron Matras and Jeanette Sakel (eds), *Grammatical Borrowing: A Cross-linguistic Survey*, pp. 551–565. Berlin: Mouton de Gruyter.

Epps, Patience, 2009. Loanwords in Hup, a Nadahup language of Amazonia. In Martin Haspelmath and Uri Tadmor (eds), *Loanwords in the World's Languages: A Comparative Handbook*. Berlin: de Gruyter Mouton.

Epps, Patience, 2012. On form and function in language contact: A case study from the Amazonian Vaupés region. In Isabelle Léglise and Claudine Chamoreau (eds), *Dynamics of Contact-induced Language Change*. Berlin: de Gruyter Mouton.

Epps, Patience, 2013. Inheritance, calquing, or independent innovation? Reconstructing morphological complexity in Amazonian numerals. In Epps, Pat-El and Huehnergard (eds), pp. 329–357.

Epps, Patience, 2014. Exploring traces of contact between Tupí-Guaraní languages and their neighbors. Talk given 29 May 2014, Amazónicas V, Belém, Brazil.

Epps, Patience, 2015. South American languages. In Claire Bowern, Patience Epps, Jane Hill and Patrick McConvell, *Languages of Hunter-Gatherers and their Neighbors: Database.* https://huntergatherer.la .utexas.edu

Epps, Patience, Claire Bowern, Cynthia Hansen, Jane Hill and Jason Zentz, 2012. On numeral complexity in hunter–gatherer languages. *Linguistic Typology* 16: 39–107.

Epps, Patience and Kelsey Neely, 2014. Movimiento y orientación en construcciones verbales: Una perspectiva amazónica [Movement and orientation in verbal constructions: An Amazonian perspective]. In Lilián Guerrero (ed.), *Movimiento y espacio en lenguas de América [Movement and Space in Languages of the Americas]*. México: Universidad Nacional Autónoma de México.

Epps, Patience, Na'ama Pat-El and John Huehnergard (eds), 2013. *Contact Among Genetically Related Languages.* Special edition of *Journal of Language Contact* 6 (2).

Epps, Patience and Kristine Stenzel (eds), 2013. *Upper Rio Negro: Cultural and Linguistic Interaction in Northwestern Amazonia.* Rio de Janeiro: Museu do Índio-FUNAI.

Eriksen, Love and Swintha Danielsen, 2014. The Arawakan matrix. In O'Connor and Muysken (eds), pp. 152–176.

Fausto, Carlos, Bruna Franchetto and Michael J. Heckenberger, 2008. Language, ritual and historical reconstruction: Towards a linguistic, ethnographical and archaeological account of Upper Xingu Society. In David K. Harrison, David S. Rood and Aryenne Dwyer (eds), *Lessons from Documented Endangered Languages*, pp. 129–158. Amsterdam: John Benjamins.

Floyd, Simeon, 2013. Semantic transparency and cultural calquing in the northwest Amazon. In Epps and Stenzel (eds), pp. 271–309.

Franchetto, Bruna (ed.), 2011. *Alto Xingu: Uma sociedade multilíngue [Upper Xingu: A Multilingual Society]*. Rio de Janeiro: Museu do Índio-FUNAI.

Gomez-Imbert, Elsa, 1993. Problemas en torno a la comparación de las lenguas Tukano orientales [Problems of comparison in Eastern Tukanoan languages]. In Maria Luisa Rodríguez de Montes (ed.), *Estado actual de la clasificación de las lenguas indígenas de Colombia [Current State of Classification of the Indigenous Languages of Colombia]*, pp. 235–267. Santafé de Bogotá: Instituto Caro y Cuervo.

Gomez-Imbert, Elsa, 1996. When animals become 'rounded' and 'feminine': Conceptual categories and linguistic classification in a multilingual setting. In John J. Gumperz and Stephen C. Levinson (eds), *Rethinking Linguistic Relativity*, pp. 438–469. Cambridge: Cambridge University Press.

Guillaume, Antoine, in press. Sistemas complejos de movimiento asociado en las lenguas Takana y Pano: Perspectivas descriptiva, tipológica e histórico-comparativa [Complex systems of associated motion in the Takanan and Panoan languages: Descriptive, typological and historical-comparative perspectives]. In A. Guillaume and P. M. Valenzuela (eds), *Estudios sincrónicos y diacrónicos sobre lenguas Pano y Takana: fonología, morfología y sintaxis [Synchronic and Diachronic Studies of Panoan and Takanan Languages: Phonology, Morphology and Syntax]*, special edition of *Amerindia*.

Guillaume, Antoine and Françoise Rose, 2010. Sociative causative markers in South American languages: A possible areal feature. In Franck Floricic (ed.), *Essais de typologie et de linguistique générale: Mélanges offerts à Denis Creissels*, pp. 383–402. Lyon: ENS Éditions.

Guirardello-Damien, Raquel, 2011. Léxico comparativo: Explorando aspectos da história trumai [Lexical comparison: Exploring aspects of Trumai history]. In Franchetto (ed.), pp. 113–154.

Haspelmath, Martin, 2004. How hopeless is genealogical linguistics, and how advanced is areal linguistics? *Studies in Language* 28 (1): 209–223.

Haynie, Hannah, Claire Bowern, Patience Epps, Jane Hill and Patrick McConvell, 2014. Wanderwörter in languages of the Americas and Australia. *Ampersand* 1: 1–18.

Heckenberger, Michael and Eduardo Góes Neves, 2009. Amazonian archaeology. *Annual Review of Anthropology* 38: 251–266.

Hill, Jonathan, 1996. Ethnogenesis in the northwest Amazon: An emerging regional picture. In *History, Power, and Identity: Ethnogenesis in the Americas, 1492–1992*, pp. 142–160. Iowa City: University of Iowa Press.

Hornborg, Alf, 2005. Ethnogenesis, regional integration, and ecology in prehistoric Amazonia: Toward a system perspective. *Current Anthropology* 46 (4): 589–620.

Hornborg, Alf and Love Eriksen, 2011. An attempt to understand Panoan ethnogenesis in relation to long-term patterns and transformations of regional interaction in western Amazonia. In Hornborg and Hill (eds), pp. 129–154.

Hornborg, Alf and Jonathan D. Hill (eds), 2011a. *Ethnicity in Ancient Amazonia: Reconstructing Past Identities from Archeology, Linguistics, and Ethnohistory*. Boulder, CO: University Press of Colorado.

Hornborg, Alf and Jonathan Hill, 2011b. Introduction. In Hornborg and Hill (eds), pp. 1–30.

Howard, Catherine Vaughan, 2001. *Wrought Identities: The Waiwai Expeditions In Search of the 'Unseen Tribes' of Northern Amazonia*. PhD dissertation, University of Chicago.

Jackson, Jean, 1983. *The Fish People: Linguistic Exogamy and Tukanoan Identity in Northwest Amazonia*. Cambridge: Cambridge University Press.

Krashnoukhova, Olga, 2012. *The Noun Phrase in the Languages of South America*. PhD dissertation, Radboud Universiteit, Nijmegen.

Lathrap, Donald, 1973. The antiquity and importance of long-distance trade relationships in the moist tropics of pre-Columbian South America. *World Archaeology* 5 (2): 170–186.

Lévi-Strauss, C., 1948. Tribes of the right bank of the Guaporé river. In J. H. Steward (ed.), *Handbook of South American Indians*, vol. 3, pp. 370–379. Washington, DC: Smithsonian Institution.

Londoño Sulkin, Carlos, 2012. *People of Substance: An Ethnography of Morality in the Colombian Amazon*. Toronto: University of Toronto Press.

Maldi, Denise, 1991. O complexo cultural do marico: Sociedades indígenas do rio Branco, Colorado e Mequens, afluentes do médio Guaporé [The marico cultural complex: Indigenous societies of the Rio Branco, Colorado, and Mequens]. *Boletim do Museu Paraense Emílio Goeldi* 7: 209–269.

Michael, Lev, William Chang and Tammy Stark, 2014. Exploring phonological areality in the circum-Andean region using a naive Bayes classifier. *Language Dynamics and Change* 4 (1): 27–86.

Michael, Lev, Tammy Stark and Will Chang (compilers), 2012. South American Phonological Inventory Database v1.1.2. Survey of California and Other Indian Languages Digital Resource. Berkeley, CA: University of California. http://linguistics.berkeley.edu/~saphon/en/

Migliazza, Ernesto, 1985. Languages of the Orinoco-Amazonia region: Current status. In Harriet E. M. Klein and Louisa R. Stark (eds), *South American Indian Languages: Retrospect and Prospect*, pp. 17–139. Austin, TX: University of Texas Press.

Muysken, Pieter, 2012. Contacts between indigenous languages in South America. In Campbell and Grondona (eds), pp. 235–258.

Muysken, Pieter, Harald Hammarström, Joshua Birchall, Rik van Gijn, Olga Krasnoukhova and Neele Müller, 2015. Linguistic areas, bottom up or top down? The case of the Guaporé-Mamoré region. In Bernard Comrie and Lucía Golluscio (eds), *Language Contact and Documentation / Contacto Lingüístico y Documentación*, pp. 205–238. Berlin: de Gruyter.

Muysken, Pieter, et al., 2014. *South American Indigenous Language Structures (SAILS) Online*. Leipzig: Online Publication of the Max Planck Institute for Evolutionary Anthropology. http://sails.clld.org

Nordenskiöld, Erland, 1922. *Deductions Suggested by the Geographical Distribution of Some Post-Columbian Words Used by the Indians of South America*. Göteborg: Elanders Boktryckeri Aktiebolag.

O'Connor, Loretta and Pieter Muysken (eds), 2014. *The Native Languages of South America*. Cambridge: Cambridge University Press.

Ospina Bozzi, Ana Maria and Elsa Gomez-Imbert, 2013. Predicados complejos en el Noroeste Amazónico: El caso del Yuhup, el Tatuyo y el

Barasana [Complex predicates in the northwest Amazon: The case of Yuhup, Tatuyo, and Barasana]. In Epps and Stenzel (eds), pp. 309–352.

de Oviedo y Valdés, Gonzalo Fernández, 1851–1855 [1535]. *Historia general de las indias [General History of the Indies]*. Madrid.

Payne, Doris, 1990. Introduction. In Doris Payne (ed.), *Amazonian Linguistics: Studies in Lowland South American Languages*, pp. 1–10. Austin, TX: University of Texas Press.

Rivière, Peter, 1984. *Individual and Society in Guiana: A Comparative Study of Amerindian Social Organization*. Cambridge: Cambridge University Press.

Rodrigues, Aryon, 2000. Panorama das línguas indígenas da Amazônia. In Francesc Queixalós and Odile Renault-Lescure (eds), *As línguas amazônicas hoje [Amazonian Languages Today]*, pp. 15–28. São Paulo: Instituto Socioambiental, Museu Parense Emílio Goeldi.

Roth, W. E., 1924. An introductory study of the arts, crafts, and customs of the Guiana Indians. In *Thirty-Eighth Annual Report of the Bureau of American Ethnology*, pp. 26–745.

Rydén, Stig, 1962. Salt trading in the Amazon Basin: Conclusions suggested by the distribution of Guaraní terms for salt. *Anthropos* 57 (3/6): 644–659.

Seifart, Frank, 2007. The prehistory of nominal classification in Witotoan languages. *International Journal of American Linguistics* 73: 411–445.

Seifart, Frank, 2011. *Bora Loans in Resígaro: Massive Morphological and Little Lexical Borrowing in a Moribund Arawakan Language*. Cadernos de Etnolingüística, Série Monografias, 2.

Seifart, Frank, 2012. The principle of morphosyntactic subsystem integrity in language contact: Evidence from morphological borrowing in Resígaro (Arawakan). *Diachronica* 29 (4): 471–504.

Seifart, Frank, Doris Fagua, Jürg Gasché and Juan Alvaro Echeverri (eds), 2009. *A Multimedia Documentation of the Languages of the People of the Center*. Online publication of transcribed and translated Bora, Ocaina, Nonuya, Resígaro, and Witoto audio and video recordings with linguistic and ethnographic annotations and descriptions. Nijmegen: DOBES-MPI.

Seifart, Frank and Doris Payne, 2007. Nominal classification in the northwest Amazon: Issues in areal diffusion and typological characterization. *International Journal of American Linguistics* 73 (4): 381–387.

Seki, Lucy, 1999. The Upper Xingu as an incipient linguistic area. In Dixon and Aikhenvald (eds), pp. 417–430.

Seki, Lucy, 2011. Alto Xingu: Uma sociedade multilíngue? In Franchetto (ed.), pp. 57–86.

Sicoli, Mark A. and Gary Holton, 2014. Linguistic phylogenies support back-migration from Beringia to Asia. *PLoS ONE* 9 (3): e91722.

Silverstein, Michael, 1981. The limits of awareness. *Working Papers in Sociolinguistics* 84. Austin, TX: Southwest Educational Development Laboratory.

Sorensen, Arthur P. Jr, 1967. Multilingualism in the Northwest Amazon. *American Anthropologist* 69: 670–684.

Stenzel, Kristine, 2005. Multilingualism in the Northwest Amazon, revisited. Memorias del Congreso de Idiomas Indígenas de Latinoamérica-II, University of Texas at Austin. www.ailla.utexas.org/site/cilla2/Stenzel_CILLA2_vaupes.pdf

Stenzel, Kristine, 2008. Kotiria 'differential object marking' in cross-linguistic perspective. *Amerindia* 32: 154–181.

Stenzel, Kristine, 2013a. Contact and innovation in Vaupés possession-marking strategies. In Epps and Stenzel (eds), pp. 353–402.

Stenzel, Kristine, 2013b. Butterflies 'leaning' on the doorframe: Expressions of location and position in Kotiria and Wa'ikhana. In Ana Maria Ospina Bozzi (ed.), *Expresión de nociones espaciales en lenguas amazónicas*, pp. 85–107. Bogotá: Instituto Caro y Cuervo/Universidad Nacional de Colombia.

Stenzel, Kristine and Elsa Gomez-Imbert, 2009. Contato linguístico e mudança linguística no noroeste amazônico: o caso do Kotiria (Wanano) [Language contact and language change in the northwest Amazon: The case of Kotiria]. *Revista da ABRALIN* 8: 71–100.

Thomason, Sarah G. and Terrence Kaufman, 1988. *Language Contact, Creolization, and Genetic Linguistics*. Amsterdam: John Benjamins.

Vidal, Alejandra and Verónica Nercesian, 2009. Loanwords in Wichí, a Mataco-Mataguayan language of Argentina. In Martin Haspelmath and Uri Tadmor (eds), *Loanwords in the World's Languages: A Comparative Handbook*, pp. 1015–1034. Berlin and New York: de Gruyter Mouton.

Vidal, Sílvia M., 2000. Kuwé Duwákalumi: The Arawak sacred routes of migration, trade, and resistance. *Ethnohistory* 47 (3/4): 635–667.

Viveiros de Castro, Eduardo, 1998. Cosmological deixis and Amerindian perspectivism. *Journal of the Royal Anthropological Institute* 4 (3): 469–488.

Viveiros de Castro, Eduardo, 2002. *A inconstância da alma selvagem [The Inconstancy of the Savage Soul]*. São Paulo (Brazil): Cosac and Naify Edições.

Viveiros de Castro, Eduardo, 2012. *Cosmological Perspectivism in Amazonia and Elsewhere*. HAU: Journal of Ethnographic Theory, Masterclass Series, vol. 1.

van der Voort, Hein, 2005. Kwaza in comparative perspective. *International Journal of American Linguistics* 71: 365–412.

Whiffen, Thomas 1915. *The North-West Amazons: Notes of Some Months Spent Among Cannibal Tribes*. London: Constable.

Zuñiga, Fernando, 2007. The discourse–syntax interface in northwestern Amazonia: Differential object marking in Makú and some Tucanoan languages. In W. Leo Wetzels (ed.), *Language Endangerment and Endangered Languages: Linguistic and Anthropological Studies with Special Emphasis on the Languages and Cultures of the Andean–Amazonian Border Area*, pp. 209–227. Leiden: University of Leiden.

33

Linguistic Areas, Linguistic Convergence and River Systems in South America

Rik van Gijn, Harald Hammarström, Simon van de Kerke,
Olga Krasnoukhova and Pieter Muysken

33.1 Introduction

The linguistic diversity of the South American continent is quite impressive. There are 576 indigenous languages attested (well enough documented to be classified family-wise), of which 404 are not yet extinct. There are 56 poorly attested languages (which nevertheless were arguably not the same as any of the 576), of which three are known to be not yet extinct (Nordhoff et al. 2013). Furthermore, there are 71 uncontacted living tribes, mainly in Brazil, which may speak anywhere between zero and 71 languages different from those mentioned (Brackelaire and Azanha 2006).

Perhaps the most impressive aspect of the linguistic diversity of South American indigenous languages is their genealogical diversity. The languages fall into some 65 isolates and 44 families (Campbell 2012a; Nordhoff et al. 2013), based on a comparison of basic vocabulary. Nearly all of the families show little internal diversity, indicative of a shallow time depth. Alongside this picture of genealogical diversity, many areal specialists have noted the widespread occurrence of a number of linguistic features across language families, suggesting either sustained contacts between groups of people or remnants from times when the situation in South America may have been genealogically more homogeneous.

We only have historical records going back about 500 years, and the archaeological record is scanty and fragmentary (Eriksen 2011). It follows that there are large tracts of South American prehistory that are unknown. Areal-typological analysis aims to address this gap by finding out which languages have been in contact and how, as evidenced by their typological features. Potentially, the location and intensity of language contact could answer questions about the (un)likelihood of deep genealogical relations and duration of interaction, and provide clues regarding the settlement of the continent. Intertwined with the goal of unravelling history is the modelling of different contact processes. We are not yet in a position to predict the linguistic outcome from a given contact scenario or vice versa (Muysken 2010). To achieve this, attested contact scenarios and attested typological feature distributions need to be confronted further.

However, there is another potentially significant set of variables that is so far largely unexplored in areal-typological linguistics, namely those related to physical geography. If physical geography mediates or even to some extent determines the location and intensity of contact in the region, as well as the dispersal of languages, specific historical events may play a less important role in accounting for the data. In the present chapter, we take up one variable from physical geography commonly thought to play an important role in South America, namely waterways.

We begin this chapter with a selective overview of previous studies in the field of areal linguistics in South America, discussing how the present study relates to them (Section 33.2). Section 33.4 describes the noun phrase structure questionnaire used for this study, and Sections 33.3 and 33.5 discuss the aspects of physical geography relevant to this study. In Section 33.6 we present the results of our survey, and in Section 33.7 we discuss the implications of our results and suggest some further lines of enquiry.

33.2   A Brief History of Areal-linguistic Studies in South America

33.2.1   Linguistic Areas

Traditional areal studies in South America have their roots in diffusionism in cultural anthropology, as reflected, for instance, in the writings of the Swedish archaeologist and anthropologist Nordenskiöld (1877–1932). A linguistic example of this approach is the work of Tessmann. Tessmann (1930: 617–627) attempted to group the languages of the Peruvian Amazon on the basis of lexical criteria (using a 33-word list). He assumes that the five largest accepted families represent 'pure tribes', and groups the remaining languages as 'mixed', depending how many lexical resemblances they show vis-à-vis words typical of the pure tribes. Areal influence is conceived here in terms of influence from large language families, as Tessmann (1930: 618) holds that 'there is a considerable number of isolates' but 'nothing is achieved by positing a family of its own for each isolate'.

A recurring theme in later work in the areal linguistics of South America is often the Andean/Amazonian divide. The dominant perception (also held in neighbouring disciplines such as anthropology, ethnohistory and archaeology) is that there is a basic two-way split in the indigenous languages of South America, between Andean (surveyed by Adelaar with Muysken 2004) and non-Andean or Amazonian (surveyed by Dixon and Aikhenvald 1999). This split is reflected in ideological constructs, with concomitant mental images, of the Andean highland societies and the Amazonian riverside village cultures, of the llama and the canoe. Andean societies are also commonly assumed to be 'more complex, with age-old sedentary habits and a highly diversified and technically well-developed architecture', to cite Adelaar (2008: 23–33).

The Peruvian linguist Alfredo Torero attempted in his final magnum opus (2002: 511–544), *Idiomas de los Andes*, to characterize the languages of the Andes typologically (see also van de Kerke and Muysken 2014). He contrasts the Andes with Mesoamerica, the Area Intermedia proposed by Constenla-Umaña (see below), and a possible Amazonian area (the latter with a question mark). The nine languages/small families taken into consideration are: Aru (Aymaran), Cunza, Cholon, Huarpe, Quechua, Uru(quilla), Mochica, Puquina and Mapuche. Torero uses 40 internal differentiation features to classify the nine languages. Out of the resulting 360 data points, only eleven are question marks. On the basis of his feature classification, Torero distinguishes a number of subareas (sometimes limited to a single language): *Nuclear* (Quechua, Aru), *Altiplano* (Uru, Puquina, Cunza, Huarpe), *Mochica, Cholon* and *Mapuche*.

The approach taken by Adelaar (2008) for the Andes is relatively hard to summarize, since it is not very systematic but at the same time very concise. Over 52 languages are taken into consideration, spanning the entire length of the continent and including the slopes on both sides of the Andes. It is clear that Adelaar conceives of the Andes in very wide terms. On the basis of his survey of structural features, Adelaar (2008: 31) concludes that 'there is still very little evidence that can be helpful for recognizing and delimiting linguistic typological areas, let alone, an Andean linguistic area that would encompass the entire region'. In fact, when contrasted with the rest of the continent, the area can be best defined in terms of negative features (after Adelaar 2008: 31):

- suffixing
- case marking
- no prosodic nasality
- no tone
- no complex vowel systems
- no nominal classifier systems
- no gender
- no stative/active systems
- no well-developed ergativity.

The Amazonian linguistic area is arguably more controversial than the Andean area. Nevertheless, specialists have observed several linguistic traits that are spread over large areas and across language families. We summarize the different characterizations of the Amazonian features in Table 33.1. Work has been done in this area by, among others, Derbyshire and Pullum (1986: 16–20), Doris Payne (1990) and Dixon and Aikhenvald (1999: 8–10). Those features that are mentioned by several authors are underlined; those features that are also found in the Andes are italicized.

The Costa Rican Chibcha specialist Constenla-Umaña (1991) has argued for a linguistic area in between the Andes and the well-known Mesoamerican area (Campbell et al. 1986), which we may call the Colombian–Central America area. He identifies almost twenty features as characteristic of the southern part of his sample, including parts of Ecuador and Peru. This part of his sample is assumed to be characterized by the features in Table 33.2.

Apart from these three major proposed areas of diffusion, proposals for smaller areas have also been made. Perhaps the best-known example of this is the Vaupés area (Aikhenvald 2002) in the border area between Colombia and Brazil, where Arawakan, Tucanoan and – to a lesser extent – Nadahup languages share a complex contact network resulting in convergence between the languages. The Guaporé-Mamoré area between the Bolivian and Brazilian border (Crevels and van der Voort 2008) is composed of two to three cultural areas. It is characterized by extreme genealogical diversity, but the languages share a number of structural traits; as argued by Crevels and van der Voort, these shared features are the result of contact. Seki (1999) argues that the upper Xingú area in central Brazil should be regarded as an incipient linguistic area on the basis of lexical borrowing and a few shared structural traits. Further cases of linguistic areas are summarized in Campbell (2012b: 301–309). It is interesting from the perspective of this chapter that these smaller areas in particular are associated with river systems.

33.2.2 Areal Typology

Until the present century, all proposals for linguistic areas, although drawn from decades of expertise in certain areas, were argued on the basis of impressions and selectively chosen feature lists. Recent studies have effectively closed the methodological gap by defining objective procedures that find and test prototypical linguistic areas, given language features and language locations as input. Muysken et al. (2015) provide a method for testing whether a proposed linguistic area actually has more homogeneity than expected by chance, and a method for finding the area delimitation that has the strongest areal signal.

Table 33.1 *Features used to classify the languages of the Amazon*

	Derbyshire and Pullum	Payne	Dixon and Aikhenvald
Word order	OS languages, noun-adjective, *possessor-possessed, noun-postposition*	Verb-initial orders	*Possessor-possessed*
Co- and subordination	No coordinating conjunctions, juxtaposition		*Subordination often through nominalization*
Alignment	(Remnants of) ergative case marking		Few oblique cases, many signs of ergative, purely nominative/accusative rare
Morphology		High degree of polysynthesis	Polysynthesis, *head-marking, agglutination, many prefixes, but more suffixes, person marking towards the periphery of the verb, many TAME categories optional*
Categories		Directional suffixes in the verb, nominal classification	Extensive semantic gender or noun class marking, *person markers in the nominal paradigm identical to the verbal markers, small number systems*
Phonology			Five vowel systems, nasalization, tone in some areas
Syntax			*Possession marked on the possessed element*, only one argument marked on the predicate, only obligatorily possessed nouns can be incorporated

Table 33.2 *Features of the Colombian–Central America area in Constenla-Umaña (1991)*

Segmental phonology	Absence of mid/high contrast in back vowels, absence of voiced/voiceless distinction in affricates, a voiceless alveolar affricate, palatal consonant subsystem, retroflex fricatives and affricates (not Quechua), mid/high contrast in front vowels (not Quechua), no glottalized sounds, no uvulars, voiceless labial fricative, roundedness opposition in back vowels (not Quechua)
Syntax	Adjective/noun order, numeral/noun order, question word in initial position, accusative case, genitive case, no nominal person marking, tense and aspect with prefixes (not Quechua)

Similarly, Michael et al. (2014) provide a slightly different method for testing whether a proposed area is distinguishable from its complement, and Chang and Michael (2014) define a method for inferring borrowing (as opposed to inheritance) and show that a series of borrowings between neighbouring languages is tantamount to finding a linguistic area.

Another set of recent studies aims to objectively test various proposals concerning feature distributions, typically involving (and calling into question) the Andes/Amazon divide, using standard statistical techniques to explore systematically completed databases. Van Gijn's survey (2014a) of the distribution of Andean and Amazonian features in the upper Amazon area shows that the transition from the Andean to the Amazonian area is gradual and complex, consistent with the intricate history of contact between the different ethnic groups of the area, and casting doubt on the reality of the Andean/Amazonian divide.

In the domain of verbal argument marking, Birchall (2014a, 2014b) examined the diverse array of verbal argument marking patterns encountered across the continent, and tested for regional distributions of certain often-discussed features. Statistical tests showed that many proposed areal distinctions in the literature are in fact not significant, and that an east/west division was often more significant than the classic Andean/Amazonian division. For instance, an inclusive/exclusive distinction in verbal argument marking does have an east/west distinction. Contrary to the suggestion by Adelaar (2008: 31), Birchall (2014a: 205–206) finds that 'the languages of the Andes show a lower distribution of clusivity in indexation than the rest of the continent' and that eastern South America shows 'a statistically significant areal distribution' of clusivity in indexation.

In the nominal domain, Krasnoukhova (2012, 2014) has also shown that in noun phrase structure there is a split between languages spoken in the western part and the eastern part of the continent, and not between the Andes and the Amazon as has been traditionally assumed. While the western part corresponds to the Andean sphere, the eastern part includes languages spoken far beyond the Amazon region. Furthermore, in a case study of semantic features encoded by demonstratives, Krasnoukhova (2014) has shown that the Chaco and the southwest Amazon region stand out on the continent for encoding verbal categories with demonstratives (a case of the 'trait-sprawl areas' suggested by Campbell, Chapter 2, this volume).

Other areal-typological studies suggest that linguistic features that are statistically over-represented in South America, as opposed to other parts of the world, do not necessarily show clear systematic patterns of diffusion within the continent. Van Gijn (2014b) showed that nominalization as a subordination strategy is significantly more pervasive in South America than would be predicted on the basis of global patterns. The patterns found within South America are most consistent with a scenario of several smaller spreads, possibly promoted by a few language families with major extensions (e.g. Quechuan, Tupían, Cariban). In the domain of tense/aspect/mood/evidentiality (TAME) systems, Müller (2014) presented evidence that there is little systematicity in either the genealogical or the areal distribution of specific features, although there are several continent-wide general patterns, including highly frequent desiderative marking.

33.3   Exploring the Role of Geography: River Systems

So far, physical geography has remained an understudied factor, both in the study of linguistic areas and of areal typology. However, several authors (e.g. Dahl et al. 2012; Evans and Levinson 2009; Hammarström and Güldemann 2014; Nettle 1999; Nichols 1990, 1992) have surmised that physical geography plays an important role in shaping patterns of diversity around the globe. This is also the picture that emerges from the overview of the linguistic area studies given above.

The present study is intended as a first step towards integrating factors of physical geography into areal-linguistic studies. We are fully aware that a direct connection between geography and linguistic diversity would grossly oversimplify the complex relation between humans, their environment, and their personal, social and cultural answers to this ecology. It is therefore not our goal to present a deterministic picture of human behaviour. Rather, we want to try and isolate the possible contribution of geography to the patterns of linguistic diversity, in order to assess the facts that are unaccounted for, and which should most probably be explained in terms of human choice and socio-cultural organization and innovation. Having thus acknowledged the relative simplicity of the model presented here, we must try to assess which aspects of geography are important to the rise and maintenance of ethnolinguistic diversity.

We conceive of the role of geography in shaping patterns of diversity as a rather indirect one. In broad terms, the physical surroundings potentially influence the migratory and contact-seeking or contact-avoiding behaviour of groups of people, which in turn influences diversification patterns and creates new contact situations. The role of geography in these processes has two sides: there is a set of factors to do with the *incentive* to spread or move, or get into contact with one's neighbours, and on the other hand a set of factors that either facilitate, or hamper or impede *mobility*, in terms of pathways and barriers.

33.3.1 Incentive Factors

Incentive factors can be described by what Nettle (1999) calls *ecological risk*, defined as 'the probability of a household facing a temporary shortfall, at whatever timescale, in food production' (1999: 79). In a constant and favourable climate and a rich environment (such as a seashore with plenty of molluscs), people are less forced to look for strategies to cope with ecological risk. If the climate is less dependable and the environment less rich, they may resort to a variety of strategies. The most important one in terms of language diversity is 'exchange', since that creates ties between peoples that become so strong that they start to identify or at least interact with each other, thus facilitating the spread of linguistic features.

What are the ecological factors that play a role in the degree of ecological risk? Nettle (1996, 1999) uses climatic data (rainfall and temperature per month) to calculate the length of the growing season. Based on these figures, each month is either included or excluded as part of the growing season. Months for which the average daily temperature is above 6 °C are included in the growing season if the average precipitation in millimetres exceeds twice the average temperature per month. The rationale behind this measure is: the longer the growing season, the lower the ecological risk and therefore the lower the incentive to seek contacts with other groups or to expand or move to other territories. Therefore linguistic diversity is expected to be especially high in areas of low ecological risk.

The growing season is a proxy for the degree of ecological risk, and as such it could be refined further on the basis of soil fertility, for example, or risk factors (especially the risk of inundation), or factors that facilitate the abundance of high-protein food (e.g. larger animals and fish), such as the presence of water and of dense forest. The notion of a growing season is an important one, but it should also be interpreted in terms of the availability of specific crops or gatherable plants.

33.3.2 Mobility Factors

Another set of factors of potential influence on linguistic diversity is concerned with mobility. It is probably true that a people with an incentive to migrate will do so, no matter what the difficulties they encounter on the way; see e.g. Nettle (1996) for a critique of explanations for linguistic diversity on the basis of topographical isolation hypotheses. It is nonetheless useful to consider the topographical context in terms of barriers or pathways of mobility, because it may still predict likely directions of spread, or perhaps highlight the fact that topographical barriers may raise the threshold for incentives to leave. Nichols (1990, 1992) observes that mountainous areas are in some cases linguistically diverse (Himalayas, Caucasus) but in others (e.g. the Andes versus the foothills and adjacent lowlands in South America) the diversity patterns are reversed. We will show that the Andes region is much more homogeneous than neighbouring areas.

   In the absence of a fully fledged theory of the interaction between topographical factors and human mobility, our approach is sketchy and tentative, and focuses on only one part of the programmatic sketch outlined above: the mobility factor of waterways. Especially in the Amazon area, the many rivers provide possibilities for faster travel over relatively long distances, and increased carrying capacity. To the present day, boats are the main means of transportation for many of the indigenous peoples of South America.

   In order to get a firmer grip on the role of physical geography in shaping patterns of diversity, we aim to answer the following three questions:

  (i)   Are river system networks congruent with land distances as the crow flies? If not, do riverine distances mirror typological distances better than distances as the crow flies?
 (ii)   Do languages on the same river system converge on the same structural profile?
(iii)   Are there specific features that spread easily along rivers?

To answer these questions, in the next two sections we give a more detailed introduction to the two major components of our study, the noun phrase database (Section 33.4) and the classification of geographical areas in South America (Section 33.5).

33.4 The Noun Phrase (NP) Database and Earlier Results

As mentioned, the structural features that we take into account in this chapter relate to NP structure. Technically speaking, the basis for the analysis is a questionnaire database, developed by Krasnoukhova (2012) in order to outline the structure of the NP in South American languages. The NP questionnaire consists of six general questions (e.g. constituent order at the clause level) and 50 questions which specifically relate to the NP. The latter group of questions is divided into 31 main questions and 19 dependent questions. The areas of the NP which are explored in the questionnaire include those listed below.

NP structure
- Constituent order within the NP. Modifier categories such as demonstratives, numerals and adjectives were all considered as semantic categories.
- Presence and realization of agreement within the NP.

Modifiers within the NP
- Articles, demonstratives.
- Adjectives, grammatical status of adjectives.
- Numerals, grammatical status of numerals.

NP related issues
- Grammatical expression and conditions on the realization of number within the NP.
- Noun categorization devices, such as classifiers, and gender and noun class systems.
- Attributive possessive constructions. The parameters under investigation include: head versus dependent marking of possession, and the presence and formal realization of (in)alienability.
- Spatial deixis, with a focus on semantic features that can be encoded by adnominal demonstratives.
- Grammatical marking of temporal distinctions within the NP.

This questionnaire was filled in by Krasnoukhova and van de Kerke for 97 languages using descriptive materials, and whenever possible using information provided by specialists working on a specific language. The language sample used for this chapter includes representatives of 30 language families and 16 isolates. When constructing the sample we paid attention to the areal distribution of languages in order to ensure an adequate geographical coverage. Table 33A.1 in the appendix lists the languages included in our sample, along with their genealogical affiliation.

In what follows, we give a summary of observations based on Krasnoukhova (2012, 2014) with respect to the areal distribution of NP features. Krasnoukhova observed that there is evidence in the NP domain for a split between languages spoken in the *western* versus the *eastern* part of the continent, and not so much the split between the Andes and the Amazon. The western group consists of languages spoken along the western part of the continent and roughly corresponds with the Andean sphere, while the eastern group includes languages spoken in the rest of the continent, and thus is not limited to the Amazon region. Namely, the eastern group includes languages spoken far beyond the Amazon region and includes, for instance, the eastern and southern part of Brazil, the Chaco and the Southern Cone. What are the linguistic features that suggest the west/east split in the NP domain?

The most robust features of the languages spoken in the western part are the following:

– word order within the NP: pre-head position for all modifiers (demonstratives, lexical possessors, numerals, property words);
– property words are morphologically nominal;
– absence of gender in NP;
– absence of gender distinction in personal pronouns;
– absence of classifiers;
– absence of temporal distinction within the NP;
– absence of a class of inalienable nouns.

The most robust features of the languages spoken in the eastern group can be condensed to the following list:

– word order within the NP, i.e. pre-head position for demonstratives, lexical possessors and numerals, and post-head position for property words;
– small or no distinct adjective class;
– property words are verbal;
– presence of gender in the NP;
– presence of classifiers, often of the multifunctional type;
– presence of temporal distinction within the NP (a less robust feature);
– presence of a class of inalienable nouns (a very robust feature).

Just to give a few concrete illustrations, for instance, hardly any language of the Andean sphere encodes property words by means of verbs, whereas languages in which property concepts are encoded by verbs are predominant in the northwest Amazon and the southwest Amazon regions; they are also found in the Chaco (e.g. Tapiete and Wichi), the eastern and southern part of Brazil (e.g. Timbira and Bororo) and in the Southern Cone (Tehuelche).

As for NP constituents, templates in which all modifiers tend to occur on one side of the noun are all found along the western edge of the continent, e.g. in Aymara, Huallaga Quechua, Imbabura Quechua, Leko, Mapuche, Tsafiki and Yanesha'. In Miraña, a language of the northwest Amazon region, all modifiers also tend to occur pre-head, therefore it constitutes an exception in this observation. Conversely, a template in which some modifiers (mainly demonstratives, possessors and numerals) always precede the head noun and some modifiers (mainly property words) always follow it, is found predominantly in languages outside the Andean sphere: e.g. Warao, Ninam, Dâw, Hup, Puinave, Urarina, Matsés, Yaminahua, Jarawara, Baure, Movima, Itonama, Mekens, Gavião, Wari', Karo, Kanoê,

Mamaindê, Sabanê, Wichí, Pilagá, Chamacoco, Bororo, Kamaiurá, Trumai and Timbira. There are a few exceptions here: the latter template is also found in three languages spoken in the northwestern part of Colombia, i.e. Ika, Nasa Yuwe and Northern Emberá.

To give one more example, a great majority of languages spoken along the western edge of the continent lack a class of inalienable nouns, whereas languages in the rest of the continent predominantly have such a class. Specifically, the following languages do not have a class of inalienable nouns: Quechua and Aymara, spoken in the Andes; Mapuche, spoken in the Southern Andes; Tsafiki, Awa Pit, Nasa Yuwe and Northern Emberá, spoken in the western part of Ecuador and Colombia. Inalienable nouns are also absent in Aguaruna, in the northern Peruvian foothills, and Shipibo-Conibo and Urarina, spoken in the Western Amazon (Peru). Exceptions from the observations are Warao (spoken in western Guiana and northeastern Venezuela) and Kwaza and Sabanê (spoken in the southwest Amazon region). All other languages in the sample have a class of inalienable nouns.

The data on the NP also show that the following features *cannot* be treated as characteristic of any particular larger area (western versus eastern part, specifically Andes versus Amazon), as they are found in the languages across the continent (see also the discussion in Campbell 2012b: 301–304):

- number distinction/marking in personal pronouns;
- number distinction/marking in the NP;
- inclusive/exclusive distinction in free personal pronouns.

Features such as 'locus of possession marking' were carefully examined for areality too, since the head-marking pattern has been proposed in the literature among the features of the 'Amazonian linguistic area' and the double-marking pattern was proposed among the features of the 'Andean linguistic area' (Dixon and Aikhenvald 1999: 8, 10). Our NP data showed no evidence for this areal division. It is correct to say that the double-marking pattern is found predominantly in the languages spoken in the Andes (specifically, among the Aymaran and many of the Quechuan variants, and in Aguaruna), but this is not the only possession strategy found in the languages spoken in the Andes. For instance, Chipaya is dependent-marking, as well as Imbabura Quechua. Likewise, there is no good evidence to generalize that Amazonian languages are predominantly head-marking for possession: both a dependent-marking and a head-marking pattern are equally common in the Amazonian languages in the sample. What was found was a much smaller areal clustering: namely, dependent-marking languages are more concentrated in the Western Amazon region, while head-marking languages are more present in the Bolivian lowlands and in the Chaco. In addition, head-marking languages are found along the western coast of South America (e.g. Tsafiki, Ika) and in the Southern Cone (e.g. Tehuelche) (see Krasnoukhova 2012 for more details).

33.5   The Major Drainage Basins of South America

The importance of rivers and river systems for the population dynamics in South America cannot be overestimated (Dunne and Mertes 2007). It is no coincidence that many proposals for linguistic areas of the continent are associated with river systems: the Vaupés-Içana (Aikhenvald 2002), the Guaporé-Mamoré (Crevels and van der Voort 2008) and the Xingú (Seki 1999). River systems, and the ecologies associated with them, to a considerable extent determine the possibilities for gathering and cultivating food and cultivating plants, and they facilitate mobility and with it contact between peoples. The effect of the ecological circumstances can be expected to be even greater for locally organized, rural economies (Nettle 1999), as is the case for most indigenous cultures of South America.

The connection between linguistic areas and river systems, mentioned above, raises the question of whether there is a more general interaction between river systems/ecologies and the degree of linguistic convergence. What we set out to do in this chapter, therefore, is to define a number of ecological zones mainly based on river systems, and look for patterns of structural diversity and convergence within each of these areas.

33.5.1   The South American Physical Space

The elements responsible for creating the ecological 'hardware', that is, the physical landscape and the basic ecological conditions of an area, are tectonism (the shaping of the Earth's crust) and climate (Orme 2007). In turn, these two constrain flora and fauna, and to a certain extent human activity. The South American continent is delimited in the northwest by the border of Colombia with Panama, and on all other sides by seas and oceans – the Caribbean Sea to the north, the South Pacific Ocean to the west and the Atlantic Ocean to the east. Broadly speaking, the physical geography of South America is dominated by three highland areas: the ancient Precambrian (prior to 541 million years ago) Guyanan and Brazilian highlands, and the much younger Andean mountain range, which only assumed its present shape in the Cretaceous period (145–166 million years ago). The rivers that spring from these highland areas flow through the vast lowland areas, forming some of the largest river systems in the world. These elements form the basis that underlies the different ecological systems of the continent.

In order to achieve a more local perspective (assuming that contact in local ecosystems or river systems becomes even more manifest), we divide the continent into several smaller regions. First, we distinguish between the very different ecosystems of the Pacific, the Andes and the Amazon. Second, we make further distinctions within the Amazon and Andean area, based on more local river systems and other factors.

33.5.2 Ecological Zones

The Andean mountain range is usually divided into a southern, central and northern part. However, there are different ways to determine the borders of these areas (Torero 2002: 13): to the south the Bolivian Altiplano may or may not be counted as part of the Southern Andes, and to the north, the Ecuadorian Andes are either included in or excluded from the Northern Andes. In line with our continental north/south divide, and with the secondary north/south divide in Western Amazonia, we put the border between the Central and Northern Andes in northern Peru and southern Colombia, where the Andean mountain range takes the shape of three parallel cordilleras. To the south, the border is determined by the very broad Bolivian Andean range, where the rivers flowing north join the Amazon but those flowing south join the Paraguay River, and eventually the Río de la Plata. Because of low language diversity to the south of the Gran Chaco, the Southern Andes and Southern Cone are considered together as a single area. The Andean areas are strictly speaking not river-defined areas, but they do form ecologically coherent areas, and they cannot easily be grouped with any of the river-based areas.

We also regard the Pacific coast as a separate area. Few Pacific coastal languages have survived, causing the focus of our Pacific area for the purposes of this chapter to be on the northern Peruvian/Ecuadorian coast, where a relatively low passage of the Andes between northern Peru and southern Ecuador made trade between the coast and the Amazon possible (Adelaar with Muysken 2004: 6).

In the northeast, we separate the Orinoco basin in Venezuela from the adjacent Guyanas and northern Brazil, and south of this area we recognize smaller river systems, which are defined in Table 33.3. The Río de la Plata basin (in particular the western part, the Gran Chaco in northern Argentina, southern Bolivia and Paraguay) and the Southern Cone plus Southern Andes are also separated. In the list that follows, we briefly outline the smaller areas and indicate which of the sample languages are spoken in each region. The numbers in the first column of the table refer to the numbers in the accompanying map (Map 33.1).

Mapping the NP questionnaire database discussed in Section 33.4 onto the geographical zones discussed in this section, we can now move to a discussion of the results.

Table 33.3 *Ecological zones of South America: regions, locations and sample languages*

	Region	Delimitation/description	Sample languages
1	Northern Andes	Colombian Andes	Arhuaco, Embera, Páez
2	Orinoco	Venezuelan Orinoco basin	Nhengatú, Ninam, Panare, Puinave
3	Guyanas	French and British Guyana, Surinam, northern Brazil	Emérillon, Hixkaryána, Papiamento, Trió, Warao
4	Pacific	Pacific coast: practically the Ecuadorian Pacific	Awa-Cuaiquer, Colorado, Mochica
5	Napo-Marañon	Ecuadorian and north Peruvian eastern slopes and lowlands	Bora, Aguaruna, Kokama, Muniche, Shuar, Urarina, Cofán, Iquito, Arabela
6	Vaupés	The Colombian–Brazilian border	Hup, Cubeo, Dâw, Desano, Tariana
7	Solimões	Western Brazil between the Jurua and Purus Rivers, and up to the Ucayali in the west	Jarawara, Matsés, Yaminahua
8	Tapajos-Madeira	River basins in southern Amazonia directly east of the Madeira-Guaporé line	Apurinã, Bororo
9	Xingú-Tocantins	Easternmost river basin in southern Amazonia	Kamaiurá, Krikati-Timbira, Trumai
10	Central Andes	Ecuadorian, Peruvian and Bolivian Andes	Aymara, Cusco Quechua, Huallaga Quechua, Uru, Chipaya
11	Huallaga-Ucayali	Central-south Peruvian lowlands	Shipibo-Conibo, Yanesha', Cholon
12	Beni-Guaporé	Area between the Beni and Guaporé Rivers in Bolivia and Rondônia	Baure, Cavineña, Gavião, Itonama, Kanoê, Karitiana, Karo, Kwazá, Lakondê, Leko, Mamainde, Moseten, Movima, Sabanê, Mekens, Warí, Yurakaré
13	Río de la Plata basin	Northern Argentina, Paraguay	Wichí, Chamacoco, Mocoví, Pilagá, Tapiete
14	Southern Cone	Central and southern Argentina and adjacent areas in Chile	Tehuelche, Mapudungun, Selknam-Ona, Gününa Küne-Puelche

33.6   Results

Given the geographical information about the various river systems, and the datasets on NP features for the languages in our sample, we are now in a position to try and answer a number of questions. As mentioned above, and repeated here for convenience, we address the following issues.

(i)   Are river system networks congruent with land distances as the crow flies? If not, do riverine distances mirror typological distances better than distances as the crow flies?

(ii)   Do languages on the same river system converge on the same structural profile?

(iii)   Are there specific features that spread easily along rivers?

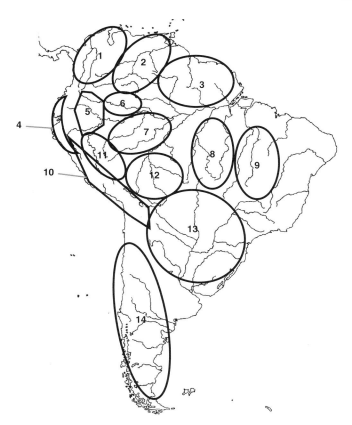

Map 33.1 Ecological zones of South America: smaller regions considered in the present study. See Table 33.3 for legend

Several methodological remarks are in order here. First, the added geographical information by itself does not help decide whether a certain feature distribution could reflect deep time geographical relationships or later contact. A river may be a conduit for exchange relations between unrelated groups as well as a path along which a population spread. Second, not all measures can be applied globally. It does not make sense to calculate river distance between two points which are not directly connected by rivers.

Our data on rivers in South America come from the freely accessible country-by-country river information from DIVA-GIS.[1] The granularity of these data is too fine for the purposes of this chapter, as it includes what appears to be every small creek on the continent. We selected the 600 largest shapes, resulting in what is impressionistically a granularity suitable for the purposes in the present chapter. This yields the river system shown in

---

[1] www.diva-gis.org/gdata

Map 33.2 River data and language locations in South America. Lines from every language location to their nearest point on a river

Map 33.2, shown at a resolution of 1/8 of a degree per point. Languages are represented with their centrepoint coordinates from Nordhoff et al. (2013).

We define river distances only for pairs of languages which are in the same drainage area, that is, languages that are actually connected by a river system. The river distance between two languages A and B is defined by the distance of A to the nearest point on a river plus the distance of B to the nearest point on a river plus the shortest river path between those two points. Map 33.2 shows a line from every language location to its nearest point on a river (based on the river data explained above). As an example,

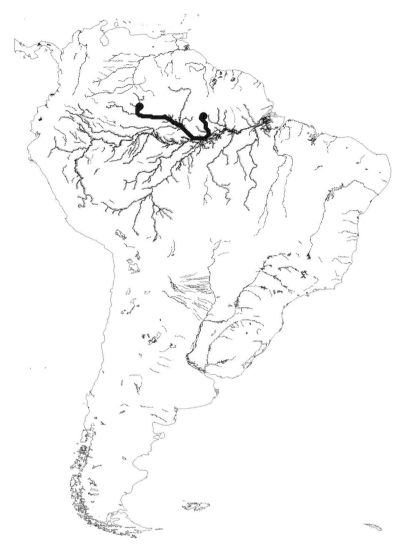

Map 33.3 The river path between the languages Hixkaryána and Nhengatu

in Map 33.3 the river path between the languages Hixkaryána and Nhengatu is indicated. The distance between Hixkaryána as the crow flies is 917 kilometres whereas the river distance, following the river path, is 1,642 kilometres.

33.6.1 River versus Bird Distances

Before relating any linguistic data to water distances, we must ask if there are any essential differences between riverine distances and distances as the crow flies. There are some logical possibilities. One possibility is that river distance for all language pairs merely prolongs the bird distance by a certain percentage. In this case, the landscape of contact effects would be the same as if there were no rivers, and the only reason to compare linguistic data and river distances would be to estimate the size of the effect, not the locus. On the other hand, it may be that some language pairs differ greatly from other pairs in terms of water distance. That is, some pairs of languages connected by a straight river path have a river distance which is very close in kilometres to their bird distance, while other pairs, that require a lengthy detour by river, have a river distance far higher than their bird distance. In this case it would be possible to test for riverine contact as a factor different from contact by proximity in general. If so, the linguistic distances should correspond better to the riverine distances than the bird distances.

Figure 33.1 shows all 510 pairs of languages for which water distances are defined, plotted against their bird distance. The water distance for most language pairs can indeed be found by adding a percentage to their bird distance, though not for all. The river distances between Cusco Quechua and Quechuan languages further north requires a very long downward route via the Madre de Dios, up the Madeira, and back up the Amazon and the Ucayali, totalling around 5,000 kilometres. Similarly, there are other pairs which require river travel down the Napo in

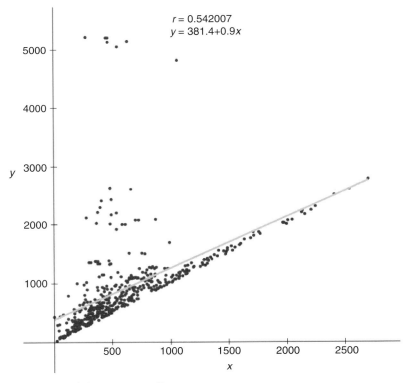

Figure 33.1 Bird versus water distance

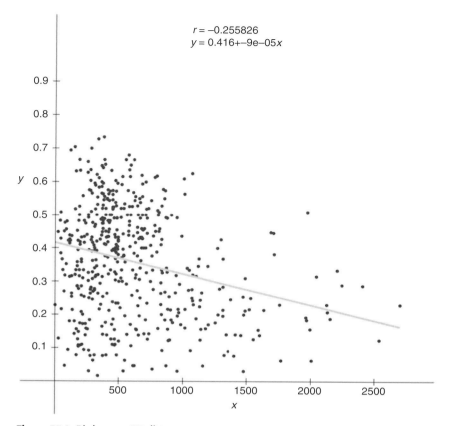

$r = -0.255826$
$y = 0.416+-9e-05x$

Figure 33.2 Bird versus NP distance

Ecuador only to turn around at the Japurá and go as far back up, totalling around 2,000 kilometres.

For the linguistic distance between a pair of languages, we use the Hamming distance, which is simply the percentage of features which do not have the same value in the two languages (see Hammarström and O'Connor 2013). For example, if 80 features are defined for the pair of languages and they agree in value for 20 of them, then the distance is $60/80 = 0.75$. The correlation between bird distance and linguistic (NP) distance is shown in Figure 33.2. The correlation between water distance and linguistic (NP) distance is shown in Figure 33.3.

The size of the correlation for bird and NP distance is $r = -0.26$, while for water and NP distance it is slightly less strong, $r = -0.23$. So there is little overall improvement in using water distances to predict NP distance. We also did a more specific test, looking only at the regions where the river systems were thought to be more significant, that is, Huallaga-Ucayali, Orinoco, Guaporé-Mamoré, Vaupés, Napo-Marañon, Tapajos-Madeira, Xingú-Tocantins and Solimões, thereby excluding pairs such as those involving the highly unnatural river route between Cusco Quechua

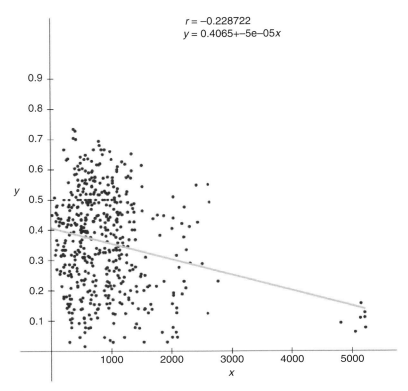

Figure 33.3 Water versus NP distance

and other Quechuan languages. In those cases, there were plausible land routes, as indeed were created during the Inca Empire.

Doing this drastically changes both bird/water distance correlations with NP distance to the values $r = 0.11$ and $r = 0.12$ respectively. So again there was no appreciable difference of water vis-à-vis bird distance.[2] We can thus answer the first question. Riverine distances are very different from distances as the crow flies for many language pairs, but the linguistic differences are not better predicted by the riverine distances.

33.6.2 Riverine Areas

While there is no simple relationship involving water distance and NP distance in our data, there may be a more indirect effect of river

[2] While we were concerned with differences between water and bird distance, the reader may have noted that the correlation in the first case was negative, i.e. that longer geographical distance predicts shorter linguistic distance. This unintuitive result is, however, due to the many pairs of languages belonging to the shallow but geographically widespread Quechua family. Quechuan languages are much more similar to other Quechuan languages far away than to many neighbouring non-Quechuan languages and, in general, much more similar to each other than a random pair of languages from the rest of the sample. In the second case the Quechuan languages were not included, and the geographic versus linguistic correlation then showed the intuitively expected positive polarity.

systems. Languages on the same river system may be hypothesized to interact both along the main waterways and cut across headwaters. Given a sufficiently long time, these languages may then influence each other structurally. The hypothesis is that they influence each other more than any set of geographically adjacent languages which do not share a river system. We thus test if the languages belonging to the same riverine area are more similar to each other than (1) random collections of the same size (Sig Random), (2) geographically coherent sets of languages of the same size (Sig Geo), and (3) random collections of languages of the same size *from different families* (Sig FamI). To generate a random geographically coherent set of languages, we start from a random language and then continue picking the geographically nearest language until the desired size has been reached. The difference between riverine areas and geographically coherent areas is merely that the riverine areas are geographically coherent sets of languages necessarily associated with a river system. To generate a random set of languages from different families, we first select a random set of families of the desired number and then select a random member from each. Table 33.4 shows the average distance of the languages within each area and the significance vis-à-vis random sets of languages, random geographically coherent sets of languages and random sets of languages from different families, of the same size as the area in question. The significance number counts the number of random sets with a higher average distance. A number of 950 or higher can be equated with a conventional significance level of 0.05.

Table 33.4 *Convergence of the NP profile in different areas of South America*

	Avg Dist[a]	Sig Random	Sig Geo	Sig FamI
Northern Andes	0.30	924	965	975
La Plata	0.47	265	114	461
Guyanas	0.43	541	612	628
Southern Cone	0.43	564	637	701
Huallaga-Ucayali	0.38	859	892	924
Central Andes	0.18	1,000	1,000	1,000
Orinoco	0.47	379	357	444
Vaupés	0.43	611	605	703
Napo-Marañon	0.40	879	907	971
Solimões	0.45	521	496	507
Xingú-Tocantins	0.33	864	910	935
Guaporé-Mamoré	0.47	157	82	304
Pacific	0.34	883	971	

[a] *Avg dist is the average distance for languages in the same area. Sig Random indicates how many (out of 1,000) random sets of languages of the corresponding size have a lower average similarity. Sig Geo indicates how many (out of 1,000) random sets of geographically coherent languages of the corresponding size have a lower average similarity. Sig FamI indicates how many (out of 1,000) random sets (of the corresponding size) of languages from different families have a lower average similarity.*

Few, if any, riverine areas show significant convergence. The only one to clearly do so is the well-known Central Andes area, where the similarity is known to be due to genealogical inheritance and intense language contact, neither involving rivers in any significant way. Also the Northern Andes and Napo-Marañon areas owe their high significance numbers to the fact that they encompass subsets of very close Quechua varieties. Interestingly, the set of riverine areas tested includes prospective and established linguistic areas like the Guaporé-Mamoré and the Vaupés, whose NP convergence is well within the bounds of similarity expected for random sets of languages. Thus we can answer the second question: merely being in the same river system is not sufficient for convergence of the entire NP profile.

33.6.3 Riverine Features

While entire typological profiles do not appear to converge in languages of the same river system, a weaker effect of rivers may be operational. Certain unstable features, not entire profiles, may spread easily along rivers. The hypothesis is that this concerns only the most unstable features, because if it concerned every feature the entire profiles would have converged. To get an idea of which features are likely to be inherently stable versus unstable, we take over the stability measure calculated in Muysken et al. (2014). This essentially measures the probability that a feature value remains the same in the transition from a proto-language to a modern language within a language family.

Suppose we define a 'riverine' feature as one which tends to have the same value in each riverine area, i.e. homogeneous within a riverine area. For example, if two-thirds of languages in an area have the same value in a certain riverine area, then the homogeneity in that area is 0.67. The overall homogeneity is the average it has across all riverine areas. (For this test, we have used only the strictly river-defined areas, excluding the Central Andes and Southern Cone areas.) We may also test for significance of homogeneity by comparing simulated random and geographically coherent sets of the same size (similar to the above). The riverine-ness of each feature is shown below (with the number of languages in the full sample for which the feature is defined, the overall homogeneity and significance of this).

Table 33.5 shows figures for how riverine a feature is, along with its stability value. Although there are a number of NP features which achieve high significance individually, notably many that concern possession, the numbers have not been controlled for multiple testing. There are about equally many that achieve a correspondingly low significance, suggesting that there are random fluctuations in both directions. Also, more importantly, there is no correlation between low stability and riverine-ness ($r \approx 0.01$).

Table 33.5 *How 'riverine' are the NP features?*

Feature[a]	No.	Hom.	Sig Random	Sig Geo	Stability
NP406: Do possessive constructions with optionally possessed nouns differ from those with obligatorily possessed nouns? (= Is alienable and inalienable possession formally distinguished?)	61	0.683	0.999	1.000	0.872
NP405: Are there nouns denoting obligatorily possessed items?	94	0.809	0.999	1.000	0.901
NP408: Does the language have a separate form for third person possessive reflexive?	34	0.824	0.996	0.998	1.000
NP160: What is the most frequent order of adjective and degree word?	31	0.807	0.994	0.998	1.000
NP13: In what way are indefinite pronouns realized?	30	0.807	0.994	0.998	1.000
NP409: Can pronominal possessors (pronoun, affix, clitic) be related to main tense and verbal person markers (pronoun, affix, clitic)?	25	0.794	0.993	0.996	0.825
NP150: What is the most frequent order of relative clause and noun?	82	0.709	0.989	0.997	0.789
NP404: In possessive constructions with a pronominal possessor, is the POSSESSED noun usually marked?	95	0.632	0.962	0.921	0.837
NP740: Is there a morphologically indicated collective marker?	81	0.691	0.947	0.962	0.869
NP305: How many distance contrasts do adnominal demonstratives encode?	91	0.668	0.900	0.951	0.757
NP304: What system of demonstratives is present in the language? (Distance-oriented system vs person-oriented system.)	80	0.725	0.891	0.920	0.820
NP307: Can adnominal demonstratives encode altitude?	92	0.974	0.889	0.872	0.968
NP508: Which word class do (the majority of) words denoting SPEED belong to?	66	0.550	0.882	0.958	0.792
NP507: Which word class do (the majority of) words denoting HUMAN PROPENSITY belong to?	67	0.587	0.866	0.882	0.861
NP402: In possessive constructions with a nominal possessor, is the POSSESSED noun usually marked?	96	0.686	0.855	0.819	0.806
NP401: In possessive constructions with a nominal possessor, is the POSSESSOR usually marked?	96	0.700	0.851	0.964	0.896

[a] The columns of the table consist, from left to right, of (i) every NP feature, (ii) the number of languages for which it is defined, (iii) its average homogeneity in riverine areas, (iv) the significance of this homogeneity with respect to randomized mirrors of the riverine areas, (v) the significance of this homogeneity with respect to geographically coherent randomized mirrors of the riverine areas, and (vi) the feature's stability value.

Table 33.5 (*cont.*)

Feature	No.	Hom.	Sig Random	Sig Geo	Stability
NP311: Can adnominal demonstratives encode gender?	93	0.837	0.830	0.826	0.975
NP230: Is there agreement between demonstrative/ determiner and the noun in the NP?	88	0.727	0.823	0.897	0.896
NP810: How many gender distinctions are realized within the NP?	94	0.853	0.822	0.926	0.922
NP312: Can adnominal demonstratives encode number?	92	0.737	0.809	0.561	0.850
NP140: What is the most frequent order of property word (adjective) and noun?	95	0.626	0.797	0.626	0.771
NP309: Can adnominal demonstratives encode movement?	93	0.928	0.782	0.854	0.963
NP12: Is nominalization the main strategy for complement clause formation?	60	0.605	0.774	0.772	0.900
NP316: What is the morphological composition of adverbial demonstratives (as compared to adnominal demonstratives)?	86	0.645	0.713	0.748	0.785
NP317: How many distance contrasts do adverbial demonstratives encode?	77	0.603	0.688	0.815	0.849
NP506: Which word class do (the majority of) words denoting PHYSICAL PROPERTY belong to?	69	0.574	0.685	0.677	0.882
NP308: Can adnominal demonstratives encode position of the referent in space or posture?	93	0.896	0.684	0.673	0.963
NP901: What kind of adposition type is most dominant?	87	0.684	0.666	0.721	0.861
NP505: Which word class do (the majority of) words denoting COLOUR belong to?	70	0.574	0.647	0.686	0.864
NP11: Is nominalization the main strategy for adverbial clause formation?	61	0.562	0.622	0.676	0.925
NP130: What is the most frequent order of possessor and possessed?	97	0.897	0.622	0.525	0.941
NP315: Do demonstratives receive different inflectional features when used pronominally or adnominally?	80	0.642	0.616	0.858	0.828
NP313: Can adnominal demonstratives encode physical properties of the referent?	92	0.879	0.609	0.585	0.942
NP720: Do nouns have a morphologically marked dual?	87	0.834	0.601	0.473	0.952
NP820: Are there any (grammaticalized) sex-markers (realized on the noun itself)?	90	0.726	0.573	0.505	0.851
NP730: Do nouns have a morphologically marked paucal form?	89	0.899	0.570	0.443	1.000
NP2: What is the pragmatically unmarked word order for a transitive clause?	94	0.632	0.544	0.561	0.798
NP314: Do adnominal demonstrative roots require further derivation?	90	0.868	0.531	0.377	0.953
NP403: In possessive constructions with a pronominal possessor, is the POSSESSOR usually marked?	96	0.635	0.523	0.726	0.831
NP310: Can adnominal demonstratives encode animacy?	93	0.836	0.481	0.275	0.950
NP9: Is there a number distinction in third person pronouns?	96	0.800	0.479	0.311	0.861
NP301: Are there indefinite articles in use?	86	0.655	0.466	0.585	0.763

Question					
NP7: Is there an inclusive/exclusive distinction in personal pronouns?	96	0.685	0.436	0.182	0.924
NP407: Is a word/morpheme meaning 'pet' (or similar) required in possessive constructions involving nouns which denote (domesticated) animals and/or food?	83	0.717	0.368	0.384	0.858
NP303: Are third person pronouns and demonstratives related?	91	0.597	0.334	0.373	0.773
NP830: Are there classifiers?	93	0.690	0.329	0.172	0.906
NP503: Which word class do (the majority of) words denoting AGE belong to?	68	0.524	0.328	0.224	0.774
NP4: Is there a copula for predicate nouns? (Only present tense clauses are taken into account.)	79	0.590	0.327	0.548	0.857
NP1020: Can temporal or aspectual distinctions with a propositional scope be marked on the head noun?	84	0.818	0.308	0.412	0.944
NP501: Is there a class of synchronically underived adjectival elements (lexemes)?	96	0.650	0.302	0.297	0.825
NP10: Is nominalization the main strategy for attributive (relative) clause formation?	70	0.579	0.259	0.338	0.913
NP1: What is the pragmatically unmarked word order for an intransitive clause?	95	0.711	0.197	0.286	0.866
NP5: Is there a copula for predicate locative phrases? (Only present tense clauses are taken into account.)	61	0.526	0.173	0.313	0.823
NP6: Is there a copula for predicate adjectives?	76	0.560	0.161	0.356	0.861
NP504: Which word class do (the majority of) words denoting VALUE belong to?	70	0.533	0.143	0.165	0.855
NP210: Is there agreement between adjective (property word) and the noun in the NP?	86	0.654	0.139	0.242	0.890
NP306: Can adnominal demonstratives encode visibility?	93	0.804	0.139	0.216	0.925
NP610: Which class do native numerals belong to?	65	0.490	0.128	0.261	0.824
NP110: What is the most frequent order of demonstrative and noun?	96	0.819	0.123	0.101	0.935
NP8: Is there a gender distinction in independent personal pronouns?	96	0.685	0.090	0.054	0.900
NP120: What is the most frequent order of numeral and noun?	93	0.663	0.089	0.071	0.906
NP710: Do nouns have a morphologically marked singular versus plural distinction?	96	0.619	0.087	0.058	0.815
NP502: Which word class do (the majority of) words denoting DIMENSION belong to?	69	0.513	0.086	0.065	0.858
NP220: Is there agreement between numeral and the noun in the NP?	83	0.655	0.079	0.103	0.932
NP302: Are there definite articles in use?	89	0.583	0.053	0.103	0.818
NP1010: Can any temporal or aspectual distinctions, restricted to NPs, be marked on the head noun?	86	0.625	0.024	0.015	0.910

We are thus inclined to answer the third question in the negative too: we find little evidence for specific features whose spread would be facilitated by rivers.

33.7 Discussion and Conclusion

The results of our study suggest that river systems do not contribute significantly to patterns of diffusion of structural NP features in South America. This is a surprising result given the fact that waterways have played such an important role in the mobility of the indigenous peoples of the continent. A few reasons for this discrepancy can be put forward, leading to a number of suggestions for further research.

First, it may be the case that structural features of the noun phrase are not very prone to diffusion through contact, perhaps due to the fact that overt NPs in South American languages with their highly synthetic verbal morphology are not altogether common. This would for instance also explain why some of the established or proposed linguistic areas associated with particular river systems do not show any significant degree of convergence either. On the other hand, Krasnoukhova (2012) does show that there are some large-scale areal patterns in South America for some of the NP-related features in her study. One suggestion for further research may nevertheless be to look at other domains of grammar.

The picture regarding word borrowing, for instance, is also quite complex. Bowern et al. (2011) report that word borrowing is not frequent among the Amazonian languages. Altogether, there is no evidence that suggests the contrary. Greenberg (1987) mentions some lexical items that have a surprisingly wide distribution, but without a systematic pattern. Muysken (2012: 252) draws attention to specific culture items that have a very wide distribution, such as the words for 'chicken' or 'hundred'. It would be good to test the distribution of specific lexical items in terms of river systems. Similarly, the spread of phonological features should be studied keeping river systems in mind. The same holds, of course, for other morphosyntactic features.

Second, it may be the case that river systems are simply less relevant to human migratory and contact patterns than is often assumed. It is probably too early to say whether or not this conclusion holds up, especially given the fact that many of the linguistic areas discussed in Campbell (2012b) for South America are connected to some river system. Furthermore, it may be a matter of finding the right scale. Even the smaller areas in our study are still rather large, and perhaps a more fine-grained analysis is required to find areal patterns of a more local nature. Finally, as mentioned in Section 33.3.2 above, waterways are only one element of a potentially much more encompassing geographical approach to linguistic diversity. Embedding the role of river systems into such a larger programmatic approach may also yield more refined results.

Third, the relation between river systems and specific structural features may simply be too indirect to yield significant results. After all, although physical geography may influence whether people decide to expand, or to contact other people, and also the directions they are most likely to travel for these purposes, there is still a large field of unknown variables that will influence the eventual patterns of structural linguistic diversity.

Fourth, rivers can unite peoples on both sides if they are easily navigable and have good communication systems. On the other hand, very large rivers or those difficult to navigate can separate peoples, in which case we have the opposite effect. So size and navigability play an important role.

Fifth, these unknowns lie within the field of human agency. Rivers exist 'in the mind' as well.[3] People may have different strategies to reduce their ecological risk, which do not necessarily involve either migration or trade (such as diversification or storage, see Nettle 1999: 80) and therefore not necessarily language contact. And even if they respond to disadvantageous ecological circumstances by mobility, this may lead to different types of encounters between peoples: they might for instance be trade-oriented or bellicose, intensive or shallow, short-term or long-term, and policies with respect to contact may vary considerably from one contact situation to another (the Vaupés area as described by Aikhenvald 2002 is a case in point).

Finally, as mentioned in Section 33.1, there is no obvious connection between contact scenarios and their linguistic outcomes to the extent that we can predict one on the basis of the other. Further research should ideally take into account as much as possible of the ethnohistorical and sociological information available.

Appendix

Table 33A.1 *Areal linguistics of South America: the language sample*

Language	ISO code	Genealogical affiliation	Region
Arhuaco	arh	Chibchan	Northern Andes
Inga	inb	Quechuan	Northern Andes
Páez	pbb	Paez	Northern Andes
Chamacoco	ceg	Zamucoan	La Plata
Ayoreo	ayo	Zamucoan	La Plata
Kadiwéu	kbc	Guaicuruan	La Plata

[3] We are grateful to Raymond Hickey for drawing our attention to this psychological component and its possible consequences for language development.

Table 33A.1 (*cont.*)

Language	ISO code	Genealogical affiliation	Region
Wichí Lhamtés Nocten	mtp	Matacoan	La Plata
Santiago del Estero Quichua	qus	Quechuan	La Plata
Maca	mca	Matacoan	La Plata
Tapiete	tpj	Tupían	La Plata
Pilagá	plg	Guaicuruan	La Plata
Toba	tob	Guaicuruan	La Plata
Mocoví	moc	Guaicuruan	La Plata
Emérillon	eme	Tupían	Guyanas
Hixkaryána	hix	Cariban	Guyanas
Trió	tri	Cariban	Guyanas
Warao	wba	Warao	Guyanas
Tehuelche	teh	Chonan	Southern Cone
Puelche	pue	Puelche	Southern Cone
Ona	ona	Chonan	Southern Cone
Mapudungun	arn	Araucanian	Southern Cone
Shipibo-Conibo	shp	Panoan	Huallaga-Ucayali
Matsés	mcf	Panoan	Huallaga-Ucayali
Yanesha'	ame	Arawakan	Huallaga-Ucayali
Cholón	cht	Hibito_Cholon	Huallaga-Ucayali
Yaminahua	yaa	Panoan	Huallaga-Ucayali
San Martín Quechua	qvs	Quechuan	Huallaga-Ucayali
Uru	ure	Uru-Chipaya	Central Andes
North Junín Quechua	qvn	Quechuan	Central Andes
Cusco Quechua	quz	Quechuan	Central Andes
Imbabura Highland Quichua	qvi	Quechuan	Central Andes
Huaylas Ancash Quechua	qwh	Quechuan	Central Andes
Ayacucho Quechua	quy	Quechuan	Central Andes
Huangascar-Topara-Yauyos Quechua	qux	Quechuan	Central Andes
Chipaya	cap	Uru-Chipaya	Central Andes
Callawalla	caw	Mixed Language	Central Andes
Pacaraos Quechua	qvp	Quechuan	Central Andes
Cajamarca Quechua	qvc	Quechuan	Central Andes
Southern Aymara	ayc	Aymaran	Central Andes
Huallaga Huánuco Quechua	qub	Quechuan	Central Andes
Jauja Wanca Quechua	qxw	Quechuan	Central Andes
South Bolivian Quechua	quh	Quechuan	Central Andes
Jaqaru	jqr	Aymaran	Central Andes
Salasaca Highland Quichua	qxl	Quechuan	Central Andes
Central Aymara	ayr	Aymaran	Central Andes
Awa-Cuaiquer	kwi	Barbacoan	Pacific
Mochica	omc	Mochica	Pacific
Northern Emberá	emp	Chocoan	Pacific
Colorado	cof	Barbacoan	Pacific
Ninam	shb	Yanomamic	Orinoco
Puinave	pui	Puinave	Orinoco
Panare	pbh	Cariban	Orinoco
Itonama	ito	Itonama	Guaporé-Mamoré
Karo (Brazil)	arr	Tupían	Guaporé-Mamoré
Leco	lec	Leko	Guaporé-Mamoré
Movima	mzp	Movima	Guaporé-Mamoré
Gavião Do Jiparaná	gvo	Tupían	Guaporé-Mamoré
Wari'	pav	Chapacuran	Guaporé-Mamoré

Table 33A.1 (*cont.*)

Language	ISO code	Genealogical affiliation	Region
Kanoê	kxo	Kanoe	Guaporé-Mamoré
Mosetén-Chimané	cas	Moseten-Chimane	Guaporé-Mamoré
Lakondê	lkd	Nambiquaran	Guaporé-Mamoré
Cavineña	cav	Tacanan	Guaporé-Mamoré
Sabanê	sae	Nambiquaran	Guaporé-Mamoré
Sakirabiá	skf	Tupían	Guaporé-Mamoré
Ese Ejja	ese	Tacanan	Guaporé-Mamoré
Reyesano	rey	Tacanan	Guaporé-Mamoré
Yuracaré	yuz	Yurakare	Guaporé-Mamoré
Baure	brg	Arawakan	Guaporé-Mamoré
Mamaindé	wmd	Nambiquaran	Guaporé-Mamoré
Yuqui	yuq	Tupían	Guaporé-Mamoré
Karitiâna	ktn	Tupían	Guaporé-Mamoré
Kwaza	xwa	Kwaza	Guaporé-Mamoré
Dâw	kwa	Nadahup	Vaupés
Nhengatu	yrl	Tupían	Vaupés
Desano	des	Tucanoan	Vaupés
Tariana	tae	Arawakan	Vaupés
Hupdë	jup	Nadahup	Vaupés
Cubeo	cub	Tucanoan	Vaupés
Bora	boa	Boran	Vaupés
Southern Pastaza Quechua	qup	Quechuan	Napo-Marañon
Urarina	ura	Urarina	Napo-Marañon
Tena Lowland Quichua	quw	Quechuan	Napo-Marañon
Iquito	iqu	Zaparoan	Napo-Marañon
Muniche	myr	Muniche	Napo-Marañon
Shuar	jiv	Jivaroan	Napo-Marañon
Siona-Tetete	snn	Tucanoan	Napo-Marañon
Cocama-Cocamilla	cod	Tupían	Napo-Marañon
Arabela	arl	Zaparoan	Napo-Marañon
Aguaruna	agr	Jivaroan	Napo-Marañon
Cofán	con	Cofan	Napo-Marañon
Bororo	bor	Bororoan	Tapajos-Madeira
Kamaiurá	kay	Tupían	Xingú-Tocantins
Canela	ram	Nuclear Macro-Je	Xingú-Tocantins
Trumai	tpy	Trumai	Xingú-Tocantins
Jamamadí	jaa	Arawan	Solimões
Apurinã	apu	Arawakan	Solimões

References

Adelaar, Willem (with Pieter Muysken), 2004. *The Languages of the Andes*. Cambridge: Cambridge University Press.

Adelaar, Willem, 2008. Towards a typological profile of the Andean languages. In Alexander Lubotsky, Jos Schaeken and Jeroen Wiedenhof (eds), *Evidence and Counter-Evidence: Essays in Honour of Frederik Kortlandt*, vol. 2: *General Linguistics*, pp. 23–33. Amsterdam: Rodopi.

Aikhenvald, Alexandra Y., 2002. *Language Contact in Amazonia*. Oxford: Oxford University Press.

Birchall, Joshua, 2014a. Verbal argument marking patterns in South American languages. In O'Connor and Muysken (eds), pp. 223–249.

Birchall, Joshua, 2014b. *Argument Realization in the Languages of South America*. Doctoral dissertation, Radboud University, Nijmegen.

Bowern, Claire, Patience Epps, Russell Gray et al., 2011. Does lateral transmission obscure inheritance in hunter–gatherer languages? *PLoS ONE* 6 (9): e25195.

Brackelaire, Vincent and Gilberto Azanha, 2006. Últimos pueblos indígenas aislados en América Latina: Reto a la supervivencia [Last isolated indigenous peoples in Latin America: The challenge of their Survival]. In *Lenguas y Tradiciones Orales de la Amazonía: ¿Diversidad en Peligro? [Languages and Oral Traditions of Amazonia: Diversity in Peril?]*, pp. 313–367. La Habana: Casa de las Américas.

Campbell, Lyle, Terrence Kaufman and Thomas C. Smith-Stark, 1986. Meso-America as a linguistic area. *Language* 62 (3): 530–570.

Campbell, Lyle, 2012a. Classification of the indigenous languages of South America. In Lyle Campbell and Verónica Grondona (eds), *The Indigenous Languages of South America: A Comprehensive Guide*, pp. 59–166. Berlin: Mouton de Gruyter.

Campbell, Lyle, 2012b. Typological characteristics of South American indigenous languages. In Lyle Campbell and Verónica Grondona (eds), *The Indigenous Languages of South America: A Comprehensive Guide*, pp. 259–330. Berlin: Mouton de Gruyter.

Campbell, Lyle, this volume, Chapter 2. Why is it so hard to define a linguistic area?

Chang, Will and Lev Michael, 2014. A relaxed admixture model of contact. *Language Dynamics and Change* 4 (1): 1–26.

Constenla-Umaña, Adolfo, 1991. *Las Lenguas del Area Intermedia: Introducción a su Estudio Areal [The Languages of the Intermediate Area: Introduction to Their Areal Study]*. San José: Editorial de la Universidad de Costa Rica.

Crevels, Mily and Hein van der Voort, 2008. The Guaporé-Mamoré region as a linguistic area. In Pieter Muysken (ed.), *From Linguistic Areas to Areal Linguistics*, pp. 151–180. Amsterdam: John Benjamins.

Dahl, Östen, J. Christopher Gillam, David G. Anderson, José Iriarte and Silvia M. Copé, 2012. Linguistic diversity zones and cartographic modeling: GIS as a method for understanding the prehistory of lowland South America. In Alf Hornborg and Jonathan David Hill (eds), *Ethnicity in Ancient Amazonia: Reconstructing Past Identities from Archaeology, Linguistics, and Ethnohistory*, pp. 211–224. Boulder, CO: University Press of Colorado.

Derbyshire, Desmond C. and Geoffrey K. Pullum, 1986. Introduction. In Desmond C. Derbyshire and Geoffrey K. Pullum (eds), *Handbook of Amazonian Languages*, vol. 1, pp. 1–28. Berlin: Mouton de Gruyter.

Dixon, R. M. W. and Alexandra Y. Aikhenvald, 1999. Other small families and isolates. In Robert M. W. Dixon and Alexandra Y. Aikhenvald (eds), *The Amazonian Languages*, pp. 341–381. Cambridge: Cambridge University Press.

Dunne, Thomas and Leal Anne Kerry Mertes, 2007. Rivers. In Thomas T. Veblen, Kenneth R. Young and Anthony R. Orme (eds), *The Physical Geography of South America*, pp. 76–90. Oxford: Oxford University Press.

Eriksen, Love, 2011. *Nature and Culture in Prehistoric Amazonia*. PhD Dissertation, Lund University.

Evans, Nicholas and Stephen C. Levinson, 2009. The myth of language universals: Language diversity and its importance for cognitive science. *Behavioral and Brain Sciences* 32 (5): 429–492.

van Gijn, Rik, 2014a. The Andean foothills and adjacent Amazonian fringe. In O'Connor and Muysken (eds), pp. 102–125.

van Gijn, Rik, 2014b. Subordination strategies in South America: Nominalization. In O'Connor and Muysken (eds), pp. 274–297.

Greenberg, Joseph H., 1987. *Language in the Americas*. Stanford, CA: Stanford University Press.

Hammarström, Harald and Loretta O'Connor, 2013. Dependency-sensitive typological distance. In Lars Borin and Anju Saxena (eds), *Approaches to Measuring Linguistic Differences*, pp. 337–360. Berlin: de Gruyter Mouton.

Hammarström, Harald and Tom Güldemann, 2014. Quantifying geographical determinants of large-scale distributions of linguistic features. *Language Dynamics and Change* 4 (1): 87–115.

van de Kerke, Simon and Pieter Muysken, 2014. The Andean matrix. In O'Connor and Muysken (eds), pp. 126–151.

Krasnoukhova, Olga, 2012. *The Noun Phrase in the Languages of South America*. Doctoral dissertation, Radboud University, Nijmegen.

Krasnoukhova, Olga, 2014. The noun phrase: Focus on demonstratives, redrawing the semantic map. In O'Connor and Muysken (eds), pp. 250–273.

Michael, Lev, Will Chang and Tammy Stark, 2014. Exploring phonological areality in the circum-Andean region using a Naive Bayes Classifier. *Language Dynamics and Change* 4 (1): 27–86.

Müller, Neele, 2014. Language internal and external factors in the development of the desiderative in South American indigenous languages. In O'Connor and Muysken (eds), pp. 203–222.

Muysken, Pieter, 2010. Scenarios for language contact. In Raymond Hickey (ed.), *The Handbook of Language Contact*, pp. 265–281. Malden, MA: Wiley-Blackwell.

Muysken, Pieter, 2012. Contacts between indigenous languages in South America. In Veronica Grondona and Lyle Campbell (eds), *Handbook of South American Historical Linguistics*, pp. 235–258. Berlin: de Gruyter Mouton.

Muysken, Pieter, Harald Hammarström, Joshua Birchall et al., 2014. The languages of South America: Deep families, areal relationships, and language contact. In O'Connor and Muysken (eds), pp. 299–322.

Muysken, Pieter, Harald Hammarström, Joshua Birchall, Rik van Gijn, Olga Krasnoukhova and Neele Müller, 2015. Linguistic areas, bottom up or top down? The case of the Guaporé-Mamoré. In Bernard Comrie and Lucia Golluscio (eds), *Language Contact and Documentation*, pp. 205–238. Berlin: de Gruyter.

Nettle, Daniel, 1996. Language diversity in West Africa: An ecological approach. *Journal of Anthropological Archaeology* 15 (4): 403–438.

Nettle, Daniel, 1999. *Linguistic Diversity*. Oxford: Oxford University Press.

Nichols, Johanna, 1990. Linguistic diversity and the first settlement of the New World. *Language* 66 (3): 475–521.

Nichols, Johanna, 1992. *Linguistic Diversity in Space and Time*. Chicago: University of Chicago Press.

Nordhoff, Sebastian, Harald Hammarström, Robert Forkel and Martin Haspelmath, 2013. Glottolog 2.1. Leipzig: Max Planck Institute for Evolutionary Anthropology. http://glottolog.org

O'Connor, Loretta and Pieter Muysken (eds), 2014. *The Native Languages of South America: Origins, Development, Typology*. Cambridge: Cambridge University Press.

Orme, Anthony R., 2007. The tectonic framework of South America. In Thomas T. Veblen, Kenneth R. Young and Anthony R. Orme (eds), *The Physical Geography of South America*, pp. 3–22. Oxford: Oxford University Press.

Payne, Doris, 1990. Morphological characteristics of Amazonian languages. In Doris Payne (ed.), *Amazonian Linguistics: Studies in Lowland South American Languages*, pp. 213–241. Austin, TX: University of Texas Press.

Seki, Lucy, 1999. The Upper Xingú as an incipient linguistic area. In R. M. W. Dixon and Alexandra Y. Aikhenvald (eds), *The Amazonian Languages*. Cambridge: Cambridge University Press, pp. 417–430.

Tessmann, Günter, 1930. *Die Indianer Nordost-Perus: Grundlegende Forschungen für eine systematische Kulturkunde*. Hamburg: Friedrichsen, de Gruyter and Co.

Torero, Alfredo, 2002. *Idiomas de los Andes: Lingüística e Historia [Languages of the Andes: Linguistics and History]*. Lima: IFEA and Editorial Horizonte.

Index